HOOVER'S
GUIDE TO
COMPUTER
COMPANIES

SECOND EDITION

Hoover's
BUSINESS
PRESS

Austin, Texas

Hoover's Guide to Computer Companies is intended to provide its readers with accurate and authoritative information about the enterprises covered in it. Hoover's asked all companies and organizations profiled to provide information for the book. Many did so; a number did not. The information contained herein is as accurate as we could reasonably make it. In many cases we have relied on third-party material that we believe to be trustworthy, but were unable to independently verify. We do not warrant that the book is absolutely accurate or without error. Readers should not rely on any information contained herein in instances where such reliance might cause loss or damage. The publisher, the editors, and their data suppliers specifically disclaim all warranties, including the implied warranties of merchantability and fitness for a specific purpose. This book is sold with the understanding that neither the publisher, the editors, nor any content contributors are engaged in providing investment, financial, accounting, legal, or other professional advice.

The financial data (How Much section) in this book are from a variety of sources. Media General Financial Services, Inc., provided selected financial data for the How Much section for publicly traded companies. For private companies and for historical information on public companies prior to their becoming public, we obtained information directly from the companies or from trade sources deemed to be reliable. Hoover's, Inc., is solely responsible for the presentation of all data. The computer industry overview was written by Eric Nee and edited by Alan Chai.

Many of the names of products and services mentioned in this book are the trademarks or service marks of the companies manufacturing or selling them and are subject to protection under US law. Space has not permitted us to indicate which names are subject to such protection, and readers are advised to consult with the owners of such marks regarding their use. Hoover's is a trademark of Hoover's, Inc.

Hoover's
BUSINESS PRESS

10 9 8 7 6 5 4 3 2 1

Publisher Cataloging-In-Publication Data

Hoover's Guide to Computer Companies — 2nd. ed.

Includes indexes.

1. Business enterprises — Directories. 2. Corporations — Directories.

HF3010   338.7

Company information and profiles from the *Hoover's* series of handbooks, guides, and directories are also available on America Online, Baseline, Bloomberg Financial Network, CompuServe, LEXIS-NEXIS, Microsoft Network, Reuters NewMedia, and on the Internet at Hoover's Online (www.hoovers.com), CNNfn (www.cnnfn.com), Farcast (www.farcast.com), IBM InfoMarket (www.infomkt.ibm.com), InfoSeek (www.infoseek.com), IBM Infosage (www.infosage.ibm.com), Pathfinder (www.pathfinder.com), PAWWS (www.pawws.com), Wall Street Journal Interactive edition (www.wsj.com), The Washington Post (www.washingtonpost.com), and others.

A catalog of Hoover's products is available on the World Wide Web (www.hoovers.com).

ISBN 1-878753-80-0

This book was produced by Hoover's Business Press using Claris Corporation's FileMaker Pro 3.0, Quark, Inc.'s Quark XPress 3.32, EM Software, Inc.'s Xdata 2.5, and fonts from Adobe's Clearface and Futura families. Cover design is by Daniel Pelavin. Electronic prepress and printing were done by Quebecor Printing (USA) Corp. in Fairfield, Pennsylvania. Text paper is 60# Postmark White.

US AND WORLD DIRECT SALES
Hoover's, Inc.
1033 La Posada Drive, Suite 250
Austin, TX 78752
Phone: 512-374-4500
Fax: 512-374-4501
e-mail: orders@hoovers.com

US BOOKSELLERS AND JOBBERS
Little, Brown and Co.
200 West Street
Waltham, MA 02154
Phone: 800-759-0190
Fax: 617-890-0875

US WHOLESALER ORDERS
Warner Publisher Services
Book Division
9210 King Palm Drive
Tampa, FL 33619
Phone: 800-873-BOOK
Fax: 813-664-8193

EUROPE
William Snyder Publishing Associates
5, Five Mile Drive
Oxford OX2 8HT
England
Phone & fax: +44-186-551-3186

HOOVER'S, INC.

Founder: Gary Hoover
Chairman, President, CEO, and Publisher: Patrick J. Spain

Senior Managing Editor — Production: George Sutton
Senior Managing Editor — Editorial: James R. Talbot
Senior Contributing Editor: Alan Chai
Editorial Coordinator: Ken Little
Senior Editor: Thomas Trotter
Associate Editor: William Cargill
Editors: Chris Barton, Paul Mitchell, Anthony Shuga
Assistant Editorial Coordinator: Melanie Lea Hall
Research Manager: Sherri M. Hale
Desktop Publishing Manager: Christina Thiele
Senior Researchers: Sarah Hallman, James A. Harris, Jr., Brian Pedder, David Ramirez
Senior Writers: Joy Aiken, Stuart Hampton, Diane Lee, Barbara M. Spain, Jeffrey A. Twining
Financial Editor: Dennis Sutton
Copyeditors: Patrice Sarath, John Willis
Fact Checkers/Proofreaders: Ramalakshmi Bollini, Allan Gill, Michael G. Laster
Elizabeth Gagne Morgan, Sarah Palmer, Marianne Tatom
Database Editors: Tweed Chouinard, Yvonne A. Cullinan, Karen Hill, Britton E. Jackson
Desktop Publishers: Trey Colvin, Michelle de Ybarrondo, Kevin Dodds, JoAnn Estrada,
Gregory Gosdin, Holly Hans Jackson, Christy Ostler
Research Assistant: Erica Taylor

Director, Hoover's Online: Matt Manning
Senior Brand Manager: Leslie A. Wolke
Online Production Manager: Richard Finley
Online Content Editor: Martha DeGrasse
Online Systems Analyst: Eric Periche
Online Editors: Kay Nichols, Perrin Patterson
Electronic Media Producers: Rick Navarro

Senior Vice President, Sales and Marketing: Dana L. Smith
Vice President, Electronic Publishing: Tom Linehan
VP Finance and Administration and CFO (HR): Lynn Atchison
Director, Corporate Communications: Jani Farlow Spede
Controller: Deborah L. Dunlap
Systems Manager: Bill Crider
Fulfillment Manager: Beth DeVore
Office Manager: Tammy Fisher
Direct Marketing Manager: Marcia Harelik
Advertising Sales Manager: Joe McWilliams
Customer Service Manager: Rhonda T. Mitchell
Shipping Coordinator: Michael Febonio
Advertising Coordinator: Michelle Swann
Communications Coordinator: Angela Young
Customer Service Representatives: John T. Logan, Darla Wenzel
Administrative Assistant: Margaux Bejarano
Communications Assistant: Becky Hepinstall
Systems Assistant: John Padwick

HOOVER'S, INC. MISSION STATEMENT

1. To produce business information products and services of the highest quality, accuracy, and readability.
2. To make that information available whenever, wherever, and however our customers want it through mass distribution at affordable prices.
3. To continually expand our range of products and services and our markets for those products and services.
4. To reward our employees, suppliers, and shareholders based on their contributions to the success of our enterprise.
5. To hold to the highest ethical business standards, erring on the side of generosity when in doubt.

Contents

List of Lists

Companies Profiled

ABOUT *HOOVER'S GUIDE TO COMPUTER COMPANIES*

There is no sitting still in the business of high tech. And just as the computer industry evolves, so do we at Hoover's. Thus we offer this 2nd edition of *Hoover's Guide to Computer Companies* — a completely updated version of our book that describes the businesses that have helped create, or were spawned by, the computer revolution.

Whether in the form of laptops connected to the Internet or microprocessors controlling our toasters, computers are part of the fabric of our lives, and at the speed of current change, information about these companies becomes even more important, not to mention more interesting.

In fact, as computers move off the desktop and into the living room and beyond, entire industries from telephone and cable to television and advertising have been forced to change their business strategies. Even our own business of distributing useful business information to consumers is changing. Electronic means will enhance everything from getting information to paying the bills, but we believe that the printed word has a place in our fast-paced world, and we will continue to make our information available whenever, wherever, and however you want it.

In this volume, we selected 250 companies to focus on for our in-depth profiles. Reflective of the growth in the industry this past year, you will find 108 of our 2-page profiles of industry leaders (e.g., America Online, IBM, and Toshiba), 30 more than in last year's book. We have included a selection of interesting, smaller companies in our one-page profile format. Some of these were already well-known (NeXT Software) and some have only recently come into public awareness (Pixar). We also include several nontechnical enterprises, including legal firms (Fenwick & West LLP), advertising agencies (Waggener Edstrom), and venture capitalists (The Paul Allen Group). All, however, have played an important role in the industry.

An additional 1,220 companies have been profiled in capsule form (335 more than in our first edition). These include every public company directly involved in the computer industry; most private computer companies with more than $50 million in revenues; and a select few smaller private companies. Because the computer industry is centered in the United States, the vast majority of companies are US-based. We have, however, included major players from Europe, Hong Kong, Israel, Japan, Korea, Singapore, Taiwan.

Although we have covered the spectrum from Acclaim Entertainment to Zoom Telephonics, there are many more company profiles we would have liked to include in this book, had space permitted. These profiles may be found on the Internet at Hoover's Online (www.hoovers.com).

Hoover's Guide to Computer Companies represents the most complete source of in-depth information on global, computer-related business enterprises available to the general public. Many of these companies have high public visibility thanks to their size, worldwide presence, technical prominence, or notoriety. Others keep a lower profile. We have tried to bring you a balanced representation of the computer greats in as concise, accurate, and readable a format as possible.

Hoover's Guide to Computer Companies is divided into the following components:

1. The first section, "Using the profiles" describes the contents of the profiles and explains how to get the most from them.

2. The second section, "The Computer Industry in Perspective," presents an overview of the industry, including a look at the past and the future as well as the current state of various industry segments.

3. The next section, "A List-Lover's Compendium," contains lists of the largest and fastest-growing companies in this book as well as selected lists from other sources to provide different viewpoints.

4. The fourth section of the book contains the 250 in-depth profiles of computer-related business enterprises. The profiles are grouped according to size, first the 108 two-page profiles of industry leaders and then the 142 one-page profiles. They are arranged alphabetically within groups.

5. The next section provides capsule summaries of 1,470 companies. If an in-depth profile also exists for a company, the page number of that

profile is included in the entry for easy reference.

6. The book concludes with 2 indexes:

- an index of companies by headquarters location

- the main index of the book, containing the names of all brands, companies, and people mentioned in the profiles.

We have provided a free CD-ROM version of the capsule summaries in this book in an easy-to-use database for both Mac and Windows users. Developed in Claris' Filemaker (a run-time copy of which is part of our software package), the program combines a simple intuitive interface (no user manual required) with a flexible search engine. You can use the software to search for specific information, to export the data to other programs, and to create mailing lists or write letters.

We trust you will find this book both informative and useful. We invite your comments via e-mail (info@hoovers.com), by phone (512-374-4500), fax (512-374-4501), or mail (1033 La Posada Drive, Suite 250, Austin, Texas, 78752).

The Editors
Austin, Texas
October 1996

Using the Profiles

ORGANIZATION

Profiles of companies in *Hoover's Guide to Computer Companies* are presented in alphabetical order. This alphabetization is generally word by word, which means that Micro Warehouse, Inc., precedes MicroAge, Inc. We have shown the full legal name of the enterprise at the top of each page, unless it is too long, in which case you will find it in front of the address in the Where section of the profile. If a company name starts with a person's first name (for example, The Paul Allen Group), it will be alphabetized under the first name, in this case "Paul" (the article is ignored). All company names (past and present) used in the profiles are indexed in the last index in the book.

Basic financial data are listed under the heading How Much: where the company's stock is traded if it is public, the ticker symbol used by the stock exchange, and the company's fiscal year-end.

The annual financial information contained in the profiles is current through fiscal year-ends occurring as late as May 1996. We have included certain nonfinancial developments, such as officer changes, through September 1996.

OVERVIEW

In the first section of the profile, we have tried to give a thumbnail description of the company and what it does. The description will usually include information on the company's strategy, reputation, and ownership. We recommend that you read this section first.

WHEN

This extended section reflects our belief that every enterprise is the sum of its history, and that you have to know where you came from in order to know where you are going. While some companies have limited historical awareness and were unable to help us much and other companies are just plain boring, we think the vast majority of the enterprises in this book have colorful backgrounds. We have tried to focus on the people who made the enterprises what they are today. We have found these histories to be full of twists and ironies; they can make for fascinating reading.

WHO

Here we list the names of the people who run the company, insofar as space allows. In the case of public companies, we have shown the ages and pay of key officers. In some cases the published data are for the previous year although the company has announced promotions or retirements since year-end. The pay represents cash compensation, including bonuses, but excludes stock option programs.

While companies are free to structure their management titles any way they please, most modern corporations follow standard practices. The ultimate power in any corporation lies with the shareholders, who elect a board of directors, usually including officers or "insiders" as well as individuals from outside the company. The chief officer, the person on whose desk the buck stops, is usually called the chief executive officer (CEO). Most times, he or she is also the chairman of the board. As corporate management has become more complex, it is common for the CEO to have a "right-hand person" who oversees the day-to-day operations of the company, allowing the CEO plenty of time to focus on strategy and long-term issues. This right-hand person is usually designated the chief operating officer (COO) and is often the president of the company. In other cases one person is both chairman and president.

A multitude of other titles exists, including chief financial officer (CFO), chief administrative officer, and vice chairman (VC). We have always tried to include the CFO, the chief legal officer, and the chief human resources or personnel officer. Our best advice is that officers' pay levels are clear indicators of who the board of directors thinks are most important on the management team. The Who section also includes the name of the company's audit-ing (accounting) firm, where available.

The people named in the profiles are indexed at the back of the book.

WHERE

Here we include the company's headquarters, street address, telephone and fax numbers, and web site, as available. The back of the book includes an index of companies by headquarters locations.

In some cases we have also included information on the geographical distribution of the company's business, including sales and profit data. Note that these profit numbers, like those in the What section below, are usually operating or pretax profits rather than net profits. Operating profits are generally those before financing costs (interest income and payments) and before taxes, which are considered costs attributable to the whole company rather than to one division or part of the world. For this reason the net income figures (in the How Much section) are usually much lower, since they are after interest and taxes. Pretax profits are after interest but before taxes.

WHAT

This section lists as many of the company's products, services, brand names, divisions, subsidiaries, and joint ventures as we could fit. We have tried to include all its major lines and all familiar brand names. The nature of this section varies by company and the amount of information available. If the company publishes sales and profit information by type of business, we have included it. The brand, division, and subsidiary names are listed in the last index in the book.

KEY COMPETITORS

In this section we have listed companies that compete with the profiled company. This feature is included as a quick way to locate similar companies and compare them.

HOW MUCH

Here we have tried to present as much data about each enterprise's financial performance as we could compile in the allocated space. While the information varies somewhat from industry to industry, and is less complete in the case of private companies that do not release these data (although we have always tried to provide annual sales and employment), the following information is generally present.

A 6-year table, with relevant annualized compound growth rates, covers:

- **Sales** — fiscal year sales (year-end assets for most financial companies)
- **Net Income** — fiscal year net income (before accounting changes)
- **Income as a percent of sales** — fiscal year net income as a percent of sales (as a percent of assets for most financial firms)
- **Earnings Per Share** — fiscal year earnings per share (EPS)
- **Stock price** — the high, low, and close (for the calendar year unless otherwise noted)
- **P/E** — high and low price/earnings (P/E) ratio
- **Dividends Per Share** — fiscal year dividends per share
- **Book Value Per Share** — Fiscal year-end book value (common shareholders' equity per share)
- **Employees** — fiscal year-end or average number of employees

All revenue numbers are as reported by the company in its annual report.

The information on the number of employees is intended to aid the reader interested in knowing whether a company has a long-term trend of increasing or decreasing employment. As far as we know, we are the only company that publishes this information in print format.

The year at the top of each column in the How Much section is the year in which the company's fiscal year actually ends. Thus a company with a February 28, 1996, year-end is shown as 1996. Stock prices for companies with year-ends between January 1 and April 30 are for the prior calendar year and are so footnoted on the chart.

In addition, we have provided in graph form a stock price history for each public company. The graphs show the range of trading between the high and the low price as well as the closing price for the year. Generally, for private companies, we have graphed net income, or, where that is unavailable, sales.

Key year-end statistics in this section generally show the financial strength of the enterprise, including:

- Debt ratio (total debt as a percent of combined total debt and shareholders' equity)
- Return on equity (net income divided by the average of beginning and ending common shareholders' equity)
- Cash, marketable securities, and short-term investments on hand
- Current ratio (ratio of current assets to current liabilities)
- Total long-term debt (including capital lease obligations)
- Number of shares of common stock outstanding (less treasury shares)
- Dividend yield (fiscal year dividends per share divided by the calendar year-end closing stock price)
- Dividend payout (fiscal year dividends divided by fiscal year EPS)
- Market value at calendar year-end (calendar year-end closing stock price multiplied by fiscal year-end number of shares outstanding)
- Research and development or a percent of sales
- Advertising as a percent of sales

Per share data have been adjusted for stock splits. The data for public companies (and private companies with public debt) have been provided to us by Media General Financial Services, Inc. Other public company information was compiled by Hoover's, which takes full responsibility for the content of this section.

In the case of private companies that do not publicly disclose financial information, we usually did not have access to such standardized data. We have gathered estimates of sales and other statistics from numerous sources.

COMPUTER Industry Overview

The Computer Industry in Perspective

THE INFORMATION AGE

In 1969, a group of engineers at Intel Corp. began development of a radical new semiconductor chip for a small Japanese calculator company. The goal was to pack all of the functionality of numerous dedicated-function chips onto a single multifunction chip. A computer on a chip. The microprocessor.

Twenty-five years later the results of that project have transformed the computer industry, and with it, much of the world. Computers, which were once confined behind glass-enclosed rooms and available only to a limited few, are now the basis for a $400 billion-a-year industry, with tens of millions sold each year.

The most powerful mainframe computer available 25 years ago can now be bought for less than $2,000 and put on a desk. Software applications for managing a business that used to be crafted by hand can now be bought through the mail for a few hundred dollars. Extensive databases of information which used to consume stacks and stacks of expensive computer tape are now available on a single CD that can fit in a folder.

We are in the midst of the Information Revolution, a period in history between the Industrial Age, which was dominated by oil, steel, and mass production, and the Information Age, which will be dominated by semiconductors, software, and customization.

The technologies and companies that are creating the Information Revolution are profiled in this book. Some of them, such as Motorola, Hewlett-Packard, and IBM, were begun earlier this century. They are the old-timers of the computer industry. Other companies, such as Microsoft, Intel, and Apple, gave birth to the personal computer revolution and are themselves less than 30 years old.

Then there are the new firms, those only a few years old, such as Netscape, Ascend, and FORE. These are the companies leading the way into the next phase of the Information Revolution, interconnecting the ever-increasing computing power now spreading throughout the globe into a worldwide web of information, entertainment, communication, and commerce.

A LOOK BACK

The computer industry is young by any historical measure. The first functioning electronic computer was not built until World War II. ENIAC, one of the first, did not become operational until 1945 and was used by the federal government in its war efforts. It was not until 1954 that the first computers were sold to private industry for business data processing.

In its short history, the computer industry has gone through 3 phases, each of which has spawned its own technologies, companies, and ways of doing business. The first was the world of mainframes, very large and very expensive computers that require legions of workers and millions of dollars to buy and run. Hence only the largest corporations and institutions could afford them. IBM came to dominate this world, but there were other firms of importance as well, including what is now Unisys, Control Data, Hitachi, Fujitsu, ICL, and Groupe Bull.

Then came the minicomputer, essentially a smaller version of the mainframe, less expensive, and easier to program. Digital Equipment Corporation (DEC) became the dominant minicomputer vendor and was joined by firms such as Wang, Data General, and Hewlett-Packard. By reducing the cost of computing, the minicomputer broadened its use, but it was still too expensive to be used for anything but business and government operations.

In the late 1970s came the personal computer, enabled by the development of the microprocessor. It further broadened the market by significantly reducing the price, size, and programming requirements. The PC gave birth to companies such as Apple, Compaq, and Dell.

Most significantly, the PC also gave rise to a wide variety of ancillary businesses in the semiconductor, software, peripheral, and communications businesses. Before the PC, the computer industry was dominated by "systems" vendors, vertically integrated companies such as IBM and DEC that supplied nearly everything in the computer. In fact, the user often didn't have a choice of buying products from another firm because the vendors used technology to tie their users into their "proprietary" products.

Today that has all changed. No single company controls the computer. The PC is a combination of interrelated standards controlled by individual companies, groups of companies, or industry standards bodies. The 2 most important standards are the microprocessor architecture, as defined by Intel, and the operating system, as defined by Microsoft. While these 2 firms wield a lot of power within the industry, theirs is in many ways less than the power that the proprietary firms used to exercise. The resulting competition between competing standards and companies is what keeps the industry vibrant and growing.

TODAY'S LEADERS

Today's computer industry can be divided into 6 major segments, all interrelated but each dominated by its own group of companies.

Semiconductors

On the strength of its control over the microprocessor market, Intel has emerged as the largest semiconductor company in the world, with revenues of more than $16.2 billion, a position it is not likely to give up soon. Even RISC chip maker Hewlett-Packard has partnered with Intel in the development of its next-generation P7 microprocessor. Because of its near monopoly over one of the key computer components, microprocessors, Intel is also among the 5 companies in the computer industry with the highest market value ($85.7 billion at this writing).

But the semiconductor market is large and growing, leaving room for a number of other

strong foreign and domestic firms. Among them are Hitachi, Toshiba, and NEC in Japan. As a group, the Japanese are the largest producers of memory chips (DRAMs), one of the biggest segments of the semiconductor market. But the largest DRAM vendors today are not Japanese firms but Korean companies, Samsung and Hyundai, signifying the emergence of Korea as a world player in semiconductors. Hyundai, in particular, has demonstrated a commitment to build market share by continuing to aggressively expand production in the face of plunging DRAM prices.

In the United States there are a number of important semiconductor firms besides Intel. These include Motorola, IBM, Texas Instruments, and National Semiconductor, all suppliers of a broad line of semiconductor products. There are also a host of more specialized semiconductor firms, most notably Advanced Micro Devices, LSI Logic, Xilinx, and Cyrix.

Computers

While still the largest computer systems company in the world, IBM continues to face a tough transition to a world dominated by personal computer technology. CEO Lou Gerstner has reduced the company's costs enough to return IBM to profitability, but it remains to be seen whether he can affect the long-term revival of the company's product lines necessary for IBM to complete its turnaround.

While IBM, DEC, and other traditional large computer system power houses struggle to find their way in the new computing paradigm, one older firm is rolling products out the door as fast as it can make them —Hewlett-Packard. The company is the 2nd largest computer firm in the US behind IBM, with annual revenues of $31.5 billion and a 5-year growth rate approaching 20% annually.

Another computer systems company growing at a remarkable rate is Compaq, which in 1994 became the largest personal computer vendor in the world. Packard Bell held the #2 spot in 1995. Apple, which once sat atop the personal computer market, appears to be fighting a losing battle with Microsoft for the allegiance of desktop users and has recast its strategy to focus on the Internet and multimedia.

While it is becoming increasingly tough for a new company to break into the top ranks of the computer systems market, there are a few firms that are managing to do it. One is Acer, a Taiwanese firm that saw its revenues increase 78% in 1995 to $5.7 billion. A plethora of hopeful computer makers, old and new, are designing low-priced "network computers" or "Internet appliances" to be introduced in 1996 and 1997.

Software

The king of the software industry, and some would argue ruler of the computer industry, is Microsoft. The company is the dominant supplier of personal computer operating systems with MS-DOS and Windows. It has used this as leverage to achieve dominance in PC applications, where it is the leading supplier of suites (Office), spreadsheets (Excel), presentation graphics (Power Point), and database software (Access and Fox Pro). From this base Microsoft is moving down into the consumer market, where it is rapidly becoming an important supplier of CD-ROM software such as its best-selling Encarta encyclopedia. The company is also moving up into the corporate market with its NT operating system intended to compete with UNIX. Now Microsoft is making its move on the Internet, rolling out a line of browsers, servers, and World Wide Web development tools.

No other independent software company comes close to matching Microsoft in size, domination of key markets, breadth of offerings, or ambition. But there are a number of other firms that play important roles in different sectors of the market. One area that has spawned a number of large firms is corporate databases. Computer Associates International and Oracle, the #2 and #3 independent software firms in the

world, respectively, both play major roles in this market, as does Informix.

In the PC software market there are a number of firms that have survived by achieving strong footholds in their respective markets. These include Novell in local area networks, Adobe Systems in graphics and desktop publishing, Autodesk in computer-aided design, and Symantec in utility software. While the software industry, like so much of the computer industry, is dominated by US firms, there is one notable exception, the German company SAP AG, the dominant supplier of client/server business applications.

There are several emerging markets that are generating a large number of new companies, and some among these may grow to become the next Oracle or Novell. One such market is educational and game software, and from this segment Brøderbund Software, Softkey, and Electronic Arts are among the most notable. Another market is communications, and here Netscape Communications stands a chance of becoming a dominant supplier of system software for the Internet, and numerous companies, including Sun Microsystems, Adobe, and Macromedia, have jumped on the bandwagon by designing "plug-in" software that adds functionality to World Wide Web browsers made by Netscape and Microsoft.

Communications

Data communication products are often called the "plumbing" of the computer industry. It's not a very sexy description, but it does reflect the importance of the business (for what's a house without plumbing?) and the amount of money and profits it generates (have you hired a plumber lately?).

The largest segment of the communications market is major corporations, which use large numbers of products to interconnect their far-flung operations and computer systems. Routers, bridges, adapters, multiplexers, hubs, switches

— these are all names of sophisticated products that allow users to send information from one computer to another.

The business market has come to be dominated by a handful of firms that have increasingly broad product offerings covering all of a company's needs. These firms are Cisco Systems (the largest, with revenues of about $4.1 billion), Cabletron, Bay Networks (the product of a merger between Wellfleet and SynOptics), and 3Com.

The growing use of multimedia communications in the business market has helped create a demand for even faster network devices, the most popular of which are asynchronous transfer mode (ATM) switches. FORE Systems is one firm that has benefited from this demand.

The small business and home market has recently begun to be a significant market as well for less sophisticated data communication products, primarily local area network cards and modems. With the growing popularity of the Internet and such services as America Online, high-speed modems are a booming market. Just take a look at U.S. Robotics, the high-flying leader in the rapidly growing modem market.

Peripherals

Products like printers, disk drives, and monitors are as essential as any to the success of the computer industry but do not get the same attention as semiconductors or software. One of the reasons is because this segment is not dominated by highly visible companies the way the others are. In fact, the biggest peripheral suppliers are subsumed within larger companies: Hewlett-Packard is the largest supplier of PC printers and IBM is the largest supplier of mass storage subsystems in the world.

Nevertheless, there are some large peripheral suppliers of note. The biggest among these are the major hard-disk drive companies, all of them American. These include Seagate, by far the largest with revenues of $8.6 billion, as well as Quantum and Western Digital. Two firms stand out among the suppliers of mass storage subsystems: EMC and Storage Technology.

Despite the prosaic nature of most of the peripheral business, there is still room for innovation. One of the areas where this is most evident is color printing. The most notable example is Electronics for Imaging, a fast-growing firm that has devised a unique way of turning a color copier into a high-speed color printer. An older firm that is having a revival in the color printing area is Tektronix.

Online and the Internet

The hottest market to emerge in recent years is online services and the Internet. These services have been around for some time, but it is only recently that they have taken off, spurred by the growing numbers of home PCs, the availability of faster and less expensive data modems, the introduction of user-friendly interfaces on these services, and, to some extent, hype.

The Internet is by far the largest of these networking services. While exact numbers of users are impossible to discern, it can be safely said that there are tens of millions of people around the world that regularly use the Internet. The Internet, which is "owned" by no one, can best be thought of as the *de facto* industry standard networking platform, based on standards such as the HTML programming language and TCP/IP protocols. Today the TCP/IP protocol transports as much data over local area networks as Novell's proprietary IPX protocol. Because of the huge potential market, thousands of companies have begun offering additional features and services on this basic platform, the Internet. In fact, the Internet is likely to spawn an industry as diverse and large as the one spawned by the IBM PC. Some of the more interesting companies to be launched so far are Yahoo!, CINET, and NETCOM On-Line Communications Services.

The "Big Three" commercial online services, America Online, CompuServe, and Prodigy, appear to have become the "Big Two," as Prodigy's decline continues. Combined, America

Online and CompuServe provide services to more than 10 million customers, up from about 4 million a year ago. Despite last year's impressive subscriber growth, the online industry appears to be threatened by the enormity and popularity of the World Wide Web. In the last year AT&T shelved plans for its Interchange online service and Microsoft and CompuServe altered their services to embrace the Internet.

THE FUTURE

As we approach the turn of the century there are 2 key trends that will have an increasingly important impact on the computer industry. The first is the continuing move of computer technology into the home, and the 2nd is the emergence of a world of interconnected digital devices, variously called the Internet, interactive TV, or online services.

Until recently the frontiers of computer and communication science were pushed by demands placed on it from the military, business, and science. Today it is the entertainment, media, and consumer markets that are driving technology ahead. Companies like Silicon Graphics are putting their best engineers into such projects as interactive TV and game machines, not high-end workstations. Venture capitalists have all but abandoned the supercomputer and scientific markets for games and entertainment. The new game machines and TV settop boxes will be as powerful as all but the latest supercomputers.

To understand the power of this trend, just look at Microsoft, the one company that has benefited from this more than any other. Many people laughed at the company's early software, calling MS-DOS a toy operating system, Windows a crude interface, and Word a lousy word processor. All of which was true. But what Microsoft understood that its critics did not was the power of volume. By creating products that could be sold inexpensively, Microsoft could dominate the high-volume markets. This volume could then be used to generate cash to develop better products that could be sold in volume as well, and so on. The end result is that Microsoft is using its base in the low end of the market not only to broaden out the mass consumer market but also to move up into the more demanding business markets.

As Microsoft goes, so goes the computer industry. It is rapidly moving out of its esoteric niches and becoming a force throughout society. Companies such as Motorola, Hewlett-Packard, Microsoft, and Intel are well on their way to becoming the most powerful companies in the world, the Standard Oils of their day.

The key difference between the Standard Oils of yesteryear and the Microsofts of today, however, is that no single company has been able to control digital technology the way Standard Oil controlled oil. Bits and bytes and the technology that created them are not natural resources to be bought and sold. Rather, they are the result of intellectual labor, open and available to everyone. Which is why the computer industry will likely remain as vibrant in the future as it has been in the past.

List-Lover's Compendium

The 200 Largest Companies by Sales in
Hoover's Guide to Computer Companies

Rank	Company	Sales ($ mil.)	Rank	Company	Sales ($ mil.)
1	Samsung Group	78,100	51	CompUSA Inc.	3,830
2	Hitachi, Ltd.	76,640	52	Gateway 2000, Inc.	3,676
3	IBM Corporation	71,940	53	Micron Technology, Inc.	3,654
4	Siemens AG	61,641	54	Intelligent Electronics, Inc.	3,588
5	Toshiba Corporation	53,047	55	SGS-Thomson Microelectronics N.V.	3,554
6	Sony Corporation	47,582			
7	NEC Corporation	45,557	56	Computer Associates International	3,505
8	Fujitsu Limited	38,976	57	Computer 2000 AG	3,465
9	Hewlett-Packard Company	31,519	58	Nintendo Co., Ltd.	3,337
10	Motorola, Inc.	27,037	59	SEGA Enterprises, Ltd.	3,228
11	Hyundai Group	23,221	60	Tech Data Corporation	3,087
12	Canon Inc.	21,026			
13	Sharp Corporation	17,102	61	Applied Materials, Inc.	3,062
14	Xerox Corporation	16,611	62	TATUNG Co.	3,000
15	Intel Corporation	16,202	63	MicroAge, Inc.	2,941
16	Compaq Computer Corporation	14,755	64	Silicon Graphics, Inc.	2,921
17	Digital Equipment Corporation	14,563	65	Western Digital Corporation	2,865
18	LG Group	13,189	66	SCI Systems, Inc.	2,674
19	Texas Instruments Incorporated	13,128	67	National Semiconductor Corp.	2,623
20	Electronic Data Systems Corp.	12,422	68	AST Research, Inc.	2,468
21	Apple Computer, Inc.	11,062	69	Advanced Micro Devices, Inc.	2,430
22	Ricoh Company, Ltd.	10,258	70	3Com Corporation	2,327
23	The General Electric Company PLC	9,760	71	Cap Gemini Sogeti S.A.	2,308
24	Microsoft Corporation	8,671	72	Tandem Computers Incorporated	2,285
25	Ingram Micro Inc.	8,617	73	Imation Corp.	2,246
26	Seagate Technology, Inc.	8,588	74	Comdisco, Inc.	2,240
27	NCR Corporation	8,162	75	Inacom Corp.	2,200
28	Best Buy Co., Inc.	7,217	76	Lexmark International Group	2,158
29	Sun Microsystems, Inc.	7,095	77	Vobis Microcomputer AG	2,131
30	Oki Electric Industry Company, Limited	6,977	78	Entex Information Services	2,100
			79	Solectron Corporation	2,066
31	Olivetti S.p.A.	6,208	80	Bay Networks, Inc.	2,057
32	Unisys Corporation	6,202	81	Novell, Inc.	2,041
33	Kyocera Corporation	5,965	82	Storage Technology Corporation	1,930
34	Merisel, Inc.	5,957	83	Science Applications	1,922
35	Arrow Electronics, Inc.	5,919	84	EMC Corporation	1,921
36	Tandy Corporation	5,839	85	SAP AG	1,887
37	Acer Incorporated	5,530	86	Vanstar Corporation	1,805
38	Compagnie des Machines Bull SA	5,440	87	Tektronix, Inc.	1,769
39	Dell Computer Corporation	5,296	88	ESCOM AG	1,642
40	AMP Incorporated	5,227	89	Racal Electronics PLC	1,617
41	Avnet, Inc.	5,208	90	SOFTBANK CORP.	1,595
42	The ASCII Group Inc.	5,100	91	Varian Associates, Inc.	1,576
43	ICL PLC	4,826	92	Safeguard Scientifics, Inc.	1,546
44	Packard Bell Electronics, Inc.	4,600	93	Amdahl Corporation	1,516
45	Quantum Corporation	4,423	94	AmeriData Technologies, Inc.	1,516
46	Computer Sciences Corporation	4,242	95	CompuCom Systems, Inc.	1,442
47	Andersen Consulting	4,224	96	Stream International Inc.	1,433
48	Oracle Corporation	4,223	97	DSC Communications Corp.	1,422
49	Reuters Holdings PLC	4,188	98	CUC International Inc.	1,415
50	Cisco Systems, Inc.	4,096	99	International Data Group	1,400
			100	Ceridian Corporation	1,333

The 200 Largest Companies by Sales in
Hoover's Guide to Computer Companies (continued)

Rank	Company	Sales ($ mil.)	Rank	Company	Sales ($ mil.)
101	Creative Technology Ltd.	1,308	151	Scitex Corporation Ltd.	729
102	Micro Warehouse, Inc.	1,308	152	PRC Inc.	720
103	Kingston Technology Corporation	1,300	153	VLSI Technology, Inc.	720
104	Lam Research Corporation	1,277	154	CSK Corporation	711
105	LSI Logic Corporation	1,268	155	Informix Corporation	709
106	Anam Group	1,254	156	FIserv, Inc.	703
107	Vishay Intertechnology, Inc.	1,224	157	GE Information Services, Inc.	700
108	Origin B.V.	1,200	158	KLA Instruments Corporation	695
109	TAD Resources International, Inc.	1,200	159	Integrated Device Technology, Inc.	680
110	Teradyne, Inc.	1,191	160	Newbridge Networks Corporation	677
111	Marshall Industries	1,165	161	Cray Research, Inc.	676
112	MagneTek, Inc.	1,162	162	Berg Electronics Corp.	667
113	Data General Corporation	1,159	163	GVC Corporation	663
114	Lotus Development Corporation	1,150	164	Adaptec, Inc.	659
115	Cirrus Logic, Inc.	1,147	165	Shared Medical Systems Corporation	651
116	Advantis	1,130			
117	Pioneer-Standard Electronics, Inc.	1,105	166	Bloomberg L.P.	650
118	Finanziaria per i Sistemi Informativi Elettronici S.p.A.	1,103	167	Tellabs, Inc.	635
			168	Global Directmail Corporation	635
119	Booz, Allen & Hamilton Inc.	1,100	169	Atmel Corporation	634
120	Intergraph Corporation	1,098	170	American Management Systems	632
121	America Online, Inc.	1,094	171	CDW Computer Centers, Inc.	629
122	Wang Laboratories, Inc.	1,090	172	Andrew Corporation	627
123	IPC Corporation	1,089	173	Lexis-Nexis	623
124	Bell Communications Research	1,080	174	Primark Corporation	617
125	Wyle Electronics	1,078	175	Compuware Corporation	614
126	Cabletron Systems, Inc.	1,070	176	Cypress Semiconductor Corporation	596
127	Taiwan Semiconductor Manufacturing Company Ltd.	1,054	177	Anacomp, Inc.	591
128	Read-Rite Corporation	1,003	178	Sterling Software, Inc.	588
129	Micron Electronics, Inc.	1,000	179	Stratus Computer, Inc.	588
130	Nobody beats the Wiz	1,000	180	International Rectifier Corporation	577
131	Future Shop Ltd.	959	181	ASM Lithography Holding NV	572
132	Sybase, Inc.	957	182	Acclaim Entertainment, Inc.	567
133	Ziff-Davis Publishing Company	950	183	Supercom, Inc.	565
134	Analog Devices, Inc.	942	184	Bell Industries, Inc.	564
135	CHS Electronics, Inc.	937	185	Comark, Inc.	563
136	Micro Electronics Inc.	930	186	SAS Institute Inc.	562
137	The Reynolds and Reynolds Co.	911	187	Xilinx, Inc.	561
138	Scribona AB	910	188	Jabil Circuit, Inc.	560
139	Volt Information Sciences, Inc.	907	189	Symbol Technologies, Inc.	555
140	MCI Systemhouse Inc.	893	190	Intuit Inc.	553
141	BDM International, Inc.	890	191	Software AG	552
142	U.S. Robotics Corporation	889	192	Cadence Design Systems, Inc.	548
143	MEMC Electronic Materials, Inc.	887	193	Autodesk, Inc.	547
144	Groupe Sligos	882	194	Sequent Computer Systems, Inc.	540
145	Diebold, Incorporated	863	195	DecisionOne Corporation	540
146	Cap Volmac Group NV	849	196	El Camino Resources, Ltd.	540
147	Memorex Telex N.V.	834	197	Mosel Vitelic Corporation	540
148	Bell & Howell Company	820	198	Policy Management Systems Corp.	537
149	CompuServe Corporation	793	199	SunGard Data Systems Inc.	533
150	Adobe Systems Incorporated	762	200	Electronic Arts Inc.	532

The 200 Largest Companies by Employees in
Hoover's Guide to Computer Companies

Rank	Company	Number of Employees
1	Siemens AG	373,000
2	Hitachi, Ltd.	331,852
3	IBM orporation	225,347
4	Samsung Group	206,407
5	Toshiba Corporation	190,000
6	Fujitsu Limited	164,364
7	NEC Corporation	151,069
8	Motorola, Inc.	142,000
9	Sony Corporation	138,000
10	Hewlett-Packard Company	102,300
11	Electronic Data Systems Corp.	96,000
12	Seagate Technology, Inc.	87,000
13	Xerox Corporation	85,200
14	The General Electric Company PLC	82,967
15	Canon Inc.	72,280
16	Texas Instruments Incorporated	59,574
17	Digital Equipment Corporation	59,100
18	Hyundai Group	50,000
19	Ricoh Company, Ltd.	50,000
20	Tandy Corporation	49,300
21	NCR Corporation	43,000
22	Sharp Corporation	42,883
23	Intel Corporation	41,600
24	AMP Incorporated	40,800
25	Andersen Consulting	38,000
26	Unisys Corporation	37,400
27	TAD Resources International, Inc.	35,000
28	Computer Sciences Corporation	33,850
29	Best Buy Co., Inc.	33,500
30	Olivetti S.p.A.	30,120
31	Volt Information Sciences, Inc.	26,800
32	SGS-Thomson Microelectronics N.V.	25,468
33	ICL PLC	24,000
34	Compagnie des Machines Bull SA	24,000
35	Compaq Computer Corporation	23,884
36	Read-Rite Corporation	23,074
37	National Semiconductor Corp.	22,400
38	Cap Gemini Sogeti S.A.	22,079
39	Oki Electric Industry Company, Inc.	21,718
40	Microsoft Corporation	20,561
41	Science Applications	20,500
42	LG Group	20,000
43	TATUNG Co.	19,491
44	Vishay Intertechnology, Inc.	17,900
45	Apple Computer, Inc.	17,615
46	Sun Microsystems, Inc.	17,400
47	Oracle Corporation	16,882
48	Reuters Holdings PLC	14,348
49	SCI Systems, Inc.	13,185
50	Kyocera Corporation	13,162

Rank	Company	Number of Employees
51	MagneTek, Inc.	13,000
52	Racal Electronics PLC	12,855
53	Advanced Micro Devices, Inc.	12,730
54	Imation Corp.	12,000
55	Solectron Corporation	11,049
56	CUC International Inc.	11,000
57	Serco Group PLC	10,791
58	Applied Materials, Inc.	10,537
59	Ceridian Corporation	10,200
60	Storage Technology Corporation	10,000
61	Origin B.V.	9,772
62	Western Digital Corporation	9,628
63	Avnet, Inc.	9,500
64	Gateway 2000, Inc.	9,300
65	Acer Incorporated	8,800
66	Computer Associates International	8,800
67	International Data Group	8,500
68	Dell Computer Corporation	8,400
69	Intergraph Corporation	8,400
70	Tandem Computers Incorporated	8,380
71	Finanziaria per i Sistemi Informativi Elettronici S.p.A.	8,315
72	FIserv, Inc.	8,222
73	Amdahl Corporation	8,200
74	Micron Technology, Inc.	8,080
75	MacTemps, Inc.	8,000
76	CompUSA Inc.	7,963
77	BDM International, Inc.	7,900
78	Wang Laboratories, Inc.	7,900
79	Anam Group	7,629
80	Tektronix, Inc.	7,619
81	Ingram Micro Inc.	7,604
82	Lexmark International Group, Inc.	7,500
83	Stream International Inc.	7,500
84	Novell, Inc.	7,272
85	NeoStar Retail Group, Inc.	7,100
86	Quantum Corporation	7,036
87	Arrow Electronics, Inc.	7,000
88	Varian Associates, Inc.	6,900
89	SAP AG	6,857
90	PRC Inc.	6,850
91	Booz, Allen & Hamilton Inc.	6,700
92	AST Research, Inc.	6,595
93	MEMC Electronic Materials, Inc.	6,400
94	Groupe Sligos	6,347
95	Silicon Graphics, Inc.	6,300
96	Bell Communications Research Inc.	6,172
97	The Reynolds and Reynolds Co.	6,036
98	Analog Devices, Inc.	6,000
99	Lotus Development Corporation	6,000
100	Bell & Howell Company	5,966

Rank	Company	Number of Employees	Rank	Company	Number of Employees
101	DSC Communications Corporation	5,860	151	AmeriData Technologies, Inc.	3,500
102	America Online, Inc.	5,828	152	CompuServe Corporation	3,500
103	Bay Networks, Inc.	5,758	153	The DII Group, Inc.	3,500
104	DecisionOne Corporation	5,600	154	Scitex Corporation Ltd.	3,500
105	Affiliated Computer Services, Inc.	5,580	155	Esterline Technologies Corporation	3,499
106	Applied Magnetics Corporation	5,500	156	Misys PLC	3,441
107	American Management Systems, Incorporated	5,400	157	Taiwan Semiconductor Manufacturing Company Ltd.	3,412
108	Berg Electronics Corp.	5,400	158	Computer Data Systems, Inc.	3,400
109	Cabletron Systems, Inc.	5,377	159	Newbridge Networks Corporation	3,400
110	CSK Corporation	5,340	160	U.S. Robotics Corporation	3,347
111	Keane, Inc.	5,338	161	Andrew Corporation	3,345
112	Teradyne, Inc.	5,200	162	Software AG	3,327
113	MCI Systemhouse Inc.	5,189	163	Future Shop Ltd.	3,266
114	Diebold, Incorporated	5,178	164	Merisel, Inc.	3,263
115	Primark Corporation	5,131	165	CACI International Inc	3,250
116	Computer Task Group, Inc.	5,014	166	Nashua Corporation	3,234
117	Data General Corporation	5,000	167	Informix Corporation	3,219
118	DST Systems, Inc.	5,000	168	QUALCOMM Incorporated	3,167
119	Entex Information Services	5,000	169	Cirrus Logic, Inc.	3,151
120	Packard Bell Electronics, Inc.	5,000	170	Innodata Corporation	3,100
121	Hutchinson Technology Inc.	4,858	171	Acxiom Corporation	3,098
122	Shared Medical Systems Corp.	4,826	172	3Com Corporation	3,072
123	Policy Management Systems Corp.	4,655	173	Aniie Group PLC	3,064
124	Rand McNally & Company	4,650	174	Cadence Design Systems, Inc.	3,028
125	Cap Volmac Group NV	4,636	175	Advantis	3,000
126	Lam Research Corporation	4,500	176	Micro Warehouse, Inc.	3,000
127	The Cherry Corporation	4,399	177	VLSI Technology, Inc.	3,000
128	SOFTBANK CORP.	4,375	178	Atmel Corporation	2,978
129	Nobody beats the Wiz	4,300	179	Komag, Incorporated	2,915
130	Vanstar Corporation	4,300	180	SunGard Data Systems Inc.	2,900
131	Cray Research, Inc.	4,225	181	Key Tronic Corporation	2,824
132	Creative Technology Ltd.	4,185	182	Tellabs, Inc.	2,814
133	Compuware Corporation	4,105	183	Intuit Inc.	2,732
134	EMC Corporation	4,100	184	National Computer Systems, Inc.	2,700
135	Memorex Telex N.V.	4,100	185	Ziff-Davis Publishing Company	2,700
136	Cisco Systems, Inc.	4,086	186	Jabil Circuit, Inc.	2,661
137	Advanced Semiconductor Materials International N.V.	4,037	187	Silicon Valley Group, Inc.	2,653
138	Sybase, Inc.	4,016	188	Tech Data Corporation	2,625
139	Lexis-Nexis	4,000	189	CompuCom Systems, Inc.	2,615
140	Flextronics International Ltd.	3,994	190	Source Services Corporation	2,600
141	International Rectifier Corporation	3,915	191	Axime SA	2,593
142	LSI Logic Corporation	3,870	192	Intelligent Electronics, Inc.	2,569
143	Elamex S.A. de C.V.	3,865	193	Computer Horizons Corporation	2,511
144	Integrated Device Technology, Inc.	3,828	194	GE Information Services, Inc.	2,500
145	Analysts International Corporation	3,770	195	KLA Instruments Corporation	2,500
146	SEGA Enterprises, Ltd.	3,758	196	Knight-Ridder Business Information Services	2,500
147	Sterling Software, Inc.	3,700	197	Vobis Microcomputer AG	2,500
148	SAS Institute Inc.	3,683	198	ADFlex Solutions, Inc.	2,465
149	Anacomp, Inc.	3,600	199	IEC Electronics Corp.	2,456
150	Safeguard Scientifics, Inc.	3,600	200	Stratus Computer, Inc.	2,441

The 200 Fastest-Growing Companies by Sales in *Hoover's Guide to Computer Companies*

Rank	Company	One-Year Sales Growth % Change	Rank	Company	One-Year Sales Growth % Change
1	Netscape Communications Corp.	11,429	51	International Network Services	185
2	Healthdyne Information	8,600	52	Shiva Corporation	183
3	Siebel Systems, Inc.	7,900	53	Mattson Technology, Inc.	182
4	Xylan Corporation	7,325	54	Level 8 Systems Inc.	181
5	Global Intellicom, Inc.	2,071	55	Vitech America, Inc.	179
6	iSTAR Internet Inc.	1,182	56	C-Cube Microsystems Inc.	177
7	CSG Systems International, Inc.	1,136	57	Hauppauge Digital, Inc.	176
8	Multimedia Games, Inc.	1,121	58	Wired Ventures, Inc.	175
9	Check Point Software Techologies	1,088	59	McAfee Associates, Inc.	174
10	Bull Run Corporation	871	60	Stratasys, Inc.	171
11	Silicon Storage Technology, Inc.	863	61	Graphix Zone, Inc.	171
12	Visioneer, Inc.	856	62	Adaptive Solutions, Inc.	170
13	Elcom International, Inc.	847	63	Cascade Communications Corp.	169
14	VISTA Information Solutions, Inc.	767	64	Novadigm, Inc.	169
15	Viisage Technology, Inc	762	65	Electrostar, Inc.	168
16	Puma Technology, Inc.	756	66	HMT Technology Corporation	167
17	Avant! Corporation	513	67	Quarterdeck Corporation	164
18	Integrated Packaging Assembly	494	68	CHS Electronics, Inc.	161
19	CD-Max, Inc.	436	69	Voice It Worldwide, Inc.	160
20	Visigenic Software, Inc.	409	70	ROSS Technology, Inc.	158
21	IDT Corporation	393	71	Creative Computers, Inc.	157
22	Ameriquest Technologies, Inc.	376	72	DSP Communications, Inc.	156
23	Wiztec Solutions Ltd.	338	73	Netsmart Technologies, Inc.	155
24	Meridian Data, Inc.	329	74	PSINet, Inc.	155
25	NETCOM On-Line Communication Services, Inc.	323	75	GSE Systems, Inc.	154
26	Polyphase Corporation	308	76	EA Industries, Inc.	153
27	SeaChange International, Inc.	307	77	T-HQ, Inc.	150
28	Open Text Corporation	300	78	1st Tech Corporation	150
29	Xeikon N.V.	290	79	Zoran Corporation	148
30	Ascend Communications, Inc.	281	80	Documentum, Inc.	145
31	Micron Electronics, Inc.	276	81	The Vantive Corporation	145
32	Intelligroup, Inc.	262	82	Red Brick Systems, Inc.	142
33	Sykes Enterprises, Inc.	247	83	Eltron International, Inc.	142
34	DecisionOne Corporation	231	84	Pure Atria Corp.	142
35	General Magic, Inc.	230	85	The Sage Group PLC	141
36	Asyst Technologies, Inc.	224	86	GT Interactive Software Corp.	140
37	ESS Technology, Inc.	216	87	Premisys Communications, Inc.	139
38	Network Appliance Corporation	215	88	Oacis Healthcare Holding Corp.	139
39	IMNET Systems, Inc.	213	89	Information Resource Engineering Inc.	138
40	America Online, Inc.	205	90	FastComm Communications	138
41	Centennial Technologies, Inc.	205	91	U.S. Robotics Corporation	135
42	Forte Software, Inc.	200	92	Sapient Corporation	133
43	Starwave Corporation	200	93	Intracorp Entertainment	131
44	7th Level, Inc.	198	94	Logic Works, Inc.	131
45	Allied Digital Technologies Corp.	193	95	Iomega Corporation	131
46	Spyglass, Inc.	189	96	Diamond Multimedia Systems	130
47	ISG International Software Group Ltd.	189	97	Workgroup Technology Corporation	128
48	PLATINUM technology, Inc.	188	98	Pen Interconnect, Inc.	127
49	4Front Software International	188	99	S3 Incorporated	125
50	SQA, Inc.	187	100	i2 Technologies, Inc.	125

The 200 Fastest-Growing Companies by Sales in
Hoover's Guide to Computer Companies (continued)

Rank	Company	One-Year Sales Growth % Change		Rank	Company	One-Year Sales Growth % Change
101	MRV Communications, Inc.	124		151	Avid Technology, Inc.	100
102	Oak Technology, Inc.	123		152	CBT Group PLC	98
103	SoftNet Systems, Inc.	122		153	Dickens Data Systems, Inc.	98
104	Cambridge Technology Partners	122		154	StorMedia, Inc.	97
105	Precision Systems, Inc.	122		155	Raster Graphics, Inc.	97
106	FORE Systems, Inc.	121		156	Infinity Financial Technology, Inc.	96
107	EPIC Design Technology, Inc.	121		157	Applied Science and	
108	Open Environment Corporation	121			Technology, Inc.	96
109	Arbor Software Corporation	118		158	Datastream Systems, Inc.	95
110	Macromedia, Inc.	117		159	Engineering Animation, Inc.	95
111	Prism Solutions, Inc.	117		160	Sync Research, Inc.	95
112	Pixar	116		161	Hummingbird Communications Ltd.	95
113	Centon Electronics, Inc.	115		162	Cerion Technologies, Inc.	93
114	PowerCerv Corporation	115		163	Verity, Inc.	93
115	Computer Integration Corp.	115		164	Natural MicroSystems Corp.	93
116	SubMicron Systems Corp.	115		165	Atria Software, Inc.	93
117	OnTrak Systems, Inc.	115		166	Security Dynamics	
118	Merkantildata AS	114			Technologies, Inc.	92
119	E*TRADE Group, Inc.	114		167	Edify Corporation	90
120	Multiple Zones International, Inc.	114		168	Brooks Automation, Inc.	90
121	Alpha Technologies Group, Inc.	113		169	Better Online Solutions Ltd.	90
122	Simple Technology Inc.	113		170	Mosel Vitelic Corporation	89
123	Astea International, Inc.	111		171	Cable Design Technologies Corp.	89
124	Intevac, Inc.	109		172	Seagate Technology, Inc.	89
125	Integrated Process Equipment	109		173	ASE Test Limited	89
126	Semitool, Inc.	107		174	Flextronics International Ltd.	89
127	Cisco Systems, Inc.	107		175	Krystaltech International Inc.	89
128	Align-Rite International, Inc.	107		176	Madge Networks N.V.	88
129	Helisys, Inc.	105		177	SoftQuad International, Inc.	88
130	Clarify, Inc.	105		178	DataWorks Corporation	88
131	Physician Computer Network, Inc.	104		179	FEI Company	87
132	NetManage, Inc.	104		180	Scopus Technology, Inc.	87
133	Rimage Corporation	104		181	ASM Lithography Holding NV	86
134	Byron Preiss Multimedia			182	Splash Technology Holdings, Inc.	86
	Company, Inc.	103		183	INCOMNET, Inc.	85
135	Plasma & Materials			184	INSO Corporation	85
	Technologies, Inc.	103		185	Applied Materials, Inc.	84
136	Integrated Silicon Solution, Inc.	103		186	Hambrecht & Quist LLP	84
137	id Software, Inc.	103		187	Cerprobe Corporation	83
138	FSI International, Inc.	103		188	Advanced Energy Industries, Inc.	82
139	Remedy Corporation	103		189	Aetrium Inc.	82
140	SS&C Technologies, Inc.	102		190	Data Dimensions, Inc.	82
141	Altera Corporation	102		191	Multicom Publishing, Inc.	82
142	PeopleSoft, Inc.	102		192	Sigma Circuits, Inc.	82
143	OMNI MultiMedia Group, Inc.	101		193	En Pointe Technologies, Inc.	82
144	SpeedFam International, Inc.	101		194	VERTEQ, Inc.	82
145	Business Objects S.A.	101		195	Legato Systems, Inc.	82
146	Databeam, Inc.	100		196	Opal, Inc.	82
147	Individual, Inc.	100		197	Cap Volmac Group NV	82
148	Multi-Media Tutorial Service	100		198	Tencor Instruments	81
149	Sarcom Inc.	100		199	VideoServer, Inc.	81
150	TriTeal Corporation	100		200	Global Village Communication, Inc.	81

The 200 Fastest Growing Companies by Employees in
Hoover's Guide to Computer Companies

Rank	Company	One-Year Emp. Growth % Change	Rank	Company	One-Year Emp. Growth % Change
1	SoftNet Systems, Inc.	1,653	51	ExecuTrain Corporation	96
2	Netscape Communications		52	Tridex Corporation	95
	Corporation	611	53	McAfee Associates, Inc.	95
3	Infoseek Corporation	545	54	M.A.I.D plc	95
4	Physician Computer Network	385	55	N2K Inc.	93
5	SOFTBANK CORP.	381	56	Information Resource	
6	SportsLine USA, Inc.	380		Engineering Inc.	91
7	Polyphase Corporation	365	57	Avid Technology, Inc.	90
8	Electronic Designs Inc.	338	58	InTime Systems International	89
9	PNY Electronics, Inc.	275	59	Logistix	89
10	Edify Corporation	246	60	New Image Industries Inc.	88
11	NETCOM On-Line		61	Iomega Corporation	88
	Communication Services, Inc.	227	62	Natural MicroSystems	
12	VISTA Information Solutions	209		Corporation	87
13	Wired Ventures, Inc.	184	63	Datastream Systems, Inc.	85
14	PSINet, Inc.	183	64	Global Village Communication	84
15	Shiva Corporation	183	65	Micro Electronics Inc.	84
16	Mattson Technology, Inc.	178	66	National TechTeam, Inc.	82
17	Simple Technology Inc.	177	67	Cascade Communications Corp.	82
18	Starwave Corporation	176	68	Attachmate Corporation	82
19	Diamond Multimedia Systems	176	69	C-Cube Microsystems Inc.	81
20	FORE Systems, Inc.	174	70	Future Shop Ltd.	80
21	Acclaim Entertainment, Inc.	171	71	CKS Group, Inc.	80
22	Quarterdeck Corporation	169	72	VMARK Software, Inc.	79
23	Ascend Communications, Inc.	164	73	Expert Software, Inc.	77
24	Asyst Technologies, Inc.	164	74	SyQuest Technology, Inc.	76
25	Eltron International, Inc.	163	75	Fulcrum Technologies Inc.	76
26	7th Level, Inc.	157	76	Jabil Circuit, Inc.	76
27	MRV Communications, Inc.	156	77	Data Broadcasting Corporation	75
28	Protosource Corporation	150	78	Sterling Information Group	75
29	Aspen Technology, Inc.	149	79	Rimage Corporation	74
30	Camelot Corporation	141	80	Viking Components	74
31	Scangraphics, Inc.	139	81	OnTrak Systems, Inc.	74
32	America Online, Inc.	135	82	Applix, Inc.	73
33	The Panda Project, Inc.	132	83	Rainbow Technologies, Inc.	73
34	U.S. Robotics Corporation	131	84	INCOMNET, Inc.	72
35	4Front Software International	130	85	SoftKey International Inc.	72
36	Alpharel, Inc.	127	86	Misys PLC	72
37	Intuit Inc.	122	87	ACT Networks, Inc.	72
38	SubMicron Systems Corporation	122	88	Gateway 2000, Inc.	71
39	Intelligent Electronics, Inc.	121	89	Wave Technologies	
40	Allied Digital Technologies Corp.	119		International, Inc.	71
41	Hummingbird Communications	118	90	Brooks Automation, Inc.	69
42	Madge Networks N.V.	110	91	Activision, Inc.	69
43	Semitool, Inc.	110	92	Solectron Corporation	68
44	PeopleSoft, Inc.	106	93	Alliance Semiconductor	
45	The Sage Group PLC	105		Corporation	68
46	Affiliated Computer Services, Inc.	99	94	All American Semiconductor	68
47	Xpedite Systems, Inc.	98	95	Cree Research, Inc.	68
48	MICROS Systems, Inc.	97	96	Acxiom Corporation	67
49	Plasma & Materials		97	Cisco Systems, Inc.	67
	Technologies, Inc.	97	98	Cerprobe Corporation	67
50	Cambridge Technology		99	QUALCOMM Incorporated	67
	Partners, Inc.	97	100	AmeriData Technologies, Inc.	67

The 200 Fastest Growing Companies by Employees in
Hoover's Guide to Computer Companies (continued)

Rank	Company	One-Year Emp. Growth % Change	Rank	Company	One-Year Emp. Growth % Change
101	Ma Laboratories	67	151	Irvine Sensors Corporation	51
102	ViewSonic Corporation	67	152	HCIA Inc.	51
103	Xircom, Inc.	67	153	Mustang Software, Inc.	51
104	Integrated Process Equipment Corporation	66	154	KLA Instruments Corporation	51
105	Compaq Computer Corporation	66	155	Macromedia, Inc.	51
			156	Tseng Labs, Inc.	51
106	Atria Software, Inc.	66	157	S3 Incorporated	51
107	Daktronics, Inc.	65	158	Lexmark International Group, Inc.	50
108	Seagate Technology, Inc.	64	159	Pervasive Software Inc.	50
109	Navarre Corporation	64	160	Stratasys, Inc.	50
110	Business Objects S.A.	64			
111	Mecklermedia Corporation	63	161	SystemSoft Corporation	50
112	Datatrend Services, Inc.	63	162	Bay Networks, Inc.	50
113	Applied Materials, Inc.	62	163	Nichols Research Corporation	49
114	Baan Company N.V.	62	164	FSI International, Inc.	49
115	Photronics, Inc.	61	165	INSO Corporation	49
116	EPIC Design Technology, Inc.	61	166	Novellus Systems Inc	49
117	ESS Technology, Inc.	60	167	Micron Technology, Inc.	48
118	Silicon Valley Group, Inc.	60	168	Sigma Circuits, Inc.	48
119	SI Diamond Technology, Inc.	59	169	Information Storage Devices	47
120	Advanced Technology Materials	59	170	Trident Microsystems, Inc.	47
121	SpeedFam International, Inc.	58	171	Amdahl Corporation	46
122	Softdesk, Inc.	58	172	Adobe Systems Incorporated	46
123	ScanSource, Inc.	58	173	Delphi Group PLC	46
124	IMNET Systems, Inc.	57	174	Boca Research, Inc.	46
125	RWD Technologies, Inc.	57	175	BTG, Inc.	46
126	Individual, Inc.	57	176	Informix Corporation	46
127	Peak Technologies Group, Inc.	57	177	TSR, Inc.	46
128	Corel Corporation	56	178	Interactive Group, Inc.	45
129	Atmel Corporation	56	179	Kingston Technology Corporation	45
130	FTP Software, Inc.	56	180	Micro-Integration Corp.	45
131	Merkantildata AS	56			
132	Renaissance Solutions, Inc.	55	181	Silicon Graphics, Inc.	45
133	VisionTek Inc.	55	182	Rocket Science Games Inc.	44
134	GaSonics International Corporation	55	183	Avant! Corporation	44
135	Micros-to-Mainframes, Inc.	55	184	Microdyne Corporation	43
			185	CBT Group PLC	43
136	Technology Solutions Company	54	186	Entex Information Services	43
137	Pinnacle Micro, Inc.	54	187	Micrion Corporation	43
138	Objective Systems Integrators	54	188	Exar Corporation	42
139	EA Industries, Inc.	54	189	MapInfo Corporation	42
140	International Microcomputer Software, Inc.	53	190	J.D. Edwards & Company	42
141	Ariel Corporation	53	191	Claremont Technology Group, Inc.	41
142	Parametric Technology Corporation	53	192	Aladdin Knowledge Systems Ltd.	41
143	Kulicke and Soffa Industries	53	193	Digi International Inc.	41
144	Open Environment Corporation	53	194	JetForm Corporation	41
145	Symantec Corporation	53	195	Credence Systems Corporation	41
146	CIBER, Inc.	52	196	XcelleNet, Inc.	40
147	SigmaTron International, Inc.	52	197	Amstrad plc	40
148	Zoom Telephonics, Inc.	52	198	Oracle Corporation	40
149	Spyglass, Inc.	52	199	CompuServe Corporation	40
150	Pomeroy Computer Resources	52	200	Maxis, Inc.	40
			201	TENERA, Inc.	40

The *Upside* 200

Rank	Company	Headquarters	Value Created 1995 ($ mil.)	Market Value 1995 ($ mil.)
1	AT&T Corp.	New York, NY	22,750.6	101,593.1
2	Intel Corp.	Santa Clara, CA	20,495.5	46,875.0
3	Hewlett-Packard Co.	Palo Alto, CA	17,232.9	42,683.5
4	Bellsouth Corp.	Atlanta, GA	16,314.5	43,173.1
5	Microsoft Corp.	Redmond, WA	15,469.1	50,982.8
6	GTE Corp.	Atlanta, GA	13,028.6	42,343.1
7	Intl. Business Machines Corp.	Armonk, NY	10,505.3	53,702.0
8	SBC Communications Inc.	San Antonio, TX	10,278.3	34,869.9
9	Ameritech Corp.	Chicago, IL	10,202.0	32,467.3
10	Cisco Systems Inc.	San Jose, CA	10,179.0	19,230.6
11	Bell Atlantic Corp.	Philadelphia, PA	7,469.7	29,169.9
12	Nynex Corp.	New York, NY	7,307.0	22,874.2
13	Electronic Data Systems Corp.	Plano, TX	6,563.2	25,048.4
14	Computer Associates Intl. Corp.	Islandia, NY	5,895.2	13,661.8
15	Oracle Systems Corp.	Redwood City, CA	5,615.4	18,363.5
16	MCI Communications	Washington, DC	5,270.0	17,765.0
17	Sun Microsystems Inc.	Mountain View, CA	5,232.2	8,563.9
18	Ericsson North America Inc.	New York, NY	4,969.3	16,943.9
19	Digital Equipment Corp.	Maynard, MA	4,393.1	9,124.2
20	Sprint Corp.	Westwood, KS	4,179.6	13,801.4
21	Micron Technology Inc.	Boise, ID	3,579.3	8,075.6
22	Ascend Communications Inc.	Alameda, CA	3,395.0	3,882.6
23	Applied Materials Inc.	Santa Clara, CA	3,069.8	6,623.2
24	3COM Corp.	Santa Clara, CA	2,886.1	6,455.8
25	Texas Instruments Inc.	Dallas, TX	2,606.8	9,546.3
26	Worldcom Inc.	Jackson, MS	2,524.4	5,627.4
27	Cabletron Systems Inc.	Rochester, NH	2,465.7	5,789.0
28	Compaq Computer Corp.	Houston, TX	2,218.8	12,529.8
29	Automatic Data Processing Inc.	Roseland, NJ	2,216.0	10,446.9
30	Pacific Telesis Group	San Francisco, CA	2,120.3	14,206.2
31	First Data Corp.	Hackensack, NJ	2,099.0	7,198.6
32	Bay Networks Inc.	Santa Clara, CA	1,988.9	3,811.8
33	Adobe Systems Inc.	San Jose, CA	1,972.1	3,791.3
34	Informix Corp.	Menlo Park, CA	1,825.2	3,928.4
35	Parametric Technology Corp.	Waltham, MA	1,821.3	3,785.0
36	Tele-Communications Inc.	Englewood, CO	1,782.2	14,311.6
37	Intuit Inc.	Menlo Park, CA	1,716.8	3,000.8
38	Seagate Technology Inc.	Scotts Valley, CA	1,711.6	3,459.5
39	C-Cube Microsystems Inc.	Milpitas, CA	1,632.0	1,924.5
40	Cadence Design Systems Inc.	San Jose, CA	1,606.3	2,388.2
41	U.S. Robotics Corp.	Skokie, IL	1,563.9	2,075.3
42	Cascade Communications Corp.	Westford, MA	1,476.9	2,315.6
43	LSI Logic corp.	Milpitas, CA	1,435.8	3,742.9
44	Stratacom Inc.	San Jose, CA	1,365.6	2,607.0
45	Glenayre Technologies Inc.	Charlotte, NC	1,365.6	2,323.6
46	America Online Inc.	Vienna, VA	1,362.1	2,173.5
47	HBO & Co.	Atlanta, GA	1,342.4	2,434.6
48	MFS Communications Inc.	Omaha, NE	1,315.1	3,416.1
49	Altera Corp.	San Jose, CA	1,238.3	2,138.1
50	Macromedia Inc.	San Francisco, CA	1,224.5	1,619.8

The *Upside* 200 (continued)

Rank	Company	Headquarters	Value Created 1995 ($ mil.)	Market Value 1995 ($ mil.)
51	Maxim Integrated Products Inc.	Sunnyvale, CA	1,204.3	2,207.9
52	Cincinnati Bell Inc.	Cincinnati, OH	1,170.6	2,291.7
53	Peoplesoft Inc.	Pleasanton, CA	1,155.8	2,060.1
54	Adtran Inc.	Huntsville, AL	1,136.4	1,963.3
55	Dell Computer Corp.	Austin, TX	1,121.0	2,747.8
56	Computer Sciences Corp.	El Segundo, CA	1,062.0	3,875.8
57	Linear Technology Corp.	Milpitas, CA	1,052.9	2,850.2
58	Madge Networks NV	Hoofddorp, CA	1,005.8	1,366.5
59	Qualcomm Inc.	San Diego, CA	978.2	2,213.9
60	Picturetel Corp.	Danvers, MA	956.1	1,324.7
61	Analog Devices Inc	Norwood, MA	899.9	2,662.0
62	Adaptec Inc.	Milpitas, CA	897.9	2,118.8
63	Total System Services Inc.	Columbus, GA	864.4	1,971.2
64	Iomega Corp.	Roy, UT	840.3	900.5
65	Tellabs Inc.	Lisle, IL	796.5	3,229.7
66	Xilinx Inc.	San Jose, CA	754.9	2,141.9
67	Paging Network Inc.	Plano, TX	747.9	2,471.8
68	BMC Software Inc.	Houston, TX	722.8	2,158.9
69	Electronics For Imaging Inc.	San Mateo, CA	719.3	1,049.0
70	Structural Dynamics Research Corp.	Milford, OH	693.5	848.8
71	ECI Telecom Ltd.	Petah Tikva, Israel	692.0	1,718.3
72	Solectron Corp.	Milpitas, CA	686.6	1,822.5
73	Fore Systems Inc.	Warrendale, PA	668.2	1,544.1
74	Ceridian Corp.	Minneapolis, MN	652.7	1,872.8
75	Frontier Corp.	Rochester, NY	649.3	2,194.8
76	ADC Telecommunications Inc	Minneapolis, MN	641.4	2,035.8
77	Conner Peripherals Inc	San Jose, CA	603.3	1,101.7
78	Comcast Corp.	Philadelphia, PA	597.6	4,347.4
79	Teradyne Inc.	Boston, MA	595.3	1,826.7
80	Synopsys Inc.	Mountain View, CA	576.1	1,357.6
81	EG&G Inc.	Wellesley, MA	558.1	1,336.8
82	Computervision Corp.	Bedford, MA	550.7	738.3
83	Gandalf Technologies Inc.	Nepean, NJ	550.6	599.0
84	Safeguard Scientifics Inc.	Wayne, PA	540.6	704.2
85	McAfee Associates Inc.	Santa Clara, CA	532.0	768.4
86	Sterling Software Inc.	Dallas, TX	527.5	1,284.0
87	Intl. Rectifier Corp.	El Segundo, CA	524.1	1,017.6
88	Cirrus Logic Inc.	Fremont, CA	515.0	1,196.7
89	Pairgain Technologies Inc.	Tustin, CA	514.7	695.8
90	Atmel Corp.	San Jose, CA	510.5	2,030.8
91	Security Dynamics Tech. Inc.	Cambridge, MA	504.1	608.0
92	Shared Medical Systems Corp.	Malvern, PA	496.1	1,247.5
93	Quarterdeck Corp.	Marina del Rey, CA	487.7	550.3
94	Cheyenne Software Corp.	Roslyn Heights, NY	480.0	1,013.3
95	Harris Corp.	Melbourne, FL	476.5	2,146.7
96	Advanced Semiconduct. Materials	Bilthoven, The Netherlands	471.7	520.6
97	Cambridge Technology Partners Inc.	Cambridge, MA	468.7	764.5
98	Tektronix Inc.	Wilsonville, OR	467.7	1,544.4
99	Komag Inc.	Milpitas, CA	458.0	1,056.3
100	System Software Associates Inc.	Chicago, IL	455.5	880.7

The *Upside* 200 (continued)

Rank	Company	Headquarters	Value Created 1995 ($ mil.)	Market Value 1995 ($ mil.)
101	American Mobile Satellite Corp.	Reston, VA	443.3	759.5
102	Diebold Inc.	North Canton, OH	434.1	1,686.7
103	BBN Corp.	Cambridge, MA	432.0	676.8
104	LCI Intl. Inc.	McLean, VA	422.4	1,215.4
105	Comdisco Inc.	Rosemont, IL	396.8	1,245.4
106	Cognos Inc.	Ottawa, MA	359.6	599.9
107	S3 Inc.	Santa Clara, CA	355.4	642.5
108	Electronic Arts Inc.	San Mateo, CA	349.7	1,328.8
109	Atria Software Inc.	Lexington, MA	347.6	549.5
110	Sungard Data Systems Inc.	Wayne, PA	347.2	1,069.7
111	Intergraph Corp.	Huntsville, AL	341.5	705.4
112	Aspect Telecommunications Corp.	San Jose, CA	340.5	680.9
113	Applied Magnetics Corp.	Goleta, CA	333.8	411.0
114	Fiserv Inc.	Brookfield, WI	332.8	1,174.7
115	Shiva Corp.	Bedford, MA	329.8	729.8
116	Arrow Electronics Inc.	Melville, NY	328.9	1,985.2
117	National SemiconductoerCorp.	Santa Clara, CA	322.4	2,717.0
118	Mitel Corp.	Kanata, Ontario	317.3	687.6
119	Avnet Inc.	Great Neck, NY	315.1	1,819.5
120	Medic Computer Systems, Inc.	Raleigh, NC	313.4	642.7
121	Kent Electronics Corp.	Houston, TX	313.3	572.4
122	C Tec Corp.	Princeton, NJ	305.3	850.8
123	Acxiom Corp.	Conway, AR	302.7	613.8
124	Excalibur Technologies Corp.	Vienna, VA	301.7	358.2
125	Lattice Semiconductor Corp.	Hillsboro, OR	299.9	616.3
126	Microchip Technology Inc.	Chandler, AZ	299.7	1,215.6
127	CompUSA Inc.	Dallas, TX	297.5	574.3
128	Vicor Corp	Andover, MA	296.0	830.9
129	Inso Corp.	Boston, MA	289.9	494.1
130	Borland Intl. Inc.	Scotts Valley, CA	284.3	452.2
131	American Management Systems Inc.	Fairfax, VA	281.6	785.9
132	Octel Communications Corp.	Milpitas, CA	278.0	779.5
133	Broderbund Software Inc.	Novato, CA	274.7	1,192.2
134	Auspex Systems Inc.	Santa Clara, CA	263.3	417.9
135	Computer Horizons Corp.	Mountain Lakes, NJ	258.9	339.3
136	Newbridge Networks Corp.	Kanata, VA	257.1	3,403.4
137	Clearnet Communications Inc.	Pickering, Ontario	249.7	491.7
138	Siliconix Inc.	Santa Clara, CA	245.3	368.5
139	GRC Intl. Inc.	Vienna, VA	243.3	345.8
140	GTech Holdings Corp.	West Greenwich, RI	243.3	1,124.4
141	Hummingbird Communications Ltd.	North York, CA	240.3	483.5
142	Veritas Software Co.	Mountain View, CA	239.9	311.6
143	Burr-Brown Corp.	Tucson, AZ	236.8	366.0
144	Stac Inc.	San Diego, CA	232.1	360.8
145	Progress Software Corp.	Bedford, MA	230.1	463.4
146	Cray Research Inc.	Eagan, MN	229.2	627.2
147	VLSI Technology Inc.	San Jose, CA	224.7	664.9
148	Symbol Technologies Inc.	Holtsville, NY	221.8	1,016.0
149	Filenet Corp.	Costa Mesa, CA	221.7	520.9
150	Dialogic Corp.	Parsippany, NJ	220.6	566.3

The *Upside* 200 (continued)

Rank	Company	Headquarters	Value Created 1995 ($ mil.)	Market Value 1995 ($ mil.)
151	Alantec Corp.	San Jose, CA	218.6	485.0
152	Compucom Systems Inc.	Dallas, TX	214.8	320.1
153	Symantec Corp.	Cupertino, CA	213.8	864.3
154	Read-Rite Corp.	Milpitas, CA	211.3	1,047.9
155	Kulicke & Soffa Industries Inc.	Willow Grove, PA	210.3	383.6
156	Gateway 2000 Inc.	North Sioux City, SD	208.1	1,773.7
157	Wang Laboratories Inc.	Billerica, MA	207.9	531.7
158	Park Electrochemical Corp.	Lake Success, NY	207.4	377.7
159	Project Software & Dev. Inc.	Cambridge, MA	200.6	275.7
160	PC DOCS Group Intl. Inc.	Toronto, Ontario	200.0	215.1
161	Lam Research Corp.	Fremont, CA	200.0	1,076.4
162	Sanmina Corp.	San Jose, CA	197.1	415.3
163	Davidson & Associates Inc.	Torrance, CA	196.8	752.9
164	Rational Software Corp.	Santa Clara, CA	193.3	280.2
165	Integrated Systems Inc.	Sunnyvale, CA	192.3	370.3
166	Sierra On-Line Inc.	Bellevue, WA	191.7	474.0
167	Wyle Electronics	Irvine, CA	190.5	428.3
168	Checkpoint Systems Inc.	Thorofare, NJ	190.0	391.7
169	Heartland Wireless Com. Inc.	Richardson, TX	188.9	330.5
170	Wind River Systems Inc.	Alameda, CA	186.7	265.2
171	Hadco Corp.	Salem, NH	186.2	273.9
172	Applix Inc.	Westborough, MA	184.1	241.8
173	Control Data Systems Inc.	Arden Hills, MN	176.0	270.9
174	Henry (Jack) & Associates	Monett, MO	175.1	288.9
175	Continuum Inc.	Austin, TX	172.2	755.6
176	Flextronics Intl. Ltd.	Singapore	171.1	348.1
177	Optical Data Systems Inc.	Richardson, TX	169.3	400.0
178	Logicon Inc.	Torrance, CA	168.8	371.4
179	Network General Corp.	Menlo Park, CA	167.8	728.6
180	Affiliated Computer Services Inc.	Dallas, TX	166.4	390.0
181	Computer Products Inc.	Boca Raton, FL	165.0	233.5
182	Microcom Inc.	Norwood, MA	162.4	288.8
183	Comverse Technology Inc.	Woodbury, NY	161.7	398.1
184	Itron Inc.	Spokane, WA	161.2	402.9
185	IMP Inc.	San Jose, CA	160.1	204.9
186	Mentor Graphics Corp.	Wilsonville, OR	154.1	937.1
187	Physician Computer Network Inc.	Morris Plains, NJ	153.8	307.6
188	Coherent Communications Sys. Corp.	Leesburg, VA	152.9	264.6
189	Global Village Communications Inc.	Sunnyvale, CA	151.7	286.8
190	Health Management Systems Inc.	New York, NY	148.9	344.9
191	Verifone Inc.	Redwood City, CA	147.7	663.4
192	Boca Research Inc.	Boca Raton, FL	147.4	223.3
193	Identix Inc.	Sunnyvale, CA	146.8	206.6
194	TCA Cable TV Inc.	Tyler, TX	144.4	678.8
195	Trident Microsystems Inc.	Mountain View, CA	141.9	272.2
196	Tencor Instruments	Mountain View, CA	140.7	669.2
197	Telxon Corp.	Akron, OH	138.7	353.5
198	Geoworks	Alameda, CA	137.9	213.9
199	Electroglas Inc.	Santa Clara, CA	136.3	427.3
200	Aliant Communications, Inc.	Lincoln, NE	133.4	683.4

Source: *Upside*, May 1996

The *DATAMATION* Global 100

Rank	Company	1995 Information Technology Revenue ($ mil.)	Rank	Company	1995 Information Technology Revenue ($ mil.)
1	IBM	71,940	51	SAP	1,887
2	Fujitsu	26,798	52	Entex Information Services	1,785
3	Hewlett-Packard	26,073	53	Bay Networks	1,700
4	NEC	19,350	54	Amdahl	1,516
5	Hitachi	16,208	55	Lexmark	1,478
6	Compaq Computer	14,800	56	SAIC	1,401
7	Digital Equipment	14,440	57	Samsung	1,400
8	Electronic Data Systems	12,422	58	Texas Instruments	1,313
9	AT&T*	11,384	59	Kingston Technology	1,300
10	Toshiba	11,380	60	Coopers & Lybrand	1,260
11	Apple Computer	11,378	61	Maxtor	1,230
12	Siemens Nixdorf	8,951	62	Data General	1,205
13	Seagate Technology	8,200	63	Stream International	1,200
14	Microsoft	7,418	64	Alcatel Business Systems	1,156
15	Matsushita	7,026	65	LM Ericsson	1,107
16	Sun Microsystems	6,500	66	Finsiel	1,103
17	Unisys	6,202	67	Cabletron Systems	1,100
18	Olivetti	6,035	68	Intergraph	1,098
19	Acer	5,700	69	Wang Laboratories	1,095
20	Canon	5,616	70	US Robotics	1,092
21	Groupe Bull	5,300	71	Sema Group	1,067
22	Dell Computer	5,296	72	Mitac	1,062
23	NTT Data	5,287	73	General Electric	1,050
24	Xerox	4,668	74	Nomura	1,042
25	Packard Bell	4,300	75	Tatung	1,032
26	Andersen Consulting	4,220	76	MCI	992
27	Quantum	4,174	77	Memorex Telex	981
28	Mitsubishi	4,145	78	Sybase	957
29	Computer Sciences	4,100	79	ALLTEL	927
30	Cap Gemini Sogeti	3,785	80	Price Waterhouse	880
31	Gateway 2000	3,676	81	Sony	847
32	Intel	3,240	82	British Telecom	838
33	Computer Associates	3,196	83	Micron Electronics	833
34	Automatic Data Processing	3,157	84	Sligos	778
35	Oki	3,071	85	Adobe Systems	762
36	Motorola	2,974	86	First Int'l Computer	725
37	Oracle	2,707	87	Informix Software	714
38	Cisco Systems	2,668	88	FiServ	703
39	Silicon Graphics	2,541	89	Cray Research	676
40	AST Research	2,349	90	Comparex	670
41	Western Digital	2,430	91	Ceridian	667
42	KPMG Peat Marwick	2,300	92	Ernst & Young	653
43	Tandem	2,285	93	Shared Medical Systems	651
44	Lockheed Martin	2,057	94	PRC	648
45	Novell	2,040	95	Newbridge Networks	641
46	Seiko Epson	2,026	96	Intec	637
47	Ricoh	1,966	97	AMS	632
48	3Com	1,963	98	Sterling Software	610
49	Storage Technology	1,929	99	Racal Electronics	604
50	EMC	1,921	100	Deloitte & Touche	600

* AT&T revenue includes NCR and Lucent Technologies
Source: *DATAMATION*; June 15, 1996

Software Magazine's Top 100 Independent Software Venders

Rank	Company	1995 Worldwide Sales ($ mil.)	Rank	Company	1995 Worldwide Sales ($ mil.)
1	Microsoft Corp.	7,271.0	51	Softlab Inc.*	74.0
2	Computer Associates International Inc.	3,196.0	52	Netscape Communications	73.2
			53	Lawson Software*	69.5
3	Oracle Corp.	2,558.0	54	Rational Software Corp.	68.6
4	Novell Inc.	1,900.0	55	Interleaf Inc.	68.1
5	SAP AG	1,350.0			
6	Sybase Inc.	786.1	56	Ross Systems Inc.	64.6
7	Adobe Systems Inc.	762.3	57	Micrografx Inc.	64.5
8	Informix Software Inc.	536.0	58	Seer Technologies Inc.	60.8
9	SAS Institute Inc.*	534.3	59	SPSS Inc.	56.8
10	Symantec Corp.	437.8	60	Business Objects S.A.	56.1
11	BMC Software Inc.	396.9	61	Hummingbird Communications Ltd.	54.3
12	Sterling Software Inc.	390.0	62	VMark Software Inc.	53.9
13	Compuware Corp.	388.7	63	Systems Union Group Ltd.*	49.4
14	Software AG*	376.0	64	Software 2000 Inc.	48.7
15	Attachmate Corp.*	347.0	65	Thomson Software Products*	48.2
16	Dun & Bradstreet Software*	285.0	66	Insignia Solutions Plc.	47.9
17	System Software Associates	280.3	67	Landmark Systems Corp.*	46.9
18	J.D. Edwards & Co.*	236.6	68	Visual Edge Software Ltd.*	45.5
19	Platinum Technology Inc.	230.4	69	Apertus Technologies Inc.	44.2
20	Candle Corp.*	230.3	70	American Software Inc.	44.1
21	Information Builders Inc.*	225.0	71	Synon Corp.*	43.9
22	PeopleSoft Inc.	211.0	72	Computron Software Inc.	43.5
23	Borland International Inc.	208.0	73	Inso Corp.	43.4
24	Claris Corp.*	183.8	74	Tivoli Systems Inc.	43.3
25	The Santa Cruz Operation Inc.	178.1	75	Pure Software Inc.	43.3
26	Progress Software Corp.	168.4	76	Caere Corp.	41.7
27	Cheyenne Software Inc.	157.6	77	Antares Alliance Group*	40.8
28	Cincom Systems Inc.*	157.0	78	PC Docs Group International	40.5
29	Boole & Babbage Inc.	150.4	79	Manugistics Group Inc.	40.0
30	Intersolv Inc.	138.7	80	Macro 4 Plc.	39.9
31	Intentia International*	137.0	81	Project Software & Development	39.6
32	The Baan Co. N.V.	131.8	82	Group 1 Software Inc.	39.6
33	Cognos Inc.	131.3	83	BGS Systems Inc.	39.4
34	FileNet Corp.	127.0	84	Platinum Software Corp.	39.0
35	NetManage Inc.	125.4	85	The Coda Group Plc.	38.9
36	FTP Software Inc.	123.0	86	Wind River Systems Inc.	38.6
37	Hyperion Software Corp.	122.1	87	Mercury Interactive Corp.	37.5
38	McDonnell Information Systems Group Plc.	122.0	88	InterSystems Corp.*	37.4
39	Banyan Systems Inc.	118.4	89	Atria Software Inc.	36.2
40	Micro Focus Group Plc.	114.2	90	New Dimension Software Ltd.	35.7
41	WRQ Inc.*	111.6	91	Cadre Technologies Inc.*	35.6
42	Wall Data Inc.	110.7	92	Programart Corp.*	33.6
43	Marcam Corp.	100.8	93	LBMS Plc.	33.6
44	Tibco Inc.*	95.0	94	Walker Interactive Systems	33.6
45	Macromedia Inc.	95.0	95	Cyborg Systems Inc.*	33.2
46	Software Engineering of America*	94.6	96	Object Design Inc.*	32.0
47	Comshare Inc.	94.1	97	Symix Systems Inc.	31.6
48	Quarterdeck Corp.	93.0	98	CheckPoint Software Technologies Ltd.*	31.0
49	McAfee Associates Inc.	90.1	99	Remedy Corp.	30.4
50	JBA Holdings Plc.	76.7	100	Consilium Inc.	30.3

* Indicates Private Company
Source: *Software Magazine*, July 1996

Computer Retail Week's Top 100 Computer Retailers

Rank	Company	Estimated Sales ($ mil.)	Rank	Company	Estimated Sales ($ mil.)
1	CompUSA	3,235.0	51	Computer Expo	40.0
2	Best Buy	2,771.0	52	Navy Resale & Services	39.9
3	Computer City SuperCenters	1,750.0	53	Specialty Retail Group*	39.0
4	Office Depot	1,600.0	54	Soundtrack/Ultimate	38.9
5	Circuit City Stores	1,570.0	55	RCS	38.2
6	Micro Center	930.0	56	Software City	36.5
7	Egghead Software	890.0	57	Computize	36.0
8	Staples	718.0	58	47th St. Photo	35.7
9	Sears	700.0	59	Fred Meyer	35.6
10	OfficeMax	671.0	60	Computer Stores Northwest	32.0
11	CDW Computer Warehouse	630.0	61	ABC Warehouse	31.1
12	Sam's Club	622.0	62	HD Computers	30.5
13	Wal-Mart	585.0	63	PC Club	30.0
14	Fry's Electronics	414.0	64	The May Company	29.8
15	Creative Computers	400.0	65	Dillard Department Stores	29.0
16	PriceCostco	397.0	66	Hastings	28.4
17	Neostar	354.7	67	H.H. Gregg Appliance	28.0
18	Elek-Tek	335.0	68	Tops Appliance City	25.0
19	Radio Shack	330.0	69	Nebraska Furniture Mart	25.0
20	Montgomery Ward	324.3	70	CW Electronics	23.6
21	PC Warehouse	321.0	71	Laptop Superstore	22.3
22	Army/Air Force Exchange	258.0	72	Access Technologies	19.5
23	Catalink Direct	233.0	73	R.C. Willey Home Furnishings	19.0
24	J&R Computer World	230.0	74	Alpha Computers	18.7
25	Nobody Beats the Wiz	187.0	75	Doppler Computer	18.0
26	Sun TV & Appliances	186.0	76	Fedco	16.8
27	Incredible Universe	182.0	77	Toys R Us	16.5
28	Electronics Boutique	176.0	78	Boscov's	16.0
29	Lechmere	161.0	79	Roberd's	15.0
30	The Good Guys!	136.0	80	DataVision	15.0
31	Future Shop	132.0	81	Rex Stores	14.4
32	Whole Earth Access	98.0	82	Dayton Hudson	14.2
33	Computer Express	90.0	83	AMS Computer Stores	14.0
34	ComputerWare	88.0	84	Barnes & Noble	13.5
35	NCA Computer Products	78.0	85	State Street Discount	9.1
36	SBI Computer Warehouse	75.0	86	ACP Superstore	8.0
37	Computer Town	73.0	87	American Appliance	8.0
38	Computer Attic SuperCenter	62.5	88	Kay-Bee Toys	7.5
39	Campo	61.0	89	Ekos Computers	7.5
40	BJ's Wholesale Club	57.1	90	Caldor	7.2
41	Kmart	56.4	91	Atlantic Computer Systems	7.0
42	Fretter	54.0	92	Foley's	6.5
43	Media Play (Musicland)	52.0	93	Borders	6.3
44	Lucky Computer	51.2	94	Baillio's	6.0
45	American TV	51.0	95	Steinberg's	5.8
46	Service Merchandise	48.0	96	Computer Warehouse of Nevada	5.2
47	Office 1 Superstore	48.0	97	Meijer	5.2
48	P.C. Richard & Son	47.2	98	Virgin Megastores	4.8
49	Target Stores	44.8	99	Apex Department Store	4.0
50	BrandsMart U.S.A.	44.0	100	Great Buys Plus	3.7

* Radio Shack Division
Souce: *Computer Retail Week*; June 3/10, 1996

COMPUTER Industry Leaders

3COM CORPORATION

OVERVIEW

3Com Park isn't the name of this San Francisco-based company's headquarters -- the company's deal to rename San Francisco sport stadium Candlestick Park is the embodiment of its new marketing strategy. 3Com (#2, after rival Cisco Systems) designs and manufactures the highly specialized interfacing and switching hardware that enables computers to communicate with each other across a LAN or a WAN. These devices include hubs (network control devices), routers (network linking devices), switches, remote access servers (for home or remote office), and network adapter cards (plug-in circuit boards that enable PCs to be linked to a network).

3Com is looking to play every side of the cyberspace explosion: the firm expects large businesses will need high-speed LAN and WAN connections to take full advantage of the Internet (which is also expected to drive millions of small businesses into the networked fold). The company has also introduced ISDN (high-speed) remote-access products for the Internet and business intranets.

3Com's acquisition of high-end competitor Chipcom (which cost $775 million and took months to digest) has expanded the company's customer base and broadened its product lines. CEO Eric Benhamou believes the nascent small-office and telecommuter market is a potential gold mine, so 3Com is developing low-end niche products (to be introduced in late 1997) and has plunked down $3.9 million to build general name recognition -- venerable Candlestick will be known as 3Com Park through the year 2000.

WHEN

Engineer Robert Metcalfe led the Xerox research team that invented Ethernet (a PC networking system that later became an industry standard) in 1973. Six years later, Metcalfe cofounded 3Com (for computer, communication, compatibility) with Greg Shaw (who left in 1985), Howard Charney, and another colleague. 3Com began as a "computer network consulting firm" before there were many PCs to network. But in 1980 Xerox agreed to share its Ethernet patent to make it an industry standard, and $1.1 million in venture capital helped get 3Com's development ball rolling. The upstart introduced its first product (an Ethernet transceiver and adapter) the next year. William Krause was hired away from Hewlett-Packard in 1981 and was made 3Com's president. Sales took off the following year after IBM introduced its 16-bit PC.

3Com went public in 1984. It did well by selling network adapter cards to large computer manufacturers and resellers. But by 1986 its manufacturing customers began integrating their own networking hardware into their machines. So Krause (who had succeeded Metcalfe as CEO) broadened the company's focus, and 3Com began providing complete computer network hardware and software systems.

In 1987 3Com acquired Bridge Communications (a supplier of internetwork bridge and router hardware) for $151 million. This gave 3Com its first direct sales force. Bridge cofounder William Carrico was made president of 3Com, but divergent corporate cultures and management styles created friction, soon prompting Carrico and Bridge cofounder Judith Estrin to leave.

3Com and Microsoft began a joint venture in 1988 to develop a networking operating system that could compete with Novell's Netware. The product fell behind schedule, and the venture ended in 1990. Metcalfe (who described working with Microsoft as "mating with a black widow spider") again wanted to lead the company in 1990, but the job of turning 3Com around was given to Eric Benhamou (a cofounder of Bridge), and Metcalfe departed.

Benhamou shed 3Com's operating system software and server businesses, reorganized the company, and concentrated on developing its prosperous line of LAN adapters, hubs, and routers. He then acquired makers of complementary products, turning first to British hub maker BICC Data Networks in 1992.

3Com purchased Star-Tek (token rings), Synernetics (LAN switches), and Pacific Monolithics (wireless LANS) the following year. The company bought Centrum Communications (remote access technology) and NiceCom (an ATM innovator) in 1994, tipping 3Com into the red.

The buying spree continued in 1995, when 3Com bought Primary Access Corp. (remote access systems) and Chipcom. In 1996 3Com acquired Axon Networks, which makes technology to monitor data flow in computer networks, and it agreed to purchase OnStream Networks for $245 million. The purchase of switch-maker OnStream would give 3Com its first significant line of ATM products.

WHO

Chairman, President, and CEO: Eric A. Benhamou, age 39, $521,518 pay
President, 3Com Systems: Robert J. Finocchio Jr., age 44, $373,758 pay (prior to promotion)
EVP Personal Connectivity Division: Douglas C. Spreng, age 51, $344,592 pay
SVP Worldwide Sales: Ralph B. Godfrey, age 54, $332,239 pay (prior to promotion)
SVP Global System Sales: Alan J. Kessler, age 37, $298,905 pay (prior to promotion)
VP Finance and CFO: Christopher B. Paisley, age 42
VP and Chief Technical Officer: John H. Hart, age 49
VP and Chief Information Officer: Tom Thomas
VP Corporate Services (HR): Debra Engel, age 43
Director Human Resources: Susan Gellen
Auditors: Deloitte & Touche LLP

WHERE

HQ: 5400 Bayfront Plaza, Santa Clara, CA 95052
Phone: 408-764-5000
Fax: 408-764-5001
Web site: http://www.3com.com

	1996 Sales	
	$ mil.	% of total
US	1,104	47
Europe	765	33
Export sales from US	457	20
Other	1	0
Total	**2,327**	**100**

WHAT

	1996 Sales
	% of total
Network systems products	57
Network adapters	39
Other	4
Total	**100**

Selected Network Products

Adapters
3Com EtherLink III (Ethernet adapter)
Fast EtherLink 10/100 (Fast Ethernet adapter)
TokenLink III (Token Ring adapter)
TokenLink Velocity (PCI adapter)
Hubs
OfficeConnect Ethernet (hubs for small offices)
SuperStack Ethernet (flexible, fault-tolerant hubs)
Remote Access
AccessBuilder 4000 Remote Access Servers (multiprotocol servers)
AccessBuilder 8000 Integrated Remote Access System (for Internet providers)
Routers
LinkConverter II SNA-to-LAN Converters
NETBuilder Remote Office 32X Routers (multiprotocol routers)
Switches
Asynchronous Transfer Mode (ATM switches)
Multifunction Stackable

KEY COMPETITORS

ADTRAN	IBM
Artisoft	Microcom
Asante	Microsoft
Ascend Communications	MRV Communications
Banyan Systems	Proteon
Bay Networks	Shiva
Cabletron	Standard Microsystems
Cisco Systems	U.S. Robotics
Digi International	Xircom
FORE Systems	

HOW MUCH

OTC symbol: COMS FYE: May 31	Annual Growth	1987	1988	1989	1990	1991	1992	1993	1994	1995	1996[1]
Sales ($ mil.)	35.0%	156	252	386	419	399	408	617	827	1,295	2,327
Net income ($ mil.)	30.7%	16	23	34	21	(28)	4	39	(29)	126	178
Income as % of sales	—	10.4%	8.9%	8.9%	4.9%	—	1.0%	6.3%	—	9.7%	7.6%
Earnings per share ($)	22.6%	0.16	0.20	0.29	0.18	(0.25)	0.04	0.30	(0.23)	0.86	1.00
Stock price – high ($)	—	6.47	5.94	7.19	4.75	3.16	7.50	12.13	26.63	53.63	52.00
Stock price – low ($)	—	3.09	3.91	2.50	1.34	1.38	2.41	4.91	10.06	22.19	35.75
Stock price – close ($)	28.9%	5.00	5.47	3.44	2.00	2.81	7.41	11.75	25.78	46.63	49.25
P/E – high	—	42	30	25	27	—	188	40	—	63	52
P/E – low	—	20	20	9	8	—	60	16	—	26	36
Dividends per share ($)	—	0.00	0.00	0.00	0.00	0.00	0.00	0.00	0.00	0.00	0.00
Book value per share ($)	19.8%	1.14	1.42	1.80	2.00	1.75	1.81	2.10	2.16	3.36	5.80
Employees	22.2%	853	1,348	1,922	2,008	1,731	1,963	1,971	2,306	3,072	5,190

[1] Stock prices are through May 31.

1996 YEAR-END

Debt ratio: 10.1%
Return on equity: 24.6%
Cash (mil.): $499
Current ratio: 2.99
Long-term debt (mil.): $110
No. of shares (mil.): 169
Dividends
  Yield: —
  Payout: —
Market value (mil.): $8,313

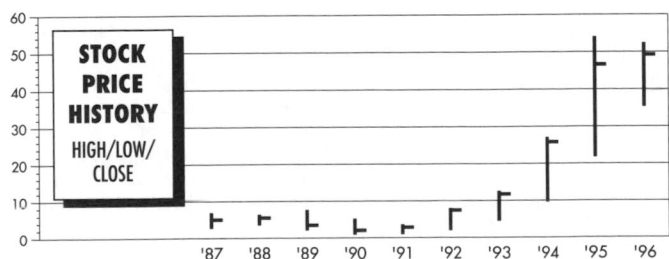

ACER INCORPORATED

OVERVIEW

Acer is the company that made the PC pretty — consumers love its curvy, colorful Aspire PCs. The company ranks 7th worldwide in personal computer sales and is Taiwan's largest exporter. Among the Acer Group's 10 subsidiaries are companies that produce computer chips, publish high-tech books and periodicals, and distribute and service Acer products around the world. Alliances are a big part of Acer's success; 3 of Acer Group's companies are joint ventures — Texas Instrument-Acer, Acer-Computec Latino America (with Computec de Mexico), and Ambit Microsystems Inc. (with Germany's Telefunken Microelectronics).

Acer uses a string of 39 just-in-time assembly plants to reach global markets: PC housings and floppy disk drives are shipped to locations around the world, motherboards are flown in to ensure that the latest technology is available, and CPUs, hard drives, and memories are purchased locally, saving on tariffs. These modular components are then quickly put together in a standardized assembly process, a strategy that helps Acer maintain quality and minimize inventory.

Chairman and CEO Stan Shih, who owns 10% of the firm, compares Acer Group companies to a client/server network, with subsidiaries operating autonomously but accessing the services of the central company (Acer Inc.). Shih says he will spin off 21 Acer units by the turn of the century, with Acer Inc. keeping a big share of each.

WHEN

Stan Shih designed Taiwan's first desktop calculator in the early 1970s. Acer's precursor, Multitech International, was launched in 1976 with $25,000 by Shih and 4 others who called themselves the "Gardeners of Microprocessing." In 1980 Multitech introduced the Dragon Chinese-language CRT terminal that won Taiwan's top design award; in 1983 it introduced an Apple II clone, a CPM machine, and its first IBM XT/PC compatible. Multitech set up AcerLand, Taiwan's first and largest franchised computer retail chain, in 1985.

A year later Multitech beat IBM and tied with Compaq to be the first to sell PCs using Intel's 386 microprocessor. The company changed its name to Acer (from the Latin word for sharp, acute, able, and facile) in 1987 and went public on the Taiwan exchange the next year.

Texas Instruments and Acer entered into a joint venture during 1989 to design and develop DRAM chips at a facility in Taiwan that was one of the world's 10 largest wafer fabricating facilities. In 1990 Acer's US subsidiary, Acer America, purchased Altos Computer Systems, a US manufacturer of multiuser and networked UNIX systems for business markets.

During the prosperous 1980s Acer had increased its management layers and slowed the decision-making process. In late 1990 the company restructured, trimming its workforce by 8% (about 400 employees), including a 2/3 cut in headquarters staff. This release of workers was an unprecedented move — being asked to resign from a job in Taiwan carries a social stigma. Shih wrote a letter to all those affected, explaining the plight of the company. The following year Acer began its decentralization plan to create a worldwide confederation of publicly owned companies. In most cases the parent company still owns around 50% of the spinoffs.

Also in 1991 Acer suffered its first loss, while its revenues were almost $1 billion. The company put itself in a hole in part by increasing its US and European marketing budgets and investing money in its $250 million joint venture with TI, and it was still affected by its $90 million purchase of Altos in 1990. Acer bounced back in 1993, with 80% of its profit coming from its DRAM joint venture with TI.

Acer's effort to have its subsidiaries Acer Peripherals and Acer Sertek listed separately on the Taiwan stock market failed in 1994 because they had inadequate histories of financial independence from the parent. That year the company formed a joint venture with Technical Systems Distribution to market Acer computers in South Africa.

The Aspire PC, available in shades of gray and green, was unveiled in 1995; within 3 months 300,000 units had sold.

In 1996 the company began introducing a host of new, inexpensive consumer electronics intended to boost the company's global market share; these included an inexpensive ($499) PC called the Basic, a personal computer for children, digital videodisk players, wide-screen TVs, and video telephones.

WHO

Chairman and CEO: Stan Shih, age 52
President: Hsienmin Lin
President and COO, Acer America: Ronald Chwang
VP Finance, Acer America: Michael Tung
VP Human Resources, Acer America: Ken Stempson
Auditors: KPMG Peat Marwick LLP

WHERE

HQ: 156 Min Sheng East Rd., Sec. 3, 6F, Taipei, 105, Taiwan
Phone: +886-2-545-5288
Fax: +886-2-545-5308
US HQ: Acer America Corporation, 2641 Orchard Pkwy., San Jose, CA 95134
US Phone: 408-432-6200
US Fax: 408-922-2933
Web site: http://www.acer.com

Acer has 80 offices in 38 countries.

	1995 Sales % of total
Taiwan	37
North America	36
Europe	11
Other regions	16
Total	**100**

WHAT

Selected Products
Acer Altos open servers
Acer Aspire home computers
AcerEntra desktop computers
AcerFax fax machines
AcerNote color notebook computers
AcerPower desktop computers
AcerView monitors

The Acer Group
Acer America Corp. (assembly, marketing, sales, and service of Acer brand products in North America)
Acer Computer BV (marketing, sales, and service of Acer brand products in Europe)
Acer Computer International Pte Ltd. (assembly, marketing, sales, and service of Acer brand products in African, Asia/Pacific, Indian, Middle Eastern, and Russian markets)
Acer Laboratories Inc. (design and manufacture of ASICs for PC motherboard makers)
Acer Market Services Ltd. (marketing, sales, and service of Acer products in China)
Acer Peripherals, Inc. (production of fax machines, keyboards, laser printers, and monitors)
Acer Sertek Inc. (distribution of professional high-tech products in Taiwan)
Acer TWP Corp. (publishing)
Acer-Computec Latino America (50%; joint venture with Computec de Mexico to manufacture, market, and service Acer products; Latin America)
Ambit Microsystems (50%; joint venture with Daimler-Benz-owned Telefunken Microelectronics of Germany to produce ASICs and other custom electronics; Taiwan)
Fora International Corp. (international high-tech products distribution)
Texas Instruments-Acer Inc. (56%; joint venture to produce DRAM chips; Asia)

KEY COMPETITORS

AMD	Gateway 2000	Packard Bell
Apple Computer	Hewlett-Packard	Philips
AST	Hitachi	Samsung
Canon	IBM	Sanyo
Compaq	Machines Bull	Siemens
DEC	Matsushita	Texas
Dell	Micron	Instruments
Fujitsu	Electronics	Toshiba

HOW MUCH

Principal exchange: Taiwan FYE: December 31	Annual Growth	1986	1987	1988	1989	1990	1991	1992	1993	1994	1995
Sales ($ mil.)	33.6%	—	—	—	689	950	985	1,260	1,883	2,397	3,925
Net income ($ mil.)	79.8%	—	—	—	6	2	(23)	2	77	118	203
Income as % of sales	—	—	—	—	0.8%	0.3%	—	0.2%	4.1%	4.9%	5.2%
Earnings per share ($)	88.8%	—	—	—	—	0.01	(0.54)	0.01	0.09	0.15	0.24
Stock price – high ($)	—	—	—	—	—	2.35	1.62	1.09	2.16	4.85	3.61
Stock price – low ($)	—	—	—	—	—	0.54	0.60	0.58	0.64	1.67	1.91
Stock price – close ($)	24.9%	—	—	—	—	0.76	0.88	0.71	2.16	3.77	2.31
P/E – high	—	—	—	—	—	235	—	109	25	33	15
P/E – low	—	—	—	—	—	54	—	58	7	11	8
Dividends per share ($)	0.0%	—	—	—	—	0.00	0.00	0.00	0.00	0.00	0.00
Book value per share ($)	16.1%	—	—	—	—	—	—	0.69	0.77	0.81	1.08
Employees	13.2%	—	—	—	5,216	5,352	5,540	5,711	7,200	9,700	11,000

1995 YEAR-END

Debt ratio: 37.3%
Return on equity: 26.8%
Cash (mil.): $365
Current ratio: 1.43
Long-term debt (mil.): $107
No. of shares (mil.): 945
Dividends
  Yield: —
  Payout: —
Market value (mil.): $2,182

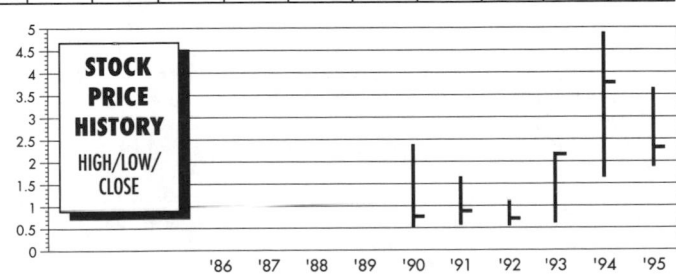

STOCK PRICE HISTORY HIGH/LOW/CLOSE

ADOBE SYSTEMS INCORPORATED

OVERVIEW

Adobe is making mud pies of the competition. Based in Mountain View, California, the company is the #3 PC software vendor behind Microsoft and Novell. Adobe, whose PostScript computer language made desktop publishing a reality in the mid-1980s, is hoping to ride its Internet software toward success in the late 1990s. Its Adobe PageMill and Adobe SiteMill programs help users easily create pages for the World Wide Web.

Adobe's other products enable computer users to create a virtually unlimited range of printable pages. Its Adobe Illustrator and PageMaker software, with advanced editing, graphics manipulation, and layout capabilities, are used to design books, consumer product packaging, even fine art. Adobe Photoshop gives users a sort of "electronic darkroom" to alter digitized photographs and design original images. Adobe also makes software for "desktop broadcasting," which enables film and video to be edited and manipulated on the computer instead of with traditional production equipment.

Adobe culminated a string of 10 acquisitions with the 1995 purchase of business and technical document software company Frame Technology. Frame has, however, proved a little hard to digest, depressing the company's earnings in early 1996.

WHEN

When Charles Geschke hired John Warnock as chief scientist for copier king Xerox's new graphics and imaging lab at its Palo Alto Research Center (a place Warnock called "the world's greatest sandbox" for technology research), he set the stage for one of the world's largest software manufacturers. While at Xerox, the pair developed the PostScript computer language, which instructs a printer how to reproduce a computer image on paper. When Xerox refused to market their product, the duo left the company and started Adobe (named after a river near their homes in San Jose, California) in 1982.

Their original plan was to produce a high-end electronic document processing system based on PostScript, but the company changed direction when Apple Computer whiz Steve Jobs hired the firm to co-design the controller board and software for his company's LaserWriter printer, which was introduced in 1985. A year later Adobe went public. Meanwhile, PostScript was pioneering the desktop publishing industry by allowing users to laser-print nearly anything they could create on the computer.

Adobe branched into the European market in 1987 with the establishment of its Adobe Systems Europe subsidiary. That year it entered the PC market by adapting PostScript for IBM's operating system. In 1989 the company started a subsidiary to market its products in the Pacific Rim.

Adobe grew in the early 1990s by acquiring other software companies, including OCR Systems and Nonlinear Technologies (1992) and AH Software and Science & Art (1993). Also in 1993 the company began licensing its PostScript software to printer manufacturers so they could use it in their products, which upped Adobe's share of the market. (The company kept control of the software that interprets the information, though, so printer-makers still have to rely on them for the programs that complete the printing system.) That year it began marketing Acrobat software, which enables users to create and distribute electronic documents over computer networks or online.

In 1994 Adobe acquired the 10-year-old Seattle-based Aldus, whose PageMaker software had been instrumental in establishing the desktop-publishing market. Since PageMaker's success depended on the font and font translator software that Adobe makes, the 2 companies had a history of cooperation predating 1990.

The company announced a deal in 1995 with Internet wunderfirm Netscape to integrate Acrobat's viewing technology (Acrobat) into Netscape's Internet software, including the Navigator browser. Also that year Adobe extended its range of publishing software by acquiring Frame Technology, whose FrameMaker software is used to publish long, complex documents such as books.

Adobe forecast in 1996 that sales of its products for the Internet would grow at a rate of 100% per year and would be focused on business-to-business sites. That year it spun off its prepress applications operations to the newly created Luminous Corporation, which planned to continue marketing Adobe's products. Adobe also agreed with imaging software leader FileNet to develop imaging standards that would enable different image file formats to be shared more easily by different computer users.

WHO

Chairman and CEO: John E. Warnock, age 55, $668,322 pay
President and Acting CFO: Charles M. Geschke, age 56, $668,322 pay
SVP and COO: David B. Pratt, age 56, $439,282 pay
SVP and General Manager, Adobe Europe: Derek J. Gray, age 46
VP, General Counsel, and Secretary: Colleen M. Pouliot, age 37
Director Human Resources: Rebecca Guerra
Auditors: KPMG Peat Marwick LLP

WHERE

HQ: 345 Park Ave., San Jose, CA 95110-2704
Phone: 415-536-6000
Fax: 415-537-6000
Web site: http://www.adobe.com

More than 6,000 North American resellers and 300 distributors in Europe and the Pacific Rim offer Adobe products.

WHAT

	1995 Sales	
	$ mil.	% of total
Product sales	579	76
Licensing fees	183	24
Total	**762**	**100**

Selected Products
Acrobat (electronic document management software)
Adobe Acrobat (document formatting software)
Adobe Art Explorer (painting and drawing software for children)
Adobe Fetch (cataloging software)
Adobe Gallery Effects (special-effects software)
Adobe Illustrator (graphics software)
Adobe PageMill (Web-page creation software)
Adobe PhotoDeluxe (personalized photo software)
Adobe Photoshop (photographic image software)
Adobe Premiere (film and video editing software)
Adobe Persuasion (presentation software)
Adobe SiteMill (Internet link repair software)
FrameMaker (document authoring software)
PageMaker (page layout software)
PostScript (page description language and interpreter)

KEY COMPETITORS

Allegro New Media
America Online
Apple Computer
Autodesk
Avid Technology
Corel
Electronics for Imaging
IBM
Interleaf
Linotype-Hell
Macromedia
Micrografx
Microsoft
Quark
SoftKey

HOW MUCH

Nasdaq symbol: ADBE FYE: November 30	Annual Growth	1986	1987	1988	1989	1990	1991	1992	1993	1994	1995
Sales ($ mil.)	45.0%	—	39	83	121	169	230	266	314	598	762
Net income ($ mil.)	34.1%	—	9	21	34	40	52	44	57	6	94
Income as % of sales	—	—	22.8%	25.3%	27.8%	23.8%	22.5%	16.4%	18.2%	1.1%	12.3%
Earnings per share ($)	24.4%	—	0.22	0.49	0.78	0.92	1.13	0.94	1.22	0.10	1.26
Stock price – high ($)	—	—	14.00	12.75	15.00	25.38	33.88	34.25	37.00	38.50	74.25
Stock price – low ($)	—	—	3.25	5.88	7.00	8.50	13.38	12.63	15.63	20.50	27.25
Stock price – close ($)	30.5%	—	7.38	12.25	10.13	14.56	32.75	15.75	22.25	29.75	62.00
P/E – high	—	—	65	26	19	28	30	36	30	—	59
P/E – low	—	—	15	12	9	9	12	13	13	—	22
Dividends per share ($)	14.0%	—	—	0.08	0.10	0.12	0.15	0.16	0.19	0.20	0.20
Book value per share ($)	34.8%	—	0.88	1.07	1.46	2.57	4.13	5.05	6.03	7.47	9.59
Employees	38.4%	—	172	291	383	508	701	887	1,000	1,584	2,319

1995 YEAR-END

Debt ratio: 0.0%
Return on equity: 16.2%
Cash (mil.): $516
Current ratio: 3.72
Long-term debt (mil.): $0
No. of shares (mil.): 73
Dividends
  Yield: 0.3%
  Payout: 15.9%
Market value (mil.): $4,516

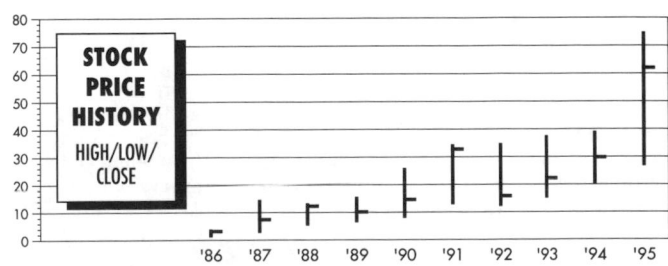

STOCK PRICE HISTORY
HIGH/LOW/CLOSE

ADVANCED MICRO DEVICES, INC.

OVERVIEW

If you like an underdog, you'll love Advanced Micro Devices (AMD). The Sunnyvale, California-based semiconductor maker is biting at the heels of top dog Intel (Intel has an 85% market share; AMD's is 9%). AMD focuses on the personal computer, computer network, and communications markets. It is the #1 supplier of integrated circuits for devices that connect computer networks, and it is a major supplier to the public communications infrastructure. AMD is also carving out a presence in wireless communications.

Despite strong sales of flash memory and programmable logic devices, the company has been chasing its tail because of the downturn in the PC market, pricing pressures, and the delayed introduction of its K5 microprocessor (a rival of Intel's Pentium chip). The K5 finally hit the market in 1996 — over a year late.

In an effort to regain its momentum, AMD acquired microprocessor developer NexGen, whose in-process designs (including a K6 model) will feed AMD's underutilized facility in Texas. AMD, which spends 16% of revenues on R&D, will break ground on a new fabrication facility in Dresden, Germany, designed to incorporate next-generation 0.25-micron chip-making technology.

WHEN

Management at Silicon Valley powerhouse Fairchild Camera & Instrument axed 30-year-old marketing whiz Jerry Sanders, reportedly for wearing a pink shirt on a sales call to IBM. So in 1969 Sanders started a semiconductor company, just as his former boss, Intel founder Robert Noyce, had done a year earlier.

Unlike Noyce, Sanders had no general management experience and was unable to raise the large amounts of capital required for semiconductor R&D. Instead, he built AMD by securing 2nd-source agreements (licenses to manufacture products designed by other chip makers) and by employing his marketing flair. The company went public in 1972. It received a $30 million cash infusion in 1977 when Siemens, anxious to get its foot in the door of the US semiconductor market, bought nearly 20% of AMD. In 1982 the company inked a 2nd-source deal with Intel, enabling AMD to manufacture exact copies of Intel's iAPX86 line of microprocessors, the "brains" of IBM and IBM-compatible PCs.

Aided by soaring demand for semiconductors in the mid-1980s, AMD became one of the nation's fastest-growing companies and began developing its own chips.

However, AMD was slow to adopt key new products and technologies. It suffered a setback in 1982 when a group of engineers left to start Cypress Semiconductor. In 1986, after prices for its old Intel microprocessor clones fell, the company closed plants and announced its first layoffs. The next year AMD bought programmable logic chip maker Monolithic Memories and began legal action against Intel for breaking the 1982 agreement for AMD to 2nd-source Intel's new 386 chips.

In 1990 Intel sued for copyright infringement when AMD introduced a version of Intel's 287 math coprocessor. Taking a swipe at Intel, Sanders sent prospective buyers Monopoly games as AMD released a 386 clone of its own design the following year; again Intel sued for copyright infringement. AMD released its 486 clone in 1993, triggering yet another lawsuit by Intel.

AMD signed a technology pact to develop microprocessors with Hewlett-Packard in 1993. The company also formed a joint venture with Fujitsu to develop, produce, and market flash memory devices. As part of the deal, Fujitsu and AMD acquired minority stakes in each other. In 1994 a federal jury handed down a decision in AMD's favor in the 287 math coprocessor case. That year AMD agreed to sell its Am486 chip to Compaq (one of Intel's biggest microchip customers).

After nearly a decade of legal wrangling, in early 1995 AMD and Intel settled their differences. Each agreed to pay damages, and AMD won a perpetual license to the microcode in Intel's 386 and 486 chips. That year AMD and chip designer Cyrix codeveloped a proposed industry standard that would make it easier to manufacture computers based on microprocessors made by different companies; it would replace the patented Intel standard now widely used. Also in 1995 the company opened its $1.2 billion wafer "megafab" in Austin, Texas.

In 1996 AMD purchased NexGen for $806 million. The purchase was intended to close the gap with Intel in processor performance. In an effort to take advantage of its strong programmable logic device business, that year AMD spun off its PLD unit as a wholly owned subsidiary.

WHO

Chairman and CEO: W. Jeremiah Sanders III, age 59, $3,005,848 pay
VC: Anthony B. Holbrook
President and COO: Richard Previte, age 61, $2,019,252 pay
SVP and Chief Marketing Executive: Stephen J. Zelencik, age 61, $848,410 pay
SVP, CFO, and Treasurer: Marvin D. Burkett, age 53, $692,897 pay
SVP Operations: Eugene D. Conner, age 52, $681,001 pay
SVP Human Resources: Stanley Winvick, age 56
Group VP, Computation Products Group: John Bourgoin
Group VP, Computation Products Group: Vinod Dham
Group VP, Communications and Components Group: Richard Forte
Group VP, Sales: Terryll R. Smith
VP and Chief Technical Officer: S. Atiq Raza, age 47
VP, General Counsel, and Secretary: Thomas M. McCoy, age 45
Auditors: Ernst & Young LLP

WHERE

HQ: One AMD Place, Sunnyvale, CA 94088-3453
Phone: 408-732-2400
Fax: 408-982-6164
Web site: http://www.amd.com
AMD has manufacturing facilities in California and Texas as well as in Japan, Malaysia, Singapore, and Thailand.

	1995 Sales		1995 Operating Income	
	$ mil.	% of total	$ mil.	% of total
North America	1,742	72	290	83
Europe	491	20	19	6
Asia	197	8	39	11
Total	**2,430**	**100**	**348**	**100**

WHAT

Selected Products
Communications and Components
Embedded control microprocessors
  AM29000 family of RISC microprocessors
Network and voice/data communications products
  Chipsets
  Development software
  Ethernet products
  Hardware evaluation tools
  Integrated circuits
  Interface software
Nonvolatile memory products
  Erasable programmable read-only memories (EPROMS)
  Flash memories
Programmable logic devices (PLDs)
Volatile memory products
  Dynamic random access memories (DRAMs)
  Static random access memories (SRAMs)

Computation Products
Integrated circuits for personal computers and local area networks
K86 microprocessors
X86 microprocessors

KEY COMPETITORS

Altera	LG Group	Philips
Atmel	LSI Logic	Samsung
Cirrus Logic	Matsushita	SGS-Thomson
Cypress	Mitsubishi	Sharp
Semiconductor	Motorola	Siemens
Fujitsu	National	Texas
Hitachi	Semiconductor	Instruments
Hyundai	NEC	Toshiba
Integrated Device	Nexgen	VLSI Technology
Technology	Nippon Electric	Xilinx
Intel	Oki	Zilog

HOW MUCH

NYSE symbol: AMD FYE: December 31	Annual Growth	1986	1987	1988	1989	1990	1991	1992	1993	1994	1995
Sales ($ mil.)	16.1%	632	997	1,126	1,105	1,059	1,227	1,515	1,648	2,135	2,430
Net income ($ mil.)	—	(96)	(48)	19	46	(54)	145	245	229	295	301
Income as % of sales	—	—	—	1.7%	4.2%	—	11.8%	16.2%	13.9%	13.8%	12.4%
Earnings per share ($)	—	(1.66)	(0.72)	0.11	0.44	(0.78)	1.52	2.49	2.24	2.92	2.81
Stock price – high ($)	—	33.50	24.88	16.88	10.50	11.38	17.75	21.50	32.88	31.75	39.25
Stock price – low ($)	—	12.88	7.50	7.13	7.13	3.63	4.00	7.38	17.00	16.75	16.13
Stock price – close ($)	2.0%	13.75	9.88	8.63	7.88	4.88	17.50	18.13	17.75	24.88	16.50
P/E – high	—	—	—	154	24	—	12	9	15	11	14
P/E – low	—	—	—	65	16	—	3	3	8	6	6
Dividends per share ($)	0.0%	0.00	0.00	0.00	0.00	0.00	0.00	0.75	0.00	0.00	0.00
Book value per share ($)	10.6%	8.11	8.41	8.07	8.51	7.73	9.32	11.86	14.63	18.19	20.09
Employees	(0.8%)	13,689	10,597	14,817	13,072	11,997	11,254	11,554	12,065	11,793	12,730

1995 YEAR-END

Debt ratio: 11.5%
Return on equity: 15.7%
Cash (mil.): $491
Current ratio: 1.76
Long-term debt (mil.): $215
No. of shares (mil.): 105
Dividends
  Yield: —
  Payout: —
Market value (mil.): $1,725

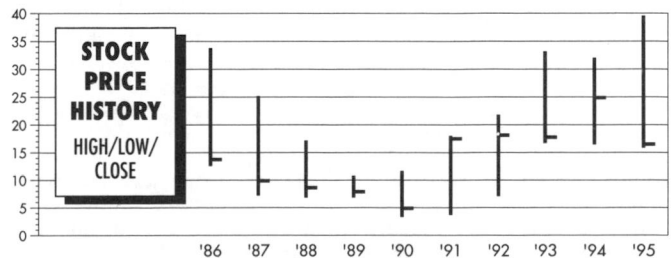

STOCK PRICE HISTORY HIGH/LOW/CLOSE

'86 '87 '88 '89 '90 '91 '92 '93 '94 '95

AMDAHL CORPORATION

OVERVIEW

Amdahl is developing new business and keeping the old; information services are silver and mainframes are gold. Headquartered in Sunnyvale, California, Amdahl's oldest friends are IBM-compatible mainframe computers and storage systems, which still account for about 60% of its sales, though volume has decreased and lower prices are hurting profits. The company also makes client/server software, open systems hardware and software, and PC servers.

Though Amdahl, which is approximately 43%-owned by Japanese computer maker Fujitsu, believes its mainframe computer business will remain healthy, it has begun to broaden its offerings by providing information-technology services. Its acquisitions of DMR Group, which provides applications development and systems integration services, and C.E. Services, a provider of data center systems support, have helped move Amdahl toward its goal of becoming a one-stop-shop for all a customer's data processing needs.

To further diversify and protect itself from the unsteady mainframe market, Amdahl has also begun to resell Sun Microsystems servers and produce its own Windows NT servers.

WHEN

In the 1960s Gene Amdahl was the principal architect of IBM's popular family of mainframe computers, the System 360. After his idea for a more advanced computer was rejected, Amdahl quit IBM in 1970 and started his own company to manufacture IBM-compatible mainframes. In view of previous failures by others, investors were reluctant to back a company challenging IBM's market dominance. But Amdahl's strategy — to make its system faster, cheaper, with high capacity, yet compatible with IBM software and peripherals — was unique, and it persuaded investors to supply enough capital to start the company. Fujitsu was one of the earliest investors. In 1975, with $47 million poured into R&D, Amdahl introduced the 470V/6, a computer compatible with IBM's largest 370 mainframe, the Model 168. IBM users could transfer to the less-expensive Amdahl V/6 and continue to use their existing software and peripherals.

Amdahl's strategy of building IBM clones with better performance for less money succeeded, and the company went public in 1976. Amdahl followed its 470V/6 with the V/7 in 1977 and a V/8 model in 1978. As Amdahl prospered by outperforming and underselling IBM, Big Blue struck back by cutting prices and announcing impending technological improvements. Potential Amdahl customers delayed purchases, drying up cash flow. By 1979 Fujitsu's interest was 34% and Gene Amdahl was gone. Seeking to diversify and bolstered by funds from a 1980 stock offering, new president Eugene White bought Tran Telecommunications (data communications products, 1980) and sought to buy Memorex (1979) and Storage Technology Corporation (1980), but Fujitsu stopped both transactions.

In 1983 Amdahl Corporation's revenues shot up 68% from the previous year to $778 million following shipments of its new 5860 mainframe and diversification into disk drives. As the US mainframe computer market matured in the 1980s, Amdahl looked toward Europe, where profit derived not merely from sales but also from a declining dollar. The company bought Key Computer Labs (scalar computing) in 1989 and launched the 5995 mainframe series in 1990.

Amdahl released Huron, an application software development package, in 1991 and licensed Sun Microsystems's SPARC (RISC) technology to further its movement toward open systems. The company formed a joint venture, Antares Alliance Group, with Electronic Data Systems (EDS, a unit of General Motors) in 1993 to develop software capable of running on both mainframes and smaller computers.

After heavy losses that year due to the slow mainframe market, Amdahl rebounded in 1994 and posted its first yearly profit since 1991. In a major reorganization, it cut manufacturing capacity in half and employment by 1/3 and wrote off about $200 million in surplus plants and equipment. That year Amdahl introduced the XPlorer 2000 database server in an alliance with Oracle, nCUBE, and Information Builders.

Amdahl acquired Canada-based DMR Group for $139 million in 1995, beating out offers from IBM and BDM International. The following year diversification continued as the company purchased Trecom, a privately held consulting and professional services company, for $145 million. Also in 1996 Amdahl announced the launch of 2 lines of Intel Pentium Pro mainframe-connectable servers, the EnVista Frontline Server and the EnVista Central Server.

WHO

Chairman, President, and CEO: John C. Lewis, age 60, $780,036 pay
EVP Enterprise Computing Group: David B. Wright, age 46, $399,800 pay
EVP, CFO, and Corporate Secretary: Bruce J. Ryan, age 52, $399,800 pay
SVP Investor Relations: William Stewart
SVP Human Resources and Corporate Development: Anthony Pozos
Chief Technical Officer; VP, Enterprise Server Development: David L. Anderson, age 48, $495,040 pay
Chief Marketing Officer; VP, Corporate Marketing: Orval J. Nutt, age 55
Auditors: Andersen Worldwide

WHERE

HQ: 1250 E. Arques Ave., Sunnyvale, CA 94088-3470
Phone: 408-746-6000
Fax: 408-773-0833
Web site: http://www.amdahl.com

Amdahl markets its products in Asia/Pacific, Europe, and much of North America. The company's products are also marketed by Fujitsu and other distributors in parts of Asia, Europe, the Middle East, and South America.

WHAT

	1995 Sales	
	$ mil.	% of total
Processors	622	41
Maintenance	475	32
Consulting	148	10
Storage products	83	5
Server equipment	77	5
Software	72	5
Other equipment	21	1
Leases	18	1
Total	**1,516**	**100**

Selected Operations

Antares Alliance Group
CrossView (service management software)
Huron ObjectStar (client/server software)

DMR Group
Applications development and maintenance
Information management consulting
Systems integration

Enterprise Computing Group
Mainframe computers
Millennium Global Servers
Spectris RAID disk array

Open Enterprise Solutions Group
SPARC server series
UTS UNIX operating systems

KEY COMPETITORS

Control Data	Machines Bull	Storage
Data General	NCR	Technology
DEC	nCUBE	Stratus
EMC Corp.	NEC	Computer
Hewlett-Packard	Olivetti	Tandem
Hitachi	Sequent	Unisys
IBM	Siemens	Wang
Intergraph	Silicon Graphics	

HOW MUCH

AMEX symbol: AMH FYE: December 31	Annual Growth	1986	1987	1988	1989	1990	1991	1992	1993	1994	1995
Sales ($ mil.)	5.1%	966	1,505	1,802	2,101	2,159	1,703	2,525	1,681	1,639	1,516
Net income ($ mil.)	(3.2%)	39	142	214	153	184	4	(7)	(589)	75	29
Income as % of sales	—	4.1%	9.4%	11.9%	7.3%	8.5%	0.3%	—	—	4.6%	1.9%
Earnings per share ($)	(5.8%)	0.41	1.37	1.99	1.39	1.66	0.04	(0.06)	(5.17)	0.63	0.24
Stock price – high ($)	—	12.88	25.06	28.00	23.38	18.88	17.88	20.63	8.50	11.13	13.63
Stock price – low ($)	—	6.75	9.56	14.06	10.75	10.00	11.63	6.63	4.38	5.25	8.13
Stock price – close ($)	(3.5%)	11.69	17.63	20.25	14.38	14.13	15.75	7.25	6.00	11.00	8.50
P/E – high	—	31	18	14	17	11	—	—	—	18	57
P/E – low	—	17	7	7	8	6	—	—	—	8	34
Dividends per share ($)	(100.0%)	0.10	0.10	0.10	0.10	0.10	0.10	0.10	0.05	0.00	0.00
Book value per share ($)	4.7%	5.19	7.32	9.51	10.80	12.44	12.38	12.12	6.90	7.51	7.83
Employees	1.2%	7,200	7,650	8,150	8,200	8,950	9,400	8,769	5,552	5,600	8,000

1995 YEAR-END

Debt ratio: 14.1%
Return on equity: 3.2%
Cash (mil.): $637
Current ratio: 2.19
Long-term debt (mil.): $131
No. of shares (mil.): 119
Dividends
  Yield: —
  Payout: —
Market value (mil.): $1,014

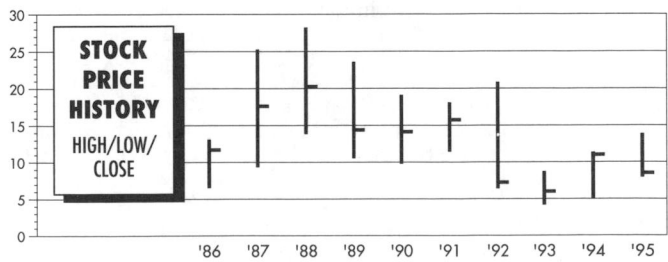

STOCK PRICE HISTORY HIGH/LOW/CLOSE

AMERICA ONLINE, INC.

OVERVIEW

America Online (AOL) is the US's — and the world's — largest and fastest-growing provider of subscription online services. Through an easy-to-use interface, its nearly 7 million members are offered access to a variety of information and services, including e-mail, electronic magazines and newspapers, stock quotes, conferences, and online classes, as well as this profile and others published by Hoover's, Inc. The Vienna, Virginia-based company hopes to duplicate its US success in Canada, Europe, and Japan. Its main obstacles are the competition for content from other online services and the rising popularity of the Internet. Many media providers are creating their own Web sites and thousands of small online services offer access to the Internet at a lower cost.

AOL is making moves to better position itself to compete for Internet access business. In one whirlwind week in March 1996, AOL announced major alliances with Netscape Communications, Microsoft, and AT&T that it hoped would significantly expand its subscriber base. The Netscape and Microsoft deals allow AOL members to use both companies' Web browsers — software for surfing the Internet — and in exchange, Microsoft said it would add AOL access to future versions of Windows 95. The 3rd agreement provides for customers of WorldNet, AT&T's Internet service, to receive discount subscriptions to AOL.

Investors in AOL include Apple Computer, Putnam Investments, and the Tribune Company. Executives and directors own about 10% of the company.

WHEN

Stephen Case was manager of new pizza development for PepsiCo's Pizza Hut (he researched new pizza toppings) when he first began using an early online service called the Source in the early 1980s. In 1983 he got a chance to get some hands-on experience when he took a marketing job with Control Video, which ran an online service for users of Atari computer games. However, Control Video soon ran into financial trouble, and the company's board fired its management. Entrepreneur Jim Kimsey was named CEO. Case helped Kimsey raise money to resurrect the company, and in 1985 Control Video was rechristened Quantum Computer Services. The company launched an online service called Q-Link for users of Commodore computers.

Q-Link proved to be a success with Commodore users, so in 1987 Quantum expanded its offerings to owners of other types of PCs, signing deals with Apple and Tandy. In 1989 the company launched a nationwide service called America Online for IBM-compatible and Apple computers. In 1991 the company changed its name to America Online.

America Online went public in 1992, the same year Case was named CEO. He focused on expanding AOL's market share, spending heavily on marketing in an effort to pass the company's biggest competitors: Prodigy and CompuServe. To boost its content, AOL signed deals with several media companies, adding features from Knight-Ridder newspapers, Time Warner's *Time* magazine, General Media International's *Omni* magazine, and Turner

Broadcasting's CNN cable news channel. Also in 1993 the company began offering a Windows version of its online software. AOL's attractive and easy-to-use interface, coupled with the growing popularity of Windows, attracted even more users to the online service. That year it announced it would begin offering Internet access.

In 1994 AOL bought multimedia developer Redgate Communications, anticipating expansion into CD-ROM and interactive TV formats, and Internet browser software maker Booklink Technologies. By the end of 1994, AOL had more than 1 million subscribers.

In 1995 it teamed up with music and publishing empire Bertelsmann to offer online services in Europe, a fledgling market. AOL also boosted its Internet-related features, buying several related businesses. Also that year AOL launched GNN, an Internet-only service for nontechnical users.

By the middle of 1996 the company had more than 6 million users. AOL offered to give subscribers refunds and millions of free hours online to settle class-action suits over claims that its time-accounting method had unfairly added minutes to many bills. In another legal fight that year, bulk e-mail company Cyber Promotions took AOL to court after AOL moved to block all junk e-mail from its system.

AOL moved from Nasdaq to the NYSE in September 1996. For fiscal 1996 AOL's sales reached $1.04 billion (with profits of $30 million), more than double the previous year's revenues.

WHO

Chairman Emeritus: James V. Kimsey, age 55
Chairman and CEO: Stephen M. Case, age 36,
  $200,000 pay
SVP; President, AOL Technologies: Michael M.
  Connors, age 53, $195,000 pay
SVP; President, AOL International: John L. Davies,
  age 45, $195,000 pay
SVP, CFO, Treasurer, and Chief Accounting Officer:
  Lennert J. Leader, age 40, $188,333 pay
SVP; President, AOL Services: Theodore J. Leonsis,
  age 39, $175,025 pay
SVP; President, AOL Enterprises: David Cole, age 42
SVP Corporate Development: Miles Gilburne, age 44
SVP Product Research: Marc S. Seriff, age 47
VP; SVP, AOL Services: Janice Brandt, age 44
VP Investor Relations: Richard Hanlon, age 47
VP, General Counsel and Secretary: Ellen M. Kirsh,
  age 47
VP Operations: Matthew Korn, age 36
VP; President, AOL Productions: Barry Schuler, age 42
VP Human Resources and Facilities: Mark Stavish,
  age 40
VP Corporate Communications: Jean N. Villanueva,
  age 35
VP Enterprise Solutions: Mark Walsh, age 41
VP; SVP, AOL Services: Audrey Y. Weil, age 35
Auditors: Ernst & Young LLP

WHERE

HQ: 8619 Westwood Center Dr., Vienna, VA 22182-2285
Phone: 703-448-8700
Fax: 703-883-1532
Web site: http://www.aol.com

WHAT

	1995 Sales	
	$ mil.	% of total
Online services	358	91
Other	36	9
Total	**394**	**100**

Selected America Online Features

Children's programming
Disney Adventures
Nintendo Power Source
Computing
Computer magazines
Public domain and
  shareware software
  programs
Education
Compton's Encyclopedia
Tutoring sessions
Entertainment
Cooking Club
Games Channel
MTV
**Global Network
  Navigator (GNN,
  Internet access)**
**Legal Pad (legal
  information and
  services)**
News
@Times (New York Times

online)
Magazines and
  newspapers
Personal Finance
Hoover's Business
  Resources (business
  profiles published by
  Hoovers, Inc.)
Morningstar (mutual
  fund information)
Motley Fool (investing)
Small Business Center
Travel and Shopping
1-800-Flowers (worldwide
  floral service)
2Market (interactive
  shopping)
Hallmark Connections
  (customized greeting
  cards)
Tower Records (CDs
  and tapes)
Travelers Corner

KEY COMPETITORS

AT&T Corp.
CompuServe
Dow Jones
MCI
Microsoft

NETCOM
News Corp.
People World
Prodigy
PSINet

Reuters
Starwave
Thomson Corp.
Time Warner

HOW MUCH

NYSE symbol: AOL FYE: June 30	Annual Growth	1986	1987	1988	1989	1990	1991	1992	1993	1994	1995
Sales ($ mil.)	60.4%	—	9	14	15	20	21	27	40	104	394
Net income ($ mil.)	—	—	0	0	(6)	0	1	4	4	6	(34)
Income as % of sales	—	—	0.2%	2.9%	—	1.0%	7.0%	13.3%	10.5%	5.9%	—
Earnings per share ($)	—	—	—	—	—	0.01	0.04	0.08	0.08	0.10	(0.99)
Stock price – high ($)	—	—	—	—	—	—	—	3.66	8.75	14.63	46.25
Stock price – low ($)	—	—	—	—	—	—	—	1.34	2.22	5.97	12.31
Stock price – close ($)	117.2%	—	—	—	—	—	—	3.66	7.31	14.00	37.50
P/E – high	—	—	—	—	—	—	—	46	117	154	—
P/E – low	—	—	—	—	—	—	—	17	30	63	—
Dividends per share ($)	—	—	—	—	—	—	—	0.00	0.00	0.00	0.00
Book value per share ($)	88.9%	—	—	—	—	—	—	0.43	0.50	1.71	2.90
Employees	115.1%	—	—	—	—	—	116	124	236	527	2,481

1995 YEAR-END

Debt ratio: 9.1%
Return on equity: —
Cash (mil.): $64
Current ratio: 1.00
Long-term debt (mil.): $19
No. of shares (mil.): 75
Dividends
  Yield: —
  Payout: —
Market value (mil.): $2,817

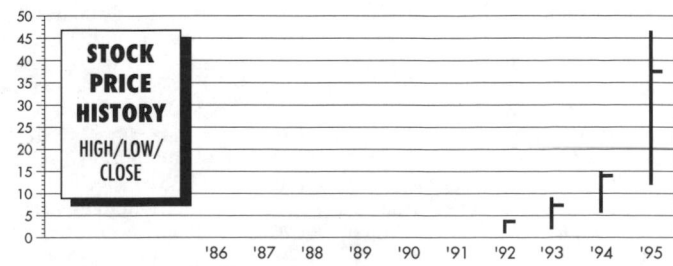

STOCK PRICE HISTORY
HIGH/LOW/CLOSE

AMERIDATA TECHNOLOGIES, INC.

OVERVIEW

How would you like to draw the organizational chart for AmeriData Technologies? The Stamford, Connecticut-based company, itself an amalgam of separate but complementary subsidiaries, is now but one of more than 2 dozen subsidiaries of GE Capital Services, which itself is a subsidiary of megaconglomerate General Electric. Now, was that perfectly clear?

The company is a leading provider of computer products, networks, and services and is ranked #1 in overall customer satisfaction among the nation's top 1,000 computer systems integrators. AmeriData rents out PC networking equipment and offers business and technology consulting services. Customers include businesses and governmental and educational organizations. AmeriData's international unit provides computer products in Europe, Mexico, and Russia.

Primarily because of the 30 businesses it has acquired and assimilated over the past several years, AmeriData is the fastest-growing computer reseller and systems integrator. The company has racked up a phenomenal 5-year growth rate of 135,647%.

Its major strategy is to consolidate its different acquisitions under the established AmeriData brand name. Another strategy is the adoption of LifeCycle Solutions, which provides a single source for design, implementation, installation, maintenance, and upgrades of customers' management information systems, thus helping clients control operating costs.

Gerald Poch, cofounder of an AmeriData predecessor and co-chairman of the company before it was bought by GE Capital, now heads a new division, Worldwide Desktop Services, which includes AmeriData.

WHEN

Gerald Poch and Leonard Fassler were in the telecommunications business in the late 1970s and early 1980s. They cofounded Sage Broadcasting (radio stations) in 1985 and 5 years later began Sage Alerting Systems (emergency-alert systems for high-risk environments).

While installing an alert system for a petrochemical customer, the 2 realized the need for a national technology integrator and decided to make that their next business. They took Sage Alerting Systems public in 1991 and the next year formed Sage DataCom as a subsidiary to provide computer products and services. The first acquisitions came later that year, partly as a test of their theories about the market and the synergies they could create. They decided to continue their acquisition strategy, but they needed a better vehicle, so they began a discreet search for a business they could buy and build their company around.

That's when Jim McCleary came along. He was looking for financing for his company, AmeriData, which had begun as a teletype repair shop in 1968. It had become one of the nation's largest and most successful regional computer systems integrators (it was one of the first IBM computer dealers), and Poch and Fassler considered it the best-managed company in the business. Sage acquired AmeriData in mid-1993 and became AmeriData Technologies in 1994. By the end of that year, it had bought and integrated more than 25

companies, including a computer rental business in Virginia. That was combined with a systems rental business from McCleary's AmeriData and spun off as AmeriData Computer Rentals in 1994. Also that year AmeriData Consulting was formed.

Co-chairmen Poch, Fassler, and McCleary thought it was important to maintain certain advantages held by the smaller companies they had bought, including being flexible enough to innovate and take chances and staying in touch with customers in order to respond quickly to changing needs.

The acquisition of Bohdan Associates (renamed AmeriData Federal Systems) promised the company a piece of Uncle Sam's information technology market. Its designation by IBM as one of 5 authorized vendors of EduQuest, a classroom network, assured AmeriData a share of EduQuest's estimated $2 billion market. In early 1995 AmeriData formed an international subsidiary, InterData Inc.; the $34 million acquisition of selected Control Data Systems businesses that year gave it operations in Canada, Mexico, and Europe.

GE Capital acquired AmeriData in mid-1996 and made it a subsidiary of its Technology Management Systems (TMS) business. The $490 million deal (approximately doubling TMS's expected revenue) gave GE Capital a foothold in Austria, Scandinavia, and the UK. Poch became chairman and CEO of a new TMS division, Worldwide Desktop Services.

WHO

Chairman and CEO, Worldwide Desktop Services:
Gerald A. Poch
President and CEO, Technology Management Systems:
Mike Ford
President and CEO, North American Desktop Services:
Perry Monych
SVP Finance, GE Capital Services: James A. Parke
SVP Human Resources, GE Capital Services: Lawrence
J. Toole
Auditors: Ernst & Young LLP

WHERE

HQ: 700 Canal St., Stamford, CT 06902
Phone: 203-357-1464
Fax: 203-357-1531
Web site: http://www.ameridata.com
AmeriData has more than 100 sales offices in the US and
provides computer products in Austria, Canada, the
Czech Republic, Greece, Mexico, Norway, Portugal,
Russia, and the UK. It also has a product distribution
facility in the UK.

	1995 Sales	
	$ mil.	% of total
US	1,442	95
Europe	53	3
Canada	11	1
Mexico	10	1
Total	**1,516**	**100**

WHAT

	1995 Sales	
	$ mil.	% of total
Computer products	1,368	90
Computer services	148	10
Total	**1,516**	**100**

Selected Products and Services

Ameridata Computer Rental
Office productivity software
System delivery, setup, checkout, and pickup of PCs and
  Unix-based workstations
Toll-free support hotline

Ameridata Consulting
Application development and systems
Architecture solutions
Business performance improvement
Business systems consulting
Document management
Internet services
Packaged system selection
Sales force automation
Testing

Ameridata Global
Intel-based desktop and server platforms
Unix workstations and multiuser systems

Ameridata Systems and Services
Engineering
Hardware and software troubleshooting
Installation of hardware and software
LANs and WANs
Network-ready configuration and network services
Online product and pricing information
Outsourcing
Personal computers, hardware, and software
Software fulfillment, licensing support, and asset
  management
Systems integration
Technical support and maintenance
Testing
Training

Selected Vendors

Adobe	Intel
Aldus	Lexmark
Apple	Microsoft
AST	Novell
Compaq	Oracle
Epson	Packard Bell
Hewlett-Packard	Radius
Hitachi	Sun Microsystems
IBM	Toshiba

KEY COMPETITORS

Andersen Consulting	Entex
American Management	Gemini Consulting
Booz, Allen	Inacom
CompuCom	Intelligent Electronics
Computer Data Systems	MCI Systemhouse
Computer Sciences	Technology Solutions
Control Data	Vanstar
EDS	

HOW MUCH

Subsidiary FYE: December 31	Annual Growth	1986	1987	1988	1989	1990	1991	1992	1993	1994	1995
Sales ($ mil.)	524.0%	—	—	—	—	—	1	6	220	1,019	1,516
Net income ($ mil.)	—	—	—	—	—	—	0	0	4	14	17
Income as % of sales	—	—	—	—	—	—	—	0.6%	1.9%	1.4%	1.1%
Employees	372.9%	—	—	—	—	—	7	100	1,600	2,100	3,500

1995 YEAR-END

Debt ratio: 68.2%
Return on equity: 12.4%
Cash (mil.): $41
Current ratio: 1.07
Long-term debt (mil.): $12

AmeriData
Technologies, Inc.

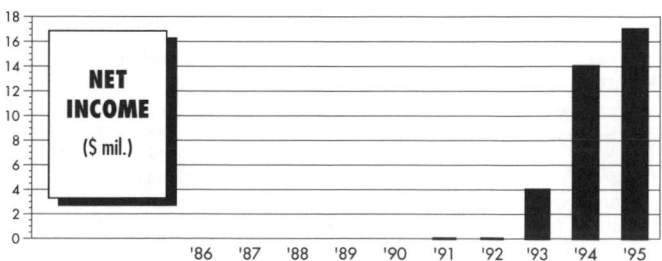

NET INCOME ($ mil.)

ANAM GROUP

OVERVIEW

South Korea's Anam Group is becoming quite the corporate octopus. Among the Seoul-based conglomerate's many arms is Anam Industrial, the world's #1 microchip package assembler. Anam Industrial counts Intel, Motorola, and Texas Instruments among its customers. The group's Amkor Electronics markets Anam chips in the US and accounts for more than 3/4 of the group's sales. Other members of Anam Group include Anam Electronics (audio and video equipment and large-screen TVs), the Electronics Boutique (a software retailer), and Amkor/Anam Pilipinas Inc. (AAPI), the group's Philippine manufacturing facilities.

Anam remains dwarfed by Korea's big corporate fish (the 4 "chaebols": Daewoo,

Hyundai, LG Group, and Samsung), but the group is growing new arms in an effort to compete. It recently purchased Yoo Bong Industries, an industrial waste processor, and Anam Electronics established a discount finance company for its consumer electronics customers. Anam has also joined with Geotek Communications, a New Jersey-based wireless telecommunications company in which Anam has invested, to bid on mobile radio licenses in Korea. Once it has established a mobile radio business in Korea, Anam wants to export the service to China and the Philippines.

Anam Industrial and Anam Electronics are publicly traded on the Korean Stock Exchange. The founding Kim family has majority holdings in both.

WHEN

The oldest of 7 children, Kim Joo-Jin ("Jim") came to the US in 1955 to study economics at the University of Pennsylvania's Wharton School; he later lectured in economics at Villanova. In 1968 Kim started Amkor Electronics as the US agent for his father's company, Anam Industrial (which had evolved from an electronics firm started in 1953 into South Korea's first semiconductor maker). To cushion its dependence on the volatile semiconductor market, Anam Industrial diversified into watchmaking in 1975. About that time Kim's wife, Agnes, began selling electronic watches and calculators from a mall kiosk near the family home in Pennsylvania.

In the 1980s Kim's brother Joo-Chai added to the family business by founding large-screen TV maker Anam Electronics, a joint venture with Japan's Matsushita Electric. Kim joined the board of California semiconductor maker VLSI Technology in 1982, and through that association the company entered the application-specific integrated circuit (ASIC) market. The company opened a branch in Tokyo in 1986 in an effort to enter the Japanese market. During the late 1980s the Kims' mall kiosk business moved into storefronts and started selling computer software and video games under the name Electronics Boutique.

The Anam Group grew along with the semiconductor industry and by 1990 had 50% of the world's semiconductor package assembly business. That year the group established AAPI in Manila when it took over a plant from Advanced Micro Devices. It also acquired

Scotland-based ITEQ Europe Ltd., Europe's leading semiconductor assembly contractor. Anam Electronics opened its 2nd plant in 1990 and began to diversify into computers, fax machines, and VCRs. During the early 1990s Anam Industrial developed tape automated bonding (TAB), a manufacturing process that improved productivity and profitability.

When the senior Kim retired in 1992, Kim Joo-Jin became head of Anam Group. With an eye toward the telecommunications market, that year Kim began investing in Geotek. Also in 1992 the Electronics Boutique began managing the 55-store Waldensoftware chain owned by Kmart. By late 1994 the Electronics Boutique had evolved into a 400-store chain with sales of $240 million, more than 60% from PCs and software.

In 1995 Amkor — a leader in ball-grid array (BGA) chip packaging, an emerging standard — said it would build the US's first independent BGA facility in Arizona. Amkor also formed a joint venture with Integral Company of Belarus to build semiconductors in Russia. (It pulled out the following year, citing the need to invest in other opportunities.)

Anam Group in 1996 said it would build a 4th semiconductor assembly plant in the Philippines with a target production of 50 million chips a month. That year the company formed a partnership with Kuala Lumpur-based Niaga Lima Sdn. Bhd. to produce semiconductor components in Malaysia. By 1996 Electronics Boutique had over 500 stores, including locations in Canada, Ireland, Puerto Rico, South Korea, and the UK.

WHO

Honorary Chairman: Kim Hyang-Soo
Chairman and CEO: Kim Joo-Jin "Jim" Kim
VC: Kim Joo-Chai
President, Anam Electronics: Kim Joon Yeon
President, Anam Industrial: Hwang In Kil
President, Amkor Electronics: John Boruch
President and CEO, Electronics Boutique: Joseph Firestone
Corporate VP Finance and Administration, Amkor Electronics: Frank Marcucci
VP Merchandising and Distribution, Electronics Boutique: Jeff Griffiths
VP Finance, Electronics Boutique: John Panichello
Managing Director, Anam Industrial: K. H. Kim
Auditors: Coopers & Lybrand L.L.P.

WHERE

HQ: 280-8, Sungsudong 2Ka, Sungdong-ku, Seoul, Korea
Phone: +82-2-460-5114
Fax: +82-2-465-2607
US HQ: Amkor Electronics, 1345 Enterprise Dr., Westchester, PA 19380
US Phone: 610-431-9600
US Fax: 610-431-5881

Anam Group has manufacturing facilities in Malaysia, the Philippines, South Korea, and the US.

WHAT

Selected Subsidiaries and Products

Amkor Electronics
Semiconductor sales and engineering

Amkor/Anam Pilipinas
Semiconductor packaging and testing

Anam Electronics
Computers
Fax machines
Modems
Televisions
VCRs

Anam Environmental Industry
Anam Industrial
Semiconductor assembly

Anam Semiconductor & Technology
Application-specific integrated circuit (ASIC) design
Lead frames
Photo masks

Electronics boutique
Retail sales of computer supplies and accessories, Education and entertainment software, Productivity and reference software, and Video games

KEY COMPETITORS

ACT Manufacturing	PCI Ltd.
AMD	Philips Electronics
Best Buy	Pioneer
CompUSA	Samsung
DII	Sanyo
Egghead	SGS-Thomson
Group Technologies	Sharp
Hitachi	Sharper Edge
IBM	Sony
Intel	Tandy Corporation
Kmart	Texas Instruments
Kyocera	Toshiba
Micron Technology	Wal-Mart
NEC	Zenith
NeoStar	Zycon

HOW MUCH

Principal exchange: Korea FYE: December 31	Annual Growth	1986	1987	1988	1989	1990	1991	1992	1993	1994	1995
Sales ($ mil.)	28.6%	—	—	—	—	—	461	613	771	977	1,260
Net income ($ mil.)	35.1%	—	—	—	—	—	9	9	14	18	30
Income as % of sales	—	—	—	—	—	—	2.0%	1.5%	1.8%	1.9%	2.4%
Earnings per share ($)	33.4%	—	—	—	—	—	0.76	0.74	1.07	1.55	2.41
Stock price – high ($)	—	—	—	—	—	—	28.16	22.04	34.90	36.33	30.12
Stock price – low ($)	—	—	—	—	—	—	18.49	12.75	19.36	26.21	20.80
Stock price – close ($)	3.8%	—	—	—	—	—	18.98	21.92	32.70	27.16	22.07
P/E – high	—	—	—	—	—	—	37	30	33	23	13
P/E – low	—	—	—	—	—	—	24	17	18	17	9
Dividends per share ($)	—	—	—	—	—	—	0.00	0.16	0.21	0.28	0.38
Book value per share ($)	4.3%	—	—	—	—	—	16.73	17.03	17.39	18.42	19.81
Employees	—	—	—	—	—	—	—	—	—	—	7,629

Note: Information presented is for Anam International only.

1995 YEAR-END

Debt ratio: 68.1%
Return on equity: 12.1%
Cash (mil.): $95
Current ratio: 0.56
Long-term debt (mil.): $199
No. of shares (mil.): 15
Dividends
  Yield: 1.7%
  Payout: 15.7%
Market value (mil.): $338

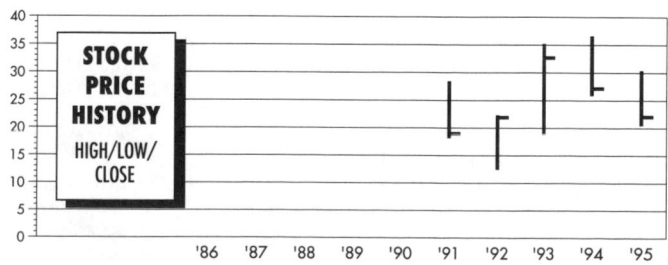

STOCK PRICE HISTORY HIGH/LOW/CLOSE

ANDERSEN CONSULTING

OVERVIEW

With offices from Auckland to Zurich, from Etobicoke to Al Khobar, Andersen Consulting stands ready to serve its multinational clientele, wherever they are. The Chicago-based consulting firm, the world's largest, is part of Andersen Worldwide, whose Arthur Andersen & Co. is the world's #1 accounting concern.

Andersen Consulting's worldwide presence lets it offer seamless service to multinational corporations, wherever the particular assignment happens to be. It is also based on the firm's technical competence: it trains its pro-

fessional staff intensively and works with major computer and software suppliers like Hewlett-Packard and Microsoft.

But the firm is also a canny marketer. Andersen Consulting's leading position helps it sell directly to top management, rather than go through lower levels. In addition, the firm has set up several hands-on exhibit areas, including New York's Financial Ideas Exchange, highlighting banking and insurance, and the Retail Place, a store-of-the-future exhibit in Chicago.

WHEN

In 1907 Arthur Andersen was working in the Chicago office of Price Waterhouse. The next year (at age 23), he became the youngest CPA in Illinois. Also in 1908 he began teaching accounting at Northwestern University, soon rising to head of the department. In addition, he worked briefly as controller at Schlitz Brewing before joining with fellow accountant Clarence DeLany to form an accounting firm, Andersen, DeLany & Co.

Establishment of the Federal Reserve and implementation of the federal income tax in 1913 aided the firm's early growth by increasing the demand for accounting services. Early clients included ITT, Briggs & Stratton, Colgate-Palmolive, and Parker Pen. In 1915 the company opened an office in Milwaukee. When DeLany left in 1918, the firm became Arthur Andersen & Co.

The enterprise grew rapidly during the 1920s and added to its list of services financial investigations, which formed the basis for its future strength in management consulting. The firm continued to expand in the 1920s, opening offices in New York (1921), Kansas City (1923), and Los Angeles (1926), among others. When financier Samuel Insull's empire collapsed in 1932, Andersen was appointed the bankers' representative and guarded the assets during the refinancing. He opened additional offices in Boston and Houston in 1937 and in Atlanta and Minneapolis in 1940.

Andersen dominated the firm until he died in 1947. He was succeeded by Leonard Spacek. During Spacek's tenure, which lasted until 1963, Arthur Andersen opened 18 more US offices and began a period of foreign expansion. The firm also began offering consulting services to its clients during this period.

True to the founder's academic background, the company has placed great emphasis on

training. It established Andersen University, its Center for Professional Education, in the early 1970s in St. Charles, Illinois. Reflecting the company's global scope, it transferred its headquarters to Geneva in 1977.

Throughout the 1970s the firm increased its consulting business. By 1979 consulting accounted for 21% of sales; 9 years later that number had risen to 40%, creating tension between the consultants and the auditors. The struggle for dominance forced a 1989 restructuring, which established Arthur Andersen and Andersen Consulting as distinct entities.

The consulting group, which initially focused on systems integration service, began developing new specialties in manufacturing, financial services, and government. The firm addressed the shift from mainframes to PCs (which saw the proliferation of computer systems to control production, transportation, and retail systems) by forming alliances with Hewlett-Packard, Sun Microsystems, and Microsoft. Beginning in 1993, it also began targeting the Asia/Pacific region for particular growth.

As it grew, Andersen Consulting found that the old accounting model (featuring a relatively short "up or out" partnership track) did not work well in a field where specialized experience and knowlege were at a premium. In 1995 the firm restructured its partnership track to provide for a longer learning curve and began providing a role for technicians uninterested in partnership. It has also begun billing on a value-provided rather than hourly basis.

In 1996 Andersen was chosen by the Frankfurt Stock Exchange's governing body, Deutsche Burse Group, to create an electronic securities trading system that can operate in conjunction with floor trading.

Chairman, Managing Partner, and CEO, Arthur Andersen & Co, SC: Lawrence A. Weinbach
Managing Partner: George T. Shaheen
Managing Partner, Americas: John Kelly
Managing Partner, Europe/Middle East/Africa/India: Vernon Ellis
Managing Partner, Asia/Pacific: Thomas E. McCarty
CFO: Michael O. Hill
Managing Director, Marketing and Communications: James E. Murphy
Managing Partner, Human Resources: Carol Meyer
General Counsel: Jon N. Ekdahl
Auditors:

WHERE

HQ: 100 S. Wacker Dr., Ste. 1070, Chicago, IL 60606
Phone: 312-507-2900
Fax: 312-507-7965
Web site: http://www.ac.com

Andersen Consulting provides management and technology consulting services through more than 149 offices in 46 countries.

	1995 Sales	
	$ mil.	% of total
Americas	2,385	56
Europe, India, Africa & Middle East	1,420	34
Asia/Pacific	419	10
Total	**4,224**	**100**

WHAT

	1995 Sales	
	$ mil.	% of total
Manufacturing industry	1,702	40
Financial services industry	1,125	27
Communications industry	573	14
Government	396	9
Utilities	282	7
Other	146	3
Total	**4,224**	**100**

Selected Services
Business consulting
Business reengineering
Customer service system design
Data system consulting and design
Energy and utility consulting
Internet sales systems research and design
Sales systems design
Securities trading system design

Representative Clients

Australian Mutual Provident Society
Bell Atlantic
Commune di Milano (Italy)
Department of Social Security (UK)
Deutsche Telekom
Dow Chemical
Ford
Harley Davidson
London Stock Exchange
Pirelli
Samsung
Singapore Power
Sony
Tenneco
USAA

KEY COMPETITORS

American Software
Arthur D. Little
Booz, Allen
Boston Consulting
Cap Gemini
CompuCom
Computer Sciences
Control Data
Coopers & Lybrand
DEC
Deloitte Touche Tohmatsu
EDS
Ernst & Young
Getronics
IBM
KPMG
Logica
Marsh & McLennan
MCI Systemhouse
McKinsey & Co.
Perot Systems
PRC
Price Waterhouse
Primark
System Software Associates

HOW MUCH

Subsidiary FYE: December 31	Annual Growth	1986	1987	1988	1989	1990	1991	1992	1993	1994	1995
Sales ($ mil.)	19.6%	—	—	—	1,442	1,561	2,340	2,723	2,876	3,220	4,224
Employees	13.7%	—	—	—	—	20,000	25,000	26,730	29,300	32,000	38,000

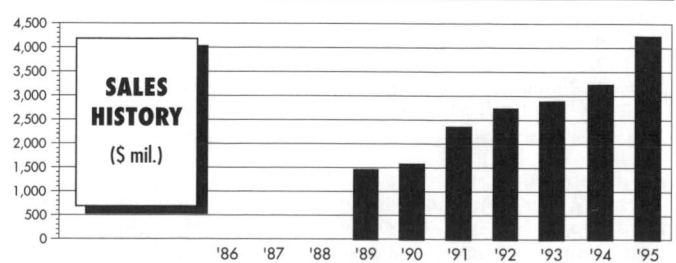

ANDERSEN CONSULTING

SALES HISTORY ($ mil.)

APPLE COMPUTER, INC.

OVERVIEW

If one bad apple can spoil the bunch, Apple CEO Gilbert Amelio may have a whole bushel basket of rotting fruit to dig through to find a tasty morsel. Amelio, credited with the turn-around at National Semiconductor, was hired in early 1996 to replace Michael Spindler as CEO at Apple. The Cupertino, California-based company is facing an orchard of problems, from shrinking market share to executive defections to outdated inventory. Once the world's largest maker of personal computers, Apple has watched its windfall shrink as makers of PCs running archrival Microsoft's Windows operating software have passed it by.

Amid rampant buyout speculation, the company entered talks with Sun Microsystems in 1996, but they failed to bear fruit. Amelio insists that he can revive the company and keep it independent. One of his first moves was to take a $350 million write down on about $1 billion in obsolete inventory. That, and a restructuring charge, helped push Apple's loss for the first half of fiscal 1996 to more than $800 million.

One hope for the future could be the Internet. Buoyed by the popularity of Apple computers among Web page designers, graphic artists, and entertainment content providers, the firm hopes to become a major provider of online products.

Amelio has also begun outsourcing some of its manufacturing business to lower costs. In 1996 it announced plans to sell a major PC, laptop, and circuit board plant to contract computer maker SCI Systems, which will supply Apple with products.

WHEN

College dropouts Steven Jobs and Stephen Wozniak founded Apple in 1976 in the Santa Clara Valley. Their plan to sell circuit boards changed to selling fully assembled microcomputers after Jobs's first sales call brought an order for 50 units. They built the Apple I in Jobs's garage and sold it without a monitor, keyboard, or casing. The demand for the Apple I made Jobs aware of the market for small computers. The Apple name (from Jobs's days on an Oregon farm) and the computer's "user-friendly" appearance appealed to non-technical buyers.

By 1977 Wozniak, who invented the Apple I, had substantially improved it by adding a keyboard, color monitor, and 8 slots for peripheral devices. The latter feature inspired numerous 3rd-party add-on devices and software programs for the new machine, the Apple II.

More than 130,000 Apple IIs had been sold by 1980, when revenues reached $117 million and Apple went public. By 1983 Wozniak had left and Jobs had hired John Sculley from PepsiCo to succeed Mike Markkula as president. (After a tumultuous power struggle, Jobs left in 1985 and started NeXT.)

Following the failure of the Apple III and Lisa computers (1983), Apple roared back with the revolutionary Macintosh. Advertised as the computer "For the Rest of Us," Macintosh incorporated a graphical user interface inspired by Xerox's Alto computer. In 1986 Apple moved into the office market with the Mac Plus and the LaserWriter printer, ushering in desktop-publishing. But the late 1980's brought new competition from Microsoft, whose Windows operating system featured a graphical interface similar to Apple's. Apple sued Microsoft in 1988, beginning a long legal battle between the 2 companies.

Apple lost a key 1992 ruling in its copyright suit against Microsoft over the "look and feel" of Mac software. After an 84% drop in earnings in 1993, the company made major changes, including upgrading its technology and trimming its workforce. Sculley departed (according to some he was forced out), Michael Spindler became CEO, and Markkula returned as chairman.

In 1994 Apple released its popular Power Mac computer, with a PowerPC microchip (developed with IBM and Motorola) that lets computers run software designed for Mac OS, Windows NT, OS/2, and AIX platforms. Also that year the company finally licensed three companies, including Power Computing, to make Mac-compatible clones.

However, the flurry of Macintosh clones that would boost the amount of software written for the Mac failed to appear. In an indication of lost confidence, mutual fund giant Fidelity Investments sold 3/4 of its almost 11% stake in Apple in 1995. The next year the company announced a layoff of 1,300 people and suspended its dividend. Also that year Apple pulled the plug on its struggling eWorld online service and agreed to bundle America Online software with some of its computers. And in 1996, to encourage the development of more Mac software, Apple licensed the rights to its current and future operating systems To Motorola and IBM.

WHO

Chairman and CEO: Gilbert F. Amelio, age 52
VC: Armas C. Mike Markkula Jr., age 53
EVP and COO: Marco Landi, age 51
EVP and CFO: Fred D. Anderson Jr., age 51
EVP R & D, Chief Technical Officer: Ellen Hancock, age 53
SVP Worldwide Operations: G. Frederick Forsyth, age 51, $622,353 pay
SVP; President, Apple Americas: James J. Buckley, age 45, $586,448 pay
SVP; President, Apple Pacific: John Floisand, age 51
SVP Macintosh Systems: Howard F. Lee
SVP Marketing: Satjiv S. Chahil, age 45
SVP, General Counsel, and Secretary: Edward B. Stead, age 48
SVP Human Resources: Pat Sharp, age 54
Auditors: Ernst & Young LLP

WHERE

HQ: One Infinite Loop, Cupertino, CA 95014
Phone: 408-996-1010
Fax: 408-974-2113
Web site: http://www.apple.com

	1995 Sales		1995 Operating Income	
	$ mil.	% of total	$ mil.	% of total
North America	6,130	56	(20)	—
Europe	2,365	21	245	36
Japan	1,822	16	46	7
Pacific	745	7	383	57
Adjustments	—	—	20	—
Total	**11,062**	**100**	**674**	**100**

WHAT

Computers
Macintosh LC
Macintosh Performa
Macintosh PowerBook
Power Macintosh

Peripherals
CD-ROM drives
Monitors
Network interfaces
Printers
Scanners

Networking and Connectivity Products
LAN connectivity products

Workgroup server systems

Personal Digital Assistant
Apple MessagePad

Software
Applications
Database management
Developer tools
Educational software
Graphics
Languages
System software Utilities

KEY COMPETITORS

Acer
Artisoft
AST
Canon
Casio
Compaq
Daewoo
Dell
Fujitsu
Gateway 2000
Hewlett-Packard
Hitachi
Hyundai
IBM
Intel
LG Group
Machines Bull
Matsushita
Micron Electronics
Microsoft
NEC
Novell
Oki
Olivetti
Packard Bell
Philips
Power Computing
Radius
Samsung
Sharp
Siemens
Silicon Graphics
Sony
Sun Microsystems
Toshiba

HOW MUCH

Nasdaq symbol: AAPL FYE: September 30	Annual Growth	1986	1987	1988	1989	1990	1991	1992	1993	1994	1995
Sales ($ mil.)	21.6%	1,902	2,661	4,071	5,284	5,558	6,309	7,087	7,977	9,189	11,062
Net income ($ mil.)	11.9%	154	218	400	454	475	310	530	87	310	424
Income as % of sales	—	8.1%	8.2%	9.8%	8.6%	8.5%	4.9%	7.5%	1.1%	3.4%	3.8%
Earnings per share ($)	12.5%	1.20	1.65	3.08	3.53	3.77	2.58	4.33	0.73	2.61	3.45
Stock price – high ($)	—	21.88	59.25	47.25	49.63	47.75	73.25	70.00	65.25	43.75	50.13
Stock price – low ($)	—	10.88	20.44	36.13	33.75	24.25	40.25	41.50	22.00	24.63	31.44
Stock price – close ($)	5.2%	20.25	42.00	40.25	35.25	43.00	56.38	59.75	29.25	39.00	31.88
P/E – high	—	18	36	15	14	13	28	16	89	17	15
P/E – low	—	9	12	12	10	6	16	10	30	9	9
Dividends per share ($)	—	0.00	0.12	0.32	0.40	0.44	0.48	0.48	0.48	0.48	0.48
Book value per share ($)	17.5%	5.54	6.63	8.17	11.77	12.54	14.92	18.46	17.45	19.94	23.60
Employees	13.6%	5,586	7,228	10,836	14,517	14,528	14,432	14,798	14,938	14,592	17,615

1995 YEAR-END

Debt ratio: 20.8%
Return on equity: 16.0%
Cash (mil.): $952
Current ratio: 2.25
Long-term debt (mil.): $303
No. of shares (mil.): 123
Dividends
 Yield: 1.5%
 Payout: 13.9%
Market value (mil.): $3,9

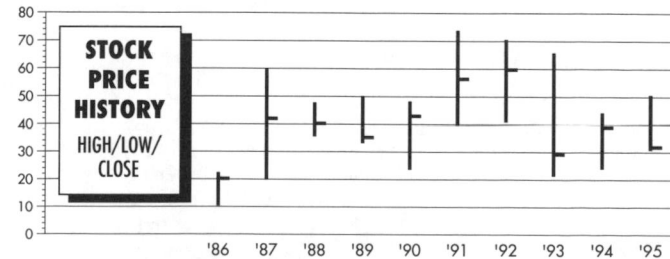

STOCK PRICE HISTORY
HIGH/LOW/CLOSE

APPLIED MATERIALS, INC.

OVERVIEW

Applied Materials is handling its success as well as its machines handle silicon wafers. The Santa Clara, California-based company is the world's #1 maker of wafer fabrication equipment used by semiconductor manufacturers. With microchips being incorporated into more and more products, many chip makers are increasing production (experts predict that more than 200 new chip factories will be built worldwide by the turn of the century). Applied's products are hot and its revenues have tripled since 1993.

The company's machines have a big share in most segments of the complex chip-making industry: deposition (layering film on wafers, 50%), etching (removing excess material from circuit patterns on the film, 32%), and ion implantation (altering electrical characteristics of certain areas of film, 20%).

Now Applied, which spends nearly 11% of revenues on R&D and engineering, has a new

product to wow the industry — a machine that polishes the surface of semiconductors to increase uniformity (a process formerly done by hand). The new machine is expected to kick revenues up several notches toward Applied's goal of $10 billion by the year 2000. Applied also has machines in development to accommodate the industry's expected move from 8-inch to 12-inch wafers and has added a rapid thermal processing (RTP) system to its line. (RTP accommodates processes that require high temperatures.)

Globalization — the company established itself in Asia back in the 1970s — has helped Applied weather the semiconductor industry's cycles. The company has developed expertise in setting up new facilities and in serving customers around the world, skills that should give it an advantage as markets take shape in China and India.

WHEN

Applied Materials was founded in 1967 in Mountain View, California, as a maker of chemical vapor deposition (CVD) systems for semiconductor wafer fabrication. After growing more than 40% annually, the company went public in 1972. Two years later, it purchased Galamar Industries, a wafer manufacturer.

In 1975 Applied suffered a 45% drop in sales as the semiconductor industry contracted along with the US economy. Financial and managerial problems plagued the company after the recession, so in 1976 James Morgan was picked to replace founder Michael McNeilly as CEO. Two years later Morgan, a former division manager for conglomerate Textron, also became chairman.

After selling Galamar (1977) and other non-core units and persuading the company's main backer, the Bank of America, to extend Applied's credit limit, Morgan announced a plan to move into Japan. Its first joint venture, Applied Materials Japan, was set up in 1979.

Morgan's hunch that Japan would become a major producer of semiconductor chips paid off. His early arrival, plus his attention to Japanese ways of doing business, put Applied way ahead of its American competitors. By going directly to its Japanese customers, the company was able to tailor its products to their needs, overcoming the industry's notorious quality problems and providing technical services that other American suppliers, who sold their products through Japanese trading

houses, were unable to offer. (Morgan even wrote a book about doing business in Japan, *Cracking the Japanese Market.*)

The computer chip industry fell into another slump in 1985, and Morgan used the slowdown as an opportunity to rev up his R&D department. With 2 separate technologies competing for the next wave of wafer-manufacturing machines, Morgan essentially bet the company on the fast but unproven one-at-a-time, multiple-chamber method (as opposed to the existing batch-process system). The result was the Precision 5000 series machine, which revolutionized the industry and catapulted Applied to the top. By 1989 the company had captured 10% of the semiconductor-equipment market.

Applied formed a joint venture with Japanese equipment maker Komatsu in 1993 to develop machinery for makers of flat panel displays. That year Applied's sales topped $1 billion for the first time. The company joined SGS-Thomson Microelectronics in 1995 to research advanced metal deposition processes, which will be used to develop future generations of chip fabricating equipment. Also in 1995 Applied sued rival Novellus, charging it had copied Applied's CVD system.

In 1996 the company received its largest order ever, for $153 million worth of machinery for the new Hyundai Electronics South Korean factory.

WHO

Chairman and CEO: James C. Morgan, age 57, $1,678,826 pay
VC: James W. Bagley, age 56, $1,357,416 pay
President; Co-chairman, Applied Komatsu Technology: Dan Maydan, age 60, $1,166,263 pay
Chairman, Applied Materials Japan; President, Applied Komatsu Technology: Tetsuo Iwasaki
SVP Worldwide Products Operations: Sasson Somekh, age 49, $736,371 pay
SVP Worldwide Business Operations: David N. K. Wang, age 49, $736,371 pay
SVP; President and CEO, Applied Materials Japan: Keisuke Yawata, age 61
SVP and CFO: Gerald F. Taylor, age 55
Group VP, Worldwide Manufacturing Operations: Joseph R. Bronson
VP Human Resources: Dana Ditmore
Auditors: Price Waterhouse LLP

WHERE

HQ: 3050 Bowers Ave., Santa Clara, CA 95054-3299
Phone: 408-727-5555
Fax: 408-748-9943
Web site: http://www.appliedmaterials.com/

Applied Materials has facilities in Israel, Japan, the UK, and the US.

	1995 Sales		1995 Operating Income	
	$ mil.	% of total	$ mil.	% of total
North America	989	32	228	28
Japan	791	26	151	19
Korea	504	17	206	25
Europe	471	15	104	13
Other Asia/ Pacific	307	10	120	15
Adjustments	—	—	(115)	—
Total	**3,062**	**100**	**694**	**100**

WHAT

Selected Processes

Deposition
Chemical vapor deposition
Epitaxial and polysilicon deposition
Physical vapor deposition

Etching (removes material on the wafer that lies outside a photoresistant pattern)

Ion Implantation (deposits ions in specific layers on a semiconductor chip using controlled electrical currents)

Rapid Thermal Processing (uses very rapid heating cycles for high-temperature processes)

Selected Products

CVD
Centura DxZ
Precision 5000 DCVD xP
Precision 5000 SACVD
  BPSG and USG
WCVD xZ

Dry Etch
Etch MxP+
HDP Dielectric Etch Centura
Metal Etch MxP Centura
Polysilicon MxP
Precision Etch 8300

Ion Implantation
Precision Implant xR series

PVD
Centura HP PVD
Endura HP PVD
Endura VHP PVD

Thermal Process
Epi Centura
Poly Centura
Precision 7700 Epi
RTP Centura

KEY COMPETITORS

Advanced Semiconductor Materials
ASMLithography
Canon
DaiNippon Screen
Esterline
Genus
Integrated Process Equipment
Lam Research
Nikon Corporation
Novellus Systems
Silicon Valley Group
Tencor Instruments
Teradyne
Tokyo Electron
Varian Associates

HOW MUCH

Nasdaq symbol: AMAT FYE: October 31	Annual Growth	1986	1987	1988	1989	1990	1991	1992	1993	1994	1995
Sales ($ mil.)	39.9%	149	174	363	502	567	639	751	1,080	1,660	3,062
Net income ($ mil.)	97.3%	1	0	40	52	34	26	40	100	221	454
Income as % of sales	—	0.7%	—	11.0%	10.4%	6.0%	4.1%	5.3%	9.3%	13.3%	14.8%
Earnings per share ($)	71.4%	0.02	0.01	0.31	0.39	0.25	0.19	0.27	0.61	1.26	2.56
Stock price – high ($)	—	2.05	4.16	4.47	4.10	5.07	4.75	9.69	20.00	27.25	59.88
Stock price – low ($)	—	1.00	1.22	2.11	2.78	2.07	2.44	4.03	8.06	18.13	18.50
Stock price – close ($)	47.5%	1.19	2.44	2.78	3.57	2.69	4.41	8.44	19.38	21.13	39.38
P/E – high	—	136	831	15	11	20	25	36	33	22	23
P/E – low	—	67	244	7	7	8	13	15	13	14	7
Dividends per share ($)	—	0.00	0.00	0.00	0.00	0.00	0.00	0.00	0.00	0.00	0.00
Book value per share ($)	30.8%	0.89	1.24	1.59	1.96	2.26	2.41	3.03	3.72	5.74	9.95
Employees	25.0%	1,415	1,406	1,765	2,651	3,281	3,543	3,909	4,739	6,497	10,537

1995 YEAR-END

Debt ratio: 16.9%
Return on equity: 33.0%
Cash (mil.): $286
Current ratio: 2.68
Long-term debt (mil.): $280
No. of shares (mil.): 179
Dividends
  Yield: —
  Payout: —
Market value (mil.): $7,059

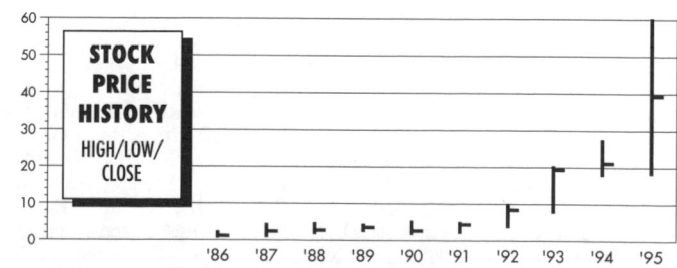

STOCK PRICE HISTORY HIGH/LOW/CLOSE

ARROW ELECTRONICS, INC.

OVERVIEW

Arrow Electronics is right on target, maintaining its position as the world's #1 distributor of electronic components and computer products. Among the Melville, New York-based company's inventory are semiconductors (2/3 of sales), computer peripherals, passive components, and interconnect products. Arrow's customers are primarily original equipment manufacturers in industries such as aviation and aerospace, computers and office equipment, industrial equipment, medical and scientific devices, and telecommunications equipment, and value-added resellers of computer systems. The company has more than 500 suppliers, with semiconductor maker Intel accounting for about 14% of products purchased and electronic components maker Texas Instruments accounting for about 10%.

The company has 5 sales groups in North America: Arrow/Schweber Electronics and Anthem Electronics (the world's leading distributor of semiconductors) sell semiconductors and industrial subsystems; Capstone Electronics sells capacitors, relay switches, power supplies, and related components; Gates/Arrow Distributing sells computers and peripherals; and Zeus Electronics sells specialized semiconductors for the military.

After rapid acquisitions allowed it to supplant rival Avnet in the top global distribution spot, Arrow has shifted its focus to ensure internal support for its operations. The company is increasing its efforts toward global coordination, including integration of its computer systems and its administrative and support functions.

WHEN

Arrow Radio began in 1935 in New York City as a used-radio-equipment outlet. In the mid-1960s the company was selling various home entertainment products and wholesaling electronic parts. However, in 1968, 3 Harvard Business School graduates got Arrow in their sights. Duke Glenn Jr., Roger Green, and John Waddell led a group of investors who acquired the company for $1 million in borrowed money. The 3 also bought a company that reclaimed lead from used car batteries.

With the money they made in the lead reclamation business, the trio expanded Arrow's inventory in its wholesale electronic distribution business. By 1971 Arrow was the 10th largest electronic parts distributor in the US. The company grew rapidly during the 1970s, primarily through internal growth. By 1977 Arrow had become the 4th largest distributor in the US. In 1979 Arrow bought the #2 US distributor, Cramer Electronics. While the purchase of the West Coast-based Cramer was financed with junk bonds and left the company deeply in debt, it also doubled its revenues. Also that year Arrow went public.

A December 1980 hotel fire killed 13 members of Arrow's senior management, including Glenn and Green, who were having a budget meeting. Waddell, who had remained at company headquarters to answer questions about a stock split announced that day, was named acting CEO. Company stock fell 19% the first day it traded after the fire and another 14% before the end of the month. In the spring of 1981, a slump hit the electronics industry. Later in 1981 Arrow's board enticed Alfred Stein to

leave Motorola to become the company's president and CEO. Waddell remained as chairman. However, Stein did not mesh with Arrow, and in early 1982 the board fired him and put Waddell in charge again. By 1983 the slump in the electronics industry was over, and Arrow was temporarily back in the black. However, another industry slump led to significant losses between 1985 and 1987.

In 1985, in a move significant to Arrow's global expansion, the company acquired a 40% interest in Germany's largest electronics distributor, Spoerle Electronic (it currently owns 70% of Spoerle). Steve Kaufman, who became CEO in 1986, continued the company's expansion, acquiring Kierulff Electronics, the 4th largest US distributor (1988), and Lex Electronics, the 3rd largest (1991).

Kaufman expanded Arrow's operations into Asia in 1993 with the acquisition of Hong Kong-based Components Agent Limited. Also that year the company acquired the semiconductor distribution business of Zeus Components for about $25 million.

Spoerle acquired Germany's HED Heinrich Electronic Distribution in 1995. Also that year Arrow acquired semiconductor distributor Anthem Electronics. Arrow continued its Pacific Rim expansion in 1995 with the acquisition of the components and distribution business of Components+Instrumentation, a New Zealand-based enterprise.

The company's Italian subsidiary, Silverstar Ltd., acquired Eurelettronica, one of Italy's biggest semiconductor distributors, in 1996.

WHO

Chairman and CEO: Stephen P. Kaufman, age 54, $1,688,295 pay
CEO, Spoerle Electronic: Carlo Giersch, age 58, $698,178 pay
EVP: Robert E. Klatell, age 50, $561,600 pay
SVP: Steven W. Menefee, age 51, $670,712 pay
SVP and CFO: Gerald Luterman, age 52
SVP: B. J. Scheihing, age 47
VP; Chairman and CEO, Anthem Electronics: Robert S. Throop, age 58, $627,765 pay
VP; President, Arrow/Schweber Electronics: Jan S. Salsgiver, age 39
VP; President, Anthem Electronics: John J. Powers III, age 41
VP; President, Capstone Electronics: Wesley S. Sagawa, age 48
VP; President, Gates/Arrow Distributing: Michael J. Long, age 37
VP Human Resources: Thomas F. Hallam
Auditors: Ernst & Young LLP

WHERE

HQ: 25 Hub Dr., Melville, NY 11747
Phone: 516-391-1300
Fax: 516-391-1640
Web site: http://www.streetlink.com/arw/
Arrow has facilities in 31 countries.

	1995 Sales		1995 Operating Income	
	$ mil.	% of total	$ mil.	% of total
North America	3,929	66	296	67
Europe	1,719	29	135	31
PacificRim	271	5	9	2
Adjustments	—	—	(17)	—
Total	**5,919**	**100**	**423**	**100**

WHAT

Selected Operations
North America
Anthem Electronics (semiconductors and computer products)
Arrow/Schweber Electronics Group (semiconductors)
Capstone Electronics (passive, electromechanical, and interconnect products)
Gates/Arrow Distributing (commercial computer products and systems)
Zeus Electronics (military and high-reliability markets)

Europe
Amitron (75%, Portugal and Spain)
Arrow Electronics Ltd. (UK)
Arrow Electronique (France)
ATD Electronica S.A. (87%, Portugal and Spain)
Exatec A/S (Scandinavia)
Field Oy (Scandinavia)
The Megachip Group (France)
Silverstar (86%, Italy)
Spoerle Electronic (70%, central Europe)
TH:s Elektronik AB (Scandinavia)

Asia/Pacific
Ally (Taiwan)
Arrow Components (New Zealand)
Components Agents Ltd. (Malaysia, Singapore, South Korea, Taiwan)
Lite-On Group (45%; China, Malaysia, Singapore, South Korea, Taiwan)
Veltek (Australia)
Zatek (Australia)

KEY COMPETITORS

Avnet
Bell Industries
Bell Microproducts
Graybar Electric
Jaco Electronics
Marshall Industries
Pioneer-Standard Electronics
Premier Industrial
Rexel
Wyle Electronics

HOW MUCH

NYSE symbol: ARW FYE: December 31	Annual Growth	1986	1987	1988	1989	1990	1991	1992	1993	1994	1995
Sales ($ mil.)	30.7%	530	562	1,006	925	971	1,044	1,622	2,536	4,649	5,919
Net income ($ mil.)	—	(35)	(8)	18	(2)	5	4	41	81	112	203
Income as % of sales	—	—	—	1.8%	—	0.5%	0.4%	2.5%	3.2%	2.4%	3.4%
Earnings per share ($)	—	(5.32)	(3.17)	1.55	(0.19)	0.44	0.28	1.54	2.43	2.31	4.03
Stock price – high ($)	—	17.13	12.13	10.75	6.75	7.00	16.50	30.50	43.13	45.13	59.75
Stock price – low ($)	—	3.00	4.88	5.38	3.13	3.63	3.63	14.38	26.50	33.63	35.13
Stock price – close ($)	24.2%	6.13	6.75	6.63	3.88	4.38	15.75	28.63	41.75	35.88	43.00
P/E – high	—	—	—	7	—	16	59	20	18	20	15
P/E – low	—	—	—	3	—	8	13	9	11	15	9
Dividends per share ($)	(100.0%)	0.15	0.00	0.00	0.00	0.00	0.00	0.00	0.00	0.00	0.00
Book value per share ($)	4.8%	15.61	14.30	12.90	12.67	12.66	11.34	11.99	14.60	18.15	23.73
Employees	13.7%	2,200	2,900	2,775	2,475	2,280	4,200	4,100	4,600	6,500	7,000

1995 YEAR-END

Debt ratio: 32.1%
Return on equity: 19.9%
Cash (mil.): $94
Current ratio: 2.37
Long-term debt (mil.): $452
No. of shares (mil.): 51
Dividends
  Yield: —
  Payout: —
Market value (mil.): $2,178

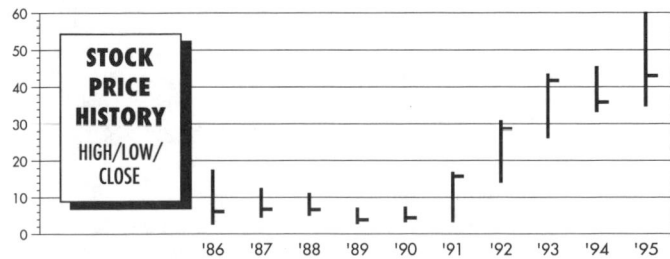

STOCK PRICE HISTORY
HIGH/LOW/CLOSE

AST RESEARCH, INC.

OVERVIEW

Computer maker AST is looking for fixes. The Irvine, California, company, whose president and CEO is former Apple executive Ian Diery, is cutting jobs while it looks for new strategies to survive the cutthroat PC market. Unprofitable since 1993, AST now operates under the watchful eye of 40%-plus owner Samsung. The South Korean industrial conglomerate has deep pockets, and it has already infused AST with $60 million.

Diery, a quick and demanding decision maker, has reduced hour-long service phone waits and broken the $1,000 price barrier with a PC model designed for sale at Wal-Marts. But

AST's underlying illness, says Diery, is its lag in new-product development in an industry where a product cycle is half a year.

Diery's cure for product development lag was to make AST an assembler of components like its competitor Dell: now instead of making motherboards it buys them from Intel. Another remedy was to sell a richer mix of more profitable portable computers: Diery wants 40% of revenues to come from these instead of the present 15%. AST is selling all its new models at prices it says are comparable to mail-order specialist Dell's.

WHEN

In 1979 friends Albert Wong, Safi Qureshey, and Tom Yuen started a high-tech consulting firm, drawing lots to see who would be president. They called the Orange County-based venture AST Associates after the initials of their first names. In 1980 they incorporated as AST Research, Inc., and the 3 Asia-born engineers, working from Yuen's garage, set out to make computer enhancement and peripheral products.

Their timing couldn't have been better. Only 4 months after IBM came out with its PC in 1981, AST had a memory enhancer. Two years later sales reached $12 million, and in 1984 AST went public, raising over $13 million.

As PCs became more sophisticated, with more built-in software features, demand for enhancement products matured. AST responded by introducing its own PC, the Premium/286 (based on Intel's 286 chip), in 1986. But it fell behind in introducing a machine based on the 386 chip in 1987.

After Wong left to start his own company in 1988, Qureshey and Yuen reorganized AST, selling divisions that made enhancement boards for Apple and DEC and cutting staff. The company was in trouble: its former marketing complacency had led to financial woes, and it reported its first loss in fiscal 1989.

By mid-year AST was back on track with 2 new 386-based computers. The company also introduced a line of PCs with the microprocessor on a separate board, allowing users to upgrade without having to buy a complete new motherboard. Also in 1989 it began emphasizing overseas business, establishing subsidiaries in Europe and the Far East.

AST introduced 12 new computers the following year, including a notebook PC priced

30-50% lower than its competitors. The company unveiled the first PC to run both NEC 9801 (the standard in Japan) and MS-DOS operating systems, making it a potential contender in the hard to crack Japanese market. That year AST and IBM announced a 5-year patent cross-licensing accord. AST launched a CAD (computer-aided design) workstation in 1991 and a multiprocessor computer in 1992. Fierce competition slowed AST's growth that year, forcing the company to restructure, and cofounder Yuen abruptly left the company.

In 1993 AST opened a new subsidiary in Singapore and launched its Pentium-based Manhattan servers and its Premmia 486-based computers. That year, when it acquired Tandy's PC manufacturing operations in an effort to increase the number of its distribution outlets (Radio Shack, Computer City, and Incredible Universe), the company began losing money.

The company formed subsidiaries in Ireland, Malaysia, Norway, and South Korea, as well as a sales and manufacturing operation in China, in 1994. It also introduced its Ascentia line of notebook computers and a new line of Advantage PCs that feature user interface software (AST Works).

To maintain its share of the PC market in 1995, AST cut prices on some servers by as much as 22%. Several executives left AST that year, and former Apple executive Ian Diery was named CEO and president. In 1996, after Samsung bought over 40% of the company and bolstered its credit, Samsung president and CEO Kwang-Ho Kim was named AST's chairman.

WHO

Chairman: Kwang-Ho Kim
President and CEO: Young-Soo Kim, age 46, $700,000 pay
SVP Americas: Gerald T. Devlin, age 50, $232,577 pay
SVP Legal and Administration and Secretary: Dennis R. Leibel, age 51, $217,820 pay
SVP Worldwide Manufacturing Operations: Gary D. Weaver, age 53, $104,100 pay
SVP Asia/Pacific and Middle East Region: Michael Willcocks, age 47
CFO: Won Suk Yang, age 49
VP, Controller, and Principal Accounting Officer: Mark P. de Raad, age 36
Director Human Resources: Candice Byrne
Auditors: Ernst & Young LLP

WHERE

HQ: 16215 Alton Pkwy., Irvine, CA 92619-7005
Phone: 714-727-4141
Fax: 714-727-8584
Web site: http://www.ast.com
AST has plants in the US (Texas), China, Ireland, and Taiwan.

	1995 Sales	
	$ mil.	% of total
Americas	453	45
Europe	383	38
Pacific Rim	180	17
Total	**1,016**	**100**

	1995 Sales	
	$ mil.	% of total
Desktop system products	753	74
Notebook computer products	168	17
Other	95	9
Total	**1,016**	**100**

WHAT

Computer Product Lines
Advantage!
Ascentia (notebook computers)
ASTVision color monitors
Bravo
GRiD (palmtop and pen-based systems)
Manhattan SMP (multiprocessor line for minicomputer/superserver marketplace)
PowerExec (notebook computers)
Premmia (desktops and servers)
Victor (desktops in Europe)

KEY COMPETITORS

Acer	NCR
Apple Computer	NEC
Canon	Olivetti
Compaq	Packard Bell
Daewoo	Power Computing
Data General	Radius
DEC	Sanyo
Dell	Sharp
Fujitsu	Silicon Graphics
Gateway 2000	Sony
Hewlett-Packard	Sun Microsystems
Hitachi	TATUNG
Hyundai	Texas Instruments
IBM	Toshiba
Machines Bull	Unisys
Matsushita	

HOW MUCH

Nasdaq symbol: ASTA FYE: December 31	Annual Growth	1986	1987	1988	1989	1990	1991	1992	1993	1994	1995[1]
Sales ($ mil.)	19.4%	206	413	457	534	689	944	1,412	2,367	2,468	1,016
Net income ($ mil.)	—	13	15	(8)	35	65	69	(54)	54	(99)	(225)
Income as % of sales	—	6.3%	3.7%	—	6.6%	9.4%	7.3%	—	2.3%	—	—
Earnings per share ($)	—	0.57	0.64	(0.32)	1.21	2.13	2.16	(1.72)	1.59	(3.07)	(5.27)
Stock price – high ($)	—	15.63	10.88	8.50	5.50	18.88	32.75	24.50	25.50	33.00	19.13
Stock price – low ($)	—	5.31	3.25	3.63	3.38	5.19	14.50	11.25	12.57	10.38	7.50
Stock price – close ($)	3.1%	6.44	3.69	3.94	5.19	18.63	16.75	21.00	22.75	14.63	8.50
P/E – high	—	27	17	—	5	9	15	—	16	—	—
P/E – low	—	9	5	—	3	2	7	—	8	—	—
Dividends per share ($)	0.0%	0.00	0.00	0.00	0.00	0.00	0.00	0.00	0.00	0.00	0.00
Book value per share ($)	5.4%	4.34	5.01	4.68	6.34	9.34	11.80	10.09	11.19	8.12	6.96
Employees	18.0%	1,350	2,242	2,281	2,312	2,960	3,560	4,509	6,977	6,595	6,006

[1] 6-month fiscal year

1995 YEAR-END

Debt ratio: 48.5%
Return on equity: —
Cash (mil.): $125
Current ratio: 1.36
Long-term debt (mil.): $126
No. of shares (mil.): 45
Dividends
  Yield: —
  Payout: —
Market value (mil.): $380

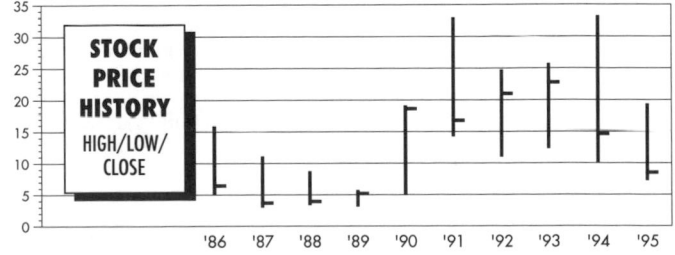

STOCK PRICE HISTORY
HIGH/LOW/CLOSE

AVNET, INC.

OVERVIEW

Avnet is nipping at the heels of rival Arrow Electronics. The Great Neck, New York-based company is the #2 (after Arrow) distributor of semiconductors and other electronic components in both the US and Europe. Its clients include original equipment manufacturers, value-added resellers, the military, and end users. Formerly #1 in the industry, Avnet continues to dog Arrow for the top spot worldwide and has recently expanded its territory with acquisitions in Asia and Europe.

Avnet's Electronic Marketing Group (EMG) accounts for 90% of the company's sales. More than half of those sales come from Hamilton Hallmark, which distributes products for top chipmakers such as Advanced Micro Devices,

Intel, Motorola, National Semiconductor, and Texas Instruments. Other Avnet units include the Electrical and Industrial Group (industrial equipment distribution and repair services) and Video Communications Group (equipment for cable and satellite television).

Among the tools Avnet is employing in its effort to win back the top spot are its POURS (point-of-use replenishment system) bar code-based inventory system and its EDI (electronic data interchange) computerized ordering system. POURS and EDI help Avnet's customers store parts and order replacements automatically. In Europe, Avnet companies communicate via a state-of-the-art multilanguage, multicurrency computer network.

WHEN

In 1921, before commercial battery-operated radios, Charles Avnet started a small ham radio replacement parts distributorship in lower Manhattan. The stock market crash in 1929 left the business strapped, and it went bankrupt in 1931. Later that decade, Avnet founded another company, making car radio kits and antennas. But competition got the best of him, and his company went bankrupt.

During WWII Charles and son Lester founded Avnet Electronic Supply to sell parts to government and defense contractors, since production of home radio sets was prohibited. After the war it bought and sold surplus electrical and electronic parts. A contract from Bendix Aviation spurred growth, and Avnet opened a West Coast warehouse. In 1955 the company incorporated as Avnet Electronics Supply Co. Sales reached $1 million that year. The company changed its name to Avnet Electronics Corp. in 1958.

Two years later Avnet made its first acquisition, British Industries Corp., and went public. The acquisitions continued throughout the 1960s with Hamilton Electro (1962), Fairmount Motor Production Co. (1963), and Valley Forge Products, (1964). Semiconductor maker Hamilton remained autonomous but buoyed Avnet's connector component business.

To reflect its diversification into motors and other products, the company again changed its name, to Avnet, Inc., in 1964. That year Charles died and Lester became chairman and president. In 1970 Lester died and director Simon Sheib became chairman and CEO.

The 1970s brought new opportunities to the company. In 1973 Intel, which had brought

out the first microprocessor, signed Avnet as a distributor, and by 1979, sales had topped $1 billion. The next year Anthony Hamilton, founder of Hamilton Electro, became CEO, and Avnet took the top spot among US distributors of electronic components.

During 1991 and 1992 Avnet spent over $100 million for acquisitions in the European market, buying Access Group (UK), F.H. Tec Composants (France), and Nortec AB (Scandinavia). In 1992 DEC signed a 15-year distribution contract with Avnet. The company outbid Wyle Laboratories for Hall-Mark Electronics, the US's 3rd largest distributor, in 1993, and acquired Penstock, the top US distributor of microwave radio frequency products, the next year.

Thanks to these acquisitions, Avnet was Europe's #2 electronics distributor in 1994 despite having had almost no European operations prior to 1990. The company continued to expand globally in 1995, acquiring German electronics distributor Setron Schiffer-Electronik, which has a presence in Eastern Europe, and buying 70% of Hong Kong distributor WKK Semiconductor.

In 1996 the company added an 80% interest in Kopp Electronics of South Africa and a 70% interest in the science and technology division of Taiwanese distributor Mercuries and Associates. That year Hamilton Hallmark signed a North American franchise distribution agreement with the big French chipmaker SGS-Thomson Microelectronics. In fiscal 1996 Avnet had sales of $5,208 million and net income of $188 million.

WHO

Chairman and CEO: Leon Machiz, age 71,
$1,660,000 pay
VC, President, and COO: Roy Vallee, age 43,
$864,000 pay
SVP and Secretary: Sylvester D. Herlihy, age 68,
$498,030 pay
SVP: Joseph W. Semmer, age 58, $487,876 pay
SVP and CFO: Raymond Sadowski, age 41
SVP and Chief Information Officer: Anthony T. DeLuca,
age 45
SVP and General Counsel: David R. Birk, age 48
SVP: Burton Katz, age 53
SVP: Keith Williams, age 47, 499,48 1 pay
VP: Steven C. Church, age 46
VP: John A. Carfora, age 49
VP: John T. Clark, age 41
VP: Patrick Jewett, age 50
VP: Donald E. Sweet, age 58
VP: Morton M. Vogel, age 65
VP: Richard Ward, age 55
VP Human Resources: Robert Zierk
Auditors: Andersen Worldwide

WHERE

HQ: 80 Cutter Mill Rd., Great Neck, NY 11021-3107
Phone: 516-466-7000
Fax: 516-466-1203
Web site: http://www.avnet.com
Avnet distributes its products worldwide.

	1995 Sales	
	$ mil.	% of total
US	3,412	79
Other countries	888	21
Total	**4,300**	**100**

WHAT

	1995 Sales	
	$ mil.	% of total
Electronic marketing	3,873	90
Video communications	246	6
Electrical & industrial	181	4
Total	**4,300**	**100**

Selected Operations

Electronic Marketing Group
Allied Electronics (electronic components to
maintenance and repair services)
Avnet Cable Technologies (cable assemblies)
Avnet Computer Marketing Group (international
distribution)
Avnet EMG International
Hamilton Hallmark (semiconductors)
Penstock (radio frequency/microwave products and
services distribution)
Time Electronics (interconnect products distribution)

Video Communications Group
Channel Master
Channel Master (UK)

Electrical and Industrial Group
Avnet Industrial (maintenance and repair organization
products and services)
Avnet Supply (electronic production line supplies)
Brownell Electro (motor repair and industrial OEM
product services)

KEY COMPETITORS

Arrow Electronics
Bell Industries
Bell Microproducts
Graybar Electric
Jaco Electronics
Marshall Industries
Nu Horizons Electronic

Pioneer-Standard
Electronics
Premier Industrial
Rexel
Richardson Electronics
Sterling Electronics
TTI
Wyle Electronics

HOW MUCH

NYSE symbol: AVT FYE: June 30	Annual Growth	1986	1987	1988	1989	1990	1991	1992	1993	1994	1995
Sales ($ mil.)	13.1%	1,416	1,539	1,817	1,919	1,751	1,741	1,759	2,238	3,548	4,300
Net income ($ mil.)	21.6%	24	23	52	54	57	62	51	69	88	140
Income as % of sales	—	1.7%	1.5%	2.9%	2.8%	3.2%	3.5%	2.9%	3.1%	2.5%	3.3%
Earnings per share ($)	19.5%	0.67	0.64	1.46	1.51	1.57	1.72	1.42	1.91	2.16	3.32
Stock price – high ($)	—	40.38	39.25	28.13	32.75	33.50	30.00	36.00	42.25	45.00	55.63
Stock price – low ($)	—	25.00	18.50	19.00	20.63	21.50	23.25	23.50	29.00	30.75	35.75
Stock price – close ($)	6.3%	25.75	23.75	22.25	31.00	25.88	27.13	34.50	39.00	37.00	44.75
P/E – high	—	60	61	19	22	21	17	25	22	21	17
P/E – low	—	37	29	13	14	14	14	17	15	14	11
Dividends per share ($)	2.0%	0.50	0.50	0.50	0.50	0.58	0.60	0.60	0.60	0.60	0.60
Book value per share ($)	5.9%	18.20	18.44	19.54	20.60	21.46	22.60	23.56	24.35	27.26	30.38
Employees	(0.3%)	9,250	9,500	10,000	8,500	7,500	7,250	6,650	6,500	8,000	9,000

1995 YEAR-END

Debt ratio: 25.3%
Return on equity: 12.0%
Cash (mil.): $49
Current ratio: 3.26
Long-term debt (mil.): $419
No. of shares (mil.): 41
Dividends
  Yield: 1.3%
  Payout: 18.1%
Market value (mil.): $1,835

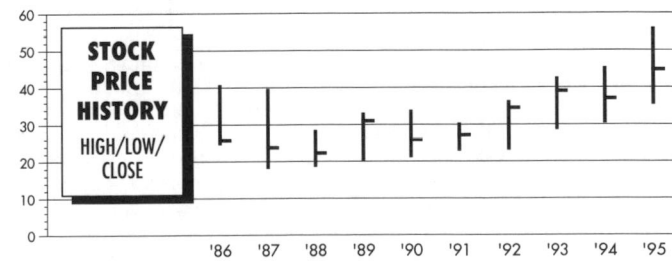

STOCK PRICE HISTORY
HIGH/LOW/CLOSE

BAY NETWORKS, INC.

OVERVIEW

Bay Networks' products direct traffic along the electronic freeways that connect computers. The Santa Clara, California-based company develops and manufactures intelligent hubs (the central "switchboards" where the cables of a computer network converge), multi-pro-tocol routers (which allow different kinds of networks, such as PCs and Macs, to interact), other LAN and WAN products, and network management software and services.

Bay Networks is the result of the 1994 merger of SynOptics, a manufacturer of hubs, and Wellfleet, a maker of routers, making it the #3 (after Cisco Systems and 3Com) manufacturer of internetworking products. The networking industry is experiencing explosive growth — estimated at 40% annually — and the distinctions among networking devices such as hubs, routers, and switches are disappearing. The industry is also constantly embracing new technologies such as transmission of video and voice. To keep up with the cost of R&D, the industry is beginning to consolidate; the merger that created Bay Networks is one example.

With the company experiencing mixed results following the merger (although revenues nearly doubled in its first 2 years), Bay Networks is looking to expand its product line by acquiring other technology firms. In 1995 it purchased Centillion Networks, a Mountain View, California-based manufacturer of Token Ring networking products, for $140 million in stock. It also agreed to acquire Xylogics, a leading supplier of routing products, for around $330 million. Both Centillion and Xylogics will function as independent operating units of Bay Networks.

WHEN

Bay Networks is the result of the $1 billion merger in 1994 of 2 networking pioneers, SynOptics Communications and Wellfleet Communications, the largest merger in the networking industry at the time. The new company's name is derived from the fact that although a continent apart, both the original companies were headquartered near bays — SynOptics near San Francisco Bay and Wellfleet near Massachusetts Bay.

SynOptics was founded by Andrew Ludwick and Ronald Schmidt, who met while working at Xerox's Palo Alto Research Center. Ludwick's job was to determine which new technologies could be marketed commercially. Schmidt developed Ethernet applications. In 1984 IBM announced a new LAN configuration based on a star-shaped cable layout, the Token Ring, that rivaled the traditional linear Ethernet layout. Ludwick and Schmidt began working on a way to convert Ethernet networks to the Token Ring layout.

With backing from Xerox, the partners opened SynOptics in 1985. Its first product, LattisNet, allowed Ethernet networks to use the star layout using special twisted-wire cables. In 1987 the company unveiled a product that would allow Ethernet networks to run on ordinary telephone lines. Revenues jumped from about $6 million that year to more than $40 million the next. SynOptics went public in 1988. By the mid-1990s competition had pared down much of its market lead. In response the company continued to develop new products, including Fiber Distribution Data Interface, the standard for high-speed data transmission.

Wellfleet was formed in 1986 by Paul Severino and Bill Siefert. The company... named for the Massachusetts town where the first transatlantic radio transmission was made in 1903. Wellfleet was a pioneer in enterprise networking, developing an expandable system architecture. The company shipped its first products in 1988 but did not make a profit until 1990. It went public in 1991 and by 1993 had $700 million in revenues.

After the 1994 merger Wellfleet CEO Severino became chairman of Bay Networks; SynOptics CEO Ludwick became president and CEO, and SynOptics cofounder Schmidt became EVP and chief technical officer.

In 1994 Bay introduced BaySIS, a switched internetworking architecture supported by a family of new products.

In early 1995 the company unveiled intelligent hub products that integrate asynchronous transfer mode (ATM) switching and Token Ring-to-ATM switching. It also bought Centillion. The company's net income rose to $206 million on sales of ¢2.1 billion in fiscal 1996. With Bay Networks troubled by product delays, bicoastal operations, soft marketing, and the departure of key engineers, Intel veteran David House replaced Severino and Ludwick in 1996 as chairman and CEO.

WHO

Chairman, President, and CEO: David L. House, age 53
EVP and Chief Technical Officer: Ronald V. Schmidt
EVP and CFO: William J. Ruehle, age 53, $382,493 pay
EVP Worldwide Field Operations and Marketing: Gary J. Bowen, age 48, $366,258 pay
SVP Operations: Jeff Allen
SVP Hub Products Business Unit: Dominic P. Orr, age 44
VP Human Resources: David M. Lietzke
Auditors: Ernst & Young LLP

WHERE

HQ: 4401 Great America Pkwy., Santa Clara, CA 95054
Phone: 408-988-2400
Fax: 408-988-5525
Web site: http://www.baynetworks.com

	1995 Sales	
	$ mil.	% of total
US	906	68
Europe	283	21
Other regions	153	11
Total	**1,342**	**100**

International Offices

Argentina	Malaysia
Australia	Mexico
Belgium	The Netherlands
Brazil	Norway
Canada	Puerto Rico
China	Singapore
Denmark	South Africa
France	South Korea
Germany	Spain
Hong Kong	Sweden
India	Switzerland
Italy	UK
Japan	United Arab Emirates

WHAT

	1995 Sales		1995 Net Income	
	$ mil.	% of total	$ mil.	% of total
Bay Networks	1,043	78	93	71
SynOptics	173	13	17	13
Wellfleet	126	9	21	16
Total	**1,342**	**100**	**131**	**100**

Selected Products

Connectivity Products
Intelligent hubs and related host modules and transceivers

Internetworking Products
Backbone Node products
Local and remote bridges, local and remote routers, and switches

Network Management Products
Optivity network management systems

Switching Products
BaySIS (Bay Switched Internetworking Services, a networking architecture that combines switching technology with hub and router technology)

KEY COMPETITORS

3Com	Hewlett-Packard
Artisoft	IBM
Asante	Lucent
Ascend Communications	Madge
Cabletron	Microcom
Cheyenne Software	Novell
Chipcom	Olicom USA
Cisco Systems	Optical Data Systems
Compaq	Proteon
DEC	U.S. Robotics
FORE Systems	Wang
FTP Software	

HOW MUCH

NYSE symbol: BAY FYE: June 30	Annual Growth	1986	1987	1988	1989[1]	1990[1]	1991[1]	1992[1]	1993[1]	1994[2]	1995
Sales ($ mil.)	61.0%	—	—	—	77	176	248	389	705	1,130	1,342
Net income ($ mil.)	56.3%	—	—	—	9	28	27	42	76	144	131
Income as % of sales	—	—	—	—	12.2%	16.0%	10.8%	10.9%	10.8%	12.7%	9.8%
Earnings per share ($)	24.1%	—	—	—	0.20	0.47	0.44	0.66	1.09	0.83	0.73
Stock price – high ($)	—	—	—	—	4.20	12.24	17.17	27.83	42.75	29.25	49.92
Stock price – low ($)	—	—	—	—	2.16	3.50	4.75	6.24	20.25	12.42	18.33
Stock price – close ($)	46.3%	—	—	—	4.20	11.41	7.03	27.10	27.88	19.67	41.13
P/E – high	—	—	—	—	21	26	39	42	39	35	68
P/E – low	—	—	—	—	11	7	11	10	19	15	25
Dividends per share ($)	—	—	—	—	0.00	0.00	0.00	0.00	0.00	0.00	0.00
Book value per share ($)	23.0%	—	—	—	1.25	1.80	2.37	3.38	5.19	3.43	4.32
Employees	45.5%	—	—	—	405	774	959	1,255	1,736	3,000	3,840

[1] Synoptics only [2] Pro forma

1995 YEAR-END

Debt ratio: 12.9%
Return on equity: 20.1%
Cash (mil.): $590
Current ratio: 3.60
Long-term debt (mil.): $111
No. of shares (mil.): 172
Dividends
  Yield: —
  Payout: —
Market value (mil.): $7,089

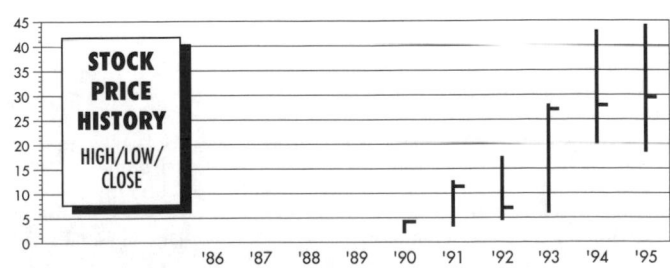

STOCK PRICE HISTORY HIGH/LOW/CLOSE

BORLAND INTERNATIONAL, INC.

OVERVIEW

Take a ride on the Borland roller coaster. Once the #3 publisher of desktop software and the self-declared "barbarians" of the software world, Borland has been hanging on for dear life during the ride it has taken the last few years. The struggling Scotts Valley, California-based company provides software development tools (including the Delphi and Borland C++ lines) and database management systems (including Paradox and Visual dBASE). The company also makes ReportSmith, a program that helps the user design and produce reports using a variety of database management sources.

With lagging sales of many of its traditional products, Borland has attempted to shift to de-velopment tools for the client/server market and for programmers of Internet and intranet software. It is working on a visual development tool for Java, the Sun Microsystems Internet programming language, and is expanding its focus to include middleware, software which helps link users of client/server systems to applications and databases.

Continuing weak results led to the resignation (after just a year and a half on the job) of CEO Gary Wetsel, whose attempt to turn the company around included cutting labor, outsourcing manufacturing, and closing international offices in addition to refocusing product lines.

WHEN

In 1982 Philippe Kahn, a mathematician and self-taught computer programmer, left his native France for America, hoping to land a job in the high-tech mecca of Silicon Valley. After an offer from Hewlett-Packard petered out (the company discovered that he had no green card or work permit), the determined Kahn and a few American friends completed work on Turbo Pascal, a program that made it easier for users to write code in the Pascal language. To market it, they launched Borland International (Kahn liked the multinational ring to it). Kahn persuaded "BYTE" magazine to run the company's first advertisement on credit, and by the end of the first month Borland had received 100,000 orders.

The company continued as a relatively small concern until the mid-1980s, when Kahn started acquiring other software makers to augment Borland's product line. He bought Analytica International in 1985 and followed with Ansa Software, which had developed the database management system Paradox, in 1987. Borland's version of Paradox (launched 2 years later) eventually helped to alter the company's direction.

But first Borland had to work through financial difficulties. In 1989 the firm reported an unexpected 2nd-quarter loss, followed by an annual loss of $3 million. Although Kahn attributed the loss to sluggish European sales, he also regarded it as a personal failure and responded by strengthening financial controls and replacing 2 high-level European managers. In 1990 Borland reported a profit of $12 million. Kahn took the company public that year with an $11.9 million offering.

In 1989 Borland came out with a new version of Paradox and introduced Quattro Pro, a high-end spreadsheet program. In 1990 the company introduced the Turbo C++ programming language. Later that year Lotus filed suit against Borland, claiming that user interfaces for Quattro and Quattro Pro violated copyrights for Lotus 1-2-3.

The company experienced yearly losses starting in 1991 when it went head-to-head with Microsoft, resulting in a price war (Borland lost). That year Borland bought long-time rival Ashton-Tate (a company twice Borland's size, with the popular dBASE database product in its applications portfolio). The acquisition was expensive and unsuccessful because of a weakening database market, and the company was slow in shipping new products.

In 1994 Borland launched dBase for Windows and Sidekick for Windows, a desktop organizing program. It also acquired ReportSmith. Kahn was blamed for many of the company's problems; he resigned in 1995 and bought Starfish Software, a Borland consumer-products division. He later bought Sidekick (a scheduling program) and Dashboard (a PC utility program) from Borland, which still owns 10% of Starfish.

Gary Wetsel, who took the helm in January 1995, temporarily brought the company into the black, then resigned in 1996 as the company forecast another quarterly loss.

Borland agreed to acquire Open Environment Corp. (a developer of network, PC, and Internet software) in 1996, but the deal was shaky because of Borland's troubled financial situation.

WHO

Chairman: William F. Miller
President and CEO: Gary Wetsel
SVP Research and Development: Paul H. Gross, age 35, $283,865 pay
SVP Corporate Affairs, Secretary, and General Counsel: Robert H. Kohn, age 39, $247,639 pay
VP International Sales and Operations: David McGlaughlin, age 58, $292,722 pay
VP and General Manager Desktop and PC-LAN Development Tools: Frank Vaculin, age 38, $264,711 pay
VP and CFO: David Mullin, age 43
VP Business Development: William H. Jordan, age 42
Director Human Resources: Marcia Bartelmie
Auditors: Price Waterhouse LLP

WHERE

HQ: 100 Borland Way, Scotts Valley, CA 95066-3249
Phone: 408-431-1000
Fax: 408-431-4141
Web site: http://www.borland.com

Borland has offices in Australia, Belgium, Brazil, Canada, Chile, Denmark, France, Germany, Hong Kong, Italy, Japan, Malaysia, the Netherlands, New Zealand, Singapore, South Korea, Spain, Sweden, Switzerland, Taiwan, the UK, and the US.

	1996 Sales		1996 Operating Income	
	$ mil.	% of total	$ mil.	% of total
US	110	51	(14)	—
Europe	57	27	15	—
Japan	31	14	7	—
Other regions	17	8	6	—
Total	**215**	**100**	**14**	**—**

WHAT

Client/Server Development Tools
Delphi Client/Server Suite
Delphi Desktop
InterBase 4.0
ReportSmith

Database Products
dBASE III PLUS
dBASE IV
dBASE for Windows
Paradox 5.0 for Windows
Paradox for DOS
Visual dBASE
Visual dBASE Client/Server
Visual dBASE Compiler

Language Products
Borland C++ 4.5 for DOS
Borland C++ 4.5 for Windows
Borland C++ and Database Tools
Borland C++ for Windows NT
Object Pascal

KEY COMPETITORS

Claris
Computer Associates
IBM
Information Builders
Microsoft
Progress Software

HOW MUCH

Nasdaq symbol: BORL FYE: March 31	Annual Growth	1987	1988	1989	1990	1991	1992	1993	1994	1995	1996
Sales ($ mil.)	24.9%	29	77	91	113	227	483	464	394	254	215
Net income ($ mil.)	24.4%	2	6	(3)	12	27	(110)	(49)	(70)	(12)	14
Income as % of sales	—	7.9%	7.2%	—	10.4%	11.8%	—	—	—	—	6.6%
Earnings per share ($)	(24.3%)	—	—	—	—	1.81	(4.29)	(1.87)	(2.62)	(0.43)	0.45
Stock price – high ($)[1]	—	—	—	—	—	32.00	83.50	86.50	27.25	16.00	20.63
Stock price – low ($)[1]	—	—	—	—	—	9.88	27.88	19.75	12.75	6.00	6.13
Stock price – close ($)[1]	(12.3%)	—	—	—	—	31.75	82.25	22.25	14.88	6.13	16.50
P/E – high		—	—	—	—	18	—	—	—	—	46
P/E – low		—	—	—	—	15	—	—	—	—	14
Dividends per share ($)	0.0%	—	—	—	—	0.00	0.00	0.00	0.00	0.00	0.00
Book value per share ($)	(2.0%)	—	—	—	—	6.09	8.82	7.12	4.48	4.49	5.50
Employees	(1.0%)	—	—	—	—	986	1,331	1,885	1,898	1,111	938

[1] Stock prices are for the prior calendar year.

1996 YEAR-END

Debt ratio: 7.8%
Return on equity: 9.7%
Cash (mil.): $90
Current ratio: 1.92
Long-term debt (mil.): $15
No. of shares (mil.): 31
Dividends
  Yield: —
  Payout: —
Market value (mil.): $514

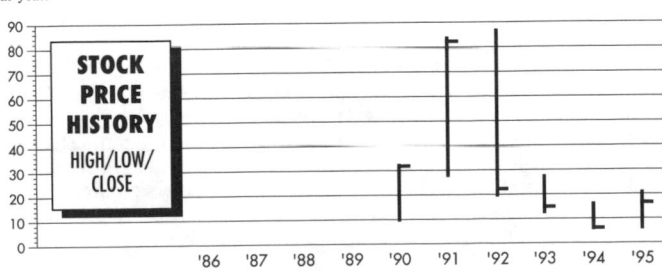

STOCK PRICE HISTORY HIGH/LOW/CLOSE

CABLETRON SYSTEMS, INC.

OVERVIEW

Cabletron is a LAN lover. The Rochester, New Hampshire-based company is a leading provider of such networking hardware as hubs, routers, and switches (devices that transfer data among computers). Its SPECTRUM software, which lets network administrators monitor and control their systems, is #3 in its market. The company also provides support. Cabletron customers include such corporate end users as Audi and Microsoft and such OEMs as Lockheed and Bull Systems.

Cabletron has climbed toward the top of the networking products ladder by combining product innovations (it produced one of the first network hubs and now spends about 10%

of revenues on R&D), an aggressive sales force that focuses on high-end corporate accounts, and a no-frills corporate culture (traveling employees must double up in hotel rooms). This combination has given Cabletron an 8-year earnings growth rate of nearly 40%. Although the company ranks 4th among networking products companies (behind Cisco Systems, 3Com, and Bay Networks), acquisitions have expanded its product lines and customer list.

Founders Robert Levine and Craig Benson each own about 13% of the company. The 2 executives pay themselves a modest salary of $52,000 each, but their combined stake in Cabletron is worth more than $1 billion.

WHEN

Cabletron got its start in 1983 when Robert Levine, an independent wire and cable salesman, needed 1,000 feet of cable for a customer's computer network. He could find only rolls of 10,000 feet. Levine's friend Craig Benson suggested they cut the cable and sell the shorter segments to business associates. By guaranteeing delivery within 48 hours (the industry norm was 90 days), they created a niche. A year later the company had 10 part-time employees. Its first-year revenues were $100,000.

The 2-man garage start-up soon began installing networks, then designing networking equipment. The company was known for parsimony: its office furniture was secondhand and its boardrooms had no chairs (which undoubtedly discouraged long meetings).

The company's rapid growth began in 1988 with MMAC (Multi Media Access Center), an intelligent wiring hub used to simplify network installation, aid in troubleshooting, and facilitate modifications. Cabletron went public in 1989. It also introduced LANVIEW network management software. LANVIEW Network Analyzer and SPECTRUM network management software debuted in 1990. That year hubs accounted for half of the company's revenues.

In 1992 Cabletron unveiled the first SCSI-to-Ethernet adapter, which allowed Macintosh users to connect to Ethernet LANs. It also introduced the industry's first bridge that links Ethernet, token ring, and WANs. The company launched MMAC intelligent hubs with asynchronous transfer mode (ATM, a networking protocol) connectivity in 1993. That year Cabletron introduced the ESX-MIM, a hub that provides bridging, routing, and fast-packet switching.

To counter the 1994 merger of rivals Synoptics and Wellfleet (now Bay Networks), that year Cabletron signed an aggressive marketing deal with Cisco that included a buyback policy, free technical service, and large discounts. The company spent $100 million and engaged 200 engineers in a 3-year project to develop the MMAC-plus, a switching hub that supports both ATM cell-based and packet-based networks. The product was unveiled in 1994.

Cabletron grew through internal development, while many of its rivals grew by acquiring complementary companies. With several rivals pulling ahead in the marketplace, in 1995 Cabletron purchased a unit of Standard Microsystems that made high-speed LAN switches. That year the company unveiled its SmartSwitch ASIC, which has allowed Cabletron to connect 4 times as many workstations on a LAN and to increase the speed of its networking products more than 5-fold. The company also released SPECTRUM 4.0, which works with networks based on Microsoft's Windows NT software. When rivals 3Com and Chipcom merged in 1995, Cabletron sought to capitalize on the situation by offering buyback incentives to 3Com and Chipcom customers.

Cabletron agreed in 1996 to acquire network switch maker Network Express and networking connector maker Zietnet, paying more than $250 million for the pair. The company also unveiled VNET Manager, software for managing virtual networks (networks that aren't connected by hard wiring), and Cabletron WebView, which lets network managers configure and manage SmartSwitches via the World Wide Web using standard Web browser software.

WHO

Chairman, COO, and Treasurer: Craig R. Benson,
age 41, $52,000 pay
President and CEO: S. Robert Levine, age 38,
$52,200 pay
Director Engineering and Manufacturing:
Christopher J. Oliver, age 35, $275,000 pay
Director Finance and CFO: David J. Kirkpatrick, age 44,
$239,952 pay
Executive Director Sales, Worldwide: Kenneth R.
Levine, age 32
Secretary: Michael D. Myerow
Director Human Resources: Linda Pepin
Auditors: KPMG Peat Marwick LLP

WHERE

HQ: 35 Industrial Way, Rochester, NH 03867
Phone: 603-332-9400
Fax: 603-332-8007
Web site: http://www.cabletron.com/

Cabletron has operations in about 30 countries, including manufacturing facilities in Ohio and Ireland and a research facility in New Hampshire.

	1996 Sales	
	$ mil.	% of total
US	757	71
Europe	215	20
Other regions	62	6
Direct foreign export	35	3
Total	**1,070**	**100**

WHAT

	1996 Sales	
	$ mil.	% of total
Network interconnection products	965	90
Test equipment & other	98	9
Cable assemblies	7	1
Total	**1,070**	**100**

Selected Products
Coaxial cable, optical fiber, and shielded and unshielded twisted-pair wire
Network interconnection equipment
Network management software (SPECTRUM)
Network test equipment
Smart hubs and switches and related products (MMAC family)

Selected Services
Certification and documentation
Consulting, design, and configuration
Project management
Project planning
Service maintenance
Testing
Training

KEY COMPETITORS

3Com	Digi	Newbridge
Artisoft	International	Networks
Asante	FORE Systems	Novell
Bay Networks	Hitachi	Optical Data
Belden	Hewlett-Packard	Systems
Cheyenne	IBM	Proteon
Software	Madge	Tandem
Cisco Systems	Microsoft	Unisys
Datapoint	Network General	
DEC	NetWorth	

HOW MUCH

NYSE symbol: CS FYE: February 28	Annual Growth	1987	1988	1989	1990	1991	1992	1993	1994	1995	1996
Sales ($ mil.)	52.8%	—	—	55	105	181	291	418	598	811	1,070
Net income ($ mil.)	45.3%	—	—	12	23	36	58	84	119	162	164
Income as % of sales	—	—	—	22.1%	21.5%	19.9%	20.0%	20.0%	19.9%	20.0%	15.4%
Earnings per share ($)	42.7%	—	—	0.19	0.35	0.54	0.83	1.19	1.68	2.27	2.29
Stock price – high ($)[1]	—	—	—	—	6.60	11.70	22.10	34.10	47.60	53.00	87.75
Stock price – low ($)[1]	—	—	—	—	3.70	2.75	10.20	16.85	29.80	33.05	37.37
Stock price – close ($)[1]	66.9%	—	—	—	3.75	11.40	21.50	33.60	45.00	46.50	81.00
P/E – high	—	—	—	—	19	22	27	29	28	23	38
P/E – low	—	—	—	—	11	5	12	14	18	15	16
Dividends per share ($)	—	—	—	—	0.00	0.00	0.00	0.00	0.00	0.00	0.00
Book value per share ($)	48.1%	—	—	—	1.02	2.01	2.90	4.09	5.94	8.22	10.77
Employees	29.9%	—	—	862	1,223	1,825	2,032	2,625	3,663	4,970	5,377

[1] Stock prices are for the prior calendar year.

1996 YEAR-END
Debt ratio: 0.0%
Return on equity: 24.1%
Cash (mil.): $254
Current ratio: 3.80
Long-term debt (mil.): $0
No. of shares (mil.): 72
Dividends
  Yield: —
  Payout: —
Market value (mil.): $5,851

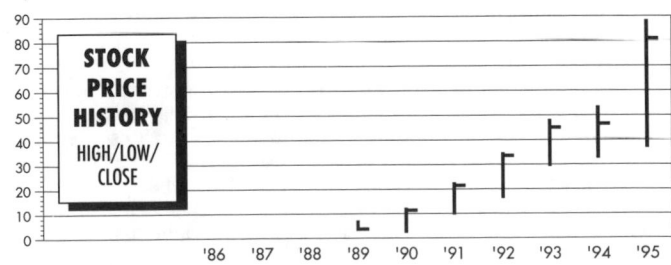

STOCK PRICE HISTORY
HIGH/LOW/CLOSE

CANON INC.

OVERVIEW

In an increasingly global market, Canon is prepared to defend its dominance. Based in Tokyo, the company is one of the world's largest makers of business machines, cameras, and equipment for semiconductor manufacturing, broadcasting, and medical treatment. Its products include fax machines, bubble-jet printers, laser printers, cameras, and color scanners. Most of Canon's revenue comes from its business machines, which include copiers, computer peripherals, and business systems. Canon's sales reflect its international thrust. In the past several years, Japanese sales have fallen from more than half of the total to about 1/3.

Canon's sales have been helped by a healthy demand for PCs in Japan and the falling price of PCs worldwide, allowing consumers to spend more on peripherals such as printers and copiers. To avoid the effects of a slowing US economy and stagnant growth in Europe, as well as weak consumer spending at home, Canon has cut costs by shifting production outside Japan and buying more parts overseas.

Canon's expectations for growth hinge on other markets in the Asia/Pacific region. It plans to set up joint ventures in the Philippines, Vietnam, and India in response to growing demand for printers and copiers there. It also continues to introduce new standards for consumer electronics, including the world's smallest compact camera and the first solar-powered camera. Canon plans to spend the balance of the decade focusing on multimedia technologies and clean energy products such as solar cells.

WHEN

Takeshi Mitarai and a friend, Saburo Uchida, formed Seiki Kogaku Kenkyusho (Precision Optical Research Laboratory) in Tokyo in 1933 to build Japan's first 35mm camera. The camera was introduced in 1935 under the brand name Kwanon (the Buddhist goddess of mercy) and later renamed Canon. In response to the military buildup before WWII, the company began building X-ray machines for the Japanese military.

After WWII the company sold its Canon cameras to US GIs stationed in Japan and adopted the name Canon Camera Company in 1947 as the brand name gained popularity. Canon diversified into business equipment, introducing the first 10-key electronic calculator (1964) and a plain-paper photocopier, independent of Xerox's patented technology (1968). Canon dropped "Camera Company" from its name in 1969.

In 1972 Canon invented the "liquid dry" system of copying, using plain paper and liquid developer, but failed to produce any new cameras in the interim and was surpassed by Minolta and Pentax as Japan's leading camera exporter. Sales were sluggish in the early 1970s, and Canon had to suspend its dividend in 1975 for the first time since WWII.

At that time Canon's managing director, Ryuzaburo Kaku, convinced Mitarai that the company's problems stemmed from indecisive leadership and weak marketing practices. Kaku turned Canon around, unleashing the electronic AE-1 in a media blitz that in 1976 included the first-ever TV commercials for any 35mm camera. With almost every feature (except focus) automated, the AE-1 made 35mm cameras accessible to even the clumsiest camera operator. Its success catapulted Canon past Minolta as the world's #1 camera maker.

In 1979 Canon introduced the highly successful NP-200, the first copier to use a dry developer. As the plain-paper copier market matured in the early 1980s, Canon shifted to making other automated office machines, including laser printers and fax machines.

Minolta again replaced Canon as the world's #1 camera maker in 1985, when it introduced the fully automated Maxxum 7000. But Canon came back in 1987, introducing the EOS (electronic optical system) autofocus camera that returned the company to preeminence in 1990.

In 1992 Canon announced a joint venture with IBM to produce portable PCs with built-in bubble-jet printers. Canon teamed up with IBM again in 1994, agreeing to develop a line of products based on the PowerPC, a chip codeveloped by IBM.

Canon introduced the world's first color ferroelectric liquid crystal display (FLCD) in 1995. The technology could replace cathode ray tubes in computer and TV screens as the industry standard. It also unveiled a camcorder that lets users operate the focus and other functions by eye movement.

In 1996 the company established a research and development center in Costa Mesa, California, for its bubble-jet printers and peripheral products.

WHO

Chairman: Ryuzaburo Kaku
President: Fujio Mitarai
EVP: Hiroshi Tanaka
Senior General Manager Finance and Accounting:
Ryozo Hirako
President and CEO, Canon U.S.A.: Haruo Murase
CFO, Canon U.S.A.: Seymour Liebman
Director Personnel, Canon U.S.A.: Annette Colarusso
Auditors: KPMG Peat Marwick

WHERE

HQ: 30-2, Shimomaruko 3-chome, Ohta-ku, Tokyo, 146,
Japan
Phone: +81-3-3758-2111
Fax: +81-3-5482-5130
US HQ: Canon U.S.A., Inc., One Canon Plaza, Lake
Success, NY 11042-1113
US Phone: 516-488-6700
US Fax: 516-328-5069
Web site: http://www.canon.co.jp/index-e.html

	1995 Sales	
	$ mil.	% of total
Japan	6,969	33
North America	6,464	31
Europe	5,908	28
Other regions	1,684	8
Total	**21,025**	**100**

WHAT

	1995 Sales	
	$ mil.	% of total
Business machines		
Copiers	7,270	35
Computer peripherals	6,820	32
Business systems	3,581	17
Cameras	1,724	8
Optical & other products	1,630	8
Total	**21,025**	**100**

Selected Products

Business Machines
Bubble-jet printers
Computers
Digital cameras
Electronic typewriters
Fax machines
Full-color copiers
Image scanners
Laser beam printers
Micrographics
Office copiers
Personal copiers
Personal information equipment
Word processors

Cameras and Accessories
8mm camcorders
Compact cameras
Lenses
Single-lens-reflex cameras

Optical and Other Products
Broadcasting equipment
Medical equipment
Semiconductor production equipment

KEY COMPETITORS

Applied Materials	IBM	Polaroid
AST	Matsushita	Ricoh
Casio	Minolta	Sanyo
Compaq	NEC	Seiko
Dell	Novellus Systems	Sharp
Eastman Kodak	Oce-wan der	Siemens
Fuji Photo	Grinten	Sony
Fujitsu	Oki Electric	Texas
General Signal	Olivetti	Instruments
Hanson	Packard Bell	Toshiba
Harris Corp.	Philips	Xerox
Hewlett-Packard	Pioneer	
Hitachi	Pitney Bowes	

HOW MUCH

Nasdaq symbol: CANNY FYE: December 31	Annual Growth	1986	1987	1988	1989	1990	1991	1992	1993	1994	1995
Sales ($ mil.)	15.8%	5,628	8,072	8,849	8,181	12,725	14,976	15,338	16,452	19,333	21,025
Net income ($ mil.)	25.7%	68	109	297	232	452	418	288	189	310	534
Income as % of sales	—	1.2%	1.4%	3.4%	2.8%	3.6%	2.8%	1.9%	1.1%	1.6%	2.5%
Earnings per share ($)	21.0%	0.55	0.80	2.05	1.49	2.88	2.61	1.88	1.20	1.79	3.05
Stock price – high ($)	—	34.19	44.31	56.94	69.50	66.00	60.13	59.00	71.13	92.50	95.38
Stock price – low ($)	—	23.75	21.03	33.06	48.84	45.13	44.25	47.25	53.50	68.63	72.00
Stock price – close ($)	13.8%	28.53	32.84	54.78	64.00	47.00	56.88	55.00	68.75	85.00	91.38
P/E – high	—	62	55	28	47	23	23	31	59	52	31
P/E – low	—	43	26	16	33	16	17	25	45	38	24
Dividends per share ($)	9.4%	0.29	0.30	0.34	0.34	0.37	0.36	0.39	0.42	0.48	0.57	0.65
Book value per share ($)	12.4%	17.25	22.43	23.01	22.82	30.45	32.65	36.67	40.55	47.05	49.32
Employees	8.2%	35,498	37,521	40,740	44,401	54,381	62,700	64,512	64,535	67,672	72,280

1995 YEAR-END

Debt ratio: 49.8%
Return on equity: 6.7%
Cash (mil.): $6,241
Current ratio: 1.51
Long-term debt (mil.): $2,894
No. of shares (mil.): 167
Dividends
  Yield: 0.7%
  Payout: 21.3%
Market value (mil.): $15,282

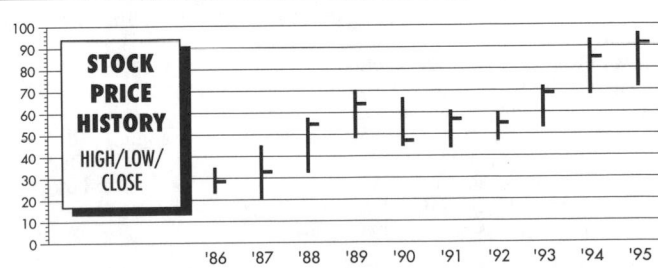

STOCK PRICE HISTORY HIGH/LOW/CLOSE

CAP GEMINI SOGETI S.A.

OVERVIEW

Cap Gemini Sogeti, Europe's largest computer services company and the world's 3rd largest, has lost its last name in a floor-to-ceiling reorganization. The company's consulting, systems management, software development, and systems integration services have been merged into a new Paris-based holding company called Cap Gemini. Cap Gemini America (headquartered in New York City with offices in more than 30 cities) is its US subsidiary. Gemini Consulting, the world's 5th largest consultant, was formerly a subsidiary but is now wholly owned by the new entity.

With technology transforming the way people work, think, learn, and live, major keys to the company's culture and strategy are training and teamwork. Its Cap Gemini Sogeti University emphasizes the radical shift from centralized computers to client/servers and the impact that has on development processes. The company focuses on creating partnerships with users and meeting their needs.

One such collaboration is the development of Year 2000 software to help companies avoid the programming glitches that will occur at the turn of the century, arising from software that uses just the last 2 digits of a year (e.g., 96) instead of the full year (1996) in specifying dates.

Under the merger, Germany's Daimler-Benz and France's CGIP each hold about 25% of Cap Gemini, and chairman and founder Serge Kampf owns about 20%.

WHEN

Serge Kampf founded software house Sogeti in 1967 at Grenoble, his hometown. He had an economics degree and had held a variety of jobs — from selling bakery ovens and computers to working for the French national telephone company. An executive with French computer company Groupe Bull, he became frustrated because he couldn't get anything done, resigned, and started his own business. Believing that the future of information technology would be in services rather than hardware, Kampf focused on providing computer services to companies outside Paris that were being overlooked by his larger competitors. He was immediately successful, and 3 years later opened a Paris branch. In 1973 Kampf changed the focus of the company, abandoning the more specialized activities of data entry and data processing for general consulting, software, and technical assistance.

Cap Gemini Sogeti was created 2 years later by merging Sogeti with 2 French software service companies, C.A.P. (Computerized Applications Programming, started in 1962) and Gemini (begun in 1969). At first it operated as a "body shop," a loose organization of freelance programmers offering temporary help to computer users. It set up a consulting team in the US in 1978 and around that time began a series of US acquisitions that led to the formation of Cap Gemini America in 1981. Meanwhile the parent had become France's leading computer services company.

The company acquired a 42% stake in French competitor Sesa in 1982; 6 years later it bought the rest as part of a new strategy to become a global operator with a range of services. The 1990 purchase of the Hoskyns Group, the UK's largest computer services company, was just one of a string of acquisitions aimed at fulfilling that goal (over a 5-year period, the company bought 22 European and American companies for a total of $1.1 billion). To raise money for his international expansion plans, Kampf sold 34% of Sogeti to German car maker Daimler-Benz for $773 million in 1991.

As Cap Gemini Sogeti expanded around the world, its decentralized network of operations rarely shared business or expertise. In 1993, on the heels of its first loss ever, the company launched Genesis, a restructuring program that set up 7 strategic business areas with dual regional and segment roles and modified product lines. (The company returned to profitability in 1995.)

The mid 1990s saw more than a dozen contracts and partnerships for Cap Gemini Sogeti. Deals in 1995 included insurer CPAs Coopers & Lybrand of the UK and French chemical conglomerate Rhone-Poulenc. The next year the company entered several US partnerships, including one with computer pioneer IBM, and signed contracts with Japan's Sumitomo Bank and British Steel, among others. Also in 1996 the company launched its Year 2000 software, which automates the task of locating dates and changing codes in computer programs, and completed the merger creating the new Cap Gemini and moving its corporate headquarters to Paris.

WHO

Executive Chairman: Serge Kampf
COO: Geoff Unwin
Chief Central Functions Officer: Paul Hermelin
Corporate Group VP and CFO: Pascal Giraud
Chairman and CEO, Gemini Consulting: Pierre Hessler
CEO, Cap Gemini America: Michel Berty
SVP Human Resources and Acting CFO, Cap Gemini America: Bruce Posner
Auditors: Coopers & Lybrand L.L.P.

WHERE

HQ: Place de l'Etoile-11, rue de Tilsitt, 75017, Paris, France
Phone: +33-1-47-54-50-00
Fax: +33-1-42-27-32-11
US HQ: Cap Gemini America, 1114 Avenue of the Americas, 29th Fl., New York, NY 10036
US Phone: 212-944-6464
US Fax: 212-719-5346
Web site: http://mark.cgs.fr

Through its various units, Cap Gemini has operations in the US, 15 European countries, Brazil, Japan, Singapore, and South Africa.

WHAT

	1995 Sales
	% of total
Finance	22
Manufacturing	19
Administration & public services	17
Telecommunications & media	12
Consumer products retail & distribution	10
Process industries	8
Travel, transport & tourism	7
Utilities	5
Total	**100**

Services
Applications management
Computing services
Consulting
Education and training
Implementation
Information systems management and maintenance
Information technology service provider
Operational improvement
Process development
Professional services
Project services
Software development
Software products
Strategic business planning
Support
Systems integration

KEY COMPETITORS

Andersen Consulting
Computer Sciences
Control Data
Coopers & Lybrand
Deloitte Touche Tohmatsu
EDS
Ernst & Young
IBM
ICL
Logica
Machines Bull
MCI
Systemhouse
Olivetti
Siemens
Unisys
Wang

HOW MUCH

Principal exchange: Paris FYE: December 31	Annual Growth	1986	1987	1988	1989	1990	1991	1992	1993	1994	1995
Sales ($ mil.)	5.1%	—	—	—	—	1,802	1,936	2,152	1,866	1,901	2,308
Net income ($ mil.)	(38.6%)	—	—	—	—	122	108	(13)	(73)	(18)	11
Income as % of sales	—	—	—	—	—	6.8%	5.6%	—	—	—	0.5%
Earnings per share ($)	(47.9%)	—	—	—	—	5.23	3.50	(0.36)	(1.69)	(0.40)	0.20
Stock price – high ($)	—	—	—	—	—	105.89	85.71	61.37	37.57	44.39	36.67
Stock price – low ($)	—	—	—	—	—	64.07	46.33	27.17	23.35	29.33	26.12
Stock price – close ($)	(16.1%)	—	—	—	—	67.78	56.37	29.87	29.58	31.84	28.11
P/E – high	—	—	—	—	—	20	24	—	—	—	180
P/E – low	—	—	—	—	—	12	13	—	—	—	128
Dividends per share ($)	—	—	—	—	—	—	—	—	0.00	1.97	0.00
Book value per share ($)	5.3%	—	—	—	—	—	—	22.65	20.87	—	26.48
Employees	3.1%	—	—	—	—	18,919	16,892	21,374	20,559	19,823	22,079

1995 YEAR-END

Debt ratio: 34.9%
Return on equity: 0.8%
Cash (mil.): $271
Current ratio: 1.55
Long-term debt (mil.): $611
No. of shares (mil.): 53
Dividends
  Yield: —
  Payout: —
Market value (mil.): $1,492

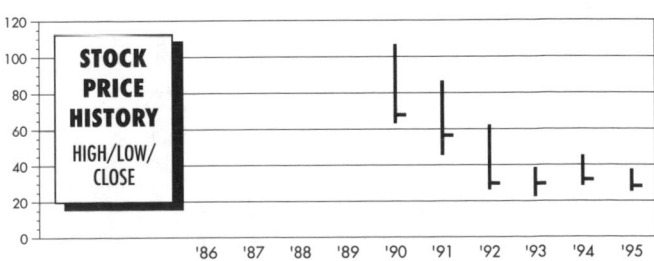

STOCK PRICE HISTORY
HIGH/LOW/CLOSE

CERIDIAN CORPORATION

OVERVIEW

Synergistic, it's not. But Ceridian's collection of defense avionics and imaging, human resources administration and management, and media marketing businesses seems to be paying off.

The Minneapolis-based company operates in 2 broad business lines. The larger and more eclectic is Information Services. This group includes the company's Human Resources Group, which provides human resources management and benefits administration services. A recent addition is Comdata, which provides information services to long-haul truckers.

These include gas purchasing cards, cash advances, and routing services. (This subsidiary also provides cash advance services for casino patrons.) The last segment is Arbitron, the radio (and, increasingly, cable) ratings service.

Ceridian's Defense Electronics division makes information-intensive electronics systems, including reconnaissance and imaging systems, avionics, and communications. Contracts with US and Canadian defense authorities account for approximately 30% of Ceridian's sales.

WHEN

In 1957 William Norris founded Control Data Corporation (CDC) to challenge IBM in mainframe computers for scientific applications. Norris, an electrical engineer who had worked as a cryptologist during WWII, helped found Engineering Research Associates (ERA) after the war. ERA was sold to Remington Rand and formed the nucleus of Sperry Rand, where Norris managed the UNIVAC division. He lured away other engineers, including Seymour Cray (who later founded Cray Computers and Cray Research) and created a line of computers so popular the company didn't need a sales department.

During the 1960s and 1970s the business was a powerhouse. It bought more than 80 companies, primarily in peripherals and data services (it began selling computer time shares in the early 1960s). The company's service segment became vastly enlarged in 1973 when, in the settlement of an antitrust suit against IBM, CDC was allowed to buy IBM's service bureau for less than market value (this business later evolved into the Human Resources Group). The company also began providing lease financing services for its customers (through the 1968 purchase of Commercial Credit Company).

During this period Norris also directed the company into social remediation projects, building facilities in low-income and minority areas and offering fringe benefits that included day care, counseling, and bail-bond services.

In the early 1980s CDC plunged into supercomputers, encountering heated competition from the Japanese. It also entered the fiercely competitive semiconductor business. But these operations sucked cash out of the organization and never became profitable.

Huge losses in 1985 prompted Norris to retire. His successor, Robert Price, tried to stanch the hemorrhaging by divesting operations, including Commercial Credit. Sales rose modestly and then fell again, and Price resigned with a golden parachute that enraged stockholders. Lawrence Perlman was brought in as CEO in 1990. He turned the company away from proprietary systems and made alliances with other manufacturers, including Silicon Graphics and Volkswagen (to develop computer-assisted engineering and manufacturing software). In 1992 CDC spun off its computer products and services subsidiary, Control Data Systems, and changed its name to Ceridian (a made-up word).

After all this, the company consisted of the human resources management and benefits administration operations, Arbitron, and defense electronics. Reaching for a common thread, the company redefined itself as a diversified information services company. Bankrolled by higher earnings at last and about $1 billion in tax credits from its past losses, Ceridian went looking for acquisitions.

In 1995 it found several. Comdata, the largest, provides truck tracking information, driver cash advances, fuel credit cards, and casino cash advances. It also bought Resumix (which makes employment skills matching software) and a UK benefits administration company.

The spree continued in 1996 with the acquisition of EAS Technologies, which makes employee time and attendance software, and Information Learning, which provides systems for answering employee questions about benefits and retirements.

WHO

Chairman, President, and CEO: Lawrence Perlman, age 57, $1,283,750 pay
EVP; President and CEO, Computing Devices International: Ronald L. Turner, age 49, $522,900 pay
EVP and CFO: John R. Eickhoff, age 55, $503,000 pay
EVP; Chairman and CEO, Comdata Holdings Corp.: George L. McTavish, age 54, $487,396 pay
EVP; President and CEO, The Arbitron Company: Stephen B. Morris, age 52, $449,289 pay
EVP; President and CEO Human Resources Group: Ronald James, age 45
VP; President, Ceridian Employer Services: George J. Klauser, age 41
VP Strategic Initiatives: James D. Miller, age 47
VP and Corporate Controller: Loren D. Gross, age 50
VP Corporate Relations and Communications: Linda J. Jadwin, age 52
VP and General Counsel: Steven J. Olson, age 55
VP Organization Resources (HR): Michael Kotten
Auditors: KPMG Peat Marwick LLP

WHERE

HQ: 8100 34th Ave. South, Minneapolis, MN 55425
Phone: 612-853-8100
Fax: 612-853-5300
Web site: http://www.ceridian.com
Ceridian has facilities in Canada, the UK, and the US.

	1995 Sales		1995 Pretax Income	
	$ mil.	% of total	$ mil.	% of total
US	1,037	78	118	87
Other countries	296	22	17	13
Total	**1,333**	**100**	**135**	**100**

WHAT

	1995 Sales	
	$ mil.	% of total
Defense electronics	510	38
Human resources data svcs.	412	31
Trucking & gaming data svcs.	274	21
Media ratings	137	10
Total	**1,333**	**100**

Selected Products and Services

Defense Electronics
Antisubmarine warfare systems
Avionics systems
Communications systems
Computing Devices International
Display subsystems
Ground subsystems
Intelligence and surveillance systems
Shipboard subsystems

Information Services
Arbitron (radio and other media ratings services, marketing databases)
Comdata (trucking information services: cash advances, billing, fuel purchasing cards, route management; cash advances to customers of gaming establishments)
Human Resources Group (benefits administration, employee assistance programs, payroll processing, payroll tax filing, personnel outsourcing, software)

KEY COMPETITORS

A.C. Nielsen
ADP
Computer Language Research
CTA
Digital Solutions
ESCO Electronics
Hughes Electronics
IBM
ITT Industries
Kelly Services
Litton Industries
Lockheed Martin
Norrell
Northrop Grumman
Olsten
Paychex
Raytheon

HOW MUCH

NYSE symbol: CEN FYE: December 31	Annual Growth	1986	1987	1988	1989	1990	1991	1992	1993	1994	1995
Sales ($ mil.)	(9.7%)	3,347	3,367	3,628	2,935	1,691	1,525	830	886	916	1,333
Net income ($ mil.)	—	(269)	25	2	(680)	3	(9)	(351)	(22)	66	59
Income as % of sales	—	—	0.7%	0.0%	—	0.2%	—	—	—	7.2%	4.4%
Earnings per share ($)	—	(6.58)	0.59	0.03	(16.11)	0.05	(0.21)	(8.24)	(0.52)	1.43	0.66
Stock price – high ($)	—	28.75	38.25	30.50	24.00	21.63	13.75	17.25	19.88	27.50	47.50
Stock price – low ($)	—	18.75	17.63	16.38	16.25	7.63	6.75	9.13	13.00	18.50	26.13
Stock price – close ($)	5.1%	26.38	21.63	19.63	18.13	8.88	10.88	15.25	19.00	26.88	41.25
P/E – high	—	—	65	—	—	—	—	—	—	19	72
P/E – low	—	—	30	—	—	—	—	—	—	13	40
Dividends per share ($)	—	0.00	0.00	0.00	0.00	0.00	0.00	0.00	0.00	0.00	0.00
Book value per share ($)	(23.1%)	23.63	24.54	24.68	9.38	10.43	10.24	(2.36)	2.41	3.99	2.23
Employees	(12.6%)	34,409	34,500	33,500	18,000	14,500	13,000	8,800	7,600	7,500	10,200

1995 YEAR-END

Debt ratio: 58.7%
Return on equity: 49.5%
Cash (mil.): $152
Current ratio: 0.94
Long-term debt (mil.): $205
No. of shares (mil.): 67
Dividends
  Yield: —
  Payout: —
Market value (mil.): $2,777

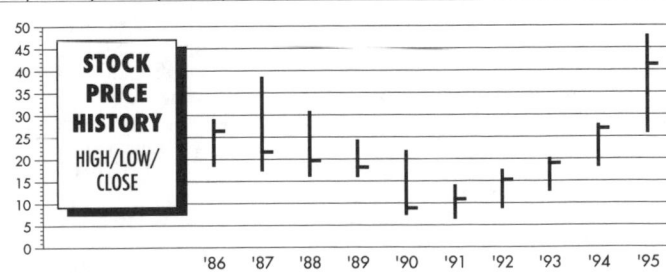

STOCK PRICE HISTORY
HIGH/LOW/CLOSE

CISCO SYSTEMS, INC.

OVERVIEW

Still a relatively young kid in the computer industry, Cisco is the world's #1 supplier of internetworking products that link local area and wide area networks (LANs and WANs). The San Jose, California-based company markets its routers, switches, dial-up access servers, and network management software in some 75 countries.

Cisco's Internetworking Operating System (Cisco IOS) software lets networks running under differing standards interoperate, creating a seamless information and communications system. A rise in scope and use of online applications and services has led to an increase in demand for the company's products, which serve as on-ramps to the Information Superhighway. Through close working relationships with telecommunications firms AT&T, British Telecom, MCI, and Sprint, Cisco is working to bridge the gap between private (corporate and government) and public (the World Wide Web and other consumer networks).

WHEN

Cisco was founded by Stanford University husband-and-wife team Leonard Bosack and Sandra Lerner in 1984. Bosack, who was manager of the school's computer science laboratory, developed technology to link his department's computer network with the network in his wife's department, the graduate school of business. Deciding there could be a market for internetworking devices, Bosack and Lerner founded Cisco with 3 colleagues, Greg Setz, Bill Westfield, and Kirk Lougheed. Bosack and Lerner mortgaged their house, bought a used mainframe, put it in their garage, and got friends and relatives to work for deferred pay. They sold their first network router in 1986.

In the beginning Cisco targeted universities, research centers, the aerospace industry, and government facilities, relying mostly on word-of-mouth advertising and contacts made via ARPANET (the precursor to the Internet). However, in 1988 the company decided to expand its marketing to include large corporations. Short of cash, Cisco turned to venture capitalist Donald Valentine of Sequoia Capital. Valentine bought a controlling stake in the company and became chairman. He hired John Morgridge, COO of laptop maker GRiD Systems, to be president and CEO.

As the market for network routers opened up in the late 1980s, Cisco, whose products had a proven track record with its customers at universities and other institutions, had a head start on competitors. In addition, the company was the first to offer reasonably priced, high-performance routers. Cisco sales exploded, jumping from $1.5 million in 1987 to $28 million in 1989.

Cisco went public in 1990. Later that year Morgridge fired Lerner, with whom he had constantly battled. Bosack quit the company, and the pair sold their stock for about $200 million. (They eventually gave about 70% of their fortune to various favorite causes.)

By 1991 Cisco's sales had reached $183 million, but the company also began to face increased competition from start-ups as well as computer giants IBM and DEC. It began to expand its product offerings and also beefed up overseas sales. In 1993 the company addressed the lower end of the router market by introducing the Cisco 2000. That year it also made its first acquisition, Crescendo Communications, a Sunnyvale, California-based networking company.

While Cisco 2000 gave the company an entry to the lower end of the router market, Cisco was still known mainly for its high-end, high-priced routers. In 1994 the enterprise intensified its presence in the low-end router market with the acquisition of PC-operated router maker Newport Systems Solutions. It also bought Kalpana, the leading maker of Ethernet switches, that year.

In 1995 the company pumped up its position in the fast-growing asynchronous transfer mode (ATM) switching market when it bought LightStream from Bolt Beranek and Newman. Also in 1995 EVP John Chambers succeeded Morgridge as president and CEO. Morgridge became chairman. Cisco earned $421 million on sales of $1.98 billion in that fiscal year.

Cisco increased its presence in the Internet connectivity market in 1996 with 2 acquisitions. One of the purchases was TGV Software, maker of MultiNet software, which lets network-computer users tap into the Internet; the other was Internet Junction, which makes software that connects Novell NetWare users with the World Wide Web and other networks. Also in 1996 Cisco acquired ATM products maker StrataCom for $4.6 billion, and it agreed to acquire Telebit Corp., a company with high-speed modem technology.

WHO

Chairman: John P. Morgridge, age 62, $294,799 pay
VC: Donald T. Valentine, age 63
President and CEO: John T. Chambers, age 46,
 $394,27 4 pay
SVP Worldwide Sales: Donald A. LeBeau, age 48,
 $345,723 pay
VP and General Manager, Core Business Unit: Frank J.
 Marshall, age 48, $321,459 pay
VP Business Development and Chief Technical Officer:
 Edward R. Kozel, age 40, $274,508 pay
VP Manufacturing: Carl Redfield, age 48, $ 259,679 pay
VP Finance and Administration, CFO, and Secretary:
 Larry R. Carter, age 52
VP North American Operations: James G. Richardson
VP Japanese Operations: Takatoshi Matsumoto
VP Quality: Karin J. Beumer
VP Human Resources: Barbara Beck
Auditors: Coopers & Lybrand L.L.P.

WHERE

HQ: 170 W. Tasman Dr., San Jose, CA 95134-1706
Phone: 408-526-4000
Fax: 408-526-4100
Web site: http://www.cisco.com

Cisco sells products in approximately 75 countries and
has Technical Assistance Centers in California, North
Carolina, Australia, and Belgium.

	1995 Sales % of total
US	58
Other countries	42
Total	**100**

WHAT

Selected Products and Services
ATM switching products
Cisco IOS software
Ethernet switches
LAN switching products
Network integration
Routers

Selected Vendor Partners
Alcatel
Cabletron Systems
Compaq
Fujitsu
Hitachi
LanOptics
NEC
Northern Telecom
Sun Microsystems
Toshiba

KEY COMPETITORS

3Com
ALANTEC
Ascend Communications
Bay Networks
Cabletron
Cascade Communications
Clearpoint
Compatible Systems
CrossComm
DEC
FORE Systems
IBM
Microcom
Optical Data Systems
Proteon
Shiva

HOW MUCH

Nasdaq symbol: CSCO FYE: Last Sunday in July	Annual Growth	1986	1987	1988	1989	1990	1991	1992	1993	1994	1995
Sales ($ mil.)	158.3%	—	1	5	28	70	183	340	649	1,243	1,979
Net income ($ mil.)	—	—	0	0	4	14	43	84	172	315	421
Income as % of sales	—	—	5.6%	7.1%	15.1%	19.9%	23.6%	24.9%	26.5%	25.3%	21.3%
Earnings per share ($)	105.8%	—	—	—	0.02	0.06	0.17	0.33	0.67	1.19	1.52
Stock price – high ($)	—	—	—	—	—	2.83	8.53	20.19	32.88	40.75	89.38
Stock price – low ($)	—	—	—	—	—	1.23	2.45	8.06	19.06	18.75	32.38
Stock price – close ($)	92.8%	—	—	—	—	2.80	8.28	18.91	32.31	35.13	74.63
P/E – high	—	—	—	—	—	47	50	61	49	34	59
P/E – low	—	—	—	—	—	21	14	24	28	16	21
Dividends per share ($)	—	—	—	—	—	0.00	0.00	0.00	0.00	0.00	0.00
Book value per share ($)	73.7%	—	—	—	—	0.32	0.56	1.02	1.92	3.29	5.06
Employees	87.5%	—	—	—	94	254	505	882	1,451	2,443	4,086

1995 YEAR-END

Debt ratio: 0.0%
Return on equity: 37.8%
Cash (mil.): $440
Current ratio: 2.95
Long term debt (mil.): $0
No. of shares (mil.): 272
Dividends
 Yield: —
 Payout: —
Market value (mil.): $20,318

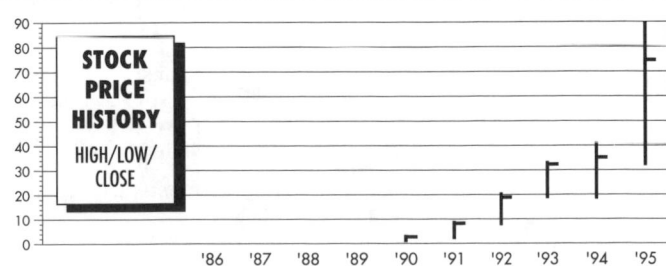

STOCK PRICE HISTORY HIGH/LOW/CLOSE

CMP PUBLICATIONS, INC.

OVERVIEW

CMP Publications is elbowing its way to the top of the mountain — in this case, the mountain of information about computers and technology. The Manhasset, New York-based company publishes 13 magazines and newspapers for technology consumers and professionals, including *HomePC, Network Computing,* and *WINDOWS Magazine, Computer Reseller News,* and *VARBusiness.* CMP holds about 24% of its market, putting it neck and neck for the #2 spot with rival Ziff-Davis (*PC Magazine, PC Week*). Both still trail the much larger International Data Group (*InfoWorld, MacWorld*).

CMP "practices what it preaches," embracing computer technology as an adjunct to traditional paper publishing. It launched MAX, a CD-ROM companion to *Computer Reseller News,* in 1994 and the following year established TechWeb, a World Wide Web site where all CMP publications can be viewed online. In early 1996 the company added a Web browser to the MAX CD-ROM, giving its users direct access to the MAX home page and advertisers' Web sites.

The company also organizes trade shows and conferences on high-technology products and issues. Its Looking Glass Consulting service assists advertisers and ad agencies in the development of advertising programs for CD-ROM and the Internet.

CMP is privately held by the founding Leeds family.

WHEN

Husband-and-wife team Gerry and Lilo Leeds founded CMP in 1971 when they began publishing *Electronic Buyers' News.* Gerry, an electronics engineer with experience in marketing, was inspired by a friend's idea to market a specialized mailing list targeted to people involved in high-tech purchasing. However, he was convinced that a newspaper would reach the audience more effectively. Before founding CMP (he had originally wanted to call the company Creative Media Publications), Gerry had started several other companies, including an organization for electronics manufacturers; Lumatron, which made high-speed sampling scopes; and Data Device (later ILC Data Device), which made operational amplifiers.

The Leedses created a prototype for *EBN* modeled after *Newsday* and *Women's Wear Daily.* Dissatisfied with the paper's first issue, they scrapped all 2,000 copies and redesigned it. As it grew, CMP continued to add trade-oriented tabloids aimed at the computer and telecommunications markets, including *CommunicationsWeek, Computer Reseller News, Electronic Engineering Times,* and *VARBusiness.* It also expanded into travel titles, launching *Tour & Travel News* in 1985.

Unsettled by growing pains, in 1986 CMP was restructured into operating groups. The Leedses turned over the operation of the company in 1988 to their oldest son, Michael. He sold most of CMP's health and travel holdings and introduced the *Long Island Monthly,* a lifestyle magazine whose start-up cost the company around $10 million before it ceased publication 2 years later. CMP published 14 titles in 1990, including *Network Computing.*

CMP consolidated its focus on technology and telecommunications in the early 1990s. It killed its trade titles, *Buildings Journal* and *Manufacturing Week.* The company left the health care market altogether in 1992. With ad sales slowing in the early 1990s, CMP added ancillary products and services such as direct marketing, research services, and trade shows.

In 1991 CMP bought a small, year-old publication called *WINDOWS/OS2* from Silicon Beach Operations. CMP added 2 more consumer magazines in 1993: *HomePC* for home computer users and *NetGuide* for the growing Internet market.

Early in 1994 CMP sold its 4-title travel publications group (including *Tour & Travel News* and *Business Travel News*) to Miller Freeman for around $20 million. With its focus firmly on high tech, later that year it launched *Interactive Age* (reporting on converging technologies) and *Informatiques,* a publication in French for MIS (management information systems) professionals. In late 1994 the company became the first high-tech publisher to launch all of its print products on the Internet.

CMP continued to expand into international markets in 1995 by introducing a German edition of *Computer Reseller News.* Also that year it folded *Interactive Age,* which had competed against Ziff-Davis's *Inter@ctive Week.*

To focus its business in the face of increasing production costs, in 1996 CMP sold both *Communications Week International* and *Communications Week International Latinamerica* to EMAP Business Communications of London.

WHO

Cochairperson: Gerard G. Leeds
Cochairperson: Lilo J. Leeds
President and CEO: Michael S. Leeds
President, CMP Publications International: Daniel H. Leeds
President, Publishing: Ken Cron
EVP and Chief Information Officer: Grace Monahan
SVP Enterprise Computing, National Accounts: Jeffrey C. Strief
VP and CFO: Joseph E. Sichler
VP and Treasurer: Pearl Turner
VP and General Counsel: Robert D. Marafioti
VP/Group Publisher, Channel Group: John Russell
VP/Group Publisher, Personal Computing Group: E. Drake Lundell
VP/Group Publisher, OEM Group: Girish Mhatre
VP Customer Services: Georgette Ross
Senior Director Trade Show and Conference Services: Peter Candito

WHERE

HQ: 600 Community Dr., Manhasset, NY 11030-3847
Phone: 516-562-5000
Fax: 516-562-7830
Web site: http://techweb.cmp.com

CMP publishes 13 magazines and trade newspapers and provides marketing and information services to the high-technology consumer and business marketplaces.

WHAT

Selected Publications and Circulation

Channel Group
Computer Reseller News (103,000)
Computer Retail Week (31,000)
VARBusiness (95,000)

Enterprise Computing Group
CommunicationsWeek (175,000)
InformationWeek (325,000)
Informatiques (France, 40,000)
Network Computing (185,550)

OEM Group
Electronic Buyers' News (61,000)
Electronic Engineering Times (131,000)
OEM Magazine (80,000)

Personal Computing Group
HomePC (400,000)
NetGuide (250,000)
WINDOWS Magazine (700,000)

Selected Conferences and Expositions
ATM (Asia/Pacific, Europe)
Client/Server Conference and Exposition
Commercial Parallel Processing Conference
CROSSROADS
Enterprise PC: Desktop Strategies for the '90s
Global Mobile
High-Tech Direct 2000
The Networked Economy Conference (US, Asia/Pacific, Europe)
Programmed Logic Devices Design
TechDecisions

KEY COMPETITORS

C/NET	Mecklermedia
Cowles Media	Organic Online
Crain Communications	Pittway
Hearst	Reed Elsevier
HyperMedia	T/SF Communications
International Data Group	Walt Disney
Lagardere	Wired Ventures
McGraw-Hill	Ziff-Davis
Modem Media	

HOW MUCH

Private company FYE: December 31	Annual Growth	1986	1987	1988	1989	1990	1991	1992	1993	1994	1995
Sales ($ mil.)	17.3%	91	111	133	157	174	178	210	259	317	382
Employees	6.7%	—	—	950	—	1,000	1,000	1,045	1,200	1,400	1,500

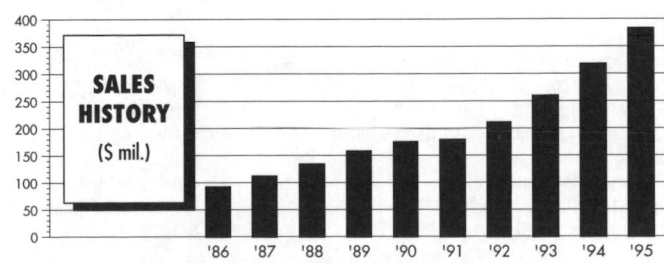

SALES HISTORY ($ mil.)

COMDISCO, INC.

OVERVIEW

Comdisco has changed its beat and is now drumming up new computer business. For more than 20 years, the Rosemont, Illinois-based company has leased mainframe computers; lately, however, equipment other than mainframes has made up nearly half of all new leases. As "big iron" usage has waned over the last decade, the firm has added personal computers and medical, manufacturing, and telecommunications equipment to its mix.

Through its Comdisco Disaster Recovery Services subsidiary, it is also the world's leading provider of emergency backup support for business services, including emergency data processing and business recovery. CEO Jack Slevin is using the business's experience in disaster recovery to move into the broader market of systems integration consulting.

The family of founder Kenneth Pontikes owns 26% of Comdisco.

WHEN

In 1969, at age 29, former IBM salesman Kenneth Pontikes borrowed $5,000 from his father to set up Computer Discount Corp. He saw a market niche in the increasing dependence of large corporations on mainframes. Gambling that companies would rather lease than pay outright for expensive equipment that might soon become obsolete, Pontikes built Computer Discount by leasing IBM mainframes. It grew quickly, recording sales of $1 million during its first year.

In 1971 the company reincorporated as Comdisco and went public. It grew rapidly until 1974, when Intel put $250 million worth of used IBM System 360 computers up for sale just after Comdisco had agreed to purchase hundreds of the same computer. The drop in prices for the 360 eliminated Comdisco's opportunity for profits, and it lost nearly $1 million that year. Comdisco Financial Services was created in 1976 to help customers finance leases of equipment from Comdisco and help them dispose of their old equipment. Four years later Comdisco Disaster Recovery Services was formed to help businesses whose computer systems were down or damaged because of flood, fire, or other misfortune. The company also began expanding overseas. Offices were set up in West Germany and Switzerland (1979), the UK (1983), and Japan (1985).

With the company's operations generating plenty of cash and the staff gaining specialized knowledge of the computer industry, Pontikes formed Comdisco Equities in 1984 to engage in stock arbitrage of potential takeover targets. However, the subsidiary was shut down after the stock market crash of 1987 produced a net loss of $80 million. Comdisco was still able to participate in high-risk computer stocks through its Venture Lease Division, which leased equipment to high-tech start-ups for a price including the right to purchase a stake in the company. (Renamed Comdisco Ventures, by 1995 it owned pieces of more than 250 start-ups, including microchip manufacturer Cyrix and software developers Sybase and Synopsys.)

As its revenues passed the $1 billion mark (1985), Comdisco looked for ways to further diversify its leasing business. Telephone equipment was added in 1985, and in 1988 the Comdisco Medical Equipment Group (now Comdisco Healthcare Group) was created to refurbish and lease medical equipment. In 1992 Comdisco Electronics Group was formed to supply used semiconductor manufacturing equipment.

Despite the company's attempts to diversify out of mainframes, the widespread switch to PCs, combined with the 1990-91 recession, cut its profits. Compounding those problems was a $70 million payment in 1994 to settle a lawsuit brought by IBM that accused Comdisco of using older IBM parts to produce computer mainframes to compete with newer IBM models. (Comdisco denied any wrongdoing.) That year Pontikes died of cancer. Pontikes was succeeded by Slevin, the company's COO.

In 1995 it purchased NetforceMTI, a private network services company. It also acquired certain assets of National Equipment Sales and Leasing and formed Comdisco Laboratory and Scientific Group to sell and lease equipment to the biotechnology, chemical, food processing, pharmaceutical, and research industries. Using NetforceMIT as the foundation, that year the company formed Comdisco Network Services. In 1996 Comdisco Healthcare received the first basic ordering agreement by the US Department of Veterans Affairs for reconditioned medical equipment. Also in 1996 Comdisco agreed to purchase the disaster recovery operations of CSC CompuSource, a unit of high-tech consulting firm Computer Sciences Corp.

WHO

President and CEO: Jack Slevin, age 59, $801,000 pay
EVP: Robert A. Bardagy, age 56, $730,000 pay
EVP: Nicholas K. Pontikes, age 31, $460,000 pay
EVP: William N. Pontikes, age 54
EVP, CFO, and Treasurer: John J. Vosicky, age 47,
  $470,000 pay
EVP: Alan J. Andreini, age 49, $400,000 pay
VP Human Resources: Lucie A. Buford
Auditors: KPMG Peat Marwick LLP

WHERE

HQ: 6111 N. River Rd., Rosemont, IL 60018
Phone: 847-698-3000
Fax: 847-518-5440
Web site: http://www.comdisco.com

Comdisco has nearly 50 offices in Canada, Europe, the
Pacific Rim, and the US.

| | 1995 Sales | |
	$ mil.	% of total
US	1,735	76
Europe	426	19
Canada	77	3
Pacific Rim	54	2
Adjustments	(52)	—
Total	**2,240**	**100**

WHAT

| | 1995 Sales | |
	$ mil.	% of total
Leasing	1,573	70
Sales	358	16
Disaster recovery	267	12
Other	42	2
Total	**2,240**	**100**

Selected Products (Sales and Leasing)
Central processing units
Electronic manufacturing, testing, and monitoring
  equipment
Medical and high-technology equipment
Laboratory equipment
Office equipment
Personal computers and workstations
Point-of-sale terminals
Telecommunications equipment
Testing equipment

Selected Operations
Comdisco Disaster Recovery Services
Comdisco Electronics Group
Comdisco Financial Services
Comdisco Healthcare Group
Comdisco Laboratory and Scientific Group
Comdisco Network Services
Comdisco Ventures

KEY COMPETITORS

Amplicon
AT&T Corp.
Forsythe McArthur
  Associates
Fujitsu
General Electric

Hitachi
IBM
Leasing Solutions
Portfolio Acquisition
Winthrop Resources

HOW MUCH

NYSE symbol: CDO FYE: September 30	Annual Growth	1986	1987	1988	1989	1990	1991	1992	1993	1994	1995
Sales ($ mil.)	3.8%	1,601	2,001	2,228	1,678	1,935	2,174	2,205	2,153	2,098	2,240
Net income ($ mil.)	2.2%	79	94	17	108	85	69	20	67	53	96
Income as % of sales	—	4.9%	4.7%	0.8%	6.4%	4.4%	3.2%	0.9%	3.1%	2.5%	4.3%
Earnings per share ($)	4.0%	1.21	1.43	0.26	1.63	1.33	1.13	0.33	0.98	0.77	1.73
Stock price – high ($)	—	15.88	23.17	15.80	21.59	18.09	18.02	15.47	14.00	16.17	23.75
Stock price – low ($)	—	7.63	7.63	10.80	13.25	9.28	11.52	8.33	8.75	11.83	14.67
Stock price – close ($)	9.5%	10.00	11.83	13.33	15.88	11.67	13.89	9.58	12.83	15.42	22.63
P/E – high	—	13	16	61	13	14	16	47	14	21	14
P/E – low	—	6	5	42	8	7	10	25	9	15	8
Dividends per share ($)	11.5%	0.09	0.12	0.15	0.15	0.15	0.17	0.18	0.18	0.23	0.24
Book value per share ($)	11.7%	5.49	7.13	6.91	8.37	9.58	10.42	10.25	11.03	11.65	14.85
Employees	9.5%	930	1,050	1,471	1,875	1,960	2,179	2,087	2,000	2,000	2,100

1995 YEAR-END

Debt ratio: 76.0%
Return on equity: 12.7%
Cash (mil.): $115
Current ratio: 0.55
Long-term debt (mil.): $1,796
No. of shares (mil.): 52
Dividends
  Yield: 1.1%
  Payout: 13.9%
Market value (mil.): $1,183

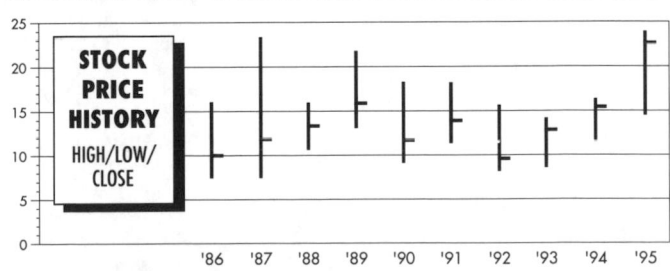

STOCK
PRICE
HISTORY
HIGH/LOW/
CLOSE

COMPAQ COMPUTER CORPORATION

OVERVIEW

Where do you go from #1? Compaq thinks there's plenty of room to grow up. The Houston-based company sold 5.7 million personal computers in 1995, making it the world's leading PC maker, with a 10% global market share. Compaq's products include desktop PCs for businesses and consumers, portable computers, and network servers.

Not content with Compaq's #1 spot in the PC market, CEO Eckhard Pfeiffer wants it to become a "full-service computer company." Compaq has already moved into the lead in the network server market. Now the company is pushing into networking via acquisitions such as networking products makers Networth (hubs and switches) and Thomas-

Conrad Corp. (interface cards and hubs). It has also entered the market for high-powered workstation computers.

Partnerships are helping Compaq's sales climb higher. The company is developing network routing products with internetworking leader Cisco Systems, PC-to-server links with German modem maker ITK, and high-speed networking chips with computer maker Texas Instruments. Compaq also has an alliance with Harman International (audio and video products), NEC (Japan's leading computer maker), and VideoLogic (video technology) to give arcade-quality graphics and high-fidelity stereo sound to Compaq computers.

WHEN

Joseph R. "Rod" Canion and 2 other ex-Texas Instruments engineers started Compaq in Houston in 1982 to manufacture and sell portable IBM-compatible computers. Compaq's first portable was developed from a prototype the 3 sketched on a paper place mat when they first discussed the product idea.

Compaq shipped its first computer in 1982 and in 1983 (the year it went public) recorded sales of $111 million — unprecedented growth for a computer start-up. Compaq's success was due in part to emphasis on leading-edge technology. In 1983 it introduced a 28-pound portable computer — 18 months before IBM did — and in 1986 it was first out with a computer based on Intel's 386 chip. However, Compaq delayed introduction of its laptop until the prototype's display and battery technologies met engineering specifications. Although introduced late (1988), the company's SLT/286 laptop with its crisp display screen became an immediate success.

To sell its products, Compaq capitalized on the extensive base of dealers and suppliers built up around the IBM PC. Rather than establish a large sales force, the company gave exclusive rights to dealers for sales and service of its products and by 1990 had a network of 3,800 retailers in 152 countries. The dealer channel proved to be effective. In 1988 Compaq became the first company to exceed the $2 billion sales mark within 6 years of its first product introduction.

In 1991 the firm bought a 13% interest in engineering workstation maker Silicon Graphics and paid $50 million for access to its graphics technology. Compaq also took a lead

role in creating a 21-company alliance, Advanced Computer Environment (ACE), to establish a standard for Reduced Instruction Set Computing (RISC) computers to compete with those of Sun and IBM.

Economic recession and stiff price competition slashed Compaq's revenues in 1991. Founder and CEO Canion (an engineer) was forced to resign; he was replaced with German-born Pfeiffer, the company's COO and a former marketing head at Texas Instruments. The next year Compaq withdrew from ACE and sold back its stake in Silicon Graphics and its 20% interest in Conner Peripherals (bought in 1986) for an $80 million profit. Late in 1992 it introduced the world's fastest PC server, the Compaq SYSTEMPRO/XL. In 1993 Compaq and Microsoft announced a joint venture to develop pen-based PCs, mobile computing, and multiprocessor computers and servers. The following year Compaq passed IBM and Apple to become the #1 PC maker.

In a major drive to boost its business, in early 1995 Compaq announced more than 100 new and redesigned PC models. In 1996 the company cut PC prices (as much as 51% on some models); introduced 5 lines of home PCs with varying features in an attempt to target consumer demand more specifically; and announced plans to boost the flagging sales of its portable PC by introducing a new family of midpriced portables. Later that year the company introduced 3 new lower priced lines for the business market.

That year it acquired a 7% stake in Raptor Systems, a maker of Internet and local area network "firewall" security software.

WHO

Chairman: Benjamin M. Rosen, age 63
President and CEO: Eckhard Pfeiffer, age 54, $3,625,000 pay
SVP Europe, Middle East, and Africa: Andreas Barth, age 51, $1,092,932 pay
SVP North America: Ross A. Cooley, age 55, $910,000 pay
SVP Corporate Operations and Quality: Gregory E. Petsch, age 45, $875,000 pay
SVP and General Manager, Consumer Products Group: Michael D. Heil, age 48
SVP and General Manager, Enterprise Computing Group: John T. Rose, age 50
SVP and General Manager, PC Products Group: Michael J. Winkler, age 51
SVP Technology, Corporate Development, and Marketing: Robert W. Stearns, age 45
SVP Human Resources: Hans W. Gutsch, age 52
CFO: Earl Mason, age 48
Auditors: Price Waterhouse LLP

WHERE

HQ: 20555 State Hwy. 249, Houston, TX 77070
Phone: 713-370-0670
Fax: 713-374-1740
Web site: http://www.compaq.com

Compaq has manufacturing facilities in Brazil, China, Singapore, the UK, and the US.

	1995 Sales	
	$ mil.	% of total
US & Canada	8,887	48
Europe	5,677	31
Other regions	3,806	21
Adjustments	(3,615)	—
Total	**14,755**	**100**

WHAT

	1995 Sales
	% of total
Commercial desktop PCs	45
PC systems	22
Portable PCs	17
Consumer/home desktop PCs	16
Total	**100**

Selected Products

Desktop PCs	Servers
Deskpro	ProLiant
Presario	ProSignia
ProLinea	
	Software
Portables	Insight Manager
Contura	SmartStart
LTE 5000	

KEY COMPETITORS

3 Com	Machines Bull
Acer	Micron Electronics
Advanced Logic Research	NCR
Apple Computer	NEC
AST	Oki
Bay Networks	Olivetti
Cisco Systems	Packard Bell
Data General	Philips
DEC	Sharp
Dell	Siemens
Fujitsu	Sony
Gateway 2000	Sun Microsystems
Hewlett-Packard	Texas Instruments
Hitachi	Toshiba
IBM	Unisys
Intel	Wang

HOW MUCH

NYSE symbol: CPQ FYE: December 31	Annual Growth	1986	1987	1988	1989	1990	1991	1992	1993	1994	1995
Sales ($ mil.)	42.1%	625	1,224	2,066	2,876	3,599	3,271	4,100	7,191	10,866	14,755
Net income ($ mil.)	38.2%	43	136	255	333	455	131	213	462	867	789
Income as % of sales	—	6.9%	11.1%	12.4%	11.6%	12.6%	4.0%	5.2%	6.4%	8.0%	5.3%
Earnings per share ($)	33.0%	0.22	0.60	1.05	1.29	1.70	0.50	0.84	1.78	3.21	2.87
Stock price – high ($)	—	3.60	13.07	10.95	18.73	22.60	24.73	16.61	25.22	42.13	56.75
Stock price – low ($)	—	1.94	3.21	6.99	9.87	11.82	7.37	7.41	13.90	24.13	31.13
Stock price – close ($)	35.1%	3.21	9.22	9.93	13.24	18.77	8.78	16.23	24.63	39.50	48.00
P/E – high	—	16	22	10	15	13	50	20	14	13	20
P/E – low	—	9	5	7	8	7	15	9	8	8	11
Dividends per share ($)	—	0.00	0.00	0.00	0.00	0.00	0.00	0.00	0.00	0.00	0.00
Book value per share ($)	35.4%	1.13	1.95	3.52	4.97	7.88	7.64	8.37	10.49	14.07	17.28
Employees	25.6%	2,200	4,000	6,900	9,500	11,400	11,600	11,300	10,541	14,372	17,055

1995 YEAR-END

Debt ratio: 6.1%
Return on equity: 19.0%
Cash (mil.): $745
Current ratio: 2.44
Long-term debt (mil.): $300
No. of shares (mil.): 267
Dividends
  Yield: —
  Payout: —
Market value (mil.): $12,816

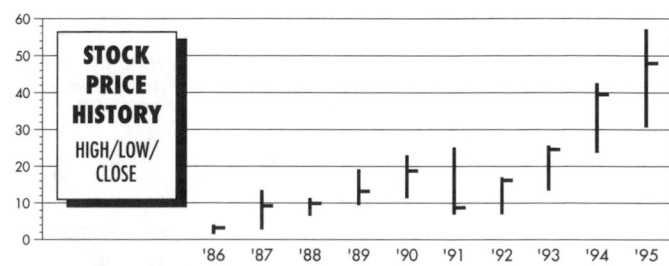

STOCK PRICE HISTORY HIGH/LOW/CLOSE

COMPUCOM SYSTEMS, INC.

OVERVIEW

CompuCom keeps big business working. At any given time, large companies have to cope with a dizzying array of desktop computer products. Dallas-based CompuCom offers personal computer hardware, software, and peripherals but makes the array a little less dizzying by also providing field engineering, network management, configuration, and other services via some 40 sales and service centers. The company stocks PC products from such manufacturers as Apple, Compaq, and IBM and software from Lotus, Microsoft, Novell, and Corel.

CompuCom is growing through such acquisitions as the Network Compatibility Group,

which sets standards for technology platforms for large enterprises.

The company is also taking its business global. It provides an International Service Desk to handle multiple languages, currencies, and licensing agreements in foreign countries. CompuCom also has an alliance with InfoPoint SA, a Paris-based systems integrator. The GlobalServe network is a worldwide alliance of service providers that gives customers a single source for purchasing, distribution, and managing their PC needs. Investment and management firm Safeguard Scientifics owns about 52% of CompuCom.

WHEN

CompuCom was founded by Stanley Sternberg in Michigan in 1981 to make factory automation products. Originally called CytoSystems, the company changed its name in 1983 to Machine Vision International (MVI) to reflect its focus on designing artificial vision systems for computers. Its main customers were Detroit automakers, who used MVI's automated inspection guidance systems to control industrial robots.

By the mid-1980s MVI was one of the largest machine vision companies in the US. In 1984 Safeguard Scientifics bought 31.5% of the company; Safeguard had been founded in 1953 by Warren Musser and Frank Diamond to raise funds for small, promising businesses. Looking to raise more capital for MVI, Safeguard and MVI's management took it public in 1985. However, MVI soon ran into trouble as the machine vision industry began to cool off. General Motors, the company's biggest customer, cut its orders, and MVI lost more than $13 million in 1986. Safeguard chairman Musser became chairman of MVI and began to shift the company's focus.

In 1987 MVI acquired New Jersey-based computer retailer TriStar Data Systems and Office Automation. The company moved its headquarters to New Jersey, adopted its present name, and shifted the thrust of its business to selling and supporting microcomputer systems.

CompuCom exited the machine vision business in 1988 to focus on computer retailing. That year the company acquired CompuShop, a Dallas-based computer retailer, from Bell Atlantic. CompuCom then moved its headquarters to Dallas. James Dixon, CEO of

CompuShop, became president of CompuCom. In 1989 the company named former CompuCraft head Avery More president and co-CEO; Dixon was named co-CEO and chairman. More made the key decision to abandon minicomputers and shift operations to a networked PC platform.

With the acquisition of the Computer Factory in 1991, the company became an authorized Apple dealer and gained a foothold in the northeastern US. Also that year it expanded its presence in the western US with the acquisition of retailer Photo & Sound Company. CompuCom considered expanding into discount superstore retailing but decided to focus on what More called its "bread and butter" — direct sales to large and medium-size corporate customers. The retail outlets of the Computer Factory were sold.

In 1992 CompuCom expanded its networking business when it bought network integrator MicroSolutions. When More left the company in 1993 to start venture capital firm Eureka Ventures, COO Ed Anderson became CEO; Dixon remained chairman.

As part of its strategy to expand its networking and service business, CompuCom has acquired several network service companies, including San Francisco-based International Micronet Systems in 1994. In 1995 it bought 3 network integrators: New Jersey-based Allerion, Houston's Trellis/Hayes/Micronet, and Minneapolis-based Benchmark Network Systems.

CompuCom introduced GlobalServe, its purchasing, distribution, and service alliance, in 1996. Also that year Charles Root replaced Dixon as chairman.

Chairman: Charles A. Root, age 63
President and CEO: Edward R. Anderson, age 49,
$726,020 pay
EVP Sales: Daniel F. Brown, age 50, $543,900 pay
SVP Finance and CFO: Robert J. Boutin, age 38,
$339,080 pay
VP and Chief Information Officer: Jack D. Dowling
VP Product Integration Networking Group: David W.
Hall
VP Distribution Services: David I. Robinson
VP Finance and Corporate Controller: M. Lazane Smith
VP Human Resources: Mark S. Esselman
Treasurer: Daniel L. Celoni
Auditors: KPMG Peat Marwick LLP

WHERE

HQ: 10100 N. Central Expwy., Dallas, TX 75231-1800
Phone: 214-265-3600
Fax: 214-265-5220
Web site: http://www.compucom.com

WHAT

	1995 Sales	
	$ mil.	% of total
Products	1,334	92
Service	101	7
Other	6	1
Adjustment	1	—
Total	**1,442**	**100**

Selected Microcomputer Brands Sold
3Com
Apple
Compaq
DEC
Hewlett-Packard
IBM
NEC
Toshiba

Selected Software Brands Sold
Lotus
Microsoft
Novell
WordPerfect

Selected Services
Configuration
Field engineering
Help desk services
Network management
Network project management

KEY COMPETITORS

AmeriData	Gateway 2000	Software
Technologies	Inacom	Spectrum
BDM	Intelligent	Tandy
CompUSA	Electronics	Corporation
Dell	Micro Warehouse	Vanstar
Entex	MicroAge	

HOW MUCH

Nasdaq symbol: CMPC FYE: December 31	Annual Growth	1986	1987	1988	1989	1990	1991	1992	1993	1994	1995
Sales ($ mil.)	98.6%	3	43	159	271	343	529	713	1,016	1,256	1,442
Net income ($ mil.)	—	(14)	0	2	2	4	5	7	11	15	21
Income as % of sales	—	—	0.2%	1.0%	0.6%	1.0%	0.9%	1.0%	1.1%	1.2%	1.4%
Earnings per share ($)	—	(1.25)	0.01	0.06	0.06	0.13	0.16	0.22	0.29	0.34	0.44
Stock price – high ($)	—	5.75	3.38	2.50	2.25	2.13	3.56	2.88	4.63	7.25	10.63
Stock price – low ($)	—	0.50	0.38	1.13	1.13	0.75	1.31	1.44	2.19	2.75	3.13
Stock price – close ($)	38.7%	0.50	2.13	1.50	1.13	1.31	2.25	2.19	4.06	3.13	9.50
P/E – high	—	—	—	42	38	16	22	13	16	21	24
P/E – low	—	—	—	19	19	6	8	7	8	8	7
Dividends per share ($)	—	0.00	0.00	0.00	0.00	0.00	0.00	0.00	0.00	0.00	0.00
Book value per share ($)	—	(0.49)	0.42	0.72	0.81	0.93	1.14	1.39	1.78	2.21	2.80
Employees	33.9%	—	253	540	590	683	1,061	1,156	1,542	1,975	2,615

1995 YEAR-END

Debt ratio: 46.5%
Return on equity: 17.8%
Cash (mil.): $4
Current ratio: 1.93
Long-term debt (mil.): $120
No. of shares (mil.): 44
Dividends
  Yield: —
  Payout: —
Market value (mil.): $419

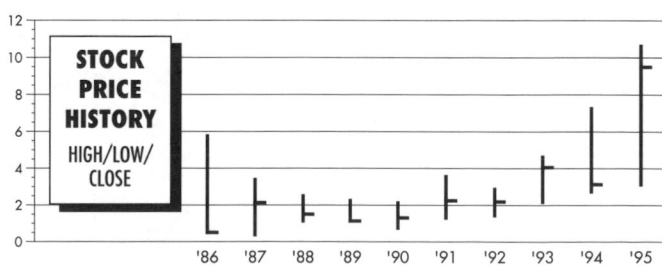

STOCK PRICE HISTORY
HIGH/LOW/CLOSE

COMPUSA INC.

OVERVIEW

Almost counted out by some analysts, Dallas-based CompUSA has risen from the mat and come back fighting. The nation's largest computer retailer, CompUSA has installed a new management team led by James Halpin and instituted a number of changes designed to transform the company from an entrepreneurial daredevil into a stable, mature corporation. In addition to decreasing the rate of new store openings (and even closing some old stores), changes included a new emphasis on training and customer services, consolidation of inventory and pricing at the corporate level, and a new focus on the home market rather than the hard-core "techie" market. In order to facilitate this change, the company began remodeling its stores to make them less intimidating to computer neophytes and adding informational programs and events.

The makeover seems to have helped. CompUSA's sales and same-store sales have risen. However, CompUSA doesn't have time to rest on its laurels. It faces stiff competition from both computer superstores, including Tandy's Computer City, and consumer electronics chains, including Best Buy and Circuit City.

CompUSA plans to continue to focus on "nontechie" computer buyers. To entice parents it has introduced to many of its stores a CompKids area, which features hundreds of edutainment software titles that kids can try before they buy.

WHEN

CompUSA was founded in 1984, when 23-year-old Mike Henochowicz (a native of South Africa and former Highland Appliance salesman) and 33-year-old Errol Jacobson invested $2,000 to open Soft Warehouse, an 800-square-foot software store near Dallas.

When the business opened, profit margins on computer programs were huge, and deep discounting, with little competition, still offered good profits. Soft Warehouse prospered by offering a wide selection of titles. In 1985 Henochowicz and Jacobson opened their first superstore in Dallas.

While the superstore concept was booming in other retail areas, it was a fairly new concept in the computer world. In the early 1980s buyers often did not know very much about computers and would go to one store to purchase hardware and another to buy software, relying on each store's technical expertise to guide their buying decisions. Soft Warehouse's one-stop-shopping concept coincided with the rise of savvy buyers who knew what they wanted. Soft Warehouse let them explore many options under one roof.

In 1988 the partners opened a 24,000-square-foot store in Atlanta. In 1989 Dubin Clark & Co., a private investment firm, bought a 50% interest in Soft Warehouse and brought in Nathan Morton, a former SVP of Home Depot, as the new COO. With the influx of capital, Morton immediately began an expansion program by opening stores in Houston, Los Angeles, Philadelphia, Miami, San Diego, and Washington, DC - all in 1989. In 1990 Morton became CEO, and Soft Warehouse attempted

an IPO but abandoned the effort when the Persian Gulf War dampened the market.

Decisions by Dell in 1990 and Apple in 1991 to sell their products through Soft Warehouse built the company's credibility. Because it was then selling computer hardware as well as software, in 1991 Soft Warehouse adopted the name CompUSA to reflect its broader product lines and national expansion. Also in 1991 CompUSA successfully launched its IPO. The 2 founders left the company about that time to pursue other interests. By 1992 the company operated 31 stores in 21 markets.

To manage its growth, CompUSA restructured in May 1993 and created an international division. Morton became chairman, while James Halpin (former president of HomeBase) was named president.

Just 7 months later, Morton resigned amid board dissatisfaction with CompUSA's poor earnings, which analysts blamed on inefficiencies stemming from rapid growth. Under Morton CompUSA had become extremely decentralized - individual stores were responsible for buying and pricing. Halpin became CEO and killed plans for an international division. He also began staff cutbacks and instituted centralized buying (decentralization had resulted in such great inefficiencies that in late 1994 the company had to auction off excess inventory).

In 1995 CompUSA opened its first stand-alone customer training centers, in Boston and Seattle. It bought PCs Compleat, a mail-order operation, in 1996. CompUSA's profits rose to $60 million in fiscal 1996 on sales of $3,830 million.

WHO

Chairman: Giles H. Bateman
President and CEO: James F. Halpin, age 43,
$451,805 pay
EVP Merchandising: Lawrence N. Mondry, age 34,
$236,000 pay
EVP and COO: Harold F. Compton, age 47
EVP, CFO, and Treasurer: James E. Skinner, age 41
SVP Human Resources, Training, and Administration:
Paul B. Poyfair, age 42
SVP Marketing and Advertising: Ronald Gilmore, age 39
VP, General Counsel, and Secretary: Mark R. Walker,
age 37
VP Real Estate: Ronald D. Strongwater, age 51
VP Human Resources: Mel McCall, age 51
Auditors: Ernst & Young LLP

WHERE

HQ: 14951 N. Dallas Pkwy., Dallas, TX 75240
Phone: 214-982-4000
Fax: 214-982-4276
Web site: http://www.compusa.com

	1995 Stores No.
California	16
Texas	7
Florida	6
New York	6
Ohio	6
Georgia	4
New Jersey	4
Illinois	3
Maryland	3
Massachusetts	3
Michigan	3
Pennsylvania	3
Virginia	3
Other states	19
Total	**86**

WHAT

Selected Products
Connectivity products
Data storage devices
Laptop computers
Microcomputers
Modems
Monitors
Printers

Selected Brands
Apple
Compaq
DEC
Dell
Hewlett-Packard
Sony
Texas Instruments
Toshiba

KEY COMPETITORS

Anam	Intelligent Electronics
Barnes & Noble	J&R Computer World
Best Buy	Kmart
CDW Computer Centers	Micro Center
Circuit City	Micro Warehouse
CompuCom	MicroAge
Dell	Montgomery Ward
Egghead	NeoStar
ELEK-TEK	OfficeMax
Entex	Price/Costco
Fretter	Sears
Fry's Electronics	Service Merchandise
Future Shop	Staples
Gateway 2000	Tandy Corporation
Global Directmail	Tiger Direct
Good Guys	Vanstar
Inacom	Wal-Mart
Inmac	

HOW MUCH

NYSE symbol: CPU FYE: June 30	Annual Growth	1986	1987	1988	1989	1990	1991	1992	1993	1994	1995
Sales ($ mil.)	75.0%	—	32	67	137	300	544	821	1,342	2,146	2,813
Net income ($ mil.)	—	—	0	2	2	2	(11)	8	12	(17)	23
Income as % of sales	—	—	0.9%	2.9%	1.2%	0.5%	—	1.0%	0.9%	—	0.8%
Earnings per share ($)	122.4%	—	—	—	0.01	0.16	(1.58)	0.62	0.67	(0.92)	1.21
Stock price – high ($)	—	—	—	—	—	—	23.75	40.50	37.00	22.25	44.38
Stock price – low ($)	—	—	—	—	—	—	15.00	19.25	17.88	6.75	14.75
Stock price – close ($)	9.7%	—	—	—	—	—	21.50	28.00	19.88	15.00	31.13
P/E – high	—	—	—	—	—	—	—	65	55	—	37
P/E – low	—	—	—	—	—	—	—	31	27	—	12
Dividends per share ($)	—	—	—	—	—	—	0.00	0.00	0.00	0.00	0.00
Book value per share ($)	—	—	—	—	—	—	(2.05)	5.55	8.80	7.91	9.01
Employees	56.5%	—	—	—	543	1,208	1,782	2,767	5,086	7,819	7,963

1995 YEAR-END

Debt ratio: 41.3%
Return on equity: 14.5%
Cash (mil.): $95
Current ratio: 1.55
Long-term debt (mil.): $155
No. of shares (mil.): 19
Dividends
  Yield: —
  Payout: —
Market value (mil.): $591

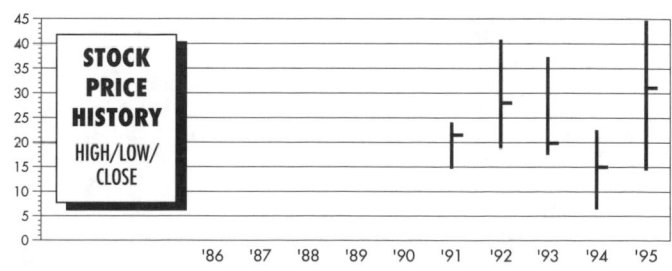

STOCK PRICE HISTORY HIGH/LOW/CLOSE

COMPUSERVE CORPORATION

OVERVIEW

CompuServe is battling for your cybersoul. The Columbus, Ohio-based company's flagship CompuServe Information Service is the world's #2 online service (after America Online). CompuServe subscribers can access services such as airline reservations, e-mail, online shopping, and stock market information (you may be reading this profile on CompuServe, where Hoover's Business Resources is part of its Basic Service). Subscribers can also play computer games, join any of 900 special interest "forums," or search through a variety of online databases and other information. In addition, the company offers SPRYNET, an Internet-only service, and WOW!, a family-oriented, set-fee (about $18 a month) service for novice users.

Through its Network Services Division, CompuServe provides network and Internet services to more than 950 corporate customers. Its corporate networking services include package tracking for Federal Express, transmission of credit data to more than 200,000 corporate clients for TRW, and VISA's point-of-sale network for credit card authorizations.

Spun off from its "stodgy" parent, tax prep firm H&R Block, CompuServe is trying to keep up with rival online services and the popularity of the Internet. It has added new features such as online banking services through an agreement with Cardinal Bancshares's Security First Network Bank. The company is also looking overseas for growth. It is the leading online service provider in Europe, where its subscribers number more than 650,000. In Japan 1.5 million subscribers use NiftyServe, CompuServe's joint venture with Fujitsu.

WHEN

In 1969, 25-year-old Jeffrey Wilkins started CompuServe to computerize his father-in-law's insurance company. Eight years later he introduced MicroNet, a mainframe computer time-sharing network that eventually became one of the first true online services.

H&R Block acquired CompuServe in 1980, providing the financial support it needed to aggressively develop online technology. Through the 1980s the company expanded globally and initiated several now-standard services, including e-mail and forums. CompuServe Network Services was established in 1982. Wilkins left CompuServe in 1985; he is currently CEO of CD-ROM publisher Metatec.

CompuServe was the first online provider to establish an international presence. Through a joint venture with Nissho Iwai and Fujitsu, the company debuted NiftyServe in 1987. During the late 1980s and early 1990s it reached agreements for expansion into Australia, Chile, Hungary, Israel, South Africa, South Korea, and Taiwan. CompuServe established its first European office, in Bristol, England, in 1991. Also that year it added an icon-based, color, graphical user interface. In 1994 the firm joined the rush to commercialize the Internet by acquiring a stake in Network Publishing, a company that established corporate Internet sites.

In 1995 CompuServe purchased SPRY, developer of the popular Internet in a Box software, and began supplying World Wide Web access to subscribers via a built-in Web browser. Late that year a German prosecutor said CompuServe was breaking the law by allowing subscribers to view certain sex-related materials. The company responded by banning 200 talk groups. In early 1996 it began offering Cyber Patrol software from Microsystems to control access to "cyberporn."

Under shareholder pressure to maximize share value, H&R Block spun off CompuServe in early 1996. The IPO raised $454 million, much less than analysts had expected. That year the online service firm announced a pact with Netscape that allows CompuServe subscribers to use Netscape's Navigator software to browse the World Wide Web, then said it would abandon its proprietary CompuServe software altogether and restructure itself in the Web's open environment. Also in 1996 the company launched WOW! and said it would offer reduced-rate access to CompuServe for users of AT&T's WorldNet online service.

In mid 1996 CompuServe announced its subscriber growth had stalled, sending its stock price into a tailspin. Competition from America Online and the Internet, a poor marketing strategy, hard-to-use software and a slow network were all blamed as culprits. The company finally introduced its much delayed CompuServe 3.0 software in late 1996. The new software featured an easier to use interface and Internet access. CompuServe also began a major equipment upgrade to give customers faster access to the network.

WHO

Chairman: Frank Salizzoni, age 58
President and CEO: Robert J. Massey, age 51, $470,358 pay
President, Online Services: Dennis D. Matteucci, age 57
President, CompuServe Europe: Steven P. Stanbrook, age 39
EVP Administration: Herbert J. Kahn, age 56, $285,673 pay
EVP Network Services Division: Peter F. Van Camp, age 40
EVP and CFO: Lawrence A. Gyenes, age 46
VP Human Resources: Judy Reinhard
Auditors: Deloitte & Touche LLP

WHERE

HQ: 5000 Arlington Centre Blvd., Columbus, OH 43220
Phone: 614-457-8600
Fax: 614-457-0348
Web site: http://www.compuserve.com
CompuServe has more than 60 offices worldwide.

	1996 Sales % of total
US	78
Other countries	22
Total	**100**

WHAT

	1996 Sales	
	$ mil.	% of total
Online services	561	71
Network services	199	25
Other	33	4
Total	**793**	**100**

Selected Operations
Interactive Services
  CompuServe Information Service (CIS, consumer online service targeted to experienced home and office users)
  NiftyServe (consumer online service, Japanese counterpart to CIS)
  SPRYNET (Internet-access-only service)
  WOW! (consumer online service targeted to the home market)

Network Services (wide area network applications, connectivity, and systems management services for business clients)

Selected CompuServe Features and Information Providers
Business Database Plus (articles from business publications)
Classified Ads (marketplace for members)
Electronic Mall (products from more than 170 merchants)
Executive News Service (clips from AP, UPI, Dow Jones, Reuters, and others)
Games (including interactive games and trivia)
GO MAPS (weather maps)
Grolier's Academic American Encyclopedia
Hoover's Company Database (business profiles published by Hoover's, Inc.)
IQuest (850 bibliographic and full-text databases)
Knowledge Index (access to the text of more than 50,000 journals and 100 popular databases)
Magazine Database Plus (articles from more than 100 popular magazines)
Movie Reviews (reviews by Roger Ebert)
New Car Showroom (information on current models)
TRAVELSHOPPER (airline schedules, fares, and booking; hotel and car rental information)

KEY COMPETITORS

America Online
ASCIINet
AT&T Corp.
BBN
Bertelsmann
Deutsche Telekom
Dow Jones
EarthLink
France Telecom
IBM
Knight-Ridder
La Tribune Desfosses
MCI
MFS Communications
Microsoft
NETCOM
PC Van
People World
Prodigy
PSINet
Reed Elsevier
Reuters
Scholastic
Starware
Thomson Corp.

HOW MUCH

Nasdaq symbol: CSRV FYE: April 30	Annual Growth	1987	1988	1989	1990	1991	1992	1993	1994	1995	1996
Sales ($ mil.)	24.3%	—	—	173	207	252	281	315	430	583	793
Net income ($ mil.)	(11.1%)	—	—	—	—	—	—	—	62	9	49
Income as % of sales	—	—	—	—	—	—	—	—	14.4%	1.5%	6.2%
Employees	32.1%	—	—	—	—	—	1,200	1,500	2,200	2,500	3,650

1996 YEAR-END

Debt ratio: 0.0%
Return on equity: 7.2%
Cash (mil.): $310
Current ratio: 3.51
Long-term debt (mil.): $0

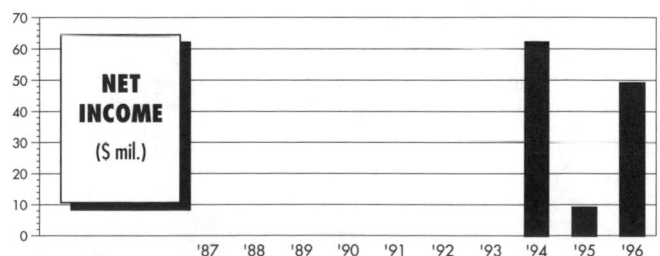

NET INCOME ($ mil.)

COMPUTER ASSOCIATES

OVERVIEW

Computer Associates (CA) is soft on business. The Islandia, New York-based business software developer is the world's #3 independent software company (Microsoft is numero uno, followed by Oracle). CA brags that it offers the broadest range of applications for the broadest range of computer platforms; it sells and services more than 500 products and claims more than 100,000 customers worldwide. Many of CA's products — which include tools for accounting, database management, network management, and manufacturing and distribution — are industry standards. Its flagship, Unicenter, gives an organization centralized control over its entire "information

technology infrastructure," including applications, databases, and computer networks.

The breadth of CA's product line is benefiting the company as sales surge for both mainframes and microcomputer networks. Marketing and development alliances — including recent pacts with Digital Equipment, Fujitsu, and Microsoft — are helping deepen the company's penetration of high-end corporate computing (95% of *FORTUNE* Global 500 companies use CA software) as well as client/server computing.

Founder and CEO Charles Wang owns 5% of CA. Swiss billionaire Walter Haefner owns 23% of the company.

WHEN

Charles Wang (pronounced "wong") and his family fled Communist China in 1952. After graduating from Queens College (New York) in 1976, Wang started a joint venture with Swiss-owned Computer Associates to sell software in the US. Wang started with 4 employees and one product, a file organizer for IBM storage systems (CA-SORT). It was a great success, and in 1980 Wang bought out his Swiss partners.

Wang soon realized that a penetrating distribution and service network, continuously fed by new products, was the key to success; acquiring existing software (and its customers) reduced risky in-house development and moved products to market sooner. CA's purchases of mostly struggling software firms produced the first independent software company to reach $1 billion in sales (1989).

The company moved beyond mainframe utilities into microcomputer software, buying the popular SuperCalc spreadsheet (1984) and BPI (accounting software, 1987); data security software, including the Top Secret program (1985); and a string of applications vendors, including Software International (financial, 1986) and Integrated Software Systems (graphics, 1986).

The 1987 purchase of chief utilities rival UCCEL made CA the world's largest independent software supplier and gave Haefner a stake in the company. It then had 64% of the tape/disk-management software market and a strong presence in banking applications and data security.

CA entered the mainframe database software market in 1988 with the purchase of Applied Data Research (ADR) from Ameritech. With

the $300 million acquisition of Cullinet in 1989, CA added the IDMS database line, software for VAX computers, and banking applications to its product line. But the incompatibility of Cullinet's IDMS software with that of ADR left customers guessing which one CA would ultimately support. This uncertainty and other problems in assimilating Cullinet caused product sales and net income to drop in 1990. In response, CA started a program to integrate its various acquisitions and began developing a way to let its software communicate regardless of hardware platform or operating system.

In the 1990s CA acquired On-Line Software, a maker of mainframe debugging software, and Pansophic Systems, a maker of AS/400 (IBM minicomputer) software applications.

CA rewrote its CA-Unicenter systems management software in 1994 for use on smaller computers. That year it acquired ASK Group, a developer of material management software.

CA acquired Legent, a rival software developer, for $1.8 billion in 1995. It also introduced CA-OpenIngres/Desktop, which integrates ASK's Ingres database software with Gupta Corp.'s database technology.

Charges related to the acquisition of Legent caused a net loss for CA in 1996. That year CA released Jasmine, a database management software system that includes multimedia and network application development tools. CA agreed that year to buy Cheyenne Software, a leading maker of data storage and network management products, for $1.2 billion.

WHO

Chairman and CEO: Charles B. Wang, age 51, $6,000,000 pay
President and COO: Sanjay Kumar, age 34, $3,900,000 pay
EVP Research and Development: Russell M. Artzt, age 49, $1,525,000
SVP Finance and CFO: Peter A. Schwartz, age 52, $975,000 pay
SVP Finance: Charles P. McWade, age 51, $440,000
SVP and Secretary: Belden A. Frease, age 57
SVP and Treasurer: Ira Zar, age 34
SVP Human Resources: Lisa Mars
Auditors: Ernst & Young LLP

WHERE

HQ: Computer Associates International, Inc., One Computer Associates Plaza, Islandia, NY 11788-7000
Phone: 516-342-5224
Fax: 516-342-5329
Web site: http://www.cai.com

Computer Associates operates in North America and through wholly owned subsidiaries in foreign 36 countries.

	1996 Sales		1996 Operating Income	
	$ mil.	% of total	$ mil.	% of total
US	2,081	53	(281)	—
Other countries	1,827	47	225	—
Adjustments	(403)	—	—	—
Total	**3,505**	**100**	**(56)**	**—**

WHAT

	1996 Sales	
	$ mil.	% of total
Products	2,775	79
Maintenance	730	21
Total	**3,505**	**100**

Selected Software Products
Application development
Automated production control
Business decision tools
CASE technologies
COBOL and testing tools
Data center administration
Database management
DB2 tools
Distributed client/server solutions
Enterprise information solutions
Financial management
Graphics tools
Manufacturing management
Security, control, and audit
Warehouse management

KEY COMPETITORS

Amdahl
Apple Computer
BMC Software
DEC
Dun & Bradstreet
Hewlett-Packard
IBM
Informix
Intuit
Microsoft
Oracle
PLATINUM technology
Seagate
Sequent
Sterling Software
Sun Microsystems
Sybase
Symantec
Wang

HOW MUCH

NYSE symbol: CA FYE: March 31	Annual Growth	1987	1988	1989	1990	1991	1992	1993	1994	1995	1996
Sales ($ mil.)	31.0%	309	709	1,030	1,296	1,348	1,509	1,841	2,418	2,623	3,505
Net income ($ mil.)	—	37	102	164	158	159	163	246	401	432	(56)
Income as % of sales	—	12.0%	14.4%	15.9%	12.2%	11.8%	10.8%	13.4%	18.7%	16.5%	—
Earnings per share ($)	—	0.25	0.42	0.65	0.57	0.57	0.61	0.96	1.56	1.71	(0.23)
Stock price – high ($)[1]	—	3.44	8.28	7.31	9.83	7.50	5.28	9.22	19.67	22.61	47.00
Stock price – low ($)[1]	—	1.81	3.05	5.31	4.67	1.94	2.78	4.83	8.94	12.17	20.83
Stock price – close ($)[1]	32.3%	3.06	7.11	7.08	5.56	3.44	5.06	9.00	17.78	21.56	37.92
P/E – high	—	14	20	11	17	13	9	10	13	13	—
P/E – low	—	7	7	8	8	3	5	5	6	7	—
Dividends per share ($)	—	0.00	0.00	0.00	0.00	0.07	0.07	0.07	0.09	0.13	0.14
Book value per share ($)	17.2%	1.47	2.10	2.97	3.54	3.99	3.71	4.19	5.08	6.57	6.12
Employees	14.0%	2,700	4,450	6,250	6,900	6,700	7,400	7,200	6,900	7,550	8,800

[1] Stock prices are for the prior calendar year.

1996 YEAR-END

Debt ratio: 49.4%
Return on equity: —
Cash (mil.): $201
Current ratio: 0.96
Long-term debt (mil.): $945
No. of shares (mil.): 242
Dividends
Yield: 0.4%
Payout: —
Market value (mil.): $9,185

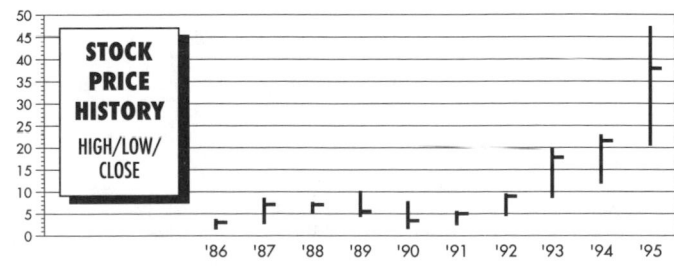

STOCK PRICE HISTORY HIGH/LOW/CLOSE

COMPUTER SCIENCES CORPORATION

OVERVIEW

Like a high-tech lifeguard, Computer Sciences Corporation (CSC) rescues corporations drowning in information. The El Segundo, California-based firm helps companies handle information by offering management consulting and such computer services as software development, data center management, and the integration of computer and communication networks. Its US clients include Hughes Aircraft and papermaker James River. Nearly 40% of the company's sales come from the US government; CSC has contracts with the Department of Labor and the Federal Emergency Management Agency, among others. Internationally the company works with

British Aerospace and the National Health Service of Scotland.

CSC is using acquisitions to enter new markets, both in the US and abroad. An agreement to buy Continuum, a leading financial IT services company with clients in 40 countries, gives CSC a foothold in the growing market for insurance and banking outsourcing. The purchase also kicks CSC to the #3 spot among computer services companies, after IBM and Electronic Data Systems. CSC will also buy American Practice Management, the US's largest health care consulting firm. An alliance with Check Point Software moves CSC into the commercial information security industry.

WHEN

CSC was founded in Los Angeles in 1959 by Fletcher Jones, director of a computer center for North American Aviation, and Roy Nutt, who worked for United Aircraft. The 2 started the company to write software programs for major computer manufacturers. CSC designed software packages for Honeywell and Univac in its early years. Jones believed the future lay in writing proprietary software that could be sold to the masses; however, the company has never succeeded at this.

In 1963 CSC became the first software company to go public. It signed a $5.5 million contract in 1996 to support NASA's computation laboratory. By 1968 annual sales had climbed to just over $53 million.

That year CSC agreed in principle to merge with Western Union; however, the deal fell through. The 2 companies had been working together for 4 years developing ways to transmit computerized information over telegraph wires. In 1969 William Hoover took over daily operations. Before joining CSC in 1964, Hoover was chief of computer applications and data systems at the Jet Propulsion Laboratory of the California Institute of Technology.

Jones, left to concentrate on strategy, began development of Infonet, a nationwide computer network, and Computicket, a system developed to sell computerized tickets to entertainment events. The cost of developing these network-based systems was crippling, and the company was forced to write off millions of dollars in losses.

When Jones died in a plane crash in 1972, Hoover became chairman of the troubled company. CSC soon bounced back with the help of a profitable government contract to supply

computer services to the General Services Administration.

Under Hoover, CSC started its transformation into a systems integrator. In 1981 the company won a $45.6 million contract for computer services at Cape Canaveral, Florida.

In 1986 CSC began diversifying in an attempt to increase its commercial operations. Also that year the company acquired Computer Partners, enhancing its operations in retail markets. In 1988 CSC bought consulting firm Index Group to compete with large accounting firms doing systems integration.

In 1991 CSC signed a 10-year, $3 billion contract with General Dynamics. The following year the EPA canceled its $347 million contract with CSC, citing problems with CSC's accounting practices. The Justice Department stepped in, and CSC agreed to pay $2.1 million to settle the charges.

The company secured an 8-year, $1.5 billion contract in 1995 to handle data processing for Hughes Aircraft. That year, after more than 2 decades, Hoover stepped down as CEO (he remained chairman) and was succeeded by Van Honeycutt, previously the president and COO. Also in 1995 CSC acquired several consulting firms. The company also purchased Germany's largest independent computer services firm, Ploenzke AG.

In 1996 CSC agreed to acquire Continuum Co. in a stock swap valued at $1.44 billion. Continuum specializes in software and computer services for financial services companies. That year the company paid $70 million to acquire 75% of Datacentralan A/S, Denmark's state-owned information service.

WHO

Chairman: William R. Hoover, age 66
President and CEO: Van B. Honeycutt, age 51, $625,000 pay
VP; Chairman, CSC Index: James A. Champy, age 54, $714,335 pay
VP; President, Consulting Group: John M. Mickel, age 56, $651,135 pay
VP; President, Integrated Business Services: Thomas R. Madison Jr., age 50, $648,731 pay
VP; President, European Group: Ronald W. Mackintosh, age 47, $572,240 pay
VP; President, Systems Group: Milton E. Cooper, age 57
VP and CFO: Leon J. Level, age 55
VP, General Counsel, and Secretary: Hayward D. Fisk, age 53
VP and Deputy General Counsel: Harvey N. Bernstein, age 49
VP Corporate Development: Lawrence Parkus, age 59
VP Corporate and Marketing Communications: C. Bruce Plowman, age 59
VP Human Resources: L. Scott Sharpe, age 57
Auditors: Deloitte & Touche LLP

WHERE

HQ: 2100 E. Grand Ave., El Segundo, CA 90245
Phone: 310-615-0311
Fax: 310-322-9805
Web site: http://www.csc.com
The company provides services throughout the US and has international offices in Australia, Belgium, Denamrk, France, Germany, the Netherlands, and the UK.

	1996 Sales	
	$ mil.	% of total
US	3,103	73
Other countries	1,139	27
Total	**4,242**	**100**

WHAT

	1996 Sales	
	$ mil.	% of total
US federal government	1,571	37
US commercial	1,532	36
International commercial	1,139	27
Total	**4,242**	**100**

Selected Services

Information Technology and Management Consulting
Business process reengineering
Computer facilities operation
Industry-specific information technology services
Information system development
Information technology strategy

Outsourcing
Applications development
Data center management
Network operations
Systems analysis

Systems Integration
Information system design, development, implementation, and integration

KEY COMPETITORS

American Management
Andersen Consulting
Arthur D. Little
Cap Gemini
Control Data
Coopers & Lybrand
Deloitte Touche Tohmatsu
EDS
Fiserv
IBM
Lockheed Martin
NCR
Perot Systems
Price Waterhouse
Unisys

HOW MUCH

NYSE symbol: CSC FY: March 31	Annual Growth	1987	1988	1989	1990	1991	1992	1993	1994	1995	1996
Sales ($ mil.)	17.0%	1,031	1,152	1,304	1,500	1,738	2,113	2,480	2,583	2,480	4,242
Net income ($ mil.)	18.0%	32	44	52	66	65	68	78	91	78	142
Income as % of sales	—	3.1%	3.8%	4.0%	4.4%	3.7%	3.2%	3.2%	3.5%	3.2%	3.3%
Earnings per share ($)	15.3%	0.69	0.91	1.09	1.36	1.34	1.37	1.55	1.77	1.55	2.48
Stock price – high ($)[1]	—	14.95	24.33	18.00	19.50	19.33	26.96	28.29	33.42	28.29	75.25
Stock price – low ($)[1]	—	9.83	13.83	12.67	15.42	12.25	15.92	19.00	23.33	19.00	46.50
Stock price – close ($)[1]	19.5%	14.14	16.83	15.83	19.25	16.29	26.96	26.08	33.25	26.08	70.25
P/E – high	—	22	27	16	14	14	20	65	19	65	30
P/E – low	—	14	15	12	11	9	12	45	13	45	19
Dividends per share ($)	—	0.00	0.00	0.00	0.00	0.00	0.00	0.00	0.00	0.00	0.00
Book value per share ($)	15.9%	6.17	7.12	8.21	9.59	10.89	12.33	13.95	15.92	13.95	23.30
Employees	7.3%	18,000	18,300	19,600	21,600	22,900	26,500	26,000	29,000	32,900	33,850

[1] Stock prices are for the prior calendar year.

1996 YEAR-END

Debt ratio: 26.7%
Return on equity: 11.5%
Cash (mil.): $105
Current ratio: 1.50
Long-term debt (mil.): $405
No. of shares (mil.): 56
Dividends
  Yield: —
  Payout: —
Market value (mil.): $3,936

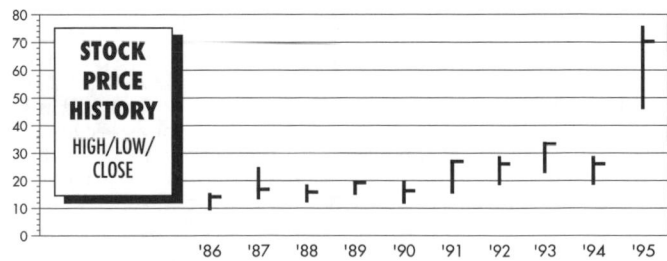

STOCK PRICE HISTORY
HIGH/LOW/ CLOSE

COMPUTERVISION CORPORATION

OVERVIEW

Computervision has redesigned itself — betting that its customers will use its software to do the same with their products. The Bedford, Massachusetts-based company is one of the world's 5 leading suppliers of CAD/CAM software. Its Electronic Product Definition (EPD) design framework enables a manufacturer to create a complex product design (e.g., a nuclear submarine) electronically. The design (or any part of it) can be altered, tested, and tooled in real time on an enterprise's engineering and manufacturing computers, across networks if necessary. The software that makes this happen includes Computervision's flagship CADDS 5 (component modeling), PELORUS (model development across multiple networks), and Product Data Management

software (such as Optegra Workflow Manager, which automates the manufacturing work process by directing the work to the right people at the right time).

Chairman Russell Planitzer has largely succeeded in returning Computervision to the forefront of CAD/CAM software development (after terminating its hardware business in the early 1990s). He has handed the president and CEO's baton to Kathleen Cote, who plans to broaden EPD's offerings, particularly for medium-sized and small companies, as well as boost sales efforts in North America. The company's main selling strategy is rooted in EPD's ability to save a customer significant design, development, and manufacturing costs (in a world where price is everything).

WHEN

Seven former Honeywell engineers founded Prime Computer in Natick, Massachusetts, in 1972 to develop powerful 32-bit superminicomputers. Older manufacturers were loath to supersede their profitable 16-bit lines; unencumbered by such ties, Prime introduced its 200 model. It was an instant success.

The company designed fully compatible product lines (such as the 50 series of minis, 1979) and networking software (PRIMENET, RINGNET). Sales jumped from $11 million in 1975 to $365 million in 1981. In 1978 Prime had become the youngest company ever listed on the NYSE.

IBM alumnus Joe Henson (president in 1982) centralized planning, expanded to the Far East, and began a growth-by-acquisition strategy that by 1988 had catapulted Prime to revenues of $1.6 billion. Henson targeted CAD/CAM software companies, buying Compeda (1982), VersaCAD (1987), and Computervision (1988); Computervision alone raised Prime's CAD/CAM market share from 3.5% to 17%. Prime purchased the CALMA mechanical design product from GE in 1988.

The company moved beyond superminis to provide platforms for its burgeoning CAD/CAM line. New computer platforms included supermicros (the EXL Series, 1987) and, from a series of joint ventures, workstations (the CADDStation and WS3600, with Sun Microsystems, 1987), mainframes (the EXL 1200 series, with Sequent Computers, 1989), and minisupers (the MXCL 5, with Cydrome, 1989). In 1990 Prime introduced a RISC-based

EXL 7000 series — the result of a partnership with MIPS Computer Systems.

Prime's defense against a hostile takeover by MAI Basic Four contributed to a $281 million loss in 1989 and forced the company to be acquired by DR Holdings, a corporation formed by New York investment firm J. H. Whitney. The acquisition left Prime with over $1 billion in debt. To reduce costs, Computervision laid off 20% of its staff and decentralized into 5 new product-based divisions in 1990. Another 800 employees were let go in 1991.

In 1992 Prime discontinued the manufacture of computer hardware. Later that year the company renamed itself Computervision (the name of its well-known CAD/CAM unit) and went public. Poor financial results led the company's board to oust CEO John Shields and replace him with chairman Russell Planitzer in 1993. Planitzer discontinued the workstation resale business that year and sold off its System 9 product (geographic mapping software) to Unisys.

Lehman Brothers sold almost all of its 22% stake in Computervision to the public in 1994. That year bankrupt DR Holdings distributed its 33% stake in the company to creditors. The restructured firm made a $10 million profit in 1994 (its first in 6 years). Nine-year company veteran Kathleen Cote was made president in 1995 and CEO in 1996. Also that year the company agreed to sell its hardware services business to an investor group. Computervision retained a minority stake in the newly created company, CV Services International.

WHO

Chairman: Russell E. Planitzer, age 52, $1,993,165 pay
President and CEO: Kathleen A. Cote, age 47,
$558,116 pay (prior to promotion)
SVP Human Resources and Organizational
Productivity: Barry F. Cohen, age 51, $547,388 pay
SVP R&D: Attilio Rimoldi, age 53, $527,849 pay
VP Worldwide Sales: Patrick L. Clark, $554,340 pay
VP Business Operations and General Counsel:
Anthony N. Fiore Jr., age 49
CFO: William A. Foniri, age 46
Auditors: Andersen Worldwide

WHERE

HQ: 100 Crosby Dr., Bedford, MA 01730-1480
Phone: 617-275-1800
Fax: 617-275-2670
Web site: http://www.cv.com

Computervision has facilities in California and Germany.

	1995 Sales	
	$ mil.	% of total
Europe	251	49
US	165	33
Pacific Rim	91	18
Total	**507**	**100**

WHAT

	1995 Sales	
	$ mil.	% of total
Software products	164	32
Software services	120	24
Other services	223	44
Total	**507**	**100**

Software Products
CADDS 5 (component-modeling software that provides
  integrated CAD/CAM for every stage of the product
  development process, from design to manufacturing)
Optegra Workflow Manager (permits organizations to
  distribute product-related data according to routing
  instructions)
PELORUS (advanced component-modeling software that
  makes it possible to develop automation applications
  across multiple networks)
Product Data Management (PDM; software designed to
  improve collaboration and information access and
  sharing throughout an enterprise)

Services
Productivity services (business consulting, customer
  education and training, design automation and PDM
  products, and implementation consulting for EPD)
Software support services

KEY COMPETITORS

Autodesk
Dassault
DEC
EDS
IBM
Intergraph
MacNeal-Schwendler
Parametric Technology
Sherpa Systems
Structural Dynamics Research

HOW MUCH

NYSE symbol: CVN FYE: December 31	Annual Growth	1986	1987	1988	1989	1990	1991	1992	1993	1994	1995
Sales ($ mil.)	(5.7%)	860	961	1,595	1,141	1,290	1,213	1,066	827	574	507
Net income ($ mil.)	(7.6%)	47	65	13	(281)	(71)	(461)	(226)	(571)	10	23
Income as % of sales	—	5.5%	6.7%	0.8%	—	—	—	—	—	1.7%	4.5%
Earnings per share ($)	—	—	—	—	—	(1.40)	(18.71)	(6.09)	(11.89)	0.20	0.43
Stock price – high ($)	—	—	—	—	—	—	—	12.38	6.50	5.38	15.50
Stock price – low ($)	—	—	—	—	—	—	—	4.00	2.13	2.50	3.63
Stock price – close ($)	38.4%	—	—	—	—	—	—	5.75	3.63	3.88	15.25
P/E – high	—	—	—	—	—	—	—	—	—	27	36
P/E – low	—	—	—	—	—	—	—	—	—	13	8
Dividends per share ($)	—	—	—	—	—	—	—	0.00	0.00	0.00	0.00
Book value per share ($)	—	—	—	—	—	—	—	1.02	(11.00)	(10.52)	(5.38)
Employees	(14.5%)	8,621	8,818	12,386	10,670	8,700	6,750	5,900	3,800	2,300	2,100

1995 YEAR-END

Debt ratio: 100.0%
Return on equity: —
Cash (mil.): $51
Current ratio: 0.69
Long-term debt (mil.): $224
No. of shares (mil.): 63
Dividends
  Yield: —
  Payout: —
Market value (mil.): $958

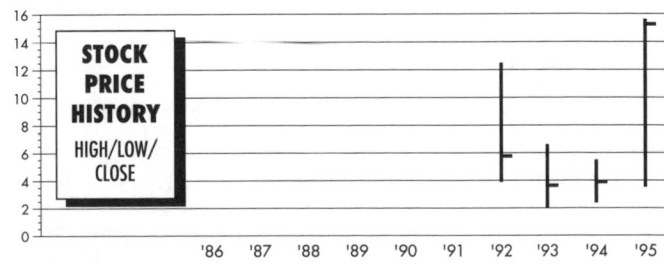

STOCK
PRICE
HISTORY
HIGH/LOW/
CLOSE

CONTROL DATA SYSTEMS, INC.

OVERVIEW

Leaving its mainframe computer manufacturing origins behind, Control Data Systems has moved ahead at warp speed toward systems integration in general and electronic commerce (virtual shopping on the Internet) in particular. The Arden Hills, Minnesota-based company helps governments and other large organizations — in financial services, telecommunications, and manufacturing — develop enterprise-wide information systems needed for creating, transmitting, accessing, and controlling business information.

The company develops software for messaging; computer-aided design, manufacturing, and engineering (CAD/CAM/CAE); and product data management (PDM). It also offers consulting services, with a special emphasis on client/servers, networking technology, and outsourcing. The US government accounts for almost 14% of sales.

The company has been narrowing its focus by getting rid of noncore operations and concentrating on intranet applications and software products for CAD, PDM, and Internet shopping. In addition, it has been aggressively seeking telecommunications partners worldwide, making agreements with Sprint, British Telecom, and China Telecom.

WHEN

William Norris, a former code breaker for the US Navy during WWII, founded Control Data Corporation (CDC) in 1957. Norris brought in several engineers from Sperry Rand, where he had headed the UNIVAC division. The new company originally planned to do R&D for the military and to manufacture components and accessories, but Seymour Cray, a gifted designer employed by the company, convinced Norris that CDC could build a mainframe to challenge giant IBM.

In 1958 CDC introduced the 1604 mainframe. Designed by Cray, the computer was a hit with the scientific community. In 1963 the company introduced another Cray-designed computer, the 6600, which was 20 times more powerful than the 1604.

The company reached a settlement with rival IBM in an antitrust case in 1973, claiming its sales had been hurt by IBM salespeople's promises of computers that existed only on paper. As part of the settlement, CDC bought IBM's Service Bureau Corporation for far less than market value.

During the 1980s CDC faced challenges to its computer business from both home and abroad. Cray Research (founded by Cray after he left CDC in 1973) surpassed the company as the dominant supercomputer maker, and Japanese competition also cut into sales. In addition, the company was slow to react as the computer industry shifted away from mainframe systems to microcomputers. In 1985 and 1986 it lost more than $800 million.

Jim Ousley, a 21-year company veteran, was named head of CDC's computer products division in 1989. His first major decision was to stop developing and selling mainframes, focusing instead on open systems and system integration. Although forsaking the company's heritage made him none too popular, Ousley saw that the division had to change with the changing times. R&D budgets were cut and employment levels were slashed.

In 1992 CDC changed its name to Ceridian and spun off its computer products and services business as Control Data Systems. Ousley became CEO of the new company. To expand its system integration business, Control Data acquired several system integrators, both in the US and abroad, in 1992. To expand its product offerings, it signed remarketing agreements in 1993 with Sun Microsystems, Hewlett-Packard, and several other computer makers.

The company continued to expand its service business in 1994, creating Enterprise Management Center (providing worldwide remote management, monitoring, and outsourcing for computer networks) and Electronic Commerce Solutions (helping businesses and organizations use the applications available via the Internet).

In 1995 the company won a contract to supply electronic-mail servers to NASA, inked multiyear deals with China Telecom and British Telecom, and announced an alliance with Sprint to provide information exchange services. It also sold its international product distribution operations in Austria, Canada, Greece, Mexico, Norway, Portugal, and the UK to AmeriData for $13.4 million. The divestiture and the decreasing emphasis on hardware led to decreased sales that year.

In 1996 the company launched InfoEngine, software that lets users locate, access, and process information on any platform on a companywide intranet.

President and CEO: James E. Ousley, age 50,
$768,000 pay
VP Europe, Middle East, and Africa Region: Dieter
Porzel, age 59, $329,618 pay
VP and CFO: Joseph F. Killoran, age 55, $312,500 pay
VP Human Resources and Administration: Ruth A.
Rich, age 52, $180,000 pay
VP Asia and Pacific Region: Arnold Nol Rutgers, age 54
VP Managed Services: Alan H. Lynchosky, age 43
**VP North America Manufacturing/Product Data
Management:** John V. Todd
VP North America Systems and Services: Michael W.
Dubyak
VP Worldwide Operations Assessment and Planning:
Wayne A. Ray
VP Technical Services: Michael G. Eleftheriou, age 50
VP Electronic Commerce Solutions: David B. Folsom,
age 48
VP Corporate Marketing and Communications: Tom
Charland
**Chief Information Officer and General Manager,
Electronic Commerce Development:** Sandie Rowe
General Counsel and Secretary: Ralph W. Beha
Auditors: KPMG Peat Marwick LLP

WHERE

HQ: 4201 Lexington Ave. North, Arden Hills, MN
55126-6198
Phone: 612-482-2401
Fax: 612-482-2791
Web site: http://www.cdc.com
Control Data Systems has sales operations in the US and
12 other countries.

WHAT

	1995 Sales	
	$ mil.	% of total
Hardware products	205	45
Software & services	175	38
Maintenance & support	75	17
Total	**455**	**100**

Consulting and Other Services
Client/server services
Managed services
Networking services

Hardware and Software Maintenance
24-hour hotline
Online diagnostic system
Spare parts

Remarketing
Hardware (Hewlett-Packard, Sun Microsystems, and
Silicon Graphics products)
Software (3Com, Banyan, Bay, Informix, Novell,
OpenVision, Oracle, Sybase, and Wingra products)

Software
CAD/CAM/CAE application products (Integrated
Computer-Aided Engineering and Manufacturing
series)
Messaging (Mail*Hub line)
Product data management application products
(Metaphase)
Web-based products (InfoEngine)

KEY COMPETITORS

AmeriData	Computer	Perot Systems
Attachmate	Sciences	SAS
BBN	EDS	Unisys
Cap Gemini	Inacom	Vanstar
CompuCom	MCI	Wang
	Memorex Telex	

HOW MUCH

Nasdaq symbol: CDAT FYE: December 31	Annual Growth	1986	1987	1988	1989	1990	1991	1992	1993	1994	1995
Sales ($ mil.)	(9.6%)	—	—	—	834	578	574	517	452	524	455
Net income ($ mil.)	—	—	—	—	(160)	19	(44)	(134)	9	(94)	9
Income as % of sales	—	—	—	—	—	3.2%	—	—	2.0%	—	1.9%
Earnings per share ($)	—	—	—	—	(15.12)	1.76	(4.14)	(12.03)	0.66	(6.87)	0.62
Stock price – high ($)	—	—	—	—	—	—	—	10.50	14.13	11.38	21.38
Stock price – low ($)	—	—	—	—	—	—	—	7.00	8.57	5.38	5.88
Stock price – close ($)	29.1%	—	—	—	—	—	—	9.13	10.13	6.88	19.63
P/E – high	—	—	—	—	—	—	—	—	21	—	34
P/E – low	—	—	—	—	—	—	—	—	13	—	9
Dividends per share ($)	—	—	—	—	—	—	—	0.00	0.00	0.00	0.00
Book value per share ($)	(20.6%)	—	—	—	—	—	—	12.76	12.88	5.96	6.39
Employees	(16.7%)	—	—	—	5,488	4,498	3,918	3,285	3,142	2,890	1,829

1995 YEAR-END

Debt ratio: 0.8%
Return on equity: 10.7%
Cash (mil.): $84
Current ratio: 2.03
Long-term debt (mil.): $0
No. of shares (mil.): 13
Dividends
  Yield: —
  Payout: —
Market value (mil.): $257

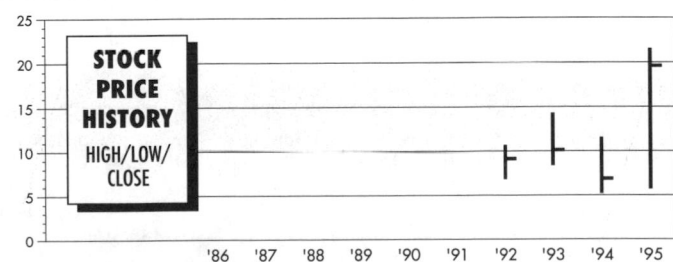

STOCK
PRICE
HISTORY
HIGH/LOW/
CLOSE

CREATIVE TECHNOLOGY LTD.

OVERVIEW

Creative Technology's corporate name may seem a little oxymoronic but its products are sound. The Singapore-based company is the world's leading maker of sound card and multimedia upgrade kits. The company's Sound Blaster sound card, a circuit board installed in a PC, enhances a computer's sound quality, while its multimedia upgrade kits include a sound card, speakers, CD-ROM drive, and software (published by others). Seven out of 10 PC audio systems worldwide are built with Sound Blaster technology. Creative Technology also makes digital video products and software.

The company has alliances, licensing agreements, and OEM relationships with a number of industry leaders, including AST Research, Dell Computer, DEC, Gateway 2000, IBM, Intel, and Microsoft. Milpitas, California-based Creative Labs, Inc., is a wholly-owned subsidiary that provides sales, marketing, and customer support in the US, Canada, and Latin America. Creative Technology also has a number of subsidiaries in Asia and Europe. Cofounders Sim Wong Hoo, Chay Kwong Soon, and Ng Kai Wa, own 28.2%, 15.1%, and 15.8% of the company, respectively.

Creative Technology is trying to parlay its position as de facto industry standard in sound products into market strength in other multimedia products. It has launched Graphics Blaster, a series of add-on multimedia graphics accelerator cards for Pentium-based systems, and it is also beefing up its R&D center in Singapore to exploit the advantages of in-house software and hardware development, semiconductor design, and high volume manufacturing. But hitting another home run like Sound Blaster has proven difficult with the field for 3-D graphics and games crowded with competitors.

WHEN

With a $6,000 investment Sim and Ng (later joined by Chay) founded Creative Technology in Singapore in 1981 to provide engineering services. In 1984 it began making Apple II clones for the Chinese market and 2 years later began producing PC clones. Most of the company's revenues came from PC design, development, and distribution. Creative Technology opened an office in the US in 1988.

With competition stiff in the PC market, Sim decided to focus on sound cards and other value-added features. The company introduced its first Sound Blaster audio card in 1989, and it soon became the industry standard. That year Creative launched PJS, an artificial intelligence-based Chinese operating system, and Views, a complementary word processor and desktop publisher with over 70,000 characters. Also in 1989 Tandy, USA, ordered a large supply of Game Blasters for its 8,000 nationwide Radio Shack stores, giving Creative a strong foothold in the US market.

That year the company launched the first of its market-dominating upgrade kits, the Sound Blaster Multimedia Upgrade Kit, a software package bundled with a high-performance CD-ROM drive, the Sound Blaster Pro, and software applications. The company went public in 1992. That year Creative set up a Beijing-based joint venture, Beijing Chuang Tong Multimedia Computer Ltd.

The growing popularity of multimedia products was music to Creative Technology's ears.

With more computers being sold with sound cards and multimedia capabilities preinstalled, the company signed deals with OEMs, including Compaq and Dell, to supply them with equipment. The company also diversified. In 1993 it acquired ShareVision Technology (video conferencing products) and E-Mu Systems (digital sound production systems).

Creative Technology also tried its hand at communication products. In 1994 it acquired modem maker Digicom and released Phone Blaster, a telecommunications product that combines voice mail, e-mail, and fax transmission, in 1995. That year it also opened a new manufacturing plant in Malaysia.

Cracks began to show in Creative's progress in 1995. The slowing of the sound board market caused a steep drop in profits and prompted the company to restructure. It terminated its product development agreement with 3DO for interactive multiplayer games and stopped production of multimedia-CD-ROM software. Cofounder Ng resigned as chief technical officer "to pursue other interests."

In 1996 Chay, the company president, also resigned for "personal reasons," leaving Sim the only cofounder in an executive position. Ng and Chay remain on the board of directors.

Creative posted a loss of $37.6 million on sales of $1.3 billion in fiscal 1996. It was hurt by tough price competition for audio cards and the costs of exiting the CD-Rom drive business.

Chairman and CEO: Sim Wong Hoo, age 40
VC: Ng Kai Wa, age 39
CFO: Patrick Verderico, age 51
President, Creative Labs, Inc. (US): W. H. Sim
Director Human Resources, Creative Labs, Inc. (US):
  Judith Martin
Auditors: Price Waterhouse LLP

WHERE

HQ: 67 Ayer Rajah Crescent #03-18, Singapore 139950
Phone: +65-773-0233
Fax: +65-773-0353
US HQ: Creative Labs, Inc., 1901 McCarthy Blvd.,
  Milpitas, CA 95035
US Phone: 408-428-6600
US Fax: 408-428-6611
Web site: http://www.creaf.com

	1995 Sales
	% of total
Americas	48
Europe	30
Other countries	22
Total	**100**

WHAT

	1995 Sales
	% of total
Upgrade kits	57
Sound cards	37
Video cards	2
Other	4
Total	**100**

Selected Products

Multimedia Upgrade Kits
Sound Blasters, CD-ROM drive, and bundled CD-ROM
  and other software applications

Audio
Sound Blaster AWE 32 (32-bit stereo sound card)
Sound Blaster Value Edition (8-bit mono sound card)

Video
Video Blaster RT300 (digital video capture)

Other
Audio communication products
Data Stream products (AeroPen and Aero Mouse 3-D
  pointer products)
Desktop videoconferencing
E-Mu products (digital music applications)
Hans Vision (Chinese language computing platform)
Software publishing

KEY COMPETITORS

Apple Computer	Compression	OPTi
Aztech Systems	Labs	Packard Bell
Boca Research	Diamond	PictureTel
Boston	Multimedia	Reveal
Technology	ESS Technology	Sony
Brite Voice	Intel	U.S. Robotics
Cardinal	Micronics	
Technologies	NEC	

HOW MUCH

Nasdaq symbol: CREAF FYE: June 30	Annual Growth	1986	1987	1988	1989	1990	1991	1992	1993	1994	1995
Sales ($ mil.)	146.2%	—	—	—	5	8	25	86	292	658	1,202
Net income ($ mil.)	154.2%	—	—	—	0	1	8	1	45	98	27
Income as % of sales	—	—	—	—	1.5%	13.0%	33.9%	0.7%	15.3%	14.9%	2.2%
Earnings per share ($)	76.3%	—	—	—	0.01	0.02	0.12	0.01	0.55	1.11	0.30
Stock price – high ($)	—	—	—	—	—	—	—	11.38	19.25	24.00	14.38
Stock price – low ($)	—	—	—	—	—	—	—	5.38	8.75	9.75	5.88
Stock price – close ($)	(4.0%)	—	—	—	—	—	—	9.75	15.88	14.25	8.63
P/E – high	—	—	—	—	—	—	—	—	35	22	48
P/E – low	—	—	—	—	—	—	—	—	16	9	20
Dividends per share ($)	—	—	—	—	—	—	—	0.00	0.00	0.00	0.00
Book value per share ($)	184.4%	—	—	—	—	—	—	0.15	1.89	3.09	3.45
Employees	106.2%	—	—	—	—	—	—	477	1,020	4,100	4,185

1995 YEAR-END

Debt ratio: 25.2%
Return on equity: 9.3%
Cash (mil.): $127
Current ratio: 2.25
Long-term debt (mil.): $102
No. of shares (mil.): 88
Dividends
  Yield: —
  Payout: —
Market value (mil.): $756

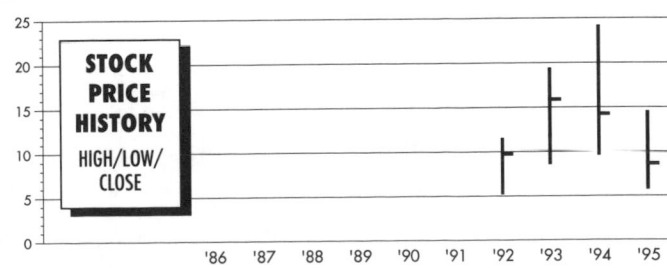

STOCK PRICE HISTORY
HIGH/LOW/CLOSE

DATA GENERAL CORPORATION

OVERVIEW

Data General (DG) continues to innovate within its niches. The Westboro, Massachusetts-based manufacturer's flagship products are its AViiON computers (used as servers or multiuser systems that support large databases and high-throughput operations) and its CLARiiON mass storage subsystems. DG also provides users worldwide with a single contact point for problems and queries regarding both hardware and software — its less glamorous service operations contribute over 1/3 of its total revenues.

A longtime money-loser, Data General for the past decade has had revenues as flat as a silicon chip. While cutting jobs, the company hopes to expand sales by forming more relationships with OEMs and creating worldwide distribution alliances, especially for its NUMA

(nonuniform memory access) server technology and systems. The UK's leading computer maker, ICL, will adopt NUMA technology for its high-end servers. Daewoo, the South Korean giant, will market AViiON servers (including the NUMALiiNE systems) and CLARiiON storage units.

DG is gearing up for a future dominated by Internet users. Its technology guru Thomas West, of minicomputer fame, heads DG's new THiiN Line Business Unit in developing a line of computers that will emphasize information storage and retrieval. DG believes that Internet-based use is driving technology in the direction of viewing information rather than processing it, and it plans to make THiiN Internet appliances available in 1997.

WHEN

Edson de Castro and 2 other engineers left minicomputer maker Digital Equipment in 1968 to form Data General. Starting with $800,000, the company developed a minicomputer targeted at distributors who would add customized software and sell it to specialized markets such as manufacturers and hospitals.

DG's first computer, the 16-bit NOVA minicomputer, quickly became a success by filling a gap in DEC's product line. The NOVA's simple design made use of the latest advances in chips and incorporated large printed circuit boards that reduced the computer's costs. With low overhead, an aggressive pricing strategy, and brash marketing, DG soon became a major contender in the minicomputer market. It later began making computers ranging from microcomputers to its $600,000 ECLIPSE, all based on the NOVA architecture. In 10 years (1969-79) DG sold over 70,000 computers. It made the *FORTUNE* 500 list in 1978.

By 1979, however, DG was slipping. Many of its rivals had already introduced 32-bit superminicomputers. In response, Data General introduced its version, called the MV8000, in 1980. The crash project to build the supermini was chronicled in Tracy Kidder's 1981 bestseller, *The Soul of a New Machine*.

Between 1980 and 1984 DG's sales climbed following the introduction of new machines and the highly rated Comprehensive Electronic Office (CEO) software, an office automation product that included electronic mail, word processing, and a filing system. In 1984 gross revenues were up 40% from 1983.

Like that of its rivals in the minicomputer industry, however, Data General's growth slowed after 1985 because of increased competition from the less expensive but powerful PCs. In response, between 1985 and the end of 1989, the company reduced its workforce and closed several plants. Nevertheless, DG's results continued to decline.

In 1989 cofounder de Castro stepped down as CEO and became chairman. He left in 1990. Ronald Skates, the new CEO, continued to pare operations, reducing employment and closing plants. Skates scuttled many R&D projects, including a high-visibility venture with Japan's NET, choosing to focus on RISC-based servers (AViiON) and maintenance of the ECLIPSE MV customer base. The AViiON product line was launched in 1989.

The company sold Nippon Data General, its Japanese distribution unit, to Omron in 1991. In 1992 it introduced its CLARiiON family of mass storage devices. It formed an alliance with software developer INSCI in 1994 to market INSCI's data storage and retrieval software with the AViiON server.

The company eliminated more than 500 jobs in 1995. However, it failed to stanch the flow of red ink despite receiving $53 million from defense contractor Northrop Grumman in settlement of a lingering lawsuit for copyright and trade secret infringement of DG's MV/ADEX software. In 1996 the company announced a new CLARiiON product — RAID 3 disk arrays that boost the performance of digital imaging applications.

WHO

President and CEO: Ronald L. Skates, age 54, $611,500 pay
SVP Advanced Development: J. Thomas West, age 56, $326,200 pay
VP: Joel Schwartz, age 53, $305,800 pay
VP and CFO: Arthur W. DeMelle, age 55, $305,800 pay
VP Manufacturing and Corporate Quality: William J. Cunningham, age 57, $305,800 pay
VP CLARiiON Business Unit: Larry D. Hemmerich
VP and General Counsel: Jacob Frank
VP Human Resources: Jonathan W. Lane
Auditors: Price Waterhouse LLP

WHERE

HQ: 4400 Computer Dr., Westborough, MA 01580
Phone: 508-898-5000
Fax: 508-898-4003
Web site: http://www.dg.com

Data General has 32 subsidiaries and 250 sales and service offices in more than 70 countries.

	1995 Sales		1995 Operating Income	
	$ mil.	% of total	$ mil.	% of total
US	745	65	(52)	—
Europe	295	25	(15)	—
Other regions	119	10	(16)	—
Adjustments	—	—	7	—
Total	**1,159**	**100**	**(76)**	**—**

WHAT

	1995 Sales	
	$ mil.	% of total
Products	757	65
Services	402	35
Total	**1,159**	**100**

Selected Products and Services

Computer
AViiON (workstations and servers)
DG/ViiSION (personal computers)
ECLIPSE MV series (minicomputers)
WALKABOUT (laptop computers)

Operating Systems
AOS/RT32
AOS/VS
DG/RDOS

Peripheral Equipment
CLARiiON (mass storage subsystems)
Communication controllers
Memory
Printers
Video display terminals

Software
CEO (integrated office automation)
CEO Connection (communications)
CEO Object Office (PC graphics interface)

Services
Applications development
Consulting
Installation support
Systems design

KEY COMPETITORS

Acer	Intel	Sony
Apple Computer	Iomega	Storage
AST	Maxtor	Technology
Compaq	NCR	Sun
DEC	NEC	Microsystems
Dell	Oki Electric	SyQuest
Fujitsu	Olivetti	Tandem
Gateway 2000	Packard Bell	Toshiba
Hewlett-Packard	Quantum Corp.	Unisys
Hitachi	Seagate	Vobis
IBM	Siemens	

HOW MUCH

NYSE symbol: DGN FYE: September 30	Annual Growth	1986	1987	1988	1989	1990	1991	1992	1993	1994	1995
Sales ($ mil.)	(1.0%)	1,268	1,274	1,365	1,314	1,216	1,229	1,116	1,078	1,121	1,159
Net income ($ mil.)	—	6	(83)	(16)	(120)	(140)	86	(63)	(60)	(88)	(47)
Income as % of sales	—	0.4%	—	—	—	—	7.0%	—	—	—	—
Earnings per share ($)	—	0.21	(3.07)	(0.55)	(4.10)	(4.65)	2.45	(1.91)	(1.73)	(2.45)	(1.23)
Stock price – high ($)	—	48.50	38.75	28.13	19.50	13.25	22.50	18.13	13.88	12.00	14.75
Stock price – low ($)	—	25.00	16.00	16.75	11.75	3.50	3.75	7.13	7.75	6.63	6.75
Stock price – close ($)	(8.3%)	29.63	23.63	18.50	12.50	4.50	16.50	11.63	9.38	10.00	13.63
P/E – high	—	—	—	—	—	—	9	—	—	—	—
P/E – low	—	—	—	—	—	—	2	—	—	—	—
Dividends per share ($)	—	0.00	0.00	0.00	0.00	0.00	0.00	0.00	0.00	0.00	0.00
Book value per share ($)	(13.0%)	25.76	21.32	21.51	17.68	13.21	15.50	13.41	10.69	8.47	7.37
Employees	(11.9%)	15,565	15,685	15,400	13,700	10,600	8,500	7,100	6,500	5,800	5,000

1995 YEAR-END

Debt ratio: 35.7%
Return on equity: —
Cash (mil.): $189
Current ratio: 1.60
Long-term debt (mil.): $153
No. of shares (mil.): 38
Dividends
  Yield: —
  Payout: —
Market value (mil.): $517

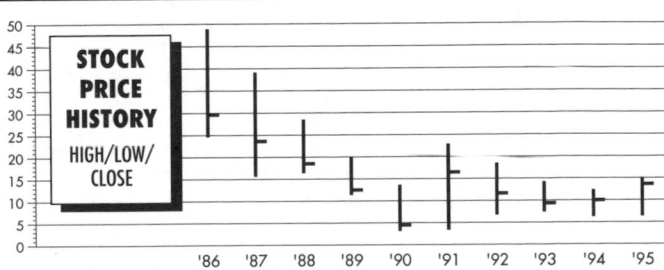

STOCK PRICE HISTORY
HIGH/LOW/CLOSE

DELL COMPUTER CORPORATION

OVERVIEW

The myth is true; some things do grow bigger in Texas. Austin-based Dell is the world's leading direct seller of computers (but only #2 in US sales, after Gatway 2000). Dell — which manufactures its own line of desktop PCs, notebook computers, and servers — also ranks among the world's largest computer makers. In addition to its computers, the company sells a variety of peripherals and software from 3rd-party manufacturers through its DellWare marketing program.

Dell's strength lies in its direct-marketing approach and in its manufacturing model. Instead of producing standardized PCs based on sales predictions, the company custom-builds computers as they are ordered. This allows it to provide the latest technology without large investments in inventory that could quickly become obsolete. With more than 30 offices around the world, the company can also customize computers to suit regional preferences.

Dell is forgoing the individual PC buyer to court the higher-margin business market. More than 90% of Dell's sales are to corporate customers, small to medium-size businesses, and governmental and educational institutions.Founder and chairman Michael Dell owns about 16% of his namesake firm.

WHEN

At age 13, Michael Dell was already a successful businessman. From his parents' home in Houston, Dell ran a mail-order stamp trading business that, within a few months, grossed over $2,000. At 16 he sold subscriptions to the *Houston Post*, and at 17 Dell bought his first BMW. When he enrolled at the University of Texas in 1983, he was thoroughly bitten by the business bug.

Dell started college as a pre-med student but found time to establish a business selling random-access memory (RAM) chips and disk drives for IBM PCs. Dell bought his products at cost from IBM dealers, who, at the time, were required to order from IBM large monthly quotas of PCs, which frequently exceeded demand. Dell resold his stock through newspapers (and later through national computer magazines) at 10-15% below retail.

By April 1984 Dell's dorm-room computer components business was grossing about $80,000 a month — enough to convince him to drop out of college. At about that time he started making and selling his own IBM clones under the brand name PC's Limited. Dell sold his machines directly to end-users rather than through retail computer outlets, as most manufacturers did. By eliminating the retail markup, Dell could sell his PCs at about 40% of the price of an IBM.

The company was plagued by management changes during the mid-1980s. Renamed Dell Computer, it added international sales offices in 1987. In 1988 it started selling to government agencies and added a sales force to serve larger customers. That year Dell went public in a $34.2 million offering.

Dell tripped in 1990, reporting a 64% drop in profits. Sales were growing — but so were costs, mostly because of Dell's efforts to design a PC using proprietary components and RISC chips. Also, the company's warehouses were oversupplied. Within a year Dell turned itself around by cutting inventories and coming out with 8 new products.

In 1990 Dell entered the retail arena by allowing Soft Warehouse Superstores (now CompUSA) to sell its PCs at mail-order prices. The company struck a similar deal in 1991 with Staples, an office supply chain. That year Dell opened a plant in Limerick, Ireland.

In 1992 Xerox agreed to sell Dell machines in 19 Latin American countries. The following year Dell opened subsidiaries in Japan and Austria and began selling PCs through Best Buy stores in 16 US states.

Dell abandoned retail stores in 1994 to refocus on its mail-order origins. The company took a $40 million charge to retool its troubled notebook computer line and later that year released its Latitude notebook to general acclaim. The company also introduced a new line of servers, called PowerEdge. Also in 1994 Dell signed deals with resellers in Indonesia and South Korea.

The company offered its first Pentium-based notebook in 1995. In 1996 Dell continued to ramp up its efforts in the Asian computer market with a new mail-order service in Hong Kong, Japan, and Singapore; a new Asia Pacific Customer Center in Malaysia; and direct-sales operations in South Korea and Taiwan.

WHO

Chairman and CEO: Michael S. Dell, age 31,
$1,300,050 pay
VC: Morton L. Topfer, age 59, $1,122,321 pay
SVP Finance and Information Systems and CFO:
Thomas J. Meredith, age 45, $643,710 pay
SVP Product and Technology Strategy: Eric F. Harslem,
age 50, $715,279 pay
SVP and General Manager, Americas: Kevin B. Rollins,
age 43
SVP and General Manager, Europe: Martyn R. Ratcliffe,
age 34
VP and General Manager, Japan: Hiroshi Fukino, age 54
VP and General Manager, Asia Pacific: Phillip E. Kelly,
age 38
General Counsel and Secretary: Thomas B. Green,
age 41
VP Human Resources: Julie A. Sackett, age 52
Auditors: Price Waterhouse LLP

WHERE

HQ: 2214 W. Braker Ln., Ste. D, Austin, TX 78758-4053
Phone: 512-338-4400
Fax: 512-728-3330
Web site: http://www.dell.com

Dell sells its products in more than 130 countries.
The company has manufacturing facilities in Ireland,
Malaysia, and the US.

	1996 Sales		1996 Operating Income	
	$ mil.	% of total	$ mil.	% of total
Americas	3,540	64	285	62
Europe	1,670	30	171	38
Asia/Pacific	344	6	(21)	—
Adjustments	(258)	—	—	—
Total	**5,296**	**100**	**435**	**100**

WHAT

	1996 Sales % of total
Desktop systems	81
Notebooks	16
Servers	3
Total	**100**

Selected Products
Computer peripherals
Desktop computers
Notebook computers
Servers
Service and support
Software

KEY COMPETITORS

Acer
Apple Computer
Canon
Compaq
CompUSA
DEC
Fujitsu
Gateway 2000
Hewlett-Packard
Hitachi
Hyundai
IBM
Machines Bull
Matsushita
Micro Warehouse
Micron Electronics
NCR
NEC
Oki
Olivetti
Packard Bell
Philips
Sharp
Siemens
Sony
Sun Microsystems
Tandy Corporation
Texas Instruments
Toshiba
Unisys

HOW MUCH

Nasdaq symbol: DELL FYE: January 31	Annual Growth	1987	1988	1989	1990	1991	1992	1993	1994	1995	1996
Sales ($ mil.)	61.7%	70	159	258	389	546	890	2,014	2,873	3,475	5,296
Net income ($ mil.)	72.6%	2	9	14	5	27	51	102	(36)	140	272
Income as % of sales	—	3.2%	5.9%	5.6%	1.3%	5.0%	5.7%	5.0%	—	4.0%	5.1%
Earnings per share ($)	51.0%	0.07	0.24	0.27	0.09	0.46	0.70	1.30	(0.53)	1.58	2.65
Stock price – high ($)[1]	—	—	—	4.20	3.55	6.30	12.08	24.19	24.94	23.69	49.38
Stock price – low ($)[1]	—	—	—	2.58	1.67	1.55	5.25	7.50	6.75	9.56	19.75
Stock price – close ($)[1]	39.7%	—	—	3.33	1.83	6.17	8.55	24.00	11.31	20.50	34.63
P/E – high	—	—	—	16	38	14	17	19	—	15	19
P/E – low	—	—	—	10	19	3	8	6	—	6	8
Dividends per share ($)	—	—	—	0.00	0.00	0.00	0.00	0.00	0.00	0.00	0.00
Book value per share ($)	34.0%	—	—	1.35	1.42	1.93	3.83	5.01	6.21	8.21	10.41
Employees	32.4%	—	—	1,175	1,500	2,050	2,970	4,650	5,980	6,400	8,400

[1] Stock prices are for the prior calendar year.

1996 YEAR-END

Debt ratio: 10.4%
Return on equity: 25.5%
Cash (mil.): $55
Current ratio: 2.08
Long-term debt (mil.): $113
No. of shares (mil.): 93
Dividends
  Yield: —
  Payout: —
Market value (mil.): $3,236

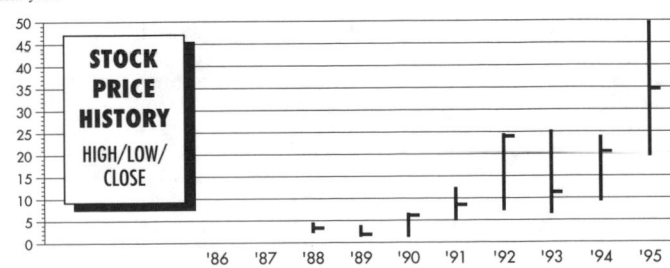

STOCK PRICE HISTORY
HIGH/LOW/CLOSE

DIGITAL EQUIPMENT CORPORATION

OVERVIEW

Like a besieged fort, early in the decade Digital Equipment Corp. (DEC) needed a cavalry to ride to its rescue. Encroaching technologies (the minicomputer pioneer was late getting into the open systems PC market) and an entrenched corporate mind-set threatened its viability in the rapidly changing computer marketplace. In the early 1990s DEC lost $5 billion. The charge that delivered DEC was led by Robert Palmer, who became CEO in 1992. Palmer has undertaken numerous restructurings, and ordered massive layoffs (more than 60,000 people) and plant closings in an effort to keep DEC competitive.

Palmer is especially effective at forging alliances. Deals with software kingpins Computer Associates, Microsoft, and Oracle, among others, are helping boost DEC's hardware and service revenues. One key alliance lets Microsoft's Windows NT operating system and other software run on machines using DEC's 64-bit (ultrafast) Alpha microprocessor. This gives users of DEC machines new software options, decreasing the likelihood they will move to other hardware products.

Despite Palmer's success, DEC is still vulnerable. The company's improved sales have depended largely on its Alpha microprocessor, but others are bringing their own 64-bit chips to market. DEC is hoping other product innovations will protect its newfound profitability. One, DEC's StrongARM embedded microprocessor (developed with Apple), is designed to power small consumer electronics such as cellular phones, handheld computers, and network computers.

WHEN

Two young MIT engineers, Kenneth Olsen and Harlan Anderson, founded DEC in 1957 to venture beyond mainframes into smaller, less expensive computers. DEC soon produced innovations popular with engineers and scientists, including the PDP-1 (the first interactive computer, 1960) and the PDP-5 (dubbed the minicomputer, 1963). The PDP-8 (1965) and later the PDP-11 (1970) provided number-crunching breakthroughs. The company's revenue and profit growth averaged 30% per year for almost 2 decades. Anderson left the company in 1966.

DEC began its networking tradition in 1974, introducing the Digital network architecture (DNA) to link its PDP-11s to local- and wide-area networks. DEC engineering whiz Gordon Bell conceived of the VAX line of computers, which allowed easy upgrades from PDPs and virtually unlimited memory; the VAX-11/780 appeared in 1977.

In 1979 Olsen pledged billions to an expanded VAX generation using all DEC-made components. The company focused the new VAXes (like the VAX 6000 mini, 1984) on the larger commercial market and extended its DECnet umbrella to provide global company/client/supplier connections. During the VAX glory days, between 1984 and 1988, sales doubled and earnings nearly quadrupled.

By 1988 DEC was embracing open systems and entering alliances to connect PCs to VAXes (Apple, Compaq), to translate VAX software to ULTRIX (DEC's version of UNIX), and to bring popular software to the VAX line (Lotus 1-2-3, dBase). DEC also took a 5% stake in MIPS Computer (which provides the reduced instruction set computing [RISC] chip for the DECstation).

DEC reported its first quarterly loss ever in 1990 and a net loss for fiscal 1991. In response the company restructured and reduced its workforce. After DEC posted a loss of more than $2 billion in 1992, Olsen resigned. He was replaced by Palmer. That year DEC agreed to buy 10% of Olivetti (office equipment, Italy) and began mail-order PC sales.

Mitsubishi agreed to manufacture DEC's new Alpha chip in 1993. In late 1994 DEC sold its RDB database software operations to Oracle for $108 million.

In 1995 the company announced a pact with Sybase, a leading developer of client/server software, to develop a system for delivering and managing interactive television services.

In 1996 DEC announced plans to spin off a stake in its AltaVista Internet software unit. That year the company said it would ship its final PDP-11 minicomputer in 1997, after more than 25 years of sales. Also in 1996 the #2 executive, Enrico Pesatori abruptly resigned; the following day DEC announced a slip in its recovery forcing a layoff of 7,000 workers (12% of the workforce). For fiscal 1996 DEC reported a loss of $111 million on sales of $14.6 billion.

WHO

Chairman, President, and CEO: Robert B. Palmer, age 55, $1,275,016 pay
VP and General Manager Components Division: Charles F. Christ, age 56, $600,006 pay
VP Advanced Technology Group and Chief Technical Officer: William D. Strecker, age 51, $560,008 pay
VP and General Manager Multivendor Customer Services Division: John J. Rando, age 43, $523,089 pay
VP Finance and CFO: Vincent J. Mullarkey, age 47
VP; President, Asia Pacific: Bobby A. F. Choonavala
VP and General Manager Systems Business Unit: Harold D. Copperman, age 49
President, Digital Europe: Hans W. Dirkmann, age 55
VP Communications: Charles B. Holleran
VP Worldwide Human Resources: Savino R. Sid Ferrales, age 45
VP and General Manager, Personal Computers: Bruce Claflin, age 44
Auditors: Coopers & Lybrand L.L.P.

WHERE

HQ: 111 Powdermill Rd., Maynard, MA 01754-1499
Phone: 508-493-5111
Fax: 508-493-8780
Web site: http://www.digital.com
DEC sells its products in more than 100 countries.

WHAT

	1995 Sales	
	$ mil.	% of total
Products	7,616	55
Services & other	6,197	45
Total	**13,813**	**100**

Selected Products and Services

Computers, Servers, and Systems
Alpha-based systems
Intel-based systems
VAX-based systems

Peripherals
Data storage products
Network components
  Hubs
  Routers
  Switches
Printers
Video terminals

Services
Education and customer training
Information systems consulting
Maintenance and support

Network design and support
Outsourcing and resource management
Project management
Systems integration
Technical and applications design

Software
Applications
Language compilers
Networking and communications products
Office and workgroup software frameworks
Operating systems
Production systems
Productivity tools
Run-time services

KEY COMPETITORS

Advanced Logic Research
Amdahl
Apple Computer
AST
Compaq
Computer Sciences
Data General
Dell
Fujitsu
Gateway 2000
Hewlett-Packard
Hitachi
IBM

ICL
Intel
Machines Bull
Matsushita
Micron Electronics
Microsoft
Motorola
NCR
NEC
Novell
Olivetti
Packard Bell
Sequent
Sharp

Siemens
Silicon Graphics
Sony
Storage Technology
Stratus Computer
Sun Microsystems
Tandem
Toshiba
Unisys
Vobis
Wang

HOW MUCH

NYSE symbol: DEC FYE: June 30	Annual Growth	1986	1987	1988	1989	1990	1991	1992	1993	1994	1995
Sales ($ mil.)	6.9%	7,590	9,389	11,475	12,742	12,943	13,911	13,931	14,371	13,451	13,813
Net income ($ mil.)	(31.0%)	617	1,137	1,306	1,073	74	(617)	(2,310)	(251)	(2,116)	22
Income as % of sales	—	8.1%	12.1%	11.4%	8.4%	0.6%	—	—	—	—	0.2%
Earnings per share ($)	(32.0%)	4.81	8.53	9.90	8.45	0.59	(5.08)	(18.50)	(1.93)	(15.43)	0.15
Stock price – high ($)	—	109.00	199.50	144.75	122.38	95.13	83.00	65.50	49.25	38.13	65.00
Stock price – low ($)	—	65.81	110.00	86.38	56.88	45.50	48.50	30.38	32.75	18.25	31.13
Stock price – close ($)	(5.3%)	104.75	135.00	98.38	82.00	54.88	55.25	33.75	34.25	33.25	64.13
P/E – high	—	23	23	15	15	161	—	—	—	—	—
P/E – low	—	14	13	9	7	77	—	—	—	—	—
Dividends per share ($)	—	0.00	0.00	0.00	0.00	0.00	0.00	0.00	0.00	0.00	0.00
Book value per share ($)	(6.8%)	44.54	49.87	59.47	66.12	66.76	61.17	38.58	36.19	23.02	23.53
Employees	(4.6%)	94,700	110,500	121,500	125,800	124,000	121,000	113,800	94,200	82,800	61,700

1995 YEAR-END

Debt ratio: 22.6%
Return on equity: 0.6%
Cash (mil.): $1,602
Current ratio: 1.71
Long-term debt (mil.): $1,013
No. of shares (mil.): 150
Dividends
  Yield: —
  Payout: —
Market value (mil.): $9,604

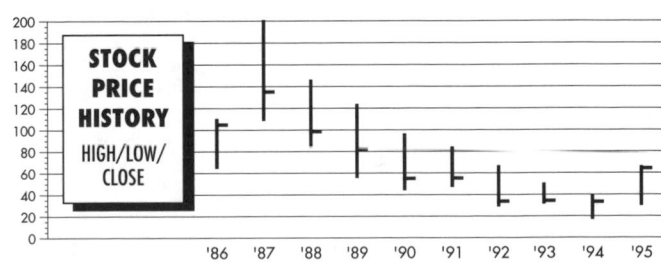

STOCK PRICE HISTORY
HIGH/LOW/CLOSE

EGGHEAD, INC.

OVERVIEW

Egghead is retreating to its retailing nest. Based in Liberty Lake, Washington (near Spokane), Egghead sells computer software, hardware, peripheral devices, and accessories directly (1-800-EGGHEAD) and through some 160 retail outlets in the US and Canada. The company also operates Elekom Corporation, a subsidiary that develops electronic commerce applications and services.

Flat same-store sales and poor bottom-line results brought on by intense competition from larger retailers and direct-sales companies have Egghead scrambling. CEO Terence Strom has attempted to seal the cracks by selling the company's corporate, government, and education division and focusing on Egghead's retail operations. The company has also closed stores to cut costs and restructured its top management to improve its product delivery.

Strom believes Egghead's future lies in its new store format. The new outlets range from 5,000-7,000 square feet, twice the size of its typical strip-mall stores, and add more hardware to an inventory dominated by software.

However, putting all of its eggs in one basket may not have been so smart. Egghead had planned an aggressive rollout of the new stores to boost sales, but inconsistent performance has led Strom to reduce new store openings so management can decide if the stores are worthy of a nationwide campaign.

Paul Allen, cofounder of Microsoft, owns 9.5% of the company.

WHEN

A stranger to the energy business, 24-year-old Victor Alhadeff nevertheless started ENI, an oil and gas tax shelter business, in 1971. In 1980 and 1981 supersalesman Alhadeff raised over $100 million in capital for ENI and its sister companies. When 1982 tax law changes and a crash in natural gas prices wiped out ENI, investors brought 23 lawsuits against Alhadeff, claiming they had been misled.

Undaunted, Alhadeff sought another business opportunity. Shopping for software for his son in 1983, he was unable to find a store to his liking and felt that the salespeople used too much jargon. His experience prompted him to open the first Egghead Discount Software store in Bellevue, Washington, in 1984. He formed a direct sales unit the same year. Despite continuing legal entanglements and few retailing credentials, Alhadeff talked investors into parting with $47 million by the time Egghead went public in 1988.

Egghead carried a broad assortment of titles and tried to make software buying a friendlier experience by adorning stores and promotional materials with Professor Egghead and ubiquitous, tooth-grinding egg puns. Not even Alhadeff's secretary could avoid them — she became known as his "eggsecutive assistant."

By the end of its 1989 fiscal year, the Egghead chain had expanded to 112 stores. But as Alhadeff pushed for more growth, nearly doubling the number of stores in fiscal 1989, poor controls led to unexpectedly high inventory shrinkage (loss or theft). High turnover left stores with personnel lacking adequate product knowledge.

With the company facing its first loss, Alhadeff resigned as president in 1989. Matthew Griffin, Stuart Sloan, and Ron Weinstein took charge, accepting $1 per year and hefty stock options as compensation.

The troika established stronger inventory controls, created profit-and-loss statements for each store, and eliminated unprofitable outlets. Egghead University, a software training business, was sold to Alhadeff in 1990. The next year Egghead returned to profitability.

Competition from computer superstores offering discounted software prices led to renewed pressure on the company. Sloan resigned as chairman in September 1992 and was succeeded by Ronald Erickson. Then Griffin resigned, and Erickson became CEO and acting president. Griffin's departure was not the last. In less than a year, another CEO came and went. Finally, Terence Strom, who had become president in July 1993, took over as CEO in August. Setting aside $4.4 million for restructuring costs, Egghead recorded a loss in 1994. That year Erickson resigned as VC.

After a nationwide search, Egghead decided to pull up stakes and move its headquarters to (and consolidate its operations in) Spokane. In July 1995 the company introduced its new store design in Beaverton, Oregon. That year it also opened 10 new stores, closed 15, and formed the Elekom subsidiary.

Texas-based Software Spectrum acquired Egghead's corporate, government, and education division in 1996.

WHO

President and CEO: Terence M. Strom, age 52, $299,994 pay
EVP Customer Offers: Peter Grossman, age 42, $230,000 pay
SVP Customer Delivery System: Ronald J. Smith, age 49, $227,943 pay
SVP Logistics and Control: Kurt S. Conklin, age 43, $202,940 pay
VP and CFO: Edward Wozniak, age 50
VP Retail Operations: Diane E. Cousineau, age 46
VP International and Strategic Planning: Kirk W. Lockhart, age 39
VP Management Information Services: Tom Collins, age 39
VP Merchandising: Jim Kalasky, age 46
Corporate Counsel: Dave Davis
VP Human Resources: Kurt S. Conklin
Auditors: Andersen Worldwide

WHERE

HQ: 22705 E. Mission, Liberty Lake, WA 99019
Phone: 509-922-7031
Fax: 509-921-7929
Web site: http://www.egghead.com

	1996 Stores
	No.
California	42
Illinois	15
New York	10
Washington	9
Massachusetts	8
New Jersey	7
Virginia	7
Maryland	6
Michigan	5
Pennsylvania	5
Other locations	50
Total	**164**

WHAT

Selected Products and Services
Accessories
Computer Select (CD-ROM-based system offering information about hardware and software products)
Computer-related books
Custom updates and "eggstras" program (CUE, customer membership program)
Hardware
Peripheral devices
Software (IBM-compatible and Apple Macintosh)
Technical support
Tutorials

Selected Subsidiary
Elekom Corp. (electronic commerce software)

KEY COMPETITORS

Anam
Best Buy
CDW Computer Centers
Circuit City
CompuCom
CompUSA
Dell
ELEK-TEK
Fry's Electronics
Gateway 2000
Good Guys
Harbinger
Kmart
Micro Warehouse
MicroAge
NeoStar
Office Depot
Staples
Sterling Commerce
Tandy Corporation
Vanstar

HOW MUCH

Nasdaq symbol: EGGS FYE: March 31	Annual Growth	1987	1988	1989	1990	1991	1992	1993	1994	1995	1996
Sales ($ mil.)	20.1%	78	201	342	456	519	665	725	778	863	404
Net income ($ mil.)	—	2	5	(12)	(8)	15	16	7	(1)	3	(11)
Income as % of sales	—	2.5%	2.3%	—	—	3.0%	2.4%	1.0%	—	0.3%	—
Earnings per share ($)	—	0.24	0.44	0.80	(0.47)	0.92	0.90	0.41	(0.03)	0.15	(0.62)
Stock price – high ($)[1]	—	—	—	21.50	14.25	18.00	22.00	30.75	11.25	12.13	14.25
Stock price – low ($)[1]	—	—	—	10.25	9.00	7.00	9.50	7.75	6.63	6.13	5.75
Stock price – close ($)[1]	(7.9%)	—	—	11.50	11.25	10.25	16.75	9.88	9.00	11.75	6.44
P/E – high	—	—	—	27	—	20	24	75	—	81	—
P/E – low	—	—	—	13	—	8	11	19	—	41	—
Dividends per share ($)	—	—	—	0.00	0.00	0.00	0.00	0.00	0.00	0.00	0.00
Book value per share ($)	3.5%	—	—	6.25	6.01	6.93	8.00	8.42	8.38	8.55	7.94
Employees	2.3%	—	—	1,955	1,708	1,772	2,000	2,700	2,500	2,600	2,300

[1] Stock prices are for the prior calendar year.

1996 YEAR-END

Debt ratio: 0.4%
Return on equity: —
Cash (mil.): $50
Current ratio: 1.73
Long-term debt (mil.): $0
No. of shares (mil.): 18
Dividends
  Yield: —
  Payout: —
Market value (mil.): $113

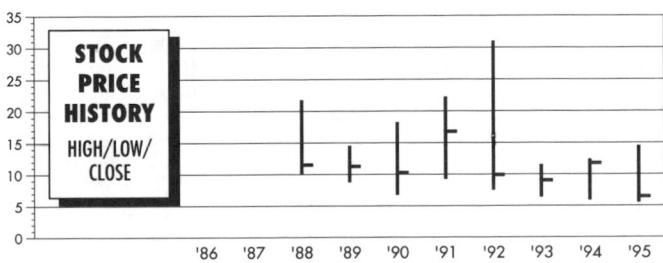

STOCK PRICE HISTORY HIGH/LOW/CLOSE

ELECTRONIC DATA SYSTEMS

OVERVIEW

IT (information technology) has sparked a global revolution, and Electronic Data Systems (EDS) is on the front lines. The Plano, Texas-based company is the world's largest independent IT management and computer services company. EDS develops, assembles, and manages complex computer and telecommunications systems for major corporate and government clients, including Citicorp, Rockwell International, and Britain's tax authority, the Inland Revenue. Its A. T. Kearney unit provides management consulting.

EDS is focused on expansion — around the world and on the World Wide Web. The company's growth closely follows that of its clients, which are developing global operations and Internet presences (EDS developed Pepsi's Web site). The company is fortifying its own presence in Africa, the Asia/Pacific region, Europe, the Middle East, and Russia with acquisitions and new contracts for clients such as the state government of South Australia and the aerospace division of the UK's Rolls-Royce.

For more than a decade EDS was a subsidiary of General Motors, and the carmaker accounts for about 30% of its revenues. EDS's recent spinoff should open up markets (e.g., other carmakers) that had been off-limits because of its relationship with its powerful parent. EDS had also been constrained financially as a subsidiary, but its independence might open the possibility for major acquisitions, particularly to shore up its telecommunications technology (the company once failed in an attempt to buy Sprint).

WHEN

After 10 years with computer powerhouse IBM, disgruntled salesman Ross Perot founded Electronic Data Systems in 1962. IBM executives had pooh-poohed Perot's idea of providing companies with electronic data processing management services that would take data management worries off clients' hands.

It took Perot 5 months to find his first customer, Collins Radio of Cedar Rapids, Iowa. EDS pioneered the long-term, fixed-price contract with snack food maker Frito-Lay in 1963, writing a 5-year contract instead of the 60- to 90-day contracts usually offered by service companies.

The company entered Medicare and Medicaid claims processing (mid-1960s), insurance company data processing (1963), and data management for banks (1968). It went on to become the #1 provider of data management services in all 3 of these markets.

EDS went public in 1968. It bought Wall Street Leasing (computer services) and established Regional Data Centers and central data processing stations, pioneering the concept of distributed processing in the early 1970s.

In 1976 EDS signed its first offshore contract, in Saudi Arabia, and also signed a contract with the government of Iran. But by 1978 Iran was 6 months behind in its payments, and EDS halted operations. When 2 EDS employees were later arrested amid the disorder of the Islamic revolution, Perot assembled a rescue team to get them out of the country.

On EDS's 22nd anniversary (and Perot's birthday) in 1984, the company was bought by General Motors for $2.5 billion. GM promised EDS its independence as well as contract work managing its lumbering data processing system. EDS prospered, but the differing managerial styles of Perot and GM chairman Roger Smith resulted in an uneasy alliance. GM bought Perot's EDS shares in 1986 for over $700 million. Perot formed competitor Perot Systems Corporation in 1988.

EDS bought UK computer services company SD-Scicon in 1990. It won an FAA contract worth $508 million in 1993. That year the company launched its management consulting service as a way of leveraging the contacts it makes in its systems business.

The company scored big in 1994 when Xerox contracted EDS to manage most of its information technology needs (worth $3 billion). That year EDS began, on a small scale, selling new house-brand personal computers.

The next year EDS acquired Chicago-based management consulting firm A. T. Kearney, paying $600 million in cash and stock. It also bought securities industry consultant FCI.

EDS won its independence from GM in mid-1996 in a spinoff that included a $500 million payment to GM and an agreement to extend the automaker more favorable contract terms in handling its computer services. That year A. T. Kearney acquired a major presence in Russia when it purchased certain assets of management consulting firm Cannon Associates's Moscow office. Also in 1996 EDS won a contract worth $250 million to support the global computer network operations of Citicorp.

WHO

Chairman, President, and CEO: Lester M. Alberthal Jr., age 52, $1,675,000 pay
VC: Gary J. Fernandes, age 52, $905,000 pay
President and COO: Jeffrey M. Heller, age 56, $935,000 pay
SVP: John R. Castle Jr., age 53, $820,000 pay
SVP: Dean Linderman, age 52, $785,000 pay
SVP and CFO: Joseph M. Grant, age 57
SVP: Paul J. Chiapparone, age 56
SVP Personnel: G. Stuart Reeves, age 56
Auditors: KPMG Peat Marwick LLP

WHERE

HQ: Electronic Data Systems Corporation, 5400 Legacy Dr., Plano, TX 75024-3105
Phone: 214-604-6000
Fax: 214-645-6798
Web site: http://www.eds.com

EDS has operations in 40 countries.

	1995 Sales % of total
US	70
Other countries	30
Total	**100**

WHAT

	1995 Sales % of total
Manufacturing	47
Financial services	14
Government	12
Communications	8
Health	7
Travel & transportation	4
Energy	3
Other	5
Total	**100**

Services	Selected Clients
Business operations management	American Express
Development of information systems	Banco Santander
Integration of information systems	Citibank
Management consulting (A. T. Kearney)	Dow Jones & Co.
Management of information systems	General Motors
	Inland Revenue (UK)
	Kooperativa Forbundet
	National Geographic
	Rockwell International
	Gruppo S&M
	Southland
	USTravel
	Xerox

KEY COMPETITORS

Andersen Worldwide	Ernst & Young
Arthur D. Little	IBM
Cap Gemini	MCI Systemhouse
Central Data	Origin
Computer Sciences	Perot Systems
Control Data	Price Waterhouse
Coopers & Lybrand	Unisys
DEC	Vanstar
Deloitte Touche Tohmatsu	

HOW MUCH

NYSE symbol: EDS FYE: December 31	Annual Growth	1986	1987	1988	1989	1990	1991	1992	1993	1994	1995
Sales ($ mil.)	12.3%	4,366	4,423	4,844	5,467	6,109	7,099	8,219	8,562	10,052	12,422
Net income ($ mil.)	15.3%	261	323	384	435	497	563	636	724	822	939
Income as % of sales	—	6.0%	7.3%	7.9%	8.0%	8.1%	7.9%	7.7%	8.5%	8.2%	7.6%
Earnings per share ($)	15.6%	0.53	0.67	0.79	0.91	1.04	1.17	1.33	1.51	1.71	1.96
Stock price – high ($)	—	12.38	12.75	11.22	14.41	20.06	33.06	34.00	35.88	39.50	52.63
Stock price – low ($)	—	6.13	6.00	8.38	10.63	12.19	17.50	25.25	26.00	27.50	36.88
Stock price – close ($)	26.5%	6.25	9.63	11.22	13.66	19.31	31.50	32.88	29.25	38.38	52.00
P/E – high	—	23	19	14	16	19	28	26	24	23	27
P/E – low	—	12	9	11	12	12	15	19	17	16	19
Dividends per share ($)	20.1%	0.10	0.13	0.17	0.24	0.28	0.32	0.36	0.40	0.48	0.52
Book value per share ($)	22.6%	1.64	2.16	2.88	3.69	4.56	5.46	6.39	7.52	8.79	10.29
Employees	8.8%	45,000	44,000	47,500	55,000	59,900	65,800	70,500	70,000	79,500	96,000

1995 YEAR-END

Debt ratio: 29.7%
Return on equity: 20.4%
Cash (mil.): $639
Current ratio: 1.34
Long-term debt (mil.): $1,853
No. of shares (mil.): 484
Dividends
  Yield: 1.0%
  Payout: 26.5%
Market value (mil.): $25,152

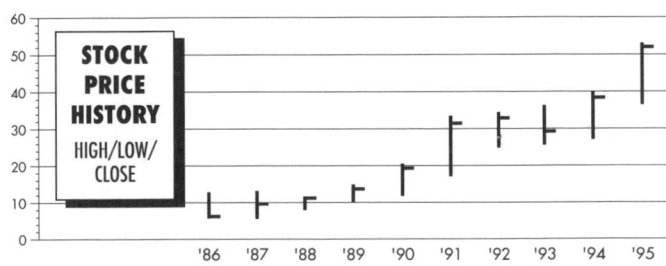

STOCK PRICE HISTORY HIGH/LOW/CLOSE

EMC CORPORATION

OVERVIEW

EMC is squarely focused on developing new computer memory products. Based in Hopkinton, Massachusetts, EMC Corporation is the #1 producer (ahead of IBM) of disk memory storage systems for mainframe computers, with about 40% of the market. These storage systems, called RAIDs, are composed of groups of standard PC floppy disks that together provide faster and less-expensive retrieval of information than IBM's dinner plate-sized storage disks. EMC markets its mainframe memory products, which provide up to one terabyte (1,000 gigabytes) of storage, under the name Symmetrix. The company's other products include storage systems for open systems and high-capacity storage solutions for IBM AS/400 computers.

EMC is working to broaden its product portfolio. It has recently entered the market for computer networking storage products with EDM (Epoch Data Manager), which combines memory backup and recovery capabilities to help protect the integrity of computer data-

bases. With the acquisition of McDATA Corporation, maker of high-performance information switching and computer connection products, EMC increased its presence in this fast-growing market.

The company is introducing memory systems that can replace file servers in situations where basic information retrieval functions (such as downloading content from the Internet or pulling up data files) do not require the main computer server to perform the command. EMC is also developing computer systems that link to a centralized memory source (like the World Wide Web) to retrieve information without needing their own internal storage system.

Company founder and chairman Dick Egan and his wife, Maureen (the company's first employee and current board member), own about 5% of EMC. Their son John is a company EVP, and Maureen's brother, private investor Paul Fitzgerald, is a director.

WHEN

EMC was founded in 1979 by former Intel executive Dick Egan and his college roommate, Roger Marino (their initials gave the company its name). Feisty entrepreneur Egan's first job was shining shoes. He served as a marine in Korea and later, while at MIT, worked on the computer system for the Apollo program for NASA. Egan also helped found Cambridge Memory Systems (later Cambex).

EMC was started with no business plan, only the idea that Egan and Marino would be better off working for themselves. At first they sold office furniture, which in short order led to contacts at technology companies and recognition that there was a niche market for add-on memory products for minicomputers.

The firm went public in 1986. Two years later Michael Ruettgers, a former COO of hightech publishing and research firm Technical Financial Services, joined the company as EVP of operations. Ruettgers spent his first year and a half at EMC dealing with a crisis that almost ruined the company: defective disk drives in some of its products were losing customers' files. Ruettgers beefed up quality control and guided EMC through the crisis period. In 1989 he became EMC's president and COO.

In the late 1980s the company expanded into data storage systems, developing one that employed small disks rather than the larger and more expensive disks and tapes used for

mainframes by IBM. EMC then separated itself from competitors by providing systems with a large cache — a temporary storage area that allows for quicker data retrieval.

EMC in 1990 pioneered RAID (redundant arrays of inexpensive disks) storage and began focusing on products for its 2 primary markets: IBM and compatible mainframes and AS/400 mid-range computers. The company introduced its original Symmetrix system, based on the new integrated cached disk array technology, in 1990.

Ruettgers became EMC's CEO in 1992. In 1993 the company acquired Epoch Systems, a provider of data management software for the UNIX market. The next year EMC bought storage products firm Array Technology and Magna Computer, a leader in tape storage technology for IBM's midrange computers. Also in 1994 EMC introduced its first ICDA-based storage product for open systems, the Centriplex series, and its sales passed the $1 billion mark.

In 1995 EMC established a subsidiary in South Africa. The next year it launched a video storage and retrieval system for the TV and film industry. The system, which can digitally store video images, could save moviemakers 1/3 of their production costs by allowing them to distribute films electronically.

WHO

Chairman: Richard J. Egan, age 60, $642,820 pay
President and CEO: Michael C. Ruettgers, age 53, $642,820 pay
EVP Sales and Marketing: John R. Egan, age 38, $497,453 pay
SVP International Sales: Raymond Fortune, age 56, $407,642 pay
SVP Enterprise Alliances: Neal M. Waddington, age 49, $374,765 pay
SVP Operations: Joel Beck, age 57
SVP Customer Service: L. Daniel Butler, age 57
SVP and Chief Staff Officer: Robert T. O'Connell, age 57
VP, CFO, and Treasurer: Colin G. Patteson
VP and General Counsel: Paul T. Dacier, age 38
VP and Controller: William J. Teuber Jr., age 44
VP Human Resources: Brian P. O'Connor
Auditors: Coopers & Lybrand L.L.P.

WHERE

HQ: 171 South St., Hopkinton, MA 01748-9103
Phone: 508-435-1000
Fax: 508-497-6961
Web site: http://www.emc.com

EMC has 54 sales offices in the US and offices in 20 other countries.

	1995 Sales	
	$ mil.	% of total
North & South America	1,230	64
Europe, Middle East & Africa	567	30
Asia/Pacific	124	6
Total	**1,921**	**100**

WHAT

	1995 Sales	
	$ mil.	% of total
Mainframe storage products	1,426	75
Open systems storage products	201	10
Other	294	15
Total	**1,921**	**100**

Selected Products

Mainframe Systems
Symmetrix series
 Model 5100 (up to 136 gigabytes)
 Model 5200 (up to 402 gigabytes)
 Model 5500 (up to one terabyte)

Open Storage Systems
Centriplex
EDM (network backup software)
Symmetrix series
 Model 3100 (up to 139 gigabytes)
 Model 3200 (up to 408 gigabytes)
 Model 3500 (up to one terabyte)

Midrange Systems
Harmonix series (ICDA-based storage systems for use with IBM AS/400 computers)
Voyager series (tape subsystems for use with IBM AS/400)

Other
Media server (video storage and retrieval)

KEY COMPETITORS

Amdahl	IBM
Compaq	Procom
Data General	Seagate
DEC	Silicon Graphics
Exabyte	Storage Tech
Fujitsu	
Hitachi	

HOW MUCH

NYSE symbol: EMC FYE: December 31	Annual Growth	1986	1987	1988	1989	1990	1991	1992	1993	1994	1995
Sales ($ mil.)	45.2%	67	127	123	132	171	232	349	783	1,378	1,921
Net income ($ mil.)	37.2%	19	28	(8)	(19)	9	13	29	127	251	327
Income as % of sales	—	27.9%	22.2%	—	—	5.2%	5.6%	8.2%	16.2%	18.2%	17.0%
Earnings per share ($)	28.5%	0.14	0.20	(0.06)	(0.13)	0.06	0.09	0.17	0.60	1.10	1.34
Stock price – high ($)	—	2.12	4.63	3.06	1.02	1.63	2.19	6.06	19.50	24.00	27.38
Stock price – low ($)	—	1.28	1.71	0.65	0.46	0.56	0.81	1.81	5.13	12.50	13.00
Stock price – close ($)	26.2%	1.89	2.63	0.90	0.54	1.33	2.08	5.94	16.50	21.97	15.38
P/E – high	—	15	23	—	—	27	24	36	33	22	20
P/E – low	—	9	9	—	—	9	9	11	9	11	10
Dividends per share ($)	—	0.00	0.00	0.00	0.00	0.00	0.00	0.00	0.00	0.00	0.00
Book value per share ($)	28.5%	0.52	0.88	0.81	0.69	0.74	0.83	1.02	2.24	3.66	4.96
Employees	29.5%	400	850	910	936	1,142	1,155	1,500	2,452	3,375	4,100

1995 YEAR-END

Debt ratio: 17.8%
Return on equity: 35.0%
Cash (mil.): $380
Current ratio: 3.67
Long-term debt (mil.): $246
No. of shares (mil.): 230
Dividends
 Yield: —
 Payout: —
Market value (mil.): $3,534

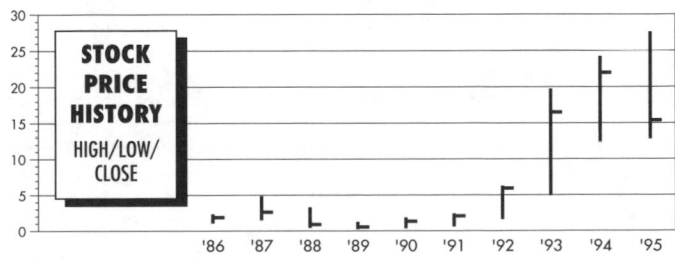

STOCK PRICE HISTORY HIGH/LOW/CLOSE

ENTEX INFORMATION SERVICES

OVERVIEW

A couple of decades ago, just having a computer earned respect for a company; now a firm has to know what to do with it. That's where Entex comes in. Headquartered in Rye Brook, New York, privately held Entex Information Services is the nation's #1 PC systems integrator, whose clients include Microsoft, Intel, and Motorola. Services include sales of PCs and other computer hardware, network configuration, system maintenance, and warranty upgrades — basically anything that has to do with a client's computer system.

Entex's role has changed. Whereas once its primary objective was to supply hardware, it now focuses more on helping customers get the most from their investments in information technology (particularly client/server networks) through an array of services such as systems management.

Entex is considering going public. It has brought in a new CFO and added a COO position to help prepare it for the possible move and has also increased its network and professional services capabilities. An investment group led by chairman Dort Cameron owns about 2/3 of the company; Microsoft also has a stake.

WHEN

David Norman founded Dataquest in 1972. Six years later it was a top US research company. Norman then sold the business to the A.C. Nielsen Co. but remained as CEO. After 4 years he realized he would never run Nielsen because it remained family managed, so he again struck out on his own.

In 1982 entrepreneur Norman wrote a 15-page business plan for a PC retail chain. In 8 weeks he had raised $3.5 million to start Businessland. Norman's next goal was a deal with IBM. Big Blue had a policy of not dealing with start-ups, and initially no one would talk to him. But he persisted, and eventually IBM agreed. Norman began opening stores and raised $21 million in additional capital backing by January 1983. By the end of that year, he made a $50 million public stock offering. After its 3rd full year, Businessland showed sales of $267 million and a small profit.

Norman then made a series of poor decisions, including angering Compaq head Joseph Canion, buying the now-defunct ComputerCraft retail chain, and agreeing to sell the NeXT computer while excluding its chief rival, the Sun Microsystems workstation. By 1991 Businessland had suffered 5 straight losing quarters. Norman attempted a comeback, slashing costs and laying off 1,000 workers, but that year Businessland succumbed to rival JWP.

JWP Inc., a 100-year-old New York-based company, entered the information services industry in 1987 with its subsidiary JWP Information Systems, Inc. JWP (the name stands for Jamaica Water Properties) was originally a waterworks operator, but by 1987 its primary business was building maintenance for large corporations and governments. In 1990 JWP Information Systems acquired Micro Financial, a 4-store PC retailer on the West Coast.

In 1991 the subsidiary purchased Businessland and was renamed JWP Businessland. The acquisition contributed to JWP's loss of almost $500 million in less than 2 years and its ultimate bankruptcy. With the additional burden of a construction industry slump, in 1993 the parent company decided to sell its PC reseller unit. Two potential buyers emerged — CompuCom Systems (a Dallas PC dealer) and an investor group that was led by Dort Cameron (formerly with Drexel Burnham Lambert) and included JWP Businessland management. The $1.7 billion subsidiary ended up in the hands of the management team.

The company was renamed Entex (short for Enterprise Technologies) and was headquartered in the same building as its former owner. Entex quickly formed an Advanced Client Services Division to increase its capability in the growing LAN/WAN integration and support business. It consolidated 3 warehouses into one automated facility with a state-of-the-art inventory control system and increased its on-site technical support staff. Entex began selling Texas Instruments personal notebook computers and printers in 1994.

Entex acquired computer reseller Random Access for $22 million in 1995. That year the company also purchased the L.E.A.D. Group of Detroit, an integrator with expertise in Lotus Notes and LAN integration. In 1996 it purchased computer network services firm FCP Technologies and joined with electronic commerce software concern Connect, Inc., to sell PCs over the Internet.

WHO

Chairman: Dort A. Cameron III
President: John A. McKenna Jr.
COO: Robert Auray Jr.
EVP and CFO: David I. Chemerow
EVP: Dale Allardyce
EVP Sales and Marketing: Anthony Ibarguen
**SVP Selective Outsourcing and Field Operations
   Services:** Thomas E. Martin
SVP Human Resources: Phillip R. Johnson
VP Corporate Communications: Herbert H. Foster III

WHERE

HQ: 6 International Dr., Rye Brook, NY 10573
Phone: 914-935-3600
Fax: 914-935-3750
Web site: http://www.entex-is.com

Entex has 60 major branch offices in the US and provides support through an international alliance in 23 countries.

WHAT

Selected Services
Asset management
Hardware sales
Infrastructure consulting
Internetworking
LAN installation services
Network configuration
System maintenance
Upgrades

Selected Business Partners
3Com
Apple
AST
AT&T
Compaq
Hewlett-Packard
IBM
Intel
Microsoft
NEC
Netscape
Novell
Toshiba

KEY COMPETITORS

Ameridata Technologies
CompuCom
Computer Horizons
CompUSA
Dell
Gateway 2000
Inacom
Intelligent Electronics
MicroAge
Software Spectrum
Tandy
Vanstar

HOW MUCH

Private company FYE: June 30	Annual Growth	1987[1]	1988[1]	1989[1]	1990[1]	1991[1]	1992	1993[2]	1994	1995	1996
Sales ($ mil.)	13.2%	687	980	1,189	1,354	1,163	1,700	1,200	1,200	1,470	2,100
Employees	7.4%	—	—	—	3,260	2,400	—	1,900	2,300	3,500	5,000

[1] Figures are for Businessland. [2] Estimated sales

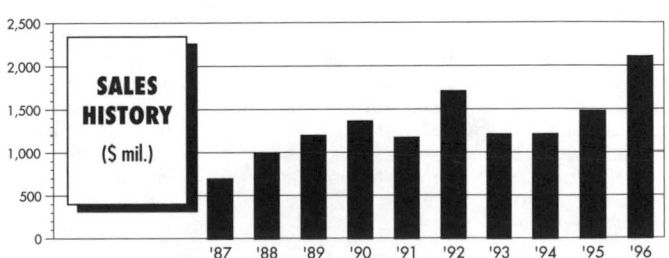

SALES
HISTORY
($ mil.)

FUJITSU LIMITED

OVERVIEW

The battleship Fujitsu is starting a slow turn toward cyberspace. Headquartered in Tokyo, Fujitsu Limited makes communications and information processing systems and electronic devices. It is Japan's leading manufacturer of mainframe computers (followed closely by IBM) and the country's #2 producer of personal computers (trailing NEC and leading Apple). Other products include computer chips, ink-jet printers, memory storage subsystems, and workstations. Strong sales, particularly in Asia, have brought Fujitsu back to profitability after major losses in recent years.

The company's presence in the online world is vast and growing. Fujitsu makes telecommunications switches used to build networks and, through a major R&D effort, plans to earn some 30% of its sales from Internet-related hardware, software, and services by 1998. It also operates Japan's leading commercial online service, Nifty-Serve, which has more than 1.5 million subscribers and runs the WorldsAway graphics-supported chat room found on the CompuServe online service.

Fujitsu has chopped the prices of its PCs (even to the point of selling for a loss) to tie up more of the market in its homeland. Underselling led to a drop in Fujitsu's PC profits, however, with the company relying on its mainframe and office computer sales to support the effort.

Fuji Electric owns 13.5% of Fujitsu.

WHEN

Siemens and Furukawa Electric created Fuji Electric in 1923 to produce electrical equipment. Fuji spun off Fujitsu, its communications division, in 1935. Originally a manufacturer of telephone equipment, Fujitsu produced antiaircraft weapons during WWII. After the war it returned to telecommunications, becoming one of 4 major suppliers to state-owned monopoly Nippon Telegraph and Telephone and benefiting from Japan's rapid economic recovery in the 1950s and 1960s.

With encouragement from Japan's Ministry of International Trade and Industry (MITI), Fujitsu entered the data processing industry by developing the country's first commercial computer in 1954. Starting in 1959 MITI erected trade barriers to protect Japan's new computer industry. In the early 1960s MITI sponsored the production of mainframe computers, directing Fujitsu to develop the central processing unit. The company expanded into the related areas of semiconductor production and factory automation in the late 1960s. Its factory automation business was spun off as Fujitsu Fanuc in 1972.

Fujitsu sought to gain market share in the 1970s by making IBM-plug-compatible computers that provided superior value to buyers. The company bought 30% of plug-compatible manufacturer Amdahl (1972) and gained badly needed technical information. In 1974 Fujitsu introduced its first plug-compatible computer and the following year began supplying Amdahl with OEM mainframe subassemblies. In 1979 Fujitsu passed IBM to become Japan's #1 computer manufacturer.

In Europe Fujitsu entered into computer marketing ventures with Siemens (1978) and ICL (1981). The company teamed with TRW (US) to sell point-of-sale systems in 1980, assuming full control of the operation in 1983. Fujitsu released its first supercomputer in 1982.

IBM accused Fujitsu of stealing proprietary operating system software technology in 1985. Fujitsu objected, citing a secret 1983 agreement under which Fujitsu had paid IBM for software information. In 1988 an arbitrator awarded IBM $237 million. It also granted Fujitsu the right to inspect certain IBM software for 10 years for a relatively small annual fee of $25-$52 million.

Fujitsu bought 80% of British mainframe maker ICL (from STC) in 1990. The next year ICL bought 50% of the European computer-maintenance operations of Bell Atlantic and all of Nokia Data Holding, the largest computer company in Scandinavia. In 1992 Fujitsu and Advanced Micro Devices built a $700 million facility in Japan to build flash memory chips, though a drop in the market has delayed its opening. Fujitsu signed a deal with Sun Microsystems in 1994 to develop microprocessors for Sun's line of workstations.

The company doubled its share of Japan's PC market in 1995 to more than 18%. In 1996 it received US patent rights for its TV plasma display technology, which it intends to license to other manufacturers. Also that year Fujitsu planned to invest nearly $1.4 billion on a logic chip plant in Japan, and it has devoted nearly half its $3.6 billion R&D budget to Internet and multimedia technologies.

WHO

Chairman: Takuma Yamamoto
President: Tadashi Sekizawa
EVP: Naoyuki Akikusa
EVP: Michio Naruto
EVP: Takeshi Maruyama
EVP: Masuo Tanaka
EVP: Keizo Fukagawa
EVP: Michio Fujisaki
President and CEO, Fujitsu America: Yoshio Honda
Director Human Resources, Fujitsu America:
Lela Chavez
Auditors: Showa Ota & Co.

WHERE

HQ: 6-1, Marunouchi 1-chome, Chiyoda-ku,
Tokyo, 100, Japan
Phone: +81-3-3216-3211
Fax: +81-3-3216-9352
US HQ: Fujitsu America, Inc., 3055 Orchard Dr.,
San Jose, CA 95134-2022
US Phone: 408-432-1300
US Fax: 408-432-1318
Web site:http://www.fujitsu.co.jp

Fujitsu operates worldwide, with offices in Abu Dhabi, Amman, Bangkok, Beijing, Bogota, Brussels, Hanoi, Harare, Honolulu, Jakarta, Kuala Lumpur, Mexico City, Munich, New Delhi, New York, Shanghai, Taipei, and Washington, DC.

WHAT

Selected Products

Communications Systems
ATM products
Optical transmission equipment
Switching systems
Teleconferencing equipment

Computer Products
Peripherals
Personal computers
Servers
Software
Storage products
Supercomputers

Electronic Devices
Gate arrays
Semiconductors

KEY COMPETITORS

Apple Computer	Motorola
AST	National Semiconductor
Canon	NEC
Compaq	Northern Telecom
Data General	Oki Electric
DEC	Philips Electronics
Dell	Samsung
Gateway 2000	Sanyo
Hewlett-Packard	Seagate
Hitachi	SGS-Thomson
Hyundai	Siemens
IBM	Silicon Graphics
Intel	Sony
LG Group	Sun Microsystems
LSI Logic	Tandem
Lucent	Texas Instruments
Machines Bull	Toshiba
Mitsubishi	Unisys

HOW MUCH

OTC symbol: FJTSY FYE: March 31	Annual Growth	1987	1988	1989	1990	1991	1992	1993	1994	1995	1996
Sales ($ mil.)	12.5%	12,270	16,460	18,005	16,117	21,134	25,879	30,143	30,479	36,603	35,490
Net income ($ mil.)	17.1%	144	339	528	548	588	92	(284)	(366)	506	595
Income as % of sales	—	1.2%	2.1%	2.9%	3.4%	2.8%	0.4%	—	—	1.4%	1.7%
Earnings per share ($)	15.4%	0.45	0.94	1.39	1.43	1.63	0.23	(0.78)	(1.01)	1.40	1.63
Stock price – high ($)[1]	—	38.13	54.13	72.13	61.88	55.00	46.52	34.16	40.80	57.66	63.34
Stock price – low ($)[1]	—	22.80	25.75	45.00	50.00	34.98	30.19	20.14	20.80	37.97	42.86
Stock price – close ($)[1]	5.7%	33.75	47.75	59.88	50.63	36.09	31.86	22.02	37.67	50.61	55.73
P/E – high	—	86	57	52	43	34	202	—	—	41	39
P/E – low	—	51	27	32	35	22	131	—	—	27	26
Dividends per share ($)	6.4%	0.27	0.32	0.34	0.38	0.38	0.38	0.35	0.39	0.56	0.47
Book value per share ($)	8.2%	14.64	19.45	20.59	19.03	22.75	24.16	26.44	28.27	34.02	29.84
Employees	7.0%	89,293	94,825	104,503	115,012	145,872	155,779	161,974	163,990	164,364	164,800

[1] Stock prices are for the prior calendar year.

1996 YEAR-END

Debt ratio: 57.1%
Return on equity: 32.7%
Cash (mil.): $4,348
Current ratio: 1.24
Long-term debt (mil.): $7,310
No. of shares (mil.): 363
Dividends
 Yield: 0.8%
 Payout: 28.9%
Market value (mil.): $20,254

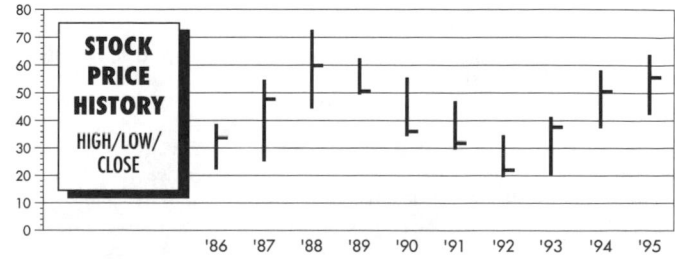

STOCK PRICE HISTORY
HIGH/LOW/CLOSE

GATEWAY 2000, INC.

OVERVIEW

If you're seeing spots, thank Gateway 2000. The North Sioux City, South Dakota-based company — which makes its own brand of IBM-compatible personal computers and is the #1 direct marketer of PCs in the US (ahead of global sales leader Dell) — ships more than 1.4 million machines a year. Each is packed in a box spotted like a cow; such spots are the firm's trademark.

Gateway is increasing its revenues nearly $1 billion a year by offering products that combine high reliability, low cost, and popular technology (for example, it was one of the first PC makers to add CD-ROM drives as a standard feature on selected products). Intel's

Pentium processor and Microsoft's Windows 95 operating system have also helped Gateway move PCs.

Some 1,200 salespeople ride herd on the company's telephone operations, offering 7-day-a-week convenience. Customers can also custom-order PCs via the Web. Most Gateway clients are individual computer users, but corporations, educational institutions, and government agencies account for more than 28% of the company's sales.

Chairman and founder Ted Waitt and his brother Norm own a majority of Gateway's stock (about 49% and 10%, respectively).

WHEN

Apparently, college and billion-dollar PC retailers don't mix. Like his main competitor, Michael Dell, Waitt dropped out of college to get into the computer business. He spoke with a friend who was working for a computer retailer, liked the sound of the job, and left school to go to work. After 9 months of on-the-job training, he quit to start his own company.

Using his grandmother's certificate of deposit as collateral, Waitt borrowed $10,000 and set up shop in his father's barn in South Dakota in 1985, founding a company called the TIPC Network with his brother Norm and Mike Hammond. TIPC sold add-on parts by phone for Texas Instruments PCs. However, Waitt's goal was to sell PCs himself, and in 1987 the 3 men jumped into the fray. Waitt and Hammond put together a fully configured computer system at a price that was near what other companies were charging for a bare-bones system, and sales took off. The next year they changed the enterprise's name to Gateway 2000 (because they believed their computers were the gateway to the 21st century).

The company's customer base was made up of sophisticated buyers who were willing to dig through computer catalogs to find the best price for the exact system they wanted, and much of the firm's success was rooted in Waitt's ability to predict which standard features customers would want.

Gateway distinguished itself from competitors with eye-catching ads. Some featured cows, while others featured Gateway employees (including one in which Waitt was dressed as Robin Hood). His idea was to sell the company — to convince potential customers that if they bought a computer from Gateway, the

firm would be around in the future to service it. When the company's eccentric ads kept popping up in computer magazines, Gateway's name started sticking in readers' minds.

The company continued to grow at breakneck speeds. In 1990 it moved to North Sioux City, South Dakota, and in 1991 Gateway topped the *Inc.* 500 list of fastest-growing private companies. That year Waitt hired Rick Snyder, head of mergers and acquisitions at accounting firm Coopers & Lybrand's Chicago office, to help him manage a company that was rapidly becoming a major player in the PC wars.

In 1992 Gateway introduced a line of notebook computers and a subnotebook, called Handbook. The company also began offering a CD-ROM product from Sony and created a new division to handle component add-ons.

Gateway made its initial public offering in late 1993. That year it opened a manufacturing and service facility in Ireland. The company expanded its catalog with software and computer peripherals in 1994. Also that year it opened a sales and support facility in Kansas City, Missouri, and showrooms in France and Germany.

In July 1995 Gateway began offering PCs through kiosks in Costco and Price Club warehouse stores. The company also started selling its products in Japan and expanded into Australia when it purchased 80% of the country's largest computer maker, Osborne Computer.

Gateway introduced the Destination, a cross between a PC and a big-screen TV (called a PC-TV), in 1996.

WHO

Chairman and CEO: Theodore W. Waitt, age 33, $838,916 pay
President and COO: Richard D. Snyder, age 37, $547,237 pay (prior to promotion)
SVP, CFO, and Treasurer: David J. McKittrick, age 50, $361,314 pay
SVP, General Counsel, and Corporate Secretary: William M. Elliott, age 61, $279,500 pay
SVP Global Products: James P. Collas, age 35, $228,691 pay
SVP Americas Group: Robert M. Spears, age 36
SVP Global Marketing: James A. Taylor, age 48
SVP Corporate Human Resources: Robert N. Beck, age 56
VP and Chief Information Officer: Robert J. Elliott, age 55
Auditors: Coopers & Lybrand L.L.P.

WHERE

HQ: 610 Gateway Dr., North Sioux City, SD 57049-2000
Phone: 605-232-2000
Fax: 605-232-2023
Web site: http://www.gw2k.com

Gateway 2000 has facilities in Australia, France, Germany, Ireland, Japan, Malaysia, and the US.

	1995 Sales		1995 Operating Income	
	$ mil.	% of total	$ mil.	% of total
US	3,211	87	235	94
Other countries	465	13	14	6
Total	**3,676**	**100**	**249**	**100**

WHAT

	1995 Sales
	% of total
Pentium products	76
Portable products	4
Other PCs, peripherals & software	20
Total	**100**

Selected Products

Personal Computers
Desktop PCs
Notebook PCs
PC-TVs
Subnotebook PCs

Add-On Products
Peripherals
    CD-ROM drives
    Fax modems
    Monitors
    Printers
Software

KEY COMPETITORS

Acer
Apple Computer
AST
Compaq
CompUSA
DEC
Dell
Hewlett-Packard
IBM
Packard Bell
Sony
Tandy Corporation
Texas Instruments
Toshiba

HOW MUCH

Nasdaq symbol: GATE FYE: December 31	Annual Growth	1986	1987	1988	1989	1990	1991	1992	1993	1994	1995
Sales ($ mil.)	155.9%	—	2	12	71	276	627	1,107	1,732	2,701	3,676
Net income ($ mil.)	—	—	—	0	4	17	39	70	100	96	173
Income as % of sales	—	—	—	2.8%	5.0%	6.0%	6.3%	6.3%	5.8%	3.6%	4.7%
Earnings per share ($)	87.7%	—	—	—	0.05	0.25	0.59	1.03	1.41	1.22	2.19
Stock price – high ($)	—	—	—	—	—	—	—	—	21.50	24.75	37.50
Stock price – low ($)	—	—	—	—	—	—	—	—	16.75	9.25	16.00
Stock price – close ($)	11.7%	—	—	—	—	—	—	—	19.63	21.63	24.50
P/E – high	—	—	—	—	—	—	—	—	15	20	17
P/E – low	—	—	—	—	—	—	—	—	12	8	7
Dividends per share ($)	—	—	—	—	—	—	—	—	0.00	0.00	0.00
Book value per share ($)	38.7%	—	—	—	—	—	—	—	3.87	5.19	7.45
Employees	132.2%	—	11	40	150	303	657	1,369	2,832	5,442	9,300

1995 YEAR-END

Debt ratio: 4.2%
Return on equity: 37.1%
Cash (mil.): $169
Current ratio: 1.65
Long-term debt (mil.): $11
No. of shares (mil.): 75
Dividends
  Yield: —
  Payout: —
Market value (mil.): $1,827

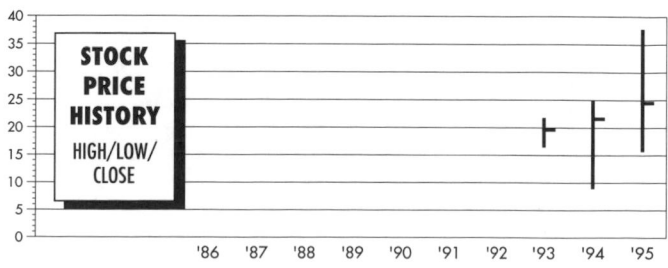

STOCK PRICE HISTORY
HIGH/LOW/CLOSE

HEWLETT-PACKARD COMPANY

OVERVIEW

HP stands for high performance, as in Hewlett-Packard. The Palo Alto, California-based electronics manufacturer is indeed performing well — its revenues were up 26%, a whopping $6.5 billion, in 1995. HP's computer printers lead the market, its workstations are 2nd only to those made by Sun Microsystems, it ranks 6th among personal computer makers, and its UNIX-based servers are benefiting from the rapid growth of client/server computing. Despite a slowdown in PC sales and price cuts by several manufacturers, HP continues to gain market share.

The company is enjoying additional growth in its lines of medical electronics and test and analysis instruments. It is also courting emerging markets through alliances. HP is developing cable TV products with ComCast, the US's #3 cable operator, and handheld devices for voice, fax, and data communications with Finland's Nokia, the #2 maker of portable phones. It is also offering Internet-related services through a marketing alliance with Internet access provider ANS, a subsidiary of America Online.

In 1996 cofounder David Packard died of pneumonia. His family owns 14% of HP. Cofounder Bill Hewlett and his family own 7% of the company.

WHEN

In 1938 Stanford engineers Hewlett and Packard, encouraged by professor Frederick Terman (considered the founder of Silicon Valley), started Hewlett-Packard out of a garage in Palo Alto with $538. Their first product was an audio oscillator. One of the first customers was Walt Disney Studios, which bought 8 audio oscillators to use in the making of *Fantasia*.

Demand for HP's electronic testing equipment during WWII spurred revenue growth from $34,000 (1940) to near $1 million (1943). During the 1950s the company expanded 50-100% each year and opened up European subsidiaries. HP entered the medical field in 1961 by acquiring Sanborn Co. and the analytical instrumentation business in 1965 with the acquisition of F&M Scientific.

In 1972 the company pioneered personal computing with the world's first hand-held scientific calculator (HP-35) and launched the HP 3000 for business computing.

Under the leadership of John Young, the founders' chosen successor (named president in 1977 and CEO in 1978), HP introduced personal computers (HP-85, 1980; HP Vectra PC, 1985), the first desktop mainframe (HP 9000, 1982), and the LaserJet printer. By 1986 Young's 5-year, $250-million open-systems effort had produced a high-performance RISC-based (reduced instruction set computing) line able to run the UNIX operating system. The company licensed its RISC chip to Hitachi and Samsung to increase the availability of applications for its products. Hewlett retired in 1987.

HP became a leader in the workstation market with the 1989 purchase of workstation pioneer Apollo Computers. Differences in technologies, however, caused problems in integrating the 2 product lines and delayed HP's workstation development.

The company bought microwave-component manufacturer Avantek in 1991. The next year the company started a joint venture with Sweden's LM Ericsson to develop telecommunications network management systems to produce devices enabling TV access to certain services (such as home banking). It also acquired the Texas Instruments line of UNIX-based computers.

In 1993 HP introduced one of the first personal communicators, the pocket-sized HP 100LX — a PC that can send and receive messages. That year Packard retired. The company paid about $50 million in 1994 for a 15% stake in Taligent, a joint venture between IBM and Apple to develop a computer operating system that uses object-oriented technology. The next year HP beat out rivals Hughes and DEC for the contract to build a $1.3 billion Tactical Advanced Computer for the US Navy.

The company combined its PC, printer, UNIX workstation, and customer support operations in 1995 to create the Computer Products Organization. The operations were consolidated to take advantage of the evolution of computing to a multiplatform environment. That year the Taligent software venture was dissolved.

In 1996 HP bought most of SecureWare, a developer of "firewalls," software security systems that protect information on computer networks. The company pulled out of a deal to build a semiconductor plant in Taiwan, saying it wanted to concentrate on wafer investments in the US.

Chairman, President, and CEO: Lewis E. Platt, age 54, $1,530,755 pay
EVP Finance and Administration and CFO: Robert P. Wayman, age 50, $807,105 pay
EVP; General Manager, Computer Organization: Richard E. Belluzzo, age 42, $576,112 pay
SVP; General Manager, Test and Measurement Organization: Edward W. Barnholt, age 52, $560,797 pay
SVP; General Manager, Worldwide Customer Support Operations: James L. Arthur, age 61
SVP; General Manager, Measurement Systems Organization: Douglas K. Carnahan, age 54
SVP; Managing Director, Geographic Operations: Alan D. Bickell, age 59
SVP Research and Development: Joel S. Birnbaum, age 58
SVP Corporate Affairs and General Counsel: S. T. Jack Brigham III, age 56
SVP Personnel: F. E. (Pete) Peterson, age 54
Auditors: Price Waterhouse LLP

WHERE

HQ: 3000 Hanover St., Palo Alto, CA 94304
Phone: 415-857-1501
Fax: 415-857-7299
Web site: http://www.hp.com

Hewlett-Packard operates major development and production facilities in the US and 16 other countries. It has sales and support offices in more than 120 countries.

	1995 Sales	
	$ mil.	% of total
US	19,691	46
Europe	12,574	30
Other regions	10,197	24
Adjustments	(10,943)	—
Total	**31,519**	**100**

WHAT

	1995 Sales	
	$ mil.	% of total
Computers, service & support	25,269	80
Electronic test & measurement equip.	3,288	10
Medical electronics & service	1,300	4
Electronic components	856	3
Chemical analysis & service	806	3
Total	**31,519**	**100**

Selected Products
Calculators and other personal information products
Computers and computer peripherals
Electronic test equipment and systems
Medical electronic equipment

Selected Services
Consulting
Customer support and maintenance
Product financing and rentals
Systems integration

KEY COMPETITORS

Acer	Gateway 2000	Radius
Apple Computer	IBM	Samsung
AST	Intel	Sharp
Baxter	Iomega	Siemens
Becton,	LG Group	Silicon Graphics
Dickinson	Machines Bull	Sony
Cabletron	3M	Sun
Casio	NCR	Microsystems
Compaq	NEC	SyQuest
C. R. Bard	Oki	Tandem
Data General	Olivetti	Texas
DEC	Packard Bell	Instruments
Dell	Philips	Toshiba
Fisher Scientific	Power	Unisys
Fujitsu	Computing	

HOW MUCH

NYSE symbol: HWP FYE: October 31	Annual Growth	1986	1987	1988	1989	1990	1991	1992	1993	1994	1995
Sales ($ mil.)	18.0%	7,102	8,090	9,831	11,899	13,233	14,494	16,410	20,317	24,991	31,519
Net income ($ mil.)	18.8%	516	644	816	829	739	755	881	1,177	1,599	2,433
Income as % of sales	—	7.3%	8.0%	8.3%	7.0%	5.6%	5.2%	5.4%	5.8%	6.4%	7.5%
Earnings per share ($)	18.4%	1.01	1.25	1.68	1.76	1.53	1.51	1.75	2.33	3.07	4.63
Stock price – high ($)	—	24.81	36.81	32.75	30.75	25.19	28.69	42.50	44.63	51.25	96.63
Stock price – low ($)	—	17.88	17.88	21.88	20.13	12.44	14.94	25.13	32.19	35.94	49.00
Stock price – close ($)	16.7%	20.94	29.13	26.63	23.63	15.94	28.50	34.94	39.50	49.94	83.75
P/E – high	—	25	29	19	17	16	19	24	19	17	21
P/E – low	—	18	14	13	11	8	10	14	14	12	11
Dividends per share ($)	22.8%	0.11	0.12	0.14	0.18	0.21	0.24	0.37	0.45	0.55	0.70
Book value per share ($)	11.8%	8.54	10.01	9.68	11.46	13.04	14.45	14.95	16.84	19.48	23.22
Employees	2.5%	82,000	82,000	87,000	95,000	92,000	89,000	92,600	96,200	98,400	102,300

1995 YEAR-END

Debt ratio: 24.7%
Return on equity: 22.4%
Cash (mil.): $2,616
Current ratio: 1.48
Long-term debt (mil.): $663
No. of shares (mil.): 510
Dividends
  Yield: 0.8%
  Payout: 15.1%
Market value (mil.): $42,709

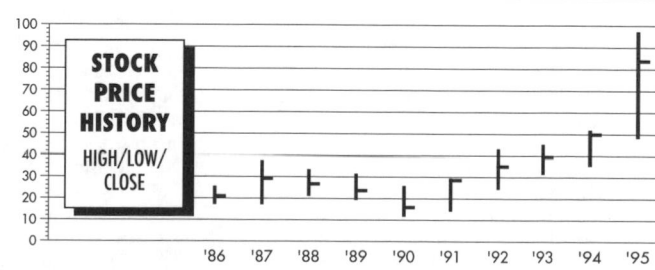

STOCK PRICE HISTORY HIGH/LOW/CLOSE

HITACHI, LTD.

OVERVIEW

Hitachi is a "hi-tech" company, but it's a low-tech one, too. The company is Japan's largest integrated maker of electrical machinery and electronic equipment and one of the world's leading manufacturers of mainframes, supercomputers, workstations, and state-of-the-art semiconductors. The conglomerate also makes power plant equipment, industrial and plant machinery, and low-tech goods, including chemicals and wire and cable. The Tokyo-based company makes a range of consumer electronic goods and has operations in financial services, general trading, printing, property management, and transportation.

Facing a slow-growing and highly competitive market in Japan, Hitachi is expanding its offshore operations. The company has restructured its consumer electronics division, shifting production of VCRs from Japan and the UK to Malaysia, and it is beefing up its marketing operations. Hitachi has moved into the notebook computer market in the US by establishing notebook PC maker Hitachi PC Corp. and hiring former Apple executive David Hancock as the new subsidiary's CEO. The firm is also strengthening its presence in China by setting up 4 joint ventures to make and sell elevators and escalators. Hitachi's sales have risen over the last 2 years, a fact not represented when sales are translated into dollars because of fluctuations in the value of the dollar against the yen.

WHEN

Namihei Odaira, an employee of Kuhara Mining in the Japanese coastal city of Hitachi, wanted to prove that Japan did not have to depend on foreigners for technology. In 1910 he began building 5-hp electric motors in Kuhara's engineering and repair shop. Japanese power companies were forced to buy Odaira's generators when WWI made imports scarce. Impressed, they reordered, and in 1920 Hitachi (meaning "rising sun") became an independent company.

During the 1920s acquisitions and growth turned Hitachi into a major manufacturer of electrical equipment and machinery. In the 1930s and 1940s, Hitachi developed vacuum tubes and light bulbs and produced radar and sonar for the Japanese war effort. Postwar occupation forces removed Odaira and closed 19 Hitachi plants. Reeling from the plant closures, war damage, and labor strife, Hitachi was saved from bankruptcy by US military contracts during the Korean War.

In the 1950s Hitachi was designated a supplier to Nippon Telegraph and Telephone (NTT), the state-owned communications monopoly. Japan's economic recovery led to strong demand for the company's communications and electrical equipment. Hitachi began mass-producing home appliances, radios, TVs, and transistors. The company spun off Hitachi Metals and Hitachi Cable in 1956 and Hitachi Chemical in 1963.

With the help of NTT, the Ministry of International Trade and Industry (MITI), and computer technology licensed from RCA, Hitachi produced its first computer in 1965. In the 1960s Hitachi began producing color TVs, built factories in Southeast Asia, and started manufacturing integrated circuits.

Hitachi launched an IBM-plug-compatible computer in 1974. It sold its computers in the US through Itel until 1979, and afterward through National Semiconductor's NAS (National Advanced Systems) unit. In 1982 FBI agents caught Hitachi staff buying documents allegedly containing IBM software secrets. Hitachi settled a civil case with IBM for around $300 to $500 million up front and $2 to $3 million per month for 8 years as compensation for the use of IBM's software.

In the late 1980s the rising Japanese yen hurt exports. Hitachi responded by focusing on burgeoning domestic markets and investing heavily in factory automation. In 1988 the company and Texas Instruments agreed to join in the costly development and production of 16-megabit DRAMs. In 1989 Hitachi bought 80% of NAS, giving it direct control of its US distribution.

Despite its rivalry with IBM, in 1991 Hitachi agreed to resell IBM notebook PCs under its own name in Japan; in 1992 the 2 companies agreed to jointly develop high-end printers. In a major restructuring move to combat sluggish consumer electronics sales, Hitachi announced in 1994 that it would merge with its marketing subsidiary, Hitachi Sales Corp. In 1995 Hitachi signed a joint venture agreement with India's Tata Group in an effort to break into India's growing middle-class market.

The company teamed up in 1996 with the US's Cheyenne Software to distribute Cheyenne's ARCserve, the leading backup system for distributed enterprise systems.

WHO

Chairman: Katsushige Mita
President: Tsutomu Kanai
President, Hitachi America: Tsuneo Tanaka
President and CEO, Hitachi PC Corp.: David Hancock
VP and CFO, Hitachi America: Shuji Nakanishi
VP and General Manager (Personnel), Hitachi America:
Iwao Hara
Auditors: KPMG Peat Marwick LLP

WHERE

HQ: 6, Kanda-Surugadai 4-chome, Chiyoda-ku, Tokyo,
101, Japan
Phone: +81-3-3258-1111
Fax: +81-3-3258-2375
US HQ: Hitachi America, Ltd., 50 Prospect Ave.,
Tarrytown, NY 10591-4698
US Phone: 914-332-5800
US Fax: 914-332-5555
Web site: http://www.hitachi.co.jp
Hitachi operates more than 70 subsidiaries worldwide.

WHAT

	1996 Sales		1996 Operating Income	
	$ mil.	% of total	$ mil.	% of total
Information systems & electronics	28,538	29	1,744	45
Power & industrial systems	23,807	25	1,076	28
Materials	12,946	13	709	18
Consumer products	8,988	9	(139)	—
Services & other	23,322	24	349	9
Adjustments	(20,961)	—	(601)	
Total	**76,640**	**100**	**3,138**	**100**

Selected Products and Services

Information Systems and Electronics
Broadcasting equipment
Computers and peripherals
Medical electronics
Semiconductors
Telephone exchanges
Test equipment

Power and Industrial Systems
Auto equipment
Elevators and escalators
HVAC equipment
Industrial robots
Power plants

Materials
Ceramic materials
Copper products
Electric wire and cable

Pipe fittings
Printed circuit boards
Rubber products
Steel and steel products

Consumer Products
Air conditioners
Dry batteries
Kitchen appliances
Microwave ovens
Refrigerators
TVs and VCRs
Vacuum cleaners

Services and Other
Financial services
General trading
Printing
Property management
Transportation

KEY COMPETITORS

Alcatel Alsthom	McDermott	Silicon Graphics
Amdahl	Microsoft	Sony
DEC	Mitsubishi	Tandem
Ericsson	Motorola	Texas
Fluor	NCR	Instruments
Fujitsu	NEC	Toshiba
GEC	Nippon Steel	United
IBM	Northern	Technologies
Intel	Telecom	Whirlpool
Machines Bull	Samsung	Yamaha
Matsushita	Siemens	

HOW MUCH

NYSE symbol: HIT FYE: March 31	Annual Growth	1987	1988	1989	1990	1991	1992	1993	1994	1995	1996
Sales ($ mil.)	9.7%	33,257	40,010	48,496	44,797	55,025	58,388	67,863	72,174	87,713	76,640
Net income ($ mil.)	7.9%	677	1,100	1,406	1,335	1,637	960	696	666	1,316	1,337
Income as % of sales	—	2.0%	2.7%	2.9%	3.0%	3.0%	1.6%	1.0%	2.0%	1.5%	1.7%
Earnings per share ($)	4.6%	2.53	3.34	4.47	3.71	4.69	2.78	2.04	1.96	3.80	3.78
Stock price – high ($)[1]	—	74.00	110.50	152.25	133.75	112.00	100.25	76.38	84.75	110.88	114.13
Stock price – low ($)[1]	—	35.50	59.25	93.13	100.00	76.75	67.50	56.00	55.50	72.00	82.88
Stock price – close ($)[1]	4.3%	69.00	90.75	129.00	105.50	82.00	74.50	59.88	73.50	98.75	100.50
P/E – high	—	29	33	34	36	24	36	37	43	29	30
P/E – low	—	14	18	21	27	16	24	28	28	19	22
Dividends per share ($)	3.7%	0.75	1.12	0.89	0.51	0.71	0.70	0.75	0.86	0.94	1.04
Book value per share ($)	8.2%	44.68	55.56	57.28	52.75	61.07	6.70	80.81	84.99	106.60	90.68
Employees	8.3%	161,325	159,910	274,508	290,811	309,757	324,929	331,505	330,637	331,673	331,852

[1] Stock prices are for the prior calendar year.

1996 YEAR-END

Debt ratio: 41.1%
Return on equity: 4.5%
Cash (mil.): $20,950
Current ratio: 1.62
Long-term debt (mil.): $11,352
No. of shares (mil.): 333
Dividends
Yield: 1.0%
Payout: 27.5%
Market value (mil.): $33,458

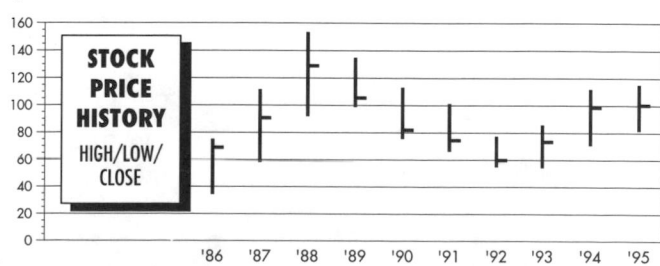

STOCK PRICE HISTORY HIGH/LOW/CLOSE

ICL PLC

OVERVIEW

ICL is following in the footsteps of rivals AT&T and Digital Equipment and all but abandoning the manufacture of personal computers. London-based ICL had ranked among Europe's top 10 PC makers, but the company has had to implement a series of restructurings since 1990 to stay afloat in the competitive PC marketplace. Now ICL is remaking itself into a computer software, systems, and services company. To that end ICL is selling more than 80% of its PC and UNIX server business to world-class computer maker Fujitsu. ICL will also sell a majority stake in its contract manufacturing unit, D2D. Fujitsu owns about 84% of ICL; Northern Telecom owns about 16%.

ICL may be playing catch-up to larger information technology service firms, but it has already established some footholds. The company is the world's #3 provider of systems for retailers, including checkout machines, and it has an 8,000-machine automatic teller network in Europe. ICL is also banking on software development, offering its TeamWARE networking product as an alternative to IBM's Lotus Notes. The company is rounding out its new business with an interactive services unit that courts the education, media, and publishing markets.

WHEN

ICL traces its roots to the Tabulator Ltd., founded in 1904 by Robert Porter and renamed British Tabulating Machine Company (BTM) in 1907. BTM imported punched-card tabulators made by the US's Tabulating Machine Company (predecessor to IBM). Its first major job was to process the results of the 1911 United Kingdom census. During the 1920s BTM began making tabulators in the UK, based on the IBM models it had been importing, although it still had to pay royalties.

In 1949 BTM and IBM ended their royalty agreement, leaving the 2 companies free to compete. Facing the prospect of going head-to-head with IBM in tabulators, BTM began research into electronic computers. In 1953 it introduced a prototype of its first computer, the HEC, which became the UK's best-selling computer during the late 1950s.

In 1959 BTM merged with Powers-Samas Accounting Machines to form International Computers and Tabulators (ICT). Founded in 1915, Powers-Samas had been one of BTM's main competitors for 4 decades. ICT struggled in the early 1960s as it lagged behind IBM in developing computers, but established itself as a major computer maker with the introduction of the 1900 model in 1964. However, heavy development costs proved to be a drag on finances, and in 1968 ICT merged with computer company English Electric to form International Computers, Ltd. (ICL).

More troubles arose in the early 1970s in the form of heavy R&D costs and a recession. Despite a reorganization and management restructuring, ICL was struggling by 1981, when it posted a $175 million loss. The company got $450 million in loan guarantees from the British government, overhauled its R&D department, and signed a deal with Fujitsu to use Fujitsu-designed semiconductors in ICL mainframes. In 1984, in an early effort to meld telecommunications and computers, the UK's Standard Telephones & Cables (STC) acquired ICL for about $500 million.

ICL moved into open systems technology in the late 1980s, and launched a new line of UNIX-based computers in 1990. Also that year STC sold an 80% stake in ICL to Fujitsu for $1.3 billion. To boost its presence in the PC business, ICL acquired computer maker Nokia Data from Finland's Nokia for $400 million in 1991. That same year Northern Telecom bought STC, acquiring the remaining 20% of ICL.

In 1994 ICL signed a deal with Computer Associates International, giving it the rights to market CA's systems-management software. Netscape tapped ICL as its first systems integrator in northern Europe in 1995. That year the company's Workplace Technologies network integration company was spun off in a management-led buyout.

In early 1996, 15-year ICL president Peter Bonfield took a job as CEO of British Telecommunications. CFO Keith Todd took over the top spot and immediately began narrowing ICL's focus.

Under a $230 million restructuring plan, the company said it would cut 1,300 jobs, sell factories, and largely withdraw from the PC market. That year the Fleming Companies, one of the US's leading supermarket distributors, began marketing ICL's point-of-sale system. ICL also recruited Sun Microsystems for its North American systems integration program.

WHO

Chairman: Peter Bonfield
CEO: T. Keith Todd
CFO, ICL Retail Systems: Peter Kelly
CEO, ICL Sorbus: Paul M. Whitwam
President, ICL Retail Systems: Rod Powell
Group Executive Director, ICL Enterprises: Richard E. Livesey-Haworth
Group Executive Director, Technology: Ninian P. D. Eadie
SVP Human Resources, ICL Retail Systems: Phil Resch
Director Interactive: W. J. Davison
Director Quality and Customer Care: J. W. Goasdoue
Director Business Strategies: N. R. Hartnell
Director Personnel: D. J. Berry
Auditors: Coopers & Lybrand L.L.P.

WHERE

HQ: ICL House, One High St., Putney, London SW15 1SW, UK
Phone: +44-181-788-7272
Fax: +44-181-785-3936
US HQ: ICL Retail Systems, 5429 LBJ Fwy., Dallas, TX 75240
US Phone: 214-716-8300
US Fax: 214-716-8586
Web site: http://www.icl.co.uk

Selected Offices

Austria	Hungary	Singapore
Belgium	India	Slovakia
Botswana	Ireland	Slovenia
Bulgaria	Italy	South Africa
Canada	Kenya	Spain
Croatia	Malawi	Sweden
Czech Republic	Malaysia	Switzerland
Denmark	The Netherlands	UK
Egypt	Nigeria	United Arab
Finland	Norway	Emirates
France	Poland	US
Germany	Portugal	Zimbabwe
Greece	Romania	
Hong Kong	Russia	

WHAT

Selected Businesses

Systems and Services
CFM (outsourcing)
ICL Enterprises (systems integration)
ICL Financial Services (banking systems)
ICL Retail Systems (in-store retail systems)
ICL Sorbus (enterprise-wide support and facilities management)
Interactive Services Business

Technology
D2D (electronics contract manufacturing)
ICL High Performance Systems (sales and service of servers for data centers)
ICL Volume Products (volume sales of personal computers and small systems)
TeamWARE Group (networking software)
Technology plc (multivendor sales and distribution)

KEY COMPETITORS

AmeriData	Hewlett-Packard
Andersen Worldwide	IBM
Cap Gemini	Logica
Computer Sciences	Olivetti
Control Data	Sema Group
DEC	Unisys
EDS	Wang

HOW MUCH

Private company FYE: December 31	Annual Growth	1986	1987	1988	1989	1990	1991	1992	1993	1994	1995
Sales ($ mil.)	12.0%	1,737	2,451	2,465	2,502	2,943	3,507	3,747	3,875	4,124	4,826
Net income ($ mil.)	—	—	—	—	—	—	58	20	(22)	3	(312)
Income as % of sales	—	—	—	—	—	—	1.7%	0.5%	—	0.1%	—
Employees	(1.4%)	—	—	—	—	—	—	25,000	24,000	24,000	24,000

1995 YEAR-END

Debt ratio: 45.8%
Return on equity: —
Cash (mil.): $185
Current ratio: 1.13
Long-term debt (mil.): $101

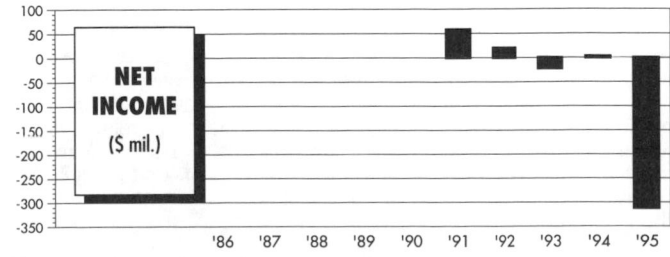

NET INCOME ($ mil.)

100										
50										
0										
-50										
-100										
-150										
-200										
-250										
-300										
-350	'86	'87	'88	'89	'90	'91	'92	'93	'94	'95

IMATION CORP.

OVERVIEW

Imation is no longer stuck to 3M. Head-quartered in Oakdale, Minnesota, Imation is the world's #1 maker of branded removable magnetic and optical-technology media (such as computer diskettes and storage tapes) for the data processing industry. Its portfolio of more than 10,000 products also includes carbonless papers, color proofing systems, disk drives, photographic films (it is a top world supplier of private-label brands), single-use cameras, and medical imaging systems (including ultrasound, magnetic resonance, and nuclear medical devices).

Imation, which emerged from Minnesota Mining and Manufacturing (3M) when the maker of Post-It Notes and Scotch tape spun off some less profitable units, is focusing short-term on key product lines such as DryView digital laser imagers, LS-120 disk drives, Rainbow color proofing systems, and Travan data cartridges. For long-term growth, the company is counting on streamlining operations and cutting costs, expanding overseas, and eliminating less profitable lines while combining the technological expertise of its diverse units to develop new offerings. Demand for Imation's products is likely to rise with data transmission rates, digital storage needs, and the use of color printing.

WHEN

Imation's ancestry stretches back to 1902, when 5 businessmen founded 3M in Two Harbors, Minnesota, to sell corundum to manufacturers for grinding wheels. Faced with stiff competition, and the realization that its mining holdings contained the nearly worthless igneous rock anorthosite instead of corundum, the company shifted gears and began making sandpaper and abrasive wheels.

Future CEO William McKnight joined 3M as a bookkeeper in 1907 and had risen to the position of president by 1929. 3M's future was assured with the development of 2 products — Scotch brand masking tape (1925) and Scotch brand cellophane tape (1930). McKnight fostered a creative atmosphere, telling company leaders in 1944: "Management that is destructively critical when mistakes are made kills initiative."

In the late 1940s McKnight implemented a vertical management structure and introduced his autonomy-for-performance philosophy. The company introduced the first commercially viable magnetic recording tape in 1947.

In 1950, after a decade of work and $1 million in development costs, 3M employee Carl Miller completed the ThermoFax copying machine, one of the company's first imaging products.

3M's offerings in the 1960s included dry-silver microfilm, photographic products, carbonless papers, overhead projection systems, and medical and dental products. The company produced backdrops for the movie *2001: A Space Odyssey*, which won an Academy Award in 1968. 3M moved into pharmaceuticals, radiology, energy control, and office markets in the 1970s and 1980s.

Lewis Lehr took over as president in 1981 and created the company's electronic and information technology and graphics technology units, which evolved into the divisions that were later spun off. He also instituted a goal of having 1/4 of earnings come from products less than 5 years old. 3M in 1984 debuted the 831 Laser Imager, the world's first laser-based diagnostic medical imaging system.

In 1990 the company moved into India, opening a tape and telecommunications products plant there. New products for 1993 included a privacy filter for personal computers and a line of overhead projectors. The next year 3M introduced brightness-enhancing plastic sheeting for portable computer displays and the Travan minicartridge, used to back up computer files.

In 1995 the company debuted the DryView laser medical imaging system, which eliminated film wet processing costs and other expenses from the imaging procedure.

Imation (a name taken from the words "information" and "imagination") was born in 1996 when 3M spun off its low-performing data storage, imaging, and printing businesses. (3M retained its industrial and consumer and life science units and discontinued its audiotape and videotape business.)

Imation in 1996 unveiled the LS-120 disk drive, which uses standard floppy disks (1.44 megabyte) as well as high-capacity 120-megabyte, 3.5" disks. That year Imation received major endorsements of the LS-120 line as Hitachi, Matsushita, and Mitsubishi began making products based on the technology.

Chairman, President, and CEO: William T. Monahan, age 49, $360,989 pay
VP Technology Development: Krzysztof K. Burhardt, age 54, $287,107 pay
VP Corporate Business Processes: David G. Mell, age 49, $211,187 pay
VP Operations: Charles D. Oesterlein, age 53, $209,414 pay
VP Marketing and Public Affairs: Dennis A. Farmer, age 52, $207,200 pay
VP International: David H. Wenck, age 52
CFO: Jill. D. Burchill, age 41
Treasurer: Deborah D. Weiss, age 40
General Counsel and Secretary: Carolyn A. Bates, age 49
Director Human Resources: Jacqueline Chase
Auditors: Coopers & Lybrand L.L.P.

WHERE

HQ: One Imation Place, Oakdale, MN 55128
Phone: 612-704-4000
Fax: 612-704-4200
Web site: http://www.imation.com

	1995 Sales		1995 Operating Income	
	$ mil.	% of total	$ mil.	% of total
US	1,129	50	(169)	—
Africa, Europe & the Middle East	804	36	56	—
Other regions	313	14	(36)	—
Total	**2,246**	**100**	**(149)**	**—**

WHAT

	1995 Sales	
	$ mil.	% of total
Information processing, management & storage	931	42
Medical & photo imaging	608	27
Information printing	542	24
Other products & services	165	7
Total	**2,246**	**100**

Selected Products and Services

Information Processing and Storage
CD-ROM replication
Computer disks
Computer tapes
Data cartridges (Travan)
Disk drives (LS-120)

Medical and Photo Imaging
Chest System (radiograph imaging)
Disposable cameras
Dry imaging products (DryView)
Film processors
Laser imaging systems (969 HQ family)
Photography film (Scotch)
X-ray film

Information Printing
Carbonless papers
Color proofing systems (Rainbow)
Image setting and graphic arts products
Printing plates

KEY COMPETITORS

Acuson
BASF
DuPont
Eastman Kodak
Elscint
Exabyte
Fuji Photo
Fujitsu
Hitachi
Hyundai
IBM
Iomega
KAO

Konica
Matsushita
Pinnacle Micro
Polaroid
Quantum Corp.
Scitex
Seagate
Sony
SyQuest
Toshiba
Western Digital
Xerox

HOW MUCH

NYSE symbol: IMN FYE: December 31	Annual Growth	1986	1987	1988	1989	1990	1991	1992	1993	1994	1995
Sales ($ mil.)	(1.4%)	—	—	—	—	—	—	—	2,308	2,281	2,246
Net income ($ mil.)	—	—	—	—	—	—	—	—	75	54	(97)
Income as % of sales	—	—	—	—	—	—	—	—	3.3%	2.4%	—
Employees	—	—	—	—	—	—	—	—	—	—	12,000

1995 YEAR-END

Debt ratio: 0.0%
Return on equity: —
Cash (mil.): $0
Current ratio: 3.22
Long-term debt (mil.): $0

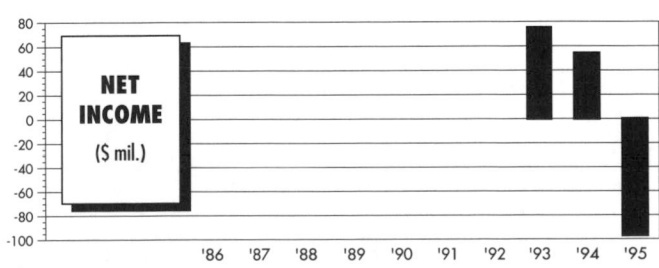

INACOM CORP.

OVERVIEW

Omaha-based InaCom is a leading provider of technology management products and services. The company sells microcomputer systems, workstations, and networking and telecommunications equipment and offers system support and systems integration services through more than 1,000 company-owned and franchised business centers around the US. Chairman Rick Inatome and his father own about 5% of the company.

InaCom distributes products from such companies as IBM, Compaq, Hewlett-Packard, Toshiba, and Apple. It also offers voice, data,

and video convergence equipment via its InaCom Communications subsidiary. The company is trying to move away from the razor-thin margins of computer reselling and concentrating on its more lucrative technology management services. Though services only generate about 5% of revenues, they account for about 45% of profits. InaCom has acquired companies that specialize in network integration services and software development, and it has also introduced a new division, InaCom Professional Services, which provides high-end consulting services.

WHEN

It was a case of computers before swine. In 1982 Valmont Industries (founded in 1946), a manufacturer of irrigation systems and other products, created ValCom to sell computers and software to the farmers that made up its customer base. The company sold PCs along with software such as Swine Management and Poultry Farm Management. However, when ValCom discovered that the hog software was not flying off the shelves along with the computers, it learned that most of its customers were not farmers but local bankers, lawyers, and store owners. They bought PCs from the company because of the extensive training and service ValCom offered with the purchase. Bill Fairfield, head of ValCom, dropped the farming software to focus on selling hardware and services to small businesses.

ValCom expanded through both company-owned and franchised computer centers, and by 1984 it had 121 stores. A year later it introduced an online system to provide its stores with product information. In 1987 Valmont spun off ValCom to the public, with Bill Fairfield as CEO, and acquired 6 retail locations in the midwestern and western US from Bell Atlantic subsidiary CompuShop Inc.

The company continued to expand. In 1988 it acquired New Jersey's #1 computer chain, Clancy-Paul, and by the end of the year had 181 computer stores in 46 states. ValCom bought the Office Works Computer Centers, with locations in Pennsylvania and North Carolina, in 1990. That year it expanded its businesses to include value-added resellers and systems integrators, giving ValCom more than 300 locations.

ValCom nearly doubled in size in 1991 when it merged with computer reseller Inacomp Computer Centers, founded in 1976 by Rick Inatome. After graduating from Michigan

State, Inatome borrowed $35,000 and opened a small computer store called Computer Mart in Clawson, Michigan. In 1979 the company became an authorized Apple dealer.

During the early 1980s the company began to focus on larger corporate accounts and changed its name to Inacomp Computer Centers. To expand its product offerings, it also became an authorized IBM dealer. Inacomp went public in 1983. The company expanded through acquisitions, buying computer store chains in California and Georgia. It also added computer rentals and opened computer superstores to serve its business customers.

Negotiations for the merger between Inacomp and ValCom began in 1989 and completed in 1991. The companies became InaCom after Inatome insisted that his company's name come first. To provide more services to businesses, InaCom added technical support for networking systems in 1992. It also signed a deal with system integration consortium ICG to expand its services worldwide. The following year InaCom acquired Sears Business Centers and shifted its emphasis to direct-to-end-user shipments, streamlining its distribution system.

InaCom acquired the computer and service businesses of Chaparral Information Systems, a networking company in 1994. InaCom posted a loss in 1994 due, in part, to the loss of a government contract. The next year the company agreed to sell and support the Cisco Systems internetworking products and the Canon Computer Systems printers and scanners.

The company continued its expansion in 1996, acquiring Nashville-based network integrator Technology Express and the education and software development group of Chaparral Information Systems.

WHO

Chairman: Rick Inatome, age 42
President and CEO: Bill L. Fairfield, age 49,
$1,102,815 pay
EVP and CFO: Dave Guenthner, age 46, $436,502 pay
**President and General Manager, Direct Operations and
Client Service Division:** Robert A. Schultz, age 53,
$506,280 pay
**Group President, Communications and Corporate
Marketing:** George DeSola, age 49, $460771 pay
**Secretary; President and General Manager, Distribution
and Operations:** Michael A. Steffan, age 44,
$445,799 pay
President and General Manager, International Division:
Cris Freiwald, age 41
VP and Corporate Treasurer: Gary L. Goldsberry, age 47
VP Corporate Resources (HR): Larry Fazzini
Auditors: KPMG Peat Marwick LLP

WHERE

HQ: 10810 Farnam Dr., Omaha, NE 68154
Phone: 402-392-3900
Fax: 402-392-3602
Web site: http://www.inacom.com

Distribution Centers
Omaha, NE
Ontario, CA
Swedesboro, NJ

WHAT

	1995 Sales	
	$ mil.	% of total
Computer products	2,047	93
Technology management services	95	4
Communication products & services	58	3
Total	**2,200**	**100**

	1995 Sales	
	$ mil.	% of total
Independently owned business centers	1,106	50
Company-owned business centers	994	45
Other	100	5
Total	**2,200**	**100**

	1995 Distribution Network	
	No.	% of total
Independent resellers	972	96
Company-owned stores	45	4
Total	**1,017**	**100**

KEY COMPETITORS

Ameriquest	Gateway 2000
ASCII	Intelligent Electronics
Bell Microproducts	Merisel
CompuCom	Micro Warehouse
CompUSA	MicroAge
Control Data	SOFTBANK
Dataflex	Tandy Corporation
Dell	Tech Data
Entex	Vanstar

HOW MUCH

Nasdaq symbol: INAC FYE: December 31	Annual Growth	1986	1987	1988	1989	1990	1991	1992	1993	1994	1995
Sales ($ mil.)	40.1%	106	164	235	359	428	680	1,015	1,545	1,801	2,200
Net income ($ mil.)	22.0%	2	4	5	6	7	3	11	12	(2)	12
Income as % of sales	—	2.2%	2.2%	2.1%	1.8%	1.6%	0.5%	1.1%	0.8%	—	0.5%
Earnings per share ($)	7.2%	0.61	0.92	1.12	1.40	1.69	0.56	1.25	1.23	(0.22)	1.14
Stock price – high ($)	—	—	10.88	10.38	11.75	17.00	18.50	14.75	25.50	21.00	15.25
Stock price – low ($)	—	—	6.25	7.25	9.38	9.25	7.00	9.25	12.75	6.88	7.00
Stock price – close ($)	8.9%	—	7.13	9.75	10.75	12.50	10.00	14.50	13.50	7.00	14.13
P/E – high	—	—	12	9	8	10	33	12	21	—	13
P/E low	—	—	7	7	7	6	13	7	10	—	6
Dividends per share ($)	—	—	0.00	0.00	0.00	0.00	0.00	0.00	0.00	0.00	0.00
Book value per share ($)	13.1%	—	5.55	6.71	8.19	9.81	11.07	12.24	13.92	13.75	14.85
Employees	35.3%	—	195	398	438	661	1,380	1,309	1,883	1,884	2,196

1995 YEAR-END

Debt ratio: 41.9%
Return on equity: 8.2%
Cash (mil.): $21
Current ratio: 1.20
Long-term debt (mil.): $24
No. of shares (mil.): 10
Dividends
  Yield: —
  Payout: —
Market value (mil.): $142

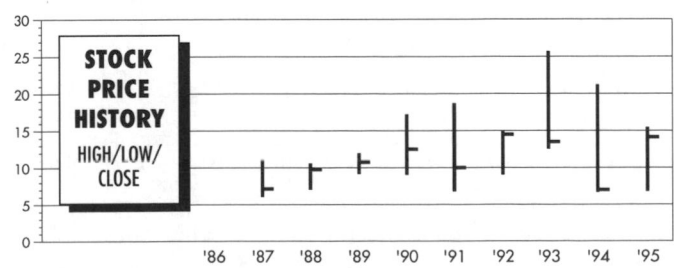

STOCK PRICE HISTORY
HIGH/LOW/CLOSE

INGRAM MICRO INC.

OVERVIEW

Ingram Micro is the largest wholesale distributor of microcomputer products in the world. The Santa Ana, California-based subsidiary of Ingram Industries offers more than 36,000 products (including desktop and notebook PCs, servers, mass storage devices, CD-ROM drives, monitors, printers, and software) to some 105,000 reseller customers in 120 countries. About 90% of its sales are generated from products supplied by Compaq, IBM, NEC, and Apple. Ingram Micro distributes its products through 8 warehouses in the US and 21 international warehouses in North America, Europe, and Asia. About 1/3 of the company's business comes from its international sales. The Ingram family owns more than 75% of the company.

Ingram Micro is the product of the 1989 merger of California-based software distributor Micro D and Ingram Industries' computer distributor Ingram Computer. The company has reaped the benefits of the decrease in personal computer prices. In a fierce price war, computer manufacturers and software makers have sold their products to distributors in bulk rather than employing their own sales forces.

With a 22% share of the domestic microcomputer distribution market, Ingram Micro's strategy is to emphasize such high-end goods as UNIX, document imaging, and networking equipment. The company is also expanding its international presence, adding a distributor in Malaysia to its Pacific Rim operations. In 1996 Ingram Micro announced plans to go public.

WHEN

There is no love lost between the former Micro D and Ingram Industries. Micro D was founded in Fountain Valley, California, in 1979 by husband-and-wife entrepreneurs Geza Csige and Lorraine Mecca. As the company grew, Mecca sought to merge the computer distributor with a partner that could take over daily operations. She relinquished control of Micro D to Linwood "Chip" Lacy in 1986 and sold her 51% share of the company to minority shareholder Ingram Distribution Group.

Sales bottomed out for Micro D in 1986, when it reported the largest quarterly loss in its history. Lacy tightened Micro D's belt and took huge charges for outdated inventory it sold at a discount and overdue payments from customers that had gone bankrupt.

At the same time, Ingram Industries was busy merging recently acquired Ingram Software Distribution Services of Buffalo, New York, and Compton, California-based Softeam. The merger made the company one of the nation's largest wholesale distributors of computer software. Lacy saw Ingram's purchase of Micro D shares as a conflict of interest, but he was too busy returning Micro D to profitability: centralizing its marketing and distribution functions, cutting costs, and expanding its market to include more small retailers, which provided higher margins. Micro D went from the 4th largest distributor of microcomputer products to first in just one year.

By the late 1980s the PC market was surging, which fueled Micro D's growth. By 1988 the firm had expanded outside the US for the first time, acquiring Ottawa, Ontario-based

Frantek Computer Products. It also signed an exclusive deal to distribute Claris software for Apple computers.

Ingram Industries offered to acquire the 41% of outstanding Micro D stock it did not own in 1988, but Lacy resisted, preferring to let Ingram wait. Though Ingram owned a majority of Micro D stock, it only controlled 3 of 7 seats on the board. Ingram was forced to play Lacy's game and finally acquired the company for a higher price early in 1989.

The new company, which controlled 20% of the computer distribution market, was called Ingram Micro D. The merger was anything but smooth, and several Micro D executives jumped ship. In 1989 the company acquired the Brussels-based software distributor Softeurop to expand its business into Europe and over the next few years established itself in Mexico and the Far East.

As the PC took hold in the US in the 1990s, Ingram Micro D became the dominant player in the industry, but relations between Lacy and the Ingram family never improved. The company shortened its name to Ingram Micro in 1991. Two years later, just as the company was hitting on all cylinders, Lacy decided to leave. To keep him at the company, Ingram Industries CEO Bronson Ingram (much to his distaste) promised to let Lacy take the company public and Ingram Micro announced its plan to go public in 1996. However, citing irreconcilable differences, Lacy resigned that year. Jerre Stead (formerly CEO of software maker Legent) signed on as Lacy's successor in 1996.

WHO

Chairman: Martha R. Ingram, age 61
VC: David R. Dukes, age 52, $465,741 pay
CEO: Jerre L. Stead, age 53
President and COO: Jeffrey R. Rodek, age 43, $659,909 pay
CFO: Michael J. Grainger, age 44
EVP; President, Ingram Micro US: Sanat K. Dutta, age 47, $477,093 pay
EVP; President, Ingram Micro Europe: John William Winkelhaus II, age 45, $381,441
SVP; President, Ingram Alliance: Douglas R. Antone, age 43
SVP; President, Ingram Micro Canada: Larry L. Elcheson, age 46
SVP Human Resources: David M. Finley, age 55
Auditors: Price Waterhouse LLP

WHERE

HQ: 1600 E. St. Andrew Place, Santa Ana, CA 92705
Phone: 714-566-1000
Fax: 714-566-7733
Web site: http://www.ingram.com

	1995 Sales	
	$ mil.	% of total
US	5,970	70
Europe	1,849	21
Other regions	798	9
Total	**8,617**	**100**

WHAT

Selected Merchandise
Business application software
CD-ROM drives
Computer supplies
Desktop and notebook PCs
Entertainment software
Mass storage devices
Modems
Monitors
Network interface cards
Networking hubs, routers, and switches
Printers
Scanners
Servers
Workstations

Selected Services
Electronic services
Financial services
Inventory management
Order fulfillment
System configuration
Tailored marketing services
Technical education
Technical support
Telesales
Warehousing

KEY COMPETITORS

Asia Source
CHS Electronics
Computer 2000
Data Storage Marketing
Inacom
Intelligent Electronics
Macrotron
Marshall Industries
Merisel
Micro Warehouse
MicroAge
Pulsar Data Systems
Softworks Development
Tech Data
Wyle Electronics

HOW MUCH

Subsidiary FYE: December 31	Annual Growth	1986	1987	1988	1989	1990	1991	1992	1993	1994	1995
Sales ($ mil.)	43.8%	—	—	—	—	—	2,017	2,731	4,044	5,830	8,617
Net income ($ mil.)	29.4%	—	—	—	—	—	30	31	50	63	84
Income as % of sales	—	—	—	—	—	—	1.5%	1.1%	1.2%	1.1%	1.0%
Employees	—	—	—	—	—	—	—	—	—	—	7,604

1995 YEAR-END

Debt ratio: 73.2%
Return on equity: 31.7%
Cash (mil.): $57
Current ratio: 1.57
Long-term debt (mil.): $844

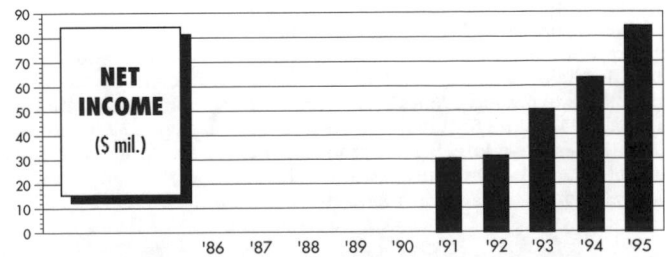

NET INCOME ($ mil.)

INTEL CORPORATION

OVERVIEW

Just how inside is Intel? Its PC microprocessors (the "brains" of a computer) have an 88% market share. The Santa Clara, California-based company is the world's top maker of integrated circuits, including microprocessors, flash memory chips, and chip sets. Intel's biggest seller is the industry-standard Pentium microprocessor. Its biggest outlet is personal computers; Intel makes about $300 for each Intel-based PC sold. The company's products are also used in communications equipment and other electronics.

To keep sales strong, preaches CEO Andrew Grove, "We need to create waves of excitement for what our product ends up in." Already the company is plotting computing's next wave, which it calls the "connected PC." These systems, based on MMX (which adds multimedia functions to microprocessors), combine high-speed PCs with advanced capabilities (such as 3-D graphics, accelerated Internet access, speech recognition, and videoconferencing) now handled by specialized chips from smaller chip shops.

Computer sales in the US are slowing, but only 1/3 of homes have PCs, and technologies such as MMX may make machines both cheaper and more powerful, spurring sales. The overseas PC market continues to boom, keeping Intel's sales solid.

WHEN

In 1968, 3 engineers from Fairchild Semiconductor created Intel in Mountain View, California, to develop large-scale integration (LSI) technology for silicon-based chips. (The company's name is a contraction of Integrated Electronics, a name that was already in use.) Robert Noyce (co-inventor of the integrated circuit, 1958) and Gordon Moore handled long-range planning, while Grove oversaw manufacturing. It was Moore who originated "Moore's Law," an industry tenet maintaining that chip capabilities double every year and a half.

Intel's sales soon mushroomed as it became a supplier of semiconductor memory for large computers (DRAM chips, which replaced magnetic core memory storage, 1970; and EPROM chips, which allowed read-only memory to be erased and reused, 1971).

This success funded Intel's microprocessor designs, which revolutionized the electronics industry. When Intel's 8088 chip was chosen for IBM's PC in 1981, Intel's place as the microcomputer standards supplier was secured.

Cutthroat pricing of DRAMs by Japanese competitors forced Grove (who succeeded Noyce as president and CEO in 1979) to close plants, cut the workforce by 30%, and withdraw from the DRAM market in 1985.

To regroup, Grove focused on proprietary PC chips. In its drive to set the industry standard, Intel licensed Advanced Micro Devices and others to produce clones of the 286, only to see AMD capture 52% of that market by 1990. In response, Intel fiercely protected the technology of its highly successful 386 (1985) and 486 chips (1989), leading AMD to sue for breach of contract in 1987. In 1990 and again in 1992, an arbitrator ruled against Intel, validating a 1982 technology exchange deal with AMD. Intel introduced a credit-card-sized, 20MB flash memory card for small PCs in 1992 and unveiled its Pentium chip in 1993.

While Intel originally dismissed concerns over a mathematical flaw discovered in the Pentium in 1994, public concern forced it to address both the flaw and its tarnished image. That year the company opened new plants in Ireland and New Mexico and broke ground on a $1.3 billion chip factory in Arizona.

Intel ramped up its motherboard operations in 1995 with a $100 million upgrade of its Dupont, Washington, plant. That year Intel and AMD settled several microcode court cases: AMD got the microcode license; Intel was awarded $58 million in past damages. Also in 1995 Intel's 6th-generation chip, the Pentium Pro, hit the market.

In late 1995 Intel beat out Cray Research and nCUBE to win a Department of Energy contract to develop the world's fastest supercomputer, which will use 6,000 Pentium Pro microprocessors, at an estimated price of $45 million.

In 1996 the company announced that it would stop making supercomputers by the end of that year. It also joined with MCI in producing a new line of servers to sell to small and medium-sized businesses for use in Internet commerce. Intel also announced plans to introduce a new modem that will allow PCs to send and receive video phone calls over standard phone lines.

Chairman: Gordon E. Moore, age 67
President and CEO: Andrew S. Grove, age 59, $2,756,700 pay
EVP and COO: Craig R. Barrett, age 56, $2,067,500 pay
SVP; General Manager, Enterprise Server Group: David L. House, age 52, $1,293,400 pay
SVP; General Manager, Technology and Manufacturing Group: Gerhard H. Parker, age 52, $1,264,500 pay
SVP; General Manager, Internet and Communications Group: Frank C. Gill, age 52, $1,255,000 pay
SVP; General Manager, Semiconductor Products Group: Robert W. Reed, age 49
VP and CFO: Andy D. Bryant, age 45
VP, General Counsel, and Secretary: F. Thomas Dunlap Jr., age 44
VP; Director, Human Resources: Kirby A. Dyess
Auditors: Ernst & Young LLP

WHERE

HQ: 2200 Mission College Blvd., Santa Clara, CA 95052-8119
Phone: 408-765-8080
Fax: 408-765-1402
Web site: http://www.intel.com

Intel has manufacturing plants in Ireland, Israel, Malaysia, the Philippines, Puerto Rico, and the US.

	1995 Sales		1995 Operating Income	
	$ mil.	% of total	$ mil.	% of total
US	14,261	55	3,315	58
Europe	5,750	22	1,383	24
Japan	1,765	7	353	6
Asia/Pacific	3,549	14	271	5
Other regions	684	2	410	7
Adjustments	(9,807)	—	(480)	—
Total	**16,202**	**100**	**5,252**	**100**

WHAT

Selected Products

Conferencing Products
ProShare Conferencing Video System 200
ProShare TeamStation group video conferencing system

Embedded Products
Memory products
Microcontrollers
Microprocessors

Flash Memory Products
SmartVoltage

Microprocessor Products
Core-logic chipsets
Intel 486
Pentium
Pentium Pro

Network Products
EtherExpress LAN adapters
Express Stackable Hubs
FastEthernet cards
NetportExpress print servers
StorageExpress backup servers

KEY COMPETITORS

3Com	Hitachi	Picture Tel
AMD	IBM	SGS-Thomson
Apple Computer	Inacom	Silicon Graphics
Cyrix	LG Group	Sun
DEC	Motorola	Microsystems
Fujitsu	National	Texas
General Electric	Semiconductor	Instruments
Harris Corp.	NEC	Toshiba

HOW MUCH

Nasdaq symbol: INTC FYE: December 31	Annual Growth	1986	1987	1988	1989	1990	1991	1992	1993	1994	1995
Sales ($ mil.)	32.8%	1,265	1,907	2,875	3,127	3,921	4,799	5,844	8,782	11,521	16,202
Net income ($ mil.)	—	(203)	248	453	391	650	819	1,067	2,295	2,288	3,566
Income as % of sales	—	—	13.0%	15.8%	12.5%	16.6%	17.1%	18.3%	26.1%	19.9%	22.0%
Earnings per share ($)	—	(0.29)	0.35	0.63	0.52	0.80	0.98	1.25	2.60	2.62	4.03
Stock price – high ($)	—	5.38	10.45	9.31	9.00	13.00	14.81	22.88	37.25	36.75	78.38
Stock price – low ($)	—	2.73	3.45	4.81	5.72	7.00	9.44	11.63	21.38	28.00	31.50
Stock price – close ($)	36.3%	3.50	6.63	5.94	8.63	9.63	12.25	21.75	31.00	31.94	56.75
P/E – high	—	—	30	15	17	16	15	18	14	14	19
P/E – low	—	—	10	8	11	9	10	9	8	11	8
Dividends per share ($)	—	0.00	0.00	0.00	0.00	0.00	0.00	0.03	0.10	0.12	0.15
Book value per share ($)	26.7%	1.76	1.90	2.88	3.46	4.50	5.42	6.50	8.97	11.22	14.79
Employees	9.6%	18,200	19,200	20,800	21,700	23,900	24,600	25,800	29,500	32,600	41,600

1995 YEAR-END

Debt ratio: 5.8%
Return on equity: 33.3%
Cash (mil.): $2,458
Current ratio: 2.24
Long-term debt (mil.): $400
No. of shares (mil.): 821
Dividends
  Yield: 0.3%
  Payout: 3.7%
Market value (mil.): $46,592

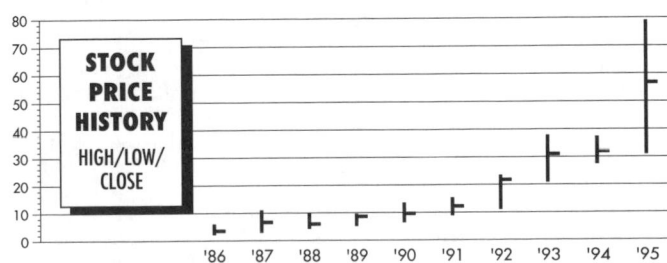

STOCK PRICE HISTORY HIGH/LOW/CLOSE

INTELLIGENT ELECTRONICS, INC.

OVERVIEW

Intelligent Electronics (IE) is working 3 times as smart. Despite hard times, the Exton, Pennsylvania-based computer distributor has a 3-pronged strategy for maintaining its leadership position in the highly competitive wholesale computer industry. IE distributes microcomputers, telecommunications products, and related software and peripherals. Customers include computer network integrators and resellers as well as corporate, governmental, and educational buyers.

To keep business growing, it is beefing up customer services, especially technology services. At the same time, the company is cutting costs and getting more efficient by consolidating warehouses and upgrading its electronic ordering system. And IE is expanding, using acquisitions — such as the purchase of computer sales and consulting company the Future Now — to widen its distribution channel.

All this is designed to help stop the flow of red ink and the dealer defections that have plagued the company.

Chairman Richard Sanford owns about 11.5% of IE.

WHEN

In 1982 Sanford, an EVP at Commodore, retired at age 38, having accumulated enough wealth to never work again. After 4 months of relaxing, Sanford was bored to tears. He went back to work — not for the money or the prestige, he said, but for the challenge. Using venture capital, he founded Intelligent Electronics, leasing space from Strawbridge & Clothier's department store in Philadelphia to sell computers under the name Todays Computers Business Centers.

With a little guidance from the department store's head, Peter Strawbridge, Sanford enlarged his customer base and acquired salesmanship and public relations savvy. In 1984, after expanding into Pittsburgh, he began franchising the company's name, products, and services. Targeting smaller "stand-alone" office supply merchants who weren't yet selling computers, Sanford succeeded by passing on bulk-purchase savings and requiring no royalty fee.

By year-end 1985 IE controlled a 45-store network and had begun to establish relationships with key suppliers. The company began selling Compaq computers in 1986 after IBM placed a moratorium on reseller authorizations. In 1987, the year the company went public, sales reached $81 million. Between 1986 and 1989, IE more than doubled the size of its retail network, to 193 stores. In 1989 the company bought 2 computer resellers, Entre Computer Centers (184 locations) and Connecting Point of America (245 locations), and subsequently became the nation's #1 reseller. It also began marketing Apple computers that year.

IE entered the retail superstore market in 1991 with the purchase of the 57-store BizMart chain. It believed that BizMart could generate high computer sales. However, computer sales never really took off, market competition proved strong, and BizMart lost $27 million in 1992. However, that year the firm won its first major outsourcing contract, with IBM's EduQuest, to provide computer services to IBM customers in primary and secondary schools.

IE sold BizMart in 1993 to Kmart's OfficeMax for $270 million. In 1994 the company announced the development of Wireless Telecom, a wholly owned subsidiary, in order to create a specialized sales channel for wireless data communications products and services. Also that year the SEC began an informal investigation of IE's alleged overcharging of suppliers for contributions earmarked for marketing. An article in the *Wall Street Journal* revealed that about half of the company's 1991 operating income came from unused marketing funds, and it raised the question of whether IE's failure to fully report the sources of its profits constituted fraud on its shareholders. Following the article, IE's stock dropped 25%.

The company settled a suit filed by former counsel Daniel Shannon in 1995. Shannon, who had been in charge of compliance with the SEC, had filed a wrongful discharge suit in 1993 after he was fired. Also in 1995 IE acquired the Future Now, its largest customer.

In 1996 IE formed XLConnect, a subsidiary that will provide internetworking solutions, local area network and wide area network installation, and other data transmission services. That year IE was stung by an industry shift toward "open sourcing," meaning vendors no longer require resellers to purchase from a designated distributor. IE is one of the last remaining high-volume distributors dependent on the old system.

WHO

Chairman, President, and CEO: Richard D. Sanford, age 52, $850,000 pay
Assistant to the Chairman: Mark Briggs, $325,000 pay
EVP: Gregory A. Pratt, age 47, $500,000 pay
SVP Fulfillment: Timothy D. Cook, age 35, $317,500 pay
SVP and CFO: Thomas J. Coffey, age 43, $277,846 pay
SVP Sales, Marketing, and Service: Susan Bailey
CEO, XLConnect: Rick Ellenberger
VP, Secretary, and Treasurer: Stephanie D. Cohen, age 34
Administrator Personnel: Sherri Haines
Auditors: Price Waterhouse LLP

WHERE

HQ: 411 Eagleview Blvd., Exton, PA 19341-1117
Phone: 610-458-5500
Fax: 610-458-6702
Web site: http://www.intelect.com

Intelligent Electronics operates distribution centers in Memphis and Denver.

WHAT

	1996 Suppliers % of total
Hewlett-Packard	25
Compaq	24
IBM	15
Apple	8
Other	28
Total	**100**

Selected Products
Local and wide area network systems
Microcomputers
Peripherals
Software
Telecommunications equipment
Workstations

Selected Services
Financing
Marketing assistance
New product evaluation
Preshipment configuration
Product promotion
Technical support

KEY COMPETITORS

CHS Electronics
Graybar Electric
Inacom
Ingram Micro
Marshall Industries
Merisel
MicroAge
Tech Data
Vanstar
Wyle Electronics

HOW MUCH

Nasdaq symbol: INEL FYE: January 30	Annual Growth	1987	1988	1989	1990	1991	1992	1993	1994	1995	1996
Sales ($ mil.)	58.4%	57	81	129	712	1,459	1,914	2,017	2,646	3,208	3,588
Net income ($ mil.)	—	1	2	5	11	29	38	2	43	8	(20)
Income as % of sales	—	1.4%	2.7%	4.0%	1.5%	2.0%	2.0%	0.1%	1.6%	0.3%	—
Earnings per share ($)	—	0.04	0.16	0.30	0.51	1.05	1.11	0.06	1.18	0.23	(0.59)
Stock price – high ($)[1]	—	—	3.13	3.13	8.56	11.88	18.75	30.38	28.00	27.63	14.63
Stock price – low ($)[1]	—	—	1.50	1.56	2.88	4.81	8.75	12.00	7.50	6.00
Stock price – close ($)[1]	15.2%	—	1.94	3.00	6.94	10.75	17.50	12.88	27.38	8.00	6.00
P/E – high	—	—	20	10	17	11	17	—	24	120	—
P/E – low	—	—	9	5	6	5	8	104	10	33	—
Dividends per share ($)	—	—	0.00	0.00	0.00	0.00	0.00	0.00	2.16	0.38	0.40
Book value per share ($)	21.8%	—	1.06	1.43	3.26	4.98	7.59	7.75	6.23	5.37	5.15
Employees	71.1%	—	35	53	765	721	2,669	526	809	1,162	2,569

[1] Stock prices are for the prior calendar year.

1996 YEAR-END

Debt ratio: 33.3%
Return on equity: —
Cash (mil.): $35
Current ratio: 1.05
Long-term debt (mil.): $80
No. of shares (mil.): 35
Dividends
  Yield: 6.7%
  Payout: —
Market value (mil.): $207

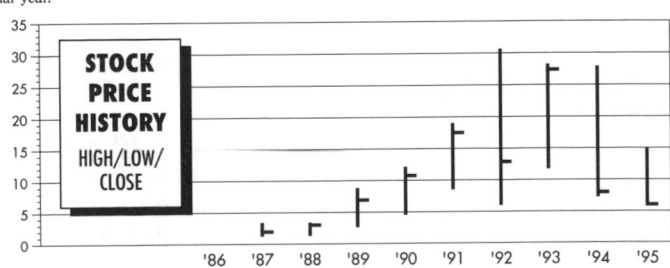

STOCK PRICE HISTORY HIGH/LOW/CLOSE
'86 '87 '88 '89 '90 '91 '92 '93 '94 '95

INTERGRAPH CORPORATION

OVERVIEW

Intergraph believes its map shows the way to profitability. While the route has been tortuous and Intergraph has had to make a couple of stops along the way (to pick up new hardware and software standards), the Huntsville, Alabama-based company is charting increased sales and continuing to win design accolades. Intergraph produces data management and graphics applications software for computer-aided design, management, and engineering (CAD/CAM/CAE). It also develops mapping and geographic information systems software.

While it continues to support customers using UNIX operating system software, Intergraph has thrown its weight behind Microsoft Windows NT as the network operating system of the future. Intergraph has also stopped building computers based on its proprietary chip and switched to Intel's Pentium microprocessors. CEO James Meadlock has declared the company's wrenching 3-year transition a success — anticipating that lower operating costs, an end to restructuring charges, and higher sales will yield a profit.

Meadlock and EVP Nancy Meadlock, his wife, own about 6% of Intergraph.

WHEN

James and Nancy Meadlock and several other former IBM coworkers (all software developers for Saturn rockets at IBM's Federal Systems Division in Huntsville, Alabama) founded M&S Computing in 1969. Its initial focus was consulting work. The first contract, a guidance system for the US Army Missile Command in Huntsville, used the real time applications that later grew into Intergraph's computer graphics business.

The company's first commercial graphics system was for mapping applications (1973). Penetration of the architecture, engineering, and construction markets followed with the introduction of a single graphics product, the Interactive Graphics Design System (IGDS). M&S packaged the software with industry-accepted hardware while competitors stuck to more restricted proprietary versions.

In the late 1970s the company began making its own computers to boost profit margins and compatibility across product lines. The company changed its name to Intergraph in 1980 and went public the following year. During the graphics boom of the early 1980s, Intergraph grew 40-60% yearly. In 1984 it introduced the competitive InterPro 32 workstation, followed by the first dual-screen workstation, Interact.

Intergraph supported open systems adopting the UNIX operating system and networking Intergraph workstations using Ethernet technology. It powered its workstations with its speedy RISC microprocessor, and it anticipated demand for generic workstations unbundled from applications graphics software.

Intergraph also absorbed key technologies, buying makers of CLIPPER (RISC) chips (1987), scanning and plotting hardware (Optotronics, 1986; AnaTech, 1987), engineering software (Tangent Systems, 50%, 1984;

82%, 1988), and software development tools (Quintus, 1989). Intergraph bought a 50% stake in Bentley Systems (creator of Intergraph's MicroStation software, 1987) and acquired struggling Daisy Cadnetix (1990), making it a leading supplier to the electronic design automation (EDA) industry.

A 2nd-generation CLIPPER chip (the C300) fueled the 3000 workstation series (1988) and the successor 6000 series (1990). In 1989 Intergraph moved into the dispatch management system and technical information management (TIM) markets. Intergraph introduced the Series 2000, a workstation for the low-end market, in 1990.

Intergraph acquired Norsk Data's Technovision CAD and ISYKON's Proren software, 2 of Germany's leading 2D mechanical design and documentation systems in 1992. The next year Intergraph began a major transition from UNIX-based products to "personal workstations" based on Intel microprocessors and Microsoft operating systems. The company posted a loss in 1993 because of lower sales and restructuring costs. As part of its reorganization, Intergraph cut its workforce by 8% and exited the microprocessor design business.

In 1994 and 1995 the company signed contracts for telecommunications systems in Australia, Saudi Arabia, and Sweden worth nearly $200 million. Intergraph acquired technical illustration software vendor InterCap Graphics Systems in 1995 and launched 2 new software products that year: Jupiter, which allows graphics modules from multiple vendors to work together, and Transcend, an advanced language translation product. It also cut 800 jobs in 1995. The next year Intergraph introduced the StudioZ RAX (a real time digital video workstation for producers of advertising and videos).

WHO

Chairman and CEO: James W. Meadlock, age 62,
$300,000 pay
EVP: Manfred Wittler, age 55, $377,865 pay
EVP: Stephen J. Phillips, age 54, $219,080 pay
EVP: Allan B. Wilson, age 47, $198,880 pay
EVP; President, Intergraph Software Solutions:
Tommy D. Steele, age 55, $196,700 pay
EVP: Robert E. Thurber, age 55
EVP; President, Intergraph Federal Systems: William
E. Salter, age 54
EVP; President, Intergraph Computer Systems: Wade
C. Patterson, age 34
EVP and CFO: Larry J. Laster, age 44
EVP: Nancy B. Meadlock, age 57
EVP; President, Intergraph Public Safety: James F.
Taylor Jr., age 51
VP Corporate Human Resources: Milford B. French
Auditors: Ernst & Young LLP

WHERE

HQ: One Industrial Park, Huntsville, AL 35894-0001
Phone: 205-730-2000
Fax: 205-730-7898
Web site: http://www.intergraph.com
Intergraph sells its systems worldwide.

	1995 Sales		1995 Operating Income	
	$ mil.	% of total	$ mil.	% of total
US	766	58	(12)	—
Europe	391	30	(28)	—
Other regions	161	12	(21)	—
Adjustments	(220)	—	7	—
Total	**1,098**	**100**	**(54)**	**—**

WHAT

	1995 Sales	
	$ mil.	% of total
Systems	710	65
Maintenance & services	388	35
Total	**1,098**	**100**

Selected Hardware
TD Series workstations
TDZ 3D graphics workstation
Web Server

Selected Software
Architecture/engineering/construction (enables users to
develop and model building concepts, produce
construction documents and manage space and assets
in a finished structure)
Civil engineering (includes tools for coordinate
geometry and for bridge, geotechnical, site, structural,
and transportation engineering)
Jupiter (allows competing CAD systems to work with
Intergraph's software without the need for translation)
Mapping and GIS (includes tools to manage data
collection and integration, spatial query and analysis,
output, and map production)
Mechanical design engineering and manufacturing
(enables the user to model production processes and
design structural integrity)

KEY COMPETITORS

AST	Hitachi	Structural
Autodesk	IBM	Dynamics
CIMLINC	Mentor Graphics	Research
Compaq	NEC	Sun
Computervision	Network Imaging	Microsystems
Data General	Olivetti	Tandem
DEC	Parametric	Unisys
Evans &	Technology	Viewlogic
Sutherland	Silicon Graphics	Wang
Fujitsu	Softdesk	

HOW MUCH

Nasdaq symbol: INGR FYE: December 31	Annual Growth	1986	1987	1988	1989	1990	1991	1992	1993	1994	1995
Sales ($ mil.)	6.8%	606	641	800	860	1,045	1,195	1,177	1,050	1,041	1,098
Net income ($ mil.)	—	70	70	88	80	63	71	8	(119)	(70)	(45)
Income as % of sales	—	11.6%	10.9%	11.0%	9.2%	6.0%	5.9%	0.7%	—	—	—
Earnings per share ($)	—	1.26	1.23	1.55	1.48	1.28	1.47	0.18	(2.56)	(1.56)	(0.98)
Stock price – high ($)	—	39.88	30.00	32.38	22.50	23.50	31.50	22.38	13.50	11.25	18.50
Stock price – low ($)	—	15.50	16.75	19.50	14.50	10.50	13.00	11.00	8.50	7.38	8.13
Stock price – close ($)	(0.8%)	17.00	24.75	21.00	17.25	13.75	17.75	13.25	10.63	8.13	15.75
P/E – high	—	32	24	21	15	18	21	124	—	—	—
P/E – low	—	12	14	13	10	8	9	61	—	—	—
Dividends per share ($)	—	0.00	0.00	0.00	0.00	0.00	0.00	0.00	0.00	0.00	0.00
Book value per share ($)	2.3%	8.80	10.06	11.72	12.58	14.36	15.80	15.49	12.98	11.66	10.76
Employees	4.4%	5,700	6,300	7,300	8,200	9,600	10,300	10,300	9,500	9,200	8,400

1995 YEAR-END

Debt ratio: 12.1%
Return on equity: —
Cash (mil.): $56
Current ratio: 1.93
Long-term debt (mil.): $37
No. of shares (mil.): 47
Dividends
  Yield: —
  Payout: —
Market value (mil.): $738

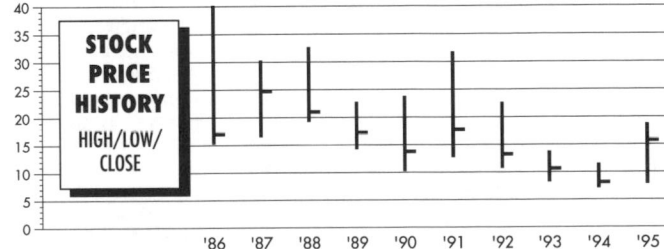

STOCK
PRICE
HISTORY
HIGH/LOW/
CLOSE

IBM

OVERVIEW

Things are rosy at Big Blue. International Business Machines (IBM) is the world's #1 provider of computer hardware, software, and services. After posting big losses in the early 1990s, it had returned to profitability by mid-decade. Said CEO Louis Gerstner, "the industry is moving our way."

Only a few years ago analysts made dire forecasts for IBM's mainstay — mainframe and midrange computers. But with customers such as airlines, insurance companies, and banks depending on mainframes, and with the booming Internet business calling on "big servers," that segment has surprised naysayers.

Software is another stable revenue source for IBM, but most of its software sales involve programs for the company's larger systems. Now IBM wants to be a player in the enterprise software market. To further that end, it acquired spreadsheet publisher Lotus (1995) and systems management software maker Tivoli Systems (1996).

IBM has de-emphasized the high-competition, low-margin PC and storage markets. And, with its OS/2 operating system a disappointment, it is looking to the interdependent areas of big computers, semiconductors, software, and service for momentum.

WHEN

In 1914 National Cash Register's star salesman, 40-year-old Thomas Watson, left to rescue the flagging Computing-Tabulating-Recording Company. Watson aggressively marketed C-T-R's Hollerith machine (a punch card tabulator) and supplied tabulators to the US government during WWI, tripling C-T-R's revenues to almost $15 million by 1920. The company became International Business Machines in 1924 and soon dominated the global market for tabulators, time clocks, and electric typewriters. It was the US's largest office machine firm by 1940, with sales approaching $50 million.

IBM perfected electromechanical calculation but initially dismissed the potential of computers. When Remington Rand's commercial computer (UNIVAC, 1951) began replacing IBM machines, IBM quickly responded. Using its superior R&D and marketing, it built a market share near 80% in the 1960s and 1970s. Competitors scattered to niches on the periphery.

In 1952 Thomas Watson Jr. became president, and the company introduced its first computer, the 701. Other triumphs achieved under him included the STRETCH systems, which eliminated vacuum tubes (1960) and the first compatible family of computers, the System/360 (1964). Accompanying innovations included the FORTRAN programming language (1957) and floppy disk storage (1971). IBM later moved into midrange systems (System/38, 1978; AS/400, 1988). The introduction of the IBM PC in 1981 kick-started the personal computer industry with its barrage of PC clones. In 1984 IBM, with partners Sears and CBS, founded Trintex, which became the Prodigy Online Service.

The shift to smaller, open systems, along with greater competition in all of IBM's segments, caused wrenching change. After posting profits of $6.6 billion in 1984, IBM began a slow slide. The company sold many noncomputer businesses, such as its copier division (to Kodak, 1988); Rolm telecommunications (to Siemens, 1988); and its typewriter, keyboard, personal printer, and supplies business, Lexmark (to Clayton & Dubilier, 1991).

In 1992 IBM set up a European unit to sell low-cost clones of its own computers and formed a joint venture with Sears called Advantis to provide voice-and-data network services. In 1993 IBM and Groupe Bull entered a joint venture to develop software. That year Gerstner, a former executive at American Express and RJR Nabisco, became IBM's CEO.

In 1994 IBM sold its Federal Systems unit, which provides computer systems and services to the government, to Loral for $1.5 billion. In a challenge to Intel's dominance of the microprocessor business, IBM agreed to manufacture computer chips designed by Cyrix.

IBM acquired software pioneer Lotus, developer of the 1-2-3 spreadsheet, for $3.52 billion in 1995. Also that year Apple released its first Power Mac computers that use the PowerPC chip developed by Apple, IBM, and Motorola.

After investing an estimated $1.2 billion, IBM and remaining partner Sears sold Prodigy to management and investors for $250 million. Also that year the company became the nation's largest to extend health benefits to partners of gay and lesbian workers.

The company agreed in 1996 to sell Celestica, a Canadian electronics manufacturing unit, to Onex Corp., a buyout firm.

WHO

Chairman and CEO: Louis V. Gerstner Jr., age 54,
$4,775,000 pay
EVP; CEO, Lotus Development: Michael D. Zisman
EVP; COO, Lotus Development: Jeffrey Papows
**SVP and Group Executive, Worldwide Sales and
Services:** Ned C. Lautenbach, age 52, $1,240,000 pay
SVP and Group Executive, Software Group: John M.
Thompson, age 53, $1,218,334 pay
SVP and CFO: G. Richard Thoman, age 51,
$1,125,000 pay
SVP and Group Executive, Technology Group: Patrick
A. Toole, age 58, $1,087,500 pay
SVP and Group Executive, Server Group: Nicholas M.
Donofrio, age 50
SVP and General Counsel: Lawrence R. Ricciardi,
age 55
SVP Human Resources: J. Thomas Bouchard,
age 55
Auditors: Price Waterhouse LLP

WHERE

HQ: International Business Machines Corporation, One
Old Orchard Rd., Armonk, NY 10504
Phone: 914-765-1900
Fax: 914-288-1147
Web site: http://www.ibm.com

	1995 Sales		1995 Net Income	
	$ mil.	% of total	$ mil.	% of total
US	37,342	40	599	14
Europe/Middle East/Africa	27,768	30	2,271	53
Asia/Pacific	16,590	18	1,098	25
Americas	11,354	12	324	8
Adjustments	(21,114)	—	(176)	—
Total	**71,940**	**100**	**4,116**	**100**

WHAT

	1995 Sales	
	$ mil.	% of total
Hardware	35,600	49
Service & maintenance	20,123	28
Software	12,657	18
Rentals & financing	3,560	5
Total	**71,940**	**100**

Business Units
Personal Systems Group
Server Group
Software Group
Technology Group
Worldwide Sales and Services

KEY COMPETITORS

Acer	Gateway 2000	Sony
Amdahl	Hewlett-Packard	Sun
Apple Computer	Hitachi	Microsystems
AST	ICL	SAP
Candle Corp.	Machines Bull	Tandem
Ceridian	Microsoft	Texas
Compaq	NCR	Instruments
Data General	NEC	Toshiba
DEC	Packard Bell	Unisys
Dell	PLATINUM	
EDS	technology	
Fujitsu	Siemens	

HOW MUCH

NYSE symbol: IBM FYE: December 31	Annual Growth	1986	1987	1988	1989	1990	1991	1992	1993	1994	1995
Sales ($ mil.)	3.6%	52,160	55,256	59,598	62,654	68,931	64,766	64,523	62,716	64,052	71,940
Net income ($ mil.)	(1.7%)	4,789	5,258	5,451	3,722	5,967	(598)	(6,865)	(7,940)	2,937	4,116
Income as % of sales	—	9.3%	9.7%	9.1%	5.9%	8.7%	—	—	—	4.6%	5.7%
Earnings per share ($)	(0.9%)	7.81	8.72	9.20	6.41	10.42	(1.05)	(12.03)	(14.02)	5.02	7.23
Stock price – high ($)	—	161.88	175.88	129.50	130.88	123.13	139.75	100.38	59.88	76.38	114.63
Stock price – low ($)	—	119.25	102.00	104.50	93.38	94.50	83.50	48.75	40.63	51.38	70.25
Stock price – close ($)	(3.0%)	120.00	115.50	121.88	94.13	113.00	89.00	50.38	56.50	73.50	91.38
P/E – high	—	21	20	14	20	12	—	—	—	15	16
P/E – low	—	15	12	11	14	9	—	—	—	10	10
Dividends per share ($)	(15.2%)	4.40	4.40	4.40	4.73	4.84	4.84	4.84	1.58	1.00	1.00
Book value per share ($)	(3.7%)	56.73	64.09	66.99	67.01	76.43	64.20	48.31	33.95	38.00	40.47
Employees	(6.4%)	407,080	389,348	387,112	383,220	373,816	344,396	301,542	256,207	219,839	225,347

1995 YEAR-END

Debt ratio: 49.4%
Return on equity: 18.5%
Cash (mil.): $7,701
Current ratio: 1.29
Long-term debt (mil.): $10,060
No. of shares (mil.): 548
Dividends
  Yield: 1.1%
  Payout: 13.8%
Market value (mil.): $50,053

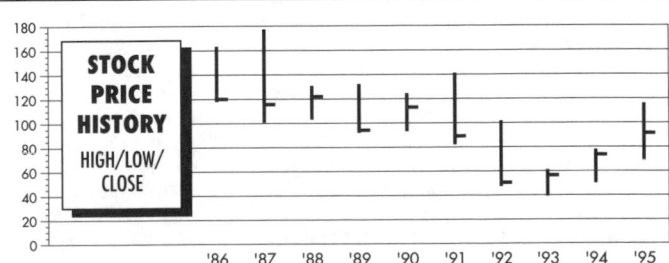

STOCK
PRICE
HISTORY
HIGH/LOW/
CLOSE

INTERNATIONAL DATA GROUP

OVERVIEW

A million dollars says Microsoft king Bill Gates has at least one International Data Group (IDG) magazine on his coffee table. Through its print products, Internet magazines, e-mail newsletters, and other media, the Boston-based company is the world's leading provider of computer information. Subsidiary IDG Communications is the world's #1 publisher of computer-related periodicals, with more than 275 magazines (including *Macworld* and *PC World*) and newspapers in 78 countries. Its publications are read by more than 90 million people each month. IDG Books Worldwide prints some 350 titles (including the *For Dummies* series and *InfoWorld*) in 28 languages. Subsidiary International Data Corporation leads the industry in computer market research and analysis. IDG World

Expositions sponsors conferences, trade shows, and other events for the computer industry.

IDG's strategy is to develop computer publications in markets throughout the world. It is also starting online-only "webzines," such as JavaWorld Magazine. IDG and Internet search service Infoseek announced in 1996 that *Macworld* would be the exclusive sponsor and content provider for Infoseek's Macintosh Directory.

Founder Patrick McGovern owns about 65% of IDG, while the employees own the rest. McGovern, known as "Chairman Pat," is listed as one of the 400 richest Americans in *Forbes* and has been known to dress up like Ben Franklin for employees in Boston and as Confucius for employees in China. He hands out Christmas bonuses personally — in cash.

WHEN

Patrick McGovern began his publishing career at the *Philadelphia Bulletin* as a paper boy. As a teenager in the 1950s he was inspired by Edmund Berkeley's book *Giant Brains; or Machines That Think*. He built a computer impressive enough to win a scholarship to MIT. While there he edited the first computer magazine, *Berkeley's Computers and Automation*.

In 1964 McGovern was interviewing the president of computer pioneer UNIVAC for *Computers and Automation* when he was inspired to start a market research service, International Data Corporation. Three years later he began International Data Group with the launch of an 8-page tabloid, *Computerworld*. At that time, according to McGovern, computer products had a 7-year life cycle, and over 75% of the computer market was in the US. (Today product life cycles are measured in months, and less than 35% of the market is US based.) McGovern introduced his new paper at a computer trade show. Within a few weeks it had 20,000 subscribers; advertisers soon started to seek out the publication. By 1968 IDG had $1 million in annual revenues.

Since its modest beginning IDG has set out to conquer the computer world. It began publishing in Japan in 1971, then expanded to Germany in 1975 and to Brazil in 1976. By 1988 the company had established a presence in Russia. Two years later, after the collapse of Communism, it started 10 publications in Russia and eastern Europe.

Two teen hackers, angry because they didn't receive a free poster with the IDG publication

Gamepro, broke into the company's voice-mail system in 1990 and erased orders from customers and messages from writers. The prank cost as much as $2.4 million in lost revenues and additional expenses.

Beset by competition from the mushrooming computer magazine marketplace in 1993, several of IDG's magazines, including *InfoWorld*, *Macworld*, and *PC World*, began losing ad pages. The company began an incentive program tied in to its new online service to help stem advertiser attrition.

In 1994 IDG traded a 4% stake in its *Multimedia World* magazine and $110,000 cash for the assets of Mecklermedia's *CD-ROM World*. The 2 publishers said they would collaborate on future projects. The following year the company said it would cease publication of *AmigaWorld*, started in 1985.

Also in 1995, as part of IDG's move away from closed systems and toward Internet-based services, it purchased a stake in online software companies Architect Software, Inc., and Netscape. That year IDG and a former IDG officer, Axel Leblois, bought Boston-based publisher World Times.

The company started producing a free e-mail weekly newsletter, *infusion*, in 1996 to provide up-to-date news and information on the networking industry. That year it purchased *PC Advisor*, the UK's fastest-growing computer magazine, and laid plans to launch *Intranet Magazine* as a tabloid-size supplement to *Network World* before spinning it off as a stand-alone publication.

WHO

Chairman and CEO: Patrick J. McGovern, age 58
President: Kelly P. Conlin, age 35
COO: James Casella, age 47
EVP Finance: William P. Murphy
VP Human Resources: Martha Stephens
Director Information Systems: Jeff Debalko
Director Corporate Communications: Chris McAndrews
Auditors: Deloitte & Touche LLP

WHERE

HQ: One Exeter Plaza, 15th Fl., Boston, MA 02116
Phone: 617-534-1200
Fax: 617-262-2300
Web site: http://www.idg.com

IDG publishes more than 275 computer magazines and newspapers in 78 countries.

WHAT

Divisions

IDG Communications
Books
Magazines
Newsletters
Newspapers
Online services

IDG Research Companies
Advisory services
Consulting
Research reports
Technology briefings

IDG World Expositions
Conferences
Special events
Trade shows

Selected Periodicals

United States
CD Review
CIO Magazine
Computerworld
Computerworld Client/Server Journal
DOS World
Federal Computer Week
GamePro
InfoWorld
Macworld
Network World
PC World
Video Event
WebMaster

Foreign
China Infoworld
Computerworld Brazil
East African Computer News (Kenya)
InfoCanada
Le Monde Informatique (France)
Macworld Denmark
PC Advisor
PC World Hong Kong
PC World Israel
PC World Vietnam
Telecom Romania
Windows World Japan

Selected Book Brands and Series

Computerworld ... For Dummies
Heavy Metal
InfoWorld
Macworld
Multimedia World
Network World
PC World
SECRETS
Type and Learn

KEY COMPETITORS

CMP Publications
Cowles Media
Gartner Group
GP Publications
Gigg Information Group
HyperMedia
McGraw-Hill
Mecklermedia
Phillips Publishing
Pittway
Seybold
SOFTBANK
Upside Publishing
Wired Ventures
Wolff New Media

HOW MUCH

Private company FYE: September 30	Annual Growth	1986	1987	1988	1989	1990	1991	1992	1993	1994	1995
Sales ($ mil.)	17.7%	—	—	—	—	620	780	840	880	1,100	1,400
Employees	17.4%	—	—	—	—	3,812	4,200	4,500	5,000	7,200	8,500

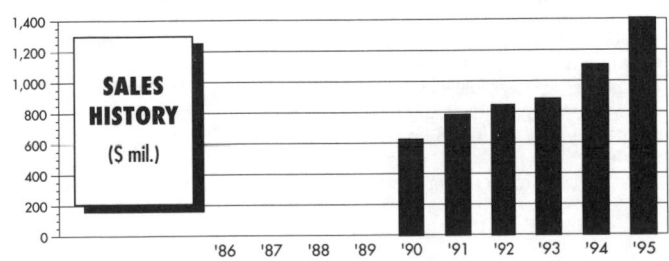

SALES HISTORY ($ mil.)

KINGSTON TECHNOLOGY CORPORATION

OVERVIEW

The Kingston duo of John Tu and David Sun hope that computer operating systems and software keep getting hungrier for memory. Based in Fountain Valley, California, Kingston Technology is the #1 maker of memory enhancement chip clusters used to increase the capacity and speed of computers, printers, and servers. The Internet's growing popularity and memory-hungry applications and systems (some platforms require more than 64 MB of storage space) have increased demand for Kingston's memory upgrades. Other products include PC peripherals, networking products, processor upgrades, and storage expansion subsystems.

The company's philosophy is that the customer comes 3rd, placing its employees and suppliers at the top of its priority list. Owners Tu and Sun occupy cubicles like the rest of the staff, and Kingston's workers, which the executives treat like family, are among the highest paid in the industry. As for the suppliers, Kingston never turns away shipments from chip vendors and does not try to renegotiate when the market price for chips dips below the company's contracted price.

Customers do not fare poorly, though. Kingston has been known to ship $500,000 worth of product on a handshake, and it once designed a memory upgrade and manufactured and installed 100 of them in a single day for a ComputerLand retailer caught short on an order. Tu and Sun (who are both on the "Forbes" list of the 400 richest people in America) have no intention of taking Kingston public, for fear it would change the company's culture.

WHEN

Kingston was founded in 1987 by Shanghai-born Tu and Taiwan-born Sun, who both moved to California in the 1970s. The pair met in 1982 and started a memory-upgrade company called Camminton Technology out of Tu's garage. At first they carried around memory chips in the back seats of their cars. Sales had reached $9 million by 1986, when they sold the business to high-tech firm AST Research for $6 million. The 2 invested their money in stock market futures but suffered heavy losses when the market crashed in 1987.

That year PC makers were producing computers that lacked the memory needed to run the latest, hottest software, and Tu and Sun sprang into action. With just $4,000 in cash, they started another company by converting inexpensive, outdated chips into memory upgrades. Tu, who was educated in Europe, wanted to call the company Kensington after the gardens in London. A mouse pad company had that name, so Kingston was chosen.

Tu had doubts about the new company and bet Sun a Jaguar that it wouldn't survive the first year of operations. Sun won the car (which he later gave to a veteran employee who had a longtime dream to own one), as Kingston's success was instantaneous; within 2 years the company had sold nearly $40 million worth of product. In 1989 Kingston began making memory system upgrades and a year later started producing processor upgrades.

The company appeared as #1 on "Inc." magazine's list of the fastest-growing private US companies in 1992. That year Kingston began marketing a selection of networking products, including Ethernet cards and token-ring adapters. The company's vendor-friendly policy panned out in 1993, when the demand for semiconductors exceeded the supply. Suppliers kept shipping to Kingston as orders from other buyers were delayed.

In 1994 the company broadened its product portfolio when it unveiled 9 new processor upgrade models. The next year demand for Kingston's upgrades kicked into high gear with Microsoft's launch of the Windows 95 operating system, which led many consumers to boost the power of their computers so they could run the software. In addition, Kingston increased its production capacity by expanding its US facilities.

The company joined with Legend Technology Limited in 1996 to develop computers for the emerging Chinese market. That year it launched the TurboChip 133 processor upgrade, which gives a 486-based computer system the processing power of a 75MHz Pentium chip. Also in 1996 Kingston increased its presence in the networking market with the introduction of 3 new plug-and-play Ethernet adapters (the EthRx series), which are installed simply by inserting them into the computer board.

WHO

President and CEO: John Tu
VP Engineering: David Sun
VP Marketing: Gary MacDonald
VP Administration (HR): Daniel Hsu
CFO: Henri Tchen

WHERE

HQ: 17600 Newhope St., Fountain Valley, CA 92708
Phone: 714-435-2600
Fax: 714-435-2699
Web site: http://www.kingston.com
Kingston Technology sells its products around the world and has manufacturing facilities in the US.

WHAT

Selected Products

Memory Products
Add-on boards
Memory modules

Networking Products
Ethernet adapters
Ethernet hubs
Token-ring adapters
Token-ring multistation access units

Portable Devices
CD-ROM adapters
Ethernet adapters
Fax/modems
Storage systems

Processor Upgrades
286 upgrades
386 upgrades
486 upgrades

Storage Subsystems
PC expansion boards
Removable subsystems
Storage chassis

KEY COMPETITORS

Adaptec
Ampex
AST
Boca Research
Centon
Microdyne
Micronics
MTI Technology
NEC
PNY Electronics
Samsung
Sequel
SMART Modular
SyQuest
Toshiba
Unigen
Viking Components
VisionTek

HOW MUCH

Private company FYE: December 31	Annual Growth	1986	1987	1988	1989	1990	1991	1992	1993	1994	1995
Sales ($ mil.)	79.6%	—	12	13	37	88	141	251	489	800	1,300
Employees	42.2%	—	—	—	—	—	110	175	255	310	450

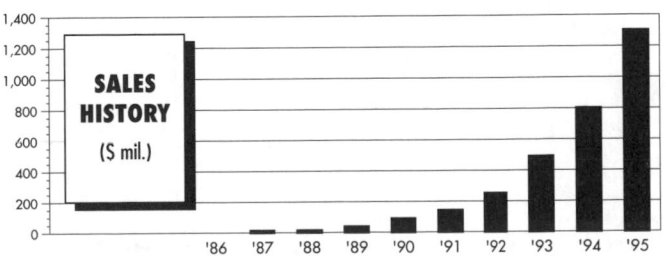

SALES HISTORY ($ mil.)

KYOCERA CORPORATION

OVERVIEW

Japan's ceramic Godzilla, Kyocera — the world's largest maker of integrated circuit (IC) ceramic packages — is beginning to throw its weight around in new markets, including portable telephones and multimedia services. In addition to IC packages (casings that provide electrical insulation and protect ICs from air, moisture, and physical shock), Kyocera is a major producer of other semiconductor and electronic components. The company's other ceramic products are used in everything from engine parts for industrial machinery to dental implants and artificial gemstones. Kyocera is a leading maker of solar cells and thermal printheads. It also makes office equipment, cordless and cellular telephones, and cameras.

Kyocera is led by its founder and chairman, Kazuo Inamori. The company (named after its home city, Kyoto, and main product, ceramics) has been prompted by slow growth in the IC package business to diversify into such areas as communications and multimedia, while developing new applications of its ceramic technologies. The rapid growth in the telecommunications markets, especially of mobile phones, has helped lift revenues.

The company has launched a new venture, Kyocera Multimedia Corp., to market database information, delivery services, and game software for consumers' TVs.

WHEN

A rebel from his youth, Kazuo Inamori was born into a poor Japanese family in 1932. At age 23 he joined Shofu Industries, a Kyoto manufacturer of ceramic insulators, quitting 3 years later after an argument with supervisors. He and 7 colleagues then started Kyoto Ceramic in 1959. Leaving an established company to start a new one was nearly unheard of in Japan, so the 8 men took a blood oath of loyalty to seal their commitment. Their first product was a ceramic insulator for cathode ray tubes. In the late 1960s the company developed the ceramic IC package that has made it a world-class supplier.

The company started manufacturing in the US in 1971 after buying Fairchild Camera & Instrument's failing plant. The firm diversified into artificial gemstones (Crescent Vert, 1977) and dental implants (New Medical, 1978). In 1979 Inamori bought control of failing Cybernet Electronics (Japanese citizens-band radio maker), using it to move Kyoto Ceramic into the production of copiers and stereos, and with West Germany's Feldmuhle (with whom it had already formed a European partnership) formed Kyocera Feldmuhle (US producer of industrial ceramics and cutting tools).

The company merged 5 subsidiaries in 1982, forming Kyocera Corporation. Another acquisition (Yashica) moved it into the production of cameras and other optical equipment in 1983. That year Kyocera ran into trouble. At the time NTT was the only legal supplier of telephones in Japan, but Inamori started marketing cordless telephones without the required approval. The government forced Kyocera to recall the phones. In 1984 when the government abolished NTT's monopoly,

Kyocera joined 24 other companies to form Daini-Denden (meaning 2nd phone company), which later changed its name to DDI. That year Inamori established the Inamori Foundation, which awards annual prizes for achievement in advanced technology, basic sciences, and creative arts.

More trouble with the government followed in 1985 when the overanxious Inamori marketed artificial bones without official approval. Kyocera got more bad press the following year when a deal to make hard disk drives for Silicon Valley's LaPine Technology fell apart, leaving LaPine out in the cold.

In 1988 Inamori reorganized Kyocera, setting up US, European, and Asian regional offices. Kyocera bought Elco (electronic connectors, US, 1989) and AVX (largest US multilayer ceramic capacitor maker, 1990).

Kyocera worked with Canon in 1992 to develop and produce video and electronic optical equipment. The company also worked with the Carl Zeiss Foundation (Germany) to make cameras and lenses.

Kyocera signed a deal with Cirrus Logic in 1994 to provide technology and integrated chips for a cordless phone project. Also that year the company announced that it would introduce a teleconferencing system for use with personal computers connected via a LAN. In 1995 Kyocera introduced the personal handy phone system (PHS) in Japan. The PHS is similar to cellular systems (but not as mobile) and costs about 1/5 as much to use.

The company's Guangdong-based optical instrument joint venture began operations in 1996, making cameras and lenses for the Chinese market.

Chairman: Kazuo Inamori
VC: Kinju Anjo
President: Kensuke Itoh
Senior Managing Director: Sadao Yamamoto
Senior Managing Director; CEO, AVX Corporation:
Marshall D. Butler
Managing Director and CFO: Yuji Itoh
Managing Director; President, Kyocera International,
Inc.: Rodney N. Lanthorne
VP Human Resources (US): George Woodworth
Auditors: Coopers & Lybrand L.L.P.

WHERE

HQ: 5-22 Kitainoue-cho, Higashino, Yamashina-ku,
Kyoto, 607, Japan
Phone: +81-75-592-3851
Fax: +81-75-501-2194
US HQ: Kyocera International, Inc., 8611 Balboa Ave.,
San Diego, CA 92123-1580
US Phone: 619-576-2600
US Fax: 619-492-1456

Kyocera has operations worldwide.

	1996 Sales		1996 Operating Income	
	$ mil.	% of total	$ mil.	% of total
Japan	3,322	56	1,017	77
US	1,109	18	150	11
Southeast Asia	768	13	67	5
Europe	718	12	71	5
Other	48	1	17	2
Adjustments	—	—	(4)	—
Total	**5,965**	**100**	**1,318**	**100**

WHAT

	1996 Sales		1996 Operating Income	
	$ mil.	% of total	$ mil.	% of total
Ceramic products	3,906	65	852	65
Electronic products	1,648	28	425	32
Optical instruments	411	7	41	3
Total	**5,965**	**100**	**1,318**	**100**

Ceramic Products
Cellular products
Electronic components
Fine ceramic parts
Semiconductor parts

Electronic Products
Cordless phones
Karaoke CD equipment
Laser printers
Videoconferencing units

Optical Instruments
Compact cameras
Still video cameras

Selected Subsidiaries and Affiliates
AVX Corporation (US)
Elco Corporation (US)
Kyocera Fineceramics SA
(France)
Taito Corporation (20%)

KEY COMPETITORS

ACX Technologies	Matsushita	Samsung
AST	Minolta	Sandvik
AT&T Corp.	Mitsubishi	Sanyo
Canon	Motorola	Seagate
Compaq	NEC	Seiko
DEC	Nokia	Sharp
Dell	NTT	Sony
Eastman Kodak	Oki	Sumitomo
Fuji Photo	Philips	Thomson SA
Hewlett-Packard	Pioneer	Toshiba
Hitachi	Pitney Bowes	Xerox
IBM	Polaroid	
	Ricoh	

HOW MUCH

NYSE symbol: KYO FYE: March 31	Annual Growth	1987	1988	1989	1990	1991	1992	1993	1994	1995	1996
Sales ($ mil.)	13.6%	1,894	2,416	2,554	2,661	3,280	3,416	3,758	4,177	5,741	5,965
Net income ($ mil.)	22.8%	120	182	224	214	229	204	209	359	500	761
Income as % of sales	—	6.3%	7.5%	8.8%	8.0%	7.0%	6.0%	5.5%	8.6%	8.7%	12.8%
Earnings per share ($)	20.1%	1.56	2.16	2.62	2.31	2.44	2.18	2.23	3.84	5.32	8.09
Stock price – high ($)[1]	—	55.39	93.90	91.04	92.71	126.00	103.00	74.50	122.88	154.25	184.00
Stock price – low ($)[1]	—	37.68	45.64	67.87	66.80	74.00	60.00	51.00	64.50	104.00	123.00
Stock price – close ($)[1]	13.4%	48.02	80.59	79.40	75.00	84.75	63.50	70.13	105.50	149.00	149.25
P/E – high	—	36	44	35	40	52	47	33	32	29	23
P/E – low	—	24	21	26	29	30	28	23	17	20	15
Dividends per share ($)	12.9%	0.36	0.51	0.55	0.50	0.53	0.64	0.78	0.78	0.85	1.07
Book value per share ($)	10.8%	26.11	31.46	32.19	32.08	38.29	41.27	47.96	56.60	71.61	65.78
Employees	(3.0%)	17,300	12,397	—	—	14,031	14,473	10,682	13,470	13,250	13,162

[1] Stock prices are for the prior calendar year.

1996 YEAR-END

Debt ratio: 9.1%
Return on equity: 13.3%
Cash (mil.): $2,775
Current ratio: 3.03
Long-term debt (mil.): $550
No. of shares (mil.): 93
Dividends
  Yield: 0.7%
  Payout: 13.2%
Market value (mil.): $13,951

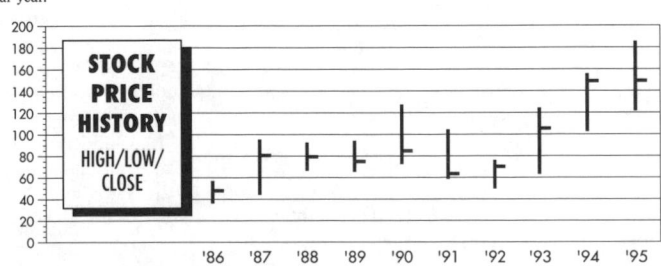

STOCK PRICE HISTORY
HIGH/LOW/CLOSE

LEXMARK INTERNATIONAL

OVERVIEW

Lexmark International Group isn't afraid to fight with its mother. The Greenwich, Connecticut-based company makes computer printers and related supplies. Its laser printers and dot-matrix printers are primarily used by businesses while its ink-jet printers are designed for the personal computing market. Lexmark also makes typewriters.

While its former parent, computer heavyweight IBM, still owns 6% of Lexmark, the expiration of a noncompetition pact allows Big Blue to go head to head with its offspring in the laser printer market. Lexmark is more concerned with market leader Hewlett-Packard,

however, and has lowered the prices and improved the quality of its printers to gain ground on the mighty HP.

Lexmark's advantage lies in the fact that unlike other major printer makers, it produces all of its own printer components. Doing so gives Lexmark a lower manufacturing cost and allows it to sell its printers at lower prices. This also means Lexmark benefits from the sales of replacement supplies for its printers, such as toner cartridges.

The Clayton, Dubilier & Rice investment group owns about 1/3 of Lexmark.

WHEN

During the late 1980s, as a horde of Davids was taking aim at Goliath IBM, the computer giant began to downsize to become more competitive. IBM cut its workforce by 100,000 between 1986 and 1992 and also began to sell off its peripheral businesses, including Lexmark ("Lex" as in "lexicon" and "mark" as in "marks on paper").

In early 1991 IBM sold Lexmark to a group led by investment firm Clayton, Dubilier & Rice for $1.5 billion. Martin Dubilier, who helped found the firm in 1978, had learned the LBO ropes as a turnaround expert for Jerome Kohlberg, founder of investment firm KKR, during the 1970s. Clayton, Dubilier's LBO of Lexmark was financed primarily with bank loans, leaving the new company over $1 billion in debt. Marvin Mann, an IBM VP with 32 years at the company, became Lexmark's chairman.

Mann took a cue from his former bosses and did some downsizing of his own at Lexmark, cutting employees from 5,000 to 3,000, primarily by reducing middle management. Mann also put more of the responsibility for running the company in the hands of his line managers, allowing them to come up with their own goals and business plans rather than take strategy from above.

While many employees were given their walking papers, Mann put up a "Help Wanted" sign in his sales department. The reason? He was creating one from scratch. As an IBM subsidiary, Lexmark had relied on Big Blue's general sales force. By the end of 1991, staff had risen to 4,000.

As another sign of Lexmark's break from IBM, where it had sometimes gotten lost in the shuffle, Mann reorganized the company into 4 operating groups and made each group's finan-

cial information available to everyone in the company.

Lexmark began to flex its muscles as an independent in 1992, when it introduced 2 laser printers for Macintosh and the first products (IBM PC-compatible keyboards) bearing its own name rather than the IBM logo. That year Lexmark's first color printer debuted and the company began producing notebook computers for OEMs. Lexmark's operating profits doubled in 1992, its 2nd year of operation, and using the additional cash flow, the company reduced its debt ahead of schedule, to about $750 million.

In 1993 the company, through Lexmark Australia, made its first acquisition when it bought Australian printer maker Gestetner Lasers, increasing Lexmark's presence in Pacific Rim markets. The company continued to add new printer products during 1993, including a series of network laser printers. It signed a licensing agreement that year with Interlink Electronics for joystick technology. Lexmark began removing the IBM logo from its products in 1994 and kicked off retail distribution of its own Lexmark-branded ink-jet printers and low-end laser printers.

Fujitsu began marketing Lexmark printers in Japan in 1995. That year Lexmark expanded its network printer management software, MarkVision, adding versions for Macintosh, UNIX, and Windows operating systems. Also in 1995 the company went public, introduced its first color laser printer (the Optra C).

In 1996 Lexmark planned to open a manufacturing plant in Mexico to help it keep up with rising demand. That year the company phased out its keyboard line.

WHO

Chairman, President, and CEO: Marvin L. Mann,
   age 62, $1,629,000 pay
EVP Operations: Paul J. Curlander, age 43,
   $882,992 pay
VP; President, Lexmark Europe: John A. Stanley,
   age 58, $844,264 pay
VP and General Manager: Donald C. Shropshire Jr.,
   age 57, $555,962 pay
VP and CFO: Gary E. Morin, age 46
VP and General Counsel: John Matuszeski, age 59
VP Human Resources: Kathleen E. Affeldt, age 47
Treasurer: John S. Garnett, age 50
Auditors: Coopers & Lybrand L.L.P.

WHERE

HQ: Lexmark International Group, Inc., 740 New Circle
   Rd. NW, Lexington, KY 40511
Phone: 606-232-2000
Fax: 606-232-2403
Web site: http://www.lexmark.com

Lexmark sells its products in over 100 countries.

	1995 Sales
	% of total
US	60
Other countries	40
Total	**100**

Manufacturing Facilities
Boulder, CO
Lexington, KY
Orleans, France
Rosyth, Scotland
Sydney, Australia

WHAT

	1995 Sales	
	$ mil.	% of total
Printers & printer supplies	1,478	69
Other office imaging products	501	23
Keyboards & other	179	8
Total	**2,158**	**100**

Selected Products

Printers
Network printers
   MarkNet
   MarkVision
   Optra series
Personal printers
   Color Jetprinter series
   Dot-matrix and Plus dot-matrix series

Printer Supplies
Ink-jet cartridges
Laser cartridges

Other Products
Coated paper
Memory chips
Typewriter ribbons and supplies
Wheelwriter typewriters

KEY COMPETITORS

Apple Computer	Nu-kote Holding
Canon	Oce-van der Grinten
Compaq	Oki Electric
Gateway 2000	Olivetti
GENICOM	QMS
Hewlett-Packard	Seiko
IBM	Smith Corona
Matsushita	Sony
Nashua	Tandy Corporation
NEC	Xerox

HOW MUCH

NYSE symbol: LXK FYE: December 31	Annual Growth	1986	1987	1988	1989	1990[1]	1991[2]	1992	1993	1994	1995
Sales ($ mil.)	1.5%	—	—	—	—	2,000	1,273	1,764	1,676	1,852	2,158
Net income ($ mil.)	—	—	—	—	—	—	(118)	(57)	(9)	(29)	32
Income as % of sales	—	—	—	—	—	—	—	—	—	—	1.5%
Earnings per share ($)	—	—	—	—	—	—	—	—	—	(0.49)	0.43
Stock price – high ($)	—	—	—	—	—	—	—	—	—	—	22.38
Stock price – low ($)	—	—	—	—	—	—	—	—	—	—	15.50
Stock price – close ($)	—	—	—	—	—	—	—	—	—	—	18.25
P/E – high	—	—	—	—	—	—	—	—	—	—	52
P/E – low	—	—	—	—	—	—	—	—	—	—	36
Dividends per share ($)	—	—	—	—	—	—	—	—	—	—	0.00
Book value per share ($)	29.0%	—	—	—	—	—	—	—	—	—	5.56
Employees	8.4%	—	—	—	—	5,000	4,000	4,000	4,000	5,000	7,500

[1] As part of IBM. [2] 9-month fiscal year.

1995 YEAR-END

Debt ratio: 33.3%
Return on equity: 9.5%
Cash (mil.): $151
Current ratio: 1.47
Long-term debt (mil.): $175
No. of shares (mil.): 70
Dividends
   Yield: —
   Payout: —
Market value (mil.): $1,281

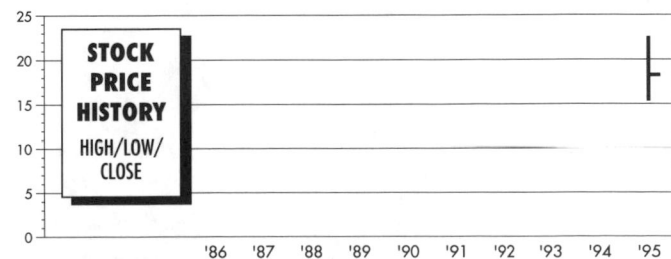

STOCK PRICE HISTORY
HIGH/LOW/CLOSE

LOGITECH INTERNATIONAL SA

OVERVIEW

Logitech is one mighty mouse maker. Based in Switzerland, Logitech International is the world's #1 producer (ahead of software powerhouse Microsoft) of computer mice and other input products, including touch pads and trackballs. The company also makes 3-D controllers, game pads, and joysticks for playing PC games and surfing the World Wide Web, as well as color scanners and digital video cameras. Logitech markets its products under its own name and also sells them to personal computer OEMs such as Apple, Compaq, Hewlett-Packard, IBM, and NEC.

Though Logitech just recently entered the joystick market, it has already attracted a hearty following for its WingMan and

WingMan Extreme joysticks. The company's Cordless MouseMan 96 can operate a computer from up to 6 feet away. New products for other markets include the PageScan Color sheetfed scanner, the TrackMan Marble pointing device, and the VideoMan color digital video camera.

To avoid high labor and overhead costs, Logitech has begun manufacturing its products in China. The rise in PC sales (which now outsell televisions in the US) has bolstered Logitech's revenues.

Founders Pierluigi Zappacosta (the company's president) and Daniel Borel (its chairman and CEO) each own more than 5% of Logitech.

WHEN

Pierluigi Zappacosta (from Italy) and Daniel Borel (from Switzerland) met while studying computer engineering at Stanford University in the 1970s. The 2 wanted to transfer the entrepreneurial feeling of California's Silicon Valley back to Europe and start a high-tech company. However, there was little venture capital to be found in Europe during that time, and no European bank would lend the amount of money the two 27-year-olds needed.

In 1981 Zappacosta and Borel obtained the rights to sell a Swiss-designed mouse in the US, and they started Logitech in California and Switzerland with Swiss backers.

Zappacosta and Borel intended Logitech to be a software company in the tradition of Microsoft. However, this vision changed quickly as the importance of the mouse and other peripherals became apparent. The company improved the manufacturing process and soon developed a cordless mouse.

Computer maker Hewlett-Packard was Logitech's first big OEM customer. Others soon followed, including computer maker Olivetti and telecommunications giant AT&T. Logitech made its first foray into the US retail market in 1986 but had only limited success. Its brand name was not recognized, and the company had a small advertising budget. The firm decided to bypass the regular retail route and offer its mouse at a deep discount through specialty computer magazines. Consumers, followed by dealers and distributors, soon took notice.

Within a short time Logitech began supplying mice to leading computer makers Apple and IBM. Apple came first, but its demands were hard to meet and the company initially

did not make any profits. With its new manufacturing facility on line in Taiwan and with an increased capacity, Logitech reached an agreement to supply IBM in 1988. That year the company went public in Switzerland because of its ties to the financial community in that country and is still traded only in Switzerland.

Logitech formed a joint venture in China in 1991 that included funding from the China National Aerotechnology Import and Export Corporation and the International Resources Technology Association of Hong Kong. That year the company purchased 51% of Simi Valley, California-based Gazelle Graphics Systems, which develops single-board digitizers and cordless digitizing pens. It also developed the first trackball for Apple's PowerBook laptop computers in 1991. Two years later the company purchased the rest of Gazelle.

Logitech announced a new design for its stationary desktop mouse, the TrackMan, for the Macintosh in 1993. The next year the company, along with cable television company TCI, invested in Seattle-based Virtual I/O, the developer of a 3-D personal video and computer display headset. Logitech eliminated 500 positions worldwide in 1994. At that time Zappacosta said that the company would begin to focus less on mice and more on input devices such as cameras and scanners.

With stiff competition and pricing pressures eroding its profits, Logitech struggled through 1995. That year it closed factories in Ireland and the US and consolidated its plants in China and Taiwan, taking a $20 million restructuring charge. With that charge behind it, Logitech returned to profitability in 1996.

WHO

Chairman and CEO: Daniel Borel
President: Pierluigi Zappacosta
VP and General Manager, American Area: Patrick Brubeck
VP Business Development and General Counsel: Margaret Wynne
VP Worldwide Human Resources: Marianne Jackson
VP Special Projects: Rory Dooley
VP, Imaging Division: Dominique Pitteloud
VP and CFO: Bary Zwarenstein
Auditors: Price Waterhouse SA

WHERE

HQ: Moulin-du-Choc, CH-1122, Romanel-sur-Morges, Switzerland
Phone: +41-21-863-51-11
Fax: +41-21-863-53-11
US HQ: Logitech Inc., 6505 Kaiser Dr., Fremont, CA 94555
US Phone: 510-795-8500
US Fax: 510-792-8901
Web site: http://www.logitech.com/

Logitech has manufacturing facilities in China and Taiwan.

	1996 Sales	
	$ mil.	% of total
Far East	199	38
North America	169	32
Europe	156	30
Adjustments	(169)	—
Total	**355**	**100**

WHAT

Selected Products

Joysticks
WingMan
WingMan Extreme

Mice
Cordless MouseMan
First Mouse
MouseMan 96
MouseMan Sensa
MouseMan Serial Bus

Trackballs
TrackMan Live!
TrackMan Marble
TrackMan Vista
TrackMan Voyager

Video Cameras and Scanners
PageScan Color
ScanMan 256
ScanMan Color
VideoMan digital camera

KEY COMPETITORS

Acer	Key Tronic
Alps Electronics	Microsoft
Ameriquest	Microtek International
Apple Computer	Mitsubishi
Brother Industries	Mitsumi
CalComp	Olivetti
Creative Technology	OMRON
Diamond Flower Electric	Packard Bell
Instrument	Plustek USA
Fujitsu	Scitex
Gateway 2000	Tech Data
IBM	

HOW MUCH

Principal exchange: Zurich FYE: March 31	Annual Growth	1987	1988	1989	1990	1991	1992	1993	1994	1995	1996
Sales ($ mil.)	36.9%	21	50	83	117	162	237	293	326	303	355
Net income ($ mil.)	30.5%	1	6	8	9	13	15	6	19	(17)	11
Income as % of sales	—	4.4%	11.2%	9.0%	7.9%	8.2%	6.4%	2.1%	5.8%	—	3.0%
Earnings per share ($)	2.0%	—	4.69	5.90	6.60	10.05	10.75	3.89	10.44	(8.80)	5.50
Stock price – high ($)[1]	—	—	—	—	59.18	68.26	67.08	80.17	148.15	178.86	114.31
Stock price – low ($)[1]	—	—	—	—	45.72	47.08	42.39	61.40	75.42	60.38	61.36
Stock price – close ($)[1]	13.4%	—	—	—	47.02	49.04	66.35	78.46	138.72	65.73	100.03
P/E – high	—	—	—	—	9	7	6	21	14	—	21
P/E – low	—	—	—	—	7	5	4	16	7	—	11
Dividends per share ($)	(0.7%)	—	—	—	1.04	1.57	1.77	1.64	1.62	0.00	1.00
Book value per share ($)	3.4%	—	—	—	35.22	41.94	46.95	34.19	50.59	37.07	43.10
Employees	18.0%	—	—	731	980	1,470	1,828	2,399	2,402	2,489	2,322

[1] Stock prices are for the prior calendar year.

1996 YEAR-END

Debt ratio: 37.0%
Return on equity: 16.0%
Cash (mil.): $29
Current ratio: 1.43
Long-term debt (mil.): $5
No. of shares (mil.): 2
Dividends
  Yield: 1.0%
  Payout: 18.2%
Market value (mil.): $163

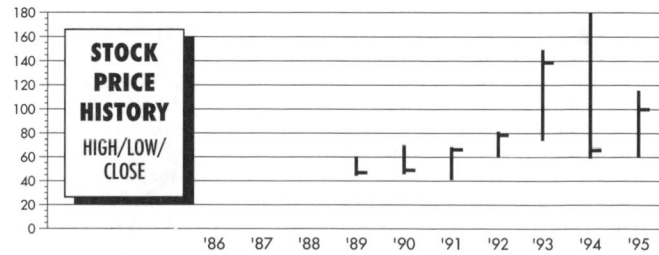

STOCK PRICE HISTORY
HIGH/LOW/CLOSE

LOTUS DEVELOPMENT CORPORATION

OVERVIEW

IBM is hoping that it won't become a lotus eater (dazed and confused) following its acquisition of Cambridge, Massachusetts-based Lotus, the pioneer spreadsheet developer (Lotus 1-2-3) and the world's #6 software vendor. Far from the earlier fear that the Internet, World Wide Web, and intranets would threaten the market share of its Notes software, Lotus is marketing Notes — with its ability to handle complex workflows — as an integral part of the intranet environment, enhancing the ability of people to collaborate across a network. Despite its high cost (about $3,000 per worker), Notes provides advantages that its upstart competitors, such as Netscape, cannot match — better security and the capacity to synchronize multiple copies of databases.

Michael Zisman and Jeffrey Papows, former SVPs of Lotus communications business group, jointly lead Lotus. Zisman's job is to persuade clients that Notes is the best intranet option on the Web.

Lotus is focusing on upgrading its core products, including developing Notes (currently the industry standard) for a variety of operating systems.

WHEN

When IBM introduced the PC in 1981, Mitch Kapor quickly saw the light and designed an electronic spreadsheet for it. He called it Lotus 1-2-3 (after the Hindu symbol of enlightenment). Soon the former Transcendental Meditation teacher's Cambridge-based company had blossomed. One year after the 1982 founding, sales were $53 million; by 1985, sales were $226 million.

Kapor brought to Lotus the values of his late- 1960s Yale undergraduate days: consensus, jeans, and T-shirts were staples. Unwieldy growth, however, prompted the structure-shy Kapor to boost star marketer Jim Manzi to president in 1984. Manzi transformed Lotus into a market-driven company and installed a management team drawn from mainframe vendor ranks after Kapor left in 1986.

When the highly touted Symphony spreadsheet and Jazz (for Macintosh PCs) drew muted responses, Manzi focused on 1-2-3. Lotus acquired a number of small 1-2-3 enhancement developers and launched several foreign language versions. In 1985 and 1986 Manzi began broadening beyond 1-2-3, buying Dataspeed (stock quote services); ISYS (developer of the OneSource CD/ROM); and Graphics Communications (graphics software).

With competing spreadsheets attacking market share, Lotus undertook the arduous 3-year development of 1-2-3 Release 3.0 (featuring 3-D graphics). Both it and a version for less powerful PCs, Release 2.2, appeared in 1989.

That year the company bought 15% of Sybase, a database management software developer, and in 1990 agreed to acquire networking software leader Novell, but the deal collapsed. Lotus did acquire Samna and its word processing software (Ami Pro) that year. Also in 1990 the company introduced Notes, which allows individuals to communicate, collaborate on projects, and coordinate their activities on a shared database.

Lotus underestimated the success of Microsoft's graphics interface software Windows 3.0, and its delay in developing a version of 1-2-3 for Windows (released in mid-1991) allowed Microsoft to cash in with its Excel spreadsheet. The company spent $32 million to buy cc:Mail and introduced 1-2-3 for Macintosh. The following year it sold its stake in Sybase for a $50 million profit. Lotus launched Improv for Windows (spreadsheet for business analysis), Notes Release 3.0, and 1-2-3 for OS/2; sold majority control of OneSource; bought Approach Software (database management software) for $15 million; and won additional claims from Borland in a 1990 suit for copyright infringement of 1-2-3, all in 1993. The next year it acquired Soft*Switch (e-mail switches) and Edge Research (applications development tools).

IBM, whose own software offerings have consistently lost out to Microsoft's, was especially attracted by Lotus's Notes workgroup software — one area not yet dominated by Bill Gates's company. Big Blue acquired Lotus for $3.5 billion in 1995. Lotus then focused on developing enhanced versions of its primary products for Microsoft's Windows 95 operating system. But by early 1996 all of Lotus's top executives were gone, including CEO Jim Manzi, who resigned after a disagreement with IBM chairman Louis Gerstner about IBM's software strategy. That year Lotus began building Lotus Notes Release 4 servers, which supports Lotus's InterNotes Web Navigator, providing direct access to the World Wide Web from inside Notes. Also in 1996 Lotus released Domino, an Internet version of Notes.

WHO

EVP and CEO, Office of the President: Michael D. Zisman
EVP and COO, Office of the President: Jeffrey Papows
SVP Worldwide Sales: Deborah Besemer
SVP Finance and CFO: J. Philip Dellasega
SVP Interenterprise Computing Group: Larry Moore
SVP Communications Product Development: Eileen Rudden
VP Lotus Marketing and Integration: Harold Bailey
General Counsel: Neal Goldman
Auditors: Price Waterhouse LLP

WHERE

HQ: 55 Cambridge Pkwy., Cambridge, MA 02142
Phone: 617-577-8500
Fax: 617-693-1299
Web site: http://www.lotus.com

WHAT

Communications Products
cc:Mail
cc:Mail Mobile for HP 100LX
Domino
InterNotes Web Navigator
Messaging Switch
Notes Release 4 and companion products (Document Imaging, In-bound Fax Gateway, and Optical Character Recognition)

Consulting and Educational Services
Lotus Consulting
Lotus Education
Lotus Institute
Technical Support

Database Management Products
Approach 96 for Windows 95

Integrated Desktop Products
SmartSuite for OS/2
SmartSuite for Windows

Personal Information Management Products
Organizer for Macintosh
Organizer for Windows

Presentation Graphics
Freelance Graphics for DOS
Freelance Graphics for OS/2
Freelance Graphics for Windows
SmartPics for Windows

Spreadsheet Products
1-2-3 for DOS
1-2-3 for Macintosh
1-2-3 for OS/2
1-2-3 for UNIX
1-2-3 for Windows
Improv for Windows

Word Processing
Ami Pro for OS/2
Ami Pro for Windows

KEY COMPETITORS

Adobe
Apple Computer
Borland
Centura Software
Computer Associates
ExcelleNet
Interleaf
Microsoft
Netscape
Network Computing Devices
Novell
Progress Software
Quark
SAS
Software AG
Software Publishing
Spyglass
Symantec
Wall Data

HOW MUCH

Subsidiary FYE: December 31	Annual Growth	1986	1987	1988	1989	1990	1991	1992	1993	1994	1995
Sales ($ mil.)	16.9%	283	396	469	556	685	829	900	981	971	1,150
Employees	17.6%	1,400	2,100	2,500	2,800	3,500	4,300	4,400	4,738	5,522	6,000

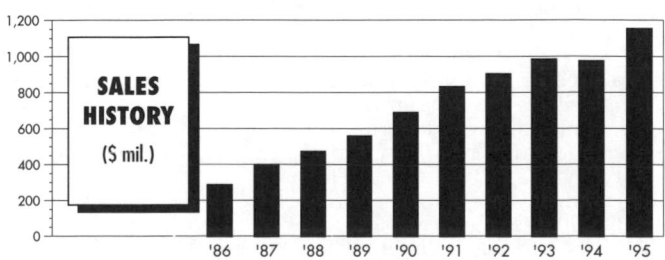

Lotus.

SALES HISTORY ($ mil.)

LSI LOGIC CORPORATION

OVERVIEW

LSI Logic styles itself the "system-on-a-chip" company. The Milpitas, California-based firm designs and makes application specific integrated circuits (ASICs). Its principal customers are OEMs in the computer, communications, and consumer products industries. Sony accounts for about 12% of the company's revenues.

LSI's systems-on-a-chip products integrate the functions of an electronic system onto a single chip, combining microprocessor engines, logic blocks (including industry-standard functions, interfaces, and protocols), and memory with the customer's own proprietary logic blocks. LSI spends about 10% of its sales on R&D and continues to introduce faster and more powerful chips. Recent innovations include the first single-chip satellite receiver for digital TV, a 4-port Ethernet controller, and the "Internet-on-a-chip," which provides the electronic brains of inexpensive Internet-access computers. The company's G10 process puts up to 49 million transistors on a chip, 5 times more than the industry's previous technology allowed.

At the core of LSI's custom-chip design process is CoreWare, the company's extensive library of industry-standard building blocks (including microprocessors, networking controllers, and video compression engines). CoreWare saves customers time and money as they develop ASICs.

Founder and CEO Wilf Corrigan owns 5% of the company's stock.

WHEN

Wilf Corrigan, an engineer and former CEO of Fairchild Camera & Instrument, founded LSI in Santa Clara, California, in 1981. Its name is the acronym for large scale integration, indicating a chip that has up to 100,000 transistors. The semiconductor industry is extremely competitive, so, to give his enterprise a fighting chance, Corrigan chose a niche market — customized chips, or ASICs. In 1982 the company formed a subsidiary, LSI Logic Europe, in the UK. LSI went public in 1983 with a record-setting $152 million IPO. That year it began building a wafer facility in Santa Clara and an assembly and test plant in nearby Fremont. Also in 1983 LSI introduced regional design centers — where customers could design their chips using company equipment and facilities — in Massachusetts and the UK. The company established affiliates in Japan and Germany in 1984.

By 1985 LSI had won big military and aerospace customers and, with sales that had raced to $140 million, was the US's leading ASIC manufacturer. That year it formed a joint venture, Nihon Semiconductor, with Kawasaki Steel Corp. During the 2nd half of the 1980s the company opened units in Canada and Korea.

By the end of the 1980s LSI was foundering, the result of its heavy investment in manufacturing facilities (the company had geared up for a boom in the chip market that had yet to materialize). When sales to the aerospace industry slumped, LSI began closing factories and cutting payrolls. The company completed its 10,000th design and opened its 39th regional design center in 1990. In 1992 it took a $102 million restructuring charge and posted its 3rd (and biggest) loss in 4 years.

A trimmer, smarter LSI emerged in 1993 — the year the company introduced the 0.5-micron CMOS ASIC chip, which Corrigan compared to "several high-performance workstations on a single chip." It also announced the first reprogrammable ATM chip and a family of Ethernet hub and router products called CASCADE.

In addition to technological breakthroughs, partnerships have been key to the firm's reemergence as a microchip market leader. TV maker Zenith and LSI began codevelopment of a chip for cable television decoder boxes in 1993. That year LSI penned 10-year technology-sharing agreements with electronic design automation leaders Synopsys and Cadence. Also that year Sony debuted its PlayStation video game system, which is based on CoreWare design.

The company started construction on a $4 billion manufacturing facility in Gresham, Oregon, in 1995. That year LSI passed the $1 billion revenue mark. Also in 1995 it bought out Kawasaki to become the sole owner of Nihon Semiconductor (now called LSI Logic Japan Semiconductor).

In 1996 LSI announced development agreements with Argonaut Software (3-D graphics accelerator products) and High Level Design Systems (development of deep submicron IC design methodologies). LSI chips were chosen that year for the set-top boxes of the EchoStar Communications DISH Network direct broadcast satellite system.

WHO

Chairman and CEO: Wilfred J. Corrigan, age 58, $1,330,769 pay
EVP LSI Logic Products: Brian L. Halla, age 49, $619,231 pay
EVP Worldwide Operations: Cyril F. Hannon, age 57, $541,923 pay
SVP Finance and CFO: Albert A. Pimentel, age 40, $451,923 pay
SVP; General Manager, International Marketing and Sales: Moshe N. Gavrielov, age 41, $391,923 pay
SVP; General Manager, North American Marketing and Sales: W. Richard Marz, age 52
VP, General Counsel, and Secretary: David E. Sanders, age 48
VP Investor Relations, Communications, and Geographic Markets Support: Bruce L. Entin, age 45
VP Human Resources: Lewis C. Wallbridge, age 52
Auditors: Price Waterhouse LLP

WHERE

HQ: 1551 McCarthy Blvd., Milpitas, CA 95035
Phone: 408-433-8000
Fax: 408-434-7715
Web site: http://www.lsilogic.com

LSI Logic has manufacturing facilities in the Far East and the US.

	1995 Sales		1995 Operating Income	
	$ mil.	% of total	$ mil.	% of total
US	1,005	40	117	37
Pacific Rim	720	29	150	47
Japan	533	21	24	7
Europe	204	8	22	7
Canada	61	2	7	2
Adjustments	(1,255)	—	(1)	—
Total	**1,268**	**100**	**319**	**100**

WHAT

	1995 Sales
	% of total
Component products	94
Design & services	6
Total	**100**

Selected Coreware Components
ATM (asynchronous transfer mode) standard for networking
Ethernet standard for networking
MiniRISC family of MIPS-based RISC central processing units
MPEG compression/decompression standard for digital video
PCI bus interfaces for the computer market
SONET standard for networking

KEY COMPETITORS

C-Cube Microsystems
Exar
Fujitsu
IBM
IMP
Integrated Circuit Systems
Motorola
NEC
Oki Electric
SGS-Thomson
Siemens
Texas Instruments
Toshiba
VLSI Technology
Xilinx

HOW MUCH

NYSE symbol: LSI FYE: December 31	Annual Growth	1986	1987	1988	1989	1990	1991	1992	1993	1994	1995
Sales ($ mil.)	14.1%	—	—	—	—	656	698	618	719	902	1,268
Net income ($ mil.)	—	—	—	—	—	(34)	8	(110)	54	109	238
Income as % of sales	—	—	—	—	—	—	1.2%	—	7.5%	12.1%	18.8%
Earnings per share ($)	—	—	—	—	—	(0.80)	0.19	(2.48)	1.05	1.85	1.75
Stock price – high ($)	—	—	—	—	—	13.00	12.50	11.13	19.25	45.38	62.50
Stock price – low ($)	—	—	—	—	—	5.13	5.38	4.88	10.25	15.50	18.25
Stock price – close ($)	39.3%	—	—	—	—	6.25	8.13	10.75	15.88	40.38	32.75
P/E – high	—	—	—	—	—	—	66	—	18	25	36
P/E – low	—	—	—	—	—	—	28	—	10	8	10
Dividends per share ($)	—	—	—	—	—	0.00	0.00	0.00	0.00	0.00	0.00
Book value per share ($)	7.5%	—	—	—	—	6.55	6.70	4.35	5.88	9.54	9.41
Employees	(2.5%)	—	—	—	—	4,401	4,000	3,450	3,370	3,750	3,870

1995 YEAR-END

Debt ratio: 18.7%
Return on equity: 27.0%
Cash (mil.): $686
Current ratio: 2.87
Long-term debt (mil.): $222
No. of shares (mil.): 129
Dividends
  Yield: —
  Payout: —
Market value (mil.): $4,235

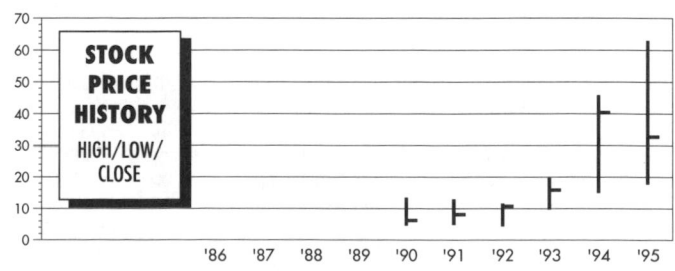

STOCK PRICE HISTORY
HIGH/LOW/CLOSE

'86 '87 '88 '89 '90 '91 '92 '93 '94 '95

COMPAGNIE DES MACHINES BULL SA

OVERVIEW

The Bull is charging again. Louveciennes, France-based Compagnie des Machines Bull is one of the top 5 manufacturers of large-scale computer systems in Europe and one of the top 4 system and network management businesses in the US. It makes mainframe computers and networking and storage systems and provides data center management and systems integration services.

After bleeding in the pen since the late 1980s, a drastically reduced workforce and elevated sales of products such as the Escala PowerPC-based multiprocessor system have helped Bull reenter the ring of profitability. Bull controls about 20% of the US's PC-market matador Packard Bell.

The French government owns 36% of the company. In addition, Bull's primary corporate investors include Japanese computing and telecommunications concern NEC, Europe's 2nd largest telecommunications services provider France Telecom, and US semiconductor producer and wireless communications innovator Motorola, each of which owns 17% of Bull.

By teaming with these and other partners, Bull plans to introduce new high-tech products such as multimedia computers and video-on-demand systems and strengthen its presence around the globe.

WHEN

Bull is named for Norwegian engineer Frederik Bull, who in 1919 invented a punch-card machine. Georges Vieillard, a French bank employee, bought the patents for Bull's machine in 1931. Vieillard, who wanted to develop a better adding machine, persuaded the owners of a punch-card supplier to finance his venture, and Compagnie des Machines Bull was incorporated in Paris in 1933.

Bull started competing with IBM in 1935, after unveiling a tabulator capable of printing up to 150 lines a minute. Bull went on to confound its American rival by pioneering the use of germanium diodes (instead of electron tubes) in its first mainframe computer, the Gamma 3 (introduced in 1952). But the battle of one-upmanship proved to be costly. Bull defaulted on a $4 million loan payment in 1964 and, faced with financial ruin, jumped at the chance when General Electric (US) offered to buy a 50% stake (later increased to 66%). The company (renamed Bull-GE) continued to lose money until 1969. It became Honeywell Bull in 1970, when GE sold its computer businesses to Honeywell.

In the meantime the French government had formed Compagnie Internationale pour l'Informatique (CII) to ensure the survival of the French computer industry (1966). In 1975 CII merged with Honeywell Bull to form CII-Honeywell Bull (CII-HB). Initially, Honeywell owned a 47% minority stake in the company, but in 1982 it accepted a gradual buyout offer from the French government. CII-HB then merged with 3 other French computer companies (Transac, Sems, and R2E) to form Groupe Bull in 1983.

Bull was shaky in the early 1980s, posting losses from 1981 through 1984, but it got back on track (for a while) under the leadership of Jacques Stern. In 1987 Bull entered a US-based 3-way mainframe computer partnership (Honeywell Bull Inc.) with Honeywell and NEC. Originally owning 42.5% of the venture, Bull upped its share to 72.2% (reducing Honeywell's share to 12.8%) and renamed the venture Bull HN Information Systems. In 1989 Bull bought Zenith's ZDS, a leading US laptop computer and PC maker.

Bull in 1991 acquired the rest of Bull HN, buying out Honeywell and NEC. The next year the EC approved a state injection of $1.3 billion into debt-laden Bull. In 1993 Bull bought a 19.9% stake in Packard Bell, then the #7 maker of PCs and the #1 supplier for the home market, and teamed it with Zenith Data Systems to jointly develop desktop PCs.

Jean-Marie Descarpentries was chosen by the government as the new CEO in 1993 (the company's 3rd CEO in as many years) and reduced Bull's Paris offices from 25 to 5 and reorganized the sprawling conglomerate.

Zenith Data Systems, the group's principal source of losses since 1989, reported a recovery in 1993. It beat out 22 rival companies to win a 3-year, $724 million contract to supply 300,000 PCs to the US government.

To improve Packard Bell's cash flow in 1996, Machines Bull and NEC provided a $650 million infusion — partly in cash and partly through Packard Bell's acquisition of subsidiary Zenith Data Systems. In exchange for the infusion the 2 companies received preferred stock that is redeemable and convertible into common Packard Bell shares.

WHO

Chairman and CEO: Jean-Marie Descarpentries
Director Finance and Administration: Camille de
  Montalivet
**President and CEO, Bull HN Information Systems
  (US):** Donald P. Zereski
CFO, Bull HN Information Systems (US): Robert Kelly
**VP Human Resources, Bull HN Information Systems
  (US):** Cecile Wright
Auditors: Bernard Montagne

WHERE

HQ: 68, route de Versailles, 78430 Louveciennes, France
Phone: +33-1-39-66-60-60
Fax: +33-1-46-96-90-92
US HQ: Bull HN Information Systems, Inc.,
  300 Concord Rd., Billerica, MA 01821
US Phone: 508-294-6000
US Fax: 508-294-4908
Web site: http://www.bull.com

	1995 Sales % of total
France	38
Other Europe	38
North America	20
Other regions	4
Total	**100**

WHAT

	1995 Sales % of total
Personal computers	23
Enterprise systems	20
Customer service	19
Systems integration & facilities management	18
Industry & emerging technologies	12
Open systems	8
Total	**100**

Selected Products and Services
Application development
Data warehousing systems
Disaster recovery
Enterprise servers
Network and system management
Open client/server networks
Personal computers
Systems integration

KEY COMPETITORS

Apple Computer	LG Group
Canon	Motorola
Cap Gemini	NCR
Compaq	NEC
Data General	Oki Electric
DEC	Samsung
Dell	Siemens
Gateway 2000	Sony
Hewlett-Packard	Sun Microsystems
Hitachi	Tandem
Hyundai	Texas Instruments
IBM	Toshiba
ICL	Unisys
Intel	

HOW MUCH

OTC symbol: CODMY FYE: December 31	Annual Growth	1986	1987	1988	1989	1990	1991	1992	1993	1994	1995
Sales ($ mil.)	7.7%	2,795	3,519	5,206	5,665	6,794	6,458	5,465	4,781	5,610	5,440
Net income ($ mil.)	4.1%	43	42	50	(46)	(1,334)	(637)	(855)	(858)	(403)	62
Income as % of sales	—	1.5%	1.2%	1.0%	—	—	—	—	—	—	1.1%
Earnings per share ($)	(30.4%)	12.56	11.29	13.20	(10.39)	(277.01)	(4.25)	(43.09)	(16.08)	(7.60)	0.48
Stock price – high ($)	—	596.78	528.69	227.76	216.43	176.82	100.39	86.00	52.46	64.51	40.20
Stock price – low ($)	—	314.10	148.64	115.53	129.86	60.90	48.26	30.05	31.31	29.38	2.47
Stock price – close ($)	(35.9%)	321.95	154.28	143.59	135.05	62.87	48.26	38.02	40.62	36.91	5.91
P/E – high	—	48	47	17	—	—	—	—	—	—	84
P/E – low	—	25	13	9	—	—	—	—	—	—	5
Dividends per share ($)	—	0.00	0.00	0.00	0.00	0.00	0.00	0.00	0.00	0.00	0.00
Book value per share ($)	(36.0%)	168.04	225.78	209.61	207.77	(43.22)	(11.20)	(24.98)	1.18	2.07	3.04
Employees	(1.2%)	26,804	26,337	45,557	43,617	44,476	39,878	35,175	31,735	27,902	24,000

1995 YEAR-END

Debt ratio: 63.9%
Return on equity: 23.7%
Cash (mil.): $477
Current ratio: 1.08
Long-term debt (mil.): $262
No. of shares (mil.): 130
Dividends
  Yield: —
  Payout: —
Market value (mil.): $767

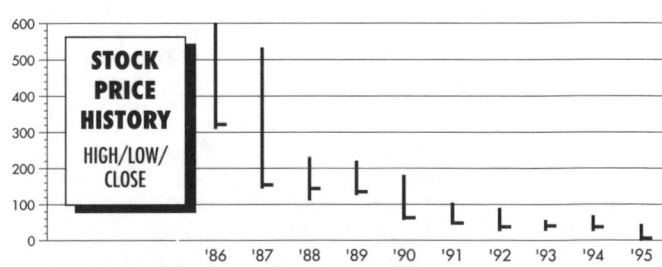

STOCK PRICE HISTORY HIGH/LOW/CLOSE

MERISEL, INC.

Merisel could be spelled Meri-sell. The El Segundo, California-based company is one of the world's largest wholesale distributors of computer hardware and software. Merisel stocks more than 25,000 products from more than 850 hardware manufacturers and software publishers. Hewlett-Packard, Microsoft, and Compaq brands account for about 16%, 14%, and 11%, respectively, of the company's sales. In addition to distributing to more than 55,000 resellers, the company supplies more than 150 franchisees of its ComputerLand retail business and more than 550 affiliates of its Datago aggregator service (which packages computer systems from large manufacturers).

With value-added services the key to an edge in the fiercely competitive distribution business, Merisel continues to develop its range of customer services, including financing, marketing, product training, and technical support programs. Heavy competition and unfruitful acquisitions have caused losses at Merisel, and it is selling assets; its Australian subsidiary was the first to go, followed by the European and Latin American operations. Talks with possible suitors failed to find a merger match for the company itself.

David Wagman owns about 7% of Merisel and Robert Leff owns about 5%; the 2 co-founded the company and both are retired.

Robert Leff, a software developer for Citibank's Transaction Technologies subsidiary, got started in the distribution business in 1980 when he bought $1,700 worth of game and entertainment software and began selling it in his spare time. He and co-worker David Wagman quit their jobs and founded Softsel Computer Products to sell software full-time.

Working out of Leff's house and using a list of authorized Apple Computer distributors as a prospect sheet, the pair had sales of $350,000 in their first year. By the end of 1981, sales had jumped to $7 million. Softsel expanded its operations, moving into Europe in 1983 to become one of the first computer distributors to expand overseas. That year Softsel introduced Softeach, a series of training seminars for computer product purchasers.

In 1985 the company moved into mass-market software. However, the computer industry slumped, and Softsel had to take back millions of dollars in returns on unsold products, leading to the company's first loss. To lower its costs the company sold its software publishing division and its unprofitable German subsidiary, saving about $10 million.

Softsel rebounded and in 1988 it went public. It also promoted Mike Pickett, who as COO had helped guide the company back into the black, to CEO. By 1989 the company had sales of more than $600 million, but it had set its sights on bigger targets. Late that year it announced plans to acquire hardware distributor Microamerica for about $80 million, making it the largest computer products distributor in the world, with sales of more than $1 billion. The acquisition included Microamerica's warehouses in Europe and Latin America.

In 1990, when the deal was completed, the companies combined their names to create Merisel. Merging the 2 corporate cultures proved problematic. California-based Softsel had a laid-back atmosphere (Leff's taste ran to Hawaiian shirts), while Boston-based Microamerica was more button-down in dress and atmosphere. As the company struggled to meld decentralized Microamerica with the centralized operations of Softsel, its costs soared while profits plummeted.

By the next year, however, profits began to recover. That year Merisel made another, more successful push into mass-market channels as the computer industry shifted away from traditional computer retailers toward big chains and warehouse stores.

Merisel became what it calls a Master Distributor, both a distributor and a reseller, when it acquired the franchise and distribution operations of ComputerLand in 1994. The deal called for the company to provide about $1 billion a year in merchandise to ComputerLand franchisees and Datago resellers.

The next year Leff and Wagman both retired from the company. Pickett, the other co-chairman, became chairman. He resigned the following year after the company posted an unexpected loss for 1995. Dwight Steffensen, a former president and COO of pharmaceuticals distributor Bergen Brunswig and a Merisel board member since 1990, was named chairman and CEO. In 1996 the company added several suppliers, including Allegro New Media (business software), FTP Software, (Internet and Web server software), Random House (entertainment software), and Zitel (storage subsystems).

WHO

Chairman and CEO: Dwight A. Steffensen, age 52
President and COO: Ronald A. Rittenmeyer, age 48
EVP Dealer, Datago, and Consumer Product Sales:
Martin D. Wolf, age 37, $241,875 pay
**SVP Worldwide Information Services and Chief
Information Officer:** Paul M. Lemerise, age 50,
$248,100 pay
SVP European Operations: Susan J. Miller-Smith,
age 43, $241,664 pay
SVP and CFO: James E. Ilson
SVP Worldwide Operations: John F. Thompson, age 51
SVP Canadian Operations: Thomas P. Reeves, age 34
**SVP Franchise and Aggregation Operations and
Asia/Pacific Operations:** Verilyn Smith, age 43
President, Merisel Latin America: Cliff Dyer
Managing Director, Merisel UK: Derek Anderson
General Counsel: Kelly Martin
Director Human Resources: Carol Baker
Auditors: Deloitte & Touche LLP

WHERE

HQ: 200 Continental Blvd., El Segundo, CA 90245-0948
Phone: 310-615-3080
Fax: 310-615-1270
Web site: http://www.merisel.com

	1995 Sales	
	$ mil.	% of total
US	4,040	67
Europe	1,051	17
Canada	573	10
Other regions	337	6
Adjustments	(44)	—
Total	**5,957**	**100**

WHAT

	1995 Sales
	% of total
Hardware & accessories	75
Software	25
Total	**100**

Hardware	Selected Suppliers
Computer systems,	3Com
including servers	Apple
Connectivity products,	AST
including modems	Compaq
Monitors	DEC
Networking products	Hayes
Plug-in boards	Hewlett-Packard
Printers	IBM
Storage devices, including	Intel
disk drives	Microsoft
Software	NEC
Desktop publishing and	Novell
graphics	Sony
Operating systems	Sun Microsystems
Spreadsheets	Texas Instruments
Word processing	Toshiba
	U.S. Robotics

KEY COMPETITORS

Ameriquest
CHS Electronics
Computer 2000
Graybar Electric
Inacom
Ingram Micro
Intelligent Electronics
Marshall Industries
MicroAge
Tech Data
Wyle Electronics

HOW MUCH

Nasdaq symbol: MSEL FYE: December 31	Annual Growth	1986	1987	1988	1989	1990	1991	1992	1993	1994	1995
Sales ($ mil.)	44.2%	—	319	465	629	1,192	1,585	2,239	3,086	5,019	5,957
Net income ($ mil.)	—	—	7	8	10	1	11	20	30	12	(84)
Income as % of sales	—	—	2.1%	1.7%	1.6%	0.1%	0.7%	0.9%	1.0%	0.2%	—
Earnings per share ($)	—	—	0.62	0.70	0.81	0.03	0.43	0.67	1.00	0.38	(2.82)
Stock price – high ($)	—	—	—	6.25	7.88	6.38	9.38	14.88	18.50	22.50	8.50
Stock price – low ($)	—	—	—	5.13	5.50	1.63	1.75	6.63	9.75	6.25	3.88
Stock price – close ($)	(4.4%)	—	—	6.00	6.13	2.38	9.13	10.13	18.38	8.00	4.38
P/E – high	—	—	—	9	10		22	22	19	59	—
P/E – low	—	—	—	7	7	54	4	10	10	16	—
Dividends per share ($)	—	—	—	0.00	0.00	0.00	0.00	0.00	0.00	0.00	0.00
Book value per share ($)	7.6%	—	—	3.10	4.08	4.71	5.13	6.79	7.56	7.95	5.17
Employees	28.4%	—	442	538	629	1,282	1,450	1,939	2,502	3,072	3,263

1995 YEAR-END

Debt ratio: 71.2%
Return on equity: —
Cash (mil.): $1
Current ratio: 1.37
Long-term debt (mil.): $321
No. of shares (mil.): 30
Dividends
  Yield: —
  Payout: —
Market value (mil.): $130

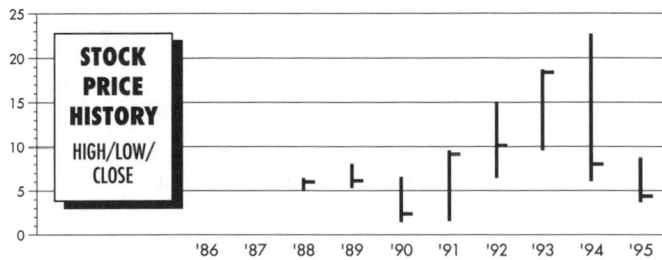

STOCK PRICE HISTORY
HIGH/LOW/CLOSE

MICRO WAREHOUSE, INC.

OVERVIEW

Micro Warehouse lets you create the computer system of your dreams without ever leaving your home. The Norwalk, Connecticut-based company sells more than 20,000 computer products, including Apple Macintoshes and PCs, peripherals, software, and accessories, primarily through its full-color monthly catalogs "MacWAREHOUSE" and "MicroWAREHOUSE." The company also sells through specialty catalogs such as "Data CommWAREHOUSE" (data communication and networking) and through outbound telemarketing to businesses. Micro Warehouse buys most of its products in large volumes directly from manufacturers (such as Apple, Toshiba, Hewlett-Packard, and Microsoft), allowing the company to set prices at 30-60% below retail. Chairman and CEO Peter Godfrey owns about 8% of the firm's stock.

Micro Warehouse's success can be partly attributed to its strong customer service, which includes a toll-free technical support line and

next-day delivery. The firm also employs more than 1,000 sales and support staff on call 24 hours a day, 7 days a week.

Nearly 1/4 of the company's sales are generated by its international markets. Micro Warehouse has been expanding its global presence via acquisition, recently purchasing a catalog retailer in the UK. The company also expanded its data communications and networking product lines by acquiring Santa Clara, California-based Inmac Corp. In addition, it has begun marketing its products on the World Wide Web, offering product descriptions and pictures of its best-selling items. Prospective buyers can download demonstration versions of selected software.

Micro Warehouse continues to diversify the selection of products in its catalogs, adding more brand-name hardware and peripherals. Previously, software accounted for most of the company's sales, but nearly 70% of revenues now come from hardware.

WHEN

Peter Godfrey got together with Robert Bartner in 1974 to run Fiona Press, a publisher of adult magazines (sold to Paragon Publishing in 1992). In 1985 they (along with Felix Dennis) founded "MacUser" magazine, which they sold to Ziff-Davis the following year. They founded Micro Warehouse in 1987 and launched "MacWAREHOUSE" to sell products to Macintosh computer users.

The company targeted consumers to build its mailing list, taking names of subscribers from technical magazines and names of registered users from its suppliers. In 1989 the firm added the "MicroWAREHOUSE" catalog to sell to PC users.

International expansion became key to the company's growth in the early 1990s. It established full-service, direct marketing operations in the UK in 1991. The next year Micro Warehouse went public and set up operations in France and Germany.

The company was distributing 30 million catalogs to almost 2 million customers by 1993. It expanded that year, introducing 4 specialty catalogs: "Data CommWarehouse," "Micro SuppliesWarehouse," "Paper design Warehouse," and "CD-ROM Warehouse." Micro Warehouse also went down under, entering Australia for the first time. Also in 1993 Micro Warehouse invested almost $5 million in its telemarketing and computer centers around

the globe, expanding its facilities and increasing employee training.

By 1994 the company had entered some European countries, Japan, Canada, and Mexico. It added 2 more specialty catalogs, "Micro SystemsWAREHOUSE" and "Home ComputerWAREHOUSE," that year.

In 1994 and 1995 Micro Warehouse focused on balancing its Macintosh- and PC-related sales and expanding internationally. It acquired Technomatic (UK) in May 1995 and Mac Direct and Castle Computing (both in Australia) 2 months later. The company also acquired Toronto-based Mac Store.

Micro Warehouse incorporated "CD-ROM WAREHOUSE" into "MacWAREHOUSE" and "MicroWAREHOUSE" and launched "Mac SystemsWAREHOUSE" in 1995. The company also discontinued certain specialty catalogs (including "Paper designWarehouse") and received authorization from Apple to market its full line of Macintosh computers.

Micro Warehouse acquired Inmac Corporation, an international catalog retailer of computer-networking products, in 1996. Inmac had operations in Canada, France, Germany, the Netherlands, Sweden, and the UK. Micro Warehouse closed a number of Inmac facilities, including its Santa Clara corporate office, and eliminated about 270 Inmac employee positions.

Chairman, President, and CEO: Peter Godfrey, age 50, $1,500,000 pay
EVP and COO: Melvin Seiler, age 53, $972,000 pay
VP Finance, CFO, and Treasurer: Steven Purcell, age 45, $772,750 pay
VP, General Counsel, and Secretary: Bruce L. Lev, age 52, $376,539 pay
VP Worldwide Marketing: Adam Shaffer, age 30, $273,154 pay
VP Mac Marketing: Deborah Cooper, age 33
VP International Business Development: Powell Crowley, age 50
VP Worldwide Advertising: Stephen F. England, age 42
VP Human Resources: Michael J. Kurtz, age 47
Auditors: KPMG Peat Marwick LLP

WHERE

HQ: 535 Connecticut Ave., Norwalk, CT 06854
Phone: 203-899-4000
Fax: 203-899-4203
Web site: http://www.warehouse.com

Micro Warehouse distributes its catalogs in 15 countries worldwide.

WHAT

Selected Brand Names
Adobe
Apple
Hayes
Hewlett-Packard
IBM
Iomega
Macromedia
Microsoft
Quark
Toshiba

Selected Catalogs
Data CommWAREHOUSE
Mac SystemsWAREHOUSE
MacWAREHOUSE
Micro SystemsWAREHOUSE
MicroWAREHOUSE

KEY COMPETITORS

Best Buy
CDW Computer Centers
Circuit City
Compaq
CompuCom
CompUSA
DAMARK International
Dell
Egghead
ELEK-TEK

Gateway 2000
Global Directmail
Inacom
Intelligent Electronics
MicroAge
NeoStar
Office Depot
Packard Bell
Tandy Corporation

HOW MUCH

Nasdaq symbol: MWHS FYE: December 31	Annual Growth	1986	1987	1988	1989	1990	1991	1992	1993	1994	1995
Sales ($ mil.)	70.6%	—	—	—	53	124	164	270	450	776	1,308
Net income ($ mil.)	159.0%	—	—	—	—	—	1	0	15	28	45
Income as % of sales	—	—	—	—	—	—	0.9%	0.1%	3.3%	3.6%	3.4%
Earnings per share ($)	61.0%	—	—	—	—	—	0.22	0.39	0.64	1.01	1.48
Stock price – high ($)	—	—	—	—	—	—	—	13.25	21.38	36.25	56.88
Stock price – low ($)	—	—	—	—	—	—	—	10.81	9.63	17.75	26.75
Stock price – close ($)	52.3%	—	—	—	—	—	—	12.25	20.81	35.00	43.25
P/E – high	—	—	—	—	—	—	—	34	33	36	38
P/E – low	—	—	—	—	—	—	—	28	15	18	18
Dividends per share ($)	—	—	—	—	—	—	—	0.00	0.00	0.00	0.00
Book value per share ($)	60.7%	—	—	—	—	—	—	2.65	3.91	8.11	10.99
Employees	62.6%	—	—	—	—	—	—	721	1,496	2,300	3,100

1995 YEAR-END

Debt ratio: 3.9%
Return on equity: 15.6%
Cash (mil.): $92
Current ratio: 4.56
Long-term debt (mil.): $0
No. of shares (mil.): 31
Dividends
 Yield: —
 Payout: —
Market value (mil.): $1,338

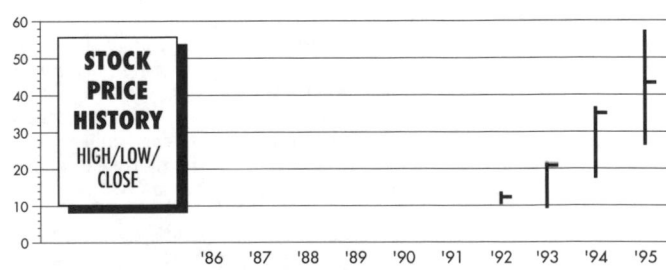

STOCK PRICE HISTORY HIGH/LOW/CLOSE

MICROAGE, INC.

OVERVIEW

MicroAge solves corporate computer conundrums. The Tempe, Arizona-based systems integrator and master reseller provides microcomputer systems, networking and telecommunications equipment, and software through its MicroAge Network of resellers and affiliates. It distributes more than 20,000 products from 500 vendors, including Apple, Compaq, DEC, Hewlett-Packard, IBM, Microsoft, and Novell. Among the services provided by MicroAge to end users are installation and technical support. Customers include corporations, institutions, and government agencies.

Through association with the MicroAge Network, resellers (including 12 owned by the company) can take advantage of MicroAge's buying power and distribution facilities. The company also provides a variety of services to resellers, including technical support, financing, shipping, and back-order management. It continues to recruit established resellers for its network.

The company took a giant step beyond the technology marketplace in early 1996 when it launched MicroAge Service Solutions to offer telephone services to business. Services include management of inbound and outbound telephone calls, 800 numbers, direct mail follow-up, simple order taking, technical support, and customer database updates. The service will operate from the company's established telephone service center in Tempe.

Cofounders Jeffrey McKeever (chairman and CEO) and Alan Hald (VC) together own more than 6% of MicroAge's stock.

WHEN

Soon after attending a convention of the World Future Society in 1976, Hald was flipping through a *Creative Computing* magazine when he came across a small ad for kit computers. He knew in a microsecond that PCs would be big sellers. At that time Hald was working at First National (later First Interstate) Bank of Arizona with McKeever and eventually convinced him that they should start a PC retail business. Each borrowed $15,000 and together opened the Byte Shop in Tempe. The company's first customer paid $691 for a build-it-yourself computer kit. By 1979 their company, called MicroAge, was the largest computer retailer-wholesaler in the US.

The company started a franchise operation in 1981 — at the same time that a recession hit. It was heading into Chapter 11 reorganization by the end of the year and filed for bankruptcy in 1982. During this difficult period an Olivetti subsidiary bought into MicroAge for $5 million, giving it a much-needed cash infusion (Olivetti sold its shares in 1990).

Olivetti's cash coupled with the rising interest in PC's (thanks to IMB's entry into the market), helped MicroAge bounce back. The company began selling Apple computers in its 157 US stores in 1985. That year IBM banned new MicroAge franchises from selling IBM products, greatly limiting the company's planned franchise expansion. To compensate, MicroAge went after independent dealers that were already authorized to sell IBM products in order to convert them to MicroAge franchises. The company went public in 1987.

In 1991 McKeever added the title of chairman to his duties as CEO, and Hald, who had been chairman, became VC. MicroAge announced a joint venture with Vertex S.A., one of the largest computer companies in Mexico, in 1992. That same year sales broke the $1 billion mark 2 days before the fiscal year-end.

In 1994 the company, along with other major resellers, was burdened with large inventories and the cost of competing for new affiliates; this led to a serious drop in its stock price. During the shortage of memory products early that year, MicroAge purchased memory products manufacturer Kelly Micro Systems.

In 1995 the company signed a master reseller agreement with computer maker Hewlett-Packard and won a 3-year, $100 million supply agreement from photographic equipment maker Eastman Kodak. That same year it formed the MicroAge Data Services division to provide computer industry information to manufacturers, sellers, and end users of high-tech products. Poor results in late 1995 forced MicroAge to sell Kelly Micro Systems and cut its payroll by 10%. Restructuring charges and financing costs hurt the company's net income that year.

In 1996 it added software developer Borland to its supplier list and signed a joint sales and marketing agreement with Canon Sales Co., the Japanese manufacturer's office equipment unit.

WHO

Chairman and CEO: Jeffrey D. McKeever, age 53,
$1,068,815 pay
VC and Secretary: Alan P. Hald, age 49, $869,331 pay
**SVP, CFO, and Treasurer; President, Headquarter
Services, MCCI:** James R. Daniel, age 48,
$320,905 pay
SVP Sales: Warren T. Mills, age 47
**VP Logistics; President, MicroAge Logistics Services,
MCCI:** John H. Andrews, age 39, $166,667 pay
**VP Services Marketing; President, MicroAge Data
Services:** Robert O'Malley, age 50
**VP Development; President, MicroAge Channel
Services, MCCI:** Wesley D. Richards, age 45
VP Legal; VP, MicroAge International, Inc.: Jeffrey A. H.
Frankel, age 42
VP Human Resources and Administration: Alan R.
Lyons
President, MicroAge Infosystems Services, Inc.:
Christopher J. Koziol, age 35
**President, MicroSource Technologies, Inc.; Chief
Technical Officer, MCCI:** Harman D. Cadis, age 38
President, MicroAge Solutions, Inc.: Jeffrey M.
Swanson, age 41
Auditors: Price Waterhouse LLP

WHERE

HQ: 2400 S. MicroAge Way, Tempe, AZ 85282-1896
Phone: 602-804-2000
Fax: 602-966-7339
Web site: http://www.microage.net

WHAT

Selected Products
Microcomputer systems
Networking equipment
Software
Telecommunications equipment
Workstations

Selected Services
Distribution services
Electronic ordering and product inquiry services
Financial services
Information services
Technical services

Selected Suppliers

3Com	IBM
Adobe	Intel
Apple	Microsoft
AT&T	NEC
Banyan	Novell
Borland	Samsung
Compaq	Toshiba
DEC	US Robotics
Hewlett-Packard	Xerox

KEY COMPETITORS

AmeriData	Hewlett-Packard
AMS	IBM
ASCII	Inacom
Avnet	Ingram Micro
CompuCom	Intelligent Electronics
Computer Sciences	Merisel
Control Data	Micro Warehouse
Dell	Price Waterhouse
Entex	Tandy Corporation
Gateway 2000	Tech Data
Government Technology	Unisys
Services	Vanstar

HOW MUCH

Nasdaq symbol: MICA FYE: October 31	Annual Growth	1986	1987	1988	1989	1990	1991	1992	1993	1994	1995
Sales ($ mil.)	37.7%	165	201	252	364	613	787	1,017	1,510	2,221	2,941
Net income ($ mil.)	—	(3)	3	4	4	7	3	5	11	16	0
Income as % of sales	—	—	1.4%	1.6%	1.2%	1.1%	0.4%	0.5%	0.7%	0.7%	0.0%
Earnings per share ($)	—	(0.77)	0.47	0.62	0.64	0.97	0.50	0.59	1.15	1.22	0.02
Stock price – high ($)	—	—	7.67	6.09	6.84	12.34	10.17	10.51	26.60	32.50	15.00
Stock price – low ($)	—	—	2.33	2.83	4.09	4.17	3.84	3.84	5.34	9.25	7.25
Stock price – close ($)	13.7%	—	2.92	4.42	4.84	6.34	7.34	5.34	25.51	11.75	8.13
P/E – high	—	—	16	10	11	13	20	18	23	27	750
P/E – low	—	—	5	5	6	4	8	7	5	8	363
Dividends per share ($)	—	—	0.00	0.00	0.00	0.00	0.00	0.00	0.00	0.00	0.00
Book value per share ($)	17.7%	—	3.19	3.70	4.19	4.73	5.29	6.56	9.13	11.76	11.74
Employees	29.5%	—	—	—	442	540	663	741	992	1,729	2,088

1995 YEAR-END

Debt ratio: 4.0%
Return on equity: 0.1%
Cash (mil.): $14
Current ratio: 1.27
Long-term debt (mil.): $4
No. of shares (mil.): 14
Dividends
  Yield: —
  Payout: —
Market value (mil.): $117

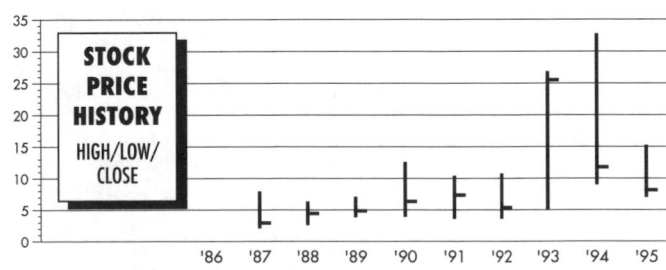

STOCK
PRICE
HISTORY
HIGH/LOW/
CLOSE

MICRON TECHNOLOGY, INC.

OVERVIEW

Steve Appleton, Micron's former and present CEO, has folded expansion plans until his chips grow in value. The Boise, Idaho-based company makes semiconductor memory products (dynamic random access memory [DRAM] and static random access memory [SRAM]), which accounted for 77% of its 1995 sales. Micron also designs and makes a broad line of PCs, including the Millennia (for high-end business users), the Powerserver (business network server), and the ZEOS Meridian (notebook), and manufactures printed circuit board assemblies.

In January 1996, amid drops in chip demand and Micron stock, a simmering internal power struggle triggered by longtime investor (and director) Allen Noble resulted in Appleton getting the boot. But within a few days, when other executives threatened to revolt, potato

potentate J. R. Simplot (who owns 6% of the firm) wooed Appleton back, and Noble resigned from the board.

Micron has made its name as a low-cost chip provider by perfecting a more cost-effective manufacturing process. By necessity, it moves more slowly than its competitors to adopt next generation chips. However, soft computer sales caused the slump in demand and price. Appleton mothballed Micron's expansion plans and stopped construction of the company's $2.5 billion chip-making facility in Utah. Micron is continuing development of 4-megabyte and 16-megabyte SRAMs. In addition, the company has begun working on a wider range of products, including a radio frequency identification chip that could be used to track luggage and parcels and a flat panel display.

WHEN

Micron Technology was founded in 1978 by twins Joe and Ward Parkinson and Doug Pitman in the basement of a dentist's office. They started out as a semiconductor design consulting firm, but their dream was to make their own chips. So in 1980 they enticed local agribusiness magnates J. R. Simplot, Allen Noble, and 2 others to invest in the company. They built their own production facility, and in 1982 sold their first 64K DRAM products.

In 1984 Micron went public and introduced its 256K DRAM. The following year Japanese chip makers began dumping chips in the US to capture market share, causing massive losses in the US DRAM industry. Micron filed an antidumping petition with the International Trade Commission, and in 1986 the US and Japan agreed to a semiconductor trade pact under which Japanese producers would sell chips at fair market value. The pact came just in time to keep Micron from folding.

By 1988 a shortage of memory chips had developed and Micron cashed in. That year the company began to diversify its product line with SRAM chips and other add-in memory products for PCs. In 1989 Micron signed an agreement with electronics manufacturer Sanyo for exclusive rights to distribute Micron's products in Japan. That year Ward Parkinson resigned as vice chairman.

In the early 1990s Korean manufacturers tried to conquer the US market using the Japanese strategy. But Micron, by then familiar

with these tactics, won a 1992 ruling that Korean chip producers were illegally dumping chips.

That same year Micron quit research consortium Sematech after disagreeing with its emphasis on chip-making equipment over the chip-making process and expanded into PC manufacturing, in part to soften the impact of the dramatic cycles in the memory chip industry. The following year the firm began raking it in when the demand for chips took off. In 1995 the company paid $405 million for Minneapolis-based PC maker ZEOS. That company was merged with two other Micron units to form Micron Electronics, Inc. Despite thin margins in the PC market, Micron hoped that access to its own chips and connections with Intel for microprocessors would give it an edge over other PC makers. In 1995 Micron Computer launched a new line of 100-megahertz Pentium-based PCs.

CEO and cofounder Joe Parkinson left in 1995 after a clash with Simplot. The COO and the CFO also left. Steve Appleton, who had started as a production operator in 1983, became the new CEO at age 34. With demand for chips booming, Micron, like other chip makers, began adding production capacity. But computer makers and other customers began using 16-megabyte memory chips instead of 4-megabyte chips and overall demand slackened late that year. Micron had earnings of $593 million in 1996 on sales of nearly $3.7 billion.

WHO

Chairman, President, and CEO: Steven R. Appleton, age 35, $1,689,540 pay
VC and Chief Technology Officer: Tyler A. Lowrey, age 42, $1,695,274 pay
VP Finance, CFO, and Secretary: Wilbur G. Stover Jr., age 42, $810,230 pay
VP Legal Affairs and General Counsel: W. Bryan Farney, age 35
VP, Quality: Edward J. Heitzeberg, age 49, $813,047 pay
VP Administration: Nancy M. Self, age 41
VP Corporate Affairs: Kipp A. Bedard, age 36
Director Human Resources: Susan Metzger
Auditors: Coopers & Lybrand L.L.P.

WHERE

HQ: 8000 S. Federal Way, Boise, ID 83707-0006
Phone: 208-368-4000
Fax: 208-368-4435
Web site: http://www.micron.com

	1995 Sales	
	$ mil.	% of total
US	2,199	74
Other countries	754	26
Total	**2,953**	**100**

WHAT

	1995 Sales	
	$ mil.	% of total
SRAMs & DRAMs	2,287	77
PC systems	429	15
Other	237	8
Total	**2,953**	**100**

Selected Products

Memory Semiconductors
DRAMs (dynamic random access memory semiconductor, in 4-megabyte and 16-megabyte configurations)
SRAMs (static random access memory semiconductors — about 5 times faster than DRAMs)

Personal Computers
Micron Home MPC
Micron Millennia
Micron PowerServer (business network server)
Micron PowerStation
ZEOS Meridian (portable notebook)
ZEOS Pantera

Selected Subsidiaries
Micron Communications, Inc.
Micron Construction, Inc.
Micron Display Technology, Inc.
Micron Electronics, Inc.
Micron Europe Limited
Micron Overseas Trading, Inc.
Micron Quantum Devices, Inc.
Micron Semiconductor Asia Pacific Inc.
Micron Semiconductor (Deutschland) GmbH

KEY COMPETITORS

Alliance Semiconductor	IBM	Olivetti
Apple Computer	Integrated Device Technology	Packard Bell
Compaq	Integrated Silicon Solution	Paradigm Technology
Cypress Semiconductor	LG Group	Philips
Dell	Machines Bull	Samsung
DEC	Matsushita	Sharp
Fujitsu	Mitsubishi	Siemens
Gateway 2000	Motorola	Tandy Corporation
Hewlett-Packard	NEC	Texas Instruments
Hitachi	Oki	Toshiba
Hyundai		

HOW MUCH

NYSE symbol: MU FYE: August 31	Annual Growth	1986	1987	1988	1989	1990	1991	1992	1993	1994	1995
Sales ($ mil.)	57.7%	49	91	301	446	333	425	506	828	1,629	2,953
Net income ($ mil.)	—	(34)	(23)	98	106	5	5	7	104	401	844
Income as % of sales	—	—	—	32.6%	23.7%	1.5%	1.2%	1.3%	12.6%	24.6%	28.6%
Earnings per share ($)	—	(0.35)	(0.19)	0.65	0.57	0.03	0.03	0.03	0.51	1.90	3.90
Stock price – high ($)	—	3.42	3.22	5.20	5.16	3.28	3.83	4.47	12.72	22.94	94.75
Stock price – low ($)	—	0.67	0.80	2.41	1.84	1.34	1.91	2.58	3.63	8.92	21.25
Stock price – close ($)	52.1%	0.91	2.95	3.16	1.95	2.03	2.83	3.78	9.30	22.06	39.63
P/E – high	—	—	—	8	9	109	128	149	25	12	24
P/E – low	—	—	—	4	3	45	64	86	7	5	5
Dividends per share ($)	—	0.00	0.00	0.00	0.00	0.00	0.00	0.01	0.01	0.06	0.15
Book value per share ($)	32.9%	0.71	0.56	1.75	2.60	2.62	2.65	2.67	3.19	5.15	9.19
Employees	25.1%	1,080	1,479	2,230	3,061	3,606	4,095	4,300	4,900	5,450	8,080

1995 YEAR-END

Debt ratio: 7.6%
Return on equity: 57.3%
Cash (mil.): $556
Current ratio: 2.11
Long-term debt (mil.): $129
No. of shares (mil.): 206
Dividends
  Yield: 0.4%
  Payout: 3.8%
Market value (mil.): $8,179

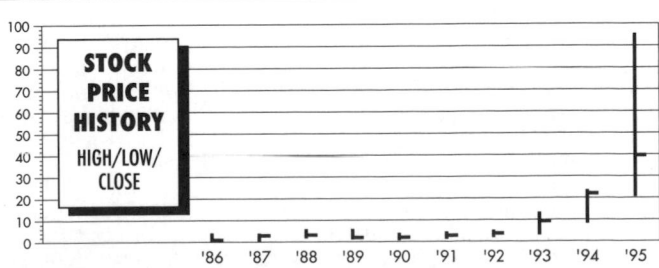

STOCK PRICE HISTORY HIGH/LOW/CLOSE

'86 '87 '88 '89 '90 '91 '92 '93 '94 '95

MICROSOFT CORPORATION

OVERVIEW

With Microsoft's operating systems controlling an estimated 80% of the world's PCs, the Redmond, Washington-based company is the 800-pound gorilla of computerdom. However, Microsoft CEO Bill Gates can't thump his chest for long because an even bigger beast is now roaming the jungle — the Internet. Microsoft is the world's #1 independent software company, and the release (and marketing hype) of Windows 95, its upgraded operating system, increased its dominance. Its software products include networking systems (Windows NT), database products (Access), spreadsheets (Excel), word processing (Word), and personal finance (Money), as well as games and reference products.

Gates is trying to make sure the burgeoning popularity of the Internet doesn't make a monkey out of Microsoft. To stave off competition from rivals such as Web browser maker Netscape and Internet software language developer Sun Microsystems, it has developed an Internet-intensive strategy. It has realigned its online service, the Microsoft Network, to allow Internet access and some free information. It has signed deals with other major online services, including America Online, CompuServe, and AT&T's WorldNet, to make Microsoft's Internet Explorer their primary web browser. And it is releasing software that allows users to develop pages easily for the Web.

But the Internet is not the only battleground for Microsoft and Netscape. At least as important is the intranet, which creates a private network using Internet software to connect people within a corporate structure. In this area, Microsoft has an edge over Netscape, since Microsoft products are already on so many corporate computers.

Microsoft is also expanding into other media. It has put together a cable TV and online news service with television network NBC and has a deal with movie studio DreamWorks SKG to develop interactive games.

Gates, the richest person in the US, owns about 24% of Microsoft. Cofounder Paul Allen owns about 10% of the company's stock and still serves on its board.

WHEN

Microsoft (originally Micro-soft) was founded in 1975 after 19-year-old William Gates dropped out of Harvard and teamed with high school friend Paul Allen to sell a version of the programming language BASIC. While Gates was at Harvard, the pair had written the language for the Altair, the first commercial microcomputer (sold by Albuquerque-based MITS, a maker of electronic kits). Gates and Allen moved to Albuquerque and set up Microsoft in a hotel room across the street to produce the program.

Microsoft moved to Gates's native Seattle area in 1979 and developed software that enabled others to write programs for PCs. Microsoft's big break came in 1980, when it was chosen by IBM, over Gary Kildall's Digital Research, to write the operating system (software that controls a computer's basic functions) for IBM's new PC. Faced with a complex task and a tight deadline, Microsoft bought the rights to QDOS (short for "quick and dirty operating system") for $50,000 from Seattle programmer Tim Paterson and renamed it the Microsoft Disk Operating System (MS-DOS).

The popularity of IBM's PC made MS-DOS an instant monopoly because other PC makers wanted to be compatible with IBM. It became the standard PC operating system in the 1980s.

Microsoft went on to develop software for IBM, Apple, and other computers. Allen fell ill with Hodgkin's disease and left Microsoft in 1983.

In the mid-1980s Microsoft introduced Windows. The company went public in 1986. In 1992 Microsoft acquired Fox Software (database management system) and released Access, a database program.

In 1993 Microsoft introduced Windows NT, a client/server product. Microsoft agreed in 1994 to modify its marketing practices in order to settle an antitrust investigation by the US Department of Justice. When the settlement moved to judicial review, it was ruled unconducive to the public good and set aside. In a victory for Microsoft, a federal appeals court in mid-1995 reinstated the 1994 antitrust settlement between Microsoft and the Justice Department. Also in 1995, after several delays, the company released Windows 95, the latest version of its operating system.

Microsoft and Tandem, a leading maker of fault-tolerant computers for networks, agreed in 1996 to make their server technology compatible. The Justice Department came calling again in 1996, launching a new investigation of Microsoft following complaints by Netscape and other Internet competitors. In fiscal 1996 Microsoft's sales rose to $8,671 million and its net income jumped to $2,195 million.

WHO

Chairman and CEO: William H. Gates III, age 39, $415,580 pay
EVP and COO: Robert J. Herbold, age 53, $740,133 pay
EVP Worldwide Sales and Support: Steven A. Ballmer, age 39, $411,974 pay
SVP; President, Microsoft Europe: Bernard P. Vergnes, age 50, $526,445 pay
SVP Law and Corporate Affairs and Secretary: William H. Neukom, age 53
SVP Consumer Systems: Craig J. Mundie, age 46
SVP Personal Systems: Brad A. Silverberg
SVP Business Systems: James E. Allchin, age 44
SVP Worldwide OEM Sales: Joachim Kempin, age 53
Group VP Applications and Content Group: Nathan P. Myhrvold, age 36
Group VP Applications and Content Group: Frank M. Pete Higgins, age 37
VP Research: Richard Rashid
VP Finance and CFO: Michael W. Brown, age 49
VP Human Resources and Administration: Michael R. Murray
Auditors: Deloitte & Touche LLP

WHERE

HQ: One Microsoft Way, Redmond, WA 98052-6399
Phone: 206-882-8080
Fax: 206-883-8101
Web site: http://www.microsoft.com
Microsoft has subsidiaries in nearly 50 countries.

	1995 Sales		1995 Operating Income	
	$ mil.	% of total	$ mil.	% of total
US	4,495	68	1,709	77
Europe	1,575	24	412	19
Other regions	558	8	91	4
Adjustments	(691)	—	(174)	—
Total	**5,937**	**100**	**2,038**	**100**

WHAT

	1995 Sales	
	$ mil.	% of total
Applications & content	3,581	60
Platforms	2,356	40
Total	**5,937**	**100**

Selected Products

Business Systems
Microsoft Mail
Microsoft Project
Microsoft Schedule+
Microsoft SQL Server
Microsoft Windows NT

Consumer Products
Microsoft Bookshelf
Microsoft Cinemania
Microsoft Dinosaurs
Microsoft Encarta
Microsoft Flight Simulator
Microsoft Mouse
Microsoft Publisher
Microsoft Works

Desktop Application Software
Microsoft Access
Microsoft Excel

Microsoft Office
Microsoft PowerPoint
Microsoft Word

Developer Products
Microsoft Access
Microsoft FoxPro
Microsoft Visual Basic & C++

Personal Systems
Microsoft MS-DOS
Microsoft Windows
Microsoft Windows 95
Microsoft Windows for Workgroups

Other
Computer books
Microsoft Network (online)
MSNBC (news)
Slate (e-zine)

KEY COMPETITORS

Adobe
America Online
Apple Computer
CompuServe
Computer Associates
Corel
DEC
Electronic Arts
Hewlett-Packard

IBM
Informix
Intuit
Logitech
Macromedia
Netscape
NeXT
Novell
Oracle
Pearson

Prodigy
Sierra On-Line
Silicon Graphics
SoftKey
Sun Microsystems
Sybase
Symantec

HOW MUCH

Nasdaq symbol: MSFT FYE: June 30	Annual Growth	1986	1987	1988	1989	1990	1991	1992	1993	1994	1995
Sales ($ mil.)	45.9%	198	346	591	804	1,183	1,843	2,759	3,753	4,649	5,937
Net income ($ mil.)	49.5%	39	72	124	171	279	463	708	953	1,146	1,453
Income as % of sales	—	19.9%	20.8%	21.0%	21.2%	23.6%	25.1%	25.7%	25.4%	24.7%	24.5%
Earnings per share ($)	43.5%	0.09	0.15	0.25	0.34	0.52	0.82	1.21	1.58	1.88	2.32
Stock price – high ($)	—	2.84	8.79	7.74	9.84	17.96	37.35	47.50	49.00	65.13	109.25
Stock price – low ($)	—	1.42	2.66	5.12	5.17	9.34	16.24	32.75	35.19	39.00	58.25
Stock price – close ($)	47.3%	2.68	6.03	5.92	9.68	16.74	37.10	42.69	40.31	61.13	87.75
P/E – high	—	32	59	31	29	35	46	39	31	35	47
P/E – low	—	16	18	21	15	18	20	27	22	21	25
Dividends per share ($)	—	0.00	0.00	0.00	0.00	0.00	0.00	0.00	0.00	0.00	0.00
Book value per share ($)	46.2%	0.30	0.50	0.78	1.14	1.80	2.59	4.03	5.75	7.88	9.18
Employees	35.5%	1,153	1,816	2,793	4,037	5,635	8,226	11,542	14,430	15,257	17,801

1995 YEAR-END

Debt ratio: 0.0%
Return on equity: 29.7%
Cash (mil.): $4,750
Current ratio: 4.17
Long-term debt (mil.): $0
No. of shares (mil.): 581
Dividends
  Yield: —
  Payout: —
Market value (mil.): $50,983

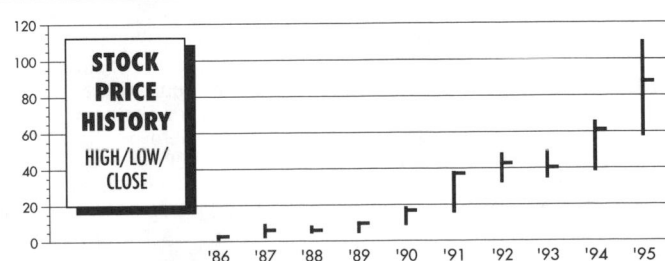

STOCK PRICE HISTORY
HIGH/LOW/CLOSE

MOTOROLA, INC.

OVERVIEW

Motorola is fomenting a global revolution in the way we communicate. The Schaumburg, Illinois-based electronics manufacturer is the world's #1 supplier of equipment for cellular telephones, paging, and 2-way radio. It is the prime contractor for the proposed IRIDIUM satellite network, which is expected to transmit voice, data, fax, and paging signals anywhere on earth starting in 1998.

And don't forget the Internet. Anticipating a market explosion as cable and phone companies enter electronic commerce, Motorola has formed an alliance with Sun Microsystems to develop products for high-speed Internet access.

Global political and economic changes have created new markets, including East Asia (in China, cellular phones are called "Motorolas"), India, and South America. New regulations will open up the European market in 1998. Motorola's strength in wireless communications — the system of choice in emerging nations because they are cheaper to set up than wired systems — is also bringing in new business.

Technology's relentless advance is also fueling change, and Motorola's commitment to innovation is significant; it spends more than 8% of revenues on research and development and owns more than 7,200 patents worldwide.

WHEN

Paul Galvin founded Galvin Manufacturing in Chicago in 1928. The following year he began producing car radio receivers and trying to develop a mobile radio for the police. Daniel Noble was a professor working on mobile design when he met Galvin, who persuaded Noble to join the company in 1940. That same year Galvin Manufacturing developed the first hand-held 2-way radio for the US Army.

In 1947 Galvin renamed the company Motorola, after its car radios. That year Noble established an Arizona research laboratory to pursue defense contracts for radio communications. Radios and TVs required vacuum tubes, which Motorola had to purchase. Noble persuaded Galvin to invest R&D dollars in solid-state devices, and in the late 1950s Motorola turned to semiconductors. The company began manufacturing integrated circuits and microprocessors, which allowed it to market outside its auto industry mainstay. Galvin died in 1959, and his son Robert became CEO. Noble continued as chairman of the science committee. In 1965 Motorola debuted the 8-track tape player for automobiles.

In the 1970s Motorola changed focus. The company launched its 6800 microprocessor and sold its TV business to Matsushita (Japan) in 1974, then began investing in the data communications market for hardware such as modems through the acquisitions of Codex (1977) and Universal Data Systems (1978). In 1987 Motorola made its last car radio.

Robert Galvin's chosen successor, George Fisher, took over in 1990 (Galvin's son Christopher became company president in 1993). That year Motorola organized the $3.4 billion Iridium project, an ambitious scheme to

create a global satellite system capable of handling digital service to hand-held telephones, faxes, and pagers without using land-based stations. In 1991 Motorola formed a partnership with IBM and Apple to develop the PowerPC chip. That year Motorola started making electronic ballasts for lighting systems.

In 1993 the company acquired Lexicus (handwriting-recognition software for pen-based computers) and purchased a 40% interest in Monterrey, Mexico-based CedeTel, a regional cellular phone service.

After Fisher jumped to Eastman Kodak in 1993, Gary Tooker became CEO. The company sold its US 800MHz mobile radio business to Nextel for a minority stake in Nextel valued at $1.7 billion.

In 1995 Motorola began shipping its hand-held Envoy wireless communicator, used to exchange electronic messages and receive stock updates. That year Motorola completed a DRAM plant in Japan (a joint venture with Toshiba). It also signed 4 technology agreements for projects in China.

In 1996 Apple gave Motorola the rights to use its current and future operating systems. Motorola also gets the right to sublicense the operating system to other computer makers likely to produce Apple clones. That year China adopted Motorola's technology as its national paging standard. In mid-year AirTouch Communications launched its long-delayed Los Angeles cellular service based on Motorola's code division multiple access (CDMA) technology, which allows transmission of more signals and provides clearer connections than older analog systems.

Chairman: William J. Weisz, age 68
VC: John F. Mitchell, age 67
VC and CEO: Gary L. Tooker, age 56, $2,020,000 pay
President and COO: Christopher B. Galvin, age 45, $1,570,000 pay
EVP; President and General Manager, General Systems Sector: Edward F. Staiano, age 59, $1,254,231 pay
EVP; President, Motorola Europe, Middle East, and Africa: James A. Norling, age 53, $1,165,000 pay
EVP; Manager, Semiconductor Products Sector: Thomas D. George, age 55, $1,090,000 pay
EVP; President and General Manager, Land Mobile Products Sector: Merle Gilmore, age 47
EVP; President and General Manager, Messaging, Information, and Media Sector: Robert L. Growney, age 53
EVP and General Manager, Automotive, Energy, and Controls Group: Frederick T. Tucker, age 55
EVP and CFO: Carl F. Koenemann, age 57
SVP, General Counsel, and Secretary: Richard H. Weise, age 60
SVP; Director Human Resources: Glenn A. Gienko, age 43
Auditors: KPMG Peat Marwick LLP

WHERE

HQ: 1303 E. Algonquin Rd., Schaumburg, IL 60196
Phone: 847-576-5000
Fax: 847-576-8003
Web site: http://www.motorola.com

Motorola has manufacturing facilities in the US and 17 foreign countries.

WHAT

	1995 Sales		1995 Operating Income	
	$ mil.	% of total	$ mil.	% of total
General systems	10,660	36	1,266	39
Semiconductors	8,539	29	1,218	37
Messaging, Information, & Media products	3,681	12	310	10
Land mobile products	3,598	12	324	10
Other products	3,346	11	131	4
Adjustments	(2,787)	—	(467)	—
Total	**27,037**	**100**	**2,782**	**100**

Operating Units
Automotive, Energy, and Controls Group
General System Sector
Government and Space Technoogy Group
Land Mobile Products Sector
Messaging, Information, and Media Sector
Semiconductor Products Sector

KEY COMPETITORS

AMD	Lucent	Robert Bosch
Canon	Matsushita	Samsung
Ericsson	Micron	Siemens
General Electric	Technology	Sony
Hewlett-Packard	Mitsubishi	Texas
Hitachi	NEC	Instruments
Hyundai	Nokia	Thomson SA
IBM	Northern	Toshiba
Intel	Telecom	Westinghouse
Kyocera	Oki	
LG Group	Philips	

HOW MUCH

NYSE symbol: MOT FYE: December 31	Annual Growth	1986	1987	1988	1989	1990	1991	1992	1993	1994	1995
Sales ($ mil.)	18.5%	5,888	6,707	8,250	9,620	10,885	11,341	13,303	16,963	22,245	27,037
Net income ($ mil.)	27.9%	194	308	445	498	499	454	576	1,022	1,560	1,781
Income as % of sales	—	3.3%	4.6%	5.4%	5.2%	4.6%	4.0%	4.3%	6.0%	7.0%	6.6%
Earnings per share ($)	25.1%	0.39	0.60	0.86	0.96	0.95	0.86	1.08	1.78	2.65	2.93
Stock price – high ($)	—	12.50	18.50	13.66	15.63	22.09	17.81	26.59	53.75	61.13	82.50
Stock price – low ($)	—	8.41	8.75	8.97	9.88	12.28	11.44	16.06	24.38	42.13	51.50
Stock price – close ($)	22.9%	8.91	12.44	10.50	14.59	13.09	16.31	26.13	46.13	58.00	57.00
P/E – high	—	33	31	16	16	23	21	25	30	23	28
P/E – low	—	22	15	10	10	13	13	15	14	16	18
Dividends per share ($)	10.7%	0.16	0.16	0.16	0.16	0.19	0.19	0.19	0.19	0.22	0.31	0.40
Book value per share ($)	14.9%	5.37	5.83	6.51	7.29	8.08	8.76	9.54	11.50	15.47	18.68
Employees	4.6%	94,400	97,700	102,000	104,000	105,000	103,000	107,000	120,000	132,000	142,000

1995 YEAR-END

Debt ratio: 24.3%
Return on equity: 17.7%
Cash (mil.): $1,075
Current ratio: 1.35
Long-term debt (mil.): $1,949
No. of shares (mil.): 591
Dividends
  Yield: 0.7%
  Payout: 13.7%
Market value (mil.): $33,710

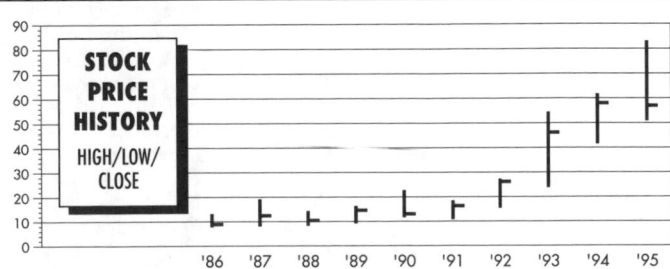

STOCK PRICE HISTORY
HIGH/LOW/CLOSE

NATIONAL SEMICONDUCTOR

OVERVIEW

National Semiconductor is hoping to send the right signals for today's high-tech marketplace. The Santa Clara, California-based company makes analog, digital, and mixed signal (combining analog and digital technologies) integrated circuits. National focuses on 4 customer segments: communications (computer networks, telephones), personal systems (computers and peripherals), consumer goods (home appliances and electronics), and industrial applications (from auto instrumentation to satellites and submarines). Its OEM customers include Compaq, General Motors, IBM, Intel, Hewlett-Packard, Samsung, and

Siemens. Analog and mixed signal devices account for about 60% of the company's revenues; logic and memory chips account for 20%.

Pricing competition in the semiconductor industry is tough, but manufacturers are finding new applications for the company's IC products. To secure its place in the industry, National has streamlined its operations and formed alliances in emerging markets such as China. The company is also focusing on building its expertise in new technologies such as those involving cryptography and wireless communications.

WHEN

National, a transistor company founded in 1959 in Danbury, Connecticut, was by 1967 struggling on only $7 million in sales. That year Peter Sprague, heir to the Sprague electric fortune, took over as chairman and hired manufacturing expert Charles Sporck away from Fairchild Semiconductor.

Sporck transferred operations to Silicon Valley, halved the transistor workforce, and plowed the savings into developing linear and digital logic chips. During the 1970s National's mass manufacturing of low-cost chips made the company the leading US semiconductor maker for a time, while its no-frills management approach led to its employees being dubbed "the animals of Silicon Valley."

The company then bought National Advanced Systems (NAS, a distributor/servicer of Hitachi mainframes; 1979) and Data Terminal Systems (point-of-sale terminals, 1983), which became Datachecker. When Japanese manufacturers dumped digital memory chips on the market in 1984 and 1985, National pulled out of the memory business. Its logic chips also suffered price squeezes, and in 1986 the company lost $148 million.

Sporck then moved to transform his low-cost commodity chipmaker into a higher-margin supplier of niche products. National bought troubled Fairchild Semiconductor in 1987 to gain superior logic chip designs and custom linear circuits for the US military.

Sluggish mainframe demand, coupled with mounting mainframe competition from IBM and Amdahl, prompted National in 1989 to sell NAS for $386 million (to a joint venture between Hitachi and EDS and Datachecker for $126 million (to ICL). It also consolidated plants and laid off 5% of its workforce.

As sales continued to decline that year, Sporck reorganized the company into 3 market-based divisions to better respond to customer needs, but the changes failed to improve results. National left the high-speed, high-density SRAM business, and in early 1991 Sporck retired after 24 years as National's president. Former Rockwell International executive Gilbert Amelio was hired as CEO and undertook another restructuring.

Late in 1992 the company obtained flash memory technology from Toshiba. By early 1993 National had ended large-scale chip production in the Silicon Valley, having shifted production to Arlington, Texas. The company also signed an agreement with Adaptive to develop ATM technology for computer networks.

In 1994 the company introduced a data-security microchip for use in pocket-size cards. The cards can be used in place of passwords to access computers and can meter transactions and keep billing records, enabling users to shop on computer networks.

National purchased SiTel Sierra, a Netherlands-based supplier of cellular and wireless products, in 1995. Also that year the company formed alliances with InfoGear (California) to develop Internet access products, and with Chartec (Denmark) to develop algorithms for charging batteries.

After Amelio left in 1996 to revive Apple Computer, National chose former LSI Logic EVP Brian Halla to head the company. Shortly thereafter National consolidated its operations into 4 divisions, resurrecting the Fairchild Semiconductor name for its discrete device and logic and memory chip operations. Fairchild is expected to be spun off.

WHO

Chairman, President, and CEO: Brian Halla, age 49
President and CEO, Fairchild Semiconductor: Kirk P.
  Pond, age 51, $560,821 pay
EVP Worldwide Sales and Marketing: Patrick J.
  Brockett, age 48, $398,369 pay
EVP Finance and CFO: Donald Macleod, age 47,
  $395,921 pay
**SVP Intellectual Property Protection and Business
  Development:** Richard L. Sanquini
SVP and Chief Technical Officer: Charles P. Carinalli,
  age 47
SVP, General Counsel, and Secretary: John M. Clark III,
  age 46
VP Human Resources: Robert G. MacLean
Auditors: KPMG Peat Marwick LLP

WHERE

HQ: National Semiconductor Corporation, 2900
  Semiconductor Dr., Santa Clara, CA 95051
Phone: 408-721-5000
Fax: 408-739-9803
Web site: http://www.nsc.com

Manufacturing facilities are located in Malaysia, the
Philippines, Singapore, the UK, and the US.

	1996 Sales	
	$ mil.	% of total
Asia	1,638	41
Americas	1,621	40
Europe	761	19
Adjustments	(1,397)	—
Total	**2,623**	**100**

WHAT

	1996 Sales
	% of total
Analog & mixed signal	60
CMOS logic	7
Bipolar logic	7
Discretes	7
Nonvolatile memory	6
Digital & other	13
Total	**100**

Company Divisions

Analog Group (analog products and wireless
  communications products)
Communications and Consumer Group (Ethernet LAN
  and WAN products, mixed signal products)
Fairchild Semiconductor (family logic, memory, and
  discrete products)
Personal Systems Group (embedded technology
  products for personal computers and workstations)

KEY COMPETITORS

Acer	Hitachi	NEC
Altera	Hyundai	NCR
AMD	IBM	Oki
Analog Devices	Intel	Philips
Apple	LG Group	Pioneer
Atmel	Linear	Samsung
Cirrus Logic	Technology	SGS-Thomson
Cypress	LSI Logic	Siemens
Semiconductor	Maxim	Siliconix
Cyrix	Integrated	Sony
Daewoo	Microchip	Standard
Dallas	Technology	Microsystems
Semiconductor	Micron	Texas
Fujitsu	Technology	Instruments
General Signal	Mitsubishi	Toshiba
Harris Corp.	Motorola	Xilinx

HOW MUCH

NYSE symbol: NSM FYE: May 31	Annual Growth	1987	1988	1989	1990	1991	1992	1993	1994	1995	1996[1]
Sales ($ mil.)	3.8%	1,868	2,470	1,648	1,675	1,702	1,718	2,014	2,295	2,379	2,623
Net income ($ mil.)	—	(29)	63	(23)	(25)	(150)	(120)	130	259	264	185
Income as % of sales	—	—	2.5%	—	—	—	—	6.5%	11.3%	11.1%	7.1%
Earnings per share ($)	—	(0.42)	0.48	(0.32)	(0.34)	(1.55)	(1.24)	0.96	1.84	1.92	1.34
Stock price – high ($)	—	22.25	15.00	10.00	8.88	9.00	14.13	21.75	25.00	33.63	23.25
Stock price – low ($)	—	9.75	8.13	6.38	3.00	3.88	6.38	10.13	14.38	16.50	13.50
Stock price – close ($)	2.9%	12.00	9.75	7.25	4.38	6.50	10.63	16.25	19.50	22.13	15.50
P/E – high	—	—	31	—	—	—	—	23	14	18	17
P/E – low	—	—	17	—	—	—	—	11	8	9	10
Dividends per share ($)	—	0.00	0.00	0.00	0.00	0.00	0.00	0.00	0.00	0.00	0.00
Book value per share ($)	3.2%	8.69	9.43	8.28	7.91	6.34	5.07	7.63	9.04	11.75	11.52
Employees	(4.0%)	29,200	37,700	32,200	32,700	29,800	27,200	23,400	22,300	22,400	20,300

[1] Stock prices are through May 31.

1996 YEAR-END

Debt ratio: 19.1%
Return on equity: 12.4%
Cash (mil.): $504
Current ratio: 1.86
Long-term debt (mil.): $351
No. of shares (mil.): 137
Dividends
  Yield: —
  Payout: —
Market value (mil.): $2,225

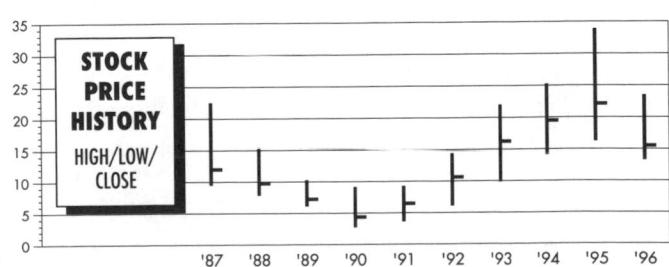

STOCK PRICE HISTORY
HIGH/LOW/CLOSE

NCR CORPORATION

OVERVIEW

Like Jonah, NCR has returned from the belly of the whale. The Dayton, Ohio-based computer company — which was acquired by telecommunications powerhouse AT&T — is being split off again just 5 years later as part a master reorganization at AT&T.

NCR's primary operating units include the Retail Systems Group (which makes point of sale terminals and barcode scanners), the Financial Systems Group (the #1 producer of ATMs, which also makes information terminals and image processing equipment that help reduce the use of paper), and the Computer Systems Group (maker of scalable business computers, massively parallel processors, and servers). The company's operations are rounded out by Worldwide Services (which provides customer service and information technology consulting) and the Systemedia Group (which makes business forms, labels, thermal transfer ribbons, and mailers).

The company is particularly concentrating on data warehousing, which offers customers the ability to consolidate and retrieve a wide variety of information across databases.

NCR focuses on the business-to-business market and has bowed out of the consumer PC race completely after a disastrous attempt to become one of the top 5 PC producers.

But the key to success as a stand-alone company will be regaining profitability — net losses in recent years have totalled nearly $4 billion — and AT&T has pumped almost $3 billion into the company to prop it up. As part of the 1996 spinoff, AT&T and its other spinoff, Lucent Technologies (telephone equipment) pledged to give NCR continuing business.

WHEN

John Patterson bought control of a Dayton cash register factory and founded National Cash Register in 1882. In 1899 Colonel Edward Deeds, (later chairman) joined NCR. He hired inventor Charles Kettering in 1904 to develop an electric cash register. (The 2 men also developed an electric automobile ignition system and left to start DELCO). By the second decade of the 20th century, NCR controlled 90% of the cash register market. In 1913 Patterson was fined by the Justice Department for anti-competitive violations — including product tampering, spying, and bribing competitors — and was sentenced to jail. But Patterson's participation in rescue efforts after Dayton was hit by a flood earned Patterson commendations from municipal authorities that helped keep him out of jail.

NCR introduced accounting machines (which prepared vouchers and audit sheets) to its product line in the early 1920s; these machines became almost as important as cash registers to the company. In the 1929 crash NCR's stock dropped from $154 to $6.87, but by 1936 the company had recovered fully.

The birth of commercial computers after WWII put new pressure on NCR. In 1952 it bought computer developer Computer Research. In 1960 it introduced mainframe computers and opened data processing centers; 3 years later it established microelectronics research facilities; and in 1968 it introduced disk-based computers. Yet NCR failed to grasp the effects of automation on what remained its primary products — cash registers and accounting machines. In 1969 NCR had record profits of $50 million; by 1971 they had plunged to $2 million.

William Anderson, who became NCR's president in 1972, was credited with saving the company. He slashed NCR's Dayton workforce by 75% and focused the company on computing with retail scanners and ATMs.

In the early 1980s NCR moved from proprietary to UNIX operating systems. It also introduced networking equipment. In 1990 NCR and Teradata agreed to codevelop parallel-processing technologies. That year NCR won a contract to supply workstations to J. C. Penney's stores.

In 1991, hoping to become one of the world's top 5 PC makers, AT&T bought NCR in a $7.4 billion hostile takeover. AT&T also acquired Teradata. But GIS never became a low-cost PC maker, and its losses became a drag on earnings after 1993. In 1994 NCR (renamed Global Information Systems — GIS) acquired a 12% stake in First Virtual Corp., a developer of electronic commerce systems. Lars Nyberg, who led a turnaround at electronics maker Philips, took over GIS in 1995 and began an expensive reorganization.

At the same time, AT&T began making plans to slim down its own operations. In 1996 it resurrected the NCR name and announced the new company's spin-off as of December 31. Also in 1996 NCR planned to team with Netscape to develop Internet commerce technology.

WHO

Chairman, CEO, and President: Lars Nyberg, age 45, $1,055,890 pay
SVP and CFO: John L. Giering, age 52, $394,476 pay
SVP and Chief Technical Officer: Dennis Roberson, age 47
SVP Worldwide Customer Support Services: Robert R. Carpenter, age 41, $472,900 pay
SVP Systemedia Group: Daniel J. Enneking, age 49
SVP Retail Systems Group: Anthony Fano, age 53, 331,383 pay
SVP Financial Systems Group: Per-Olof Loof, age 46
SVP Computer Systems Group: William J. Eisenman, age 50, 329,382 pay
SVP, Americas Region: Raymond G. Carlin, age 41
SVP, Europe and Middle East/Africa Region: Jose Luis Solla, age 48
SVP, Asia/Pacific Region: Hideaki Takahashi, age 48
SVP Worldwide Professional Services and Information Systems Operations: Alice H. Lusk, age 48
SVP and Chief Quality Officer: Robert A. Davis, age 46
SVP Public Relations: Michael P. Tarpey, age 51
SVP and General Counsel: Jonathan S. Hoak, age 47
SVP Global Human Resources and Chief Strategy Officer: Richard H. Evans, age 50
Auditors: Coopers & Lybrand L.L.P.

WHERE

HQ: 1700 S. Patterson Blvd., Dayton, OH 45479
Phone: 513-445-2078
Fax: 513-445-1893
Web site: http://www.ncr.com

NCR has more than 1,000 offices and more than 50 development and manufacturing facilities in over 130 countries.

	1995 Sales	
	$ mil.	% of total
US	3,577	44
Europe/Middle East/ Africa	2,551	31
Japan	1,008	12
Other Asia/Pacific	533	7
Other	493	6
Total	**8,162**	**100**

WHAT

	1995 Sales	
	$ mil.	% of total
Customer service and consulting	2,979	37
Computer products		
Servers	1,724	21
Computers	1,087	13
Financial products	1,026	13
Business supplies	577	7
Retail products	424	5
Other	354	4
Total	**8,162**	**100**

Group Operations

Computer Systems Group (develops and markets computer systems based on the WorldMark family of midrange servers)

Financial Systems Group (develops and markets software and systems for financial delivery systems, banking data warehousing, and payment systems/item processing)

Retail Systems Group (develops and markets computer-based systems for food, general merchandise, and hospitality retailers)

Systemedia Group (makets specialty papers for ATMs and point-of-sale devices)

Worldwide Services (provides data warehousing services and network and systems design and support services)

KEY COMPETITORS

Andersen Worldwide	NEC
BancTec	Olivetti
Cap Gemini	Omron Electronics
DEC	Pyramid Technology
Dell	Reynolds and Reynolds
Diebold	Sequent
DST	SNI
EDS	Sony
Fujitsu	Spectra-Physics
Hewlett-Packard	Standard Register
Hitachi	Sun Microsystems
IBM	Symbol Technologies
ICL	Tandem
Machines Bull	Unisys
Metrologic	Wallace Computer

HOW MUCH

Division FYE: December 31	Annual Growth	1986	1987	1988	1989	1990	1991	1992	1993	1994	1995
Sales ($ mil.)	5.9%	4,882	5,614	5,990	5,596	6,285	6,335	7,135	7,262	8,459	8,162
Net income ($ mil.)	—	—	—	—	—	—	—	—	(1,287)	(203)	(2,280)
Income as % of sales	—	—	—	—	—	—	—	—	—	—	—
Employees	(18.1%)	—	—	—	—	—	—	—	—	46,250	37,900

1995 YEAR-END:
Debt ratio: 51.2%
Return on equity: —
Cash (mil.): $338
Current ratio: 1.14
Long-term debt (mil.): $330

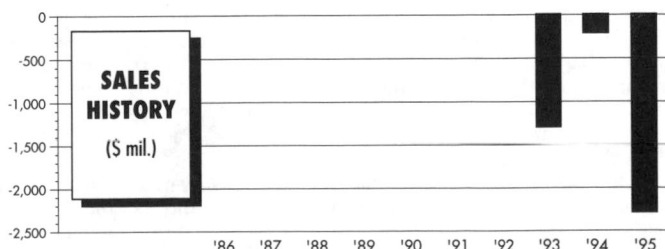

SALES HISTORY
($ mil.)

0										
-500										
-1,000										
-1,500										
-2,000										
-2,500	'86	'87	'88	'89	'90	'91	'92	'93	'94	'95

NEC CORPORATION

OVERVIEW

NEC has its irons in several high-tech fires. The Tokyo-based company has been Japan's leading PC maker for several years. Worldwide, it ranks 2nd in computer chips, 4th in computers, and 5th in telecommunications products. With the popularity of multimedia PCs, the Internet, and new telecommunications technologies — all requiring higher-grade memory chips — NEC's products are hot.

Nec is staying true to its prescient vision of "C & C," the convergence of computers and communications, which NEC has been preaching for 2 decades. It has formed BIGLOBE, an Internet communications service, and created a subsidiary, Holon Net Corp., to develop products for the Internet market.

With computers making up the bulk of NEC's sales, the company moved to strengthen its position by merging its international operations with US computer maker Packard Bell to create Packard Bell NEC, the world's #4 PC company. At home, where both foreign and domestic rivals are stealing customers, NEC is moving to bolster its presence by investing in new technologies, such as advanced color plasma display panels. To position itself better to respond to market needs, the company has reorganized its computer operations into separate units for notebook computers, desktop PCs, and international operations.

On the chip side, NEC has ramped up production of flash memory chips (chips that retain data even when power is turned off) to counter the sagging sales of 16-megabit dynamic random access memory (DRAM) chips.

WHEN

A group of Japanese investors led by Kunihiko Iwadare formed Nippon Electric Company (NEC) in a joint venture with Western Electric (US) in 1899. Starting as an importer of telephone equipment, NEC soon became a manufacturer and major supplier to Japan's Communications Ministry. Western Electric sold its stake in NEC in 1925. ITT (US) began acquiring shares and owned 59% of NEC before selling its stake in the 1960s.

After Nippon Telegraph and Telephone (NTT) was formed in 1952, NEC became one of its 4 leading suppliers. The postwar need to repair Japan's telephone systems and the country's continuing economic recovery resulted in strong demand from NTT. In the 1950s and 1960s, NTT business represented over 50% of sales, even though NEC had expanded overseas, diversified into home appliances, and formed a computer alliance with Honeywell (US). In 1968 NTT began working with NEC, Hitachi, and Fujitsu to develop computers for use in telecommunications.

In the 1970s Honeywell's lagging position in computers hurt NEC; the company recovered through in-house development efforts and a mainframe venture with Toshiba. In 1977 CEO Koji Kobayashi articulated his vision of NEC's future as an integrator of computers and communications through semiconductor technology. Now generally accepted, Kobayashi's thoughts were revolutionary at the time.

A joint effort between the Japanese government and private industry to develop VLSI (very large-scale integration) chips took place in NEC's labs in the 1970s. NEC invested heavily in R&D and capacity expansion and became the world's largest independent semiconductor manufacturer in 1985. The company produced the world's first 4-megabit DRAM chip in 1986.

The company enjoyed great success in the Japanese PC market, garnering over 50% of the market in the 1980s despite a proprietary operating system. NEC's portable IBM clones were also well received internationally. NEC passed IBM to become Japan's #2 computer maker (after Fujitsu) in 1986 and entered into a mainframe computer partnership (now Bull HN Information Systems) with Honeywell and France's Machines Bull in 1987.

In 1992 NEC sold its 5 millionth PC-9800 series PC in Japan. In that year Compaq challenged NEC with a cheap, Japanese-language PC that uses the IBM standard, forcing NEC to cut its PC prices. The rising yen and the sluggish Japanese economy also hurt NEC's income in 1992 and 1993.

In 1995 the company acquired 20% of US computer maker Packard Bell for $170 million. The following year NEC merged most of its PC business outside Japan with Packard Bell, transferring about $300 million in assets to the US company. The deal created the world's 4th largest PC maker, called NEC Packard Bell. Also in 1996 NEC created Holon Net Corp., a US subsidiary, to produce hardware and software for Internet and intranet markets.

WHO

Chairman: Tadahiro Sekimoto
President: Hisashi Kaneko
SVP; President and CEO, NEC America: Mineo Sugiyama
CFO: Yoshihiro Suzuki
SVP Human Resources: Hirokazu Akiyama
Auditors: Price Waterhouse LLP

WHERE

HQ: 7-1, Shiba 5-chome, Minato-ku, Tokyo, 108-01, Japan
Phone: +81-3-3454-1111
Fax: +81-3-3798-1510
US HQ: NEC America, Inc., 8 Old Sod Farm Rd., Melville, NY 11747-3112
US Phone: 516-753-7000
US Fax: 516-753-7041
Web site: http://www.nec.co.jp

In Japan, NEC operates a network of 89 consolidated subsidiaries, 62 plants, and more than 430 sales offices. Outside Japan the company operates 102 subsidiaries and affiliates in 31 countries.

WHAT

Selected Products
Communications Systems and Equipment
CATV systems
Cellular phones
Defense electronic systems
Digital switching systems
Fiber-optic submarine cable systems
Mobile communications systems
Network management systems
Pagers
Satellite communication systems
Television and radio broadcast equipment

Computers and Industrial Electronics Systems
Internet services
Mainframe computers
Medical electronic equipment
Peripherals
Personal computers
Servers
Software products
Systems integration services
Workstations

Electron Devices
Color display tubes
Electrical connectors
Electron tubes
Gate arrays
Linear ICs
Memories
Transistors

Other Operations
Auto electronics
Home appliances
Lighting
Televisions
VCRs

KEY COMPETITORS

Alcatel Alsthom	GE	Northern
Apple Computer	GTE	Telecom
Atmel	Hewlett-Packard	Philips
Compaq	Hitachi	Samsung
Cypress	IBM	Siemens
Semiconductor	Intel	Silicon Graphics
Data General	Lucent	Sony
DEC	Matsushita	Sun
Dell	Micron	Microsystems
EMC	Technology	Texas
Ericsson	Motorola	Instruments
Fujitsu	Nokia	Toshiba
Gateway 2000		Unisys

HOW MUCH

Nasdaq symbol: NIPNY FYE: March 31	Annual Growth	1987	1988	1989	1990	1991	1992	1993	1994	1995	1996
Sales ($ mil.)	10.5%	16,803	21,893	23,247	21,771	26,306	28,428	30,605	35,096	43,326	41,376
Net income ($ mil.)	24.1%	103	205	323	497	361	112	(407)	81	406	721
Income as % of sales	—	0.6%	0.9%	1.4%	2.3%	1.4%	0.4%	—	0.2%	0.9%	1.7%
Earnings per share ($)	22.1%	0.35	0.70	1.30	1.54	1.14	0.36	(1.06)	0.26	1.32	2.11
Stock price – high ($)[1]	—	78.50	89.88	90.50	80.75	71.50	62.75	50.00	50.50	64.75	75.25
Stock price – low ($)[1]	—	30.25	45.13	67.63	60.13	45.75	42.50	24.63	24.50	38.75	45.13
Stock price – close ($)[1]	(0.5%)	63.88	73.50	78.50	65.50	47.50	48.25	26.88	38.13	57.00	61.00
P/E – high	—	284	128	70	52	63	174	—	194	49	36
P/E – low	—	86	85	52	39	40	118	—	94	29	21
Dividends per share ($)	26.8%	0.06	0.28	0.30	0.26	0.30	0.32	0.34	0.39	0.42	0.51
Book value per share ($)	9.3%	11.97	16.29	17.41	16.75	20.36	21.49	22.79	24.90	29.55	26.64
Employees	4.7%	101,227	102,452	104,022	114,599	117,994	128,320	140,969	147,910	151,069	152,719

[1] Stock prices are for the prior calendar year.

1996 YEAR-END

Debt ratio: 67.4%
Return on equity: 9.2%
Cash (mil.): $4,487
Current ratio: 1.14
Long-term debt (mil.): $9,386
No. of shares (mil.): 308
Dividends
  Yield: 0.8%
  Payout: 24.2%
Market value (mil.): $18,804

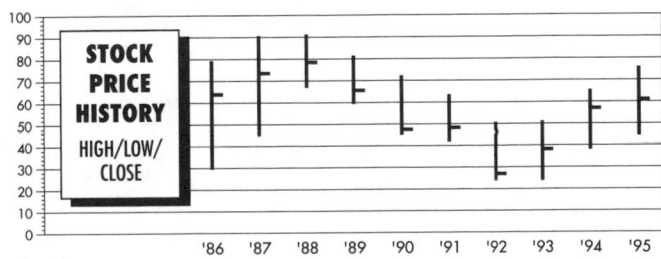

STOCK PRICE HISTORY
HIGH/LOW/CLOSE

NINTENDO CO., LTD.

OVERVIEW

Sixty-four to 32 would win a basketball game, but will it win back Nintendo's dominance in the video game market? Based in Kyoto, Japan, Nintendo, once the clear frontrunner, is battling for the industry lead. Though the 16-bit Super Nintendo Entertainment Center is still the #1 video game system on the market, more powerful (32-bit) machines made by rivals Sega and Sony, as well as PC games, are cutting into its market share. Nintendo also makes the handheld Game Boy electronic game machine and the 32-bit Virtual Boy 3D game.

Nintendo (which, loosely translated, means "leave luck to heaven") isn't going to step off the hill without a fight. It is attacking the competition with a 64-bit system, the N64, which has been unveiled to rave reviews. With 3D graphics and games like Super Mario 64, TetrisPhear, and WaveRace 64, Nintendo hopes the new system will woo consumers back from its competitors. Naysayers, however, point out that the system is based on outdated cartridge technology. Critics also lambaste Nintendo for charging game makers exorbitant licensing fees, about 5 times as much as Sega or Sony charges.

The founding Yamauchi family owns 11% of the company.

WHEN

Nintendo was founded in 1889 as the Marufuku Company to make and sell "hanafuda" Japanese game cards. Its success was furthered in the early 20th century when "hanafuda" became a major gambling pastime. In 1907 the company began producing Western playing cards. It became the Nintendo Playing Card Company in 1951 and began making theme cards under a licensing agreement with Disney in 1959. The company took its current name in 1963.

During the 1950s and 1960s, Hiroshi Yamauchi, scion of the founding family, took the company public and diversified into new areas (including a "love" hotel). Nintendo entered the budding field of video games in the late 1970s by licensing Magnavox's Pong technology. Then it moved into arcade games. The company established its US subsidiary, Nintendo of America, in 1980; its first hit was Donkey Kong (roughly translated, "silly monkey"). Its next hit was Super Mario Bros. (named after Nintendo of America's warehouse landlord).

Nintendo released Famicom, a technologically advanced home video game system, in Japan in 1983. With its high-quality sound and graphics, Famicom was a smash, selling 15.2 million consoles and more than 183 million game cartridges in Japan alone.

Meanwhile, in 1983 and 1984, the US home game market crashed, sending pioneer Atari up in flames. Nintendo persevered, successfully launching Famicom in the US in 1986 as the Nintendo Entertainment System (NES).

To prevent a barrage of independently produced, low-quality software (which had contributed to Atari's demise), the company established stringent licensing policies for its software developers. Licensees were required to have approval of every game design, buy the blank cartridges from the company, agree not to make the game for any of Nintendo's competitors, pay development and marketing costs, and pay Nintendo royalties for the honor of developing a game. Designers chafed under these conditions, but they were part of Nintendo's strategy.

As the market became increasingly saturated, Nintendo sought new products, releasing Game Boy in 1989 and the Super Family Computer game system (Super NES in the US) in 1991.

In the 1990s Nintendo was hit by an outcry against violent games. However, the company declined to participate in a ratings system devised by SEGA because its own games were usually less violent (one reason for declining sales) than SEGA's.

Donkey Kong Country (introduced in 1994) sold 7 million cartridges worldwide in the first 3 months it was on the market. That year, in a quest for new games, Nintendo broke with tradition by making design alliances with companies like Silicon Graphics and began giving other designers more favorable deals. One of the resulting products, a 3D virtual reality system called Virtual Boy (created with Reflection Technology), was rolled out in 1995. It was the company's first 32-bit product.

Nintendo launched the much-touted N64 game system in Japan in 1996, about 6 months behind schedule. Release of the system in the US was planned for later in the year. Nintendo also teamed with Microsoft and Nomura Research Institute to begin developing a satellite-delivered Internet system for Japan.

WHO

President: Hiroshi Yamauchi
Senior Managing Director: Katsunori Tanimoto
Senior Managing Director: Akio Tsuji
Managing Director: Hiroyuki Fukuda
Managing Director: Yasuhiro Onishi
Managing Director: Masaharu Matsumoto
Managing Director: Hiroshi Imanishi
Managing Director: Kimio Mariko
Managing Director; Chairman, Nintendo of America: Howard C. Lincoln
Managing Director; President, Nintendo of America: Minoru Arakawa
CFO, Nintendo of America: Bruce Holdren
Personnel Director, Nintendo of America: Bev Mitchell
Auditors: Chuo Audit Corporation

WHERE

HQ: 60 Fukuine Kamitakamatsu-cho, Higashiyama-ku, Kyoto, 605, Japan
Phone: +81-75-541-6111
Fax: +81-75-531-7996
US HQ: Nintendo of America Inc., 4820 150th Ave. NE, Redmond, WA 98052-9733
US Phone: 206-882-2040
US Fax: 206-882-3585
Web site: http://www.nintendo.co.jp/

The company has offices and plants in Japan and major subsidiaries in Australia, Belgium, Canada, France, Germany, Hong Kong, the Netherlands, Spain, the UK, and the US.

	1996 Sales	
	$ mil.	% of total
Japan	1,880	56
Other countries	1,457	44
Total	**3,337**	**100**

WHAT

Game Consoles
Game Boy
N64
Super Nintendo Entertainment System
Virtual Boy

Selected Games
Body Harvest
Cruis'n USA
Donkey Kong Country
PilotWings 64
Street Fighter II
Super Mario 64
TetrisPhear
Vegas Stakes
Vertical Force
WaveRace 64
Yoshi's Island
Zelda series

KEY COMPETITORS

3DO
Acclaim Entertainment
Activision
Broderbund
Electronic Arts
GT Interactive
LucasArts
Matsushita
Microsoft
NEC
Philips
SEGA
Sierra On-Line
Sony
Walt Disney
WMS Industries

HOW MUCH

OTC symbol: NTDOY FYE: March 31	Annual Growth	1987	1988	1989	1990[2]	1991	1992	1993	1994	1995	1996
Sales ($ mil.)	14.4%	992	1,638	2,193	1,522	3,463	4,405	5,681	4,825	4,666	3,337
Net income ($ mil.)	14.1%	173	243	258	209	489	655	771	511	468	565
Income as % of sales	—	17.4%	14.8%	11.8%	13.7%	14.1%	14.9%	13.6%	10.6%	9.7%	16.9%
Earnings per share ($)	14.3%	0.15	0.21	0.23	0.18	0.43	0.58	0.68	0.45	0.41	0.50
Stock price – high ($)[1]	—	—	—	—	12.55	18.89	16.52	12.28	22.02	10.88	10.30
Stock price – low ($)[1]	—	—	—	—	4.94	9.36	9.06	8.20	7.14	6.50	6.33
Stock price – close ($)[1]	(0.2%)	—	—	—	9.63	12.89	11.70	10.61	8.03	6.75	9.50
P/E – high	—	—	—	—	68	44	29	18	49	26	21
P/E – low	—	—	—	—	27	22	16	12	16	16	13
Dividends per share ($)	26.0%	—	—	—	0.03	0.03	0.06	0.08	0.09	0.10	0.12
Book value per share ($)	19.8%	—	—	—	1.43	2.12	2.18	3.10	3.81	4.61	4.22
Employees[3]	4.8%	—	—	684	730	777	825	943	924	927	952

[1] Stock prices are for the prior calendar year. [2] 7-month fiscal year [3] Headquarters only

1996 YEAR-END

Debt ratio: 0.0%
Return on equity: 11.3%
Cash (mil.): $4,505
Current ratio: 4.21
Long-term debt (mil.): $0
No. of shares (mil.): 142
Dividends
  Yield: 1.2%
  Payout: 23.6%
Market value (mil.): $1,346

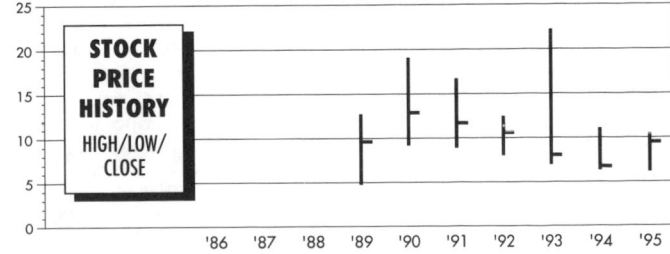

STOCK PRICE HISTORY HIGH/LOW/CLOSE

NOVELL, INC.

OVERVIEW

Computer networks are everywhere, and 63% of all networks run on Novell software. The Orem, Utah-based company's flagship product is the NetWare network operating system, which has been licensed to more than 50 million users. It also makes GroupWise groupware products (for groups of users working on a project) and LAN Workplace and LANalyzer for connecting and managing local area networks.

With the Internet, rival software developer Microsoft's powerful NT server operating system, and newer networking technologies putting pressure on NetWare sales, Novell is redefining its role in the networking marketplace. It has embraced the Internet, amending its software with options that help NetWare customers connect their LANs to the Net. In 1996 it licensed Java, Sun Microsystems's Internet development language, to speed its development of Internet capabilities for Novell software.

Novell's renewed focus on networking comes after an unsuccessful attempt to widen its scope that included the purchase of WordPerfect Corp., maker of a popular word processing program, and Digital Research, which made a PC operating system. Both programs competed directly with top-selling programs from software developer Microsoft (MS Word and MS-DOS), and both failed to dent Microsoft's market share.

Novell has partnerships with such technology leaders as AT&T, Hewlett-Packard, and IBM to help develop its Smart Global Network, where everything from appliances to cars to telephones is networked. The company is already working with AT&T to create a global data network on a scale with the telephone system.

Former Novell CEO Ray Noorda owns 7%; WordPerfect cofounder Alan Ashton owns about 4%.

WHEN

Novell Data Systems started out in 1980 as a Provo, Utah-based maker of PC peripherals. In 1981 Safeguard Scientifics, a high-tech venture capital firm, bought a 55% stake in Novell (raised to 88% in 1982). By 1983 the company had already been through 8 presidents and was nearly defunct. Safeguard provided 51% of the capital needed for revival and brought in as CEO turnaround artist Raymond Noorda, who invested $125,000 of his own money in the new Novell (then equal to a 33% stake).

When Noorda took over, Novell was already working on solutions to PC networking. He designated one machine in the network as a file server to manage the network and to control access to shared devices, such as disk drives and printers. Novell introduced NetWare, the first LAN software based on file server technology, in 1983.

After going public in 1985, Novell began acquiring other companies to enhance and expand its product line, including Santa Clara Systems (microcomputer work-stations, 1987), CXI (computer products, 1987), SoftCraft (programming tools, 1987) 60% of Indisy Software (electronic messaging systems, 1988), Excelan (networking software and related equipment, 1989), and the remaining 40% of Indisy (1990). In 1988 Novell announced it would drop production of most hardware. In 1989 it released NetWare 386, which took advantage of

Intel's 386 chip and ran on UNIX and Macintosh operating systems.

In 1990 software developer Lotus, at Noorda's instigation, moved to acquire the company, but Novell's directors nixed the deal. In 1991 Novell acquired Digital Research (PC operating software) and Univel (UNIX products). That year the company bought interests in former AT&T unit UNIX Systems Laboratories and object-oriented software tool developer Serius. Novell acquired the remaining shares of both UNIX Systems Laboratories and Serius in 1993.

Noorda stepped down in 1994 and was succeeded by Robert Frankenberg, an experienced Hewlett-Packard executive. Novell transferred its database products (NetWare SQL, Xtrieve) that year to Btrieve Technologies, a company in which Novell holds a minority stake, and acquired Borland's Quattro Pro spreadsheet and WordPerfect Corp.

To focus on its increasingly competitive market, Novell sold its WordPerfect subsidiary to Corel Corp. in early 1996 (for about $124 million, well below the $855 million it paid for the company in 1994). In addition the company sold its UnixWare product line to Santa Cruz Operation. In late 1996 Frankenberg resigned after the company posted flat sales for several quarters in a row. The company named former Hewlett-Packard CEO John Young Chairman and began a search for a new CEO.

WHO

Chairman: John A. Young, age 48, $813,166 pay
EVP Worldwide Sales: Joseph A. Marengi, age 42, $552,618 pay
EVP and CFO: James R. Tolonen, age 46, $498,529 pay
EVP and COO: Mary M. Burnside, age 48, $489,489 pay
EVP NetWare Systems Group: Richard W. King, age 39, $352,462 pay
EVP Information Access and Management Group: Steven Markman, age 50
EVP Applications Group: Jeffrey H. Waxman, age 49
SVP Corporate Research and Development and Chief Technology Officer: Glen Ricart, age 46
SVP, General Counsel, and Corporate Secretary: David R. Bradford, age 45
SVP Human Resources: Jennifer Konecny-Costa
Auditors: Ernst & Young LLP

WHERE

HQ: 1555 N. Technology Way, Orem, UT 84057
Phone: 801-222-6000
Fax: 801-222-7077
Web site: http://www.novell.com

Novell markets its products through 40 offices in the US and 60 offices in foreign countries.

WHAT

	1995 Sales
	% of total
Network systems	57
Personal productivity applications	20
Access & management	12
Groupware applications	4
Education & service	7
Total	**100**

Selected Products

Groupware
GroupWise (integrated document management, e-mail, forms, group calendaring, online conferencing, and scheduling)

Information Access and Management
LAN Workplace TCP/IP (for connecting PCs to UNIX systems and the Internet)
LANalyzer (for monitoring, analyzing, and troubleshooting NetWare networks)
ManageWise (for management of the Novell environment)
NetWare Connect (for remote access to NetWare networks)
NetWare for SAA (for connecting NetWare and IBM mainframe environments)
NetWare Mobile (for remote access to networks)
NetWare Navigator (for centralized, automated software and data distribution for Novell networks)

Systems
NetWare 3, NetWare 4 (network operating systems)
NetWare Symmetrical Processing (for use on multiprocessor hardware)
Novell Embedded Systems Technology development kits
TUXEDO System (for development of distributed client/server applications)

KEY COMPETITORS

Apple Computer	Datapoint	Oracle
Artisoft	DEC	PLATINUM
Banyan Systems	Digi	technology
Bay Networks	International	Santa Cruz
Cheyenne	Hewlett-Packard	Operation
Software	IBM	Sun
Computer	Madge	Microsystems
Associates	Microsoft	Wang

HOW MUCH

Nasdaq symbol: NOVL FYE: October 31	Annual Growth	1986	1987	1988	1989	1990	1991	1992	1993	1994	1995
Sales ($ mil.)	42.9%	82	183	281	422	498	640	933	1,123	1,998	2,041
Net income ($ mil.)	47.9%	10	20	30	49	94	163	249	(35)	207	338
Income as % of sales	—	12.4%	11.1%	10.8%	11.5%	19.0%	25.4%	26.7%	—	10.3%	16.6%
Earnings per share ($)	35.1%	0.06	0.10	0.14	0.19	0.34	0.55	0.81	(0.11)	0.56	0.90
Stock price – high ($)	—	1.64	3.69	4.02	4.72	8.50	32.38	33.50	35.25	26.25	23.25
Stock price – low ($)	—	0.88	1.50	2.22	3.03	3.44	7.63	22.50	17.00	13.75	13.75
Stock price – close ($)	27.4%	1.61	3.00	3.75	3.88	8.25	30.00	28.50	20.75	17.13	14.25
P/E – high	—	27	37	29	25	25	59	41	—	47	26
P/E – low	—	15	15	16	16	10	14	28	—	25	15
Dividends per share ($)	—	0.00	0.00	0.00	0.00	0.00	0.00	0.00	0.00	0.00	0.00
Book value per share ($)	33.0%	0.40	0.47	0.62	0.89	1.41	2.08	3.12	3.23	4.08	5.22
Employees	34.4%	507	1,138	1,584	2,120	2,419	2,843	3,637	4,335	7,914	7,272

1995 YEAR-END

Debt ratio: 0.0%
Return on equity: 19.8%
Cash (mil.): $1,321
Current ratio: 4.18
Long-term debt (mil.): $0
No. of shares (mil.): 372
Dividends
 Yield: —
 Payout: —
Market value (mil.): $5,295

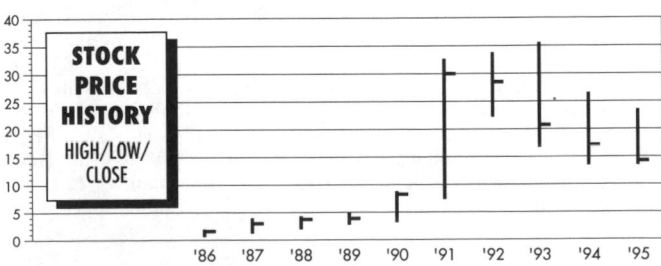

STOCK PRICE HISTORY HIGH/LOW/CLOSE

OKI ELECTRIC

OVERVIEW

Its name may appear in red on its products, but Oki is back in the black after 3 consecutive money-losing years, despite a relatively high Japanese yen and flat yen-denominated sales. The Tokyo-based company has cut its operating expenses but not its R&D expenditures, which were up almost 13% despite the string of bad years and amount to over 5% of its annual sales.

Oki manufactures and markets information processing systems (computer, control, networking, and telemetry), as well as telecommunications products and an array of electric components from motorcycle ignition parts to memory chips. The company foresees increasing demand for large-scale integrated circuits

(LSIs) as markets grow for PCs, peripherals, and mobile communications equipment, and it is adding to its production capacity with a new plant in Japan. Its R&D budget may also help: Oki has developed a wire using a copper alloy for LSIs that lasts 35 times longer than ones made of pure copper.

Believing that multimedia applications will play into its strengths in data transmission technology, Oki plans to prune production costs and broaden its technological base. Intending to build relations with Asian companies, it has begun buying 16-megabit DRAMs from Taiwan's Nan Ya Technology and plans to buy 64-megabit DRAMs from it when technology is transferred or added to Nan Ya's own.

WHEN

Oki dates back to 1881, when engineer Kibataro Oki, formerly of Japan's Department of Industry, founded Meikosha Company in Tokyo. Originally formed to manufacture and sell telephones, Meikosha was soon producing telegraphs, bells, and medical equipment. The company's main manufacturing plant adopted the name Oki Electric Plant in 1889; the marketing division began operating under the name Oki & Company in 1896.

In 1907, a year after the death of Kibataro Oki, the Oki groups were united as a limited partnership, divided again in 1912, then ultimately recombined in 1917 as Oki Electric Company. Oki continued to expand its product line to include automatic switching equipment (1926) and electric clocks (1929).

Oki produced communications equipment for the Japanese military during WWII but shifted back to civil production after the war, starting work on the teleprinter and adding consumer goods, such as portable stoves. The company adopted its present name in 1949.

It entered the semiconductor and computer industries in the 1950s, joining Fujitsu, Hitachi, Toshiba, Nippon Electric Company, and Mitsubishi as one of Japan's Big 6 electronic makers by 1960. It began developing overseas businesses, particularly in Latin America, where it built communications networks in Honduras (1962) and Bolivia (1966) and radio networks in Brazil (1971).

Oki formed a computer software division in 1970 and started building PCs in 1981. The company continued as a major supplier of telecommunications equipment to the

Japanese government until the mid-1970s, when the government increased purchases from other companies. The loss of government business eroded both sales and profits for Oki, resulting in a $7 million loss in 1978. Former NTT executive Masao Miyake took over as Oki's president, initiating a dramatic reorganization of the company into 15 highly focused and profitable business units.

Oki later consolidated its US operations, forming Oki America (1984). But a new financial crisis followed in the mid-1980s, when the bottom fell out of the semiconductor market, and earnings plummeted into the red in 1986.

The following year Oki set up a division to provide oceanographic services (Oki Seataec). As a major provider of ATMs and bank computer systems, Oki enjoyed a ninefold increase in profits in 1989, sparked by growth in the Japanese financial industry. That year Oki strengthened its position as one of the world's leading suppliers of computer systems and ATMs to the banking and financial sector by entering an agreement with Sun Microsystems that gives Oki access to Sun's financial software. In 1990 Oki and Hewlett-Packard formed a joint venture in Puerto Rico to build printed circuit boards.

Oki signed an agreement with the French electronics firm Matra MHS to help develop computer chips in 1992 and 2 years later established a new subsidiary, Oki Data Corp., to handle its printer and fax machine operations. In 1996 Oki created a California unit, Silicon Dynamics, to create products for US telecommunications and multimedia markets.

WHO

President and CEO: Shiko Sawamura
EVP: Minoru Imai
EVP: Tadao Higashi
Senior Managing Director: Yasunori Nishizawa
Auditors: Showa Ota & Co.

WHERE

HQ: Oki Electric, 7-12,Toranomon 1-chome, Minato-ku, Tokyo, 105, Japan
Phone: +81-3-3501-3111
Fax: +81-3-3581-5522
US HQ: Oki America, Inc., 3 University Plaza, Hackensack, NJ 07601
US Phone: 201-646-0011
US Fax: 201-646-9229
Web site: http://www.oki.com/OkiEle.html

Oki has operations in 19 countries. Its products are sold worldwide.

WHAT

	1995 Sales	
	$ mil.	% of total
Info. processing systems	2,754	40
Electronic devices	2,174	31
Telecommunications systems	1,806	26
Other	243	3
Total	**6,977**	**100**

Information Processing Systems
Banking systems (ATMs)
Client server systems
Earthquake observation and early-warning systems
OCR systems
Personal computers
Point-of-sale systems
Printers
Ticket-issuing systems
Traffic control systems
Underwater imaging systems
Water resource control systems
Workstations

Electronic Devices
Application-specific ICs
Memories
Microprocessors
Optoelectronic devices
Solid-state disk cards
Telecommunications and voice synthesis LSIs

Telecommunications Systems
Cellular telephones
Central-office switching systems
Fax machines
Fiber optics
LANs
Modems
Multimedia-multiplex systems
PBX systems
Radio equipment
Teleconferencing
Voice and fax mail systems

KEY COMPETITORS

Alcatel Alsthom	Hughes	Octel Communi-
Arrow	Electronics	cations
Electronics	IBM	Olivetti
Brother	ITOCHU	Philips
Canon	Lexmark	Pioneer
Compression	International	Racal Electronics
Labs	Lucent	Ricoh
DEC	Machines Bull	Sanyo
Diebold	Mannesmann	Seiko
Ericsson	Matsushita	Sharp
Fujitsu	Mitsubishi	Siemens
General	Motorola	Silicon Graphics
Instrument	NEC	Sony
Hewlett-Packard	Nokia	Tektronix
Hitachi	Northern	Toshiba
Honeywell	Telecom	

HOW MUCH

Principal exchange: Tokyo FYE: March 31	Annual Growth	1987	1988	1989	1990	1991	1992	1993	1994	1995	1996
Sales ($ mil.)	10.7%	2,797	3,637	4,184	3,991	4,687	5,122	5,567	6,325	7,300	6,977
Net income ($ mil.)	35.4%	15	28	115	104	70	(4)	(287)	(17)	359	230
Income as % of sales	—	0.5%	0.8%	2.8%	2.6%	1.5%	—	—	—	4.9%	3.3%
Earnings per share ($)	32.6%	0.03	0.05	0.21	0.18	0.12	(0.01)	(0.47)	(0.02)	0.58	0.38
Stock price – high ($)[1]	—	5.73	7.08	8.68	7.98	8.96	6.55	5.27	5.60	9.26	9.42
Stock price – low ($)[1]	—	3.70	3.77	4.71	5.93	4.14	3.99	2.52	3.09	5.92	4.11
Stock price – close ($)[1]	8.4%	4.19	5.09	7.27	7.60	4.94	4.51	2.94	5.27	7.82	8.65
P/E – high	—	187	129	41	45	76	—	—	—	16	25
P/E – low	—	121	69	22	34	35	—	—	—	10	11
Dividends per share ($)	14.9%	0.02	0.05	0.05	0.04	0.05	0.06	0.03	0.00	0.00	0.07
Book value per share ($)	10.8%	1.20	1.58	1.64	1.64	2.25	2.35	2.22	2.46	3.46	3.01
Employees	1.3%	19,375	18,659	18,440	19,331	20,278	21,593	23,463	22,585	23,568	21,718

[1] Stock prices are for the prior calendar year.

1996 YEAR-END

Debt ratio: 59.9%
Return on equity: 11.6%
Cash (mil.): $2,716
Current ratio: 1.70
Long-term debt (mil.): $2,042
No. of shares (mil.): 612
Dividends
  Yield: 0.8%
  Payout: 17.4%
Market value (mil.): $5,297

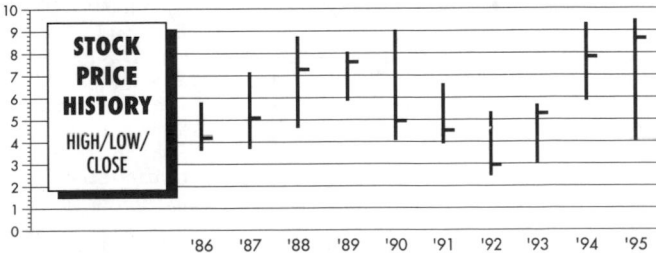

STOCK PRICE HISTORY
HIGH/LOW/CLOSE

OLIVETTI S.P.A.

OVERVIEW

Olivetti is saying "ciao" to PCs. Poor computer sales and massive restructuring charges have kept the Ivrea, Italy-based information and telecommunications company in the red for years. Now, along with the ouster of long-time chairman Carlo De Benedetti, the company has decided to give the boot to its PC business. Olivetti has higher hopes for Omnitel, its venture with a host of international partners into the booming Italian cellphone service market.

Olivetti's most recent configuration includes 5 businesses: Omnitel, Olivetti Telemedia (a variety of other telecommunications services), Olivetti Lexikon (copiers, fax machines, printers, and accessories), Olivetti

Systems and Services (consulting and network integration and support), and, at least for now, Olivetti Personal Computers.

Once #1 in Europe, Olivetti's PC unit now has the 7th largest share of the continental market and has been draining away more money than the company made from its other operations. Omnitel, however received 300,000 subscribers in its first 7 months. Meanwhile, through Olivetti Telemedia, the company and partner Bell Atlantic have formed Infostrada, a joint venture that will string the Internet along the Appian Way.

De Benedetti remains a major influence at Olivetti, as he and his family still own about 15% of the company.

WHEN

Camillo Olivetti founded Olivetti in Ivrea in 1908 to produce the first Italian-made typewriter (introduced in 1911). The company later diversified into office furniture (1930), teleprinters (1938), and adding machines (1940). The company went public in 1932. Camillo's son Adriano, general manager since 1933, led Olivetti into computers, which resulted in Italy's first mainframe in 1959. That year Olivetti bought control of ailing US typewriter maker Underwood (founded by John Thomas Underwood in 1896), which later became Olivetti Corporation of America (OCA).

Adriano died in 1960, and his family sold most of its stake in Olivetti to the Pirelli/Fiat syndicate in 1964. General Electric bought Olivetti's mainframe business that year. Because the company was slow to switch from mechanical to electric office equipment in the 1960s, earnings stagnated; Olivetti suspended its dividend in 1974.

Former Fiat executive Carlo De Benedetti invested $17 million in the company in 1978. As CEO, he slashed debt (and the payroll) while increasing R&D spending eightfold between 1978 and 1984. Olivetti introduced its first electronic typewriter in 1978 and bought Swiss typewriter maker Hermes Precisa International in 1981.

OCA, in the meantime, had suffered through more than a decade of losses. De Benedetti hoped to end this by selling OCA to Dallas-based Docutel (ATMs) in exchange for a 46% stake in the company in 1982. When the losses continued, Olivetti bought the rest of Docutel and used it to establish Olivetti USA in 1985.

Olivetti unveiled its first PC in 1982. AT&T bought a 25% stake in Olivetti in 1983, and

Toshiba bought 20% of its Japanese operations in 1985. De Benedetti hoped these moves would increase Olivetti's market share, but competition from low-priced PCs got the better of it. AT&T traded its stake in Olivetti to De Benedetti for 18.6% of his holding company, Compagnie Industriali Riunite, in 1989.

Meanwhile, Olivetti bought 80% of the UK's Acorn Computers Group (1985) and Volkswagen's ailing office-products maker Triumph-Adler (1986). Olivetti boosted its stake in bank automation by buying Bunker Ramo (1986) and I.S.C. Systems Corporation (1989). The company's cell phone unit, Omnitel, got its start in 1989. World minicomputer demand softened in the late 1980s; in 1991 Olivetti posted its first loss in 13 years.

Olivetti tried to restore its reputation for innovative product development by introducing a high-end workstation PC using RISC technology, followed by the Quaderno, a subnotebook PC with voice recording capability.

De Benedetti was convicted in 1992 for bankruptcy fraud in the scandal surrounding the 1982 Banco Ambrosiano collapse (he is still appealing his 4-1/2-year sentence). Francesco Caio, who led the Omnitel startup, was named CEO of Olivetti in July 1996, and dominant shareholder De Benedetti soon resigned as chairman. A subsequent dispute over accounting methods led to the departure of Caio after 70 days as CEO. He was replaced by auto parts executive and De Benedetti disciple Roberto Colaninno, who soon announced plans to sell Olivetti's PC business and a stake in Omnitel to raise cash.

WHO

Chairman: Carlo De Benedetti
CEO: Francesco Caio
CFO: Angelo Fornasari
Secretary of the Board: Piera Rosiello
President, Olivetti USA: Salomon Suwalsky
CFO, Olivetti USA: Dave Frasier
Manager Human Resources, Olivetti USA: Kelle Adams
Auditors: Coopers & Lybrand S.a.s.

WHERE

HQ: Via Jervis 77, 10015, Ivrea, Italy
Phone: +39-125-52-5
Fax: +39-125-52-20-08
US HQ: Olivetti USA, Inc., 765 Hwy. 202 South,
Bridgewater, NJ 00807-6945
US Phone: 908-526-8200
US Fax: 908-526-8405
Web site: http://www.olivetti.it

Olivetti has partly or wholly owned subsidiaries in 30
countries including Italy.

WHAT

	1995 Sales	
	$ mil.	% of total
Systems & services	3,606	58
Office products	1,267	20
Personal computers	849	14
Telemedia	107	2
Other	379	6
Total	**6,208**	**100**

Selected Products
ATMs
Banking peripherals
Cash registers
Cellular phones
Copiers
Office products
Personal computers
Echos P notebook PC
Envision multimedia personal computer
Plain-paper fax machines
Printers
Workstations
Clerical Workstation
Power Workstation

Selected Services
OliPro (consulting, systems analysis)
OliService (network integration and support)

Selected Subsidiaries and Affiliates
Acorn Computer Group Plc (48.3%, UK)
IEPRO — Industria Electronica de Productos de Oficina
SA (44%, Mexico)
Olivetti Corporation of Japan
Olivetti Personal Computers SpA
Olivetti Telemedia SpA
Omnitel Gestioni SpA
Omnitel Pronto Italia SpA (70%)
Omnitel-Sistemi Radiocellulari Italiani SpA (59%)
Syntax Processing SpA
Triumph-Adler Leasing GmbH (Germany)

KEY COMPETITORS

Alcatel Alsthom	GEC	Pitney Bowes
Apple Computer	Harris Corp.	Siemens
AST	Hewlett-Packard	Silicon Graphics
AT&T Corp.	Hitachi	STET
Compaq	IBM	Sun
Data General	IRI	Microsystems
DEC	Machines Bull	Tandem
Dell	NCR	Unisys
Deutsche	NEC	Vobis
Telekom	Oce-van der	
Fujitsu	Grinten	
Gateway 2000	Packard Bell	

HOW MUCH

OTC symbol: OLIVY FYE: December 31	Annual Growth	1986	1987	1988	1989	1990	1991	1992	1993	1994	1995
Sales ($ mil.)	1.4%	5,473	6,375	6,435	7,132	8,019	7,501	5,430	5,028	5,568	6,208
Net income ($ mil.)	—	423	347	272	160	53	(401)	(440)	(271)	(417)	(1,008)
Income as % of sales	—	7.7%	5.4%	4.2%	2.2%	0.7%	—	—	—	—	—
Earnings per share ($)	—	0.82	0.63	0.50	0.29	0.09	(0.66)	(0.88)	(0.23)	(0.29)	(0.54)
Stock price – high ($)	—	—	—	—	—	6.00	3.88	2.80	6.00	1.91	1.44
Stock price – low ($)	—	—	—	—	—	2.72	1.98	1.17	0.80	1.09	0.64
Stock price – close ($)	(22.2%)	—	—	—	—	2.80	2.11	1.48	1.25	1.27	0.80
P/E – high	—	—	—	—	—	67	—	—	—	—	—
P/E – low	—	—	—	—	—	30	—	—	—	—	—
Dividends per share ($)	(100.0%)	0.24	0.29	0.26	0.27	0.24	0.00	0.00	0.00	0.00	0.00
Book value per share ($)	(24.0%)	5.29	6.14	5.59	5.53	5.98	5.17	3.04	1.23	0.86	0.45
Employees	(7.2%)	59,091	58,087	57,560	56,937	53,679	46,484	40,401	35,171	33,867	30,120

1995 YEAR-END

Debt ratio: 100.0%
Return on equity: —
Cash (mil.): $769
Current ratio: 1.82
Long-term debt (mil.): $1,748
No. of shares (mil.): 3,526
Dividends
Yield: —
Payout: —
Market value (mil.): $2,810

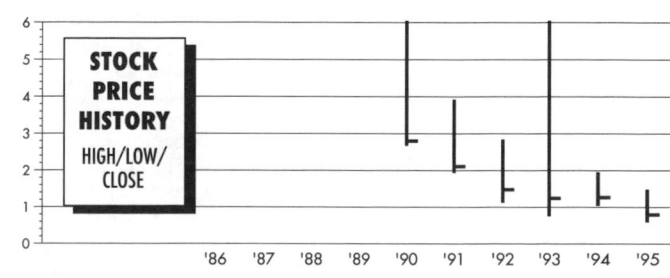

STOCK PRICE HISTORY
HIGH/LOW/CLOSE

ORACLE CORPORATION

OVERVIEW

Those who claim second sight when it comes to the computer industry are predicting a profitable future for Oracle. As the world's #1 vendor of relational database software, the Redwood City, California-based company has already made a fortune telling corporate computers how to gather information.

Now Oracle chairman and CEO Lawrence Ellison is forecasting a role for the company in such emerging technologies as interactive television and electronic commerce. Ellison is also touting network computers, low-cost terminals designed for Internet access (and independence from Microsoft's Windows operating system). At the same time, the growing client/server market is heralding sales growth for the company's application software; nearly 20% of all US offices now have Oracle's client/server applications. Oracle is targeting

corporate intranets as a major growth engine, developing server software, development tools, and applications for the enterprise-wide networks.

Alliances with key information technology companies are helping expand Oracle's industry presence. Sun Microsystems, IBM, and Netscape have joined Oracle to create a software standard for network computers; NEC and Oracle have formed a partnership to provide systems integration services in Japan; and DEC and Oracle are offering a new software-and-hardware package to speed the processing times for large databases. The company also has joined telecom superstar MCI and Rupert Murdoch's News Corp. in a joint venture to develop an online information service.

Ellison, owns about 23% of Oracle.

WHEN

Ellison, Robert Miner, and Edward Oates founded Oracle in 1977 to create a relational database management system for minicomputers according to theoretical specifications published by IBM. Ellison, who grew up on Chicago's South Side, studied physics at the University of Chicago and dropped out to seek his fortune in Silicon Valley in the 1960s. Working first for Ampex and then Amdahl, he was part of the team that developed the first IBM-compatible mainframe. Miner, a programmer with more than 14 years of experience, was mostly responsible for developing Oracle DBMS, introduced in 1979. One of Oracle's early advantages was its ability to tailor its products to run on many brands of computers of all sizes -- from PCs to mainframes.

Oracle went public in 1986 and began to make inroads into government circles. Within 2 years Oracle had a healthy 36% share of the government PC database market. It also added financial management, graphics, and human-resource management software.

Oracle's rapid growth came at a great cost. The firm developed a reputation as a leader in "vaporware," products announced but never developed. Software was released prematurely, bug-ridden, and lacking promised features. Oracle also offered generous payment terms, which led to uncollectible receivables. Duplicate billings and the booking of unconsummated sales inflated revenues. Profits were further increased by capitalizing, rather than expensing, R&D costs.

The company recorded a loss for fiscal 1991, accompanied by a downward restate for past years. Its stock nosedived. Oracle laid off 400 employees, including 6 executives, and revised its growth estimates.

Recognizing (with help from the board) that Oracle had passed the entrepreneurial stage, Ellison got company funding on solid ground by granting Nippon Steel an option to buy 25% of its Japanese operations. He also brought in Raymond Lane, formerly of Booz, Allen, giving him 6 months to reorganize. Lane streamlined and centralized the company and imposed strict performance standards. In 1992, solidly convalescent, Oracle launched Oracle7, a network database featuring simplified information access.

Sales at Oracle hit the $2 billion mark in fiscal 1994, helping secure its position as the #1 maker and distributor of DBMS software. That year British Telecom chose Oracle to provide software for its London cable network and nCUBE to provide the servers.

In 1995 the company unveiled Personal Oracle7, a desktop version of its business database software. The following year it paid $100 million for Information Resources, including the Express family of online analysis tools. That year Oracle won an order from the US Department of Defense to create one of the world's largest human-resource databases, consisting of nearly 2 million current and retired military personnel and their dependents.

Chairman, President, and CEO: Lawrence J. Ellison, age 51, $2,330,882 pay
EVP; President, Worldwide Operations: Raymond J. Lane, age 49, $1,525,127 pay
EVP and CFO: Jeffrey O. Henley, age 51, $1,088,648 pay
EVP Product Division: Dirk A. Kabcenell, age 44, $708,305 pay
SVP Corporate Development: David J. Roux, age 39, $699,992 pay
SVP, General Counsel, and Corporate Secretary: Raymond L. Ocampo Jr., age 43
SVP Human Resources: Phillip E. Wilson
VP and Corporate Controller: Thomas A. Williams, age 44
Auditors: Andersen Worldwide

WHERE

HQ: 500 Oracle Pkwy., Redwood City, CA 94065
Phone: 415-506-7000
Fax: 415-506-7200
Web site: http://www.oracle.com
Oracle has operations in 95 countries worldwide.

	1996 Sales		1996 Operating Income	
	$ mil.	% of total	$ mil.	% of total
US	1,816	43	714	75
Europe/ Middle East/Africa	1,541	37	114	12
Asia/Pacific	605	14	82	8
Other Americas	261	6	46	5
Total	**4,223**	**100**	**956**	**100**

WHAT

	1996 Sales	
	$ mil.	% of total
Licenses & other	2,296	54
Services	1,967	46
Total	**4,223**	**100**

Selected Products

Application development and business technology tools
Application design
Application development
Data access tools

Client/server business applications
Administration module

Distribution module
Finance module
Human resources module
Manufacturing module

Server technologies
Connectivity products
Distributed database servers
Gateways

Selected Services

Consulting
Education

Software updates
Technical support

KEY COMPETITORS

American Management Systems
American Software
Baan
BMC Software
Borland
Business Objects
Cognos
Computer Associates
Computer Data Systems

Conner Peripherals
DEC
Forte
Hyperion Software
IBM
Informix
Microsoft
NCR
Novell
PeopleSoft
Progress Software

PLATINUM technology
SAP
Sequent
Software AG
Sybase
Symantec
System Software Associates
Unisys
Wang

HOW MUCH

Nasdaq symbol: ORCL FYE: May 31	Annual Growth	1987	1988	1989	1990	1991	1992	1993	1994	1995	1996[1]
Sales ($ mil.)	47.1%	131	282	584	971	1,028	1,179	1,503	2,001	2,967	4,223
Net income ($ mil.)	49.7%	16	43	82	117	(12)	62	142	284	442	603
Income as % of sales	—	12.2%	15.2%	14.0%	12.0%	—	5.3%	9.4%	14.2%	14.9%	14.3%
Earnings per share ($)	44.2%	0.03	0.07	0.14	0.19	(0.02)	0.10	0.22	0.43	0.67	0.90
Stock price – high ($)	—	2.07	2.47	5.73	6.31	3.69	6.36	16.78	20.67	32.50	36.67
Stock price – low ($)	—	0.58	1.31	2.11	1.09	1.22	2.67	5.92	11.67	17.78	26.33
Stock price – close ($)	39.9%	1.61	2.17	5.20	1.75	3.22	6.31	12.78	19.61	28.25	33.13
P/E – high	—	62	34	41	33	—	64	76	48	49	41
P/E – low	—	17	18	15	6	—	27	27	27	27	29
Dividends per share ($)	—	0.00	0.00	0.00	0.00	0.00	0.00	0.00	0.00	0.00	0.00
Book value per share ($)	44.4%	0.16	0.25	0.41	0.66	0.56	0.69	0.83	1.15	1.86	4.38
Employees	40.7%	1,072	2,207	4,148	6,811	7,466	8,160	9,247	12,058	16,882	23,113

[1] Stock prices are through May 31.

1996 YEAR-END

Debt ratio: 0.2%
Return on equity: 29.6%
Cash (mil.): $841
Current ratio: 1.57
Long-term debt (mil.): $1
No. of shares (mil.): 656
Dividends
  Yield: —
  Payout: —
Market value (mil.): $21,724

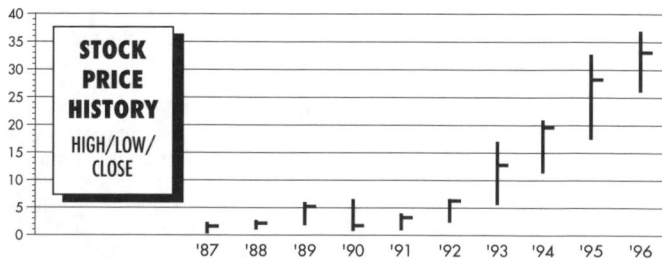

STOCK PRICE HISTORY HIGH/LOW/CLOSE

ORIGIN B.V.

OVERVIEW

Left brain vs. right brain; reason vs. intuition; establishment vs. counterculture. These are the cultural conflicts facing the newly formed Origin B.V., an information technology (IT) development and consulting firm. The Eindhoven, Netherlands-based company is the result of a long-anticipated merger between the systems subsidiary of Philips NV (the concretized left brain) and another Philips NV affiliate, Origin/BSO, which developed software (the more creative right brain). Philips NV owns about 82% of the company.

Origin's IT Services unit provides systems integration management and consulting services and project management. Its IT Systems Management offers company reengineering, outsourcing and facilities management, EDI, and other applied technical services. The company operates more than 120 offices in almost 30 countries in Europe, the Americas, and the Asia/Pacific region.

All operations were expected to be fully merged by 1997. When the merger became effective in 1996, company officials noted the possibility of taking Origin public once it has a proven business record of its own — sometime during or after 1998.

WHEN

Founded as a light bulb maker in 1891, Philips clambered into the computer age in 1958, when it opened a computer science lab. Five years later the company opened its first computer center, which it trumpeted as "unique in Europe." As computing capacities grew, the number of facilities and internal computer-based organizations increased. Eventually there were 48 computer centers providing data and information services to the company and outside clients. Different company units ended up competing for business.

To eliminate this cannibalization, in 1989 Philips consolidated several units (Information Systems and Automation, Data Process, and Corporate and National Communications) as Philips Communications & Processing Services (Philips C&P). Philips gained a 41% interest in software developer BSO in 1990 as part of the formation of BSO/Origin.

BSO had been founded in 1976 by Eckart Wintzen, a former Philips programmer. He had set up a Dutch computer subsidiary for GTE, which the company discontinued and sold to Wintzen. He named it Bureau voor Systeem Ontwikkeling (BSO — bureau for systems development). Wintzen used his Utrecht-based company to express his political and environmental views. One of the company's notable software products was an internally used program that assessed the economic cost of BSO's effects on the environment — demonstrating the impact of using plastic cups, for example — which was explained in the annual report.

The company expanded rapidly during the 1980s with an unusual "cell" structure. When an office reached a critical size (about 65 people), it split in half and opened a new office.

This autonomous, decentralized structure sufficed within Europe, but it could not support far-flung operations, so BSO sought a larger ally — Philips's internal software department (PASS), which was already a client.

In 1990, the year BSO and PASS formed the alliance BSO/Origin, Philips lost nearly $500 million. As part of a general reorganization, it launched Philips C&P and PASS as independent (but wholly owned) entities that would build their own nonaffiliated client bases.

By 1993 BSO/Origin and Philips C&P had agreed in principle to merge in order to provide full systems and software services. Studies confirmed the fit of the 2 companies operationally, but there was anxiety about how the cultures would meld (noted by the company as right brain/left brain conflict). By 1994 BSO/Origin's results had begun to lag because of the effects of rapid expansion (during 1993 and 1994 it opened 20 offices). Eschewing the idea of taking on an ailing partner, Philips C&P delayed the merger for a year while BSO/Origin turned itself around.

One of the factors that contributed to BSO/Origin's 1995 rejuvenation was winning a contract to manage facilities for British Coal. The companies also spent 1995 threading their way through the complex maze of Dutch merger regulations and attempting to reconcile the companies' vastly different internal cultures.

Philips C&P merged with BSO/Origin in 1996 to form Origin BV. The new company's first big deal was a contract with the UK's Imperial Chemical Industries to provide system support and management services for ICI's European operations.

WHO

CEO: Geoffrey Carroll
COO: Thomas M. Butler
CFO: Wil C. J. T. van Gorp
Director Human Resources: Mattjis Kropholler
President and CEO, Origin IT Services US: Tony
Stepanski
CFO, Origin IT Services US: Robert Rhode
Manager Human Resources, Origin IT Services US:
Alyson Zanden
Auditors: KPMG Peat Marwick

WHERE

HQ: Euclideslaan 2, NL 3584 BN, Utrecht, The
Netherlands
Phone: +31-30-586800
Fax: +31-30-2586710
US HQ: Mountain Heights Center, 430 Mountain Ave.,
Murray Hill, NJ 07974-2732
US Phone: 908-508-1700
US Fax: 908-508-0882
Web site: http://www.origin.nl

Origin has offices in 28 countries in the Americas, the
Asia/Pacific region, and Europe.

	1995 Sales	
	$ mil.	% of total
The Netherlands	466	39
Other Europe	429	36
South America	126	10
North America	126	10
Asia/Pacific	42	4
Other	11	1
Total	**1,200**	**100**

WHAT

	1995 Sales		1995 Pretax Income	
	$ mil.	% of total	$ mil.	% of total
BSO/Origin	622	52	9	30
Philips C&P	578	48	22	70
Total	**1,200**	**100**	**31**	**100**

Selected Services

Origin IT Services
Application facilities management
Consulting
Project management
Systems integration

Origin IT Systems Management
Electronic Data Interchange (Internet and electronic
payment systems)
Network management
Outsourcing and facilities management
Technical Automation Services (computer assisted
design and engineering data management systems)
Transformational Services (company reengineering)

Selected Subsidiaries and Affiliates
Hyperion (66%; transaction processing software)
ICA MFG/PRO
ICA SAP
ICA Support Services
ICA Triton Consultancy Group
ISES International (with KPMG; Information
Technology management training)
Philips Home Services

KEY COMPETITORS

American Management	Control Data
Andersen Consulting	Coopers & Lybrand
Arthur D. Little	Deloitte Touche Tohmatsu
Bain & Co.	EDS
Booz, Allen	Ernst & Young
Boston Consulting	Getronics
Cap Gemini	ICL PLC
Celsius Industrier	Logica
CompuCom	McKinsey & Co.
Computer Sciences	Perot Systems
Computer Task Group	

HOW MUCH

Private company FYE: December 31	Annual Growth	1986	1987	1988	1989	1990	1991	1992	1993	1994	1995
Sales ($ mil.)	22.2%	—	—	—	—	—	539	617	629	860	1,200
Employees	18.9%	—	—	—	—	—	—	—	—	8,216	9,772

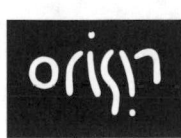

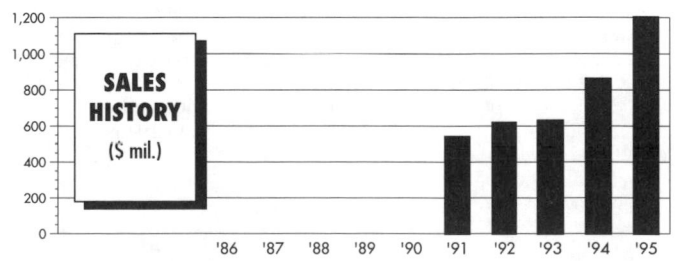

SALES HISTORY ($ mil.)

PACKARD BELL ELECTRONICS, INC.

OVERVIEW

The global competition for computer dollars is getting even hotter. Sacramento, California-based Packard Bell, the US's top seller of home PCs, has merged with Japanese PC leader NEC's personal computer operations outside Japan and China. The new company becomes the world's 4th largest PC firm (after Compaq, IBM, and Apple). The deal boosted NEC's 20% share of privately held Packard Bell to 35-40%. French computer maker Groupe Bull owns 20%, while company cofounders including CEO Beny Alagem (who remains in charge) control the rest.

Packard Bell has led the US's competitive home PC market with about a 13% share. The company pioneered the idea of selling PCs through retail channels — its distributors include Wal-Mart, Sears, Price/Costco, and Montgomery Ward. NEC, which has had so-so success marketing its machines outside Japan and China, has coveted an entree into the US market.

Despite its strong sales, Packard Bell has struggled recently. The company blames its 1995 red ink on capital investments, while analysts say the company has sacrificed profitability to undercut the competition. Packard Bell, which has a shaky reputation for quality and customer support, has had to call on Bull, NEC, and chip maker Intel for cash infusions. NEC has contributed production support to improve quality. As part of an investment by Bull, in 1996 Packard Bell acquired that company's Zenith Data Systems subsidiary (notebook computers and servers).

WHEN

Israeli immigrants Alagem (formerly a member of the Israeli intelligence community), Jason Barzilay, and Alex Sandel, owners of a computer component distribution company, decided to enter the PC business in the mid-1980s. With so many upstarts doing the same thing, they wanted something to give their company credibility. They found that something in late 1985 when Alagem acquired the Packard Bell name from Teledyne for less than $100,000. The original Packard Bell made radios beginning in the 1920s and later moved into TV manufacturing, but by the mid-1980s it was defunct. Having the name of a company that had been around since the 1920s gave their products an instant heritage, and the inferences consumers might make with respect to the better-known Hewlett-Packard and Bell Telephone didn't hurt. Alagem, Barzilay, and Sandel founded their computer company, Packard Bell, in 1986.

The next year the new company shipped its first PCs to mass-market retail stores, a channel its competitors had avoided because of the risks of high return rates. As part of its strategy of making its products as user-friendly as possible, Packard Bell loaded its machines with operating systems, applications, and entertainment software. In 1988 the firm became the first PC maker to offer toll-free technical support, and in 1989 it became the first to provide on-site service in customers' homes.

By 1990 the company had more than $500 million in sales and was earning high marks for the reliability of its machines (but poor marks for customer support, which it consequently has been trying to beef up). In 1991 Packard Bell moved into Europe, opening a marketing headquarters in Paris and a factory in the Netherlands.

In 1992 Packard Bell began offering fully configured multimedia systems. That year it announced plans to go public, but when it posted less-than-stellar financial numbers (partly because of a high number of returns), investors balked and the IPO was withdrawn. However, to compete with IBM and Compaq, who were beginning to move in on its turf, Packard Bell needed cash, so in 1993 it sold 19.9% of itself to Groupe Bull.

After the Northridge, California, earthquake destroyed its headquarters in 1994, the company moved to Sacramento, where it converted an old Army depot into its new home. That year Packard Bell added several software products, including children's storybook titles. In 1995 it launched Spectria, a line of multimedia PCs with built-in monitors.

In mid-1996 Packard Bell and NEC (1995 sales of $43 billion) announced a merger of their PC operations, a deal that included the transfer to $300 million in NEC assets to Packard Bell. That year Packard Bell introduced its Platinum line of computers, including a 166-megahertz Pentium model.

Chairman, President, and CEO: Beny Alagem, age 43
COO: Roger A. Nordby
CFO: Phil Handley
President, International Operations: Brent Cohen
VP Marketing: Mal D. Ransom
Director Human Resources: Karen Schmidt

WHERE

HQ: One Packard Bell Way, Sacramento, CA 95828-0903
Phone: 916-388-0101
Fax: 916-388-1109
Web site: http://www.packardbell.com

Packard Bell has manufacturing and distribution facilities in Australia, Brazil, Canada, France, Israel, Japan, Hong Kong, Singapore, and the US.

WHAT

Selected Products

Packard Bell
Desktop PCs
Monitors
Multimedia PCs

Zenith Data Systems
Commercial servers
Desktop PCs
Laptop computers
Wireless remote PC interfaces

KEY COMPETITORS

Acer
Advanced Logic Research
Amstrad
Apple Computer
AST
Compaq
DEC
Dell
Fujitsu
Gateway 2000
Hewlett-Packard
Hitachi
Hyundai
IBM
Machines Bull
Matsushita
Micron Electronics
NCR
Oki
Olivetti
Power Computing
Sharp
Siemens
Sony
Tandy Corporation
Texas Instruments
Toshiba
Vobis

HOW MUCH

Private company FYE: December 31	Annual Growth	1986	1987	1988	1989	1990	1991	1992	1993	1994	1995
Sales ($ mil.)	57.9%	—	—	188	338	518	676	925	1,250	3,000	4,600
Net income ($ mil.)	—	—	—	—	—	—	5	—	48	99	—
Income as % of sales	—	—	—	—	—	—	0.7%	—	3.8%	3.3%	—
Employees	35.7%	—	—	—	—	—	—	2,000	2,600	4,000	5,000

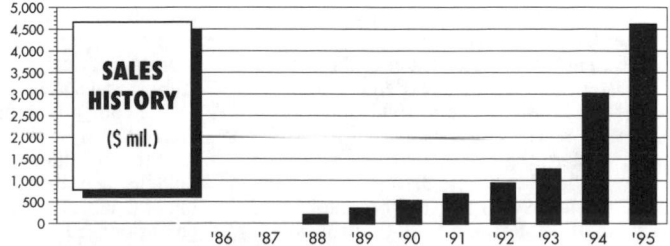

SALES HISTORY ($ mil.)

QUANTUM CORPORATION

OVERVIEW

When it comes to computer storage, Quantum saves the data. The Milpitas, California-based company makes disk drives — the main storage units of computers — for 9 of the 10 top computer makers. Compaq accounts for about 12% of Quantum's sales, while Apple accounts for about 11%. Quantum was the #1 disk drive maker until the 1996 merger of #2 Seagate and #3 Conner Peripherals. However, Quantum still has 23% of the $22 billion hard disk market.

Quantum blames its recent red ink on a slowdown in personal computer sales and difficulty competing with rival Seagate in the high-end drive sector. To regain its momentum, Quantum phased out its plants in California and Malaysia (including a layoff of

2,250 workers) and transferred its remaining manufacturing to Japanese firm Matsushita-Kotobuki Electronics (MKE), which already made Quantum's low-end drives. This frees Quantum to concentrate on design and marketing.

Despite slow PC sales, markets for workstations and servers are robust, and applications such as graphics and multimedia are increasingly storage-intensive. To keep its customers' interest, Quantum keeps breaking storage capacity barriers — it introduced the first 3.8 gigabyte, 3-disk desktop drive. The company has also entered the retail channel, selling PC drives through CompUSA stores and Multiple Zone mail order catalogs.

WHEN

Founded in 1980 by a group including David Brown and James Patterson, Quantum was almost immediately successful. It began manufacturing 8" hard disk drives in early 1981 and, in its first year of business, reported $14 million in sales. Plus Development was founded in 1983 as Quantum's sales, marketing, and R&D arm.

Apple became a customer during 1986. The next year Plus Development was awarded a patent for its Hardcard, a "hard-disk-on-a-card" that slides into floppy disk drives. Hardcard revenues rose from about $10 million in 1986 to more than $60 million in 1987. However, Quantum fell behind in the hard disk drive market in 1987, losing 8-inch and 5.25-inch drive sales as the industry began moving to 3.5-inch models. CEO Stephen Berkley repositioned the company to concentrate on this emerging market. By turning over manufacturing to Japan's MKE, a leader in robotics manufacturing and a subsidiary of Matsushita Electric, Quantum saved time and money in getting its first 3.5-inch models, the ProDrive Series, to market in 1988.

On the strength of its 3.5-inch drives, Quantum acquired a host of new customers, including Sun Microsystems, AT&T, Hewlett-Packard, Unisys, Intel, and Zenith.

NEC paid almost $3 million to the company in a patent infringement settlement in 1988. Another suit was settled in 1990, and this time Quantum received net proceeds of $3.7 million from Western Digital.

By 1990, 3.5-inch disk drives were accounting for almost 90% of Quantum's sales. William Miller, formerly with Control Data,

succeeded Berkley as CEO in 1992. Quantum and MKE renewed their long-term agreement whereby Quantum has the exclusive right to design and market worldwide and MKE has the exclusive right to manufacture worldwide. Also that year Quantum folded Plus Development into Quantum Commercial Products, a new unit established to better meet buyers' needs.

Quantum lost market share as demand exceeded supply in 1992. Less than a year later, though, demand faltered and the worst price wars in the industry's history began.

In 1994 Quantum opened an international repair center in Malaysia, and the company bought the disk, tape, and solid-state drive and thin film head operations of Digital Equipment Corp. (DEC) that year. The $348 million purchase, which included DEC's cutting-edge magneto-resistive recording head technology, expanded the company's mainframe and minicomputer product lines.

In 1995 Quantum opened PT Quantum Peripherals Indonesia to manufacture thin film recording heads; the plant had belonged to DEC. That year both Compaq and Silicon Graphics added Quantum storage as an optional feature on their high-end systems. Also in 1995 Quantum and software developer Symantec agreed to codevelop S.M.A.R.T. (self-monitoring analysis and reporting technology) storage and software products.

The company returned to the 5.25-inch drive market in 1996 after a 16-year hiatus with its introduction of the Bigfoot drive family. That year charges related to the restructuring of Quantum's high-capacity drive operations led to a loss for the year.

WHO

Chairman: Stephen M. Berkley
President and CEO: Michael A. Brown
EVP Worldwide Sales: William F. Roach
EVP Hard Disk Drive Operations: Mark Jackson
President Workstation System Storage Group and Chief Technical Officer: Kenneth Lee
President Recording Heads Group: William Robinette
EVP Finance, CFO and Secretary: Joseph T. Rodgers
President and General Manager Desktop and Portable Storage Group: Young K. Sohn
VP Human Resources: Deborah E. Barber
Auditors: Ernst & Young LLP

WHERE

HQ: 500 McCarthy Blvd., Milpitas, CA 95035
Phone: 408-894-4000
Fax: 408-894-3218
Web site: http://www.quantum.com

Quantum has manufacturing facilities in Colorado and Massachusetts and overseas in Indonesia. Its manufacturing partner, Matsushita-Kotobuki Electronics, has facilities in Ireland, Japan, and Singapore.

	1996 Sales		1996 Operating Income	
	$ mil.	% of total	$ mil.	% of total
US	2,602	53	(167)	—
Europe	2,187	44	337	—
Other regions	161	3	(117)	—
Adjustments	(527)	—	(166)	—
Total	**4,423**	**100**	**(113)**	**—**

WHAT

Operating Divisions and Products

Desktop and Portable Storage Group (hard disk drives for desktop and portable systems)

Recording Heads Group (thin film inductive and magnetoresistive recording heads)

Specialty Storage Products Group (linear tape drives and solid state disk drives)

Workstation and Systems Storage Group (disk drives for high-end desktop systems, minicomputers, servers, storage subsystems, and servers)

KEY COMPETITORS

Amdahl
Data General
EMC Corp.
Exabyte
Fujitsu
Hewlett-Packard
Hyundai
IBM
Imation
Iomega
Kingston Technology
Seagate
Storage Technology
Syquest
Toshiba
Western Digital

HOW MUCH

Nasdaq symbol: QNTM FYE: March 31	Annual Growth	1987	1988	1989	1990	1991	1992	1993	1994	1995	1996
Sales ($ mil.)	49.2%	121	189	208	446	878	1,128	1,697	2,131	3,368	4,423
Net income ($ mil.)	—	9	(3)	13	47	74	47	94	3	82	(90)
Income as % of sales	—	7.3%	—	6.2%	10.6%	8.4%	4.2%	5.5%	0.1%	2.4%	—
Earnings per share ($)	—	0.21	(0.08)	0.30	1.14	1.69	1.05	1.77	0.06	1.52	(1.74)
Stock price – high ($)[1]	—	6.00	7.50	3.06	10.67	17.18	18.18	18.00	17.75	20.25	28.50
Stock price – low ($)[1]	—	3.56	1.81	2.17	2.90	5.92	8.88	11.13	9.38	11.63	13.75
Stock price – close ($)[1]	14.9%	4.63	2.81	2.96	7.25	12.42	11.38	15.25	14.13	15.13	16.13
P/E – high	—	29	—	10	9	10	17	10	296	13	—
P/E – low	—	17	—	7	3	4	9	6	156	8	—
Dividends per share ($)	—	0.00	0.00	0.00	0.00	0.00	0.00	0.00	0.00	0.00	0.00
Book value per share ($)	16.0%	2.65	2.59	2.82	4.14	6.09	7.19	9.19	9.22	11.04	10.05
Employees	29.3%	696	508	531	763	1,445	1,752	2,455	2,984	7,265	7,036

[1] Stock prices are for the prior calendar year.

1996 YEAR-END

Debt ratio: 52.5%
Return on equity: —
Cash (mil.): $165
Current ratio: 1.86
Long-term debt (mil.): $598
No. of shares (mil.): 54
Dividends
 Yield: —
 Payout: —
Market value (mil.): $874

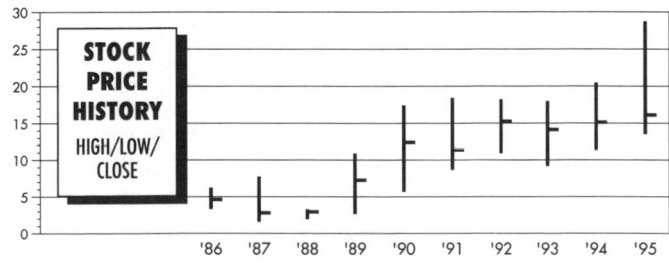

STOCK PRICE HISTORY HIGH/LOW/CLOSE

RACAL ELECTRONICS PLC

OVERVIEW

Racal Electronics is continuing to move its tuning knob back and forth, deleting and adding businesses in an effort to bring in higher profits. The Berkshire, UK-based conglomerate (with about 70 subsidiaries worldwide) has 5 operating groups in 3 principal markets — defense electronics, maritime and industrial services, and voice and data communications. The Data Communications group (which accounts for more than 40% of the company's sales) designs, builds, and manages high-speed WANs, radio data networks, and telephone systems. Racal's other business groups include Radio Communications (combat radio equipment), Defence Radar and Avionics (electronic surveillance, navigation, and radar systems for military aircraft and warships), and Marine and Energy (navigation

and radar systems for the merchant marine and offshore oil industry).

After years of tweaking, chairman Sir Ernest Harrison still appears to consider Racal a work in progress. The company is spending $30 million to radically restructure the Data Products division (a unit of the Data Communications group) in hopes of making it profitable: the division's manufacturing operations are being consolidated into the US, and 17 subsidiaries are being wrapped into one. Meanwhile, Racal is looking far and wide for complementary businesses to buy.

The company is Europe's leading supplier of electronic warfare systems, and the order backlog of its Defence Radar and Avionics group has exceeded $400 million.

WHEN

Ray Brown and Calder Cunningham merged their names and talents to form Racal (a consulting firm) in 1950. The company introduced its first proprietary product, the RA 17 radio receiver, 7 years later. Cunningham died in 1958, but Brown carried on, launching the company's IPO in 1961 and developing the Squadcal, a lightweight military man-pack radio that went into production in 1966. That same year Brown handed the reins over to Ernest Harrison, who had started with the company as an accountant.

Harrison soon had Racal on a fast growth track. The company bolstered its tactical radio business in 1969 by acquiring British Communications Corp. That year Racal also formed a partnership with US data communications firm Milgo Electronic Corp. Racal's sales reached $25 million the following year.

In 1977 Racal bought out Milgo for $60 million, then added modem manufacturer Vadic Corp. Racal made another lateral move in 1980 by acquiring Decca Ltd. (avionics, marine electronics, and radar) for $250 million. This helped make Racal a one-stop shop for all of a country's electronic warfare needs. By 1982 the company's sales had reached $1 billion, but profits were uneven.

Racal branched out in 2 ways: it won a UK cellular telephone license in 1983 and entered the building security business with its purchase of Chubb and Son PLC in 1984. Its timing couldn't have been better, since military export sales soon began to weaken, and tough competition hurt its data communications

business. Indeed, Harrison turned away from the problem children to focus on the logistical nightmare of building a nationwide cellular phone network. But Vodaphone soon proved the wisdom of the investment risk, accounting for about 1/3 of the company's profits by 1988.

Takeover rumors swirled in 1990, so Harrison announced plans to spin off the Chubb and Telecom units, then lead a management buyout of Racal. Shareholders howled, forcing him to back off the idea of taking Racal private. In August of the following year Racal spun off its cellular business as Vodaphone Group PLC. The next day British industrial conglomerate Williams Holdings PLC launched a hostile takeover bid for Racal. Shareholders refused to sell, however, and the attempt failed. Racal spun off its security business as Chubb Security PLC in 1992.

The company went on a shopping spree in 1994, buying Canadian radio equipment maker Spilsbury Communications, information technology security firm ACS Ventures, and Singapore-based submersibles manufacturer Techno Transfer.

In 1995 Racal bought the Sensors division (radar and other electronic systems) from Thorn EMI and acquired British Rail Telecommunications. The following year the company's Hermes Europe Railtel BV joint venture was given permission to build a telecommunications network alongside railway lines throughout Europe. Racal also planned to provide a managed Internet business service through another joint venture.

WHO

Chairman: Sir Ernest Harrison, $1,027,624 pay
CEO: David C. Elsbury, $807,340 pay
Director, Specialised Businesses, Marine and Energy: Martin R. Richardson, $392,442 pay
Director, Company Secretary, and Legal Services: David Whittaker, $353,126 pay
Director, Defence Radar, Avionics: Barton J. Clarke, $348,159 pay
Director, Data Communications: Paul G. Kozlowski
Director, Finance: Andrew R. Wood
CFO: J. M. Kaye
SVP Finance, Racal-Datacom: Charles Kuehne
SVP Human Resources, Racal-Datacom: Dan Bronson
Auditors: Deloitte & Touche LLP

WHERE

HQ: Western Rd., Bracknell, Berkshire, RG12 1RG, UK
Phone: +44-1-344-481-222
Fax: +44-1-344-541-19
US HQ: The Racal Corp., 1601 Harrison Pkwy, Sunrise, FL 33323-2899
US Phone: 954-846-1601
US Fax: 954-846-4942

Racal has subsidiaries and associated companies in Australia, Belgium, Bermuda, Canada, China, Denmark, France, Germany, Hong Kong, Italy, Malaysia, the Netherlands, New Zealand, Norway, Saudi Arabia, Singapore, South Africa, Sweden, the US, and the UK.

	1996 Sales	
	$ mil.	% of total
UK	933	58
North & South America	419	26
Rest of Europe	168	10
Asia & Australia	78	5
Africa	9	1
Adjustments	10	—
Total	**1,617**	**100**

WHAT

	1996 Sales	
	$ mil.	% of total
Data communications	656	41
Defense radar & avionics	276	17
Radio communications	246	15
Specialized businesses	242	15
Marine & energy	187	1
Adjustments	10	—
Total	**1,617**	**100**

Selecteed Products and Services

Channel Tunnel communications infrastructure
Electronic surveillance
Marine electronics
Navigation systems
Professional recording systems
Radar
Remotely operated underwater survey vehicles
Satellite-based inflight telephone
    and data communications systems for airlines
Secure communication for point-of-sale terminals

KEY COMPETITORS

Alcatel Alsthom	Lockheed Martin
Alcatel SEL AG	Lucent
Alliant Techsystems	Nokia Group
Banner Aerospace	Philips Kommunikations
Boeing	Industrie
Bremer Vulkan	Rockwell International
California Microwave	STET
Ceridian	Tadiran Limited
Ericsson	Texas International
GE	VSEL

HOW MUCH

OTC symbol: RCALY FYE: March 31	Annual Growth	1987	1988	1989	1990	1991	1992	1993	1994	1995	1996
Sales ($ mil.)	(3.7%)	2,262	2,959	3,296	3,521	3,118	1,633	1,434	1,359	1,541	1,617
Net income ($ mil.)	(7.8%)	146	218	195	184	146	(49)	43	23	62	70
Income as % of sales	—	6.5%	7.4%	5.9%	5.2%	4.7%	—	3.0%	1.7%	4.0%	4.4%
Earnings per share ($)	(8.7%)	1.16	1.72	1.52	1.41	1.03	(0.36)	0.31	0.16	0.44	0.51
Stock price – high ($)[1]	—	—	—	—	—	—	9.88	23.86	7.77	8.34	9.03
Stock price – low ($)[1]	—	—	—	—	—	—	8.50	4.38	4.50	5.55	6.38
Stock price – close ($)[1]	(2.7%)	—	—	—	—	—	9.88	4.83	5.70	6.97	8.84
P/E – high	—	—	—	—	—	—	—	77	48	19	18
P/E – low	—	—	—	—	—	—	—	14	28	12	13
Dividends per share ($)	1.4%	—	—	—	—	—	0.17	0.13	0.13	0.16	0.18
Book value per share ($)	(6.9%)	—	—	—	—	—	6.20	5.61	5.63	6.13	4.66
Employees	(9.8%)	32,418	31,910	33,702	37,414	38,461	34,501	12,564	11,779	11,325	12,855

[1] Stock prices are for the prior calendar year.

1996 YEAR-END

Debt ratio: 53.5%
Return on equity: 9.3%
Cash (mil.): $264
Current ratio: 2.41
Long-term debt (mil.): $711
No. of shares (mil.): 142
Dividends
  Yield: 2.1%
  Payout: 36.3%
Market value (mil.): $1,255

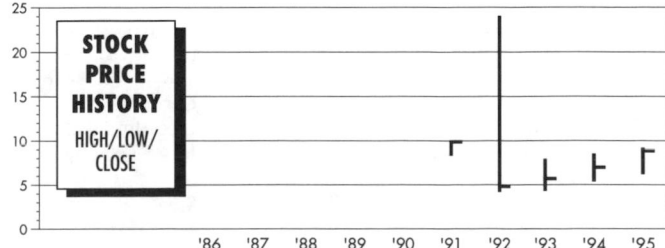

STOCK PRICE HISTORY
HIGH/LOW/CLOSE

'86 '87 '88 '89 '90 '91 '92 '93 '94 '95

READ-RITE CORPORATION

OVERVIEW

For Read-Rite, 2 heads are better than one. Based in Milpitas, California, Read-Rite is the world's #1 producer of magnetic recording heads used in rigid disk drives. The company also makes a 2nd type of head — thin-film magnetoresistive tape heads — used in 1/4-inch cartridge (QIC) tape drives.

Read-Rite's heads record and retrieve information from the surface of computer disks and are sold to disk drive manufacturers. Other products include head gimbal assemblies (HGAs, recording head combined with a suspension arm and related components) and headstack assemblies (modules that include a collection of HGAs and other parts). Western Digital, Quantum, and Seagate account for about 80% of the company's sales.

Making disk drive heads is a complicated process that requires lots of expensive equip-ment; consequently, only a few companies do it. Read-Rite maintains its 25% share of the market by controlling costs through volume manufacturing and by being a low-cost supplier to the OEMs. It has also initiated a just-in-time production process and has begun to use new technologies to operate more efficiently and improve its yield.

Though tape drive makers' profits are slumping from lower prices, Read-Rite is thriving on record demand for its components. It has begun to diversify from the disk drive business. It has purchased a stake in Redwood MicroSystems, a maker of miniature silicon micro-machined valves and actuators used in automobiles, consumer appliances, instrumentation, and other equipment and is working with Redwood to develop valves for other applications.

WHEN

Peter Bischoff and Jack Osborne left Memorex and in 1983 founded Read-Rite to manufacture heads for computer disk drives using a thin-film technology similar to the process used to make semiconductors. Through the 1980s the company struggled with high development and equipment costs and stiff competition. Following the 1989 release of the microslider (a smaller and more efficient version of the device that carries the head over a rotating disk to process information) Read-Rite became profitable, though it still depended on a single customer, Conner Peripherals (now part of Seagate), for a large majority of its sales, and its market was being threatened by Japanese competitors.

For Read-Rite, 1991 was a defining year. That year it went public and started a joint venture (called Read-Rite SMI Corporation) with Japan's #3 steel company, Sumitomo Metal Industries, to make disk drive components for that country. Also that year Read-Rite entered the market for headstack assemblies when it bought a Malaysian assembly plant from disk drive maker Maxtor. In addition, the company began producing thin-film heads in Thailand and introduced the nanoslider, an improved version of the microslider.

The SMI joint venture turned its first profit in 1993, but the disk drive industry hit a slide. Read-Rite was rocked by falling prices and order cancellations as the market shifted to higher-capacity drives, leaving the company with slim profits.

The firm focused on transforming itself into a low-cost supplier during the mid-1990s. It built its own fabrication plant (in Fremont, California) in 1994 to give it more control over the manufacturing process. That year it acquired Sunward Technologies, a leading supplier of ferrite metal recording heads, in a stock swap.

Read-Rite and Komag signed a deal in 1995 to jointly develop advanced disks and heads. A rise in the demand for business and personal computers boosted Read-Rite's sales to more than $1 billion. To keep up with growing demand, the company increased manufacturing capacity at its plants. Also in 1995 sales of the company's Tripad thin-film inductive proximity recording head (which enables faster and denser information storage) increased Read-Rite's presence in the market for high-capacity disk drives. However, two of the company's largest customers, Seagate and Quantum, began to produce their own heads in 1995, placing them in direct competition with Read-Rite.

The company in 1996 started producing magnetoresistive recording heads for 3.5" disk drives with one gigabyte capacity. Read-Rite agreed that year to purchase assets of Censtor Corporation, a San Jose-based developer of recording technology for disk drives. Read-Rite's 1996 R&D effort was focused on developing magnetic heads that will store up to 4 gigabytes of information on a single 3.5" disk.

WHO

Chairman and CEO: Cyril J. Yansouni, age 53, $1,020,000 pay
President and COO: Frederic Schwettmann, age 55, $691,200 pay
EVP R&D: Peter G. Bischoff, age 55, $388,080 pay
EVP Operations: Michael A. Klyszeiko, age 56, $380,160 pay
SVP Customer Programs: Alan S. Lowe, age 34
VP Finance and CFO: John T. Kurtzweil, age 39
VP, General Counsel, and Secretary: Rex S. Jackson, age 35
VP Human Resources: Sherry F. McVicar, age 43
Auditors: Ernst & Young LLP

WHERE

HQ: 345 Los Coches St., Milpitas, CA 95035
Phone: 408-262-6700
Fax: 408-956-3205
Web site: http://www.readrite.com

	1995 Sales	
	$ mil.	% of total
Far East	821	82
US	182	18
Total	**1,003**	**100**

WHAT

	1995 Sales
	% of total
Head gimbal assemblies	50
Headstack assemblies	48
Tape heads	2
Total	**100**

Selected Products
Ferrite metal-in-gap (MIG) heads
Head gimbal assemblies (HGAs, magnetic recording head assemblies)
Headstack assemblies (HSAs, multiple HGAs combined with other components)
Tape heads (tape heads for use in QIC drives)
Thin-film heads (thin-film magnetoresistive heads used in QIC tape drives)

	1995 Sales
	% of total
Western Digital	37
Quantum	29
Seagate (Conner)	13
Maxtor	11
Micropolis	5
Other companies	5
Total	**100**

KEY COMPETITORS

Applied Magnetics	Lafe
DMC	Matsushita
Fujitsu	NEC
Hitachi	Sony
IBM	Tandon
Kaifa	TDK
Komag	Yamaha

HOW MUCH

Nasdaq symbol: RDRT FYE: September 30	Annual Growth	1986	1987	1988	1989	1990	1991	1992	1993	1994	1995
Sales ($ mil.)	72.6%	—	—	—	38	74	177	389	482	639	1,003
Net income ($ mil.)	123.3%	—	—	—	1	7	23	47	1	20	124
Income as % of sales	—	—	—	—	1.6%	8.9%	13.0%	12.1%	0.2%	3.1%	12.3%
Earnings per share ($)	110.4%	—	—	—	0.03	0.33	1.04	1.59	0.02	0.43	2.60
Stock price – high ($)	—	—	—	—	—	—	15.88	32.00	31.25	19.88	49.50
Stock price – low ($)	—	—	—	—	—	—	11.75	14.13	8.63	10.88	14.00
Stock price – close ($)	12.0%	—	—	—	—	—	14.75	31.25	15.00	18.56	23.25
P/E – high	—	—	—	—	—	—	15	20	—	46	19
P/E – low	—	—	—	—	—	—	11	9	—	25	5
Dividends per share ($)	—	—	—	—	—	—	0.00	0.00	0.00	0.00	0.00
Book value per share ($)	6.4%	—	—	—	—	—	8.82	6.84	8.03	8.81	11.31
Employees	94.7%	—	—	—	423	893	2,500	7,522	10,448	18,472	23,074

1995 YEAR-END

Debt ratio: 23.0%
Return on equity: 26.4%
Cash (mil.): $262
Current ratio: 2.52
Long-term debt (mil.): $137
No. of shares (mil.): 48
Dividends
  Yield: —
  Payout: —
Market value (mil.): $1,106

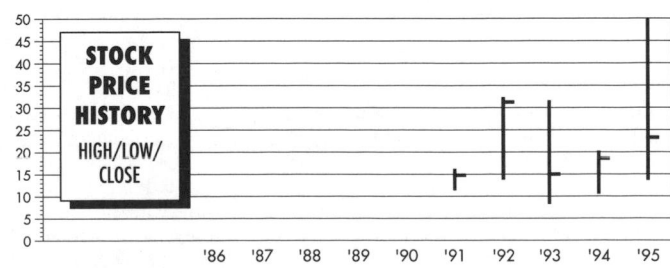

STOCK PRICE HISTORY
HIGH/LOW/CLOSE

SAMSUNG GROUP

OVERVIEW

South Korea's largest "chaebol" (industrial group), Seoul-based Samsung consists of 28 companies, including manufacturers such as Samsung Aerospace and Samsung Fine Chemicals and service companies such as Samsung Fire & Marine Insurance. The core of Samsung's rise to prominence is Samsung Electronics Co. (SEC), which brings in well over half of the group's profits. The company is the world's #1 maker of computer memory chips, principally dynamic random access memory (DRAM) chips.

The microchip market is notoriously volatile, however. A mid-decade slump in chip prices has eroded Samsung's profits, causing investments in other group companies to be put on hold. Still, chairman Lee Kun-Hee is depending on alliances, diversification, and globalization to mitigate the group's dependence on chips.

Samsung has decentralized its operations by setting up regional headquarters whose managers have more decision-making authority. Among the group's technology-sharing alliances are pacts with General Instrument (for digital television), Motorola (for personal digital assistants), and USA Video (for set-top cable television boxes). Recent group ventures include Samsung Motors, which is set to bring cars to market before the turn of the century. Samsung has even joined with rival "chaebol" Hyundai to bid on a license to provide personal communications services (PCS, a wireless telephone service) to the Korean market.

WHEN

In 1936 Japan-educated Lee Byung-Chull began operating a rice mill in Korea, then under Japanese rule. By 1938 Lee had begun trading in dried fish and had incorporated as Samsung (Korean for "Three Stars"). WWII did not inflict widespread destruction on Korea, and, by the end of the war, Samsung had transportation and real estate adjuncts.

The Korean War, however, destroyed nearly all Samsung assets. Using the profits from a surviving brewery and importing goods for UN personnel, Lee reconstructed Samsung in South Korea. He formed the highly profitable Cheil Sugar Company, at the time the country's only sugar refinery, in 1953. Establishment of textile, banking, and insurance ventures followed.

When a 1961 coup brought Park Chung Hee to power in South Korea, Lee, known for his wealth and ties to the former government, was accused of illegal profiteering. A 1966 smuggling scandal involving one of Lee's sons led to another scandal, but charges were dropped when Lee agreed to give the government an immense fertilizer plant he was building. Despite the setback, Samsung continued to grow, diversifying into paper, department stores, and publishing.

Lee established Samsung Electronics with help from Sanyo in 1969. The company grew rapidly as a result of the South Korean government's export drive and low wage rates. It gained engineering know-how by disassembling Western-designed electronic goods. It then produced inexpensive, private-label, black-and-white televisions and, later, color televisions, VCRs, and microwave ovens for General Electric, Sears, and others.

In concert with the government's industrialization push, the "chaebol" formed Samsung Shipbuilding (1974), Samsung Petrochemical (1977), and Samsung Precision Industries (aircraft engines and maintenance, 1977). Exports and a higher domestic standard of living helped group sales reach $3 billion in 1979.

In the 1980s Samsung began exporting electronic goods under its own name in an effort to increase margins. Success in low-end products encouraged the company to export up-market items. When Lee died in 1987, his son Lee Kun-Hee assumed control. After years of importing technology and spending freely on R&D, in 1990 Samsung became a world leader in chip production.

In 1992 Samsung acquired Werk fur Fernschelektronik (of the former East Germany). Encouraged by the Korean government, Samsung agreed to cooperate with fellow Korean "chaebol" Goldstar (now LG Group) to obtain foreign technology to develop liquid crystal displays.

In 1995 the Lee family paid $300 million for an 11% interest in fledgling entertainment powerhouse DreamWorks SKG.

The company acquired a 49.9% share of struggling PC maker AST Research in 1996 and installed Samsung CEO Kim Kwang-Ho as AST chairman. That year Samsung chairman Lee was caught in a corruption scandal that resulted in a death sentence for former South Korean ruler Chun Doo Hwan. Lee received a 2-year suspended sentence for bribery.

WHO

Chairman: Lee Kun-Hee, age 53
VC: Soh Byong Hae
CEO: Song Bo Soon
President, Samsung Electronics America, Inc.: Song Kiryong
President and CEO, Samsung Electronics: Kim Kwang Ho
CEO, Samsung America: M. S. Lee
Treasurer, Samsung America: J. K. Kang
General Manager Human Resources, Samsung America: Robert Schachter
EVP, Samsung Electronics America, Inc.: Kim Insoo
President and CEO, Samsung North America: Song Bo-Son
VP, Samsung North America: Moon Sung Cho
Auditors: Samil Accounting Corp.

WHERE

HQ: CPO Box 1580, Seoul, Korea
Phone: +82-2-724-0361
Fax: +82-2-724-0198
US HQ: Samsung America, Inc., 105 Challenger Rd., Ridgefield Park, NJ 07660
US Phone: 201-229-6050
US Fax: 201-229-6058
Web site: http://www.samsung.com

WHAT

	1995 Group Sales	
	$ mil.	% of total
Electronics	26,700	31
Financial & insurance	19,800	23
Machinery	5,400	6
Chemicals	2,100	2
Other companies	33,000	38
Total	**87,000**	**100**

Selected Group Companies

Electronics
Samsung Corning Co., Ltd.
Samsung Display Devices Co., Ltd.
Samsung Electronics Co., Ltd.

Finance and Insurance
Samsung Finance Co.
Samsung Fire & Marine Insurance Co., Ltd.
Samsung Life Insurance Co., Ltd.
Samsung Securities Co., Ltd.

Machinery
Samsung Aerospace Industries, Ltd.
Samsung Heavy Industries Co., Ltd.

Chemicals
Samsung Fine Chemicals Co., Ltd.
Samsung Petrochemical Co., Ltd.

Samsung-BP Chemicals Co., Ltd.

Other
Cheil Communications Inc.
Hotel Shilla Co., Ltd.
Innovative Design Lab of Samsung
The Joong-Ang Daily News
Samsung Art & Design Institute
Samsung Economic Research Institute
Samsung Entertainment Group
Samsung Fashion Institute
Samsung Foundation of Culture
Samsung Medical Center
Samsung Motors Co., Ltd.

KEY COMPETITORS

Daewoo
DuPont
Exxon
GE
Hitachi
Hyundai
ITOCHU
LG Group
Litton Industries
Marubeni

Micron Technology
Mitsubishi
Mitsui
NEC
Philips
Sharp
Sony
Sumitomo
Tokio Marine and Fire
Toshiba

HOW MUCH

Industrial group FYE: December 31	Annual Growth	1986	1987	1988	1989	1990	1991	1992	1993	1994	1995
Sales ($ mil.)	32.3%	7,000	22,000	29,400	34,200	40,900	43,900	48,900	51,300	63,900	87,000
Net income ($ mil.)	39.8%	187	259	498	511	330	348	375	521	1,681	3,802
Income as % of sales	—	2.7%	1.2%	1.7%	1.5%	0.8%	0.8%	0.8%	1.0%	2.6%	4.4%
Employees	5.1%	—	—	—	—	182,000	183,000	189,000	191,000	206,407	233,000

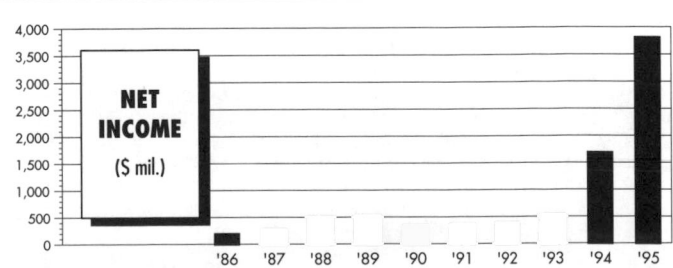

NET INCOME ($ mil.)

SAP AG

OVERVIEW

Die U.S. ist das Mutterland der Datenverarbeitung — "the US is the motherland of data processing." That may be true, but Walldorf, Germany-based SAP is oozing with profits soaked up in the client/server software market. The company controls about 1/3 of the worldwide market for corporate client/server application programs, used to integrate and process information in areas including product distribution, finance, human resources, and manufacturing. SAP's 2 main product lines are R/2, software for mainframes, and R/3, UNIX-based software for servers and workstations. The increased popularity of client/server systems in the corporate world has fueled strong sales of the company's products.

Though SAP dominates the client/server software market, competition is increasing as the market expands. Challengers such as Oracle (with about 10% of the market), Marcam, and System Software Associates are trying to win over customers by pointing out potential weaknesses in SAP's flagship R/3 program. The product, they claim, is hard to install, customize, or integrate with existing software systems. SAP's rivals also point out that the R/3 has become outdated, which could require costly upgrades or modifications.

To stay ahead, SAP is adding Internet and telephone capabilities to its R/3 software. With a company's internal computer system linked to the World Wide Web, customers can check prices and availability of products, distributors can verify inventory, and sales staff can access account information and other important data.

SAP is far from the typical German company. A sense of the entrepreneurial pervades the company's small-town headquarters, giving it an almost California feel. While most German employees wear suits to work, SAP's offices are more casual, with employees donning sandals and choosing their own schedules. Three of the 4 SAP founders retain control of about 2/3 of the company's shares.

WHEN

Software engineers Hans-Werner Hector, Dietmar Hopp, Hasso Plattner, and Klaus Tschira (all of whom are on the "Forbes" list of the world's most wealthy, with over $7 billion among them) started SAP in 1972 when the project they were working on for IBM was being moved to another unit. The 4 agreed to write a program for IBM customer Imperial Chemical Industries (UK), and SAP (named for the IBM project they left — Systems, Applications and Projects), was formed.

The group worked nights on borrowed computers until business picked up. Their first year they launched a real-time accounting transaction processing program, called R/1. Seven years later, they adapted the program to create R/2 mainframe software, used to link a company's external databases and communication systems.

The company went public in 1988. That year it decided to tap the client/server market and began a massive R&D project to create its next generation of software. Over the next 4 years SAP invested more than $650 million to develop a program that didn't share a single line of code with its predecessors. In 1992, as sales of its R/2 mainframe software lagged, SAP introduced its R/3 client/server software.

Still basically a stranger outside Europe, SAP built a technology development center that year in Foster City, California, to attract attention from the Silicon Valley crowd. To support the push into the US, the company launched a $2 million advertising campaign in 1993 (though it wasn't supported by the board). The gamble paid off as sales soared past projections, making the company the world's leading developer of client/server software. Also in 1993 SAP introduced a Japanese version of R/3 and agreed with Microsoft to make R/3 compatible with Windows NT.

By 1995 the US had become SAP's largest market, accounting for 30% of its sales, 3 points ahead of the company's homeland. That year it teamed with Microsoft, Netscape, and Sun Microsystems to make R/3 software compatible with the Internet.

SAP opened an office in Singapore in 1996 to boost the company's presence in Asia; it also upped its stake in IntelliCorp, which makes business modeling software used with R/3, to 14%. That year, apparently unwittingly, co-founder Hector signed away control of about 10% of SAP's common shares, possibly undermining takeover barriers.

Chairman: Bernd Thiemann
Chairman Administration, Sales and Consulting, Germany: Dietmar Hopp
Deputy Chairman Business Development and Technology: Hasso Plattner
VP Training: Hans-Werner Hector
VP Logistics Development: Claus E. Heinrich
VP Financials Development and Industry Solutions: Henning Kagermann
VP Human Resources Development: Klaus Tschira
CEO, SAP America, Inc.: Paul Wahl
Auditors: Andersen Worldwide

WHERE

HQ: Neurottstrasse 16, 69190, Walldorf, Germany
Phone: +49-6227-34-0
Fax: +49-6227-34-12-82
US HQ: SAP America, Inc., 701 Lee Rd., Ste. 200, Wayne, PA 19087
US Phone: 610-725-4500
US Fax: 610-725-4555
Web site: http://www.sap.com

SAP has offices, partners, and subsidiaries in more than 50 countries.

	1995 Sales	
	$ mil.	% of total
America	659	35
Germany	555	30
Rest of Europe	434	23
Asia/Australia	195	10
Africa	31	2
Total	**1,875**	**100**

WHAT

	1995 Sales	
	$ mil.	% of total
Product sales	1,345	72
Consulting	347	19
Training	157	8
Other	26	1
Total	**1,875**	**100**

Selected Products
R/2 (software for mainframes)
R/3 (UNIX-based software for servers and workstations)

KEY COMPETITORS

Amdahl
Borland
Computer Associates
Dun & Bradstreet
Marcam
Microsoft
Oracle
PeopleSoft, Inc.
Progress Software
Santa Cruz Operation
SAS
Software AG
Sybase
System Software Associates
Wang

HOW MUCH

Principal exchange: Frankfurt FYE: December 31	Annual Growth	1986	1987	1988	1989	1990	1991	1992	1993	1994	1995
Sales ($ mil.)	51.8%	—	—	101	217	333	465	513	634	1,182	1,875
Net income ($ mil.)	53.6%	—	—	14	41	54	81	78	84	181	282
Income as % of sales	—	—	—	13.8%	19.0%	16.3%	17.4%	15.3%	13.3%	15.4%	15.0%
Earnings per share ($)	42.8%	—	—	0.23	0.47	0.62	0.89	0.78	0.84	1.79	2.78
Stock price – high ($)	—	—	—	—	21.90	29.19	22.37	22.77	21.28	68.41	189.18
Stock price – low ($)	—	—	—	—	13.28	18.24	16.32	17.70	13.80	22.85	69.55
Stock price – close ($)	41.6%	—	—	—	19.18	18.45	18.42	21.77	20.65	66.15	154.40
P/E – high	—	—	—	—	47	47	25	29	25	38	68
P/E – low	—	—	—	—	28	30	18	23	16	13	25
Dividends per share ($)	30.8%	—	—	—	0.18	0.20	0.24	0.22	0.25	0.55	0.90
Book value per share ($)	34.4%	—	—	—	1.78	3.38	3.93	5.53	5.80	7.88	10.51
Employees	30.8%	—	—	—	1,367	2,138	2,685	3,157	3,648	5,229	6,857

1995 YEAR-END

Debt ratio: 6.3%
Return on equity: 30.2%
Cash (mil.): $277
Current ratio: 4.15
Long-term debt (mil.): $29
No. of shares (mil.): 101
Dividends
 Yield: 0.6%
 Payout: 32.5%
Market value (mil.): $15,631

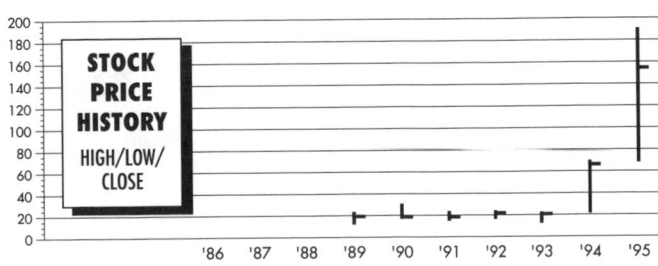

STOCK PRICE HISTORY
HIGH/LOW/CLOSE

SAS INSTITUTE INC.

OVERVIEW

Cary, North Carolina-based SAS Institute, regarded as one of the world's most user-friendly software companies, has customers in more than 100 countries. It is best known for its SAS System, a suite of information delivery software that allows users to access, manage, analyze, and present data. The SAS System includes tools for financial analysis, market research, and report writing, among other things. Customers include many big-name companies, including AT&T, Intel, and Sony.

SAS Institute is moving full steam ahead in the data warehousing market. The latest version of SAS System, dubbed the Orlando Release, furthers the software's ability to store and allow manipulation of information. SAS Institute is introducing industry-specific soft-

ware with its packaged products for human resources reporting and financial consulting and reporting.

The company provides basic technical support for its more than 3 million customers, as well as organizing conferences, councils, and user groups where customers can get assistance and feedback from SAS's staff. The institute also distributes ballots and surveys for customer input. It is an industry leader in research and development, reinvesting an average of 37% of its revenues. The company has a reputation as an excellent place to work and has a 4% turnover rate, compared to the national industry average of 15%. It also claims to have the nation's largest childcare center.

WHEN

The SAS Institute was started in 1976 by 2 North Carolina State University professors, James Goodnight and John Sall. The 2 had developed their own mainframe statistical analysis software package, which gained popularity at other southern campuses. Eventually, the package's popularity led the professors to go out on their own. By 1994 almost all the top 100 companies in the *FORTUNE* 500 had site license agreements for SAS Institute software.

Inc. magazine named the SAS Institute as one of the fastest-growing private companies in the US in 1982. The firm began rewriting SAS System software to make it hardware independent in 1984. While rewriting the package in C language, the company ran into a problem — none of the commercial C compilers supported the IBM 370 mainframe architecture. It then began developing MultiVendor Architecture in C to allow the package to be hardware and platform-independent. That year Intel sold its SYSTEM 2000 DBMS to SAS Institute.

The company acquired Lattice Inc., a prominent maker of C language code translators, to assist with adapting SAS software to the PC environment in 1986. The next year the complete version of SAS System for the PC was released and in 1988 the institute unveiled systems for UNIX platforms.

In 1989 SAS released JMP software for the Apple Macintosh, developed a cooperative software program with IBM and began consulting services. Also that year *Working Mother* maga-

zine declared the institute one of the 10 best in the US for working mothers.

By 1990 the company completed its redesign of all SAS System software so it would be completely hardware independent in the mainframe and minicomputer platforms. Later that year SAS System was released for the OS/2 environment. The institute also introduced a new menu-driven, task-oriented interface to the SAS System that allowed those with limited computer experience to access it.

SAS's revenues continued to increase in 1991, despite a weak global economy. That year it participated with DEC in its efforts to develop systems software for its new family of RISC-based processors. The company released its first vertical market product for the pharmaceutical and biotech industries in 1992 and in 1993 introduced software for building customized executive information systems. It released a version of its SAS/Access communications software, which ties its data analysis tools more closely to client/server applications, the following year.

The Orlando Release, an expanded version of the SAS System's data warehousing capabilities, was delivered in late 1995. The next year SAS entered an agreement with Big 6 accounting firm KPMG Peat Marwick. The accounting firm will use SAS's Rapid Warehousing program to evaluate warehouse implementation strategies for clients.

President and CEO: James H. Goodnight
SVP: John Sall
CFO: Greyson Quarles
Director Information Systems: Charlie Dunham
Director North American Sales and Marketing: Barrett R. Joyner
Director Human Resources: David Russo
Auditors:

WHERE

HQ: SAS Campus Dr., Cary, NC 27513
Phone: 919-677-8000
Fax: 919-677-8123
Web site: http://www.sas.com

SAS Institute has offices, subsidiaries, and distributors in about 60 countries and districts.

	1995 Sales % of total
North America	51
Europe	38
Asia/Pacific	11
Total	**100**

Regional Locations

Atlanta	Detroit	New York
Austin	Hartford, CT	Orlando, FL
Bedminster, NJ	Houston	Philadelphia
Boston	Indianapolis	Phoenix
Carey, NC	Kansas City, MO	Pittsburgh
Chicago	Los Angeles	Rockville, MD
Cincinnati	Minneapolis	St. Louis
Dallas	Nashville	San Francisco
Denver	New Orleans	Seattle

SAS International Locations

Australia	Indonesia	Portugal
Austria	Italy	Singapore
Belgium	Japan	Slovenia
Canada	Malaysia	South Africa
China	Mexico	South Korea
Denmark	Middle East	Spain
Finland	The Netherlands	Sweden
France	New Zealand	Switzerland
Germany	Norway	Taiwan
Hong Kong	Philippines	Thailand
Hungary	Poland	UK

WHAT

SAS System Features
Applications development
Data access
Data analysis
Data management
Data presentation

Selected Customers

American Airlines	DuPont
Apple Computer	Ford
AUDI	General Dynamics
Banc One	General Mills
Bank of America	General Motors
Black & Decker	Georgia-Pacific
BMW	Hershey
Boeing	Hewlett-Packard
Boise Cascade	Honda
Campbell Soup	IBM
Chase Manhattan	J. P. Morgan
Chrysler	Kellogg
Citicorp	McDonald's
Coca-Cola	McDonnell Douglas
Colgate-Palmolive	McGraw-Hill
Corning	Novell
Daimler-Benz	PepsiCo
Delta Air Lines	Philip Morris
Deutsche Bank	Procter & Gamble
Dun & Bradstreet	Rockwell International
	Rolls-Royce
	Sanyo Electric
	Sun Microsystems
	Turner Broadcasting
	United Airlines
	Washington Post
	Xerox

KEY COMPETITORS

Borland
Computer Associates
Dun & Bradstreet
IBM
Infodata Systems
Microsoft
Novell
Oracle
Progress Software
SAP
Sybase
System Software Associates
VMARK Software

HOW MUCH

Private company FYE: December 31	Annual Growth	1986[1]	1987[1]	1988	1989	1990	1991	1992	1993	1994	1995
Sales ($ mil.)	21.4%	98	130	170	206	240	295	366	420	482	562
Employees	12.1%	1,077	1,344	1,537	1,970	2,237	2,386	2,600	2,897	3,260	3,000

[1] Estimated

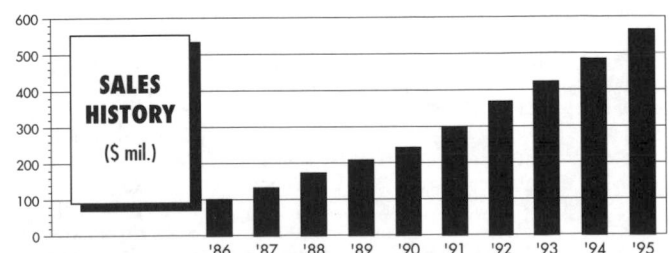

SALES HISTORY ($ mil.)

SCI SYSTEMS, INC.

OVERVIEW

Call SCI the unknown computer company. Although it is one of the largest computer manufacturers, SCI isn't well known because it contracts its services to big-name companies. Among the logos on SCI-made machines are those of Dell, Conner Peripherals, Hewlett-Packard (HP), and IBM. In 1995 HP alone accounted for 39% of the company's business.

SCI builds computers and hundreds of other electronic products and parts for a long list of mostly anonymous customers. The company runs one of the world's largest surface-mount technology operations (SMT fixes components to both sides of a circuit board, instead of a single side). Its flexible and superefficient assembly lines can build a PC in 45 seconds.

With PC sales booming and HP hustling to become a top vendor, in 1995 SCI's order backlog doubled to nearly $2 billion.

Also in 1995 SCI agreed to acquire the contract manufacturing business of Digital Equipment Corp. (DEC), including DEC's Maine plant and contract accounts. SCI will also supply DEC with networking electronics products that DEC had previously made at the plant.

Founder and CEO Olin King owns 4.4% of the company.

WHEN

Olin King (a former employee at Wernher von Braun's army rocket center) and 2 friends started Space Craft Inc., later SCI Systems, in 1961 in Huntsville, Alabama. The 3 men combined their $21,000 in savings with $300,000 in venture capital and started the company to do contract engineering for NASA.

Initially the company specialized in building electronics systems for the Saturn rocket and later for other NASA and military missile and satellite programs. Its product line expanded to include subsystems for military aircraft (e.g., cockpit controls for the F-15 fighter plane) and military surface systems.

SCI's major breakthrough came in 1976 with a contract from IBM to produce sub-assemblies for IBM terminals. The contract helped the company get its start in subcontracting for OEMs. SCI continued to do work for the US government, but it also began to build everything from white blood cell analyzers to coin sorters.

When IBM went to work on its personal computer, introduced in 1981, it turned to SCI with a $30 million contract for the PC's first batch of circuit boards. IBM shipped 100,000 PCs in 1981. In 1984 that number had grown to 2.3 million — all outfitted with SCI boards. SCI's contracts with IBM, which extended to other parts and subassemblies for the PC, accelerated SCI's sales. The company was ranked as the 8th fastest-growing electronics company in the US in 1985, based on its sales growth between 1981 and 1985. SCI's 1985 sales totaled $538 million.

In an attempt to reduce its reliance on IBM contracts, which accounted for 60% of sales in 1982-83, SCI expanded into making entire microcomputers (1984) and selling them to companies like Kodak, which resold them under its label. However, microcomputer sales could not compensate for SCI's loss when IBM cut its orders for circuit boards in 1985. SCI's sales dropped 12% in 1986.

The company's sales bounced back in 1987 after SCI negotiated a new contract with IBM for circuit boards for IBM's PS/2 computers, but the experience of a dropoff in IBM contracts sent SCI looking for new customers.

SCI built additional facilities in the US and overseas and moved quickly into a leadership position among SMT manufacturers. Because of the high cost of surface-mount production, companies rely on subcontractors such as SCI to supply surface-mount boards.

In 1990 SCI added capacity by increasing to 100% its holdings in Adelantos de Tecnologia (Mexico) and Cambridge Computer (UK). The company opened a new plant in Canada and acquired a California manufacturing facility from Tandem Computers in 1992, and the next year it expanded its plant in Guadalajara, Mexico, to meet increased demand.

In 1994 SCI bought Hewlett-Packard's Surface Mount Centre in Grenoble, France. Also in 1994 the company reached an agreement to sell Cambridge Computer.

NEC signed up SCI in 1995 for a contract worth over $100 million to provide a family of computer products. That year SCI completed an expansion and began production at its Grenoble manufacturing facility. It also added a new plant in Asia. Apple announced in 1996 that as part of its cost-saving measures it agreed to sell its manufacturing plant in Fountain, Colorado, to SCI. SCI will continue to make products for Apple in the Colorado factory through an outsourcing arrangement. SCI's profits rose to $81 million on sales of $4.5 billion for fiscal 1996.

Chairman and CEO: Olin B. King, age 60, $611,183 pay
President and COO: A. Eugene Sapp Jr., age 58, $446,347 pay
SVP Commercial Division, Western Region: David F. Jenkins, age 57, $232,774 pay
SVP Commercial Division, Central Region: Jerry F. Thomas, age 53, $209,581 pay
SVP Government Division: Richard A. Holloway, age 52, $179,357 pay
SVP Commercial Division, Eastern Region: Jeffrey L. Nesbitt, age 43
SVP Commercial Division, Asian Region: Peter M. Scheffler, age 43
SVP Commercial Division, European Region: Alexander A. C. Wilson, age 57
VP: Bruce R. Anderson
VP: C. T. Chua
VP: George J. King
VP Personnel: Francis X. Henry
Treasurer: Ronald G. Sibold
Auditors: Ernst & Young LLP

WHERE

HQ: 2101 W. Clinton Ave., Huntsville, AL 35805
Phone: 205-882-4800
Fax: 205-882-4804
Web site: http://www.sci.com/
SCI has plants in Canada, France, Hong Kong, Ireland, Mexico, Singapore, Thailand, the UK, and the US.

	1995 Sales	
	$ mil.	% of total
US	1,582	56
Other countries	1,092	44
Total	**2,674**	**100**

WHAT

Commercial Division
Component testing
Computer-aided design services
Engineering support
Pin-in-hole circuit board assembly
Surface-mount circuit board assembly

Government Division
Advanced Airborne Test Instrumentation System
Apache Longbow helicopter weapons, systems computers, and communication interface units
Digital Non-Secure Voice Terminal
Distributed Data Acquisition System for the Titan IV Launch Vehicle

Selected Subsidiaries
Adelantos de Tecnologia SA de CV (Mexico)
Cambridge Computer, Ltd. (UK)
Consolidated Communications Corp. (50%)
Norlite Technology, Inc. (Canada)
SCI Ireland Limited
SCI Manufacturing Singapore Pte. Ltd.
SCI Systems (Thailand) Limited
SCI Technology, Inc.

KEY COMPETITORS

Allegheny	Hitachi	SigmaTron
Teledyne	Honeywell	Solectron
AlliedSignal	Hughes	Texas
AMP	Electronics	Instruments
AST	IEC Electronics	Thomson SA
Benchmark	Intel	Tyco
Electronics	Loral	International
Comptronix	Oki	
DII	PCI Ltd.	
General Signal	Raytheon	
Group	Rockwell	
Technologies	International	
Harris Corp.	Sanmina	

HOW MUCH

Nasdaq symbol: SCIS FYE: June 30	Annual Growth	1986	1987	1988	1989	1990	1991	1992	1993	1994	1995
Sales ($ mil.)	21.3%	470	553	774	987	1,179	1,129	1,045	1,697	1,852	2,674
Net income ($ mil.)	13.9%	14	16	19	21	2	4	4	27	21	45
Income as % of sales	—	2.9%	2.9%	2.5%	2.1%	0.2%	0.3%	0.4%	1.6%	1.1%	1.7%
Earnings per share ($)	9.8%	0.67	0.77	0.91	1.00	0.11	0.16	0.18	1.07	0.76	1.56
Stock price – high ($)	—	13.84	22.75	15.00	15.88	13.13	10.13	18.50	23.38	22.25	38.00
Stock price – low ($)	—	9.00	11.50	10.88	8.00	5.25	5.88	6.50	14.38	12.63	17.00
Stock price – close ($)	11.4%	11.75	13.25	15.00	8.63	8.25	6.50	18.25	17.63	18.00	31.00
P/E – high	—	21	30	17	16	119	63	103	22	29	24
P/E – low	—	13	15	12	8	48	37	36	13	17	11
Dividends per share ($)	—	0.00	0.00	0.00	0.00	0.00	0.00	0.00	0.00	0.00	0.00
Book value per share ($)	9.7%	5.53	6.39	7.27	8.11	8.42	8.87	9.17	10.27	11.16	12.75
Employees	10.9%	5,185	6,660	8,970	8,578	10,694	9,762	9,512	10,811	12,027	13,185

1995 YEAR-END

Debt ratio: 31.7%
Return on equity: 13.8%
Cash (mil.): $10
Current ratio: 1.60
Long-term debt (mil.): $156
No. of shares (mil.): 27
Dividends
  Yield: —
  Payout: —
Market value (mil.): $851

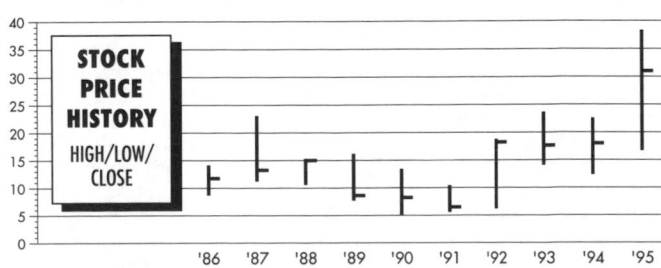

STOCK PRICE HISTORY
HIGH/LOW/CLOSE

SCIENCE APPLICATIONS INTERNATIONAL

OVERVIEW

Dr. Strangelove's brain trust is eagerly embracing the commercial market for its high-tech expertise. San Diego-based Science Applications International Corporation (SAIC) specializes in solving complex scientific and engineering problems for DOD and civilian customers. The highly decentralized firm performs computer systems integration, software development, and environmental studies and develops sophisticated electronic hardware (such as chemical testing equipment). Much of the manufacturing goes to subcontractors.

Chairman Robert Beyster credits SAIC's 90% employee ownership as a primary reason for its success in transforming itself from a defense contractor without peer (but with a captive market) to a nearly $2 billion (in sales) firm ably competing among a host of rivals such as TRW and Andersen Consulting. SAIC's

stock (which is internally traded) is priced using a performance-based formula that reflects changes in net income and competitors' P/Es. The employees' well-being is tied directly to the firm's long-term profitability.

Overall, defense-related contracts accounted for nearly half of SAIC's work in 1994. It probably doesn't hurt that the company's board rivals the Pentagon's in concentration of brass. Among others, former Defense Secretary Melvin Laird and former NSA Director Bobby Ray Inman are SAIC directors, while Defense Secretary William Perry and CIA Director John Deutch are former directors.

Nevertheless, the firm is broadening its focus by targeting medical technologies, computer systems integration, environmental remediation, and transportation. SAIC is also extending its capabilities through acquisitions.

WHEN

Physicist Robert Beyster worked at Los Alamos National Laboratory in the 1950s, then was hired by General Atomic in 1957 to establish and manage its Traveling Wave Linear Accelerator. When the company was sold to Gulf Oil in 1968, research priorities changed and Beyster left. He founded Science Applications Inc. (SAI) the following year, landing consulting contracts from Los Alamos and Brookhaven National Laboratories.

Within the first year, Beyster instituted an employee ownership plan in which stock became available to all those judged to be doing a superior job. Beyster's idea was to share the nascent success of SAI as well as raise capital. His stake declined from 100% to 10%.

In 1970 the company established an office in Washington, DC. Despite a recession, SAI continued to grow during the 1970s. The firm's policy was to support new researchers for their first year, after which they had to bring in enough work to support their position or be released. While this may have created an entrepreneurial atmosphere, it also fostered cloistered divisions.

SAI's sales rose to $100 million by 1979. The following year the company was restructured and became a subsidiary of the Science Applications International Corporation, a new holding company.

During the 1980s the defense buildup, an emphasis on high-tech weaponry, and the firm's high-level Pentagon connections brought in contracts for submarine warfare

systems, artificial intelligence work, and technical development for the Strategic Defense Initiative (better known as Star Wars). These larger contracts required a greater concentration of resources, so SAI reorganized again.

In 1984 SAI was merged into SAIC, and by the following year a new layer of management was added to coordinate the company's autonomous divisions. Cost consciousness in Washington and new competition put added pressure on the company. Nevertheless, the company continued to grow.

As defense spending slowed with the end of the Cold War in 1989, SAIC began casting a wider net, winning a contract for an electronic toll collection system in Florida, for example. By 1991 computer systems integration and consulting accounted for 25% of SAIC's sales. That year the firm pleaded guilty to fraud charges relating to a government contract and paid $1.3 million in fines.

In 1994 SAIC acquired several companies, including Syntonic (transportation communications). During 1994 and 1995 SAIC was accused of fraud by a former employee regarding a $9 million air force contract. In 1995 it acquired majority interests in Tesci and Danet, (European telecommunications software companies). In addition, Admiral William Owens (retired vice chairman of the Joint Chiefs of Staff) became a VC on SAIC's board. Analysts speculated that Owens would succeed Beyster.

WHO

Chairman and CEO: J. Robert Beyster, age 71
President and COO: Lorenz A. Kull
VC and EVP: J. W. McRary
VC: William A. Owens, age 55
VC: V. N. Cook
VC: W. E. Zisch
EVP: S. J. Dalich
EVP: J. H. Warner Jr.
SVP: W. M. Layson
SVP: David Overskei, age 46
SVP and CFO: William A. Roper
VP Human Resources: Bernard Theull
Auditors: Price Waterhouse LLP

WHERE

HQ: Science Applications International Corporation, 10260 Campus Point Dr., San Diego, CA 92121
Phone: 619-546-6000
Fax: 619-546-6634
Web site: http://www.saic.com

SAIC and its subsidiaries have more than 400 offices in 45 states and other countries.

WHAT

Selected Products and Services
Bioremediation of contaminated soils
Color liquid crystal display panel backlighted by an ultraviolet lamp
Electronic toll and traffic management systems
Fuel cell propulsion systems for vehicles
Global atmospheric modeling
Lightweight, small-particle accelerator to generate radioisotopes for positron emission tomography (medical PET scans)
Radio frequency identification systems that track cars, buses, trucks, planes, and their cargo
Solar thermal power systems
Thermal neutron analysis system (advanced explosives detection for airline passenger luggage)

Selected Contracts
3-dimensional modeling to determine the effects of space radiation on personnel and materials for NASA
Compact disc plus graphics software development for the entertainment industry

Conversion of high-powered electron beam used to simulate nuclear weapon effects into a system for removing sulfur dioxide and nitrogen oxides from coal-fired power plant emissions
Fingerprint identification system for the FBI
Integrated technologies for simulating warfare across a theater of operations for DOD
Lightweight computer equipment for the US Army
Marine and freshwater sediment sampling for the Army Corps of Engineers
Medical records computerization for DOD
Occupational safety and environmental services for NASA's Ames Research Center

Selected Subsidiaries
American Systems Engineering Corp. (components and technical support for US Navy ships)
Bull, Inc. (conducts quarterly stock trades among SAIC employees)
Carl T. Jones Corp. (communications consulting)
General Sciences Corp. (professional meteorological information processing systems)
JHK and Associates (transportation planning and engineering)
Network Solutions (integrates telephones, video, and computer communications)
R.E. Right Environmental (environmental site assessment and consulting)
SAIC Canada
SAIC Columbia, Limitada
SAIC de Mexico, SA de CV
SAIC-MIR (establishment of American business contacts with former Soviet scientists, Russia)

KEY COMPETITORS

AlliedSignal	Groundwater Protection
Amtech Corporation	IBM
Andersen Consulting	Johnson Controls
BDM International	Kalsler Holding
Black & Decker	Loral
Boeing	Operation Simulation
Booz, Allen	Raytheon
Computer Sciences	Titan Corp.
Control Data	TRW
EDS	Unisys

HOW MUCH

Private company FYE: January 31	Annual Growth	1987	1988	1989	1990	1991	1992	1993	1994	1995	1996
Sales ($ mil.)	15.3%	600	694	865	1,022	1,163	1,285	1,504	1,671	1,922	2,156
Net income ($ mil.)	13.7%	18	22	26	31	33	34	38	42	49	57
Income as % of sales	—	3.0%	3.0%	3.0%	3.0%	2.9%	2.6%	2.5%	2.5%	2.5%	2.7%
Employees	14.0%	6,500	8,600	10,000	11,000	12,000	13,510	15,839	17,800	20,500	21,100

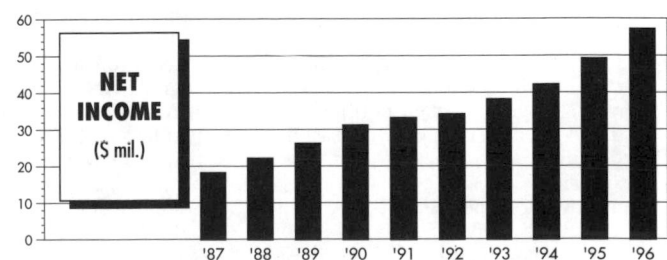

NET INCOME ($ mil.)

SCITEX CORPORATION LTD.

OVERVIEW

Desktop publishing has forced Scitex to reinvent itself. Based in Herzlia, Israel, the company is a leading manufacturer of digital information systems primarily for the graphic arts, digital printing, and digital video markets. It is integrating its industry-standard printing technology such as continuous-tone and line-work formats into such popular publishing software as Adobe Photoshop and QuarkXPress. It also emphasizes its software, producing one of the best systems for trapping (the precise positioning of colors on the printed page) available for Macintosh computers.

Scitex has seen sales drop in North and South America, the company's largest market.

(Almost all of its sales are from outside Israel.) The slow development of a new dealer distribution network contributed to Scitex America's poor performance. The firm has also experienced problems because of low selling prices of prepress equipment, higher unit sales of lower margin items such as input devices and servers, and high manufacturing costs associated with new product introductions, including the Iris Realist line of printers.

Scitex's largest shareholders, with about 13% each, are International Paper, CEI (Clal Electronics Industries Ltd.), and entities controlled by the Recanati family of Israel.

WHEN

Ephraim Arazi, an Israeli who had worked for Itek (optical systems) in the US, went back to Israel after the Six Day War. There he founded Scientific Technology (1968) to produce systems for the Israeli military. After growing weary of the defense sphere, which was burdened with controls and regulations, he found a civilian application: automated scanners to design patterns for jacquard knits. With the help of Arthur Low, a Canadian, Arazi turned the company, Scitex (founded in 1971), into a success and opened a US distribution company. When the fad for patterned knits faded around 1975, the company applied the same technology to developing prints for woven fabrics. Its first European office opened in 1974, and it began selling its products in Japan 2 years later.

With their North American background, Arazi and Low were more aware than most Israeli executives of the importance of marketing, and by the mid-1970s marketing expenditures were keeping pace with R&D costs. They particularly emphasized the importance of elaborate exhibits at trade shows.

But fabric printing was a somewhat limited market, and in the late 1970s the company began to apply its technology to graphics and printing. Here at last was a true growth industry. Its first system, Response 300, was introduced in 1979. It was expensive, which meant that it could only pay for itself if used nearly continuously, and only major printing operations could use it economically. And as they did, color illustrations improved and became less expensive.

Company sales exploded. In the early 1980s sales grew 100% every 2 years, and the work force doubled every 3 years. By 1985, however,

growth slowed, and the company was in trouble. Although there were layoffs, across-the-board pay reductions kept them to minimum. Major shareholders poured more money into the company, sales staff worked to prevent customers from being lured away by fear-mongering competitors, and R&D continued hot and heavy. By 1987 the company was on track, and it returned to profitability in 1988.

By the next year Scitex had recovered enough to be attractive to a major investor like UK media magnate Robert Maxwell, who bought 27% of the company. He believed Scitex should become a major multinational company and that his new interest represented an attractive synergy with his printing holdings. Two years later Maxwell was overextended. By then his share of Scitex was reduced to 19% and the company's 1991 US stock offering allowed him to dispose of his remaining interest. The firm used proceeds of the sale to fund acquisitions that included a minority interest in P.INK, a German developer of print production software in 1994.

The advent of less expensive desktop publishing products made Scitex's workstations, which sold for up to $1.5 million each, obsolete. Scitex president and CEO Arie Rosenfeld resigned in 1995 and was replaced by former EVP Yoav Chelouche. That year Scitex reorganized into 3 divisions: Graphic Arts, Scitex Digital Printing, and Scitex Digital Video.

After a disappointing performance caused in part by a maturing graphic arts market, Scitex named a new management team and laid off about 250 employees in 1996. In addition, investor Davidi Gilo attempted a hostile takeover bid that was ultimately refused.

WHO

Chairman: Dov Tadmor, age 66
VC: David Wainshal, age 60
President and CEO: Yoav Z. Chelouche, age 42
SEVP; President, Graphic Arts Group: Shimon Alon, age 46
EVP and CFO: Giora Bitan, age 41
President, Scitex Digital Video, Inc.: Randolph J. Hood, age 47
President, Scitex Digital Printing, Inc.: Dwight T. Johnson, age 56
CEO, Scitex America Corp.: George M. Carlisle
Corporate VP, Operations: Shlomo Shamir, age 49
VP Marketing, Graphic Arts Group: David Ofek, age 44
VP Human Resources and Organization, Graphic Arts Group: Ilan Gonen, age 52
General Manager, Scitex Israel: Gil Nitzan, age 57
Corporate Secretary: David Shulman, age 49
Auditors: Kesselman & Kesselman

WHERE

HQ: Hamada St., Industrial Park, Herzlia B, 46103, Israel
Phone: +972-9-597-222
Fax: +972-9-502-922
US HQ: Scitex America Corp., 8 Oak Park Dr., Bedford, MA 01730
US Phone: 617-275-5150
US Fax: 617-275-3430
Web site: http://www.scitex.com

	1995 Sales	
	$ mil.	% of total
North & South America	303	41
Europe	296	41
Japan	72	10
Other regions	58	8
Total	**729**	**100**

WHAT

	1995 Sales	
	$ mil.	% of total
Equipment		
Imagesetters	162	22
Inkjet printers	162	22
Workstations & servers	124	17
Scanners & digital cameras	85	12
Video systems & devices	43	6
Service & supplies	153	21
Total	**729**	**100**

Selected Products

Billboard Color Digital Printing Systems	Image Input
Scitex Outboard (printer)	Leaf (scanners)
Design and layout software	Smart (scanners)
Digital Video	Networking and Telecommunications
InMix (video workstations)	Output
Editing Systems	Dolev (imagesetters)
Blaze96 (workstation)	Proofing
Prismax S (workstation)	Iris (printers)

Billboard Color Digital Printing Systems
Scitex Outboard (printer)
Design and layout software
Digital Video
  InMix (video workstations)
Editing Systems
  Blaze96 (workstation)
  Prismax S (workstation)

Image Input
  Leaf (scanners)
  Smart (scanners)
Networking and Telecommunications
Output
  Dolev (imagesetters)
Proofing
  Iris (printers)
Short Run Color Digital Printing Systems
  Spontane (on-demand color digital printing)

KEY COMPETITORS

Adobe
Avid Technology
Bayer
Barco
Bull Run Gold Mines
Dai Nippon Printing
Delphax Systems
Discreet Logic
Domino Printing Sciences
DuPont
Fuji Photo
General Electric
IBM
Linotype-Hell
Philips
Quark
Siemens
Sony
Tektronix

HOW MUCH

Nasdaq symbol: SCIXF FYE: December 31	Annual Growth	1986	1987	1988	1989	1990	1991	1992	1993	1994	1995
Sales ($ mil.)	20.8%	133	159	192	238	352	430	550	663	704	729
Net income ($ mil.)	0.3%	(34)	(5)	15	35	77	101	122	94	64	(35)
Income as % of sales	—	—	—	7.7%	14.9%	21.9%	23.4%	22.3%	14.2%	9.1%	—
Earnings per share ($)	—	(1.54)	(0.21)	63.00	1.00	2.10	2.70	3.02	2.10	1.49	(0.81)
Stock price – high ($)	—	4.88	2.56	4.06	8.63	21.13	39.25	44.13	44.38	26.88	24.75
Stock price – low ($)	—	1.19	0.88	1.06	3.63	7.38	13.50	31.50	22.25	15.25	12.00
Stock price – close ($)	24.7%	1.88	1.06	4.06	8.50	15.13	35.50	42.75	24.75	16.63	13.63
P/E – high	—	—	—	6	9	10	15	15	21	18	—
P/E – low	—	—	—	2	4	4	5	10	11	10	—
Dividends per share ($)	6.8%	0.00	0.00	0.00	0.00	0.07	0.40	0.48	0.52	0.52	0.52
Book value per share ($)	18.7%	3.49	3.35	4.23	4.79	6.51	8.76	15.07	16.78	17.52	16.37
Employees	10.1%	—	—	—	—	—	—	—	2,970	3,470	3,600

1995 YEAR-END

Debt ratio: 0.4%
Return on equity: —
Cash (mil.): $155
Current ratio: 3.20
Long-term debt (mil.): $0
No. of shares (mil.): 43
Dividends
  Yield: 3.8%
  Payout: —
Market value (mil.): $583

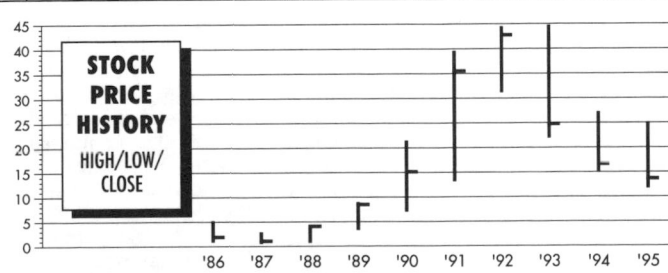

STOCK PRICE HISTORY HIGH/LOW/ CLOSE

SEAGATE TECHNOLOGY, INC.

OVERVIEW

Seagate Technology has driven to the top of its industry on a road of acquisitions. The Scotts Valley, California-based computer disk drive maker boosted its market share from 19% to 35% with its 1996 purchase of long-time rival Conner Peripherals. Seagate makes more than 150 hard-disk drive models for notebook and desktop computers, workstations, and supercomputers. The company's products are sold primarily to original equipment manufacturers, distributors, and value-added resellers.

Fueled by its numerous purchases (the Conner acquisition added tape drives to the company's hardware lines), Seagate is recasting itself as the "data technology company." Seagate is also positioning itself as a supplier of components — including custom integrated circuits, motors, and recording heads — to other manufacturers.

Networking and systems management software is another market in which Seagate is revving its engine. To strengthen its software package, the company has acquired more than a dozen software companies since 1994. CEO Alan Shugart says he wants to build a $1 billion software business by 1999.

WHEN

Seagate Technology was founded in 1979 by Shugart, an 18-year IBMer who had made floppy disks standard on microcomputers at Shugart Associates; manufacturing expert Tom Mitchell, formerly of Commodore and Memorex; design engineer Douglas Mahon; and Finis Conner. Seagate pioneered the downsizing of mainframe hard disk drives for PCs; the resulting drive had 30 times more storage than floppy disks, faster access times, and much higher long-term reliability.

Seagate's first product, a 5.25" hard disk, sold briskly. With IBM as a customer, Seagate had grabbed half of the market for small disk drives by 1982; by 1984 sales had reached $344 million. But Seagate's heavy dependence on IBM showed its double edge as eroding IBM PC demand prompted it to cut orders. Sales in 1985 dropped to $215 million and profits to $1 million (from $42 million the year before). Seagate transferred its manufacturing to Singapore and cut its California workforce in half. Finis Conner left Seagate in 1985 to start his own disk drive company, Conner Peripherals.

The company sped up its vertical integration to ensure availability of critical components and reduce time to market. Seagate purchased Grenex (thin-film magnetic media, 1984), Aeon (aluminum substrates, 1987), and Integrated Power Systems (custom semiconductors, 1987).

With revenues more than doubling in 1986 and again in 1987 (to $958 million), Seagate spent $290 million to increase 5.25" production, ignoring signs of a coming 3.5" drive standard. The strong market in 1988 for the smaller drives prompted Seagate's quick shift to 3.5" production.

Seagate purchased Imprimis from Control Data (1989), thus making itself the world's premier independent drive maker. The acquisition nearly doubled Seagate's size and made it a leader in high-capacity (greater than one gigabyte) drives. In 1993 Seagate acquired a 25% interest in SunDisk, a leader in flash memory storage systems.

Seagate and Hitachi signed an agreement in 1994 to share their mass-storage technologies. That year the company began pursuing its software initiative in earnest, acquiring software companies Palindrome and Crystal Computer Services. It also expanded its recording head operations with the purchase of Applied Magnetics' magnetic recording head operations.

Seagate paid just over $1 billion for Conner Peripherals in early 1996. Compaq president Rod Canion had been an early backer of Conner Peripherals, which from the start had banked on 3.5" disk drives. By 1987, its first full year of sales, company revenues reached $113 million; Compaq bought 90% of its products. Conner Peripherals went public in 1988. The company created its Arcada software for data management on client/server networks in 1993. By the time of its acquisition, Conner Peripherals was a leading maker of disk and tape drives, storage systems, and software.

Following the Conner acquisition, Seagate merged that company's Arcada Holdings software subsidiary with Palindrome to form Seagate Storage Management Group. That year Seagate continued to expand its software offering by acquiring several management software companies, including Calypso Software Systems and OnDemand Software.

Seagate earned $213 million on sales of $8.6 billion in fiscal 1996.

WHO

Chairman, President, and CEO: Alan F. Shugart, age 64, $1,122,718 pay
EVP, CFO, Chief Administrative Officer, and Secretary: Donald L. Waite, age 62, $773,505 pay
EVP; COO, Recording Heads Group: Brendan C. Hegarty, age 52, $767,738 pay
EVP; COO, Storage Products Group: Ronald D. Verdoorn, age 44, $715,809 pay
EVP Worldwide Sales, Marketing, and Product Line Management: Bernardo A. Carballo, age 46, $706,578 pay
EVP Corporate Development; COO, Seagate Software: Stephen J. Luczo, age 38
EVP; COO, Recording Media Operations: William D. Watkins
SVP and Chief Technical Officer, Data Storage Products Group: Hossein M. Moghadam, age 51
SVP Corporate Materials: Robert A. Sandie, age 59
VP Human Resources: Annette Surtees
Auditors: Ernst & Young LLP

WHERE

HQ: 920 Disc Dr., Scotts Valley, CA 95066
Phone: 408-438-6550
Fax: 408-438-6172
Web site: http://www.seagate.com

Seagate has sales offices in 14 countries. The company's primary manufacturing facilities are located in Malaysia, Singapore, Thailand, the UK, and the US.

	1995 Sales $ mil.	1995 Sales % of total	1995 Operating Income $ mil.	1995 Operating Income % of total
US	2,672	59	47	13
Far East	1,868	41	326	87
Total	**4,540**	**100**	**373**	**100**

WHAT

	1995 Sales % of total
Customers	
OEMs	72
Systems integrators & distributors	28
Total	**100**

Selected Products
Mainframe and supercomputer applications
Networking and systems management software
Rigid disk drives
  2.5" drives for notebook computers
  3.5" drives for desktop and midrange computers
  5.25" drives for high-end computers, including multimedia applications
Solid-state flash memory devices

KEY COMPETITORS

BCE	Matsushita
Canon	Maxtor
Cheyenne Software	Microsoft
Computer Associates	Mitsubishi
Data General	NEC
DEC	Novell
EMC	Quantum Corp.
Fujitsu	Oracle
Hewlett-Packard	Read-Rite
Hitachi	Storage Technology
IBM	SyQuest
Intel	Toshiba
Iomega	Unisys
Komag	Western Digital

HOW MUCH

NYSE symbol: SEG FYE: June 30	Annual Growth	1986	1987	1988	1989	1990	1991	1992	1993	1994	1995
Sales ($ mil.)	29.0%	460	958	1,266	1,372	2,413	2,677	2,875	3,044	3,500	4,540
Net income ($ mil.)	25.0%	35	140	77	0	117	63	63	195	225	260
Income as % of sales	—	7.5%	14.6%	6.1%	0.0%	4.9%	2.3%	2.2%	6.4%	6.4%	5.7%
Earnings per share ($)	17.4%	0.72	2.81	1.54	0.01	1.92	0.95	0.92	2.71	2.83	3.06
Stock price – high ($)	—	20.75	45.13	23.00	15.50	19.75	19.88	22.38	25.13	28.75	54.75
Stock price – low ($)	—	7.13	10.13	6.63	8.88	5.63	7.13	9.00	13.13	18.63	23.63
Stock price – close ($)	10.6%	19.13	14.88	8.63	15.00	11.75	9.13	19.63	23.75	24.00	47.50
P/E – high	—	29	16	15	—	10	21	24	9	10	18
P/E – low	—	10	4	4	—	3	8	10	5	7	8
Dividends per share ($)	—	0.00	0.00	0.00	0.00	0.00	0.00	0.00	0.00	0.00	0.00
Book value per share ($)	19.0%	4.41	7.36	8.89	8.85	10.64	11.76	12.63	15.34	18.24	21.16
Employees	30.9%	4,700	8,900	16,000	30,000	40,000	38,000	42,000	43,000	43,000	53,000

1995 YEAR-END

Debt ratio: 26.3%
Return on equity: 18.1%
Cash (mil.): $1,247
Current ratio: 2.69
Long-term debt (mil.): $540
No. of shares (mil.): 73
Dividends
  Yield: —
  Payout: —
Market value (mil.): $3,460

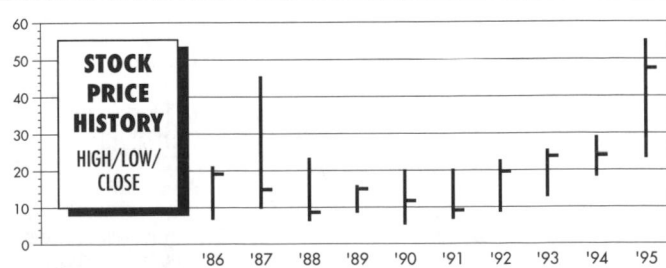

STOCK PRICE HISTORY
HIGH/LOW/CLOSE

SEGA ENTERPRISES, LTD.

OVERVIEW

Facing cutthroat competition from rivals Nintendo and Sony, SEGA, the Tokyo-based maker of consumer video games and amusement centers and machines, isn't playing games. The #2 video game maker (after Sony), SEGA has knocked $100 off the price of its SegaSaturn 32-bit home video game system in answer to price cuts on Sony's PlayStation. Sega faces an even stiffer challenge from Nintendo's 64-bit game system, Ultra 64. In spite of this, SEGA is staying in the game by offering commercial as well as consumer versions of its games. Its latest move is Net Link, a device that, when combined with the SegaSaturn and a TV, provides Internet access.

SEGA is the largest Japanese maker of portable video games and amusement machines for video arcades. It has established 1,100 amusement centers all over Japan in addition to a handful of centers in France, the UK, and Thailand. The company also sells PICO, an electronic learning aid for children.

Alliances could help SEGA recapture the industry's top spot. Its joint venture with Time Warner and Tele-Communications, Inc. (TCI), the SEGA TV cable channel, provides SEGA home video game system owners with access, via their TVs, to many game titles. The company has also joined forces with 4 other major Japanese communications, electronics, and entertainment companies (NTT, Sony, Yamaha, and Victor) to form GrR HomeNet Corp., a joint venture intended to put electronic games, karaoke, and other products online.

WHEN

One of the originators of the Japanese electronic games industry was born in New York. David Rosen, who is still a SEGA director, returned to Japan following a military stint there during the Korean War. He planned to marry his Japanese girlfriend and start an art export business. However, Rosen Enterprises, founded in 1951, became more profitable in 1954 when it began importing instant photo booths made in the US. Rosen recognized the need for a quick method of making ID cards, which were used for numerous purposes in Japan. He modified the machines to improve the photo quality, and they became quite successful. However, the Japanese became concerned about the US company and its advanced technology, and Rosen decided to offer licensing of his machines to Japanese operators — perhaps the first franchise operation in Japan.

As Japan's economy improved, Rosen, after much persistence, imported coin-operated games into the country in 1957, later opening the first big bowling alley in Tokyo. In 1965, after becoming dissatisfied with US amusement game quality, he acquired a US company that made jukeboxes in Japan. The combined companies were renamed SEGA Enterprises (short for SErvice GAmes). It developed the popular game Periscope and began challenging US games. In 1970 conglomerate Gulf + Western Industries acquired SEGA. The buyout led to Rosen's joining the board of Gulf + Western's Paramount Pictures.

In the early 1980s, as the video game industry floundered, Gulf + Western sold off SEGA's US operations. Rosen then assembled a group of Japanese investors, including software firm

CSK, to buy SEGA's Japanese operation, which was a subsidiary of the US company. In 1984 SEGA again was a Japanese company; investors paid only $38 million.

Initially SEGA was eclipsed by Nintendo's 8-bit system, released in Japan in 1985. However, SEGA beat its rival to Europe with its own 8-bit game player. The rivalry continued in 1989 when SEGA introduced Genesis, the 16-bit game player. By 1991, when Nintendo finally came out with a 16-bit system, SEGA had already sold more than one million Genesis systems. The company also came out with ads that year portraying the SEGA system as the one the "cool" guys in the neighborhood were playing. This coolness quotient grew when the Genesis version of the game Mortal Kombat, released in 1993, allowed players to rip off heads and pull out hearts. Nintendo's version was sanitized, and the SEGA version outsold Nintendo's 2 to one.

In 1994 SEGA opened its first full-scale high-tech park, Joypolis, in Yokohama and launched the SEGA TV channel in the US and Japan. The company released its SegaSaturn system in 1995. That year it teamed up with software developer Softbank to distribute interactive entertainment and PC software and hardware in the US.

SEGA lost its top gamesmaker spot to Sony in 1996. That year it set up a joint venture with US film studios MCA and DreamWorks SKG to develop amusement centers in the US. Also in 1996 SEGA entered the Internet arena with the debut of Net Link, which allows Sega Saturn users to receive e-mail, browse the Web, or, of course, play games.

WHO

Director and Chairman: Isao Okawa
Representative Director, President, and CEO: Hayao Nakayama
Representative Director and EVP: Shoichiro Irimajiri
EVP: Tokuzo Komai
Senior Managing Director, Consumer Products Domestic: Ren Mori
Senior Managing Director, Consumer Products Overseas: Naoyoshi Takeshita
Senior Managing Director, Amusement Machine Marketing: Takenori Ogata
Senior Managing Director, Administration: Katsuhiko Nishimura
Managing Director, R&D: Hisashi Suzuki
President and CEO, SEGA of America Inc.: Tom Kalinske
CFO, SEGA of America Inc.: Shinobu Toyoda
Group Director Human Resources, SEGA of America Inc.: Steve Goveia
Auditors: Chuo Audit Corporation

WHERE

HQ: 2-12, Haneda 1-chome, Ohta-ku, Tokyo, 144, Japan
Phone: +81-3-5736-7034
Fax: +81-3-5736 7058
US HQ: SEGA of America Inc., 255 Shoreline Dr., Ste. 200, Redwood City, CA 94065
US Phone: 415-508-2800
US Fax: 415-802-3063
Web site: http://www.segaoa.com

	1996 Sales % of total
Japan	73
Other countries	27
Total	**100**

WHAT

	1996 Sales	
	$ mil.	% of total
Consumer products	1,943	54
Amusement machines	894	25
Amusement centers	781	21
Total	**3,618**	**100**

Selected Products

Video Game Players
Game Gear
Mega Drive 2 and Mega CD2
PICO
SegaSaturn

Copyrighted Video Games
DAYTONA USA
Doom (id Software)
Lion King (Walt Disney Co.)
SONIC & Knuckles
Star Wars Arcade (Lucasfilm Ltd.)
Victory Goal
Virtua Fighter
Virtua Racing

Other
Net Link (Internet access device)

KEY COMPETITORS

3DO	Electronic Arts	Mattel
7th Level	Hasbro	Microsoft
Acclaim	id Software	NEC
Entertainment	Interplay	Nintendo
Accolade	Productions	Philips
Activision	JTS	Sony
Blockbuster	LucasArts	Walt Disney
Broderbund	Matsushita	WMS Industries
Cyan		

HOW MUCH

OTC symbol: SEGNY FYE: March 31	Annual Growth	1987	1988	1989	1990	1991	1992	1993	1994	1995	1996
Sales ($ mil.)	33.6%	266	396	416	498	758	1,605	3,019	3,432	3,731	3,618
Net income ($ mil.)	39.5%	2	19	22	31	59	105	244	225	158	40
Income as % of sales	—	0.9%	4.7%	5.2%	6.2%	7.7%	6.6%	8.1%	6.6%	4.2%	1.1%
Earnings per share ($)	(32.8%)	—	—	—	—	—	—	0.33	0.57	0.39	0.10
Stock price – high ($)[1]	—	—	—	—	—	—	—	—	27.38	21.33	14.63
Stock price – low ($)[1]	—	—	—	—	—	—	—	—	17.50	11.44	8.25
Stock price – close ($)[1]	(18.4%)	—	—	—	—	—	—	—	20.75	14.39	13.80
P/E – high	—	—	—	—	—	—	—	—	48	54	150
P/E – low	—	—	—	—	—	—	—	—	31	29	85
Dividends per share ($)	24.0%	—	—	0.02	0.01	0.02	0.03	0.06	0.09	0.11	0.09
Book value per share ($)	3.8%	—	2.74	2.66	2.20	2.54	2.23	3.20	3.99	4.89	3.69
Employees	13.5%	1,199	1,343	1,454	1,695	1,786	2,324	3,034	3,492	3,862	3,758

[1] Stock prices are for the prior calendar year.

1996 YEAR-END

Debt ratio: 58.4%
Return on equity: 16.5%
Cash (mil.): $1,104
Current ratio: 2.33
Long-term debt (mil.): $1,361
No. of shares (mil.): 403
Dividends
  Yield: 0.6%
  Payout: 90.8%
Market value (mil.): $5,555

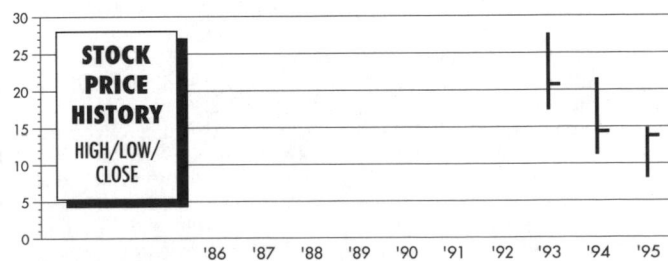

STOCK PRICE HISTORY HIGH/LOW/CLOSE

SGS-THOMSON

OVERVIEW

SGS-THOMSON can translate "semiconductor" into any language. The French-Italian company is incorporated in the Netherlands, has its headquarters in Paris, and operates worldwide. It is Europe's 2nd largest chip maker (after Philips) and the world's leading supplier of analog integrated circuits (ICs), mixed-signal (analog/digital) ICs, power ICs (hybrid chips that combine high speed and high voltage with low power consumption), and MPEG-2 decoder chips (used for transmitting video). SGS-THOMSON offers more than 3,000 kinds of semiconductor products to OEMs in the automotive, computer, consumer electronics, industrial instrumentation, and telecommunications markets.

An aggressive product development program is key to SGS-THOMSON's campaign to win a larger share of the semiconductor market. The company is focusing on differentiated ICs (dedicated products, semicustom devices, and microcontrollers) for fast-growing segments of the electronics marketplace, including cable TV, multimedia computers, and satellite communications. It keeps manufacturing costs low by expanding production facilities in low-wage areas such as eastern Asia and North Africa.

SGS-THOMSON is owned by CAE-Industrie (a corporation controlled by the French Atomic Energy Commission), France Telecom (France's state-controlled telephone company), Thomson SA (France's state-owned industrial conglomerate), I.R.I. (Italy's state-owned Istituto per la Ricostruzione Industriale S.p.A.), and Comitato SIR. Both the French and Italian governments are pursuing privatization to reduce the company's dependence on government funds.

WHEN

SGS-THOMSON was formed in 1987 through the merger of SGS Microelettronica, a state-owned Italian chip maker, and the non-military electronics arm of Thomson SA. The merger created the world's 12th largest chip maker. Included in the deal were 2 US operations: SGS Semiconductor, in Phoenix, and Thomson Components-Mostek, in Carrollton, Texas.

Microelettronica was part of Finmeccanica, formed in 1948 as the engineering subsidiary of the Italian state industrial holding company IRI (which enjoyed the support of Benito Mussolini after its creation in 1933).

Thomson SA traces its roots to shortly before the turn of the century. A group of French businessmen acquired patents from General Electric predecessor Thomson-Houston Electric and created Compagnie Francaise Thomson-Houston to produce power-generation equipment. In 1986 Thomson bought the assets of US semiconductor maker Mostek from United Technologies.

Both Thomson SA and Microelettronica were struggling at the time of their merger. Pasquale Pistorio, a veteran of Motorola who became head of SGS in 1980, was named president of the new company. To jumpstart the organization, he began shutting and selling factories, trimming management, and laying off European workers while shifting jobs to the Mediterranean and Asia. During the 1980s the company joined Jessi (the Joint European Semiconductor Silicon research program),
which offered funding and tax incentives to help European companies remain competitive in the semiconductor industry. SGS-THOMSON lost $300 million in its first 2 years of operation, made a small profit in 1989, then stumbled again as recession spread across Europe.

To secure a place for SGS-THOMSON in the semiconductor marketplace, Pistorio began making acquisitions. In 1989 the company acquired 32-bit microprocessor technology when it bought UK-based INMOS from British conglomerate Thorn-EMI. It also purchased the microwave semiconductor business of Microwave Semiconductor. Pistorio began forging alliances with major chip buyers as well, including Alcatel-Alsthom, Hewlett-Packard, and Sony, and started making x86 microprocessors for Cyrix in 1992.

By the following year SGS-THOMSON had become the world's #1 maker of erasable programmable read-only memories (EPROMs). It went public in 1994.

SGS-THOMSON opened its largest software design center outside Europe, near New Delhi, in 1995. The following year the company formed product development alliances, with Applied Materials and Hyundai Electronics and signed a licensing pact with Samsung. Also in 1996 it shipped its billionth smartcard IC (chips attached to credit cards that hold encoded information) and its 5 millionth MPEG decoder IC.

WHO

Chairman: Bruno Steve, age 54
VC: Jean-Pierre Noblanc, age 57
President and CEO: Pasquale Pistorio
Corporate VP and CFO: Maurizio Ghirga
Corporate VP Central Research and Development: Joel Monnier
Corporate VP Strategic Planning and Human Resources: Alain Dutheil
Corporate VP, Front-end Manufacturing and Americas Region (US): Laurent Bosson
VP Marketing and Sales, Americas Region: Richard Pieranunzi
Auditors: Andersen Worldwide

WHERE

HQ: SGS-Thomson, Technoparc du Pays de Gex, B.P. 112, 165, rue Edouard Branly, 01630, Saint Genis Pouilly, France
Phone: +33-50-40-26-40
Fax: +33-50-40-28-60
US HQ: SGS-THOMSON Microelectronics Inc., 1310 Electronics Dr., Carrollton, TX 75006-5039
US Phone: 214-466-6000
US Fax: 214-466-8130
Web site: http://www.st.com

SGS-THOMSON has manufacturing facilities in Africa, Asia, Europe, and North America.

	1995 Sales % of total
Europe	46
Asia/Pacific	26
Americas	24
Japan	4
Total	**100**

WHAT

	1995 Sales	
	$ mil.	% of total
Dedicated products	1,351	38
Discrete & standard ICs	838	23
Memory products	662	19
Programmable products	535	15
Other	168	5
Total	**3,554**	**100**

Selected Products

Dedicated Products Group
Audio power amplifiers
Graphic equalizer ICs
MPEG image decoder ICs
Power ICs and intelligent power ICs

Discrete and Standard ICS
Discrete power devices
Power transistors
Radio frequency products
Standard logic ICs

Memory Products
Dynamic random access memories (DRAMs)
Static random access memories (SRAMs)
Erasable programmable read-only memories (EPROMs)
Flash memories

Programmable Products Group
Digital signal processors (DSPs)
Microcontrollers
Mixed-signal semicustom devices

KEY COMPETITORS

AMD	Motorola	Sanyo
Fujitsu	National	Siemens
Hitachi	Semiconductor	Texas
Intel	NEC	Instruments
Matsushita	Philips	Toshiba
Mitsubishi	Samsung	

HOW MUCH

NYSE symbol: STM FYE: December 31	Annual Growth	1986	1987	1988	1989	1990	1991	1992	1993	1994	1995
Sales ($ mil.)	19.8%	—	—	—	1,200	1,355	1,374	1,568	2,038	2,640	3,554
Net income ($ mil.)	136.6%	—	—	—	3	(97)	(103)	3	160	363	526
Income as % of sales	—	—	—	—	0.3%	—	—	0.2%	7.9%	13.8%	14.8%
Earnings per share ($)	96.9%	—	—	—	0.07	(2.07)	(1.93)	0.06	1.92	3.04	4.08
Stock price – high ($)	—	—	—	—	—	—	—	—	—	22.75	57.50
Stock price – low ($)	—	—	—	—	—	—	—	—	—	21.63	22.50
Stock price – close ($)	76.9%	—	—	—	—	—	—	—	—	22.75	40.25
P/E – high	—	—	—	—	—	—	—	—	—	7	14
P/E – low	—	—	—	—	—	—	—	—	—	7	6
Dividends per share ($)	—	—	—	—	—	—	—	—	—	0.00	0.00
Book value per share ($)	38.3%	—	—	—	—	—	—	—	—	13.93	19.26
Employees	9.5%	—	—	—	—	—	17,730	17,813	19,898	21,800	25,523

1995 YEAR-END

Debt ratio: 20.7%
Return on equity: 24.3%
Cash (mil.): $758
Current ratio: 1.46
Long-term debt (mil.): $201
No. of shares (mil.): 138
Dividends
  Yield: —
  Payout: —
Market value (mil.): $5,563

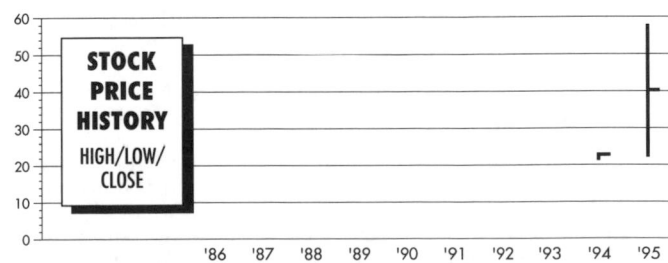

STOCK PRICE HISTORY HIGH/LOW/CLOSE

SIEMENS AG

OVERVIEW

Able-bodied Siemens is keeping its many divisions shipshape and is making money around the world. Its wholly owned subsidiary, Siemens Nixdorf Informationssysteme (SNI) is one of Europe's largest computer companies. It makes PCs, servers, peripherials, main frames, software, and offers systems integration and other services. Siemens, based in Munich, Germany, has operations in communications, components, energy, health care, information, lighting, transportation, and other industries. The company has offices in approximately 180 countries, making everything from power plants in Egypt to communications equipment in Thailand. No slouch in the US, Siemens operates 15 separate companies and

80 manufacturing and assembly locations with a workforce of more than 47,000.

Siemens Nixdorf has streamlined its operations and bounced back from years of losses. It is growing in the US through acquisitions and has doubled its size with the purchase of Pyramid Technology, a maker of high-performance enterprise servers. Pyramid is a partner of Oracle, a leader in the development of information management software.

Despite the strong German mark and tight competition worldwide, Siemens is posting profits in all its geographic regions. Growth is especially strong in the robust markets of Southeast Asia.

WHEN

In 1847 Werner von Siemens, an electrical engineer, teamed with a craftsman, Johann Halske, to make telegraphs as Siemens & Halske in Germany. The firm's first major project linked Berlin and Frankfurt with the first long-distance telegraph system in Europe (1848). In 1870 the company completed the 6,600-mile India Line running from London to Calcutta. It made the first transatlantic cable to connect Ireland and the US in 1874.

The Siemens history of firsts includes Europe's first electric power transmission system (1876), the world's first electrified railway (1879), and one of the first elevators (1880). In 1896 the company patented the world's first X-ray tube and completed the first European subway, in Budapest.

Despite losses in WWI, Siemens recovered, forming Osram, a German light bulb cartel, with AEG and Auer (1919) and entering into a venture with Furukawa Electric called Fuji Electric (1923). It developed radios and traffic lights in the 1920s and began production of electron microscopes in 1939.

Siemens suffered heavy losses in WWII but staged a quick recovery, developing silicates for semiconductors, data processing equipment, and the world's first implantable pacemaker in the 1950s. The company formed joint ventures with Bosch (Bosch-Siemens Hausgerate; appliances, 1967) and AEG (Kraftwerk Union; nuclear power, 1969), among others. It profited from Germany's protectionist telecommunications policies, but its computer ventures with RCA and Philips were disappointing.

In 1981 Karlheinz Kaske became the first CEO from outside the Siemens family. Under his direction the company entered into joint

ventures with Philips, Intel, and Advanced Micro Devices. In 1988 and 1989 it bought Bendix Electronics (US), Rolm Systems (manufacturing and development), 50% of Rolm Company (marketing and services, PBXs; US), and the telecommunications businesses of Plessey (UK). It completed the Rolm acquisition in 1992.

In 1990 Siemens and German computer maker Nixdorf combined their computer businesses, forming SNI. Nixdorf had started as a small calculator company in 1952. Heinz Nixdorf used radio tubes to power his innovative product, which he was soon selling to major telecommunications companies. In the mid-1960s the company began making small computers. In the following decades it expanded into ATMs, retail scanners, software, and telecommunications products.

The company acquired Sylvania's lamp business from GTE in 1993 and merged it with the Osram companies in the US and Canada, forming Osram Sylvania.

In 1994 Siemens entered into a joint venture with the China National Posts and Telecommunications Industry Corp. to produce fiber-optic cable. The following year SNI signed a marketing alliance with Microsoft and won a $41 million contract to develop networking software for Deutsche Telekom, Germany's state telecommunications monopoly.

In 1996 Siemens announced that its Power Generation Group will build a $500 million plant in Pakistan and a $380 million electronic components plant in Portugal. Also that year Siemens Nixdorf bought a 10% stake in German computer retailer Vobis Microcomputer AG.

WHO

Chairman: Hermann Franz
President and CEO: Heinrich von Pierer
Director Research and Development: Hans Gunter Danielmeyer
Director Finance: Karl-Hermann Baumann
Director Human Resources: Werner Maly
President and CEO, Siemens Nixdorf: Gerhard Schulmeyer
President and CEO, Siemens Corp. (US): Albert Hoser
President and CEO, Siemens Nixdorf (US): Edward A. Blechschmidt, age 43
Auditors: KPMG Deutsche Treuhand-Gesellschaft AG Wirtschaftsprufungsgesell

WHERE

HQ: Wittelsbacherplatz 2, D-80333, Munich, Germany
Phone: +49-89-2-34-28-12
Fax: +49-89-2-34-28-25
US HQ: Siemens Corp., 1301 Avenue of the Americas, New York, NY 10019-6022
US Phone: 212-258-4000
US Fax: 212-767-0580
Web site: http://www.siemens.de

	1995 Sales	
	$ mil.	% of total
Germany	26,289	43
Other Europe	16,073	26
Americas	9,844	16
Asia/Pacific	5,984	10
Other regions	3,451	5
Total	**61,641**	**100**

WHAT

	1995 Sales	
	$ mil.	% of total
Communications	12,775	22
Industry	12,483	20
Energy	9,124	15
Information	7,904	13
Transportation	5,347	9
Health care	4,672	7
Components	4,070	7
Lighting	3,742	6
Other products & services	1,524	1
Total	**61,641**	**100**

Selected Operating Groups
Automotive systems
Defense electronics
Drives and standard products
Industrial and building systems
Medical engineering
Power generation
Power transmission and distribution
Public communication networks
Semiconductors
Transportation systems

KEY COMPETITORS

ABB
Alcatel Alsthom
AT&T Corp.
DEC
Electrolux
ENI
Ericsson
Fried. Krupp
Fujitsu
General Electric
Hewlett-Packard
Hitachi
IBM
Intel
IRI
ITT Industries
Machines Bull
Mannesmann
Matsushita
Motorola
NEC
Nokia
Olivetti
Philips
Robert Bosch
Rolls-Royce
Samsung
Sanyo
Thomson SA
Toshiba
Westinghouse

HOW MUCH

OTC symbol: SMAWY FYE: September 30	Annual Growth	1986	1987	1988	1989	1990	1991	1992	1993	1994	1995
Sales ($ mil.)	10.8%	24,466	32,769	33,478	36,181	42,278	48,190	48,492	47,019	54,586	61,641
Net income ($ mil.)	7.5%	757	775	743	872	1,035	1,220	1,109	1,038	1,141	1,447
Income as % of sales	—	3.1%	2.4%	2.2%	2.4%	2.4%	2.5%	2.3%	2.2%	2.1%	2.3%
Earnings per share ($)	4.0%	3.23	3.19	3.04	3.55	4.01	4.75	3.95	3.95	4.13	4.60
Stock price – high ($)	—	—	—	—	—	93.75	85.63	89.45	93.77	91.75	110.25
Stock price – low ($)	—	—	—	—	—	65.64	66.13	68.56	69.78	76.08	92.75
Stock price – close ($)	7.2%	—	—	—	—	77.92	76.25	76.25	87.88	83.73	110.25
P/E – high	—	—	—	—	—	23	18	23	25	22	24
P/E – low	—	—	—	—	—	16	14	17	19	18	20
Dividends per share ($)	6.4%	1.04	1.53	1.35	1.30	1.47	1.72	1.61	1.50	1.68	1.81
Book value per share ($)	5.2%	32.99	41.29	38.79	42.38	43.09	43.96	39.78	39.39	47.62	51.94
Employees	0.3%	363,000	359,000	353,000	365,000	373,000	402,000	413,000	391,000	379,000	373,000

1995 YEAR-END

Debt ratio: 22.1%
Return on equity: 9.7%
Cash (mil.): $18,676
Current ratio: 1.45
Long-term debt (mil.): $1,976
No. of shares (mil.): 275
Dividends
  Yield: 1.6%
  Payout: 39.2%
Market value (mil.): $30,319

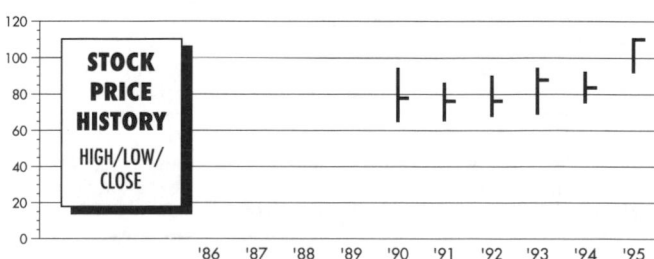

STOCK PRICE HISTORY
HIGH/LOW/CLOSE

SILICON GRAPHICS, INC.

OVERVIEW

Silicon Graphics — it brings fake things to life. The Mountain View, California-based company is the world's #1 maker of supercomputers used by engineers, scientists, and Hollywood special-effects artists. Silicon Graphics is probably best known for its graphics subsystems, which enable computers to process 3-D imagery and real-time animation without slowing the performance of more general computing tasks. Work done on the company's computers was used to make computer-generated images seem like the real thing in the movies *Forrest Gump* and *Jurassic Park*.

Silicon Graphics is moving from the movie theater to the Internet, as its graphics technology has been chosen as the industry standard for creating "virtual malls" and other 3-D sites on the World Wide Web. To get the nod, the company had to beat out industry bully Microsoft, which it did by making its technology compatible with current software.

The purchase of computer firm Cray Research has bolstered the Silicon Graphics position in the high-performance marketplace but has done little to help the company in the market for PC graphics cards, which are allowing PCs to replace high-end workstations. The firm's challenge lies in adapting its mainframe technology to create more products for the PC market.

WHEN

Professor James Clark left Stanford University in 1981 to develop and market 3-D computer graphics technology. The next year he formed Silicon Graphics, and the company introduced the first 3-D terminal (IRIS 1000) and IRIS Graphics Library in 1983 (he had chosen the name IRIS because it related to color and vision). Clark in 1984 developed the first 3-D workstation, which retailed for $75,000. Former Hewlett-Packard executive Edward McCracken joined Silicon Graphics as president that year. By 1986 (the year it went public), Silicon Graphics led in its niche — making high-end 3-D workstations for technical and scientific markets.

The company pioneered the use of RISC chips (developed by MIPS Computer Systems) in 1987. The workstation market grew 63% that year, so while the firm's sales doubled, its share of the workstation market was a tiny 4%. The company released the Personal IRIS and the IRIS POWER series of workstations and supercomputers in 1988 and raised $68.4 million for R&D by selling a 20% stake to systems integration company Control Data (it bought back most of it for $53.3 million the next year). After hoarding its 3-D technology for 6 years, Silicon Graphics licensed IRIS Graphics Library to IBM in 1988, hoping to encourage developers to write software for Silicon Graphics machines.

The company's share of the workstation market reached 5.4% in 1990. To develop its place in the fast-growing Japanese market, Silicon Graphics formed an alliance with steel maker NKK in 1990, under which NKK distributed Silicon Graphics products in Japan in return for an ownership interest in the company.

In 1991 Silicon Graphics introduced the first RISC-based PC, the IRIS Indigo. It licensed IRIS General Library to Microsoft and joined Compaq in a product development agreement, selling the PC maker for $135 million in company stock. In 1992 Compaq's technology deal with Silicon Graphics fell apart, and it sold back its stake in Silicon Graphics for $150 million. That year the company bought microprocessor maker MIPS.

In search of diversity and greater market penetration, in 1993 Silicon Graphics introduced smaller, less-expensive ($10,000 and under) systems, including the Indy (a desktop system with a digital color video camera), the Onyx (an advanced graphics supercomputer), and the Indigo2 (a workstation).

Unable to direct the future of the company he founded, in 1994 Jim Clark left to start Netscape with Marc Andreessen.

Silicon Graphics and DreamWorks SKG teamed up in 1995 to create a $50 million state-of-the-art digital animation studio to accommodate 500 animators. Also that year subsidiary MIPS Technologies debuted Magic Carpet, its first multimedia chip set to be designed for games and other interactive consumer products.

Silicon Graphics bought unprofitable Cray Research for about $740 million in stock and cash in 1996. It subsequently sold Cray's business computer unit to networking products specialist Sun Microsystems. The company's earnings in fiscal 1996 reached $245 million on sales of $2.8 billion.

WHO

Chairman and CEO: Edward R. McCracken, age 51, $1,445,671 pay
Chairman, Silicon Graphics World Trade Corp.: Robert R. Bishop, age 52, $855,772 pay
EVP Worldwide Field Operations: Gary L. Lauer, age 42, $676,807 pay
SVP East Asia: Teruyasu Sekimoto, age 56, $778,773 pay
SVP; President, Alias/Wavefront: Robert K. Burgess, age 38
SVP; President, Silicon Studio, Inc.: Michael Ramsay, age 45
SVP Finance and CFO: Stanley J. Meresman, age 48
SVP Research and Development and Chief Technology Officer: Forest Baskett, age 52
VP Business Development, General Counsel, and Secretary: William M. Kelly, age 42
VP Human Resources: Kirk Froggatt
Auditors: Ernst & Young LLP

WHERE

HQ: 2011 N. Shoreline Blvd., Mountain View, CA 94043
Phone: 415-960-1980
Fax: 415-390-6220
Web site: http://www.sgi.com

Silicon Graphics has more than 70 offices in North America and about 60 offices in 30 other countries.

	1995 Sales		1995 Operating Income	
	$ mil.	% of total	$ mil.	% of total
US	1,250	56	190	58
Europe	607	27	115	35
Pacific/Americas	371	17	21	7
Adjustments	—	—	(19)	—
Total	**2,228**	**100**	**307**	**100**

WHAT

	1995 Sales
	% of total
Products	89
Service	11
Total	**100**

Selected Products

Applications Software	Graphics Subsystems
Alias Studio	Extreme
Explore	Impact
Power Animator	Reality Engine
Wavefront Composer	XZ

Desktop Workstation	High-end Systems
Indigo2	Challenge
Indy	Onyx
POWER Indigo2	POWER Challenge
WebFORCE	POWER Onyx

Selected Operations

Alias/Wavefront (develops digital design tools)
Cray Research (manufactures supercomputers)
MIPS Technologies, Inc. (designs microprocessors)
Silicon Studio, Inc. (provides software for entertainment content development)

KEY COMPETITORS

Apple Computer
Data General
DEC
Fujitsu
Hewlett-Packard
Hitachi
IBM
Intel
Intergraph
Machines Bull
Microsoft
Motorola
National Semiconductor
NCR
NEC
Novell
Sun Microsystems
Texas Instruments
Toshiba
Unisys
Wang

HOW MUCH

NYSE symbol: SGI FYE: June 30	Annual Growth	1986	1987	1988	1989	1990	1991	1992	1993	1994	1995
Sales ($ mil.)	55.5%	42	86	153	264	420	550	867	1,091	1,482	2,228
Net income ($ mil.)	69.0%	2	6	12	12	32	33	(118)	88	141	225
Income as % of sales	—	4.6%	6.5%	8.0%	4.4%	7.7%	6.0%	—	8.0%	9.5%	10.1%
Earnings per share ($)	43.4%	0.05	0.12	0.22	0.17	0.40	0.37	(1.10)	0.60	0.91	1.28
Stock price – high ($)	—	3.56	6.88	6.13	7.31	10.22	12.19	14.88	24.75	33.13	45.63
Stock price – low ($)	—	3.00	2.81	3.44	3.56	4.50	5.56	7.06	11.75	18.75	26.88
Stock price – close ($)	26.8%	3.25	4.06	4.69	7.31	6.75	11.31	14.31	24.75	31.16	27.63
P/E – high	—	71	57	28	43	26	33	—	41	36	36
P/E – low	—	60	23	16	21	11	15	—	20	21	21
Dividends per share ($)	—	0.00	0.00	0.00	0.00	0.00	0.00	0.00	0.00	0.00	0.00
Book value per share ($)	—	(1.03)	1.06	2.24	2.45	3.01	3.97	3.61	4.56	6.37	8.28
Employees	38.7%	331	605	1,055	1,483	2,099	2,500	3,575	3,750	4,357	6,300

1995 YEAR-END

Debt ratio: 20.1%
Return on equity: 20.3%
Cash (mil.): $516
Current ratio: 2.63
Long-term debt (mil.): $287
No. of shares (mil.): 160
Dividends
  Yield: —
  Payout: —
Market value (mil.): $4,434

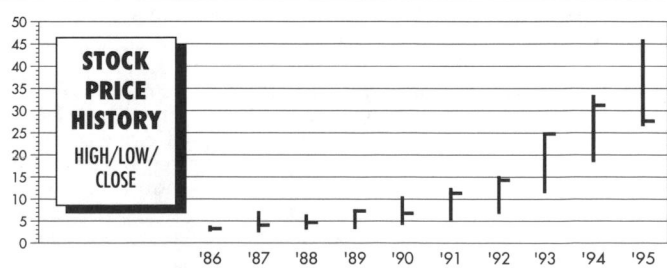

STOCK PRICE HISTORY HIGH/LOW/ CLOSE

SOFTBANK CORP.

OVERVIEW

It took a descendant of Korean immigrant laborers to bring US-style business to Japan. SOFTBANK is Japan's #1 seller of software and network products and the world's #1 publisher of high-tech magazines. But it operates largely outside Japan's traditional old-boy network of business relationships. Its founder and controlling stockholder, Masayoshi Son, is a rare animal in Japan: a self-made man and an ethnic Korean who built his business despite considerable racial prejudice.

SOFTBANK controls about 51% of the Japanese software distribution network, supplying products to many of the country's largest computer outlets. The company also publishes computer-related magazines in Japan and owns significant portions of several Japanese subsidiaries of large computer-related US corporations, including Novell and Cisco Systems.

SOFTBANK has moved into the US market on a large scale. It owns COMDEX, the sponsor of the largest computer industry trade shows in the world. SOFTBANK also owns Ziff-Davis Publishing, the world's leading publisher of computer-related magazines.

But Son is also a wheeler-dealer, aiming to have a hand in all forms of digital distribution, and the company has invested in US Internet companies, including CyberCash (secured payment systems) and Yahoo!. SOFTBANK owns 37% of Yahoo! and has engineered joint ventures to translate Yahoo!'s Internet interface into Japanese and other languages to make the Internet easier for non-English speakers to use.

Because of an ambitious growth program, the company is loaded with debt and vulnerable to changes in exchange rates between Japan and the US.

WHEN

Son grew up on the wrong side of the tracks on the island of Kyushu using the name Yasumoto to conform to the Japanese policy of "assimilation." In the early 1970s, the 16-year-old came to the US, in part to escape prejudice, and began using his Korean name. Thanks to Japanese educational rigor, Son was able to test out of a US high school within 3 weeks, and he entered the University of California at Berkeley. While there, he invented the prototype of what became the Sharp Wizard (a handheld organizer). Bankrolled by the nearly $1 million that Sharp paid him for his patent, Son returned to Japan after graduation.

After assessing his options, Son decided to go into the then embryonic PC software distribution industry. SOFTBANK was founded and got its first big break in 1981 when Joshin Denki, one of Japan's largest consumer electronics retailers, signed a distribution agreement with Son. Son used this agreement to gain exclusive distribution rights with many of the companies whose software he distributed. He soon got a loan from Dai-Ichi Kangyo Bank, but the bank, beset by its own problems, called the loan (Son managed to get financing from a government bank). Son also came down with hepatitis. Sidelined for 3 years, he had every department in the company organized as an autonomous profit center whose managers were responsible for performance.

Son returned to the business in 1986. In 1990 SOFTBANK formed a joint venture with Novell to sell networking products in Japan. The company went public in 1994 and began trading over the counter (in doing so, it gave a lift to Japan's off-exchange market, the equivalent of Nasdaq).

In 1994, as part of an evolving plan to control digital data delivery, Son attempted to buy Ziff-Davis. But he could not pay cash, so the owners sold the publishing business to Forstmann Little. Son ended up with the trade show division and then in 1995 augmented it with the purchase of computer trade show chieftain COMDEX. He continued to pursue Ziff-Davis Publishing and finally got it with an over-the-top bid of $2.1 billion (Forstmann paid $1.4 billion for it).

SOFTBANK invested in US Internet companies CyberCash and Yahoo! in 1996. That year it joined with Rupert Murdoch's News Corp. to buy 21% of TV Asahi, which will help provide programming for Murdoch's satellite TV projects in Asia.

All of these acquisitions are intended to be synergistic in the long term (following the model of a *keiretsu*, in which partner companies provide goods, services, and business for each other). As part of the plan, in 1996 SOFTBANK and Dentsu (Japan's largest advertising company) formed an Internet advertising joint venture.

WHO

President and CEO: Masayoshi Son, age 39
EVP: Takayuki Yabe
EVP: Takashi Eguchi
EVP, Publishing Division: Goro Hashimoto
EVP, Software and Network Sales Division: Ken Miyauchi
EVP and CFO, Corporate Strategy Division: Yoshitaka Kitao
EVP Human Resources: Toshitada Kobayashi
VC, SOFTBANK Holdings Inc. (US): Ronald D. Fisher
Auditors: Chuo Audit Corp.

WHERE

HQ: 24-1, Nihonbashi Hakozaki-cho, Chuo-ku, Tokyo, 103, Japan
Phone: +81-3-5642-8000
Fax: +81-3-5641-3401
US HQ: SOFTBANK Holdings Inc., 10 Langley Rd., Ste. 403, Newton Center, MA 02159
US Phone: 617-928-9300
US Fax: 617-928-9301
Web site: http://www.softbank.co.jp

WHAT

	1996 Sales		1996 Operating Income	
	$ mil.	% of total	$ mil.	% of total
Software & net-work products	1,126	71	43	32
Publishing	242	15	26	20
Exhibitions	163	10	64	48
Other	64	4	0	0
Total	**1,595**	**100**	**133**	**100**

Selected Operations

Alexander & Load Inc. (telemarketing for PC-related firms)
Mediabank Corp. (60%, R&D of interactive communications systems)
Novell Japan Ltd. (20%)
Phoenix Publishing Systems, Inc. (80%; software publishing services, including instruction manuals)
SOFTBANK Holdings Inc.
SOFTBANK COMDEX, Inc. (planning and operating trade shows)
SOFTBANK Exposition and Conference Co. Inc. (planning and operating trade shows)
SOFTBANK Korea Co. Ltd. (46%)
SOFTBANK Network Center Corp. (network consulting, training and support)
SOFTBANK Technologies, Inc. (software development and sales)
SoftVenture Capital, Inc. (computer-related investments)
CyberCash, Inc. (10%)
Yahoo! Inc. (37%)
Ziff-Davis Publishing Co. (computer-oriented publications)

KEY COMPETITORS

America Online
Asian Sources Media
CMP Publications
CSK
Ingram Micro
International Data Group
Mecklermedia
Reed Elsevier
Sendai Media Group

HOW MUCH

Principal exchange: Tokyo FYE: March 31	Annual Growth	1987	1988	1989	1990	1991	1992	1993	1994	1995	1996
Sales ($ mil.)	42.1%	—	—	—	—	275	330	449	624	1,119	1,595
Net income ($ mil.)	122.1%	—	—	—	—	1	1	5	9	24	54
Income as % of sales	—	—	—	—	—	0.5%	0.3%	1.2%	1.5%	2.1%	3.4%
Earnings per share ($)	67.0%	—	—	—	—	0.09	0.03	0.16	0.27	0.63	1.17
Stock price – high ($)[1]	—	—	—	—	—	—	—	—	—	109.06	179.81
Stock price – low ($)[1]	—	—	—	—	—	—	—	—	—	71.58	33.91
Stock price – close ($)[1]	53.1%	—	—	—	—	—	—	—	—	92.63	141.85
P/E – high	—	—	—	—	—	—	—	—	—	174	153
P/E – low	—	—	—	—	—	—	—	—	—	114	29
Dividends per share ($)	—	—	—	—	—	—	—	—	—	0.00	0.10
Book value per share ($)	85.8%	—	—	—	—	—	—	—	—	12.36	22.97
Employees	95.0%	—	—	—	—	—	—	—	590	630	909	4,375

[1] Stock prices are for the prior calendar year.

1996 YEAR-END

Debt ratio: 76.5%
Return on equity: 6.5%
Cash (mil.): $173
Current ratio: 1.18
Long-term debt (mil.): $3,512
No. of shares (mil.): 49
Dividends
  Yield: 0.1%
  Payout: 8.5%
Market value (mil.): $6,892

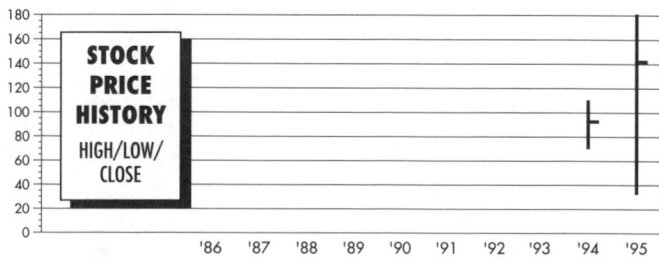

STOCK PRICE HISTORY HIGH/LOW/CLOSE

SOLECTRON CORPORATION

OVERVIEW

Choosy computer makers who want their motherboards in a jiffy choose Solectron. The Milpitas, California-based company is the #2 provider of contract manufacturing services to original equipment manufacturers (Alabama-based SCI Systems is #1). Solectron's premanufacturing, manufacturing, and postmanufacturing services span the process from product design to systems assembly to warehousing. Its facilities use leading manufacturing processes, including surface-mount technology and emerging processes such as tape-automated bonding and chip-on-substrate manufacturing.

The company builds electronic systems and subsystems for customers in a variety of industries, including avionics, communications, computers, consumer electronics, industrial and medical instrumentation, semiconductor applications, and software. Its roster reads like a "Who's Who" of electronics manufacturers and includes Apple Computer, Applied Materials, Exabyte, Hewlett-Packard, Intel, and Sun Microsystems. Its 10 largest customers accounted for 70% of its 1995 revenues, with IBM alone responsible for 21%.

Solectron's success (sales were up 42% in 1995) is the result of the increasing trend by electronics makers to outsource specialized manufacturing jobs — and of the company's own obsession with quality. It has been a consistent winner of industry quality awards, including the prestigious Malcolm Baldrige Award (in 1991).

Plant expansions and acquisitions both have fueled Solectron's climb close to the top of the rapidly consolidating electronics manufacturing industry. By the beginning of 1996 the company had more than 2 million square feet of manufacturing space on 3 continents.

WHEN

Solectron began in 1977 as a small electronics assembly job shop. It was founded by Roy Kusumoto, who had also worked for computer game systems maker Atari and cofounded Optical Diodes Inc. The company's original mission was to provide peak-period manufacturing services for the Silicon Valley's burgeoning electronics industry. It also intended to become involved in solar energy (the name Solectron reflects both industries) but never developed its solar connection.

With Solectron struggling, Kusumoto brought in Winston Chen as EVP in 1978; he became president the next year. Chen, a native of Taiwan with doctorates in applied physics and applied mechanics, had held technology management positions at IBM. Known for an obsession with quality, he believed that success lay in blending the best of Japanese management methods with American freedom to innovate. In 1980, the year after Chen became president, Solectron netted $400,000. Chen became CEO in 1984. During the late 1980s former Vermont Micro Systems head Charles Dickinson served as Solectron's chairman.

In 1987 Kusumoto left to take a position with Sanwa Electric. The following year Koichi Nishimura joined Solectron as COO. Nishimura, who has doctorates in engineering and materials science, was also an IBM veteran and had once been Chen's boss. Nishimura brought experience in the design and development of disk files, thin-film technology, and process equipment.

Solectron went public in 1989, raising only $7 million, or $1.50 a share. Intent on improving Solectron's performance, Chen and Nishimura adopted the Malcolm Baldrige National Quality Award guidelines; the company won the award 2 years later.

In 1990 Nishimura took over as Solectron's president. The following year he became co-CEO with Chen, who remained chairman. That year the company opened its first foreign manufacturing facility, in Malaysia.

In 1992 it bought plants in Charlotte, North Carolina, and Bordeaux, France, from IBM. That year the company opened a business development office in Japan, and Nishimura took over as CEO.

In 1993 Solectron bought a printed circuit board assembly plant in Everett, Washington, from Hewlett-Packard and a plant in Scotland from Philips. It also increased production space at its Malaysian plant. The company also expanded its business to include custom design and development work.

Dickinson again became chairman in 1994 when Chen retired to head the Paramitas Foundation, a charity he established. In 1995 Solectron purchased Hewlett-Packard's printed-circuit assembly plant in Boeblingen, Germany. In 1996 it acquired Fine Pitch Technology, a provider of prototype services, and Texas Instruments's custom manufacturing services in Texas and Malaysia. It also agreed to buy chip designer Force Computers.

WHO

Chairman; President, Solectron Europe: Charles A. Dickinson, age 71, $500,000 pay
President and CEO: Koichi Nishimura, age 57, $787,500 pay
SVP; President, Solectron North America: Walter W. Wilson, age 51, $485,991 pay
SVP; President, Solectron Asia: Ken Tsai, age 52, $403,731, pay
SVP, CFO, and Secretary: Susan S. Wang, age 44, $401,000 pay
SVP; President, Solectron Washington, Inc.: Leslie T. Nishimura, age 51
SVP and Chief Materials Officer: Steven T. Ng, age 40
SVP and Chief Technology Officer: Saeed Zohouri, age 44
President, Solectron Japan: Shinji Ayao
VP; President, Solectron Europe: David Kynaston
VP Human Resources: Thomas Morelli
Auditors: KPMG Peat Marwick LLP

WHERE

HQ: 777 Gibraltar Dr., Milpitas, CA 95035
Phone: 408-957-8500
Fax: 408-956-6075
Web site: http://www.oakridge.com/Solectron/index.html
Solectron has manufacturing facilities in France, Germany, Malaysia, the UK, and the US.

	1995 Sales	
	$ mil.	% of total
US	1,281	62
Europe	534	26
Asia	251	12
Total	**2,066**	**100**

WHAT

Selected Services

Premanufacturing
Component engineering
Concurrent engineering
Design engineering
Interconnection and packaging consulting
Product prototyping
Test development

Manufacturing
Concurrent engineering
Materials management
Packaging
Printed circuit and flex assembly
Software duplication
Systems integration
Testing

Postmanufacturing
Fulfillment
Printed circuit board assembly
Product upgrades
Repair and refurbishment

KEY COMPETITORS

AST
Benchmark Electronics
Comptronix
Cyberguard
DEC
EA Industries
Flextronics
Group Technologies
Hitachi
IBM
IEC Electronics
Jabil
Jaco Electronics
Kent Electronics
Nam Tai
PCI Ltd.
Sanmina
SCI Systems
Zycon

HOW MUCH

NYSE symbol: SLR FYE: August 31	Annual Growth	1986	1987	1988	1989	1990	1991	1992	1993	1994	1995
Sales ($ mil.)	54.2%	42	60	93	130	205	265	407	836	1,457	2,066
Net income ($ mil.)	—	(3)	2	3	4	7	9	14	31	56	80
Income as % of sales	—	—	2.5%	3.2%	3.3%	3.6%	3.5%	3.6%	3.7%	3.8%	3.9%
Earnings per share ($)	—	(0.19)	0.09	0.18	0.23	0.31	0.35	0.44	0.75	1.18	1.62
Stock price – high ($)	—	—	—	—	1.84	4.38	9.13	18.69	29.75	34.00	45.13
Stock price – low ($)	—	—	—	—	1.50	1.72	2.16	8.13	16.56	23.38	22.13
Stock price – close ($)	69.8%	—	—	—	1.84	2.22	8.69	18.69	28.38	27.50	44.13
P/E – high	—	—	—	—	8	14	26	42	40	29	28
P/E – low	—	—	—	—	6	6	6	18	22	20	14
Dividends per share ($)	—	—	—	—	0.00	0.00	0.00	0.00	0.00	0.00	0.00
Book value per share ($)	52.9%	—	—	—	0.85	1.48	1.86	3.16	6.42	8.01	10.85
Employees	35.0%	—	—	1,350	1,550	2,000	2,131	2,979	4,545	6,568	11,049

1995 YEAR-END

Debt ratio: 6.1%
Return on equity: 18.3%
Cash (mil.): $149
Current ratio: 1.96
Long-term debt (mil.): $30
No. of shares (mil.): 50
Dividends
  Yield: —
  Payout: —
Market value (mil.): $2,188

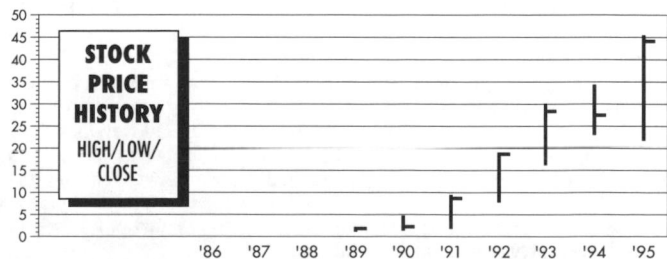

STOCK PRICE HISTORY
HIGH/LOW/CLOSE

STORAGE TECHNOLOGY CORPORATION

OVERVIEW

StorageTek spells relief I-B-M. With headquarters in Louisville, Colorado, Storage Technology has 80% of the worldwide market for robotic tape-handling systems, such as the one used in its PowderHorn cartridge library (which handles up to 6,000 computer data storage tapes). Other data storage and retrieval products include direct access storage devices, rotating magnetic disk systems, and tape drives. The company also makes such networking products as channel extenders, routers, security encryption devices, and switches.

With increased competition trimming its profits, the company set out to increase its sales volume. Salvation came as it reached an agreement with IBM to supply the computer powerhouse with mainframe computer storage products to be sold under the IBM name. The deal also calls for the 2 companies to cooperate on research and development of new storage technology.

StorageTek isn't just relying on its agreement with IBM to help dig it out of a hole. It is looking beyond the mainframe market and using its information storage know-how to develop new products. These include electronic video storage systems for TV broadcasters and shared-space storage libraries, which allow small companies to share the memory capacity of a large data storage system.

WHEN

A group of 4 former IBM engineers founded Storage Technology in Colorado in 1969 to fill a niche in tape drives for IBM-compatible mainframe computers. One of the founders, a Palestinian refugee named Jesse Aweida, led the company to the top of its industry.

Heady growth inspired StorageTek to become a full-line supplier of peripherals. Acquisitions included Promodata (1973), Disk Systems (1974), Microtechnology (1979), and Documation (1980). The company also began developing an IBM-compatible mainframe computer and an optical laser disk. Sales climbed from $4 million in 1971 to $922 million in 1981, making StorageTek the world's leading supplier of tape drives (with a 55% market share for IBM-compatible tape drives) and disk drives (35%) and the 9th largest company in the computer industry.

In 1982, however, delayed expansion projects ate capital while providing no return. In addition, malfunctions on disk drives installed earlier resulted in costly replacements and damage to the company's reputation. Aweida's termination of several product lines could not prevent a cash-flow crisis, and in late 1984 StorageTek filed for bankruptcy.

Aweida stepped down, and turnaround artist Ryal Poppa (who became CEO in 1985) sliced $85 million in expenses by eliminating 2 layers of management, 5,000 workers, and the mainframe and optical disk projects. Although the company was still awash in red ink, Poppa persuaded creditors to fund his vision of automated tape storage at a fraction of disk drive prices. The resulting 4400 ACS (Automated Cartridge System) was instrumental to the company's success after its 1987 emergence from bankruptcy. The company's Library Server software allowed the ACS to work with most high-performance computers, reducing StorageTek's dependence on IBM machines.

The company purchased Aspen Peripherals in 1989 to enter the midrange tape market. Aspen president Jesse Aweida did not rejoin the company he had helped found.

In 1991 StorageTek merged its nonimpact printer operations into a venture with Siemens Nixdorf (sold to Siemens Nixdorf in 1994). In 1992 the company agreed to buy Swedish storage system distributor Edata. Later in the year StorageTek expanded its midrange computer (AS/400) product line by acquiring Lago Systems and Prime Solutions. Also in 1992 DEC and StorageTek established Rocky Mountain Magnetics (with StorageTek owning 19%) to develop magneto-resistive thin-film heads.

Poor European results, heavy price competition in the midrange market, and new product development expenses pushed StorageTek nearly $130 million into the red in 1993. The company restructured, reorganized its distribution and service operations, and overhauled its product line, returning to profitability in 1994. (Additional restructuring charges led to another loss the next year.)

In 1995 StorageTek opened its new manufacturing and R&D center in Toulouse, France. The plant manufactures the TimberLine tape subsystems. That year the company broadened its presence in the booming network computing market with the purchase of Minneapolis-based Network Systems Corp.

David Weiss replaced Poppa as CEO in 1996. StorageTek sold its midrange products unit that year and planned to lay off 1,500 workers as part of further cost-cutting.

WHO

Chairman, President, and CEO: David E. Weiss, age 51, $333,943 pay (prior to promotion)
EVP Worldwide Field Operations: John V. Williams, age 52, $275,001 pay
EVP; General Manager Network Systems: Lowell Thomas Gooch, age 51, $255,539 pay
EVP and CFO: David E. Lacey, age 49
VP, General Counsel, and Secretary: W. Russell Wayman, age 51, $199,424 pay
VP Human Resources: Laurie Dodd
Auditors: Price Waterhouse LLP

WHERE

HQ: 2270 S. 88th St., Louisville, CO 80028-4309
Phone: 303-673-5151
Fax: 303-673-2296
Web site: http://www.stortek.com

StorageTek has manufacturing facilities in Colorado, Florida, Minnesota, Puerto Rico, France, and the UK. The company sells its products worldwide.

	1995 Sales % of total
US	59
Other countries	41
Total	**100**

WHAT

	1995 Sales	
	$ mil.	% of total
Nearline products	1,198	62
Online products	376	19
Networking products	209	11
Other products	147	8
Total	**1,930**	**100**

Selected Products
Nearline tape libraries
  4410 ACS
  PowderHorn
  RedWood
  Silverton
  Timberline
  Wolf Creek
Online random access data products
  Arctic Fox
  Iceberg
  Kodiak
Networking products
  Channel extenders
  Routers
  Security encryption devices
  Switchers

KEY COMPETITORS

Amdahl	Fujitsu
Ameriquest	Hewlett-Packard
Compaq	Hitachi
Data General	Kingston Technology
DEC	NEC
EMC Corp.	Seagate
Exabyte	Siemens

HOW MUCH

NYSE symbol: STK FYE: December 31	Annual Growth	1986	1987	1988	1989	1990	1991	1992	1993	1994	1995
Sales ($ mil.)	12.0%	696	750	874	983	1,141	1,585	1,522	1,405	1,625	1,930
Net income ($ mil.)	—	17	19	44	36	71	93	16	(128)	29	(154)
Income as % of sales	—	2.4%	2.5%	5.1%	3.7%	6.2%	5.9%	1.0%	—	1.8%	—
Earnings per share ($)	—	4.80	1.30	1.90	1.40	2.22	2.33	0.37	(2.98)	0.66	(2.91)
Stock price – high ($)	—	73.75	50.00	36.25	22.50	35.25	51.50	78.00	45.00	41.50	33.25
Stock price – low ($)	—	17.50	11.25	12.50	9.25	11.00	17.75	18.38	18.00	25.00	17.88
Stock price – close ($)	(4.2%)	35.00	18.75	17.50	11.75	21.50	39.88	20.75	31.88	29.00	23.88
P/E – high	—	15	39	19	16	16	22	—	—	63	—
P/E – low	—	4	9	7	7	5	8	—	—	38	—
Dividends per share ($)	—	0.00	0.00	0.00	0.00	0.00	0.00	0.00	0.00	0.00	0.00
Book value per share ($)	—	(5.21)	10.23	1.25	13.12	16.14	21.80	22.25	23.62	24.13	18.06
Employees	1.7%	8,608	8,865	8,498	9,300	9,100	10,100	10,100	10,100	10,300	10,000

1995 YEAR-END

Debt ratio: 31.8%
Return on equity: —
Cash (mil.): $265
Current ratio: 1.77
Long-term debt (mil.): $364
No. of shares (mil.): 53
Dividends
  Yield: —
  Payout: —
Market value (mil.): $1,273

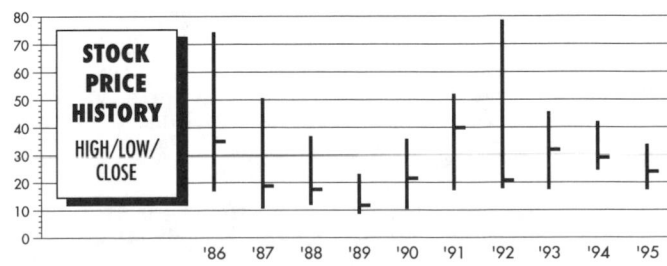

STOCK PRICE HISTORY HIGH/LOW/CLOSE

SUN MICROSYSTEMS, INC.

OVERVIEW

Sun Microsystems is burning up the Internet. The Mountain View, California-based company's Java programming language is adding a kick to Web pages by letting users add animation and real-time video. But Sun built its reputation on hardware — workstations, servers, and microprocessors — and service. Sun's UNIX-based servers run about half the networks that make up the Internet, while its microprocessors power its own and others' workstations and servers. Commercial accounts make up 1/3 of Sun's revenues.

Easy-to-learn, platform-independent, and free on the Internet, Java is a bona fide sensation. Many experts expect Java to radically change computing by allowing software applications to be used from the Internet. This so threatens Microsoft's market dominance that

the software superstar has jumped on the growing Java bandwagon, agreeing to add Java code to Windows 95. Java is also incorporated in the Netscape Web browser and is part of a standard established by several industry leaders for "network computers," inexpensive machines to be used solely for Internet access.

Sun continues to debut hardware innovations as well. Its UltraSPARC microprocessor doubles the processing power of its predecessor, the SuperSPARC, while picoJAVA is a microprocessor designed to exploit Java programming for small devices such as cellular phones, pagers, and printers. The company's Ultra Enterprise workstations return it to its roots: hardware for engineers and scientists.

WHEN

The four 27-year-olds who founded Sun Microsystems in 1982 saw great market potential for workstations that could share data using the UNIX operating system so popular with scientists and engineers.

German-born Andreas Bechtolsheim, a Stanford engineering graduate student, had built a workstation from spare parts for his numerical problems. Two Stanford MBA graduates, Scott McNealy and India-born Vinod Khosla, liked Bechtolsheim's creation, and they tapped Berkeley's UNIX guru William Joy to supply the software. Khosla was president and McNealy was director of manufacturing of the new company.

By adopting AT&T's UNIX operating system, Sun's workstations, unlike those of industry pioneer Apollo, networked easily with the hardware and software of other vendors from the outset. Sun, able to offer lower prices than the competition by using existing technologies, zoomed to more than $500 million in sales in just 5 years. In 1984 Khosla retired; he was succeeded by McNealy.

Sun went public in 1986 and the next year signed with AT&T to develop an enhanced UNIX operating system. The product that emerged in late 1989 established a de facto high-end UNIX standard (System V, Release 4.0). Sun's development of the fast and highly adaptable SPARC microprocessor (which uses a simplified reduced instruction set computer [RISC] design) gave its SPARCstation 2 (1990) minicomputer power.

Sun licensed SPARC to stimulate low-cost, high-volume production of its systems and

thus increase the number of available 3rd-party applications. PC programs such as Lotus 1-2-3, WordPerfect, and Borland's dBASE IV for Sun systems broadened Sun's commercial market.

In 1993 the company announced plans to sell microprocessors and other computer chips in an effort to become a one-stop technology shop. The next year Sun and IBM began modifying Solaris software (the leading UNIX operating system) for PowerPC-based machines.

The US Army tapped Sun in 1995 to supply about 28,000 workstations and servers over a 10-year-period for a new tactical command and control system. That same year, co-founder Bechtolsheim left Sun to form Granite Systems, a networking equipment developer. In mid-1995 Sun unveiled the Hot Java browser and a new Internet server called Netra. It also introduced Internet products for the x86 platform (Internet Gateway) and for PCs (SolarNet).

Sun failed in early 1996 in an attempt to acquire stumbling Apple Computer. Also that year the 4 creators of Java left Sun to form a networking products company called Marimba; Sun and Motorola created an alliance to develop high-speed Internet access systems for home PCs; and Apple, IBM, and Microsoft added their names to those supporting Java as a programming standard.

In 1996 Sun also bought the business computer unit of Cray Research as the supercomputer maker's other operations were being acquired by Silicon Graphics. Sun's profits rose to $476 million on sales of $7,095 million in 1996.

Chairman, President, and CEO: Scott G. McNealy, age 40, $3,000,000 pay
President, Sun Microsystems Computer Co.: Edward J. Zander, age 48, $900,000 pay
VP Worldwide Field Operations, Sun Microsystems Computer Co.: Joseph P. Roebuck, age 59, $781,648 pay
VP Corporate Planning and Development and Chief Information Officer: William J. Raduchel, age 49, $699,769 pay
VP and CFO: Michael E. Lehman, age 45
VP, General Counsel, and Secretary: Michael H. Morris, age 47
VP Human Resources: Kenneth M. Alvares, age 51
President, SunService: Lawrence W. Hambly, age 49
President, SunExpress: Dorothy A. Terrell, age 50
President, SunSoft: Janpieter T. Scheerder
President, SPARC Technology Business: Chester J. Silvestri, age 46
Chief Technology Officer: Greg M. Papadopoulos
Auditors: Ernst & Young LLP

WHERE

HQ: 2550 Garcia Ave., Mountain View, CA 94043-1100
Phone: 415-960-1300
Fax: 415-969-9131
Web site: http://www.sun.com

Sun has more than 160 sales and service offices in the US and 38 foreign countries.

	1995 Sales		1995 Operating Income	
	$ mil.	% of total	$ mil.	% of total
US	3,136	53	242	47
Europe	1,491	25	251	48
Other regions	1,275	22	27	5
Adjustments	—	—	(20)	—
Total	**5,902**	**100**	**500**	**100**

WHAT

Software
Developer products
Enterprise management products
Networking products
Operating system (Solaris)
PC desktop integration products

Servers
Netra
SPARCcenter 2000
SPARCserver

Storage
SPARCstorage Array 100 series

Workstations
SPARCstation
SPARC Xterminal 1

Operating Companies
SPARC Technology Business (SPARC microprocessors)
Sun Microsystems Computer Co. (SPARC workstations and servers)
SunExpress, Inc. (distribution of software, accessories, and 3rd-party products)
SunService (UNIX service and support)
SunSoft, Inc. (develops and markets Solaris, a UNIX operating system, and other software)

KEY COMPETITORS

Advanced Logic Research	IBM	Oracle
AMD	Intel	Sequent
Ceridian	Intergraph	Siemens
Compaq	LG Group	Sony
Cyberguard	Machines Bull	Symantec
Data General	Microsoft	Tandem
DEC	National Semiconductor	Unisys
Fujitsu	nCUBE	Wang
Hewlett-Packard	NEC	Wyse Technology
Hitachi	NCR	

HOW MUCH

Nasdaq symbol: SUNW FYE: June 30	Annual Growth	1986	1987	1988	1989	1990	1991	1992	1993	1994	1995
Sales ($ mil.)	44.9%	210	538	1,052	1,765	2,466	3,221	3,589	4,309	4,690	5,902
Net income ($ mil.)	45.7%	12	36	66	61	111	190	173	157	196	356
Income as % of sales	—	5.7%	6.8%	6.3%	3.4%	4.5%	5.9%	4.8%	3.6%	4.2%	6.0%
Earnings per share ($)	35.2%	0.12	0.28	0.45	0.38	0.61	0.93	0.86	0.75	1.01	1.81
Stock price – high ($)	—	6.03	11.09	10.13	11.38	18.56	19.31	18.06	20.50	18.81	51.44
Stock price – low ($)	—	2.81	6.00	6.69	6.81	7.50	10.38	11.25	10.56	9.13	14.94
Stock price – close ($)	25.3%	6.00	8.38	8.31	8.63	10.69	14.19	16.81	14.56	17.75	45.63
P/E – high	—	50	40	23	30	30	21	21	27	19	28
P/E – low	—	23	21	15	18	12	11	13	14	9	8
Dividends per share ($)	—	0.00	0.00	0.00	0.00	0.00	0.00	0.00	0.00	0.00	0.00
Book value per share ($)	30.5%	0.98	1.79	2.56	3.94	5.00	6.29	7.43	8.04	8.67	10.77
Employees	14.8%	4,200	7,100	7,090	10,208	11,500	12,480	12,800	13,253	13,282	14,498

1995 YEAR-END

Debt ratio: 7.8%
Return on equity: 19.0%
Cash (mil.): $1,228
Current ratio: 2.20
Long-term debt (mil.): $91
No. of shares (mil.): 197
Dividends
  Yield: —
  Payout: —
Market value (mil.): $8,900

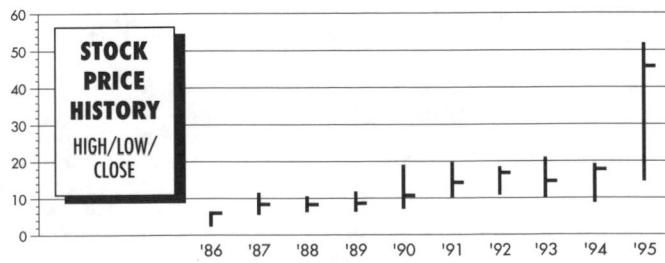

STOCK PRICE HISTORY HIGH/LOW/CLOSE

TANDEM COMPUTERS INCORPORATED

OVERVIEW

Tandem can tolerate glitches in its market but not in its computers. The Cupertino, California-based company's fault-tolerant computers feature redundant systems to ensure against failure. These computers are used to manage the majority of the world's critical financial transactions, including 80% of all automatic teller transactions, 66% of all credit card transactions, and 90% of the world's stock market transactions. Top telecommunications companies worldwide depend on Tandem's servers for uninterrupted service. The enterprise also supplies network hardware and software through its subsidiary, UB Networks.

Tandem has seen some rough spots recently, the result of manufacturing difficulties, pricing pressures, and its transition to an open-standard architecture. But the naming of new CEO Roel Pieper, former head of UB Networks, and the introduction of the new interconnect architecture, ServerNet, mark management's attempt to reinvigorate company growth.

Strategic alliances have been integral to Tandem's success. Recently telecommunications equipment maker Ericsson began incorporating Tandem technology into its products, software giant Microsoft agreed to support ServerNet as an industry standard, NEC said it would codevelop servers with Tandem for the Windows NT market, and database software leader Oracle Corp. began converting its Oracle 7 software to the ServerNet platform.

WHEN

Tandem Computers was started in 1974 by James Treybig, a former marketing manager at Hewlett-Packard and limited partner in venture capital firm Kleiner, Perkins, Caufield & Byers. Treybig pioneered a way to link computers to work in tandem so that if one failed, another would take over without interruption. Tandem introduced its first fail-safe minicomputer, the NonStop16, in 1976.

Tandem's computers quickly became a success. Revenues doubled each year from 1976 to 1981. Designed to process continuous, online transactions quickly, the computers were popular with banks, brokerage firms, manufacturers, and hospitals. By 1987 Tandem was a $1 billion company with 130 offices worldwide.

Although Tandem dominated the fail-safe computer market in the 1970s, it faced stiff competition in the early 1980s from such companies as Stratus Computer. The company's earnings were flat from 1982 to 1985, forcing a reassessment of both its product line and its business methods. By 1987 Tandem had tightened its management control and substantially revamped and expanded its product line. Sales grew 35% that year. Contributing to the rise in sales were Tandem's 1987 introduction of a smaller CLX minicomputer and announcement of a more versatile database software product, NonStop SQL.

Tandem expanded into complementary specialty areas through its acquisition of Atalla (1987, data security products), Integrated Technology (1988, telecommunications software), and Ungermann-Bass (1988, network specialists; now UB Networks). The 1989 introduction of the NonStop Cyclone moved Tandem into the mainframe market, enabling it to compete head-on with IBM's comparable machine at 1/3 the cost.

The company continued its expansion in the early 1990s, buying Array Technology (fault-tolerant mass storage systems), Applied Communications (finance and telecommunications software), MPACT EDI (software developer for Tandem products), and 50% of NetWorth (LAN software and hardware). But Tandem refused to make its systems compatible with other operating systems, forcing its clients to use only the company's software. Eventually this stance brought client defections, falling profits, and losses in 1992 and 1993. The company made a key strategic move when it switched to open-system technologies. The tactic led to more than $500 million in restructuring charges, but it worked and the company returned to profitability in 1994. That year Tandem introduced Himalaya, a new line of lower-priced computer servers.

In 1995 Tandem teamed up with Silicon Graphics (high-end graphics workstations and software) and with Spyglass (developer of the Mosaic Web browser) to provide financial transaction security on the Internet. Treybig stepped down as president and CEO; he was succeeded by Pieper in early 1996.

In 1996 Tandem joined with GTE to develop anti-fraud products for the telecommunications industry. Also that year to cut operating costs so that the company could reduce prices and stimulate sales growth, Tandem laid off more than 800 workers, almost 10% of its workforce. Tandem and Microsoft agreed in 1996 to make their server technology compatible.

WHO

Chairman: Thomas J. Perkins, age 63
President and CEO: Roel Pieper, age 39, $336,520 pay
(prior to promotion)
SVP; General Manager, Systems Development Group:
Kurt L. Friedrich, age 46, $377,109 pay
SVP; General Manager, Solutions Products Group:
Donald E. Fowler, age 57, $370,130 pay
**SVP; General Manager, Tandem Sales and Support
Group:** Gerald L. Peterson, age 50, $369,800 pay
SVP and COO: Robert C. Marshall, age 64
SVP and CFO: David J. Rynne, age 55
VP, General Counsel, and Secretary: Josephine T. Parry,
age 47
**VP Systems Development; General Manager, Austin
Unit Operations:** Lawrence A. Laurich, age 52
VP Human Resources: Philip Johnson
Auditors: Ernst & Young LLP

WHERE

HQ: 19333 Vallco Pkwy., Cupertino, CA 95014-2599
Phone: 408-285-6000
Fax: 408-285-0035
Web site: http://www.tandem.com

Tandem has more than 180 offices worldwide.

	1995 Sales	
	$ mil.	% of total
US	1,149	50
Europe	578	25
Japan	339	15
Other regions	219	10
Total	**2,285**	**100**

WHAT

	1995 Sales	
	$ mil.	% of total
Products	1,846	81
Services & other	439	19
Total	**2,285**	**100**

Server Products
Integrity server family (UNIX-based servers)
NonStop Himalaya servers (parallel processing servers)
Tandem NonStop Kernel (open-platform operating
system)

Other Products
Networking hardware and software products (UB
Networks)
PC-compatible computers
Printing products
Storage devices
UNIX-based workstations and servers

KEY COMPETITORS

3Com	Hitachi
Amdahl	IBM
Apple Computer	Machines Bull
Asante	NCR
Bay Networks	NEC
Cabletron	Proteon
Cisco Systems	Sequent
Concurrent Computer	Sequoia Services
Data General	Silicon Graphics
DEC	Storage Technology
Deluxe	Stratus Computer
Fujitsu	Sun Microsystems
Hewlett-Packard	Unisys

HOW MUCH

NYSE symbol: TDM FYE: September 30	Annual Growth	1986	1987	1988	1989	1990	1991	1992	1993	1994	1995
Sales ($ mil.)	12.9%	768	1,036	1,315	1,633	1,866	1,922	2,037	2,031	2,108	2,285
Net income ($ mil.)	6.0%	64	106	95	118	122	35	(41)	(530)	170	108
Income as % of sales	—	8.3%	10.2%	7.2%	7.2%	6.5%	1.8%	—	—	8.1%	4.7%
Earnings per share ($)	2.6%	0.72	1.08	0.96	1.17	1.13	0.33	(0.38)	(4.72)	1.50	0.91
Stock price – high ($)	—	19.63	37.38	29.50	26.38	30.13	17.63	15.88	16.88	19.13	19.75
Stock price – low ($)	—	9.75	17.56	12.38	14.75	8.88	9.13	9.88	8.50	10.50	10.00
Stock price – close ($)	(5.2%)	17.13	27.50	16.88	23.00	11.63	11.25	15.00	10.88	17.13	10.63
P/E – high	—	27	35	31	23	27	53	—	—	13	22
P/E – low	—	14	16	13	13	8	28	—	—	7	11
Dividends per share ($)	—	0.00	0.00	0.00	0.00	0.00	0.00	0.00	0.00	0.00	0.00
Book value per share ($)	5.1%	6.09	7.74	8.92	9.69	11.41	11.54	11.18	6.48	8.13	9.51
Employees	4.3%	5,719	7,007	8,624	9,548	10,936	11,167	10,784	9,963	8,466	8,380

1995 YEAR-END

Debt ratio: 11.3%
Return on equity: 10.5%
Cash (mil.): $121
Current ratio: 1.45
Long-term debt (mil.): $76
No. of shares (mil.): 117
Dividends
  Yield: —
  Payout: —
Market value (mil.): $1,241

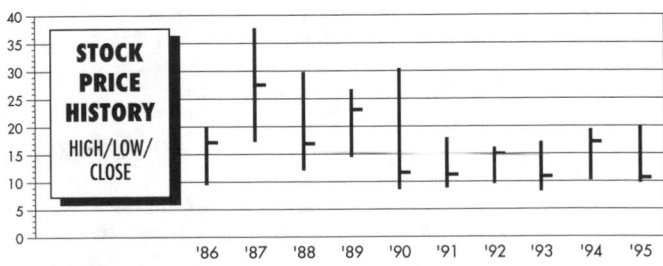

STOCK PRICE HISTORY
HIGH/LOW/CLOSE

TANDY CORPORATION

OVERVIEW

Unlike the cosmic version, Tandy's incredible universe isn't ever-expanding. Operating almost 7,000 stores in the US, Tandy is focusing on its 3 retail operations — Radio Shack, Incredible Universe, and Computer City — after selling most of its manufacturing operations and closing more than 200 VideoConcepts and McDuff stores. Radio Shack, offering a broad selection of electronic goods as well as repair services, represents more than half of the company's sales. Computer City stores offer computers, software, and related products at discount prices. Tandy's latest retail format is the Incredible

Universe chain of "gigastores," each the size of 3 football fields, which sell an array of electronics (including appliances, cameras, and computers) and software.

The company has announced a series of measures in response to low consumer demand at its Computer City and Incredible Universe stores. The latter has been forced to close 2 stores and cut jobs in an effort to streamline costs. Computer City stores now feature a price guarantee and safeguards against stock runouts. The company also created a new division to consolidate purchasing for its 3 retail chains.

WHEN

During the 1950s Charles Tandy expanded his family's small Fort Worth leather business (founded in 1919) into a nationwide chain of leathercraft and hobby stores. By 1960 Tandy Corporation stock was being traded on the NYSE. In the early 1960s Tandy began to expand into other retail areas, buying Leonard's, a Fort Worth department store.

In 1963 Tandy purchased Radio Shack, a nearly bankrupt electronic parts supplier with a mail-order business and 9 retail stores in the Boston area. Tandy collected part of the $800,000 owed the company and began expanding, stocking the stores with quick turnover items and putting 8-9% of sales revenue into advertising. Between 1961 and 1969 Tandy's sales grew from $16 million to $180 million, and earnings rose from $720,000 to $7.7 million, with the bulk of the growth due to the expansion of Radio Shack. Between 1968 and 1973 Tandy expanded from 172 to 2,294 stores; Radio Shack provided over 50% of Tandy's sales and 80% of earnings in 1973.

The company sold its department store operations to Dillard in 1974. The next year Tandy spun off to shareholders its leather products business as Tandy Brands and its hobby and handicraft business as Tandycrafts, focusing Tandy Corporation on the consumer electronics business. During 1976 the boom in CB radio sales pushed income up 125% as Tandy opened 1,200 stores. In 1977 it introduced the first mass-marketed personal computer, the TRS-80, which became the #1 PC on the market. In 1979, the year after Charles Tandy died, there were 5,530 McDonald's, 6,805 7-Elevens, and 7,353 Radio Shacks.

The company in 1984 introduced the Tandy 1000, the first IBM-compatible PC priced under $1,000. Since 1984 Tandy has expanded

through acquisitions — Scott/McDuff and VideoConcepts in 1985, GRiD Systems in 1988, and Victor Technologies in 1990.

In 1987 Tandy spun off its foreign retail operations as InterTAN. Realizing that Radio Shack had nearly exhausted its expansion possibilities, the company focused on alternate retail formats such as GRiD Systems Centers and in 1991 opened Computer City and the Edge in Electronics. That year Tandy introduced name-brand products into Radio Shack stores. The company also increased its manufacturing and R&D capacity and focused on such emerging technologies as digital audio recording and multimedia computing.

Tandy sold Memtek Products (magnetic tape), O'Sullivan Industries (ready-to-assemble furniture), LIKA (printed circuit boards), and its computer manufacturing and marketing operations in 1993. As part of the restructuring, Tandy began to scale back 2 mall retail operations, VideoConcepts and McDuff Electronics.

In 1994 Radio Shack stores began offering repair services under the name the Repair Shop at Radio Shack. The service fixes VCRs, audio equipment, and computers that are no longer under manufacturer warranty.

The company announced in 1995 that it would close all its VideoConcepts mall stores and half its McDuff electronics stores. Also that year it sold its credit card business to SPS Services (a subsidiary of Dean Witter, Discover), and Radio Shack introduced an expanded in-store catalog for hard-to-find electronic equipment and parts.

In 1996 Tandy planned to open about 110 new Radio Shack stores, almost 20 Computer City stores, and 2 or 3 new Incredible Universe "gigastores."

WHO

Chairman and CEO: John V. Roach, age 57, $918,339 pay

President; President, Radio Shack: Leonard H. Roberts, age 47, $697,693 pay

SVP and Secretary: Herschel C. Winn, age 64, $431,749 pay

SVP, Tandy Retail Services: Robert M. McClure, age 60, $343,200 pay

SVP and CFO: Dwain H. Hughes, age 48, $249,888 pay

VP and Controller: Richard L. Ramsey, age 50

VP Law: Frederick W. Padden, age 63

VP and Treasurer: Loren K. Jensen, age 35

VP Tax: Mark W. Barfield, age 38

VP Corporate Relations: Lou Ann Blaylock, age 57

VP Corporate Development: Ronald L. Parrish, age 53

VP Human Resources: George Berger

Auditors: Price Waterhouse LLP

WHERE

HQ: 1800 One Tandy Center, Fort Worth, TX 76102
Phone: 817-390-3700
Fax: 817-390-2647
Web site: http://www.tandy.com

Tandy operates or franchises more than 6,800 Radio Shacks throughout the US; operates 99 Computer City stores in the US, Canada, and Europe; and has 17 Incredible Universe stores in the US. The company also operates 14 distribution centers and 139 service centers in the US. Tandy has 9 manufacturing plants in the US and one manufacturing plant in China.

WHAT

	Stores
	No.
Radio Shack	
Company-owned	4,831
Dealer/franchise	2,005
Computer City SuperCenters	99
Incredible Universe	17
Total	**6,952**

	1995 Sales
	% of total
Consumer electronics	46
Electronic parts, accessories & specialty equipment	33
PCs, peripherals, software & accessories	11
Other	10
Total	**100**

KEY COMPETITORS

Anam
Barnes & Noble
Best Buy
CDW Computer Centers
Circuit City
CompuCom
CompUSA
Dell
Egghead
ELEK-TEK
Entex
Fry's Electronics
Future Shop
Gateway 2000
Global Directmail
Good Guys
Inacom
Intelligent Electronics
J & R Music World
Kmart
Matsushita
Micro Warehouse
MicroAge
Montgomery Ward
NeoStar
Office Depot
OfficeMax
Phillps
Price/Costco
Sears
Service Merchandise
Sharper Image
Staples
Sun Television & Appliances
Tiger Direct
Vanstar
Wal-Mart

HOW MUCH

NYSE symbol: TAN FYE: December 31	Annual Growth	1986	1987	1988	1989	1990	1991	1992	1993	1994	1995
Sales ($ mil.)	7.5%	3,036	3,452	3,794	4,181	4,500	4,562	4,680	4,103	4,944	5,839
Net income ($ mil.)	0.4%	198	242	316	324	290	206	184	84	218	205
Income as % of sales	—	6.5%	7.0%	8.3%	7.7%	6.5%	4.5%	3.9%	2.1%	4.4%	3.5%
Earnings per share ($)	3.9%	2.22	2.70	3.54	3.64	3.54	2.58	2.24	1.01	2.91	3.12
Stock price – high ($)	—	45.00	56.50	48.63	48.75	41.13	36.50	31.75	50.75	50.63	64.38
Stock price – low ($)	—	30.50	28.00	31.50	37.00	23.50	23.38	22.25	24.63	30.75	36.50
Stock price – close ($)	(0.3%)	42.50	33.00	41.00	39.13	29.25	28.88	29.75	49.50	50.00	41.50
P/E – high	—	20	21	14	13	12	14	14	50	17	21
P/E – low	—	14	10	9	10	7	9	10	24	11	12
Dividends per share ($)	—	0.00	0.25	0.55	0.60	0.60	0.60	0.60	0.60	0.63	0.74
Book value per share ($)	5.9%	14.57	15.38	18.10	20.13	21.78	23.56	22.17	22.21	22.66	24.32
Employees	3.6%	36,000	39,000	37,000	38,000	40,000	40,000	37,000	42,000	45,800	49,300

1995 YEAR-END

Debt ratio: 15.2%
Return on equity: 14.6%
Cash (mil.): $143
Current ratio: 2.13
Long-term debt (mil.): $141
No. of shares (mil.): 62
Dividends
  Yield: 1.8%
  Payout: 23.7%
Market value (mil.): $2,562

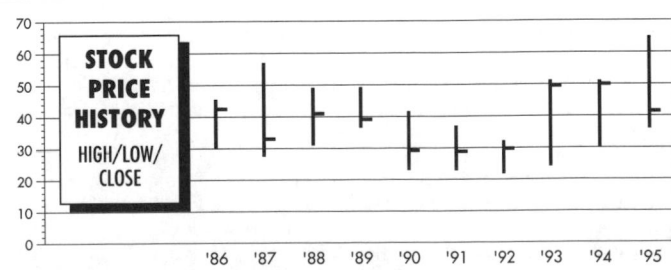

STOCK PRICE HISTORY
HIGH/LOW/CLOSE

TATUNG CO.

OVERVIEW

TATUNG, whose founder dedicated the company to "honesty, integrity, industry, and frugality" is an 80-year-old success. Taiwan's largest consumer electronics manufacturer, TATUNG is involved with a broad range of products, from televisions and telephones to refrigerators and escalators. "Electronic products are the company's biggest sellers, accounting for about 2/3 of its revenues. TATUNG makes TVs, VCRs, stereos, workstations, PCs, monitors, telephone systems, fax machines, and a variety of other products. The company is also a major supplier of computer components to US PC maker Packard Bell. In addition, it manufactures home appliances and industrial equipment and imports products made by others, including Hoover and Toshiba.

TATUNG has more than 2 dozen subsidiaries. Its domestic units include 90%-owned Chunghwa Picture Tubes, the world's largest cathode-ray tube maker, as well as TATUNG Fujitsu (a joint venture with the Japanese computer maker) and TATUNG Otis Elevator (a joint venture with the US-based elevator maker). In the US, TATUNG Co. of America makes monitors, graphics boards, PCs, and consumer electronics, while TATUNG Telecom Corp. develops telecommunications equipment. A new joint venture, with control systems maker Honeywell, will manufacture semiconductors in the US. Among TATUNG's other international subsidiaries are companies in Germany, Indonesia, Japan, Korea, Malaysia, Singapore, Thailand, and the UK.

Two education foundations, Tatung Institute of Technology and Tatung Senior High School, together own 11% of the company.

WHEN

TATUNG began as Hsieh Chih, a construction company founded in 1918 by Lin Shan-Chih. The company completed more than 600 construction projects in 30 years, including the Building of the Executive Yuan (the building that houses the ministerial offices of Taiwan's national government).

Lin later shifted the enterprise's emphasis to electric products. In 1949 the company began producing electric fans, and in 1950 it changed its name to TATUNG (Chinese for "great harmony") . When Lin set up his estate, he endowed the Tatung Schools Company. The Tatung Institute of Technology was established in 1956 to provide hands-on training in factories and offices for Taiwanese students. The company's industrial publishing subsidiary was formed in 1959.

During the 1960s TATUNG expanded further into home appliances and electronics, introducing refrigerators (1961), air conditioners (1964), and televisions (1964) to its product line. Taiwan Telecommunications was formed in 1966.

Lin died in 1971. During that decade the company began to expand overseas. It established a subsidiary in the US in 1972 and began making electric fans there 2 years later. In 1973 the company formed a joint venture with Japanese computer manufacturer Fujitsu. TATUNG also established offices in Singapore (1972), Japan (1975), and South Korea (1979).

The company's joint venture with Otis Elevator was formed in 1983. TATUNG continued to expand overseas during the 1980s, establishing subsidiaries in the UK (1981) and Germany (1985). California-based TATUNG Electric Co. of America was formed in 1988. During that period the company continued to move production overseas, shipping the finished goods back to Taiwan as imports.

Despite its industry-leading karaoke machines, TATUNG's profits slipped in the early 1990s as Taiwan's economy slowed. However, the company rebounded, signing a deal with Packard Bell in 1991 to supply the PC marketer with 100,000 PCs a month. In 1994 it formed an alliance with telecommunications company QUALCOMM to develop cellular phone systems for the Taiwanese market.

The following year TATUNG's subsidiary Chunghwa Picture Tubes signed a deal to manufacture large picture tubes for Toshiba. The company also announced that it would enter the semiconductor manufacturing industry and was looking for a joint venture partner.

TATUNG expanded its electronics line in 1996 when it began making computer motherboards. Other new products in TATUNG's lineup include set-top boxes for cable TV, CD-ROM drives, digital video disks, and network computers. The company was also negotiating with Apple Computer to license that company's MAC OS operating system, which would allow TATUNG to manufacture Mac clones.

TATUNG also announced in 1996 that it had formed a joint venture agreement with Honeywell to build a $100 million semiconductor plant in Minnesota.

WHO

Chairman: Lin Tingsheng
President: Lin Weishan
President, TATUNG Co. of America: Hsin-chu Liu
CFO, TATUNG Co. of America: Michael Lai
Director Information Systems, TATUNG Co. of America: Thomas Tpsai
Manager Personnel, TATUNG Co. of America: Irma Castillo

WHERE

HQ: 22 Chungshan North Rd., Sec. 3
Taipei 104, Taiwan
Phone: +886-2-592-5252
Fax: +886-2-591-5185

Selected International Subsidiaries
Makolin Electronics (Malaysia) SDN. BHD.
P.T. Tatung Budi Indonesia
Tatung Co. of America, Inc. (US)
Tatung Co. of Japan, Inc.
Tatung Co. of Thailand, Inc.
Tatung International (Deutschland) GmbH (Germany)
Tatung Electric Co. of America, Inc. (US)
Tatung Electronics (Singapore) PTE. Ltd.
Tatung Science and Technology, Inc. (US)
Tatung (UK) Ltd.

WHAT

Selected Products
Air conditioners
Cables
Copiers
Elevators and Escalators
Fans
Fax machines
Furniture
Keyboards
Laminates
Meters and switches
Microwave ovens
Monitors
Motors
PCs
Printers
Refrigerators
Resins
Silicon wafers
Stereos
Telecommunication systems
Telephones
Televisions
VCRs
Washers
Workstations

KEY COMPETITORS

Acer	Honeywell	Sanyo
Canon	Hyundai	Sharp
Casio	IBM	Shinlee
Compaq	Kyocera	Siemens
Daewoo	Lucent	Sony
Dell	Technologies	Sun
Emerson	Matsushita	Microsystems
Fujitsu	NCR	Yamaha
GEC	NEC	Zenith
General Electric	Oki	
Hitachi	Pioneer	

HOW MUCH

Principal exchange: Tawain FYE: December 31	Annual Growth	1986	1987	1988	1989	1990	1991	1992	1993	1994	1995
Sales (NT$ mil.)	16.3%	—	—	29,399	31,066	27,767	44,808	52,042	54,431	64,842	84,698
Net income (NT$ mil.)	26.3%	—	—	1,288	1,408	216	405	1,216	3,509	5,391	6,606
Income as % of sales	—	—	—	4.4%	4.5%	0.8%	0.9%	2.3%	6.4%	8.3%	7.8%
Earnings per share (NT$)	66.1%	—	—	—	—	—	—	0.62	1.80	2.42	2.84
Stock price – high (NT$)	—	—	—	—	—	—	—	12.86	38.97	47.48	43.87
Stock price – low (NT$)	—	—	—	—	—	—	—	8.60	8.83	28.13	31.35
Stock price – close (NT$)	63.0%	—	—	—	—	—	—	9.33	38.97	40.97	40.40
P/E – high	—	—	—	—	—	—	—	21	22	20	15
P/E – low	—	—	—	—	—	—	—	14	5	12	11
Dividends per share (NT$)	—	—	—	—	—	—	—	0.00	0.00	0.00	0.00
Book value per share (NT$)	21.4%	—	—	—	—	—	—	8.45	9.84	13.21	15.11
Employees	(1.8%)	—	—	—	—	21,300	19,967	19,168	18,690	17,869	19,491

1995 YEAR-END

Debt ratio: 46.6%
Return on equity: 34.9%
Cash (mil.): $6,386
Current ratio: 1.10
Long-term debt (mil.): $9,516
No. of shares (mil.): 2,325
Dividends
  Yield: -
  Payout: -
Market value (mil.): $3,104

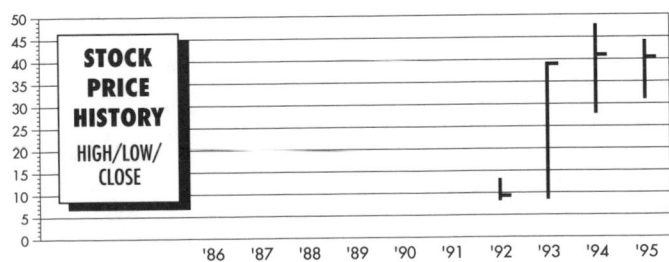

STOCK PRICE HISTORY HIGH/LOW/CLOSE

TECH DATA CORPORATION

OVERVIEW

With annual sales growth topping 25% for more than a decade, it's no wonder Tech Data likes being a middleman. The Clearwater, Florida-based company is one of the nation's top distributors of personal computer hardware and software. Tech Data handles more than 28,000 items, including computer peripherals, networking and communications products, storage devices, and complete computer systems. Among its customers are more than 50,000 value-added resellers (VARs) and retail stores in the Americas and France. The company's 600 suppliers include such top manufacturers as Apple, Compaq, IBM, Toshiba, and Xerox, and such leading software publishers as Corel, Microsoft, and Novell.

One of Tech Data's strengths is its attention to small VARs that cannot afford the vol-

ume purchasing requirements of leading manufacturers. Tech Data buys in large quantities and offers volume discounting. The company also offers a variety of support services, including advertising assistance, product support, and training.

Tech Data one-upped its rivals in 1995 when, through a deal with MCI, it became the first distributor to resell telephone line service employing advanced data transmission technologies such as asynchronous transfer mode, frame relay, and ISDN. The pact lets Tech Data resellers package line services with their computer networks. Both the VAR and Tech Data earn monthly usage fees on the services.

Chairman Steven Raymund owns about 10% of the company's stock.

WHEN

Tech Data grew out of an electronics distribution business founded by Edward Raymund, a USC graduate who started out as a representative for electronic products manufacturers. By the early 1960s he had established an industrial electronics distribution business in Florida. In 1973 he incorporated that business as Tech Data.

In 1981 Raymund's 25-year-old son, Steven, who had earned master's degrees in economics and international politics from Georgetown University's School of Foreign Service, joined Tech Data on a temporary basis to work on the company's catalog. At that time Tech Data sold diskettes and other computer supplies to local companies and had about $2 million in revenues.

Steven's favored status at the company angered a group of managers. Shortly after he arrived at Tech Data, they copied the company's client list and walked out. The defection nearly sank Tech Data, but Steven stayed on when his father handed him 2/3 of the company. With the PC industry beginning to take off, Steven worked to position Tech Data as a middleman between computer and peripheral manufacturers and VARs.

Steven Raymund was named COO in 1984 and CEO in 1986. That year the company went public.

In 1990 fast growth strained Tech Data's resources, and earnings slumped. Raymund cut inventory and management costs to revive the company's upward growth. The following year he became chairman.

Tech Data began to distribute software in 1992 and by 1993 it had become the #1 distributor of Novell's networking software. That year the company signed up Microsoft and inked a distribution deal for IBM's PS/ValuePoint and ThinkPad computer systems.

In early 1994 Tech Data purchased U.S. Software Resource, a distributor of more than 500 business and entertainment software titles. The acquisition increased Tech Data's software list and added high-profile publishers such as Borland and WordPerfect to its suppliers. It also boosted Tech Data's presence in the major software retail chains.

Later that year Tech Data, which already distributed products to South America and the Caribbean from its Miami center, acquired Paris-based Softmart International, France's largest distributor of wholesale computer products ($136 million in 1994 revenues). The Softmart purchase (for stock valued at about $22 million) increased Tech Data's international sales to about 10% of revenues and made it the #4 distributor worldwide.

Also in 1994 Tech Data began selling Lotus's business software and DEC's Alpha-based workstations and servers. Tech Data won US distribution rights for Apple subsidiary Claris Corp.'s software line in 1995.

The company became a dealer for Axil Computer in 1996; Axil makes clones of Sun Microsystems's SPARC-based workstations. That year the company also began distributing Xerox's laser printers.

WHO

Chairman Emeritus: Edward C. Raymund
Chairman and CEO: Steven A. Raymund, age 40
VC, President, and COO: A. Timothy Godwin, age 46
SVP Human Resources: Lawrence W. Hamilton, age 38
SVP Finance and CFO: Jeffery P. Howells, age 39
SVP Sales and Marketing: Peggy K. Caldwell, age 50
SVP Logistics and Chief Information Officer: James T. Pollard, age 49
VP and Worldwide Controller: Joseph B. Trepani, age 35
VP and General Manager Latin America: Yuda Saydun, age 43
VP and General Counsel: David R. Vetter, age 37
VP Taxes: Charles V. Dannewitz
VP, Treasurer and Secretary: Arthur W. Singleton
VP MIS: Bruce D. Eden
VP Worldwide Credit Services: Patrick O. Connelly
Auditors: Price Waterhouse LLP

WHERE

HQ: 5350 Tech Data Dr., Clearwater, FL 34620
Phone: 813-539-7429
Fax: 813-538-7054

Tech Data has distribution centers in 6 states and in Canada and France.

	1996 Sales		1996 Operating Income	
	$ mil.	% of total	$ mil.	% of total
US	2,655	86	49	88
Other countries	432	14	7	12
Total	**3,087**	**100**	**56**	**100**

WHAT

	1996 Sales
	% of total
VARs	70
Corporate resellers, franchisees & retails	30
Total	**100**

Major Products Distributed	
Disk drives	Corel
Microcomputers	DEC
Networks	Epson
Printers	Hewlett-Packard
Software	IBM
Terminals	Intel
	Kingston
Selected Brands Distributed	Lotus
3Com	Microsoft
Adobe	NEC Technologies
Apple	Novell
Bay Networks	Okidata
Canon	Quarterdeck
Cisco	SCO
Compaq	Seagate
Computer Associates	Symantec
	Toshiba
	U.S. Robotics
	Xerox

KEY COMPETITORS

Ameriquest	Ingram Micro
Baker & Taylor	Intelligent Electronics
CHS Electronics	Marshall Industries
Computer 2000	Merisel
Graybar Electric	MicroAge
Inacom	Wyle Electronics

HOW MUCH

Nasdaq symbol: TECD FYE: January 31	Annual Growth	1987	1988	1989	1990	1991	1992	1993	1994	1995	1996
Sales ($ mil.)	51.8%	72	149	247	348	442	647	979	1,532	2,418	3,087
Net income ($ mil.)	30.5%	2	4	8	3	7	12	20	30	35	22
Income as % of sales	—	2.8%	2.8%	3.2%	0.9%	1.5%	1.8%	2.0%	2.0%	1.4%	0.7%
Earnings per share ($)	19.8%	0.11	0.22	0.35	0.13	0.27	0.44	0.63	0.83	0.91	0.56
Stock price – high ($)[1]	—	2.04	4.31	4.00	4.19	2.69	7.81	15.19	18.38	22.13	17.88
Stock price – low ($)[1]	—	1.21	1.63	2.50	1.91	1.00	1.75	6.63	10.63	14.00	8.25
Stock price – close ($)[1]	27.7%	1.66	2.63	3.25	1.94	2.06	7.00	15.13	18.00	17.00	15.00
P/E – high	—	19	20	11	32	10	18	24	22	24	32
P/E – low	—	11	8	7	15	4	4	11	13	15	15
Dividends per share ($)	—	0.00	0.00	0.00	0.00	0.00	0.00	0.00	0.00	0.00	0.00
Book value per share ($)	33.2%	0.57	0.78	1.68	1.62	2.07	3.05	3.70	5.76	6.90	7.53
Employees	36.2%	163	293	426	556	573	690	1,025	1,350	2,265	2,625

[1] Stock prices are for the prior calendar year.

1996 YEAR-END

Debt ratio: 50.6%
Return on equity: 7.4%
Cash (mil.): $1
Current ratio: 1.27
Long-term debt (mil.): $9
No. of shares (mil.): 38
Dividends
  Yield: —
  Payout: —
Market value (mil.): $569

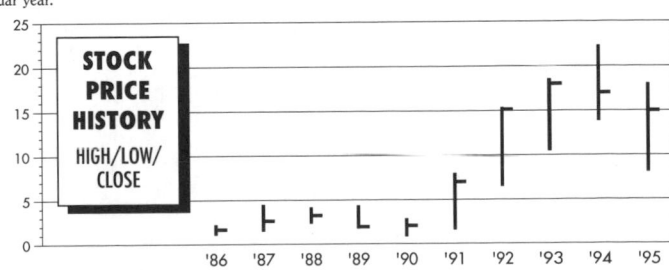

STOCK PRICE HISTORY
HIGH/LOW/CLOSE

TEKTRONIX, INC.

OVERVIEW

As data, video, and voice technologies are converging, Tektronix is reemerging. Headquartered in Wilsonville, Oregon, the company is the world's #1 maker of oscilloscopes (instruments used in the aerospace, communications, and computer industries to make fine measurements of high-speed electrical signals) as well as TV measurement and testing equipment. It also produces color printers, networking devices, and video studio-production equipment. Tektronix's sales have recovered following a slump in the early 1990s.

The combination of data, video, and voice signals on a single network, such as the Internet, has created a demand for products that can simultaneously process these various signal types. The need for new products has led to a boost in sales of the company's measurement tools, which are used to help design such high-tech gear. To keep up with emerging technologies, Tektronix is working to elevate its presence in the markets for network access, multisignal processing, and video compression equipment.

The company sees excellent growth potential for its color printers. It is betting that solid-ink printers, such as its Phaser line, which can quickly and inexpensively print on any paper with good color definition, will overtake ink-jet and color laser printers in the marketplace, though it continues to produce the others using components from other manufacturers.

Textronix is also excited about its disk storage system, video editing and switching equipment, and other products for the entertainment industry, which have been posting strong gains due to an increase in digital broadcasting.

WHEN

Tektronix was founded as Tekrad in 1946 by WWII veterans Melvin Murdock, Glenn Leland, Miles Tippery, and Charles Howard Vollum. Their initial plan was to manufacture, sell and repair electronic equipment. When another firm registered a name similar to Tekrad, the company changed its name to Tektronix. The company's first oscilloscope was built from electronic parts purchased from government surplus sales. When released in 1946, the device was superior to any oscilloscope on the market, and within 2 years the company was selling to major electronics firms, including Hewlett-Packard, RCA, and Bell Laboratories.

During the 1950s the company began developing "Tek culture," a casual workplace environment in which all employees communicated on a first-name basis. The company provided excellent benefits, encouraged the pursuit of individual interests, and kept company rules to a minimum.

The growing popularity of television and FM radio fueled demand for the company's products in the 1950s. Tektronix introduced plug-in oscilloscopes, which could be adapted for different uses, in 1954. The firm went public in 1963 and by the end of the decade it controlled 75% of the world's oscilloscope market.

Tektronix sold its first cathode ray tube (CRT) terminals in 1970. The company's 1974 purchase of the Grass Valley Group, a video special-effects electronic systems company, finally reduced its reliance on the oscilloscope.

The company passed the $1 billion mark in sales in 1981, though its slow transformation from analog to digital technology left it behind the competition. In the early 1980s earnings fell more than 40%, leading to layoffs and the loss of top executives and engineers who left to start their own companies. In 1985 Tektronix starting making color printers. That year it purchased CAE Systems, which released a workstation computer in 1986 that flopped. CAE shifted to developing software, but that effort stalled also. Tektronix finally sold CAE in 1988, after losing about $200 million.

Facing a $93 million loss in 1990, Tektronix's board seized control. Turnaround specialist Jerome Meyer, brought in as president and promoted to chairman, slashed jobs, sold off noncore businesses, and focused on 3 product areas: test and measurement equipment, TV measuring and production equipment, and terminals and printers.

In 1995 Tektronix broadened its product offerings with the purchase of communication test equipment manufacturer Microwave Logic and nonlinear editing systems designer Lightworks Editing Systems. Also that year the firm's Color Printing & Imaging Division introduced PhaserLink, a World Wide Web-based tool used to configure and troubleshoot Tektronix's printers over the Internet. In addition, the company in 1996 unveiled the Phaser line of color printers with 2-sided printing capabilities.

WHO

Chairman, President, and CEO: Jerome J. Meyer, age 58, $1,153,625 pay
VC: William D. Walker, age 65
SVP and CFO: Carl W. Neun, age 52, $577,580 pay
SVP Corporate Development and Secretary: John P. Karalis, age 58, $384,795 pay
VP; President, Measurement Business Division: Daniel Terpack, age 55, $621,196 pay
VP; President, Video and Networking Division: Lucie J. Fjeldstad, age 52, $516,495 pay
VP; President, European Operations: John W. Vold, age 66
VP; President, Color Printing & Imaging Division: Gerald Perkel, age 40
VP Total Quality and Human Resources: Robert M. Baughman
Auditors: Deloitte & Touche LLP

WHERE

HQ: 26600 SW Parkway Ave., Wilsonville, OR 97070
Phone: 503-627-7111
Fax: 503-627-5502
Web site: http://www.tek.com

| | 1996 Sales | |
	$ mil.	% of total
US	891	50
Europe	471	27
Other regions	407	23
Total	**1,769**	**100**

WHAT

| | 1996 Sales | |
	$ mil.	% of total
Measurement business	812	46
Color printing & imaging	562	32
Video & networking products	395	22
Total	**1,769**	**100**

Selected Products

Measurement Business
Cable testers
Logic analyzers
Oscilloscopes
RF and wireless test instruments
Video and audio test instruments

Color Printing and Imaging
Color printers
Ink and other printer supplies

Video and Networking
Netstations (network graphics terminals)
Signal processing and distribution equipment
Studio production equipment
Transmission systems
Video disk recorders
Video editing systems

KEY COMPETITORS

ADC Telecommunications	Dynamics Corporation of America	NEC Network Computing Devices
Apple	Dynatech	Pioneer
Avid Technology	Fast Multimedia	QMS
Canon	Fluke	Scitex
Cohu	Fuji Photo	Sony
Data General	Hewlett-Packard	Wavetek
DEC	LeCroy	Xerox
Discreet Logic	MTS Systems	

HOW MUCH

NYSE symbol: TEK FYE: Last Saturday in May	Annual Growth	1987	1988	1989	1990	1991	1992	1993	1994	1995	1996[1]
Sales ($ mil.)	2.7%	1,396	1,412	1,433	1,408	1,331	1,297	1,302	1,318	1,472	1,769
Net income ($ mil.)	4.4%	68	11	19	(93)	48	20	(58)	61	81	100
Income as % of sales	—	4.9%	0.8%	1.3%	—	3.6%	1.5%	—	4.6%	5.5%	5.6%
Earnings per share ($)	6.0%	1.78	0.35	0.66	(3.19)	1.66	0.67	(1.94)	2.00	2.63	3.00
Stock price – high ($)	—	43.25	30.13	24.25	19.25	30.88	22.88	27.88	40.50	61.88	49.13
Stock price – low ($)	—	20.50	19.00	16.13	11.63	16.00	16.50	20.13	23.63	31.38	29.75
Stock price – close ($)	4.9%	24.75	20.38	17.88	18.50	19.75	20.13	23.50	34.25	49.13	38.00
P/E – high	—	24	86	37	—	19	34	—	20	24	16
P/E – low	—	12	54	24	—	10	25	—	12	12	10
Dividends per share ($)	0.0%	0.60	0.60	0.60	0.60	0.60	0.60	0.60	0.60	0.60	0.60
Book value per share ($)	(1.0%)	22.67	11.67	17.18	13.24	14.65	14.87	14.27	15.51	19.17	20.66
Employees	(9.0%)	—	—	—	13,941	11,947	11,334	9,840	8,468	7,619	7,929

[1] Stock prices are through May 31

1996 YEAR-END

Debt ratio: 26.7%
Return on equity: 15.6%
Cash (mil.): $37
Current ratio: 2.06
Long-term debt (mil.): $202
No. of shares (mil.): 33
Dividends
 Yield: 1.6%
 Payout: 20.0%
Market value (mil.): $1,242
R&D as % of sales: 9.3%

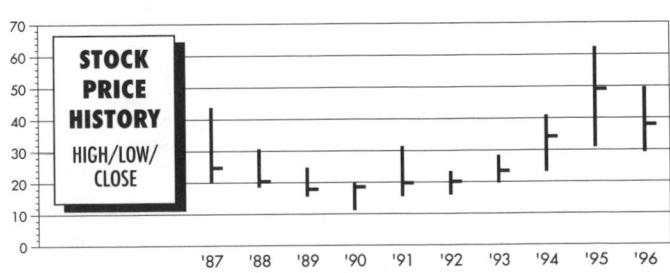

STOCK PRICE HISTORY
HIGH/LOW/CLOSE

TERADYNE, INC.

OVERVIEW

Consumer appetite for electronics and telecommunications devices determines Teradyne's success in the ATE market. Headquartered in Boston, Teradyne is the world's #1 manufacturer of automated test equipment (ATE), which is used to analyze semiconductor chips and circuit boards used in aerospace equipment, automobiles, computers, defense electronics, and telephone systems.

Teradyne is broadening its product offerings to help protect itself from the cyclical nature of its business — as evidenced by periodic decreases in the demand for semiconductors and cutbacks in defense spending — and from stiff competition in its core markets. The company

purchased Megatest Corporation, giving Teradyne a strong presence in the flash memory and logic testing market. The acquisition of Hammer Technologies moved Teradyne into the computerized telecommunications systems testing market, which is poised for rapid growth as computers become more prevalent in the telephone services industry. In addition, Teradyne has entered the networking systems testing market with the purchase of Midnight Networks and has started a unit to develop software development tools.

Teradyne is also boosting its presence in international markets, primarily in Europe and Japan, where its sales have been skyrocketing.

WHEN

College pals Nicholas DeWolf and Alexander d'Arbeloff (who met in an alphabetical ROTC lineup) founded Teradyne in 1960 to develop an industrial grade of electronic test equipment. The name was selected as a combination of tera (meaning 10 to the 12th power in the metric system) and dyne (a unit of force); to the founding duo, it meant, "rolling a 15,000-ton boulder uphill." The company established its headquarters in a loft over Joe & Nemo's hot dog stand in downtown Boston. Its first product was an automatic tester (called a go/no-go diode tester) for semiconductor diodes, the first of which was sold to Raytheon for $5,000.

The company grew rapidly by first understanding what its customers did, then building a machine to fit their needs. Teradyne introduced other products, including testers for integrated circuits, resistors, transistors, and zener diodes, in the 1960s. In the latter part of the decade, the firm began using computers to speed up the testing process, which in essence created the ATE industry. Teradyne started Teradyne Components (later Teradyne Connection Systems) in 1968 to produce electronics connection assemblies.

Teradyne went public in 1970. That year saw the first slump in the semiconductor industry, as decreased demand from Teradyne's top customers convinced the company to diversify its customer base and led to the laying off of 15% of its workforce. DeWolf left Teradyne in 1971, leaving d'Arbeloff to run the company. The market quickly recovered, and the company began to grow and prosper again. In 1972 it began working on a telephone system testing device called 4Tel. However, the market re-

versed itself again, and in 1975 the firm again cut its staff by 15%.

The company was buoyed in 1981 by a $35 million sale of a 4Tel testing system to GTE. Trouble hit again in the mid-1980s, as Teradyne laid off another 140 workers and suffered back-to-back losses. Meanwhile, Japanese companies had taken over the US semiconductor market, leaving Teradyne short of customers for its testers.

The company fought back in the late 1980s by lowering prices to undercut the competition and by pushing hard into the Japanese market. In addition, Teradyne formed its computer-aided engineering (CAE) group by purchasing and combining Aida Corporation and Case Technologies.

By 1989 Teradyne had recovered, posting a profit of $10 million that year and looking abroad to shore up its operations.

The cycle continued in the early 1990s as military spending fell, leading to further staff cuts, salary freezes, and even a temporary suspension of production. In 1993 Teradyne won a $63 million contract from the German national telephone system and introduced an upgraded line of ATE. The next year, Teradyne started its Software and Systems Test unit, which released its first product, the TestMaster software development tool, in 1995.

High demand for PCs in 1995 elevated the sales of the company's semiconductor testing equipment, helping lead the company to top $1 billion in sales for the first time. In 1996 George Chamillard succeeded d'Arbeloff as president, though the cofounder retained his titles of chairman and CEO.

Chairman and CEO: Alexander V. d'Arbeloff, age 68, $757,207 pay
VC and EVP: James A. Prestridge, age 64, $483,215 pay
VC, EVP, and CFO: Owen W. Robbins, age 66, $483,215 pay
President and COO: George W. Chamillard, age 57, $457,094 pay
VP: George V. d'Arbeloff, age 51, $360,876 pay
VP: Michael A. Bradley, age 47
VP: Ronald J. Dias, age 52
VP: John E. Halter, age 62
VP and Treasurer: Stuart M. Osattin, age 50
Corporate Director of Personnel: James Dawson
Auditors: Coopers & Lybrand L.L.P.

WHERE

HQ: 321 Harrison Ave., Boston, MA 02118
Phone: 617-482-2700
Fax: 617-422-2910
Web site: http://www.teradyne.com

Teradyne has sales and services offices in Asia/Pacific, Europe, Japan, and North America.

	1995 Sales % of total
US	48
Other countries	52
Total	**100**

WHAT

	1995 Sales % of total
Semiconductor test systems	69
Backplane connection systems	13
Circuit-board test systems	11
Telecommunications test systems	7
Total	**100**

Selected Products
Backplane connection systems
In-circuit testers
Logic test systems
Memory test systems
Software development tools

KEY COMPETITORS

Credence Systems
Dynatech
Fluke
KLA Instruments
LTX
Oak Industries
Plexus
Schlumberger
Tektronix
Telemetrix
Toray Industries

HOW MUCH

NYSE symbol: TER FYE: December 31	Annual Growth	1986	1987	1988	1989	1990	1991	1992	1993	1994	1995
Sales ($ mil.)	14.5%	351	378	462	484	459	509	530	555	677	1,191
Net income ($ mil.)	—	(12)	(21)	(3)	10	(21)	18	23	35	71	159
Income as % of sales	—	—	—	—	2.1%	—	3.6%	4.2%	6.3%	10.5%	13.4%
Earnings per share ($)	—	(0.21)	(0.38)	(0.06)	0.18	(0.36)	0.29	0.34	0.49	0.96	1.89
Stock price – high ($)	—	14.81	18.25	8.88	7.38	5.56	8.44	10.19	14.81	17.13	42.88
Stock price – low ($)	—	7.81	6.69	5.31	4.94	1.88	3.06	5.00	6.50	10.19	16.06
Stock price – close ($)	13.3%	8.19	8.06	5.88	5.50	3.50	7.94	7.69	13.88	16.94	25.13
P/E – high	—	—	—	—	42	—	29	30	30	18	23
P/E – low	—	—	—	—	28	—	11	15	13	11	8
Dividends per share ($)	—	0.00	0.00	0.00	0.00	0.00	0.00	0.00	0.00	0.00	0.00
Book value per share ($)	6.2%	5.34	4.91	4.84	5.01	4.63	4.89	5.22	5.89	6.79	9.20
Employees	0.9%	4,800	4,700	4,700	4,700	4,400	4,300	4,100	4,000	4,000	5,200

1995 YEAR-END

Debt ratio: 3.7%
Return on equity: 23.9%
Cash (mil.): $276
Current ratio: 3.22
Long-term debt (mil.): $19
No. of shares (mil.): 83
Dividends
  Yield: —
  Payout: —
Market value (mil.): $2,076

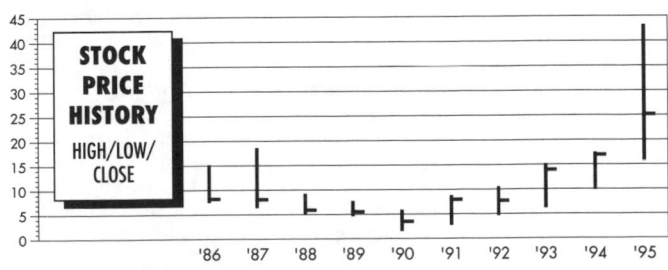

STOCK PRICE HISTORY HIGH/LOW/CLOSE

TEXAS INSTRUMENTS INCORPORATED

OVERVIEW

Texas Instruments (TI), long a sleeper in the volatile computer chip industry, has awakened. The Dallas-based company has moved into 7th place among the world's chip makers. It leads the market in digital signal processors (specialized chips used in personal computers and cellular phones). Semiconductors account for about 75% of TI's sales and more than 90% of its profits. The company's latest milestone in chip development is a 0.18-micron transistor; a thumbnail-size chip can hold as many as 125 million of these tiny transistors. The breakthrough will allow TI to consolidate memory, microprocessor, and other functions onto a single chip.

While the company's defense industry revenues are shrinking (about 17% of sales, down from 27% in 1992), its calculators are setting sales records. On the other hand, new market-

ing efforts have yet to turn around its recently streamlined notebook computer and software segment.

Continuity will be a central issue for TI as the decade ends. Fluctuating chip prices — especially a steep drop that began in late 1995 — have rocked the industry, including TI. In mid-1996 the company's chairman, president, and CEO, Jerry Junkins (credited by many with building TI into a force in the semiconductor industry), died unexpectedly. He was replaced by company outsider James Adams (a former president of Southwestern Bell) as chairman and Thomas Engibous (formerly president of TI's Semiconductor Group) as president and CEO. Also in 1996 many of TI's royalty-producing cross-licensing agreements expired, forcing the company to renegotiate or look for ways to replace the lost income.

WHEN

"Doc" Karcher and Eugene McDermott founded Geophysical Service Inc. (GSI) in Newark, New Jersey, in 1930 to develop reflective seismology, a new technology used to explore for oil and gas deposits. In 1934 GSI moved its headquarters to Dallas.

During WWII, GSI began making submarine detectors for the US Navy. It established a defense division in 1946. The company changed its name to Texas Instruments in 1951 and was listed on the NYSE in 1953.

TI started manufacturing transistors in 1952 after buying a license from Western Electric. TI invested about $2 million in an effort to reduce the price of the germanium transistor, which made possible the pocket transistor radio (1954). The firm produced the first commercial silicon transistor in 1954, and company engineer Jack Kilby (with Intel founder Bob Noyce) invented the integrated circuit in 1958. By 1959 TI's semiconductor manufacturing division accounted for half of its total sales.

Other TI breakthroughs included terrain-following airborne radar (1958), forward-looking infrared (FLIR) systems (1964), hand-held calculators (1967), single-chip microcomputers (1971), and the LISP (list processing language) chip, a 32-bit microcomputer for artificial intelligence applications (1987).

TI moved into consumer products in the 1970s with calculators, digital watches, and home computers. Although the company developed the basic technologies for these

products, its inability to follow through in the face of low-cost foreign competition led it to abandon its digital watch and PC businesses. Attempts to meet competitors' prices, as well as plunging semiconductor prices, led to TI's first annual loss in 1983.

TI's Kilby patent for the integrated circuit (named after the coinventor of the IC) was upheld in Japan in 1989, and all major Japanese electronics firms except Fujitsu pay royalties to TI.

In tough times TI leveraged its dynamic random access memory (DRAM) chip know-how in a number of strategic alliances that include a joint venture (26%) with Canon, Hewlett-Packard, and the Singapore Economic Development Board to make 4-megabit DRAMs (TECH, 1991) and an agreement with Hitachi to research and develop 256-megabit DRAM chips (1993). In 1994 TI and Hitachi announced plans to build a $500 million DRAM chip plant in Richardson, Texas.

In 1995 the company debuted its patented "digital mirror device," which gives big-screen TVs, computer monitors, and other display panels a super-clear picture.

In 1996 TI sued Samsung Electronics in an effort to force the company to resume paying patent fees to TI. The 2 companies are battling over a 5-year cross-licensing agreement that expired at the end of 1995. Also in 1996 TI sold its custom manufacturing business to contract manufacturer Solectron for $130 million.

WHO

Chairman: James R. Adams, age 57
VC: William P. Weber, age 55, $1,154,250 pay
VC: William B. Mitchell, age 60, $1,023,750 pay
President and CEO: Thomas J. Engibous, age 43, $1,369,750 pay (prior to promotion)
EVP: William F. Hayes, age 52, $1,071,750 pay
EVP; President, Defense Systems and Electronics Group: Gary D. Clubb, age 49
EVP; President, Semiconductor Group: Richard K. Templeton, age 37
EVP: David D. Martin, age 56
SVP, CFO, and Treasurer: William A. Aylesworth, age 53
SVP, Secretary, and General Counsel: Richard J. Agnich, age 52
VP: Elwin L. Skiles Jr., age 54
VP and Corporate Controller: Marvin M. Lane Jr., age 61
VP Human Resources: Charles F. Nielson, age 58
Auditors: Ernst & Young LLP

WHERE

HQ: 13500 N. Central Expwy., Dallas, TX 75243
Phone: 214-995-2011
Fax: 214-995-4360
Web site: http://www.ti.com

Texas Instruments has manufacturing operations in the US and 18 other countries.

	1995 Sales		1995 Pretax Income	
	$ mil.	% of total	$ mil.	% of total
US	8,224	49	1,204	70
East Asia	5,944	35	287	17
Europe	2,571	15	230	13
Other regions	126	1	(2)	—
Adjustments	(3,737)	—	(100)	—
Total	**13,128**	**100**	**1,619**	**100**

WHAT

	1995 Sales		1995 Pretax Income	
	$ mil.	% of total	$ mil.	% of total
Components	9,480	72	1,830	91
Digital products	1,852	14	(59)	—
Defense systems & electronics	1,740	13	172	9
Metallurgical materials	183	1	2	—
Adjustments	(127)	—	(326)	—
Total	**13,128**	**100**	**1,619**	**100**

Selected Products
Clad metals
Defense suppression missiles
Electrical and electronic control devices
Electronic calculators
Electronic warfare systems
Missile guidance and control systems
Mobile computing products
Navigation systems
Precision-engineered parts and electronic connectors
Printers
Radar systems
Semiconductor devices

KEY COMPETITORS

AMD	Honeywell	NEC
Apple Computer	Hyundai	Oki
Canon	Intel	Raytheon
Casio	IBM	Rockwell
EG&G	LG Group	International
Emerson	LSI Logic	Samsung
Fujitsu	Micron	Sharp
General Electric	Technology	Siemens
Harris Corp.	Motorola	Thomson SA
Hewlett-Packard	National	Toshiba
Hitachi	Semiconductor	

HOW MUCH

NYSE symbol: TXN FYE: December 31	Annual Growth	1986	1987	1988	1989	1990	1991	1992	1993	1994	1995
Sales ($ mil.)	11.4%	4,974	5,595	6,295	6,522	6,567	6,784	7,440	8,523	10,315	13,128
Net income ($ mil.)	44.3%	40	257	366	292	(39)	(409)	247	476	691	1,088
Income as % of sales	—	0.8%	4.6%	5.8%	4.5%	—	—	3.3%	5.6%	6.7%	8.3%
Earnings per share ($)	45.7%	0.19	1.48	2.03	1.52	(0.46)	(2.70)	1.25	2.54	3.64	5.63
Stock price – high ($)	—	24.70	40.13	30.00	23.38	22.00	23.81	26.13	42.13	44.75	83.75
Stock price – low ($)	—	17.13	18.13	17.25	14.06	11.25	13.00	15.00	22.88	30.50	34.38
Stock price – close ($)	11.3%	19.69	27.88	20.50	17.94	19.00	15.38	23.31	31.75	37.44	51.50
P/E – high	—	130	27	15	15	—	—	21	17	12	15
P/E – low	—	90	12	9	9	—	—	12	9	8	6
Dividends per share ($)	7.3%	0.34	0.35	0.36	0.36	0.36	0.36	0.36	0.36	0.47	0.64
Book value per share ($)	7.5%	11.25	10.98	10.68	12.05	11.23	9.68	10.46	12.75	16.40	21.62
Employees	(2.8%)	77,270	77,984	75,685	73,854	70,318	62,939	60,557	59,048	56,333	59,574

1995 YEAR-END

Debt ratio: 16.9%
Return on equity: 30.5%
Cash (mil.): $1,553
Current ratio: 1.73
Long-term debt (mil.): $804
No. of shares (mil.): 189
Dividends
  Yield: 1.2%
  Payout: 11.4%
Market value (mil.): $9,754

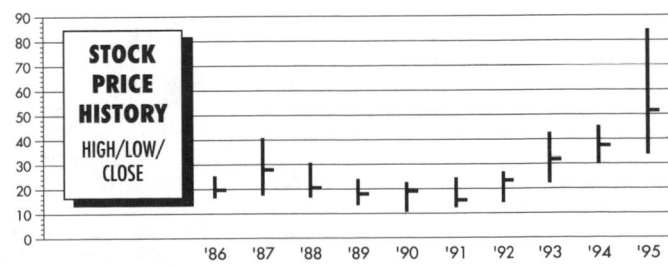

STOCK PRICE HISTORY HIGH/LOW/CLOSE

TOSHIBA CORPORATION

OVERVIEW

The appointment of Taizo Nishimuro as president of Tokyo-based electronics and energy equipment giant Toshiba has signaled a major shift for the company. In a break from the tradition of appointing the president from its heavy electrical divisions, Nishimuro came to the title with a background in multimedia and sales. Significantly, in terms of international operations, Nishimuro is the first head of the company to have lived in the US.

Toshiba manufactures a range of products including electronic devices such as batteries, diodes, DRAMs, power transistors, SRAMs, and X-ray tubes; heavy electrical apparatus for rolling stock, locomotives, elevators, escalators, switchgear, and industrial motors, and power generating equipment; and consumer electronics such as air conditioners, cameras, and TVs.

Despite fierce competition in the multimedia area, and a drop in demand for semiconductors, Nishimuro sees information technology, communications systems, and semiconductor divisions as the key to the company's growth. It is hoping the launch of its digital video disc player in 1996 will set the industry standard and become a consumer electronics blockbuster.

The company is also pursuing international alliances as a means of growth. Its joint venture partners include IBM (visual displays), Motorola (semiconductors), Time Warner (cable TV), and France-based Thomson Multimedia (video cassette recorders).

WHEN

Two Japanese electrical equipment manufacturers came together in 1939 to create Toshiba. Tanaka Seizo-sha, Japan's first telegraph equipment manufacturer, was founded in 1875 by Hisashige Tanaka, the so-called Edison of Japan. In the 1890s the company started making heavier electrical equipment, such as transformers and electric motors, adopting the name Shibaura Seisakusho Works in 1893. Seisakusho went on to pioneer the making of hydroelectric generators (1894) and X-ray tubes (1915) in Japan.

The other half of Toshiba, Hakunetsusha & Company, was founded by Dr. Ichisuke Fujioka and Shoichi Miyoshi as Japan's first incandescent lamp maker (1890). Renamed Tokyo Electric Company (1899), the firm developed the coiled filament light bulb (1921), Japan's first radio receiver and cathode ray tube (1924), and the internally frosted glass light bulb (1925). In 1939 it merged with Shibaura Seisakusho to form Tokyo Shibaura Electric Company (Toshiba).

Toshiba was the first company in Japan to make fluorescent lamps (1940), radar (1942), broadcasting equipment (1952), and digital computers (1954). Production of TVs began in 1949, the same year the company was listed on the Tokyo exchange. Even so, through the 1970s it was considered an also-ran, trailing other Japanese keiretsu (business groups) in size, market share, sales skills, and brand recognition. Part of the problem was a traditional and bureaucratic management that impeded technological innovation.

Then electrical engineer Shoichi Saba became president in 1980. Saba invested heavily in Toshiba's information and communications segments. As a result the company became the first in the world to produce the powerful one-megabit DRAM chip (1985). In 1986 Toshiba unveiled the popular T3100 laptop computer. In the meantime Saba (named chairman in 1986) pushed Toshiba into joint ventures with Siemens (1985) and Motorola (1986) to exchange microcomputer and memory-chip technology.

But in 1987 Toshiba incurred the wrath of the US government. A subsidiary sold submarine sound-deadening equipment to the USSR, resulting in threats of US sanctions and a precipitous decline in US sales and its stock price. Chairman Saba and President Sugichiro Watari resigned in shame.

With Joichi Aoi at the helm, Toshiba has become a leader among Japanese companies in establishing a global presence. Toshiba and GE linked up in 1991 to promote cooperative business ventures in Asia in large home appliances. Easing years-long trade tensions between Japan, the US, and Europe, Toshiba, IBM, and Siemens inked an 8-year, $1 billion deal in early 1992. Also that year Toshiba, IBM, and Apple announced a joint venture to make multimedia equipment and software. Toshiba invested in the US entertainment industry, buying a $500 million stake in Time Warner.

Toshiba opened a plant in China in 1995 to make cellular phones for the US market. The following year the company signed a deal with India-based HCL to distribute Toshiba's computer notebooks in India. That year Nishimuro, a former US-based Toshiba sales executive, was appointed president.

WHO

Chairman: Fumio Sato
President and CEO: Taizo Nishimuro, age 60
SEVP: Atsumi Uchiyama
SEVP: Hideharu Egawa
SEVP: Masaichi Koga
SEVP: Tetsuya Yamamoto
President and CEO, Toshiba America: Takeshi Okatomi
SVP Finance, Toshiba America: Katsufumi Nomura
Director Human Resources, Toshiba America: Lynne Kennedy
Auditors: Price Waterhouse LLP

WHERE

HQ: 1-1, Shibaura 1-chome, Minato-ku, Tokyo, 105-01, Japan
Phone: +81-3-3457-2105
Fax: +81-3-3456-4776
US HQ: Toshiba America, Inc., 1251 Avenue of the Americas, 41st Fl., New York, NY 10020
US Phone: 212-596-0600
US Fax: 212-593-3875
Web site: http://www.toshiba.com

	1996 Sales	
	$ mil.	% of total
Japan	43,889	77
Other countries	12,869	23
Adjustments	(8,455)	—
Total	**48,303**	**100**

WHAT

	1996 Sales	
	$ mil.	% of total
Information/communication systems & electronic devices	27,819	54
Heavy electrical apparatus	11,109	22
Consumer products & other	12,313	24
Adjustments	(2,938)	—
Total	**48,303**	**100**

Selected Products

Information/Communication Systems and Electronic Devices
DRAMs
Lithium ion secondary batteries
Nickel metal-hydride rechargeable batteries
Optical devices
Power transistors
SRAMs
X-ray tubes

Heavy Electrical Apparatus
Boiling water reactor power plants
Electric equipment for rolling stock, locomotives elevators, escalators, switchgear
Gas insulated switchgear
Industrial motors
Nuclear fuel reprocessing facilities
Power generating equipment
Superconducting magnets
Transformers

Consumer and Other Products
Air conditioners
CCD color cameras
CD-ROM drives
Color TV sets
Digital still cameras
HDTV systems
Microwave ovens
Personal computers
Refrigerators
Rice cookers
Vacuum cleaners
Video projectors
Videocassette recorders
Washing machines

KEY COMPETITORS

ABB	General Signal	Nokia
Alcatel Alsthom	Hitachi	Oki
Canon	Honeywell	Philips
Casio	Hyundai	Raytheon
Daewoo	IBM	Ricoh
Electrolux	Ingersoll-Rand	Sanyo
Emerson	Kyocera	Seiko
Ericsson	Lucent	Sharp
Fuji Photo	Machines Bull	Siemens
Fujitsu	Matsushita	Sony
GEC	Minolta	Sun
General Electric	NEC	Microsystems

HOW MUCH

Principal exchange: Tokyo FYE: March 31	Annual Growth	1987	1988	1989	1990	1991	1992	1993	1994	1995	1996
Sales ($ mil.)	8.7%	22,705	28,787	28,627	26,942	34,645	36,866	41,705	46,695	53,829	48,303
Net income ($ mil.)	15.4%	235	489	899	835	857	297	179	118	502	853
Income as % of sales	—	1.0%	1.7%	3.1%	3.1%	2.5%	0.8%	0.4%	0.3%	0.9%	1.8%
Earnings per share ($)	13.5%	0.08	0.16	0.28	0.25	0.25	0.09	0.06	0.04	0.15	0.25
Stock price – high ($)[1]	—	—	—	—	6.67	6.69	5.42	7.02	8.42	10.14	7.56
Stock price – low ($)[1]	—	—	—	—	4.66	4.41	4.03	4.75	6.08	7.74	4.60
Stock price – close ($)[1]	6.4%	—	—	—	5.19	5.05	5.08	6.06	7.23	8.35	7.54
P/E – high	—	—	—	—	26	26	60	126	228	67	30
P/E – low	—	—	—	—	18	17	44	85	164	51	18
Dividends per share ($)	6.7%	0.05	0.06	0.06	0.06	0.07	0.08	0.09	0.10	0.11	0.09
Book value per share ($)	9.9%	1.49	1.97	2.15	2.17	2.61	2.77	3.11	3.38	3.91	3.48
Employees	108.2%	121,000	122,000	125,000	142,000	162,000	168,000	173,000	174,000	190,000	186,000

[1] Stock prices are for the prior calendar year.

1996 YEAR-END

Debt ratio: 64.1%
Return on equity: 7.2%
Cash (mil.): $7,642
Current ratio: 1.05
Long-term debt (mil.): $9,362
No. of shares (mil.): 3,219
Dividends
  Yield: 1.3%
  Payout: 36.8%
Market value (mil.): $24,280

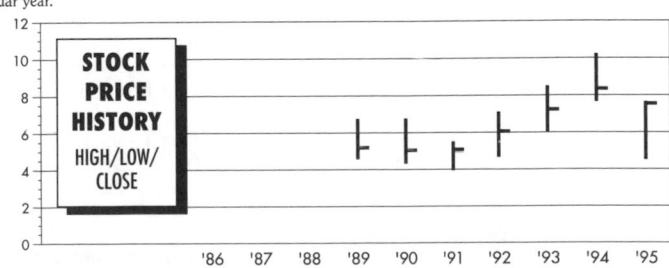

STOCK PRICE HISTORY
HIGH/LOW/CLOSE

UNISYS CORPORATION

OVERVIEW

Like a circus lion tamer, Unisys helps big organizations control their information beast. The Blue Bell, Pennsylvania-based information management company provides computer hardware, software, and services to such clients as Air France, Pacific Bell, and the US Department of Justice. The US government accounts for 9% of Unisys's revenues.

Now the question is, can Unisys find its market niche? The company originally provided mainframe computers and defense electronics. However, as the market has moved to client/server computing, Unisys has scrambled to keep up with the technology shift. Unisys (which has reorganized 5 times in 7 years) has laid plans for another overhaul. In 1996 the company said it would eliminate more than 20% of its workforce.

New products, including the Aquanta line of personal computers and the ClearPath server (which combines mainframe, Microsoft Windows NT, and UNIX systems on a single platform), may herald Unisys's turnaround.

WHEN

Unisys was formed in 1986 when struggling mainframe computer giant Burroughs swallowed fellow mainframe manufacturer Sperry Corporation. Burroughs traced its roots back to American Arithmometer (St. Louis, 1886), later Burroughs Adding Machine (Detroit, 1905), and Burroughs Corporation (1953). Burroughs entered data processing by purchasing Electrodata (1956) and many others, including Memorex (1982).

Sperry was the product of a 1955 merger of Sperry Gyroscope (founded in 1910 by Elmer Sperry) and Remington Rand, an old-line typewriter manufacturer and maker of the first commercially viable computer, the UNIVAC. Sperry bought RCA's faltering computer unit in 1971.

In 1986 Burroughs president Michael Blumenthal sought to achieve efficiency in parts and development by merging Burroughs's small database managers with Sperry's defense-related number crunchers. The new company was called Unisys, a condensation of "United Information Systems."

As president of Unisys, Blumenthal quickly disposed of $1.8 billion in assets (Sperry Aerospace and Marine divisions and Memorex), closed plants, and cut jobs. He promised continued support for Sperry's flagship 1100 line of mainframes and nurtured Burroughs's prized "A" series of computers. The initial results were positive, with 1986's $43 million loss followed by 1987's $578 million profit.

Amid an industry trend toward stronger, smaller systems, Unisys in 1988 equipped its U line of servers with the open UNIX operating system and moved to networked smaller systems, acquiring Timeplex (voice/data networks) and Convergent (UNIX-based workstations).

The Justice Department in 1988 launched an investigation of illegal defense procurement practices committed by Sperry prior to its merger with Burroughs. Unisys settled the charges in 1991 by agreeing to pay $54 million over 5 years, forgo $46 million in fees and profits, and make contingency payments of up to $90 million through 1997, based on asset sales and net income.

Plummeting mainframe demand in 1989 and 1990 caught Unisys in transition and led to heavy losses. Blumenthal left Unisys in 1990. Continuing losses prompted additional layoffs in 1991. Unisys's product line was pared and 7 of its 15 plants were closed.

Unisys and Intel entered a joint venture in 1993 to develop a parallel processing computer using Intel's Pentium chip. In 1994 the company won a $127 million contract by the Savings Bank of the Russian Federation to provide an information management system.

Unisys and Intel unveiled the OPUS megacomputer (the name is an acronym for Open Parallel Unisys Servers) in 1995. OPUS uses parallel processing technology to speed computations. Also that year Unisys won contracts worth $119 million to provide data storage for the IRS, voice mail for a Colombian state, and an oil spill management system for Texas A&M University. The company sold its defense unit to Loral in 1995 for $862 million in cash to be used to boost its commercial business.The company ended the year with losses that resulted in part from charges for its latest restructuring.

In 1996 shareholders rejected a proposal to split Unisys into 3 companies (computer manufacturing, consulting, and services). That year legal woes continued to mount over the past few years several states (including Iowa and Massachusetts) have sued or penalized the company, alleging substandard performance for work ranging from state insurance payments to motor-voter network development.

WHO

Chairman and CEO: James A. Unruh, age 54, $800,004 pay
EVP; President, Computer Systems Group: Alan G. Lutz, age 50, $493,336 pay
EVP; President, Information Services Group: Lawrence C. Russell, age 57
EVP; President, Global Customer Services: Gerald A. Gagliardi, age 48
SVP; President, Pacific Asia Americas Group; and VP, Information Technology and: Dewaine L. Osman, age 61, $377,923 pay
SVP, General Counsel, and Secretary: Harold S. Barron, age 59, $381,250 pay
SVP, Strategic Business Development: Malcolm D. Coster, age 51
VP Worldwide Human Resources: David O. Aker, age 49
Auditors: Ernst & Young LLP

WHERE

HQ: Township Line & Union Meeting Rds., Blue Bell, PA 19422-9945
Phone: 215-986-4011
Fax: 215-986-2312
Web site: http://www.unisys.com

	1995 Sales	
	$ mil.	% of total
US	3,127	44
Europe/Africa	2,119	30
Americas/Pacific	1,845	26
Adjustments	(889)	—
Total	**6,202**	**100**

WHAT

	1995 Sales
	% of total
Computer Systems Group	40
Global Customer Services Group	30
Information Services Group	30
Total	**100**

	1995 Sales	
	$ mil.	% of total
Products	2,646	43
Services	2,198	35
Equipment maintenance	1,358	22
Total	**6,202**	**100**

Selected Products and Services

Departmental servers
Desktop systems
Enterprise servers and systems
Equipment maintenance
Information services
Software
Systems integration

KEY COMPETITORS

Amdahl	MicroAge
Andersen Worldwide	Microsoft
Apple Computer	NCR
Computer Associates	NEC
Control Data	Oracle
Data General	Price Waterhouse
DEC	Siemens
EDS	Silicon Graphics
Fujitsu	Sony
Gartner Group	Storage Technology
Hewlett-Packard	Sun Microsystems
Hitachi	Tandem
IBM	Wang
Machines Bull	

HOW MUCH

NYSE symbol: UIS FYE: December 31	Annual Growth	1986	1987	1988	1989	1990	1991	1992	1993	1994	1995
Sales ($ mil.)	(2.0%)	7,432	9,713	9,902	10,097	10,111	8,696	8,422	7,743	7,400	6,202
Net income ($ mil.)	—	(43)	578	681	(639)	(437)	(1,393)	296	214	(20)	(745)
Income as % of sales	—	—	6.0%	6.9%	—	—	—	3.5%	2.8%	—	—
Earnings per share ($)	—	(0.54)	2.93	3.27	(4.71)	(3.45)	(9.37)	1.04	1.37	(0.11)	(4.35)
Stock price – high ($)	—	28.81	48.38	39.00	30.50	17.13	6.88	11.75	13.88	16.50	11.75
Stock price – low ($)	—	19.16	24.00	25.00	12.38	1.75	2.13	4.13	9.88	8.25	5.50
Stock price – close ($)	(16.1%)	26.63	33.63	28.13	14.75	2.50	4.13	10.13	12.63	8.63	5.50
P/E – high	—	—	17	12	—	—	—	11	10	—	—
P/E – low	—	—	8	8	—	—	—	4	7	—	—
Dividends per share ($)	(100.0%)	0.87	0.89	0.96	1.00	0.75	0.00	0.00	0.00	0.00	0.00
Book value per share ($)	(22.9%)	17.43	20.90	22.23	15.49	11.79	2.69	4.12	6.57	6.02	1.68
Employees	(10.2%)	98,300	92,500	93,000	82,300	75,300	60,300	54,300	49,000	46,300	37,400

1995 YEAR-END

Debt ratio: 50.4%
Return on equity: —
Cash (mil.): $1,120
Current ratio: 1.02
Long-term debt (mil.): $1,533
No. of shares (mil.): 172
Dividends
  Yield: —
  Payout: —
Market value (mil.): $948

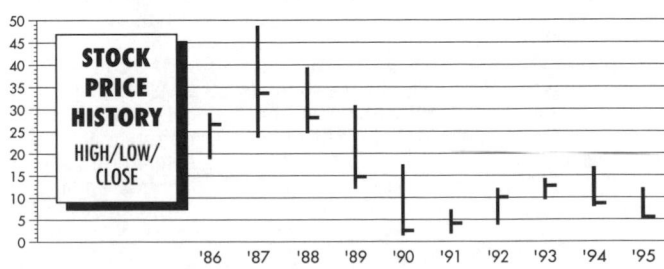

STOCK PRICE HISTORY HIGH/LOW/CLOSE

VANSTAR CORPORATION

OVERVIEW

Sometimes you do have to reinvent the wheel. Once the country's largest computer retailer, Pleasanton, California-based Vanstar (formerly ComputerLand) is now a leading provider of computer services and products to *FORTUNE* 1,000 companies. Its "life cycle management" and consulting services take customers from the network design stage, through installation and servicing, to upgrades, and finally to disposal of used computers. But more than 85% of Vanstar's sales come from providing corporate clients with PCs, peripherals, and networking and software products from more than 700 vendors. LAN sales account for over half of its business. Vanstar also offers hardware maintenance agreements, telephone support for hardware and software, and training programs.

In accomplishing its transition, Vanstar has had to overcome ComputerLand's old image (which had declined during the management upheavals of the mid-1980s), rid itself of retail locations, and downsize staff and office space.

The company continues to grow through acquisitions, especially in adding service capabilities. Another key strategy has been to form alliances with major companies to expand its services, products, and global outreach.

Vanstar recently went public, albeit to a lukewarm reception. Still the largest shareholder (with 35%) is investment firm Warburg, Pincus Capital Co., which bought ComputerLand with chairman William Tauscher and investor Richard Bard in 1987. Tauscher owns 6%.

WHEN

In 1973 William Millard, a computer consultant working under the name IMS Associates, met Philip Reed, a car dealer needing a computer program to track sales and inventory. They agreed that Millard would develop and Reed would finance the software.

The software was never developed. Rather, the two decided to sell a computer kit through magazine ads. It was a hit, and they followed it with a preassembled model. They remained strapped for cash, however, and in 1976 received a $250,000 loan from Boston-based Marriner & Co., which received a note convertible into 20% of IMS stock.

Reed left in 1976, after differing with Millard on the direction and management of the company. That year franchise consultant John Martin-Musumeci sold Millard on the idea of franchise retailing. The operation, Computer Shack, was a hit because it sold the new Apple computer as well.

Millard reshuffled the businesses to try to limit the Marriner note to IMS (and its successor company, IMSAI) but failed. He succeeded in shielding Computer Shack from IMSAI's debts, and in 1979 IMSAI went bankrupt, wiping out Reed's investment.

Renamed ComputerLand in 1977 (because of rumblings from Radio Shack), the company prospered after the 1981 introduction of the IBM PC. In the early 1980s the novelty of PCs drove sales to ever greater heights, and Millard steadily raised franchise fees, causing franchisee friction.

In 1981 Martin-Musumeci, through his new company, Micro/Vest, bought the Marriner note and split it with Reed. When Millard refused to recognize his right to the stock, Martin-Musumeci sued and won the stock plus punitive damages in 1985. Unable to pay for the appeal of the $141 million award, Millard sold out to the Warburg group 2 years later.

The new management, led by Tauscher, intended to go public in 1988, but the market was unenthusiastic. Instead, ComputerLand began to reposition itself as a reseller to businesses and as a provider of service and support. In 1991, to build its customer service base, it bought NYNEX Business Centers. The following year it acquired TRW's customer service division.

The repositioning was expensive; sales fell in the early 1990s, and the cost of the acquisitions dragged down earnings. But the acquisitions provided the basis for its new service orientation. By 1993 ComputerLand was in the midst of a credit crunch. This was eased, though, by the 1994 sale of its US retail and franchise operations and the US rights to the "ComputerLand" name to Merisel for $110 million.

The company changed its name to Vanstar in 1994. It also sold several international franchise subsidiaries and bought Ziff-Davis's training division. Vanstar went public in 1996; entered into alliances with MCI, Groupe Bull, and Ingram Micro; and bought Mentor Technologies and Dataflex.

WHO

Chairman and CEO: William Y. Tauscher, age 45,
$580,008 pay
VC and CFO: Jeffrey S. Rubin, age 52
President and COO: Jay Amato, age 36, $281,254 pay
SVP and General Manager Product Operations: Ahmad
Manshouri, age 55, $224006 pay
SVP Operations: Robert C. Kuntzendorf, age 50,
$209,006 pay
SVP Sales: Richard N. Anderson, age 39, $202,508 pay
SVP and Chief Technology Officer: Thanos M. Triant,
age 50
SVP and General Manager Learning Network: Coleman
D. Sisson, age 38
SVP and General Manager Professional Services:
Daniel S. Maher, age 44
SVP Management Information Services: Michael J.
Moore, age 44
SVP Networking Services: Chris M. Laney, age 38
SVP Service: William R. Waas, age 48
SVP, General Counsel, and Secretary: H. Christopher
Covington, age 45
VP Human Resources: Judith Marshall
Auditors: Ernst & Young LLP

WHERE

HQ: 5964 W. Las Positas Blvd., Pleasanton, CA 94588
Phone: 510-734-4000
Fax: 510-734-4802
Web site: http://www.vanstar.com.
Vanstar has more than 100 sales and service offices in
the US. It also has distribution centers in Indiana and
California and a repair facility in New Jersey.

WHAT

	1996 Sales	
	$ mil.	% of total
Products	1,578	87
Support services	138	8
Networking services	58	3
Other services	30	2
Total	**1,804**	**100**

Selected Manufacturers
3Com
Apple
Bay Networks
Compaq
Groupe Bull
Hewlett-Packard
IBM
Intel
Lexmark
Microsoft
NEC
Novell
Sun Microsystems
Toshiba

Selected Services
Deployment
  Cabling and connectivity
  Configuration
  Distribution
  Installation
  Procurement
Design and consulting services
  Asset management
  Communications
  Disaster recovery planning
  Outsourcing
Enhancement and migration services
  Assistance in moving to new hardware and software
  Training and education services
Operation and support services
  Maintenance and repair
  Move assistance
  National help desk
  Network monitoring
  Upgrades

KEY COMPETITORS

AmeriData
Andersen Consulting
The Asset Group
Bell Atlantic
Compaq
CompuCom
DEC
EDS
Entex
Hewlett-Packard
Inacom
Intelligent Electronics
MicroAge
Office Depot
OfficeMax
Tandem
Technology Solutions
Unisys
Wang

HOW MUCH

NYSE symbol: VST FYE: April 30	Annual Growth	1987	1988	1989	1990	1991	1992	1993	1994	1995	1996
Sales ($ mil.)	0.7%	1,700	2,039	2,630	3,000	1,500	2,000	2,200	1,200	1,187	1,805
Net income ($ mil.)	—	—	—	—	—	—	—	—	—	1	17
Income as % of sales	—	—	—	—	—	—	—	—	—	0.1%	1.0%
Employees	14.7%	—	—	—	—	2,069	3,763	3,295	3,088	3,200	4,100

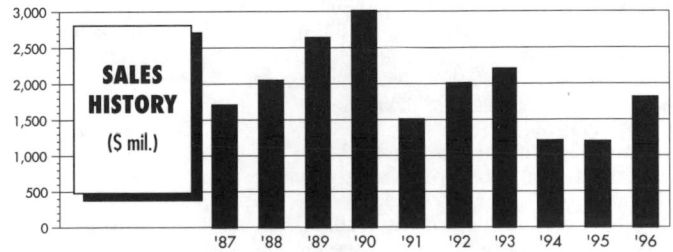

Vanstar

SALES HISTORY
($ mil.)

VISHAY INTERTECHNOLOGY, INC.

OVERVIEW

Vishay Intertechnology is aggressive about passive components. The Malvern, Pennsylvania-based company is the US's and Europe's leading maker of passive electronic components such as capacitors and resistors. These tiny but vital devices modify the flow of electricity through a circuit. As integrated circuits become more sophisticated, they require more passive components. High-powered microprocessors such as Intel's Pentium chip and the telecommunications industry's switch from analog to digital technology are driving demand for passive components. Vishay's components are found in products ranging from autos and aircraft to computers, medical instruments, and satellites. Its customers are a diverse group of electronics OEMs, including Apple, Bosch, Hewlett-Packard, Intel, Motorola, and Siemens.

Vishay became an industry top gun by acquiring competitors and integrating them smoothly into the company's operations. However, Vishay has wisely retained its acquisitions' established brand names, which include Dale and Sprague in the US and Draloric and Sfernice in Europe. To cut costs, the company has moved much of its production to low-wage countries such as the Czech Republic, Mexico, and Portugal. It also has plants in France, Germany, and Israel. The latter, whose business incentives contribute to Vishay's bottom line, accounts for 10% of the company's production.

Cofounder and chairman Felix Zandman and Luella Slaner, the widow of his partner and cousin (Alfred Slaner), control 67% of Vishay's voting stock.

WHEN

Felix Zandman, a native of Poland and a Holocaust survivor, earned his doctorate in physics from the Sorbonne. As a student Zandman developed PhotoStress, a plastic coating that revolutionized stress testing of airplane wings and rail cars. In the mid-1950s Zandman was recruited to work for the Budd Co., a Philadelphia-based steelmaker. During that period he developed a revolutionary resistor whose performance wasn't affected by temperature.

In 1962 Zandman borrowed $200,000 from his cousin, apparel maker Alfred Slaner, to start Vishay. The company was named after the family's ancestral village in Lithuania. With James Starr (now deceased), Zandman made significant developments in resistors. Vishay opened its first manufacturing facility in Israel in 1969. It went public in 1974. By the early 1980s the company had become a world leader in the development and manufacturing of ultraprecise resistors and resistive sensors.

Vishay evolved from a small company into a major player in passive components by a series of acquisitions of electronics component makers. In 1985 the company bought 50% of Dale Electronics (US), a resistor maker 3 times Vishay's size. The company soon added Draloric Electronic (1987, Germany), the remaining 50% of Dale (1988), and Sfernice (1988, France).

In 1992 Vishay purchased parts of the American Annuity Group, formerly Sprague Technologies. Sprague, a specialist in compact, highly stable tantalum capacitors, had been the US's top capacitor maker for several

decades. In 1993 Vishay completed its purchase of capacitor and resistor maker Roederstein (Germany, begun in 1992). Both Sprague and Roederstein boosted Vishay's presence in the rapidly growing field of surface-mount chip making technology, while the Roederstein purchase made Vishay the only maker of thick-film chip resistors in Europe and North America. When the market for small specialty tantalum capacitors heated up, the company in 1993 acquired the tantalum capacitor segment of Philips Electronics North America. In 1994 Vishay added Vitramon, the multilayer ceramic chip capacitor business of rival Thomas & Betts.

Vishay, which has had a limited presence in Asia, made a strong push into that market in 1995 by purchasing a 49% share of Japanese passive components maker Nikkohm. That year the company unveiled a resistor chip that helps extend the life of lithium batteries used in portable electronics such as laptop computers. The chip is already being used by electronics OEMs Matsushita, Sanyo, and Sony.

Zandman himself has become a celebrity. In 1995 his autobiography, "Never the Last Journey," a harrowing tale of Zandman's survival under the Nazis as a teenager in Poland, sold out its initial printing of 25,000 copies.

In 1996 Vishay courted rival capacitor maker KEMET Electronics in a takeover bid but was rejected. That year the company entered a partnership that will develop China's deposits of tantalum ore and produce tantalum capacitors in China.

WHO

Chairman, President, and CEO: Felix Zandman, age 67, $1,626,970 pay
VC and EVP: Avi D. Eden, age 48
EVP, Chief Business Development Officer, and SVP Marketing and Sales: Donald G. Alfson, age 50, $345,000 pay (prior to promotion)
EVP and COO: Gerald Paul, age 47, $335,900 pay (prior to promotion)
EVP and CFO: Richard N. Grubb, age 49, $216,900 pay (prior to promotion)
SVP: Robert A. Freece, age 55
VP; President and CEO, Measurements Group, Inc.: Henry V. Landau, age 49, $334,718 pay
VP; President, Vishay Israel Ltd.: Abraham Inbar, age 67
VP and Secretary: William J. Spires, age 54
Auditors: Ernst & Young LLP

WHERE

HQ: 63 Lincoln Hwy., Malvern, PA 19355-2120
Phone: 610-644-1300
Fax: 610-296-0657
Web site: http://vishay.com/vishay

Vishay has more than 50 manufacturing facilities in Europe, Israel, and the US.

	1995 Sales		1995 Operating Income	
	$ mil.	% of total	$ mil.	% of total
US	671	43	60	37
Europe	643	41	32	19
Israel	220	14	67	41
Other regions	33	2	5	3
Adjustments	(343)	—	—	—
Total	**1,224**	**100**	**164**	**100**

WHAT

Selected Products
Aluminum and specialty ceramic capacitors
Film capacitors
Fixed resistors
Inductors
Multilayer ceramic chip (MLCC) capacitors
Plasma displays
Potentiometers
Tantalum capacitors
Thermistors

KEY COMPETITORS

KAO
KEMET
Kyocera
Matsushita
Murata
NEC
Ohmite
ROHM
TDK
Yageo

HOW MUCH

NYSE symbol: VSH FYE: December 31	Annual Growth	1986	1987	1988	1989	1990	1991	1992	1993	1994	1995
Sales ($ mil.)	40.1%	59	109	176	416	446	442	664	856	988	1,224
Net income ($ mil.)	28.1%	10	16	8	18	23	21	30	43	59	93
Income as % of sales	—	17.3%	14.2%	4.6%	4.3%	5.2%	4.7%	4.6%	5.0%	6.0%	7.6%
Earnings per share ($)	20.5%	0.32	0.34	0.49	1.11	1.40	1.14	1.55	1.82	2.40	1.71
Stock price – high ($)	—	5.23	6.09	7.77	15.48	18.13	18.72	32.17	34.23	49.88	42.27
Stock price – low ($)	—	3.58	3.16	4.03	10.27	7.83	9.59	13.38	23.11	29.81	21.88
Stock price – close ($)	24.5%	4.16	4.73	6.66	12.69	10.97	14.81	29.48	31.86	46.67	30.00
P/E – high	—	16	18	16	14	13	16	21	19	21	25
P/E – low	—	11	9	8	9	6	8	9	13	12	13
Dividends per share ($)	—	0.00	0.00	0.00	0.00	0.00	0.00	0.00	0.00	0.00	0.00
Book value per share ($)	23.5%	2.33	2.83	3.15	8.23	11.22	12.08	16.32	17.74	21.45	15.56
Employees	12.2%	—	—	—	9,000	8,500	11,500	14,400	14,200	16,800	18,000

1995 YEAR-END

Debt ratio: 24.1%
Return on equity: 12.6%
Cash (mil.): $20
Current ratio: 2.80
Long-term debt (mil.): $229
No. of shares (mil.): 58
Dividends
  Yield: —
  Payout: —
Market value (mil.): $1,751

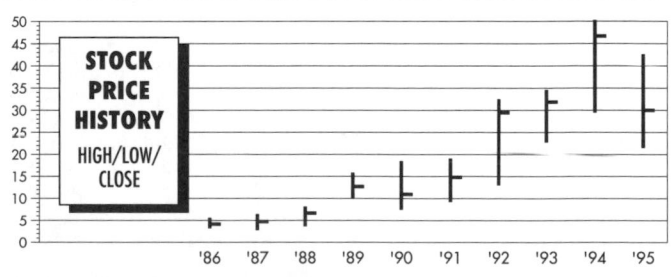

STOCK PRICE HISTORY
HIGH/LOW/CLOSE

WANG LABORATORIES, INC.

OVERVIEW

Massachusetts-based Wang Laboratories has reinvented itself. Left behind as computer users switched to PCs, the company has moved away from dedicated systems and into services and applications for a variety of computers. The new company is focusing on software, systems consulting, and systems management for paper-intensive organizations like banks, hospitals, insurance companies, and government agencies (sales to federal agencies accounted for 16% of its 1995 fiscal year sales). Wang still provides support and updates for its proprietary VS computer systems.

Wang has been shopping for alliances and acquisitions to expand its product line and geographic markets. In mid-1995 software giant Microsoft invested $90 million to buy rights to Wang's electronic document technology for its Windows 95 and Windows NT operating sys-

tems, agreeing to jointly promote Wang's products. It also designated Wang as one of its 5 global support centers. With the purchase of Groupe Bull's US customer service operations in early 1995, Wang had doubled its capability to supply customer service to other companies. Wang also bought Bull's systems-integration business and its operations in Australia, Canada, Mexico, and New Zealand. The purchase resulted in a hefty charge against revenues that left Wang with a loss in fiscal year 1995.

The alliance with Microsoft means Wang has an opportunity to sell its expensive server software, which manages the flow of electronic documents across a LAN. Microsoft now owns 10% of the company; Paris-based Bull has a 4.9% stake in Wang and a seat on its board.

WHEN

In 1951, with $600 in savings, An Wang started Wang Laboratories in Boston. An Wang had come to the US from China in 1945 to earn a PhD at Harvard. While working for Harvard's Computation Laboratory, he patented a magnetic pulse device that led to the development of memory cores. The small rings of iron were the central components of computer memory until replaced by microchips in the late 1960s. IBM bought Wang's patent in 1956 for $500,000.

Wang's next success came from engineering custom digital devices (e.g., the first digitally programmed scoreboard in New York's Shea Stadium). Another was the successful semi-automatic typesetter (Linasec) that Wang developed in 1963 under contract, which increased sales to over $1 million in 1964.

Adhering to An Wang's philosophy of "find a need and fill it," the company entered the calculator business, introducing an innovative desktop calculator, the LOCI, in 1965. The subsequent demand for Wang calculators caused the company to go public in 1967 to finance its expansion.

In the mid-1970s Wang relinquished the calculator business to its competitors and entered the word-processor market. Wang introduced the first screen-based (TV-like display) word processor in 1976, and by 1978 it had become the largest supplier of screen-based systems. Wang introduced its VS minicomputer series in 1977.

But Wang's peak years coincided with the advent of the microcomputer age, an event that An Wang failed to recognize until 1983, when, in an effort to stop customers from switching to competitive technologies, he announced a bevy of new products, many of which did not exist. The company lost credibility with customers, and its fortunes reversed as proprietary systems lost favor and market demand shifted from minicomputers to networked PCs. Wang appointed his son Fred as his successor in 1986, a disastrous move that resulted in Fred's firing in 1989. In 1990 An Wang died from cancer of the esophagus.

In 1991, as Wang was finishing its 3rd straight year of declining sales, the company announced an alliance to remarket selected IBM systems, in turn receiving from IBM fresh capital of up to $100 million. Wang lost $1.9 billion from 1989 through 1992, and demand for its word processors and minicomputers all but disappeared. With $540 million in debt, the company filed for bankruptcy in 1992. Chairman and CEO Richard Miller resigned early in 1993 after 3 years with the company.

In 1995 Wang moved into the North American headquarters of Groupe Bull in Billerica, Massachusetts. In another 1995 alliance, Kodak agreed to use Wang's software in its Imagelink document management systems. Later that year Wang bought closely held software developer Sigma Imaging Systems for $20 million. Wang's sales rose to $1,090 million in 1996, but it posted a loss of about $1 million.

WHO

Chairman and CEO: Joseph M. Tucci, age 48, $1,048,000 pay
President and Chief Technology Officer: Donald P. Casey, age 49, $1,027,000 pay
EVP and CFO (Acting HR): Franklyn A. Caine, age 45
SVP; President, Customer Services Business: William P. Ferry, age 43, $467,649 pay
SVP: James J. Hogan, age 53, $406,600 pay
SVP: Stephen G. Jerritts, age 69
SVP; President, International Business: Jeremiah van Vuuren, age 52
SVP; General Manager, Workflow/Imaging Business Group: Bruce A. Ryan, age 53
SVP; President, Software Business: Robert Weiler, age 44
SVP Business Development: David Goulden, age 36
SVP; President, Wang Federal, Inc.: Ronald E. Cuneo, age 52
SVP, General Counsel, and Secretary: Albert A. Notini, age 38
VP and Treasurer: Richard L. Buckingham, age 49
Auditors: Ernst & Young LLP

WHERE

HQ: 600 Technology Park Dr., Billerica, MA 01821-4130
Phone: 508-967-5000
Fax: 508-967-0436
Web site: http://www.wang.com

	1995 Sales		1995 Pretax Income	
	$ mil.	% of total	$ mil.	% of total
US	453	48	(37)	—
Europe	307	33	11	—
Asia/Pacific	134	14	(18)	—
Other Americas	52	5	(13)	—
Adjustments	—	—	3	—
Total	**946**	**100**	**(54)**	**—**

WHAT

	1995 Sales	
	$ mil.	% of total
Product sales	365	39
Service & other income	581	61
Total	**946**	**100**

Products and Services

Customer Services
Network integration
Nonpropietary systems support and maintenance
Service and maintenance for VS systems (Wang's proprietary hardware/software products)

Software
OPEN/coldplus (storage and retrieval)
OPEN/image (imaging)
OPEN/workflow (work management)
Windows 95 and Windows NT image processing

Solutions Integration (for US government)
Network integration
Systems integration
TEMPEST (secure systems)
ZONE (secure systems)

KEY COMPETITORS

Andersen	DEC	Proteon
Consulting	EDS	Safeguard
Apple Computer	FileNet	Scientifics
Bell Atlantic	Fiserv	Sybase
Cap Gemini	Hewlett-Packard	Systems &
Centura Software	IBM	Computer
Cisco Systems	Infodata Systems	Technology
Compaq	NCR	Vanstar
Computer	Novell	Xerox
Associates	Oracle	
Computer	Perot Systems	
Horizons	PRC	

HOW MUCH

Nasdaq symbol: WANQ FYE: June 30	Annual Growth	1986	1987	1988	1989	1990	1991	1992	1993	1994[1]	1995
Sales ($ mil.)	(10.7%)	2,615	2,751	2,952	2,910	2,497	2,093	1,896	1,247	855	946
Net income ($ mil.)	—	51	(71)	93	(424)	(716)	(386)	(357)	(197)	6	(66)
Income as % of sales	—	2.0%	—	3.2%	—	—	—	—	—	0.7%	—
Earnings per share ($)	32.5%	—	—	—	—	—	—	—	(1.15)	0.20	(2.02)
Stock price – high ($)	—	—	—	—	—	—	—	—	19.00	21.88	19.50
Stock price – low ($)	—	—	—	—	—	—	—	—	15.00	9.13	9.88
Stock price – close ($)	(1.1%)	—	—	—	—	—	—	—	17.00	10.13	16.63
P/E – high	—	—	—	—	—	—	—	—	—	109	—
P/E – low	—	—	—	—	—	—	—	—	—	46	—
Dividends per share ($)	—	—	—	—	—	—	—	—	0.00	0.00	0.00
Book value per share ($)	(12.4%)	—	—	—	—	—	—	—	8.44	8.26	6.48
Employees	(15.6%)	31,650	30,300	31,500	26,800	20,200	16,800	12,850	6,560	5,900	6,900

[1] Earnings for 9-month fiscal year

1995 YEAR-END

Debt ratio: 6.6%
Return on equity: —
Cash (mil.): $181
Current ratio: 1.12
Long-term debt (mil.): $23
No. of shares (mil.): 34
Dividends
  Yield: —
  Payout: —
Market value (mil.): $564

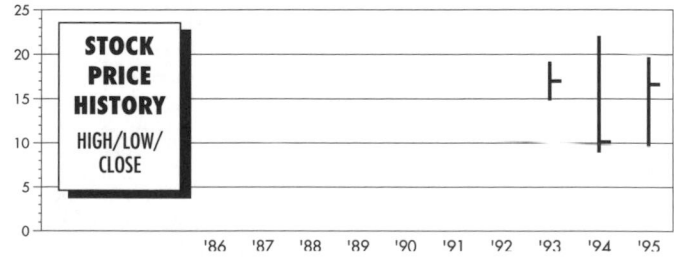

STOCK PRICE HISTORY HIGH/LOW/CLOSE

WESTERN DIGITAL CORPORATION

OVERVIEW

With the introduction of its high-performance gigabyte (GB) drives, Western Digital is moving to the front of the hard disk pack. The Irvine, California-based company is the #3 US manufacturer of hard drives for PCs (after Seagate and Quantum), including some of the highest-capacity drives (1-, 1.3-, and 1.6 GBs) in the retail marketplace. It also makes input/output (I/O) products - semiconductors, boards, and software that allow a CPU to work with peripherals such as printers and modems. The company's primary customers include OEMs such as Compaq, DEC, Gateway 2000, Hewlett-Packard, and IBM and retail distributors such as Computer City, and CompUSA,

Competition within the disk drive industry has been brutal, exemplified by bloody price wars in recent years. However, the release of the new Windows 95 operating system plus the growing popularity of multimedia computing and online services, with their increased storage needs, have galvanized sales of high-performance storage devices and driven Western Digital's revenues to record levels.

Western Digital is working to keep one step ahead of the marketplace. In late 1994 it opened a new research and development center in Minnesota (the company spent over 6% of 1995 revenues on R&D). In 1995 Western Digital's High-Performance Storage Group began building a new manufacturing facility in Singapore, near another plant already supplying its Personal Storage Group.

In addition, Western Digital expects that sales of its multimedia products unit to Philips Electronics will help it to focus its resources on its 2 core product lines. The company unveiled several new I/O products in 1995.

WHEN

Western Digital was founded in 1970 as a manufacturer of specialized semiconductors and electronic calculators. The company filed for Chapter 11 bankruptcy in late 1976. However, it reorganized and emerged successfully in 1978. Roger Johnson, after a succession of executive positions at Memorex, Measurex, System Development, and Burroughs, came to Western Digital as EVP and COO in 1982. At that point company revenues were only $34 million; it had bought a number of ill-fitting computer and electronics businesses. By 1984 Johnson, who had acquired the titles of president and CEO, sold off several companies to concentrate on storage control devices. By 1987 Western Digital's sales topped $460 million annually. A contract with IBM contributed significantly to the dramatic increase.

Anticipating a change in computer technology that would result in disk drive makers building storage control into the drives themselves, Western Digital soon had to shift its efforts toward making disk drives or face becoming a small semiconductor company. In 1988 the company acquired the disk drive operations of Tandon Corporation for $56 million. While Tandon was considered a second-rate manufacturer using aging technology, Western Digital leaders felt $56 million was a modest price to enter the drive business. Unfortunately, Tandon's drives continued to sell well for a period following the acquisition, creating a false sense of security and leading to a delay in the development of more competitive drives. The

profit for the fiscal year ending in June 1990 was $24.1 million with over $1 billion in sales. By year's end the market for storage controller boards had essentially disappeared; losses caused a company restructuring that in turn violated Western Digital's credit agreements.

In 1991 the US economy slowed and the disk drive industry began a price war. That year Western Digital sold its profitable LAN business to Standard Microsystems. The company appeared close to bankruptcy.

As the PC market improved in 1992, so did Western Digital's prospects. However, still short of cash, it reduced its workforce by 20% and made an effort to improve collection time. A big boost came in September 1992, when the company introduced its Architecture I product line, which offered drives with a commonality of parts. In 1993 Western Digital's IPO and sale of its wafer factory to Motorola reduced its high debt. That same year the Clinton administration appointed CEO Roger Johnson head of the General Services Administration.

In 1994 (its first profitable year since 1990) Western Digital became the first company to ship an inch-high, 3-platter, 3.5" enhanced drive with a 1-GB capacity. The company released its 1.6-GB Caviar drive — the largest drive of its kind available — in mid-1995 and announced that AT&T Global Information Solutions, Dell, and Gateway 2000 would feature the drive in their new systems. Western Digital had a net income of $97 million on sales of $2.87 billion in fiscal 1996.

WHO

Chairman, President, and CEO: Charles A. Haggerty, age 54, $1,136,469 pay
EVP Personal Storage Group: Kathryn A. Braun, age 44, $530,749 pay
EVP, CFO, and Chief Administrative Officer: D. Scott Mercer, age 44, $451,680 pay
EVP Microcomputer Products Group: Kenneth E. Hendrickson, age 54, $420,779 pay
SVP Engineering: Marc H. Nussbaum, age 39, $385,146 pay
President, Western Digital Japan: Toshio Yasui
VP Worldwide Sales: David W. Schafer, age 43
VP and Treasurer: Duston M. Williams, age 37
VP Law and Secretary: Michael A. Cornelius, age 53
VP Human Resources: Scott T. Hughes, age 32
Auditors: KPMG Peat Marwick LLP

WHERE

HQ: 8105 Irvine Center Dr., Irvine, CA 92718
Phone: 714-932-5000
Fax: 714-932-6096
Web site: http://www.wdc.com

Western Digital has sales offices and technical support available throughout Asia, Europe, and the US. It has manufacturing facilities in California, Malaysia, and Singapore.

	1995 Sales	
	$ mil.	% of total
United States	1,596	75
Europe	485	23
Asia	50	2
Total	**2,131**	**100**

WHAT

	1995 Sales
	% of total
Hard drive products	91
Microcomputer products	9
Total	**100**

Selected Products

Hard Drive Products
2.5" CaviarLite drives (2 disks, 200 megabytes)
3.5" Caviar drives
　AC2540 (2 disks, 541 megabytes)
　AC2700 (2 disks, 731 megabytes)
　AC31000 (3 disks, 1.084 gigabytes)
　AC1365 (1 disk, 365 megabytes)
　AC1425 (1 disk, 428 megabytes)
　AC2850 (2 disks, 854 megabytes)
　AC31200 (3 disks, 1.282 gigabytes)
　AC31600 (3 disks, 1.625 gigabytes)
　AC2635 (2 disks, 640 megabytes)

I/O Products
Areal density products
Hard disk controller products
Host controller products
Media interface products
Systems logic products

KEY COMPETITORS

Adaptec	Quantum Corp.
Ameriquest	Samsung
Chips and Technologies	Seagate
Hitachi	Sequel
IBM	Sharp
Intel	Siemens
Matsushita	StreamLogic
Maxtor	Toshiba

HOW MUCH

NYSE symbol: WDC FYE: June 30	Annual Growth	1986	1987	1988	1989	1990	1991	1992	1993	1994	1995
Sales ($ mil.)	25.4%	278	463	768	992	1,074	986	938	1,225	1,540	2,131
Net income ($ mil.)	21.7%	21	43	43	34	24	(134)	(73)	(25)	73	123
Income as % of sales	—	7.4%	9.3%	5.6%	3.5%	2.3%	—	—	—	4.7%	5.8%
Earnings per share ($)	10.3%	1.02	1.65	1.51	1.18	0.82	(4.59)	(2.49)	(0.79)	1.70	2.47
Stock price – high ($)	—	20.00	32.63	17.88	15.25	14.88	6.75	8.75	10.50	20.38	22.13
Stock price – low ($)	—	9.88	11.63	11.00	5.75	4.00	2.00	2.50	3.63	8.63	13.13
Stock price – close ($)	(0.4%)	18.50	16.25	14.75	8.38	4.88	2.63	8.63	9.13	16.75	17.88
P/E – high	—	20	20	12	13	18	—	—	—	12	9
P/E – low	—	10	7	7	5	5	—	—	—	5	5
Dividends per share ($)	—	0.00	0.00	0.00	0.00	0.00	0.00	0.00	0.00	0.00	0.00
Book value per share ($)	7.9%	4.81	7.83	9.26	10.38	11.02	6.34	3.84	3.71	6.42	9.53
Employees	13.0%	2,541	3,422	6,582	6,394	7,607	6,740	6,906	7,322	6,593	7,647

1995 YEAR-END

Debt ratio: 0.0%
Return on equity: 32.4%
Cash (mil.): $308
Current ratio: 1.98
Long-term debt (mil.): $0
No. of shares (mil.): 50
Dividends
　Yield: —
　Payout: —
Market value (mil.): $888

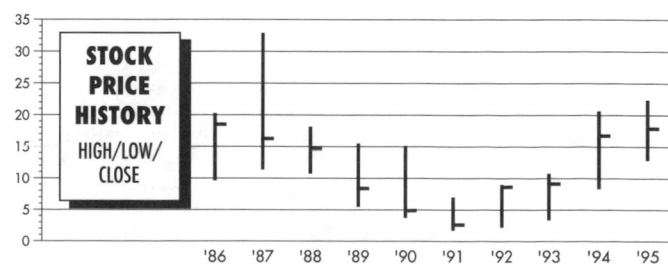

STOCK PRICE HISTORY HIGH/LOW/CLOSE

XEROX CORPORATION

OVERVIEW

Xerox, long synonymous with "copy," wants to mean more to paper pushers. The Stamford, Connecticut-based firm is focused on the $200 billion global document processing market, which encompasses most of the things you can do with a document electronically. In fact, Xerox's Document Centre System copies, faxes, prints, and scans.

New products are pushing the company's growth. These include innovative color copiers and networking printing systems. After its legendary Palo Alto Research Center introduced new technology for high-resolution electronic displays, Xerox formed Dpix to develop flat-panel displays using the new technology.

The company's return to document handling comes after a failed foray into finance during the 1980s. Over the past few years, Xerox has aggressively restructured, cut its workforce by 12,000, and sold its noncore businesses (including acquisitions in finance, desktop publishing, and investment banking). Charges for restructuring have left the company in the red for 3 of the last 4 years.

Xerox operates globally through 80%-owned Rank Xerox (British leisure and recreation conglomerate Rank owns 20%) and through Fuji Xerox, which Rank Xerox co-owns with Japan's Fuji Photo Film.

WHEN

The Haloid Company was incorporated in 1906 to make and sell photographic paper. In 1935 it bought Rectigraph, a photocopier company. This purchase led Haloid to acquire a license for a new process called electrophotography (later renamed xerography from the ancient Greek words for dry and writing) from the Battelle Memorial Institute in 1947. Battelle had backed inventor Chester Carlson, who had labored since 1937 to perfect a process of transferring electrostatic images from a photoconductive surface to paper.

Haloid commercialized the process, introducing the Model A copier in 1949 and the Xerox Copyflo in 1955. By the next year xerographic products represented 40% of the company's sales. The firm became Haloid Xerox in 1958 and in 1959 introduced the Xerox 914, the first simplified office copier. That machine took the world by storm, beating out such competing technologies as mimeograph (A.B. Dick), thermal paper (3M), and damp copy (Kodak). Revenues soared from $37 million in 1960 to $268 million in 1965. The firm dropped Haloid from its name in 1961.

Xerox branched out in the 1960s, buying 3 publishing firms and one computer company; all were later sold or disbanded.

In the 1970s Xerox bought companies that made printers (Diablo, 1972), plotters (Versatec, 1975), and disk drives (Shugart, 1977; sold in 1984); it also bought record carrier Western Union International (1979; sold in 1982). In 1974 the FTC, believing Xerox was too dominant in its market, forced the company to license its xerographic technology to other manufacturers.

In the 1980s Xerox bought companies in optical character recognition (Kurzweil, 1980),

scanning and fax (Datacopy, 1988), and desktop publishing (Ventura, 1990; sold to Corel in 1993). It also diversified into financial services, buying insurance companies (Crum and Forster, 1983) and investment banking companies (Van Kampen Merritt, 1984; sold in 1993), among others.

After becoming CEO in 1990, Paul Allaire embarked on a major restructuring program to focus Xerox's operations on document processing. With an eye to future alliances, the firm signed agreements to supply print engines to computer companies Compaq (1992) and Apple (1993). The Apple contract was a particular coup, as Canon, a chief US competitor, had been Apple's sole print engine supplier since 1985.

A surge of new products accompanied more cost cutting, indicating better use of its R&D centers. Xerox's R&D had a reputation for great inventions (the laser printer, PC networking, the graphical computer screen) but slow implementation.

In 1995 Xerox introduced a new family of networked color laser printers and a host of software products, including DocuWeb and InterDoc, which allow documents to be printed via the Internet.

Leveraged buyout firm Kohlberg Kravis Roberts agreed to buy Xerox's 5 insurance businesses for an estimated $2.6 billion in 1996, but backed uot before the deal closed, leaving many analysts wondering if the units were in worse financial shape than previously expected. That year Xerox formed a joint venture with Korean electronics megamanufacturer LG Electronics to make multimedia-related office equipment.

WHO

Chairman and CEO: Paul A. Allaire, age 57, $4,166,832 pay
EVP and CFO: Barry D. Romeril, age 52, $1,418,421 pay
EVP Operations: Addison B. Rand, age 51, $1,411,352 pay
EVP and Chief Staff Officer: William F. Buehler, age 56, $1,271,269 pay
EVP; Chairman and CEO, Xerox Financial Services: Stuart B. Ross, age 58
SVP Corporate Strategic Services: Allan E. Dugan, age 55, $1,168,482 pay
SVP Corporate Research and Technology: Mark B. Myers, age 57
SVP and General Counsel: Richard S. Paul, age 54
VP; President, Desktop Products Group: James H. Lesko, age 44
VP, Treasurer, and Secretary: Eunice M. Filter, age 55
VP and Controller: Philip D. Fishbach, age 54
VP Human Resources and Quality: Hector J. Motroni
Auditors: KPMG Peat Marwick LLP

WHERE

HQ: 800 Long Ridge Rd., Stamford, CT 06904
Phone: 203-968-3000
Fax: 203-968-4559
Web site: http://www.xerox.com

Xerox, in conjunction with jointly owned subsidiaries Rank Xerox and Fuji Xerox, operates offices, manufacturing plants, and other facilities worldwide.

	1995 Sales $ mil.	1995 Sales % of total	1995 Operating Income $ mil.	1995 Operating Income % of total
US	9,444	50	288	25
Europe	5,722	31	409	36
Other regions	3,510	19	446	39
Adjustments	(2,065)	—	—	—
Total	**16,611**	**100**	**1,143**	**100**

WHAT

	1995 Sales $ mil.	1995 Sales % of total
Sales	8,799	53
Service & rentals	6,804	41
Equipment financing	1,008	6
Total	**16,611**	**100**

Selected Products
Copiers (black-and-white and color)
Document Centre Systems (digital fax/printer/scanner/copiers)
Facsimile products
PC and workstation software
Printers (including electrostatic, ink jet, and laser document printers and high-end, high-volume production printers)
Scanners

KEY COMPETITORS

3M
AM International
Canon
Casio
Eastman Kodak
GEC
General Binding
Harris Corp.
Hewlett-Packard
Hitachi
Lexmark International
Machines Bull
Matsushita
Minolta

Mitsubishi
Moore Corp.
Nashua
NEC
Oce-van der Grinten
Olivetti
Pitney Bowes
Polaroid
Ricoh
Sharp
Siemens
Wang

HOW MUCH

NYSE symbol: XRX FYE: December 31	Annual Growth	1986	1987	1988	1989	1990	1991	1992	1993	1994	1995
Sales ($ mil.)	6.6%	9,355	10,320	31,234	33,148	17,973	17,830	18,261	17,410	17,837	16,611
Net income ($ mil.)	—	423	578	388	704	243	454	(1,074)	(126)	794	(472)
Income as % of sales	—	4.5%	5.6%	1.2%	2.1%	1.4%	2.5%	—	—	4.5%	—
Earnings per share ($)	—	3.85	5.35	3.50	6.41	1.66	3.86	(3.32)	(1.84)	6.44	(5.26)
Stock price – high ($)	—	72.25	85.00	63.00	69.00	58.88	69.75	82.25	90.00	112.75	144.63
Stock price – low ($)	—	48.63	50.00	50.25	54.38	29.00	35.25	66.50	69.88	87.75	96.50
Stock price – close ($)	9.6%	60.00	56.63	58.38	57.25	35.50	68.50	79.25	89.38	99.00	137.00
P/E – high	—	19	16	18	11	36	18	—	—	18	—
P/E – low	—	13	9	14	9	18	9	—	—	14	—
Dividends per share ($)	—	3.00	3.00	3.00	3.00	3.00	3.00	3.00	3.00	3.00	3.00
Book value per share ($)	(3.2%)	48.00	51.00	52.22	54.66	54.76	55.36	40.76	38.15	39.41	35.79
Employees	(1.8%)	100,400	99,200	100,000	99,000	99,000	100,900	99,300	97,000	87,600	85,200

1995 YEAR-END

Debt ratio: 74.2%
Return on equity: —
Cash (mil.): $130
Current ratio: 1.40
Long-term debt (mil.): $7,867
No. of shares (mil.): 108
Dividends
  Yield: 2.2%
  Payout: —
Market value (mil.): $14,843

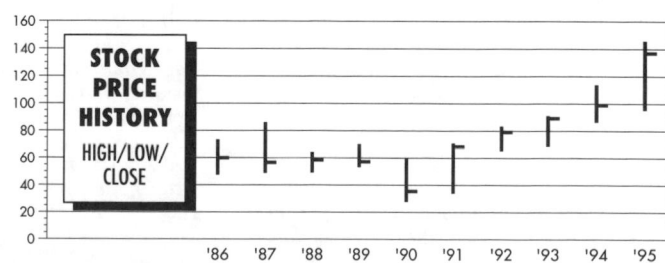

STOCK PRICE HISTORY
HIGH/LOW/CLOSE

ZIFF-DAVIS PUBLISHING COMPANY

OVERVIEW

Ziff-Davis has a big byte of the computer magazine market. The New York City-based company publishes such top computer magazines as *PC Magazine*, *FamilyPC*, and *MacUser*. Its magazines have an estimated global circulation of nearly 6 million. Other units publish newsletters (the Cobb Group), conduct market research (Computer Intelligence Infocorp), perform Benchmark testing (Ziff-Davis Benchmark Operation), produce management training products (Logical Operations), and provide online services (ZDNet).

In early 1996 the company was acquired by Tokyo-based SOFTBANK, Japan's top publisher of computer magazines and books from investment firm Frostmann Little for $2.1 billion.

Ziff-Davis has been busy since its acquisition by SOFTBANK. It announced the creation of ZDTV, an independent unit that will produce television and Internet programming. It also formed a new Internet advertising representative group with Interactive Marketing Inc. (initial clients include the National Football League and Playboy) and started USWeb, a Web site development and consulting service.

SOFTBANK is Japan's largest distributor of computer software and peripherals. Its founder and 61% owner is 39-year-old Masayoshi Son, who has been called "Japan's Bill Gates." The Ziff-Davis purchase moves Son closer to his goal of building SOFTBANK into the leading global provider of computer infrastructure services, including distributing, publishing, and trade shows.

WHEN

William Ziff (a famed WWI flyer, author, and lecturer) and Bernard Davis founded Ziff-Davis Publishing in 1927 with the publication of *Popular Aviation* (now *Flying*). The pair concentrated on hobby- and leisure-related publications. When Ziff died of a heart attack in 1953, Ziff-Davis was publishing *Modern Bride*, *Popular Electronics*, and *Popular Photography*, among others.

Ziff's 24-year-old son Bill Jr. gave up a promising career in academia to take over the company. In 1956 he bought out Davis and began an unprecedented buying spree, seeking out niche markets in which a continuous supply of new products and services would keep readers interested.

In 1973 Ziff acquired the publishing arm of paper products company Boise Cascade, inheriting, among other titles, *Psychology Today*. By the mid-1980s his enterprise published about 35 magazines, including *Car & Driver*, *Yachting*, and *Travel Weekly*, and owned 6 television stations.

During the 1980s, Ziff's battle with prostate cancer hampered the company's growth and most of its holdings were sold. The television stations were sold for $100 million in 1983. In 1985, 12 trade magazines went to Rupert Murdoch for $350 million, and 12 consumer magazines were sold to CBS for $363 million. Ziff also passed ownership of the company to his 3 sons and 3 nephews.

The firm did keep its computer magazines, which were already among the strongest in the industry. In 1988, having beaten cancer, Ziff

resumed chairmanship of the renamed Ziff Communications; by the early 1990s the company was the US's #1 publisher of computer magazines. In 1993 it began expanding into trade shows, newsletters, and electronic services. That year Bill Ziff retired at age 63.

In 1994 Ziff's successors decided the market had peaked and put Ziff Communications up for sale. The surprise winner of the bidding for Ziff-Davis Magazines was Forstmann Little, which beat out SOFTBANK and media companies Time Warner and Bertelsmann.

SOFTBANK was founded in 1981 by Son, who, as a teenager, made his first million exporting video games from Japan to the US. SOFTBANK is Japan's largest distributor of computer software, peripherals, and systems and its leading publisher of high-tech magazines. Its publishing division, created just 6 months after SOFTBANK was founded, issues Japanese versions of leading computer magazines. Despite losing its bid for Ziff-Davis in 1994, SOFTBANK did pick up the company's trade show business, ZD Expos.

In 1996 Ziff-Davis joined with Yahoo!, the online search service, and converted *ZD Internet Life* magazine into *Yahoo! Internet Life*. That year Ziff-Davis created 3 new US divisions: US Publications (Business Media, Consumer Media, and Magazine Networks), Interactive Media and Development (ZDNet and a newly created Internet Publishing Group), and Training and Support Publishing (Logical Operations and the Cobb Group).

WHO

Chairman and CEO: Eric Hippeau
CFO: Tim O'Brien
President, US Publications: Ronni Sonnenberg
President, Interactive Media and Development: Jeff Ballowe
President, Training and Support Publishing; President, Logical Operations Group: William Rosenthal
President, Business Media: Claude Sheer
President, Consumer Media: J. Scott Briggs
President, Computer Intelligence/Infocorp: Bob Brown
President, International Media Group: J. B. Holston III
VP Human Resources: Rajna Brown

WHERE

HQ: One Park Ave., New York, NY 10016-5801
Phone: 212-503-3500
Fax: 212-503-4599
Web site: http://www.zd.com

Ziff-Davis publishes 12 magazines in the US and 10 in foreign countries. The company licenses or syndicates its editorial content to 56 other publications.

WHAT

US Publications
Computer Gaming World
Computer Life
Computer Shopper
FamilyPC (with the Walt Disney Co.)
Inter@ctive Week (with Inter@ctive Enterprises)
MacUser
MacWEEK
PC Computing
PC Magazine
PC WEEK
Windows Sources
Yahoo! Internet Life

Foreign Publications
China
  PC Magazine (with Richina Media)
France
  PC Direct
  PC Expert
Germany
  PC Direkt
  PC Professional
  Pl@net

Mexico
  PC Computing en Espanol (with Editorial Televisa)
UK
  Computer Life
  PC Direct
  PC Magazine

Other Operations
The Cobb Group newsletters
  Inside NetWare
  Inside OS/2
  Inside the Internet
  Inside Visual Basic
Computer Intelligence Infocorp (market research)
Logical Operations (management training)
USWeb (World Wide Web site development and consulting service)
ZD Europe (European magazine operations)
  ZD Deutschland
  ZD France
  ZD UK
ZDNet (online information)
ZDTV (production of television and Internet programming)
Ziff-Davis Benchmark Operation (Benchmark testing)

KEY COMPETITORS

Bronner Slosberg
CMP Publications
C/NET
Cowles Media
HyperMedia
International Data Group
International Post
McGraw-Hill
Mecklermedia
Modem Media
New York Times
Pittway
Reed Elsevier
Sendai Media Group
Times Mirror
Wired Ventures

HOW MUCH

Subsidiary FYE: December 31	Annual Growth	1986	1987	1988	1989	1990	1991	1992	1993	1994	1995
Sales ($ mil.)	20.7%	175	145	200	240	889	436	620	718	852	950
Employees	2.3%	2,200	—	—	—	—	3,100	4,100	4,300	2,800	2,700

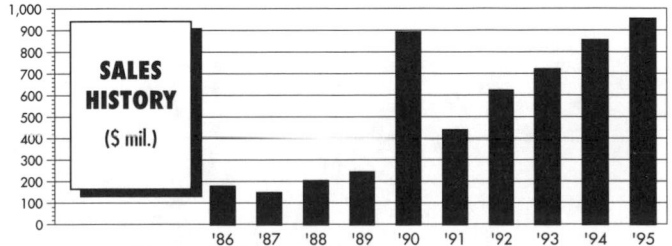

SALES HISTORY ($ mil.)

| | '86 | '87 | '88 | '89 | '90 | '91 | '92 | '93 | '94 | '95 |

COMPUTER **Selected Industry Players**

7TH LEVEL, INC.

OVERVIEW

Like T.F. Gumby, the head-bandaged character in many a Monty Python episode, your brain may hurt from hours of playing 7th Level's Monty Pythonesque programs. The Richardson, Texas-based multimedia software company is aiming high, mixing big-name performers with proprietary production techniques and top animators to create titles including Monty Python's Complete Waste of Time, a CD-ROM with clips from the classic BBC television series; TuneLand, an interactive cartoon featuring comedian Howie Mandel; and Ace Ventura, a CD-ROM game featuring Hollywood star Jim Carrey. The company also produces educational and children's software, including the popular game Battle Beast. Entec Associates (which includes Michael Milken as a general partner) owns about 16% of 7th Level. CEO George Grayson owns 11%, and president Robert Ezrin and EVP Scott Page each own 5%.

Grayson, a founder of graphics software company Micrografx, launched 7th Level in 1993 and gathered creative talent including Ezrin (a record producer for Pink Floyd) and musician Page. The enterprise created a proprietary interactive software development system called TopGun, which speeds production of CD-ROMs, in 1993. The company released its first title, TuneLand, in 1994 and went public.

7th Level is forging strategic alliances with other media groups, such as QDE (a joint venture among media heavyweights Quincy Jones, David Salzman, and Time Warner) and Walt Disney, to codevelop multimedia products. It also plans to test the South Korean market by setting up a joint venture with 2 Korean firms.

Monty Python moved into cyberspace in 1996 when 7th Level introduced its satirical, cartoon-rich Web site — www.pythonline.com — on the auspicious (and unusual) date of June 36th.

WHO

Chairman and CEO: George D. Grayson, age 40, $143,576 pay
President: Robert A. Ezrin, age 47, $300,500 pay
COO: David R. Henkel, age 44, $287,500 pay
EVP Production: W. Scott Page, age 44, $152,583 pay
CFO: David W. Craig, age 52
VP Sales: Jeffery Croson, age 37
VP Research and Development: Doug Gillespie, age 34
Manager Personnel and Human Resources: Sherry Denning
Auditors: KPMG Peat Marwick LLP

WHERE

HQ: 1110 E. Collins Blvd., Ste. 122, Richardson, TX 75081
Phone: 214-498-8100   **Fax:** 214-437-2717
Web site: http://www.7thlevel.com

WHAT

Software Products

Arcade Style Games	Education
Arcade America	The Great Word Adventure
Battle Beast	Peter and the Wolf
Take Your Best Shot	TuneLand
Comedic Strategy Games	
Monty Python and the Quest for the Holy Grail	**Graphic Adventure Games**
	Ace Ventura: Pet Detective
Monty Python's Complete Waste of Time	**Other**
	Battle Beast Baseball Cap
	Battle Beast Mouse Pad
	Monty Python T-shirt

KEY COMPETITORS

3DO	Digital Pictures	Microsoft
Acclaim	Educational	Nintendo
Entertainment	Insights	Rocket Science
Accolade	Electronic Arts	Games
Activision	id Software	SEGA
Aristo	Interplay	SoftKey
International	Productions	Sony
Brøderbund	JTS	Spectrum
CUC	Knowledge	HoloByte
International	Adventure	Trilobyte
Cyan	LucasArts	

HOW MUCH

Nasdaq symbol: SEVL FYE: December 31	Annual Growth	1990	1991	1992	1993	1994	1995
Sales ($ mil.)	290.5%	—	—	—	0.8	4.1	12.2
Net income ($ mil.)	—	—	—	—	(6.1)	(6.5)	(14.6)
Income as % of sales	—	—	—	—	—	—	—
Earnings per share ($)	—	—	—	—	(0.90)	(0.85)	(1.33)
Stock price – high ($)	—	—	—	—	—	11.00	22.63
Stock price – low ($)	—	—	—	—	—	4.75	5.00
Stock price – close ($)	—	—	—	—	—	5.25	14.00
P/E – high	—	—	—	—	—	—	—
P/E – low	—	—	—	—	—	—	—
Dividends per share ($)	—	—	—	—	—	0.00	0.00
Book value per share ($)	—	—	—	—	—	1.89	3.69
Employees	97.6%	—	—	—	52	79	203

1995 YEAR-END
Debt ratio: 1.4%
Return on equity: —
Cash (mil.): $40
Current ratio: 9.02
Long-term debt (mil.): $1
No. of shares (mil.): 13
Dividends
  Yield: —
  Payout: —
Market value (mil.): $183

ACCLAIM ENTERTAINMENT, INC.

OVERVIEW

Playing is serious business for Acclaim Entertainment, one of the US's largest independent makers of entertainment software for SEGA and Nintendo game systems. Acclaim's games, mainly targeted for 11- to 17-year-old boys, include WWF Raw, NFL Quarterback Club, and The Simpsons. The company's Acclaim Comics is a major publisher of comic books. Founders Gregory Fischbach and James Scoroposki own 14% and 13% of Acclaim's stock, respectively.

Acclaim was founded in 1986 to design and sell video games, mostly for Nintendo's NES system. The company went public in 1988 and 2 years later acquired LJN Toys from MCA. In 1989 Acclaim began making software for Nintendo's Game Boy.

In 1992 the company entered the SEGA game market by buying Mirrorsoft, a European designer of software for SEGA's Genesis and Game Gear systems. While Acclaim sank $3 million that year into a failed television venture, it benefited from a price war between Nintendo and SEGA that caused both companies to lower their prices.

The company diversified into comic books with the purchase of Voyager Communications (renamed Acclaim Comics) in 1994. That year it contracted with Warner Bros. Studios to create special effects for the movie Batman Forever using video game technology.

The company is vulnerable to technological advances in its market. The rise of interactive PC games for home use and the introduction of 32- and 64-bit systems has made some of its products obsolete, which contributed to a slight decline in earnings in 1995.

In late 1995 the company acquired Lazer-Tron (which makes coin-operated redemption games) and video-game makers Probe Entertainment and Sculptured Software.

WHO

Co-chairman and CEO: Gregory E. Fischbach, age 53, $3,550,000 pay
Co-chairman, EVP, Secretary, and Treasurer: James Scoroposki, age 47, $2,850,000 pay
President, COO, and General Manager: Robert Holmes, age 42, $2,900,000 pay
EVP Finance and CFO: Anthony R. Williams, age 37, $270,000 pay
VP Planning and Operations (HR): John Ma
Attorney: Bernard Fischbach, age 49
Auditors: Grant Thornton

WHERE

HQ: One Acclaim Plaza, Glen Cove, NY 11542
Phone: 516-656-5000   **Fax:** 516-656-2040

WHAT

	1995 Sales
	% of total
16-bit game software	74
CD software	10
Portable game software	10
Other	6
Total	**100**

Selected Software Titles
Batman Forever
Mortal Kombat II
NBA Jam
NFL Quarterback Club
The Simpsons
StarGate
True Lies
Warlock

KEY COMPETITORS

3DO	Cyan	SEGA
7th Level	id Software	Sony
Accolade	Interplay	Spectrum
Activision	Productions	HoloByte
Brøderbund	JTS	Trilobyte
Electronic Arts	LucasArts	WMS Industries
Cuc	Microsoft	
International	Nintendo	

HOW MUCH

Nasdaq symbol: AKLM FYE: August 31	Annual Growth	1990	1991	1992	1993	1994	1995
Sales ($ mil.)	32.0%	141.5	122.1	214.6	327.1	480.8	566.7
Net income ($ mil.)	25.8%	14.2	(5.8)	13.8	28.2	45.1	44.8
Income as % of sales	—	10.0%	—	6.4%	8.6%	9.4%	7.9%
Earnings per share ($)	11.0%	0.51	(0.21)	0.37	0.63	1.00	0.86
Stock price – high ($)	—	10.67	4.25	12.26	31.75	27.25	28.63
Stock price – low ($)	—	2.08	1.92	3.00	10.67	12.88	10.75
Stock price – close ($)	30.7%	3.25	3.08	12.09	21.25	14.38	12.38
P/E – high	—	21	—	33	50	27	33
P/E – low	—	4	—	8	17	13	13
Dividends per share ($)	—	0.00	0.00	0.00	0.00	0.00	0.00
Book value per share ($)	37.9%	1.41	1.17	1.85	2.60	4.45	7.03
Employees	60.5%	75	89	133	193	295	800

1995 YEAR-END
Debt ratio: 8.5%
Return on equity: 17.9%
Cash (mil.): $45
Current ratio: 2.59
Long-term debt (mil.): $0
No. of shares (mil.): 46
Dividends
  Yield: —
  Payout: —
Market value (mil.): $573

ADAPTEC, INC

OVERVIEW

Adaptec may operate in the periphery on your desktop, but it's right in the middle of several computer industry hot spots. Based in Milpitas, California, Adaptec makes small computer system interface (SCSI, pronounced "scuzzy") systems, which are used to connect peripherals to computers. It also produces input/output (I/O) software and Fast Ethernet networking devices, which help route information through computer systems. Adaptec's sales are buzzing as high-performance peripherals (such as memory drives, recordable CDs, and scanners) and PC networks soar in popularity.

Formed in 1981, Adaptec shipped its first SCSI product in 1983. It went public in 1986 and shipped its first SCSI host adapter a year later. In 1989 the company developed ASPI (advanced SCSI programming interface), which Novell adopted for its NetWare networking software in 1991 and IBM adopted for the OS/2 operating system in 1992.

Adaptec abandoned its laser printer controller business in 1993 because of competition. Also that year it acquired Trantor Systems (SCSI host adapters) and started a subsidiary in Tokyo. The next year Adaptec launched a new line of SCSI host adapters and the first drive-manager chip for high-volume hard drives.

The company has been positioning itself for the future through acquisitions, which in 1995 included Future Domain (which makes CD-ROM connection devices), Trillium Research (maker of Apple-compatible connection devices), and Incat Systems Software USA (which produces I/O software for recordable CD peripherals). In 1996 Adaptec bought Western Digital's Connectivity Systems Group and Corel's CD Creator software, agreed to buy computer networking devices maker Cogent Data Technologies, and purchased software maker Data Kinesis.

WHO

Chairman: John G. Adler, age 59, $1,052,135 pay
President and CEO: F. Grant Saviers, age 51, $1,001,462 pay
COO: Robert M. Stephens, age 50
VP and General Manager: John D. Hamm, age 36, $490,461 pay
VP Finance, CFO, and Assistant Secretary: Paul G. Hansen, age 48, $489,115 pay
VP Operations: Sam Kazarian, age 53, $458,212 pay
VP and General Manager: Subramanian Sundaresh, age 39, $420,57 7 pay
VP and Treasurer: Christopher G. O'Meara, age 38
VP Administration (HR): Daniel W. Bowman, age 51
Auditors: Price Waterhouse LLP

WHERE

HQ: 691 S. Milpitas Blvd., Milpitas, CA 95035
Phone: 408-945-8600   **Fax:** 408-262-2533
Web site: http://www.adaptec.com

WHAT

Selected Products	Subsidiaries
Accelerator cards	Adaptec Europe SA
ASPI software	(Belgium)
CD software	Adaptec GmbH (Germany)
Enterprise computing	Adaptec Japan Ltd.
systems	Adaptec SA (France)
Fast Ethernet cards	Adaptec Singapore
Mass storage controllers	Adaptec U.K.
Network interface cards	
SCSI host adapters	
Wireless networking	
connectors	

KEY COMPETITORS

3Com	Lannet
Asante	Microware Systems
CMD Technology	Olicom
3Com	Parity Systems
FORE Systems	Standard Microsystems
Fujitsu	U.S. Robotics
IBM	

HOW MUCH

Nasdaq symbol: ADPT FYE: March 31	Annual Growth	1991	1992	1993	1994	1995	1996
Sales ($ mil.)	38.6%	128.9	150.3	311.3	372.2	466.2	659.3
Net income ($ mil.)	53.3%	12.2	14.6	49.4	59.0	93.4	103.4
Income as % of sales	—	9.5%	9.7%	15.9%	15.9%	20.0%	15.7%
Earnings per share ($)	44.5%	0.30	0.35	0.96	1.10	1.70	1.89
Stock price – high ($)[1]	—	6.03	4.84	15.50	19.94	24.38	48.38
Stock price – low ($)[1]	—	2.22	2.13	4.28	9.25	14.00	21.75
Stock price – close ($)[1]	77.8%	2.31	4.38	13.00	19.88	23.63	41.00
P/E – high	—	20	14	16	18	14	26
P/E – low	—	7	6	5	8	8	12
Dividends per share ($)	—	0.00	0.00	0.00	0.00	0.00	0.00
Book value per share ($)	31.9%	2.42	2.82	4.44	5.69	7.19	9.66
Employees	26.8%	644	721	1,316	1,582	1,697	2,111

[1] Stock prices are for the prior calendar year.

1996 YEAR-END
Debt ratio: 9.5%
Return on equity: 23.4%
Cash (mil.): $296
Current ratio: 3.57
Long-term debt (mil.): $4
No. of shares (mil.): 53
Dividends
  Yield: —
  Payout: —
Market value (mil.): $2,174
R&D as % of sales: 13.3%

ADVENT SOFTWARE, INC.

OVERVIEW

Tracking investments is old hat to Advent. The San Francisco-based company is a leading provider of software products that automate and integrate the investment management process. Advent offers a broad range of products, including software for trading and order management (Moxy), handling of client accounts and contacts (Axys and Qube), and major portfolio management and accounting (WinDx). Advent also offers consulting, systems integration, programming, and training to support its products. The company's customers include investment advisors, brokerage firms, banks, universities, and corporations. Cofounder and CEO Stephanie DiMarco owns about 18% of the company.

DiMarco was a financial analyst in her early 20s when she was asked to oversee the job of putting back-office operations on computer. The IBM PC came out soon afterword, and DiMarco foresaw a promising market, starting Advent in 1985 with programmer Steve Strand. The following year the company sold its first product, Professional Portfolio, designed to help small and mid-size investment firms with accounting, compliance, and record keeping. Annual sales were over $4 million by 1990. The company introduced Axys, the first Windows-based portfolio management system software, in 1993. That year DiMarco bought out Strand. In 1994 and 1995 the company added software for investment firms of all sizes and for a broader range of functions, with new products including Axys Advantage (for small investment managers) and Geneva (a high-end, portfolio management system for complex global accounting systems).

Advent went public in late 1995. The next year the company bought Data Exchange, Inc., (a maker of portfolio and trade order software) for $4.8 million.

WHO

Chairman, President, and CEO: Stephanie G. DiMarco, age 38
CFO: Irv H. Lichtenwald, age 40
VP Sales and Professional Services: Peter M. Caswell, age 39
VP Technology: Lily S. Chang, age 47
VP Marketing: John J. Griffin, age 45
Manager Human Resource: Lisa Ebersole
Auditors: Coopers & Lybrand LLP

WHERE

HQ: 301 Brannan St., 6th Fl., San Francisco, CA 94107-1849
Phone: 415-543-7696   **Fax:** 415-543-5070
Web site: http://www.advent.com

WHAT

	1995 Sales	
	$ mil.	% of total
License	12.0	46
Maintenance & other	10.0	39
Professional services & other	4.0	15
Total	**26.0**	**100**

Selected Products
Axys (Windows-based portfolio management)
Axys Advantage (investment management for small investment managers)
Geneva (high-end portfolio management system for complex global accounting requirements)
Moxy (trading and order management)
Qube (client contact and management)
WinDx (portfolio accounting)

Selected Services
Consulting
Programming
Systems integration
Training

KEY COMPETITORS

Applix
Best Programs
Checkfree
CSK
Melson Technologies
PMC International
SS&C Technologies
SunGard Data Systems
Symix
Thomson Corp.

HOW MUCH

Nasdaq symbol: ADVS FYE: December 31	Annual Growth	1990	1991	1992	1993	1994	1995
Sales ($ mil.)	34.9%	—	—	10.6	16.2	20.1	26.0
Net income ($ mil.)	51.8%	—	—	0.8	1.3	1.1	2.8
Income as % of sales	—	—	—	7.2%	7.8%	5.3%	10.9%
Earnings per share ($)	46.5%	—	—	0.14	0.24	0.17	0.44
Stock price – high ($)	—	—	—	—	—	—	24.75
Stock price – low ($)	—	—	—	—	—	—	14.00
Stock price – close ($)	—	—	—	—	—	—	17.75
P/E – high	—	—	—	—	—	—	56
P/E – low	—	—	—	—	—	—	32
Dividends per share ($)	—	—	—	—	—	—	0.00
Book value per share ($)	—	—	—	—	—	—	5.03
Employees	21.0%	—	—	—	144	173	211

1995 YEAR-END
Debt ratio: 0.0%
Return on equity: 8.5%
Cash (mil.): $35
Current ratio: 4.20
Long-term debt (mil.): $0
No. of shares (mil.): 7
Dividends
  Yield: —
  Payout: —
Market value (mil.): $122
R&D as % of sales: 16.2%

ALTERA CORPORATION

OVERVIEW

Altera's success is highly logical. The San Jose, California-based company is a leading maker of high-density programmable logic devices (PLDs) — standard integrated circuits that customers program using software also provided by Altera. The company's products, based on complementary metal-oxide semiconductor (CMOS) technology, require less power than other chips and are used by more than 23,000 customers worldwide, (primarily makers of communications, computer, and industrial equipment). The chips are gaining popularity over custom logic chips because they allow manufacturers to cut development costs and time to market.

The company was formed in 1983 by a group of former Fairchild Semiconductor managers, including Rodney Smith, a British-born applications engineer who is Altera's chairman. In 1984 the business became Altera Corp. (Altera is short for "alterable") and introduced its first generation of chips. The company went public in 1988 and bought a minority interest in Cypress Semiconductor's wafer fabrication facility.

Altera introduced new generations of chips in 1988, 1991, and 1992. The company faltered in 1992 when business in Japan slowed, and aggressive pricing by rivals led Altera to drop its chip prices. In late 1994 Altera acquired Intel's PLD business, increasing the company's market share to 20%.

In 1995 Altera introduced the MAX 9000 family of erasable PLDs. That year the company's sales more than doubled on the strength of its MAX 7000 family of erasable PLDs. The chip's popularity was spurred by a 30% price drop.

Altera introduced the industry's largest-capacity chip — the 10K100, which has 10 million transistors — in 1996.

WHO

Chairman, President, and CEO: Rodney Smith, age 55, $817,814 pay
VP Operations: Denis Berlan, age 46, $490,689 pay
VP Sales: Peter Smyth, age 58, $465,525 pay
VP Development Engineering: Clive McCarthy, age 49, $440,361 pay
VP Administration: Paul Newhagen, age 46, $436,322 pay
VP Finance and CFO: Nathan Sarkisian, age 37
VP Human Resources: John R. Fitzhenry, age 46
Auditors: Price Waterhouse LLP

WHERE

HQ: 2610 Orchard Pkwy., San Jose, CA 95134-2020
Phone: 408-894-7000   **Fax:** 408-428-0463
Web site: http://www.altera.com

WHAT

	1995 Sales
	% of total
Communications	55
Computer	17
Industrial	17
Other	11
Total	**100**

Selected Products
Development system software (MAX+PLUS II)
Classic family (general-purpose PLDs)
FLASHlogic
FLEX family
Function-specific PLDs
Integrated circuits
MAX family

KEY COMPETITORS

AMD	Lattice	SGS-Thomson
Atmel	Semiconductor	Texas
Cypress	LSI Logic	Instruments
Semiconductor	Microchip	Toshiba
Integrated	Technology	Xilinx
Device	Motorola	Zilog
Technology	National	
	Semiconductor	

HOW MUCH

Nasdaq symbol: ALTR FYE: December 31	Annual Growth	1990	1991	1992	1993	1994	1995
Sales ($ mil.)	38.7%	78.3	106.9	101.5	140.3	198.8	401.6
Net income ($ mil.)	45.3%	13.4	17.8	11.5	21.2	14.6	86.9
Income as % of sales	—	17.1%	16.7%	11.3%	15.1%	7.3%	21.6%
Earnings per share ($)	41.2%	0.34	0.44	0.28	0.51	0.34	1.91
Stock price – high ($)	—	7.44	14.25	18.00	16.81	21.56	70.88
Stock price – low ($)	—	3.38	4.56	4.06	5.94	10.81	19.63
Stock price – close ($)	56.0%	5.38	14.13	6.44	16.38	20.94	49.75
P/E – high	—	22	32	64	33	63	37
P/E – low	—	10	10	15	12	32	10
Dividends per share ($)	—	0.00	0.00	0.00	0.00	0.00	0.00
Book value per share ($)	30.1%	1.57	2.06	2.38	2.98	3.68	5.86
Employees	18.9%	370	446	477	527	667	881

1995 YEAR-END
Debt ratio: 55.4%
Return on equity: 42.0%
Cash (mil.): $365
Current ratio: 3.02
Long-term debt (mil.): $256
No. of shares (mil.): 44
Dividends
  Yield: —
  Payout: —
Market value (mil.): $2,167
R&D as % of sales: 8.4%

AMERICAN POWER CONVERSION

OVERVIEW

American Power Conversion (APC) believes in "better safe than sorry." The West Kingston, Rhode Island-based company is the leading maker of uninterruptible power supplies (UPSs) and surge protectors, devices that protect information on computers from power surges or outages. APC's products are sold through computer distributors such as Ingram Micro (which accounts for about 10% of sales).

Company VPs Emanuel Landsman and Neil Rasmusssen and director Ervin Lyon founded APC in 1981 to make solar-powered products. To keep from going under in 1982, however, the company started making lead backup batteries, used mainly in PCs. The market was then too small to attract the notice of big-league electronics firms, yet required too much sophistication to allow just any battery company to enter. APC went public in 1988 and the next year established a European subsidiary, APCE, in Paris. Chairman Rodger Dowdell owns 10.5% of APC; Rasmussen owns 6%.

Emerging countries, in which power is often unreliable, are providing a hot market for APC. In 1994 the company's plant in Galway, Ireland, began operating, serving Europe and Russia.

APC's growth is also being fueled by the global proliferation of computers and power-sensitive devices for telecommunications and data storage. The company lost ground in 1995 when IBM formed an alliance with rival Best Power and when Hewlett-Packard began producing its own UPSs. However, as the only power supply maker certified for Microsoft's Windows 95, APC increased production in 1995 in anticipation of its release.

In 1996 APC's market toughened, and the company's growth shifted to the low-margin home PC market. That year APC introduced a travel-size surge protector, SurgeArrest Notebook, for mobile computing.

WHO

Chairman, President, and CEO: Rodger B. Dowdell Jr., age 46, $608,000 pay
CFO: Donald M. Muir, age 39
VP Engineering: Neil E. Rasmussen, age 41, $403,180 pay
VP Operations and Treasurer: Edward W. Machala, age 42, $403,180 pay
VP Worldwide Business Development: David P. Vieau
VP and Clerk: Emanuel E. Landsman, age 59, $182,600 pay
VP Marketing: John P. DiPippo, age 30
Manager Human Resources: Lisa Defruscio
Auditors: KPMG Peat Marwick LLP

WHERE

HQ: American Power Conversion Corporation, 132 Fairgrounds Rd., West Kingston, RI 02892
Phone: 401-789-5735 **Fax:** 401-788-2710
Web site: http://www.apcc.com

	1995 Sales		1995 Operating Income	
	$ mil.	% of total	$ mil.	% of total
US	310.7	60	69.8	67
Other countries	204.6	40	33.9	33
Total	**515.3**	**100**	**103.7**	**100**

WHAT

Selected Products

Protection Devices
Electrical surge protection products
Power conditioning products
Uninterruptible power supply products

Software
PowerChute plus

KEY COMPETITORS

Chloride Group	General Signal
Emerson	Hewlett-Packard
Exide Electronics	MagneTek
Fiskars OY AB	Silcon
General Electric	

HOW MUCH

Nasdaq symbol: APCC FYE: December 31	Annual Growth	1990	1991	1992	1993	1994	1995
Sales ($ mil.)	54.2%	59.2	93.6	157.5	250.3	378.3	515.3
Net income ($ mil.)	49.5%	9.3	15.6	27.8	48.6	71.3	69.5
Income as % of sales	—	15.7%	16.7%	17.7%	19.4%	18.8%	13.5%
Earnings per share ($)	46.4%	0.11	0.17	0.31	0.53	0.77	0.74
Stock price – high ($)	—	2.42	7.06	14.38	24.75	30.50	25.88
Stock price – low ($)	—	0.61	1.78	5.19	10.50	14.50	9.13
Stock price – close ($)	33.0%	2.28	6.69	14.00	23.75	16.38	9.50
P/E – high	—	22	42	46	47	40	35
P/E – low	—	6	11	17	20	19	12
Dividends per share ($)	—	0.00	0.00	0.00	0.00	0.00	0.00
Book value per share ($)	59.6%	0.30	0.51	0.87	1.45	2.29	3.11
Employees	49.2%	316	461	731	914	1,990	2,340

1995 YEAR-END
Debt ratio: 0.0%
Return on equity: 27.7%
Cash (mil.): $39
Current ratio: 5.36
Long-term debt (mil.): $0
No. of shares (mil.): 93
Dividends
 Yield: —
 Payout: —
Market value (mil.): $886
R&D as % of sales: 2.6%
Advertising as % of sales: 4.5%

ANACOMP, INC.

OVERVIEW

Anacomp doesn't care about the big picture. The Indianapolis-based company, fresh out of bankruptcy, is the world's leading maker of COM (computer output microfilm) systems, which convert digital information to microfilm and microfiche. Other products include magnetic storage tape and cartridges. Though it also makes CD systems used to record, store, and retrieve digital information, Anacomp has lagged somewhat in its efforts to expand beyond outdated micrographics technology.

Anacomp was founded in 1968 by Ronald Palmara, a computer engineer and former Purdue University professor, to develop micrographics products. He led the company in a foray into the banking software business, but the project went way over budget and was the subject of numerous delays. Palmara was diagnosed with cancer in 1982, and 2 years later, in failing health, he named Louis Ferrero to replace him as CEO. Palmara died in 1985 and the company lost money for the 3rd straight year.

Ferrero canceled the banking software project, sold Anacomp's stake in a TV station, and bought microfilm equipment companies DatagraphiX (from General Dynamics) and Consolidated Micrographics. In 1988 the company bought Xidex, a struggling microfilm and disk maker, for $400 million but was unable to turn the manufacturer around. In the early 1990s Anacomp began to look for more-sophisticated applications for its COM products. It acquired Graham Magnetics, a maker of computer tape products, in 1994. The next year Lang Lowrey succeeded Ferrero as CEO.

Still reeling from its purchase of Xidex, Anacomp went through bankruptcy protection in 1996. That year an investor group, Questor Partners Fund (including financier Dan Lufkin and turnaround titan Jay Alix), offered to buy up to 44% of Anacomp's stock.

WHO

Chairman, President, and CEO: P. Lang Lowrey III, age 42, $377,442 pay
VC: Richard D. Jackson
President, U.S. Group: Thomas R. Simmons, age 48, $272,874 pay
President, European Group: Hasso Jenss, age 52, $244,777 pay
President, Anacomp Worldwide Operations Group: Thomas W. Murrel, age 55
President, International Group: Gary M. Roth, age 53
EVP and CFO: Donald L. Viles, age 49
VP Human Resources: Patricia J. Wilkins
Auditors: Andersen Worldwide

WHERE

HQ: 11550 N. Meridian St., PO Box 40888, Indianapolis, IN 46240
Phone: 317-844-9666 **Fax:** 317-848-1360
Web site: http://www.anacomp.com

Anacomp markets its products in 65 countries.

	1995 Sales	
	$ mil.	% of total
US	404.2	68
Other countries	187.0	32
Total	**591.2**	**100**

WHAT

Selected Products
CD-ROM systems
Computer output microfilm systems
Open reel tape
Recordable CDs
Tape cartridges
Writable/erasable magneto-optical disks

KEY COMPETITORS

A. Messerli	Fuji Photo
AGFA	Hoechst
BASF	Imation
Eastman Kodak	Micrographic Technology
First Image	Rexham Graphics

HOW MUCH

Nasdaq symbol: ANCO FYE: September 30	Annual Growth	1990	1991	1992	1993	1994	1995
Sales ($ mil.)	(1.9%)	652.2	635.4	628.9	590.2	592.6	591.2
Net income ($ mil.)	—	9.6	29.2	24.8	16.4	4.8	(240.5)
Income as % of sales	—	1.5%	4.6%	3.9%	2.8%	3.5%	—
Earnings per share ($)	—	0.20	0.64	0.58	0.39	0.10	(5.22)
Stock price – high ($)	—	4.75	4.63	5.38	4.63	4.25	2.38
Stock price – low ($)	—	1.38	1.25	3.00	2.38	1.75	0.02
Stock price – close ($)	(39.7%)	1.75	3.88	4.38	4.00	2.00	0.14
P/E – high	—	24	7	9	12	43	—
P/E – low	—	7	2	5	6	18	—
Dividends per share ($)	—	0.00	0.00	0.00	0.00	0.00	0.00
Book value per share ($)	20.9%	(1.58)	(0.67)	0.19	0.34	1.09	(4.08)
Employees	(6.4%)	5,000	4,600	4,500	4,200	4,400	3,600

1995 YEAR-END
Debt ratio: 100.0%
Return on equity: —
Cash (mil.): $19
Current ratio: 0.30
Long-term debt (mil.): $0
No. of shares (mil.): 46
Dividends
  Yield: —
  Payout: —
Market value (mil.): $7

ANALOG DEVICES, INC.

OVERVIEW

Analog Devices is IC hot. The company is a leading producer of integrated circuits (ICs); its biggest sellers are analog chips, which translate phenomena such as pressure, temperature, and sound into electronic signals. Its customers are primarily OEMs in the automotive, communications, computer, consumer electronics, medical and scientific instrumentation, and military/aerospace markets. Analog anticipates growing sales as multimedia technologies and wireless communications become more prevalent.

Analog was founded in 1965 by Ray Stata and Matthew Lorber and made operational amplifiers used to strengthen electrical signals. Lorber left the company after it went public in 1968. Analog began to expand, first into analog-to-digital converters that could be used for controlling machinery or for taking measurements. In 1969 it began funding research in semiconductors, and through the next decade it shifted to semiconductor manufacturing. Profits began to decline by the mid-1980s as Japanese competitors began to eat up market share. Analog looked for new ways to compete and saw opportunities in computer and communications products. In 1989 CEO Stata began investing heavily in voice processing technology.

Analog introduced its first digital signal processor chips for PCs in 1992. Two years later the company introduced a high-performance 32-bit chip used in multimedia applications.

Analog isn't subject to the whims of the computer market; less than 10% of the company's chips are used in PCs. With demand growing, in 1996 the company began converting a former Polaroid factory near Boston into a chip plant. That year Analog said it would build a new research and development facility in Tel Aviv, and it bought Mosaic Microsystems, a British developer of chips for wireless communications.

WHO

Chairman and CEO: Ray Stata, age 61, $1,197,441 pay
President and COO: Jerald G. Fishman, age 50, $1,159,679 pay
VP Sales: Brian P. McAloon, age 45, $483,082 pay
VP Finance and CFO: Joseph E. McDonough, age 48, $424,365 pay
VP Human Resources: Ross Brown, $173,598 pay
Auditors: Ernst & Young LLP

WHERE

HQ: One Technology Way, Norwood, MA 02062-9106
Phone: 617-329-4700   **Fax:** 617-326-8703
Web site: http://www.analog.com

WHAT

	1995 Sales
	% of total
Standard-linear ICs	64
System-level ICs	24
Assembled products	8
Hard disk drive ICs	4
Total	**100**

Selected Products

Standard-function Linear and Mixed-signal ICs	**System-level ICs**
Amplifiers	Linear-only devices
Analog signal-processing devices	Mixed-signal devices
Comparators	**Assembled Products**
Data converters	Hybrid products
Interface circuits	Multichip modules
Power management ICs	Printed-board modules
Voltage references	**Hard-disk Drive ICs**

KEY COMPETITORS

Brooktree
Burr-Brown
Cirrus Logic
Cyberguard
Exar
Hitachi
Linear Technology
Maxim
Integrated Products
Motorola
National Semiconductor
NEC
Sierra Semiconductor
Siliconix
Texas Instruments
Toshiba

HOW MUCH

NYSE symbol: ADI FYE: Last Saturday in October	Annual Growth	1990	1991	1992	1993	1994	1995
Sales ($ mil.)	14.2%	485.2	537.7	567.2	666.3	773.5	941.5
Net income ($ mil.)	—	(12.9)	8.2	14.9	44.5	74.5	119.3
Income as % of sales	—	—	1.5%	2.6%	6.7%	9.6%	12.7%
Earnings per share ($)	—	(0.13)	0.07	0.14	0.39	0.65	1.00
Stock price – high ($)	—	4.39	5.56	7.22	12.44	16.33	26.33
Stock price – low ($)	—	2.44	2.89	3.83	6.72	10.39	13.33
Stock price – close ($)	51.6%	2.94	4.22	7.22	10.94	15.61	23.58
P/E – high	—	—	76	52	32	25	26
P/E – low	—	—	39	27	17	16	13
Dividends per share ($)	—	0.00	0.00	0.00	0.00	0.00	0.00
Book value per share ($)	12.3%	3.25	3.32	3.47	3.91	4.63	5.81
Employees	1.0%	5,700	5,200	5,200	5,300	5,400	6,000

1995 YEAR-END
Debt ratio: 11.2%
Return on equity: 20.3%
Cash (mil.): $151
Current ratio: 2.07
Long-term debt (mil.): $80
No. of shares (mil.): 113
Dividends
  Yield: —
  Payout: —
Market value (mil.): $2,661
R&D as % of sales: 14.3%

ANALYSTS INTERNATIONAL

OVERVIEW

Analysts International Corporation (AiC) offers service with a :-). The Minneapolis-based company provides computer software-related services — including systems analysis and design, custom programming, and specialized training — to more than 700 corporate and government clients. IBM is its largest client, accounting for more than 10% of 1995 revenues. AiC maintains 27 branch offices in 19 states.

The company was founded in 1966 by Frederick Lang (current CEO) and Victor Benda (current president and COO), who had both worked at UNIVAC. Among the firm's earliest clients were Reliance Electric and the Jet Propulsion Laboratory. By AiC's 2nd full year of operation, it had exceeded $1 million in revenues. During the 1970s, as companies became increasingly dependent on computers for everything from data processing to inventory control, AiC continued to add branches and services. By the end of the decade it had 23 branches. In the 1980s the company provided its services to such clients as Ameritech, NationsBank, and Vulcan Chemicals.

AiC has continued to expand its client list during the 1990s, adding Cargill, Goodyear Tire & Rubber, IBM spin-off Lexmark International, and Owens-Corning.

In 1995 AiC added 280 new clients. It completed a major outsourcing agreement with U S WEST and created a new division, AiC TechWest, to handle the project. That year the company began providing consulting, programming, and technical support services to TransQuest, a joint venture between Delta Air Lines and NCR (formerly AT&T Global Information Solutions), and it won a new 2-year contract to provide technical services to IBM. AiC's earnings rose to $12.4 million on sales of $329.5 million in fiscal 1996.

WHO

Chairman and CEO: Frederick W. Lang, age 71, $556,956 pay
President and COO: Victor C. Benda, age 64, $489,780 pay
VP, Treasurer, and CFO: Gerald M. McGrath, age 56, $225,862 pay
VP Program Management: Richard A. Ferrera
VP National Marketing: George R. Zak
Secretary and General Counsel: Thomas R. Mahler, age 49, $225,862 pay
Payroll and Benefits Supervisor (HR): Lori Buegler
Auditors: Deloitte & Touche LLP

WHERE

HQ: Analysts International Corporation, 7615 Metro Blvd., Minneapolis, MN 55439-3050
Phone: 612-835-5900   **Fax:** 612-835-4924
Web site: http://www.analysts.com

AiC has offices in Canada, the UK, and the US.

WHAT

	1995 Sales % of total
Electronics	27
Telecommunications	17
Services	12
Manufacturing	11
Financial	7
Oil & chemical	6
Merchandising	4
Food	4
Insurance/health care	4
Power & utility	2
Transportation	2
Government	1
Other	3
Total	**100**

KEY COMPETITORS

Andersen Consulting
CGA
Computer Data Systems
Computer Horizons
Computer Task Group
DEC
IBM
Keane

HOW MUCH

Nasdaq symbol: ANLY FYE: June 30	Annual Growth	1990	1991	1992	1993	1994	1995
Sales ($ mil.)	15.2%	107.5	116.8	129.6	159.7	176.0	218.4
Net income ($ mil.)	13.5%	6.0	5.6	5.4	8.3	8.0	11.3
Income as % of sales	—	5.6%	4.8%	4.1%	5.2%	4.5%	5.2%
Earnings per share ($)	12.5%	0.86	0.79	0.76	1.15	1.10	1.55
Stock price – high ($)	—	15.67	12.17	17.33	23.83	20.75	33.00
Stock price – low ($)	—	6.67	7.92	10.33	15.00	14.50	19.75
Stock price – close ($)	25.9%	9.50	10.83	16.83	18.00	20.50	30.00
P/E – high	—	18	15	23	21	19	21
P/E – low	—	8	10	14	13	13	13
Dividends per share ($)	10.2%	0.32	0.37	0.37	0.40	0.48	0.52
Book value per share ($)	17.0%	2.84	3.28	3.69	4.48	5.14	6.22
Employees	13.3%	1,700	1,750	2,070	2,270	2,600	3,170

1995 YEAR-END
Debt ratio: 10.6%
Return on equity: 27.6%
Cash (mil.): $13
Current ratio: 3.33
Long-term debt (mil.): $5
No. of shares (mil.): 7
Dividends
  Yield: 1.7%
  Payout: 33.5%
Market value (mil.): $218

APPLIED MAGNETICS CORPORATION

OVERVIEW

Applied Magnetics has finally attracted a profit — its first this decade. The Goleta, California-based company manufactures recording heads for rigid disk drives, including standard ferrite heads and advanced thin-film and magnetoresistive heads. Conner Peripherals (acquired by Seagate in 1996) accounted for 41% of 1995 revenues, and Maxtor for 19%; Quantum Corp. and Western Digital are also important customers. Founder and chairman emeritus Harold Frank controls about 5.3% of the company's shares.

Frank started Applied Magnetics in 1957 as a manufacturer of magnetic tape recording heads. It went public 10 years later. Starting in the early 1970s, the company pioneered development of thin-film technology. With the popularization of the personal computer, Applied Magnetics became a major supplier of disk drive heads, with operations worldwide. It weathered the industry's shifts between periods of intense demand requiring increased manufacturing capacity and periods of slow PC sales and dampened demand. In 1988 the company acquired Magnetic Data, a Minnesota-based disk-drive maintenance firm.

Losses dogged Applied Magnetics through the first half of the 1990s. Heavy investment in magnetoresistive technology, manufacturing problems with thin-film heads, and a slump in the industry contributed to the losses. In 1993 the company restructured, cut its payroll, and sold its laser disk drive, magnetic data, and optical products units. In 1994 Applied Magnetics sold its tape-head operations to Seagate for $21.5 million.

The firm's 1995 profit was attributed to increased demand for thin-film products and implementation of operating efficiencies in 1994. Frank also stepped down as chairman in 1995 after heading the enterprise for 38 years.

WHO

Chairman, President, CEO, CFO, and Secretary: Craig D. Crisman, age 54, $62,500 pay
General Manager: John E. Ross, age 50, $252,968 pay
Corporate Controller: Peter T. Altavilla, age 42
Director Human Resources: David Swanson
Auditors: Andersen Worldwide

WHERE

HQ: 75 Robin Hill Rd., Goleta, CA 93117
Phone: 805-683-5353   **Fax:** 805-967-8227
Web site: http://www.mol-usa.com/recruit/app-mag.htm

	1995 Sales	
	$ mil.	% of total
US	271.9	93
Other countries	20.7	7
Total	**292.6**	**100**

WHAT

Selected Products
Ferrite disk heads
Magnetoresistive (MR) disk heads
Thin-film disk heads

KEY COMPETITORS

Alps Electric
Fujitsu
IBM
NEC
Read-Rite
Seagate
TDK
Yamaha

HOW MUCH

NYSE symbol: APM FYE: September 30	Annual Growth	1990	1991	1992	1993	1994	1995
Sales ($ mil.)	(4.5%)	368.3	455.5	297.9	335.9	275.9	292.6
Net income ($ mil.)	—	(10.0)	(18.3)	(25.1)	(43.7)	(52.7)	1.7
Income as % of sales	—	—	—	—	—	—	0.6%
Earnings per share ($)	—	(0.62)	(1.12)	(1.51)	(2.17)	(2.39)	0.08
Stock price – high ($)	—	15.00	13.00	11.88	14.50	7.50	19.00
Stock price – low ($)	—	6.38	4.38	5.00	4.88	2.13	2.50
Stock price – close ($)	17.3%	8.38	5.75	10.50	5.50	3.50	18.63
P/E – high	—	—	—	—	—	—	238
P/E – low	—	—	—	—	—	—	31
Dividends per share ($)	—	0.00	0.00	0.00	0.00	0.00	0.00
Book value per share ($)	(14.9%)	10.33	9.16	7.60	6.84	4.46	4.60
Employees	(12.0%)	—	9,183	7,407	7,259	5,531	5,500

1995 YEAR-END
Debt ratio: 40.2%
Return on equity: 1.7%
Cash (mil.): $48
Current ratio: 0.96
Long-term debt (mil.): $3
No. of shares (mil.): 23
Dividends
  Yield: —
  Payout: —
Market value (mil.): $420
R&D as % of sales: 11.5%

APPLIX, INC.

OVERVIEW

Master of the quick change, Westboro, Massachusetts-based Applix makes real-time software tools and applications. Its products let users access, analyze, and communicate rapidly changing information, such as stock market data or database information. The company is the leading provider of real-time systems in the financial services market (including securities trading), which accounts for nearly half its revenues. Another big customer is the US Army, which uses the company's Applixware system for command and control activities.

Applix was founded in 1983 by Indian immigrant and Data General veteran Jit Saxena to develop and market UNIX-based software applications. The company introduced its first offering, office automation product Alis, in 1986. Aster*x, its next generation of UNIX software, was released in 1991 and accounted for over half the company's revenue. Applix entered the real-time software market in 1993 with Applixware, which was based on the Aster*x technology but had additional applications and increased emphasis on real-time decision support capabilities. The costs of rolling out the new software led to a loss, but in less than a year Applix had grabbed the top spot in the securities market.

In 1994 the company introduced Applix Real Time, which incorporated live data feeds into spreadsheets, and formed marketing relationships with users such as Reuters and Dow Jones. The company acquired customer information management software maker Target Systems the following year.

It is expanding its products in the network computing market by developing an application that will deliver Applixware through Sun Microsystems' Java Internet language.

WHO

President and CEO: Jitendra S. Saxena, age 50, $340,687 pay
EVP Sales and Marketing: Richard J. Davis, age 52, $288,081 pay
VP Finance and Administration, CFO, and Treasurer: Patrick J. Scannell Jr., age 42, $190,475 pay
VP Product Development: Craig Cervo, age 49, $190,475 pay
VP Technology: Barry M. Zane, age 40, $158,737 pay
Director Human Resources: Betty Kochergin
Auditors: Coopers & Lybrand L.L.P.

WHERE

HQ: 112 Turnpike Rd., Westborough, MA 01581-2831
Phone: 508-870-0300   **Fax:** 508-366-9313
Web site: http://www.applix.com

WHAT

Selected Products

Applix Enterprise
Applix HelpDesk (customer support system)
Applix Service (problem-management application)

Applixware Real Time Application Server
Applix Data (provides access to regional database management systems)
Applix Real Time (links live data feeds to spreadsheets)

Applixware Real Time Desk
Applix Builder (creates real-time decision support applications)
Applix HTML Author (Web document developer)
Applix Presents (presentation tool)
Applix Spreadsheets (spreadsheet with charts, graphs, and financial functions)
Applix Words (customizable word processor)

KEY COMPETITORS

Advent Software	Microsoft
Astea Intl	Novell
Clarify	Oracle
IBM	Remedy
Investment Intelligence	Scopus Technology
Systems	Sybase
MarketArts	

HOW MUCH

Nasdaq symbol: APLX FYE: December 31	Annual Growth	1990	1991	1992	1993	1994	1995
Sales ($ mil.)	37.8%	6.5	7.1	11.8	12.2	18.5	32.3
Net income ($ mil.)	7.0%	0.5	0.0	0.8	(0.4)	1.4	0.7
Income as % of sales	—	8.0%	0.5%	6.6%	—	7.6%	2.1%
Earnings per share ($)	(4.9%)	0.09	0.01	0.12	(0.34)	0.20	0.07
Stock price – high ($)	—	—	—	—	—	6.63	28.75
Stock price – low ($)	—	—	—	—	—	4.75	6.19
Stock price – close ($)	—	—	—	—	—	6.50	27.25
P/E – high	—	—	—	—	—	33	411
P/E – low	—	—	—	—	—	24	88
Dividends per share ($)	—	—	—	—	—	0.00	0.00
Book value per share ($)	—	—	—	—	—	0.49	0.44
Employees	34.2%	—	—	—	130	135	234

1995 YEAR-END
Debt ratio: 0.7%
Return on equity: 7.3%
Cash (mil.): $25
Current ratio: 2.01
Long-term debt (mil.): $0
No. of shares (mil.): 21
Dividends
 Yield: —
 Payout: —
Market value (mil.): $582
R&D as % of sales: 12.9%

ASCEND COMMUNICATIONS, INC.

OVERVIEW

Ascend hooked its rising star to workplace changes, but it's now going at warp speed as it rides the growth of the Internet, which now constitutes about 30% of its business. The Alameda, California-based firm makes remote networking access products that allow users to dial up a central computer from home, on the road, or in field offices. Its gadgetry — mainly network access equipment — works with existing digital and analog networks by adjusting the bandwidth, which controls information traffic, as needed. Ascend's rapid growth has come from providing products to Internet service providers, including UUNET and BBN, and telecommunications companies, including AT&T and MCI.

Ascend was founded in 1989 by Robert Ryan and 3 former employees of Hayes Microcomputer to build connecting devices for Integrated Service Digital Network phone lines. When companies were slow to embrace ISDN, Ryan redirected the company to create videoconferencing products. The company launched Multiband (its first product line) in 1991, MAX in 1992, and the Pipeline series in 1993. Ascend went public in 1994, and the company shifted away from its focus on the videoconferencing access market toward remote and Internet access. Ryan stepped down as chairman and CEO for health reasons in 1995.

To bolster its top-selling MAX line, in 1995 the company purchased DaynaLINK remote access products and related technology from Dayna Communications. The next year Ascend announced 2 acquisitions: Morning Star Technologies, a provider of Internet security, and NetStar, a maker of high-speed computer switches. The company also teamed with rival Cisco Systems in 1996 to develop technology to ease the flow of traffic on the Internet.

WHO

President and CEO: Mory Ejabat, age 46, $463,103 pay
VP Finance and CFO: Robert K. Dahl, age 55, $401,803 pay
SVP International Sales and General Manager International Operations: Curtis N. Sanford, age 37, $333,465 pay
SVP North American Sales: Michael Hendren, age 49, $331,029 pay
VP Engineering and Chief Technology Officer: Jeanette Symons, age 33, $283,000 pay
Manager Human Resources: Roy Rettberg
Auditors: Ernst & Young LLP

WHERE

HQ: 1275 Harbor Bay Pkwy., Alameda, CA 94502
Phone: 510-769-6001   **Fax:** 510-814-2300
Web site: http://www.ascend.com

WHAT

	1995 Sales
	% of total
MAX products	63
Pipeline products	20
Multiband products	15
Other	2
Total	**100**

Selected Products
MAX (WAN access and integrated voice, video, and data access)
Pipeline products (telecommuting, remote office access, and Internet access)
Multiband products (videoconferencing networks)

KEY COMPETITORS

3Com	Global Village
ADTRAN	GTI
Bay Networks	Motorola
Cabletron	Newbridge Networks
Cisco Systems	Northern Telecom
Datapoint	Shiva
Gandalf Technologies	U.S. Robotics
General DataComm	Zoom Telephonics

HOW MUCH

Nasdaq symbol: ASND FYE: December 31	Annual Growth	1990	1991	1992	1993	1994	1995
Sales ($ mil.)	331.5%	0.1	3.2	7.2	16.2	39.3	149.6
Net income ($ mil.)	—	(3.1)	(2.4)	(3.8)	1.3	8.7	30.6
Income as % of sales	—	—	—	—	8.3%	22.1%	20.4%
Earnings per share ($)	274.2%	—	—	—	0.02	0.09	0.28
Stock price – high ($)	—	—	—	—	—	5.56	40.63
Stock price – low ($)	—	—	—	—	—	1.41	4.94
Stock price – close ($)	—	—	—	—	—	5.09	40.56
P/E – high	—	—	—	—	—	59	145
P/E – low	—	—	—	—	—	15	18
Dividends per share ($)	—	—	—	—	—	0.00	0.00
Book value per share ($)	—	—	—	—	—	0.46	2.69
Employees	86.9%	—	—	—	87	115	304

1995 YEAR-END
Debt ratio: 0.0%
Return on equity: 18.0%
Cash (mil.): $211
Current ratio: 6.98
Long-term debt (mil.): $0
No. of shares (mil.): 110
Dividends
  Yield: —
  Payout: —
Market value (mil.): $4,465
R&D as % of sales: 6.4%

ATMEL CORPORATION

OVERVIEW

Atmel has the memory of a pachyderm and the logic of a Vulcan. The San Jose-based integrated circuit maker produces nonvolatile memory chips (ICs that retain information without power) and logic chips (which process information). Its customers include OEMs in the automotive, avionics, computer, industrial instrument, and telecommunications markets. Motorola accounts for about 17% of Atmel's revenues. Chairman George Perlegos and his brother Gust, a VP, own 12% of the company.

A former design engineer for Intel and co-founder of chip maker Seeq Technology, George Perlegos founded Atmel (short for Advanced Technology for Memory and Logic) in 1984. The enterprise started with a $30,000 investment and a $5.1 million design contract from General Instrument, soon adding military and blue-chip corporate contracts. Atmel bought a wafer plant in Colorado Springs from Honeywell in 1989. The company went public in 1991, the same year it introduced the first 3-volt "flash" memory.

Atmel built its business by developing fast, power-efficient chips — perfect for portable electronics. The company acquired Concurrent Logic, a maker of field programmable gate arrays (a user-programmable chip), in 1993. A year later Atmel became the #1 producer of electrically erasable programmable ROM chips when it bought Seeq's chip business.

In 1995 the company announced a new process to produce wireless logic chips.

In an effort to strengthen its product line, in 1995 Atmel licensed SRAM (static random access memory) technology from Paradigm Technology for use in creating multimedia chips. It purchased RISC technology (which uses shorter instruction sets for faster processing) from Norwegian chip maker Nordic VLSI in 1996.

WHO

Chairman, President, and CEO: George Perlegos, age 46, $403,538 pay
VP and General Manager: Gust Perlegos, age 48, $350,462 pay
VP Technology: Tsung-Ching Wu, age 45, $316,486 pay
VP Finance and Administration and CFO: Kris Chellam, age 45, $293,252 pay
VP; General Manager, ASIC Operations: Jack Peckham, age 54, $283,416 pay
VP Manufacturing: Ralph Bohannon
VP Planning and Information Systems: Mikes N. Sisois, age 50
VP Marketing: B. Jeffrey Katz, age 52
Director Human Resources: Valerie Menager
Auditors: Coopers & Lybrand L.L.P.

WHERE

HQ: 2325 Orchard Pkwy., San Jose, CA 95131
Phone: 408-441-0311   **Fax:** 408-436-4200
Web site: http://www.atmel.com

WHAT

Selected Products

Logic Products
Application-specific integrated circuits (ASICs)
Erasable programmable logic devices (EPLDs)
Field programmable gate arrays (FPGAs)
Microcontrollers

Nonvolatile Memory Products
Electrically erasable programmable read-only memories (EEPROMS)
Erasable programmable read-only memories (EPROMS)
Flash memories

KEY COMPETITORS

Altera	Integrated Silicon	National
AMD	Solution	Semiconductor
Catalyst	Intel	Orbit
Semiconductor	Lattice	Semiconductor
Cirrus Logic	Semiconductor	VLSI Technology
Cypress	LSI Logic	Xicor
Semiconductor	Microchip	Xilinx
Integrated Device	Technology	
Technology		

HOW MUCH

Nasdaq symbol: ATML FYE: December 31	Annual Growth	1990	1991	1992	1993	1994	1995
Sales ($ mil.)	52.5%	76.9	120.4	139.8	221.7	375.1	634.2
Net income ($ mil.)	93.4%	4.2	10.3	13.9	30.0	59.5	113.7
Income as % of sales	—	5.5%	8.6%	10.0%	13.5%	15.8%	17.9%
Earnings per share ($)	66.8%	—	0.15	0.19	0.37	0.67	1.16
Stock price – high ($)	—	—	4.72	4.25	9.66	18.81	36.75
Stock price – low ($)	—	—	1.69	1.91	3.88	8.25	15.38
Stock price – close ($)	78.2%	—	2.22	4.09	8.66	16.75	22.38
P/E – high	—	—	31	22	26	28	32
P/E – low	—	—	11	10	10	12	13
Dividends per share ($)	—	—	0.00	0.00	0.00	0.00	0.00
Book value per share ($)	37.2%	—	1.71	1.88	2.63	3.95	6.06
Employees	24.2%	1,006	872	991	1,282	1,907	2,978

1995 YEAR-END
Debt ratio: 13.1%
Return on equity: 24.0%
Cash (mil.): $180
Current ratio: 1.57
Long-term debt (mil.): $89
No. of shares (mil.): 97
Dividends
  Yield: —
  Payout: —
Market value (mil.): $2,175
R&D as % of sales: 11.0%

ATTACHMATE CORPORATION

OVERVIEW

Attachmate does what it says; it connects computers by providing information access software and services to companies and government agencies worldwide. The Bellevue, Washington-based company concentrates on Internet and intranet (corporatewide systems) products and consulting services; through its Advantage Internet Services Consulting Group (ICG), it analyzes a client's current company process, then designs, implements, and supports a new intranet system to help employees share information. Attachmate has kicked around the idea of going public but remains the world's largest privately held software company, with chairman Frank Pritt holding a stake of about 70%.

Pritt founded Attachmate in late 1982. The day he quit his job at Harris Corp. to design a new product (desktop-to-mainframe connectivity software), Pritt saw his idea advertised by Digital Communications Associates (DGA) in a trade journal. Pritt decided to ignore the competition and start his company anyway, using his retirement money and becoming the sole stockholder. He pioneered a trade-in policy for competitors' products that became a standard in the industry. The privately held company grew rapidly (beating out competitors partly by offering more product features), realizing $5 million in sales in 1986. By 1991 sales were over $100 million.

Attachmate formed key partnerships with Lotus Development, Microsoft, Powersoft, and Novell in 1993. The following year the company achieved a major coup with its takeover of competitor DCA, which made Attachmate the 7th largest personal computer software company, with about a 35% share of the PC-to-IBM mainframe connectivity market.

In late 1995, in a key step in its aggressive pursuit of Internet and intranet market opportunities, Attachmate acquired the Wollongong Group, developer of the innovative Internet access software product EMISSARY.

In 1996 Attachmate introduced Open Mind 3.0, a suite of intranet software that includes electronic conferencing, document management, and publishing as well as the EMISSARY Desktop Browser that it picked up in the Wollongong acquisition.

WHO

Chairman: Frank W. Pritt, age 53
President and CEO: James Lindner
EVP and CFO: Bill Boisvert
EVP Worldwide Sales and Support: Barry Horn
EVP Products: Paul Rodwick
EVP Intranet Products: Herb Martin
VP Product Marketing: Bill Patterson
VP Strategic Relations: Todd Mavis
VP Human Resources: Pam Pride
Auditors: Deloitte & Touche LLP

WHERE

HQ: 3617 136 th Ave. SE, Bellevue, WA 98006
Phone: 206-644-4010   **Fax:** 206-747-9924
Web site: http://www.atm.com

Attachmate has offices in over 50 cities in North America. It also has locations in Australia, Austria, Belgium, Brazil, Denmark, Finland, France, Germany, Hong Kong, Ireland, Italy, Japan, Korea, Latin America, Malaysia, the Netherlands, Norway, Portugal, Singapore, South Africa, Spain, Sweden, Switzerland, and the UK.

WHAT

Selected Product Lines
EMISSARY (Internet access and publishing software)
EXTRA! (Intranet access)
IRMA/CIREL (Hardware connectivity adapters)
KEA! (connectivity solutions for DEC, UNIX, and Hewlett-Packard products)
NETWIZARD (software distribution/management)
OPENMIND (Intranet software)
PATHWAY TCP/IP (networking applications)
RALLY!/SELECT (IBM AS/400 application, database clients)
RLN (remote access software/hardware)
SUPPORTWARE! (enterprise support and consulting)

KEY COMPETITORS

Apertus
Banyan Systems
BBN
FTP Software
IBM
Locus Computing
Microsoft
Netscape
Network Management
Novell
Software AG
Walker Richer & Quinn
Wall Data

HOW MUCH

Private company FYE: December 31	Annual Growth	1990	1991	1992	1993	1994	1995
Sales ($ mil.)	37.5%	79.4	103.2	121.7	145.1	373.0	390.6
Employees	52.9%	—	—	560	993	1,100	2,000

AUTODESK, INC.

OVERVIEW

Autodesk is a cad no more. The San Rafael, California-based firm has signaled a broader product focus by changing its Nasdaq stock symbol from ACAD (a reference to its main product, AutoCAD) to ADSK. Autodesk is #1 in the design-automation software market and its AutoCAD software is used primarily by architects and engineers for design, modeling, drafting, and mapping. The company has also created a separate division for its multimedia group. The new division, Kinetix, develops products for film, games, and the World Wide Web.

John Walker founded Autodesk in 1982 as a diversified PC software supplier. The name came from a software application the company never succeeded in selling. But when Walker bought the software for AutoCAD (computer-aided design) from inventor Michael Riddle, Autodesk took off. While competitors went after more complex computer systems, Autodesk focused on PC software. When PC sales boomed in the early 1980s, the firm was there to take advantage of a growing software market. It went public in 1985.

Carol Bartz, a former Sun Microsystems executive, took over as CEO in 1992 and implemented a back-to-basics approach. She sold the company's interests in AMIX (an online information company) and terminated its support of Xanadu (an advanced database networking project) that year to focus on design automation.

In 1994 Walker resigned, and the firm lost a trade-secret lawsuit to Vermont Microsystems and was ordered to pay $25.5 million. (Autodesk has appealed.) The company launched Release 13 of AutoCAD in 1995. In 1996 Autodesk acquired software developer Creative Imaging Technologies in a bid to enter the interior decorating market.

WHO

Chairman, President, and CEO: Carol A. Bartz, age 47, $704,284 pay
VP Finance, Administration, and Data Publishing and CFO: Eric B. Herr, age 48, $434,926 pay
VP Mechanical CAD Market Group and Asia/Pacific: Dominic J. Gallello, age 41, $375,500 pay
VP Americas: Godfrey R. Sullivan, age 42, $364,858 pay
VP Europe: Michael E. Sutton, age 51, $312,306 pay
VP AEC/FM Market Group and Advanced Products Group, and Chief Technology Officer: John E. Lynch, age 39
VP Business Development and General Counsel: Marcia K. Sterling, age 52
VP Human Resources: Stephen McMahon, age 54
Auditors: Ernst & Young LLP

WHERE

HQ: 111 McInnis Pkwy., San Rafael, CA 94903
Phone: 415-507-5000   **Fax:** 415-507-5100
Web site: http://www.autodesk.com

WHAT

Selected Products

Design Automation
Computer-aided design software (AutoCAD Designer, AutoCAD LT, AutoCAD OEM, AutoCAD Release 13, AutoCAD Runtime Extension, AutoSketch, AutoSurf,)

Multimedia
Graphics software (3D Studio, 3D Studio MAX, AutoVision)

KEY COMPETITORS

3D Systems	Environmental	Parametric
Adobe	Systems	Technology
CAD/CAM	Research	PC DOCS
Solutions	Fractal Design	Sense 8
Caligari	IBM	Silicon Graphics
Computervision	Intergraph	Stratasys
Corel	KETIV	Structural
Dassault Aviation	Technologies	Dynamics
Documentum	Microsoft	Research
	Network Imaging	Visio Corp

HOW MUCH

Nasdaq symbol: ADSK FYE: January 31	Annual Growth	1991	1992	1993	1994	1995	1996
Sales ($ mil.)	18.1%	237.9	284.9	367.7	418.7	465.3	546.9
Net income ($ mil.)	9.1%	56.8	57.8	43.9	62.2	56.6	87.8
Income as % of sales	—	23.9%	20.3%	11.9%	14.8%	12.2%	16.1%
Earnings per share ($)	8.9%	1.15	1.15	0.88	1.25	1.14	1.76
Stock price – high ($)[1]	—	30.13	31.13	28.25	28.38	41.50	53.00
Stock price – low ($)[1]	—	16.00	14.75	11.63	18.50	21.13	31.25
Stock price – close ($)[1]	6.2%	25.38	17.25	23.13	22.50	39.63	34.25
P/E – high	—	26	27	32	23	36	30
P/E – low	—	14	13	13	15	19	18
Dividends per share ($)	3.7%	0.20	0.23	0.24	0.24	0.24	0.24
Book value per share ($)	10.6%	4.47	5.44	5.58	6.25	6.85	7.39
Employees	11.4%	1,102	1,272	1,565	1,788	1,788	1,894

[1] Stock prices are for the prior calendar year.

1996 YEAR-END
Debt ratio: 0.0%
Return on equity: 26.4%
Cash (mil.): $193
Current ratio: 2.41
Long-term debt (mil.): $0
No. of shares (mil.): 46
Dividends
  Yield: 0.7%
  Payout: 13.6%
Market value (mil.): $1,588
R&D as % of sales: 14.4%

BAAN COMPANY N.V.

OVERVIEW

Think "bond" and remove the "d" and you get Baan, a company that bonds its clients' works operations together with software. With dual headquarters in Menlo Park, California, and Ede, the Netherlands, Baan is a leading provider of open systems, client/server-based Enterprise Resource Planning (ERP) software (used to monitor and manage a company's operations); it is fighting Oracle to be the world's #2 ERP provider (after Germany's SAP). Baan's flagship TRITON products integrate such functions as distribution, finance, inventory, manufacturing, procurement, project management, sales, and transportation. Founder Jan Baan calls TRITON a "software bridge" — companies gather information, and then, using a relational database, apply the information throughout the company. A charitable foundation formed by Baan and his brother Paul owns 48% of the company; financier General Atlantic Partners owns 15%.

Jan Baan was a Dutch college dropout with a mediocre career (food-processing clerk, controller, accounting consultant), but he and his wife had saved a handsome sum from buying and selling several homes. In 1978, with $250,000, he started Baan Co., a consulting firm specializing in financial engineering. He began software development the next year to improve clients' factory efficiency.

Paul Baan joined the company in 1981, and it shipped its first software the next year. It began development of TRITON in 1987, rolling out the first products in 1989. Although initial US expansion efforts were unsuccessful, a $20-million contract with Boeing in 1994 led to the establishment of a 2nd headquarters in California. The company went public in 1995. In 1996 it acquired Canada's Berclain Group, a global leader in manufacturing scheduling software.

WHO

Chairman and CEO: Jan Baan, age 49
VC: J. G. Paul Baan, age 45
President and COO: Tom C. Tinsley, age 42
EVP Americas Operations: Amal M. Johnson, age 43
SVP Research and Development: Laurens van der Tang, age 30
VP Finance: Jan Westerhoud, age 43
VP Human Resources: Gerrit van Munster, age 32
General Counsel and Secretary: Wim H. Heijting, age 30
Auditors: Ernst & Young LLP

WHERE

HQ: Zonneoordlaan 17, 6710 BG, Ede, The Netherlands
Phone: +31-342-428-888   **Fax:** +31-342-428-822
US HQ: 4600 Bohannon Dr., Menlo Park, CA 94025
US Phone: 415-462-4949   **US Fax:** 415-462-4951
Web site: http://www.baan.com

WHAT

	1995 Sales	
	$ mil.	% of total
License	113.0	52
Maintenance & service	79.9	37
Hardware & other	23.3	11
Total	**216.2**	**100**

Selected Products	
TRITON Applications	TRITON OrgWare
Distribution	TRITON Tools
Enterprise	
Finance	**Selected Services**
Manufacturing	Education and training
Project	Project management and
Service	implementation
Transportation	Technical support

KEY COMPETITORS

Andersen	Dun &	SAP
Consulting	Bradstreet	Sybase
Computer	EDS	System Software
Associates	J. D. Edwards	Associates
Computron	Marcam	Wall Data
Software	Oracle	Wang
	PeopleSoft, Inc.	

HOW MUCH

Nasdaq symbol: BAANF FYE: December 31	Annual Growth	1990	1991	1992	1993	1994	1995
Sales ($ mil.)	44.9%	33.8	35.2	46.8	63.4	122.9	216.2
Net income ($ mil.)	—	(1.2)	1.3	6.8	(2.1)	1.2	15.3
Income as % of sales	—	—	3.7%	14.6%	—	1.0%	7.1%
Earnings per share ($)	—	(0.03)	0.04	0.20	(0.06)	0.03	0.34
Stock price – high ($)	—	—	—	—	—	—	24.56
Stock price – low ($)	—	—	—	—	—	—	10.63
Stock price – close ($)	—	—	—	—	—	—	22.63
P/E – high	—	—	—	—	—	—	72
P/E – low	—	—	—	—	—	—	31
Dividends per share ($)	—	—	—	—	—	—	0.00
Book value per share ($)	—	—	—	—	—	—	2.65
Employees	38.4%	—	—	—	796	943	1,525

1995 YEAR-END
Debt ratio: 1.9%
Return on equity: 15.3%
Cash (mil.): $36
Current ratio: 2.21
Long-term debt (mil.): $2
No. of shares (mil.): 43
Dividends
 Yield: —
 Payout: —
Market value (mil.): $976
R&D as % of sales: 8.6%

BBN CORPORATION

OVERVIEW

Adopting a ball as a new logo is great when things are bouncing along, but BBN's only upward kick in 3 years resulted from the 1995 sale of subsidiary LightStream Corp., a maker of ATM network switches. Cambridge, Massachusetts-based BBN (formerly Bolt Beranek and Newman) is investing much of the $80 million in proceeds in its internetworking products and services. BBN also produces commercial speech recognition software and performs structural acoustic design consulting. CEO George Conrades implemented a major restructuring in 1996 to focus more upon Internet-related products and services.

Founded in 1948 by MIT professors Richard Bolt and Leo Beranek (who were soon joined by Robert Newman, an MIT graduate student), the firm's first job was to help with the acoustic design of the UN General Assembly hall. It expanded into military work, including communications and network software. In 1964 it introduced the first computer-based communication system, and in 1969 it created ARPANET, a government computer network that has evolved into the Internet. In the 1970s it introduced Telenet, the first packet-switching network (which can route e-mail).

With government budget-cutting hurting sales, the company hired Conrades (the former head of IBM's US sales) in 1994. That year the company acquired SURAnet and BARRNET (Internet service providers). In 1995 it signed a deal with AT&T to provide the telecommunications giant's customers Internet access through BBN Planet. Also in 1995 it signed an agreement to develop and support America Online's high-speed dial-up access service. BBN's sales rose to $234.3 million in fiscal 1996, but it lost $49.9 million, primarily because of restructuring charges and investments related to its Internet expansion.

WHO

Chairman, President, and CEO: George H. Conrades, age 56, $400,000 pay (prior to promotion)
SVP, CFO, and Treasurer: Ralph A. Goldwasser, age 48, $207,500 pay
VP: John T. Kish Jr., age 39, $350,000 pay
VP; General Manager and President, BBN Planet: Paul R. Gudonis
VP Human Resources: Steven P. Heinrich
Auditors: Coopers & Lybrand L.L.P.

WHERE

HQ: 150 Cambridge Park Dr., Cambridge, MA 02140
Phone: 617-873-2000   **Fax:** 617-873-5011
Web site: http://www.bbn.com

	1995 Sales	
	$ mil.	% of total
US	191.0	89
Other countries	24.0	11
Total	**215.0**	**100**

WHAT

	1995 Sales	
	$ mil.	% of total
Internetworking	88.3	41
Collaborative systems & acoustic technologies	87.3	41
Data analysis software	39.4	18
Total	**215.0**	**100**

KEY COMPETITORS

Advantis
Computer Sciences
Control Data
General Electric
IBM
Kurzweil Applied Intelligence
Loral
MCI
MFS Communications
MindSpring
MITRE
NETCOM
PSINet
Raytheon
SAIC
Sprint
Sterling Software
Titan Corp.
Unisys
Voice Control
WorldCom

HOW MUCH

NYSE symbol: BBN FYE: June 30	Annual Growth	1990	1991	1992	1993	1994	1995
Sales ($ mil.)	(3.9%)	261.9	270.6	258.0	233.5	196.1	215.0
Net income ($ mil.)	—	(34.8)	9.1	4.2	(32.3)	(7.8)	64.8
Income as % of sales	—	—	3.4%	1.6%	—	—	30.2%
Earnings per share ($)	—	(1.91)	0.49	0.24	(2.05)	(0.48)	3.61
Stock price – high ($)	—	7.63	9.38	6.75	14.75	21.50	48.75
Stock price – low ($)	—	3.88	4.38	3.63	4.25	10.00	14.63
Stock price – close ($)	56.5%	4.38	5.38	4.75	12.00	14.88	41.13
P/E – high	—	—	19	28	—	—	14
P/E – low	—	—	9	15	—	—	4
Dividends per share ($)	(100.0%)	0.06	0.06	0.06	0.03	0.00	0.00
Book value per share ($)	15.1%	2.33	2.54	2.66	0.63	0.44	4.71
Employees	(3.3%)	2,367	2,284	2,086	1,663	1,694	2,000

1995 YEAR-END
Debt ratio: 47.1%
Return on equity: 144.4%
Cash (mil.): $111
Current ratio: 2.81
Long-term debt (mil.): $74
No. of shares (mil.): 18
Dividends
  Yield: —
  Payout: —
Market value (mil.): $721
R&D as % of sales: 11.8%

BELL MICROPRODUCTS INC.

OVERVIEW

Ring-a-ding-ding. Bell Microproducts doesn't do phones, but the distributor of high-tech computer components is ringing up record sales. The San Jose-based company distributes semiconductor and computer products from more than 70 manufacturers to original equipment manufacturers and value-added resellers (more than 1/3 of Bell's sales come from IBM and Quantum products). But Bell has also been building its own value-added services operations, especially contract manufacturing. Founder and CEO Donald Bell owns 8% of the company.

Bell had worked for a number of electronics distributors before leading the group that founded his namesake company in 1987. The company primarily sold semiconductors until 1990, when demand slumped and its profits sank. Bell began to diversify its product line and in 1991 created the value-added services division. The company expanded that unit in 1993 when it acquired manufacturers Quadrus and Adlar Turnkey, and it was selected as an authorized distributor of IBM Microelectronics products. That year Bell went public.

The company plans to expand its product lines as well as capitalize on manufacturers' growing use of outsourcing. In 1994 it acquired semiconductor distributor Vantage Components and certain assets of UNIX Central, a UNIX reseller. The next year it added a center to configure programmable semiconductor products to customer specifications. It also added 25 product lines, including new imaging products, and entered the document management business with a new value-added distribution program.

In 1996, Bell planned to relocate its contract manufacturing operations to more than double its space and add more capacity.

WHO

Chairman, President, and CEO: W. Donald Bell, age 58, $414,757 pay
SVP Computer Products Marketing: Philip M. Roussey, age 53, $211,047 pay
SVP Commercial Sales: John Higgins
SVP Industrial Sales: William A. Murphy, age 45
VP Operations: Robert J. Sturgeon, age 42, $147,238 pay
CFO, Corporate Controller, and Secretary: Remo E. Canessa, age 38, $105,452 pay
Manager Human Resources: Linda Teague
Auditors: Price Waterhouse LLP

WHERE

HQ: 1941 Ringwood Ave., San Jose, CA 95131-1721
Phone: 408-451-9400   **Fax:** 408-451-1600
Web site: http://www.bellmicro.com

Bell Microproducts has 19 sales or warehouse locations throughout the US. Its contract manufacturing facility is in California.

WHAT

	1995 Sales % of total
Computer products	48
Semiconductor products	36
Value-added services	14
Other	2
Total	**100**

KEY COMPETITORS

Arrow Electronics	Milgray	Richardson
Avnet	Nu Horizons	Electronics
Bell Industries	Electronic	SCI Systems
Graybar	Pioneer-Standard	Solectron
Electronics	Electronics	Sterling
Inacom	Premier	Electronics
Jaco Electronics	Industrial	TTI
Marshall	Reptron	Wyle Electronics
Industries	Electronics	
Merisel	Rexel	

HOW MUCH

Nasdaq symbol: BELM FYE: December 31	Annual Growth	1990	1991	1992	1993	1994	1995
Sales ($ mil.)	60.0%	33.0	33.7	65.5	125.3	250.8	346.3
Net income ($ mil.)	—	(1.1)	0.1	0.6	2.1	5.1	4.0
Income as % of sales	—	—	0.4%	0.9%	1.7%	2.0%	1.2%
Earnings per share ($)	—	(0.59)	0.03	0.14	0.45	0.86	0.48
Stock price – high ($)	—	—	—	—	10.00	16.00	14.25
Stock price – low ($)	—	—	—	—	6.75	7.50	7.00
Stock price – close ($)	(2.5%)	—	—	—	7.63	10.75	7.25
P/E – high	—	—	—	—	22	19	30
P/E – low	—	—	—	—	15	9	15
Dividends per share ($)	—	—	—	—	0.00	0.00	0.00
Book value per share ($)	41.0%	—	—	—	3.77	7.02	7.50
Employees	59.3%	45	64	94	238	351	462

1995 YEAR-END
Debt ratio: 49.2%
Return on equity: 6.7%
Cash (mil.): $3
Current ratio: 4.02
Long-term debt (mil.): $60
No. of shares (mil.): 8
Dividends
  Yield: —
  Payout: —
Market value (mil.): $60

BMC SOFTWARE, INC.

OVERVIEW

If you can't beat 'em, join 'em. Houston-based BMC Software has transformed itself from a company that provides software for mainframe computers — enabling clients to manage data more efficiently using a single powerful computer — into a major player in both the IBM mainframe and open systems (used in networks of smaller computers) markets. BMC's transformation has been prompted by its corporate customers' rapid shift to the more flexible client/server technology used in networking. However, many of these companies continue to rely to some degree on mainframes, and about 90% of BMC's revenues are still generated from this part of its business. The company has a software portfolio of 83 mainframe and 27 open systems products.

BMC was launched in 1979 by Scott Boulett, John Moores, and Dan Cloer (whose last initials gave the company its name). Its first product was the 3270 SuperOptimizer, a utility that dramatically improved terminal input/output operations. BMC, which went public in 1988, originally geared its products to corporations and institutions with large, sophisticated database systems.

The 1994 purchase of PATROL Software added UNIX-based open systems products to BMC's line and marked its extension beyond mainframes. To support its product expansion, BMC has invested heavily in R&D and has beefed up its partnership strategy with complementary hardware, software, and network vendors. In 1995 the company opened an office in Washington, DC, to focus on the government market. It also unveiled its MetaSUITE software for open systems.

The following year BMC announced an alliance with software giant Sun Microsystems to provide customers with integrated software for managing Lotus Notes on Solaris Servers.

WHO

Chairman, President, and CEO: Max P. Watson Jr., age 50, $840,970 pay
EVP and COO: Douglas J. Erwin, age 43, $670,857 pay
SVP North American Sales and Marketing: Richard P. Gardner, age 42, $489,385 pay
SVP Research and Development: James E. Juracek, age 50, $482,030 pay
Chief Accounting Officer and Corporate Controller: Kevin M. Klausmeyer, age 37
Director Human Resources: Johnnie Horn
Auditors: Andersen Worldwide

WHERE

HQ: 2101 CityWest Blvd., Houston, TX 77042-2827
Phone: 713-918-8800 **Fax:** 713-918-8000
Web site: http://www.bmc.com

WHAT

Selected Products

Mainframe
CICS Integrity Series (protection of customer information control systems)
IMS Application Enhancements (improves performance and availability of application programs)
IMS Database Utilities (tools to organize and back up information management systems)
TRIMAR Fast Path Series (speeds operations and maintenance)

Open Systems
MetaSuite series (general database management)
SQL BackTracks (backup and recovery)

KEY COMPETITORS

Computer Associates
Compuware
Hewlett-Packard
IBM
Oracle
Software AG
Sybase
System Software Associates

HOW MUCH

Nasdaq symbol: BMCS FYE: March 31	Annual Growth	1991	1992	1993	1994	1995	1996
Sales ($ mil.)	25.2%	139.5	188.7	238.5	288.5	345.0	428.9
Net income ($ mil.)	27.5%	31.4	48.6	65.4	56.5	77.5	105.6
Income as % of sales	—	22.5%	25.8%	27.4%	19.6%	22.5%	24.6%
Earnings per share ($)	26.2%	0.63	0.94	1.25	1.08	1.52	2.02
Stock price – high ($)[1]	—	15.13	37.38	39.50	42.06	35.50	51.50
Stock price – low ($)[1]	—	8.88	13.50	18.63	19.38	20.13	26.69
Stock price – close ($)[1]	23.3%	15.00	33.00	36.25	24.00	28.44	42.75
P/E – high	—	24	40	32	39	23	25
P/E – low	—	14	14	15	18	13	13
Dividends per share ($)	—	0.00	0.00	0.00	0.00	0.00	0.00
Book value per share ($)	30.1%	2.06	2.91	4.26	4.86	6.06	7.68
Employees	19.5%	593	782	909	987	1,185	1,444

[1] Stock prices are for the prior calendar year.

1996 YEAR-END
Debt ratio: 0.0%
Return on equity: 30.6%
Cash (mil.): $100
Current ratio: 1.02
Long-term debt (mil.): $0
No. of shares (mil.): 50
Dividends
  Yield: —
  Payout: —
Market value (mil.): $2,136
R&D as % of sales: 13.8%

BRØDERBUND SOFTWARE, INC.

OVERVIEW

Brøderbund is bundling fun and education. The Novato, California-based firm is a leading publisher and distributor of entertainment, educational, and personal productivity software. Its titles include the geography "edutainment" program Where in the World Is Carmen Sandiego? (which inspired the Emmy-winning PBS series), the adventure game Myst (developed by Cyan), and Print Shop, which lets computer users create cards, posters, and flyers.

Brothers Doug and Gary Carlston started Brøderbund (a hybrid Scandinavian word meaning "brotherhood") in 1980 to market some computer games Doug had programmed while practicing law. (Doug owns 10% of Brøderbund; Gary left the company in 1989.) Brøderbund's first big hit came in 1984 with Print Shop. The next year it released Where in the World Is Carmen Sandiego?, which teaches geography by having users track down a spy-turned-thief. The company went public in 1991. The following year it acquired PC Globe, an electronic atlas publisher, and expanded its list of affiliated labels (software it exclusively distributes for other publishers). The company formed a joint venture with Random House in 1994 to create Living Books, a line of interactive children's storybook CD-ROMs.

In 1995 Brøderbund completed the transfer of its product line to CD-ROM. It also acquired Banner Blue Software, including its the top-selling genealogy software program, Family Tree Maker.

In 1996 the company completed an agreement for its Alien Tales program to be made into a television series produced by DIC Entertainment, the same production house that made Carmen Sandiego an Emmy winner. Former direct-marketing executive Joseph Durrett replaced Doug Carlston as CEO in 1996.

WHO

Chairman: Douglas G. Carlston, age 48, $790,881 pay
CEO: Joseph Durrett, age 51
President and COO: William M. McDonagh, age 39, $638,354 pay
SVP Brøderbund Studios: Harry R. Wilker, age 49, $454,093 pay
SVP Marketing and Sales: Jan L. Gullet, age 41
VP Business Development, General Counsel, and Secretary: Thomas L. Marcus, age 42, $376,138 pay
VP Sales: Rodney D. Haden, age 45, $286,779 pay
VP Finance and CFO: Michael J. Shannahan, age 47
VP Engineering: M. W. Mantle
Director Human Resources: Patsy Murphy
Auditors: Ernst & Young LLP

WHERE

HQ: 500 Redwood Blvd., Novato, CA 94948-6121
Phone: 415-382-4400 **Fax:** 415-382-4582
Web site: http://www.broderbund.com

WHAT

	1995 Sales
	% of total
Print Shop	30
Entertainment	24
Living Books	13
Carmen Sandiego	10
Early Learning	10
Other	13
Total	**100**

KEY COMPETITORS

3DO	Gametek	Nintendo
Accolade	Golden Books	Scholastic
Activision	id Software	3EGA
Davidson &	Knowledge	Sierra On-Line
Associates	Adventure	SoftKey
Edmark	LucasArts	Sony
Educational	Maxis	Spectrum
Insights	Microsoft	HoloByte
Electronic Arts	National	T-HQ
Expert Software	Geographic	

HOW MUCH

Nasdaq symbol: BROD FYE: August 31	Annual Growth	1990	1991	1992	1993	1994	1995
Sales ($ mil.)	27.8%	50.4	55.8	75.1	95.6	111.8	171.6
Net income ($ mil.)	62.4%	3.2	7.1	9.7	13.6	11.1	36.2
Income as % of sales	—	6.3%	12.7%	12.9%	14.3%	9.9%	21.1%
Earnings per share ($)	58.9%	0.17	0.38	0.49	0.68	0.55	1.72
Stock price – high ($)	—	—	13.25	24.63	29.63	47.25	78.75
Stock price – low ($)	—	—	6.25	9.25	14.88	15.75	42.25
Stock price – close ($)	51.6%	—	11.50	21.25	17.75	46.75	60.75
P/E – high	—	—	35	50	44	86	46
P/E – low	—	—	16	19	22	29	25
Dividends per share ($)	—	—	0.00	0.00	0.00	0.00	0.00
Book value per share ($)	30.0%	—	2.19	2.38	3.26	4.09	6.25
Employees	20.1%	—	271	338	402	438	563

1995 YEAR-END
Debt ratio: 0.0%
Return on equity: 34.6%
Cash (mil.): $127
Current ratio: 4.68
Long-term debt (mil.): $0
No. of shares (mil.): 21
Dividends
 Yield: —
 Payout: —
Market value (mil.): $1,253
R&D as % of sales: 13.3%

CADENCE DESIGN SYSTEMS, INC.

OVERVIEW

Cadence is trying to beat a bitter rival. The San Jose-based firm is the world's leading provider of electronic design automation (EDA) software, used in designing the integrated circuits and electronics in telephones, computers, and other devices. Cadence has also begun offering IC product development services to help customers reduce costs and time-to-market. However, the outcome of its copyright infringement and industrial espionage suit against Avant! (the #2 EDA software developer) is of paramount importance to customers who must decide whose highly specialized software to buy.

Cadence arose from the 1988 merger of 2 software firms: ECAD (formed in 1982) and SDA Systems (founded in 1983). It pursued the goal of becoming the world's leading EDA software supplier by enlarging and improving the range of software it developed in-house as well as by acquiring other companies, including Tangent Systems (1989), Gateway Design Automation (1989), and Automated Systems (1990, sold in 1993).

In 1991 Cadence swallowed competitor Valid Logic Systems to become the #1 company in the field. A long assimilation (and lackluster marketing) contributed to a loss in 1993. Management brought in a new CFO and a new COO to get product development back on track, established a new consulting unit (Spectrum Services), and reorganized foreign operations.

In 1995 the company bought Unisys's IC and electronic systems design group. Later that year Cadence sued Avant!, charging it with stealing its "place and route" code (which accounts for about 55% of Cadence's sales). Avant! countersued in 1996. That year Cadence agreed to buy High Level, a Canadian maker of IC design tools.

WHO

Chairman: Donald L. Lucas, age 66
President and CEO: Joseph B. Costello, age 42, $1,353,500 pay
EVP, CFO, and Secretary: H. Raymond Bingham, age 50, $659,000 pay
SVP Worldwide Sales: John F. Olsen, age 44, $653,900 pay
SVP Spectrum Services: M. Robert Leach, age 48, $571,069 pay
SVP and Principal Technologist: James E. Solomon, age 59, $406,750 pay
SVP Human Resources: Scott W. Sherwood
Auditors: Andersen Worldwide

WHERE

HQ: 555 River Oaks Pkwy., San Jose, CA 95134
Phone: 408-943-1234   **Fax:** 408-943-0513
Web site: http://www.cadence.com

WHAT

	1995 Sales	
	$ mil.	% of total
Products	292.2	53
Maintenance	190.3	35
Service	65.9	12
Total	**548.4**	**100**

Selected Products and Services
Allegro (printed circuit board layout design)
Analog Workbench (system design)
Design development and support
Dracula (physical design verification)
Ensemble (place and route software)
SiliconQuest (deep sub-micron design aid)
Synergy (circuit synthesis)
Verilog XL (digital simulation)
Virtuoso FastChip (automates layout process)

KEY COMPETITORS

Avant! Corp
DII
EPIC Design
Mentor Graphics

Orbit Semiconductor
Synopsys
Viewlogic
Zuken-Redac

HOW MUCH

NYSE symbol: CDN FYE: December 31	Annual Growth	1990	1991	1992	1993	1994	1995
Sales ($ mil.)	7.9%	374.4	379.5	418.7	368.6	429.1	548.4
Net income ($ mil.)	—	(9.3)	(22.4)	55.4	(12.8)	36.6	97.3
Income as % of sales	—	—	—	13.2%	—	8.5%	17.7%
Earnings per share ($)	—	(0.26)	(0.56)	1.20	(0.30)	0.84	1.05
Stock price – high ($)	—	28.50	34.63	29.88	24.38	21.75	28.25
Stock price – low ($)	—	13.25	14.50	13.13	8.25	10.25	8.56
Stock price – close ($)	3.2%	23.88	25.13	21.38	11.63	20.63	28.00
P/E – high	—	—	—	25	—	26	27
P/E – low	—	—	—	11	—	12	8
Dividends per share ($)	—	0.00	0.00	0.00	0.00	0.00	0.00
Book value per share ($)	(13.5%)	5.30	4.48	5.67	5.01	4.64	2.56
Employees	12.6%	1,676	2,588	2,500	2,476	2,449	3,028

1995 YEAR-END
Debt ratio: 2.3%
Return on equity: 62.7%
Cash (mil.): $97
Current ratio: 1.03
Long-term debt (mil.): $2
No. of shares (mil.): 2
Dividends
  Yield: —
  Payout: —
Market value (mil.): $1,467

CAMBRIDGE TECHNOLOGY

OVERVIEW

"Fixed price, fixed time" is the key to success for Cambridge Technology Partners. The Massachusetts-based company, one of the few IT (information technology) consultants to give its customers up-front guarantees on how much it will cost and how long it will take to do a job, is the fastest-growing company in Massachusetts (with a growth rate of more than 50% a year).

Cambridge, which has long foreseen the replacement of mainframes by client-servers, primarily helps *FORTUNE* 1,000 companies design new networked computers to replace their older, increasingly inefficient systems. Well-grounded in software development, Cambridge listens to its clients' business needs and then helps build consensus within client firms for a specific solution. This is sometimes accomplished through rapid-solutions workshops, where all parties are put together in a room until they decide what they want to build. Cambridge also works with companies on building intranets, as well as helping them with Internet and electronic-commerce technology.

Safeguard Scientifics, Radnor Venture Partners, and Cambridge Technology Group established Cambridge Technology Partners in 1991 to carry on certain activities that were previously done by Cambridge Technology Group. CEO James Sims was a cofounder. The company went public in 1993 and changed its name to Cambridge Technology Partners (Massachusetts), Inc. Safeguard Scientifics still owns 22% of Cambridge's stock.

In 1995 the company acquired the Systems Consulting Group (package software evaluation and implementation) and Axiom Management Consulting (business process redesign consulting). The company now has facilities in Germany, Ireland, the Netherlands, Norway, Sweden, and the UK.

WHO

Chairman: Warren V. Musser, age 69
VC: Jean C. Tempel, age 52
CEO and President: James K. Sims, age 49, $730,000 pay
EVP and President, Cambridge Technology Partners (North America): Robert L. Gett, age 45, $510,000 pay
SVP Finance, CFO, Treasurer, and Secretary: Arthur M. Toscanini, age 53, $295,000 pay
SVP Marketing: Christopher H. Greendale, age 44, $285,000 pay
SVP International Operations: William A. Seibel, age 43, $255,000 pay
SVP Human Resources: Susan J. Loker, age 51
Auditors: Coopers & Lybrand L.L.P.

WHERE

HQ: Cambridge Technology Partners, Inc., 304 Vassar St., Cambridge, MA 02139
Phone: 617-374-9800   **Fax:** 617-374-8300
Web site: http://www.ctp.com

WHAT

Selected Services
Application software development
Business process redesign
Custom management systems
Network services
Training services

KEY COMPETITORS

Andersen	Coopers &	Keane
Worldwide	Lybrand	KPMG
BDM	Datastream	MCI
International	Systems	Systemhouse
Business	DEC	Perot Systems
Systems Group	Deloitte Touche	Price Waterhouse
CACI	Tohmatsu	Systems &
International	EDS	Computer
Cap Gemini	Ernst & Young	Technology
CIBER	Hewlett-Packard	Unisys
Computer Data	IBM	
Systems	Innovative	
Computer	Technical	
Sciences	Systems	

HOW MUCH

Nasdaq symbol: CATP FYE: December 31	Annual Growth	1990	1991	1992	1993	1994	1995
Sales ($ mil.)	52.2%	16.2	10.6	19.2	32.7	59.7	132.4
Net income ($ mil.)	—	(0.9)	(0.3)	1.3	3.4	6.6	12.7
Income as % of sales	—	—	—	6.7%	10.3%	11.1%	9.6%
Earnings per share ($)	—	—	(0.04)	0.11	0.26	0.46	0.76
Stock price – high ($)	—	—	—	—	17.75	23.75	61.00
Stock price – low ($)	—	—	—	—	7.00	14.00	21.25
Stock price – close ($)	91.1%	—	—	—	15.75	22.25	57.50
P/E – high	—	—	—	—	68	52	80
P/E – low	—	—	—	—	27	30	28
Dividends per share ($)	—	—	—	—	0.00	0.00	0.00
Book value per share ($)	98.8%	—	—	—	0.85	2.19	3.36
Employees	87.0%	—	—	—	308	546	1,077

1995 YEAR-END
Debt ratio: 0.7%
Return on equity: 32.3%
Cash (mil.): $15
Current ratio: 2.61
Long-term debt (mil.): $0
No. of shares (mil.): 15
Dividends
  Yield: —
  Payout: —
Market value (mil.): $846

CASCADE COMMUNICATIONS CORP.

OVERVIEW

If Internet dominance is the bait, Cascade Communications has the switch. The company makes wide area network (WAN) switches based on high-speed broadband network technologies. It serves some of the world's largest commercial Internet service providers and estimates that up to 70% of Internet traffic passes through its switches. The switch vendor has become one of the world's fastest-growing data communications companies, largely owing to the deregulation of the phone industry, which caused nonvoice traffic to surge through newly deployed public carrier phone networks (85% of the company's customer base). Calling on Cascade's technology, Bell Atlantic and U S WEST ring up about 30% of the company's sales.

The Westford, Massachusetts-based company was founded in 1990 as Nexgencom by Gururaj "Desh" Deshpande, a founder of local area network (LAN) products maker Coral Network. Nexgencom became Cascade in 1991.

In 1992 Daniel Smith, a former Proteon executive, became CEO, succeeding Deshpande, who became EVP. The company went public in 1994 as one of the hottest-selling high-tech stocks of the year. Cascade's sales surged 169% in 1995, mainly attributed to the increased demand for broadband packet equipment. Favored by local exchange carriers and Internet service providers seeking cost-efficient datacom services, the company's B-STDX line of higher-speed, greater-capacity switches accounted for more than 90% of 1995 sales.

Cascade entered partnerships with Motorola and IBM in 1996. Also that year Cascade paid $175 million for Arris Networks, a developer of remote access technology. Networking leader Cisco Systems owns 6% of the company but plans to sell its stake following its 1996 purchase of WAN rival StrataCom.

WHO

Chairperson: Victoria A. Brown, age 48
President and CEO: Daniel E. Smith, age 46, $275,854 pay
EVP Marketing and Customer Service: Gururaj Deshpande, age 45, $212,554 pay
VP Worldwide Sales: Michael A. Champa, age 44, $278,981 pay
VP Finance and Administration, CFO, Treasurer, and Secretary: Paul E. Blondin, age 45, $164,139 pay
VP Operations: John E. Dowling, age 42, $158,150 pay
VP Engineering: Hassan M. Ahmed, age 38
VP Marketing: Robert N. Machlin, age 38
Director Human Resources: Mary Cogan
Auditors: Coopers & Lybrand L.L.P.

WHERE

HQ: 5 Carlisle Rd., Westford, MA 01886
Phone: 508-692-2600   **Fax:** 508-692-9214
Web site: http://www.casc.com

	1995 Sales	
	$ mil.	% of total
US	113.3	84
Europe/Africa	11.7	9
Pacific Rim/Asia	8.4	6
North & South America (excluding US)	1.4	1
Total	**134.8**	**100**

WHAT

Selected Products
B-STDX 8000/9000 Switch Family (high-performance multiservice WAN switches)
Cascade 500 ATM (high-capacity ATM switches)
CascadeView Network Management Systems (WAN/LAN network management applications)
STDX 6000 (multiservice WAN switches for smaller networks)

KEY COMPETITORS

Bay Networks
Cisco Systems
FORE Systems
General DataComm
General Signal

IBM
Newbridge Networks
Northern Telecom
StrataCom

HOW MUCH

Nasdaq symbol: CSCC FYE: December 31	Annual Growth	1990	1991	1992	1993	1994	1995
Sales ($ mil.)	452.3%	—	—	0.8	7.0	50.1	134.8
Net income ($ mil.)	—	—	—	(3.1)	(2.6)	9.3	25.4
Income as % of sales	—	—	—	—	—	18.6%	18.8%
Earnings per share ($)	—	—	—	(0.15)	(0.12)	0.12	0.28
Stock price – high ($)	—	—	—	—	—	10.83	30.83
Stock price – low ($)	—	—	—	—	—	3.50	9.55
Stock price – close ($)	—	—	—	—	—	10.30	28.42
P/E – high	—	—	—	—	—	94	110
P/E – low	—	—	—	—	—	30	34
Dividends per share ($)	—	—	—	—	—	0.00	0.00
Book value per share ($)	—	—	—	—	—	0.64	1.03
Employees	235.2%	1	15	29	72	232	423

1995 YEAR-END

Debt ratio: 0.0%
Return on equity: 36.6%
Cash (mil.): $61
Current ratio: 3.71
Long-term debt (mil.): $0
No. of shares (mil.): 84
Dividends
  Yield: —
  Payout: —
Market value (mil.): $2,381
R&D as % of sales: 15.4%

CDW COMPUTER CENTERS, INC.

OVERVIEW

You can send mail through your computer, so why not get your computer through the mail? Based in Buffalo Grove, Illinois, CDW is the nation's largest catalog-based direct-market retailer of PC- and Windows-based products. The company offers more than 20,000 hardware and software items, networking products, and accessories for PCs and Apple computers. Windows- and DOS-based products generate 90% of the company's sales.

CDW sends out more than 30 million catalogs a year to businesses, institutions, and home business users. Its business customers account for almost 3/4 of sales.

CEO Michael Krasny and company president Gregory Zeman own 60% and 12% of the company, respectively.

Krasny started CDW (Computer Discount Warehouse) in 1983 at age 29. Weary of selling used cars at his father's Chicago lot, Krasny quit but soon ran out of money and was forced to sell his personal computer. A classified ad in the *Chicago Tribune* generated phenomenal response, and Krasny sold his computer almost instantly. When calls kept coming in, Krasny bought more computers and sold them to people responding to the original ad, and his mail-order business was underway. The company launched its first catalog in 1987 and opened its first retail showroom in Chicago in 1989. CDW went public in 1993.

Widespread interest in the Internet has provided a booming market for computer upgrades; CDW sales have grown with the demand for high-speed modems, high-capacity storage devices, and new software packages. Though the paint is still drying at CDW's latest headquarters, continued growth has already led the firm to build additional space for telemarketing, a warehouse, a showroom, and corporate offices.

WHO

Chairman, CEO, Secretary, and Treasurer:
Michael P. Krasny, age 42, $1,044,370 pay
President: Gregory C. Zeman, age 37, $817,177 pay
CFO: Harry J. Harczak Jr., age 39, $255,108 pay
VP Sales: Daniel B. Kass, age 39, $616,352 pay
VP Purchasing: Paul A. Kozak, age 31, $306,996 pay
VP Finance, Controller, and Chief Accounting Officer:
Daniel F. Callen, age 38
VP Advertising: Donald M. Gordon, age 55
VP MIS: James R. Shanks, age 31
VP Human Resources: Mary C. Gerlits, age 37
Auditors: Coopers & Lybrand L.L.P.

WHERE

HQ: 1020 E. Lake Cook Rd., Buffalo Grove, IL 60089
Phone: 847-465-6000   **Fax:** 847-465-6800
Web site: http://www.cdw.com

WHAT

	1995 Sales % of total
Notebook & laptop computers	22
Printers	14
Desktop computers	12
Software	11
Data storage devices	9
Video products	8
Add-on boards/memory	8
Network products	7
Communications	5
Other accessories	4
Total	**100**

KEY COMPETITORS

Best Buy	Fry's Electronics	Micro Warehouse
Circuit City	Gateway 2000	MicroAge
CompuCom	Inacom	NeoStar
CompUSA	Inmac	Tandy
Dell	Intelligent	Corporation
Egghead	Electronics	Tiger Direct
ELEK-TEK	Micro Center	Vanstar

HOW MUCH

Nasdaq symbol: CDWC FYE: December 31	Annual Growth	1990	1991	1992	1993	1994	1995
Sales ($ mil.)	49.9%	83.1	101.5	138.6	270.9	413.3	628.7
Net income ($ mil.)	75.7%	1.2	3.7	1.3	12.6	12.1	20.1
Income as % of sales	—	1.4%	3.7%	0.9%	4.7%	2.9%	3.2%
Earnings per share ($)	26.1%	—	—	—	0.90	0.91	1.43
Stock price – high ($)	—	—	—	—	14.25	34.75	63.50
Stock price – low ($)	—	—	—	—	6.75	13.38	30.50
Stock price – close ($)	70.1%	—	—	—	14.00	34.13	40.50
P/E – high	—	—	—	—	16	38	44
P/E – low	—	—	—	—	8	15	21
Dividends per share ($)	—	—	—	—	0.00	0.00	0.00
Book value per share ($)	107.4%	—	—	—	1.72	4.05	7.40
Employees	46.3%	80	100	135	247	390	536

1995 YEAR-END
Debt ratio: 0.0%
Return on equity: 24.8%
Cash (mil.): $57
Current ratio: 4.57
Long-term debt (mil.): $0
No. of shares (mil.): 14
Dividends
  Yield: —
  Payout: —
Market value (mil.): $581
Advertising as % of sales: 1.5%

CHEYENNE SOFTWARE, INC.

OVERVIEW

Cheyenne Software has elected to join a larger tribe. The company is the #1 producer of data storage management solutions for LAN-based systems. It also makes software for network imaging, communications, management, and security. OEMs that pre-install Cheyenne software include Hewlett-Packard, IBM, and Intel. Cheyenne is being acquired by Computer Associates, the world's #2 independent software company.

The company's founders were still looking for a name as they flew to Delaware to file for incorporation in 1983. Overhearing their conversation, the flight attendant suggested Cheyenne, from the model of airplane on which they were flying. The company went public in 1985. It acquired Freeman-Owings and FA Components, both computer distributors, in 1987. Cheyenne introduced its flagship product, ARCserve, a data storage manager for Novell networks, in 1989; it entered into an OEM agreement with Hewlett-Packard and into a partnership with Novell in 1990.

Cheyenne introduced InocuLAN and FAXserve in 1992, and the next year it formed a subsidiary, Cheyenne Communications, to focus on network communications. In 1994 Cheyenne introduced ARCserve for Mac and acquired NETstor, an HSM (hierarchical storage management) software developer. The company introduced BitWare for Windows, a fax, voice mail, and data communications software package, in 1995. That year it formed a technology and marketing alliance with Computer Associates and acquired 2 small storage management software developers, Chile Pepper and Media Blitz.

In 1996 Cheyenne accepted Computer Associates' $1.2 billion offer for the company. That fiscal year Cheyenne earned $27 million on sales of $174 million.

WHO

Chairman, President, and CEO: ReiJane Huai, age 36, $205,000 pay
EVP, Senior Financial Officer, and Treasurer: Elliot Levine, age 59, $180,000 pay
EVP Sales and Secretary: Alan W. Kaufman, age 57, $180,000 pay
EVP Business Development: James P. McNiel, age 32, $180,000 pay
EVP: Yuda Doron, $159,653 pay
VP Engineering: Robert Daly
Director Human Resources: Andy Boyland
Auditors: KPMG Peat Marwick LLP

WHERE

HQ: 3 Expressway Plaza, Roslyn Heights, NY 11577
Phone: 516-484-5110   **Fax:** 516-484-7106
Web site: http://www.cheyenne.com

	1995 Sales	
	$ mil.	% of total
US	68.3	53
Europe	48.8	38
Canada	2.2	2
Other regions	8.6	7
Total	**127.9**	**100**

WHAT

	1995 Sales	
	$ mil.	% of total
Distribution	94.1	74
OEM	15.3	12
Other	18.5	14
Total	**127.9**	**100**

Selected Products
ARCserve (network data storage management)
Bit Software (network communications)
FAXserve (network communications)
InocuLAN (network security)
Monitrix (network management)

KEY COMPETITORS

Artisoft	McAfee Associates	Seagate
Banyan Systems	Microsoft	Symantec
BMC Software	MTI Technology	
Legato Systems	Novell	

HOW MUCH

AMEX symbol: CYE FYE: June 30	Annual Growth	1990	1991	1992	1993	1994	1995
Sales ($ mil.)	137.3%	1.7	7.2	17.9	56.7	97.7	127.9
Net income ($ mil.)	—	(2.1)	2.1	9.1	20.6	32.5	38.5
Income as % of sales	—	—	29.1%	50.8%	40.7%	33.3%	30.1%
Earnings per share ($)	—	(0.06)	0.06	0.24	0.53	0.82	0.97
Stock price – high ($)	—	2.44	5.30	15.89	26.83	30.25	27.88
Stock price – low ($)	—	0.96	2.19	4.17	10.90	6.00	12.38
Stock price – close ($)	60.7%	2.44	5.15	13.39	18.50	13.75	26.13
P/E – high	—	—	88	66	51	37	29
P/E – low	—	—	36	17	21	7	13
Dividends per share ($)	—	0.00	0.00	0.00	0.00	0.00	0.00
Book value per share ($)	55.1%	0.33	0.37	0.75	1.62	2.71	2.96
Employees	60.1%	59	170	107	229	430	621

1995 YEAR-END
Debt ratio: 0.0%
Return on equity: 34.8%
Cash (mil.): $31
Current ratio: 5.93
Long-term debt (mil.): $0
No. of shares (mil.): 39
Dividends
 Yield: —
 Payout: —
Market value (mil.): $1,027
R&D as % of sales: 12.8%

COMPUWARE CORPORATION

OVERVIEW

While betting that digital dinosaurs (mainframes) will stay in vogue with some users (airlines and banks, for example), Compuware is hedging. The Farmington Hills, Michigan-based company dominates the market for automated testing, fault diagnosis, debugging, and file and data management software for large mainframe systems, and also provides consulting services. CEO and cofounder Peter Karmanos continues to move away from dependence on the static mainframe market (although significant opportunity remains there for the firm because few mainframe users have yet bought such diagnostic software) by acquiring providers of similar software and services for the thriving client/server market. Karmanos owns 17% of the firm and cofounder Thomas Thewes owns 5%.

Karmanos, Thewes, and Allen Cutting pooled their tax refunds (a total of $9,000) and founded Compuware in 1973. The consulting firm became a troubleshooter for diverse mainframe problems. It entered the software market in 1977 with Abend-AID, an automatic fault diagnosis tool. Two years later it launched MBX Xpediter/TSO (interactive analysis and debugging tools), and in 1983 it introduced File-AID (file and data management products). By the late 1980s the company was growing rapidly — particularly overseas — and software accounted for 65% of sales. Compuware went public in 1992. Karmanos used part of the $111.5 million in proceeds to strengthen the company's position in the mainframe arena and in 1994 acquired Uniface Holding, a Dutch client/server development tool firm.

Compuware acquired Direct Technology (automated software testing) and CoroNet Systems (systems management tools) in 1995 and Adams & Reynolds (client/server services) in 1996.

WHO

Chairman and CEO: Peter Karmanos Jr., age 53, $636,000 pay
President and COO: Joseph A. Nathan, age 43, $530,000 pay
SVP Professional Services: John N. Shevillo, age 60, $424,000 pay
SVP Enterprise Systems: Stephen H. Fagan, age 41, $350,000 pay
SVP Marketing and Communications: W. James Prowse, age 53, $320,000 pay
SVP Worldwide Sales: Henry A. Jallos, age 47, $320,000 pay
SVP, CFO, Chief Accounting Officer, and Treasurer: Ralph A. Caponigro, age 64
SVP Administration: Denise A. Knobblock, age 40
VP, General Counsel, and Secretary: Thomas Costello Jr., age 42
VP Human Resources: Shiela McKinnon
Auditors: Deloitte & Touche

WHERE

HQ: 31440 Northwestern Hwy., Farmington Hills, MI 48334-2564
Phone: 810-737-7300   **Fax:** 810-737-7108
Web site: http://www.compuware.com

Compuware has 15 sales offices in the US and overseas.

WHAT

	1996 Sales	
	$ mil.	% of total
Software license fees	226.7	37
Professional service fees	203.7	33
Maintenance fees	184.0	30
Total	**614.4**	**100**

KEY COMPETITORS

Andersen Consulting
BMC Software
Centura Software
Computer Associates
EDS

IBM
Informix
PLATINUM technology
Sybase
VIASOFT

HOW MUCH

Nasdaq symbol: CPWR FYE: March 31	Annual Growth	1991	1992	1993	1994	1995	1996
Sales ($ mil.)	34.1%	141.8	175.0	234.9	330.3	533.9	614.4
Net income ($ mil.)	36.3%	9.4	(24.5)	34.9	59.1	62.1	44.2
Income as % of sales	—	6.7%	—	14.8%	17.9%	11.6%	7.2%
Earnings per share ($)	—	—	(0.79)	1.07	1.52	1.30	0.99
Stock price – high ($)[1]	—	—	—	26.25	34.25	49.25	43.00
Stock price – low ($)[1]	—	—	—	24.00	19.25	24.50	17.50
Stock price – close ($)[1]	(10.4%)	—	—	25.75	26.00	36.00	18.50
P/E – high	—	—	—	25	23	38	43
P/E – low	—	—	—	22	13	19	18
Dividends per share ($)	—	—	—	0.00	0.00	0.00	0.00
Book value per share ($)	16.2%	—	—	4.80	6.43	7.39	7.54
Employees	31.4%	—	1,627	1,808	2,774	4,105	4,844

[1] Stock prices are for the prior calendar year.

1996 YEAR-END
Debt ratio: 0.0%
Return on equity: 13.5%
Cash (mil.): $108
Current ratio: 1.64
Long-term debt (mil.): $0
No. of shares (mil.): 42
Dividends
  Yield: —
  Payout: —
Market value (mil.): $783
R&D as % of sales: 10.4%

CORBIS CORPORATION

OVERVIEW

At Corbis, image is everything. The Bellevue, Washington-based company (owned by Microsoft CEO Bill Gates) maintains the world's largest collection of digitized visual content, with some 700,000 images reproduced in electronic form. The library contains scanned copies of prints, artistic and journalistic photographs, and associated text. Corbis plans to expand the collection to include video, audio, graphics, and other media. The images are licensed for use in traditional print publications and in various types of electronic communications media.

The company's Bettmann division handles rights to the famed Bettmann Archive, which contains more than 16 million images, including such classic photos as the exploding Hindenberg and a skirt-clad Marilyn Monroe over a subway air vent. The Corbis Media division supplies stock images (including Mathew Brady's Civil War photographs, Picasso paintings, and images of historic events from NASA and the Smithsonian) for use by advertisers, graphic designers, and print and electronic publishers. The Corbis Publishing division develops CD-ROMs (releases include Volcanoes: Life on the Edge and Paul Cezanne: Portrait of My World) and documentary products for the World Wide Web.

In 1989 Gates founded Interactive Home Systems (later Continuum Productions) and began buying the rights to digitize images from museums, archival collections, and other sources. The company changed its name in 1995 to Corbis Corporation (corbis is Latin for "woven basket" and symbolizes the company as a container for high-quality images). That year Corbis bought the Bettmann Archive and the rights to the artwork and other images of Russia's Hermitage Museum. Such moves prompted concern about the extent of Corbis's (and Gates's) control over world art treasures.

Corbis acquired exclusive rights in 1996 to use selections from photographer Ansel Adams's works (some 40,000 images, including many of the wilderness and the American West) for CD-ROM and online distribution. Also that year it reached a licensing agreement with Mariners' Museum in Newport News, Virginia (with 650,000 photographic images).

WHO

President and CEO: Doug Rowan
VP Finance and Operations: Tony Rojas
VP Business and Legal Affairs: Steve Davis
Director Sales and Marketing: Mike Martucci
Director Technology: Steve White
General Manager and Executive Producer, Corbis Productions: Curtis Wong
General Manager, Corbis Publishing: Nana Kuo
Marketing Manager: Scott Sedlik
Sales Manager: Mark Daniel
Manager Human Resources: Tica Gordon

WHERE

HQ: 15395 SE 30th Place, Ste. 300, Bellevue, WA 98007
Phone: 206-641-4505   **Fax:** 206-746-1618
Web site: http://www.corbis.com

WHAT

Divisions
Bettmann (handles rights to the Bettmann Archive, which contains more than 16 million images)
Corbis Media (licenses visual content and stock photography for use by advertisers, graphic designers, and print and electronic publishers)
Corbis Publishing (publishes CD-ROM and online documentary consumer products)

Selected Image Archive Subjects
Fine arts
Geography
History
Natural history
Sciences
Technology
World cultures

KEY COMPETITORS

Agence France-Presse
Archive Photos
Associated Press
Dorling Kindersley
EMME Interactive
IBM
Image Bank
Image Smith
Index Stock Photography
Knight-Ridder
LookingGlass Technologies
Media Photographers Copyright Agency
Photodisc
Picture Network International
StarPress
Times Mirror

HOW MUCH

Private company FYE: December 31	Annual Growth	1990	1991	1992	1993	1994	1995
Estimated sales ($ mil.)	—	—	—	—	—	0.0	8.0
Employees	—	—	—	—	—	270	270

COREL CORPORATION

OVERVIEW

"We are setting this up to be a Pepsi-Coke situation," says Corel CEO Michael Cowpland. Since Corel's 1996 purchase of WordPerfect Corporation from Novell (which is expected to triple Corel's revenue and vastly expand its product line), Cowpland believes his company can compete on the same level with Microsoft. However Corel, which until now has been primarily a one-product company (CorelDRAW), still has a long way to go to match the fizz in Microsoft's formula. To that end it has introduced several all-in-one programs that include WordPerfect packaged with a spreadsheet, e-mail, and graphic capabilities (among other programs). Cowpland owns about 14% and Novell owns almost 15% of Corel.

Corel was founded in 1985 by Cowpland (former head of Canadian telecommunications company Mitel) as a systems integrator for desktop publishing products. As it developed enhancements for these applications, Corel began creating graphics software. In 1989 the company introduced CorelDRAW, its first illustration program, and went public in Canada.

Corel software has evolved into a package of artist's tools, including a bitmap paint program and photo editor (PHOTO-PAINT) and an animation module (MOVE). Corel's line of CD-ROM products includes Corel GALLERY (a clip-art image library) and Corel Professional Photos (25 royalty-free photo CDs).

The company closed its systems integration business in 1991. In 1992 Corel began trading on Nasdaq. The following year the company acquired the popular Ventura Publisher page layout software and bundled it with the Corel 5 design package.

Corel unveiled several new products in 1996, including CorelCAD (3-D computer-aided design program) and CorelVIDEO (video conferencing).

WHO

Chairman, President, and CEO: Michael C. J. Cowpland, age 52, $163,895 pay
Director Finance and CFO: Charles A. Norris, age 49
Secretary/Treasurer: Paul C. LaBarge, age 45
Chief Engineer: Patrick R. Beirne, age 41, $136,882 pay
Director Graphics Software: Eid Eid, age 38, $156,617 pay
Director Sales and Marketing: Arlen Bartsch, age 36, $119,037 pay
Director Operations: Kerry Williams, age 33, $114,348 pay
General Counsel and Director Corporate and Legal Services: Lisa Kenkel, age 32
Auditors: KPMG Peat Marwick LLP

WHERE

HQ: 1600 Carling Ave., Ottawa, ON, K1Z 8R7 Canada
Phone: 613-728-3733   **Fax:** 613-761-9176
Web site: http://www.corel.com

WHAT

Selected Products
Corel GALLERY (clip art)
Corel Office Professional (all-in-one business program)
Corel PHOTO-PAINT (photo-editing and painting program)
Corel Presentations (creates presentation materials)
Corel Print House (clip art, fonts, and photos)
Corel Quattro Pro (spreadsheet)
Corel VENTURA (page layout program)
Corel WordPerfect Suite (all-in-one business program)
CorelDRAW (vector illustration program)
CorelFLOW (creates flow charts, diagrams, and schematics)

KEY COMPETITORS

Adaptec	Fractal Design	Microsoft
Adobe	Hewlett-Packard	Quark
Apple Computer	IBM	Software
Autodesk	Interleaf	Publishing
Borland	Lotus	Xyvision
Claris	Macromedia	
Deneba	Micrografx	

HOW MUCH

Nasdaq symbol: COSFF FYE: November 30	Annual Growth	1990	1991	1992	1993	1994	1995
Sales ($ mil.)	68.4%	25.1	46.0	70.1	104.9	164.3	196.4
Net income ($ mil.)	66.9%	5.8	9.6	8.7	20.8	32.5	14.5
Income as % of sales	—	23.3%	20.8%	12.4%	19.9%	19.8%	7.4%
Earnings per share ($)	42.4%	0.18	0.28	0.24	0.49	0.67	0.30
Stock price – high ($)	—	—	—	5.75	13.58	16.75	19.50
Stock price – low ($)	—	—	—	4.71	3.58	10.66	10.13
Stock price – close ($)	64.2%	—	—	5.13	13.09	13.81	13.00
P/E – high	—	—	—	24	28	25	65
P/E – low	—	—	—	19	7	16	34
Dividends per share ($)	—	—	—	0.00	0.00	0.00	0.00
Book value per share ($)	14.6%	—	—	1.87	2.47	2.46	3.97
Employees	29.3%	—	—	275	331	380	594

1995 YEAR-END:
Debt ratio: 0.0%
Return on equity: 8.0%
Cash (mil.): $81.8
Current ratio: 7.50
Long-term debt (mil.): $0.0
No. of shares (mil.): 49.3
Dividends
  Yield: 0.0
  Payout: —
Market value (mil.): $640.9
R&D as % of sales: 13.9%
Advertising as % of sales: 28.1%

CORNERSTONE IMAGING, INC.

OVERVIEW

Cornerstone Imaging is cleaning up the office environment. Based in San Jose, California, the company is one of the leading manufacturers of systems for document image processing (DIP). Its products include subsystems (such as DIP-specific integrated circuits and high-resolution monitors) and software products such as InputAccel (which converts documents into electronic images) that improve scanning, display, printing, and storage of document images. Cornerstone's primary customers come from such document-heavy industries as banking and insurance and from the US government.

Stephen Sheafor, a former chip designer with Hewlett-Packard, founded Cornerstone in 1986 to provide consulting to the PC industry. The company soon began developing hardware to upgrade the imaging capabilities of PCs. It introduced its first grayscale-based system (including software and monitor) in 1987 and a color system in 1992. That year Sheafor invented the ImageAccel integrated circuit (the heart of Cornerstone's imaging display controller), which greatly improved image quality. The company went public in 1993.

Cornerstone has diversified its DIP product line through acquisitions and product development, purchasing Pixel Translations, a developer of scanner control software, in 1994 and instituting InputAccel, an open industry standard for document scanning now supported by more than 60 vendors.

In 1995 the company acquired Pegasus Disk Technologies, a developer of software for managing data stored on CD-ROM and optical disc drives. Database management innovator Oracle chose Cornerstone to provide the document imaging components for its Oracle Interoffice software in 1996.

WHO

Chairman: E. David Crockett, age 59
President and CEO: Thomas T. van Overbeek, age 46, $292,500 pay
CFO and Secretary: John Finegan, age 46, $190,125 pay
Chief Technical Officer: Stephen J. Sheafor, age 46, $112,940 pay
VP and General Manager, Display Business Unit: Kenneth E. Westrick, age 38, $194,333 pay
VP Operations: George Yule Jr., age 56, $185,050 pay
VP Software Development: Johannes P. Schmidt, age 31, $169,167 pay
VP Software Business Unit: Kimra Hawley-Foster, age 39
Manager Human Resources: Denise Wescott
Auditors: Coopers & Lybrand L.L.P.

WHERE

HQ: 1710 Fortune Dr., San Jose, CA 95131
Phone: 408-435-8900 **Fax:** 408-435-8998
Web site: http://www.corimage.com

WHAT

Selected Products

Hardware
Display subsystems (DIP subsystems based on the company's ImageAccel integrated circuit and including software, and a large-screen, high-resolution color or grayscale monitor)

Software
InputAccel (automates conversion of documents into electronic images)
PixTools (provides applications with advanced scan, display, and print functionality)

KEY COMPETITORS

Control Data
FileNet
IBM
Network Imaging
Radius
Raster Graphics

Scan-Optics
Sigma Designs
SoftNet
ViewStar
Wang

HOW MUCH

Nasdaq symbol: CRNR FYE: December 31	Annual Growth	1990	1991	1992	1993	1994	1995
Sales ($ mil.)	52.9%	10.9	14.0	23.2	43.6	70.2	91.2
Net income ($ mil.)	—	(0.6)	0.3	0.9	3.8	4.8	6.2
Income as % of sales	—	—	2.2%	3.7%	8.7%	6.9%	6.8%
Earnings per share ($)	—	(0.39)	0.06	0.15	0.61	0.66	0.81
Stock price – high ($)	—	—	—	—	16.75	26.00	25.75
Stock price – low ($)	—	—	—	—	12.75	10.00	11.50
Stock price – close ($)	(0.9%)	—	—	—	14.75	15.25	14.50
P/E – high	—	—	—	—	28	39	32
P/E – low	—	—	—	—	21	15	14
Dividends per share ($)	—	—	—	—	0.00	0.00	0.00
Book value per share ($)	30.4%	—	—	—	3.15	4.22	5.36
Employees	39.0%	—	—	82	101	162	220

1995 YEAR-END
Debt ratio: 0.0%
Return on equity: 17.8%
Cash (mil.): $10
Current ratio: 3.61
Long-term debt (mil.): $0
No. of shares (mil.): 7
Dividends
  Yield: —
  Payout: —
Market value (mil.): $106
R&D as % of sales: 8.6%

CSK CORPORATION

OVERVIEW

CSK's profitability is washing away as the demand for mainframe computers continues to recede. Not yet caught up with the change from mainframes to PCs and LANs, the company is struggling to keep its head above water. Headquartered in Tokyo, CSK is an information processing and computer services firm. It analyzes, constructs, and maintains corporate computer networks and provides related consulting services and software. CSK also supplies instructional software for the Internet and distributes a Japanese version of Netscape's Navigator Web browser. In addition, CSK contracts for some of Microsoft's customer service work in Japan.

CSK was founded in 1968 by Isao Okawa to provide computer services to Japanese companies. During the 1980s the business began to expand, creating a database management company in 1982 and a research institute in 1983. CSK began trading on Nasdaq as a foreign company that year. The company concentrated on its native Japan until 1990, when it acquired Micrognosis (a networking innovator) from Control Data (a systems integration firm).

CSK began to struggle in the early 1990s as Japan's recession led many potential customers to cut back on computer systems development. With cutbacks in the financial services industry, subsidiary Micrognosis has also been treading water.

In 1995 CSK began pursuing business in high-growth multimedia markets with the establishment of its Technology Business Group and its Electronic Commerce and Mobile System divisions. It also formed SegaSoft (a joint venture with game maker SEGA) to develop multimedia software for the Internet. The following year the company established an overseas headquarters in the US to help attract more business in North America.

WHO

Chairman and President: Isao Okawa
VC: Yasuichi Toda
VC: Kazuro Ito
EVP: Keizo Fujimoto
EVP: Masahiro Aozono
EVP: Kenshi Kashima
Senior Managing Director, Accounting and Finance: Norikazu Suzuki
Chairman and CEO (US): Takuma Amano
VP Human Resources, Finance, and Administration (US): Greg O'Brien
Auditors: Chuo Audit Corporation

WHERE

HQ: Shinjuku Sumitomo Bldg., 27th Fl., 2-6-1 Nishi-Shinjuku, Shinjuku-ku, Tokyo, 163-02, Japan
Phone: +81-3-3344-1811 **Fax:** +81-3-3344-1874
US HQ: Micrognosis, Inc., 100 Saw Mill Rd., Danbury, CT 06810
US Phone: 203-730-5300 **US Fax:** 203-730-5451
Web site: http://www.csk.co.jp

WHAT

	1996 Sales % of total
Computer services	
Programming & software development	47
Facilities management	12
Other	6
Computer & other product sales	34
Building leasing	1
Total	**100**

KEY COMPETITORS

Andersen Worldwide	Merisel
CompuCom	NEC
DEC	Origin
EDS	Toshiba
Entex	Unisys
Fujitsu	Vanstar
IBM	Wang
Inacom	

HOW MUCH

Nasdaq symbol (SC): CSKKY FYE: March 31	Annual Growth	1991	1992	1993	1994[2]	1995	1996
Sales ($ mil.)	(0.3%)	721.7	699.8	676.6	316.9	639.2	710.6
Net income ($ mil.)	(11.5%)	41.7	24.6	15.4	16.6	21.1	22.6
Income as % of sales	—	5.8%	3.5%	2.3%	5.2%	3.3%	3.2%
Earnings per share ($)	(11.9%)	0.66	0.38	0.24	0.26	0.33	0.35
Stock price – high ($)[1]	—	48.00	43.50	19.00	31.50	38.00	34.00
Stock price – low ($)[1]	—	25.00	25.25	16.75	16.50	25.00	24.00
Stock price – close ($)[1]	3.4%	27.88	27.50	16.75	20.50	33.50	33.00
P/E – high	—	73	113	79	122	116	97
P/E – low	—	38	66	70	64	76	68
Dividends per share ($)	1.9%	0.10	0.10	0.11	0.11	0.13	0.11
Book value per share ($)	2.5%	16.65	17.05	19.65	21.73	24.40	18.88
Employees	(6.8%)	7,592	8,215	6,905	6,097	5,441	5,340

[1] Stock prices are for the prior calendar year. [2] 6-month fiscal year

1996 YEAR-END

Debt ratio: 42.8%
Return on equity: 1.6%
Cash (mil.): $648
Current ratio: 1.32
Long-term debt (mil.): $400
No. of shares (mil.): 64
Dividends
  Yield: 0.3%
  Payout: 31.8%
Market value (mil.): $2,116

CYAN, INC.

OVERVIEW

The phenomenal success of Myst, the #1 CD-ROM fantasy game, has allowed Cyan to say sayonara to its earlier role as a small-time software producer of children's games. The Mead, Washington-based company, founded by brothers Rand and Robyn Miller and their friend Chris Brandkamp, launched Myst through software publisher Brøderbund in 1993; it promptly sold 500,000 copies in the first year on the market. By 1996 Myst had become the first CD-ROM entertainment title to sell 2 million units.

The software equivalent of a cult-classic art film, Myst creates a colorful, artistic, interactive fantasy game that takes place on Myst Island. It incorporates 3-D animation and advanced sound and music technology with intriguing story lines and puzzles. Unlike other popular CD-ROMs, Myst is neither goal oriented nor violent; it emphasizes intellectual exploration and aesthetics over the traditional adventure format. Cyan's other games are The Manhole, Cosmic Osmo, and Spelunx and the Caves of Mr. Seudo.

The sons of a nondenominational preacher who traveled from church to church and state to state, Rand and Robyn (and 2 other brothers) moved regularly and grew up in an environment that encouraged debate and intellectual exploration. As adults the 2 brothers joined forces to develop a line of innovative children's computer games, founding Cyan in Brandkamp's garage in the mid-1980s. Robyn specialized in artwork; Rand worked on programming. The Manhole (an underground-world game) was released in 1987. This was followed by Cosmic Osmo (a space fantasy, 1990) and Spelunx (a science and nature exploration game, 1992). All sold respectably and received critical acclaim.

Moving into games for older audiences, Cyan got the backing of Japan's Sunsoft (a 5% owner) to help develop Myst.

The demands of public relations, a Disney contract (for Myst novels, products, and a film), and other distractions have delayed the brothers getting to work on Myst II. Originally scheduled to be under development 3 months after the first version was launched, it now has a 1997 release date.

WHO

President: Rand Miller, age 36
VP Operations and CFO: Chris Brandkamp
VP: Robyn Miller, age 29
Business Coordinator: Bonnie Staub
Director Human Resources: Heather Ferguson

WHERE

HQ: 14617 Newport Hwy., Mead, WA 99021
Phone: 509-468-0807
Fax: 509-467-2209
Web site: http://www.cyan.com

WHAT

Software Products
Cosmic Osmo
The Manhole
Myst
Spelunx and the Caves of Mr. Seudo

Software Product Under Development
Myst II

KEY COMPETITORS

3DO
7th Level
Acclaim Entertainment
Accolade
Activision
Aristo International
CUC International
Davidson & Associates
Digital Pictures
Educational Insights
Electronic Arts
GT Interactive
id Software
Interplay Productions
JTS
Knowledge Adventure
LucasArts
Microsoft
Nintendo
Rocket Science Games
SEGA
SoftKey
Sony
Spectrum HoloByte
Trilobyte

HOW MUCH

Private company FYE: December 31	Annual Growth	1990	1991	1992	1993	1994	1995
Sales ($ mil.)	—	—	—	—	—	9.0	12.0
Employees	58.1%	—	—	—	8	9	20

CYAN

CYBERSOURCE CORPORATION

OVERVIEW

Instead of driving to the computer store to buy that new software, why not just download it to your PC? That's what CyberSource would like you to do. Based in Menlo Park, California, the company is the first to offer electronic software distribution over the Internet. software.net, the company's Web site, is the largest software superstore on the Internet, offering more than 15,000 products from 600 publishers. Many titles can be downloaded via modem, including software from Symantec, Claris, NetManage, Novell, Quarterdeck, and IBM. CyberSource also offers Internet Commerce Services, which provides secure transaction processing for companies doing business online.

CyberSource was founded in late 1994 by CEO William McKiernan, former president of antivirus specialists McAfee Associates, and ex-CompuServe executive Jim Hogan. The company's software.net site was a traditional mail-order catalog online until 1995, when it began offering several titles by "electronic delivery." CyberSource gave out about 20 software titles free of charge, including Symantec's Norton Utilities program. After 30 days the downloaded program would delete itself unless the customer paid for it.

As security concerns have given online credit card transactions a degree of uncertainty, CyberSource has developed its Fraud Screen Technology to validate credit transactions with banks. Its Electronic Distribution Technology (EDT) encrypts digital content for secure transmission. The password to decrypt the package is sent separately via e-mail. Several companies, including QUALCOMM, Insignia, and Wall Data, have contracted CyberSource to conduct their online transactions. CyberSource continues to expand by offering Web sites that focus on niche markets, such as the Windows 95 Product Center and Internet Product Center.

In 1996 the company signed an agreement with the US Department of Defense to offer electronic ordering and distribution of software to federal employees for the first time. CyberSource has also joined with Microsoft to offer the latter's discount products via software.net's new Microsoft Government Express! Center.

WHO

President and CEO: William S. McKiernan
VP and Chief Technical Officer: John Pettit
CFO: Blake Burke
Director Human Resources: Brook Lenox

WHERE

HQ: 1050 Chestnut St., Ste. 200, Menlo Park, CA 94025
Phone: 415-462-5522   **Fax:** 415-473-3066
Web site: http://www.software.net

	1995 Sales
	% of total
US	65
Europe	25
Japan	8
Australia & New Zealand	2
Total	**100**

WHAT

Selected Software Publishers

Claris	Novell
FTP	QUALCOMM
IBM	Quarterdeck
Microsoft	Symantec
NetManage	Verity

Selected Services
Hewlett-Packard Solutions Center
Internet Product Center
License Express Center (volume purchase discounts from such publishers as Microsoft and Wall Data)
Reusable Software Component Marketplace
software.net (Internet-based software superstore)
Windows 95 Product Center

Other Services
Electronic Distribution Technology (EDT: encryption technology to ensure secure transmission of financial data)
Internet Commerce Services (secure transactions via the Internet)

KEY COMPETITORS

ASAP Software	Intelligent Systems
CDW Computer Centers	Micro Warehouse
CINET	NeoStar
CompuCom	Office Depot
CompUSA	Oracle
Egghead	Software Spectrum
ELEK-TEK	Staples
Fry's Electronics	Tandy Corporation
Global Directmail	Vanstar
InfoNow	

HOW MUCH

Private company FYE: December 31	Annual Growth	1990	1991	1992	1993	1994	1995
Sales ($ mil.)	—	—	—	—	—	0.0	1.0
Employees	—	—	—	—	—	10	20

CyberSource Corporation

CYPRESS SEMICONDUCTOR

OVERVIEW

Cypress Semiconductor is branching out. The San Jose-based, high-performance microchip maker has recently added specialty memory chips for cellular phones and high-speed networks. Cypress's major customers include computer, electronics, and telecommunications makers such as AT&T, Compaq, IBM, and Motorola.

Founder and CEO T. J. Rodgers left AMD in 1982 to start Cypress, taking Lowell Turriff, an AMD marketing VP, with him. The 2 companies have been feuding ever since.

Cypress went public in 1986. The company's growth has been fueled by funding start-up operations such as Ross Technology (SPARC microprocessors; sold 1993) and Aspen Semiconductor (ECL, PLDs, and SRAMs), which operates independently but is controlled by Cypress. In 1992 a price war and the late delivery of a key product, hyperSPARC, resulted in a drop in sales and Cypress's first annual loss as a public company.

New products helped Cypress return to profitability in 1994. Strategic acquisitions followed, including Contaq Microsystems, a PC chipset maker, and IC Designs, a maker of PC timing products.

Cypress opened its 4th plant, in Minnesota, in 1995. As memory chip prices began to fall in early 1996, Cypress's customer mix helped the company withstand the pricing crunch. However, by midyear Cypress was feeling the effects of the continuing slide and said it would delay construction on its 5th chip factory. That year Rodgers won media attention for his public response to the suggestion of a shareholder and Catholic nun that he put more qualified women and minorities on Cypress's board. Rodgers replied that choosing board members based on race and gender is "a lousy way to run a company."

WHO

Chairman: Pierre Lamond, age 65
President and CEO: Thurman John Rodgers, age 48, $524,523 pay
VP Marketing and Sales: J. Daniel McCranie, age 52, $503,344 pay
VP Research and Development: Antonio R. Alvarez, age 39, $367,636 pay
VP Wafer Fabrication; President, Cypress Semiconductor (Minnesota), Inc.: Lothar Maier, age 41, $342,047 pay
VP Finance and Administration and CFO: Emmanuel Hernandez, age 40, $333,852 pay
VP Human Resources: Joyce Sziebert
Auditors: Price Waterhouse LLP

WHERE

HQ: Cypress Semiconductor Corporation, 3901 N. First St., San Jose, CA 95134-1599
Phone: 408-943-2600   **Fax:** 408-943-6859
Web site: http://www.cypress.com

WHAT

	1995 Sales by OEM Application
	% of total
Telecommunications	29
Datacommunications	27
Computers	22
Computer peripherals	17
Other	5
Total	**100**

KEY COMPETITORS

Altera	Micron	SGS-Thomson
AMD	Technology	Sharp
Atmel	Motorola	Texas
Fujitsu	National	Instruments
Hitachi	Semiconductor	Toshiba
Integrated Device	OPTi	VLSI Technology
Technology	Philips	Waferscale
Integrated Silicon	Quality	Integration
Solution	Semiconductor	Xilinx
Intel	Samsung	

HOW MUCH

NYSE symbol: CY FYE: December 31	Annual Growth	1990	1991	1992	1993	1994	1995
Sales ($ mil.)	21.5%	225.2	286.8	272.2	304.5	406.4	596.1
Net income ($ mil.)	25.3%	33.2	34.2	(21.0)	8.0	50.5	102.5
Income as % of sales	—	14.8%	11.9%	—	2.6%	12.4%	17.2%
Earnings per share ($)	19.9%	0.44	0.43	(0.28)	0.11	0.60	1.09
Stock price – high ($)	—	7.81	12.25	9.19	8.38	12.06	27.75
Stock price – low ($)	—	4.06	5.44	3.69	4.31	6.56	10.75
Stock price – close ($)	18.1%	5.50	8.56	4.63	6.81	11.56	12.63
P/E – high	—	18	29	—	80	20	25
P/E – low	—	9	13	—	41	11	10
Dividends per share ($)	—	0.00	0.00	0.00	0.00	0.00	0.00
Book value per share ($)	11.4%	3.38	3.95	3.63	3.75	4.54	5.79
Employees	3.1%	1,595	1,945	1,529	1,262	1,423	1,859

1995 YEAR-END
Debt ratio: 16.9%
Return on equity: 24.8%
Cash (mil.): $162
Current ratio: 2.18
Long-term debt (mil.): $96
No. of shares (mil.): 82
Dividends
 Yield: —
 Payout: —
Market value (mil.): $1,029
R&D as % of sales: 12.3%

DALLAS SEMICONDUCTOR

OVERVIEW

Forget diamond chips, dahling; now you can wear a ring with a computer chip. Niche microchip products such as the digital decoder ring (which, among other things, can activate special sensors connected to computer controlling building access) are the specialty of Texas-based Dallas Semiconductor. The company makes more than 200 proprietary products and over 1,000 variations for manufacturers of consumer electronics, personal computers, scientific instrumentation, and telecommunications products, among others. Leading electronics distributor Avnet accounts for around 10% of the firm's sales.

Dallas Semiconductor was formed in 1984 by a group from Dallas-based chip maker Mostek. Mostek had floundered in the early 1980s in part because it offered too few products for a too-small client base. The company's Mostek alumni include Chairman C. V. Prothro and SVP Chao Mai, who own 9% and 3% of the company, respectively. Its technical prowess includes combining lithium cells with its chips, which gives them added life, and using direct laser writing to program the chips, which provides a higher level of precision. Dallas Semiconductor went public in 1987.

New products for 1995 included a family of plug-and-play timekeepers for personal computers and a battery identification chip that monitors battery temperature and the status of its charge. The following year Dallas Semiconductor debuted a sensor/actuator chip that can perform control functions in devices such as burglar alarms, irrigation control, thermostats, and vending machines.

Also that year, it developed the Crytographic i Button (a computer chip encased in stainless steel) which can be used for the secure transfer of electronic communications.

WHO

Chairman, President, and CEO: C. V. Prothro, age 53, $1,556,875 pay
SVP: Chao C. Mai, age 60, $648,813 pay
VP Marketing and Product Development: Michael L. Bolan, age 49, $401,562 pay
VP Computer Products: F. A. Scherpenberg, age 49, $376,094 pay
VP Sales and Strategic Marketing: Douglas L. Powell, age 71, $342,232 pay
VP Finance: Alan P. Hale, age 35
VP Human Resources: Gay Vencill
Auditors: Ernst & Young LLP

WHERE

HQ: 4401 S. Beltwood Pkwy., Dallas, TX 75244-3292
Phone: 214-450-0400 **Fax:** 214-450-3748
Web site: http://www.dalsemi.com

WHAT

Selected Products
Automatic identification chips
Integrated battery backup
Intelligent sockets
Microcontrollers
Multiport memories
Nonvolatile SRAMs
Silicon timed circuits
SIP Stik Prefab subassemblies
Software authorization chips
System extensions
Telecommunications chips
Timekeeping chips

KEY COMPETITORS

Alliance Semiconductor
Analog Devices
Atmel
Burr-Brown
Catalyst Semiconductor
Cypress Semiconductor
Integrated Device
  Technology
Integrated Silicon Solution

Intel
Microchip Technology
Motorola
National Semiconductor
Sharp
Siliconix
Texas Instruments
Xicor

HOW MUCH

NYSE symbol: DS FYE: December 31	Annual Growth	1990	1991	1992	1993	1994	1995
Sales ($ mil.)	18.5%	100.0	103.8	20.2	156.9	181.4	233.3
Net income ($ mil.)	21.6%	13.8	14.7	18.6	25.6	29.7	36.7
Income as % of sales	—	13.8%	14.2%	5.5%	16.3%	16.4%	15.7%
Earnings per share ($)	18.7%	0.56	0.58	0.71	0.95	1.09	1.32
Stock price – high ($)	—	9.63	12.38	4.50	19.00	20.13	24.88
Stock price – low ($)	—	4.13	5.38	7.00	11.75	13.38	15.00
Stock price – close ($)	27.6%	6.13	7.88	3.38	15.50	16.63	20.75
P/E – high	—	17	21	20	20	18	19
P/E – low	—	7	9	10	12	12	11
Dividends per share ($)	—	0.00	0.00	0.00	0.00	0.00	0.10
Book value per share ($)	16.9%	4.08	4.69	5.47	6.53	7.66	8.89
Employees	9.0%	701	662	696	748	821	1,078

1995 YEAR-END
Debt ratio: 0.0%
Return on equity: 17.1%
Cash (mil.): $69
Current ratio: 4.31
Long-term debt (mil.): $0
No. of shares (mil.): 26
Dividends
  Yield: 0.5%
  Payout: 7.6%
Market value (mil.): $549
R&D as % of sales: 12.3%

DATAFLEX CORPORATION

OVERVIEW

Dataflex is a direct marketer of computer equipment, but servicing that equipment has become the fastest growing part of the company's business. Edison, New Jersey-based Dataflex targets major corporations for its sales of PCs, peripherals, and related equipment. IBM and Compaq products represent 31% and 13%, respectively, of its revenues, and the company is the country's top volume dealer of Hewlett-Packard computers. To support its sales, Dataflex offers an increasing variety of systems integration, product maintenance, technical support, and training programs. Dataflex has sold 40% of the company to Recovery Equity Partners, an investment firm specializing in turnarounds, and has undergone a major restructuring to consolidate recent purchases.

Dataflex was founded in 1976 by office equipment repairman and salesman Jeffrey Lamm after he noticed that IBM made more money from servicing its products than from selling them. By 1981 Dataflex was bringing in $2.5 million in sales with 8 field technicians. The company went public that year.

Until 1994 Dataflex was working with clients exclusively in Connecticut, New Jersey, New York, and Pennsylvania. That year the firm expanded nationally by acquiring Granite Computer Products (Alameda, California), Advantage Systems (Bensenville, Illinois), Sunland Computer Services (Tempe, Arizona), and Hagen Computer Systems (Tucson, Arizona). In 1995, it acquired National Data Products (Clearwater, Florida).

After bulking up with acquisitions, Dataflex agreed in 1996 to sell assets and liabilities from its Western Region unit to systems integrator Vanstar. It also sold its Valtron disk drive repair unit to an investor group led by the unit's operating president.

WHO

Chairman and CEO: Richard C. Rose, age 47, $583,816 pay
President: Philip Doganiero, age 38
SVP: Ann Marie Bernet
SVP Finance and CFO: Raymond DioGuardi, age 40
Director Human Resources: David Castel
Auditors: Price Waterhouse LLP

WHERE

HQ: 3920 Park Ave., Edison, NJ 08820
Phone: 908-321-1100   **Fax:** 908-321-6590
Web site: http://www.dataflex.com

WHAT

Selected Operations

Sales
Application software
Desktop PCs
Individual components
Laptop PCs
Monitors
Operating systems
Peripherals
Servers

Services
Consulting services

Equipment maintenance
  and repair
Help desk support
Network installation
System integration
Training

Selected Vendors
Apple
Compaq
Hewlett-Packard
IBM
Microsoft

KEY COMPETITORS

AmeriData
BDM International
Bell Atlantic
Brandon Systems
CDI
CompuCom
Computer Sciences
Control Data
Data General

DecisionOne
Dell
Entex
Gateway 2000
IBM
Inacom
Memorex Telex
MicroAge
Vanstar

HOW MUCH

Nasdaq symbol: DFLX FYE: March 31	Annual Growth	1991	1992	1993	1994	1995	1996
Sales ($ mil.)	38.5%	92.6	89.6	67.6	102.4	273.9	472.1
Net income ($ mil.)	—	4.6	4.0	1.0	0.8	2.1	(6.3)
Income as % of sales	—	4.9%	4.5%	1.4%	0.8%	0.8%	—
Earnings per share ($)	—	1.33	1.09	0.28	0.25	0.45	(1.22)
Stock price – high ($)[1]	—	12.75	17.00	16.75	6.50	10.75	10.13
Stock price – low ($)[1]	—	5.25	8.50	4.00	3.50	5.75	3.00
Stock price – close ($)[1]	(16.8%)	8.50	15.25	6.00	6.13	8.88	3.38
P/E – high	—	10	16	60	26	24	—
P/E – low	—	4	8	14	14	13	—
Dividends per share ($)	—	0.00	0.00	0.00	0.00	0.00	0.00
Book value per share ($)	(0.4%)	5.93	7.01	7.42	7.68	7.17	5.82
Employees	35.9%	175	—	183	220	1,032	811

[1] Stock prices are for the prior calender year.

1996 YEAR-END
Debt ratio: 73.2%
Return on equity: —
Cash (mil.): $0.5
Current ratio: 1.70
Long-term debt (mil.): $54.1
No. of shares (mil.): 5.5
Dividends
  Yield: —
  Payout: —
Market value (mil.): $18.5

DATAWARE TECHNOLOGIES, INC.

OVERVIEW

Dataware Technologies can turn a roomful of paper into a couple of shiny discs. The Cambridge, Massachusetts-based software developer makes CD-ROM and text management software that enables customers to record and distribute large amounts of information, such as newspaper archives, research databases, and company documents. One of Dataware's newest additions to its software family is NetAnswer, which allows customers to send large amounts of information over the Internet. CEO Kurt Mueller and COO Jeffrey Nyweide own 8% and 6% of the company, respectively.

Mueller, former general manager of Lotus Development's West German subsidiary, was convinced that CD-ROMs would take off just as music CDs had, and he wanted to provide the tools that would allow nonprogrammers to develop CD-ROMs. In 1986 he teamed with software developer Jim Kearney to found Dataware 2000 in Germany. Three years later, Mueller moved the company to the US and renamed it Dataware Technologies. It focused on high-end users, selling easy-to-use software to customers who wanted to do in-house publishing. Dataware more than doubled its sales in 1992 when it acquired CD-ROM tools company Reference Technology. It went public in 1993.

Since the company went public, it has expanded its product lines and marketing operations through acquisitions. In 1994 it bought its Swedish and Canadian distributors, PCD Consult, and expanded into information management and online delivery when it acquired BRS Software Products, a document management software company.

Dataware acquired Ledge Multimedia (Multimedia services and software) in 1995 and S Cube SRL, a Milan based software company, the next year.

WHO

Chairman and CEO: Kurt Mueller, age 39, $162,825 pay
President and COO: Jeffrey O. Nyweide, age 40, $151,363 pay
CFO: Chris Lorch
SVP Eurasian Operations: Wolfgang P. Ruth, age 45,
Office Manager: Sue Martin
Auditors: Coopers & Lybrand L.L.P.

WHERE

HQ: 222 Third St., Ste. 3300, Cambridge, MA 02142
Phone: 617-621-0820   **Fax:** 617-621-0307
Web site: http://www.dataware.com

WHAT

	1995 Sales	
	$ mil.	% of total
Software license fees	20.0	49
Services	18.9	46
Systems integration	2.2	5
Total	**41.1**	**100**

Software Products
BRS/Search (information management)
CD Answer (database retrieval)
CD Author (database authoring)
CD Author Advanced Design Library
NETANSWER (internet management)

Services	**Systems Integration**
CD-ROM Production Services	Distribution services
Consulting	Hardware resale
Internet Hosting Services	Maintenance services
Maintenance Services	Software premastering
Project management	
Software support	

KEY COMPETITORS

Asymetrix	Fulcrum Technologies
CACI International	Macromedia
Claris	Metatec
Excalibur Technologies	Microsoft
FileNet	Thomson Corp.

HOW MUCH

Nasdaq symbol: DWTI FYE: December 31	Annual Growth	1990	1991	1992	1993	1994	1995
Sales ($ mil.)	71.1%	2.8	5.8	13.7	19.3	32.4	41.1
Net income ($ mil.)	—	(1.8)	(1.9)	(0.6)	(1.7)	1.1	1.7
Income as % of sales	—	—	—	—	—	3.4%	4.2%
Earnings per share ($)	—	(1.87)	(1.55)	(0.44)	(0.52)	0.18	0.26
Stock price – high ($)	—	—	—	—	23.50	14.25	16.25
Stock price – low ($)	—	—	—	—	7.75	7.25	8.00
Stock price – close ($)	(1.5%)	—	—	—	8.50	11.50	8.25
P/E – high	—	—	—	—	—	79	63
P/E – low	—	—	—	—	—	40	31
Dividends per share ($)	—	—	—	—	0.00	0.00	0.00
Book value per share ($)	3.8%	—	—	—	4.79	4.87	5.16
Employees	41.9%	—	—	112	170	274	320

1995 YEAR-END
Debt ratio: 0.9%
Return on equity: 5.7%
Cash (mil.): $8
Current ratio: 2.14
Long-term debt (mil.): $0
No. of shares (mil.): 6
Dividends
  Yield: —
  Payout: —
Market value (mil.): $52
R&D as % of sales: 12.3%

DIAMOND MULTIMEDIA SYSTEMS, INC.

OVERVIEW

Diamond is finding the competition in the computer peripherals market a little rough. The San Jose-based company makes graphics accelerators, hardware that helps computers process power-sapping sound and graphics. Diamond also makes fax/modems and ISDN digital telephone adapters (for network access). Though sales have been rising, increased competition in the peripherals industry and costs related to acquisitions have left Diamond with a ruby-red bottom line. Investor groups Summit Partners and TA Associates own 15% and 9% of the company, respectively, while founder Chong-Moon Lee owns about 8%.

A descendant of King Sei-Jung (who Lee says created the Korean language in the 14th century), Lee started Diamond Computer Systems in 1982 to explore the possibility of running Apple software on IBM computers. The attempt failed, costing Lee his house, his marriage, and $2.7 million. In 1987 a member of IBM's board suggested to Lee that he find a niche for himself in multimedia. Renamed Diamond Multimedia Systems, the company's first product in the relatively new industry was a software driver, which Lee sold to computer maker Gateway 2000. Diamond made its hardware products domestically, so it beat its Asian competitors to the marketplace. Through the early 1990s the company focused on high-performance graphics accelerators.

In 1994 Lee sold stakes in Diamond to Summit Partners and TA Associates. The next year he took the company public. Also in 1995 Diamond bought Supra Corporation (fax/modems) and SPEA Software (accelerators) and launched a telecommunications system that offered fax, modem, telephone, voice mail, and other capabilities in a single unit. In 1996 the company introduced its first ISDN device for PCs.

WHO

Chairman: Chong-Moon Lee, age 68
President and CEO: William J. Schroeder, age 51, $450,000 pay
SVP and CFO: Gary B. Filler, age 55, $360,270 pay
SVP and Chief Technical Officer: Hyung Hwe Huh, age 43, $339,308 pay
SVP Worldwide Sales: C. Scott Holt, age 54, $325,890 pay
VP and General Counsel: Frank G. Hausmann
Controller (HR): Song Kim
Auditors: Coopers & Lybrand L.L.P.

WHERE

HQ: 2880 Junction Ave., San Jose, CA 95134-1922
Phone: 408-325-7000   **Fax:** 408-325-7070
Web site: http://www.diamondmm.com

	1995 Sales % of total
US	65
Other countries	35
Total	**100**

WHAT

Selected Products	Graphics accelerators
3D accelerators	Stealth
Diamond EDGE 3D	Viper
Fire GL	Internet products
Fax/modems	Internet Kit
Supra	ISDN adapters
TeleCommander	Supra NetCommander
	Supra Simple

KEY COMPETITORS

3Com	Oki Electric
ATI Technologies	PairGain
Boca Research	S3
Cirrus Logic	STB Systems
Creative	Trident
Technology	Microsystems
Hayes	Tseng Labs
Microcomputer	U.S. Robotics
IEC Electronics	Weitek
Number Nine	Western Digital
Visual	

HOW MUCH

Nasdaq symbol: DIMD FYE: December 31	Annual Growth	1990	1991	1992	1993	1994	1995
Sales ($ mil.)	84.7%	—	40.2	74.5	130.3	203.3	467.6
Net income ($ mil.)	—	—	4.1	7.1	12.4	20.1	(41.3)
Income as % of sales	—	—	10.1%	9.5%	9.5%	9.9%	—
Earnings per share ($)	—	—	0.19	0.34	0.59	0.96	(1.55)
Stock price – high ($)	—	—	—	—	—	—	43.00
Stock price – low ($)	—	—	—	—	—	—	16.50
Stock price – close ($)	—	—	—	—	—	—	35.88
P/E – high	—	—	—	—	—	—	—
P/E – low	—	—	—	—	—	—	—
Dividends per share ($)	—	—	—	—	—	—	0.00
Book value per share ($)	—	—	—	—	—	—	6.02
Employees	110.6%	—	—	80	125	271	747

1995 YEAR-END
Debt ratio: 12.5%
Return on equity: —
Cash (mil.): $106
Current ratio: 2.49
Long-term debt (mil.): $12
No. of shares (mil.): 35
Dividends
  Yield: —
  Payout: —
Market value (mil.): $1,244
R&D as % of sales: 2.3%
Advertising as % of sales: 2.0%

DIGITAL PICTURES

OVERVIEW

Dishing out a mix of sports (Slam City with Scottie Pippen) and ghoulishness (Corpse City), Digital Pictures serves up the staples of the teenage software diet. But the San Mateo, California-based game maker caters to younger children too (Kids on Site). The private company is a pioneer in the field of realistic interactive games and has developed 16 CD-ROMs for computers and game systems. Each game is developed as a feature film complete with dialogue and music.

Tom Zito, formerly a technology and entertainment reporter for the "Washington Post," founded interactive toy maker Axlon in 1984 (with colleague Nolan Bushnell) and Isix, which developed an interactive TV system, in 1986. In 1991 Zito founded Digital Pictures, which broke new ground when its entry into the CD-ROM game market brought the realism of movies to a genre dominated by cartoon characters. When the company launched its first titles (Night Trap and Sewer Shark) in 1992, they became the top-selling SEGA CD titles that year. (Night Trap was held up as a prime example in a Senate subcommittee hearing on videogame violence in 1993.) The company released Ground Zero Texas and Prize Fighter in 1993. To ensure quality productions, Digital Pictures entered into an agreement that year to use Directors Guild of America members to direct its live-action productions.

The company in 1994 formed Digital Kids to produce interactive titles for younger children. Its first, Kids On Site (a construction site game), was released that year, as was Slam City. In 1995 the company released Supreme Warrior and Quarterback Attack with Mike Ditka.

But it was Slump City for Digital Pictures in 1995, when weak sales were compounded by the company's off-target strategy to develop titles only for the SEGA Saturn machine that Christmas season when Sony's PlayStation was pulling in better sales. The company laid off 40% of its workforce in 1996. It also announced plans to drop its console games entirely and focus on the PC and Macintosh markets.

WHO

President and CEO: Tom Zito, age 47
CFO: Mark Carlson, age 30
VP Business Development and General Counsel: Nancy Dusseau, age 40
VP Engineering: Mark Klein, age 38
VP Product Development: Amanda Lathroum, age 31
VP Education: Michael P. Carter, age 49
VP Sales: Melanie Mroz, age 31
Senior Product Manager: Garrett Glover, age 49
Manager Human Resources: N. Brucker
Auditors:

WHERE

HQ: 1825 S. Grant St., Ste. 900, San Mateo, CA 94402
Phone: 415-345-5300   **Fax:** 415-286-8811
Web site: http://www.digipix.com

WHAT

Selected Software Titles
Corpse Killer
Double Switch
Ground Zero Texas
Kids on Site
Maximum Surge
Night Trap
Quarterback Attack with Mike Ditka
Sewer Shark
Slam City with Scottie Pippen

KEY COMPETITORS

3DO
Acclaim Entertainment
Accolade
Activision
Brøderbund
CUC International
Electronic Arts
GT Interactive
id Software
Interplay Productions
JTS
LucasArts
Maxis
Microsoft
Nintendo
Sanctuary Woods
SEGA
Sony
Spectrum HoloByte
Spelling Entertainment
WMS Industries

HOW MUCH

Private company FYE: December 31	Annual Growth	1990	1991	1992	1993	1994	1995
Sales ($ mil.)	—	—	—	—	—	—	10.0
Employees	—	—	—	—	—	—	35

THE DII GROUP, INC.

OVERVIEW

DII (pronounced "D-eye") offers a smorgasbord of electronics-making tools. The Colorado-based company (formerly called DOVatron International) supplies a variety of electronics manufacturing products and services through 5 business units. The largest, accounting for 3/4 of revenues, is DOVatron Manufacturing, a leading contract electronics manufacturer (CEM). Among DII's major customers is Standard Microsystems, which accounts for about 12% of the company's revenues.

DII got its start in 1970 as a division of Universal Instruments Corp. (a subsidiary of industrial conglomerate Dover Corp.). In 1987 it became Dover Electronics, a stand-alone operating unit within Dover. In 1993 Dover Electronics was spun off, with Ronald Budacz, who had been president of the unit since 1988, leading the way. The spinoff went public as DOVatron International in a $50 million offering.

DOVatron expanded rapidly by acquiring other CEMs. In 1994 it doubled its workforce with the purchases of California CEM, the Theilen Group, Mexican CEM Sistemas Inteligentes Ceretronik, California circuit board maker Multilayer Technology, and Test Technology, a Singapore-based developer of in-circuit test hardware and software.

Undercapitalized customers led to a $7.2 million after-tax charge in 1994. The following year the company expanded its testing capabilities by acquiring TTI Testron, the US's leading maker of integrated-circuit test-fixture equipment (which connects the chip being tested to the testing device).

DOVatron changed its name to the DII Group in 1996. That year the company agreed to acquire Orbit Semiconductor, a California-based maker of application-specific integrated circuits (ASICs), in a $111 million stock swap.

WHO

Chairman and CEO: Ronald R. Budacz, age 49, $525,000 pay
SVP and CFO: Carl R. Vertuca Jr., age 49, $300,000 pay
SVP; President, DOVatron Manufacturing Worldwide: Dermott O'Flanagan, age 44, $275,000 pay
SVP Sales and Marketing: Ronald R. Snyder, age 39, $187,000 pay
SVP; SVP Materials and Information Systems, DOVatron Manufacturing Worldwide: Carl A. Plichta, age 45, $145,000 pay
Director Human Resources: Connie Renfrew
Auditors: KPMG Peat Marwick LLP

WHERE

HQ: 6273 Monarch Park Pl., Ste. 200, Niwot, CO 80503
Phone: 303-652-2221 **Fax:** 303-652-0602

WHAT

	1995 Sales
	% of total
DOVatron Manufacturing	75
Multek	17
Cencorp, IRI & TTI	8
Total	**100**

Operating Companies

Cencorp, Inc. (niche assembly machine tools)
DOVatron Manufacturing (contract assembly of electronic circuits)
IRI International (process tooling)
Multilayer Technology, Inc. (MulTek, complex printed circuits)
TTI Testron, Inc. (in-circuit testing equipment)

KEY COMPETITORS

ACT Manufacturing
Anam
Benchmark Electronics
CMC Industries
Comptronix
Electronic Fab
Group Technologies
Hadco
IEC Electronics
Jabil
Jaco Electronics
Kent Electronics
PCI Ltd.
Sanmina
SCI Systems
SigmaTron
Solectron
Teradyne
Zycon

HOW MUCH

Nasdaq symbol: DIIG FYE: December 31	Annual Growth	1990	1991	1992	1993	1994	1995
Sales ($ mil.)	53.5%	39.3	51.7	101.1	131.8	208.0	335.4
Net income ($ mil.)	26.7%	5.0	4.5	6.3	6.3	3.7	16.3
Income as % of sales	—	12.8%	8.7%	6.3%	4.8%	1.8%	4.8%
Earnings per share ($)	25.4%	—	0.78	1.11	1.07	0.46	1.93
Stock price – high ($)	—	—	—	—	30.25	32.25	35.50
Stock price – low ($)	—	—	—	—	14.75	18.00	17.50
Stock price – close ($)	10.8%	—	—	—	27.50	25.75	33.75
P/E – high	—	—	—	—	28	70	18
P/E – low	—	—	—	—	14	39	9
Dividends per share ($)	—	—	—	—	0.00	0.00	0.00
Book value per share ($)	9.8%	—	—	—	11.11	11.35	13.40
Employees	70.8%	—	—	—	1,200	2,400	3,500

1995 YEAR-END
Debt ratio: 48.6%
Return on equity: 16.3%
Cash (mil.): $45
Current ratio: 2.04
Long-term debt (mil.): $86
No. of shares (mil.): 8
Dividends
  Yield: —
  Payout: —
Market value (mil.): $274

ELECTRONIC ARTS INC.

OVERVIEW

Electronic Arts (EA) can really push your buttons. The San Mateo, California-based creator and distributor of recreational software makes live-action sports and adventure video games, such as PGA TOUR Golf and Wing Commander for 14 different game systems. It also produces the audio and visual components used in its products. While nearly 60% of its sales come from video cartridges (for Sega and Nintendo systems), EA is focusing on producing more of its titles on CD-ROM.

After 4 years with Apple Computer, video game pioneer Trip Hawkins left in 1982, raised $5 million from private investors, and founded a company that would explore the entertainment potential of PCs. The result was a variety of video games. In 1990 EA began designing games for the Sega Genesis video game system, and sales exploded.

In 1992 the company bought Origin Systems, an Austin, Texas, software publisher, and formed a joint venture with a unit of consumer electronics business JVC to market EA products in Japan. A merger attempt by gamemaker Brøderbund Software failed in 1994, the same year Hawkins resigned to devote time to his new venture, game system maker 3DO. (Hawkins still owns 5% of EA.) Also in 1994 EA expanded its direct distribution capabilities in Europe with the purchase of Spanish software supplier DROSoft.

In 1995 the company announced it would gradually sell off its 18% stake in 3DO, which developed the first 32-bit CD-ROM game system, as it evolves into a competitor in the market for video games. Also that year EA purchased Germany-based video game distributor Kingsoft and acquired Bullfrog Productions, a UK-based video game developer. EA purchased entertainment software developer Manley & Associates in 1996.

WHO

Chairman, President, and CEO: Lawrence F. Probst III, age 46, $480,571 pay
EVP Marketing: William B. Gordon, age 46, $293,232 pay
SVP and Chief Financial and Administrative Officer (HR): E. Stanton McKee Jr., age 51, $330,435 pay
SVP International: Mark S. Lewis, age 46, $301,801 pay
SVP North American Sales and Distribution: Nancy L. Smith, age 43, $293,235 pay
VP, General Counsel, and Secretary: Ruth A. Kennedy
Auditors: KPMG Peat Marwick LLP

WHERE

HQ: 1450 Fashion Island Blvd., San Mateo, CA 94404-2064
Phone: 415-571-7171   **Fax:** 415-513-7160
Web site: http://www.ea.com

WHAT

	1995 Sales
	% of total
Cartridge products	60
CD-ROM products	21
Affiliated labels	10
PC floppy disk products	5
Licensing	4
Total	**100**

Selected Titles	
FIFA International Soccer	Road Rash
John Madden Football	Shock Wave
NBA Live 95	U.S. Navy Fighters
PGA TOUR Golf	Wing Commander III

KEY COMPETITORS

3DO	Digital Pictures	SEGA
7th Level	GT Interactive	Sony
Acclaim	id Software	Spectrum
Entertainment	Interplay	HoloByte
Accolade	Productions	Trilobyte
Activision	JTS	WMS Industries
Brøderbund	LucasArts	
CUC	Microsoft	
International	Nintendo	

HOW MUCH

Nasdaq symbol: ERTS FYE: March 31	Annual Growth	1991	1992	1993	1994	1995	1996
Sales ($ mil.)	39.2%	101.8	162.1	298.4	418.3	493.3	531.9
Net income ($ mil.)	34.8%	9.1	15.7	30.9	44.7	55.7	40.5
Income as % of sales	—	8.9%	9.7%	10.4%	10.7%	11.3%	7.6%
Earnings per share ($)	26.7%	0.23	0.37	0.65	0.90	1.07	0.75
Stock price – high ($)[1]	—	4.22	9.63	21.75	42.00	33.50	42.25
Stock price – low ($)[1]	—	1.53	2.22	9.19	19.75	12.75	15.38
Stock price – close ($)[1]	62.0%	2.34	9.56	20.63	30.00	19.25	26.13
P/E – high	—	18	26	34	47	31	56
P/E – low	—	7	6	14	22	12	21
Dividends per share ($)	—	0.00	0.00	0.00	0.00	0.00	0.00
Book value per share ($)	39.7%	1.15	1.56	2.39	3.61	4.66	6.11
Employees	38.0%	300	470	910	1,077	1,172	1,500

[1] Stock prices are for the prior calendar year.

1996 YEAR-END
Debt ratio: 0.0%
Return on equity: 14.5%
Cash (mil.): $186
Current ratio: 2.98
Long-term debt (mil.): $0
No. of shares (mil.): 53
Dividends
  Yield: —
  Payout: —
Market value (mil.): $1,378
R&D as % of sales: 18.7%

ELECTRONICS FOR IMAGING, INC.

OVERVIEW

Electronics for Imaging (EFI) is hastening black-and-white computer printers to a fiery death. The San Mateo, California-based company designs computer network servers and associated software that let a color laser copier work like a high-performance color printer. EFI dominates the market it created. It sells its principal product, the Fiery XJ series, exclusively to OEMs such as Canon, Kodak, and Xerox. CEO Dan Avida (who designed the Fiery server) is seeking to expand the company's reach. In late 1995 it introduced the Fiery XJe, a chip board that can be embedded into desktop printers, enabling them to print much faster while maintaining high quality.

Efi Arazi, an MIT-trained engineer (and founder of Scitex Corp., a digital printer manufacturer in Israel), started EFI in 1988. He acquired exclusive rights to an MIT patent that formed EFI's core technology: the EfiColor Color Management System. The company spent millions on R&D before shipping its first Fiery server in August 1991. To finance growth, EFI went public the next year. Its secondary strategy of selling its EfiColor and Cachet Color Editor software alone failed, so in 1993 the company scrapped Cachet and decided to sell EfiColor bundled with the Fiery Color Server, making the development and marketing of the Fiery series top priority.

In early 1995 EFI introduced the Fiery XJ series, which was twice as fast as its predecessor and easily upgraded. The company expects competition to heat up as office copier and high-volume offset press manufacturers improve their technologies and begin to encroach on EFI's market. EFI has agreements with OEM pack leaders Canon and Digital Equipment Corp. for EFI product distribution within their new desktop printers.

WHO

Chairman: Efraim Efi Arazi, age 58, $300,000 pay
President and CEO: Dan Avida, age 32, $435,840 pay (prior to promotion)
EVP: Jeffrey Lenches, age 48, $304,241 pay
VP Manufacturing and Support: Fred Rosenzweig, age 39, $148,603 pay
VP Strategic Relations: Eric Saltzman, age 33
VP Human Resources: Janice Smith
VP Finance: David Warner
Auditors: Price Waterhouse LLP

WHERE

HQ: 2855 Campus Dr., San Mateo, CA 94403
Phone: 415-286-8600   **Fax:** 415-286-8544
Web site: http://www.efi.com

	1995 Sales % of total
US	52
International	48
Total	**100**

WHAT

Selected Products
EfiColor Color Management System (software to manage color adjustment, compensation, and translation; incorporated in Fiery servers)
Fiery XJ 300 Color Server (high-performance hardware to convert color laser photocopiers into plain-paper color printers)
Fiery XJ 250 Color Server (midrange model)
Fiery XJ 170 Color Server (low-end model)
Fiery XJe (embedded controller card for OEM installation in desktop printers)

KEY COMPETITORS

Adobe	DICE-Net	Olivetti
Apple Computer	Eastman Kodak	QMS
Canon	Fractal Design	Quark
ColorAge	Hewlett-Packard	Radius
ColorBus	Indigo N.V.	Scitex
Crossfield Electronics	Linotype-Hell	Tektronix
Data Translation	Microsoft	
	Oki	

HOW MUCH

Nasdaq symbol: EFII FYE: December 31	Annual Growth	1990	1991	1992	1993	1994	1995
Sales ($ mil.)	148.8%	2.0	16.4	53.7	89.5	130.4	190.5
Net income ($ mil.)	—	(4.1)	0.6	6.6	12.8	21.3	37.5
Income as % of sales	—	—	3.8%	12.3%	14.2%	16.3%	19.7%
Earnings per share ($)	—	(0.41)	0.05	0.37	0.52	0.86	1.41
Stock price – high ($)	—	—	—	11.88	11.25	14.75	50.13
Stock price – low ($)	—	—	—	6.88	7.00	6.63	12.00
Stock price – close ($)	64.2%	—	—	9.88	8.25	13.75	43.75
P/E – high	—	—	—	32	22	17	36
P/E – low	—	—	—	19	13	8	9
Dividends per share ($)	—	—	—	0.00	0.00	0.00	0.00
Book value per share ($)	38.6%	—	—	2.47	3.81	4.73	6.57
Employees	38.9%	43	85	129	173	192	222

1995 YEAR-END
Debt ratio: 0.0%
Return on equity: 27.0%
Cash (mil.): $144
Current ratio: 6.14
Long-term debt (mil.): $0
No. of shares (mil.): 25
Dividends
  Yield: —
  Payout: —
Market value (mil.): $1,093
R&D as % of sales: 6.8%

ELEK-TEK, INC.

OVERVIEW

ELEK-TEK is struggling to keep up with the big boys. Based in Skokie, Illinois, the company is a regional marketer of microcomputer hardware, software, and related accessories via 8 Midwestern superstores and direct marketing and mail-order operations. The company has been pressured in recent years by increasingly intense competition from national superstores such as CompUSA, Circuit City, and Best Buy. Cofounder Morton Goldman and former CEO Cameron Estes own 31.6% and 39% of the company, respectively.

In 1979, when PCs were in their infancy, Hal Goldman (then in his mid-20s) went into the mail-order computer business with his father, Morton. ELEK-TEK soon became a well-known and well-regarded reseller, and it opened a single retail outlet. In 1982 the company opened its first "superstore" in Lincolnwood, Illinois. The concept was a success, but growth was slow; it did not open another store until 1987. Nevertheless, ELEK-TEK dominated the Chicago market against such national competition as Radio Shack and ComputerLand, 2 new stores that opened in 1991 and 1992. ELEK-TEK went public in 1993 and used the proceeds to pay down debt, open a store in Indianapolis, and remodel its stores to further differentiate them from national warehouse-type stores, which by 1993 had penetrated the Chicago market.

In 1994 the company opened a store in Kansas and one in Colorado. That year it suffered a blow when Hal Goldman killed himself and Morton retired. SVP Cameron Estes, heir to much of Hal Goldman's stock in the company, became CEO.

Cameron Estes retired as chairman and CEO in 1996, and Richard Rodriguez, a former Creative Computers executive, took the helm.

WHO

Chairman: Harvey Kinzelberg, age 51
CEO, President, COO, and Secretary:
  Richard L. Rodriguez, age 36
VP and CFO: Miguel A. Martinez, age 41
VP Retail: Rory K. Zaks, age 39
Director Human Resources: Jane McCarthy
Auditors: Coopers & Lybrand L.L.P.

WHERE

HQ: 7350 N. Linder Ave., Skokie, IL 60077
Phone: 847-677-7660   **Fax:** 847-677-1081
Web site: http://www.elek-tek.com

	1995 Stores
	No.
Illinois	4
Colorado	1
Indiana	1
Kansas	1
Total	**7**

WHAT

	1995 Sales	
	$ mil.	% of total
Retail	160.4	48
Direct sales	108.4	32
Mail order	69.2	20
Total	**338.0**	**100**

KEY COMPETITORS

Applied	Data Storage	Micro Warehouse
Computer	Marketing	MicroAge
Technology	Dataflex	NeoStar
Best Buy	Egghead	Office Depot
CDW Computer	Gateway 2000	PC and Mac
Centers	Global	Connection
Circuit City	Directmail	Software
CompUSA	Inmac	Spectrum
Creative	Intelligent	Staples
Computers	Electronics	Tandy
DAMARK	Liuski	Corporation
International	International	

HOW MUCH

Nasdaq symbol: ELEK FYE: December 31	Annual Growth	1990	1991	1992	1993	1994	1995
Sales ($ mil.)	19.6%	138.4	148.7	176.8	222.2	305.6	338.0
Net income ($ mil.)	—	2.7	1.7	2.1	6.1	3.5	(0.3)
Income as % of sales	—	1.9%	1.2%	1.5%	2.7%	1.1%	—
Earnings per share ($)	—	—	—	0.51	0.78	0.55	(0.05)
Stock price – high ($)	—	—	—	—	17.75	19.00	8.50
Stock price – low ($)	—	—	—	—	9.25	7.00	2.75
Stock price – close ($)	(60.5%)	—	—	—	17.63	8.50	2.75
P/E – high	—	—	—	—	23	35	—
P/E – low	—	—	—	—	12	13	—
Dividends per share ($)	—	—	—	—	0.00	0.00	0.00
Book value per share ($)	52.3%	—	—	—	2.97	3.51	3.46
Employees	6.5%	—	—	—	788	882	893

1995 YEAR-END
Debt ratio: 58.6%
Return on equity: —
Cash (mil.): $8
Current ratio: 1.15
Long-term debt (mil.): $5
No. of shares (mil.): 6
Dividends
  Yield: —
  Payout: —
Market value (mil.): $17

FENWICK & WEST LLP

OVERVIEW

For computer companies in need of legal counsel, the advice might be, "go West, young nerd, go West" — Fenwick & West. The Palo Alto, California-based law firm, with some 50 partners, is one of the most prominent law firms in Silicon Valley. It specializes in areas of particular interest to high-tech companies, including intellectual property, licensing, export and customs issues, and antitrust law.

The firm was founded in 1972 by 4 young escapees from New York's Cleary, Gottlieb, Steen & Hamilton. Seeking a land where they could settle down and raise their families, William Fenwick, Donald Davis, Joel Kellman, and Blakeney Stafford moved to northern California and hung out their shingle as Davis, Stafford, Kellman & Fenwick. The firm grew along with the computer industry. In the late 1980s it became involved in one of the industry's biggest patent and copyright cases when it represented Apple in its copyright infringement suit against Microsoft. Apple claimed that Microsoft had copied the "look and feel" of its "point-and-click graphical user interface operating system when creating Windows. (Most of Apple's claims were eventually dismissed.)

Diversifying into another hot new area in 1992, the firm set up the first FDA practice on the West Coast to shepherd emerging biotech companies through drug approval and regulation processes. After undergoing several name changes through its history to reflect shifts in top personnel, the firm that year was renamed Fenwick & West (Henry West had come aboard in 1975). It joined forces with Weissmann, Wolff, Bergman, Coleman & Silverman (a Beverly HIlls entertainment practice) in 1994 to form the Interactive Law Group — a joint venture to serve companies eager to join the interactive market.

The company handled several high-profile cases in 1996. One, for Sun Microsystems, involved seeking out companies throughout the US that use the word "java" or variations thereof to determine whether they infringe on Sun's Java trademarks. Another was a tax case hinging on whether the ailing Apple manufactured computers in Ireland or merely assembled them there between 1989 and 1991.

WHO

Member Managing Committee: Frederick R. Chilton
Member Managing Committee: Gordon Davidson
Member Managing Committee: Timothy K. Roake
Chairman, Intellectual Property Group: David L. Hayes
Chairman, International Practice Group:
  Fred M. Greguras
Chairman, Tax Group: James P. Fuller
Chairman, Litigation Group: David Slaby
Chairman, Corporate Group: Dennis De Broeck
Partner Litigation Group: William A. Fenwick
Of Counsel: Henry West
Chief Administrative Officer and CFO: Patricia M. Rock
Recruitment Administrator (HR): Carol Ida

WHERE

HQ: 2 Palo Alto Sq., Palo Alto, CA 94306
Phone: 415-494-0600   **Fax:** 415-494-0674
Web site: http://www.fenwick.com

Fenwick & West has offices in Palo Alto and San Francisco, California, and Washington, DC.

WHAT

Selected Areas of Practice	Representative Clients
Business litigation	@Home
Civil litigation	Amdahl
Computer law	Cisco Systems
Corporate	Claris
FDA law	Electronic Arts
Incorporation	Hitachi
Intellectual property	Intuit
International law	Matsushita
Labor law	Mitsubishi
Patents	Sharp
Patent litigation	Sun Microsystems
Securities	Toshiba

Tax
Trusts and Estates

KEY COMPETITORS

Brobeck, Phleger & Harrison
Cooley Godward, Castro Huddleson & Tatum
Gray Cary Ware & Freidenrich
Heller Ehrman White & McAuliffe
McCutcheon, Doyle, Brown & Enersen
Orrick, Herrington & Sutcliffe
Pillsbury, Madison & Sutro
Townsend & Townsend
Venture Law Group
Wilson, Sonsini, Goodrich & Rosati

HOW MUCH

Partnership FYE: December 31	Annual Growth	1990	1991	1992	1993	1994	1995
Sales ($ mil.)	15.9%	24.4	27.6	29.8	33.1	37.8	51.0
Employees	6.4%	183	204	239	210	240	250

■ FENWICK & WEST

FILENET CORPORATION

OVERVIEW

FileNet is the Swiss Army knife of the software industry, specializing in products that perform a variety of functions. The Costa Mesa, California-based company's "Foundation for Enterprise Document Management" is a family of products that allows users to manage electronic information in any form, including text, scanned images, faxes, spreadsheets, graphics, electronic forms, computer-aided design drawings, and video. FileNet, which claims to be the first software company to offer a software suite of this kind, has been busy making acquisitions that have substantially broadened its product line.

Taking advantage of improvements in optical scanning equipment, Theodore Smith founded FileNet in 1982 with funding from venture capitalists. The company went public in 1987. Throughout most of the 1980s its hardware and software dominated the document-imaging market. In the late 1980s, however, as technology improved further, scanning became much simpler and more common, and many new competitors entered the arena. Growth slowed and FileNet lost market share, largely because its proprietary systems were incompatible with other systems and were more expensive than other scanning hardware.

The company began to remake itself in 1992, changing from a hardware producer to primarily a software company. That year restructuring costs drove FileNet into the red, but the strategy paid off and in 1993 FileNet turned profitable again.

FileNet bolstered its market presence in 1995 by acquiring Watermark Software, a developer of document-imaging applications, and in 1996 with its acquisitions of enterprise document software maker Saros and International Financial Systems Limited, maker of Greenbar archiving software.

WHO

Chairman, President, and CEO: Theodore J. Smith, age 66, $473,909 pay
SVP Finance and CFO: Mark S. St. Clare, age 49, $253,282 pay
SVP International: Lewis H. Carpenter Jr., age 42, $223,091 pay
SVP Engineering and Chief Technology Officer: Bruce Waddington, age 45, $221,733 pay
VP Human Resources: Audrey N. Schaeffer
Auditors: Deloitte & Touche LLP

WHERE

HQ: 3565 Harbor Blvd., Costa Mesa, CA 92626-1420
Phone: 714-966-3400   **Fax:** 714-966-3232
Web site: http://www.filenet.com

WHAT

	1995 Sales	
	$ mil.	% of total
Software	106.2	49
Service	63.1	29
Hardware	46.2	22
Total	**215.5**	**100**

Selected Software Products
Ensemble (administrative workflow tool)
FileNet WorkGroup
Greenbar Software (stores and retrieves computer-generated output reports)
Image Management Services Software
Watermark Enterprise Series (intranet software system)
WorkFlo (business application development software)

KEY COMPETITORS

BancTec	NCR
Caere	Open Text
Computron Software	Optika
Cornerstone Imaging	PC DOCS
Documentum	Unisys
IBM	ViewStar
Interleaf	Wang

HOW MUCH

Nasdaq symbol: FILE FYE: December 31	Annual Growth	1990	1991	1992	1993	1994	1995
Sales ($ mil.)	15.9%	102.9	122.5	138.3	158.8	179.7	215.5
Net income ($ mil.)	31.2%	3.8	8.1	(8.0)	7.8	16.1	14.8
Income as % of sales	—	3.7%	6.6%	—	4.9%	8.9%	6.9%
Earnings per share ($)	23.7%	0.37	0.75	(0.76)	0.71	1.37	1.07
Stock price – high ($)	—	21.50	25.00	37.50	23.00	29.25	51.00
Stock price – low ($)	—	5.00	6.75	10.50	8.75	14.25	25.25
Stock price – close ($)	40.8%	8.50	24.88	22.75	21.50	27.00	47.00
P/E – high	—	58	33	—	32	21	48
P/E – low	—	14	9	—	12	10	24
Dividends per share ($)	—	0.00	0.00	0.00	0.00	0.00	0.00
Book value per share ($)	8.8%	6.77	7.59	6.87	7.71	9.42	10.34
Employees	7.9%	770	854	1,006	885	940	1,126

1995 YEAR-END
Debt ratio: 0.2%
Return on equity: 12.5%
Cash (mil.): $69
Current ratio: 2.97
Long-term debt (mil.): $0
No. of shares (mil.): 13
Dividends
  Yield: —
  Payout: —
Market value (mil.): $607
R&D as % of sales: 9.0%

FISERV, INC.

OVERVIEW

FIserv probably works for you. The #2 financial data processor (after EDS) in the US, FIserv provides check clearing, funds transfer, credit card administration, and data processing outsourcing services to more than 5,000 client institutions worldwide.

The company was founded in 1984 by George Dalton and Leslie Muma. Dalton had headed Milwaukee's Midland Bank's data processing operations since the mid-1960s. When First Bank System of Minneapolis bought Midland, Dalton teamed with Muma, who ran Sunshine State Systems, to buy Midland's data processing subsidiary and form FIserv. Later rounds of venture investment and public stock offerings (it went public in 1986) reduced their interests in the company to less than 3%.

The key to FIserv's success has been the ability of Dalton and Muma to choose good acquisition candidates: operations that are well run and mostly profitable, with strong management that is willing to stay on. As it grew, the company diversified, adding cash management, credit card embossing, item processing services, and retirement plan management. It has also taken advantage of the trend toward outsourcing and now provides data processing site management services. The company has also expanded its software offerings.

In 1995 it bought Information Technology, Inc., in a transaction that left ITI's chairman, Donald Dillon, holding about 5% of FIserv's stock. Charges related to the acquisition pushed FIserv into the loss column in 1995. That year Chase Manhattan Bank awarded FIserv a 12-year outsourcing contract for check processing. In 1996, however, Chase merged with Chemical Banking, jeopardizing the contract. After negotiations, the new Chase agreed to allow FIserv to provide check processing services for 3 years.

WHO

Chairman and CEO: George D. Dalton, age 67, $615,000 pay
VC, President, and COO: Leslie M. Muma, age 51, $555,000 pay
VC; President, Information Technology, Inc.: Donald F. Dillon, age 55
SEVP, CFO, and Treasurer: Kenneth R. Jensen, age 52, $430,000 pay
EVP; Group Executive, Savings and Community Bank Group: Norman J. Balthasar, age 49, $322,000 pay
EVP; Group Executive, Bank and Credit Union Group: Frank R. Martire, age 48, $306,000 pay
EVP, General Counsel, and Secretary: Charles W. Sprague, age 46
SVP Corporate Human Resources: Jack P. Bucalo, age 58
Auditors: Deloitte & Touche LLP

WHERE

HQ: 255 Fiserv Dr., Brookfield, WI 53045
Phone: 414-879-5000   **Fax:** 414-879-5013
Web site: http://streetlink.com/fisv/

WHAT

Selected Operating Units

Bank and Credit Union Group (data processing, software systems, outsourcing)
BankLink (cash management services)
Data-Link Systems (mortgage banking services)
Fiserv EFT (electronic funds transfer services)

Industry Products and Services Group
Cadre, Inc. (disaster recovery service)
Information Technology, Inc. (banking software and services)
NEC Card Services (credit card fulfillment services)

Savings and Community Bank Group (data processing resource management)

KEY COMPETITORS

ALLTEL
BISYS
Concord EFS
EDS

First Data
IBM
National Data
Perot Systems

PMT Services
Symitar

HOW MUCH

Nasdaq symbol: FISV FYE: December 31	Annual Growth	1990	1991	1992	1993	1994	1995
Sales ($ mil.)	30.9%	183.2	281.3	332.1	454.7	536.6	703.4
Net income ($ mil.)	—	13.8	18.3	23.0	30.7	37.7	(59.9)
Income as % of sales	—	7.5%	6.5%	6.9%	6.8%	6.7%	—
Earnings per share ($)	—	0.47	0.56	0.67	0.80	0.95	(1.36)
Stock price – high ($)	—	8.96	16.89	17.50	23.75	23.75	31.00
Stock price – low ($)	—	5.70	8.00	13.67	16.75	18.00	21.00
Stock price – close ($)	26.6%	9.22	16.78	16.88	19.25	21.50	30.00
P/E – high	—	19	30	26	30	25	—
P/E – low	—	12	14	20	24	19	—
Dividends per share ($)	—	0.00	0.00	0.00	0.00	0.00	0.00
Book value per share ($)	13.3%	5.18	4.47	5.67	7.93	8.96	9.67
Employees	27.7%	2,418	3,655	3,750	6,300	6,195	8,222

1995 YEAR-END
Debt ratio: 46.8%
Return on equity: —
Cash (mil.): $60
Current ratio: —
Long-term debt (mil.): $381
No. of shares (mil.): 45
Dividends
  Yield: —
  Payout: —
Market value (mil.): $1,347

FORE SYSTEMS, INC.

OVERVIEW

FORE Systems is foremost among makers of networking products based on ATM (asynchronous transfer mode, a high-speed, high-volume networking protocol). Warrendale, Pennsylvania-based FORE makes both hardware and software to help companies create LANs and WANs. It sells primarily to corporate end users; customers include AT&T, Ford, General Electric, Motorola, and Sprint.

The company was founded in 1990 by 4 Carnegie Mellon researchers studying computer technologies: Francois Bitz, Onat Menzilcioglu, Robert Sansom, and Eric Cooper (their first initials gave FORE its name). It shipped its initial products, a line of ATM adapter cards, in 1991 and unveiled its ATM switching products the following year. FORE went public in 1994. The founders together own about 16% of the company's stock.

FORE secured its leading-edge position by developing alliances with other developers of high-tech applications, including Cabletron and Northern Telecom. In 1994 the company joined with Microsoft and Tele-Communications, Inc. (the US's largest cable operator), to test an interactive television system, including home shopping and movies on demand.

In 1995 FORE moved to counter the threat of Ethernet, a rival technology, by acquiring Applied Network Technology, a developer of Ethernet switching products. That year it also bought RainbowBridge Communications, a developer of network routing software, and Cell-Access Technology, a supplier of digital-access products.

The company acquired Alantec, a leading vendor of Ethernet products, in 1996. That year it formed an alliance with telecommunications equipment maker General Instrument to develop a system for home use that delivers computer images without a time delay.

WHO

Chairman and CEO: Eric C. Cooper, age 37, $256,157 pay
President: Onat Menzilcioglu, age 37, $224,750 pay
VP Engineering: Francois J. Bitz, age 36, $182,313 pay
VP Engineering and Secretary: Robert D. Sansom, $182,313 pay
VP Sales and Marketing: Michael I. Green, age 48, $210,709 pay
VP Finance, CFO, and Treasurer: Thomas J. Gill, age 38
VP Human Resources: Thomas Armour
Auditors: Price Waterhouse LLP

WHERE

HQ: 174 Thorn Hill Rd., Warrendale, PA 15086-7586
Phone: 412-772-6600   **Fax:** 412-772-6500
Web site: http://www.fore.com

WHAT

Selected ATM Products
CellPath WAN multiplexers (aggregate network traffic onto wide area transmission lines)
ForeRunner ATM adapter cards (allow computers to communicate over ATM networks)
ForeRunner ATM switches (workgroup, LAN backbone, and WAN-access switches for up to 96 computers or other networking devices)
ForeThought software (includes control software for FORE's ATM switches and the device driver for its ATM adapter cards)
ForeView software (network management)
PowerHub LAN switches (intelligent switches for Ethernet, Fast Ethernet, FDDI, and ATM networks)

KEY COMPETITORS

3Com
Bay Networks
Cabletron
Cascade
  Communications
Cisco Systems
DEC
Digital Link
DSC Commun-ications

FastComm Commun-
  ications
General DataComm
IBM
Interphase
Newbridge Networks
Sun Microsystems
Xylan

HOW MUCH

Nasdaq symbol: FORE FYE: March 31	Annual Growth	1991	1992	1993	1994	1995	1996
Sales ($ mil.)	372.4%	0.1	1.0	5.5	23.5	75.6	235.2
Net income ($ mil.)	—	0.0	0.1	0.3	2.1	7.4	9.7
Income as % of sales	—	—	8.9%	5.4%	8.8%	9.7%	4.1%
Earnings per share ($)	48.3%	—	—	—	0.05	0.14	0.11
Stock price – high ($)[1]	—	—	—	—	—	17.88	33.88
Stock price – low ($)[1]	—	—	—	—	—	5.00	12.75
Stock price – close ($)[1]	—	—	—	—	—	16.88	29.75
P/E – high	—	—	—	—	—	132	308
P/E – low	—	—	—	—	—	37	116
Dividends per share ($)	—	—	—	—	—	0.00	0.00
Book value per share ($)	—	—	—	—	—	1.05	3.82
Employees	88.4%	—	—	146	165	357	977

[1] Stock prices are for the prior calendar year.

1996 YEAR-END
Debt ratio: 0.0%
Return on equity: 4.5%
Cash (mil.): $296
Current ratio: 4.52
Long-term debt (mil.): $0
No. of shares (mil.): 88
Dividends
  Yield: —
  Payout: —
Market value (mil.): $2,618
R&D as % of sales: 13.3%

FRANKLIN ELECTRONIC PUBLISHERS

OVERVIEW

Fair dinkum, mate! You soon won't have to drive your ute (utility vehicle) to the uni (university) to check out the *Macquarie Dictionary* (the authoritative guide to Australian English). Franklin, the world's #1 electronic book publisher, is developing an electronic version. The Burlington, New Jersey-based company has sold more than 12 million "electronic books." These handheld, battery-powered keyboard devices allow readers to access selected portions on a liquid crystal display screen. Franklin electronic books and IC-ROM cards include thesauruses, dictionaries, encyclopedias, and medical publications, as well as the Bible.

The company was founded as Franklin Computer, a maker of general-purpose PCs, in 1981. Under the leadership of Morton David, who was appointed CEO in 1984, the business moved steadily into the electronic publishing market. In 1986 it introduced an $80 spellchecker called Spelling Ace, one of the very first electronic books released in the US. Franklin Computer introduced increasingly sophisticated versions of thesauruses and dictionaries in 1987 and 1988, capturing around 80% of the market. Facing growing competition in the electronic publishing arena from companies such as Apple, Seiko, Sharp, and Sony, Franklin Computer increased the range and quality of its products. In 1990 the company adopted its current name.

Franklin expanded internationally in 1992 when it opened a UK office. That year the company launched its first medical product, the Med-Spell MED-55 dictionary.

In 1995 Franklin teamed up with Intuit to build a mobile, wallet-sized version of Intuit's personal-finance software, Quicken. In 1996 it bought the electronic portion of Insilco's Rolodex organizer line.

WHO

Chairman, President, and CEO: Morton E. David, age 58, $804,000 pay
EVP: Michael R. Strange, age 47, $227,500 pay
SVP and Secretary: Gregory J. Winsky, age 45, $227,500 pay
President, Medical Division: Bruno Bieler
Managing Director, Franklin Electronic Publishers (Europe) Ltd.: Michael Kemp, $222,160 pay
VP Finance and Treasurer: Kenneth H. Lind, age 42, $222,500 pay
VP Manufacturing: Barry J. Lipsky, age 44
VP Sales: Regina A. Casey, age 38
VP International Sales: Peter J. Hudson
Auditors: Feldman Radin & Co.

WHERE

HQ: Franklin Electronic Publishers, Incorporated, One Franklin Plaza, Burlington, NJ 08016
Phone: 609-261-4800   **Fax:** 609-387-7420
Web site: http://www.franklin.com

	1996 Sales	
	$ mil.	% of total
US	70.2	70
Other countries	30.6	30
Total	**100.8**	**100**

WHAT

Selected Titles
Betty Crocker's Cookbook
Concise Columbia Encyclopedia
Franklin Personal Organizer
Holy Bible
Merriam-Webster's Collegiate Dictionary
Parker's Wine Guide
The Pocket PDR (Physicians' Desk Reference)

KEY COMPETITORS

Apple Computer
Aurora Impex
Casio
Hewlett-Packard
MathSoft
Psion
Royal Business Products
Seiko
Sharp
Sony
Texas Instruments
U.S. Robotics

HOW MUCH

NYSE symbol: FEP FYE: March 31	Annual Growth	1991	1992	1993	1994	1995	1996
Sales ($ mil.)	13.1%	54.4	53.8	65.4	66.1	83.3	100.8
Net income ($ mil.)	—	(5.9)	3.1	7.1	8.1	12.4	10.4
Income as % of sales	—	—	5.8%	10.9%	12.3%	14.9%	10.3%
Earnings per share ($)	—	(0.89)	0.44	0.92	1.06	1.52	1.25
Stock price – high ($)[1]	—	6.25	7.25	16.25	19.75	21.50	44.25
Stock price – low ($)[1]	—	3.00	1.38	5.63	10.75	10.50	20.25
Stock price – close ($)[1]	56.6%	3.13	5.88	15.25	13.25	21.13	29.50
P/E – high	—	—	17	18	19	14	35
P/E – low	—	—	3	6	10	7	16
Dividends per share ($)	—	0.00	0.00	0.00	0.00	0.00	0.00
Book value per share ($)	25.9%	2.64	3.18	4.22	5.33	9.15	8.34
Employees	13.3%	166	156	170	206	271	310

[1] Stock prices are for the prior calendar year.

1996 YEAR-END
Debt ratio: 0.0%
Return on equity: 17.3%
Cash (mil.): $11
Current ratio: 3.61
Long-term debt (mil.): $0
No. of shares (mil.): 8
Dividends
  Yield: —
  Payout: —
Market value (mil.): $232

FRY'S ELECTRONICS INC.

OVERVIEW

Fry's may be the best-kept secret in computer retailing outside California. Based in Palo Alto, the closely-held company operates only 10 stores, but it is still among the largest computer retailers in the US. Fry's approaches the computer superstore business as an opportunity to entertain the customer. Each store features a theme, complete with characters, from ancient Egypt to "Alice in Wonderland."

Even more unique than the decor is the variety of products they sell, which range from silicon chips to potato chips, from "technical" magazines (including "Playboy") to beer, from PCs, software, printers, and other computer peripherals and supplies to over-the-counter drugs such as No Doz. Fry's Electronics stores are well known as a one-stop shopping place for its techno-nerd customers.

The 3 brothers, David, John, and Randy Fry, who founded and own Fry's Electronics have not gotten completely away from their retail roots. Their father, Charles, started Fry's Food Stores supermarket chain in South Bay, California; the chain was sold before the family went into the electronics business. All 3 brothers have executive positions with the company, which is very private — the brothers work behind locked doors and refuse to speak to the press or industry analysts. The chain was started in Sunnyvale in 1985; a 2nd store was added in Fremont in 1988. The Palo Alto store was completed in 1990 with the corporate headquarters next door. The first Los Angeles-area store opened in 1992 and the 2nd one the following year. The Campbell, California, store also opened in 1993.

In 1994 the Los Angeles computer retail market began to see increased competition from nationwide discount computer superstores. Fry's responded by opening a new store in Woodland Hills, California, in 1995 with an "Alice in Wonderland" theme. It was the first Southern California Fry's Electronics store to offer appliances and an expanded music department.

Fry's went on a frenzy in 1996, opening new California stores in Burbank, San Jose, and Anaheim Hills.

WHO

President: John Fry
EVP and General Manager: Randy Fry
VP Business Development: Kathryn Kolder
Chief Information Officer: David Fry
Director Special Operations: Omar Siddiqui
Director Computer Merchandising and Operations:
  Charley Yandell
Director Software Merchandising and Operations:
  Ed Sturr
Manager Human Resources: Katherine Bleisae
Auditors:

WHERE

HQ: 382 Portage Ave., Palo Alto, CA 94306-2244
Phone: 415-496-6100   **Fax:** 415-496-6093

Store Locations (all in California)
Anaheim Hills
Burbank
Campbell
Fountain Valley
Fremont
Manhattan Beach
Palo Alto
San Jose
Sunnyvale
Woodland Hills

WHAT

Selected Computer Products	Other Products
Computer chips	Audio compact discs
Motherboards	Beer
PCs	Magazines
Peripherals	Over-the-counter
Software	medicines
	Potato chips
	Soda
	Stereos
	Video systems

KEY COMPETITORS

Best Buy
CDW Computer Centers
Circuit City
CompUSA
Dell
Gateway 2000
Good Guys
Micro Center
Micro Warehouse
Office Depot
Tandy Corporation
Vanstar

HOW MUCH

Private company	Annual Growth	1990	1991	1992	1993	1994	1995
Estimated sales ($ mil.)	28.7%	—	—	—	250.0	327.0	414.0
Employees	7.4%	—	—	—	1,300	1,500	1,500

GARTNER GROUP INC.

OVERVIEW

Clara Bow, the original "It Girl" may be long gone, but IT is still sexy. IT — information technology — is highly desirable, but, like sex, leaves many confused. Gartner Group is the industry's Dr. Ruth, providing reviews, advice and recommendations on other companies' computer hardware and software, communications, and related high-tech industries and products. The Stamford, Connecticut-based company provides IT research and reports to subscribers who pay between $19,000 and $100,000 annually. Clients include corporations, IT product vendors, and Wall Street analysts. Gartner also provides consulting services and conducts seminars and conferences on IT topics.

The company was founded by computer analyst Gideon Gartner in 1979. Two years after its 1986 IPO, it was acquired by ad agency Saatchi & Saatchi in that company's futile bid to become a business services powerhouse. Management and investors purchased the company in a leveraged buyout in 1990 and forced out Gartner almost immediately. The company went public again in 1993. (In 1995, with the end of the noncompetition agreement that was part of his separation package, Gartner founded a competing, lower-cost IT research service, Giga Information Group.)

In its drive toward the top of the IT information market, Gartner Group is absorbing complementary companies. It purchased New Science Associates, an IT information provider, and Real Decisions, a supplier of benchmarking services for data center operators, in 1993; 2 years later it bought Dataquest, a company partly owned by Gartner Group's majority stockholder, Dun & Bradstreet.

The company has worked to widen the scope of its coverage, targeting applications and equipment of interest to finance and health care companies. Despite its high-tech focus, Gartner Group was late getting online, waiting until 1995, when it joined AT&T's Interchange OnLine Network. In 1996 it finally debuted on the Internet.

WHO

Chairman, President, and CEO: Manuel A. Fernandez, age 49, $807,000 pay
EVP Sales and Marketing and Chief Marketing Officer; President, Gartner Group Di: E. Follett Carter, age 53, $424,000 pay
EVP Operations and COO; President, Gartner Group Research: William T. Clifford, age 49, $380,000 pay
EVP, CFO, Secretary, and Treasurer: John F. Halligan, age 48, $375,000 pay
EVP Interactive Services: Bruce Barlag
SVP Human Resources: Lindon Smith
Auditors: Price Waterhouse LLP

WHERE

HQ: 56 Top Gallant Rd., Stamford, CT 06904-2212
Phone: 203-964-0096   **Fax:** 203-316-1100
Web site: http://www.gartner.com

WHAT

	1995 Sales	
	$ mil.	% of total
Subscription services	194.4	85
Consulting, conferences & other	34.8	15
Total	**229.2**	**100**

Selected Services
Conference sponsorship
Consulting
Interactive services
   (@vantage,
   GartnerFLASH, Internet
   services)

Research and report
   subscriptions

Selected Subsidiaries
Dataquest
Real Decisions

KEY COMPETITORS

Cowles Media
Forrester Research
Giga Information Group
Intelliquest
International Data Group
Jupiter Communications

McGraw-Hill
META Group
Phillips Publihsing
Seybold
Paul Viajan Associates
Zeitech

HOW MUCH

Nasdaq symbol: GART FYE: September 30	Annual Growth	1990	1991	1992	1993	1994	1995
Sales ($ mil.)	24.9%	75.4	84.4	100.4	122.5	169.0	229.2
Net income ($ mil.)	—	(15.9)	(10.4)	(5.5)	4.0	15.0	25.5
Income as % of sales	—	—	—	—	3.3%	8.9%	11.1%
Earnings per share ($)	10.2%	—	0.19	(0.10)	0.05	0.17	0.28
Stock price – high ($)	—	—	—	—	4.66	9.88	24.13
Stock price – low ($)	—	—	—	—	3.09	4.00	8.88
Stock price – close ($)	135.7%	—	—	—	4.31	9.75	23.94
P/E – high	—	—	—	—	93	60	88
P/E – low	—	—	—	—	62	24	32
Dividends per share ($)	—	—	—	—	0.00	0.00	0.00
Book value per share ($)	113.2%	—	—	—	0.22	0.59	1.00
Employees	25.5%	—	473	572	614	912	1,175

1995 YEAR-END
Debt ratio: 7.3%
Return on equity: 38.0%
Cash (mil.): $91
Current ratio: 1.03
Long-term debt (mil.): $0
No. of shares (mil.): 86
Dividends
   Yield: —
   Payout: —
Market value (mil.): $2,048

GENERAL MAGIC, INC.

OVERVIEW

If General Magic doesn't pull off its next trick, it may find itself doing a disappearing act. The Sunnyvale, California-based company has developed 2 object-oriented software programs, Magic Cap (which combines e-mail, fax, paging, and telephone capabilities) and Telescript (which creates intelligent software "agents" to perform various tasks for computer network users, such as data searching). When major customers Sony (which owns 7% of the firm) and AT&T (6%) abandoned products that use the company's programs, General Magic waved its wand and turned itself into an Internet company (intending to leverage the power of its software online).

Marc Porat (who owns 8% of the company), Andrew Hertzfeld (7%), and William Atkinson worked at Apple (which owns 10%), where Hertzfeld and Atkinson helped develop the Macintosh operating system. They wanted to invent a communication system contained in an instrument the user could take anywhere. In 1990 Apple set them up in their own company, General Magic. With backing from parties including AT&T, Sony, and Motorola (6%) they set to work. Three years and $53 million later they unveiled a prototype, which was skeptically received, and in 1994 there was finally a product. By then, however, Apple had come out with the Newton. Worse, the point-and-click office interface that General Magic envisioned had already appeared in Microsoft's Bob.

General Magic went public in 1995, but customers' product sales languished.

In 1996 Sony and AT&T terminated products that used General Magic software. Later that year General Magic decided to convert its know-how into Internet products. Porat stepped down as CEO, replaced by Steve Markman (who helped Novell make its software compatible with the Internet).

WHO

Chairman: Marc Porat, age 48, $175,481 pay
President and CEO: Steve Markman, age 51
VP and General Manager, Worldwide Field Operations Division: William Keating, age 39, $150,000 pay
VP and General Manager, Magic Cap Division: Steven Schramm, age 36, $136,365 pay
VP Magic Cap Technologies and Software Wizard: Andrew Hertzfeld, age 42
VP Business Affairs and General Counsel: Michael Stern, $133,019 pay
VP Internet Business Development: Tony Rutkowski, age 52
VP Human Resources: Stephen Hams
Controller and Acting CFO: Wendy Olszewski
Auditors: KPMG Peat Marwick LLP

WHERE

HQ: 420 N. Mary Ave., Sunnyvale, CA 94086
Phone: 408-774-4000   **Fax:** 408-774-4010
Web site: http://www.genmagic.com

WHAT

	1995 Sales	
	$ mil.	% of total
Software licenses	9.9	70
Other	4.3	30
Total	**14.2**	**100**

Selected Products
Magic Cap (integrates e-mail, fax, paging, telephone, and other communication methods)
Presto!Links and Presto!Mail (mobile Internet platform)
Tabriz Agent Tools (software developer tools for creating agent-based applications at Tabriz Web sites)
Telescript (object-oriented software)

KEY COMPETITORS

Edify
FTP Software
Geoworks
Microsoft
Oracle
ParcPlace-Digitalk
Verity

HOW MUCH

Nasdaq symbol: GMGC FYE: December 31	Annual Growth	1990	1991	1992	1993	1994	1995
Sales ($ mil.)	—	—	0.0	0.0	0.0	2.5	14.2
Net income ($ mil.)	—	—	(3.6)	(10.1)	(17.4)	(21.5)	(20.6)
Income as % of sales	—	—	—	—	—	—	—
Earnings per share ($)	—	—	—	—	—	—	(0.84)
Stock price – high ($)	—	—	—	—	—	—	32.00
Stock price – low ($)	—	—	—	—	—	—	9.88
Stock price – close ($)	—	—	—	—	—	—	10.33
P/E – high	—	—	—	—	—	—	—
P/E – low	—	—	—	—	—	—	—
Dividends per share ($)	—	—	—	—	—	—	0.00
Book value per share ($)	—	—	—	—	—	—	3.45
Employees	—	—	—	—	—	161	208

1995 YEAR-END
Debt ratio: 2.2%
Return on equity: —
Cash (mil.): $105
Current ratio: 13.08
Long-term debt (mil.): $1
No. of shares (mil.): 26
Dividends
  Yield: —
  Payout: —
Market value (mil.): $274
R&D as % of sales: 136.2%

GLOBAL VILLAGE

OVERVIEW

Global Village has a new Window on the world. The Sunnyvale, California-based company has made its name and fortune supplying fax modems for Macintoshes, produced by now troubled Apple Computer. While the majority of Global Village's sales are still derived from its OneWorld, PowerPoint, and TelePort products (all designed for Apples), CEO Neil Selvin has planted the seeds for an even larger customer base of PC users. Global Village is also expanding its international presence and its stable of technologies through acquisitions and partnerships. Investor Michael O'Neill owns 5% of the company.

Founded in 1989 by chairman Len Lehmann and 2 others, the company took its name from Marshall McLuhan's metaphor of a world made small and interconnected by a vast electronic communications network. In 1992 Global signed a deal with Apple allowing the company to develop software for Apple products. Global brought in Neil Selvin (formerly director of marketing at Apple for PowerBook products) as president and CEO in 1993. Global's strongest market edge is that it is the only maker of integrated fax servers for Macintoshes. Global went public in 1994.

That year Global broke out of its Mac-only mold with the $13.5 million acquisition of SoftNet, a developer of communications software for DOS, Windows, and OS/2 PCs (networked or stand-alone).

In 1996 Global Village introduced FocalPoint; hailed by some analysts as the first truly integrated communication software, it includes fax, e-mail, Internet, voice-mail, and paging capabilities. Also that year the company formed a new subsidiary (GlobalCenter) from its Internet services division, and Internet service provider UUNET bought a 20% interest in the unit.

WHO

Chairman: Leonard A. Lehmann, age 41
President and CEO: Neil Selvin, age 42, $423,629 pay
VP Finance, CFO, and Secretary: James M. Walker, age 47, $247,337 pay
VP and General Manager, Communications Systems Division: Charles R. Oppenheimer, age 37, $254,171 pay
VP Operations: James Brown, age 41, $217,795 pay
VP Sales: Douglas Dennerline, age 37, $197,083 pay
VP Customer Satisfaction: Marsha Raulston, age 47
Manager Human Resources: Mary Cravalho
Auditors: KPMG Peat Marwick LLP

WHERE

HQ: Global Village Communication, Inc., 1144 E. Arques Ave., Sunnyvale, CA 94086-4602
Phone: 408-523-1000   **Fax:** 408-523-2287
Web site: http://www.globalvillag.com

WHAT

Selected Products
Apple Macintosh desktop computer modems
Apple PowerBook notebook computer modems
GlobalCenter Internet access service
GlobalFax 2.5 software
Integrated communications software for individual PCs
Integrated communications software for PC workgroups
Integrated communications systems for Macintosh workgroups
ISDN products

KEY COMPETITORS

3Com	GVC
Apex Data	Hayes
Ascend Communications	Matsushita
Attachmate	Motorola
Bay Networks	Multi-Tech Systems
Boca Research	NEC
Brooktrout Technology	Shiva
DATA RACE	U.S. Robotics
Diamond Multimedia	Zoom Telephonics

HOW MUCH

Nasdaq symbol: GVIL FYE: March 31	Annual Growth	1991[2]	1992	1993	1994	1995	1996
Sales ($ mil.)	210.6%	0.5	4.2	22.9	46.6	80.0	144.5
Net income ($ mil.)	—	(0.5)	(0.7)	1.5	4.3	(6.2)	8.8
Income as % of sales	—	—	—	6.5%	9.2%	(0.45)	6.1%
Earnings per share ($)	—	(0.13)	(0.19)	0.12	0.37	(0.45)	0.49
Stock price – high ($)[1]	—	—	—	—	—	12.50	25.75
Stock price – low ($)[1]	—	—	—	—	—	5.75	8.88
Stock price – close ($)[1]	—	—	—	—	—	9.13	19.38
P/E – high	—	—	—	—	—	—	53
P/E – low	—	—	—	—	—	—	18
Dividends per share ($)	—	—	—	—	—	0.00	0.00
Book value per share ($)	—	—	—	—	—	2.53	2.86
Employees	33.4%	—	—	125	122	225	297

1996 YEAR-END
Debt ratio: 0.2%
Return on equity: 20.7%
Cash (mil.): $38
Current ratio: 2.29
Long-term debt (mil.): $0
No. of shares (mil.): 17
Dividends
  Yield: —
  Payout: —
Market value (mil.): $324
R&D as % of sales: 11.3%

[1] Stock prices are for the prior calendar year. [2] 15-month period.

GT INTERACTIVE SOFTWARE CORP..

OVERVIEW

Although GT Interactive Software has plenty of Cayres (founding family members), the New York City-based publisher is doing just fine. The company has served up a steady diet of scary, bloody, and fast action computer games to consumers, primarily through such mass merchandisers as Kmart, Target, and Wal-Mart. Its game titles include id Software's Doom, Hexen, and Quake, as well as Williams's Mortal Kombat 3. The company also caters to the children's and edutainment markets, selling such titles as Fun 'n Games and Just Me and My Dad. In addition GT Interactive publishes reference titles, including Charlton Heston's New Testament. The company has modeled its business on film studios and record companies, distributing the work of independent software developers through retail channels.

Before establishing the company in 1992, Joseph Cayre and his brothers Kenneth and Stanley had founded GoodTimes Home Video (GTHV), a publisher and distributor of prerecorded videotapes, in 1984. Former GTHV executive Ronald Chaimowitz also cofounded GT Interactive. The firm's first published software product, id Software's Wolfenstein 3-D, was released in 1993.

The company acquired Slash Corp., a major publisher, repackager, and distributor of value-priced software, in 1995. The company is also expanding internationally, including a joint venture deal with SOFTBANK, the top distributor of PC software in Japan. GT Interactive went public in 1995. The Cayre family holds more than 61% of the company's shares.

The company went on an acquisition spree in 1996, buying Wizard Works Group, a publisher of cut-price software; Form Gen, the publisher of PC game Duke Nukem 3D; and Humongous Entertainment, a developer of children's software titles.

WHO

Chairman: Joseph J. Cayre, age 54
President and CEO: Ronald Chaimowitz, age 48, $300,000 pay
EVP and General Manager, International Division and Business Affairs: Harry M. Rubin, $310,000 pay
EVP: Jack J. Cayre, age 23, $208,000 pay
SVP Finance and Administration and CFO: Andrew Gregor, age 47
SVP Publishing: Chris Garske, age 40
VP Operations: Harry Steck, age 51, $289,000 pay
Publisher, Slash Division: Charles F. Bond, age 39
Director Human Resources: Harry Glanz
Auditors: Andersen Worldwide

WHERE

HQ: 16 E. 40th St., New York, NY 10016
Phone: 212-726-6500   **Fax:** 212-726-6590
Web site: http://www.gtinteractive.com

WHAT

Selected Software Titles

Edutainment	
Buzzy the Knowledge Bug	Duke Nukem 3D
Freddi Fish	Hexen
Fun 'n Games	Island Casino
Just Me and My Dad	Quake
Just Me and My Mom	Mortal Kombat 3
Putt-Putt	Vampire, The Masquerade

Entertainment	Reference
Alien Central	Charlton Heston's New
Barb Wire	Testament
Doom	DC Comics 60th
Dreggs	Anniversary
	Internet the Easy Way

KEY COMPETITORS

3DO	Cyan	Nintendo
7th Level	Electronic Arts	SEGA
Acclaim	Interplay	SoftKey
Entertainment	Productions	Sony
Accolade	Knowledge	Spectrum
Activision	Adventure	HoloByte
Brøderbund	LucasArts	Trilobyte
CUC	Maxis	Walt Disney
International	Microsoft	WMS Industries

HOW MUCH

Nasdaq symbol: GTIS FYE: December 31	Annual Growth	1990	1991	1992	1993	1994	1995
Sales ($ mil.)	345.1%	—	—	—	10.3	85.2	204.1
Net income ($ mil.)	374.3%	—	—	—	0.8	11.6	18.0
Income as % of sales	—	—	—	—	8.2%	13.6%	8.8%
Earnings per share ($)	—	—	—	—	—	—	—
Stock price – high ($)	—	—	—	—	—	—	16.50
Stock price – low ($)	—	—	—	—	—	—	5.50
Stock price – close ($)	—	—	—	—	—	—	14.00
P/E – high	—	—	—	—	—	—	—
P/E – low	—	—	—	—	—	—	—
Dividends per share ($)	—	—	—	—	—	—	0.00
Book value per share ($)	—	—	—	—	—	—	2.04
Employees	—	—	—	—	—	—	597

1995 YEAR-END
Debt ratio: 7.4%
Return on equity: 19.8%
Cash (mil.): $92
Current ratio: 1.65
Long-term debt (mil.): $8
No. of shares (mil.): 59
Dividends
  Yield: —
  Payout: —
Market value (mil.): $830

HAMBRECHT & QUIST LLP

OVERVIEW

Investment banker Hambrecht & Quist (H&Q) has walked the talk. One of the leading underwriters of public offerings for emerging growth companies (it has handled offerings for about 400 companies, including technology firms such as Apple Computer, Genentech, Netscape Communications, and Convergent Technologies), San Francisco-based H&Q went public itself in 1996. About 16% of the firm was sold in an offering that valued H&Q at $350 million. Founder William Hambrecht was left with control of about 13% of company stock, president and CEO Daniel Case with 9%, and VC William Timken 7%. Besides underwriting public offerings, H&Q also provides research, sales and trading services, merger and acquisition advisory services, and venture capital.

In 1968 Hambrecht and George Quist teamed up to start an investment firm that would specialize in high-tech companies. Their initial investment fund included their own money and funds from other private investors who were enthusiastic about getting in on the ground floor of the burgeoning computer and technology businesses that were starting up in the Silicon Valley.

Hambrecht and Quist were at the right place at the right time with lots of money, so their firm prospered. Quist, who was the cautious, methodical business manager, died in 1982, and Hambrecht, the glad-handing dealer, was unleashed. As the 1990s dawned, H&Q's reputation had been hurt by its spotty track record, and its share of the high-tech IPO market had declined. Hambrecht brought in Case, who stabilized the firm's reputation and expanded its focus both by industry and by region. Case also expanded H&Q into new services, such as merger and acquisition advising.

In 1994, with little fanfare, the firm launched a new brokerage to underwrite IPOs for small companies ($15-$25 million in sales) beyond the startup phase. In 1996 H&Q opened an office in London to provide its services to European companies in such industries as electronic technology, health care, and biotechnology.

WHO

Chairman; Chairman, H&Q LLC: William R. Hambrecht, age 60, $1,233,688 pay
VC; VC H&Q LLC: William R. Timken, age 60, $940,000 pay
President and CEO; President and CEO, H&Q LLC: Daniel H. Case III, age 38, $2,300,000 pay
EVP; Director Institutional Equity, H&Q LLC: Paul L. Barney Hallingby, age 49, $1,147,000 pay
Managing Director; Co-Director Investment Banking, H&Q LLC: Cristina M. Morgan, $1,665,363 pay
Managing Director; Co-Director Investment Banking, H&Q LLC: David M. McAuliffe, age 47
CFO; Managing Director and CFO, H&Q LLC: Raymond J. Minehan, age 54
General Counsel and Secretary; Managing Director, General Counsel, and Secretary, H&Q LLC: Steven N. Machtinger, age 46
Director of Research; Managing Director, H&Q LLC: Bruce M. Lupatkin, age 40
Director Human Resources: K. C. Egan
Auditors: Andersen Worldwide

WHERE

HQ: One Bush St., San Francisco, CA 94104
Phone: 415-576-3300   **Fax:** 415-576-3624
Web site: http://www.hamquist.com

WHAT

	1995 Sales	
	$ mil.	% of total
Investment banking	70.4	32
Principal transactions	53.4	24
Net investment gains	33.9	16
Agency commissions	24.6	11
Corporate finance fees	20.7	9
Other	17.0	8
Total	**220.0**	**100**

KEY COMPETITORS

Accel Partners
Alex. Brown
Asset
   Management
Austin Ventures
Bear Stearns
Brentwood
   Associates
Institutional
   Venture
   Partners

Jefferies Group
Kleiner Perkins
Lehman
   Brothers
Mayfield Fund
Menlo Ventures
Montgomery
   Securities
Morgan Stanley
Norwest Venture
   Capital

Paine Webber
Piper Jaffray
Safeguard
   Scientifics
Salomon
Sequoia Capital
Sutter Hill
Volpe, Welty

HOW MUCH

NYSE symbol: HMQ FYE: September 30	Annual Growth	1990	1991	1992	1993	1994	1995
Sales ($ mil.)	28.1%	—	81.8	125.5	110.5	119.3	220.0
Net income ($ mil.)	—	—	(9.9)	9.7	15.3	15.9	49.4
Income as % of sales	—	—	—	7.8%	13.8%	13.3%	22.5%
Employees	14.5%	—	291	327	350	426	500

1995 YEAR-END
Debt ratio: 30.2%
Return on equity: 64.6%
Cash (mil.): $35
Current ratio: 1.22
Long-term debt (mil.): $39

HAYES MICROCOMPUTER PRODUCTS

OVERVIEW

After demodulating all the way into bankruptcy, Hayes has been connected to an Asian lifeline and may yet recover. The Norcross, Georgia-based company is the 2nd largest US designer and manufacturer of computer modems (after U.S. Robotics). Cofounder and chairman Dennis Hayes won US Bankruptcy Court approval to sell 49% of his company to Asian investors Acma Ltd., Kaifa Technologies, and Wongs Ltd for $35 million. The new owners offered credit, access to low-cost factories, and an open door to booming Asian markets. In return Hayes relinquished his role as CEO to high-tech manufacturing guru Joseph Formichelli. Hayes still owns 49.5% of the firm.

A former engineer for Financial Data Sciences, Hayes founded Hayes Microcomputer in 1978. At the time most PCs were made from kits, but he saw an opportunity to get in on the ground floor of the burgeoning PC business. He chose modems because he had experience with telecommunications and computers. Hayes's partner, Dale Heatherington, retooled existing technology to make the company's products compatible with kit computers. Hayes and Heatherington, with 3 other employees, began building modems by hand at the rate of 5 per day. When IBM introduced its first PC in 1981, Hayes Microcomputer had the modem field largely to itself. Business skyrocketed, and the Hayes name became synonymous with modems.

By the mid-1980s competition from mail-order houses began to take a bite out of the company's sales, so it began offering lower-priced modems to compete. However, the company lost ground to even cheaper clones during the late-1980s. The company restructured in 1990, but it continued to struggle.

According to Hayes, the company ran into trouble in 1994 when manufacturing was unable to meet orders, leaving the company short of cash. But analysts agree that the CEO's inability to delegate authority led inexorably to the company's fall.

In 1996 Hayes dodged takeover attempts by rivals U.S. Robotics and Diamond Multimedia. In April of that year, he sold nearly half of his company to the Asian consortium and bounced out of bankruptcy court.

WHO

Chairman: Dennis C. Hayes, age 46
President and CEO: Joseph Formichelli, age 53
CFO: James Jones
Chief Technical Officer: Alan Clark
Marketing Manager: Larry J. Hancock
VP Operations: P. K. Chan
Business Unit Manager Software and LAN Connectivity Products: Ken Karegeannes
Business Unit Manager PC Modem Group: Alan Adamson
Business Unit Manager Advanced Network Systems: Ash Dittiavaki
Director Human Resources: Bruce Meyers
Auditors:

WHERE

HQ: Hayes Microcomputer Products, Inc., 5835 Peachtree Corners East, Norcross, GA 30092-3405
Phone: 770-840-9200   **Fax:** 770-441-1213
Web site: http://www.hayes.com

Hayes has 26 regional offices in the US and in Australia, Canada, China, Denmark, France, Germany, Japan, Mexico, and the UK.

WHAT

Selected Products
ACCURA 288 (bundled modem)
Century 2 Rack System (multiple modems for business offices)
ESP Communications Accelerator
OPTIMA Business Modems (single, high-quality modem with features such as fax-on-demand, Caller ID, dial-back security, distinctive ring, and multiple voice mailbox system)
OPTIMA PCMCIA modems
Smartcom Message Center (Windows-based communications package; includes voice, fax, and data features)
ULTRA 144 Modem

KEY COMPETITORS

Analogic	Motorola
Asante	Multi-Tech Systems
Brooktrout Technology	Racal Electronics
DATA RACE	Symantec
Global Village	U.S. Robotics
GVC	Zoom Telephonics
IBM	
Lucent	

HOW MUCH

Private company FYE: September 30	Annual Growth	1990	1991	1992	1993	1994	1995
Sales ($ mil.)	28.0%	80.0	125.0	150.0	195.0	246.9	275.0
Employees	12.9%	600	450	800	889	1,100	1,100

HUTCHINSON TECHNOLOGY

OVERVIEW

Hutchinson Technology thinks thin. Not Twiggy-thin — more like 2-millionths of an inch thin. The Hutchinson, Minnesota-based company is the world's largest maker of suspension assemblies for disk drives, with a 70% market share. Suspension assemblies position the read-write head above the spinning disk in a disk drive, typically at a height of about 2-millionths of an inch (1,500 times thinner than a piece of paper). The company supplies nearly every US disk drive maker, including Seagate and Read-Rite. Cofounder and CEO Jeffrey Green owns 8% of the company.

Green and Jon Geiss, who met when they lived in the same apartment building in Minneapolis, founded Hutchinson Industrial Corporation in 1965 in Geiss's hometown of Hutchinson. The company set up shop in a converted chicken coop and began providing photoetching services. Its first big contract was to provide circuit boards for mainframe computer maker Sperry (now Unisys). In 1975 it signed its first deal with computer behemoth IBM, beginning a long relationship. In 1982, after a dispute with Green, Geiss left the company. That same year the company changed its name to Hutchinson Technology. During the early 1980s it expanded its operations to produce a wide range of disk drive products.

As disk drive technology speeds forward, Hutchinson must develop suspension assemblies for smaller read-write heads. Smaller heads can read and write more data tracks, increasing a disk drive's memory and speed. In 1994 the company shifted to assemblies for "nano" heads (one-billionth of an inch) and in 1995 it began production of "pico" heads (one-trillionth of an inch).

In 1996 Hutchinson announced plans to build a metal stamping plant in St. Paul, Minnesota.

WHO

Chairman and CEO: Jeffrey W. Green, age 55, $573,258 pay
President and COO: Wayne M. Fortun, age 46, $516,380 pay
VP, CFO, Treasurer, and Secretary: John A. Ingleman, age 49, $243,170 pay
VP Administration: Richard C. Myers, age 55, $220,899 pay
VP Disk Drive Components Business Development: R. Scott Schaefer, age 42, $207,702 pay
VP Disk Drive Components Operations: Beatrice A. Graczyk, age 47
VP Human Resources: Rebecca A. Albrecht, age 42
Auditors: Andersen Worldwide

WHERE

HQ: Hutchinson Technology Incorporated, 40 W. Highland Park, Hutchinson, MN 55350
Phone: 320-587-3797   **Fax:** 320-587-1892

	1995 Sales	
	$ mil.	% of total
US	199.5	66
Other countries	100.5	34
Total	**300.0**	**100**

WHAT

	1995 Sales	
	$ mil.	% of total
Suspension assemblies	292.1	97
Etched & stamped components	7.9	3
Total	**300.0**	**100**

KEY COMPETITORS

Applied Magnetics
K. R. Precision
Magnacomp
Nippon Hatsujo Kogyo

HOW MUCH

Nasdaq symbol: HTCH FYE: September 30	Annual Growth	1990	1991	1992	1993	1994	1995
Sales ($ mil.)	19.6%	122.4	143.3	160.3	198.7	238.8	300.0
Net income ($ mil.)	31.8%	5.3	4.5	12.8	8.6	5.9	21.1
Income as % of sales	—	4.3%	3.1%	8.0%	4.3%	2.5%	7.0%
Earnings per share ($)	23.4%	1.34	1.12	2.72	1.58	1.08	3.84
Stock price – high ($)	—	13.50	15.00	45.25	51.25	41.00	91.00
Stock price – low ($)	—	5.50	8.25	14.00	19.00	21.50	23.50
Stock price – close ($)	35.5%	9.25	15.00	42.88	29.25	24.75	42.25
P/E – high	—	10	13	17	32	38	24
P/E – low	—	4	7	5	12	20	6
Dividends per share ($)	—	0.00	0.00	0.00	0.00	0.00	0.00
Book value per share ($)	24.7%	7.29	8.44	14.88	16.64	17.74	21.98
Employees	12.9%	2,648	2,798	3,332	4,108	4,575	4,858

1995 YEAR-END
Debt ratio: 24.7%
Return on equity: 19.7%
Cash (mil.): $32
Current ratio: 2.50
Long-term debt (mil.): $35
No. of shares (mil.): 5
Dividends
  Yield: —
  Payout: —
Market value (mil.): $230
R&D as % of sales: 5.0%

HYPERION SOFTWARE CORPORATION

OVERVIEW

Hyperion Software helps businesses balance their checkbooks. The Stamford, Connecticut-based firm is the #3 developer of financial software for client/server networks (after Oracle and SAP). Its products — including accounting, budgeting, and forecasting software — are used by more than 2,300 corporations in 25 countries. CEO James Perakis owns 5.8% of Hyperion's stock.

The company was founded as IMRS in 1981 by Robert Thomson and shipped its first product, Micro Control, in 1983. Perakis came aboard as CEO in 1985. Thomson eased out of the business, stepping down as president in 1987, but remains a consultant and director. Demand for the company's Hyperion products has been driven by the spread of PC networks. In 1988 IMRS began standardizing the development of its software around Windows. The next year IMRS bought FASTAR, a competing product, from Hoechst Celanese. The company went public in 1991 and that year released its Hyperion line of Windows software (it now has more than 80% of the Windows market for financial software).

IMRS realized early on that business information could be handled on LANs. It has grown internationally by designing multilingual programs so that multinational companies can use the same programs everywhere. One of its most effective means of promotion is forming alliances with the consulting arms of the Big 6 accounting firms, which recommend its products to clients.

In 1995 IMRS changed its name to capitalize on the success of its Hyperion product line. Later that year it released Hyperion Financials, a corporate accounting software package. In fiscal 1996 Hyperion had sales $172.8 million and net income of $9.5 million.

WHO

Chairman, President, and CEO: James A. Perakis, age 51, $360,000 pay
EVP: Terence W. Rogers, age 53, $312,000 pay
SVP: David M. Sample, age 47, $341,000 pay
SVP and CFO: Lucy Rae Ricciardi, age 53
VP Hyperion Enterprise Business Group:
Gordon O. Rapkin, age 40, $208,000 pay
VP Products and Services and Secretary:
Craig M. Schiff, age 40, $192,000 pay
Director Human Resources: Paul Avalone
Auditors: Ernst & Young LLP

WHERE

HQ: 900 Long Ridge Rd., Stamford, CT 06902-1247
Phone: 203-703-3000   **Fax:** 203-595-8500
Web site: http://www.hysoft.com

WHAT

	1995 Sales	
	$ mil.	% of total
Software licenses	78.0	57
License renewals & services	59.1	43
Total	**137.1**	**100**

Selected Products
Hyperion Enterprise and Micro Control (financial data consolidation and reporting)
Hyperion Financials (business transaction collecting and reporting)
Hyperion OnTrack (graphical data presentation)
Hyperion Pillar (budgeting and forecasting)

KEY COMPETITORS

American Software
Computer Associates
Consilium
Fourth Shift
IBM
Marcam

Oracle
PeopleSoft, Inc.
Ross Systems
SAP
System Software
  Associates

HOW MUCH

Nasdaq symbol: HYSW FYE: June 30	Annual Growth	1990	1991	1992	1993	1994	1995
Sales ($ mil.)	41.6%	24.1	34.3	46.0	61.0	84.4	137.1
Net income ($ mil.)	48.1%	1.7	2.7	4.2	4.3	8.5	12.1
Income as % of sales	—	6.9%	7.7%	9.1%	7.0%	10.0%	8.9%
Earnings per share ($)	36.1%	0.15	0.23	0.31	0.29	0.55	0.70
Stock price – high ($)	—	—	11.00	12.50	13.88	20.13	28.38
Stock price – low ($)	—	—	6.00	6.88	5.63	9.00	15.63
Stock price – close ($)	21.5%	—	9.75	12.38	12.75	19.75	21.25
P/E – high	—	—	48	41	49	37	41
P/E – low	—	—	26	23	20	17	22
Dividends per share ($)	—	—	0.00	0.00	0.00	0.00	0.00
Book value per share ($)	50.1%	—	0.88	2.56	2.93	2.81	4.47
Employees	34.8%	190	262	335	419	580	846

1995 YEAR-END
Debt ratio: 11.9%
Return on equity: 19.4%
Cash (mil.): $46
Current ratio: 1.60
Long-term debt (mil.): $9
No. of shares (mil.): 16
Dividends
  Yield: —
  Payout: —
Market value (mil.): $341
R&D as % of sales: 15.3%

ID SOFTWARE, INC.

OVERVIEW

Game players don't have to be psycho or psyched up to have their egos captivated by id Software's adventure games from the dark side — but it helps. The Mesquite, Texas-based company's bloodcurdling titles include Doom (its best-selling demon-infested game series), Quake, and Commander Keen: Aliens Ate My Babysitter. id's marketing strategy is to release a fully featured portion of a game as shareware (available on the Internet, via major online services, or from id's bulletin board) for free. The theory is that players, hooked by the free sample, will run to the retail store and buy the complete program. So far, the strategy has worked. The Doom series is one of the most successful shareware programs in history. The company has gone a step further by releasing software that allows Quake players to compete with each other over the Internet.

Friends John Carmack, Adrian Carmack (no relation), and John Romero worked together as programmers at Softdisk Publishing in Shreveport, Louisiana. With a 4th friend, Tom Hall, they created the first Commander Keen game, Invasion of the Vorticons (starring child genius Billy Blaze), and released it as shareware in late 1990. One month later the quartet launched id Software, named for Freud's psychic seat of pleasure. (Hall has since left to pursue other interests.) The 2nd in the Commander Keen series, Goodbye, Galaxy!, debuted in 1991. The release of Wolfenstein 3-D followed in 1992. The game's 3-D graphics raised the standard for the entire industry.

Doom, the first product released on id's own label, was introduced in 1993. An estimated 100 million players downloaded the shareware, with one in 10 paying for the more advanced version. Doom II: Hell on Earth shipped straight to retail in 1994 with 500,000 copies (worth $25 million) presold. GT Interactive Software markets and distributes the company's products.

id is continuing to expand the multiplayer capabilities of its games and has licensed Doom to an interactive arcade developer, Austin Virtual Gaming. The company pushed the limits in 1996 with the shareware launch of Quake, a scary shoot-'em-up game with state-of-the-art 3-D effects.

WHO

Biz Guy: Jay Wilbur, age 34
Director of Marketing and Biz Guy #2: Mike Wilson
Lead Programmer: John Carmack
Programmer and Game Designer: John Romero
Computer Artist: Adrian Carmack
Computer Artist: Kevin Cloud
Game Programmer: Michael Abrash
Network Programmer: John Cash
Game Designer: Sandy Peterson
Level Designer, Entity Programmer, and Teacher of Beatings: American McGee
Level Designer: Tim Willits
Support Director: Barrett "Bear" Alexander
Project Manager: Shawn Green
Office Assistant and id Mom: Donna Jackson

WHERE

HQ: Town East Tower, 18601 LBJ Fwy., Ste. 615, Mesquite, TX 75150
Phone: 214-613-3589   **Fax:** 214-686-9288
Web site: http://www.idsoftware.com

WHAT

Selected Software Products
Commander Keen: Aliens Ate My Babysitter
Commander Keen: Goodbye, Galaxy!
Commander Keen: Invasion of the Vorticons
Doom: Knee Deep in the Dead
Doom II: Hell on Earth
Heretic
Heretic II
Hexen: Beyond Heretic
Quake
Spear of Destiny
Strife
Wolfenstein 3-D

KEY COMPETITORS

3DO	Knowledge Adventure
7th Level	LucasArts
Acclaim Entertainment	Maxis
Accolade	Microsoft
Activision	Nintendo
Aristo International	Rocket Science Games
Brøderbund	SEGA
Cyan	Sony
Digital Pictures	Spectrum HoloByte
Electronic Arts	T-HQ
Interplay Productions	Trilobyte
JTS	

HOW MUCH

Private company FYE: December 31	Annual Growth	1990	1991	1992	1993	1994	1995
Sales ($ mil.)	149.9%	—	—	1.0	3.0	7.7	15.6
Employees	44.3%	—	3	5	6	10	13

IN FOCUS SYSTEMS, INC.

OVERVIEW

With new products for the home and office, this company is bringing focus to the future of projection technology. Based in Wilsonville, Oregon, In Focus Systems is the world's leading maker of multimedia equipment that projects content from computers, laser disc players, and VCRs onto viewing screens. Unlike the Japanese companies that dominate the industry, In Focus concentrates on all areas of the market, not just the high-tech, high-priced segments. Its Triple Super Twist Nematic technology, which applies monochrome LCD technology to color LCDs, enabled the company to introduce the industry's lowest-priced color LCD. Although its products are typically used for business meetings and presentations, the company is increasing its attention on the home entertainment market.

Paul Gulick and 2 partners set up In Focus in 1986 as an information display system maker. A year later it shipped its first product, PC Viewer, a computer-driven LCD projection panel. In 1989 the company pioneered the first true-color LCD projection panel. In Focus went public the next year.

In Focus has concentrated on making its products smaller, cheaper, and simpler to operate than those of its competitors. In 1992 it set up Motif, a joint venture with Motorola to make low-cost LCDs. The company introduced the portable PanelBook series, projection display devices no larger than notebook computers in 1993. In 1995 joint venture Motif's mandate was changed to licensing the company's passive matrix LCD technology to manufacturers of display screens for handheld games, PCs, and wireless communications devices. The following year In Focus introduced an updated projector model designed to produce better colors, clearer images, and improved video performance.

WHO

Chairman, President, and CEO: John V. Harker, age 61, $453,134 pay
VP Sales, Marketing, and Service: Mark E. Reed, age 45, $213,014 pay
VP Information Services, CFO, and Treasurer: Michael D. Yonker, age 38, $211,952 pay
VP Business Management and Corporate Development: Allen H. Alley, age 41, $201,420 pay
VP Operations: Lyle W. Jordan, age 51, $173,454 pay
VP, General Counsel, and Secretary: Douglas S. Robertson, age 49
VP Human Resources: Susan L. Thompson, age 38
Auditors: Andersen Worldwide

WHERE

HQ: 27700B SW Parkway Ave., Wilsonville, OR 97070-9215
Phone: 503-685-8888   **Fax:** 503-685-8889
Web site: http://www.infs.com

	1995 Sales	
	$ mil.	% of total
US	123.9	61
Europe	49.6	25
Other regions	29.3	14
Total	**202.8**	**100**

WHAT

Selected Products

Color LCD Projection Panels
PanelBook 550 (active-matrix projection panel)
PanelBook 750 (high-resolution panel)
PowerView 950 (very high-resolution projection panel)

Projection Systems
LitePro 560 (active-matrix, data-only projector)
LitePro 570 (projector with sound system and full-motion capability)
LitePro 580 (multimedia projector with stereo sound)

KEY COMPETITORS

ASK LCD	IBM	Proxima
Davis Liquid Crystals	Leisengang	Sarif
Eastman Kodak	Matsushita	Seiko
General Electric	Mitsubishi	Sharp
Hitachi	nVIEW	Toshiba

HOW MUCH

Nasdaq symbol: INFS FYE: December 31	Annual Growth	1990	1991	1992	1993	1994	1995
Sales ($ mil.)	40.8%	36.7	49.5	59.8	73.5	123.1	202.8
Net income ($ mil.)	32.8%	5.5	4.7	3.9	6.0	10.4	22.7
Income as % of sales	—	15.0%	9.5%	6.5%	8.2%	8.4%	11.2%
Earnings per share ($)	18.4%	0.85	0.53	0.42	0.53	0.89	1.98
Stock price – high ($)	—	11.75	28.75	13.50	19.25	31.00	38.00
Stock price – low ($)	—	10.25	5.50	6.00	8.75	10.25	17.75
Stock price – close ($)	26.9%	11.00	7.50	12.25	15.00	26.06	36.13
P/E – high	—	14	54	32	36	35	19
P/E – low	—	12	10	14	17	12	9
Dividends per share ($)	—	0.00	0.00	0.00	0.00	0.00	0.00
Book value per share ($)	20.0%	3.59	4.34	5.89	6.34	7.47	8.93
Employees	29.1%	109	156	164	185	391	391

1995 YEAR-END
Debt ratio: 0.0%
Return on equity: 24.7%
Cash (mil.): $49
Current ratio: 3.78
Long-term debt (mil.): $0
No. of shares (mil.): 11
Dividends
 Yield: —
 Payout: —
Market value (mil.): $395
R&D as % of sales: 3.8%

INFORMIX CORPORATION

OVERVIEW

Informix puts information at your fingertips. The Menlo Park, California-based company is one of the largest database management software companies in the US. It develops open systems software that can handle vast amounts of information and can be accessed from a variety of computer systems. It also produces software that allows for easy data transfer from personal computers to mainframes and makes development tools for client/server production applications.

Informix was founded in 1980 by Roger Sippl, who had been diverted from the study of medicine by a bout with Hodgkin's disease. Sippl scraped up enough capital to start his own company. It grew quickly and went public in 1986. In 1988 Informix introduced OnLine Dynamic Server, the parallel database server that is its core product. That year it merged with Innovative Software, of Kansas City, Missouri but instead of lower costs and more business, Informix wound up with duplicated operations and an inflated organization. Realizing that Informix had outgrown his ability to run it, Sippl brought in Phillip White as CEO in 1989. White turned the organization around. In 1992 Sippl, an entrepreneur at heart, stepped down as chairman and went on to found Visigenic Software.

Informix expanded its global presence in 1994 when it acquired distributors NextWare (Malaysia) and Garmhausen and Partners (Germany). In 1995 Informix purchased Stanford Technology Group to take advantage of the burgeoning market for data warehouse products.

The company acquired Illustra Information Technologies in 1996 in its bid to take the lead in the fast growing market for multimedia database products for use on the Internet.

WHO

Chairman, President, and CEO: Phillip E. White, age 53, $821,667 pay
SVP Product Management and Development: Mike Saranga, age 58, $397,333 pay
SVP Finance and CFO: Howard H. Graham, age 48, $444,333 pay
SVP International: D. Kenneth Coulter, age 51, $421,202 pay
SVP Japan Operations: Edwin C. Winder, age 46, $352,392 pay
VP Legal and Corporate Services, General Counsel, and Secretary: David H. Stanley, age 49
VP Human Resources: Ira H. Dorf, age 55
Auditors: Ernst & Young LLP

WHERE

HQ: 4100 Bohannon Dr., Menlo Park, CA 94025
Phone: 415-926-6300   **Fax:** 415-926-6564
Web site: http://www.informix.com

WHAT

	1995 Sales	
	$ mil.	% of total
License fees	536	76
Services	173	24
Total	**709**	**100**

Selected Software
Connectivity products (INFORMIX-Gateway, INFORMIX-STAR)
Database application development products (INFORMIX-NewEra, INFORMIX-4GL)
Object-relational products (Illustra Server, Illustra DataBlade)

KEY COMPETITORS

Centura Software
Computer Associates
Dynasty Technology
Forte Software
IBM

Microsoft
Object Design
Oracle
PLATINUM technology
Progress Software

Red Brick Systems
Software AG
Spyglass
Sybase

HOW MUCH

Nasdaq symbol: IFMX FYE: December 31	Annual Growth	1990	1991	1992	1993	1994	1995
Sales ($ mil.)	37.2%	146.1	179.8	283.6	352.9	468.7	709.0
Net income ($ mil.)	—	(23.1)	12.2	47.8	56.1	66.2	105.3
Income as % of sales	—	—	6.8%	16.9%	15.9%	14.1%	14.9%
Earnings per share ($)	—	(0.23)	0.11	0.38	0.42	0.49	0.76
Stock price – high ($)	—	2.19	1.98	9.44	13.63	16.06	34.38
Stock price – low ($)	—	0.44	0.33	1.66	6.69	7.13	14.56
Stock price – close ($)	121.7%	0.56	1.72	9.06	10.63	16.06	30.00
P/E – high	—	—	19	25	33	33	45
P/E – low	—	—	3	4	16	15	19
Dividends per share ($)	—	0.00	0.00	0.00	0.00	0.00	0.00
Book value per share ($)	54.1%	0.36	0.48	1.06	1.60	2.10	3.13
Employees	21.0%	1,242	1,121	1,445	1,718	2,212	3,219

1995 YEAR-END
Debt ratio: 0.3%
Return on equity: 30.2%
Cash (mil.): $252
Current ratio: 2.09
Long-term debt (mil.): $1
No. of shares (mil.): 135
Dividends
  Yield: —
  Payout: —
Market value (mil.): $4,060
R&D as % of sales: 11.2%

INSO CORPORATION

OVERVIEW

This sentunce uSe kould some hlpe frum INSO's prawducks. Headquartered in Boston, INSO (formerly InfoSoft) makes document proofing programs such as International CorrectSpell and CorrectText Grammar Correction System. Its software is loaded into some 50 million computers around the world as parts of such programs as Microsoft Word and Office and Lotus WordPro and Notes. The company also produces Inso Search Wizard, a software tool used to perform targeted searches of the World Wide Web that weed out nonrelevant information. In addition, INSO makes Quick View software, used to view and print files from online sources without having to first download them to the computer's memory system. Sales to software god Microsoft account for about half of the company's revenues. Publisher Houghton Mifflin owns nearly 34% of INSO.

The company was formed in 1982 as the Software Division of Houghton Mifflin. It developed the first commercial spell-checking system and created reference materials based on Houghton Mifflin's print products and products licensed from others. In 1990 the company hired Steven Vana-Paxhia, a former marketing director with Macmillan, to head the Software Division. With the software unit growing beyond Houghton Mifflin's core operations, the company spun it off as InfoSoft in 1994. It adopted the name INSO the next year.

To grab a bigger market share, the company purchased file viewing technology firm Systems Compatibility in 1995 and computer graphics concern ImageMark Software Labs in 1996. That year INSO introduced new products of its own, including CyberSpell (e-mail spelling checker), InWords (expanded dictionary), and SciWords (science dictionary).

WHO

President and CEO: Steven R. Vana-Paxhia, age 48, $296,703 pay
VP Business Development: Kirby A. Mansfield, age 41, $191,458 pay
VP; General Manager, Tools and Technologies: Jeffery J. Melvin, age 35, $191,458 pay
VP Engineering: Sunanda Mathai, age 44, $183,699 pay
VP, CFO, and Treasurer: Betty J. Savage, age 37, $174,691 pay
VP, General Counsel, and Secretary: Bruce G. Hill
Director Human Resources: Judith Tavano-Finkle
Auditors: Ernst & Young LLP

WHERE

HQ: 31 St. James Ave., Boston, MA 02116-4101
Phone: 617-753-6500   **Fax:** 617-753-6666
Web site: http://www.inso.com

INSO's software is used in approximately 50 million computers around the world.

WHAT

Selected Products

Information Management
ImageStream (file importer and exporter)
Inso Search Wizard (Internet search tool)
IntelliScope (multilingual search enhancer)
Outside In (file viewer for OEMs)
Quick View Plus (file viewer and printer)

Tools and Technologies
CorrectEnglish (for non-native English writers)
CorrectText Grammar Correction System (English grammar proofer)
CyberSpell (e-mail spelling checker)
International CorrectSpell (spelling checker)
International ProofReader (multilingual proofer)
SciWords (science dictionary)

KEY COMPETITORS

Corel
Encyclopædia Britannica
Lagardere
Lotus
Microlytics

Novell
Research Information
Sherpa Systems
SoftArt
SoftKey

HOW MUCH

Nasdaq symbol: INSO FYE: December 31	Annual Growth	1990	1991	1992	1993	1994	1995
Sales ($ mil.)	48.5%	6.0	7.7	9.5	13.8	23.5	43.4
Net income ($ mil.)	64.4%	0.5	1.1	1.6	2.6	5.7	6.0
Income as % of sales	—	7.5%	14.1%	16.4%	18.7%	24.1%	13.8%
Earnings per share ($)	51.8%	—	—	0.14	0.23	0.48	0.49
Stock price – high ($)	—	—	—	—	—	17.88	47.50
Stock price – low ($)	—	—	—	—	—	8.57	16.53
Stock price – close ($)	—	—	—	—	—	17.57	42.50
P/E – high	—	—	—	—	—	37	97
P/E – low	—	—	—	—	—	18	34
Dividends per share ($)	—	—	—	—	—	0.00	0.00
Book value per share ($)	—	—	—	—	—	2.38	5.80
Employees	45.6%	—	—	—	83	118	176

1995 YEAR-END
Debt ratio: 7.8%
Return on equity: 11.7%
Cash (mil.): $63
Current ratio: 4.46
Long-term debt (mil.): $0
No. of shares (mil.): 13
Dividends
  Yield: —
  Payout: —
Market value (mil.): $551
R&D as % of sales: 20.4

INTEGRATED DEVICE TECHNOLOGY

OVERVIEW

Business is looking chipper for chip maker Integrated Device Technology (IDT). The Santa Clara, California-based company's high-performance semiconductors, microprocessors, and modules are incorporated into communications equipment, computers and computer networking products, and other office electronics. Its products include static random access memories (SRAMs), logic circuits, RISC microprocessors, and specialty memory products produced using CMOS technology. Many of the world's leading electronics OEMS are IDT customers; Apple Computer accounts for about 12% of the company's revenues.

IDT was founded in 1980 by a group of engineers (mostly from Hewlett-Packard) to develop high-performance chips using the then-emerging CMOS technology. The new company's primary targets were the military and high-speed commercial markets. Its first product, an SRAM chip, was shipped in early 1982. In 1986 the company combined bipolar and CMOS technology in a process called BiCMOS; it introduced the first BiCMOS SRAM chip 2 years later. The following year IDT entered the RISC microprocessor market when it licensed MIPS Technologies's proprietary architecture. After profits fell in 1990-91 and the company posted a loss in 1992, IDT shifted its focus to commercial rather than military markets; profits rebounded in fiscal 1993.

In 1995 IDT formed a new subsidiary, Centaur Technology, to manufacture RISC chips.

IDT introduced its Fusion Memory technology the next year. Fusion Memory substantially increases the amount of memory that can be built into a single chip. Also in 1996 manufacturing operations began at the company's 8-inch wafer fabrication plant in Oregon.

WHO

Chairman: D. John Carey, age 59
President and CEO: Leonard C. Perham, age 52, $1,710,603 pay
VP Research and Development and Chief Technology Officer: Chuen-Der Lien, age 40, $605,605 pay
VP Sales and Marketing: Daniel L. Lewis, age 47, $451,864 pay
VP Worldwide Manufacturing: L. Robert Phillips, age 51, $432,200 pay
VP Wafer Operations: Wiliam B. Cortelyou, age 40
VP Assembly and Test: Robin H. Hodge, age 56
VP, General Counsel, and Secretary: Jack Menache, age 52
VP Finance and CFO: William D. Snyder, age 51
VP Human Resources: Thomas B. Wroblewski
Auditors: Price Waterhouse LLP

WHERE

HQ: Integrated Device Technology, Inc., 2975 Stender Way, Santa Clara, CA 95054
Phone: 408-727-6116   **Fax:** 408-492-8674
Web site: http://www.idt.com

WHAT

	1996 Sales % of total
SRAM products	46
Communications products	27
Logic circuits	17
Microprocessors	10
Total	**100**

KEY COMPETITORS

Alliance Semiconductor	Lattice Semiconductor
AMD	Micron Technology
Atmel	National Semiconductor
Cypress Semiconductor	NEC
Integrated Silicon Solutions	Paradigm Technology
Intel	SGS-Thompson
	Texas Instruments

HOW MUCH

Nasdaq symbol: IDTI FYE: March 31	Annual Growth	1991	1992	1993	1994	1995	1996
Sales ($ mil.)	27.9%	198.6	202.7	236.3	330.5	422.2	679.5
Net income ($ mil.)	151.3%	1.2	(32.8)	5.3	40.2	78.3	120.2
Income as % of sales	—	0.6%	—	2.3%	12.2%	18.5%	17.7%
Earnings per share ($)	116.9%	0.03	(0.63)	0.09	0.60	1.04	1.44
Stock price – high ($)[1]	—	4.00	4.88	3.88	9.88	17.19	33.50
Stock price – low ($)[1]	—	1.63	1.56	1.75	3.13	8.00	12.25
Stock price – close ($)[1]	50.1%	1.69	2.25	3.13	8.56	14.81	12.88
P/E – high	—	160	—	43	16	17	23
P/E – low	—	65	—	19	5	8	9
Dividends per share ($)	—	0.00	0.00	0.00	0.00	0.00	0.00
Book value per share ($)	22.2%	2.60	1.97	2.07	3.36	5.44	7.09
Employees	13.3%	2,052	2,159	2,414	2,615	2,965	3,828

[1] Stock prices are for the prior calendar year.

1996 YEAR-END
Debt ratio: 28.9%
Return on equity: 24.9%
Cash (mil.): $261
Current ratio: 2.78
Long-term debt (mil.): $219
No. of shares (mil.): 78
Dividends
 Yield: —
 Payout: —
Market value (mil.): $998
R&D as % of sales: 19.6%

INTUIT INC.

OVERVIEW

Intuit has a feeling there's money to be made on the Internet. The Menlo Park, California-based company is the #1 maker of accounting (QuickBooks), personal finance (Quicken), and tax (MacInTax and TurboTax) software. Its Quicken Visa Card with IntelliCharge transmits expenditure data to the cardholder via modem. But Intuit's new focus is Internet banking.

Chairman Scott Cook spent 3 years at Procter & Gamble and 4 years at Bain & Co. consulting. In 1983 he decided to apply his brand of management skills to the Market research showed that people wanted an easy-to-use personal finance software package. The result was Quicken, introduced in 1984. Cook owns 19% of Intuit. By 1990 Quicken was the market leader. Intuit released QuickBooks in 1992 and went public in 1993. The following year it acquired ChipSoft, a tax preparation software developer, Best Programs (tax preparation software), and National Payment Clearinghouse (automated bill payment services).

In 1995 software giant Microsoft tried to buy Intuit but was halted by a Justice Department antitrust lawsuit. Also that year the firm launched its online banking service through 21 of the largest national financial institutions Intuit entered the world's 2nd largest PC market — Japan — with the purchase of Tokyo-based financial software firm Milky Way KK. Expenses related to the failed Microsoft merger and subsequent acquisitions led Intuit to a loss in 1995. In 1996 Intuit said it would sell its electronic transaction processing operations to CheckFree. Intuit's sales rose to $538 million in fiscal 1996 but it again posted a loss (of $21 million) that included nearly $49 million in acquisition-related costs.

WHO

Chairman: Scott D. Cook, age 43
President and CEO: William V. Campbell, age 55
EVP: William H. Harris Jr., age 39
CFO: James J. Heeger, age 39
General Counsel: Catherine L. Valentine, age 43
VP Sales: Alan A. Gleicher, age 43
VP Human Resources: Michael A. Ahearn, age 48
Auditors: Ernst & Young LLP

WHERE

HQ: 155 Linfield Ave., Menlo Park, CA 94025
Phone: 415-322-0573   **Fax:** 415-329-2788
Web site: http://www.intuit.com

WHAT

	1995 Sales	
	$ mil.	% of total
Software	342.9	87
Supplies	52.8	13
Total	**395.7**	**100**

Personal Finance Software
Quicken (DOS, Windows, and Macintosh)
Quicken Financial Planner (retirement planning)

Small Business Accounting Software
QuickBooks
QuickPay (payroll add-on)

Tax Preparation Software
MacInTax
TurboTax

Other Software Products
Golf Digest's Scorecard
Medical Drug Reference
Quicken Family Lawyer
QuickVerse (Biblical references)

Services
Online banking & bill payment
Payroll Tax Table Update Service
Quicken Visa Card with IntelliCharge (credit management)

KEY COMPETITORS

Best Programs	FMR	NEBS
Charles Schwab	H&R Block	Sterling
Checkfree	IBM	Commerce
Citicorp	Lacerte Software	Taasc
Computer Associates	Microsoft	Visa
	Moore	

HOW MUCH

Nasdaq symbol: INTU FYE: July 31	Annual Growth	1990	1991	1992	1993	1994[1]	1995
Sales ($ mil.)	64.3%	33.1	44.5	83.8	121.4	194.1	395.7
Net income ($ mil.)	—	3.6	4.3	5.3	8.4	(176.6)	(45.4)
Income as % of sales	—	10.8%	9.6%	6.3%	6.9%	—	—
Earnings per share ($)	—	0.18	0.21	0.25	0.37	(5.22)	(1.11)
Stock price – high ($)	—	—	—	—	23.25	36.63	89.25
Stock price – low ($)	—	—	—	—	12.00	13.50	28.94
Stock price – close ($)	91.3%	—	—	—	21.31	33.38	78.00
P/E – high	—	—	—	—	63	—	—
P/E – low	—	—	—	—	32	—	—
Dividends per share ($)	—	—	—	—	0.00	0.00	0.00
Book value per share ($)	70.7%	—	—	—	2.20	4.83	6.41
Employees	90.1%	110	175	484	589	1,228	2,732

[1] 10-month fiscal year

1995 YEAR-END
Debt ratio: 1.5%
Return on equity: —
Cash (mil.): $191
Current ratio: 2.64
Long-term debt (mil.): $4
No. of shares (mil.): 44
Dividends
  Yield: —
  Payout: —
Market value (mil.): $3,422
R&D as % of sales: 13.5%
Advertising as % of sales: 4.3%

IOMEGA CORPORATION

OVERVIEW

Iomega wants to put some zip into the disk drive market. Based in Roy, Utah, Iomega's drives, including the extremely popular Zip models, bridge the gap between the high capacity and rapid access of hard disk systems and the flexibility of floppy disk drives. Chairman David Dunn owns about 14% of Iomega.

David Bailey and David Norton started the company (an offshoot of an IBM research facility in Tucson) as Databyte Corporation in 1980, changing the name to Iomega later that year. Its first product, the Bernoulli Box (developed and abandoned by IBM), was a disk drive system used by the government. In 1983 Iomega launched the Bernoulli storage drive for PC users. Storing up to 30 times the data of a contemporary floppy disk, the drive was an instant success. That year Iomega went public. Sales zoomed 18-fold between 1983 and 1986 — then trouble hit. Poor management and lagging sales led to a $37 million loss in 1987. The firm closed its plants for 4 months, fired nearly half its employees, and began to focus on tape backup systems.

In 1993 Kim Edwards, an executive with battery maker Gates Energy, was named CEO. He challenged the company's engineers to design a data storage product that would appeal to the mass market. The answer — the 100-megabyte Zip drive — was released in 1995. That year, the company also released the Jaz drive, which holds 10 times the data of the Zip.

In an effort to make Zip drives the next industry-standard storage system, Iomega has pushed hard in retail channels and has signed deals with several major computer makers, in 1996. In another developments include promises from American Megatrends and Phoenix Technologies make software allowing a PC to start up using a Zip drive rather than a standard hard drive.

WHO

Chairman: David J. Dunn, age 65
President and CEO: Kim B. Edwards, age 48, $400,000 pay
SVP Finance and CFO: Leonard C. Purkis, age 47
SVP and Chief Internal Operating Officer: Leon J. Staciokas, age 67, $377,792 pay
SVP Strategic Business Development: Anton J. Radman Jr., age 43, $293,305 pay
SVP Europe: Srini Nageshwar, age 53, $262,968 pay
SVP Operations: M. Wayne Stewart, age 50
VP Sales: Edward D. Briscoe, age 33
Director Human Resources: Dan Henrie
Auditors: Andersen Worldwide

WHERE

HQ: 1821 W. Iomega Way, Roy, UT 84067
Phone: 801-778-1000   **Fax:** 801-778-3190
Web site: http://www.iomega.com
Iomega has facilities around the world.

WHAT

Selected Products
Bernoulli drives and disks (removable storage systems)
Ditto Easy tape backup drives and cartridges (420 MB-3,200 MB)
Jaz drives and disks (1000 MB)
Zip drives and disks (100 MB)

Selected OEM Contracts

Acer	NEC
IBM	Packard Bell

KEY COMPETITORS

Compaq	3M
Exabyte	Mitsumi
Fujitsu	Pinnacle Micro
Hewlett-Packard	Quantum Corp.
Hitachi	Seagate
Hyundai	Seiko
IBM	SyQuest
JTS	Toshiba
Matsushita	Western Digital

HOW MUCH

Nasdaq symbol: IOMG FYE: December 31	Annual Growth	1990	1991	1992	1993	1994	1995
Sales ($ mil.)	24.6%	120.4	136.6	139.2	147.1	141.4	362.2
Net income ($ mil.)	(9.5%)	14.0	12.3	4.7	(16.9)	(1.9)	8.5
Income as % of sales	—	11.6%	9.0%	3.4%	—	—	2.6%
Earnings per share ($)	(10.2%)	0.12	0.10	0.04	(0.16)	(0.02)	0.07
Stock price – high ($)	—	0.83	1.20	1.50	1.09	0.59	8.95
Stock price – low ($)	—	0.41	0.64	0.64	0.31	0.27	0.55
Stock price – close ($)	62.3%	0.72	1.14	0.98	0.34	0.55	8.11
P/E – high	—	7	12	38	—	—	128
P/E – low	—	4	5	16	—	—	8
Dividends per share ($)	0.0%	0.00	0.00	0.00	0.00	0.00	0.00
Book value per share ($)	2.0%	0.48	0.57	0.61	0.46	0.44	0.53
Employees	10.6%	1,006	1,153	1,270	1,077	886	1,667

1995 YEAR-END
Debt ratio: 50.6%
Return on equity: 15.2%
Cash (mil.): $1
Current ratio: —
Long-term debt (mil.): $4
No. of shares (mil.): 118
Dividends
  Yield: —
  Payout: —
Market value (mil.): $954
R&D as % of sales: 6.0%
Advertising as % of sales: 3.3%

JABIL CIRCUIT, INC.

OVERVIEW

Jabil Circuit designs, manufactures, and assembles circuit boards and electronic component systems for computers, peripheral equipment, and automobile instrumentation. The St. Petersburg, Florida-based company's sales and income were up in 1995, in part because of the strong performance of its operations in Scotland, which were profitable for the first time. Jabil focuses on long-term manufacturing agreements with original equipment manufacturers of products including portable and desktop computers, color ink-jet printers, hard disk and tape drives, digital cellular telephones, and automotive instrumentation. Hewlett Packard, Quantum, and NEC Technologies accounted for 28%, 17%, and 14% of net revenues, respectively, in 1995. CEO (and founder's son) William Morean and his family control 48% of the company's shares, while president Thomas Sansone has 8%.

Jabil was named for founders James Golden and Bill Morean. They started the company in suburban Detroit in 1966 to assemble circuit boards, primarily replacement assemblies for computer manufacturer Control Data, and incorporated in 1969. It entered the automotive electronics business in 1979 through a high-volume manufacturing agreement with General Motors. In 1983 the firm moved its headquarters to St. Petersburg. Jabil opened a manufacturing facility in Scotland in 1993 to better serve its European customers. Also that year the company went public.

The company announced in 1995 that it would expand into Asia with the opening the next year of a manufacturing plant in Penang, Malaysia. Jabil suffered a setback early in 1996 when disk-drive manufacturer Quantum canceled production orders worth some $60 million for high-end drive components.

WHO

Chairman and CEO: William D. Morean, age 40, $200,000 pay
President: Thomas A. Sansone, age 46, $200,000 pay
CFO: Ronald J. Rapp, age 43, $144,978 pay
VP Business Development: Timothy L. Main, age 37, $212,232 pay
Secretary and General Counsel: Linda V. Moore, age 48
Treasurer: Chris A. Lewis, age 35
Director Human Resources: Fred McCoy
Auditors: KPMG Peat Marwick LLP

WHERE

HQ: 10800 Roosevelt Blvd., St. Petersburg, FL 33716
Phone: 813-577-9749 **Fax:** 813-579-8529
Jabil has manufacturing facilities in California, Florida, and Michigan and in Malaysia and the UK.

	1995 Sales
	% of total
US	79
Other countries	21
Total	**100**

WHAT

Selected Services

Circuit design	System assembly
Mechanical design	System testing
Production design	Volume board assembly
Prototype assembly	

KEY COMPETITORS

ACT Manufacturing
Avex
Benchmark Electronics
DII
Flextronics
Group Technologies
IEC Electronics
Intel
Merix
SCI Systems
Solectron
Texas Instruments

HOW MUCH

Nasdaq symbol: JBIL FYE: August 31	Annual Growth	1990	1991	1992	1993	1994	1995
Sales ($ mil.)	35.1%	124.3	232.6	173.1	334.7	375.8	559.5
Net income ($ mil.)	46.0%	1.1	10.3	3.2	8.1	2.6	7.3
Income as % of sales	—	0.9%	4.4%	1.8%	2.4%	0.7%	1.3%
Earnings per share ($)	39.2%	0.09	0.86	0.27	0.59	0.17	0.47
Stock price – high ($)	—	—	—	—	10.00	9.38	23.00
Stock price – low ($)	—	—	—	—	5.75	3.50	3.75
Stock price – close ($)	24.6%	—	—	—	7.25	4.00	11.25
P/E – high	—	—	—	—	17	55	49
P/E – low	—	—	—	—	10	21	8
Dividends per share ($)	—	—	—	—	0.00	0.00	0.00
Book value per share ($)	8.6%	—	—	—	3.42	3.57	4.03
Employees	34.7%	600	—	—	997	1,516	2,661

1995 YEAR-END
Debt ratio: 64.7%
Return on equity: 13.1%
Cash (mil.): $6
Current ratio: 1.18
Long-term debt (mil.): $28
No. of shares (mil.): 15
Dividends
  Yield: —
  Payout: —
Market value (mil.): $166
R&D as % of sales: 0.3%

JTS CORPORATION

OVERVIEW

Disk drive maverick JTS has gotten into the game. Headquartered in San Jose, JTS Corporation makes Palladium 3.5-inch disk drives for desktop computers and Nordic 3-inch disk drives used in mobile computers. Through its merger with Atari, the company now also makes the Jaguar video game system and games for PCs. JTS believes its Nordic drives, though wider than standard drives for notebook computers, have an advantage since they are thinner and cheaper and can store nearly twice as much information.

Jugi Tandon, inventor of the double-sided floppy disk drive, started the company in 1994 as JT Storage to develop low-cost drives. Fellow drive veteran Tom Mitchell invested in the company and became CEO, and drive maker Western Digital invested $10 million. The new enterprise developed a 3-inch disk drive (for portable computers) that can use metal-in-gap ferrite heads, which are considerably less expensive than the thin-film heads required to make 2.5 inch drives.

JT Storage began selling its Palladium and Nordic disk drives in 1995. In 1996 the company went public, adopted the name JTS, and merged with Atari to get an infusion of cash from the gaming dinosaur's considerable reserves. Atari was established in Sunnyvale, California, in 1972 by Nolan Bushnell, an engineer who produced his first video arcade game while tinkering with microcomputers at home. The company's 2nd arcade game, Pong, became an overwhelming success.Other video game hits included Asteriods, Missile Command, and Pac-Man. A waning interest in video games in the mid-1980s slowed sales, and later in the decade competition mounted. Sales continued to slide in the 1990s. In a failed comeback attempt in 1993, Atari launched the Jaguar 64-bit media entertainment system.

Atari in 1996 began updating the graphics and sound of its library of 1980s-vintage video games, such as Asteroids and Pac-Man. But when the merger with JTS was announced, Atari cut most of its staff. Also in 1996 JTS began supplying hard disk drives to Compaq for use in that company's PCs.

WHO

Chairman: Jugi Tandon
President and CEO: Tom Mitchell
EVP and COO: Ken Wing
EVP Finance and Administration and CFO:
  W. Virginia Walker
EVP: Amit Chaokshi
VP Marketing: Richard Retmeyer
Chief Technical Officer: Steve Kaczeus
Manager Human Resources: Margaret Carey
Auditors: Andersen Worldwide

WHERE

HQ: 166 Baypointe Pkwy., San Jose, CA 95134
Phone: 408-468-1800   **Fax:** 408-468-1801

JTS has manufacturing, marketing, and other facilities in the US, Europe, India, and the Far East.

WHAT

Selected Products
Jaguar video game systems
Nordic disk drives (3-inch format, 840MB-1.8GB)
Palladium disk drives (3.5-inch format, 850MB-2.4GB)
PC video games

KEY COMPETITORS

Acclaim Entertainment
Electronic Arts
Fujitsu
Hitachi
IBM
Iomega
Ma Labs
Nintendo
Seagate
SEGA
Sequel
Siliconix
Sony
StreamLogic
Quantum Corp.
Toshiba

HOW MUCH

AMEX symbol: JTS FYE: January 31	Annual Growth	1991	1992	1993	1994	1995	1996
Sales ($ mil.)	—	—	—	—	—	—	18.8
Net income ($ mil.)	—	—	—	—	—	—	(33.1)
Income as % of sales	—	—	—	—	—	—	—
Employees	—	—	—	—	—	—	1,300

1996 YEAR-END
Debt ratio: 100.0%
Return on equity: —
Cash (mil.): $1
Current ratio: 0.44
Long-term debt (mil.): $0
R&D as % of sales: 71.2%

KEY TRONIC CORPORATION

OVERVIEW

Spokane, Washington-based Key Tronic is the world's largest producer of keyboards for personal computers, terminals, and workstations, featuring ergonomic designs that allow easier, faster input with less user fatigue. The company sells its products to more than 170 original equipment manufacturers. Hewlett-Packard, Microsoft, and Compaq accounted for 23%, 19%, and 12% of 1995 sales, respectively.

Key Tronic was founded in 1969 by Lewis Zirkle, who had worked for more than 20 years at General Electric in various engineering and manufacturing positions. In 1975 the company developed and marketed a capacitance keyboard (a lower-cost keyboard), the first major independent supplier to do so. By 1981 Key Tronic was a leader in manufacturing ergonomic keyboards. The company went public in 1983. In 1987 it developed new technology that reduced costs by using a smaller circuit board and fewer components.

Hard times hit in 1991 and 1992 as overseas competition and a failed attempt to produce a computer notebook contributed to net losses for both years. Turnaround artist Stanley Hiller stepped in as CEO in 1992; he owns 19% of the company. Key Tronic acquired Honeywell's keyboard operations in 1993 and moved a large part of its production to Honeywell's former plant in Ciudad Juarez, Mexico, in 1994.

Fred Wenninger, a former Hewlett-Packard executive, took over as CEO and president that year, replacing Hiller, who remains chairman. In 1996, Key Tronic had sales of $201 million and posted a loss of $1.8 million. The company was hurt by poor results in Europe and that year it closed its Irish manufacturing operations and moved them to Mexico, resulting in a charge of more than $2 million.

WHO

Chairman: Stanley Hiller Jr., age 70
President and CEO: Fred Wenninger, age 56
SVP Operations: Jack W. Oehlke, age 49, $244,871 pay
VP Engineering: Craig D. Gates, age 36
VP Quality Assurance: Richard T. Tinsley, age 47, $200,676 pay
VP Finance and Treasurer: Ronald F. Klawitter, age 43, $194,410 pay
Director Human Resources: Keith C. Clement
Auditors: Deloitte & Touche LLP

WHERE

HQ: 4424 N. Sullivan Rd., Spokane, WA 99216
Phone: 509-928-8000   **Fax:** 509-927-5248
Web site: http://www.keytronic.com/index.htm

	1995 Sales	
	$ mil.	% of total
US	124.3	60
Other countries	83.2	40
Total	**207.5**	**100**

WHAT

	1995 Sales	
	$ mil.	% of total
Keyboards	185.3	89
Nonkeyboard products	22.2	11
Total	**207.5**	**100**

Selected Keyboard Products
ConnectKey
EuroTech
IBM's ThinkPad 701C Butterfly
KB 101, KB 101 Plus, KT 2000
Microsoft's Natural
ProTouch

KEY COMPETITORS

Alps Electric
Astronics
BTC
Cherry
Chicony
Cybex
Fujitsu
Lexmark International
Mitsumi
NMB
Se-Jin
Siletek/Litcon

HOW MUCH

Nasdaq symbol: KTCC FYE: June 30	Annual Growth	1990	1991	1992	1993	1994	1995
Sales ($ mil.)	8.2%	140.2	141.0	124.0	123.3	159.5	207.5
Net income ($ mil.)	24.0%	1.5	(7.7)	(7.5)	3.8	(1.1)	4.4
Income as % of sales	—	1.0%	—	—	3.1%	—	2.1%
Earnings per share ($)	19.0%	0.18	(1.00)	(0.96)	0.42	(1.19)	0.43
Stock price – high ($)	—	5.50	5.50	10.75	14.25	11.50	6.31
Stock price – low ($)	—	3.63	1.88	2.13	5.75	5.75	7.75
Stock price – close ($)	13.9%	4.38	2.13	10.38	8.25	10.50	8.38
P/E – high	—	31	—	—	34	—	10
P/E – low	—	20	—	—	14	—	18
Dividends per share ($)	—	0.00	0.00	0.00	0.00	0.00	0.00
Book value per share ($)	(3.1%)	7.09	6.00	5.22	5.54	5.38	6.06
Employees	7.5%	2,127	2,241	1,618	2,085	2,244	3,056

1995 YEAR-END
Debt ratio: 39.8%
Return on equity: 9.2%
Cash (mil.): $5
Current ratio: 2.07
Long-term debt (mil.): $29
No. of shares (mil.): 9
Dividends
  Yield: —
  Payout: —
Market value (mil.): $71
R&D as % of sales: 3.0%

KLA INSTRUMENTS CORPORATION

OVERVIEW

If the chips are down, then KLA Instruments is in trouble. The San Jose, California-based company is a leader in the field of yield management and process monitoring systems used to reduce defects in integrated circuits. KLA is the world's largest supplier of such systems to the wafer and reticle inspection and optical metrology equipment markets. The company has manufacturing facilities in San Jose as well as in Israel and Switzerland.

KLA was founded in 1975 by Silicon Valley entrepreneurs Kenneth Levy and Robert Anderson to develop semiconductor manufacturing inspection systems. In the late 1970s it introduced its RAPID reticle inspection system, which utilized advanced optical and image processing technology to test the templates used to etch circuit designs onto silicon wafers. The company went public in 1980. In 1984 KLA introduced the WISARD automated wafer inspection system. When US semiconductor demand faltered in the mid-1980s, the company ramped up its sales to growing markets in Europe and Japan. KLA introduced its 2nd generation wafer inspection system, which was 100 times faster that previous systems, in 1990.

KLA poured $64 million into R&D in 1991 and 1992 (22% of sales) to get its new products to market. In 1994 the company acquired Metrologix, a San Jose-based maker of advanced electron beam measurement equipment, for $16 million.

The next year KLA launched an electron-beam metrology system that doubles wafer production to 40 wafers per hour. Also in 1995 the company signed a joint deal with Samsung to apply electron microscope technology to the detection of defects on advanced microchips. KLA's profits rose to $120.9 million on sales of $694.9 million in fiscal 1996.

WHO

Chairman and CEO: Kenneth Levy, age 52, $589,307 pay
President and COO: Kenneth L. Schroeder, age 49, $566,095 pay
SVP Strategic Business Development: Samuel Harrell, age 55
VP Finance and Administration and CFO: Robert J. Boehlke, age 54, $389,908 pay
Group VP Wafer and Reticle Inspection: Arthur P. Schnitzer, age 52, $327,385 pay
VP Corporate Sales: Michael D. McCarver, age 49, $274,556 pay
VP and Chief Technical Officer: Bin-Ming Ben Tsai, age 37
VP Human Resources: Virginia J. DeMars, age 53
Auditors: Price Waterhouse LLP

WHERE

HQ: 160 Rio Robles, PO Box 49055, San Jose, CA 95161-9055
Phone: 408-468-4200   **Fax:** 408-434-4266
Web site: http://hrweb.kla.com/empl/index.htm

	1995 Sales	
	$ mil.	% of total
Japan	159.2	36
US	138.9	31
Asia/Pacific	96.4	22
Western Europe	47.9	11
Total	**442.4**	**100**

WHAT

Selected Business Units
Metrology (electron-beam and optical)
Reticle Inspection Systems (RAPID)
Scanning Electron Microscope Inspection Systems (SEMSpec)
Software Productivity and Analysis Systems (PRISM)
Wafer Probing Systems

KEY COMPETITORS

Hitachi
Industrial Technologies
Integrated Process
  Equipment
Orbot Systems
Schlumberger
Semitool
Tektronix

HOW MUCH

Nasdaq symbol: KLAC FYE: June 30	Annual Growth	1990	1991	1992	1993	1994	1995
Sales ($ mil.)	22.3%	161.6	148.4	156.0	167.2	243.7	442.4
Net income ($ mil.)	44.2%	9.4	(10.6)	(13.8)	7.0	30.2	58.6
Income as % of sales	—	5.8%	—	—	4.2%	12.4%	13.2%
Earnings per share ($)	35.8%	0.52	(0.57)	0.75	0.35	1.37	2.40
Stock price – high ($)	—	6.25	7.25	6.88	14.13	27.00	48.75
Stock price – low ($)	—	2.88	4.00	3.00	5.13	12.25	23.25
Stock price – close ($)	42.9%	4.38	5.56	6.13	13.88	24.50	26.06
P/E – high	—	12	—	9	40	20	20
P/E – low	—	6	—	4	15	9	10
Dividends per share ($)	—	0.00	0.00	0.00	0.00	0.00	0.00
Book value per share ($)	18.9%	6.79	6.18	5.51	5.85	9.95	16.11
Employees	8.5%	1,100	1,100	1,000	1,000	1,135	1,654

1995 YEAR-END
Debt ratio: 5.7%
Return on equity: 18.6%
Cash (mil.): $119
Current ratio: 2.72
Long-term debt (mil.): $0
No. of shares (mil.): 25
Dividends
  Yield: —
  Payout: —
Market value (mil.): $654
R&D as % of sales: 6.4%

KLEINER PERKINS CAUFIELD & BYERS

OVERVIEW

"Follow the cash" are watchwords at Kleiner Perkins Caufield & Byers (KPCB). The Menlo Park, California-based partnership is one of the leading venture capital firms in Silicon Valley. Since its inception, KPCB has invested about $1 billion in more than 200 companies, about 90 of which have gone public.

The company was founded in 1972 by Eugene Kleiner, a cofounder of Fairchild Semiconductor, and Thomas Perkins, the first general manager of Hewlett-Packard's computer division. Their expertise lured investors to their fund, which they invested in start-up high-tech companies. The firm grew with the computer industry in Silicon Valley. Frank Caufield, a career venture capitalist, and Brook Byers, a specialist in life science businesses, soon became partners. But the highest profile partner doesn't have his name on the shingle. John Doerr, who joined in 1980, has coordinated most of the firm's electronics investments.

One of the firm's unique characteristics is its company network. Likened to a Japanese "keiretsu," KPCB's investments are grouped into collections of companies that work cooperatively within 2 broad groups: Life Sciences (biotech, diagnostics, and medical equipment) and Information Sciences (software, computers and peripherals, interactive media, communications, and mobile computing and communications). Acuson, Genentech, Intuit, Compaq, and Sun Microsystems are some of its successes. The company has also had some clunkers, including Cellular Data, Dynabook, and Rose Communications.

KPCB missed out on the birth of cellular communications but is leading the charge onto the Internet. Its investment in Web wunderkind Netscape paid off with a fabulously successful IPO in 1995, and the streak continued in 1996 when it took Excite! (an Internet search service) public. These successes demonstrated the smarts behind KPCB's strategy while showing the potential value of Internet stocks.

Also in 1996 KPCB launched Java Fund, a $100 million venture capital fund focused exclusively on investing in companies developing products using the new Java programming language.

WHO

Partner: Alexander E. Barkas
Partner: Brook H. Byers
Partner: Frank J. Caufield
Partner: Kevin R. Compton
Partner (CFO): Michael S. Curry
Partner: L. John Doerr
Partner: William Randolph Hearst III
Partner: Cynthia Healy
Partner: Vinod Khosla
Partner: E. Floyd Kvamme
Partner: Joseph S. Lacob
Partner: Bernard J. Lacroute
Partner: James P. Lally
Partner: Douglas J. MacKenzie
Partner: Ted Schlein
Partner: David Schnell
Partner: Russ Siegelman

WHERE

HQ: 2750 Sand Hill Rd., Menlo Park, CA 94025
Phone: 415-233-2750   **Fax:** 415-233-0300
Web site: http://www.kpcb.com

WHAT

Recent Investments

Information Sciences
@Home (Internet services via cable TV systems)
Power Computing (Macintosh-compatible computers)
Sportsline (online sports information service)

Life Sciences
Cardiac Mariners (low-dose digital X-ray systems)
Corrixa (vaccine development)
Sunshine Medical (noninvasive glucose monitoring)

KEY COMPETITORS

Accel Partners
Advent International
Applied Technology
Asset Management
Austin Ventures
Brentwood Associates
Capital Southwest
Greylock Management
Hambrecht & Quist
Hummer Winblad
Inman & Bowman
Matrix Partners
Mayfield Fund
Menlo Ventures
New Enterprise
Safeguard Scientifics
Sequoia Capital
Summit
Sutter Hill
TA Associates
Trinity Ventures
Venrock Associates
Ziff Brothers

HOW MUCH

Private company FYE: December 31	Annual Growth	1990	1991	1992	1993	1994	1995
Total capital under management ($ mil.)	41.4%	—	—	—	500.0	825.0	1,000.0
Number of partners	7.4%	—	—	—	13	14	15

KOMAG, INCORPORATEAD

OVERVIEW

Based in Milpitas, California, Komag is the #1 manufacturer of thin-film media for computer hard disks. While spinning more than 150 times faster than a 45-rpm record, Komag's disks are scanned by a magnetic head to magnetically record or retrieve information from a network file server, workstation, or other computer system. Disk drive manufacturers Seagate Technology, Quantum, and Hewlett-Packard account for about 80% of Komag's sales.

Tu Chen and Scott Chen (no relation) founded Komag in 1983. Four years later the company formed a joint venture with Vacuum Metallurgical and Asahi Glass to build and sell thin-film media products in Japan as well as supply them to Komag for resale. Komag went public that year and in 1991 acquired Dastek, a maker of inductive thin-film heads (which scan disks). In 1989 Komag exited the thin-film head business to focus on disks.

Komag has benefited from a series of joint ventures and alliances. In fact, the company has cooperated openly with competitors, especially in the realm of research and development, a strategy long practiced in Japan that helps companies save money by sharing the costs of R&D. In 1994 Komag's joint venture with Asahi (Asahi Komag) formed Headway Technologies with Hewlett-Packard to develop magnetoresistive heads. The next year the company signed an agreement with Read-Rite to develop better disk-to-head interfaces.

The increase in computer sales and the need to upgrade existing data storage systems are driving up demand for Komag's disk media. The company has responded with plans to increase its manufacturing capacity by 250% by the end of 1997 with new plants in California and Malaysia.

WHO

Chairman: Tu Chen, age 60, $1,436,619 pay
President and CEO: Stephen C. Johnson, age 53, $1,436,619 pay
SVP Marketing and Sales: T. Hunt Payne, age 53, $692,882 pay
SVP and COO: Willard Kauffman, age 60, $673,699 pay
SVP, CFO, and Secretary: William L. Potts Jr., age 49, $496,968 pay
VP Human Resources: Kathryn A. McGann, age 50
Auditors: Ernst & Young LLP

WHERE

HQ: 275 S. Hillview Dr., Milpitas, CA 95035
Phone: 408-946-2300   **Fax:** 408-946-1126
Web site: http://www.komag.com

	1995 Sales		1995 Operating Income	
	$ mil.	% of total	$ mil.	% of total
US	344.2	67	55.7	45
Far East	168.0	33	67.6	55
Adjustments	—	—	5.8	—
Total	**512.2**	**100**	**129.1**	**100**

WHAT

Selected Products
95-mm disks for 3.5-inch hard drives
130-mm disks for 5.25-inch hard drives

Selected Affiliates and Subsidiaries
Asahi Komag Co., Ltd. (50%, Japan)
Headway Technologies, Inc. (less than 20%)
Komag Material Technology, Inc. (80%, disk substrates)
Komag Technology Partners (holds Asahi Komag)

KEY COMPETITORS

Fuji Photo
Hewlett-Packard
Hitachi
HMT Technology
Hoya
IBM
Mitsubishi
Read-Rite
Seagate
Showa Denko
StorMedia
Western Digital

HOW MUCH

Nasdaq symbol: KMAG FYE: December 31	Annual Growth	1990	1991	1992	1993	1994	1995
Sales ($ mil.)	27.9%	149.9	279.2	326.8	385.4	392.4	512.2
Net income ($ mil.)	51.5%	13.4	15.4	16.9	(9.9)	58.5	106.8
Income as % of sales	—	8.9%	5.5%	5.2%	—	14.9%	20.9%
Earnings per share ($)	37.2%	0.44	0.38	0.40	(0.23)	1.27	2.14
Stock price – high ($)	—	8.06	12.25	11.63	12.00	14.44	37.44
Stock price – low ($)	—	4.25	5.38	5.38	6.88	7.88	11.13
Stock price – close ($)	31.2%	5.94	7.50	8.75	8.88	13.06	23.06
P/E – high	—	18	32	29	—	11	17
P/E – low	—	10	14	13	—	6	5
Dividends per share ($)	—	0.00	0.00	0.00	0.00	0.00	0.00
Book value per share ($)	23.6%	3.93	4.93	5.90	5.87	7.23	11.33
Employees	13.6%	1,542	2,637	3,090	3,497	2,635	2,915

1995 YEAR-END
Debt ratio: 0.0%
Return on equity: 23.6%
Cash (mil.): $214
Current ratio: 4.56
Long-term debt (mil.): $0
No. of shares (mil.): 51
Dividends
  Yield: —
  Payout: —
Market value (mil.): $1,170
R&D as % of sales: 4.6%

LAM RESEARCH CORPORATION

OVERVIEW

Lam Research is one impressive manufacturer of semiconductor processing equipment. The Fremont, California-based company makes 2 types of systems vital to the chip making process: deposition products, which apply thin layers of film to silicon wafers, and etch products, which cut tiny circuitry patterns into that film. It is neck and neck with Applied Materials for the top spot in the etcher market, each with about 1/3 of the total. Lam Research sells its equipment to chip makers around the world, including IBM, Samsung, and Intel. The latter alone accounted for 11% of 1995 sales.

Chinese immigrant David Lam started the business in 1980 to use plasma chemistry to improve the process for making semiconductors. The company introduced its first product, the AutoEtch, in 1982 and went public in 1984. Lam left the firm in 1985. Two years later it introduced its top-selling Rainbow line of dry-etch equipment. In 1992 the company introduced Transformer Coupled Plasma, a technology that offered fine detail at a low cost. It signed a development agreement in 1994 with the U.S. Display Consortium to develop equipment for making more advanced circuits for flat-panel displays.

Lam Research achieved 0.25-micron processing capability in 1995, which enabled manufacturers to process smaller, more powerful, and less-expensive chips than with traditional 0.5-micron technology. The company reached another milestone that year when it introduced a system capable of processing 300mm wafers, which have more than 2 1/2 times the surface area of standard 8-inch wafers. Also that year VP Hsui-Sheng "Way" Tu was promoted to president, succeeding Roger Emerick, who remained chairman and CEO. Lam had sales of $1,276 million and profits of $141 million in fiscal 1996.

WHO

Chairman and CEO: Roger D. Emerick, age 56, $965,070 pay
President: Hsui-Sheng Way Tu, age 38
EVP: Robert C. Fink, age 60
SVP Finance and CFO (HR): Henk J. Evenhuis, age 52, $362,346 pay
SVP: Raymond L. Degner, age 51, $355,232 pay
VP, Metal Etch Business Unit: Thomas O. Yep, age 56, $333,517 pay
VP and Chief Technical Officer: Alexander M. Voshchenkov, age 50
VP Worldwide Sales: Rick Friedman
Auditors: Ernst & Young LLP

WHERE

HQ: 4650 Cushing Pkwy., Fremont, CA 94538
Phone: 510-659-0200   **Fax:** 510-572-6454
Web site: http://www.lamrc.com

	1995 Sales	
	$ mil.	% of total
US	820.4	86
Japan	52.9	6
Europe	38.6	4
Asia/Pacific	38.2	4
Adjustments	(139.5)	—
Total	**810.6**	**100**

WHAT

Selected Products

Deposition products (chemical vapor deposition using various gases to deposit thin film layers on a silicon wafer)

Etch products (plasma etching using ionized gases to define the lines and patterns of an integrated circuit)

KEY COMPETITORS

Allied Technology Materials
Advanced Semiconductor Materials
Applied Materials
ASM Lithography
Canon
Esterline
Genus
Hitachi
Novellus Systems
Silicon Valley Group
Tegal
Teradyne
Tokyo Electron
Varian Associates

HOW MUCH

Nasdaq symbol: LRCX FYE: June 30	Annual Growth	1990	1991	1992	1993	1994	1995
Sales ($ mil.)	41.9%	140.9	144.0	171.4	265.0	493.7	810.6
Net income ($ mil.)	—	(8.8)	6.1	9.9	18.9	37.8	89.2
Income as % of sales	—	—	4.2%	5.8%	7.1%	7.7%	11.0%
Earnings per share ($)	—	(0.51)	0.33	0.49	0.79	1.55	3.06
Stock price – high ($)	—	6.00	9.17	14.34	36.75	46.75	73.38
Stock price – low ($)	—	2.00	2.58	6.92	12.92	22.75	35.25
Stock price – close ($)	69.7%	3.25	8.34	13.92	32.50	37.25	45.75
P/E – high	—	—	28	29	47	30	24
P/E – low	—	—	8	14	16	15	12
Dividends per share ($)	—	0.00	0.00	0.00	0.00	0.00	0.00
Book value per share ($)	35.6%	3.16	3.50	4.78	5.63	7.51	14.49
Employees	35.0%	804	925	1,083	1,640	2,226	3,600

1995 YEAR-END
Debt ratio: 20.8%
Return on equity: 31.2%
Cash (mil.): $101
Current ratio: 2.79
Long-term debt (mil.): $96
No. of shares (mil.): 27
Dividends
  Yield: —
  Payout: —
Market value (mil.): $1,248
R&D as % of sales: 15.8%

LINEAR TECHNOLOGY CORPORATION

OVERVIEW

Linear Technology Corporation (LTC) makes products that let digital and analog electronic signals converse. The Milpitas, California-based company manufactures linear (analog) integrated circuits (ICs) for use in automotive, industrial, multimedia, satellite, and telecommunications applications. Linear ICs make up about 15% of the total IC market. LTC sells more than 4,700 different products, primarily to original equipment manufacturers (OEMs).

In 1981 CEO Robert Swanson persuaded 5 of his fellow employees at National Semiconductor to join him in a new venture. Starting as an alternative to National, LTC had to defend itself against a series of National suits over trade secrets and patent infringement. The company benefited from a linear IC shortage in the mid-1980s and used profits to develop proprietary products for laptop computers and data processing equipment.

LTC directs its R&D efforts (equivalent to 9% of 1995 revenues) to products that use little power but operate at high speed. Rather than depend on high-volume sales of a single product, LTC makes a broad range of products that it markets to many different OEMs and targets high-growth markets such as laptop and desktop computers and cellular phones.

The company is expecting improved efficiency as the result of its new fabrication lines and facilities. It opened a new factory in Singapore in 1994. In 1995 a plastic-assembly facility was added in Malaysia, ground was broken for a new wafer fabrication plant in Washington State (due to open in 1996), and capacity was expanded at the company's Milpitas factory. Also in 1995 LTC added 100 new OEM accounts.

Linear posted profits of $134 million on sales of $378 million in fiscal 1996.

WHO

President and CEO: Robert H. Swanson Jr., age 56, $907,389 pay
VP and COO: Clive B. Davies, age 52, $752,604 pay
VP Engineering: Robert C. Dobkin, age 51, $710,622 pay
VP Finance and CFO: Paul Coghlan, age 50, $699,431 pay
VP International Sales: Hans J. Zapf, age 55, $453,659 pay
VP Quality and Reliability: Paul Chantalat, age 45
VP Marketing: Thomas D. Recine, age 57
Manager Human Resources: Steve Marcey
Auditors: Ernst & Young LLP

WHERE

HQ: 1630 McCarthy Blvd., Milpitas, CA 95035-7487
Phone: 408-432-1900 **Fax:** 408-434-0507
Web site: http://www.linear-tech.com/

	1995 Sales	
	$ mil.	% of total
North America	135.5	51
Europe	58.2	22
Japan	26.4	10
Other regions	44.9	17
Total	**265.0**	**100**

WHAT

Selected Products

Amplifiers	Interface circuits
Buffers	Switched capacitor filters
Comparators	Voltage references
Data converters	Voltage regulators

KEY COMPETITORS

AMD	Maxim Integrated Products
Analog Devices	Motorola
Brooktree	National Semiconductor
Burr-Brown	NEC
Coherent Communications	Sierra Semiconductor
Exar	Siliconix
General Electric	Texas Instruments
IBM	Unitrode
Integrated Circuit Systems	

HOW MUCH

Nasdaq symbol: LLTC FYE: June 30	Annual Growth	1990	1991	1992	1993	1994	1995
Sales ($ mil.)	28.5%	75.6	94.2	119.4	150.9	200.5	265.0
Net income ($ mil.)	49.6%	11.3	16.9	25.0	36.4	56.8	84.7
Income as % of sales	—	14.9%	18.0%	20.9%	24.2%	28.3%	32.0%
Earnings per share ($)	45.5%	0.17	0.24	0.35	0.49	0.75	1.11
Stock price – high ($)	—	3.59	8.19	12.75	19.75	25.75	45.63
Stock price – low ($)	—	2.06	3.09	7.88	10.38	18.25	23.00
Stock price – close ($)	65.5%	3.16	8.19	12.75	19.38	24.75	39.25
P/E – high	—	21	34	36	40	34	41
P/E – low	—	12	13	23	21	24	21
Dividends per share ($)	—	0.00	0.00	0.00	0.08	0.12	0.14
Book value per share ($)	31.9%	1.05	1.33	1.76	2.28	3.08	4.19
Employees	16.2%	637	729	802	870	1,004	1,350

1995 YEAR-END
Debt ratio: 0.0%
Return on equity: 31.8%
Cash (mil.): $250
Current ratio: 5.67
Long-term debt (mil.): $0
No. of shares (mil.): 74
Dividends
  Yield: 0.4%
  Payout: 12.6%
Market value (mil.): $2,888
R&D as % of sales: 9.0%

LIUSKI INTERNATIONAL, INC.

OVERVIEW

Some companies go the extra mile to compete effectively — Liuski went about 1,000. The company distributes microcomputers and peripherals primarily to smaller value-added resellers (VARs), consultants, and business clients and offers its own brand of personal computers and notebooks, Magitronic. The firm relocated its corporate headquarters from Long Island to Norcross, Georgia, (outside Atlanta) and reduced the number of distribution centers from 10 to 4, pushing the company into the loss column and decreasing employment by more than 100.

The company was founded in 1984 by Hsing-Yen Liu (who took the more Americanized first name of Morries after moving to the US from Taiwan). Liu had taken some technical training in the US, but he was stymied in a computer career by his lack of an engineering degree. He turned to sales instead, and after a short period of selling small items imported from Taiwan, he began selling imported computer parts and accessories. In naming the company, of which he owns 42%, Liu modified his own name to Liuski to Americanize it.

Liuski has grown explosively since its founding, thanks to Liu's strategy of targeting smaller VARs and emphasizing lower prices. In its early days the company chose to offer less service to achieve lower prices, but after going public in 1991, it began to upgrade its service side as well.

Magitronic experienced delays and parts shortages as a result of the relocation. The company is now focusing on winning back disgruntled customers by getting its new assembly line workers trained and back on schedule. It is also introducing new lines of Magitronic computers, such as its high-end Mercury powerbooks.

WHO

Chairman and CEO: Morries Liu, age 47, $172,459 pay
President and COO: Manuel C. Tan, age 40, $175,950 pay
EVP Sales and Marketing: Shirley Lee, age 34
SVP Sales and Marketing: Mike Hong, $129,375 pay
SVP Finance and CFO (Human Resources): Mark Rafuse, age 32
Auditors: BDO Seidman

WHERE

HQ: 6585 Crescent Dr., Norcross, GA 30071
Phone: 770-447-9454   **Fax:** 770-447-8266
Web site:
http://www.stockprofiles.com/~hastings/lski/index.htm

	1995 Sales	
	$ mil.	% of total
Southeast	148.0	37
Midwest & Southwest	100.3	25
Northeast (including Toronto)	98.8	26
West	36.2	9
Mail order	7.4	2
Pacific	4.4	1
Total	**395.1**	**100**

WHAT

Selected Merchandis
Communications (modems and fax boards)
Hard drives
Magitronic computers and accessories
Monitors
Multimedia
Networking products
Notebooks
Printers
Software
Tape backup systems

KEY COMPETITORS

Ameriquest
Apple Computer
CDW Computer Centers
Compaq
Dell
Gateway 2000
Global
Directmail
IBM
Ingram Micro
Merisel
Micro Warehouse
MicroAge
NCR
NEC
NeoStar
Tech Data
Toshiba

HOW MUCH

Nasdaq symbol: LSKI FYE: December 31	Annual Growth	1990	1991	1992	1993	1994	1995
Sales ($ mil.)	25.0%	129.7	136.7	212.1	293.1	365.1	395.1
Net income ($ mil.)	—	1.3	1.9	3.2	3.6	1.0	(1.1)
Income as % of sales	—	1.0%	1.4%	1.5%	1.2%	0.3%	—
Earnings per share ($)	—	0.64	0.77	1.00	0.91	0.23	(0.24)
Stock price – high ($)	—	—	7.75	11.50	13.38	13.63	5.50
Stock price – low ($)	—	—	5.38	5.88	8.75	3.88	2.38
Stock price – close ($)	(13.8%)	—	6.00	8.75	11.00	4.13	3.31
P/E – high	—	—	10	12	15	59	—
P/E – low	—	—	7	6	10	17	—
Dividends per share ($)	—	—	0.00	0.00	0.00	0.00	0.00
Book value per share ($)	18.3%	—	3.07	4.07	6.01	6.26	6.01
Employees	11.2%	—	—	375	537	644	516

1995 YEAR-END
Debt ratio: 45.1%
Return on equity: —
Cash (mil.): $0
Current ratio: 2.25
Long-term debt (mil.): $22
No. of shares (mil.): 4
Dividends
 Yield: —
 Payout: —
Market value (mil.): $15

MACROMEDIA, INC.

OVERVIEW

Macromedia has filled its studio with all the digital tools a cyberartist could want: pen, paintbrush, sound, and video, software tools enable developers to create multimedia applications for CD-ROM, film, the Internet, print, and videotape. The company has focused on marketing over the Internet, direct mail advertising, and agreements with big kids like Microsoft to push sales skyward. However, Apple Computer's woes have slowed demand from Macromedia's biggest customers: graphic designers. Former Altsys executives James Von Ehr and Kevin Crowder own about 9% and 5% of the company, respectively.

The company was created in 1992 from the merger of Authorware and MacroMind/Paracomp. Michael Allen founded Authorware in 1985 to make multimedia authoring software. MacroMind, which developed multimedia software tools for PCs (set up by Marc Canter in 1984) and Paracomp, a creator of design and visualization software products (founded in 1986 by William Woodward), had merged in 1991. Macromedia purchased Farallon Computing's SoundEdit and MacRecorder technology in 1992 and went public in 1993. The following year it acquired Altsys, maker of the popular FreeHand illustration program.

In 1995 Macromedia bought Fauve Software (for its xRes image editing software and Matisse paint program) and joined Netscape to integrate the company's Director multimedia playback software into the Netscape Navigator Web browser. Macromedia also bought OSC (digital audio production software) in 1995. The company debuted Shockwave, an application that enables Macromedia software-based productions to be used on the Web, in 1996. It also acquired iband (software for designing and linking Web pages).

WHO

Chairman, President, and CEO: John C. Colligan, age 41, $354,789 pay
SVP Engineering: Norman Meyrowitz, age 36
VP Worldwide Sales: Susan Gordon Bird, age 36, $314,439 pay
VP Operations, CFO, and Secretary: Richard B. Wood, age 47, $244,833 pay
VP Corporate Marketing and Customer Support: Miles C. Walsh, age 44, $240,833 pay
VP Product Development/JAVA: James R. Von Ehr II, age 45
Director Human Resources: Denise Minaberry
Auditors: KPMG Peat Marwick LLP

WHERE

HQ: 600 Townsend St., San Francisco, CA 94103
Phone: 415-252-2000   **Fax:** 415-626-0554
Web site: http://www.macromedia.com

WHAT

Selected Software Development Products
DECK II (multitrack recording)
Extreme 3D (software for designing 3D images and animation)
Fontographer (software for designing and modifying fonts) FreeHand (graphic design, illustration, and page layout software)
Macromedia xRes 2.0 (software for designing high-resolution images)
Shockwave (compression standard technology for playing audio and graphics files created with Macromedia tools over the World Wide Web)
SoundEdit 16 (software-only recording studio)

KEY COMPETITORS

Adobe	Innovex
Asymetrix	International Computers &
Avid Technology	Telecom
Chyron	Metatec
Corel	Micrografx
Dynatech	Microsoft
Evans & Sutherland	Netscape
Horizons Technology	Silicon Graphics
IBM	Sun Microsystems

HOW MUCH

Nasdaq symbol: MACR FYE: March 31	Annual Growth	1991	1992	1993	1994	1995	1996
Sales ($ mil.)	50.1%	15.3	24.7	25.3	30.1	53.7	116.7
Net income ($ mil.)	—	(7.6)	(12.0)	(0.2)	3.1	6.5	23.0
Income as % of sales	—	—	—	—	10.4%	12.2%	19.7%
Earnings per share ($)	—	—	—	(0.02)	0.15	0.19	0.59
Stock price – high ($)	—	—	—	—	8.88	13.88	63.75
Stock price – low ($)	—	—	—	—	6.38	3.75	10.56
Stock price – close ($)	149.7%	—	—	—	8.38	12.75	52.25
P/E – high	—	—	—	—	61	73	108
P/E – low	—	—	—	—	44	20	18
Dividends per share ($)	—	—	—	—	0.00	0.00	0.00
Book value per share ($)	84.1%	—	—	—	1.08	1.28	3.66
Employees	37.7%	80	138	151	155	262	396

1996 YEAR-END
Debt ratio: 0.0%
Return on equity: 26.6%
Cash (mil.): $117
Current ratio: 6.44
Long-term debt (mil.): $0
No. of shares (mil.): 36
Dividends
 Yield: —
 Payout: —
Market value (mil.): $1,903
R&D as % of sales: 17.2%

MADGE NETWORKS N.V.

OVERVIEW

Madge Networks isn't out to find missing links; it prefers to forge better links connecting the networks of corporations and other large enterprises. One of the largest networking vendors in the world, the Netherlands-based company offers the gamut of end-to-end products, including hubs, switches, adapters, and enterprise network management software. Customers include Sony, Ford, the Swiss Bank, and the US Navy, with more than 60% of sales coming outside the Americas. Although the company is intent on building a technically sophisticated direct-sales force, it relies heavily on distributors such as Tech Data and Ingram Micro, each of which accounts for about 10% of sales. Founder Robert Madge owns about 44% of the company.

A self-taught programmer who once oversaw the design of a chess-playing robot, Madge founded the business in 1986 as Madge Networks Ltd. in a converted barn on his family's farm in England. Enhancing IBM's token-ring systems, the enterprise introduced its first product in 1987 and licensed its token-ring software in 1988 to Microsoft. Madge went public in 1993, the same year it moved its main office to the Netherlands.

In 1994 the company signed a deal with Whitetree Network Technologies to develop asynchronous transfer mode products, capable of handling multimedia and video conferencing, for desktop PCs.

The firm bought Lannet Data Communications, a Tel Aviv-based maker of Ethernet switching systems in a 1995 stock swap valued at about $346 million. The next year it signed a technology licensing agreement with Cisco Systems. Also in 1996, in a deal valued at $165 million, the company bought Teleos Communications, a pioneer in WAN access switches.

WHO

Chairman and CEO: Robert H. Madge, age 44, $468,000 pay
COO and Group President: Marc E. Jones, age 38, $374,848 pay
SVP Corporate Development: Cynthia J. Ringo, age 43, $225,814 pay
SVP Products Division: Benny Hanigal, age 46, $212,296 pay
CFO: Kevin R. Evins, age 38
President, Japan: Toshihiro Yoshida, age 45, $348,472 pay
President, Americas: Richard K. Ellinger, age 48
President, Europe: Brian J. McBride, age 40
President, Asia: Raymond Lee, age 39
VP Manufacturing and Logistics: Michael D. Wilson
VP Human Resources: Ivy Ang
Auditors: Ernst & Young LLP

WHERE

HQ: Transpolis Schiphol Airport, Polaris Ave. 23, NL-2132 JH Hoofddorp, The Netherlands
Phone: +31-2356-855-2 **Fax:** +31-2356-855-27
US HQ: 2310 N. First St., San Jose, CA 95131-1011
US Phone: 408-955-0700 **US Fax:** 408-955-0970
Web site: http://www.madge.com

WHAT

	1995 Sales	
	$ mil.	% of total
Desktop products	232.2	58
Shared-media infrastructure products	102.5	25
Switched-media infrastructure products	62.9	16
Other	4.4	1
Total	**402.0**	**100**

KEY COMPETITORS

3Com	Cisco Systems	IBM
Auspex Systems	CrossComm	Newbridge
Bay Networks	DEC	Networks
Cabletron	Fibronics	Olicom USA
Cascade	International	Proteon
Communications	FORE Systems	

HOW MUCH

Nasdaq symbol: MADGF FYE: December 31	Annual Growth	1990	1991	1992	1993	1994	1995
Sales ($ mil.)	82.8%	19.7	33.4	78.8	145.4	213.3	402.0
Net income ($ mil.)	(12.9%)	1.2	2.5	7.5	16.5	23.7	0.6
Income as % of sales	—	6.0%	7.4%	9.5%	11.4%	11.1%	0.2%
Earnings per share ($)	(27.5%)	0.05	0.09	0.27	0.56	0.74	0.01
Stock price – high ($)	—	—	—	—	15.00	19.63	48.63
Stock price – low ($)	—	—	—	—	18.00	9.88	11.50
Stock price – close ($)	72.7%	—	—	—	15.00	11.69	44.75
P/E – high	—	—	—	—	27	27	—
P/E – low	—	—	—	—	32	13	—
Dividends per share ($)	—	—	—	—	0.00	0.00	0.00
Book value per share ($)	46.8%	—	—	—	2.00	2.71	4.31
Employees	20.5%	579	700	—	—	—	1,473

1995 YEAR-END
Debt ratio: 1.6%
Return on equity: 0.4%
Cash (mil.): $112
Current ratio: 1.98
Long-term debt (mil.): $2
No. of shares (mil.): 40
Dividends
  Yield: —
  Payout: —
Market value (mil.): $1,773
R&D as % of sales: 11.0%

MAXIS, INC.

OVERVIEW

Simulating and stimulating, Maxis's software games are for architects and kids of all ages. The Walnut Creek, California-based company's simulation games include SimCity, a city-building game. Other products include adventure games Coral Reef, Daring to Fly, and Gift Maker; and children's games Marty and the Trouble With Cheese and Zaark and the Night Team.

The company was founded by self-described toy nut and computer whiz Jeff Braun of Los Angeles. As head of Interactive Softworks, Braun had helped develop a font manager for the Commodore Amiga PC. Realizing the potential of the consumer PC market, Braun and software programmer Will Wright decided to tap into it, and they launched Maxis in 1987. They developed an urban simulation game and persuaded established software maker Brøderbund to distribute the product.

SimCity debuted in 1989 and pulled in $3 million in sales in its first year. SimCity simulated designing and building a city, and it encouraged learning through risk taking, experimentation, and play, allowing players to develop the game in whichever direction they chose. The company expanded its product line in 1990 with SimEarth and 1991 with SimAnt and SimLife. Braun hired Disney executive Sam Poole as VP of sales in 1992. In 1993 Maxis severed its distribution relationship with Brøderbund, repackaged SimCity, and scored record sales. SimFarm was also a big hit with the school market that year. Maxis went public in 1995. Braun owns 29% of the company, and Wright owns about 12%.

Maxis branched into fast-action entertainment in 1995 with the launch of Full Tilt! Pinball. The following year it signed a deal with Ringling Bros. and Barnum and Bailey to develop SimCircus.

WHO

Chairman: Jeffrey B. Braun, age 40, $300,600 pay
President and CEO: Samuel L. Poole, age 48, $234,305 pay (prior to promotion)
VP and CFO: Fred M. Gerson, age 45, $197,925 pay
VP Product Development: Joseph M. Scirica, age 50, $178,133 pay
VP Business Development: Douglas B. Litke, age 46, $160,495 pay
VP Operations: Valentine Garcia, age 50, $134,900 pay
VP Marketing: Robin D. Harper, age 44
VP Sales: M. Ileana Seander, age 39
VP Human Resources: Deborah L. Gross, age 44
VP and General Counsel: Robert R. Derber, age 39
Auditors: Ernst & Young LLP

WHERE

HQ: 2121 N. California Blvd., Ste. 600, Walnut Creek, CA 94596-3572
Phone: 510-933-5630   **Fax:** 510-927-3736
Web site: http://www.maxis.com

WHAT

Selected Software Products

Full Tilt! Pinball	RoboSport
Daring to Fly	SimAnt
Gift Maker	SimCity 2000
Klik & Play	SimEarth
Marty and the Trouble	SimFarm
With Cheese	SimHealth
SimTown	SimLife
Zaark and the Night Team	Unnatural Selection
A-Train	

KEY COMPETITORS

3DO	Electronic Arts	SEGA
Acclaim	GT Interactive	SoftKey
Entertainment	id Software	Sony
Accolade	Interplay	Spectrum
Activision	Productions	HoloByte
Brøderbund	JTS	Spelling
CUC International	Knowledge	Entertainment
Cyan	Adventure	Trilobyte
Digital Pictures	LucasArts	Walt Disney
Educational	Microsoft	WMS Industries
Insights	Nintendo	

HOW MUCH

Nasdaq symbol: MXIS FYE: March 31	Annual Growth	1991	1992	1993	1994	1995	1996
Sales ($ mil.)	39.7%	10.4	10.6	13.9	23.3	38.1	55.4
Net income ($ mil.)	36.7%	1.3	0.7	0.1	1.8	3.6	6.2
Income as % of sales	—	12.1%	7.1%	0.5%	7.5%	9.5%	11.2%
Earnings per share ($)	47.0%	—	0.12	0.01	0.20	0.40	0.56
Stock price – high ($)	—	—	—	—	—	—	50.00
Stock price – low ($)	—	—	—	—	—	—	17.75
Stock price – close ($)	—	—	—	—	—	—	38.00
P/E – high	—	—	—	—	—	—	89
P/E – low	—	—	—	—	—	—	32
Dividends per share ($)	—	—	—	—	—	—	0.00
Book value per share ($)	—	—	—	—	—	—	5.21
Employees	33.2%	50	71	95	120	152	210

1996 YEAR-END
Debt ratio: 0.0%
Return on equity: 13.0%
Cash (mil.): $43
Current ratio: 5.50
Long-term debt (mil.): $0
No. of shares (mil.): 11
Dividends
  Yield: —
  Payout: —
Market value (mil.): $418
R&D as % of sales: 15.2%

MCAFEE ASSOCIATES, INC.

OVERVIEW

Virus — the word sends chills up the spines of most people in the computer world. But not those at McAfee Associates. The Santa Clara, California-based company is an industry leader in PC network security and network management software. Its main product, VirusScan, provides protection for Windows, Macintosh, DOS, and OS/2 systems and sifts out viruses during disk activities (such as program executions, startups, and shutdowns). The company sells its products through a direct sales force and through resellers, distributors, and retailers. It also offers its software for a 30-day trial period over the Internet.

John McAfee, a former systems consultant for Lockheed, started the company in 1989 to sell his antivirus software. But normal retail channels were too difficult for a small entrepreneur to crack, so he marketed his product on computer bulletin boards as shareware, depending on the honesty of his users to pay for the product if they found it useful. Enough of them did to make the company a success. And the success was compounded as satisfied personal users (who were often in positions of authority in their businesses) recommended it for use in their companies' systems.

In 1992, the year of its IPO, the enterprise benefited by playing on fears of the Michelangelo virus. The bug, which still strikes every March 6, provides an annual surge in profits for the company.

The next year Bill Larson replaced McAfee as CEO and quickly focused on acquisitions and movement into the growing network management industry. The company bought Saber Software in 1995, making it the largest supplier of PC LAN management software. In 1996 the company made a $1 billion bid to acquire Cheyenne Software but dropped it after a bitter fight with Cheyenne.

WHO

Chairman, President, and CEO: William L. Larson, age 40, $449,684 pay
VP Worldwide Channel Sales: Dennis Cline, age 35, $192,642 pay
VP Operations: Richard D. Kreysar, age 40, $165,763 pay
VP International Operations: Peter Watkins, age 41, $143,284 pay
VP Finance, Corporate Controller, and Treasurer: Prabhat Goyal, age 41
VP Professional Services and Corporate Development and Secretary: R. Terry Duryea, age 49
Controller, Secretary, and Chief Accounting Officer (HR): Robert J. Schwei
Auditors: Coopers & Lybrand L.L.P.

WHERE

HQ: 2710 Walsh Ave., Ste. 200, Santa Clara, CA 95051
Phone: 408-988-3832   **Fax:** 408-970-9727
Web site: http://www.mcafee.com

WHAT

Selected Products
BootShield (boot repair software)
NetShield (antivirus utility for Novell NetWare and
Vycor Enterprise (problem management, resolution, and prevention)
WebScan (virus protection)
WebStor (backup protection)
Network Management Tools
BrightWorks (enterprise asset management suite)
LANInventory (hardware and software asset audits)
Saber LAN Workstation (network management software)
SaberTools (centralized management)
ServerStor (data backup system)
SiteExpress (distribution solution)
SiteMeter (enterprise software)
VirusScan (virus detection software)

KEY COMPETITORS

Cheyenne	Microsoft	Seagate
Software	Novell	Symantec
Datawatch	Oracle	
Intel	Progress Software	

HOW MUCH

Nasdaq symbol: MCAF FYE: December 31	Annual Growth	1990	1991	1992	1993	1994	1995
Sales ($ mil.)	123.9%	1.6	6.9	13.7	17.9	32.9	90.1
Net income ($ mil.)	90.1%	0.6	3.2	6.4	7.3	1.4	14.9
Income as % of sales	—	38.5%	45.6%	46.5%	40.8%	4.2%	16.6%
Earnings per share ($)	62.5%	0.06	0.29	0.57	0.61	0.11	0.68
Stock price – high ($)	—	—	—	23.25	20.25	20.25	35.25
Stock price – low ($)	—	—	—	13.00	4.25	6.50	6.67
Stock price – close ($)	19.8%	—	—	17.00	7.50	20.25	29.25
P/E – high	—	—	—	41	33	184	52
P/E – low	—	—	—	23	7	59	10
Dividends per share ($)	—	—	—	0.00	0.00	0.00	0.00
Book value per share ($)	49.4%	—	—	0.93	1.64	1.97	3.10
Employees	118.7%	5	15	34	47	128	250

1995 YEAR-END
Debt ratio: 0.0%
Return on equity: 29.7%
Cash (mil.): $55
Current ratio: 2.53
Long-term debt (mil.): $0
No. of shares (mil.): 21
Dividends
  Yield: —
  Payout: —
Market value (mil.): $600
R&D as % of sales: 10.4%

MECKLERMEDIA CORPORATION

OVERVIEW

Mecklermedia has given itself a subtitle: The Internet Media Company. Circulation for the Westport, Connecticut-based publisher's flagship magazine, *Internet World,* hit 250,000 in late 1995, and the company has added 2 new publications, *Web Developer* and *Web Week.* Mecklermedia's site on the World Wide Web, iWorld, is a top source of online Internet information, receiving more than a million hits a week. The firm also conducts trade shows in nearly a dozen countries for Internet and World Wide Web users and developers. Founder and CEO Alan Meckler owns about 31% of the company; VP James Mulholland III and his family own about 15%.

Meckler started the Meckler Corporation in 1971 to publish library science journals and reference books. As information technology evolved in the 1980s, the company moved into new areas, such as CD-ROMs. In the early 1990s the firm sold many of its scholarly library titles and began focusing on the Internet, CD-ROM technology, and virtual reality. It launched *Internet World* in 1993. That year the Mulhollands purchased about 1/3 of Meckler Corporation. The company became Mecklermedia in December 1993 and went public in 1994. It launched MecklerWeb (now iWorld) in 1994 with plans to charge as much as $50,000 to help companies develop online advertising. When advertisers failed to materialize, Alan Meckler limited the service to putting Mecklermedia magazines online and selling advertising.

In 1995 Mecklermedia sold off several more directories, publications, and trade shows as it continued to focus on the Internet. That year it launched an Internet book publishing project. In 1996 the company formed Mecklermedia Internet Consulting.

WHO

Chairman, President, and CEO: Alan M. Meckler, age 50, $191,000 pay
SVP Internet Business Development: Bill H. Washburn, age 49, $100,100 pay
EVP and CFO: Christopher S. Cardell, age 36
President and COO, Trade Show Group: Carl S. Pugh
Executive Director of Development, iWorld: Tristan Louis
Director Technology: Lance Rosen
Auditors: Andersen Worldwide

WHERE

HQ: 20 Ketchum St., Westport, CT 06880
Phone: 203-226-6967 **Fax:** 203-454-5840
Web site: http://www.iworld.com

WHAT

	1995 Sales	
	$ mil.	% of total
Magazines & journals	8.1	56
Trade shows	5.3	37
Books & directories	0.6	4
Mailing list rentals	0.5	3
Total	**14.5**	**100**

Selected Products and Events

Books
Official Internet World books (with International Data Group and McGraw-Hill Books International)

Online
Internet World Forum (on CompuServe)

iWorld (WWW site)

Publications
Internet World magazine
Web Developer magazine
Web Week trade magazine

Trade Shows
Internet World
Web Developer

KEY COMPETITORS

CMP Publications
Cowles Media
Flipside Publishing
HyperMedia
International Data Group
Red Flash Internet
Reed Elsevier
Sendai Media Group
SOFTBANK
United News & Media
Upside Publishing
VNU
Wired Ventures
Wolff New Media

HOW MUCH

Nasdaq symbol (SC): MECK FYE: September 30	Annual Growth	1990	1991	1992	1993[1]	1994	1995
Sales ($ mil.)	43.6%	—	—	4.9	4.4	8.3	14.5
Net income ($ mil.)	48.1%	—	—	(0.4)	(0.1)	(2.0)	(1.3)
Income as % of sales	—	—	—	—	—	—	—
Earnings per share ($)	6.7%	—	—	(0.14)	(0.03)	(0.32)	(0.17)
Stock price – high ($)	—	—	—	—	—	6.50	24.38
Stock price – low ($)	—	—	—	—	—	2.13	2.63
Stock price – close ($)	—	—	—	—	—	3.44	16.00
P/E – high	—	—	—	—	—	—	—
P/E – low	—	—	—	—	—	—	—
Dividends per share ($)	—	—	—	—	—	0.00	0.00
Book value per share ($)	—	—	—	—	—	0.43	2.14
Employees	51.2%	—	—	—	35	49	80

[1] 9-month fiscal year

1995 YEAR-END
Debt ratio: 0.1%
Return on equity: —
Cash (mil.): $19
Current ratio: 2.94
Long-term debt (mil.): $0
No. of shares (mil.): 8
Dividends
  Yield: —
  Payout: —
Market value (mil.): $134
Advertising as % of sales: 33.9%

MEMOREX TELEX N.V.

OVERVIEW

Although Memorex Telex combines 2 well-known business names, the company is but a shadow of its former selves. A Dutch company that is headquartered in Irving, Texas, it was formerly a developer and manufacturer of computer hardware, primarily for the mainframe market. However, it is becoming a provider of networking and storage solutions and information technology services. It now buys virtually all of its products from other manufacturers for resale to *FORTUNE* 1000 corporations, government agencies, and major medical facilities, among other customers.

Founded in 1961 by Laurence Spitters, an executive with audiotape maker Ampex, Memorex made computer tape and audiotape (known for the slogan "Is it live? Or is it Memorex?"). In the late 1960s it began making disk drives for IBM mainframes and other large computer systems. By the mid-1970s, with tape drive competition heating up, Memorex began to lose ground, and in 1981 it sold its audiotape business to Tandy. That year the company was acquired by Burroughs (now Unisys). Several European managers of Memorex acquired the company in a 1986 LBO. It adopted its present name after buying computer terminal maker Telex in 1988.

By 1992 Memorex Telex was struggling with a US recession and stiff competition and filed for bankruptcy. A slow US recovery and a European recession caused continued losses, however, and it filed for bankruptcy again in 1994. The company made a profit that year but posted losses again in 1995 and 1996 as it struggled to transform itself. Layoffs continued, and the closing of its Raleigh, North Carolina, facility in 1996 completed its 3-year plan to get out of manufacturing and concentrate on sales. It sold its Asia/Pacific operations to Kanematsu in mid-1996.

WHO

Chairman and CEO: Peter H. Dailey, age 66
VC and CFO: David J. Faulkner, age 57, $626,125 pay
SVP Enterprise Storage: Ron Bulin
SVP North American Sales: George Bennett
SVP Operations: Brad Sowers
SVP and Corporate Treasurer: Greg Wood
SVP and Legal Counsel: Anthony Barbieri
VP Finance for North American Operations: Bill Keys
VP Human Resources: Peg O'Neal
Auditors: Ernst & Young LLP

WHERE

HQ: 545 E. John Carpenter Fwy., Irving, TX 75062-3931
Phone: 214-444-3500   **Fax:** 214-444-3501
Web site: http://www.mtc.com

WHAT

	1996 Sales	
	$ mil.	% of total
Networks	397	48
Services	346	41
Storage	66	8
Other	25	3
Total	**834**	**100**

Selected Products

Networks
Connectivity products
Desktop products
Servers

Services
Education services

Integration services

Storage
Automated tape libraries
Multiplatform disk and tape cartridge subsystems

KEY COMPETITORS

Ameriquest
BDM
  International
Cap Gemini
CompuCom
Computer
  Sciences
Control Data
DEC

EDS
EMC Corp.
Hewlett-Packard
Hitachi
IBM
ICL
MCI
  Systemhouse
Odetics

Perot Systems
Quantum Corp.
Systems &
  Computer
  Technology
Unisys
Vanstar
Wang

HOW MUCH

Nasdaq symbol: MEMXY FYE: March 31	Annual Growth	1991	1992	1993	1994	1995	1996
Sales ($ mil.)	(14.9%)	1,870.0	1,499.0	1,326.0	1,016.0	909.8	834.1
Net income ($ mil.)	—	(271.0)	104.0	(396.0)	227.0	(108.0)	(246.7)
Income as % of sales	—	—	7.0%	—	22.4%	—	—
Earnings per share ($)	—	—	—	—	—	(4.32)	(9.84)
Stock price – high ($)[1]	—	—	—	—	—	8.25	2.53
Stock price – low ($)[1]	—	—	—	—	—	0.44	0.44
Stock price – close ($)[1]	—	—	—	—	—	0.75	0.75
P/E – high	—	—	—	—	—	—	—
P/E – low	—	—	—	—	—	—	—
Dividends per share ($)	—	—	—	—	—	0.00	0.00
Book value per share ($)	—	—	—	—	—	(1.23)	(11.06)
Employees	(11.2%)	—	—	—	5,200	4,500	4,100

[1] Stock prices are for the prior calendar year.

1996 YEAR-END
Debt ratio: 100.0%
Return on equity: —
Cash (mil.): $27
Current ratio: 0.51
Long-term debt (mil.): $5
No. of shares (mil.): 25
Dividends
  Yield: —
  Payout: —
Market value (mil.): $19
R&D as % of sales: 1.5%

MENTOR GRAPHICS CORPORATION

OVERVIEW

Mentor Graphics has acquired electronic design automation (EDA) abilities that go beyond designing hardware. The Wilsonville, Oregon-based company's EDA software is used to design integrated circuits (ICs) and the systems that include them. However, Mentor believes that as systems shrink, the demand for Integrated System Design (a comprehensive design approach that includes hardware design, embedded software design, and testing) will quickly rise. So the company has been shopping for software design technology.

Mentor was founded in 1981 by a group from Tektronix to market desktop computers to design engineers. Throughout the 1980s it was a leader in EDA software, but by the early 1990s it was in trouble. Sales fell because of delays in upgrade releases and a worldwide recession. In 1992 Mentor began phasing out hardware sales, further disrupting operations. Wally Rhines, a 21-year veteran of Texas Instruments, became CEO in 1993, and the firm acquired CheckLogic (IC design testing software) that year.

Mentor has built a catalog of over 150 software tools for design engineers, including MCM (multichip module) and board design and system simulation, and IC design and simulation. The company provides education and consulting services as well as full design services.

Mentor bought ANACAD (analog and mixed signal design tools) in 1994. The company's merger that year with Model Technology, a simulation tool firm, helped reestablish Mentor as a leading EDA software supplier. Mentor acquired 5 companies in 1995, including Exemplar Logic (which provided it with field-programmable gate array design tools).

In 1996 Mentor moved into software design with the purchase of embedded software tool developer Microtec Research.

WHO

Chairman: Jon A. Shirley, age 57
President and CEO: Walden C. Rhines, age 49, $983,050 pay
SVP and CFO: R. Douglas Norby, age 60, $523,015 pay
VP Human Resources and the Workplace: Frank S. Delia, age 49, $280,796 pay
VP General Counsel, and Secretary: Dean Freed, age 37
Corporate Controller and Chief Accounting Officer: Richard Trebing, age 36
Treasurer: Dennis Weldon, age 47
Auditors: KPMG Peat Marwick LLP

WHERE

HQ: 8005 SW Boeckman Rd., Wilsonville, OR 97070-7777
Phone: 503-685-7000   **Fax:** 503-685-1202
Web site: http://www.mentorg.com

WHAT

	1995 Sales	
	$ mil.	% of total
System & software	195.3	51
Service & support	189.2	49
Total	**384.5**	**100**

Selected Products

ASIC/FPGA (software to design application-specific integrated circuits and field-programmable gate arrays)	AutoLogic II
	IC Station
	MicroRoute
	MCM/PCB (software that enables designers to determine the functionality of a multichip module or printed circuit board)
FPGA Station	
Idea Station	
Top-Down Design Solver	
IC design flow (enables customers to create IC designs)	Board Station
	Manufacturing Advisor
	Physical Test Manager

KEY COMPETITORS

Avant! Corp	Intergraph	Viewlogic
Cadence	Orbit	Zuken
Computervision	Semiconductor	
EPIC Design	Synopsys	

HOW MUCH

Nasdaq symbol: MENT FYE: December 31	Annual Growth	1990	1991	1992	1993	1994	1995
Sales ($ mil.)	(2.4%)	435.2	400.1	350.8	339.8	348.3	384.5
Net income ($ mil.)	16.2%	23.6	(61.6)	(50.9)	(32.1)	27.5	49.9
Income as % of sales	—	5.4%	—	—	—	7.9%	13.0%
Earnings per share ($)	10.7%	0.53	(1.43)	(1.13)	(0.69)	0.53	0.88
Stock price – high ($)	—	26.00	19.00	22.25	15.50	17.25	22.88
Stock price – low ($)	—	9.00	11.50	5.25	7.88	9.38	12.38
Stock price – close ($)	7.6%	12.63	14.75	8.13	13.75	15.25	18.25
P/E – high	—	49	—	—	—	33	26
P/E – low	—	17	—	—	—	18	14
Dividends per share ($)	(3.9%)	0.22	0.24	0.24	0.18	0.18	0.18
Book value per share ($)	(6.5%)	7.70	6.14	4.86	4.11	4.66	5.50
Employees	(5.5%)	2,700	2,400	2,200	2,100	2,000	2,039

1995 YEAR-END
Debt ratio: 16.8%
Return on equity: 18.3%
Cash (mil.): $201
Current ratio: 2.96
Long-term debt (mil.): $53
No. of shares (mil.): 56
Dividends
  Yield: 1.0%
  Payout: 20.5%
Market value (mil.): $1,014
R&D as % of sales: 18.9%

MICRO ELECTRONICS INC.

OVERVIEW

"We're not greedy," says Micro Electronics founder and president John Baker. "We don't need it all" — just a 50% share of computer, software, and peripheral sales to upper-middle-class professionals with kids. But the Hilliard, Ohio-based company (which operates 11 Micro Center stores) has already declared itself the leader in catering to this group through its "technical retailing" concept, which involves intensive training (4-8 weeks) before sales people get out on the floor. Micro Center is by far the largest of Micro Electronics' 7 divisions, which also include manufacturing (WinBook notebook and PowerSpec desktop computers), mail order, and training operations.

Baker became interested in computers in 1976, when he read an article about microcomputing. Determined to learn more, he took a job with Radio Shack. By 1980 Baker was a store manager, but he left after a disagreement with the company about marketing. That year he and another Radio Shack refugee, Bill Bayne, pooled their resources and opened the first Micro Center. The store was a success and within a few years had grown from 1,200 square feet to 44,000. The resulting company, Micro Electronics, soon added mail order and manufacturing operations.

By 1988 there were only 2 Micro Center stores, both in Ohio. Initially, Baker expanded slowly, insisting that the business finance its growth internally, without significant debt. "What grows fast, dies fast," he has said. "We won't die fast." Nevertheless, the company's retail operations have grown quickly in the 1990s.

Baker has been repeatedly approached to sell the company or take it public, but he has refused because of his belief in his long-term business plan (which extends until the turn of the century) and his expectation that a change in control would derail that strategy.

Micro Electronics opened a storefront training center in Chicago in 1995 and expects to add several others around the US.

Micro Center plans to double its store count to 22 by the end of 1997, with stores slated to open in Chicago, Southern California, the San Francisco Bay area, and metropolitan New York.

WHO

CEO: Dale Brown
President: John F. Baker
CFO: James Koehler
VP Marketing; President, WinBook Computer Corp.: Richard Mershad
Director Retail Sales, Micro Center: Henry Gleissner
Manager Human Resources: Deanna Lyon

WHERE

HQ: 4119 Leap Rd., Hilliard, OH 43026
Phone: 614-850-3000   **Fax:** 614-850-3001
Web site: http://www.micro-strip.com

Micro Electronics operates Micro Center stores in Tustin, CA; Marietta, GA; Cambridge, MA; Columbus, Mayfield Heights, Sharonville, and Westerville, OH; St. David, PA; Dallas and Houston; and Fairfax, VA. The company operates a training center in Chicago and has a purchasing and engineering office in Taiwan.

WHAT

	1995 Sales
	% of total
Retail sales	83
Nonretail sales	15
Service & support	2
Total	**100**

Selected Operations	Selected Products
Corporate sales	Computers
MEI/Micro Center (mail-order sales)	Peripherals
	Software
Micro Center (retail stores)	**Brand Names**
Training	PowerSpec
WinBook Computer Corp. (desktop and laptop computer manufacturing)	WinBook

KEY COMPETITORS

Best Buy	MicroAge
CDW Computer Centers	Montgomery Ward
Circuit City	NeoStar
CompuCom	OfficeMax
Dell	Price/Costco
Egghead	Sears
Gateway 2000	Service Merchandise
Global Directmail	Staples
Good Guys	Tandy Corporation
Intelligent Electronics	Vanstar
Kmart	Wal-Mart

HOW MUCH

Private company FYE: December 31	Annual Growth	1990	1991	1992	1993	1994	1995
Sales ($ mil.)	32.5%	—	—	400.0	515.0	780.0	930.0
Employees	26.0%	—	—	900	—	980	1,800

MCC

OVERVIEW

MCC's new strategy of developing short-term collaborations (as opposed to long-term projects that are then spun off) is starting to show results — just in the nick of time. Microelectronics and Computer Technology Corporation (MCC), an Austin-based consortium, has been faltering, losing members as well as a $27 million lawsuit. But a new CEO and a new focus seem to be helping the group, which is made up of more than 15 major companies banded together for research and development.

In 1982, when Control Data founder William Norris conceived of a research consortium, the US computer industry was gripped by the fear of a "mainframe gap" between the US and Japan after the announcement that Japanese researchers were working on a super-computer that could function like a human mind. Founding members, including AMD, Motorola, and DEC, put up $500,000 each to establish a center for long-term research. Under its first CEO, Bobby Ray Inman (former CIA chief and later, briefly, a secretary of defense nominee), the consortium pursued pure research.

MCC's funding peaked at about $65 million in 1987, by which time it was clear that the future was in networks rather than in giant computers; the Japanese had also begun to look less invincible. In the lean, mean world of the 1990s, "unproductive research" looked pointless. Under its next 2 leaders, Grant Dove and Craig Fields, MCC sought to get a return from research by launching spinoffs. Its first, a data conversion software company (Evolutionary Technologies, with revenues now over $10 million), was formed in 1991; 6 others followed.

But members were furious when MCC was sued by Staktek Corp. because MCC's RTB Technologies had appropriated someone else's idea for a stacked chip. MCC lost the case in 1994, about the time John McRary was named CEO. He worked out a settlement, began cutting $8 million in costs, and pledged to downplay spinoffs and concentrate on transferring productive technology to members. The first such transfer, the Quality Enabling Software Technology Project (QUEST), was introduced in 1996.

WHO

Chairman, President, and CEO: John W. McRary
SVP and CFO: George J. Roberts
VP Strategic Business Services: Albert Wargo
Chief Technical Officer: Erik Mettala
Director Human Resources: Jeanne Jackson

WHERE

HQ: Microelectronics & Computer Technology Corporation, 3500 West Balcones Center Dr., Austin, TX 78759
Phone: 512-343-0978   **Fax:** 512-338-3892
Web site: http://www.mcc.com

WHAT

Spinoffs
Corporate Memory Systems, Inc. (groupware tools, 1991)
Cycorp (knowledge-base systems, 1995)
Evolutionary Technologies, Inc. (data exchange, 1991)
Pavilion Technologies, Inc. (process control software, 1992)
Savantage, Inc. (electronic design automation software, 1994)
Tamarack Storage Devices, Inc. (holographic storage, 1992)
TradeWave (Internet software, 1995)

Current Research Areas
Ball-grid array evaluations
Computer industry recycling studies
Distributed object-oriented software
Evaluation of foreign technology development
Intuitive computer interfaces
Multichip systems
Network infrastructure
Software quality

Member Companies

3M	Lockheed Martin
AMD	Motorola
Ceridian	National Semiconductor
Eastman Chemical	NCR
Eastman Kodak	Nortel
DuPont	Raytheon
General Electric	SBC Communications
Harris Corp.	Science Applications
Hewlett-Packard	Texas Instruments
Hughes Aircraft	

HOW MUCH

Consortium FYE: December 31	Annual Growth	1990	1991	1992	1993	1994	1995[1]
Sales ($ mil.)	—	50.8	—	—	—	40.0	45.0
Employees	—	—	—	—	—	200	120

[1] Estimate

MICRONICS COMPUTERS, INC.

OVERVIEW

Micronics Computers makes personal computer system boards for original equipment manufacturers as well as for distributors and value-added resellers of PCs. The Fremont, California-based company's products consist of a microprocessor (central processing unit, or CPU), supporting circuitry, and optional cache memory (reserved for use by the CPU). The firm primarily produces boards using Intel's Pentium and Pentium Pro CPUs. It also assembles basic systems, composed of a system board, power supply, and case. Through subsidiary Orchid Technology, Micronics offers Kelvin and Fahrenheit graphics enhancement products that improve a computer's performance with multimedia and other advanced applications, such as desktop publishing and computer-aided design (CAD). A major account, Australia-based Osborne Computers, declared bankruptcy that year and failed to pay $11.9 million it owed the company. That factor, along with excessive inventory, left Micronics with a loss for the year.

Harvey Wong, Minsiu Huang, and Dean Chang started the firm in 1986 to assemble system boards for personal computers. It went public in 1991. That year Micronics helped develop the VESA (Video Electronics Standards Association) Local Bus, which increased data processing speed and permitted cards from various manufacturers to be added to a wide range of system boards. Huang left the board of directors later in 1991. He returned in 1992, the same year Wong and Chang retired from the board. The firm acquired its Orchid subsidiary in 1994 to make add-on enhancements for its system boards.

In 1995, COO Shanker Munshani was promoted to CEO when Steve Kitrosser stepped down. Kitrosser remained as chairman.

WHO

Chairman: Steven P. Kitrosser, age 52
President and CEO: Shanker Munshani, age 40, $155,013 pay
VP Worldwide Operations: David J. Nealon, age 56, $162,318 pay
VP Finance and CFO: Robert Mahoney
VP Worldwide Sales: Larry Lummis, age 60
VP Marketing; President, Orchid Technology: Greg Reznick, age 40
Director Human Resources: Ron Victor
Auditors: KPMG Peat Marwick LLP

WHERE

HQ: 232 E. Warren Ave., Fremont, CA 94539-7085
Phone: 510-651-2300   **Fax:** 510-651-5666
Web site: http://streetlink.com/mcrn/

	1995 Sales	
	$ mil.	% of total
US & Canada	169.9	73
Asia/Pacific	41.8	18
Europe	22.4	9
Total	**234.1**	**100**

WHAT

Selected Products
Basic systems (system board, power supply, and case)
Kelvin and Fahrenheit graphics products (multimedia enhancement boards)
Pentium and Pentium Pro system boards (CPUs)

KEY COMPETITORS

AMD	Creative	Intel
American	Technology	Kingston
Megatrends	Cyrix	Technology
AST	Diamond	Ma Labs
Aureal	Multimedia	Micron
Semiconductor	Fujitsu	Technology
Chips and	GST	Mylex
Technologies	Integrated Circuit	Pycon
	Systems	SCI Systems

HOW MUCH

Nasdaq symbol: MCRN FYE: September 30	Annual Growth	1990	1991	1992	1993	1994	1995
Sales ($ mil.)	23.5%	81.5	133.9	155.0	182.2	163.6	234.1
Net income ($ mil.)	—	4.3	9.4	8.2	10.1	2.3	(12.8)
Income as % of sales	—	5.3%	7.0%	5.3%	5.6%	1.4%	—
Earnings per share ($)	—	0.51	1.05	0.74	0.90	0.20	(0.95)
Stock price – high ($)	—	—	9.75	8.75	7.50	6.13	5.88
Stock price – low ($)	—	—	6.00	2.88	4.38	3.50	3.25
Stock price – close ($)	(19.3%)	—	8.25	4.50	6.13	4.38	3.50
P/E – high	—	—	9	12	8	31	—
P/E – low	—	—	6	4	5	18	—
Dividends per share ($)	—	—	0.00	0.00	0.00	0.00	0.00
Book value per share ($)	4.7%	—	3.45	4.24	5.11	5.15	4.14
Employees	11.4%	—	—	265	263	409	366

1995 YEAR-END
Debt ratio: 5.2%
Return on equity: —
Cash (mil.): $5
Current ratio: 2.33
Long-term debt (mil.): $0
No. of shares (mil.): 14
Dividends
  Yield: —
  Payout: —
Market value (mil.): $48
R&D as % of sales: 3.1%

MICROTOUCH SYSTEMS, INC.

OVERVIEW

MicroTouch gives the concept of user-friendly a whole new meaning. Headquartered in Methuen, Massachusetts, MicroTouch Systems is the world's #1 maker of touchscreen monitors, which allow users to control a computer by touching the screen with their fingers. Touchscreens are used in information kiosks, industrial and medical equipment, gaming machines, point-of-sale terminals, and other systems. MicroTouch founder Jim Logan owns nearly 10% the company.

A veteran of Arthur Andersen and Chemical Bank, Logan saw a touchscreen in use and started MicroTouch in 1982 to explore other uses for the technology. At first the company combined other manufacturers' touchscreens with off-the-shelf computers. Then it began making its own touchscreens using its own capacitive sensing technology, which uses static electricity from users' fingers to activate the screen. One of the first markets for the company's products was the gambling industry, which used MicroTouch screens to make user-friendly gaming machines.

In 1992 the company went public. That year the gambling market stalled, and MicroTouch lost a large segment of its sales. In response, the company diversified, finding uses for its products in automated-teller machines, cash registers, information kiosks, and factory automation. With sales recovering in 1994, MicroTouch expanded its technology base. That year it purchased Visage's TouchMate line of desktop and industrial touchscreens and Moonstone Designs' ThruGlass technology. The next year the firm expanded, developing Prospector, a touch-guided browser for the World Wide Web, with Spyglass.

In 1996 MicroTouch introduced a line of screens that used a pen-like pointer to control the computer.

WHO

Chairman: James D. Logan, age 43, $167,500 pay
President and CEO: D. Westervelt Davis, age 48
VP Operations: Ted M. Miller, $151,000 pay
VP Finance & Administration, CFO, and Treasurer: Geoffrey P. Clear
VP and General Manager European Operations: Robert J. Senior, $141,724 pay
VP Research & Development: Bernard O. Geaghan, $126,100 pay
Manager Human Resources: Annemarie Bell
Auditors: Andersen Worldwide

WHERE

HQ: 300 Griffin Brook Park Dr., Methuen, MA 01844-1873
Phone: 508-659-9000   **Fax:** 508-659-9100
Web site: http://www.microtouch.com

MicroTouch has manufacturing facilities in Australia, the UK, and the US and sales offices in France, Germany, Japan, Taiwan, and the US.

	1995 Sales	
	$ mil.	% of total
US	53.0	69
Other countries	23.7	31
Total	**76.7**	**100**

WHAT

Selected Products
Kiosks (housing units with built-in touchscreens)
PrivacyTouch (screens for confidential transactions)
Prospector (touch-guided Internet browser)
QuickPoint (sensors that retrofit standard monitors into touchscreens)
ThruGlass (screens for use with thick glass)
TouchMate (desktop and industrial screens)
TouchPen (finger- or stylus-driven computer interfaces)

KEY COMPETITORS

AMP	Metromedia	Telxon
Key Tronic	Raychem	Wells-Gardner
Logitech	Sulcus Computer	Electronics

HOW MUCH

Nasdaq symbol: MTSI FYE: December 31	Annual Growth	1990	1991	1992	1993	1994	1995
Sales ($ mil.)	43.5%	12.6	18.9	30.5	31.0	58.9	76.7
Net income ($ mil.)	35.7%	0.5	1.1	2.3	2.2	5.7	2.3
Income as % of sales	—	4.2%	5.7%	7.5%	7.1%	9.6%	3.0%
Earnings per share ($)	22.0%	0.10	0.21	0.38	0.31	0.75	0.27
Stock price – high ($)	—	—	—	10.13	8.88	47.50	45.25
Stock price – low ($)	—	—	—	6.38	4.38	5.88	11.50
Stock price – close ($)	20.1%	—	—	7.00	6.88	45.00	12.13
P/E – high	—	—	—	27	29	63	168
P/E – low	—	—	—	17	14	8	43
Dividends per share ($)	—	—	—	0.00	0.00	0.00	0.00
Book value per share ($)	48.8%	—	—	2.50	2.83	8.37	8.23
Employees	34.4%	—	—	197	217	377	478

1995 YEAR-END
Debt ratio: 0.0%
Return on equity: 3.5%
Cash (mil.): $37
Current ratio: 5.43
Long-term debt (mil.): $0
No. of shares (mil.): 8
Dividends
  Yield: —
  Payout: —
Market value (mil.): $94
R&D as % of sales: 6.5%

NCUBE CORPORATION

OVERVIEW

Thanks to nCUBE, you could be watching movies on your telephone. Headquartered in Foster City, California, nCUBE makes digital media servers used to deliver video-on-demand, provide access to digital libraries, and process sound, images, and video for business training, home shopping, and other uses.

Stephen Colley left Intel, where he had helped develop the 32-bit microprocessor, and founded nCUBE in 1983 to develop massively parallel systems technology. This technology, in essence a giant server, links small processing chips with individual memories to allow a computer to work on multiple tasks simultaneously without getting bogged down by inadequate memory paths, as mainframe computers tend to do. In 1987, when Colley met Oracle cofounder Larry Ellison, his primary clientele was academic and governmental. Ellison was so impressed that in 1989 he invested a reported $60 million in nCUBE, gaining control of the company (he owns 90%) and buying the leverage to put Oracle people into nCUBE management. The company has since dominated the commercial market.

Cooperation between Oracle and nCUBE has allowed Ellison to coordinate the companies' strategies with an emphasis on emerging multimedia technology, featuring not only database access but also video and audio capacities and the ability to search and manipulate textual information between databases. Ellison's position has also raised questions of whether he has used Oracle (a public company) to benefit nCUBE.

In 1994 Japan Electric Power Development bought an nCUBE MPP computer to be used for electric power simulation. The next year nCUBE focused on making equipment to run Oracle's media server software and unveiled the industry's first digital media server. Dubbed Metromedia, the video server makes possible the transmission of interactive TV content by combining audio, images, text, and video on a single server. In 1996 nCUBE supplied media servers to Telephone Video of America, which plans to offer video-on-demand services, and penned deals to develop interactive multimedia services with telecommunications companies in 4 other countries.

WHO

Chairman: Stephen Colley
CEO: Ronald A. Dilbeck
SVP Worldwide Sales: Craig Ramsey
VP Finance and Administration and CFO: Alan Beauchamp
VP Marketing: J. Scott Carr
VP Software Engineering: Peter Madams
VP Manufacturing and Service: Robin Walker
VP Human Resources: Sandra Chroman
General Manager European Operations: Peter Wusten

WHERE

HQ: 110 Marsh Dr., Foster City, CA 94404-1184
Phone: 415-593-9000   **Fax:** 415-508-5408
Web site: http://www.ncube.com
nCUBE maintains facilities in Australia, Germany, Japan, and the UK.

WHAT

Selected Products

MediaCUBE Servers
MediaCUBE 30 (entry-level server)
MediaCUBE 300 (scalable server)
Metromedia (multimedia server)
nABLE (end-to-end server)

nCUBE 2S servers
M5 (entry-level server)
M10 (scalable server)
nVision (end-to-end server)

KEY COMPETITORS

Advanced Logic Research
Amdahl
Auspex Systems
Convex Computer
Fujitsu
Hitachi
IBM
Intel
NEC
Netframe Systems
Sequent
Storage Technology
Sun Microsystems
Tricord Systems
Unisys

HOW MUCH

Private company FYE: October 31	Annual Growth	1990	1991	1992	1993	1994	1995
Sales ($ mil.)	45.2%	—	9.0	17.1	22.5	40.0	40.0
Employees	26.5%	—	—	—	100	180	160

nCUBE

NEOSTAR RETAIL GROUP, INC.

OVERVIEW

NeoStar Retail Group is burning less brightly these days. With sales fizzling, the Grapevine, Texas-based software retailer — which owns the Babbage's and Software Etc. mall store chains — has filed for bankruptcy protection. The company had soared on sales of Super Nintendo and Sega Genesis games before mass-market retailers began stealing its fire. Leonard Riggio (head of bookstore chain Barnes & Noble) and Dutch retailer Vendex (a major Barnes & Noble shareholder) own 13% and 14% of NeoStar, respectively.

NeoStar was created in 1994 from the merger of Software Etc. and Babbage's. Software Etc. began as a division of B. Dalton Bookseller in 1984. Riggio and Vendex acquired B. Dalton in 1986, and in 1987 established Software Etc. as a separate entity. Software Etc. went public in 1992. Babbage's was founded by former Harvard Business schoolmates James McCurry and Gary Kusin in 1983. The company, named for 19th century mathematician Charles Babbage (considered the father of the computer), went public in 1988.

Both companies focused on mall retailing: Babbage on game software, Software Etc. on a broader variety of PC software. Both saw growth spurred by the rising popularity of Nintendo and Sega game systems and by falling PC prices. The 2 merged in an effort to stave off growing competition from big retail chains like Best Buy and Wal-Mart.

Neostar opened 122 stores in 1995. Amid flat sales the following year, several senior executives left, including president Daniel DeMatteo, who was replaced by chairman and CEO McCurry. Following the bankruptcy filing, McCurry was replaced as chairman by company director Thomas Plaskett, who is also chairman of Greyhound Lines.

WHO

Chairman, President, and CEO: James B. McCurry, age 47, $400,000 pay
EVP Store Operations: Alan Bush
VP, Software Etc. Stores: Stanley A. Hirschman, age 48, $323,950 pay
VP Merchandising and Marketing: Roxanne M. Koepsell, age 37, $290,625 pay
VP, Babbage's Stores: Mary P. Evans, age 36
VP Distribution: Ron E. Freeman, age 48
VP and Controller: J. Braxton Carter II, age 37
VP Personnel: Michael A. Ivanich, age 44, $195,000 pay
CFO, Secretary, and Treasurer: Opal P. Ferraro, age 41
Auditors: Ernst & Young LLP

WHERE

HQ: 2250 William D. Tate Ave., Grapevine, TX 76051
Phone: 817-424-2000   **Fax:** 817-424-2002
Web site: http://www.software-etc.com

WHAT

	1996 Sales % of total
Video game systems & software	34
PC entertainment & educational software	26
PC productivity software	18
PC supplies & accessories	13
Computer books & magazines	8
Videos	1
Total	**100**

KEY COMPETITORS

Anam
Best Buy
Borders
CDW Computer Centers
Circuit City
Comark
CompUSA
Egghead
Fry's Electronics
Kmart

Micro Warehouse
Micro Electronics
OfficeMax
Software Spectrum
Staples
Stream International
Tandy Corporation
Toys "R" Us
Wal-Mart

HOW MUCH

Nasdaq symbol: NEOS FYE: February 3	Annual Growth	1991[2]	1992[2]	1993[2]	1994[2]	1995	1996
Sales ($ mil.)	34.3%	117.5	151.9	203.4	247.0	503.7	513.5
Net income ($ mil.)	—	(8.5)	1.6	5.7	5.7	(4.6)	0.1
Income as % of sales	—	—	1.1%	2.8%	2.3%	—	0.0%
Earnings per share ($)	—	(2.10)	0.15	0.83	0.72	(0.31)	0.01
Stock price – high ($)[1]	—	—	—	19.00	23.25	10.50	18.50
Stock price – low ($)[1]	—	—	—	7.13	8.88	9.50	6.00
Stock price – close ($)[1]	(25.7%)	—	—	18.00	9.88	10.25	7.38
P/E – high	—	—	—	23	32	—	—
P/E – low	—	—	—	9	12	—	—
Dividends per share ($)	—	—	—	0.00	0.00	0.00	0.00
Book value per share ($)	53.3%	—	—	1.56	3.99	5.55	5.62
Employees	31.2%	1,825	2,025	2,280	2,953	6,150	7,100

[1] Stock prices are for the prior calendar year. [2] Software Etc.

1996 YEAR-END
Debt ratio: 16.0%
Return on equity: 0.1%
Cash (mil.): $5
Current ratio: 1.25
Long-term debt (mil.): $12
No. of shares (mil.): 15
Dividends
  Yield: —
  Payout: —
Market value (mil.): $110

NETCOM

OVERVIEW

Like a comet, fast-moving NETCOM is blazing a trail as a leading Internet service provider. The San Jose, California-based company supplies direct Internet access to about 500,000 subscribers, while its NetCruiser web browser software offers a graphical point-and-click format for accessing the Internet's resources, including the World Wide Web and e-mail.

The company was founded in 1988 by Robert Rieger, an information services engineer for Lockheed, who had let other students in his night school class use his equipment to access the Internet. He began charging for the service, using the proceeds to buy more equipment. In 1991 Rieger quit his job at Lockheed, incorporated the business in 1992, mortgaged his house, and relocated from his den to a more commercial site in San Jose.

NETCOM grew, opening more points of presence with data lines leased from Wil-tel and concentrating on California and larger cities in the US. It soon attracted the interest of venture capitalists, who helped finance its expansion. In 1994 NETCOM went public in a well-received IPO, using the more than $22 million in proceeds primarily to finance expansion.

That year the company agreed to allow Auto-Graphics to sell NETCOM access to schools and libraries in the US and Canada. In 1995 David Garrison, formerly of Skytel, took over as president. NETCOM's subscriber growth increased more than 300% that year.

In 1996 founder Rieger left the company. NETCOM also announced plans to provide service in the UK. Also in 1996, NETCOM became the first independent Internet service provider to be included in Microsoft's Internet Referral server program. Users of Microsoft's Internet Explorer Web browser can subscribe to NETCOM by clicking on on icon on their PC desktop.

WHO

Chairman, President, and CEO: David W. Garrison, age 40, $263,112 pay
SVP Strategic Partnerships: Donald P. Hutchison, age 39, $242,938 pay
SVP, CFO, and Secretary: Clifton T. Weatherford, age 49
SVP Marketing: John E. Zeisler, age 43
SVP Customer Support: Eric V. Goffney, age 42
President, International: Eric W. Spivey, age 35
VP and Chief Technology Officer: Rick C. Francis, age 34, $185,948 pay
VP Operations: Robert E. Tomasi, age 44
Manager Human Resources: Irene Meister
Auditors: Ernst & Young LLP

WHERE

HQ: NETCOM On-Line Communication Services, Inc., 3031 Tisch Way, 2nd Fl., San Jose, CA 95128
Phone: 408-556-3233   **Fax:** 408-556-3250
Web site: http://www.netcom.com

	1995 Points of Presence	
	No.	% of total
California	41	20
Florida	12	6
Illinois	11	5
New Jersey	11	5
Other states & Canada	135	64
Total	**210**	**100**

WHAT

Selected Products and Services
Internet connection services
NetCruiser software

KEY COMPETITORS

America Online	IBM	Netscape
AT&T Corp.	IDT	Pacific Telesis
BBN	MCI	Prodigy
BT	MFS Communi-	PSINet
CompuServe	cations	Sprint
EarthLink	MindSpring	

HOW MUCH

Nasdaq symbol: NETC FYE: December 31	Annual Growth	1990	1991	1992[1]	1993	1994	1995
Sales ($ mil.)	407.9%	—	—	0.4	2.4	12.4	52.4
Net income ($ mil.)	—	—	—	0.0	0.2	(0.1)	(14.1)
Income as % of sales	—	—	—	—	0.2%	—	—
Earnings per share ($)	—	—	—	—	—	(0.02)	(1.68)
Stock price – high ($)	—	—	—	—	—	29.25	91.50
Stock price – low ($)	—	—	—	—	—	16.75	19.00
Stock price – close ($)	—	—	—	—	—	28.38	36.00
P/E – high	—	—	—	—	—	—	—
P/E – low	—	—	—	—	—	—	—
Dividends per share ($)	—	—	—	—	—	0.00	0.00
Book value per share ($)	—	—	—	—	—	4.16	16.71
Employees	118.9%	—	—	—	106	153	508

[1] 4-month fiscal year

1995 YEAR-END
Debt ratio: 0.0%
Return on equity: —
Cash (mil.): $146
Current ratio: 8.66
Long-term debt (mil.): $0
No. of shares (mil.): 11
Dividends
  Yield: —
  Payout: —
Market value (mil.): $400

NETSCAPE COMMUNICATIONS

OVERVIEW

Mountain View, California-based Netscape is the leading developer of software that supports information exchange and other transactions over corporate intranets and the Internet. Because its Navigator software (and its predecessor Mosaic) was distributed free of charge, it has become the dominant browser for the World Wide Web. Other products include Netscape Commerce Server, which provides a secure method of paying for Internet purchases, as well as software products that offer commercial data management, publishing, and electronic shopping services.

Computer wunderkind Marc Andreessen was instrumental in writing Mosaic, an Internet software program developed at the University of Illinois-Champaign. In 1994 he joined James Clark, founder of Silicon Graphics, to start Mosaic Communications. (However, the university also licensed Mosaic to other companies, including Spyglass.) That year the company, facing legal action from the university, became Netscape.

In 1995 Microsoft licensed Mosaic from Spyglass for inclusion in its new Windows 95 operating system and began a major assault on Netscape's turf. A group of media and computer companies, including Hearst Corp. and Times Mirror, acquired an 11% stake in Netscape the same year. In addition, Netscape formed an alliance with Sun Microsystems in which its products would be integrated into SunSoft's server software. Netscape went public in 1995 in one of the hottest IPOs of the decade. Clark, the chairman, owns 23.1%.

In an ongoing war with Microsoft to rule the Internet applications market, in 1996 Netscape agreed to acquire InSoft.

In addition, Netscape has announced plans to focus on a new battlefield, software for corporate intranets.

WHO

Chairman: James H. Clark, age 52, $100,000 pay
President and CEO: James L. Barksdale, age 53, $96,154 pay
VP Sales and Field Operations: Conway Rulon-Miller, age 45, $447,125 pay
VP Product Development: Richard M. Schell, age 46, $215,000 pay
VP Product Development: James C. J. Sha, age 45, $200,000 pay
VP Technology: Marc Andreessen, age 24
VP and CFO: Peter L. S. Currie, age 39
VP, General Counsel, and Secretary: Roberta R. Katz
VP Human Resources: Kandis Malefyt, age 41
Auditors: Ernst & Young LLP

WHERE

HQ: Netscape Communications Corporation, 501 E. Middlefield Rd., Mountain View, CA 94043
Phone: 415-254-1900   **Fax:** 415-528-4125
Web site: http://home.netscape.com

WHAT

Selected Products

Netscape Commerce Server (electronic commerce)
Netscape Communications Server (publishing)
Netscape Mail Server (e-mail)
Netscape Merchant System (management for virtual shopping)
Netscape Navigator Gold (Internet browser)
Netscape News Server (chat room)
Netscape Proxy Server (security)\
Netscape Publishing System (publishing software)

KEY COMPETITORS

Adobe	Infosafe	Oracle
America Online	Macromedia (CA)	Quarterdeck
Apple Computer	Microsoft	Spyglass
CompuServe	NetManage	Sun
DEC	Network	Microsystems
Edify	Computing	Sybase
FTP Software	Devices	Symantec
Hewlett-Packard	Novell	Verity
IBM	OneWave	VocalTec

HOW MUCH

Nasdaq symbol: NSCP FYE: December 31	Annual Growth	1990	1991	1992	1993	1994[1]	1995
Sales ($ mil.)	—	—	—	—	—	0.7	80.7
Net income ($ mil.)	—	—	—	—	—	(8.5)	(3.4)
Income as % of sales	—	—	—	—	—	—	—
Earnings per share ($)	—	—	—	—	—	(0.25)	(0.05)
Stock price – high ($)	—	—	—	—	—	—	71.33
Stock price – low ($)	—	—	—	—	—	—	22.88
Stock price – close ($)	—	—	—	—	—	—	68.63
P/E – high	—	—	—	—	—	—	—
P/E – low	—	—	—	—	—	—	—
Dividends per share ($)	—	—	—	—	—	—	0.00
Book value per share ($)	—	—	—	—	—	—	2.14
Employees	—	—	—	—	—	102	725

[1] 9-month fiscal year

1995 YEAR-END
Debt ratio: 1.4%
Return on equity: —
Cash (mil.): $149
Current ratio: 3.43
Long-term debt (mil.): $1
No. of shares (mil.): 81
Dividends
  Yield: —
  Payout: —
Market value (mil.): $5,563
R&D as % of sales: 30.9%

NEWBRIDGE NETWORKS CORPORATION

OVERVIEW

Newbridge Networks is bridging the global communications gap. The Kanata, Ontario-based company makes equipment for both private and public networks transmitting data, images, video, and voice. Most of the company's revenues come from its networking switches and routers and related support services. Newbridge sells its products in more than 75 countries. Its customers include major telecoms AT&T and Cable & Wireless and equipment makers Alcatel Alsthom and Siemens. Founder and CEO Terence Matthews owns 25% of the company.

A cofounder of telecommunications equipment company Mitel, Matthews founded Newbridge (named for the Welsh town where he was born) in 1986. At the time, most networking companies offered proprietary systems that were difficult for global companies to integrate across international phone lines. Matthews focused on designing an open system that could be used on all the world's major telephone systems. The idea was a hit with multinational customers, and sales topped $55 million after just 3 years. Newbridge in 1989 went public. To increase its marketing abilities, it signed alliances with partners including Hewlett-Packard and AT&T. In 1994 it signed a deal with MCI, linking its networking products with MCI's voice and data communication services.

Newbridge won several substantial overseas contracts in 1995, including awards from 75 telephone companies in China. That year it acquired controlling interests in Advanced Computer Communications, a maker of LAN bridges and routers, and Transistemas S.A., an Argentina-based systems integrator. In 1996 Newbridge and Siemens announced an alliance to develop products for ATM (asynchronous transfer mode) networks.

WHO

Chairman and CEO: Terence H. Matthews, age 53, C$148,800 pay
President and COO: Peter Sommerer, age 47, C$194,372 pay
EVP; General Manager, Americas Region: F. Michael Pascoe, age 44, C$234,872 pay
EVP; General Manager, European Region: John D. Everard, age 47, C$215,987 pay
EVP Operations: Bruce W. Rodgers, age 41, C$153,635 pay
EVP and CFO: Peter D. Charbonneau, age 42
EVP Research and Development: Scott W. Marshall, age 42
EVP Business Units: Conrad W. Lewis, age 43
Director Human Resources: Michael Gaffney
Auditors: Deloitte & Touche LLP

WHERE

HQ: 600 March Rd., Kanata, ON, K2K 2E6, Canada
Phone: 613-591-3600 **Fax:** 613-591-3680
US HQ: Newbridge Networks Inc., 593 Herndon Pkwy., Herndon, VA 22070-5241
US Phone: 703-834-3600
US Fax: 703-471-7080
Web site: http://www.newbridge.com

WHAT

	1996 Sales
	% of total
Networking multiplexers	
& switches & related services	99
Other	1
Total	**100**

KEY COMPETITORS

Alcatel Alsthom	Ericsson	NEC
Ascom Holding	FORE Systems	Northern Telecom
Banyan Systems	Fujitsu	Proteon
Bay Networks	General	Siemens
Cabletron	DataComm	StrataCom
Cisco Systems	IBM	Tellabs
DSC Communi-	IPC Information	Unisys
cations	Lucent	

HOW MUCH

NYSE symbol: NN FYE: April 30	Annual Growth	1991	1992	1993	1994	1995	1996
Sales ($ mil.)	39.2%	129.3	152.1	242.0	399.6	590.4	676.6
Net income ($ mil.)	—	(10.3)	8.2	47.2	114.1	138.9	149.0
Income as % of sales	—	—	5.4%	19.5%	28.6%	23.5%	22.0%
Earnings per share ($)	—	(0.15)	0.12	0.61	1.37	1.64	1.74
Stock price – high ($)[1]	—	7.75	4.84	21.63	73.88	68.75	45.38
Stock price – low ($)[1]	—	1.50	1.56	3.81	19.13	26.50	25.00
Stock price – close ($)[1]	91.0%	1.63	3.81	20.63	54.75	38.25	41.38
P/E – high	—	—	40	36	54	42	26
P/E – low	—	—	13	6	14	16	14
Dividends per share ($)	—	0.00	0.00	0.00	0.00	0.00	0.00
Book value per share ($)	44.2%	1.26	1.31	2.87	4.24	6.05	7.86
Employees	—	—	—	—	2,155	2,955	3,400

[1] Stock prices are for the prior calendar year.

1996 YEAR-END
Debt ratio: 0.3%
Return on equity: 25.7%
Cash (mil.): $334.7
Current ratio: 4.94
Long-term debt (mil.): $0.6
No. of shares (mil.): 84.3
Dividends
  Yield: —
  Payout: —
Market value (mil.): $3,490

NEXT SOFTWARE, INC.

OVERVIEW

And now for its NeXT act.... Redwood City, California-based NeXT Software's object-oriented (OO) products, such as the NEXTSTEP operating system, enable developers to write programs in a fraction of the usual time (since OO software greatly reduces the need to write thousands of lines of code every time a change is made). Looking ahead, CEO Steven Jobs believes the myriad companies establishing sites on the World Wide Web will need custom application software in order to interact with customers. So NeXT has launched WebObjects, which shortens the time it takes to build a "dynamic" Web site from months to hours. Some analysts believe success in this arena could launch NeXT's eventual IPO. The present owners include Jobs, Ross Perot, Sun Microsystems, and Canon.

Jobs started NeXT Computer in 1985 after he was kicked out of Apple Computer — the company he cofounded. Four years later NeXT shipped its first product, the elegant NEXT Cube PC. Although its advanced technology was applauded, the high-priced Cube was sluggish and could not be networked. In 1990 NeXT introduced the NeXTstation family, offering faster machines.

After investing an estimated $200 million in start-up capital, NeXT had captured 7% of the US UNIX workstation market by 1992. But after selling just 50,000 workstations, NeXT stopped making hardware to focus on developing its NEXTSTEP operating system. The company modified NEXTSTEP in 1993 to run on Intel and Motorola processors and formed joint ventures with Hewlett-Packard and Sun Microsystems.

The next year NeXT continued to line up support for NEXTSTEP and OpenStep, introducing products for SunSoft's Solaris and Hewlett-Packard's HP/UX operating systems, among others. Sales more than tripled in 1994, as NeXT began shipping its new OO software design tools.

In 1995 brokerage powerhouse Merrill Lynch agreed to buy $8 million in OO software and consulting services from NeXT. Early the next year, the upstart changed its name to NeXT Software.

WHO

Chairman and CEO: Steven Jobs
VP Worldwide Sales: Mitchell Mandich, age 47
VP General and Administration and CFO:
  Dominique Trempont
VP Professional Services: Sina Tamaddon
VP Engineering: Avadis Tevanian Jr
Head of Human Resources: Paul Bianchi
Auditors: KPMG Peat Marwick LLP

WHERE

HQ: 900 Chesapeake Dr., Redwood City, CA 94063
Phone: 415-366-0900   **Fax:** 415-780-3929
Web site: http://www.next.com

NeXT also has offices in Boston, Chicago, New Jersey, New York, and Washington, DC, and in Germany and the UK.

WHAT

Selected Products

D'OLE (Distributed OLE; allows software developers to use Windows-based development tools such as PowerBuilder and Visual Basic to create distributed applications that can run across Windows and UNIX platforms)

Enterprise Objects Framework (EOF; object-oriented development tool for relational database applications)

NEXTSTEP (object-oriented operating system, including numerous bundled applications)

NEXTSTEP Developer (object-oriented development tool for advanced client/server applications; bundled with Objective C, C++, ANSI C, and PostScript Level II languages)

Portable Distributed Objects (PDO; a dynamic object-oriented development tool that enables objects to be distributed across a variety of server platforms)

WebObjects (a suite of server-based development tools for building platform-independent applications for the World Wide Web; compatible with a number of standards, including Java and JavaScript)

Selected Customers

Chrysler	Motorola
DreamWorks SKG	NASA
MCI	Reebok
Merrill Lynch	The Sharper Image
Mitsubishi	Walt Disney

KEY COMPETITORS

Apple Computer	INTERSOLV	ParcPlace-
Borland	Microsoft	Digitalk
Carnegie Group	Novell	
IBM		

HOW MUCH

Private company FYE: December 31	Annual Growth	1990	1991	1992	1993	1994	1995
Sales ($ mil.)	9.7%	29.0	128.0	140.0	14.3	49.7	46.0
Employees	(16.3%)	—	570	530	240	250	280

NOVELLUS SYSTEMS INC

OVERVIEW

Novellus can really lay it on. The San Jose-based company is a leading maker of chemical vapor deposition (CVD) equipment used to deposit dielectric (insulating) layers and some metal layers during the semiconductor manufacturing process. The company's products are known for their high capacity and production quality; prices start at around $1 million. Each of the world's top 20 semiconductor makers has bought Novellus equipment.

Founded in 1984, Novellus got its name from the Latin for novel or unique. The company ran out of money soon after it built a prototype CVD system. Robert Graham, an executive at semiconductor equipment maker Applied Materials, suggested his company buy Novellus. When Applied declined, Graham resigned and joined Novellus as its president and CEO. Graham, who had started Intel's Japan operations, immediately began searching for distributors in that country. Novellus shipped its first product, Concept One, in 1987, and the company went public in 1988. It introduced the Concept One-W in 1990 to address the tungsten CVD market.

Novellus outsources the manufacture of major subassemblies in order to minimize fixed costs and capital expenditures. The company's only manufacturing responsibilities are final assembly and testing, allowing it to concentrate on product design. Novellus maintains close relationships with a handful of trusted suppliers.

Countering some critics' accusations that the company was slow to introduce new technologies, in 1994 and 1995 Novellus introduced the Concept Two Dual Altus for advanced tungsten deposition and the Concept One Maxus for nitride film deposition.

In 1996 Graham retired and Novellus president and CEO Richard Hill was named chairman.

WHO

Chairman, President, and CEO: Richard S. Hill, age 44, $771,348 pay (prior to promotion)
EVP Sales and Marketing: Peter Hanley, age 56, $531,251 pay
VP Finance and Administration, CFO, and Secretary: William J. Wall, age 49, $425,841 pay
VP Engineering: Jeffrey Benzing, age 39, $403,609 pay
VP Operations: John Chenault, age 47, $362,267 pay
VP and Chief Technical Officer: Alain Harrus, age 40
VP Human Resources: Linus Cordes, age 58
Auditors: Ernst & Young LLP

WHERE

HQ: 3970 N. First St., San Jose, CA 95134
Phone: 408-943-9700   **Fax:** 408-943-3422

WHAT

Dielectric PECVD Systems
Concept One (deposits CVD dielectric films on wafers)
Concept One Maxus (dual-capacity CVD deposition and capacity for gap fill using fluorinated TEOS)
Concept Two Sequel (high-capacity, thin-film deposition)
Concept Two Dual Sequel (dual-chamber system used to deposit thick dielectric films)
Concept Two Sequel-S (compact system for depositing both thick and thin films)

Dielectric High-density Plasma Systems
Speed (HDP deposition system)
Speed/Sequel (dual-chamber HDP deposition system)

Metal CVD Systems
Concept One-W (deposits blanket tungsten metal films used to connect multiple metal layers)
Concept Two Altus (combines tungsten processing with advanced wafer handling for increased productivity)
Concept Two Dual Altus (dual-chamber system for tungsten applications)

KEY COMPETITORS

Applied Materials
Applied Science
Genus
Lam Research
Mattson
Technology
Semitool
SpeedFam
Varian Associates

HOW MUCH

Nasdaq symbol: NVLS FYE: December 31	Annual Growth	1990	1991	1992	1993	1994	1995
Sales ($ mil.)	41.0%	67.1	80.0	69.8	113.5	224.7	373.7
Net income ($ mil.)	42.6%	14.0	16.8	6.2	16.1	44.9	82.5
Income as % of sales	—	20.9%	21.0%	8.9%	14.2%	20.0%	22.1%
Earnings per share ($)	36.7%	1.01	1.15	0.44	1.10	2.72	4.82
Stock price – high ($)	—	18.00	27.25	26.50	37.00	56.50	87.25
Stock price – low ($)	—	5.44	10.50	7.75	14.00	25.75	42.75
Stock price – close ($)	36.3%	11.50	21.25	18.25	34.25	50.00	54.00
P/E – high	—	18	24	60	34	21	18
P/E – low	—	5	9	18	13	9	9
Dividends per share ($)	—	0.00	0.00	0.00	0.00	0.00	0.00
Book value per share ($)	32.6%	4.18	5.73	6.04	7.45	13.25	17.11
Employees	28.0%	230	265	306	371	530	790

1995 YEAR-END
Debt ratio: 2.6%
Return on equity: 33.9%
Cash (mil.): $150
Current ratio: 3.46
Long-term debt (mil.): $0
No. of shares (mil.): 16
Dividends
  Yield: —
  Payout: —
Market value (mil.): $861
R&D as % of sales: 11.0%

PARAMETRIC TECHNOLOGY

OVERVIEW

Parametric Technology has a model sales curve. The Waltham, Massachusetts-based firm is the world leader in mechanical CAD/CAM/CAE (computer-aided design, manufacturing, and engineering) software. Its premier product, Pro/ENGINEER, is used by manufacturers to create 3-dimensional computer models of new products such as air conditioners and Tomahawk Cruise Missiles (speeding development and cutting costs). In 1995 CEO Steven Walske assembled a new group of SVPs and increased the company's global sales force by 43%.

Samuel Geisberg, a former geometry professor at Leningrad University, fled the USSR in 1974. After working for CAD software development firms Computervision and Applicon, he founded Parametric Technology in 1985 to remedy flaws that he perceived in mechanical design. At the time, designers were limited by geometric models described in unfamiliar mathematical terms, computers dedicated to specific tasks and disparate databases. The first Pro/ENGINEER product was shipped in 1988, and the company went public the next year. The company built its market strength by pushing advanced technology that its rivals lacked, by marketing to engineers in a range of businesses, and by keeping prices under $10,000 (half the price of competitors' products). In 1994 Geisberg retired as chairman and took up the position of senior scientist.

In 1995 Parametric Technology acquired surface-modeling software from Evans & Sutherland Computer. The purchase of software designer Rasna Corp. gave it entree into the mechanical analysis field (computer model simulations). In 1996 the company licensed one of the products of software developer ICAM Technologies as a means of connecting its software to customers' machine tools.

WHO

Chairman and CEO: Steven C. Walske, age 43, $800,000 pay
President and COO: C. Richard Harrison, age 40, $750,000 pay
SVP Sales and Distribution: Michael E. McGuinness, age 35, $558,362 pay
SVP Marketing: Marc J. L. Dulude, age 35
SVP Finance and Administration, CFO, and Treasurer: Edwin J. Gillis, age 47
SVP Research and Development: Thomas W. Jensen, age 42
VP Finance: James F. Kelliher, age 36, $123,865 pay
VP Administration, Corporate Counsel, and Clerk: Martha L. Durcan, age 36
Director Human Resources: Carl Ockerbloom
Auditors: Coopers & Lybrand L.L.P.

WHERE

HQ: Parametric Technology Corporation, 128 Technology Dr., Waltham, MA 02154
Phone: 617-398-5000 **Fax:** 617-398-6000
Web site: http://www.ptc.com

WHAT

	1995 Sales	
	$ mil.	% of total
License	288.3	73
Service	106.0	27
Total	**394.3**	**100**

Selected Products
Pro/ACCESS (allows customer to use information from a variety of sources in the Pro/ENGINEER environment)
Pro/ENGINEER (mechanical design)
Pro/MANUFACTURING (tool and manufacturing process design)
Pro/MECHANICA (model simulation)

KEY COMPETITORS

Andersen	Dassault	MacNeal-
Consulting	EDS	Schwendler
Autodesk	IBM	Structural
Cadence	Intergraph	Dynamics
Computervision		Research
		Synopsys

HOW MUCH

Nasdaq symbol: PMTC FYE: September 30	Annual Growth	1990	1991	1992	1993	1994	1995
Sales ($ mil.)	72.9%	25.5	44.2	86.7	163.1	244.3	394.3
Net income ($ mil.)	69.1%	5.6	10.3	21.1	42.9	66.9	77.4
Income as % of sales	—	22.1%	23.4%	24.3%	26.3%	27.4%	19.6%
Earnings per share ($)	61.3%	0.11	0.19	0.38	0.75	1.14	1.20
Stock price – high ($)	—	5.21	15.31	28.13	44.75	40.25	36.28
Stock price – low ($)	—	2.50	3.75	12.63	22.50	21.50	16.00
Stock price – close ($)	49.2%	4.50	15.06	26.50	38.75	34.50	33.25
P/E – high	—	47	81	74	60	35	30
P/E – low	—	23	20	33	30	19	13
Dividends per share ($)	—	0.00	0.00	0.00	0.00	0.00	0.00
Book value per share ($)	58.1%	0.60	0.85	1.51	2.69	4.25	5.93
Employees	57.4%	203	305	525	899	1,281	1,960

1995 YEAR-END
Debt ratio: 0.0%
Return on equity: 25.2%
Cash (mil.): $308
Current ratio: 5.53
Long-term debt (mil.): $0
No. of shares (mil.): 63
Dividends
 Yield: —
 Payout: —
Market value (mil.): $2,080
R&D as % of sales: 10.5%

THE PAUL ALLEN GROUP

OVERVIEW

So much money — so little time. Paul Allen, cofounder of Microsoft, is a computer billionaire with a sense of his own mortality. His mission is not only to invest in companies that promote a "wired world" (in which all people are united through interconnecting communications and information systems), but to leave that world a little better than he found it through charitable contributions.

The Paul Allen Group is the umbrella organization for Allen's ventures. Vulcan Ventures, his investment arm, holds his approximately 10% interest in Microsoft and mostly minority stakes in about 30 other companies. Most provide computer, multimedia or communications products and services, but he also has interests in PETsMART (pet supplies), and the Portland Trail Blazers basketball team.

Allen and Bill Gates, schoolmates in Seattle, started Microsoft in 1975. While Gates ran the business side, Allen was responsible for technical issues, helping design or put together many of the company's biggest successes including MS-DOS, Microsoft Word, and the Microsoft mouse. Diagnosed with Hodgkin's disease in 1983, Allen left Microsoft but retained about 13% of the company and a seat on its board. With his cancer in remission in 1985, Allen founded Asymetrix. But by then he was less intent on devoting his life to business and he chose to spread the wealth by helping small start-ups.

Allen started Interval Research, a "wired world" think tank, and Starwave, which develops multimedia software, in 1992. He also invested in America Online (AOL) that year, later selling his stock when he failed to win a seat on the company's board. The next year Allen bought 80% of Ticketmaster, the US's top ticket agency.

Allen invested in (interactive entertainment), in 1994, and added Storyopolis (multimedia programming for children) in 1995. Also that year, Allen agreed to invest $500 million in entertainment company DreamWorks SKG.

The following year Allen made a rare acquisition outside the high-tech or media worlds with the purchase of an interest in Capstone Turbine Corp., which makes power turbines.

WHO

Chairman: Paul G. Allen
President and CEO: Vern Raburn
President, Vulcan Ventures: Bill Savoy
President, Vulcan Northwest: Jody Patton
Controller, Vulcan Northwest: Frank Kraus
Director Human Resources, Vulcan Northwest:
    Pam Faber

WHERE

HQ: 110 110th Ave. NE, Ste. 530, Bellevue, WA 98004
Phone: 206-453-6101   **Fax:** 206-453-1985
Web site: http://www.starwave.com

WHAT

Selected Investments
3D/EYE Inc. (3D technologies)
Asymetrix Corp. (multimedia development software)
Attachmate (connectivity products)
Brøderbund Software Inc. (edutainment software)
Capstone Turbine Corp.
C/Net: The Computer Network (computer information television cable channel and online service)
DreamWorks SKG (entertainment company)
Egghead, Inc. (software retailer)
Harbinger*EDI Services (transaction and inventory control software)
Metricom, Inc. (wireless data transmission products)
PETsMART, Inc. (retail pet supply stores)
Portland Trail Blazers (professional basketball team)
Starwave Corp. (multimedia consumer software)
Storyopolis (children's film, television, and multimedia programming)
Telescan Inc. (online investor information)
Ticketmaster Corp. (computerized ticket service)
Trilobyte (multimedia entertainment software)
Vulcan Ventures (investments)

KEY COMPETITORS

Accel Partners	Inman &	Mayfield Fund
Austin Ventures	Bowman	Menlo Ventures
Boston Ventures	Institutional	Safeguard
Brentwood	Venture	Scientifics
Associates	Partners	Sutter Hill
Hummer	Kleiner Perkins	Trinity Ventures
Winblad	Matrix Partners	

HOW MUCH

Private company FYE: December 31	Annual Growth	1990	1991	1992	1993	1994	1995
Est. new investments	6.3%	—	—	5	6	9	6
Employees	82.6%	—	—	—	3	14	10

ASYMETRIX

PEOPLESOFT, INC.

OVERVIEW

Pleasanton, California-based Peoplesoft is the leading maker of human resource and financial administration client/server software. In addition to businesses, PeopleSoft sells to the public sector and has its sights on the larger, more competitive world of manufacturing software. But as the company has grown and repositioned itself, some customers have found customer service quality beginning to lag.

PeopleSoft was founded by Dave Duffield and Ken Morris, former Integral Systems employees who quit when the board of the mainframe-based human resource management supplier rejected Duffield's ideas for PC network-based human resource software. Duffield and Morris founded PeopleSoft and in 1988 delivered the market's first high-end client/server human resource software. After the 1991 settlement of a copyright infringement suit brought by Integral, in 1992 (the year it went public) PeopleSoft introduced a 2nd business line, financial applications. Duffield owns about 32% of the company and Morris owns about 2%.

The software maker has continued to refine its products for applications in the medical industry and government, but the Holy Grail of the field is enterprisewide applications (fulfilling all of a company's data tracking needs). In order to compete with Germany's SAP, the enterprisewide software leader, PeopleSoft has added purchasing and distribution software.

In 1995 PeopleSoft announced an alliance with Spider Technologies that allows its software to interact with the Internet through Spider's NetDynamics product. As part of its overseas expansion, the company established a European headquarters in Munich in 1996.

WHO

Chairman, President, and CEO: David A. Duffield, age 55, $326,800 pay
SVP Worldwide Operations: Albert W. Duffield, age 52, $285,950 pay
SVP Application Development and Customer Services: Margaret L. Taylor, age 44, $285,950 pay
SVP and Chief Technology Officer: Kenneth R. Morris, age 45, $243,820 pay
SVP Finance and Administration, CFO, and Secretary: Ronald E. F. Codd, age 40, $243,600 pay
Director Human Resources: Larry Butler
Auditors: Ernst & Young LLP

WHERE

HQ: 4440 Rosewood Dr., Pleasanton, CA 94588
Phone: 510-225-3000   **Fax:** 510-225-3100
Web site: http://www.peoplesoft.com

WHAT

	1995 Sales	
	$ mil.	% of total
License fees	134.6	59
Services	93.0	41
Total	**227.6**	**100**

Selected Software

Distribution Management Systems	PeopleSoft Billing
PeopleSoft Inventory	PeopleSoft Budgets
PeopleSoft Purchasing	**Human Resource Management Systems**
Financial Management Systems	PeopleSoft Benefits Administration
PeopleSoft Asset Management	PeopleSoft Payroll

KEY COMPETITORS

Baan	Dun &	Lawson Software
Ceridian	Bradstreet	Oracle
Computer	Fourth Shift	Platinum
Associates	Humanic Design	Software
Computron	Hyperion	SAP
Software	Software	System Software
Cyborg Systems	Integral Systems	Associates

HOW MUCH

Nasdaq symbol: PSFT FYE: December 31	Annual Growth	1990	1991	1992	1993	1994	1995
Sales ($ mil.)	106.2%	6.1	17.1	31.6	58.2	112.9	227.6
Net income ($ mil.)	136.2%	0.4	1.6	4.4	8.4	14.5	29.4
Income as % of sales	—	6.9%	9.1%	13.8%	14.5%	12.9%	12.9%
Earnings per share ($)	93.3%	0.02	0.05	0.12	0.17	0.28	0.54
Stock price – high ($)	—	—	—	8.00	10.13	19.75	47.00
Stock price – low ($)	—	—	—	5.63	5.88	6.50	15.00
Stock price – close ($)	82.6%	—	—	7.06	7.81	18.88	43.00
P/E – high	—	—	—	67	61	71	87
P/E – low	—	—	—	47	36	23	28
Dividends per share ($)	—	—	—	0.00	0.00	0.00	0.00
Book value per share ($)	40.4%	—	—	1.15	1.55	1.95	3.18
Employees	93.1%	50	75	188	362	651	1,341

1995 YEAR-END

Debt ratio: 0.8%
Return on equity: 23.5%
Cash (mil.): $126
Current ratio: 1.56
Long-term debt (mil.): $1
No. of shares (mil.): 49
Dividends
  Yield: —
  Payout: —
Market value (mil.): $2,121
R&D as % of sales: 15.8%

PEROT SYSTEMS CORPORATION

OVERVIEW

The largest privately held information technology company, Perot Systems develops and integrates office automation, software, and telecommunications systems for clients in industries ranging from insurance to manufacturing. Once primarily a systems integration company and then focusing on outsourcing, the company, founded by occasional presidential contender Ross Perot, appears to be transitioning into a computer power in the global financial segment (its partnership with Swiss Bank and other European operations could soon account for over half its global revenues).

Perot Systems is moving into new fields — its 7-year deal with Tenet Healthcare is one of the first times that computer operations for the health care industry have been outsourced. A Perot family trust owns about 40% of the company, but Perot is not involved in day-to-day operations.

In 1988, 4 years after he sold EDS (founded in 1962), Perot began Perot Systems as a systems integration service. When it added outsourcing, the company quickly signed up $1.2 billion worth of new business. The company began to flounder just as quickly, in part, some said, because it had promised more than it could deliver. Also Perot alienated Mexicans with anti-NAFTA political rhetoric just as his company was working on deals with Volkswagen de Mexico and Multibanco Mercentil Probursa. In 1992 former Perot aide and EDS executive Mort Meyerson became CEO and began leading the company away from computer outsourcing to higher-margin consulting services.

Perot Systems acquired the Custom Development Division of financial software company Platinum Software Corp. in 1994. The next year, its outsourcing unit became the first information technology services provider to receive ISO 9001 certification for computer facilities management. Also in 1995, former IBM strategist James Cannavino became president. A year later, he became CEO.

In a 1996 alliance, the company won a $250 million contract to run the data processing operations of Swiss Bank Corp., which took about a 1/4 stake in Perot Systems.

WHO

President and CEO: James A. Cannavino
CFO: John Vonesh
Chief, Office of Technology: Bill Harmon
General Counsel: Peter Altabef
Director Human Resources: Carol Barnett

WHERE

HQ: 12377 Merit Dr., Ste. 1100, Dallas, TX 75251
Phone: 214-383-5600   **Fax:** 214-383-4157
Web site: http://www.ps.net

WHAT

Selected Products and Services
Application performance tuning
Business reengineering
Change management
Controls engineering services
d.b.Express data visualization software
Executive information/decision support systems
Internet/intranet home page services
ProBanx Financial System software
Software development and maintenance
Systems integration
Technology consulting
Telecommunications engineering and operations
Virtual prototyping
Workflow and imaging systems

Selected Clients
Barclays Intermortgage Bank (UK)
Cadillac Plastic and Chemical Company
East Midlands Electricity (UK)
Europcar (France)
Kelsey-Hayes
M&G Group
MCI
NationsBank
Robert Plan Corp.
Rouge Steel Co.
Swiss Bank Corp.
Tenet Healthcare
University of Texas Southwestern Medical Center
Volkswagen of America

KEY COMPETITORS

Affiliated Computer
Andersen Consulting
BISYS
Cambridge Technology
Cap Gemini
CIBER
CompuCom
Computer Data Systems
Computer Sciences
Deloitte Touche Tohmatsu
EDS
Fiserv
MCI Systemhouse
Systems & Computer Technology
Technology Solutions
Wang

HOW MUCH

Private company FYE: December 31	Annual Growth	1990	1991	1992	1993	1994	1995
Sales ($ mil.)	40.4%	—	90.0	247.0	280.0	320.0	350.0
Employees	34.3%	550	800	1,500	—	2,300	2,400

PEROT SYSTEMS CORPORATION

PINNACLE MICRO, INC.

OVERVIEW

Pinnacle Micro hopes the computer CD does to the floppy disk what the audio CD did to the vinyl record. Based in Irvine, California, Pinnacle produces optical storage systems, which use lasers to record and read computer data. Uses for the company's memory systems, which are much more powerful than traditional floppy disk systems, include commercial editing, desktop publishing, medical imaging, and network data storage. Technical problems stalled the release of a major new product, the Apex 4.6 gigabyte optical drive, causing a skid in Pinnacle's financial well-being. The founding Blum family owns about 55% of the company.

William Blum and his son Scott started Pinnacle in 1987 after William retired from a 30-year career in computer sales and marketing. They began by marketing add-on memory boards but soon switched to reselling Sony's magneto-optical drives. In response to customer complaints that Sony's drive was too slow and too expensive, Pinnacle developed a new product that combined the capacity and speed of hard drives with the removability of a CD. Pinnacle introduced its line of optical drives in 1992 and went public the next year. In 1994 auditors discovered accounting irregularities that forced the company to restate its financial results.

Pinnacle's rapid growth has mirrored that of the multimedia market as users have looked for better ways to store memory-hungry audio and video information. In 1995 the company introduced its first rewritable optical drive, which allows users to store computer files on CDs instead of floppy disks, and signed an agreement to market the new CD drive and other products through retailer CompUSA. The next year, as product development problems continued, director Larry Goelman replaced William Blum as CEO.

WHO

Chairman, President, and CEO: Lawrence Goelman, age 55
EVP: Scott A. Blum, age 32, $161,192 pay
EVP and CFO: Roger Hay, age 46
SVP Corporate Development: James G. Hanley, age 34, $156,453 pay
VP, General Counsel, and Secretary: Jonathan B. Eddison, age 43
Director Human Resources: Chuck McGee
Auditors: BDO Seidmann LLP

WHERE

HQ: 19 Technology Dr., Irvine, CA 92718
Phone: 714-789-3000   **Fax:** 714-789-3150
Web site: http://www.pinnaclemicro.com

	1995 Sales
	% of total
US	65
Other countries	35
Total	**100**

WHAT

Selected Products
10Xtreme CD-ROM drive
CD-ROM recorders
　Explorer CD Recorder
　RCD 5040 Recordable CD (external)
　RCD 5040i Recordable CD (internal)
Optical hard drives
　Sierra (1.3 gigabytes)
　Tahoe (640 megabytes)
　Vertex (2.6 gigabytes)
Optical media
　OMD (230/120, 650/600, and 1300/1200 megabytes)
　OMDR (2.6/2.3 gigabytes)

KEY COMPETITORS

Canon	Iomega	Sharp
EMC Corp.	Matsushita	Sony
Fujitsu	NEC	SyQuest
Hewlett-Packard	Plasmon Data	Toshiba
Hitachi	Quantum Corp.	Western Digital
Hyundai	Ricoh	
IBM	Seagate	

HOW MUCH

Nasdaq symbol: PNCL FYE: December 31	Annual Growth	1990	1991	1992	1993	1994	1995
Sales ($ mil.)	49.4%	11.0	14.9	22.9	39.2	65.4	81.8
Net income ($ mil.)	—	0.7	0.8	0.9	1.9	2.7	(2.5)
Income as % of sales	—	6.3%	5.4%	3.9%	4.9%	4.2%	—
Earnings per share ($)	—	0.19	0.23	0.22	0.42	0.52	(0.31)
Stock price – high ($)	—	—	—	—	22.50	20.50	19.67
Stock price – low ($)	—	—	—	—	10.00	9.25	5.83
Stock price – close ($)	(10.2%)	—	—	—	18.00	9.50	14.50
P/E – high	—	—	—	—	54	39	—
P/E – low	—	—	—	—	24	18	—
Dividends per share ($)	—	—	—	—	0.00	0.00	0.00
Book value per share ($)	(19.2%)	—	—	—	3.26	3.63	2.13
Employees	40.3%	—	—	—	94	120	185

1995 YEAR-END
Debt ratio: 0.1%
Return on equity: —
Cash (mil.): $4
Current ratio: 2.12
Long-term debt (mil.): $0
No. of shares (mil.): 8
Dividends
　Yield: —
　Payout: —
Market value (mil.): $114
R&D as % of sales: 6.1%

PIXAR

OVERVIEW

Plenty of movie studios shoot on location, but few have traveled to Pixar's location — cyberspace. The Richmond, California-based company's *Toy Story* was the world's first computer-animated feature film. Pixar created the film using its proprietary software systems Marionette (modeling, animating, and lighting), Ringmaster (production management), and RenderMan (image rendering). It also makes television commercials and CD-ROMs and sells its RenderMan software to film studios, visual effects companies, and others. CEO Steven Jobs (a cofounder of Apple Computer) owns 80% of the company.

Pixar began in the early 1980s as part of Lucasfilm, where filmmaker George Lucas assembled a team to develop computer graphics systems. Among those team members were computer scientist Edwin Catmull and animator John Lasseter. In 1986, 2 years after he left Apple, Jobs acquired the division for $10 million. The new company was named Pixar after its first product, the Pixar Image Computer, a 3-D graphics system. Pixar and Disney signed a deal in 1986 to jointly develop the Computer Animated Production System (CAPS), which uses computers to digitally color hand-drawn animation. In 1988 Lasseter won an Oscar for best short film (animated) for the computer-animated *Tin Toy*. In 1991 it began work on *Toy Story*, with Lasseter directing. Meanwhile, the company's commercial business was garnering awards, winning Clios in both 1993 and 1994.

Disney and Pixar released *Toy Story* in 1995, and the movie received both critical acclaim and box office success (grossing more than $300 million by mid-1996). Jobs took the company public just weeks after the film release in one of the hottest offerings of the year.

WHO

Chairman and CEO: Steven P. Jobs, age 40
EVP and Chief Technical Officer: Edwin E. Catmull, age 50, $182,646 pay
EVP, CFO, and Secretary: Lawrence B. Levy, age 36
VP Creative Development: John Lasseter, age 38, $235,463 pay
VP Feature Film Production: Ralph J. Guggenheim, age 44, $160,411 pay
VP Interactive Products: Pamela J. Kerwin, age 46
Technical Director, Feature Films: William T. Reeves, age 44, $172,430 pay
Director Human Resources: Lisa Ellis
Auditors: KMPG Peat Marwick LLP

WHERE

HQ: 1001 W. Cutting Blvd., Richmond, CA 94804
Phone: 510-236-4000   **Fax:** 510-236-0388
Web site: http://www.pixar.com

WHAT

Software Systems
Marionette (modeling, animating, and lighting)
RenderMan (rendering to create photo-realistic image synthesis)
Ringmaster (production management)

Selected Commercials	Selected Films
Coca-Cola	*Luxo Jr.*
Fresca	*Tin Toy*
GummiSavers	*Toy Story*
Levi's Jeans	
Listerine	

KEY COMPETITORS

DreamWorks SKG	LucasFilm	Silicon Graphics
Four Media	MCA	Sony
IBM	MGM	Time Warner
Jim Henson Productions	Microsoft	Viacom
Laser Pacific Media	Netter Digital	Walt Disney
	News Corp.	
	Samuel Goldwyn	
	Savoy Pictures	

HOW MUCH

Nasdaq symbol: PIXR FYE: December 31	Annual Growth	1990	1991	1992	1993	1994	1995
Sales ($ mil.)	28.9%	3.4	7.3	4.2	6.8	5.6	12.1
Net income ($ mil.)	—	(9.7)	(0.9)	(3.4)	(1.2)	(2.4)	1.6
Income as % of sales	—	—	—	—	—	—	13.2%
Earnings per share ($)	—	—	—	—	—	(0.06)	0.04
Stock price – high ($)	—	—	—	—	—	—	49.50
Stock price – low ($)	—	—	—	—	—	—	22.00
Stock price – close ($)	—	—	—	—	—	—	28.88
P/E – high	—	—	—	—	—	—	—
P/E – low	—	—	—	—	—	—	—
Dividends per share ($)	—	—	—	—	—	—	0.00
Book value per share ($)	—	—	—	—	—	—	3.73
Employees	34.5%	—	51	64	75	86	167

1995 YEAR-END
Debt ratio: 1.7%
Return on equity: 1.1%
Cash (mil.): $144
Current ratio: 14.73
Long-term debt (mil.): $0
No. of shares (mil.): 38
Dividends
  Yield: —
  Payout: —
Market value (mil.): $1,106
R&D as % of sales: 33.6%

PLATINUM TECHNOLOGY, INC.

OVERVIEW

PLATINUM technology must have a gold card. The Oakbrook Terrace, Illinois-based firm has been on an extended shopping spree, buying more than 40 infrastructure software and other computer-related businesses and technologies to become a well-rounded provider of client/server programs.

Long dependent on mainframe database software, PLATINUM is combining its holdings to create the PLATINUM Open Enterprise Management System (POEMS). POEMS combines data warehousing, systems management, and other product suites to enable a company to integrate its multiple software platforms (including MVS, UNIX, and Windows) into a custom environment. However, PLATINUM has posted losses recently because of expenses related to the costs of acquisitions, marketing, and R&D. CEO Andrew "Flip" Filipowski owns about 7% of the company.

Filipowski started PLATINUM (with several partners) in 1987 after being forced out of DBMS Inc., a software firm he had founded in 1979 (DBMS was acquired by Computer Associates in 1990). PLATINUM's aim was to improve DB2, IBM's relational database manager that supplanted older hierarchical systems. Filipowski gained market share by deeply discounting his product. PLATINUM went public in 1991.

In the mid-1990s PLATINUM began to expand beyond mainframe database software by acquiring a range of companies, including AIB Software (multiplatform application development and testing tools), Prodea Software (business intelligence tools and data warehousing), and Software Interfaces (data access, conversion, and reporting utilities).

The company formed subsidiary PLATINUM Solutions in 1996 to offer enterprise-scale systems integration products and services.

WHO

Chairman, President, and CEO: Andrew J. Filipowski, age 45, $520,000 pay
EVP Product Development and COO:
Paul L. Humenansky, age 38, $330,000 pay
EVP, CFO, and Treasurer: Michael P. Cullinane, age 46, $330,000 pay
EVP Sales: Thomas A. Slowey, age 35, $210,000 pay
EVP International Operations: Paul A. Tatro, age 39, $210,000 pay
Director Human Resources: Jennifer Werneke
Auditors: KPMG Peat Marwick LLP

WHERE

HQ: 1815 S. Meyers Rd., Oakbrook Terrace, IL 60181
Phone: 708-620-5000   **Fax:** 708-691-0710
Web site: http://www.platinum.com

WHAT

	1995 Sales	
	$ mil.	% of total
Software	154.1	56
Maintenance	76.3	28
Professional services	45.5	16
Total	**275.9**	**100**

Selected Products

Database Management
Easy DBA (database administration)
Database Analyzer (performance analyzer)
Data Navigator (application development)

Systems Management
DBVision (performance management)
AutoXpert (job and process management)
AutoSecure (security management)

KEY COMPETITORS

American Software
BMC Software
Borland
Candle Corp.
Computer Associates
Computer Data Systems
Compuware
IBM
Informix
Oracle
Progress Software
SAP
Sequent
Software AG
Sun Microsystems
Sybase

HOW MUCH

Nasdaq symbol: PLAT FYE: December 31	Annual Growth	1990	1991	1992	1993	1994	1995
Sales ($ mil.)	78.6%	15.2	28.8	49.0	62.2	95.7	275.9
Net income ($ mil.)	—	2.2	5.1	9.3	3.0	(3.2)	(112.5)
Income as % of sales	—	14.5%	17.7%	19.0%	4.8%	—	—
Earnings per share ($)	—	0.14	0.25	0.43	0.14	(0.16)	(2.81)
Stock price – high ($)	—	—	23.50	25.25	25.00	23.75	26.00
Stock price – low ($)	—	—	9.00	11.25	7.25	10.00	13.50
Stock price – close ($)	(3.6%)	—	21.25	20.25	10.75	22.63	18.38
P/E – high	—	—	94	59	179	—	—
P/E – low	—	—	36	26	52	—	—
Dividends per share ($)	—	—	0.00	0.00	0.00	0.00	0.00
Book value per share ($)	20.6%	—	2.57	3.13	3.46	5.43	5.44
Employees	115.5%	71	163	245	382	743	3,300

1995 YEAR-END
Debt ratio: 0.7%
Return on equity: —
Cash (mil.): $115
Current ratio: 1.99
Long-term debt (mil.): $2
No. of shares (mil.): 51
Dividends
Yield: —
Payout: —
Market value (mil.): $942
R&D as % of sales: 5.0%

POLICY MANAGEMENT SYSTEMS

OVERVIEW

Policy Management provides peace of mind to the ones who provide it to everyone else — insurance companies. The Columbia, South Carolina-based company offers software, administration, and information services to insurance and financial services companies. Its software products automate most insurance processing functions, including underwriting, claims handling and accounting. Its services include business-needs analysis; insurance, data processing, and project management consulting; and training.

Before it was incorporated in 1980, the company operated as a division of Seibels, Bruce & Company. It went public in 1981 and quickly gathered market share, but by 1986 the market was saturated. The cyclical nature of the business led Policy Management Systems to offer products and services to life and health insurance industry segments that year.

Policy Management bought Data Corporation, a provider of health insurance software, in 1991. Two years later it acquired life insurance data processor CYBERTEK (for $60 million) and Vital Data, a subsidiary of a Norwegian life insurer. Policy Management purchased Creative Insurance System Pty, of the UK, and Australia's Creative Computer Services in 1994, giving it access to midrange property and casualty business abroad.

The company sold its Health Insurance Systems division in 1995. That year Policy Management acquired Creative Group Holdings, a provider of software products and services principally to midsize general insurance companies. It also bought micado, a German provider of object-oriented client-server products to insurance and financial services companies, and the next year formed PMSmicado, a separate company.

WHO

Chairman, President, and CEO: G. Larry Wilson, age 49, $784,310 pay
EVP, Secretary, and General Counsel: Stephen G. Morrison, age 46, $520,700 pay
EVP and CFO: Timothy V. Williams, age 46, $387,858 pay
EVP: Donald A. Coggiola, age 56, $357,368 pay
EVP: David T. Bailey, age 49, $312,455 pay
Manager Personnel: G. C. Pundt
Auditors: Coopers & Lybrand L.L.P.

WHERE

HQ: Policy Management Systems Corporation, One PMSC Ctr., Intersection of Hwy. 27 & Hwy. 21 North, Blythewood, SC 29016
Phone: 803-735-4000   **Fax:** 803-735-5544
Web site: http://www.pmsc.com

WHAT

Selected Services
Business-needs analysis (coordination of company software with the customer's strategic plan)
Consulting (insurance, data processing, and project management consulting)
Education (company product training)
Information (review of underwriting risks)

Selected Software Products
Billing and Collection Management System (insurance policy billing and receivables management)
Financial Management System (general ledger software)
Management Information System (client/server-based data generation and manipulation system)
Pension and Life Insurance System (individual life insurance and pension plan processing)
Underwriting Workstation (stores and manages policy information in a central location to improve underwriting accuracy and consistency)

KEY COMPETITORS

ALLTEL	Delphi	IBM
Andersen	Information	Perot Systems
Consulting	DST	
Computer	EDS	
Sciences	Fiserv	

HOW MUCH

NYSE symbol: PMS FYE: December 31	Annual Growth	1990	1991	1992	1993	1994	1995
Sales ($ mil.)	9.2%	346.1	415.4	497.1	453.1	492.7	537.3
Net income ($ mil.)	(39.2%)	37.2	47.6	59.4	(56.1)	(9.7)	3.1
Income as % of sales	—	10.7%	11.5%	11.9%	—	—	0.6%
Earnings per share ($)	(38.4%)	1.80	2.14	2.55	(2.46)	0.46	0.16
Stock price – high ($)	—	43.50	66.38	83.50	87.25	47.75	54.25
Stock price – low ($)	—	30.00	39.38	59.75	21.63	25.75	37.75
Stock price – close ($)	2.8%	41.50	66.25	82.13	31.00	42.00	47.63
P/E – high	—	24	31	33	—	104	339
P/E – low	—	17	18	23	—	56	236
Dividends per share ($)	—	0.00	0.00	0.00	0.00	0.00	0.00
Book value per share ($)	3.3%	16.72	21.56	24.40	21.07	19.47	19.69
Employees	2.1%	4,204	4,403	4,363	4,786	4,678	4,655

1995 YEAR-END
Debt ratio: 4.2%
Return on equity: 0.8%
Cash (mil.): $40
Current ratio: 1.93
Long-term debt (mil.): $15
No. of shares (mil.): 19
Dividends
 Yield: —
 Payout: —
Market value (mil.): $926

POWER COMPUTING CORPORATION

OVERVIEW

An apple has finally fallen far from the tree. The first company to bring a Macintosh clone to market is based in Round Rock, Texas — a long way from Apple's Cupertino, California, headquarters. Power Computing builds Mac clones that are faster and cheaper than the real thing and also aims to surpass the notoriously lax Apple in customer service.

Although Power Computing sold 100,000 units in its first year of operations (surpassing the first-year performance of PC cloners like Dell and Compaq), it remains to be seen whether Apple's belated decision to license its operating system (which many consider superior to Windows) will halt the decline of the Mac's share of the personal computing market.

In 1993 executives at Italy's Olivetti decided that it was only a matter of time before Apple was driven by declining market share to begin licensing its operating system to other makers. The company found other investors and recruited industry wunderkind Steve Kahng to design a Macintosh clone. Kahng had become an industry legend by designing Daewoo's pioneering PC clone, Leading Edge Model D. Using cheaper, mostly non-Mac parts, Kahng and several former Apple product engineers came up with a workable prototype, which he showed to Apple. Apple had hoped to find a better-known licensing partner but ended up choosing Power Computing because no one more desirable came forward.

As soon as the licensing deal was announced in late 1994, Kahng began production with contract manufacturers. Within 6 months Power Computing had settled in Austin because it was able to negotiate for free administrative space by contracting with then-troubled, now-defunct computer maker CompuAdd. The first machines shipped in the spring of 1995. The following year the company moved its facilities to nearby Round Rock.

Power Computing had begun to cannibalize Apple sales by 1996. But Power Computing views itself as an Apple partner, rather than competitor, and has sought to minimize direct competition with Apple by emphasizing mail-order sales and production of machines for sale under other labels.

WHO

Chairman: Enzo Torresi
President and CEO: Steve Kahng
CFO: Song Kim
SVP Sales and Marketing: Geoff Burr
VP Engineering: Jon Fitch
VP International: Tom Howard
Director Human Resources: Kay Secord

WHERE

HQ: 2555 North Interstate 35, Round Rock, TX 78664
Phone: 512-246-7807   **Fax:** 512-388-6798
Web site: http://www.powercc.com

Power Computing has facilities in Round Rock, Texas, and Cupertino, California.

WHAT

Selected Products
Power/Center series
PowerTower series
PowerWave series

KEY COMPETITORS

Acer	Micron Electronics
Apple Computer	NEC
Canon	Packard Bell
Compaq	Sharp
DayStar	Siemens
DEC	Sony
Dell	Radius
Fujitsu	Texas Instruments
Gateway 2000	Toshiba
Hewlett-Packard	Unisys
Hitachi	
Hyundai	
IBM	
Machines Bull	
Matsushita	
Micro Electronics	

HOW MUCH

Private company FYE: June 30	Annual Growth	1991	1992	1993	1994	1995	1996
Sales ($ mil.)	—	—	—	—	—	0.0	250.0
Employees	—	—	—	—	—	20	300

PRODIGY SERVICES COMPANY

OVERVIEW

This prodigiously problematic progeny of Sears and IBM is going to go it alone. In May 1996 CEO Ed Bennett and other Prodigy executives joined cellular/Internet investment group International Wireless (largely owned by Mexican industrial firm Grupo Carso) in an agreement to acquire the company from IBM and Sears. For the estimated $250 million purchase price — far below the billion-plus dollars invested in Prodigy by its sellers — the new owners have taken over an online also-ran that even its management has described as "slow, lame, and ugly." White Plains, New York-based Prodigy was the first consumer online service in the US, but it has a reputation for poor graphics and slow service, and with under 2 million subscribers it lags far behind rivals America Online and CompuServe.

Prodigy was founded in 1984 as a joint venture by IBM, Sears, and CBS (which dropped out in 1986). Originally called Trintex and led by former IBM executive Theodore Papes, the company launched its first service in 1988. Trintex marketed itself as a shopping and banking service for households, particularly for time-pressured women. It changed its name to Prodigy in 1989 and the next year made its national debut. However, by 1992 Prodigy users were more interested in e-mail and bulletin boards than shopping online. The company started to charge for e-mail, leading many users to switch to CompuServe and AOL.

In 1994 Prodigy began a major overhaul of its service, adding slicker graphics. In 1995 former MTV chief Bennett took over as CEO. That year Prodigy became the first major online service to offer access to the World Wide Web.

In 1996 Prodigy announced plans to lay off 115 employees as part of its strategy to concentrate on the Internet. Shortly after the takeover, Bennett resigned his posts to take over as head of the newly created investment firm, Prodigy Ventures. Although all involved characterized the change as voluntary, some industry observers felt that International Wireless had been unhappy with the pace of change at Prodigy. International Wireless executives Greg Carr and Paul DeLacey took over as Prodigy's chairman and CEO, respectively.

WHO

Chairman: Greg Carr
President and CEO: Paul DeLacey
EVP and COO: William J. Lansing
EVP and General Manager, Internet Services: Gerry Mueller
SVP Content: Josh Grotstein
SVP Communications: Barry Kluger
SVP and General Manager New Product Development: Scott Danielson
VP and CFO: J. Mark Hattendorf
VP and General Counsel: Marc Jacobson
Director Human Resources: Nicolas Lapko

WHERE

HQ: 445 Hamilton Ave., White Plains, NY 10601
Phone: 914-448-8000   **Fax:** 914-448-8083
Web site: http://www.prodigy.com

WHAT

Selected Services
Bulletin boards
Business and finance news
Chat groups
Consumer Reports
Downloadable software
E-mail
Entertainment news
Horoscopes
Internet access
Movie/video reviews
Music reviews
National and world news
Online shopping
Reference materials
Sports news
Travel guides and reservation system
Weather forecasts

KEY COMPETITORS

America Online
ASCIINet
AT&T Corp.
CompuServe
Dow Jones
MCI
MFS Communications
Microsoft
NETCOM
PC Van
People World
PSINet

HOW MUCH

Private company FYE: December 31	Annual Growth	1990	1991	1992	1993	1994	1995
Estimated sales ($ mil.)	35.6%	48.0	119.0	150.0	180.0	200.0	220.0
Employees	(44.1%)	—	—	1,050	800	600	485

PRODIGY.

QUARK, INC.

OVERVIEW

Quark has written a real page-turner. The Denver-based company's flagship software, QuarkXPress, is the leading page layout software, an application that helps designers assemble text and graphics into documents such as books, brochures, or newsletters. QuarkXPress has more than half of the desktop publishing market worldwide and is available for both PCs and Macintosh computers and in 24 languages. The firm is jumping from the printed page to the Internet with the release of QuarkImmedia, its Web site authoring software. Founder and chairman Tim Gill and CEO Fred Ebrahimi each own 50% of Quark.

In 1981 Gill, then 27, founded Quark after being laid off from a job at a Denver music software company. He believed "Quark" (named after the subatomic particle that got its name from James Joyce's *Finnegans Wake*) would stand out in the classified sections of magazines. Gill wrote a word processing program, called Word Juggler, for the Apple III computer, beating the competition (including Apple) to market by 6 months. Several other word processing products followed. In 1986 Gill sold half the company to Ebrahimi and handed over administrative and sales duties. The firm introduced QuarkXPress the next year. In 1992 it introduced a Windows version of QuarkXPress, launched the Quark Publishing System, and introduced QuarkXPress Passport, a multilingual version. A lower-priced configuration of its Quark Publishing System for editorial management debuted in 1994.

The company announced 2 new software programs in 1995, QuarkImmedia and QuarkXPosure. QuarkImmedia lets designers add multimedia components such as sound and video to files created in QuarkXPress for use on CD-ROMs or the Web; QuarkXPosure is electronic image manipulation software. Amid ongoing rumors that it is preparing to go public, in 1996 the company acquired a stake in Colossal Pictures, a San Francisco-based film and video special-effects and design studio whose clients include Coca-Cola and electronic game maker SEGA. The purchase moves Quark further into the realm of multimedia and is expected to help boost recognition of QuarkImmedia.

WHO

Chairman; SVP Research and Development:
Timothy E. Gill, age 41
President and CEO: Farhad Fred Ebrahimi, age 56
CFO: Kenneth J. Collins, age 48
VP Research and Development: Raymond Fink
VP Product Management: Wayne Yamamoto, age 38
Manager Public Relations: Bob Monzel
Director Human Resources: D. Witonsky

WHERE

HQ: 1800 Grant St., Denver, CO 80203
Phone: 303-894-8888   **Fax:** 303-894-3399
Web site: http://www.quark.com

Quark has international offices in Denmark, France, Germany, Ireland, Japan, and the UK.

WHAT

Selected Products
Quark Publishing System (editorial management system for workgroups)
QuarkCopyDesk (word processing and editing)
QuarkDispatch
  QuarkDispatch Administrator (configuring)
  QuarkDispatch FileManager (archiving)
  QuarkDispatch Planner (assigning and tracking)
  QuarkDispatch XTension to QuarkXPress (connects QuarkXPress to publishing system)
QuarkImmedia (high-end multimedia and Internet design and viewing software)
QuarkXPosure (image editing)
QuarkXPress (page layout)
QuarkXPress Passport (multilingual system that supports 10 languages)

Selected Publications Produced Using Quark Products
The Calgary Herald (Canada)
Die Woche (Germany)
Esquire
FORTUNE
Hoover's MasterList of Major U.S. Companies
Info-Matin (France)
La Repubblica (Italy)
Macy's catalog
The New York Times
Rolling Stone
Time
The Wall Street Journal

KEY COMPETITORS

Adobe
ColorAge
Corel
Deneba
Electronics for

Imaging
Interleaf
Linotype-Hell
Lotus
Microsoft

Multi-Ad
Services
Scitex
SoftKey

HOW MUCH

Private company FYE: June 30	Annual Growth	1990	1991	1992	1993	1994	1995
Sales ($ mil.)	46.1%	30.0	50.0	80.0	120.0	168.0	200.0
Employees	53.7%	70	200	—	420	520	600

QUARTERDECK CORPORATION

OVERVIEW

By seizing other ships, Quarterdeck has not only avoided a watery grave, but launched a new flotilla. The California-based firm develops, markets, and supports Internet, telecommunications, and utility software. Quarterdeck has been feverishly acquiring companies, products, and services to broaden its offerings. Investors Warren White and Michael Siewruk own about 7% and 6% of the firm's shares, respectively.

Quarterdeck Office Systems was founded in a garage (yes, really) in 1982 by Therese Myers and Gary Pope to develop software to enhance a PC's performance. Although Microsoft was its main rival, Quarterdeck was also dependent on the Windows maker. It went public in 1991.

Sales of its QEMM memory manager software continued to be strong through the early 1990s, but when Microsoft began improving Windows's memory management software, Quarterdeck's sales plummeted. The head of a consulting firm, King Lee, took over from Myers in a 1994 shake-up. In 1995 Gaston Bastiaens, a former general manager at Apple Computer, replaced Lee as president and CEO. That year the company changed its name to Quarterdeck Corporation.

Quarterdeck turned to Internet users for a new revenue source. Quarterdeck acquired Internetware (Internet software for Novell networks), Prospero Systems Research (Internet chat software), and StarNine Technologies (Internet server and e-mail software).

Continuing its Internet-related acquisitions in 1996, Quarterdeck announced it would buy Datastorm Technologies (communications software) and Future Labs Inc. (document-sharing products). Bastiaens resigned unexpectedly in September 1996. Later that year the company announced it would lay off 40% of its workforce as part of a restructuring aimed at curbing mounting losses.

WHO

Chairman: Frank W. T. LaHaye, age 66
Temporary Office of the President: King R. Lee and Anatoly Tikhman
SVP Worldwide Sales: James D. Moise, age 40, $334,069 pay
SVP and General Manager Internet Services: Stephen W. Tropp, age 40, $217,736 pay (prior to promotion)
SVP and General Counsel: Bradley D. Schwartz
SVP and CFO: Frank R. Greico
VP Internet Products: Emerick M. Woods, age 40, $264,884 pay
VP Strategic Business Development and Chief Technology Officer: Robert D. Kutnick, age 38
Director Human Resources: Teresa Hammond
Auditors: KPMG Peat Marwick LLP

WHERE

HQ: 13160 Mindanao Way, Marina del Rey, CA 90292-9705
Phone: 310-309-3700 **Fax:** 310-309-4218
Web site: http://www.qdeck.com

WHAT

Selected Products

Internet
Quarterdeck WebAuthor
Quarterdeck WebServer

Memory Management and Utilities
CleanSweep 95
MagnaRAM 2

Telecommunications and Collaborative Computing
eXpertise
Quarterdeck Mosaic
WebTalk

KEY COMPETITORS

Adobe	Frontier	NetManage
Apple Computer	Technologies	Netscape
Asymetrix	FTP Software	Novell
CompuServe	IBM	SoftQuad
ForeFront	ichat	Symantec
	Microsoft	

HOW MUCH

Nasdaq symbol: QDEK FYE: September 30	Annual Growth	1990	1991	1992	1993	1994	1995
Sales ($ mil.)	21.9%	26.3	48.0	55.0	44.9	26.8	70.7
Net income ($ mil.)	(8.2%)	6.3	12.0	9.1	1.2	(21.2)	4.1
Income as % of sales	—	23.8%	25.0%	16.6%	2.8%	—	5.8%
Earnings per share ($)	(14.0%)	0.34	0.63	0.45	0.06	(1.06)	0.16
Stock price – high ($)	—	—	23.75	26.63	4.50	4.13	39.50
Stock price – low ($)	—	—	11.50	3.63	1.94	1.88	2.75
Stock price – close ($)	4.3%	—	23.25	4.13	2.19	3.13	27.50
P/E – high	—	—	38	59	75	—	34
P/E – low	—	—	18	8	32	—	2
Dividends per share ($)	—	—	0.00	0.00	0.00	0.00	0.00
Book value per share ($)	(7.4%)	—	1.92	2.43	2.46	1.40	1.41
Employees	43.0%	89	190	302	291	198	532

1995 YEAR-END
Debt ratio: 0.5%
Return on equity: 13.1%
Cash (mil.): $23
Current ratio: 2.18
Long-term debt (mil.): $0
No. of shares (mil.): 20
Dividends
  Yield: —
  Payout: —
Market value (mil.): $550
R&D as % of sales: 12.0%

RADIUS INC.

OVERVIEW

Radius hopes the bruised Apple market comes full circle. Headquartered in Sunnyvale, California, the company manufactures peripheral equipment used to create and alter audio, graphics, and video on Apple computers. Its digital editing systems, graphics cards, and other products are used primarily in the publishing and professional multimedia industries. Radius lost a piece of its market pie when Apple began including graphics capabilities in its PowerPCs. However, while Apple computers remain popular in the publishing world, their declining market share overall could spell more trouble for Radius.

The enterprise was founded in 1985 by Michael Boich, who sold his house to set up the company. An alumnus of the Macintosh development team of Apple cofounder Steve Jobs, Boich went after a niche neglected by Apple — monitors. Radius soon became the top independent provider of high-resolution displays for the Mac. It went public in 1990. Boich stepped down as CEO in 1993. The next year the company merged with rival SuperMac Technologies, which helped Radius enter the Windows graphics market. Also in 1994 it bought VideoFusion (video effects and editing software), but profits were hurt by accounting charges from buyouts and the settling of 2 class-action lawsuits, which alleged improprieties that caused stock price declines at both SuperMac and Radius.

In 1995 Radius began producing Apple clones based on the Macintosh operating system. But with sales of its high-margin graphics cards on a skid, it cut its payroll nearly in half. The next year Radius sold its monochrome monitor unit to Electrohome Ltd. and agreed to sell its Mac cloning unit to UMAX Data Systems to form UMAX Computer Corp., in which it will retain a 20% interest.

WHO

Chairman, President, and CEO: Charles W. Berger, age 41, $323,700 pay
VP Engineering and Chief Technology Officer: Gregory M. Millar, age 39, $347,700 pay
VP Sales and Marketing: J. Daniel Shaver, $318,734 pay
VP and General Manager, Europe: Keith M. Harris, age 37, $209,181 pay
VP and General Manager, Pacific, Asia, and Latin America: Douglas W. C. Boake, age 30, $200,615 pay
VP Human Resources: Dawn Thompson
CFO: Dennis J. Dunnigan, age 40
Auditors: Ernst & Young LLP

WHERE

HQ: 215 Moffett Park Dr., Sunnyvale, CA 94089
Phone: 408-541-6100   **Fax:** 408-541-6150
Web site: http://www.radius.com

WHAT

Selected Products

Accelerated Color Graphics Products
ColorEngine
PhotoEngine
PrecisionColor
Thunder and ThunderColor

Color Reference Displays
PrecisionView 21
PressView

Color Server Products
Splash MX
Splash TX

Digital Video Systems and Software
QuickFlix!
Radius Telecast
Video Vision Studio
VideoFusion

KEY COMPETITORS

Apple Computer	Compression	Diamond
ATI Technologies	Labs	Multimedia
Avid Technology	Data Translation	Matrox

HOW MUCH

Nasdaq symbol: RDUSC FYE: September 30	Annual Growth	1990	1991	1992	1993	1994	1995
Sales ($ mil.)	22.7%	110.6	118.6	159.6	134.9	324.8	308.1
Net income ($ mil.)	—	6.2	3.7	7.1	(18.0)	(77.5)	(131.7)
Income as % of sales	—	5.6%	3.1%	4.4%	—	—	—
Earnings per share ($)	—	1.06	0.54	1.00	(2.64)	(5.70)	(8.75)
Stock price – high ($)	—	21.00	21.00	25.00	18.25	18.25	15.00
Stock price – low ($)	—	11.00	10.00	7.50	6.25	7.38	1.88
Stock price – close ($)	(29.7%)	11.50	19.75	8.75	15.25	8.50	1.97
P/E – high	—	20	39	25	—	—	—
P/E – low	—	10	19	8	—	—	—
Dividends per share ($)	—	0.00	0.00	0.00	0.00	0.00	0.00
Book value per share ($)	—	7.42	8.00	9.05	6.41	2.54	(3.33)
Employees	(5.5%)	315	347	416	366	539	237

1995 YEAR-END
Debt ratio: 100.0%
Return on equity: —
Cash (mil.): $5
Current ratio: 0.59
Long-term debt (mil.): $1
No. of shares (mil.): 17
Dividends
 Yield: —
 Payout: —
Market value (mil.): $34
R&D as % of sales: 6.3%

S3 INCORPORATED

OVERVIEW

S3 doesn't make razors, but it can shave off some of the time you wait for your computer to process images and sound. The Santa Clara, California-based company's products, called graphics accelerators, work with a PC's central processing unit by handling weighty graphics information, thereby freeing the CPU to deal with general computing functions. S3 also makes graphics and video accelerators for both 2-D and 3-D images as well as sound and image processors, which enhance a computer's full-motion video capabilities. S3's sales are benefiting from computer users' thirst for faster and better graphics.

By the time Dado Banatao and Ronald Yara founded S3 in 1989, starting companies was old hat. (The name S3 stands for "start-up number 3.") The pair had previously founded a short-lived business called Mostron and then semiconductor maker Chips & Technologies. They originally envisioned company #3 as a maker of superfast PCs, but the venture capitalists to whom they pitched the idea suggested they just concentrate on making graphics accelerators. Banatao and Yara agreed and set out to make the fastest accelerator they could. In 1991 S3 introduced the world's first single-chip graphical user interface accelerator. Signing up several major computer makers, including Hewlett-Packard (which bought S3's accelerator sight unseen), gave the company a running start. With the huge success of Microsoft's Windows operating system, which increased demand for the company's products, S3's sales took off. In 1993 the company went public.

S3 is concentrating on the entry-level home PC market, offering products such as the Trio64UV+ multimedia accelerator (launched in 1995). It introduced its first accelerator for notebook PCs, the Aurora64V+, in 1996.

WHO

Chairman: Diosdado P. Banatao, age 49, $923,149 pay
President and CEO: Gary J. Johnson, age 36, $549,794 pay
SVP Finance and CFO: George A. Hervey, age 49, $528,606 pay
SVP Engineering/Operations: Jackson K. C. Hu, age 46, $523,897 pay
SVP Strategic Marketing and Secretary: Ronald T. Yara, age 48, $512,754 pay
SVP Sales: Harry L. Dickinson, age 46
VP Operations: Paul G. Franklin, age 52
VP Human Resources: Cecilia A. Hayes, age 39
Auditors: Deloitte & Touche LLP

WHERE

HQ: 2770 San Tomas Expwy., Santa Clara, CA 95051-0968
Phone: 408-980-5400   **Fax:** 408-980-5444
Web site: http://www.s3.com/

	1995 Sales
	% of total
US	56
Other countries	44
Total	**100**

WHAT

Selected Products
2-D graphics and video accelerators
3-D graphics and video accelerators
MPEG decoders and audio processors

Selected Brand Names
Aurora 64V+
Trio 64UV+
ViRGE
Vision

KEY COMPETITORS

ATI Technologies	Evans &	Trident
Chips and	Sutherland	Microsystems
Technologies	Number Nine	Tseng Labs
Cirrus Logic	Visual	Weitek
Diamond	Silicon Graphics	Western Digital
Multimedia	STB Systems	

HOW MUCH

Nasdaq symbol: SIII FYE: December 31	Annual Growth	1990	1991	1992	1993	1994	1995
Sales ($ mil.)	212.9%	—	3.3	30.6	113.0	140.3	316.3
Net income ($ mil.)	—	—	(4.9)	4.4	15.1	5.5	35.4
Income as % of sales	—	—	—	14.4%	13.4%	3.9%	11.2%
Earnings per share ($)	34.2%	—	—	0.31	0.41	0.14	0.75
Stock price – high ($)	—	—	—	—	10.31	9.63	21.94
Stock price – low ($)	—	—	—	—	4.75	3.25	7.56
Stock price – close ($)	44.5%	—	—	—	8.44	7.88	17.63
P/E – high	—	—	—	—	25	69	29
P/E – low	—	—	—	—	12	23	10
Dividends per share ($)	—	—	—	—	0.00	0.00	0.00
Book value per share ($)	59.9%	—	—	—	1.72	1.89	4.40
Employees	—	—	—	—	—	—	449

1995 YEAR-END
Debt ratio: 13.9%
Return on equity: 25.8%
Cash (mil.): $94
Current ratio: 2.59
Long-term debt (mil.): $24
No. of shares (mil.): 47
Dividends
  Yield: —
  Payout: —
Market value (mil.): $825
R&D as % of sales: 13.3%

SANDISK CORPORATION

OVERVIEW

SanDisk resulted from a flash of inspiration: store computer data on a memory chip instead of a rotating disk. The Sunnyvale, California-based company makes storage products based on nonvolatile — or flash — memory. SanDisk's integrated circuits retain data when power is off, whereas other memory chips lose data as soon as power is lost. SanDisk has an industry-leading 32% share of the flash memory market. Its products include removable and embedded memory cards and are used in products ranging from cellular phones and laptop computers to medical devices and aircraft. The company's customers include AT&T, Boeing, Hewlett-Packard, and Mitsubishi. Seagate, which also makes computer storage products, owns about 28% of the company. SanDisk president Harari owns about 7%.

SanDisk was founded as SunDisk in 1988 by Eli Harari, an expert on nonvolatile memory technology and a veteran of Honeywell, Intel, and Hughes. SunDisk's first product, based on a 4-megabit flash chip, was developed with AT&T Bell Labs and released in 1991. The company has been an innovator in flash memory technology, earning more than 28 patents. Seagate bought 25% of the company in 1993.

SunDisk was being confused with Sun Microsystems, so in 1995 it changed its name to SanDisk. The company went public later that year. It also introduced the industry's smallest Type II flash storage card, the CompactFlash ("Type II" designates a PC card slot size).

In 1996 Canon and Eastman Kodak both debuted digital cameras that store pictures on SanDisk memory cards. That year SanDisk continued its development work on a double-density (D2) flash that stores 2 bits of information in each memory cell. The company hopes to begin D2 production in 1997.

WHO

Chairman: Irwin Federman, age 60
President and CEO: Eli Harari, age 50, $388,603 pay
SVP Marketing and Sales: Leon Malmed, age 58, $297,747 pay
SVP Operations and Technology: Daniel Auclair, age 49, $242,466 pay
SVP Finance and Administration, CFO, and Secretary: Cindy Burgdorf, age 48, $231,462 pay
VP Human Resources: Marianne Jackson, age 40, $125,428 pay
Auditors: Ernst & Young LLP

WHERE

HQ: 140 Caspian Ct., Sunnyvale, CA 94089
Phone: 408-542-0500   **Fax:** 408-542-0403
Web site: http://www.sandisk.com

	1995 Sales	
	$ mil.	% of total
US	27.2	43
Japan	24.3	39
Other Far East	8.1	13
Europe	3.2	5
Total	**62.8**	**100**

WHAT

Selected Products
CompactFlash (reduced-size removable storage cards)
Flash Chipsets (sets of ATA controller and flash memory chips or multiple memory chips)
FlashDisk (removable storage cards)
FlashDrives (1.3" and 1.8" embedded storage products)

KEY COMPETITORS

AMD
Atmel
Cirrus Logic
Hitachi
IBM
Intel
Mitsubishi

M-Systems Flash Disk
  Pioneers
Samsung
Silicon Storage
TDK
Toshiba

HOW MUCH

Nasdaq symbol: SNDK FYE: December 31	Annual Growth	1990	1991	1992	1993	1994	1995
Sales ($ mil.)	120.7%	1.2	2.9	22.4	20.6	35.4	62.8
Net income ($ mil.)	—	(3.7)	(8.4)	(6.0)	(10.0)	(4.3)	9.1
Income as % of sales	—	—	—	—	—	—	14.4%
Earnings per share ($)	—	—	—	—	—	(0.23)	0.43
Stock price – high ($)	—	—	—	—	—	—	31.00
Stock price – low ($)	—	—	—	—	—	—	13.50
Stock price – close ($)	—	—	—	—	—	—	15.00
P/E – high	—	—	—	—	—	—	72
P/E – low	—	—	—	—	—	—	31
Dividends per share ($)	—	—	—	—	—	—	0.00
Book value per share ($)	—	—	—	—	—	—	3.29
Employees	—	—	—	—	—	—	208	255

1995 YEAR-END
Debt ratio: 0.1%
Return on equity: 14.0%
Cash (mil.): $68
Current ratio: 4.44
Long-term debt (mil.): $0
No. of shares (mil.): 22
Dividends
  Yield: —
  Payout: —
Market value (mil.): $330
R&D as % of sales: 12.8%

THE SANTA CRUZ OPERATION, INC.

OVERVIEW

The Santa Cruz Operation (SCO) wants UnixWare (its version of the Unix operating system for servers) to foil the plans of 800-pound gorilla Microsoft. The California-based software company is the leading provider of Unix operating systems for Intel microprocessor-based computers. With Windows NT threatening to become the only network operating system, Compaq and other computer makers have lined up behind SCO's effort to establish its version of Unix as the "standard." Network software maker Novell owns 16.5% of the firm.

SCO was founded in 1979 by father and son Larry and Doug Michels, who own about 20% of the company. Larry was a defense industry management consultant who had founded a credit card verification company (sold to TRW in 1969). Doug was a college student with his own computer consulting business. The pair merged their companies, and in 1983 SCO introduced its first UNIX-based products.

But the products were slow to catch on, and the company nearly went broke. It survived by taking on outside investors, including rival Microsoft, which owns 11% of the company. Larry Michels resigned in 1992, under a cloud of sexual harassment charges, and was succeeded by Swedish-born Lars Turndal. The company went public in 1993.

In 1994 SCO formed a joint marketing venture with Tomen (a Japanese trading firm). The company acquired Visionware Ltd., a British developer of PC-to-UNIX connectivity software, for $14.8 million (which it charged against earnings in 1995).

The company acquired Novell's Unix business in late 1995. The next year it announced a 64-bit operating system development deal with Hewlett-Packard, and it introduced an Internet server product.

WHO

President and CEO: Alok Mohan, age 47, $333,720 pay
EVP and Chief Technical Officer: Douglas L. Michels, age 41, $294,113 pay
SVP and Managing Director, Europe and International: John Bernard Hulme, age 50, $267,976 pay
SVP Products: Scott McGregor, age 39, $246,374 pay
SVP and General Manager, The Americas: Edwin Adams, age 51, $224,348 pay
SVP Operations and CFO: John Jarvis, age 51
VP Marketing: David McCrabb, age 47
VP Human Resources: Jack Moyer, age 46
Auditors: KPMG Peat Marwick LLP

WHERE

HQ: 400 Encinal St., Santa Cruz, CA 95060
Phone: 408-425-7222   **Fax:** 408-458-4227
Web site: http://www.sco.com

WHAT

	1995 Sales	
	$ mil.	% of total
Licenses	177.5	89
Services	21.8	11
Total	**199.3**	**100**

Selected Products and Services
Consulting
IXI Eye2eye (networked applications environment)
SCO classes
SCO OpenServer Desktop System
SCO OpenServer Enterprise System
SCO OpenServer Host System
SCO POS Toolkit
SCO Security Services
Visionware X.Vision (PC X server and terminal emulator)

KEY COMPETITORS

Data General
DEC
Hewlett-Packard
IBM
Microsoft
Olivetti
Sun Microsystems

HOW MUCH

Nasdaq symbol: SCOC FYE: September 30	Annual Growth	1990	1991	1992	1993	1994	1995
Sales ($ mil.)	13.3%	106.9	135.6	163.7	178.2	184.1	199.3
Net income ($ mil.)	—	(3.5)	(11.1)	8.5	13.8	14.2	(6.1)
Income as % of sales	—	—	—	5.2%	7.8%	7.7%	—
Earnings per share ($)	—	(0.15)	(0.46)	0.32	0.47	0.45	(0.20)
Stock price – high ($)	—	—	—	—	13.00	11.50	15.00
Stock price – low ($)	—	—	—	—	4.75	4.88	5.50
Stock price – close ($)	(3.8%)	—	—	—	6.75	9.38	6.25
P/E – high	—	—	—	—	28	26	—
P/E – low	—	—	—	—	10	11	—
Dividends per share ($)	—	—	—	—	0.00	0.00	0.00
Book value per share ($)	5.5%	—	—	—	2.39	2.93	2.66
Employees	(2.0%)	1,249	1,358	1,163	1,208	1,205	1,128

1995 YEAR-END
Debt ratio: 0.0%
Return on equity: —
Cash (mil.): $47
Current ratio: 2.47
Long-term debt (mil.): $0
No. of shares (mil.): 31
Dividends
  Yield: —
  Payout: —
Market value (mil.): $193
R&D as % of sales: 16.7%

SECURITY DYNAMICS

OVERVIEW

Computer hackers beware: Security Dynamics Technologies is on the job. The Cambridge, Massachusetts-based company provides software and hardware security products for computers and networks. Its primary product, SecurID Tokens, prevents unauthorized access by requiring the user to enter a PIN number along with a random access code displayed on a hand-held card or token. Display codes, which are changed every 60 seconds, are then transmitted along with the PIN to a control module that manages user access.

The company, which is the market leader in smart card security systems, has acquired encryption software developer RSA Data Security. A leading provider of security products for Internet software developers, RSA licenses tool kits to Microsoft, Netscape, and others, and it manufactures RSA Secure, an end-user encryption system. Jim Bidzos, former president of RSA and current EVP at Security Dynamics, owns 17.5% of the company.

Security Dynamics was started in 1984 by Kenneth Weiss, inventor of the SecurID technology. At first, the company was primarily a research and development firm, but it moved into production of SecurID tokens and access control module (ACM) hardware in 1986. The company introduced its ACM software for mainframes and minicomputers in 1988 and its ACM software for intranets in 1991.

Security Dynamics has benefited from the increasing number of LANs and WANs, and attributes its success to the growing number of users with access to corporate intranets and confidential data. The company's purchase of RSA was part of its strategy to improve its position in the growing Internet and electronic commerce markets by tapping into RSA's Internet-focused customer base.

WHO

Chairman, President, and CEO: Charles R. Stuckey Jr., age 53, $473,434 pay
EVP, Treasurer, and CFO: Arthur W. Coviello Jr., age 42
VP Sales, The Americas: Robert W. Fine, age 53, $272,973 pay
VP Marketing: James M. Geary, age 39, $187,681 pay
VP Operations: Linda E. Saris, age 43, $139,719 pay
Director Human Resources: Vivian Vitale
Auditors: Deloitte & Touche LLP

WHERE

HQ: Security Dynamics Technologies, Inc., One Alewife Ctr., Cambridge, MA 02140
Phone: 617-547-7820   **Fax:** 617-354-8836
Web site: http://www.securid.com

WHAT

SecurID Tokens
SecurID Card (credit-card sized with LCD)
SecurID PINPAD Card (credit-card sized with keypad)
SecurID Key Fob (token for keychain)
ACE/SERVER (security software for client/server networks)

Access Control Module (software for host-based production)
DEC Open VMS/VAX and Alpha environments
IBM/MVS mainframe
CRAY/UNICOS supercomputers

Access Control Module (hardware for host-based systems)
ACM/1600 HS (for 16 RS/232 ports)
ACM/400 HS (for mid-sized computer environments)
ACM/100 HS (for small systems)

KEY COMPETITORS

Cylink
Digital Pathway
Information Resources
Leemah Datacom
Lucent
Machines Bull

Northern Telecom
Rainbow Technologies
Secure
Schlumberger
V-ONE

HOW MUCH

Nasdaq symbol: SDTI FYE: December 31	Annual Growth	1990	1991	1992	1993	1994	1995
Sales ($ mil.)	44.7%	5.3	6.1	8.9	12.1	17.6	33.6
Net income ($ mil.)	80.8%	0.3	0.5	1.2	1.7	2.3	5.8
Income as % of sales	—	6.2%	7.6%	13.6%	13.8%	13.2%	17.2%
Earnings per share ($)	55.6%	—	—	—	0.19	0.25	0.46
Stock price – high ($)	—	—	—	—	—	10.13	58.25
Stock price – low ($)	—	—	—	—	—	7.00	8.81
Stock price – close ($)	—	—	—	—	—	9.31	54.50
P/E – high	—	—	—	—	—	41	127
P/E – low	—	—	—	—	—	28	19
Dividends per share ($)	—	—	—	—	—	0.00	0.00
Book value per share ($)	—	—	—	—	—	2.59	7.06
Employees	—	—	—	—	—	94	162

1995 YEAR-END
Debt ratio: 0.0%
Return on equity: 9.4%
Cash (mil.): $90
Current ratio: 15.06
Long-term debt (mil.): $0
No. of shares (mil.): 14
Dividends
  Yield: —
  Payout: —
Market value (mil.): $733
R&D as % of sales: 12.0%

SEMATECH, INC.

OVERVIEW

With government funding coming to an end, research consortium SEMATECH has two options: declare itself successful in its mission to make US semiconductors premier in the world and gracefully quit, or find a new mission. The Austin-based consortium has no intention of quitting — it has issued a new mission statement, formed a separate organization inviting international participation, and bumped up its dues 30% to cover lost funding. Member companies say their return is $4.40 for each dollar spent on the organization, and US makers now hold 43% of the world's semiconductor market, compared with Japan's 37%. SEMATECH (for SEmiconductor MAnufacturing TECHnology) funds research into areas such as lithography and materials processing to improve semiconductor manufacturing techniques.

In 1986, when Secretary of Defense Caspar Weinberger learned that half the chips in an F-16's fire-control radar came from Japan, he wanted to find a way to improve US technology. By that year Japan had overtaken the US and had become #1 in semiconductor manufacturing. Enter the Semiconductor Industry Association (SIA), a group of leading US manufacturers. SIA directors, led by Robert Noyce (coinventor of the semiconductor), founded SEMATECH in 1987 with $100 million per year for 5 years from the DOD's Defense Advance Research Projects Agency and another $100 million per year from 14 member companies.

While SEMATECH made technological advances, critics complained that it benefited only the largest companies and that these members dominated the agenda; in 1991 Micron Technology and LSI Logic, the 2 smallest members, dropped out. In 1992 SEMATECH's government funding was extended, although it was lowered to $90 million a year. That year the US became #1 in semiconductor manufacturing again.

In 1994 SEMATECH announced it would phase out its federal backing by 1998. A planned slashing of federal funding to $39 million got scuttled in 1996, and SEMATECH received $89 million.

WHO

Chairman, President, and CEO: William J. Spencer
VC: Robert W. Galvin
COO: Jim Owens
Chief Administrative Officer: Frank Squires
General Counsel: Robert Falstad
Director Communications: Ann Marett
Director Critical Materials, Information, and Planning Department: Bill Swiss
Director Finance: Dan Damon
Director Human Resources: Mike Foster
Director Information Systems: Renee Inge
Director Supplier Relations: Randy Buchanan
Director Total Quality: Phil Pierce
Auditors: General Accounting Office

WHERE

HQ: 2706 Montopolis Dr., Austin, TX 78741-6499
Phone: 512-356-3500   **Fax:** 512-356-3086
Web site: http://www.sematech.org/public/home.html

WHAT

SEMATECH Focus Technical Advisory Boards	Consortium Members
Assembly & Packaging	AMD
Contamination-Free Manufacturing	DEC
Critical Materials	Hewlett-Packard
Design	IBM
Environment, Safety & Health	Intel
Equipment Modeling	Lucent Technologies
Factory Integration & Productivity Analysis	Motorola
Lithography	National Semiconductor
Manufacturing Systems	Rockwell International
Materials & Bulk Processes	Texas Instruments
Multi-Level Metal	United States Department of Defense
Operational Modeling	
Plasma Etch	
Strategic Technology	
Technology Computer-Aided Design (TCAD)	
Test	

HOW MUCH

Research consortium FYE: December 31	Annual Growth	1990	1991	1992	1993	1994	1995
Annual budget ($ mil.)	(2.1%)	200.0	200.0	200.0	200.0	180.0	180.0
Employees	(3.1%)	701	729	723	742	841	600

SEQUENT COMPUTER SYSTEMS, INC.

OVERVIEW

Sequent is reaching down to lift its business higher. Headquartered in Beaverton, Oregon, Sequent Computer Systems is the world's #1 vendor of high-end UNIX systems used for decision support, Internet business communications, and online transaction processing. Its open systems are used by such multilocation businesses as Japan's FamilyMart convenience stores, Dean Witter credit card services, and petroleum refiner and marketer Unocal. The company is broadening its offerings by developing servers for PC networks.

Karl "Casey" Powell and Scott Gibson started the enterprise in 1983 to develop symmetric multiprocessing (SMP) computers. The next year the company released the first SMP version of UNIX. Sequent in 1986 unveiled a UNIX SMP system capable of linking up to 30 microprocessors. The company went public in 1987. Sequent benefited from the inherent superiority of SMP for relational database management systems, which were replacing hierarchical databases in the late 1980s. In 1991 it launched the NetWare system, which enabled thousands of PCs to be linked on a single network. That year sales slipped as a recession caused customers to put off large purchases. The company restructured, emphasized sales of systems costing less than $100,000, and laid off 450 employees. Gibson left in 1992, after sales and profits rebounded.

Sequent widened its market base in 1994 by tying up a deal with Sybase whereby that company's Replication Server would run on Sequent's Symmetry SMP systems. It purchased Dutch software firm Open Tool International, a maker of mainframe-to-UNIX migration tools, in 1995. The next year Sequent planned to acquire Chen Systems (founded by Steve Chen, veteran of mainframe maker Cray Research and founder of Supercomputer Systems).

WHO

Chairman and CEO: Karl Casey Powell Jr., age 52, $630,210 pay
President and COO: John McAdam, age 45, $428,336 pay
SVP Finance and Legal and CFO: Robert S. Gregg, age 42, $268,254 pay
VP Worldwide Customer Services: Robert A. Brooks
VP Human Resources: Diane M. Williams
Auditors: Price Waterhouse LLP

WHERE

HQ: 15450 SW Koll Pkwy., Beaverton, OR 97006-6063
Phone: 503-626-5700   **Fax:** 503-578-9890
Web site: http://www.sequent.com

WHAT

	1995 Sales	
	$ mil.	% of total
Products	395.9	73
Service & other	144.4	27
Total	**540.3**	**100**

Selected Products
Client/server application software
Communications hardware and software
Corporate digital libraries
Internet Accelerator
Symmetry 5000 Series servers
UNIX-based SMP systems

Selected Services
Hardware maintenance
Systems administration
System design and implementation

KEY COMPETITORS

Amdahl	IBM	Silicon Graphics
Data General	McKinsey & Co.	Stratus
DEC	NEC	Computer
EDS	Perot Systems	Sun
Fujitsu	Pyramid	Microsystems
Hewlett-Packard	Technology	Tandem
Hitachi	Siemens	Unisys

HOW MUCH

Nasdaq symbol: SQNT FYE: December 31	Annual Growth	1990	1991	1992	1993	1994	1995
Sales ($ mil.)	16.8%	248.8	213.3	307.3	353.8	450.8	540.3
Net income ($ mil.)	13.3%	18.8	(48.7)	14.4	(7.5)	33.1	35.1
Income as % of sales	—	7.6%	—	4.7%	—	7.3%	6.5%
Earnings per share ($)	5.1%	0.81	(2.10)	0.55	(0.26)	1.03	1.04
Stock price – high ($)	—	34.00	19.75	22.00	24.00	20.63	25.94
Stock price – low ($)	—	12.50	7.50	11.13	11.25	11.13	13.75
Stock price – close ($)	(4.2%)	18.00	13.75	20.88	15.25	19.75	14.50
P/E – high	—	42	—	40	—	20	25
P/E – low	—	15	—	20	—	11	13
Dividends per share ($)	—	0.00	0.00	0.00	0.00	0.00	0.00
Book value per share ($)	1.6%	9.83	7.26	7.68	8.05	9.29	10.63
Employees	4.4%	1,719	1,364	1,600	1,700	1,810	2,129

1995 YEAR-END
Debt ratio: 12.5%
Return on equity: 10.9%
Cash (mil.): $102
Current ratio: 2.54
Long-term debt (mil.): $9
No. of shares (mil.): 33
Dividends
 Yield: —
 Payout: —
Market value (mil.): $482
R&D as % of sales: 7.6%

SHIVA CORPORATION

OVERVIEW

Shiva is helping office workers find new lives as telecommuters. With 24% of the market, Bedford, Massachusetts-based Shiva is the leading provider of remote-access hardware and software — products that let computer users at home or on the road connect to office computers via telephone lines. Founders Daniel Schwinn and Frank Slaughter own about 8% and 6% of the company, respectively.

MIT graduates Schwinn and Slaughter founded Shiva in 1985. They chose the name (after a type of laser) because it didn't sound too "techie," only later discovering it was the name of the many-armed Hindu god of destruction and rebirth. In the beginning the company concentrated on making communication products for AppleTalk networks. In 1987 Shiva introduced NetModem, the first dial-in remote-access product for the Macintosh. It began a shift toward multi-platform, remote-access products in the early 1990s. It licensed the FastPath router from Novell in 1990 and introduced the NetModem/E in 1991 and the LanRover/L in 1992.

Shiva grew rapidly, thanks to its innovative technology and the growing popularity of the "virtual" office. However, the company had trouble managing its growth and expansion beyond Apple products. In 1993 it hired Frank Ingari, VP of marketing at Lotus Development, as CEO to help guide its rapid expansion. Shiva went public in 1994 in one of the most successful IPOs of the year. The firm entered a new market in 1995 when it acquired UK-based Spider Systems, a maker of telephone switching devices that allow phone companies to route calls onto the Internet. Costs associated with the Spider acquisition left Shiva with a loss for the year. Shiva bought AirSoft, a California-based developer of remote-access software, the following year.

WHO

Chairman, President, and CEO: Frank A. Ingari, age 46, $577,200 pay
SVP Worldwide Sales and Marketing: Steven J. Benson, age 37, $350,760 pay
SVP Finance and Administration, CFO, and Treasurer: Cynthia M. Deysher, age 38, $245,000 pay
SVP Research and Development: Guy A. Daniello, age 51
VP Sales North and South America: Maria A. Cirino, age 32, $252,363 pay
VP Operations; General Manager, Edinburgh: Dennis R. Chateauneuf, age 42, $213,666 pay
VP Strategic Planning: Jean-Pierre Boespflug, age 41
VP Human Resources: Jane Callanan, age 39
Auditors: Price Waterhouse LLP

WHERE

HQ: 28 Crosby Dr., Bedford, MA 01730
Phone: 617-270-8300   **Fax:** 617-270-8599
Web site: http://www.shiva.com

WHAT

	1995 Sales	
	$ mil.	% of total
Remote-access products	83.1	71
Other communications products	24.0	20
Services	10.6	9
Total	**117.7**	**100**

Selected Products
LanRover family (remote-access communications servers)
NetModem (communications server for small offices and workgroups)
ShivaIntegrator (remote-access system for ISDN networks)
ShivaPort (communications server for Ethernet networks)

KEY COMPETITORS

3Com
Ascend Communications
Bay Networks
Cisco Systems
Gandalf Technologies
Global Village
U.S. Robotics
Zoom Telephonics

HOW MUCH

Nasdaq symbol: SHVA FYE: December 31	Annual Growth	1990	1991	1992	1993	1994	1995
Sales ($ mil.)	48.7%	16.2	28.0	23.5	29.5	41.6	117.7
Net income ($ mil.)	—	1.2	(1.0)	(4.7)	0.2	2.7	(2.9)
Income as % of sales	—	7.4%	—	—	0.7%	6.4%	—
Earnings per share ($)	—	—	(0.23)	(0.99)	0.03	0.28	(0.22)
Stock price – high ($)	—	—	—	—	—	43.00	77.50
Stock price – low ($)	—	—	—	—	—	26.50	27.00
Stock price – close ($)	—	—	—	—	—	39.88	72.75
P/E – high	—	—	—	—	—	154	—
P/E – low	—	—	—	—	—	95	—
Dividends per share ($)	—	—	—	—	—	0.00	0.00
Book value per share ($)	—	—	—	—	—	3.55	8.97
Employees	39.6%	—	128	123	146	172	486

1995 YEAR-END
Debt ratio: 0.9%
Return on equity: —
Cash (mil.): $102
Current ratio: 5.23
Long-term debt (mil.): $1
No. of shares (mil.): 14
Dividends
 Yield: —
 Payout: —
Market value (mil.): $992
R&D as % of sales: 11.6%

SILICON VALLEY BANCSHARES

OVERVIEW

Finding a bank is no snap for "preprofit" companies — particularly for high-tech businesses most bankers don't understand. But Silicon Valley Bancshares understands. The Santa Clara-based company provides lines of credit and cash management, factoring (lending against receivables), and foreign exchange services for start-up enterprises. It serves 1,500 clients in 30 states. In addition to electronics, software, and biotech companies, Silicon Valley Bancshares clients include wineries and religious institutions.

Silicon Valley Bank was founded in 1983 by Roger Smith to provide banking services to young technology companies clustered around San Jose. It was an astute move into a fast-growing niche, and with early customers like networking supernova Cisco Systems, the bank prospered during the 1980s techno-boom. In 1990 the bank moved eastward to Boston's Route 128 technology ghetto and later northward into Oregon and Washington. It also diversified into residential and commercial real estate lending.

The recession hit California late but hard and found Silicon Valley Bancshares with an overextended loan portfolio. In 1992 the bank booked a loss because of nonperforming loans. The next year it was put under federal supervision. The company brought in new management and demoted Smith from chairman to VC. (He left the company altogether in 1995.) It began diversifying into executive banking for venture capitalists and clients' upper management, foreign exchange, and factoring services.

Silicon Valley Bancshares turned around in 1995, partly because that year's IPO frenzy allowed it to cash in on warrants it had taken from young companies as collateral. In 1996 the regulatory supervision was lifted.

WHO

Chairman: Daniel J. Kelleher, age 53
President and CEO: John C. Dean, age 48, $379,521 pay
EVP Strategic Financial Services Group:
James F. Forrester, age 52, $235,703 pay
EVP, Chief Credit Officer, and General Counsel:
A. John Busch, age 41, $220,704 pay
EVP Special Projects: Richard H. Harding, age 51, $218,450 pay
EVP, CFO, and Chief Information Officer:
Glen Blackmon, age 40, $217,781 pay
EVP Human Resources and Administration:
Glen G. Simmons, age 54, $217,781 pay
Auditors: KPMG Peat Marwick LLP

WHERE

HQ: 3003 Tasman Dr., Santa Clara, CA 95054-1191
Phone: 408-654-7282   **Fax:** 408-383-5298
Web site: http://www.sivb.com

WHAT

	1995 Sales	
	$ mil.	% of total
Loan interest	79.8	70
Other interest	21.5	19
Sale of client warrants	8.2	7
Letters of credit & foreign exchange	3.0	3
Other	1.3	1
Total	**113.8**	**100**

Selected Services
Asset-based financing — Executive banking
Cash management — Factoring
Commercial banking — Foreign exchange

KEY COMPETITORS

Bank of Milpitas
Bank of Santa Clara
Bank of the West
California Bancshares
California Business Bank
Comerica
Cupertino National
Heritage Bank of Commerce
Imperial Bancorp
Mid-Peninsula Bank
Pacific Bank
South Valley National Bank
Wells Fargo

HOW MUCH

Nasdaq symbol: SIVB FYE: December 31	Annual Growth	1990	1991	1992	1993	1994	1995
Assets ($ mil.)	15.9%	673.0	869.5	959.3	992.3	1,161.5	1,407.6
Net income ($ mil.)	12.4%	10.1	12.3	(2.20)	1.6	9.1	18.2
Income as % of assets	—	1.5%	1.4%	—	0.2%	0.8%	1.3%
Earnings per share ($)	4.5%	1.59	1.71	(0.28)	0.20	1.06	1.98
Stock price – high ($)	—	15.18	15.86	14.76	12.25	13.50	26.13
Stock price – low ($)	—	6.34	7.93	5.75	7.88	9.00	13.00
Stock price – close ($)	20.0%	9.63	13.09	8.25	10.13	13.50	24.00
P/E – high	—	10	9	—	61	13	13
P/E – low	—	4	5	—	39	8	7
Dividends per share ($)	—	0.05	0.06	0.03	0.00	0.00	0.00
Book value per share ($)	12.2%	6.59	8.57	8.36	8.48	9.08	11.71
Employees	16.2%	164	175	219	291	312	348

1995 YEAR-END
Equity as % of assets: 7.5%
Return on assets: 1.4%
Return on equity: 19.9%
Long-term debt (mil.): $0.0
No. of shares (mil.): 9.0
Dividends
 Yield: —
 Payout: —
Market value (mil.): $215
Sales (mil.): $113.8

SILICON VALLEY GROUP, INC.

OVERVIEW

Silicon Valley Group (SVG) makes the machines that make the chips that power the machines that run the world. The San Jose, California-based company's automated wafer processing equipment is used by leading semiconductor manufacturers in the complex process of making integrated circuits. The firm's operations include SVG Lithography Systems (photolithography products), Thermco Systems (oxidation/diffusion and low-pressure chemical vapor deposition products), and Track Systems (photoresist processing products). In 1995 customers Motorola, Intel, and SGS-Thomson together accounted for nearly half the company's revenues. IBM, Intel, Motorola, and Texas Instruments are all investors in SVG, and SEMATECH, the federally funded research consortium, owns 6%.

SVG was founded in 1977. As Japan began to dominate high-tech electronics manufacturing during the 1980s, US companies found it increasingly hard to compete. It was during this period that SVG chose former Hewlett-Packard engineer Papken Der Torossian, a Syrian-reared US citizen of Armenian extraction, as its president. He spearheaded the company's acquisitions of Anicon (chemical vapor deposition systems, 1987), Thermco Systems (diffusion/oxidation systems, 1988), and Perkin-Elmer's optical lithography group (now SVGL, photolithography exposure products, 1990). With the market slumping in the early 1990s, Der Torossian consolidated SVG's operations, cut its workforce, and began looking for strategic alliances in the Japanese market.

In 1995 the Thermco Systems Division signed a deal with Motorola to develop temperature control technology for thermal reactors used in processing silicon wafers. In early 1996 SVG announced that it would build a 160,000-square-foot plant in San Jose.

WHO

Chairman and CEO: Papken S. Der Torossian, age 56, $859,841 pay
VP Finance and CFO: Russell G. Weinstock, age 52, $345,660 pay
VP; President, SVG Lithography Systems, Inc.: Edward A. Dohring, age 62, $336,226 pay
VP; President, Track Systems Division: Robert J. Richardson, age 49, $326,368 pay
VP Worldwide Sales and Service: Steven L. Jensen, age 46, $302,979 pay
VP; President, Thermco Systems Division: Jeffrey M. Kowalski, age 42
VP Corporate Technology: Edmond R. Ward, age 55
VP Human Resources: Boris Lipkin
Auditors: Deloitte & Touche LLP

WHERE

HQ: 2240 Ringwood Ave., San Jose, CA 95131
Phone: 408-434-0500   **Fax:** 408-434-0216
Web site: http://www.svg.com

WHAT

Selected Products
Micrascan (photolithography exposure system)
Oxidation/diffusion and LPCVD (low-pressure chemical vapor deposition) processing equipment
Photoresist processing equipment

Product Divisions
SVG Lithography Systems, Inc.
Thermco Systems Division (oxidation/diffusion and LPCVD products)
Track Systems Division (photoresist processing products)

KEY COMPETITORS

Applied Materials
ASM Lithography
Canon
DaiNippon
   Screen
Esterline
Kokusai

Lam Research
Nikon
   Corporation
Novellus Systems
Semitool
Tencor
   Instruments

Tokyo Electron
Tylan General
Ultratech
   Stepper
Varian Associates
Watkins-Johnson

HOW MUCH

Nasdaq symbol: SVGI FYE: September 30	Annual Growth	1990	1991	1992	1993	1994	1995
Sales ($ mil.)	20.2%	184.3	234.8	192.5	240.6	319.9	462.0
Net income ($ mil.)	54.7%	4.4	1.6	(0.3)	4.5	16.8	39.0
Income as % of sales	—	2.4%	0.7%	—	1.9%	5.3%	8.4%
Earnings per share ($)	30.2%	0.42	0.12	(0.03)	0.22	0.84	1.57
Stock price – high ($)	—	13.75	11.25	8.00	12.88	21.25	49.38
Stock price – low ($)	—	4.00	5.13	4.50	6.00	9.25	18.38
Stock price – close ($)	32.2%	6.25	6.75	6.13	9.88	20.63	25.25
P/E – high	—	33	94	—	59	25	31
P/E – low	—	10	43	—	27	11	12
Dividends per share ($)	—	0.00	0.00	0.00	0.00	0.00	0.00
Book value per share ($)	17.0%	6.34	7.01	7.04	7.26	8.87	13.88
Employees	9.4%	1,690	1,605	1,416	1,441	1,663	2,653

1995 YEAR-END
Debt ratio: 0.4%
Return on equity: 15.0%
Cash (mil.): $181
Current ratio: 3.26
Long-term debt (mil.): $1
No. of shares (mil.): 25
Dividends
   Yield: —
   Payout: —
Market value (mil.): $637
R&D as % of sales: 8.7%

SILICONIX INCORPORATED

OVERVIEW

Siliconix's tiny components play a big role in electronic systems. The Santa Clara, California-based company makes power transistors and integrated circuits used for motion control and power management in cars, communications systems, computers, and hard disk drives. It also makes components such as analog switches, analog multiplexers, and low-power transistors used to sense and route signals. Power MOSFETs, components that provide high-efficiency power conversion and load switching for battery-powered devices such as cellular phones and laptop computers, account for more than half of Siliconix's sales. German conglomerate Daimler-Benz owns 80% of the company.

Founded in 1962, Siliconix enjoyed a quarter-century of profitability, primarily on the strength of military contracts. During the late 1980s, however, military spending shrank and the company lost a patent infringement lawsuit. In 1990 it filed for bankruptcy, and Richard Lee, one of the company's founders, stepped down as CEO. Soon after, Daimler-Benz doubled its 38% stake in Siliconix and the company became part of TEMIC, Daimler-Benz's semiconductor consortium. That relationship gave Siliconix access to customers such as IBM and General Motors, and by 1992 it had returned to profitability.

Siliconix developed a proprietary technology that gouges "trenches" in silicon wafers and can double the number of transistors that can fit on a chip. That led to its 1994 debut of Lite Foot, a tiny but powerful discrete power transistor for portable PCs.

In 1996 Siliconix began marketing a chip designed to reduce the potential for damage to electronic circuit boards that can be plugged into electronic equipment while it is still turned on.

WHO

Chairman: Robert L. Wehrli, age 74
President and CEO: Richard J. Kulle, age 51, $591,398 pay
EVP Technology and Silicon Operations: King Owyang, age 50, $483,686 pay
VP and CFO: Jurgen F. Biehn, age 54, $405,274 pay
VP Marketing: G. Thomas Simmons, age 54, $387,750 pay
Senior Director Human Resources: Vickie Ruiz
Auditors: KPMG Peat Marwick LLP

WHERE

HQ: 2201 Laurelwood Rd., Santa Clara, CA 95056-0951
Phone: 408-988-8000   **Fax:** 408-970-3950
Web site: http://www.questlink.com/spnsz/sx/sx.html

WHAT

	1995 Sales	
	$ mil.	% of total
Discrete devices	186.1	74
Integrated circuits	64.2	26
Total	**250.3**	**100**

Selected Products

Discrete Devices (generate or regulate electronic signals)
Power MOSFETs
Small-signal field-effect transistors
  DMOS EFETs
  JFETs
  MOSFETs (Lite Foot and Little Foot models)

Integrated Circuits (components grouped on a microchip to perform a specific function)
Motor control ICs
Power conversion and interface ICs
Signal processing ICs

KEY COMPETITORS

Analog Devices
Burr-Brown
California Micro Devices
Diodes
Elantec
Exar
Linear Technology
Micrel
National Semiconductor
TriQuint
Unitrode

HOW MUCH

Nasdaq symbol: SILI FYE: December 31	Annual Growth	1990	1991	1992	1993	1994	1995
Sales ($ mil.)	13.8%	131.2	140.2	156.2	170.3	196.5	250.3
Net income ($ mil.)	—	(35.1)	(2.2)	4.6	7.2	10.6	24.2
Income as % of sales	—	—	—	3.0%	4.2%	5.4%	9.7%
Earnings per share ($)	—	(3.12)	(0.23)	0.46	0.73	1.07	2.43
Stock price – high ($)	—	3.75	4.25	8.75	9.75	13.50	40.50
Stock price – low ($)	—	0.44	2.00	3.25	5.00	6.25	11.50
Stock price – close ($)	71.4%	2.50	3.25	7.50	6.75	12.38	37.00
P/E – high	—	—	—	19	13	13	17
P/E – low	—	—	—	7	7	6	5
Dividends per share ($)	—	0.00	0.00	0.00	0.00	0.00	0.00
Book value per share ($)	14.6%	4.58	4.52	4.77	5.50	6.61	9.06
Employees	(6.7%)	1,797	1,247	1,202	1,211	1,172	1,269

1995 YEAR-END
Debt ratio: 31.4%
Return on equity: 31.0%
Cash (mil.): $28
Current ratio: 1.53
Long-term debt (mil.): $41
No. of shares (mil.): 10
Dividends
  Yield: —
  Payout: —
Market value (mil.): $369
R&D as % of sales: 7.6%

GROUPE SLIGOS

OVERVIEW

Groupe Sligos helped put the "electronic" in Europe's electronic cash system. The Paris-based company, one of Europe's largest information management services firms, provides systems integration, software, and related services to major banks, such as Credit Lyonnais (France), Banca Commerciale Italiana, and Commerzbank (Germany), and to major banking networks, such as Europay, MasterCard, and Visa. Sligos personalizes checks, makes credit cards (including smart cards, which contain data on microchips), and processes more than 150 million bank statements annually. Sligos is more than 50% owned by Groupe Consortium de Realisation, a holding company for Credit Lyonnais's devalued property assets. The public owns about 40%.

Sligos resulted from the 1973 merger of Sliga, Credit Lyonnais's data-processing services subsidiary founded in 1970, and Cegos Informatique, a data processing consultant started in 1962. In 1981 it debuted the first bank/retailer network-switching system. It acquired Soliac, France's largest credit card maker, in 1983. Sligos went public on the Paris Bourse in 1986 and 2 years later acquired a majority stake in CMG, one of France's premier computer engineering companies.

During the early 1990s Sligos concentrated on creating an international presence, gaining majority interests in banking systems companies such as Hoell (51%, Germany), Nexus (51%, UK; increased to 89%, 1993), and O'Dati (100%, Spain). In 1995 Credit Lyonnais transferred ownership of Sligos to Consortium de Realisation.

In 1996 Sligos said it would join with CyberCash, a US-based Internet payment company, to develop a secure Internet payment method targeting the European market. That year the company sold CMG to Infopoint.

WHO

Chairman and CEO: Henri Pascaud
VP Administration and Finance: Frederic Brunet

WHERE

HQ: Immeuble Ile-de-France-3, place de la Pyramide, 92067, Paris, Cedex 49, France
Phone: +33-1-49-00-90-00   **Fax:** +33-1-47-73-07-63

WHAT

	1995 Sales % of total
Information systems	43
Payment services	32
Telecommunications & networking	13
Cards & checks	12
Total	**100**

Selected Services

Cards and Checks
Card manufacturing and related services (Soliac subsidiary)
Check personalization services (Citadel, Satel, and Sati subsidiaries)

Information Systems
Facilities management
Support services
Systems integration

Payment Services
Bankcards
Checks and interbank payment tickets
Corporate services
Electronic printing

Telecommunications and Networking (Marben subsidiary)

KEY COMPETITORS

Axime
Banco Bilbao
Barclays
BDM International
Cap Gemini
Clondalkin Group
Dean Witter, Discover
Deluxe
Fiserv
GZS
IBM
MasterCard
Memorex Telex
NCR
Siemens
Visa

HOW MUCH

Principal exchange: Paris FYE: December 31	Annual Growth	1990	1991	1992	1993	1994	1995
Sales ($ mil.)	8.7%	579.2	618.2	678.4	664.2	769.0	879.2
Net income ($ mil.)	11.9%	31.4	33.5	31.3	27.1	(27.2)	16.7
Income as % of sales	—	5.4%	5.4%	4.6%	4.1%	—	1.9%
Earnings per share ($)	(16.4%)	6.69	6.89	6.44	5.07	(4.46)	2.73
Stock price – high ($)	—	107.84	107.03	92.26	95.42	118.04	103.28
Stock price – low ($)	—	78.43	77.48	45.22	59.96	59.21	72.32
Stock price – close ($)	(0.6%)	85.00	94.13	66.12	93.23	67.64	82.30
P/E – high	—	16	16	14	19	—	38
P/E – low	—	12	11	7	12	—	26
Dividends per share ($)	9.2%	1.18	1.40	1.45	1.52	1.69	1.83
Book value per share ($)	3.6%	41.10	47.06	49.01	46.06	44.39	49.06
Employees	4.9%	4,986	5,421	5,718	6,230	6,256	6,347

1995 YEAR-END
Debt ratio: 23.0%
Return on equity: 5.8%
Cash (mil.): $93.2
Current ratio: 1.37
Long-term debt (mil.): $67.3
No. of shares (mil.): 6.1
Dividends
 Yield: 2.2%
 Payout: 67.2%
Market value (mil.): $505.1

SMART MODULAR TECHNOLOGIES, INC.

OVERVIEW

Thanks to SMART, portable computer users can fax or e-mail their bright ideas from remote locations around the globe, completely untethered from wirelines. Headquartered in Fremont, California, SMART Modular Technologies is the world's #1 maker of PC data/fax modem cards (which enable a notebook computer to link with a cellular phone) and memory enhancement modules.

The skyrocketing demand for the company's products is being fueled by the proliferation of home and business PCs and the prevalence of memory-thirsty applications and graphics programs. Electronics OEMs Cisco Systems, IBM, and Hewlett-Packard account for more than 35% of SMART's sales. CEO Ajay Shah and CFO Lata Krishnan (his wife) together own about 35% of the company; VP Mukesh Patel owns nearly 25%.

Smart was founded in 1989 by Shah (a marketer who left Korean chip-maker Samsung when the company resisted his urging that it enter the memory module market), corporate accountant Krishnan, and engineer Patel. The company began by making surface-mounted single in-line memory modules (SIMMS). SMART became profitable just a few months after its founding.

The company moved into the specialty memory and PC card memory markets in 1991. Two years later it unveiled a line of PC card communications devices, which enabled portable computers to connect to a network over a phone line.

SMART in 1995 purchased Apex Data, which makes traditional and wireless data/fax modems and other PC card connectivity products. That year SMART went public. In 1996 the company aquired Newark, California-based RISQ Modular Systems, which makes embedded processor modules for electronic devices.

WHO

Chairman, President, and CEO: Ajay Shah, age 36, $2,518,345 pay
VP and General Manager Memory Product Line: Mukesh Patel, age 37, $1,944,010 pay
VP Sales and Product Manager Memory Product Line: Alan Marten, age 36, $896,979 pay
VP Finance and Administration, CFO, and Secretary: Lata Krishnan, age 34, $469,125 pay
VP Research and Development: Pranatharthi Haran, age 36, $175,312 pay
Director Human Resources: Misha Wyatt
Auditors: Andersen Worldwide

WHERE

HQ: 4305 Cushing Pkwy., Fremont, CA 94538
Phone: 510-623-1231   **Fax:** 510-623-1434
Web site: http://www3.techstocks.com/profiles/SMOD.html

WHAT

Selected Products

DRAM Memory Enhancement Modules	**Level 2 Cache SRAM Memory Enhancement Modules**
Adaptable Memory Socket Concept	Industrial SRAM modules
Workstation/server DRAM modules	Intel COASt-compliant cache modules
Flash Memory Enhancement Modules	**Portable Computer Memory and Communications Cards**
DRAM-like Flash SIMMs	ATA Flash PC cards
Standard Flash SIMMs	ClipperCom World data/fax modems
Synchronous Flash SIMMs	Linear Flash PC cards

KEY COMPETITORS

Cincinnati Microwave
Cypress Semiconductor
Diamond Multimedia
Kingston Technology
Hayes Microcomputer
IBM
Integrated Device Technology
Lucent
Ma Labs
Micron Technology
Motorola
PNY Electronics
U.S. Robotics

HOW MUCH

Nasdaq symbol: SMOD FYE: October 31	Annual Growth	1990	1991	1992	1993	1994	1995
Sales ($ mil.)	92.8%	10.3	14.1	16.0	80.8	163.8	274.6
Net income ($ mil.)	69.5%	0.9	1.0	0.3	3.3	6.0	12.6
Income as % of sales	—	8.3%	7.2%	1.8%	4.1%	3.7%	4.6%
Earnings per share ($)	59.4%	0.07	0.08	0.02	0.23	0.37	0.72
Stock price – high ($)	—	—	—	—	—	—	12.75
Stock price – low ($)	—	—	—	—	—	—	9.50
Stock price – close ($)	—	—	—	—	—	—	10.63
P/E – high	—	—	—	—	—	—	18
P/E – low	—	—	—	—	—	—	13
Dividends per share ($)	—	—	—	—	—	—	0.00
Book value per share ($)	—	—	—	—	—	—	—
Employees	—	—	—	—	—	—	354

1995 YEAR-END
Debt ratio: 19.4%
Return on equity: 63.0%
Cash (mil.): $13
Current ratio: 1.34
Long-term debt (mil.): $2
No. of shares (mil.): 15
Dividends
  Yield: —
  Payout: —
Market value (mil.): $156
R&D as % of sales: 1.9%

SOFTKEY INTERNATIONAL INC.

OVERVIEW

SoftKey plays hardball. The Cambridge, Massachusetts-based company, a leading publisher of consumer software (with more than 500 titles), has gone after acquisitions with a vengeance, adding software publishers such as Compton's NewMedia and the Learning Company to its team. Chairman and CEO Michael Perik owns 5% of the company. Tribune Co., publisher of the *Chicago Tribune*, owns 22.5%.

The company was created in 1994 by the merger of SoftKey Software, Spinnaker Software, and WordStar International. SoftKey Software, founded in Canada in 1983 by Kevin O'Leary (a former marketer for Nabisco's pet foods unit), focused on personal productivity programs. Spinnaker was founded by David Seuss in 1982 to manufacture educational software. WordStar was founded in 1978 (as MicroPro International) by Seymour Rubinstein to develop word processing programs and other software. The new company combined WordStar's strengths in international distribution and direct mail, Spinnaker's alliances with PC vendors, and SoftKey's broad product line and retail connections. Perik, SoftKey Software's CEO, was chosen to head the new firm, which began trading on Nasdaq in 1994. That year it introduced its moderately priced Platinum line, the first consumer software sold in jewel case-only packaging and displayed on racks to encourage impulse purchases.

SoftKey made several acquisitions in 1995 and won a hostile takeover battle, paying $606 million in cash in early 1996 for the Learning Company, a leading educational software publisher. Late that year SoftKey agreed to merge with another top educational software publisher, Minnesota Educational Computing Corp, and announced plans to change its name to Learning Company.

WHO

Chairman and CEO: Michael J. Perik, age 38, $300,000 pay
President: Kevin O'Leary, age 41, $300,000 pay
CFO: R. Scott Murray, age 32, $260,000 pay
COO: Les Schmidt, age 41
EVP: Edward J. Sattizahn, $220,833 pay
EVP, SoftKey Software: Robert Gagnon, age 58
President, International: David E. Patrick, age 40, $181,008 pay
VP, General Counsel, and Secretary: Neal S. Winneg
VP Human Resources: Mary De Saint Croix
Auditors: Coopers & Lybrand L.L.P.

WHERE

HQ: One Athenaeum St., Cambridge, MA 02142
Phone: 617-494-1200   **Fax:** 617-225-0318
Web site: http://www.softkey.com

WHAT

	1995 Sales	
	$ mil.	% of total
Retail	75.7	45
Direct response	26.2	16
International	25.6	15
OEMs	20.0	12
Tax software & services	19.5	12
Total	**167.0**	**100**

Selected Titles
Compton's Interactive Encyclopedia
The Family Doctor
The Hubble Space Telescope
Instant Astrologer
Key Gourmet
PC Paintbrush
PFS: First Publisher
Sports Illustrated Swimsuit Calendar

KEY COMPETITORS

Accolade
Adobe
Borland
Brøderbund
Claris
Corel
Creative Technology
Edmark
Electronic Arts
Encyclopaedia Britannica
Gametek
id Software
Intuit
Knowledge Adventure
Lotus
LucasArts
Maxis
Microsoft
Nintendo
SEGA
Software Publishing

HOW MUCH

Nasdaq symbol: SKEY FYE: December 31	Annual Growth	1990	1991	1992	1993	1994	1995
Sales ($ mil.)	23.6%	57.8	76.0	119.5	134.3	121.3	167.0
Net income ($ mil.)	—	—	(6.4)	(5.0)	(53.4)	21.1	(66.0)
Income as % of sales	—	—	—	—	—	17.4%	—
Earnings per share ($)	—	—	—	—	—	1.04	(2.65)
Stock price – high ($)	—	—	—	—	—	27.25	51.75
Stock price – low ($)	—	—	—	—	—	9.75	20.38
Stock price – close ($)	—	—	—	—	—	25.50	23.13
P/E – high	—	—	—	—	—	26	—
P/E – low	—	—	—	—	—	9	—
Dividends per share ($)	—	—	—	—	—	0.00	0.00
Book value per share ($)	—	—	—	—	—	2.54	6.71
Employees	11.4%	—	—	—	625	450	775

1995 YEAR-END
Debt ratio: 70.2%
Return on equity: —
Cash (mil.): $78
Current ratio: 1.17
Long-term debt (mil.): $501
No. of shares (mil.): 32
Dividends
  Yield: —
  Payout: —
Market value (mil.): $739
R&D as % of sales: 7.5%

SOFTWARE AG

OVERVIEW

SOFTWARE AG is slipping down the charts, but it's still in the Top 10. The Darmstadt, Germany-based private company is among the world's largest software makers. Its products include software for application engineering (NATURAL), client/server functions (ENTIRE), and database management (ADABAS). The company could use a hit, however, as its sales have stagnated and its losses are mounting.

SOFTWARE AG was founded in 1969 by Peter Schnell, Peter Page, and 4 other engineers. It originally made products for mainframe computers, introducing ADABAS in 1971. Former CACI International executive John McGuire founded SOFTWARE AG of North America in 1972 as an independent distributor. The company established an Asian subsidiary in Japan 2 years later. In 1987, under Page's direction, SOFTWARE AG began a program to expand into enterprise client/server products. The German parent purchased SOFTWARE AG of North America in 1988 and returned it to private ownership.

In 1990 SOFTWARE AG introduced its first nonmainframe product, the client/server software package ENTIRE. The following year McGuire was dismissed from SOFTWARE AG of North America by the parent company.

CEO Page resigned in 1992 over management differences, and Schnell, who had been sole owner, transferred ownership of SOFTWARE AG to 2 foundations. The company is structured as a private trust, after the philosophy of optical instrument pioneer Carl Zeiss. Shares are held by the foundations to prevent a takeover, and some 70% of profits must be used for R&D and investment.

In 1994 SOFTWARE AG introduced its Open Data Warehouse package, which allows companies to combine data from multiple sources into a single database.

SOFTWARE AG formed a partnership with Microsoft in 1995 to increase the distribution of the latter's OLE data-linking technology. After losing $8 million in 1994, SOFTWARE AG lost $33 million in 1995. The next year the company announced Peter Schnell's resignation, along with plans to cut its workforce by 10%.

WHO

President and CEO: Erwin W. Koenigs
VP Sales and Marketing: Romin Neumeister
President and CEO, Software AG of North America: Michael J. King
CFO, Software AG of North America: Harry McCreery
EVP, Software AG of North America: Joseph J. Agro
VP Technical, Software AG of North America: Marius Abel
VP Human Resources, Software AG of North America: William Cripe
Auditors: Dr. E.G. Breng

WHERE

HQ: Uhlandstrasse 12, D-64297, Darmstadt, Germany
Phone: +49-6151-92-0   **Fax:** +49-6151-92-1191
US HQ: 11190 Sunrise Valley Dr., Reston, VA 22091
US Phone: 703-860-5050   **US Fax:** 703-391-6975
Web site: http://www.softwareag.com

	1995 Sales
	% of total
Europe	65
USA	22
Other	13
Total	**100**

WHAT

Selected Products and Services
ADABAS (database management system)
Data warehousing (integrated tools that make operational data accessible for analysis and decision support)
ENTIRE (client/server software)
ESPERANT (graphical query and reporting)
NATURAL (professional application development tool based on the NATURAL language)
NATURAL Engineering Workbench (modeling and analysis software tool for data warehouse development)

KEY COMPETITORS

Amdahl
BMC Software
Centura Software
Computer Associates
Data General
DEC
IBM
Informix
Microsoft
Novell
Oracle
PLATINUM technology
Sequent
Sterling Software
Sybase
Unisys

HOW MUCH

Private company FYE: December 31	Annual Growth	1990	1991	1992	1993	1994	1995
Sales ($ mil.)	10.7%	—	367.3	381.7	328.9	533.0	552.0
Employees	4.4%	—	2,359	2,822	2,716	2,800	2,800

SOFTWARE SPECTRUM, INC.

OVERVIEW

These days businesses not only demand software performance, they also expect service. Software Spectrum provides both. Based in Garland, Texas, the company offers about 38,000 business software titles and peripherals as well as services that include consulting, application development, training, and technical support. Software Spectrum is one of the largest business software resellers in the US, selling primarily to large companies through its direct sales force. It reaches small and medium-sized businesses through telemarketing and catalogs. CEO Judy Sims and her husband, Richard, who is SVP, together own 8.6% of the company.

Frank Tindle (a director who owns 5.8% of the company) and the Simses, all CPAs, founded Software Spectrum in 1983 as the Software Store, a computer software retail operation located in a Dallas shopping center. When customers failed to come to her, Judy Sims started calling on local businesses, including Ross Perot's Electronic Data Systems. She landed the EDS account and soon added GTE, Mobil, and others. By concentrating on "FORTUNE" 500 companies and other major corporations with large numbers of PCs, Software Spectrum leveraged its sales efforts, expanding later to smaller businesses. The company adopted its present name in 1991, just prior to going public.

The company acquired Software Alternatives, a microcomputer software supplier in Canada, in 1995. The following year it went Down Under, purchasing the Essentially Group Limited, an information technology company in Australia and New Zealand. It also opened a new office in London, its first in Europe.

WHO

Chairman, President, and CEO: Judy O. Sims, age 43
EVP and COO: Keith R. Coogan, age 44
SVP: Richard G. Sims, age 42
VP Sales and Marketing: Roger J. King, age 43
VP and Chief Information Officer: Robert B. Mercer, age 44
VP Finance, Treasurer and Secretary: Deborah A. Nugent, age 42
VP Customer Operations: Lisa M. Stewart, age 33
Director Human Resources: Sue Zurber
Auditors: Grant Thornton LLP

WHERE

HQ: 2140 Merritt Dr., Garland, TX 75041
Phone: 214-840-6600   **Fax:** 214-864-7878
Web site: http://www.swspectrum.com

WHAT

Selected Merchandise and Services	Seminars
	Software
Accessories	Software library
Consulting	Spreadsheet
Database software	Training
E-mail	Utilities
Groupware	Word processing
Languages	
Operating systems	
Peripherals (modems, expansion cards, keyboards)	

KEY COMPETITORS

CDW Computer Centers	Global Directmail	Staples Stream
CompuCom	Ingram Micro	International
CompUSA	Merisel	Tandy
DEC	Micro Warehouse	Corporation
Egghead	NeoStar	Vanstar
ELEK TEK	Office Depot	
Fry's Electronics	Random Access	

HOW MUCH

Nasdaq symbol: SSPE FYE: March 31	Annual Growth	1991	1992	1993	1994	1995	1996
Sales ($ mil.)	27.5%	118.5	158.9	219.5	283.1	352.1	398.5
Net income ($ mil.)	31.2%	1.9	3.8	6.3	7.0	8.8	7.4
Income as % of sales	—	1.6%	2.4%	2.9%	2.5%	2.5%	1.8%
Earnings per share ($)	14.2%	0.89	1.28	1.70	1.66	2.08	1.73
Stock price – high ($)	—	—	17.75	29.25	30.75	23.50	26.50
Stock price – low ($)	—	—	9.50	14.75	20.00	9.25	14.00
Stock price – close ($)	5.3%	—	17.50	22.75	22.00	15.00	21.50
P/E – high	—	—	14	17	19	11	15
P/E – low	—	—	7	9	12	4	8
Dividends per share ($)	—	—	0.00	0.00	0.00	0.00	0.00
Book value per share ($)	24.3%	—	7.24	12.03	13.72	15.64	17.30
Employees	33.0%	201	303	388	514	667	835

[1] Stock prices are for the prior calendar year.

1996 YEAR-END
Debt ratio: 0.0%
Return on equity: 10.6%
Cash (mil.): $37
Current ratio: 1.81
Long-term debt (mil.): $0
No. of shares (mil.): 4
Dividends
  Yield: —
  Payout: —
Market value (mil.): $91

STERLING SOFTWARE, INC.

OVERVIEW

Dallas-based Sterling and its subsidiaries sell more than 150 software products for electronic commerce, systems management, application development, and reengineering used by some 40,000 customers worldwide. The company also provides technical, scientific, and professional services to certain sectors of the federal government (NASA and the US Department of Defense) and ranks as one of the largest software firms in the world. In addition to its presence in the US and Canada, Sterling is a major player in Europe and the Pacific Rim.

Sam Wyly, Charles Wyly, Phillip Moore, and Sterling Williams (who inspired the company name) — all former executives with University Computing — founded Sterling in 1981 and took it public 2 years later. Following a strategy of high growth through acquisitions, the company acquired Informatics General (software, 1985), Knowledge Systems Concepts (professional engineering services to the US military, 1992), and National Systems (banking EDI products, 1992), among others. The Wyly family controls about 5% of the company's stock.

In 1994 Sterling acquired KnowledgeWare, a leading provider of applications development software and services. While the acquisition doubled the size of Sterling's application management group, it also included a host of lawsuits brought against KnowledgeWare for allegedly misrepresenting its financial status. Sterling established an indemnity account to cover losses that could result from litigation still pending against KnowledgeWare. Costs related to the acquisition cut deeply into Sterling's profits in 1995.

The following year Sterling spun off its electronic commerce division (its largest revenue-generating business segment) as Sterling Commerce.

WHO

Chairman: Sam Wyly, age 61, $1,300,000 pay
VC: Charles J. Wyly Jr., age 62, $650,000 pay
President and CEO: Sterling L. Williams, age 52, $1,200,000 pay
EVP: Warner C. Blow, age 58, $621,610 pay
EVP Business Development: Werner L. Frank, age 66
EVP and Chief Technology Officer: Phillip A. Moore
EVP, CFO, General Counsel, and Secretary: Jeannette P. Meier, age 48
Auditors: Ernst & Young LLP

WHERE

HQ: 8080 N. Central Expwy., Ste. 1100, Dallas, TX 75206-1895
Phone: 214-891-8600   **Fax:** 214-739-0535
Web site: http://www.sterling.com

WHAT

	1995 Sales	
	$ mil.	% of total
Products	239.9	41
Services	188.3	32
Product support	160.0	27
Total	**588.2**	**100**

Selected Products
CLEAR:Access (query and reporting)
CLEAR:Manage (balances query loads, optimizes data warehouses, and provides automation services)
KEY:Workgroup (Windows-based object-oriented application development environment)
STAR:Flashpoint (builds integrated graphical applications in a Windows environment)
VISION:Results (information management and report generation system for IBM mainframes)

KEY COMPETITORS

ARI Network	General Electric
BMC Software	IBM
Borland	Microsoft
BT Financial	System Software
Computer Associates	Associates
DEC	TCI International

HOW MUCH

NYSE symbol: SSW FYE: September 30	Annual Growth	1990	1991	1992	1993	1994	1995
Sales ($ mil.)	24.1%	200.2	224.4	259.3	411.8	473.4	588.2
Net income ($ mil.)	(2.8%)	10.5	12.7	13.8	(33.4)	49.9	9.1
Income as % of sales	—	5.3%	5.6%	5.3%	—	12.3%	1.6%
Earnings per share ($)	(15.4%)	0.90	1.05	1.19	(2.00)	2.31	0.39
Stock price – high ($)	—	11.00	24.88	25.25	33.63	36.88	62.38
Stock price – low ($)	—	5.50	7.38	13.75	17.63	25.00	32.88
Stock price – close ($)	49.0%	8.50	24.63	21.00	28.38	36.75	62.38
P/E – high	—	12	24	21	—	16	160
P/E – low	—	6	7	12	—	11	84
Dividends per share ($)	—	0.00	0.00	0.00	0.00	0.00	0.00
Book value per share ($)	(0.2%)	13.31	14.50	10.14	5.47	8.54	13.16
Employees	14.3%	1,900	2,000	2,150	2,800	3,000	3,700

1995 YEAR-END
Debt ratio: 26.0%
Return on equity: 3.5%
Cash (mil.): $241
Current ratio: 2.00
Long-term debt (mil.): $117
No. of shares (mil.): 27
Dividends
  Yield: —
  Payout: —
Market value (mil.): $1,651
R&D as % of sales: 10.9%

STRATUS COMPUTER, INC.

OVERVIEW

Stratus is trying to remain aloft by applying its expertise in continuously available computing to computer networks. The Marlborough, Massachusetts, maker of fault-tolerant computer systems has been plagued by declining operating margins and pressure from workstation-based competitors. Its response has included new products such as the RADIO line of networked systems. "Continuously-available" computing means just that: Stratus's systems use redundant and self-monitoring hardware that detects and automatically corrects errors. Its computers come with an offer of one month's free maintenance if the customer experiences a single second's system downtime.

Bill Foster, Bob Freiburghouse, and Gardner Hendrie started Stratus in 1980. The next year they introduced the Stratus/32, the world's first hardware-based, continuous-availability computer. The company went public in 1983; in 1985 it inked an OEM agreement with IBM but by 1991 had to restructure operations and cut dependence on OEM sales. Its worldwide sales force targeted industries that depend on uninterrupted computing, including finance, telecommunications, travel, and health care.

Stratus acquired 3 software companies in 1993: Shared Financial Systems (now Shared Systems; financial applications software), BellSouth Systems Integration (now SoftCom Systems; connectivity software), and Isis Distributed Systems (products for distributed computing). Stratus acquired TCAM Systems (security industry software) in 1994 and UK banking software and professional services company AST/Transact in 1995.

Responding to lower earnings and operating margins, in 1995 the company announced plans to cut 500 jobs. The following year Stratus released its RADIO cluster-based PC superserver.

WHO

Chairman and CEO: William E. Foster, age 51, $415,012 pay
VP Finance and CFO: Robert E. Donahue, $240,000 pay
VP; CFO, ISIS Distributed Systems: Paul R. Jones, $230,000 pay
VP Worldwide Sales: J. Donald Oldham, $200,000 pay
VP and General Counsel: Eileen Casal
VP Human Resources: John F. Young
Auditors: Ernst & Young LLP

WHERE

HQ: 55 Fairbanks Blvd., Marlborough, MA 01752
Phone: 508-460-2000   **Fax:** 508-481-8945
Web site: http://www.stratus.com

WHAT

	1995 Sales
	% of total
Telecommunications	33
Financial services	31
Retail	10
Gaming	7
Other	19
Total	**100**

Products
Continuum
RADIO (fault-tolerant system architecture)
StrataLINK (intermodal communications bus)
StrataNET (wide-area network operating system)
Stratus FTX (UNIX V.4-compliant operating system)
Stratus Virtual Operating System (VOS; proprietary operating system)
XA/R Continuous Processing Systems (hardware systems)

KEY COMPETITORS

Compaq	Sequent
DEC	Sequoia Services
Hewlett-Packard	Sun Microsystems
IBM	Tandem

HOW MUCH

NYSE symbol: SRA FYE: December 31	Annual Growth	1990	1991	1992	1993	1994	1995
Sales ($ mil.)	7.8%	403.9	448.6	486.3	513.7	576.6	587.9
Net income ($ mil.)	(14.1%)	37.0	49.7	56.9	16.6	61.0	17.3
Income as % of sales	—	9.2%	11.1%	11.7%	3.2%	10.6%	2.9%
Earnings per share ($)	(16.2%)	1.77	2.22	2.43	0.70	2.47	0.73
Stock price – high ($)	—	29.00	50.63	54.25	41.25	39.88	39.88
Stock price – low ($)	—	14.63	20.75	29.50	20.25	22.88	23.00
Stock price – close ($)	8.4%	23.13	49.75	33.88	31.38	38.00	34.63
P/E – high	—	16	23	22	59	16	55
P/E – low	—	8	9	12	29	9	32
Dividends per share ($)	—	0.00	0.00	0.00	0.00	0.00	0.00
Book value per share ($)	12.9%	11.15	14.18	17.03	18.13	20.31	20.49
Employees	0.5%	2,381	2,492	2,622	2,610	2,878	2,441

1995 YEAR-END
Debt ratio: 2.1%
Return on equity: 3.6%
Cash (mil.): $155
Current ratio: 3.40
Long-term debt (mil.): $5
No. of shares (mil.): 23
Dividends
  Yield: —
  Payout: —
Market value (mil.): $808
R&D as % of sales: 14.3%

SYBASE, INC.

OVERVIEW

Sybase hopes that new and improved products will be the bridge over its troubled waters. The Emeryville, California-based company specializes in client/server software and services. It was the first to offer high-performance relational database management systems, which allow a large number of users to access information simultaneously, using different applications. It also offers consulting and technical support services. Sybase has gone from technical leader to laggard in the past year, suffering from the effects of its out-of-date System 10 family of database products.

Chairman Mark Hoffman (an engineer and West Point graduate) and EVP Robert Epstein founded Sybase in 1984. The company merged with SQL Solutions, an integrated consulting concern, in 1990 and went public in 1991. It acquired Gain Technology, which made tools used to design multimedia applications, the next year. Sybase prospered through a 7-year relationship with Microsoft, which codeveloped and sold versions of Sybase's operating systems and products (the 2 firms parted company in 1994). Other factors that helped Sybase gain ground on its main rival, Oracle, were its willingness to outspend Oracle on R&D and its commitment to customer service. Sybase introduced System 10 in 1993, but the product was too slow to keep up with larger systems. Competitors Oracle and Informix ate away at its market share with more technically advanced systems. The company acquired software developer Powersoft, which makes application development tools, in 1995.

Also in 1995, Sybase introduced SQL Server 11, a speedier version of its database software, but the company's deteriorating earnings led David Peterschmidt to step down as COO. The next year Sybase planned to lay off about 10% of its workforce.

WHO

Chairman: Mark B. Hoffman, age 49, $435,667 pay
COO (acting): Mike Forster
President and CEO: Mitchell E. Kertzman, age 47
EVP: Robert S. Epstein, age 43
SVP Worldwide Services: Michael W. Bealmear, age 48, $568,306 pay
SVP: David Litwack, age 49, $400,644 pay
CFO: Jack L. Acosta
VP, General Counsel, and Secretary:
  Laurie Bartlett Keating, age 42
VP Worldwide Human Resources: Juanita Lott, age 46
Auditors: Ernst & Young LLP

WHERE

HQ: 6475 Christie Ave., Emeryville, CA 94608
Phone: 510-596-3500   **Fax:** 510-658-9441
Web site: http://www.sybase.com

WHAT

	1995 Sales	
	$ mil.	% of total
License fees	615.7	64
Services	340.9	36
Total	**956.6**	**100**

Selected Products
Enterprise CONNECT (middleware)
New Media Products (Internet tools)
Powersoft Powerbuilder (database application tools)
SQL Server 11 (database management for OLTP applications)
Sybase IQ (interactive query)
Sybase IQ Anywhere (database management for PCs)
Sybase MPP (massively parallel processing for large data warehouse applications)
Sybase web.works (architecture for internet systems)

KEY COMPETITORS

Apple Computer	Informix
Attachmate	Microsoft
Borland	Novell
Computer Associates	Oracle
IBM	Wang

HOW MUCH

Nasdaq symbol: SYBS FYE: December 31	Annual Growth	1990	1991	1992	1993	1994	1995
Sales ($ mil.)	56.1%	103.1	159.4	264.6	426.7	693.8	956.6
Net income ($ mil.)	—	(6.0)	7.0	23.7	44.1	75.2	(19.5)
Income as % of sales	—	—	4.4%	9.0%	10.3%	10.8%	—
Earnings per share ($)	—	(0.20)	0.19	0.48	0.86	1.38	(0.27)
Stock price – high ($)	—	—	10.63	24.88	43.50	57.00	55.00
Stock price – low ($)	—	—	7.50	10.25	22.75	35.25	19.88
Stock price – close ($)	36.5%	—	10.38	24.63	42.00	52.00	36.00
P/E – high	—	—	56	52	51	41	—
P/E – low	—	—	40	21	27	26	—
Dividends per share ($)	—	—	0.00	0.00	0.00	0.00	0.00
Book value per share ($)	29.8%	—	2.13	2.63	3.99	6.53	6.05
Employees	44.9%	919	1,068	1,627	2,528	4,016	5,865

1995 YEAR-END
Debt ratio: 0.0%
Return on equity: —
Cash (mil.): $224
Current ratio: 1.44
Long-term debt (mil.): $0
No. of shares (mil.): 73
Dividends
  Yield: —
  Payout: —
Market value (mil.): $2,615
R&D as % of sales: 15.9%

SYMANTEC CORPORATION

OVERVIEW

What's next from Cupertino? Cappuccino? To take advantage of the Internet's growth, Cupertino, California-based Symantec has been serving up Java (Sun Microsystem's Internet and intranet programming language) with its "Cafe" development environment for Windows 95 and NT. The company is the industry leader in desktop utility software for PCs and Macintosh. Utility software, which maintains and improves the efficiency of computers, helps users back up programs, detect and eliminate viruses, and compress files, among other things. Symantec's best known product line is Norton (advanced utilities, security utilities, and network/communications utilities). The company also offers fax software (WinFax PRO and DosFax PRO), contact management, and development tools.

Gary Hendrix, an artificial intelligence expert, founded Symantec in 1982. CEO Gordon Eubanks, a former student of the late industry pioneer Gary Kildall and founder of C&E Software, bought the company 2 years later. Realizing that Symantec could not go head-to-head against Microsoft and Lotus, Eubanks began buying niche-market software companies. A year after going public in 1989, Symantec merged with Peter Norton Computing, the DOS utilities market leader. Symantec bought 11 companies between 1990 and 1994, when it acquired rival Central Point software for $64 million.

The spree continued into 1995 with the purchase of Delrina (WinFax). It was an attempt to cash in on Windows 95 utilities, which, according to Eubanks, was a mistake that left the company with a $40 million loss for the year. Gun-shy from the Delrina purchase, Symantec is cutting back on aquisitions and concentrating on its growing Internet and Windows NT systems in 1996.

WHO

President and CEO: Gordon E. Eubanks Jr., age 49, $537,842 pay
EVP Worldwide Operations and CFO: Robert R. B. Dykes, age 46, $406,181 pay
EVP Desktop Products: John C. Laing, age 45, $385,551 pay
EVP Applications and Development Tools: Eugene Wang, $310,680 pay
EVP Communications Products: Dennis Bennie, age 43
SVP Business Development: Mark Bailey, age 37
VP and General Manager, Peter Norton Group: Ellen Taylor, $267,218 pay
VP Networking and Client/Server Technology Group: Ted Schlein, age 32
VP Worldwide Sales: Dana E. Siebert, age 36
VP Communication Products: Christopher Calisi
VP, General Counsel, and Secretary: Derek Witte
VP Human Resources: Joe Shepela
Auditors: Ernst & Young LLP

WHERE

HQ: 10201 Torre Ave., Cupertino, CA 95014-2132
Phone: 408-253-9600   **Fax:** 408-253-3446
Web site: http://www.symantec.com

WHAT

Selected Products	Development tools
Advanced utilities (The Norton Utilities)	Fax (WinFax PRO)
Consumer/productivity applications	Network/communications utilities
Contact management	Security utilities

KEY COMPETITORS

Apple Computer	IBM	Phoenix
Borland	Intel	Technologies
Centura Software	JetForm	Quarterdeck
Cheyenne Software	McAfee Associates	Touchstone Research Lab
Computer Associates	Microcom	Traveling Software
Global Village	Microsoft	
Goldmine Software	Novell	

HOW MUCH

Nasdaq symbol: SYMC FYE: March 31	Annual Growth	1991	1992	1993	1994	1995	1996
Sales ($ mil.)	31.3%	116.3	216.6	206.0	267.7	334.9	454.4
Net income ($ mil.)	—	9.4	18.7	(11.5)	(11.1)	28.5	(39.8)
Income as % of sales	—	8.1%	8.6%	—	—	8.5%	—
Earnings per share ($)	—	0.47	0.77	(0.49)	(0.37)	0.71	(0.76)
Stock price – high ($)[1]	—	14.75	44.75	51.00	20.50	19.63	33.25
Stock price – low ($)[1]	—	7.50	13.00	5.88	9.25	9.88	16.13
Stock price – close ($)[1]	11.7%	13.38	44.50	13.63	18.25	17.50	23.25
P/E – high	—	31	58	—	—	28	—
P/E – low	—	16	17	—	—	14	—
Dividends per share ($)	—	0.00	0.00	0.00	0.00	0.00	0.00
Book value per share ($)	8.5%	2.10	3.35	2.91	2.59	2.99	3.16
Employees	29.7%	600	1,086	1,012	1,204	1,442	2,200

[1] Stock prices are for the prior calendar year.

1996 YEAR-END
Debt ratio: 7.9%
Return on equity: —
Cash (mil.): $129
Current ratio: 2.32
Long-term debt (mil.): $15
No. of shares (mil.): 54
Dividends
  Yield: —
  Payout: —
Market value (mil.): $1,247
R&D as % of sales: 9.7%
Advertising as % of sales: 9.7%

SYNOPSYS, INC.

OVERVIEW

Synopsys provides brush, paint, and canvas for the Rembrandts of microchip design. The Mountain View, California-based company's design automation software is used to create integrated circuits and other complex electronic systems. It also provides software that tests designs in theory before they reach the production line, as well as software that offers libraries of design code to significantly reduce design time. Leading electronics firms from Fujitsu to Motorola use Synopsys software, which is based on logic synthesis, a technology that translates the language that engineers use to design a chip into a language that semiconductor companies can use to manufacture the chip.

Aart de Geus, a former manager of General Electric's Advanced Computer-Aided Engineering Group, founded Optimal Solutions in 1986 with a group of researchers and funding from GE. The group built the prototype of a product that helped chip designers save a significant amount of time by automating much of the design work. The company, which changed its name to Synopsys (synthesis and optimization systems), was the first to provide synthesis products on a commercial level. It went public in 1992 and 2 years later introduced Behavioral Compiler software, a breakthrough tool that lets engineers design chips by function rather than by structure.

In 1995 Synopsys acquired design software developers Arkos Design Systems and Silicon Architects, including the latter's proprietary cell-based array integrated circuit architecture. That year the company announced major software contracts with chip maker Cirrus Logic and electronics manufacturer Hewlett-Packard. Synopsys formed a 6-year development agreement with IBM in 1996. The 2 companies intend to develop new technologies for designing complex integrated circuits.

WHO

Chairman: Harvey C. Jones Jr., age 42
President and CEO: Aart J. de Geus, age 41, $420,277 pay
EVP: William W. Lattin, age 55, $324,775 pay
SVP Design Reuse Group: Prakash Bhalerao, age 46, $766,661 pay
SVP Design Tools Group: Chi-Foon Chan, age 46, $346,199 pay
SVP Worldwide Field Operations: Alain J. Labat, age 40, $227,050 pay
SVP Finance and Operations and CFO: A. Brooke Seawell, age 48
SVP Human Resources and Facilities: Sally DeStefano
Auditors: KPMG Peat Marwick LLP

WHERE

HQ: 700 E. Middlefield Rd., Mountain View, CA 94043-4033
Phone: 415-962-5000   **Fax:** 415-965-8637
Web site: http://www.synopsys.com

WHAT

	1995 Sales	
	$ mil.	% of total
Products	180.9	68
Services	84.6	32
Total	**265.5**	**100**

Selected Software Products
Design reuse (DesignWare library of design modules and Cell-Based Array architecture libraries)
Design tools (Design Compiler core synthesis product and other high-level design products)
Verification products (simulation tools and hardware and software models)

KEY COMPETITORS

Altera	Mentor Graphics	Teradyne
Avant! Corp	NCR	Unisys
Cadence	Parametric	Viewlogic
Computervision	Technology	
DEC	Quickturn	
IBM	Design	
Intergraph	Schlumberger	

HOW MUCH

Nasdaq symbol: SNPS FYE: September 30	Annual Growth	1990	1991	1992	1993	1994	1995
Sales ($ mil.)	64.4%	22.1	40.5	63.0	108.0	196.0	265.5
Net income ($ mil.)	49.9%	4.0	3.5	7.1	13.2	15.8	30.3
Income as % of sales	—	18.2%	8.7%	11.3%	12.2%	8.0%	11.4%
Earnings per share ($)	33.0%	0.18	0.14	0.24	0.42	0.42	0.75
Stock price – high ($)	—	—	—	17.75	26.38	24.38	38.50
Stock price – low ($)	—	—	—	11.13	12.88	16.50	21.38
Stock price – close ($)	30.0%	—	—	17.31	22.63	21.88	38.00
P/E – high	—	—	—	74	64	58	51
P/E – low	—	—	—	46	31	39	29
Dividends per share ($)	—	—	—	0.00	0.00	0.00	0.00
Book value per share ($)	29.6%	—	—	2.15	2.83	3.39	4.68
Employees	58.7%	138	229	412	590	1,022	1,388

1995 YEAR-END
Debt ratio: 0.0%
Return on equity: 20.0%
Cash (mil.): $210
Current ratio: 2.28
Long-term debt (mil.): $0
No. of shares (mil.): 39
Dividends
  Yield: —
  Payout: —
Market value (mil.): $1,481
R&D as % of sales: 22.1%

SYQUEST TECHNOLOGY, INC.

OVERVIEW

SyQuest is caught in a cyclone. Based in Fremont, California, SyQuest Technology is the world's #1 manufacturer of removable cartridge hard drives, but it's getting blown around by mounting competition from Iomega and others. The company makes removable hard drives for memory-intensive desktop publishing and multimedia applications as well as small-office and home-office markets. About 2/3 of its sales are in Asia. Founder Syed Iftikar, who has been ousted as chairman, owns about 14% of the company.

Iftikar designed rigid magnetic disk drives and helped found Seagate Technology, but he left that company to pursue the potential of removable cartridge drives. He started SyQuest (short for "Syed's quest") in 1982. The firm survived its early years partly from the proceeds of Iftikar's Seagate stock. During the 1980s SyQuest developed an Apple-compatible removable drive based on the leading fixed-drive system, and sales grew steadily. The enterprise went public in 1991. That year the company started making hard drives for the PC market. As personal computers have gotten smaller, so have SyQuest drives. In 1995 the company introduced a 1.8" cartridge drive for notebook computers and personal digital assistants.

By the mid-1990s, however, intense competition in the hard drive industry led to falling income, which caused the downtrodden firm to cut prices. In 1996 SyQuest laid off 60% of its workers, and the company's total assets dropped below $1 million, prompting NASDAQ to warn of pulling the firm's stock off the market.

That year SyQuest hoped to get back on track with the release of the EZFlyer 230MB hard drive, which has more than twice the storage capacity of Iomega's Zip drive. Also in 1996 COO Edwin Harper relieved Iftikar as chairman and CEO of the troubled firm.

WHO

Chairman and CEO: Edwin L. Harper
EVP Global Operations: Louis C. Passaro, age 52
VP Business Development: Kenneth S. Hardesty, age 51, $245,620 pay
VP Human Resources: Robert E. Lyon, age 53, $127,778 pay
VP Investor Relations and Acting VP Finance and CFO: James E. Graber, age 51
Auditors: Ernst & Young LLP

WHERE

HQ: 47071 Bayside Pkwy., Fremont, CA 94538
Phone: 510-226-4000   **Fax:** 510-226-4100
Web site: http://www.syquest.com

	1995 Sales		1995 Pretax Income	
	$ mil.	% of total	$ mil.	% of total
Far East	369.4	65	6.0	—
North America	194.8	35	(19.8)	—
Adjustments	(264.7)	—	(1.7)	—
Total	**299.5**	**100**	**(15.5)**	**—**

WHAT

	1995 Sales
	% of total
5.25" products	60
3.5" products	40
Total	**100**

Selected Products
EZFlyer 230MB (3.5" data intensive drive)
SyJet 1.3GB (3.5" high performance drive)
SyQuest EZ135 (3.5" small-office or home-office drive)
SyQuest SQ3270 (laptop or desktop 3.5" drive)
SyQuest SQ5110C (removable hard disk cartridge)
SyQuest SQ5200C (200 megabyte hard disk drive)

KEY COMPETITORS

Apple Computer	IBM	Quantum Corp.
Fujitsu	Iomega	Seagate
Hewlett-Packard	Matsushita	Sony
Hitachi	Mitsubishi	Toshiba
Hyundai	NEC	

HOW MUCH

Nasdaq symbol: SYQT FYE: September 30	Annual Growth	1990	1991	1992	1993	1994	1995
Sales ($ mil.)	30.1%	80.5	115.1	174.9	206.4	221.0	299.5
Net income ($ mil.)	—	7.2	6.0	13.6	15.2	5.1	(11.8)
Income as % of sales	—	9.0%	5.2%	7.8%	7.4%	2.3%	—
Earnings per share ($)	—	0.75	0.63	1.17	1.23	0.43	(1.07)
Stock price – high ($)	—	—	15.50	28.50	25.50	19.50	19.63
Stock price – low ($)	—	—	12.50	14.50	8.75	8.50	8.88
Stock price – close ($)	(10.4%)	—	15.50	25.50	10.25	17.75	10.00
P/E – high	—	—	25	24	21	45	—
P/E – low	—	—	20	12	7	20	—
Dividends per share ($)	—	—	0.00	0.00	0.00	0.00	0.00
Book value per share ($)	18.7%	—	3.70	6.73	7.97	9.37	7.35
Employees	31.0%	624	780	1,087	1,157	1,367	2,409

1995 YEAR-END
Debt ratio: 0.0%
Return on equity: —
Cash (mil.): $30
Current ratio: 1.86
Long-term debt (mil.): $0
No. of shares (mil.): 11
Dividends
  Yield: —
  Payout: —
Market value (mil.): $113
R&D as % of sales: 8.0%

SYSTEM SOFTWARE ASSOCIATES, INC.

OVERVIEW

You might have a smokestack or 2, but that doesn't mean you can't be high tech. Chicago-based System Software Associates (SSA) targets its integrated information systems primarily at industrial firms. The company's Business Planning and Control System line consists of over 40 products designed to assist with manufacturing, distribution, finance,and electronic data interchange (EDI) operations. Pursuing a strategy of offering the most extensive line of integrated, open, client/server enterprise software applications, the company focuses on object-oriented systems that run on multiple servers including the IBM AS/400, UNIX-based IBM RS/6000, and the HP 9000. Founder and CEO Roger Covey holds about 32% of the stock.

Founded in 1981, SSA grew by offering products for IBM's AS minicomputers and by developing strong relationships with affiliates (software and professional services firms that market SSA products after being trained by SSA). The company went public in 1987, using the proceeds to acquire 3 of its affiliates.

In 1994 SSA entered into an alliance with Hewlett-Packard (a leader in commercial UNIX systems) to provide solutions to business problems worldwide. That same year, after a 3-year absence during which he studied Chinese art, Covey got back in the CEO saddle again.

SSA teamed up with Harbinger Corp. (commerce software) to develop AS/400 products in 1995. That year the company acquired Softwright, the leading provider of business object technology and systems in Europe,and in 1996 bought Canada-based Vector System Analysis (enterprise resource planning). The company also formed a partnership with AT&T to provide complete enterprise process design, including systems integration and implementation and outsourcing services.

WHO

Chairman and CEO: Roger E. Covey, age 41, $469,917 pay
President and COO: Terence H. Osborne, age 57, $516,683 pay
VP North America: Terry E. Notari, age 57, $326,187 pay
VP and CFO: Joseph J. Skadra, age 54, $284,000 pay
Director Human Resources: Mark Ugol
Auditors: Price Waterhouse LLP

WHERE

HQ: 500 W. Madison St., 32nd Fl., Chicago, IL 60661
Phone: 312-258-6000   **Fax:** 312-474-7500
Web site: http://www.ssax.com/

WHAT

	1995 Sales	
	$ mil.	% of total
License fees	270.0	69
Client services & other	124.4	31
Total	**394.4**	**100**

Business Planning and Control System (BPCS) Product Applications
Configurable Ledger (financial reporting)
Customer Order Processing
Integration Development Kernel (develops interfaces between application database and EDI messages)
Master Production Scheduling (identifies future production and procurement actions)
User/Vision (retrieves information for the BPCS client/server)

Interoperable Tool Set Products
Gen/HPUX (regenerates applications to run within UNIX-based environments)
Rapid Systems Development (enables information systems to be developed in shorter cycles)

KEY COMPETITORS

American Software
Andersen Worldwide
BMC Software
BT
Computer Associates
Dun & Bradstreet
General Electric
Oracle
PeopleSoft, Inc.
Sterling Software

HOW MUCH

Nasdaq symbol: SSAX FYE: October 31	Annual Growth	1990	1991	1992	1993	1994	1995
Sales ($ mil.)	26.0%	124.2	149.1	228.8	263.4	334.4	394.4
Net income ($ mil.)	15.8%	16.4	16.7	26.6	23.4	15.4	34.1
Income as % of sales	—	13.2%	11.2%	11.6%	8.9%	4.6%	8.6%
Earnings per share ($)	21.2%	0.31	0.42	0.66	0.57	0.38	0.81
Stock price – high ($)	—	8.52	11.03	16.89	17.00	12.00	30.50
Stock price – low ($)	—	3.78	3.70	7.89	6.67	9.17	10.25
Stock price – close ($)	22.1%	8.00	10.33	15.67	10.17	10.50	21.75
P/E – high	—	28	26	26	30	32	38
P/E – low	—	12	9	12	12	19	13
Dividends per share ($)	—	0.00	0.00	0.08	0.08	0.08	0.08
Book value per share ($)	21.2%	1.42	1.73	2.02	2.51	2.83	3.71
Employees	29.0%	560	760	1,260	1,560	1,790	2,000

1995 YEAR-END
Debt ratio: 19.5%
Return on equity: 25.2%
Cash (mil.): $57
Current ratio: 1.56
Long-term debt (mil.): $34
No. of shares (mil.): 42
Dividends
  Yield: 0.4%
  Payout: 9.9%
Market value (mil.): $915
R&D as % of sales: 10.2%

SYSTEMSOFT CORPORATION

OVERVIEW

SystemSoft has transcended its role as computer hardware-operating system linguist to become a doctor as well. The Natick, Massachusetts-based company's system-level software, enables a PC's operating system software (such as Windows) to communicate with its hardware. The firm dominates the PCMCIA card (also known as PC card) software market. PC cards have been used primarily in portable computers, but the market is expected to explode as desktop computer makers adopt them and they migrate to devices like cellular phones. After watching PC manufacturers' technical support calls (and costs) skyrocket, CEO Robert Angelo set out to develop a "call avoidance" software (System Wizard) that, when activated by the computer user, would automatically detect, diagnose, and fix most PC problems. Intel owns 9% of the company and accounts for about 10% of its sales.

Four executives of system software developer Phoenix Technologies (Angelo, Jeffrey Bobzin, Jonathan Joseph, and William O'Connell) left Phoenix in 1990 to form SystemSoft. From the beginning, the new company concentrated on the portable computer market. Its first hit was its power management software, which reduces the battery use of portable computers. SystemSoft then began developing system software for PCMCIA plug-in cards. In 1993 the company introduced CardView, a configuration tool used during PCMCIA card installation, and entered licensing agreements with Microsoft and Intel. SystemSoft went public in 1994.

In late 1994 it introduced CardWizard, which automatically configures PCMCIA cards for end users. The following year SystemSoft acquired Ventura Micro. SystemSoft launched SystemWizard in mid-1996.

WHO

Chairman, President, and CEO: Robert F. Angelo, age 49
SVP Strategic Accounts and Emerging Markets: William J. O'Connell, age 38
SVP, PC Software Division: Jonathan L. Joseph, age 38
VP Worldwide Sales: Thomas W. Higgins, age 33
VP Finance, Treasurer, and CFO: David P. Sommers
VP, Secretary and General Counsel: Steven A. Berns
Director Human Resources: Randi Nichols
Auditors: Coopers & Lybrand L.L.P.

WHERE

HQ: 2 Vision Dr., Natick, MA 01760
Phone: 508-651-0088   **Fax:** 508-651-8188
Web site: http://www.systemsoft.com

SystemSoft also has branch offices in California and Taiwan.

WHAT

| | 1996 Sales | |
	$ mil.	% of total
Software license fees	16.2	66
Engineering services	5.8	24
Related party	2.5	10
Other	0.1	0
Total	**24.6**	**100**

Selected Products and Services

Software
BIOS (basic input/output system) software
Microsoft Flash File System (allows a PCMCIA flash memory card to act like a hard disk drive)
Call-Avoidance (SystemWizard; automatically diagnoses and fixes most common PC problems)
PCMCIA card software
Plug and Play (permits PCs to automatically recognize and configure add-on peripherals and components)
Power management

Engineering Services
Software customization

KEY COMPETITORS

American Megatrends
Award Software
Phoenix Technologies
Sterling Software

HOW MUCH

Nasdaq symbol: SYSF FYE: January 31	Annual Growth	1991	1992	1993	1994	1995	1996
Sales ($ mil.)	98.4%	0.8	2.9	6.3	9.2	15.2	24.6
Net income ($ mil.)	—	(1.3)	(3.5)	(3.1)	(0.5)	1.6	3.6
Income as % of sales	—	—	—	—	—	10.7%	14.6%
Earnings per share ($)	—	(0.31)	(0.84)	(0.75)	(0.13)	0.22	0.32
Stock price – high ($)[1]	—	—	—	—	—	10.75	18.13
Stock price – low ($)[1]	—	—	—	—	—	5.50	7.00
Stock price – close ($)[1]	—	—	—	—	—	9.00	11.25
P/E – high	—	—	—	—	—	49	57
P/E – low	—	—	—	—	—	25	22
Dividends per share ($)	—	—	—	—	—	0.00	0.00
Book value per share ($)	—	—	—	—	—	1.80	2.25
Employees	34.8%	—	—	—	76	92	138

[1] Stock prices are for the prior calendar year

1996 YEAR-END
Debt ratio: 0.0%
Return on equity: 17.4%
Cash (mil.): $11
Current ratio: 8.19
Long-term debt (mil.): $0
No. of shares (mil.): 11
Dividends
  Yield: —
  Payout: —
Market value (mil.): 118
R&D as % of sales: 20.8%

TENCOR INSTRUMENTS

OVERVIEW

Imagine the commissions for a Tencor sales rep. Headquartered in Mountain View, California, Tencor Instruments makes computer chip inspection equipment that sells for about $1 million per unit. The company controls about 30% of the semiconductor wafer inspection market. Its products, which are used to identify defective wafers and help control the semiconductor manufacturing process, include particle and contamination detection systems, automated thin film monitoring equipment, and resistivity measurement and surface profiling systems.

Czechoslovak-born native Karel Urbanek started Tencor in 1976 to make semiconductor measurement and test instruments. Tencor's first product was the Alpha-Step film layer profiler. The firm followed up in 1981 with the launch of the Surfscan laser-based particle contamination detector. Seven years later Tencor moved into the patterned-wafer inspection market and in 1989 unveiled its first thin film measurement system. CEO Jon Tompkins (formerly of laser systems manufacturer Spectra-Physics) joined the company in 1991, the year Urbanek died of cancer.

In 1993, the year it went public, Tencor acquired film stress measurement system manufacturer Flexus. The next year it bought measurement system maker Prometrix and acquired wafer inspection technology from Censor AG and Park Scientific.

The company has focused on making its products accurate, cost-effective, and easy to use — a strategy that has earned it respect in the semiconductor industry. In 1995 Tencor became the exclusive reseller of laser imaging defect analysis equipment and software made by Uniphase's Ultrapointe subsidiary. Tencor established a sales and service office in Taiwan in 1996.

WHO

Chairman, President, and CEO: Jon D. Tompkins, age 55, $729,590 pay
VC and EVP: Richard J. Elkus Jr., age 61, $374,400 pay
EVP and COO: Graham J. Siddall, age 49, $433,654 pay
SVP Finance and Administration and CFO (HR): Bruce R. Wright, age 47, $386,680 pay
VP; President, Tencor Japan: Seiji Yoshii, age 58, $471,037 pay
Auditors: Price Waterhouse LLP

WHERE

HQ: 2400 Charleston Rd., Mountain View, CA 94043
Phone: 415-969-6767 **Fax:** 415-968-9482
Web site: http://streetlink.com/tncr/

WHAT

	1995 Sales % of total
Wafer inspection systems	47
Film measurement systems	32
Metrology systems	16
Other	5
Total	**100**

Selected Products

Wafer Inspection Division	Metrology Division
Surfscan (wafer inspection systems)	M-Gage (wafer characterization)
SwiftAccess (yield management and defect data analysis)	Sonogage (wafer characterization)
	Tencor (surface profiling and thin film stress measurement systems)
Film Measurement Division	
Omnimap (resistivity measurement systems)	
Prometrix (thin film measurement systems)	

KEY COMPETITORS

ADE Corp
Hitachi
Inspex
Integrated Process Equipment

KLA Instruments
Orbotech
Schlumberger
Tektronix

HOW MUCH

Nasdaq symbol: TNCR FYE: December 31	Annual Growth	1990	1991	1992	1993	1994	1995
Sales ($ mil.)	45.2%	51.1	53.5	57.7	72.1	182.3	330.2
Net income ($ mil.)	72.3%	4.3	6.2	2.7	5.1	24.3	65.3
Income as % of sales	—	8.3%	11.6%	4.7%	7.1%	13.3%	19.8%
Earnings per share ($)	40.6%	0.38	0.55	0.22	0.33	0.90	2.09
Stock price – high ($)	—	—	—	—	7.00	23.81	48.75
Stock price – low ($)	—	—	—	—	3.75	5.81	17.69
Stock price – close ($)	97.5%	—	—	—	6.25	19.25	24.38
P/E – high	—	—	—	—	21	27	23
P/E – low	—	—	—	—	11	6	8
Dividends per share ($)	—	—	—	—	0.00	0.00	0.00
Book value per share ($)	63.6%	—	—	—	3.50	5.27	9.37
Employees	77.1%	—	—	—	418	837	1,311

1995 YEAR-END
Debt ratio: 11.4%
Return on equity: 30.2%
Cash (mil.): $164
Current ratio: 3.32
Long-term debt (mil.): $3
No. of shares (mil.): 31
Dividends
  Yield: —
  Payout: —
Market value (mil.): $750
R&D as % of sales: 10.1%

U.S. ROBOTICS CORPORATION

OVERVIEW

U.S. Robotics is counting on a digital future. The US's #1 maker of modems, the Skokie, Illinois-based company designs and manufactures the hardware that makes it possible for computers to communicate with each other, whether over a phone line (analog modems), in an office (local area network [LAN] cards and hubs), or from outside the office (remote access servers).

The firm's new Courier I-Modem fuses 2 technologies: it has an analog modem that can be used on regular phone lines and an adapter that allows the device to connect directly with the much faster ISDN digital feed provided (at a premium) by regional telephone companies.

In 1975 CEO Casey Cowell, a University of Chicago economics graduate, teamed up with fellow Chicago graduates Paul Collard (who later left the firm) and Steve Muka (who died in 1985) to go into the budding computer field. U.S. Robotics (named after a company in Isaac Asimov's *I, Robot*) first produced an acoustic coupler that connected computers over phone lines via the handsets. In 1976 an FCC ruling allowed non-AT&T products to be plugged into phone lines, freeing the company to move into modems. It grew quickly, first as a distributor and after 1988 as a manufacturer. U.S. Robotics went public in 1991, and it has been riding the streaking Internet growth curve by providing ever faster, lower-priced modems for PCs. The company introduced its first ISDN products in 1995 and acquired Megahertz (credit card-sized modems and LAN adapter cards), ISDN Systems (LAN connection devices), and Palm Computing (handheld computer software). In 1996 the company acquired Amber Wave Systems, opening a door to the Ethernet switching market. Later that year it bought Israeli-based LAN switch maker Scorpio Communications.

WHO

Chairman, President, and CEO: Casey G. Cowell, age 43, $2,799,000 pay
EVP and COO: John McCartney, age 43, $1,739,400 pay (prior to promotion)
EVP Strategy and Corporate Development: Jonathan N. Zakin, age 46, $1,739,400 pay
SVP and General Manager Corporate/Systems: Ross W. Manire, age 44, $1,449,500 pay
VP and General Manager Personal Communications: Michael Seedman, age 39, $825,205 pay
VP, General Counsel, and Secretary: George A. Vinyard
VP Finance and CFO: Mark Remissong, age 43
VP Human Resources: Elizabeth S. Ryan
Auditors: Grant Thornton LLP

WHERE

HQ: 8100 N. McCormick Blvd., Skokie, IL 60076-2999
Phone: 847-982-5010　**Fax:** 847-933-5551
Web site: http://www.usr.com

WHAT

Selected Products
ConferenceLink Conference Speakerphones
Courier I-Modems with ISDN/V.34
Megahertz PC Card Ethernet Adapters
Megahertz PC Card Modems (PCMCIA card modems)
Palm Computing software (for handheld computers)
Sportster Faxmodems
Total Control Enterprise Network Hubs (LAN hubs)

KEY COMPETITORS

3Com	Intel
Apex Data	Microcom
Apple	Microdyne
Ascend Communications	Motorola
Bay Networks	Multi-Tech
Boca Research	Oki Electric
Cincinnati Microwave	PairGain
DATA RACE	Proteon
Digi International	Shiva
General DataComm	Standard Microsystems
Global Village	System Connection
GVC Technologies	Tandem
Hayes Microcomputer	Xircom
IBM	Zoom Telephonics

HOW MUCH

Nasdaq symbol: USRX FYE: September 30	Annual Growth	1990	1991	1992	1993	1994	1995
Sales ($ mil.)	73.6%	56.4	78.8	112.4	189.2	378.7	889.3
Net income ($ mil.)	69.6%	4.7	7.3	10.9	17.0	26.4	66.0
Income as % of sales	—	8.4%	9.3%	9.7%	9.0%	7.0%	7.4%
Earnings per share ($)	47.8%	0.22	0.39	0.50	0.70	1.03	1.55
Stock price – high ($)	—	—	8.38	12.13	17.63	23.00	110.50
Stock price – low ($)	—	—	6.13	6.69	8.50	12.00	19.63
Stock price – close ($)	82.0%	—	8.00	10.25	17.31	21.63	87.75
P/E – high	—	—	21	24	25	22	71
P/E – low	—	—	16	13	12	12	13
Dividends per share ($)	—	—	0.00	0.00	0.00	0.00	0.00
Book value per share ($)	62.9%	—	1.43	3.12	4.67	5.98	10.06
Employees	60.3%	316	402	479	755	1,451	3,347

1995 YEAR-END
Debt ratio: 13.4%
Return on equity: 23.3%
Cash (mil.): $232.8
Current ratio: 3.21
Long-term debt (mil.): $65.7
No. of shares (mil.): 42.2
Dividendss
　Yield: —
　Payout: —
Market value (mil.): $3,702.5
R&D as % of sales: 5.9%

VLSI TECHNOLOGY, INC.

OVERVIEW

Think of VLSI as a silicon tailor. The San Jose, California-based microchip company makes application-specific integrated circuits (ASICs) to fit its customers' needs. It also makes application-specific standard products (ASSPs) for off-the-rack chip buyers. COMPASS Design Automation, a wholly owned subsidiary, supplies design services and software tools for chip designers. Nearly half of the company's revenues come from the personal computer market, and Apple Computer is its largest customer. As VLSI's X86 chips for IBM-compatible PCs are supplanted by newer models, it anticipates more sales to the communications and digital entertainment markets. Microchip maker Intel owns nearly 6% of the company.

VLSI was founded in 1980 to make memory chips (its name is the industry acronym for "very large scale integration"). The company went public in 1983. After it lost money in 1990, VLSI shifted its focus from memory chips to ASICs. Intel bought nearly 20% of VLSI in 1992, hoping to improve its chips and capture a larger share of the X86 market. In 1993 Apple canceled $20 million in orders for VLSI chips when demand for PowerPC-based Macintosh computers supplanted orders for machines with VLSI chipsets.

The company signed a 5-year agreement with electronic design software vendor Mentor Graphics in 1995 to codevelop ASIC designs. It also joined with AT&T to develop data security chips for such devices as networked PCs, cellular phones, and cable television decoder boxes.

VLSI was hit with a double whammy in 1996: price slashing in the weak domestic semiconductor market and problems at Apple. The company is concentrating on the communications industry to help boost sales. That year VLSI teamed up with IBM to develop chipsets for IBM products based on the Apple operating system.

WHO

Chairman, President, and CEO: Alfred J. Stein, age 63, $1,257,096 pay
SVP Finance and CFO: Gregory K. Hinckley, age 49, $460,962 pay
SVP and General Manager, VLSI Products: Donald L. Ciffone, age 40, $394,777 pay
SVP; President, COMPASS Design Automation: Dieter J. Mezger, age 52, $314,069 pay
SVP Worldwide Sales and Marketing: Bernd U. Braune
SVP, General Counsel, and Secretary: Larry Grant
VP Human Resources: Eugene E. Tange
Auditors: Ernst & Young LLP

WHERE

HQ: 1109 McKay Dr., San Jose, CA 95131
Phone: 408-434-3100   **Fax:** 408-263-2511
Web site: http://www.vlsi.com

WHAT

Selected Products

Communications
Networking products
Wireless products

Computers
Products for Apple and Apple-compatible computers and peripherals
System-logic chipsets and components for PCs based on X86 and competing architectures

Consumer Digital Entertainment Products
Entertainment applications of graphics technology
Secure information products

KEY COMPETITORS

Cadence	Mitsubishi
Exar	Motorola
Fujitsu	NEC
GE	Oki
Hitachi	Samsung
IBM	Synopsys
Integrated Circuit Systems	Texas Instruments
Intel	Toshiba
LG Group	Viewlogic
LSI Logic	Xilinx

HOW MUCH

Nasdaq symbol: VLSI FYE: December 31	Annual Growth	1990	1991	1992	1993	1994	1995
Sales ($ mil.)	17.3%	324.8	413.4	428.5	515.9	587.1	719.9
Net income ($ mil.)	—	(12.7)	9.9	(32.2)	15.9	31.7	46.0
Income as % of sales	—	—	2.4%	—	3.1%	5.4%	6.4%
Earnings per share ($)	—	(0.52)	0.37	(1.12)	0.50	0.84	1.05
Stock price – high ($)	—	12.25	12.25	10.50	18.88	16.38	39.13
Stock price – low ($)	—	3.00	4.25	6.00	6.50	10.25	11.63
Stock price – close ($)	32.1%	4.50	7.63	8.13	10.75	12.00	18.13
P/E – high	—	—	33	—	42	19	37
P/E – low	—	—	12	—	14	12	11
Dividends per share ($)	—	0.00	0.00	0.00	0.00	0.00	0.00
Book value per share ($)	13.9%	5.86	6.10	5.56	6.03	6.95	11.24
Employees	7.4%	2,087	2,315	2,379	2,659	2,728	2,986

1995 YEAR-END
Debt ratio: 30.1%
Return on equity: 11.7%
Cash (mil.): $366
Current ratio: 3.02
Long-term debt (mil.): $219
No. of shares (mil.): 47
Dividends
  Yield: —
  Payout: —
Market value (mil.): $855
R&D as % of sales: 12.5%

V-ONE CORPORATION

OVERVIEW

"Safety first" is spelled V-ONE. Rockville, Maryland-based V-ONE Corporation is a leading provider of security-oriented technology products. These include the SmartWorld campus card (for ID, security, library privileges, food and vending, telephone calls, and access to academic and financial records), Wallet Technology (for secure transactions over the Internet), and SmartWall (for protection of corporate and government networks).

The company is a pioneer in smart card and firewall (which protects a network from outside intruders) technology. V-ONE has the only smart card-based network security system available off-the-shelf and its SmartWall is used by US military and intelligence agencies and "FORTUNE" 100 corporations. Founder and CEO James Chen owns 58% of the company; Hai Hua Cheng, majority owner of Scientek (which invested in V-ONE), owns 16%.

Chen founded V-ONE in 1993 (as Virtual Open Network Environment Corporation) to help organizations maintain security while using open networks. Late the next year the company introduced its first products: SmartCAT card-reading software and SmartWall (a combination of SmartCAT and firewall technologies).

The SmartGATE client/server system was launched in 1995 to ensure data exchange and safe transactions in industries such as banking, financial trading, health care, insurance, and publishing. Also that year the company hired Marcus Ranum (considered the "father of the commercial firewall") as chief scientist.

In addition to augmenting and integrating its product lines with existing network security systems, the company is developing alliances. Such alliances include deals with Web software maker Spyglass and database management applications maker Oracle.

In 1996 the company was chosen by the National Security Agency to develop network protection for its Defense Messaging System. The company, which has not yet made a profit, filed in 1996 to go public. Also that year it changed its name to V-ONE.

WHO

President and CEO: James F. Chen, age 45, $18,000 pay
Chief Scientist: Marcus J. Ranum, age 33
SVP Engineering: Jieh-Shan Wang, age 41
VP Indirect Channels: Robert W. Rybicki, age 51
VP Technology: Frederick J. Hitt, age 52
VP Business Development: William C. Wilson, age 41
VP Direct Sales: Barnaby M. Page, age 32
Treasurer and Acting CFO: Chansothi Um, age 27
Secretary: Charles C. Chen, age 41
Manager Personnel: Dan Davis
Auditors: Coopers & Lybrand L.L.P.

WHERE

HQ: 1803 Research Blvd., Ste. 305, Rockville, MD 20850
Phone: 301-838-8900   **Fax:** 301-838-8909
Web site: http://www.v-one.com/

WHAT

Selected Products
NetChart (online stock performance analysis)
Online Registration (client/server token for access)
SmartCAT (smart card client software)
SmartGATE (client/server security)
SmartWall (firewall defense)
Wallet Technology (secured payment transactions)

Alliances
Digital Pathways
Florida State University
Fortified Networks
General Electric Information Services

Network Systems
Oracle
RSA Data Security
Security Dynamics
Software.com
Spyglass
Trusted Information Systems

Selected Customers
BancOne
Bear, Stearns
Fuji Capital Markets
National Security Agency
State of Utah
US Navy
Virtual Networks
Visa

KEY COMPETITORS

Checkpoint Systems
Cylink
DEC
Harris Corp.
IBM
Milkyway Networks
Morningstar Technologies
Netscape

Open Market
Raptor Systems
Secure
Security Dynamics
Sun Microsystems
Trusted Information Systems

HOW MUCH

Private company FYE: December 31	Annual Growth	1990	1991	1992	1993	1994	1995
Sales ($ mil.)	231.7%	—	—	—	0.1	0.1	1.1
Net income ($ mil.)	—	—	—	—	0.0	(0.4)	(1.0)
Income as % of sales	—	—	—	—	—	—	—
Employees	—	—	—	—	—	—	52

1995 YEAR-END
Debt ratio: 100.0%
Return on equity: —
Cash (mil.): $1
Long-term debt (mil.): $0
R&D as % of sales: 25.2%

WAGGENER EDSTROM

OVERVIEW

You might not have heard of Corbis Corp. But you will — if Waggener Edstrom does its job. The Portland, Oregon-based public relations firm specializes in providing publicity to computer and interactive media companies. Its most famous client is Microsoft, which accounts for a large portion of its business (Microsoft's CEO Bill Gates owns Corbis, which owns the digital rights to more than 16 million visual images).

President and CEO Melissa Waggener founded the Waggener Group in 1983, luring public relations professionals from electronics company Tektronix and PR firm Regis McKenna. The Waggener Group signed 7 clients and billed $1 million its first year. Meanwhile, another Tektronix PR alumnus, Pam Edstrom, was working as PR director for a small, yet promising, software firm called Microsoft. When Edstrom joined the Waggener Group in late 1983, she brought the Microsoft account with her. In 1986 the firm added microchip manufacturer AMD to its stable. (Frustrated by AMD's bureaucracy, they soon took the unusual step of firing AMD as a client.) That year the Waggener Group helped orchestrate coverage of Microsoft's initial public offering, scoring a "FORTUNE" cover story. Edstrom's name was added to the company in 1990. Between 1991 and 1993 billings nearly doubled, topping $13 million; they more than doubled again by 1995, reaching $27 million.

As the Internet became more important, the firm expanded its in-house design operation, which had designed print materials, into the electronic arena. In 1995 the company rechristened this operation Zebra Design. This business also designs Web pages and Web-ready promotional materials and provides services not only within the company but for outside clients as well.

Waggener Edstrom keeps pace with its high-tech clientele with its own sophisticated systems and is linked electronically with its clients. The firm maintains an extensive database of press contacts, with information on the presumed attitudes of individual press members, based on the level of acceptance of Waggener Edstrom's releases.

WHO

President and CEO: Melissa Waggener
SVP: Pamela Edstrom
COO: James D. Buchanan
VP and Associate: Jody Peake
VP Professional Development: Julie Allport
VP Client Services: Claire Lematta
VP Client Services: Marianne Allison
VP Client Services: Alison O'Brien
Director Technology Services: Rod Iwata
VP Human Resources: Michael Bigelow

WHERE

HQ: 6915 SW Macadam Ave., Ste. 300, Portland, OR 97219-2396
Phone: 503-245-0905   **Fax:** 503-244-7261
Web site: http://www.wagged.com

Waggener Edstrom has offices in Santa Clara, California; Portland, Oregon; and Belleview, Washington.

WHAT

Agency Focus

Communications	Microcomputer Software
Cable	Applications
Cellular	Database
Fiber-optic linkage	Graphics
Mobile computing	Networking
Satellite	Systems
Telephony	Utilities
Wireless data voice	

Computer Technologies
Components
Engineering design
Enterprise computing
PC hardware and
  technologies
Peripherals

Consumer Technologies
Education
Entertainment and games
Home computing
Multimedia platforms
Personal communications
Publishing

Sciences
Environmental
Health and medical

Selected Clients
AT&T Corp.
Corbis
Microsoft
PrintPak
SAP
Starwave
Trilobyte

KEY COMPETITORS

Elgin/Syferd/DDB
  Needham
Harris Savage Massey
Hill and Knowlton
Insync Partners
Ketchum Communications

KPR
KVP
Miller Communications
Regis McKenna
Sterling Communications
Van Sickle, Ouellette

HOW MUCH

Private company FYE: December 31	Annual Growth	1990	1991	1992	1993	1994	1995
Sales ($ mil.)	37.5%	5.5	7.2	10.1	13.4	16.5	27.0
Employees	31.8%	—	65	84	114	158	196

WALL DATA, INCORPORATED

OVERVIEW

Even if you have 2 left feet, Wall Data will still make you feel like dancing. The Kirkland, Washington-based company makes software (RUMBA, SALSA) and offers product services and support (ONESTEP). Accounting for more than 80% of Wall Data's revenues is its flagship family of products, RUMBA, which allows PC users to access information on a variety of systems, from minicomputers to mainframes, regardless of the type of host computer, platform, or network involved. Its up-and-coming new product, SALSA, lets nonprogrammers create their own custom business applications using Windows. ONESTEP Services provides product upgrades and support; options such as software maintenance are also available.

John Wall, a 24-year-old computer techie, founded the company in 1982 to market PC connectivity tools. Lack of management depth hampered Wall Data until 1988, when former Qume Corp. president James Simpson was hired as CEO for his marketing and management experience. Simpson refocused development on connectivity software that would work with Windows. The first RUMBA product was released in 1989. Wall Data went public in 1993.

Wall Data created the SALSA business unit in 1994 to develop products for databases using the new Semantic Object Modeling (SOM) technology that it partially funded. SOM allows a company to structure data in its own language rather than in a database application language. Although sales were up in 1995, the company's revenue growth rate fell, primarily because major customers postponed purchases in anticipation of Windows 95.

In 1996 the company launched its SALSA software and ARPEGGIO Information Publisher, its application family that combines database query tools with the ability to publish information through the Web or intranets.

WHO

Chairman and CEO: James Simpson, age 58, $375,000 pay
President and Chief Technology Officer: John R. Wall, age 38, $211,250 pay (prior to promotion)
EVP: Kevin B. Vitale, age 38
VP, General Counsel, and Secretary: Alexandra A. Brookshire, age 41, $163,750 pay
VP Worldwide Sales, Service, and Distribution: Richard A. Doerr, age 53
VP Finance, CFO, and Treasurer: Richard Van Hoesen
VP Wall Data Europe: Thomas Weanie
VP Asia Pacific/Latin America: Mike Rogers
VP Product Development: Marvin Mall
VP SALSA Products: Eileen Gittins
VP Human Resources: Fran Safier
Auditors: Ernst & Young

WHERE

HQ: 17769 NE 78th Pl., Redmond, WA 98052-4992
Phone: 206-814-9255   **Fax:** 206-814-4300
Web site: http://www.walldata.com

WHAT

Selected Products and Services	RUMBA software family
ARPEGGIO Information	SALSA software family
Publisher software	**OEM Partners**
family	Apple Computer
ONESTEP Services	Cisco Systems
(provides product	CompuServe
upgrades for RUMBA	DEC
software products,	IBM
support, and	Microsoft
maintenance)	3M
R&R Report Writer	Novell
software	Olivetti
	Sun Microsystems

KEY COMPETITORS

Apertus	IBM
Attachmate	Microsoft
Boole & Babbage	NetManage
Centura Software	Netsoft
EICON Technology	Novell
FTP Software	Sun Microsystems

HOW MUCH

Nasdaq symbol: WALL FYE: December 31	Annual Growth	1990	1991	1992	1993	1994	1995
Sales ($ mil.)	90.6%	4.4	14.6	31.8	64.6	101.2	110.7
Net income ($ mil.)	—	(1.6)	1.0	4.4	9.5	14.2	7.3
Income as % of sales	—	—	6.8%	13.8%	14.7%	14.0%	6.5%
Earnings per share ($)	—	(2.29)	0.19	0.56	1.00	1.40	0.74
Stock price – high ($)	—	—	—	—	42.50	60.00	55.50
Stock price – low ($)	—	—	—	—	12.75	29.25	14.50
Stock price – close ($)	(35.9%)	—	—	—	40.13	39.75	16.50
P/E – high	—	—	—	—	43	43	75
P/E – low	—	—	—	—	13	21	20
Dividends per share ($)	—	—	—	—	0.00	0.00	0.00
Book value per share ($)	13.7%	—	—	6.35	7.12	8.90	9.34
Employees	52.4%	—	—	221	388	654	783

1995 YEAR-END
Debt ratio: 0.0%
Return on equity: 8.8%
Cash (mil.): $52
Current ratio: 3.32
Long-term debt (mil.): $0
No. of shares (mil.): 9
Dividends
  Yield: —
  Payout: —
Market value (mil.): $148
R&D as % of sales: 17.8%

WILSON SONSINI GOODRICH & ROSATI

OVERVIEW

Silicon Valley isn't just for computer geeks anymore. A service sector has grown to cater to high-tech companies, and when legal issues arise, more than 1/3 of the area's biggest companies turn to Palo Alto-based Wilson Sonsini Goodrich & Rosati. The firm specializes in areas of interest to these companies, including intellectual property and securities matters. Wilson Sonsini is unusual in that it also performs merger and IPO valuations, maintains a fund of stocks in client companies, and has partners on the boards of some of its clients.

Founded as McCloskey, Wilson & Mosher in 1961, the firm, which took its present name in 1978, remained relatively small until the 1980s. Then Silicon Valley's computer industry took off. In 1980 (when it had fewer than 30 lawyers) it helped Apple go public, and between 1985 and 1990 it handled more high-tech public offerings than any other law firm. Wilson Sonsini gained a reputation for billing more hours per partner than almost any other area firm. In 1991, to beef up its relatively small intellectual property practice, the firm lured Gary Reback from archrival Fenwick & West. In 1993, however, Wilson Sonsini was dealt a blow when several of its partners left to form a rival firm, Venture Law Group, to specialize in start-ups. By the mid 1990s it had almost 300 attorneys.

In 1994 the firm, on behalf of a group of anonymous clients, wrote a brief opposing a settlement of a Justice Department antitrust action against Microsoft. Some believed the brief played a part in Judge Stanley Sporkin's refusal to ratify the settlement (his decision was overturned).

But one of the firm's highest-profile cases had nothing to do with technology. Between 1991 and 1995 Wilson Sonsini represented inmates in a case involving abusive practices at Pelican Bay State Prison. It won and was immediately embroiled in litigation with the State of California over payment of its legal bills. The firm accepted $3.5 million after billing about $8 million.

In 1996 the firm continued to build its intellectual property practice by recruiting new partners from outside the firm.

WHO

Chairman: Larry W. Sonsini
Managing Partner: Alan Austin
VP Operations: Jim Kurpius
VP Finance: Harvey Schloss
Partner: John Goodrich
Recruiting Administrator: Lynette Baranski
Auditors:

WHERE

HQ: 650 Page Mill Rd., Palo Alto, CA 94304-1050
Phone: 415-493-9300   **Fax:** 415-493-6811
Web site: http://www.wsgr.com

WHAT

Areas of Practice
Antitrust law
Business litigation
Civil litigation
Computer law
Corporate planning
Environmental law
Estate planning
Incorporation
Intellectual property
Interactive new media
International and domestic arbitration
Labor law
Patent law
Real estate law
Securities litigation
Securities registration
Tax law
Venture capital fund formation
Venture financings
White-collar criminal defense
Wills

Selected Clients
Hewlett-Packard
Netscape
Novell
Octel Communications
Seagate
Sun Microsystems

KEY COMPETITORS

Brobeck, Phelger & Harrison
Cooley Godward
Fenwick & West
Gray Cary

Heller, Ehrman
Orrick, Herrington
Pillsbury Madison & Sutro
Townsend & Townsend
VLG

HOW MUCH

Partnership FYE: January 31	Annual Growth	1991	1992	1993	1994	1995	1996
Sales ($ mil.)	9.4%	72.7	75.5	82.5	91.5	101.2	114.1
Employees	5.8%	548	605	615	661	693	726

WILSON SONSINI GOODRICH & ROSATI
ATTORNEYS AT LAW

WIND RIVER SYSTEMS, INC.

OVERVIEW

Ever turned off an alarm clock, played a video game, or used an automatic teller machine? Chances are a Wind River product was involved. The Alameda, California-based firm makes software development systems and tools for customers building software for microprocessors (those complex computers inside everyday products). Tornado, the company's flagship product, is used to develop embedded applications for Windows and UNIX systems and includes the VxWorks operating system and communications and development tools. Chairman Jerry Fiddler and chief technical officer David Wilner own about 20% and 14% of the company, respectively.

A 1970s trip to the Wind River Mountains by Fiddler inspired the name of the enterprise, which he and Wilner started in 1981 as a consulting firm. Recognizing the growing demand for embedded system tools, they changed the company's focus in 1987 and started making their own products. They began shipping the VxWorks operating system that year, primarily for scientific and engineering applications at first and later for financial and manufacturing applications.

Wind River went public in 1993 but soon hit lean times. Ronald Abelmann took Fiddler's place as CEO in 1994 and turned the company around by restructuring and cutting jobs.

As embedded software systems become more complex, many companies are choosing to outsource the work. Wind River is positioning itself to grab a share of this growing market by allying with semiconductor and embedded device manufacturers. In 1996 Intel agreed to supply an evaluation copy of the Tornado system to customers purchasing Intel microprocessors.

WHO

Chairman: Jerry L. Fiddler
President and CEO: Ronald A. Abelmann
CTO and Secretary: David N. Wilner
Managing Director, European Operations: Graham Shenton
SVP Sales: Robert L. Wheaton
VP Finance and CFO: Richard W. Kraber
VP Engineering: David G. Fraser
Director Human Resources: Kathy Doyle
Auditors: Price Waterhouse LLP

WHERE

HQ: 1010 Atlantic Ave., Alameda, CA 94501
Phone: 510-748-4100   **Fax:** 510-814-2010
Web site: http://www.wrs.com

WHAT

	1995 Sales	
	$ mil.	% of total
Products	31.2	71
Services	12.8	29
Total	**44.0**	**100**

Selected Products
StethoScope (real-time data visualization, profiling, and debugging tool)
Tornado (development environment for embedded applications for UNIX and Windows)
VxSim Embedded System Simulator (prototyping and simulation tool for UNIX)
VxWorks Options (virtual memory interface and multiprocessing package)
WindC++ Object-Oriented Language Support (real-time C++ development tools)
WindView (diagnostic and analysis tool)

Selected Services
Engineering Services
Technical Support
Training Classes

KEY COMPETITORS

Applied Microsystems
Integrated Systems
Mentor Graphics
Microware Systems

HOW MUCH

Nasdaq symbol: WIND FYE: January 31	Annual Growth	1991	1992	1993	1994	1995	1996
Sales ($ mil.)	26.7%	—	17.1	25.1	27.3	32.1	44.0
Net income ($ mil.)	48.9%	—	1.1	1.7	0.3	2.5	5.4
Income as % of sales	—	—	6.4%	6.9%	1.2%	7.7%	12.2%
Earnings per share ($)	33.6%	—	0.11	0.17	0.03	0.17	0.35
Stock price – high ($)[1]	—	—	—	—	9.17	6.25	20.42
Stock price – low ($)[1]	—	—	—	—	3.33	2.92	5.33
Stock price – close ($)[1]	113.8%	—	—	—	4.25	5.75	19.42
P/E – high	—	—	—	—	344	36	59
P/E – low	—	—	—	—	125	17	15
Dividends per share ($)	—	—	—	—	0.00	0.00	0.00
Book value per share ($)	12.6%	—	—	—	1.86	2.08	2.36
Employees	23.3%	—	90	144	180	170	208

[1] Stock prices are for the prior calendar year.

1996 YEAR-END
Debt ratio: 0.0%
Return on equity: 17.6%
Cash (mil.): $30
Current ratio: 3.25
Long-term debt (mil.): $0
No. of shares (mil.): 14
Dividends
  Yield: —
  Payout: —
Market value (mil.): $270

WIRED VENTURES, INC.

OVERVIEW

When the world you're covering spins faster than a stock analyst's head at the mention of the word "Internet," you have got to be a little unconventional. San Francisco-based Wired Ventures has made a name for itself by chronicling the ever-changing, ever-growing online community. Reflecting the cyberculture it follows, the company's flagship magazine, *Wired*, offers irreverent but technologically savvy articles and a splashy graphic style. It also offers an online version of its cyber-chronicle, HotWired, on the World Wide Web.

Wired Ventures is trying to expand its brand into other media, including books and television. To raise the cash for the move the company has twice filed to go public in May 1996, hoping to take advantage of Wall Street's white hot interest in cyber-related stocks. It filed for an IPO valuing the company at around $415 million. However, after Wall Street's interest in Internet stocks cooled in the summer of 1996, Wired delayed the offering. In October it announced it would try again, but at a price that valued the company at about $250 million. That offering was also pulled. Cofounders Louis Rossetto and Jane Metcalfe each own about 18% of the company. Advance Publications own 13%. Metcalfe and Rossetto attempted to publish a tech-culture magazine, "Electric Pencil," in Europe in the 1980s, but the venture failed. They brought their idea to the US and recruited MIT Media Lab founder Nicholas Negroponte as a financial backer and eventual contributor. The magazine's first issue hit newsstands in 1993. In March of that year upscale magazine publisher Conde Nast bought a 17% stake in the company. The magazine had a circulation of 240,000 by 1995.

Wired's online sister, HotWired, which features shorter info-bites and pieces not available in the magazine, debuted in 1994, receiving more than 100,000 connections and 4,000 subscribers its first day, growing to 235,000 subscribers the next year. In 1996 HotWired unveiled HotBot, a search engine that combs the complete text of all documents on the Web.

WHO

CEO; Editor and Publisher, *Wired*; **Editor-in-Chief,** *HotWired*: Louis Rossetto, age 46, $88,558 pay
President: Jane Metcalfe, age 34, $88,558 pay
CFO and Secretary: Jeffrey Simon, age 34, $110,000 pay
VP Interactive: Andrew Anker, age 32, $140,369 pay
VP Corporate and Business Development: Rex O. Ishibashi, age 32, $110,000 pay
VP and Chief Technology Officer: Jacquard W. Guenon
VP Operations: Todd Sotkiewicz
Executive Editor, *Wired*: Kevin Kelly
Managing Editor, *HotWired:* Albert F. "Chip" Bayers III
Publisher *Hardwired*: Peter Rutten

WHERE

HQ: 520 Third St., 4th Fl., San Francisco, CA 94107-1815
Phone: 415-222-6200   **Fax:** 415-222-6209
Web site: http://www.hotwired.com

WHAT

Wired **Selected Features**
Deductible Junkets (information technology conferences)
Electric Word (technology news)
Fetish (product news)
Geek Page (changing technology news)
Net Surf (online directory)
Raw Data (trivia)
Reality Check (news features)
Street Cred (product news)

Hotwired Selected Features
Cocktail (lounge culture)
Dream Jobs (career opportunities)
Pop (art, literature & music)
Webmonkey (browser enhancement)

Selected Hardwired Books
Digerati: Encounters with the Cyber Elite, by John Brockman
Mind Grenades by John Plunkett and Louis Rossetto
Wired Style: Principles of English Usage in the Digital Age, by the editors of *Wired*

KEY COMPETITORS

CMP Publications	Lycos	Upside Publishing
C/NET	McGraw-Hill	Verity
Excite	Mecklermedia	Wolff New Media
HyperMedia	Open Text	Yahoo
Infoseek	Sendai Media Group	Ziff-Davis
International Data Group	Simon & Schuster	

HOW MUCH

Private company FYE: December 31	Annual Growth	1990	1991	1992	1993	1994	1995
Sales ($ mil.)	195.4%	—	—	—	2.9	9.2	25.3
Net income ($ mil.)	155.0%	—	—	—	(1.0)	(3.5)	(6.5)
Income as % of sales		—	—	—	—	—	—
Employees		—	—	—	—	—	284

1995 YEAR-END
Debt ratio: 100.0%
Return on equity: —
Cash (mil.): $7
Current ratio: 0.90
Long-term debt (mil.): $1

WYSE TECHNOLOGY INC.

OVERVIEW

San Jose, California-based Wyse Technology, the leading world supplier of advanced display terminals, says it is bringing Internet access and Windows applications to users more cheaply than PCs can. Aimed at home, school, and public access markets, its Winterm terminals cost about $500 and can provide some basic PC functions when linked with a server computer or online service provider.

Wyse is a melting pot story: Hong Kong-born Bernard Tse met his future wife, Taiwan-born Grace, at the University of Illinois. They moved to San Jose where they teamed with Larry Lummis, Jim Shaw, and Chuck Comiso, got a stake from Altos Computer, and started Wyse Technologies. Manufacturing terminals in Taiwan, they undersold giants like IBM, and Wyse soon became the US's #1 terminal seller, going public in 1986. Wyse's fortunes fell when it entered the fierce competition of the 1980s PCs market; after losses and layoffs, in 1990 Tse and the others agreed to sell the company to Channel International, a Taiwanese consortium that includes the Taiwanese government.

Under its new management, led by former Texas Instruments SVP Morris Chang, Wyse refocused on monitors and terminals, including devices to help mainframe systems operate like PC networks. By 1992 the company had turned around, and in 1994 it announced its departure from the computer manufacturing business, coincident with the end of a 1989 PC technology licensing agreement with IBM. The Taipei government takes an aggressive part in developing the island's industry, and Wyse's well-developed distribution channels in the US and elsewhere, seen as avenues for distribution of Taiwanese electronics, fit with Taipei's move to globalize Taiwanese industry.

Wyse expanded beyond simple terminals in late 1995 when it unveiled its Winterm product, designed to work like a PC when used with a Windows NT-based server. The next year the company launched a pilot project with on-line provider Moose Logic Technologies to provide Internet access. It also debuted its Boogie Board, a $500 computer with a 486 chip and built-in Web browser that uses Java to deliver Windows applications.

WHO

Chairman: Morris Chang
President and CEO: Doug Chance
CFO: Ken Czaja
General Counsel: David Renton
SVP Sales and Marketing: Roy Graham
VP Human Resources and Administration:
Frederick M. Chancellor
Auditors: Andersen Worldwide

WHERE

HQ: 3471 N. First St., San Jose, CA 95134-1803
Phone: 408-473-1200   **Fax:** 408-473-1222
Web site: http://www.wyse.com

International sales offices are located in Canada, China, France, Germany, Hong Kong, Italy, Singapore, Taiwan, the UK, and the US.

WHAT

Selected Products
Color monitors
Color terminals
Computers
Keyboards
Monochrome terminals

Brand Names
Boogie Board
Link MC
Qume
T2000 (licensed thin-client computing design)
Winterm
Wyse

KEY COMPETITORS

Amdahl
Apple Computer
Compaq
DEC
Falco Data
Falcon Systems
Hewlett-Packard
IBM

ITOCHU
Network Computing
    Devices
Sequent
Sun Microsystems
Tandem
Tektronix
TeleVideo Systems

HOW MUCH

Private company FYE: March 31	Annual Growth	1991	1992	1993	1994	1995	1996
Sales ($ mil.)	(9.0%)	480.0	480.0	481.6	400.0	290.0	300.0
Employees	(6.9%)	2,000	2,000	2,000	2,000	1,500	1,400

XILINX, INC.

OVERVIEW

Xilinx is the place for microchip do-it-your-selfers. The San Jose, California-based company makes field programmable gate arrays (FPGAs) and complex programmable logic devices (CPLDs), 2 kinds of integrated circuits that Xilinx customers can program to perform specific functions. The company also provides the software needed for programming the chips. Xilinx's chips are used by electronics makers in the data processing, industrial control, instrumentation, military, networking, and telecommunications markets.

In 1984 Bernie Vonderschmitt, then 60, joined with former colleagues Ross Freeman and Jim Barnett to start Xilinx when Zilog, their employer, rejected the idea of investing in a programmable chip operation. The company introduced the first FPGA, the XC2000 family, the next year. Successive products featured more "logic gates" providing more computing power. The XC3000, with up to 5,000 usable logic gates, was offered in 1987, and the XC4000, with up to 20,000 usable logic gates, was released in 1990. The company went public that year and three years later unveiled the world's first 25,000-gate FPGA.

Xilinx, which minimizes its overhead by contracting out its chip manufacturing, advanced $42 million in 1994 to longtime contractor Seiko Epson to build a new FPGA plant in Japan. The company acquired FPGA software developer NeoCAD the next year and will incorporate NeoCAD's technology into its own software. Also in 1995 the company formed a joint venture with United Microelectronics to build a new wafer plant.

Xilinx opened a new plant in Ireland in 1996 and announced partnerships to build plants in Japan and Taiwan. That year it lowered the price on some FPGAs by more than 50% as it ramped up production on higher-performance chips.

WHO

Chairman: Bernard V. Vonderschmitt
CEO: Willem P. Roelandts
SVP Worldwide Sales: R. Scott Brown
SVP Finance and CFO: Gordon M. Steel
VP Operations: C. Frank Myers
VP Strategic Plans and Programs and Secretary: Robert C. Hinckley
VP and CTO: William S. Carter
VP Software Product Development: David W. Bennett
VP Product Technology: Evert A. Wolsheimer
VP Human Resources: Christine C. Taylor
Auditors: Ernst & Young LLP

WHERE

HQ: 2100 Logic Dr., San Jose, CA 95124-3400
Phone: 408-559-7778   **Fax:** 408-559-7114
Web site: http://www.xilinx.com

WHAT

	1996 Sales
	% of total
XC4000	45
Other PLDs	40
Software	3
Other	12
Total	**100**

Selected Products

Programmable Logic Devices
Complex programmable logic devices (CPLDs)
Erasable programmable read-only memories (EPROMs)
Field programmable gate arrays (FPGAs)
Hardwire devices (mask-programmed integrated circuits)

Support Software
Foundation support software
XACTstep development system software

KEY COMPETITORS

Actel
Altera
AMD
Atmel

Cypress Semiconductor
Lattice Semiconductor
National Semiconductor

HOW MUCH

Nasdaq symbol: XLNX FYE: March 31	Annual Growth	1991	1992	1993	1994	1995	1996
Sales ($ mil.)	41.9%	97.6	135.8	178.0	256.4	355.1	560.8
Net income ($ mil.)	44.9%	15.9	21.3	27.2	41.3	59.3	101.5
Income as % of sales	—	16.3%	15.7%	15.3%	16.1%	16.7%	18.1%
Earnings per share ($)	41.0%	0.23	0.30	0.38	0.57	0.80	1.28
Stock price – high ($)[1]	—	5.66	10.82	10.32	18.15	20.65	55.50
Stock price – low ($)[1]	—	3.16	4.16	4.83	7.83	9.66	18.08
Stock price – close ($)[1]	46.1%	4.58	8.66	8.41	15.90	19.73	30.50
P/E – high	—	25	36	27	32	26	43
P/E – low	—	14	14	13	14	12	14
Dividends per share ($)	—	0.00	0.00	0.00	0.00	0.00	0.00
Book value per share ($)	33.0%	1.23	1.57	1.83	2.52	3.47	5.12
Employees	29.3%	332	482	544	689	868	1,201

[1] Stock prices are for the prior calendar year

1996 YEAR-END
Debt ratio: 40.5%
Return on equity: 33.1%
Cash (mil.): $378
Current ratio: 5.25
Long-term debt (mil.): $250
No. of shares (mil.): 72
Dividends
  Yield: —
  Payout: —
Market value (mil.): $2,194
R&D as % of sales: 11.5%

YAHOO! INC.

OVERVIEW

In Gulliver's Travels Yahoos were a dirty and backward people. Now they're trying to clean up on the Internet. Sunnyvale, California-based Yahoo! is one of the premier services for getting around the World Wide Web. Its free navigational guide is available on several online networks and browsers. Among companies providing content to Yahoo! are Ziff-Davis, Reuters, Rogers Communications and Hoover's, Inc. (publisher of this profile). Advertising accounts for more than 90% of the company's income.

While graduate students at Stanford, David Filo and Jerry Yang developed the Yahoo! (an acronym for "Yet Another Hierarchical Officious Oracle") search engine to compile a list of their favorite Internet sites. They set up their own Web index site in 1994, and it was soon being accessed by thousands of web surfers each day. Marc Andreessen, who had written the original Mosaic web browser and cofounded Netscape Communications, and Randy Adams, president of the Internet Shopping Network, stepped in to help Filo and Yang commercialize the service. Yahoo! hired Timothy Koogle, the former head of Intermec, a maker of data collection and communications products, as CEO. (Filo and Yang both have the title of Chief Yahoo.) In late 1995 Yahoo! and Ziff-Davis announced that they would codevelop products for delivery online, on CD-ROM, and in print.

Despite its meager revenues and minimal operating history, the company's estimated valuation at the time of its 1996 initial public offering was a staggering $300 million. Following the offering, investment firm Sequoia Capital owned about 20% of the company, and David Filo and Jerry Yang each owned about 20%. Other shareholders included Reuters New Media and SOFTBANK.

A 1996 partnership with software firm Agents, Inc. led to My Yahoo!, which lets users customize the search engine to retrieve content directly related to their personal interests.

WHO

President and CEO: Timothy Koogle, age 44, $68,750 pay
Chief Yahoo: Jerry Yang, age 27
Chief Yahoo and Acting VP Engineering and Operations: David Filo, age 29
SVP Business Operations: Jeff Mallett, age 31
SVP Finance and Administration and CFO: Gary Valenzuela, age 39
Auditors: Price Waterhouse LLP

WHERE

HQ: 3400 Central Expressway, Ste. 201, Santa Clara, CA 95051
Phone: 408-731-3300   **Fax:** 408-731-3301
Web site: http://www.yahoo.com

WHAT

Selected Products
Yahoo! (search engine for indexing the location of information on the Web)
My Yahoo! (customized searches)
Regional guides online
Yahoo! Canada (regional guide, with Rogers Communications)
Yahoo! Internet Life (online and print magazine, with Ziff-Davis)
Yahoo! Japan (Japanese-language guide, with Softbank Corp.)
Yahooligans! (Internet navigational guide for children ages 8-14)

Selected Search Categories
Arts
Business and Economy
Computers and Internet
Education
Entertainment
Government
Health
News
Recreation
Reference
Regional
Science
Social Science
Society and Culture

KEY COMPETITORS

America Online
CompuServe
DEC
Excite
Individual
Infonautics
Infoseek
Lycos
Open Text
Wired Ventures
Wolff New Media

HOW MUCH

Nasdaq symbol: YHOO FYE: December 31	Annual Growth	1990	1991	1992	1993	1994	1995[1]
Sales ($ mil.)	—	—	—	—	—	—	1.4
Net income ($ mil.)	—	—	—	—	—	—	(0.6)
Income as % of sales	—	—	—	—	—	—	—
Employees	—	—	—	—	—	—	39

[1] 10-month fiscal year

1995 YEAR-END
Cash (mil.): $5.3
Current ratio: 8.14
Long-term debt (mil.): $0.1
R&D as % of sales: 17.8%
Advertising as % of sales: 9.2%

ZILOG, INC.

OVERVIEW

Zilog has more chips than a Toll House cookie. The Campbell, California-based company makes more than 2,000 models of application-specific standard product (ASSP) chips. Its customers are OEMs in the communications, computer, and consumer electronics markets, including AT&T, Motorola, and Texas Instruments.

Founded in 1974 by Intel whiz kids Ralph Ungermann (cofounder of networking products maker Ungermann-Bass, now part of computer maker Tandem) and Federico Faggin, Zilog came up with one of the first mass-produced 8-bit microprocessors (the Z80). It also secured corporate funding from Exxon. But when IBM, which was shopping for a microprocessor to power its first generation of PCs, chose Intel's product over Zilog's, the company became a money loser. Exxon bought Zilog out in 1981. Edgar Sack was called in to turn the company around in 1984, and he led a management buyout in 1989. Zilog went public in 1991. Venture capital firm Warburg, Pincus owns 28% of the company.

Zilog has looked overseas for business opportunities. In 1994 the company announced its first shipment of television controls to China, and the following year it signed an agreement with semiconductor distributor Memec for that company to sell Zilog's products in several Asian countries.

Through its proprietary Superintegration Library methodology, Zilog mixes and matches combinations of cores (microprocessors and peripheral circuits) and cells (logic and memory circuits) onto a piece of silicon.

Zilog said in 1996 it would spend $50 million on a new process research facility. That year the company introduced a television controller that includes the so-called V-chip (which lets viewers block some channels).

WHO

Chairman, President, and CEO: Edgar A. Sack, age 65, $912,916 pay
SVP Worldwide Sales: Thomas C. Carson, age 55, $320,235 pay
SVP Operations: Michael J. Bradshaw, age 46, $300,807 pay
SVP Technology: Richard L. Moore, age 61
VP Consumer Products Division: Alan Secor, age 62, $300,767 pay
VP; General Manager, Data Communications Division: John James Magill, age 50
VP and CFO: Robert E. Collins
VP, General Counsel, and Secretary: Richard R. Pickard
VP Human Resources: Sally M. Baumwell, age 51
Auditors: Ernst & Young LLP

WHERE

HQ: 210 E. Hacienda Ave., Campbell, CA 95008-6600
Phone: 408-370-8000   **Fax:** 408-370-8056
Web site: http://www.zilog.com

WHAT

Selected Products

Consumer Products	Data Communications
Battery charger controllers	Data communications
Database processors	controllers
Digital telephone	Embedded controllers
answering device	Fax/modem controllers
controllers	
IR (infrared) remote	**Intelligent Peripherals**
controllers	Keyboard controllers
Microcontrollers	Mouse and trackball
ROM DSPs (digital signal	controllers
processors)	Pointing device controllers
TV controllers	

KEY COMPETITORS

Elantec
Exar
IMP
VLSI Technology

HOW MUCH

NYSE symbol: ZLG FYE: December 31	Annual Growth	1990	1991	1992	1993	1994	1995
Sales ($ mil.)	21.5%	100.0	110.1	145.7	202.7	233.3	265.1
Net income ($ mil.)	42.2%	7.3	10.5	16.0	26.8	34.9	42.5
Income as % of sales	—	7.3%	9.5%	11.0%	13.2%	15.0%	16.0%
Earnings per share ($)	25.5%	0.67	0.76	0.95	1.43	1.80	2.09
Stock price – high ($)	—	—	13.51	23.01	40.75	37.75	54.13
Stock price – low ($)	—	—	6.67	11.67	19.00	24.75	28.25
Stock price – close ($)	28.3%	—	13.51	22.84	30.50	29.50	36.63
P/E – high	—	—	18	24	28	21	26
P/E – low	—	—	9	12	13	14	14
Dividends per share ($)	—	—	0.00	0.00	0.00	0.00	0.00
Book value per share ($)	33.1%	—	4.56	6.68	9.25	11.49	14.33
Employees	5.6%	1,200	1,280	1,449	1,460	1,429	1,574

1995 YEAR-END
Debt ratio: 0.0%
Return on equity: 17.3%
Cash (mil.): $82
Current ratio: 2.55
Long-term debt (mil.): $0
No. of shares (mil.): 20
Dividends
 Yield: —
 Payout: —
Market value (mil.): $713
R&D as % of sales: 9.2%

ZOOM TELEPHONICS, INC.

OVERVIEW

Modem maker Zoom wants you to be able to talk and share data at the same time. The Boston-based company makes PC communications devices such as its ComStar Speakerphone/FaxModem, which can simultaneously send and receive voice and data over one phone line. Zoom is building its international sales and targeting OEMs amid the rising communications expectations of PC users around the world. Founders Frank Manning and Peter Kramer own about about 10% and 7% of the company, respectively. Pat Manning owns about 6%.

Manning and Kramer started Zoom in 1977 to sell speed dialers that Manning had designed while he was a student at MIT. The company marketed the dialers to customers of MCI and Sprint, who needed to dial a long string of numbers to access their long-distance services. In 1985 regulators eliminated the need for a long-distance access code; Zoom's sales plummeted, but they rebounded when the company changed gears and concentrated on making and selling modems.

Unable to find enough financing in the US, in 1988 Zoom went public on the Vancouver Stock Exchange. The company withdrew at the end of 1991, when it began trading on Nasdaq.

In 1993 Zoom began selling a modem that integrated voice processing and fax technology; it entered the fast-growing PCMCIA (also known as PC card) modem market in 1994.

The next year the company introduced HotScan as a feature on its new Zoom/Voice FaxModem, enabling a fax machine to be used as a computer scanner.

In 1996 the company entered the remote access market via its acquisition of Tribe Computer Works.

WHO

Chairman, President, and CEO: Frank B. Manning, age 47, $88,750 pay
EVP: Peter R. Kramer, age 44
VP Finance and CFO: Steven T. Shedd, age 43
VP Operations: Deena M. Randall, age 42
VP Engineering: Dana Whitney, age 33
VP Sales and Marketing: Terry J. Manning, age 44
VP Strategic Business Development: Eugene Chang, age 42
Chief Accounting Officer: Stephen P. Golden, age 38
Director Human Resources: Marty Levin
Auditors: KPMG Peat Marwick LLP

WHERE

HQ: 207 South St., Boston, MA 02111
Phone: 617-423-1072   **Fax:** 617-338-5015
Web site: http://www.zoomtel.com

WHAT

Selected Fax/Modems

External	Zoom/FaxModem VFP
Zoom/FaxModem V.34X	14.4V (14.4 kbps,
(28.8 kbps, Internet	Caller ID, Internet
software)	software, voice mail)
Internal	**PCMCIA**
Internet Complete 28.8	Zoom/PCMCIA V.34C
(28.8 kbps, Internet	(28.8 kbps, Internet
software, Internet	software)
extras)	
Zoom/ComStar 28.8	
(28.8 kbps, Caller ID,	
full-duplex	
speakerphone, Internet	
software, Plug & Play)	

KEY COMPETITORS

Active Voice	Global Village	NCR
Apex Data	GVC	Oki
Boca Research	Technologies	Racal Electronics
Brooktrout	Hayes	System
Technology	Microcomputer	Connection
DATA RACE	Motorola	U.S. Robotics
Diamond	Multi-Tech	
Multimedia	Systems	

HOW MUCH

Nasdaq symbol: ZOOM FYE: December 31	Annual Growth	1990	1991	1992	1993	1994	1995
Sales ($ mil.)	49.5%	13.0	25.6	41.9	55.2	68.2	97.0
Net income ($ mil.)	32.4%	1.5	2.3	3.6	3.8	2.8	6.1
Income as % of sales	—	11.5%	9.0%	8.6%	6.9%	4.1%	6.3%
Earnings per share ($)	29.4%	0.27	0.40	0.62	0.63	0.47	0.98
Stock price – high ($)	—	3.00	16.25	18.25	20.00	14.25	20.75
Stock price – low ($)	—	2.00	3.13	9.63	9.75	5.88	6.75
Stock price – close ($)	45.8%	3.00	15.75	17.25	11.25	7.88	19.75
P/E – high	—	11	41	29	32	30	21
P/E – low	—	7	8	16	15	13	7
Dividends per share ($)	—	0.00	0.00	0.00	0.00	0.00	0.00
Book value per share ($)	52.1%	0.54	1.02	1.94	2.70	3.21	4.40
Employees	38.6%	49	75	97	110	165	251

1995 YEAR-END
Debt ratio: 8.4%
Return on equity: 26.0%
Cash (mil.): $0
Current ratio: 2.08
Long-term debt (mil.): $0
No. of shares (mil.): 6
Dividends
 Yield: —
 Payout: —
Market value (mil.): $123
R&D as % of sales: 1.9%

Key Computer Companies

1MAGE SOFTWARE, INC.

6486 S. Quebec St.
Englewood, CO 80111
Phone: 303-694-9180
Fax: 303-796-0587

CEO: David R. DeYoung
CFO: Mary Anne DeYoung
HR: Mary Anne DeYoung
Employees: 20

1995 Sales: $3.0 million
1-Yr. Sales Change: (34.8%)
Exchange: Nasdaq (SC)
Symbol: ISOL

Computers - electronic document imaging software

1ST TECH CORPORATION

12201 Technology Blvd., Ste. 130
Austin, TX 78727
Phone: 512-258-3570
Fax: 512-258-3689

CEO: Gary Pankonien
CFO: —
HR: Nancy Marshall
Employees: —

1995 Sales: $105.0 million
1-Yr. Sales Change: 150.0%
Ownership: Privately Held

Electrical components - computer memory components

II-VI INCORPORATED

375 Saxonburg Blvd.
Saxonburg, PA 16056
Phone: 412-352-4455
Fax: 412-352-4980

CEO: Carl J. Johnson
CFO: James Martinelli
HR: Kathy Kinnamon
Employees: 415

1996 Sales: $37.9 million
1-Yr. Sales Change: 36.3%
Exchange: Nasdaq
Symbol: IIVI

Electrical components - optical & electro-optical components, devices & materials for infrared, near-infrared, visible & x-ray/gamma-ray instruments & applications

3COM CORPORATION

5400 Bayfront Plaza
Santa Clara, CA 95052
Phone: 408-764-5000
Fax: 408-764-5001

CEO: Eric A. Benhamou
CFO: Christopher B. Paisley
HR: Debra Engel
Employees: 5,190

1996 Sales: $2,327.1 million
1-Yr. Sales Change: 79.7%
Exchange: OTC
Symbol: COMS

Computers - local-area network (LAN) routers, hubs, remote access-servers, switches & adapters

 See pages 26–27 for a full profile of this company.

3D SYSTEMS CORPORATION

26081 Avenue Hall
Valencia, CA 91355
Phone: 805-295-5600
Fax: 805-295-0249

CEO: Arthur B. Sims
CFO: Gordon L. Almquist
HR: Gordon L. Almquist
Employees: 273

1995 Sales: $62.6 million
1-Yr. Sales Change: 44.6%
Exchange: Nasdaq
Symbol: TDSC

Instruments - stereolithographic systems that create 3-dimensional models from CAD/CAM-generated specifications

3NET SYSTEMS, INC.

629 J St.
Sacramento, CA 95814
Phone: 916-498-3900
Fax: 916-498-3900

CEO: George Van Derven
CFO: George Van Derven
HR: —
Employees: 39

1996 Sales: $1.8 million
1-Yr. Sales Change: (21.7%)
Exchange: OTC
Symbol: TNET

Computers - integrated computer network systems for hospitals, commercial & insurance laboratories & physician clinics

4FRONT SOFTWARE INTERNATIONAL, INC.

5650 Greenwood Plaza Blvd., Ste. 107
Englewood, CO 80111
Phone: 303-721-7341
Fax: 303-220-1818

CEO: Anil Doshi
CFO: Craig Kleinman
HR: —
Employees: 175

1996 Sales: $32.2 million
1-Yr. Sales Change: 187.5%
Exchange: Nasdaq
Symbol: FFST

Computers - software & hardware sales, consulting, service & support, specializing in systems integration

7TH LEVEL, INC.

1110 E. Collins Blvd., Ste. 122
Richardson, TX 75081
Phone: 214-498-8100
Fax: 214-437-2717

CEO: George D. Grayson
CFO: David W. Craig
HR: Sherry Denning
Employees: 203

1995 Sales: $12.2 million
1-Yr. Sales Change: 197.6%
Exchange: Nasdaq
Symbol: SEVL

Computers - interactive software (TuneLand), screen savers (Take Your Best Shot) & games (Battle Beast)

 See page 244 for a full profile of this company.

ACCENT SOFTWARE INTERNATIONAL LTD.

28 Pierre Koenig St.
Jerusalem 93469, Israel
Phone: +972-2-793-723
Fax: +972-2-793-731

CEO: Robert S. Rosenschein
CFO: Avi Basher
HR: —
Employees: 116

1995 Sales: $5.1 million
1-Yr. Sales Change: 168.4%
Exchange: Nasdaq (SC)
Symbol: ACNTF

Computers - multilingual application software

ACCESS SOLUTIONS INTERNATIONAL, INC.

650 Ten Rod Rd.
North Kingstown, RI 02852
Phone: 401-295-2691
Fax: 401-295-1851

CEO: Hector D. Wiltshire
CFO: Thomas E. Gardner
HR: Louise Henry
Employees: 31

1995 Sales: $3.1 million
1-Yr. Sales Change: 520.0%
Ownership: Privately Held

Computers - optical data COLD (computer output to laser disk) storage systems, including hardware (Optical Archiving System, ODSM, GIGAPAGE) & software for storing large quantities of information

ACCLAIM ENTERTAINMENT, INC.

One Acclaim Plaza	CEO: Gregory E. Fischbach	1995 Sales: $566.7 million
Glen Cove, NY 11542	CFO: Anthony R. Williams	1-Yr. Sales Change: 17.9%
Phone: 516-656-5000	HR: John Ma	Exchange: Nasdaq
Fax: 516-656-2040	Employees: 800	Symbol: AKLM

Computers - video games (WWF Raw, NFL Quarterback Club, The Simpsons), PC CD-ROM games (StarGate, Batman Forever) & comic books (Ninjak, Bloodshot)

 See page 245 for a full profile of this company.

ACCOLADE INC.

5300 Stevens Creek Blvd.	CEO: Jim Barnett	1995 Sales: $31.4 million
San Jose, CA 95129	CFO: Jill Anderson	1-Yr. Sales Change: (27.8%)
Phone: 408-985-1700	HR: Jill Higgins	Ownership: Privately Held
Fax: 408-246-0885	Employees: 95	

Computers - interactive game software (Jack Nicklaus Golf, Charles Barkley Basketball)

ACE*COMM CORPORATION

209 Perry Pkwy.	CEO: George T. Jimenez	1996 Sales: $20.0 million
Gaithersburg, MD 20877	CFO: George T. Jimenez	1-Yr. Sales Change: 61.3%
Phone: 301-258-9850	HR: Kim Schulze	Exchange: Nasdaq
Fax: 301-921-0434	Employees: 137	Symbol: ACEC

Computers - operations support systems for functions including billing data collection, network surveillance & management & alarm processing for networks deployed by telecommunications service providers

ACER INCORPORATED

156 Min Sheng East Rd., Sec. 3, 6F	CEO: Stan Shih	1995 Sales: $3,925.0 million
Taipei 105, Taiwan	CFO: Michael Tung	1-Yr. Sales Change: 63.7%
Phone: +886-2-545-5288	HR: Ken Stempson	Exchange: Taiwan
Fax: +886-2-545-5308	Employees: 11,000	

Computers - PCs (#1 maker in Taiwan); peripherals & semiconductor components

 **See pages 28–29 for a full profile of this company.**

ACT MANUFACTURING, INC.

108 Forest Ave.	CEO: John A. Pino	1995 Sales: $115.7 million
Hudson, MA 01749	CFO: Douglass C. Greenlaw	1-Yr. Sales Change: 34.8%
Phone: 508-562-1200	HR: Dodie Cavazza	Exchange: Nasdaq
Fax: 508-568-1904	Employees: 655	Symbol: ACTM

Electrical components - electronic interconnection assemblies

ACT NETWORKS, INC.

188 Camino Ruiz	CEO: Martin Shum	1996 Sales: $28.4 million
Camarillo, CA 93012-6741	CFO: Melvin L. Flowers	1-Yr. Sales Change: 37.9%
Phone: 805-388-2474	HR: Deborah Lyons	Exchange: Nasdaq
Fax: 805-388-3504	Employees: 158	Symbol: ANET

Computers - integrated WAN access products designed to work with terrestrial & wireless media

ACTEL CORPORATION

955 E. Arques Ave.	CEO: John C. East	1995 Sales: $108.5 million
Sunnyvale, CA 94086-4533	CFO: David M. Sugishita	1-Yr. Sales Change: 42.8%
Phone: 408-739-1010	HR: Michelle A. Begun	Exchange: Nasdaq
Fax: 408-739-1540	Employees: 297	Symbol: ACTL

Electrical components - field programmable gate arrays (ACT1, ACT2, ACT3) & associated software development tools (Activator)

ACTIVE VOICE CORPORATION

2901 Third Ave., Ste. 500	CEO: Robert L. Richmond	1996 Sales: $45.1 million
Seattle, WA 98121-9800	CFO: Jose S. David	1-Yr. Sales Change: 22.2%
Phone: 206-441-4700	HR: Debbie Faulkner	Exchange: Nasdaq
Fax: 206-441-4784	Employees: 177	Symbol: ACVC

Telecommunications equipment - computer-based voice-processing systems (Repartee, Replay, Replay Plus, TeLANophy)

ACTIVISION, INC.

11601 Wilshire Blvd.	CEO: Robert A. Kotick	1996 Sales: $61.4 million
Los Angeles, CA 90025	CFO: Brian G. Kelly	1-Yr. Sales Change: 50.9%
Phone: 310-473-9200	HR: Joe Gamez	Exchange: Nasdaq
Fax: 310-479-4005	Employees: 189	Symbol: ATVI

Computers - interactive entertainment software & multigame CD-ROMs

ACXIOM CORPORATION

301 Industrial Blvd.	CEO: Charles D. Morgan Jr.	1996 Sales: $269.9 million
Conway, AR 72032	CFO: Robert S. Bloom	1-Yr. Sales Change: 33.3%
Phone: 501-336-1000	HR: Cindy Childers	Exchange: Nasdaq
Fax: 501-336-3913	Employees: 3,098	Symbol: ACXM

Business services - mailing lists, integration list processing & related software; mail-order automation software, data products, data warehousing & decision abort; CD-ROM telephone directories (ProCD)

A.D.A.M. SOFTWARE, INC.

1600 Riveredge Pkwy., Ste. 800	CEO: Robert S. Cramer Jr.	1996 Sales: $6.4 million
Atlanta, GA 30328	CFO: Robert A. DiProva	1-Yr. Sales Change: 12.3%
Phone: 770-980-0888	HR: Christine H. Finch	Exchange: Nasdaq
Fax: 770-955-3088	Employees: 72	Symbol: ADAM

Computers - educational multimedia software that provides anatomical, medical, scientific & health-related information for academic & consumer markets

ADAPTEC, INC.

691 S. Milpitas Blvd.	CEO: F. Grant Saviers	1996 Sales: $659.3 million
Milpitas, CA 95035	CFO: Paul G. Hansen	1-Yr. Sales Change: 41.4%
Phone: 408-945-8600	HR: Daniel W. Bowman	Exchange: Nasdaq
Fax: 408-262-2533	Employees: 2,111	Symbol: ADPT

Computers - small computer system interface (SCSI) hardware & software

 See page 246 for a full profile of this company.

ADAPTIVE SOLUTIONS, INC.

1400 NW Compton Dr., Ste. 340	CEO: John D. Heightley	1995 Sales: $10.8 million
Beaverton, OR 97006	CFO: John C. Carveth	1-Yr. Sales Change: 170.0%
Phone: 503-690-1236	HR: —	Exchange: Nasdaq (SC)
Fax: 503-690-1249	Employees: 64	Symbol: ADSO

Computers - massively parallel pattern recognition computing products

ADE CORPORATION

77 Rowe St.	CEO: Robert C. Abbe	1996 Sales: $65.6 million
Newton, MA 02166	CFO: Mark D. Shooman	1-Yr. Sales Change: 45.5%
Phone: 617-969-0600	HR: —	Exchange: Nasdaq
Fax: —	Employees: 269	Symbol: ADEX

Electronics - automated measurement, defect detection & handling equipment for making semiconductor wafers & devices & computer disks

ADFLEX SOLUTIONS, INC.

2001 W. Chandler Blvd.	CEO: Rolando C. Esteverena	1995 Sales: $101.2 million
Chandler, AZ 85224	CFO: Dale J. Bartos	1-Yr. Sales Change: 30.2%
Phone: 602-963-4584	HR: R. Charles Furniss	Exchange: Nasdaq
Fax: 602-786-8280	Employees: 2,465	Symbol: AFLX

Electrical components - flexible copper-based circuits to connect electronic components in PCs, disk drives, cellular phones & other consumer products

ADOBE SYSTEMS INCORPORATED

345 Park Ave.
San Jose, CA 95110-2704
Phone: 415-536-6000
Fax: 415-537-6000

CEO: John E. Warnock
CFO: Charles M. Geschke
HR: Rebecca Guerra
Employees: 2,319

1995 Sales: $762.3 million
1-Yr. Sales Change: 27.5%
Exchange: Nasdaq
Symbol: ADBE

Computers - font (PostScript) & desktop publishing (PageMaker) software

 See pages 30–31 for a full profile of this company.

ADVANCED ENERGY INDUSTRIES, INC.

1625 Sharp Point Dr.
Fort Collins, CO 80525
Phone: 970-221-4670
Fax: 970-221-5583

CEO: Douglas S. Schatz
CFO: Richard P. Beck
HR: Susan C. Schell
Employees: 574

1995 Sales: $94.7 million
1-Yr. Sales Change: 82.5%
Exchange: Nasdaq
Symbol: AEIS

Machinery - power conversion & control systems for the manufacture of semiconductors, flat panel displays & data storage & other industrial thin-film equipment

ADVANCED LOGIC RESEARCH, INC.

9401 Jeronimo Rd.
Irvine, CA 92718
Phone: 714-581-6770
Fax: 714-581-9240

CEO: Gene Lu
CFO: Ronald J. Sipkovich
HR: Irene Martinez
Employees: 475

1995 Sales: $192.4 million
1-Yr. Sales Change: 4.1%
Exchange: Nasdaq
Symbol: AALR

Computers - network servers, high-performance workstations & entry-level PCs

ADVANCED MICRO DEVICES, INC.

One AMD Place
Sunnyvale, CA 94088-3453
Phone: 408-732-2400
Fax: 408-982-6164

CEO: W. Jeremiah Sanders III
CFO: Marvin D. Burkett
HR: Stanley Winvick
Employees: 12,730

1995 Sales: $2,429.7 million
1-Yr. Sales Change: 13.8%
Exchange: NYSE
Symbol: AMD

Electrical components - microprocessors, flash memories, programmable logic devices, integrated circuits & networking devices

 See pages 32–33 for a full profile of this company.

ADVANCED SEMICONDUCTOR MATERIALS INTERNATIONAL N.V.

Jan Steenlaan 9
NL-3723 BS Bilthoven, The Netherlands
Phone: +31-30-281-836
Fax: +31-30-287-469

CEO: Arthur H. del Prado
CFO: Hans Peter Hukshorn
HR: —
Employees: 4,037

1995 Sales: $418.6 million
1-Yr. Sales Change: 52.9%
Exchange: Hong Kong

Semiconductor devices; wafer fabrication equipment

AFFILIATED COMPUTER SERVICES, INC.

2828 N. Haskell	CEO: Darwin Deason	1996 Sales: $396.5 million
Dallas, TX 75204	CFO: Mark A. King	1-Yr. Sales Change: 26.6%
Phone: 214-841-6111	HR: Pam McMahan	Exchange: Nasdaq
Fax: 214-821-8315	Employees: 5,580	Symbol: ACSA

Computers - data processing outsourcing; ATM network (MoneyMaker); information management systems

AG ASSOCIATES

4425 Fortran Dr.	CEO: Arnon Gat	1995 Sales: $62.7 million
San Jose, CA 95134-2300	CFO: Susan Salvesen	1-Yr. Sales Change: 55.6%
Phone: 408-745-1790	HR: Madonna Bolano	Exchange: Nasdaq
Fax: 408-935-2737	Employees: 237	Symbol: AGAI

Machinery - semiconductor manufacturing equipment

ALADDIN KNOWLEDGE SYSTEMS LTD.

15 Beit Oved St., PO Box 11141	CEO: Yanki Margalit	1995 Sales: $11.3 million
Tel Aviv 61110, Israel	CFO: Nurit Benjamini	1-Yr. Sales Change: 52.7%
Phone: +972-3-5375795	HR: Eyla Margalit	Exchange: Nasdaq
Fax: +972-3-5375796	Employees: 113	Symbol: ALDNF

Computers - software & hardware systems for preventing unauthorized copying of software (Hardlock, HASP, CodeSafe, OpenHASP, TimeHASP)

ALBARA CORPORATION

610 S. Frazier	CEO: Real Provencher	1995 Sales: $1.6 million
Conroe, TX 77301	CFO: Real Provencher	1-Yr. Sales Change: (27.3%)
Phone: 409-539-2992	HR: —	Exchange: OTC
Fax: 409-539-4141	Employees: 14	Symbol: ALBR

Retail - Macintosh laser printer accessories & software

ALIGN-RITE INTERNATIONAL, INC.

2428 Ontario St.	CEO: James L. MacDonald	1996 Sales: $33.3 million
Burbank, CA 91504	CFO: Petar N. Katurich	1-Yr. Sales Change: 106.8%
Phone: 818-843-7220	HR: Liz Ashual	Exchange: Nasdaq
Fax: 818-566-3042	Employees: 191	Symbol: MASK

Electrical components - photomasks used to produce integrated circuits, thin-film magnetic recording heads, flat panel displays & circuit boards

ADVANCED TECHNOLOGY MATERIALS, INC.

7 Commerce Dr.	CEO: Eugene G. Banucci	1995 Sales: $30.0 million
Danbury, CT 06810-4169	CFO: Daniel P. Sharkey	1-Yr. Sales Change: 51.5%
Phone: 203-794-1100	HR: Phyllis Banucci	Exchange: Nasdaq
Fax: 203-792-8040	Employees: 173	Symbol: ATMI

Electrical components - diamond & silicon carbide semiconductors; thin-film precursors

ADVANCED VOICE TECHNOLOGY

639 Lexington Ave.	CEO: Gwyeth Smith	1995 Sales: $0.7 million
New York, NY 10017	CFO: Philip Brettschneider	1-Yr. Sales Change: —
Phone: 212-599-2062	HR: —	Exchange: Nasdaq (SC)
Fax: 212-697-5910	Employees: 17	Symbol: HMWK

Computers - hardware & software applications that allow teachers & school administrators to communicate with parents & students on a daily basis

ADVANTIS

231 N. Martingale Rd.	CEO: Syd N. Heaton	1995 Sales: $1,130.0 million
Schaumburg, IL 60173	CFO: Patrick M. Kerin	1-Yr. Sales Change: —
Phone: 847-240-3000	HR: James P. Doyle	Ownership: Joint Venture
Fax: 847-340-3868	Employees: 3,000	

Telecommunications services - data communications & networking services (joint venture between IBM & Sears)

ADVENT SOFTWARE, INC.

301 Brannan St., 6th Fl.	CEO: Stephanie G. DiMarco	1995 Sales: $26.0 million
San Francisco, CA 94107-1849	CFO: Irv H. Lichtenwald	1-Yr. Sales Change: 29.4%
Phone: 415-543-7696	HR: Lisa Ebersole	Exchange: Nasdaq
Fax: 415-543-5070	Employees: 211	Symbol: ADVS

Computers - software, data interfaces & related services for investment portfolio management (Axys, Geneva, WinDx), trade order management (Moxy) & client contact & management (Qube)

 See page 247 for a full profile of this company.

AETRIUM INC.

2350 Helen St.	CEO: Joseph C. Levesque	1995 Sales: $47.6 million
North St. Paul, MN 55109	CFO: Darnell L. Boehm	1-Yr. Sales Change: 82.4%
Phone: 612-770-2000	HR: Michael Jaeb	Exchange: Nasdaq
Fax: 612-770-7975	Employees: 134	Symbol: ATRM

Machinery - semiconductor manufacturing equipment

ALL AMERICAN SEMICONDUCTOR, INC.

16115 NW 52nd Ave.	CEO: Paul Goldberg	1995 Sales: $180.8 million
Miami, FL 33014	CFO: Howard L. Flanders	1-Yr. Sales Change: 78.8%
Phone: 305-621-8282	HR: Denise Topfer	Exchange: Nasdaq
Fax: 305-620-7831	Employees: 571	Symbol: SEMI

Electrical components - wholesale semiconductors

ALLEGRO NEW MEDIA, INC.

16 Passaic Ave., Unit 6	CEO: Barry A. Cinnamon	1995 Sales: $1.4 million
Fairfield, NJ 07004	CFO: Mark E. Leininger	1-Yr. Sales Change: 40.0%
Phone: 201-808-1992	HR: —	Exchange: Nasdaq (SC)
Fax: 201-808-2645	Employees: 36	Symbol: ANMI

Publishing - interactive how-to, business & instructional CD-ROMs (Learn To Do, Berlitz Executive Travel, Entrepreneur Magazine, Business Reference, InPrint Art Library)

ALLIANCE SEMICONDUCTOR CORPORATION

3099 N. First St.	CEO: N. Damodar Dan Reddy	1996 Sales: $201.1 million
San Jose, CA 95134	CFO: Ronald K. Shelton	1-Yr. Sales Change: 68.6%
Phone: 408-383-4900	HR: Peggy Maxfield	Exchange: Nasdaq
Fax: 408-383-4999	Employees: 74	Symbol: ALSC

Electrical components - high-speed SRAM & DRAM memory semiconductors

ALLIED DIGITAL TECHNOLOGIES CORP.

7375 Woodward Ave.	CEO: William H. Smith	1995 Sales: $119.8 million
Detroit, MI 48202-3145	CFO: Charles P. Kavanagh	1-Yr. Sales Change: 192.9%
Phone: 313-871-2222	HR: Larry Henry	Exchange: AMEX
Fax: 313-871-4120	Employees: 1,490	Symbol: ADK

Business services - CD, audio- & videocassette duplication services

ALLSTAR SYSTEMS, INC.

6401 Southwest Fwy.	CEO: James H. Long	1995 Sales: $91.1 million
Houston, TX 77074	CFO: Donald R. Chadwick	1-Yr. Sales Change: 42.1%
Phone: 713-795-2000	HR: —	Ownership: Privately Held
Fax: 713-795-2036	Employees: 279	

Computers - computer & telecommunications hardware & software products & related services

ALPHA MICROSYSTEMS

2722 S. Fairview	CEO: Douglas J. Tullio	1996 Sales: $32.8 million
Santa Ana, CA 92704	CFO: Michael J. Lowell	1-Yr. Sales Change: (15.5%)
Phone: 714-957-8500	HR: Bill Mitchell	Exchange: Nasdaq
Fax: 714-957-8705	Employees: 321	Symbol: ALMI

Computers - open systems computers (Eagle 100, AM 4000, Falcon add-in processors) & specialized software (PANDA, FOCUS, SWORDS)

ALPHA SOLARCO INC.

510 E. University Dr.	CEO: Edward C. Schmidt	1996 Sales: $1.0 million
Phoenix, AZ 85004	CFO: Edward C. Schmidt	1-Yr. Sales Change: (72.2%)
Phone: 602-252-3055	HR: —	Exchange: Nasdaq (SC)
Fax: 602-252-8053	Employees: 5	Symbol: ASCO

Electrical components - photovoltaic solar cell & solar thermal technology

ALPHA TECHNOLOGIES GROUP, INC.

750 Lexington Ave., 27th Fl.	CEO: Lawrence Butler	1995 Sales: $64.1 million
New York, NY 10022-1208	CFO: Johnny J. Blanchard	1-Yr. Sales Change: 113.0%
Phone: 212-446-5258	HR: Steve Chupik	Exchange: Nasdaq
Fax: —	Employees: 693	Symbol: ATGI

Electrical components - standard heat sinks for microprocessors, connectors, back-panels, cables & cable assemblies

ALPHANET SOLUTIONS, INC.

7 Ridgedale Ave.	CEO: Stan Gang	1995 Sales: $74.0 million
Cedar Knolls, NJ 07927	CFO: Gary S. Finkel	1-Yr. Sales Change: 5.0%
Phone: 201-267-0088	HR: Kim Cataldo	Exchange: Nasdaq
Fax: 201-267-8675	Employees: 206	Symbol: ALPH

Computers - information technology products & services, including computer hardware & software

ALPHAREL, INC.

9339 Carroll Park Dr.	CEO: Stephen P. Gardner	1995 Sales: $12.7 million
San Diego, CA 92121	CFO: John W. Low	1-Yr. Sales Change: 33.7%
Phone: 619-625-3000	HR: Amy Fager	Exchange: Nasdaq
Fax: 619-546-7671	Employees: 193	Symbol: AREL

Computers - document management software & automation systems

ALPHATRONIX INCORPORATED

4022 Stirrup Creek Dr., Ste. 315
Durham, NC 27703-9000
Phone: 919-544-0001
Fax: 919-544-4079

CEO: Robert P. Freese
CFO: Dennis B. Phillips
HR: Suzanne Jones
Employees: 65

1995 Sales: $6.0 million
1-Yr. Sales Change: (33.3%)
Ownership: Privately Held

Computers - software & systems for storage management

ALTAVISTA INTERNET SOFTWARE, INC.

30 Porter Rd.
Littleton, MA 01460
Phone: 508-486-2700
Fax: 508-486-2878

CEO: Ilene H. Lang
CFO: Robert E. Hult
HR: James E. Toale
Employees: 186

1996 Sales: $3.6 million
1-Yr. Sales Change: 260.0%
Exchange: Nasdaq
Symbol: ALTV

Computers - online services, software products for emerging Internet & Intranet business environments;
licenses internet services to major telecommunications & media companies

ALTERA CORPORATION

2610 Orchard Pkwy.
San Jose, CA 95134-2020
Phone: 408-894-7000
Fax: 408-428-0463

CEO: Rodney Smith
CFO: Nathan Sarkisian
HR: John R. Fitzhenry
Employees: 881

1995 Sales: $401.6 million
1-Yr. Sales Change: 102.0%
Exchange: Nasdaq
Symbol: ALTR

Electrical components - programmable logic devices (Flex 8000) & software tools

 See page 248 for a full profile of this company.

ALTERNATIVE RESOURCES CORPORATION

75 Tri-State Intl., Ste. 100
Lincolnshire, IL 60069
Phone: 847-317-1000
Fax: 847-317-1008

CEO: Larry I. Kane
CFO: Bradley K. Lamers
HR: Silvia U. Masini
Employees: 208

1995 Sales: $154.2 million
1-Yr. Sales Change: 63.2%
Exchange: Nasdaq
Symbol: ALRC

Personnel - temporary staffing services to information-service-related operations

ALTRON INCORPORATED

One Jewel Dr.
Wilmington, MA 01887-3390
Phone: 508-658-5800
Fax: 508-988-0900

CEO: Samuel Altschuler
CFO: Peter D. Brennan
HR: Dennis Sokol
Employees: 1,047

1995 Sales: $143.9 million
1-Yr. Sales Change: 38.1%
Exchange: Nasdaq
Symbol: ALRN

Electrical components - printed circuit boards, backplanes & interconnect systems

AMATI COMMUNICATIONS CORPORATION

3801 Zanker Rd., PO Box 5143	CEO: James Steenbergen	1996 Sales: $12.1 million
San Jose, CA 95150-5143	CFO: James Steenbergen	1-Yr. Sales Change: 0.8%
Phone: 408-433-3300	HR: Lalo Valdez	Exchange: Nasdaq
Fax: 408-433-0260	Employees: 34	Symbol: AMTX

Computers - network connectivity products for use in IBM-compatible PCs in local area networks & in bridge products for interconnecting Token-Ring networks

AMDAHL CORPORATION

1250 E. Arques Ave.	CEO: John C. Lewis	1995 Sales: $1,516.4 million
Sunnyvale, CA 94088-3470	CFO: Bruce J. Ryan	1-Yr. Sales Change: (7.5%)
Phone: 408-746-6000	HR: Anthony Pozos	Exchange: AMEX
Fax: 408-773-0833	Employees: 8,000	Symbol: AMH

Computers - software for client/server applications & business processes; information technology services; mainframes & storage devices; open systems hardware & software

 See pages 34–35 for a full profile of this company.

AMERICA ONLINE, INC.

8619 Westwood Center Dr.	CEO: Stephen M. Case	1996 Sales: $1,093.9 million
Vienna, VA 22182-2285	CFO: Lennert J. Leader	1-Yr. Sales Change: 177.6%
Phone: 703-448-8700	HR: Mark Stavish	Exchange: NYSE
Fax: 703-883-1532	Employees: 5,828	Symbol: AOL

Computers - Internet access & online services, including e-mail, conferencing, software, computing support, interactive magazines & newspapers & online classes

 See pages 36–37 for a full profile of this company.

AMERICAN MANAGEMENT SYSTEMS, INCORPORATED

4050 Legato Rd.	CEO: Paul A. Brands	1995 Sales: $632.4 million
Fairfax, VA 22033	CFO: Frank A. Nicolai	1-Yr. Sales Change: 37.5%
Phone: 703-267-8000	HR: —	Exchange: Nasdaq
Fax: 703-267-8555	Employees: 5,400	Symbol: AMSY

Consulting - business analysis, information systems management, software programming & systems design & development, primarily for telecommunications firms, financial institutions & government agencies

AMERICAN MEDICAL ALERT CORP.

3265 Lawson Blvd.	CEO: Howard M. Siegel	1995 Sales: $6.2 million
Oceanside, NY 11572	CFO: Howard M. Siegel	1-Yr. Sales Change: 14.8%
Phone: 516-536-5850	HR: Howard M. Siegel	Exchange: Nasdaq (SC)
Fax: 516-536-5276	Employees: 84	Symbol: AMAC

Computers - emergency-response system sales, rental, installation & monitoring services

AMERICAN MEGATRENDS, INC.

6145-F Northbelt Pkwy.	CEO: Subramonian Shankar	1995 Sales: $90.0 million
Norcross, GA 30071	CFO: Victor Kannan	1-Yr. Sales Change: —
Phone: 770-263-8181	HR: Xina Tuerke	Ownership: Privately Held
Fax: 770-263-9381	Employees: 165	

Computers - BIOS software & system boards for PCs

AMERICAN POWER CONVERSION CORPORATION

132 Fairgrounds Rd.	CEO: Rodger B. Dowdell Jr.	1995 Sales: $515.3 million
West Kingston, RI 02892	CFO: Donald M. Muir	1-Yr. Sales Change: 36.2%
Phone: 401-789-5735	HR: Lisa Defruscio	Exchange: Nasdaq
Fax: 401-788-2710	Employees: 2,340	Symbol: APCC

Electrical products - uninterruptible power supplies, electrical surge protection devices & battery backups for computer systems

 See page 249 for a full profile of this company.

AMERICAN SOFTWARE, INC.

470 E. Paces Ferry Rd. NE	CEO: James C. Edenfield	1996 Sales: $77.6 million
Atlanta, GA 30305	CFO: Peter W. Pamplin	1-Yr. Sales Change: (2.4%)
Phone: 404-261-4381	HR: Ryan Lenox	Exchange: Nasdaq
Fax: 404-264-5514	Employees: 606	Symbol: AMSWA

Computers - supply chain management software used on IBM mainframes & UNIX open client/server computers

AMERIDATA CONSULTING

2550 University Ave. West, Ste. 180	CEO: David Mitchell	1995 Sales: $26.0 million
St. Paul, MN 55114	CFO: Joy Nipe	1-Yr. Sales Change: —
Phone: 612-642-2100	HR: Mary Ellen Leary	Ownership: Privately Held
Fax: 612-642-2101	Employees: 200	

Computers - consulting services

AMERIDATA TECHNOLOGIES, INC.

700 Canal St.	CEO: Gerald A. Poch	1995 Sales: $1,515.6 million
Stamford, CT 06902	CFO: James A. Parke	1-Yr. Sales Change: 48.7%
Phone: 203-357-1464	HR: Lawrence J. Toole	Ownership: Subsidiary
Fax: 203-357-1531	Employees: 3,500	

Computers - systems integration, networking services, technical support, maintenance, rental & other services (subsidiary of GE Capital Services)

 See pages 38–39 for a full profile of this company.

AMERIQUEST TECHNOLOGIES, INC.

6100 Hollywood Blvd., Seventh Fl.
Hollywood, FL 33024
Phone: 954-967-2397
Fax: 954-967-1134

CEO: Michael Dressen
CFO: Donald W. Resnick
HR: Susan Jackson
Employees: 497

1995 Sales: $416.6 million
1-Yr. Sales Change: 375.6%
Exchange: NYSE
Symbol: AQS

Computers - data storage enhancement products; distribution of hard disk drive subsystems

AMISTAR CORPORATION

237 Via Vera Cruz
San Marcos, CA 92069-2698
Phone: 619-471-1700
Fax: 619-471-3942

CEO: Stuart C. Baker
CFO: William W. Holl
HR: Joann Jensen
Employees: 144

1995 Sales: $25.4 million
1-Yr. Sales Change: 41.1%
Exchange: Nasdaq
Symbol: AMTA

Machinery - semiconductor manufacturing equipment

AMISYS MANAGED CARE SYSTEMS, INC.

30 W. Gude Dr., 5th Fl.
Rockville, MD 20850
Phone: 301-251-8600
Fax: 301-279-2253

CEO: Kevin R. Brown
CFO: Robert J. Sullivan
HR: Kathy H. Lyons
Employees: 182

1995 Sales: $31.8 million
1-Yr. Sales Change: —
Exchange: Nasdaq
Symbol: AMCS

Computers - managed health care information systems for payors & providers

AMP INCORPORATED

PO Box 3608
Harrisburg, PA 17105-3608
Phone: 717-564-0100
Fax: 717-780-6130

CEO: William J. Hudson Jr.
CFO: Robert Ripp
HR: Philip G. Guarneschelli
Employees: 40,800

1995 Sales: $5,227.2 million
1-Yr. Sales Change: 29.8%
Exchange: NYSE
Symbol: AMP

Electrical connectors - splices, connectors, cable & panel assemblies, networking units, sensors, switches, electro-optic devices, touch screen data entry systems & tooling

AMPEX CORPORATION

500 Broadway
Redwood City, CA 94063-3199
Phone: 415-367-2011
Fax: 415-367-2905

CEO: Edward J. Bramson
CFO: Craig L. McKibben
HR: Richard J. Jacquet
Employees: 531

1995 Sales: $95.7 million
1-Yr. Sales Change: (24.8%)
Exchange: AMEX
Symbol: AXC

Electrical products - magnetic recording (DST tape drives), digital image processing & digital storage equipment, including robotic library systems

AMPLICON, INC.

5 Hutton Centre Dr., Ste. 500	CEO: Patrick E. Paddon	1996 Sales: $257.2 million
Santa Ana, CA 92707	CFO: S. Leslie Jewett	1-Yr. Sales Change: 24.6%
Phone: 714-751-7551	HR: Lavone Jackson	Exchange: Nasdaq
Fax: 714-751-7557	Employees: 195	Symbol: AMPI

Leasing - midrange computers, peripherals, workstations, PC networks, telecommunications equipment, CAD/CAM equipment, office automation equipment & computer software

AMSTRAD PLC

Brentwood House, 169 Kings Rd.	CEO: Alan Sugar	1996 Sales: $329.3 million
Brentwood, Essex CM14 4EF, UK	CFO: A. G. Dean	1-Yr. Sales Change: (24.1%)
Phone: +44-1-277-228-888	HR: —	Exchange: London
Fax: +44-1-277-211-350	Employees: 1,103	

Computers - PCs & other electronic products, including satellite receivers & dishes, fax machines, telephones, printers & audio equipment

AMTECH SYSTEMS, INC.

131 S. Clark Dr.	CEO: Jong S. Whang	1995 Sales: $11.4 million
Tempe, AZ 85281	CFO: Robert T. Hass	1-Yr. Sales Change: 7.5%
Phone: 602-967-5146	HR: —	Exchange: Nasdaq (SC)
Fax: 602-968-3763	Employees: 43	Symbol: ASYS

Machinery - wafer processing systems used in the manufacture of semiconductors

AMX CORPORATION

11995 Forestgate Dr.	CEO: Joe Hardt	1996 Sales: $32.7 million
Dallas, TX 75243	CFO: David Chisum	1-Yr. Sales Change: 39.7%
Phone: 214-644-3048	HR: Karen Thomas	Exchange: Nasdaq
Fax: 214-907-2753	Employees: 167	Symbol: AMXX

Computers - integrated remote-control systems & software for commercial, educational & residential uses

ANACOMP, INC.

11550 N. Meridian St., PO Box 40888	CEO: P. Lang Lowrey III	1995 Sales: $591.2 million
Indianapolis, IN 46240	CFO: Donald L. Viles	1-Yr. Sales Change: (0.2%)
Phone: 317-844-9666	HR: Patricia J. Wilkins	Exchange: Nasdaq
Fax: 317-848-1360	Employees: 3,600	Symbol: ANCO

Computers - microfilming & data storage services on paper, microfilm & microfiche

 See page 250 for a full profile of this company.

ANADIGICS, INC.

35 Technology Dr.	CEO: Ronald Rosenzweig	1995 Sales: $51.5 million
Warren, NJ 07059	CFO: John F. Lyons	1-Yr. Sales Change: 48.0%
Phone: 908-668-5000	HR: Andrea S. Foster	Exchange: Nasdaq
Fax: 908-668-5068	Employees: 315	Symbol: ANAD

Electrical components - gallium arsenide semiconductors

ANALOG DEVICES, INC.

One Technology Way	CEO: Ray Stata	1995 Sales: $941.5 million
Norwood, MA 02062-9106	CFO: Joseph E. McDonough	1-Yr. Sales Change: 21.7%
Phone: 617-329-4700	HR: Ross Brown	Exchange: NYSE
Fax: 617-326-8703	Employees: 6,000	Symbol: ADI

Electrical components - linear, mixed-signal & digital integrated circuits, primarily for OEMs in the communications, computer, instrumentation, military/aerospace & consumer electronics industries

 See page 251 for a full profile of this company.

ANALOGY, INC.

9205 SW Gemini Dr.	CEO: Gary P. Arnold	1996 Sales: $21.7 million
Beaverton, OR 97008	CFO: Terrence A. Rixford	1-Yr. Sales Change: 33.1%
Phone: 503-626-9700	HR: Nancy Martell	Exchange: Nasdaq
Fax: 503-643-3361	Employees: 160	Symbol: ANLG

Computers - high-performance software & model libraries for the top-down design & behavioral simulation of mixed-signal & mixed-technology systems

ANALYSTS INTERNATIONAL CORPORATION

7615 Metro Blvd.	CEO: Frederick W. Lang	1996 Sales: $329.5 million
Minneapolis, MN 55439-3050	CFO: Gerald M. McGrath	1-Yr. Sales Change: 50.9%
Phone: 612-835-5900	HR: Lori Buegler	Exchange: Nasdaq
Fax: 612-835-4924	Employees: 3,770	Symbol: ANLY

Computers - system design & programming services for large corporate clients

 See page 252 for a full profile of this company.

ANAM GROUP

280-8, Sungsudong 2ka, Sungdong-ku	CEO: Kim Joo-Jin "Jim" Kim	1995 Sales: $1,260.0 million
Seoul, Korea	CFO: Frank Marcucci	1-Yr. Sales Change: 29.0%
Phone: +82-2-460-5114	HR: —	Exchange: Korea
Fax: +82-2-465-2607	Employees: 7,629	

Electrical components - #1 global assembler of semiconductors; contract semiconductor packaging; software & video game stores (Electronics Boutique)

 See pages 40–41 for a full profile of this company.

ANCOR COMMUNICATIONS, INCORPORATED

6130 Blue Circle Dr.
Minnetonka, MN 55343
Phone: 612-932-4000
Fax: 612-932-4037

CEO: Stephen C. O'Hara
CFO: Lee B. Lewis
HR: —
Employees: 57

1995 Sales: $4.7 million
1-Yr. Sales Change: (2.1%)
Exchange: Nasdaq (SC)
Symbol: ANCR

Electrical components - switches, adapters & integrated circuits

ANDATACO

10140 Mesa Rim Rd.
San Diego, CA 92121-2914
Phone: 619-453-9191
Fax: 619-453-9294

CEO: W. David Sykes
CFO: Wendell Keivens
HR: Ligaya Bowman
Employees: 225

1995 Sales: $100.0 million
1-Yr. Sales Change: 19.6%
Ownership: Privately Held

Computers - SPARC workstations & UNIX peripheral products

ANDERSEN CONSULTING

100 S. Wacker Dr., Ste. 1070
Chicago, IL 60606
Phone: 312-507-2900
Fax: 312-507-7965

CEO: Lawrence A. Weinbach
CFO: Michael O. Hill
HR: Carol Meyer
Employees: 38,000

1995 Sales: $4,224.0 million
1-Yr. Sales Change: 31.2%
Ownership: Subsidiary

Consulting - management & technology consulting services (subsidiary of Arthur Andersen & Co.)

 See pages 42–43 for a full profile of this company.

ANDREW CORPORATION

10500 W. 153rd St.
Orland Park, IL 60462
Phone: 708-349-3300
Fax: 708-349-5943

CEO: Floyd L. English
CFO: Charles R. Nicholas
HR: —
Employees: 3,345

1995 Sales: $626.5 million
1-Yr. Sales Change: 12.2%
Exchange: Nasdaq
Symbol: ANDW

Telecommunications equipment - coaxial cables, microwave antennas for point-to-point communication systems & other special purpose antennas

ANICOM, INC.

6133 River Rd., Ste. 410
Rosemont, IL 60018-5171
Phone: 847-518-8700
Fax: 788-518-8791

CEO: Scott C. Anixter
CFO: Donald C. Welchko
HR: Lee Smela
Employees: 110

1995 Sales: $29.4 million
1-Yr. Sales Change: 64.2%
Exchange: Nasdaq
Symbol: ANIC

Computers - wire, cable, fiber optics & computer network & connectivity products

ANIIE GROUP PLC

161 Fleet Rd.
Fleet, Hampshire GU13 8PD, UK
Phone: +44-1-252-811-805
Fax: +44-1-252-811-806

CEO: Jon M. Richards
CFO: Simon A. Hunt
HR: —
Employees: 3,064

1996 Sales: $341.7 million
1-Yr. Sales Change: (20.0%)
Exchange: London

Computers - data communications & software systems; electronics; magazine publishing &
aerospace systems

ANSOFT CORPORATION

4 Station Square, Ste. 660
Pittsburgh, PA 15219-1119
Phone: 412-261-3200
Fax: 412-471-9427

CEO: Nicholas Csendes
CFO: Thomas A. N. Miller
HR: —
Employees: 65

1996 Sales: $8.7 million
1-Yr. Sales Change: 40.3%
Exchange: Nasdaq
Symbol: ANST

Computers - electromagnetic field simulation software for electrical & electronic engineering
design applications

ANSYS, INC.

201 Johnson Rd.
Houston, PA 15342-1300
Phone: 412-746-3304
Fax: 412-746-9494

CEO: Peter J. Smith
CFO: John M. Sherbin
HR: Peg Peters
Employees: 200

1995 Sales: $39.6 million
1-Yr. Sales Change: —
Exchange: Nasdaq
Symbol: ANSS

Computers - software for design analysis & for use by engineering analysts & design engineers

ANTARES ALLIANCE GROUP

17304 Preston Rd., Ste 1200
Dallas, TX 75252
Phone: 972-447-5500
Fax: 972-447-5783

CEO: J. Larry Fillmer
CFO: Jacob Smit
HR: —
Employees: 400

1995 Sales: $55.0 million
1-Yr. Sales Change: 17.0%
Ownership: Privately Held

Computers - Engineering software that allows software developers to build & distribute scalable applications
piece by piece

AOC INTERNATIONAL USA LTD.

311 Sinclair Frontage Rd.
Milpitas, CA 95035-5443
Phone: 800-343-5777
Fax: 408-956-1516

CEO: Jason Hsuan
CFO: Janny Pollard
HR: Ann Warner
Employees: 27

1995 Sales: $86.8 million
1-Yr. Sales Change: —
Ownership: Privately Held

Computers - PC monitors

APERTUS TECHNOLOGIES INCORPORATED

7275 Flying Cloud Dr.	CEO: Robert D. Gordon	1996 Sales: $49.3 million
Eden Prairie, MN 55344	CFO: Sue Hogue	1-Yr. Sales Change: (9.7%)
Phone: 612-828-0300	HR: Lori Cocking	Exchange: Nasdaq
Fax: 612-828-0723	Employees: 297	Symbol: APTS

Computers - communications software for mainframe & client/server platforms

APPLE COMPUTER, INC.

One Infinite Loop	CEO: Gilbert F. Amelio	1995 Sales: $11,062.0 mil.
Cupertino, CA 95014	CFO: Fred D. Anderson Jr.	1-Yr. Sales Change: 20.4%
Phone: 408-996-1010	HR: Pat Sharp	Exchange: Nasdaq
Fax: 408-974-2113	Employees: 17,615	Symbol: AAPL

Computers - personal computers, printers & peripheral products

 See pages 44–45 for a full profile of this company.

APPLIED CELLULAR TECHNOLOGY, INC.

James River Professional Ctr., Ste. 3	CEO: Richard D. Sullivan	1995 Sales: $2.3 million
Nixa, MO 65714	CFO: Gary A. Gray	1-Yr. Sales Change: 666.7%
Phone: 417-725-9888	HR: —	Exchange: Nasdaq (SC)
Fax: 417-725-5350	Employees: 35	Symbol: ACTC

Computers - software development tools & radio frequency wireless data communications systems

APPLIED COMPUTER TECHNOLOGIES CORPORATION

113 E. Main	CEO: Kent Hudson	1995 Sales: $19.1 million
Coats, NC 27521	CFO: Kent Hudson	1-Yr. Sales Change: —
Phone: 910-897-6612	HR: Don Denning	Exchange: Nasdaq (SC)
Fax: 910-897-3326	Employees: 54	Symbol: ACTI

Computers - maintenance-management systems

APPLIED COMPUTER TECHNOLOGY

2573 Midpoint Dr.	CEO: Bud Prentice	1995 Sales: $19.1 million
Fort Collins, CO 80525	CFO: Cindy Koehler	1-Yr. Sales Change: 63.2%
Phone: 970-490-1849	HR: Glenda Chermak	Ownership: Privately Held
Fax: 970-490-1439	Employees: 60	

Retail - microcomputer systems & related peripheral products

APPLIED MAGNETICS CORPORATION

75 Robin Hill Rd.	CEO: Craig D. Crisman	1995 Sales: $292.6 million
Goleta, CA 93117	CFO: Craig D. Crisman	1-Yr. Sales Change: 6.1%
Phone: 805-683-5353	HR: David Swanson	Exchange: NYSE
Fax: 805-967-8227	Employees: 5,500	Symbol: APM

Computers - magnetic recording heads for rigid disk drives

 See page 253 for a full profile of this company.

APPLIED MATERIALS, INC.

3050 Bowers Ave.	CEO: James C. Morgan	1995 Sales: $3,061.9 million
Santa Clara, CA 95054-3299	CFO: Gerald F. Taylor	1-Yr. Sales Change: 84.5%
Phone: 408-727-5555	HR: Dana Ditmore	Exchange: Nasdaq
Fax: 408-748-9943	Employees: 10,537	Symbol: AMAT

Machinery - semiconductor manufacturing equipment (#1 worldwide)

 See pages 46–47 for a full profile of this company.

APPLIED MICRO CIRCUITS CORP.

6195 Lusk Blvd.	CEO: Roger Smullen	1995 Sales: $47.0 million
San Diego, CA 92121	CFO: Joel Holliday	1-Yr. Sales Change: (6.0%)
Phone: 619-450-9333	HR: Frank Garbayo	Ownership: Privately Held
Fax: 619-450-9885	Employees: 247	

Electronic components - ASICs for computer & communications markets

APPLIED MICROSYSTEMS CORPORATION

5020 148th Ave. NE	CEO: Robert L. Deinhammer	1995 Sales: $31.0 million
Redmond, WA 98052	CFO: A. James Beach	1-Yr. Sales Change: 20.6%
Phone: 206-882-2000	HR: Gale Mowrer	Exchange: Nasdaq
Fax: 206-883-3049	Employees: 210	Symbol: APMC

Computers - hardware-assisted software tools for the design, debugging & testing of embedded software

APPLIED SCIENCE AND TECHNOLOGY, INC.

35 Cabot Rd.	CEO: Richard S. Post	1996 Sales: $39.1 million
Woburn, MA 01801-1053	CFO: John M. Tarrh	1-Yr. Sales Change: 95.5%
Phone: 617-933-5560	HR: John M. Tarrh	Exchange: Nasdaq
Fax: 617-933-0750	Employees: 115	Symbol: ASTX

Machinery - semiconductor manufacturing equipment

APPLIED TECHNOLOGY

One Cranberry Hill
Lexington, MA 02173
Phone: 617-862-8622
Fax: 617-862-8367

CEO: David Boucher
CFO: Kathleen Chapman
HR: —
Employees: 5

1996 Sales: —
1-Yr. Sales Change: —
Ownership: Privately Held

Venture capital investment firm specializing in broadcasting, high technology, information services,
publishing & software companies

APPLIED VOICE TECHNOLOGY, INC.

11410 NE 122nd Way
Kirkland, WA 98034
Phone: 206-820-6000
Fax: 206-820-4040

CEO: Richard J. LaPorte
CFO: Roger A. Fukai
HR: Angelena Hughes
Employees: 110

1995 Sales: $31.3 million
1-Yr. Sales Change: 8.7%
Exchange: Nasdaq
Symbol: AVTC

Computers - telephone, fax & e-mail software products that automate call answering (CallXpress 3)

APPLIX, INC.

112 Turnpike Rd.
Westborough, MA 01581-2831
Phone: 508-870-0300
Fax: 508-366-9313

CEO: Jitendra S. Saxena
CFO: Patrick J. Scannell Jr.
HR: Betty Kochergin
Employees: 234

1995 Sales: $32.3 million
1-Yr. Sales Change: 74.6%
Exchange: Nasdaq
Symbol: APLX

Computers - software that analyzes real-time information, including news feeds, stock quotes & sales data
(Real Time)

 See page 254 for a full profile of this company.

ARBOR SOFTWARE CORPORATION

1325 Chesapeake Terrace
Sunnyvale, CA 94089
Phone: 408-727-5800
Fax: 408-727-7140

CEO: James A. Dorrian
CFO: Stephen V. Imbler
HR: Nicole Epstein
Employees: 130

1996 Sales: $25.1 million
1-Yr. Sales Change: 118.3%
Exchange: Nasdaq
Symbol: ARSW

Computers - client/server multidimensional database software for business planning & analysis

AREL COMMUNICATIONS AND SOFTWARE LTD.

14 Hamapuach St.
Rehovot 76341, Israel
Phone: +972-8-361118
Fax: +972-8-361086

CEO: Rachel Ben-Nun
CFO: Ilan Sheena
HR: —
Employees: 45

1995 Sales: $6.3 million
1-Yr. Sales Change: 53.7%
Exchange: Nasdaq
Symbol: ARLCF

Computers - message-switching WAN software (ARCOM)

ARI NETWORK SERVICES, INC.

330 E. Kilbourn Ave.
Milwaukee, WI 53202-3166
Phone: 414-278-7676
Fax: 414-283-4357

CEO: Brian E. Dearing
CFO: Lynn Hasemeister
HR: Lynn Hasemeister
Employees: 77

1995 Sales: $5.3 million
1-Yr. Sales Change: —
Exchange: Nasdaq
Symbol: ARIS

Computers - computer-based agricultural information networks & sales automation software

ARIEL CORPORATION

2540 Rte. 130
Cranbury, NJ 08512-3507
Phone: 609-860-2900
Fax: 609-860-1155

CEO: Anthony M. Agnello
CFO: Gerard E. "Rod" Dorsey
HR: Linda Colmenares
Employees: 75

1995 Sales: $9.5 million
1-Yr. Sales Change: 37.7%
Exchange: Nasdaq (SC)
Symbol: ADSP

Computers - computer hardware & software based on DSP (digital signal processing) technology

ARISTO INTERNATIONAL CORPORATION

152 W. 57th St., 29th Fl.
New York, NY 10019
Phone: 212-586-2400
Fax: 212-586-1652

CEO: Mouli Cohen
CFO: Tony J. Burger
HR: Grace Russo
Employees: 35

1995 Sales: $0.2 million
1-Yr. Sales Change: —
Exchange: Nasdaq (SC)
Symbol: ATSP

Computers - entertainment & video game software for CD-ROM-based PCs & dedicated video games

ARROW ELECTRONICS, INC.

25 Hub Dr.
Melville, NY 11747
Phone: 516-391-1300
Fax: 516-391-1640

CEO: Stephen P. Kaufman
CFO: Gerald Luterman
HR: Thomas F. Hallam
Employees: 7,000

1995 Sales: $5,919.4 million
1-Yr. Sales Change: 27.3%
Exchange: NYSE
Symbol: ARW

Electronics - distribution of semiconductors, computer parts & related equipment (#1 worldwide) to industrial & commercial customers

 **See pages 48–49 for a full profile of this company.**

ARTISOFT, INC.

2202 N. Forbes Blvd.
Tucson, AZ 85745
Phone: 520-670-7100
Fax: 520-670-7101

CEO: William C. Keiper
CFO: Curtis J. Scheel
HR: Walker Williams
Employees: 363

1996 Sales: $61.0 million
1-Yr. Sales Change: (27.6%)
Exchange: Nasdaq
Symbol: ASFT

Computers - LAN software (LANtastic) & network management, backup, multiplatform connectivity, modem sharing, remote access & telephony software

ASANTÉ TECHNOLOGIES, INC.

821 Fox Ln.	CEO: Jeff Yuan-Kai Lin	1995 Sales: $60.9 million
San Jose, CA 95131	CFO: Robert Sheffield	1-Yr. Sales Change: (23.9%)
Phone: 408-435-8388	HR: Bette Young	Exchange: Nasdaq
Fax: 408-432-1117	Employees: 161	Symbol: ASNT

Computers - networking products, including adapters & hubs for increasing data transmission speed over Ethernet networks

ASCEND COMMUNICATIONS, INC.

1275 Harbor Bay Pkwy.	CEO: Mory Ejabat	1995 Sales: $149.6 million
Alameda, CA 94502	CFO: Robert K. Dahl	1-Yr. Sales Change: 280.7%
Phone: 510-769-6001	HR: Roy Rettberg	Exchange: Nasdaq
Fax: 510-814-2300	Employees: 304	Symbol: ASND

Computers - WAN access products (MAX, Pipeline)

 See page 255 for a full profile of this company.

THE ASCII GROUP INC.

7475 Wisconsin Ave., Ste. 350	CEO: Alan D. Weinberger	1995 Sales: $5,100.0 million
Bethesda, MD 20814-3412	CFO: Alan D. Weinberger	1-Yr. Sales Change: 9.7%
Phone: 301-718-2600	HR: Jennifer Daniels	Ownership: Privately Held
Fax: 301-718-0435	Employees: 20	

Computers - hardware & software distribution to systems integrators, value-added resellers & computer stores

ASE TEST LIMITED

2/F, 25 Kai-Far Rd.	CEO: David Pan	1995 Sales: $35.7 million
Kaohsiung, Taiwan	CFO: Joseph Tung	1-Yr. Sales Change: 88.9%
Phone: +886-7-363-6641	HR: —	Exchange: Nasdaq
Fax: —	Employees: 656	Symbol: ASTSF

Electrical components - integrated circuit testing services for semiconductor manufacturers

ASECO CORPORATION

500 Donald Lynch Blvd.	CEO: Carl S. Archer Jr.	1996 Sales: $41.6 million
Marlborough, MA 01752	CFO: Sebastian J. Sicari	1-Yr. Sales Change: 42.5%
Phone: 508-481-8896	HR: Frank Coen	Exchange: Nasdaq
Fax: 508-481-0369	Employees: 132	Symbol: ASEC

Electronics - semiconductor test handlers

ASHTECH, INC.

1170 Kifer Rd.
Sunnyvale, CA 94086
Phone: 408-524-1400
Fax: 408-524-1629

Global positioning systems

CEO: Chuck Bosenburg
CFO: Ali Mahdavi
HR: Iris Barger
Employees: 300

1995 Sales: $36.0 million
1-Yr. Sales Change: 12.5%
Ownership: Privately Held

ASHTON TECHNOLOGY GROUP, INC.

10420 Little Patuxent Pkwy., Ste. 490
Columbia, MD 21044-3559
Phone: 410-715-8732
Fax: 410-715-8735

Computers - online transaction systems (Universal Trading System)

CEO: Raymond T. Tate
CFO: Raymond T. Tate
HR: —
Employees: 38

1995 Sales: $0.0 million
1-Yr. Sales Change: —
Exchange: Nasdaq (SC)
Symbol: ASTN

ASIA SOURCE, INC.

48289 Fremont Blvd.
Fremont, CA 94538
Phone: 510-226-8000
Fax: 510-226-8858

Retail - wholesale computer parts & services

CEO: Marcel Liang
CFO: Larry Leong
HR: Crystal Yuan
Employees: 300

1996 Sales: $426.0 million
1-Yr. Sales Change: 30.7%
Ownership: Privately Held

ASM LITHOGRAPHY HOLDING NV

De Run 1110
5503 La Veldhoven, The Netherlands
Phone: +31-40-580800
Fax: +31-40-580333

Electrical components - microlithography, including wafer steppers that allow chip manufacturers to create microscopic circuitry patterns on semiconductor wafers

CEO: Willem D. Maris
CFO: Gerard S.A.J. Verdonschot
HR: —
Employees: 1,123

1995 Sales: $572.3 million
1-Yr. Sales Change: 86.1%
Exchange: Nasdaq
Symbol: ASMLF

ASPECT DEVELOPMENT, INC.

1300 Charleston Rd.
Mountain View, CA 94043
Phone: 415-428-2700
Fax: 415-968-4335

Computers - business client/server software & reference data products (Explore, VIP)

CEO: Romesh Wadhwani
CFO: David S. Dury
HR: Gary Barbato
Employees: 197

1995 Sales: $13.7 million
1-Yr. Sales Change: 61.2%
Exchange: Nasdaq
Symbol: ASDV

ASPECT TELECOMMUNICATIONS CORPORATION

1730 Fox Dr.
San Jose, CA 95131-2312
Phone: 408-441-2200
Fax: 408-441-2260

CEO: James R. Carreker
CFO: William R. Hahn
HR: Shelley C. Brown
Employees: 640

1995 Sales: $199.0 million
1-Yr. Sales Change: 35.2%
Exchange: Nasdaq
Symbol: ASPT

Telecommunications equipment - automated call distribution equipment

ASPEN TECHNOLOGY, INC.

10 Canal Park
Cambridge, MA 02141
Phone: 617-577-0100
Fax: 617-577-0722

CEO: Lawrence B. Evans
CFO: Mary Dean Palermo
HR: Ann McDonald
Employees: 1,040

1996 Sales: $103.6 million
1-Yr. Sales Change: 80.2%
Exchange: Nasdaq
Symbol: AZPN

Computers - CAE software products for the chemicals, petroleum, pharmaceuticals, metals & minerals, food & consumer products, pulp & paper & electric power industries

AST RESEARCH, INC.

16215 Alton Pkwy.
Irvine, CA 92619-7005
Phone: 714-727-4141
Fax: 714-727-8584

CEO: Young-Soo Kim
CFO: Won Suk Yang
HR: Candice Byrne
Employees: 6,595

1995 Sales: $2,467.8 million
1-Yr. Sales Change: 4.2%
Exchange: Nasdaq
Symbol: ASTA

Computers - personal computers, notebooks, memory expansion boards, graphic adapters & color monitors

 **See pages 50–51 for a full profile of this company.**

ASTEA INTERNATIONAL, INC.

455 Business Ctr. Dr.
Horsham, PA 19044
Phone: 215-682-2500
Fax: 215-682-2515

CEO: Zack B. Bergreen
CFO: Leonard W. von Vital
HR: —
Employees: 280

1995 Sales: $43.0 million
1-Yr. Sales Change: 110.8%
Exchange: Nasdaq
Symbol: ATEA

Computers - inventory tracking, order entry & parts requisitioning software

ASTRO-MED, INC.

600 E. Greenwich Ave.
West Warwick, RI 02893
Phone: 401-828-4000
Fax: 401-821-5314

CEO: Albert W. Ondis
CFO: Eugene S. Libby
HR: Michael Ragosta
Employees: 377

1996 Sales: $43.9 million
1-Yr. Sales Change: 14.9%
Exchange: Nasdaq
Symbol: ALOT

Computers - high-speed printers & printer accessories

ASYMETRIX CORP.

110 110th Ave. NE, Ste. 700
Bellevue, WA 98004-5840
Phone: 206-462-0501
Fax: 206-455-3071

CEO: Paul Allen
CFO: John Atherly
HR: Shirley Carder
Employees: 75

1995 Sales: $22.5 million
1-Yr. Sales Change: 40.6%
Ownership: Privately Held

Computers - learning, decision support & multimedia authoring tools (ToolBook) & database customizing software

ASYST TECHNOLOGIES, INC.

48761 Kato Rd.
Fremont, CA 94538
Phone: 510-661-5000
Fax: 510-661-5166

CEO: Mihir Parikh
CFO: Richard C. Yonker
HR: Deborah A. Partridge
Employees: 560

1996 Sales: $120.4 million
1-Yr. Sales Change: 223.7%
Exchange: Nasdaq
Symbol: ASYT

Filtration products - mini-environment systems designed to reduce contamination in cleanrooms for semiconductor manufacturing

ATEC GROUP, INC.

1952 E. Jericho Tpke.
Northport, NY 11731
Phone: 516-462-6700
Fax: 516-462-6223

CEO: Surinder Rametra
CFO: Ashok Rametra
HR: —
Employees: —

1996 Sales: $81.8 million
1-Yr. Sales Change: 71.8%
Exchange: Nasdaq (SC)
Symbol: ATEC

Retail - computer hardware, software & related services

@HOME CORP.

385 Ravendale Dr.
Mountain View, CA 94043
Phone: 415-833-4950
Fax: —

CEO: Thomas A. Jermoluk
CFO: Ken Goldman
HR: Ken Goldman
Employees: 15

1995 Sales: $0.0 million
1-Yr. Sales Change: —
Ownership: Privately Held

Computers - Internet & other online services access via cable TV wires

ATI TECHNOLOGIES INC.

33 Commerce Valley Dr. East
Thornhill, ON L3T 7N6, Canada
Phone: 905-882-2600
Fax: 905-882-2620

CEO: K.Y. Ho
CFO: Lance McIntosh
HR: —
Employees: 640

1995 Sales: $267.7 million
1-Yr. Sales Change: 57.6%
Exchange: Toronto

Computers - component & board-level graphics accelerators; integrated circuits

ATMEL CORPORATION

2325 Orchard Pkwy.	CEO: George Perlegos	1995 Sales: $634.2 million
San Jose, CA 95131	CFO: Kris Chellam	1-Yr. Sales Change: 69.1%
Phone: 408-441-0311	HR: Valerie Menager	Exchange: Nasdaq
Fax: 408-436-4200	Employees: 2,978	Symbol: ATML

Electrical components - high-performance semiconductors using CMOS technology

 See page 256 for a full profile of this company.

ATRIA SOFTWARE, INC.

20 Maguire Rd.	CEO: Paul H. Levine	1995 Sales: $40.1 million
Lexington, MA 02173-3104	CFO: Elliot M. Katzman	1-Yr. Sales Change: 92.8%
Phone: 617-676-2400	HR: Diane Brownlie	Exchange: Nasdaq
Fax: 617-676-2410	Employees: 216	Symbol: ATSW

Computers - software that manages software development (ClearCase)

ATTACHMATE CORPORATION

3617 136th Ave. SE	CEO: James Lindner	1995 Sales: $390.0 million
Bellevue, WA 98006	CFO: Bill Boisvert	1-Yr. Sales Change: 4.6%
Phone: 206-644-4010	HR: Pam Pride	Ownership: Privately Held
Fax: 206-747-9924	Employees: 2,000	

Computers - supplier of PC-to-mainframe software (#1 worldwide) for building secure intranets

 See page 257 for a full profile of this company.

AUDIONET, INC.

2929 Elm St.	CEO: Todd Wagner	1995 Sales: $0.0 million
Dallas, TX 75226	CFO: Joe Autem	1-Yr. Sales Change: —
Phone: 214-748-6660	HR: Joe Autem	Ownership: Privately Held
Fax: 214-748-6657	Employees: 9	

Computers - live audio broadcasts over the Internet, including radio & TV broadcasts, music, sports events & stock market analysis & information

AULT INCORPORATED

7300 Boone Ave. North	CEO: Frederick M. Green	1996 Sales: $33.8 million
Minneapolis, MN 55428-1028	CFO: Carlos S. Montague	1-Yr. Sales Change: 24.7%
Phone: 612-493-1900	HR: Judy Sand	Exchange: Nasdaq (SC)
Fax: 612-493-1911	Employees: 276	Symbol: AULT

Electrical products - external power supplies, battery chargers & transformers for modems, telephone systems, computer peripherals and medical equipment

AUREAL SEMICONDUCTOR INC.

4245 Technology Dr.	CEO: Kenneth Kokinakis	1995 Sales: $47.7 million
Fremont, CA 94538	CFO: David J. Domeier	1-Yr. Sales Change: (67.6%)
Phone: 510-770-8600	HR: Roberta Riga	Exchange: OTC
Fax: 510-770-8648	Employees: 263	Symbol: AURL

Computers - multimedia peripheral equipment, including sound & video boards

AURORA ELECTRONICS, INC.

2030 Main St., Ste. 1120	CEO: Jim C. Cowart	1995 Sales: $141.9 million
Irvine, CA 92714	CFO: John P. Grazer	1-Yr. Sales Change: 17.9%
Phone: 714-660-1232	HR: Peggy Edgington	Exchange: AMEX
Fax: 714-851-8414	Employees: 419	Symbol: AUR

Electronics - distribution of computer service parts & memory upgrade & expansion products

AURUM SOFTWARE, INC.

3385 Scott Blvd.	CEO: Mary E. Coleman	1995 Sales: $10.5 million
Santa Clara, CA 95054	CFO: Christopher L. Dier	1-Yr. Sales Change: 78.0%
Phone: 408-986-8100	HR: Rusty Huelet	Ownership: Privately Held
Fax: 408-654-3400	Employees: 137	

Computers - sales & marketing information software (Aurum Customer Enterprise)

AUSPEX SYSTEMS, INC.

5200 Great America Pkwy.	CEO: Bruce N. Moore	1996 Sales: $162.6 million
Santa Clara, CA 95054	CFO: Kent L. Robertson	1-Yr. Sales Change: 40.7%
Phone: 408-986-2000	HR: Terry Dyckman	Exchange: Nasdaq
Fax: 408-986-2020	Employees: 515	Symbol: ASPX

Computers - UNIX-based network file servers for the technical workstation market

AUSTIN COMPUTER SYSTEMS INC.

10300 Metric Blvd.	CEO: David Scull	1995 Sales: $200.0 million
Austin, TX 78758	CFO: Benny Galloway	1-Yr. Sales Change: —
Phone: 512-339-3500	HR: —	Ownership: Privately Held
Fax: 512-339-3508	Employees: 147	

Computers - desktop computers, notebooks & servers

AUSTIN VENTURES, L.P.

1300 Norwood Tower, Ste. 1300	CEO: Jeffery C. Garvey	1996 Sales: —
Austin, TX 78701	CFO: John E. Nicholson	1-Yr. Sales Change: —
Phone: 512-479-0055	HR: —	Ownership: Privately Held
Fax: 512-476-3952	Employees: 13	

Financial - venture capital investment firm specializing in high-tech & communications companies

AUTODESK, INC.

111 McInnis Pkwy.	CEO: Carol A. Bartz	1996 Sales: $546.9 million
San Rafael, CA 94903	CFO: Eric B. Herr	1-Yr. Sales Change: 17.5%
Phone: 415-507-5000	HR: Stephen McMahon	Exchange: Nasdaq
Fax: 415-507-5100	Employees: 1,894	Symbol: ADSK

Computers - CAD automation software (AutoCAD, AutoCAD LT, AutoSketch, AutoCAD Designer)

 See page 258 for a full profile of this company.

AUTOLOGIC INFORMATION INTERNATIONAL, INC.

1050 Rancho Conejo Blvd.	CEO: William Shaw	1995 Sales: $104.4 million
Thousand Oaks, CA 91360	CFO: Manuel Marrero	1-Yr. Sales Change: —
Phone: 805-498-9611	HR: —	Exchange: Nasdaq
Fax: 805-499-1167	Employees: 450	Symbol: AIII

Computers - image-setting & publication system software & equipment

AUTO-TROL TECHNOLOGY CORP.

12500 N. Washington St.	CEO: Howard B. Hillman	1995 Sales: $25.6 million
Denver, CO 80241-2400	CFO: David C. O'Brien	1-Yr. Sales Change: (26.9%)
Phone: 303-252-2107	HR: Lisa Jayne	Exchange: Nasdaq (SC)
Fax: 303-252-2249	Employees: 353	Symbol: ATTC

Computers - interactive computer graphics hardware & software

AVANT! CORPORATION

1208 E. Arques Ave.	CEO: Gerald C. Hsu	1995 Sales: $38.0 million
Sunnyvale, CA 94086	CFO: John P. Huyett	1-Yr. Sales Change: 512.9%
Phone: 408-738-8881	HR: Bella D'Mar Shimun	Exchange: Nasdaq
Fax: 408-738-0244	Employees: 206	Symbol: AVNT

Computers - integrated circuit design automation software (ArcCell, ArcGate)

AVID TECHNOLOGY, INC.

One Park West
Tewksbury, MA 01876
Phone: 508-640-6789
Fax: 508-640-1366

CEO: William J. Miller
CFO: Jonathan H. Cook
HR: Judith M. Oppenheim
Employees: 1,476

1995 Sales: $406.7 million
1-Yr. Sales Change: 99.7%
Exchange: Nasdaq
Symbol: AVID

Computers - digital, nonlinear film-, video- & audio-editing systems

AVNET, INC.

80 Cutter Mill Rd.
Great Neck, NY 11021-3107
Phone: 516-466-7000
Fax: 516-466-1203

CEO: Leon Machiz
CFO: Raymond Sadowski
HR: Robert Zierk
Employees: 9,500

1996 Sales: $5,207.8 million
1-Yr. Sales Change: 21.1%
Exchange: NYSE
Symbol: AVT

Electronics - parts distribution (#2 worldwide) for industrial & military customers; TV & audio
equipment manufacturing

 See pages 52–53 for a full profile of this company.

AW COMPUTER SYSTEMS, INC.

9000A Commerce Pkwy.
Mt. Laurel, NJ 08054
Phone: 609-234-3939
Fax: 609-234-9377

CEO: Charles W. Welch Jr.
CFO: Robert O'Connor
HR: —
Employees: 42

1995 Sales: $3.4 million
1-Yr. Sales Change: (27.7%)
Exchange: Nasdaq
Symbol: AWCSA

Computers - custom-designed software (AWare) & hardware for point-of-sale retailers

AWARD SOFTWARE INTERNATIONAL, INC.

777 E. Middlefield Rd.
Mountain View, CA 94043
Phone: 415-968-4433
Fax: 415-964-9747

CEO: George C. Huang
CFO: Kevin J. Berry
HR: Margaret Huang
Employees: 89

1995 Sales: $9.1 million
1-Yr. Sales Change: 35.8%
Ownership: Privately Held

Computers - system management software & services worldwide for designers & manufacturers of
motherboards, PC systems & other embedded devices

AWARE, INC.

One Oak Park
Bedford, MA 01730
Phone: 617-276-4000
Fax: 617-276-4001

CEO: James C. Bender
CFO: Richard P. Moberg
HR: Jennifer Tyrrell
Employees: 32

1995 Sales: $3.3 million
1-Yr. Sales Change: (13.2%)
Exchange: Nasdaq
Symbol: AWRE

Computers - telecommunications software, chipsets & modems for increasing the speed of data
transmission over conventional copper telephone lines for residential & business customers

AXENT TECHNOLOGIES, INC.

2400 Research Blvd., Ste. 200
Rockville, MD 20850
Phone: 301-258-5043
Fax: 301-330-5756

CEO: Richard A. Lefebvre
CFO: John C. Becker
HR: Arlene
Employees: 129

1995 Sales: $14.7 million
1-Yr. Sales Change: 70.9%
Exchange: Nasdaq
Symbol: AXNT

Computers - enterprise-wide information security solutions for client/server computing (OmniGuard)

AXIME SA

137, boulevard Voltaire
75011 Paris, France
Phone: +33-1-40-09-33-00
Fax: +33-1-43-56-26-02

CEO: Bernard Bourigeaud
CFO: Dominique Illien
HR: —
Employees: 2,593

1996 Sales: $435.9 million
1-Yr. Sales Change: 3.2%
Exchange: Paris

Computers - data processing & systems & facilities management

BAAN COMPANY N.V.

Zonneoordlaan 17
6710 BG Ede, The Netherlands
Phone: +31-342-428-888
Fax: +31-342-428-822

CEO: Jan Baan
CFO: Jan Westerhoud
HR: Gerrit van Munster
Employees: 1,525

1995 Sales: $216.2 million
1-Yr. Sales Change: 75.9%
Exchange: Nasdaq
Symbol: BAANF

Computers - client/server-based planning software

 See page 259 for a full profile of this company.

BANCTEC, INC.

4435 Spring Valley Rd.
Dallas, TX 75244
Phone: 214-450-7700
Fax: 214-450-7867

CEO: Grahame N. Clark Jr.
CFO: Raghavan Rajaji
HR: Jim Wimberley
Employees: 2,274

1995 Sales: $297.5 million
1-Yr. Sales Change: 20.2%
Exchange: NYSE
Symbol: BTC

Optical character recognition - computerized systems for processing financial transaction documents (ImageFirst)

BANYAN SYSTEMS INCORPORATED

120 Flanders Rd.
Westborough, MA 01581
Phone: 508-898-1000
Fax: 508-898-1755

CEO: David C. Mahoney
CFO: Jeffrey D. Glidden
HR: Ann Smith
Employees: 692

1995 Sales: $129.7 million
1-Yr. Sales Change: (13.6%)
Exchange: Nasdaq
Symbol: BNYN

Computers - network operating systems (VINES) & related software accessories, including network directories (StreetTalk) & network management, administration, security & messaging products

BARRA, INC.

1995 University Ave., Ste. 400	CEO: Andrew Rudd	1996 Sales: $61.0 million
Berkeley, CA 94704	CFO: James D. Kirsner	1-Yr. Sales Change: 17.8%
Phone: 510-548-5442	HR: Carmel Galvin	Exchange: Nasdaq
Fax: 510-548-4374	Employees: 371	Symbol: BARZ

Computers - software & information services used to analyze, manage & trade portfolios of equity, fixed income, derivatives & other financial instruments

BARRISTER INFORMATION SYSTEMS CORPORATION

465 Main St.	CEO: Henry P. Semmelhack	1996 Sales: $13.7 million
Buffalo, NY 14203	CFO: Richard P. Beyer	1-Yr. Sales Change: (10.5%)
Phone: 716-845-5010	HR: Donna L. Lonca	Exchange: AMEX
Fax: 716-845-5033	Employees: 179	Symbol: BIS

Computers - legal software products; computer equipment marketing

BASE TEN SYSTEMS, INC.

One Electronics Dr.	CEO: Myles M. Kranzler	1995 Sales: $18.3 million
Trenton, NJ 08619	CFO: Edward J. Klinsport	1-Yr. Sales Change: (5.2%)
Phone: 609-586-7010	HR: —	Exchange: Nasdaq
Fax: 609-586-1593	Employees: 168	Symbol: BASEB

Computers - safety critical software, secure communications applications; software that controls pharmaceutical manufacturing processes, medical screening & image processing

BAY NETWORKS, INC.

4401 Great America Pkwy.	CEO: Andrew K. Ludwick	1996 Sales: $2,056.6 million
Santa Clara, CA 95054	CFO: William J. Ruehle	1-Yr. Sales Change: 53.2%
Phone: 408-988-2400	HR: David M. Lietzke	Exchange: NYSE
Fax: 408-988-5525	Employees: 5,758	Symbol: BAY

Computers - internetworking equipment, LAN hub products & management systems (merger of Wellfleet Communications & Synoptics Communications)

 See pages 54–55 for a full profile of this company.

BBN CORPORATION

150 Cambridge Park Dr.	CEO: George H. Conrades	1996 Sales: $234.3 million
Cambridge, MA 02140	CFO: Ralph A. Goldwasser	1-Yr. Sales Change: 9.0%
Phone: 617-873-2000	HR: Steven P. Heinrich	Exchange: NYSE
Fax: 617-873-5011	Employees: 2,000	Symbol: BBN

Computers - internetworking services & products, collaborative systems & acoustic technologies, data analysis & process optimization software products; Internet access services (BBN Planet)

 See page 260 for a full profile of this company.

BDM INTERNATIONAL, INC.

1501 BDM Way	CEO: Philip A. Odeen	1995 Sales: $890.0 million
McLean, VA 22102-3204	CFO: C. Thomas Faulders III	1-Yr. Sales Change: 15.0%
Phone: 703-848-5000	HR: Ron Kinsley	Exchange: Nasdaq
Fax: 703-848-5006	Employees: 7,900	Symbol: BDMI

Computers - systems & software integration, technical services & enterprise management operations

BE, INC.

800 El Camino Real, Ste. 300	CEO: Jean-Louis Gassee	1995 Sales: $0.0 million
Menlo Park, CA 94025	CFO: Wes Saia	1-Yr. Sales Change: —
Phone: 415-462-4100	HR: —	Ownership: Privately Held
Fax: 415-462-4129	Employees: 40	

Computers - PCs & related software for digital video, digital audio, image processing, 3-D & communications applications (BeBox)

BELL & HOWELL COMPANY

5215 Old Orchard Rd.	CEO: William J. White	1995 Sales: $820.0 million
Skokie, IL 60077-1076	CFO: Nils A. Johansson	1-Yr. Sales Change: 13.8%
Phone: 847-470-7660	HR: Maria T. Rubly	Exchange: NYSE
Fax: 847-470-9825	Employees: 5,966	Symbol: BHW

Diversified operations - information access, including to periodicals & scholarly papers in electronic & microfilm formats (UMI) & to technical reference information; commercial mail processing systems

BELL COMMUNICATIONS RESEARCH INC.

445 South St.	CEO: George H. Heilmeier	1995 Sales: $1,079.5 million
Morristown, NJ 07960-6438	CFO: Rod L. Everhart	1-Yr. Sales Change: 2.5%
Phone: 201-740-3000	HR: Gwen P. Taylor	Ownership: Privately Held
Fax: 201-740-6877	Employees: 6,172	

Consulting - engineering & consulting services; applied research; telecommunications & information networking software

BELL INDUSTRIES, INC.

11812 San Vicente Blvd.	CEO: Theodore Williams	1995 Sales: $564.3 million
Los Angeles, CA 90049-5069	CFO: Tracy A. Edwards	1-Yr. Sales Change: 13.4%
Phone: 310-826-2355	HR: Robert Walker	Exchange: NYSE
Fax: 310-447-3265	Employees: 1,400	Symbol: BI

Electronics - distribution of electronic components (including semiconductors & microcomputers), graphic arts supplies & equipment & motor-vehicle products

BELL MICROPRODUCTS INC.

1941 Ringwood Ave.
San Jose, CA 95131-1721
Phone: 408-451-9400
Fax: 408-451-1600

CEO: W. Donald Bell
CFO: Remo E. Canessa
HR: Linda Teague
Employees: 462

1995 Sales: $346.3 million
1-Yr. Sales Change: 38.1%
Exchange: Nasdaq
Symbol: BELM

Electronics - parts distribution to computer industry

 See page 261 for a full profile of this company.

BELL TECHNOLOGY GROUP LTD.

611 Broadway, Ste. 415
New York, NY 10012
Phone: 212-982-0800
Fax: 212-979-2999

CEO: Marc H. Bell
CFO: Robert Bell
HR: —
Employees: 50

1995 Sales: $8.7 million
1-Yr. Sales Change: 33.8%
Exchange: Nasdaq (SC)
Symbol: BELT

Reatil - computer systems & networks; computer system installation services

BENCHMARK ELECTRONICS, INC.

3000 Technology Dr.
Angleton, TX 77515
Phone: 409-849-6550
Fax: 409-848-5270

CEO: Donald E. Nigbor
CFO: Cary T. Fu
HR: Nora Garton
Employees: 568

1995 Sales: $97.4 million
1-Yr. Sales Change: (0.8%)
Exchange: AMEX
Symbol: BHE

Electrical components - printed circuit boards

BENCHMARQ MICROELECTRONICS, INC.

17919 Waterview Pkwy.
Dallas, TX 75252
Phone: 214-437-9195
Fax: 214-437-9198

CEO: Darrell C. Coker
CFO: Reginald B. McHone
HR: —
Employees: 180

1995 Sales: $29.2 million
1-Yr. Sales Change: 27.0%
Exchange: Nasdaq
Symbol: BMRQ

Electrical components - mixed-signal integrated circuits & electronic modules for portable & power-sensitive electronic systems

BERG ELECTRONICS CORP.

101 S. Hanley Rd.
St. Louis, MO 63105
Phone: 314-726-1323
Fax: 314-746-2276

CEO: James N. Mills
CFO: David M. Sindelar
HR: Larry Bacon
Employees: 5,400

1995 Sales: $667.2 million
1-Yr. Sales Change: 26.8%
Exchange: NYSE
Symbol: BEI

Electrical connectors - high-density connector systems & products for computers & other electronic devices

BERKELEY SYSTEMS, INC.

2095 Rose St.	CEO: Julia Wainwright	1995 Sales: $25.0 million
Berkeley, CA 94709	CFO: Gary Iwatani	1-Yr. Sales Change: —
Phone: 510-540-5535	HR: Rene Alexander	Ownership: Privately Held
Fax: 510-540-5115	Employees: 115	

Computers - entertainment software (You Don't Know Jack), screen savers (After Dark), software for visually impaired & power management technology (EcoLogic)

BEST BUY CO., INC.

7075 Flying Cloud Dr.	CEO: Richard M. Schulze	1996 Sales: $7,217.4 million
Eden Prairie, MN 55344	CFO: Allen U. Lenzmeier	1-Yr. Sales Change: 42.1%
Phone: 612-947-2000	HR: Joseph M. Joyce	Exchange: NYSE
Fax: 612-947-2422	Employees: 33,500	Symbol: BBY

Retail - consumer electronics & prerecorded music

BETTER ONLINE SOLUTIONS LTD.

100 Bos Rd.	CEO: Israel Gal	1995 Sales: $5.5 million
20179 Teradion, Israel	CFO: David Azran	1-Yr. Sales Change: 89.7%
Phone: +972-4-999-0333	HR: —	Exchange: Nasdaq (SC)
Fax: +972-4-999-0334	Employees: 68	Symbol: BOSCF

Computers - networking & connectivity products, primarily for use with IBM mid-range computers

BGS SYSTEMS, INC.

128 Technology Ctr.	CEO: Harold S. Schwenk Jr.	1996 Sales: $41.1 million
Waltham, MA 02254-9111	CFO: Norman Bilodeau	1-Yr. Sales Change: 16.1%
Phone: 617-891-0000	HR: Sharon Burton	Exchange: Nasdaq
Fax: 617-890-0000	Employees: 242	Symbol: BGSS

Computers - benchmarking software for measuring & predicting computer system performance

BIGBOOK, INC.

448 Bryant St., Ste. 150	CEO: Kris Hagerman	1995 Sales: $3.0 million
San Francisco, CA 94107	CFO: —	1-Yr. Sales Change: 0.0%
Phone: 415-284-9886	HR: —	Ownership: Privately Held
Fax: 415-284-9888	Employees: —	

Computers - online yellow pages-style directory

BITSTREAM INC.

215 First St.
Cambridge, MA 02142
Phone: 617-497-6222
Fax: 617-868-0784

CEO: C. Raymond Boelig
CFO: James D. Hart
HR: Ahmed Awada
Employees: 62

1995 Sales: $9.0 million
1-Yr. Sales Change: (8.2%)
Ownership: Privately Held

Computers - digital typefaces & related software

BITWISE DESIGNS, INC.

Rotterdam Industrial Park, Bldg. 50
Schenectady, NY 12306
Phone: 518-356-9741
Fax: 518-356-9749

CEO: John T. Botti
CFO: Dennis H. Bunt
HR: Debby Lauer
Employees: 51

1996 Sales: $30.6 million
1-Yr. Sales Change: 28.0%
Exchange: Nasdaq (SC)
Symbol: BTWS

Computers - PCs & document imaging systems; wholesale computers & peripherals

BKC SEMICONDUCTORS INCORPORATED

6 Lake St.
Lawrence, MA 01841-3011
Phone: 508-681-0392
Fax: 508-681-9135

CEO: Albert A. Magdall
CFO: Gerald T. Billadeau
HR: Sandie Victor
Employees: 109

1995 Sales: $11.3 million
1-Yr. Sales Change: (0.9%)
Exchange: Nasdaq (SC)
Symbol: BKCS

Electrical components - semiconductor diodes for signal switching, voltage conversion, rectification & surge suppression in electronic circuits

BLACK BOX CORPORATION

1000 Park Dr.
Lawrence, PA 15055
Phone: 412-746-5500
Fax: 412-746-0746

CEO: Jeffery M. Boetticher
CFO: Frederick C. Young
HR: Richard Mandia
Employees: 600

1996 Sales: $193.4 million
1-Yr. Sales Change: 17.4%
Exchange: Nasdaq
Symbol: BBOX

Retail - mail-order sales of communications, networking & related computer connectivity products

BLOOMBERG L.P.

499 Park Ave.
New York, NY 10022
Phone: 212-318-2000
Fax: 212-980-4585

CEO: Michael R. Bloomberg
CFO: Wolf Boehm
HR: Geri Ingram
Employees: 2,000

1995 Est. Sales: $650.0 mil.
1-Yr. Sales Change: 18.2%
Ownership: Privately Held

Business services - online financial information; print, radio & TV news network

BLUE CHIP COMPUTERWARE, INC.

27-B Dubon Ct.	CEO: Victor M. Caron	1995 Sales: $5.4 million
Farmingdale, NY 11735	CFO: Chris Mallious	1-Yr. Sales Change: (72.6%)
Phone: 516-777-7130	HR: —	Exchange: Nasdaq (SC)
Fax: 516-777-7133	Employees: 68	Symbol: BCHPE

Diversified operations - neon product manufacturing; marketing of pager franchises (Beeper USA); sales & installation of computer systems

BLUERIDGE TECHNOLOGIES, INC.

664 H. Zachary Taylor Hwy.	CEO: John Jamieson	1995 Sales: $5.0 million
Flint Hill, VA 22627	CFO: —	1-Yr. Sales Change: 25.0%
Phone: 540-675-3015	HR: —	Ownership: Privately Held
Fax: 540-675-3130	Employees: 27	

Computers - document management software for use with Macintosh, Windows & the Internet (OPTIX Network)

BLYTH HOLDINGS INC.

989 E. Hillsdale Blvd., Ste. 400	CEO: Michael J. Minor	1996 Sales: $13.7 million
Foster City, CA 94404	CFO: Stephen R. Lorentzen	1-Yr. Sales Change: (18.0%)
Phone: 415-571-0222	HR: Barbara Hailey	Exchange: Nasdaq
Fax: 415-571-1132	Employees: 119	Symbol: BLYH

Computers - application development software for workgroup & enterprise-wide client/server computing environments

BMC SOFTWARE, INC.

2101 CityWest Blvd.	CEO: Max P. Watson Jr.	1996 Sales: $428.9 million
Houston, TX 77042-2827	CFO: Stephen B. Solcher	1-Yr. Sales Change: 24.3%
Phone: 713-918-8800	HR: Johnnie Horn	Exchange: Nasdaq
Fax: 713-918-8000	Employees: 1,444	Symbol: BMCS

Computers - maintenance & support services for systems software products

 **See page 262 for a full profile of this company.**

BOCA RESEARCH, INC.

1377 Clint Moore Rd.	CEO: Anthony F. Zalenski	1995 Sales: $143.0 million
Boca Raton, FL 33487	CFO: R. Michael Brewer	1-Yr. Sales Change: 71.1%
Phone: 561-997-6227	HR: Martha A. Ritchason	Exchange: Nasdaq
Fax: 561-997-0918	Employees: 386	Symbol: BOCI

Computers - add-on circuit boards used with IBM & IBM-compatible PCs

BOOLE & BABBAGE, INC.

3131 Zanker Rd.	CEO: Paul E. Newton	1995 Sales: $154.4 million
San Jose, CA 95134-1933	CFO: Arthur F. Knapp Jr.	1-Yr. Sales Change: 17.1%
Phone: 408-526-3000	HR: Janet Thomas	Exchange: Nasdaq
Fax: 408-526-3055	Employees: 754	Symbol: BOOL

Computers - enterprise automation software for managing distributed computer systems in multivendor, multiplatform computing environments

BOOZ, ALLEN & HAMILTON INC.

8283 Greensboro Dr.	CEO: William F. Stasior	1996 Sales: $1,100.0 million
McLean, VA 22102	CFO: Martha Clark Goss	1-Yr. Sales Change: 11.2%
Phone: 703-902-5000	HR: Paul F. Anderson	Ownership: Privately Held
Fax: 703-902-3333	Employees: 6,700	

Consulting - professional management & technology consulting services

BOREALIS TECHNOLOGY CORPORATION

923 Tahoe Blvd., Ste. 211	CEO: Curtis Faith	1995 Sales: $0.7 million
Incline Village, NV 89451	CFO: Tim Arnold	1-Yr. Sales Change: (30.0%)
Phone: 702-832-0300	HR: Bob Gill	Exchange: Nasdaq (SC)
Fax: 702-832-7753	Employees: 31	Symbol: BRLS

Computers - sales automation software that allows sales processes & information exchanges between mobile computer users & central information systems containing enterprise-wide customer databases

BORLAND INTERNATIONAL, INC.

100 Borland Way	CEO: Whitney G. Lynn	1996 Sales: $215.2 million
Scotts Valley, CA 95066-3249	CFO: —	1-Yr. Sales Change: (15.3%)
Phone: 408-431-1000	HR: Marcia Bartelmie	Exchange: Nasdaq
Fax: 408-431-4141	Employees: 1,111	Symbol: BORL

Computers - software development tools, including programming language software & database management systems (Paradox, Visual dBase)

 See pages 56–57 for a full profile of this company.

BOSTON TECHNOLOGY, INC.

100 Quannapowitt Pkwy.	CEO: John C. W. Taylor	1996 Sales: $105.3 million
Wakefield, MA 01880	CFO: Carol B. Langer	1-Yr. Sales Change: 18.2%
Phone: 617-246-9000	HR: A. K. Wnorowski	Exchange: Nasdaq
Fax: 617-246-4510	Employees: 559	Symbol: BSTN

Telecommunications equipment - voice messaging system (CO ACCESS)

BOXHILL SYSTEMS CORPORATION

161 Avenue of the Americas	CEO: Philip Black	1995 Sales: $41.0 million
New York, NY 10013	CFO: Richard Tom	1-Yr. Sales Change: —
Phone: 212-989-4455	HR: —	Ownership: Privately Held
Fax: 212-989-6817	Employees: 100	

Computers - redundant arrays of independent disks (RAID) storage subsystems for
Sun Microsystems servers

BRENTWOOD ASSOCIATES

3000 Sand Hill Rd., Bldg. 3, Ste. 230	CEO: John L. Walecka	1996 Sales: —
Menlo Park, CA 94025	CFO: Hilary G. Lottenberg	1-Yr. Sales Change: —
Phone: 415-854-7691	HR: —	Ownership: Privately Held
Fax: 415-854-9513	Employees: 32	

Financial - venture capital investment specializing in computer- & medical-related technologies

BRILLIANT DIGITAL ENTERTAINMENT, INC.

6355 Topanga Canyon Blvd., Ste. 513	CEO: Mark Dyne	1996 Sales: $2.1 million
Woodland Hills, CA 91367	CFO: Mark Miller	1-Yr. Sales Change: 162.5%
Phone: 818-346-3653	HR: —	Ownership: Privately Held
Fax: 818-712-0810	Employees: 27	

Computers - interactive CD-ROM software (KidStory Series) & digitally animated stories for use on the
Internet & CD-ROM, as well as on TV & home video

BRITE VOICE SYSTEMS, INC.

7309 E. 21st St.	CEO: Stanley G. Brannan	1995 Sales: $97.1 million
Wichita, KS 67206-1083	CFO: Glenn A. Etherington	1-Yr. Sales Change: 46.5%
Phone: 316-652-6500	HR: Tamila Phillips	Exchange: Nasdaq
Fax: 316-652-6800	Employees: 582	Symbol: BVSI

Telecommunications equipment - voice processing systems which integrate audiotex, voice response, voice
recognition, voice/fax messaging & interactive computer applications

BROADBAND TECHNOLOGIES, INC.

4024 Stirrup Creek Dr.	CEO: Salim A. L. Bhatia	1995 Sales: $22.7 million
Research Triangle Park, NC 27709	CFO: Timothy K. Oakley	1-Yr. Sales Change: (15.9%)
Phone: 919-544-0015	HR: Loretta Woodall	Exchange: Nasdaq
Fax: 919-544-3459	Employees: 308	Symbol: BBTK

Telecommunications equipment - electronics & software

BROADVISION, INC.

333 Distel Circle
Los Altos, CA 94022
Phone: 415-943-3600
Fax: 415-943-3699

CEO: Pehong Chen
CFO: Randall C. Bolten
HR: Judy Pace
Employees: 79

1995 Sales: $0.5 million
1-Yr. Sales Change: —
Exchange: Nasdaq
Symbol: BVSN

Computers - Website-creation software (One-To-One)

BROADWAY & SEYMOUR, INC.

128 S. Tryon St.
Charlotte, NC 28202
Phone: 704-372-4281
Fax: 704-344-3543

CEO: Alan C. Stanford
CFO: David Finley
HR: Mary Stokes
Employees: 940

1995 Sales: $114.7 million
1-Yr. Sales Change: (13.7%)
Exchange: Nasdaq
Symbol: BSIS

Computers - item & imaging processing software (VisualImpact) for financial institutions

BROCK INTERNATIONAL, INC.

2859 Paces Ferry Rd., Ste. 1000
Atlanta, GA 30339
Phone: 770-431-1200
Fax: 770-431-1201

CEO: Richard T. Brock
CFO: Richard T. Brock
HR: Alex Richards
Employees: 229

1995 Sales: $28.0 million
1-Yr. Sales Change: (8.8%)
Exchange: Nasdaq
Symbol: BROC

Computers - software for sales force automation

BRØDERBUND SOFTWARE, INC.

500 Redwood Blvd.
Novato, CA 94948-6121
Phone: 415-382-4400
Fax: 415-382-4582

CEO: Joseph Durrett
CFO: Michael J. Shannahan
HR: Patsy Murphy
Employees: 563

1995 Sales: $171.6 million
1-Yr. Sales Change: 53.5%
Exchange: Nasdaq
Symbol: BROD

Computers - educational & game software & CD-ROMs (Carmen Sandiego, Myst, Print Shop)

 See page 263 for a full profile of this company.

BROOKS AUTOMATION, INC.

15 Elizabeth Dr.
Chelmsford, MA 01824
Phone: 508-262-2400
Fax: 508-262-2500

CEO: Robert J. Therrien
CFO: Stanley D. Piekos
HR: Barbara Chouinard
Employees: 255

1995 Sales: $45.7 million
1-Yr. Sales Change: 90.4%
Exchange: Nasdaq
Symbol: BRKS

Machinery - central wafer handling systems & modules, including vacuum transfer robots, vacuum cassette elevator load locks, vacuum alignment & thermal conditioning modules & related software

BROOKTROUT TECHNOLOGY, INC.

410 First Ave.	CEO: Eric R. Giler	1995 Sales: $34.4 million
Needham, MA 02194-2722	CFO: Robert C. Leahy	1-Yr. Sales Change: 46.4%
Phone: 617-449-4100	HR: Lisbeth Mag	Exchange: Nasdaq
Fax: 617-449-9009	Employees: 93	Symbol: BRKT

Telecommunications equipment - facsimile & voice processing systems including multichannel fax boards & fax-on-demand retrieval technology

BTG, INC.

1945 Old Gallows Rd.	CEO: Edward H. Bersoff	1996 Sales: $213.6 million
Vienna, VA 22182	CFO: John M. Hughes	1-Yr. Sales Change: 36.9%
Phone: 703-556-6518	HR: Winder Heller	Exchange: Nasdaq
Fax: 703-556-9290	Employees: 923	Symbol: BTGI

Data collection & systems - modular, open-information computer-based systems

BTU INTERNATIONAL, INC.

23 Esquire Rd.	CEO: Paul J. van der Wansem	1995 Sales: $58.3 million
North Billerica, MA 01862-2596	CFO: Thomas P. Kealy	1-Yr. Sales Change: 34.6%
Phone: 508-667-4111	HR: Donald Masson	Exchange: Nasdaq
Fax: 508-667-9068	Employees: 406	Symbol: BTUI

Electrical components - thermal-processing equipment & related process controls for use in the electronics & power generation industries & solder-reflow furnaces for printed circuit board surface-mount applications

BUFFTON CORPORATION

226 Bailey Ave., Ste. 101	CEO: Robert H. McLean	1995 Sales: $19.2 million
Fort Worth, TX 76107	CFO: Robert Korman	1-Yr. Sales Change: (54.8%)
Phone: 817-332-4761	HR: Robert Korman	Exchange: AMEX
Fax: 817-877-0420	Employees: 155	Symbol: BFX

Computers - electronic filter/surge suppression products, power supply/power conversion products & power distribution systems (Current Technology); PVC fittings; restaurants

BULL RUN CORPORATION

4370 Peachtree Rd. NE	CEO: Robert S. Prather Jr.	1995 Sales: $27.2 million
Atlanta, GA 30319-3099	CFO: Samuel P. Davis Jr.	1-Yr. Sales Change: 871.4%
Phone: 404-266-8333	HR: —	Exchange: Nasdaq
Fax: 404-261-9607	Employees: 130	Symbol: BULL

Computers - heavy-duty printers (Documax, Performax) used in multiuser computer environments for heavy-duty, print-intensive applications

BUREAU OF ELECTRONIC PUBLISHING, INC.

619 Alexander Rd.	CEO: Larry Shiller	1995 Sales: $3.1 million
Princeton, NJ 08540	CFO: William P. Fox	1-Yr. Sales Change: 10.7%
Phone: 609-514-1600	HR: Brent Subkowsky	Exchange: Nasdaq
Fax: 609-514-1818	Employees: 26	Symbol: BEPI

Publishing - interactive multimedia CD-ROMs for the consumer & library/education markets (d/b/a Thynx: Inside the White House, Much Ado About Shakespeare, Multimedia World Factbook)

BURR-BROWN CORPORATION

6730 S. Tucson Blvd.	CEO: Syrus P. Madavi	1995 Sales: $269.2 million
Tucson, AZ 85706	CFO: John L. Carter	1-Yr. Sales Change: 38.6%
Phone: 520-746-1111	HR: Seth Slaughter	Exchange: Nasdaq
Fax: 520-548-6133	Employees: 1,839	Symbol: BBRC

Electrical components - analog & mixed-signal ICs, digital-to-analog converters, analog signal processing & data conversion ICs & personal computer instrumentation (PCI)

BUSINESS OBJECTS S.A.

Tour Chantecoq, 5, rue Chantecoq	CEO: Bernard Liautand	1995 Sales: $60.6 million
92808 Puteaux Cedex, France	CFO: Robert P. Verheecke	1-Yr. Sales Change: 100.7%
Phone: +33-1-41-25-21-21	HR: —	Exchange: Nasdaq
Fax: +33-1-41-25-21-20	Employees: 350	Symbol: BOBJY

Computers - software tools for client/server computer access

B.V.R. TECHNOLOGIES LIMITED

One Korazin St.	CEO: Yaron Sheinman	1995 Sales: $10.5 million
Givatayim 53583, Israel	CFO: Elior Brin	1-Yr. Sales Change: (37.5%)
Phone: +972-357-1567	HR: —	Exchange: Nasdaq (SC)
Fax: —	Employees: 92	Symbol: BVRTF

Computers - training & computer-based simulation systems for the aircraft & related industries; 2-way wireless communication & location networks

BYRON PREISS MULTIMEDIA COMPANY, INC.

24 W. 25th St., 10th Fl.	CEO: Byron Preiss	1995 Sales: $6.3 million
New York, NY 10010	CFO: James R. Dellomo	1-Yr. Sales Change: 103.2%
Phone: 212-989-6252	HR: Clairce Levine	Exchange: Nasdaq (SC)
Fax: 212-989-6550	Employees: 49	Symbol: CDRM

Computers - interactive multimedia software on CD-ROM & other multimedia formats for educational, entertainment & professional uses

CABLE DESIGN TECHNOLOGIES CORPORATION

Foster Plaza 7, 661 Andersen Dr.
Pittsburgh, PA 15220
Phone: 412-937-2300
Fax: 412-937-9690

CEO: Paul M. Olson
CFO: Kenneth O. Hale
HR: Jack Winter
Employees: 867

1996 Sales: $357.4 million
1-Yr. Sales Change: 89.2%
Exchange: Nasdaq
Symbol: CDTC

Wire & cable products - copper, fiber optics & composite electronic data transmission cables for LAN, WAN, multimedia, building automation, computer interconnect & security system applications

CABLE-SAT SYSTEMS, INC.

2105 Hamilton Ave., Ste. 140
San Jose, CA 95125
Phone: 408-879-6600
Fax: 408-559-8793

CEO: Abraham Ostrovsky
CFO: Benjamin T. Maltby
HR: —
Employees: 12

1995 Sales: $0.0 million
1-Yr. Sales Change: —
Ownership: Privately Held

Computers - software (TRUE COLOR FAX) that allows computers to send & receive color fax images

CABLETRON SYSTEMS, INC.

35 Industrial Way
Rochester, NH 03867
Phone: 603-332-9400
Fax: 603-332-8007

CEO: S. Robert Levine
CFO: David J. Kirkpatrick
HR: Linda Pepin
Employees: 5,377

1996 Sales: $1,069.7 million
1-Yr. Sales Change: 31.9%
Exchange: NYSE
Symbol: CS

Computers - LAN & WAN connectivity hardware & software, including network interconnection products such as repeaters, bridges, cable assemblies, test equipment & network management software (SPECTRUM)

 See pages 58–59 for a full profile of this company.

CACI INTERNATIONAL INC

1100 N. Glebe Rd.
Arlington, VA 22201
Phone: 703-841-7800
Fax: 703-841-7882

CEO: J. P. "Jack" London
CFO: Samuel R. Strickland
HR: Samuel R. Strickland
Employees: 3,250

1996 Sales: $244.6 million
1-Yr. Sales Change: 5.0%
Exchange: Nasdaq
Symbol: CACI

Computers - information retrieval & management consulting services, including enterprise process redesign, systems engineering, software reuse & development & litigation support services

CADENCE DESIGN SYSTEMS, INC.

555 River Oaks Pkwy.
San Jose, CA 95134
Phone: 408-943-1234
Fax: 408-943-0513

CEO: Joseph B. Costello
CFO: H. Raymond Bingham
HR: Scott W. Sherwood
Employees: 3,028

1995 Sales: $548.4 million
1-Yr. Sales Change: 27.8%
Exchange: NYSE
Symbol: CDN

Computers - electronic design automation software (Allegro, Synergy, Verilog-XL)

 See page 264 for a full profile of this company.

CAERE CORPORATION

100 Cooper Ct.	CEO: Robert G. Teresi	1995 Sales: $51.9 million
Los Gatos, CA 95030	CFO: Blanche M. Sutter	1-Yr. Sales Change: (12.2%)
Phone: 408-395-7000	HR: Claire Brown	Exchange: Nasdaq
Fax: 408-354-2743	Employees: 223	Symbol: CAER

Optical character recognition hardware & software

CAL-ABCO

6041 Variel Ave.	CEO: Alex Sandel	1995 Est. Sales: $300.0 mil.
Woodland Hills, CA 91367	CFO: Joe Budenholzer	1-Yr. Sales Change: 9.1%
Phone: 818-704-9100	HR: Molly McVeigh	Ownership: Privately Held
Fax: 818-704-7733	Employees: 25	

Retail - microcomputer distribution

CALCOMP TECHNOLOGY INC.

8500 Cameron Rd.	CEO: Michael S. Bennett	1996 Sales: $64.3 million
Austin, TX 78754-3999	CFO: David G. Osowski	1-Yr. Sales Change: (18.1%)
Phone: 512-835-0900	HR: Kay Secord	Exchange: Nasdaq
Fax: 512-339-1490	Employees: 194	Symbol: CLCP

Computers - digitizing tablets, pen plotters, ink-jet printers, scanners & graphics cutters

CALDERA, INC.

931 W. Center St.	CEO: Bryan Sparks	1996 Sales: $10.0 million
Orem, UT 84057-5203	CFO: Bryan Sparks	1-Yr. Sales Change: 0.0%
Phone: 801-229-1675	HR: Ransom Love	Ownership: Privately Held
Fax: 801-229-1579	Employees: —	

Computers - operating system (Linux) for desktop computers (owned by former Novell CEO Ray Noorda)

CALIFORNIA MICRO DEVICES CORPORATION

215 Topaz St.	CEO: Jeffrey C. Kalb	1996 Sales: $39.9 million
Milpitas, CA 95035-5430	CFO: John E. Trewin	1-Yr. Sales Change: 68.4%
Phone: 408-263-3214	HR: Zareen Mohta	Exchange: Nasdaq
Fax: 408-263-7846	Employees: 297	Symbol: CAMD

Electrical components - semiconductor ICs, thin-film passive components & mixed analog/digital products

CAM DATA SYSTEMS, INC.

17520 Newhope St., Ste. 100	CEO: Geoffrey D. Knapp	1995 Sales: $14.7 million
Fountain Valley, CA 92708	CFO: Paul Caceres Jr.	1-Yr. Sales Change: 11.4%
Phone: 714-241-9241	HR: Nadine Arrona	Exchange: Nasdaq (SC)
Fax: 714-241-9893	Employees: 102	Symbol: CADA

Computers - inventory management, point-of-sale & accounting systems

CAMBEX CORPORATION

360 Second Ave.	CEO: Joseph F. Kruy	1995 Sales: $35.2 million
Waltham, MA 02154	CFO: Sheldon M. Schenkler	1-Yr. Sales Change: (13.1%)
Phone: 617-890-6000	HR: Joseph F. Kruy	Exchange: Nasdaq
Fax: 617-890-2899	Employees: 140	Symbol: CBEX

Computers - direct-access storage products, including central, expanded & controller cache memory, disk array systems & disk & tape subsystems, which are used with IBM mainframe & client server computers

CAMBRIDGE TECHNOLOGY PARTNERS, INC.

304 Vassar St.	CEO: James K. Sims	1995 Sales: $132.4 million
Cambridge, MA 02139	CFO: Arthur M. Toscanini	1-Yr. Sales Change: 121.8%
Phone: 617-374-9800	HR: Susan J. Loker	Exchange: Nasdaq
Fax: 617-374-8300	Employees: 1,077	Symbol: CATP

Computers - information-technology consulting & software-development services

 See page 265 for a full profile of this company.

CAMELOT CORPORATION

17770 Preston Rd.	CEO: Daniel Wettreich	1996 Sales: $3.0 million
Dallas, TX 75252	CFO: Shirley A. Green	1-Yr. Sales Change: 150.0%
Phone: 214-733-3005	HR: —	Exchange: Nasdaq (SC)
Fax: 214-733-4308	Employees: 82	Symbol: CAML

Retail - CD-ROM distribution (Maxmedia Distributing) & retail sales (Mr. CD-ROM); Internet telephone software (Digiphone)

CANDLE CORPORATION

2425 Olympic Blvd.	CEO: Aubrey Chernick	1995 Sales: $230.3 million
Santa Monica, CA 90404	CFO: Don Mellert	1-Yr. Sales Change: 8.1%
Phone: 310-829-5800	HR: Bonnie MacNeill	Ownership: Privately Held
Fax: 310-582-4287	Employees: 1,200	

Computers - systems management software for IBM mainframes

CANMAX INC.

150 W. Carpenter Fwy.
Irving, TX 75039
Phone: 214-541-1600
Fax: 214-541-1155

CEO: Roger D. Bryant
CFO: Philip M. Parsons
HR: Linda Leckey
Employees: 99

1995 Sales: $9.0 million
1-Yr. Sales Change: (7.2%)
Exchange: Nasdaq (SC)
Symbol: CNMX

Computers - software systems, hardware & licensing of 3rd-party software to convenience store & gas station operators for accounting & inventory

CANON INC.

30-2, Shimomaruko 3-chome, Ohta-ku
Tokyo 146, Japan
Phone: +81-3-3758-2111
Fax: +81-3-5482-5130

CEO: Fujio Mitarai
CFO: Seymour Liebman
HR: Annette Colarusso
Employees: 72,280

1995 Sales: $21,025.5 mil.
1-Yr. Sales Change: 8.8%
Exchange: Nasdaq
Symbol: CANNY

Office equipment - copiers, peripherals, computer equipment, photographic equipment & telecommunications devices; laser & inkjet printers, facsimile machines, cameras & camcorders

 See pages 60–61 for a full profile of this company.

CANTERBURY CORPORATE SERVICES, INC.

Rte. 70 & Hartford Rd.
Medford, NJ 08055-3503
Phone: 609-953-0044
Fax: 609-953-0062

CEO: Stanton M. Pikus
CFO: Kevin J. McAndrew
HR: Jean Z. Pikus
Employees: 401

1995 Sales: $28.3 million
1-Yr. Sales Change: (5.7%)
Exchange: Nasdaq
Symbol: XCEL

Schools - vocational training, seminar training & software & management training for individuals & corporations; specialty printing & business maintenance services

CAP GEMINI SOGETI S.A.

Place de l'Etoile-11, rue de Tilsitt
75017 Paris, France
Phone: +33-1-47-54-50-00
Fax: +33-1-42-27-32-11

CEO: Serge Kampf
CFO: Pascal Giraud
HR: Bruce Posner
Employees: 22,079

1995 Sales: $2,307.8 million
1-Yr. Sales Change: 21.4%
Exchange: Paris

Computers - IT services, including advising, contracting, systems integration & management for major companies & public sector agencies

 See pages 62–63 for a full profile of this company.

CAP VOLMAC GROUP NV

Daltonlaan 300, Postbus 2575
NL-3500 GN Utrecht, The Netherlands
Phone: +31-30-526-526
Fax: +31-30-543-143

CEO: C. J. A. Van Breugel
CFO: —
HR: —
Employees: 4,636

1995 Sales: $849.0 million
1-Yr. Sales Change: 81.5%
Exchange: Amsterdam

Computers - business process redesign & customized packaged software

CAPITOL MULTIMEDIA, INC.

7315 Wisconsin Ave., Ste. 800 East	CEO: Robert I. Bogin	1996 Sales: $4.3 million
Bethesda, MD 20814	CFO: Catherine K. Hoopes	1-Yr. Sales Change: (6.5%)
Phone: 301-907-7000	HR: Igor Razboff	Exchange: Nasdaq (SC)
Fax: 301-907-7005	Employees: 160	Symbol: CDIM

Computers - educational interactive consumer software & business applications focusing on the children's market within the CD-ROM interactive software industry

CARNEGIE GROUP, INC.

5 PPG Place	CEO: Dennis Yablonsky	1995 Sales: $25.7 million
Pittsburgh, PA 15222	CFO: John W. Manzetti	1-Yr. Sales Change: 43.6%
Phone: 412-642-6900	HR: Pauline Nadeau	Exchange: Nasdaq
Fax: 412-642-6906	Employees: 209	Symbol: CGIX

Computers - client/server software development services

CASCADE COMMUNICATIONS CORP.

5 Carlisle Rd.	CEO: Daniel E. Smith	1995 Sales: $134.8 million
Westford, MA 01886	CFO: Paul E. Blondin	1-Yr. Sales Change: 169.1%
Phone: 508-692-2600	HR: Mary Cogan	Exchange: Nasdaq
Fax: 508-692-9214	Employees: 423	Symbol: CSCC

Computers - WAN switches & network-interface modules

 See page 266 for a full profile of this company.

CASTELLE

3255-3 Scott Blvd.	CEO: Arthur H. Bruno	1995 Sales: $25.1 million
Santa Clara, CA 95054	CFO: Randall I. Bambrough	1-Yr. Sales Change: 28.7%
Phone: 408-496-0474	HR: —	Exchange: Nasdaq
Fax: 408-496-0502	Employees: 83	Symbol: CSTL

Computers - network enhancement software & hardware & related services

CATALYST INTERNATIONAL, INC.

8989 N. Deerwood Dr.	CEO: Vaemond H. Crane	1995 Sales: $20.7 million
Milwaukee, WI 53223	CFO: Lisa Sanregret	1-Yr. Sales Change: 27.8%
Phone: 414-362-6800	HR: Sarah Oberhofer	Exchange: Nasdaq
Fax: 414-377-6263	Employees: 210	Symbol: CLYS

Computers - warehouse management software (Catalyst Warehouse Management System)

CATALYST SEMICONDUCTOR, INC.

2231 Calle de Luna
Santa Clara, CA 95054
Phone: 408-748-7700
Fax: 408-980-8209

CEO: C. Michael Powell
CFO: Donald B. Witmer
HR: Gayle Silva
Employees: 67

1996 Sales: $60.2 million
1-Yr. Sales Change: 23.4%
Exchange: Nasdaq
Symbol: CATS

Electrical components - nonvolatile semiconductor memory products for the computer, consumer electronics, telecommunications, automotive, industrial control & instrumentation markets

CATS SOFTWARE INC.

1870 Embarcadero Rd.
Palo Alto, CA 94303
Phone: 415-321-3000
Fax: 415-321-3050

CEO: Rod A. Beckstrom
CFO: G. Bradford Solso
HR: Steve Weinberg
Employees: 80

1995 Sales: $22.3 million
1-Yr. Sales Change: 20.5%
Exchange: Nasdaq
Symbol: CATX

Computers - financial risk management software (CAtalyst)

CAYENNE SOFTWARE, INC.

8 New England Executive Park East
Burlington, MA 01803
Phone: 617-273-9003
Fax: 617-229-9904

CEO: Peter J. Boni
CFO: Eugene DiDonato
HR: Maria Fraguso
Employees: 236

1996 Sales: $32.0 million
1-Yr. Sales Change: (3.9%)
Exchange: Nasdaq
Symbol: CAYN

Computers - application development & database-management tools & interfacing products

CBT GROUP PLC

2(b) Clonskeagh Sq.
Dublin 14, Ireland
Phone: +353-1-283-0077
Fax: —

CEO: William G. McCabe
CFO: John M. Fortune
HR: —
Employees: 259

1995 Sales: $36.9 million
1-Yr. Sales Change: 98.4%
Exchange: Nasdaq
Symbol: CBTSY

Computers - interactive business education & training software

CCC INFORMATION SERVICES, INC.

444 Merchandise Mart
Chicago, IL 60654-1005
Phone: 312-222-4636
Fax: 312-527-2298

CEO: David M. Phillips
CFO: Leonard L. Ciarrocchi
HR: Kathy Sfikas
Employees: 824

1995 Sales: $115.5 million
1-Yr. Sales Change: 25.7%
Exchange: Nasdaq
Symbol: CCCG

Computers - automotive claims software & communication services

C-CUBE MICROSYSTEMS INC.

1778 McCarthy Blvd.	CEO: Alexandre A. Balkanski	1995 Sales: $124.6 million
Milpitas, CA 95035	CFO: James G. Burke	1-Yr. Sales Change: 176.9%
Phone: 408-944-6300	HR: Jackie Darius	Exchange: Nasdaq
Fax: 408-944-8132	Employees: 254	Symbol: CUBE

Electrical components - digital video-compression processor (VideoRISC) chips & software

CD-MAX, INC.

11480 Sunset Hills Rd., Ste. 110	CEO: Robert A. Wiedemer	1996 Sales: $13.4 million
Reston, VA 20190	CFO: Philip J. Gross	1-Yr. Sales Change: 436.0%
Phone: 703-471-5755	HR: —	Exchange: Nasdaq (SC)
Fax: 703-471-2806	Employees: 19	Symbol: MAXX

Computers - professional & financial software, billing services to publishers of CD-ROM programs, enables publishers to sell information from a CD-ROM database on per-use basis

CDW COMPUTER CENTERS, INC.

1020 E. Lake Cook Rd.	CEO: Michael P. Krasny	1995 Sales: $628.7 million
Buffalo Grove, IL 60089	CFO: Harry J. Harczak Jr.	1-Yr. Sales Change: 52.1%
Phone: 847-465-6000	HR: Mary C. Gerlits	Exchange: Nasdaq
Fax: 847-465-6800	Employees: 536	Symbol: CDWC

Retail - computers, peripherals & software

 See page 267 for a full profile of this company.

CE SOFTWARE HOLDINGS, INC.

1801 Industrial Circle	CEO: Richard Skeie	1995 Sales: $12.9 million
West Des Moines, IA 50265	CFO: Curtis W. Lack	1-Yr. Sales Change: 13.2%
Phone: 515-221-1801	HR: Grant Young	Exchange: Nasdaq
Fax: 515-221-1806	Employees: 91	Symbol: CESH

Computers - message products, including an e-mail program (Quick Mail), utility & application products (QuicKeys, ProKey, CalendarMaker) & scheduling products (Network Scheduler)

CEGELEC ESCA CORPORATION

11120 NE 33rd Place	CEO: Alain Steven	1995 Sales: $30.4 million
Bellevue, WA 98004-1448	CFO: Deborah J. Beatenbough	1-Yr. Sales Change: 1.7%
Phone: 206-822-6800	HR: Clifford J. Lentz	Ownership: Privately Held
Fax: 206-889-1700	Employees: 201	

Computers - software & systems for the utility industries

CELLULAR TECHNICAL SERVICES COMPANY, INC.

2401 Fourth Ave., Ste. 808
Seattle, WA 98121-1438
Phone: 206-443-6400
Fax: 206-443-1550

CEO: Stephen Katz
CFO: Michael E. McConnell
HR: Robert Dahut
Employees: 95

1995 Sales: $12.6 million
1-Yr. Sales Change: 26.0%
Exchange: Nasdaq
Symbol: CTSC

Telecommunications equipment - integrated real-time information management systems for the cellular communication industry

CEMAX-ICON, INC.

47281 Mission Falls Ct.
Fremont, CA 94539
Phone: 510-770-8612
Fax: 510-440-9137

CEO: Terry Ross
CFO: Gregory C. Patti
HR: Jean Qian
Employees: 107

1995 Sales: $17.0 million
1-Yr. Sales Change: 3.0%
Ownership: Privately Held

Computers - medical image information systems that electronically acquire, archive, distribute & display medical images throughout hospitals, outpatient facilities & integrated delivery networks

CENTENNIAL TECHNOLOGIES, INC.

37 Manning Rd.
Billerica, MA 01821
Phone: 508-670-0646
Fax: 508-670-9025

CEO: Emanuel Pinez
CFO: James M. Murphy
HR: Patty O'Neil
Employees: 119

1996 Sales: $37.8 million
1-Yr. Sales Change: 204.8%
Exchange: AMEX
Symbol: CTN

Computers - PC cards (memory & data/fax) for products in industrial & commercial applications; laser printer font cartridges

CENTON ELECTRONICS, INC.

20 Morgan
Irvine, CA 92718
Phone: 714-855-9111
Fax: 714-855-0579

CEO: Eugene Miscionne
CFO: John N. Bui
HR: Jerry Wasson
Employees: 140

1995 Sales: $310.0 million
1-Yr. Sales Change: 115.3%
Ownership: Privately Held

Computers - supplier of PC memory boards

CENTURA SOFTWARE CORPORATION

1060 Marsh Rd.
Menlo Park, CA 94025
Phone: 415-321-9500
Fax: 415-321-5471

CEO: Samuel M. Inman
CFO: Richard A. Gelhaus
HR: Joanne Webster
Employees: 406

1995 Sales: $65.7 million
1-Yr. Sales Change: 1.9%
Exchange: Nasdaq
Symbol: CNTR

Computers - database management systems software

CERIDIAN CORPORATION

8100 34th Ave. South	CEO: Lawrence Perlman	1995 Sales: $1,333.0 million
Minneapolis, MN 55425	CFO: John R. Eickhoff	1-Yr. Sales Change: 45.5%
Phone: 612-853-8100	HR: Ronald James	Exchange: NYSE
Fax: 612-853-5300	Employees: 10,200	Symbol: CEN

Data collection & services; payroll & payroll-related services, human resource information & benefit management services; electronic systems for defense agencies

 See pages 64–65 for a full profile of this company.

CERION TECHNOLOGIES, INC.

1401 Interstate Dr.	CEO: David A. Peterson	1995 Sales: $28.2 million
Champaign, IL 61821-1090	CFO: Richard A. Clark	1-Yr. Sales Change: 93.2%
Phone: 217-359-3700	HR: Minor Jackson	Exchange: Nasdaq
Fax: 217-359-3702	Employees: 483	Symbol: CEON

Computers - metallic platforms of magnetic thin film disks used in hard disk drives, network servers, add-on storage devices & storage upgrades

CERNER CORPORATION

2800 Rockcreek Pkwy.	CEO: Neal L. Patterson	1995 Sales: $186.9 million
Kansas City, MO 64117-2551	CFO: Marc G. Naughton	1-Yr. Sales Change: 19.9%
Phone: 816-221-1024	HR: John Reedy	Exchange: Nasdaq
Fax: 816-474-1742	Employees: 1,091	Symbol: CERN

Computers - patient information software & systems for health care providers

THE CERPLEX GROUP, INC.

1382 Bell Ave.	CEO: James T. Schraith	1995 Sales: $144.3 million
Tustin, CA 92680	CFO: James R. Eckstaedt	1-Yr. Sales Change: 13.7%
Phone: 714-258-5600	HR: Robert P. Bunce	Exchange: Nasdaq
Fax: 714-258-5296	Employees: 1,500	Symbol: CPLX

Computers - repair services for computers, peripherals & circuit boards

CERPROBE CORPORATION

600 S. Rockford Dr.	CEO: C. Zane Close	1995 Sales: $26.1 million
Tempe, AZ 85281	CFO: Robert K. Bench	1-Yr. Sales Change: 82.5%
Phone: 602-967-7885	HR: Grady Brown	Exchange: Nasdaq
Fax: 602-967-7758	Employees: 299	Symbol: CRPB

Electronics - semiconductor test equipment

CERTRON CORPORATION

1545 Sawtelle Blvd.	CEO: Marshall I. Kass	1995 Sales: $3.9 million
Los Angeles, CA 90025	CFO: Marshall I. Kass	1-Yr. Sales Change: (51.2%)
Phone: 310-914-0300	HR: Jonathan Kass	Exchange: Nasdaq (SC)
Fax: 310-914-0310	Employees: 73	Symbol: CRTN

Audio & video home products - video- & audiocassettes; computer diskettes & media storage products

CFI PROSERVICES, INC.

400 SW Sixth Ave.	CEO: Matthew W. Chapman	1995 Sales: $36.8 million
Portland, OR 97204	CFO: Fred Hall	1-Yr. Sales Change: 12.9%
Phone: 503-274-7280	HR: Kathy Holmquist	Exchange: Nasdaq
Fax: 503-274-7284	Employees: 328	Symbol: PROI

Computers - electronic banking software (Personal Branch) for financial institutions

CFM TECHNOLOGIES, INC.

1336 Enterprise Dr.	CEO: Roger A. Carolin	1995 Sales: $23.4 million
West Chester, PA 19380	CFO: Lorin J. Randall	1-Yr. Sales Change: 47.2%
Phone: 610-696-8300	HR: Will Dukes	Exchange: Nasdaq
Fax: 610-696-8309	Employees: 159	Symbol: CFMT

Machinery - wet processing equipment for cleaning, etching & photoresist stripping for use in semiconductor & flat-panel display manufacturing

CHATCOM, INC.

9600 Topanga Canyon Blvd.	CEO: James B. Mariner	1996 Sales: $14.8 million
Chatsworth, CA 91311-5803	CFO: John Grady	1-Yr. Sales Change: (1.3%)
Phone: 818-709-1778	HR: Cheryl Smithey	Exchange: Nasdaq (SC)
Fax: 818-882-1424	Employees: 71	Symbol: CHAT

Computers - remote-access products for multiuser systems & networks

CHECK POINT SOFTWARE TECHOLOGIES LTD.

35 Jabotinsky St.	CEO: Gil Shwed	1995 Sales: $9.5 million
Ramat Gan 52511, Israel	CFO: Hagi Schwartz	1-Yr. Sales Change: 1,088%
Phone: +972-3-613-1833	HR: —	Exchange: Nasdaq
Fax: +972-3-575-9256	Employees: 49	Symbol: CHKPF

Computers - security software (FireWall-1) for network connectivity

CHECKFREE CORPORATION

8275 N. High St.	CEO: Peter J. Kight	1995 Sales: $49.3 million
Columbus, OH 43235-1497	CFO: —	1-Yr. Sales Change: 25.4%
Phone: 614-825-3000	HR: —	Exchange: Nasdaq
Fax: 614-825-3307	Employees: 442	Symbol: CKFR

Financial - electronic banking & payment services

CHECKMATE ELECTRONICS INC.

1011 Mansell Rd., Ste. C	CEO: Jerry P. Malec	1995 Sales: $29.2 million
Roswell, GA 30076	CFO: John J. Neubert	1-Yr. Sales Change: 69.8%
Phone: 770-594-6000	HR: Dolores Moore	Exchange: Nasdaq
Fax: 770-594-6006	Employees: 143	Symbol: CMEL

Optical character recognition - check readers, payment-authorization devices & signature verification systems

THE CHERRY CORPORATION

3600 Sunset Ave.	CEO: Peter B. Cherry	1996 Sales: $424.7 million
Waukegan, IL 60087-3298	CFO: Dan A. King	1-Yr. Sales Change: 25.2%
Phone: 847-662-9200	HR: Nancy Guarascio	Exchange: Nasdaq
Fax: 847-360-3545	Employees: 4,399	Symbol: CHERB

Electrical components - switches, keyboards, keyboard switches, gas-discharge displays, electronic automotive products, linear integrated circuits & electronic automotive products

CHEYENNE SOFTWARE, INC.

3 Expressway Plaza	CEO: ReiJane Huai	1996 Sales: $174.1 million
Roslyn Heights, NY 11577	CFO: Elliot Levine	1-Yr. Sales Change: 36.1%
Phone: 516-484-5110	HR: Andy Boyland	Exchange: AMEX
Fax: 516-484-7106	Employees: 778	Symbol: CYE

Computers - LAN & WAN software products

See page 268 for a full profile of this company.

CHIPS AND TECHNOLOGIES, INC.

2950 Zanker Rd.	CEO: James F. Stafford	1996 Sales: $150.8 million
San Jose, CA 95134	CFO: Timothy R. Christoffersen	1-Yr. Sales Change: 43.9%
Phone: 408-434-0600	HR: A. J. Newman	Exchange: Nasdaq
Fax: 408-434-9315	Employees: 209	Symbol: CHPS

Electrical components - PC interface devices, including CRT display controllers, Windows accelerators & IBM-compatible VGA color graphics boards for flat-panel displays

CHS ELECTRONICS, INC.

2153 NW 86th Ave.	CEO: Claudio Osorio	1995 Sales: $936.7 million
Miami, FL 33122	CFO: Craig Toll	1-Yr. Sales Change: 160.8%
Phone: 305-716-8273	HR: Anna Perez	Exchange: Nasdaq (SC)
Fax: 305-593-1585	Employees: 968	Symbol: CHSE

Retail - wholesale microcomputer & networking products, including software

CIBER, INC.

5251 DTC Pkwy., Ste. 1400	CEO: Bobby G. Stevenson	1996 Sales: $156.9 million
Englewood, CO 80011-2742	CFO: Mac J. Slingerlend	1-Yr. Sales Change: 43.8%
Phone: 303-220-0100	HR: Dana Harr	Exchange: Nasdaq
Fax: 303-220-7100	Employees: 1,532	Symbol: CIBR

Computers - system analysis, design & maintenance, specialized on-site consulting services & technical education & training

CIMATRON LTD.

11 Gush Etzion St.	CEO: Meir Yoeli	1995 Sales: $13.6 million
Girat Shmnel, Israel	CFO: Efi Lebel	1-Yr. Sales Change: 49.5%
Phone: +972-3-531-2121	HR: —	Exchange: Nasdaq (SC)
Fax: +972-3-531-2140	Employees: 117	Symbol: CIMTF

Computers - engineering & CAD software

CINCOM SYSTEMS INC.

2300 Montana Ave.	CEO: Thomas M. Nies	1995 Sales: $157.0 million
Cincinnati, OH 45211-3899	CFO: Tom Perazzo	1-Yr. Sales Change: 4.2%
Phone: 513-662-2300	HR: Bill Ohr	Ownership: Privately Held
Fax: 513-481-8332	Employees: 979	

Computers - database, LAN, office & manufacturing automation software

CIPRICO INC.

2800 Campus Dr.	CEO: Robert H. Kill	1995 Sales: $16.0 million
Plymouth, MN 55441	CFO: Cory J. Miller	1-Yr. Sales Change: 22.1%
Phone: 612-551-4000	HR: Jeanne N. Vencill	Exchange: Nasdaq
Fax: 612-559-8799	Employees: 80	Symbol: CPCI

Computers - computer data storage subsystems, controllers & related software

CIRCUIT SYSTEMS, INC.

2350 E. Lunt Ave.	CEO: D. S. Patel	1996 Sales: $65.1 million
Elk Grove Village, IL 60007	CFO: Dilip S. Vyas	1-Yr. Sales Change: 9.2%
Phone: 847-439-1999	HR: William Blair	Exchange: Nasdaq
Fax: 847-437-5910	Employees: 530	Symbol: CSYI

Electrical components - single-sided, double-sided & multilayer printed circuit boards

CIRRUS LOGIC, INC.

3100 W. Warren Ave.	CEO: Michael L. Hackworth	1996 Sales: $1,146.9 million
Fremont, CA 94538	CFO: Thomas F. Kelly	1-Yr. Sales Change: 29.0%
Phone: 510-623-8300	HR: William H. Bennett	Exchange: Nasdaq
Fax: 510-624-7140	Employees: 3,151	Symbol: CRUS

Electrical components - integrated circuits for desktop & portable computing

CISCO SYSTEMS, INC.

170 W. Tasman Dr.	CEO: John T. Chambers	1996 Sales: $4,096.0 million
San Jose, CA 95134-1706	CFO: Larry R. Carter	1-Yr. Sales Change: 107.0%
Phone: 408-526-4000	HR: Barbara Beck	Exchange: Nasdaq
Fax: 408-526-4100	Employees: 4,086	Symbol: CSCO

Computers - multiprotocol routers & software

 See pages 66–67 for a full profile of this company.

CITATION COMPUTER SYSTEMS, INC.

424 S. Woods Mill Rd., Ste. 200	CEO: J. Robert Copper	1996 Sales: $25.1 million
Chesterfield, MO 63017	CFO: Richard Neece	1-Yr. Sales Change: 7.3%
Phone: 314-579-7900	HR: Ann Prenatt	Exchange: Nasdaq
Fax: 314-579-7990	Employees: 161	Symbol: CITA

Business services - LAN-based information systems software for hospitals, group practice/clinics, reference laboratories & nursing homes nationwide

CITRIX SYSTEMS, INC.

210 University Dr., Ste. 700	CEO: Roger W. Roberts	1995 Sales: $14.6 million
Coral Springs, FL 33071	CFO: James J. Felcyn Jr.	1-Yr. Sales Change: 44.6%
Phone: 954-755-0559	HR: —	Exchange: Nasdaq
Fax: 954-255-1175	Employees: 77	Symbol: CTXS

Computers - multiuser application server products designed for Windows operating systems

CKS GROUP, INC.

10441 Bandley Dr.
Cupertino, CA 95014
Phone: 408-366-5100
Fax: 408-366-5120

CEO: Mark D. Kvamme
CFO: Carlton H. Baab
HR: Sharon Fitzsimmons
Employees: 187

1995 Sales: $34.8 million
1-Yr. Sales Change: 52.0%
Exchange: Nasdaq
Symbol: CKSG

Business services - marketing services, including media marketing programs designed for the World Wide Web, online services & other digital formats

CLAREMONT TECHNOLOGY GROUP, INC.

1600 NW Compton Dr., Ste. 210
Beaverton, OR 97006
Phone: 503-690-4000
Fax: 503-690-4004

CEO: Paul J. Cosgrave
CFO: Dennis M. Goett
HR: Clark Ackerman
Employees: 519

1996 Sales: $47.3 million
1-Yr. Sales Change: 73.3%
Exchange: Nasdaq
Symbol: CLMT

Computers - information technology solutions for business-wide processes, including customer service, order processing, billing & logistics for large corporations & government organizations in the US & abroad

CLARIFY, INC.

2702 Orchard Pkwy.
San Jose, CA 95134
Phone: 408-428-2000
Fax: 408-428-0633

CEO: David A. Stamm
CFO: Ray M. Fritz
HR: Tanya Morrow
Employees: 144

1995 Sales: $20.9 million
1-Yr. Sales Change: 104.9%
Exchange: Nasdaq
Symbol: CLFY

Computers - adaptable client/server application software

CLARINET COMMUNICATIONS CORP.

4880 Stevens Creek Blvd., Ste. 206
San Jose, CA 95129-1034
Phone: 408-296-0366
Fax: 408-296-1668

CEO: Brad Templeton
CFO: Roy E. Folk
HR: Marilyn Foust
Employees: 22

1995 Est. Sales: $2.0 mil.
1-Yr. Sales Change: 100.0%
Ownership: Privately Held

Publishing - electronic news publication (e.News: Internet's first & largest news publication)

CLARIS CORPORATION

5201 Patrick Henry Dr., PO Box 58168
Santa Clara, CA 95052-8168
Phone: 408-987-7000
Fax: 408-987-3931

CEO: Daniel Eilers
CFO: Rob Selvi
HR: Roberta Linsky
Employees: 700

1995 Sales: $183.8 million
1-Yr. Sales Change: 16.8%
Ownership: Subsidiary

Computers - software (ClarisWorks, FileMaker Pro; subsidiary of Apple Computer)

CMC INDUSTRIES, INC.

4950 Patrick Henry Dr.
Santa Clara, CA 95054
Phone: 408-982-9999
Fax: 408-982-9922

CEO: David S. Lee
CFO: Lanny N. Lambert
HR: Regina G. Brown
Employees: 1,242

1996 Sales: $164.7 million
1-Yr. Sales Change: 14.1%
Exchange: Nasdaq
Symbol: CMCI

Electrical products - monitor board assemblies, subassemblies, telephones & central office switches

CMD TECHNOLOGY, INC.

One Vanderbilt
Irvine, CA 92718
Phone: 714-454-0800
Fax: 714-455-1656

CEO: Simon Huang
CFO: Kirk Andrews
HR: Cheryl Bagra
Employees: 187

1995 Sales: $58.8 million
1-Yr. Sales Change: 68.0%
Ownership: Privately Held

Computers - computer data storage & data input/output solutions, including SCSI adapters, IDE controllers, RAID devices & storage servers for PCs & mainframes

CMG INFORMATION SERVICES, INC.

187 Ballardvale St., Ste. B110
Wilmington, MA 01887-7000
Phone: 508-657-7000
Fax: 508-988-0046

CEO: David S. Wetherell
CFO: Andrew J. Hajducky III
HR: Susan Michelinie
Employees: 237

1995 Sales: $2.7 million
1-Yr. Sales Change: (86.1%)
Exchange: Nasdaq
Symbol: CMGI

Data collection & systems - information-based products & services; investments in Internet-related technology (Lycos)

CML MICROSYSTEMS PLC

One Wheaton Rd., Industrial Estate East
Witham, Essex CM8 3TD, UK
Phone: +44-1-376-513-833
Fax: +44-1-376-518-247

CEO: George W. Gurry
CFO: Nigel G. Clark
HR: —
Employees: 287

1996 Sales: $26.4 million
1-Yr. Sales Change: (17.8%)
Exchange: London

Monolithic integrated circuits; data communication equipment; road traffic control equipment

CMP PUBLICATIONS, INC.

600 Community Dr.
Manhasset, NY 11030-3847
Phone: 516-562-5000
Fax: 516-562-7830

CEO: Michael S. Leeds
CFO: Joseph E. Sichler
HR: —
Employees: 1,500

1995 Sales: $382.0 million
1-Yr. Sales Change: 20.5%
Ownership: Privately Held

Publishing - technology & computer-related publications (HomePC, InformationWeek, NetGuide, WINDOWS magazine, Interactive Age); trade shows, convention management & online services

 See pages 68–69 for a full profile of this company.

C/NET, INC.

150 Chestnut St.
San Francisco, CA 94111
Phone: 415-395-7800
Fax: 415-395-9205

CEO: Halsey M. Minor
CFO: Shelby W. Bonnie
HR: Nancy Guilbert
Employees: 164

1995 Sales: $3.5 million
1-Yr. Sales Change: —
Exchange: Nasdaq
Symbol: CNWK

Computers - Internet (c/net.com, shareware.com, search.com) & TV-based programming (c/net central)

COGNEX CORPORATION

One Vision Dr.
Natick, MA 01760-2059
Phone: 508-650-3000
Fax: 508-650-3333

CEO: Robert J. Shillman
CFO: John J. Rogers Jr.
HR: Jo Ann Woodyard
Employees: 307

1995 Sales: $104.5 million
1-Yr. Sales Change: 67.2%
Exchange: Nasdaq
Symbol: CGNX

Machinery - computerized quality-control systems

COGNITRONICS CORPORATION

3 Corporate Dr.
Danbury, CT 06810-4130
Phone: 203-830-3400
Fax: 203-830-3405

CEO: Brian J. Kelley
CFO: Garrett Sullivan
HR: Janet Freund
Employees: 80

1995 Sales: $17.5 million
1-Yr. Sales Change: 19.9%
Exchange: AMEX
Symbol: CGN

Computers - voice processing & optical scanning peripherals

COGNOS INCORPORATED

3755 Riverside Dr.
Ottawa, ON K1G 4K9, Canada
Phone: 613-738-1440
Fax: 613-738-0002

CEO: Renato Zambonini
CFO: Donnie M. Moore
HR: Fiona Jameson
Employees: 986

1996 Sales: $151.5 million
1-Yr. Sales Change: 24.3%
Exchange: Nasdaq
Symbol: COGNF

Computers - information systems software tools (PowerPlay, PowerHouse, Impromptu, Axiant)

COHU, INC.

5755 Kearny Villa Rd.
San Diego, CA 92123-1170
Phone: 619-277-6700
Fax: 619-277-0221

CEO: Charles A. Schwan
CFO: John H. Allen
HR: Linda Jacobson
Employees: 900

1995 Sales: $178.8 million
1-Yr. Sales Change: 74.1%
Exchange: Nasdaq
Symbol: COHU

Machinery - semiconductor manufacturing equipment

COMARCO, INC.

22800 Savi Ranch Pkwy., Ste. 214
Yorba Linda, CA 92687
Phone: 714-282-3832
Fax: 714-283-0604

CEO: Don M. Bailey
CFO: Thomas P. Baird
HR: Evelyn M. Evans
Employees: 700

1996 Sales: $69.8 million
1-Yr. Sales Change: 2.2%
Exchange: Nasdaq
Symbol: CMRO

Computers - systems engineering, integration & product support; engineering analysis & test engineering; wireless communications products

COMARK, INC.

444 Scott Dr.
Bloomingdale , IL 60108
Phone: 708-924-6670
Fax: 708-924-6790

CEO: Chuck Rolande
CFO: Phil Courtland
HR: Chris Schuver
Employees: 605

1995 Sales: $563.0 million
1-Yr. Sales Change: 37.0%
Ownership: Privately Held

Retail - software, computer & peripherals

COMDIAL CORPORATION

1180 Seminole Trail
Charlottesville, VA 22901
Phone: 804-978-2525
Fax: 804-978-2512

CEO: William G. Mustain
CFO: Wayne R. Wilver
HR: —
Employees: 849

1995 Sales: $94.8 million
1-Yr. Sales Change: 23.0%
Exchange: Nasdaq
Symbol: CMDL

Telecommunications equipment - telephone systems, terminals & related equipment

COMDISCO, INC.

6111 N. River Rd.
Rosemont, IL 60018
Phone: 847-698-3000
Fax: 847-518-5440

CEO: Jack Slevin
CFO: John J. Vosicky
HR: Lucie A. Buford
Employees: 2,100

1995 Sales: $2,240.0 million
1-Yr. Sales Change: 6.8%
Exchange: NYSE
Symbol: CDO

Leasing - new & used computer & other high-technology equipment; disaster recovery services (emergency data processing backup); technology planning & asset management services

 **See pages 70–71 for a full profile of this company.**

COMET SOFTWARE INTERNATIONAL LTD.

13 Noah Moses St.
Tel Aviv 67442, Israel
Phone: +972-3-696-6110
Fax: —

CEO: Shmuel Sternfeld
CFO: Gadi Zilberdik
HR: —
Employees: 111

1995 Sales: $4.5 million
1-Yr. Sales Change: —
Exchange: Nasdaq
Symbol: CMTTF

Computers - computer information management systems, including health care software

COMFORCE CORPORATION

2001 Marcus Ave.
Lake Success, NY 11042
Phone: 516-352-3200
Fax: 516-352-3382

CEO: Austin A. Iodice
CFO: James D. Doering
HR: Robert Gruber
Employees: 22

1995 Sales: $2.4 million
1-Yr. Sales Change: (93.0%)
Exchange: AMEX
Symbol: CFS

Personnel - telecommunications & computer staffing & consulting services

COMMUNICATION INTELLIGENCE CORPORATION

275 Shoreline Dr., 5th Fl.
Redwood Shores, CA 94065-1413
Phone: 415-802-7888
Fax: 415-802-7777

CEO: James Dao
CFO: John Doerner
HR: Karen Kellenbach
Employees: 74

1995 Sales: $2.3 million
1-Yr. Sales Change: (36.1%)
Exchange: Nasdaq (SC)
Symbol: CICI

Computers - software primarily for pen-based computers (Handwriter Recognition System, Handwriter Dynamic Signature Verification, PenDOS, PenMac)

COMNET CORPORATION

4200 Parliament Place, Ste. 600
Lanham, MD 20706-1860
Phone: 301-918-0400
Fax: 301-731-0360

CEO: Robert S. Bowen
CFO: Charles A. Crew
HR: Trent Lutz
Employees: 256

1996 Sales: $45.9 million
1-Yr. Sales Change: 21.1%
Exchange: Nasdaq
Symbol: CNET

Computers - health care & direct marketing software

COMPAQ COMPUTER CORPORATION

20555 State Hwy. 249
Houston, TX 77070
Phone: 713-370-0670
Fax: 713-374-1740

CEO: Eckhard Pfeiffer
CFO: Earl Mason
HR: Hans W. Gutsch
Employees: 17,055

1995 Sales: $14,755.0 mil.
1-Yr. Sales Change: 35.8%
Exchange: NYSE
Symbol: CPQ

Computers - PCs (#1 worldwide); peripherals & software (TabWorks)

 **See pages 72–73 for a full profile of this company.**

COMPOSITECH LTD.

120 Ricefield Ln.
Hauppauge, NY 11788
Phone: 516-436-5200
Fax: 516-436-5203

CEO: Fred E. Klimpl
CFO: Samuel S. Gross
HR: —
Employees: 47

1995 Sales: $0.1 million
1-Yr. Sales Change: (98.0%)
Exchange: Nasdaq (SC)
Symbol: CTEK

Electrical components - copper-clad fiberglass epoxy laminates used to make printed circuit boards

COMPUCOM SYSTEMS, INC.

10100 N. Central Expwy.
Dallas, TX 75231-1800
Phone: 214-265-3600
Fax: 214-265-5220

CEO: Edward R. Anderson
CFO: Robert J. Boutin
HR: Mark S. Esselman
Employees: 2,615

1995 Sales: $1,441.6 million
1-Yr. Sales Change: 14.8%
Exchange: Nasdaq
Symbol: CMPC

Retail - computers; LAN & WAN installation & other services

 See pages 74–75 for a full profile of this company.

COMPUSA INC.

14951 N. Dallas Pkwy.
Dallas, TX 75240
Phone: 214-982-4000
Fax: 214-982-4276

CEO: James F. Halpin
CFO: James E. Skinner
HR: Paul B. Poyfair
Employees: 7,963

1996 Sales: $3,829.8 million
1-Yr. Sales Change: 36.1%
Exchange: NYSE
Symbol: CPU

Retail - computers & peripheral equipment, including PCs, laptops, monitors, modems, printers & software
(#1 in US)

 See pages 76–77 for a full profile of this company.

COMPUSERVE CORPORATION

5000 Arlington Centre Blvd.
Columbus, OH 43220
Phone: 614-457-8600
Fax: 614-457-0348

CEO: Robert J. Massey
CFO: Lawrence A. Gyenes
HR: Judy Reinhard
Employees: 3,650

1996 Sales: $793.2 million
1-Yr. Sales Change: 36.1%
Exchange: Nasdaq
Symbol: CSRV

Computers - online information service & Internet access provider

 See pages 78–79 for a full profile of this company.

COMPUTATIONAL SYSTEMS, INCORPORATED

835 Innovation Dr.
Knoxville, TN 37932
Phone: 423-675-2110
Fax: 423-675-3100

CEO: Ronald G. Canada
CFO: Bryan J. Collier
HR: J. Gribben
Employees: 320

1995 Sales: $41.8 million
1-Yr. Sales Change: 34.0%
Exchange: Nasdaq
Symbol: CSIN

Computer - integrated predictive maintenance products & services for large-scale continuous-run
manufacturing facilities

COMPUTER 2000 AG

Wolfratshauser Strasse 84
81379 Munich, Germany
Phone: +49-89-7-24-90-0
Fax: +49-89-7-24-90-200

CEO: Klaus Laufen
CFO: —
HR: —
Employees: 1,966

1995 Sales: $3,464.5 million
1-Yr. Sales Change: 39.3%
Exchange: Frankfurt

Retail - distribution of PC hardware & software products & systems

COMPUTER ASSOCIATES INTERNATIONAL, INC.

One Computer Associates Plaza	CEO: Charles B. Wang	1996 Sales: $3,504.6 million
Islandia, NY 11788-7000	CFO: Peter A. Schwartz	1-Yr. Sales Change: 33.6%
Phone: 516-342-5224	HR: Lisa Mars	Exchange: NYSE
Fax: 516-342-5329	Employees: 8,800	Symbol: CA

Computers - data processing management & personal finance software

 See pages 80–81 for a full profile of this company.

COMPUTER CONCEPTS CORP.

80 Orville Dr.	CEO: Daniel DelGiorno Sr.	1995 Sales: $16.3 million
Bohemia, NY 11716	CFO: George Aronson	1-Yr. Sales Change: 19.0%
Phone: 516-244-1500	HR: Cathy Athans	Exchange: Nasdaq (SC)
Fax: 516-563-8085	Employees: 131	Symbol: CCEE

Computers - systems management & information delivery software products, including end-user data access tools for personal & client/server environments

COMPUTER DATA SYSTEMS, INC.

One Curie Ct.	CEO: Peter A. Bracken	1996 Sales: $251.1 million
Rockville, MD 20850-4389	CFO: Wyatt D. Tinsley	1-Yr. Sales Change: 13.8%
Phone: 301-921-7000	HR: Francine DeVenoge	Exchange: Nasdaq
Fax: 301-948-9328	Employees: 3,400	Symbol: CDSI

Computers - system integration, software engineering, development & maintenance, database support & other related services

COMPUTER GENERATED SOLUTIONS, INC.

1675 Broadway	CEO: Philip Friedman	1995 Sales: $35.9 million
New York, NY 10019	CFO: Fred B. Schlossberg	1-Yr. Sales Change: 45.3%
Phone: 212-408-3800	HR: Lumei Rosales	Ownership: Privately Held
Fax: 212-977-7474	Employees: 900	

Computers - products & services, including software (ACS Optima Software), technical training, full-service on-site & remote help desk support & call management services

COMPUTER HORIZONS CORPORATION

49 Old Bloomfield Ave.	CEO: John J. Cassese	1995 Sales: $200.1 million
Mountain Lakes, NJ 07046-1495	CFO: Bernhard Hubert	1-Yr. Sales Change: 31.5%
Phone: 201-402-7400	HR: Michelle Friedberg	Exchange: Nasdaq
Fax: 201-402-7988	Employees: 2,511	Symbol: CHRZ

Computers - computer systems integration & services, including contract staffing, MIS outsourcing & information system reengineering

COMPUTER INTEGRATION CORPORATION

7900 Glades Rd.	CEO: Ronald G. Farrell	1996 Sales: $450.0 million
Boca Raton, FL 33434	CFO: John F. Chiste	1-Yr. Sales Change: 115.1%
Phone: 561-482-6678	HR: —	Exchange: Nasdaq (SC)
Fax: 561-483-5638	Employees: 500	Symbol: CICC

Retail - microcomputers, workstations & related products

COMPUTER LANGUAGE RESEARCH, INC.

2395 Midway Rd.	CEO: Stephen T. Winn	1995 Sales: $110.7 million
Carrollton, TX 75006	CFO: Charles W. Hill	1-Yr. Sales Change: 2.0%
Phone: 214-250-7000	HR: J. D. Hatch	Exchange: Nasdaq
Fax: 214-250-8181	Employees: 946	Symbol: CLRI

Business services - tax processing services & software to businesses (Fast-Tax)

COMPUTER LEARNING CENTERS, INC.

11350 Random Hills Rd., Ste. 240	CEO: Reid R. Bechtle	1996 Sales: $46.1 million
Fairfax, VA 22030	CFO: Charles L. Cosgrove	1-Yr. Sales Change: 17.3%
Phone: 703-359-9333	HR: Sharon Devine	Exchange: Nasdaq
Fax: 703-359-8225	Employees: 441	Symbol: CLCX

Schools - computer-related education & training

COMPUTER MANAGEMENT SCIENCES, INC.

8133 Baymeadows Way	CEO: Jerry W. Davis	1995 Sales: $27.8 million
Jacksonville, FL 32256	CFO: Anthony V. Weight	1-Yr. Sales Change: 41.8%
Phone: 904-737-8955	HR: Jose Jozik	Exchange: Nasdaq
Fax: 904-737-6376	Employees: 357	Symbol: CMSX

Computers - information technology & custom software-development services

COMPUTER MARKETPLACE, INC.

1490 Railroad St.	CEO: L. Wayne Kiley	1996 Sales: $30.0 million
Corona, CA 91720	CFO: Thomas Iwanski	1-Yr. Sales Change: (4.8%)
Phone: 909-735-2102	HR: Jackie Mahoney	Exchange: Nasdaq (SC)
Fax: 909-735-5717	Employees: 113	Symbol: MKPL

Retail - wholesale new & used computer equipment

COMPUTER NETWORK TECHNOLOGY CORPORATION

605 N. Highway 169, Ste. 800	CEO: Bruce T. Coleman	1995 Sales: $78.8 million
Minneapolis, MN 55441	CFO: John R. Brintnall	1-Yr. Sales Change: (0.9%)
Phone: 612-797-6000	HR: Holly Kennedy	Exchange: Nasdaq
Fax: 612-797-6813	Employees: 408	Symbol: CMNT

Computers - network products for LAN systems (CHANNELink, Brixton)

COMPUTER PEOPLE INC.

1960 E. Grand Ave., Ste. 555	CEO: Larry Stuesser	1995 Sales: $60.0 million
El Segundo, CA 90245	CFO: —	1-Yr. Sales Change: —
Phone: 310-335-4810	HR: —	Ownership: Privately Held
Fax: 310-335-4822	Employees: 600	

Computers - LAN & WAN network integration, project management, document imaging & workflow solutions

COMPUTER PRODUCTS, INC.

7900 Glades Rd., Ste. 500	CEO: Joseph M. O'Donnell	1995 Sales: $191.4 million
Boca Raton, FL 33434-4105	CFO: Richard J. Thompson	1-Yr. Sales Change: 23.6%
Phone: 561-451-1000	HR: Colleen Thomas	Exchange: Nasdaq
Fax: 561-451-1050	Employees: 1,600	Symbol: CPRD

Electrical components - power supplies & power conversion products for electronic equipment requiring precise & constant voltage level

COMPUTER SCIENCES CORPORATION

2100 E. Grand Ave.	CEO: Van B. Honeycutt	1996 Sales: $4,242.4 million
El Segundo, CA 90245	CFO: Leon J. Level	1-Yr. Sales Change: 71.1%
Phone: 310-615-0311	HR: L. Scott Sharpe	Exchange: NYSE
Fax: 310-322-9805	Employees: 33,850	Symbol: CSC

Consulting - information technology consulting, systems integration & outsourcing

 See pages 82–83 for a full profile of this company.

COMPUTER TASK GROUP, INCORPORATED

800 Delaware Ave.	CEO: Gale S. Fitzgerald	1995 Sales: $339.4 million
Buffalo, NY 14209-2094	CFO: James R. Boldt	1-Yr. Sales Change: 12.5%
Phone: 716-882-8000	HR: Vincent J. Gallenti	Exchange: NYSE
Fax: 716-887-7246	Employees: 5,014	Symbol: TSK

Consulting - information technology services, including staffing & project management

COMPUTERVISION CORPORATION

100 Crosby Dr.
Bedford, MA 01730-1480
Phone: 617-275-1800
Fax: 617-275-2670

CEO: Kathleen A. Cote
CFO: William A. Foniri
HR: Barry F. Cohen
Employees: 2,100

1995 Sales: $507.1 million
1-Yr. Sales Change: (11.6%)
Exchange: NYSE
Symbol: CVN

Computers - CAD/CAM/CAE software (CADDS), object-oriented design automation tools (PELORUS) & object-oriented enterprise data management programs (Optegra)

 See pages 84–85 for a full profile of this company.

COMPUTONE CORPORATION

1100 Northmeadow Pkwy., Ste. 150
Roswell, GA 30076
Phone: 770-475-2725
Fax: 770-664-1510

CEO: Tom Anderson
CFO: Gregg Alba
HR: Kim Rideout
Employees: 56

1996 Sales: $9.7 million
1-Yr. Sales Change: (33.6%)
Exchange: Nasdaq (SC)
Symbol: CMPT

Computers - hardware & software connectivity products for WANs & LANs

COMPUTRAC, INC.

222 Municipal Dr.
Richardson, TX 75080
Phone: 214-234-4241
Fax: 214-234-6280

CEO: Harry W. Margolis
CFO: Cheri L. White
HR: Lynda K. Thomas
Employees: 52

1996 Sales: $5.3 million
1-Yr. Sales Change: (22.1%)
Exchange: AMEX
Symbol: LLB

Computers - integrated computer systems & software applications designed for the legal profession (CompuTrac OPEN!)

COMPUTRON SOFTWARE, INC.

301 Rte. 17 North
Rutherford, NJ 07070
Phone: 201-935-3400
Fax: 201-935-4531

CEO: Adrian Peters
CFO: Richard C. Yonker
HR: Theresa Santualli
Employees: 159

1995 Sales: $55.5 million
1-Yr. Sales Change: 58.6%
Exchange: Nasdaq
Symbol: CTRN

Computers - client/server financial, workflow & archival data management software for applications in large organizations

COMPUWARE CORPORATION

31440 Northwestern Hwy.
Farmington Hills, MI 48334-2564
Phone: 810-737-7300
Fax: 810-737-7108

CEO: Peter Karmanos Jr.
CFO: Ralph A. Caponigro
HR: Shiela McKinnon
Employees: 4,844

1996 Sales: $614.4 million
1-Yr. Sales Change: 15.1%
Exchange: Nasdaq
Symbol: CPWR

Computers - integrated systems software, including series file & data management software, interactive debugging & analysis software, fault diagnosis & automated testing products

 See page 269 for a full profile of this company.

COMSHARE, INCORPORATED

555 Briarwood Circle
Ann Arbor, MI 48108
Phone: 313-994-4800
Fax: 313-994-5895

CEO: T. Wallace Wrathall
CFO: Kathryn A. Jehle
HR: Kevin McGrath
Employees: 695

1996 Sales: $119.0 million
1-Yr. Sales Change: 9.8%
Exchange: Nasdaq
Symbol: CSRE

Computers - decision-support software & related services

COMTRADE INC.

15314 E. Valley Blvd.
City of Industry, CA 91746
Phone: 818-961-6688
Fax: 818-961-6749

CEO: Christopher Luke
CFO: Allen Chang
HR: Sherry Shen
Employees: 150

1995 Sales: $195.0 million
1-Yr. Sales Change: 50.0%
Ownership: Privately Held

Retail - mail-order sales of PCs

COMTREX SYSTEMS CORPORATION

102 Executive Dr.
Moorestown, NJ 08057-4224
Phone: 609-778-0090
Fax: 609-778-9322

CEO: Jeffrey C. Rice
CFO: Lisa J. Mudrick
HR: Lisa J. Mudrick
Employees: 44

1996 Sales: $5.0 million
1-Yr. Sales Change: (12.3%)
Exchange: Nasdaq (SC)
Symbol: COMX

Computers - point-of-sale electronic information systems, related peripherals & software

COMVERSE TECHNOLOGY, INC.

170 Crossways Park Dr.
Woodbury, NY 11797
Phone: 516-677-7200
Fax: 516-677-7355

CEO: Kobi Alexander
CFO: Igal Nissim
HR: Teri Caperna
Employees: 1,008

1995 Sales: $145.9 million
1-Yr. Sales Change: 47.7%
Exchange: Nasdaq
Symbol: CMVT

Computers - integrated voice & fax mail systems (TRILOGUE) & data surveillance CD products

CONCENTRA CORPORATION

21 North Ave.
Burlington, MA 01803-3301
Phone: 617-229-4600
Fax: 617-229-4700

CEO: Lawrence W. Rosenfeld
CFO: Gerald M. Schimmoeller
HR: Pauline DeMario
Employees: 129

1996 Sales: $20.7 million
1-Yr. Sales Change: 2.5%
Exchange: Nasdaq
Symbol: CTRA

Computers - engineering automation software (The ICAD System)

CONCEPTRONIC, INC.

6 Post Rd.
Portsmouth, NH 03801
Phone: 603-431-6262
Fax: 603-431-3303

CEO: Garry A. Prime
CFO: William D. Gray
HR: William D. Gray
Employees: 93

1995 Sales: $15.0 million
1-Yr. Sales Change: 11.1%
Exchange: Nasdaq (SC)
Symbol: CNCP

Machinery - semiconductor manufacturing & repair equipment

CONCURRENT COMPUTER CORPORATION

2 Crescent Place
Oceanport, NJ 07757
Phone: 908-870-4500
Fax: 908-870-4861

CEO: John T. Stihl
CFO: Roger J. Mason
HR: David L. Vienneau
Employees: 900

1996 Sales: $95.8 million
1-Yr. Sales Change: (31.6%)
Exchange: Nasdaq
Symbol: CCUR

Computers - real-time computer systems & solutions

CONNECT, INC.

515 Ellis St.
Mountain View, CA 94043-2242
Phone: 415-254-4000
Fax: 415-254-4800

CEO: Thomas P. Kehler
CFO: Joseph G. Girata
HR: Steve Auerbach
Employees: 116

1995 Sales: $8.6 million
1-Yr. Sales Change: 7.5%
Exchange: Nasdaq
Symbol: CNKT

Computers - software & services, including user registration, multimedia catalog & content
management, merchandising, order management & security & payment processing for interactive
Internet-based commerce

CONSILIUM, INC.

640 Clyde Ave.
Mountain View, CA 94043
Phone: 415-691-6100
Fax: 415-691-6130

CEO: Thomas A. Tomasetti
CFO: Richard H. Van Hoesen
HR: Linda Kato-Ujihara
Employees: 210

1995 Sales: $33.9 million
1-Yr. Sales Change: 21.5%
Exchange: Nasdaq
Symbol: CSIM

Computers - software for real-time management of factory floor materials, equipment, personnel,
specifications/work instructions & facility conditions

CONTINENTAL CIRCUITS CORP.

3502 E. Roeser Rd.
Phoenix, AZ 85040
Phone: 602-268-3461
Fax: 602-268-0208

CEO: Frederick G. McNamee III
CFO: Thomas E. Linnen
HR: Robert A. Kosciusko
Employees: 1,016

1996 Sales: $108.4 million
1-Yr. Sales Change: 13.6%
Exchange: Nasdaq
Symbol: CCIR

Electrical components - multilayer surface-mount circuit boards for the computer, communications,
instrumentation & industrial controls industries

CONTROL DATA SYSTEMS, INC.

4201 Lexington Ave. North	CEO: James E. Ousley	1995 Sales: $454.8 million
Arden Hills, MN 55126-6198	CFO: Joseph F. Killoran	1-Yr. Sales Change: (13.2%)
Phone: 612-482-2401	HR: Ruth A. Rich	Exchange: Nasdaq
Fax: 612-482-2791	Employees: 1,829	Symbol: CDAT

Computers - systems integration & consulting

 See pages 86–87 for a full profile of this company.

COOPER & CHYAN TECHNOLOGY, INC.

1601 Saratoga-Sunnyvale Rd.	CEO: John R. Harding	1995 Sales: $17.7 million
Cupertino, CA 95014	CFO: Robert D. Selvi	1-Yr. Sales Change: 63.9%
Phone: 408-366-6966	HR: Brian Fay	Exchange: Nasdaq
Fax: 408-252-9565	Employees: 112	Symbol: CCTI

Computers - software tools that help designers route the interconnections among the electronic devices on printed circuit boards & integrated cicuits

CORBIS CORPORATION

15395 SE 30th Place, Ste. 300	CEO: Doug Rowan	1995 Est. Sales: $8.0 mil.
Bellevue, WA 98007	CFO: Tony Rojas	1-Yr. Sales Change: —
Phone: 206-641-4505	HR: Tica Gordon	Ownership: Privately Held
Fax: 206-746-1618	Employees: 270	

Computers - multimedia CD-ROMs (A Passion for Art: Renoir, Cezanne, Matisse, and Dr. Barnes); digital image licensing (Bettmann archive) - owned by Bill Gates

 See page 270 for a full profile of this company.

COREL CORPORATION

1600 Carling Ave.	CEO: Michael C. J. Cowpland	1995 Sales: $196.4 million
Ottawa, ON K1Z 8R7, Canada	CFO: Charles A. Norris	1-Yr. Sales Change: 19.5%
Phone: 613-728-3733	HR: Lisa Kenkel	Exchange: Nasdaq
Fax: 613-761-9176	Employees: 594	Symbol: COSFF

Computers - graphics (CorelDRAW), desktop publishing (CorelVENTURA) & word processing software (WordPerfect); consumer CD-ROMs (CD HOME series)

 See page 271 for a full profile of this company.

CORNERSTONE IMAGING, INC.

1710 Fortune Dr.	CEO: Thomas T. van Overbeek	1995 Sales: $91.2 million
San Jose, CA 95131	CFO: John Finegan	1-Yr. Sales Change: 29.9%
Phone: 408-435-8900	HR: Denise Wescott	Exchange: Nasdaq
Fax: 408-435-8998	Employees: 220	Symbol: CRNR

Computers - document image processing (DIP) display subsystems (#1 worldwide)

 See page 272 for a full profile of this company.

COTELLIGENT GROUP, INC.

101 California St., Ste. 2050
San Francisco, CA 94111
Phone: 415-439-6400
Fax: 415-439-6888

CEO: James R. Lavelle
CFO: Duane W. Bell
HR: James R. Lavelle
Employees: 700

1996 Sales: $64.0 million
1-Yr. Sales Change: 28.0%
Exchange: Nasdaq
Symbol: COTL

Computers - consulting & contract programming services

C.P. CLARE CORPORATION

430 Bedford St.
Lexington, MA 02173-1548
Phone: 617-863-8700
Fax: 617-863-8707

CEO: Arthur R. Buckland
CFO: Jacqueline D. Arthur
HR: —
Employees: 1,198

1996 Sales: $127.9 million
1-Yr. Sales Change: 33.2%
Exchange: Nasdaq
Symbol: CPCL

Electrical components - electromagnetic & semiconductor switches & relays

C-PHONE CORP

6714 Netherlands Dr.
Wilmington, NC 28405
Phone: 910-395-6100
Fax: 910-395-6108

CEO: Daniel P. Flohr
CFO: Paul H. Albritton
HR: Paul H. Albritton
Employees: 43

1996 Sales: $1.8 million
1-Yr. Sales Change: 80.0%
Exchange: Nasdaq
Symbol: CFON

Computers - PC-based desktop videoconferencing system (C-Phone)

CRAY RESEARCH, INC.

655A Lone Oak Dr.
Eagan, MN 55121
Phone: 612-452-6650
Fax: 612-683-3599

CEO: Robert H. Ewald
CFO: Steve Snyder
HR: Karalyn J. Harrington
Employees: 4,225

1995 Sales: $676.2 million
1-Yr. Sales Change: (26.6%)
Ownership: Subsidiary

Computers - supercomputers, superservers, massively parallel processing units & associated software, peripherals, maintenance & support (subsidiary of Silicon Graphics)

CREATIVE COMPUTER APPLICATIONS, INC.

26115-A Mureau Rd.
Calabasas, CA 91302
Phone: 818-880-6700
Fax: 818-880-4398

CEO: Steven M. Besbeck
CFO: Steven M. Besbeck
HR: Carol Bessel
Employees: 54

1995 Sales: $5.9 million
1-Yr. Sales Change: 3.5%
Exchange: AMEX
Symbol: CAP

Computers - clinical information systems for hospitals, clinics & reference laboratories

CREATIVE COMPUTERS, INC.

2645 Maricopa St.
Torrance, CA 90503
Phone: 310-787-4500
Fax: 310-222-5800

CEO: Frank Khulusi
CFO: Richard Finkbeiner
HR: Kathy Ressler
Employees: 743

1995 Sales: $420.9 million
1-Yr. Sales Change: 157.1%
Exchange: Nasdaq
Symbol: MALL

Retail - mail-order sales of Apple Macintosh hardware, software & peripheral products (MacMall)

CREATIVE TECHNOLOGY LTD.

67 Ayer Rajah Crescent #03-18
Singapore 139950
Phone: +65-773-0233
Fax: +65-773-0353

CEO: Sim Wong Hoo
CFO: Patrick Verderico
HR: Judith Martin
Employees: 4,185

1996 Sales: $1,308.1 million
1-Yr. Sales Change: 8.8%
Exchange: Nasdaq
Symbol: CREAF

Computers - interactive CDs (A Brief History of Time), sound & video multimedia products (Sound Blaster) & voice recognition software (Voiceassist)

 See pages 88–89 for a full profile of this company.

CREDENCE SYSTEMS CORPORATION

3500 W. Warren Ave.
Fremont, CA 94538
Phone: 510-657-7400
Fax: 510-623-2560

CEO: Elwood H. Spedden
CFO: Richard Y. Okumoto
HR: —
Employees: 499

1995 Sales: $176.8 million
1-Yr. Sales Change: 69.8%
Exchange: Nasdaq
Symbol: CMOS

Electronics - automatic semiconductor test equipment

CREE RESEARCH, INC.

2810 Meridian Pkwy., Ste. 176
Durham, NC 27713
Phone: 919-361-5709
Fax: 919-361-4630

CEO: F. Neal Hunter
CFO: Alan J. Robertson
HR: Brenda M. Erickson
Employees: 176

1996 Sales: $17.0 million
1-Yr. Sales Change: 53.2%
Exchange: Nasdaq
Symbol: CREE

Electrical components - silicon carbide-based semiconductors & blue-light-emitting diodes

CROSSCOMM CORPORATION

450 Donald Lynch Blvd.
Marlborough, MA 01752
Phone: 508-481-4060
Fax: 508-229-5535

CEO: William Johnson
CFO: Douglas Bryant
HR: Victoria Lias
Employees: 342

1995 Sales: $44.3 million
1-Yr. Sales Change: (11.9%)
Exchange: Nasdaq
Symbol: XCOM

Computers - internetworking platform equipment (XL line) for fail-safe routing, hub, LAN & ATM switched services

CSG SYSTEMS INTERNATIONAL, INC.

5251 DTC Pkwy.	CEO: Neal C. Hansen	1995 Sales: $96.4 million
Englewood, CO 80111	CFO: David I. Brenner	1-Yr. Sales Change: 1,136%
Phone: 303-796-2850	HR: Mark Whitehouse	Exchange: Nasdaq
Fax: 303-796-2878	Employees: 713	Symbol: CSGS

Computers - customer management software for the telecommunications industry

CSI COMPUTER SPECIALISTS, INC.

2275 Research Blvd.	CEO: Donald C. Weymer	1995 Sales: $6.8 million
Rockville, MD 20850	CFO: —	1-Yr. Sales Change: 19.3%
Phone: 301-921-8860	HR: —	Exchange: Nasdaq (SC)
Fax: —	Employees: —	Symbol: CSIS

Computers - installation & removal services, computer upgrade services & maintenance & repair services

CSK CORPORATION

2-6-1 Nishi-Shinjuku, Shinjuku-ku	CEO: Isao Okawa	1996 Sales: $710.6 million
Tokyo 163-02, Japan	CFO: Norikazu Suzuki	1-Yr. Sales Change: 11.2%
Phone: +81-3-3344-1811	HR: Greg O'Brien	Exchange: Nasdaq (SC)
Fax: +81-3-3344-1874	Employees: 5,340	Symbol: CSKKY

Business services - software development & sales, facilities management & data-entry services; building leasing

 See page 273 for a full profile of this company.

CSP INC.

40 Linnell Circle	CEO: David S. Botten	1996 Sales: $16.5 million
Billerica, MA 01821	CFO: Gary W. Levine	1-Yr. Sales Change: (10.8%)
Phone: 508-663-7598	HR: Rose Doyon	Exchange: Nasdaq
Fax: 508-663-0150	Employees: 105	Symbol: CSPI

Computers - molecular & cell biology imaging systems & add-in processor boards for workstations

CUC INTERNATIONAL INC.

707 Summer St.	CEO: Walter A. Forbes	1996 Sales: $1,415.0 million
Stamford, CT 06901	CFO: Cosmo Corigliano	1-Yr. Sales Change: 35.4%
Phone: 203-324-9261	HR: Fran Johnson	Exchange: NYSE
Fax: 203-348-4528	Employees: 11,000	Symbol: CU

Retail - membership-based consumer services, shopping, travel, dining & other services & products offered by mail order, phone & online network (Comp-U-Card); educational & game software (Sierra On-LIne)

CYAN, INC.

14617 Newport Hwy.	CEO: Rand Miller	1995 Sales: $12.0 million
Mead, WA 99021	CFO: Chris Brandkamp	1-Yr. Sales Change: 33.3%
Phone: 509-468-0807	HR: Heather Ferguson	Ownership: Privately Held
Fax: 509-467-2209	Employees: 20	

Computers - CD-ROM games (Myst)

 See page 274 for a full profile of this company.

CYBERCASH, INC.

2100 Reston Pkwy., Ste. 430	CEO: William N. Melton	1995 Sales: $0.1 million
Reston, VA 22091	CFO: Gene Riechers	1-Yr. Sales Change: —
Phone: 703-620-4200	HR: —	Exchange: Nasdaq
Fax: 703-620-4215	Employees: 65	Symbol: CYCH

Computers - payment-processing software & service that enables financial transactions between individuals, businesses & financial institutions over the Internet

CYBERGUARD CORPORATION

2101 W. Cypress Creek Rd.	CEO: Robert L. Carberry	1996 Sales: $37.4 million
Fort Lauderdale, FL 33309	CFO: Daniel S. Dunleavy	1-Yr. Sales Change: (17.1%)
Phone: 954-974-1700	HR: Debbie Kirwan	Exchange: Nasdaq
Fax: 954-977-5580	Employees: 74	Symbol: CYBG

Computers - real-time (microsecond-response) systems (Night Hawk)

CYBERMEDIA, INC.

3000 Ocean Park Blvd., Ste. 2001	CEO: Unni S. Warrier	1995 Sales: $4.8 million
Santa Monica, CA 90405	CFO: Jeffrey W. Beaumont	1-Yr. Sales Change: 2,300%
Phone: 310-581-4700	HR: Andrea Thompson	Ownership: Privately Held
Fax: 310-581-4720	Employees: 104	

Computers - service & support software products for Windows-based PC users, including software to diagnose & resolve problems (First Aid)

CYBERSOURCE CORPORATION

1050 Chestnut St., Ste. 200	CEO: William S. McKiernan	1995 Sales: $1.0 million
Menlo Park, CA 94025	CFO: Blake Burke	1-Yr. Sales Change: —
Phone: 415-462-5522	HR: Brook Lenox	Ownership: Privately Held
Fax: 415-473-3066	Employees: 20	

Retail - software distribution over the Internet & by mail

 See page 275 for a full profile of this company.

CYBEX CORPORATION

4912 Research Dr.	CEO: Stephen F. Thornton	1996 Sales: $25.0 million
Huntsville, AL 35805	CFO: Doyle C. Weeks	1-Yr. Sales Change: 37.4%
Phone: 205-430-4000	HR: Julie Yarbrough	Exchange: Nasdaq
Fax: 205-430-4030	Employees: 108	Symbol: CBXC

Computers - keyboard, video monitor & mouse switch & extension products (KVM) to allow up to 4 users to control up to 144 IBM-compatible, Macintosh & Sun computers (standalone or server) on a LAN

CYBORG SYSTEMS INC.

2 N Riverside Plaza, 12th Fl.	CEO: Michael D. Blair	1995 Sales: $41.5 million
Chicago, IL 60606	CFO: Joe Heery	1-Yr. Sales Change: —
Phone: 312-454-1865	HR: Marcy Hardman	Ownership: Privately Held
Fax: 312-930-1033	Employees: 350	

Computers - professional software used in HR, payroll & time management environments

CYLINK CORPORATION

910 Hermosa Ct.	CEO: Lewis C. Morris	1995 Sales: $34.9 million
Sunnyvale, CA 94086	CFO: John Daws	1-Yr. Sales Change: 31.2%
Phone: 408-735-5800	HR: Peggy Eger	Exchange: Nasdaq
Fax: 408-735-6643	Employees: 265	Symbol: CYLK

Computers - network information-security software

CYPRESS SEMICONDUCTOR CORPORATION

3901 N. First St.	CEO: Thurman John Rodgers	1995 Sales: $596.1 million
San Jose, CA 95134-1599	CFO: Emmanuel Hernandez	1-Yr. Sales Change: 46.7%
Phone: 408-943-2600	HR: Joyce Sziebert	Exchange: NYSE
Fax: 408-943-6859	Employees: 1,859	Symbol: CY

Electrical components - semiconductors, including logic devices, SRAM & multichip modules, primarily for mainframes & workstations

 See page 276 for a full profile of this company.

CYRIX CORPORATION

2703 N. Central Expwy.	CEO: Gerald D. Jerry Rogers	1995 Sales: $210.3 million
Richardson, TX 75080-0118	CFO: Timothy W. Kinnear	1-Yr. Sales Change: (14.5%)
Phone: 214-968-8388	HR: Margaret Quinn	Exchange: Nasdaq
Fax: 214-699-9857	Employees: 389	Symbol: CYRX

Electrical components - microprocessors & math coprocessors for IBM-compatible computers

DAISYTEK INTERNATIONAL CORPORATION

500 N. Central Expwy.	CEO: David A. Heap	1996 Sales: $464.2 million
Plano, TX 75074	CFO: Mark C. Layton	1-Yr. Sales Change: 31.5%
Phone: 214-881-4700	HR: Deborah D'Artra	Exchange: Nasdaq
Fax: 214-881-0145	Employees: 348	Symbol: DZTK

Office equipment & supplies - wholesale nonpaper computer supplies, including laser toner, ink-jet cartridges, printer ribbons & diskettes

DAKTRONICS, INC.

331 32nd Ave., PO Box 5128	CEO: Aelred J. Kurtenbach	1996 Sales: $52.5 million
Brookings, SD 57006-5128	CFO: Paul J. Weinand	1-Yr. Sales Change: 25.3%
Phone: 605-697-4000	HR: Carla Gatzke	Exchange: Nasdaq
Fax: 605-697-4700	Employees: 721	Symbol: DAKT

Computers - programmable information display systems for sports facilities, government & commercial applications

DALLAS SEMICONDUCTOR CORPORATION

4401 S. Beltwood Pkwy.	CEO: C. V. Prothro	1995 Sales: $233.3 million
Dallas, TX 75244-3292	CFO: Alan P. Hale	1-Yr. Sales Change: 28.6%
Phone: 214-450-0400	HR: Gay Vencill	Exchange: NYSE
Fax: 214-450-3748	Employees: 1,078	Symbol: DS

Electrical components - integrated circuits & semiconductor-based subsystems

 See page 277 for a full profile of this company.

DAMARK INTERNATIONAL, INC.

7101 Winnetka Ave. North	CEO: Mark A. Cohn	1995 Sales: $500.0 million
Brooklyn Park, MN 55428	CFO: Arlyn J. Lomen	1-Yr. Sales Change: 4.7%
Phone: 612-531-0066	HR: Linda Medin	Exchange: Nasdaq
Fax: 612-531-0481	Employees: 1,036	Symbol: DMRK

Retail - mail-order sales of discounted consumer merchandise, including computers & consumer electronics

D&H DISTRIBUTING CO.

2525 N. Seventh St., PO Box 5967	CEO: Israel Schwab	1995 Sales: $430.0 million
Harrisburg, PA 17110	CFO: Robert Miller	1-Yr. Sales Change: —
Phone: 717-236-8001	HR: Dawn Eichelberger	Ownership: Privately Held
Fax: 717-255-7838	Employees: 325	

Computers - microcomputer distribution

DASSAULT SYSTEMES S.A.

9 Quai Marcel Dassault, B.P. 310	CEO: Charles Edelstenne	1995 Sales: $227.9 million
92156 Suresnes Cedex, France	CFO: Thibault de Tersant	1-Yr. Sales Change: 26.1%
Phone: +33-1-40-99-40-99	HR: —	Exchange: Nasdaq
Fax: +33-1-42-04-45-81	Employees: 1,066	Symbol: DASTY

Computers - design, manufacturing & engineering software, including a 3-dimensional computer modeling system (Catia)

DATA BROADCASTING CORPORATION

3490 Clubhouse Dr., PO Box 7443	CEO: Alan J. Hirschfield	1995 Sales: $74.2 million
Jackson, WY 83001	CFO: Mark F. Imperiale	1-Yr. Sales Change: 11.7%
Phone: 307-733-9742	HR: Eileen Gilbert	Exchange: Nasdaq
Fax: 307-733-4935	Employees: 658	Symbol: DBCC

Business services - real-time stock market quotes, customized portfolio tracking & investor information

DATA DIMENSIONS, INC.

777 108th Ave. Northeast	CEO: Larry W. Martin	1995 Sales: $6.2 million
Bellevue, WA 98004	CFO: William H. Parsons	1-Yr. Sales Change: 82.4%
Phone: 206-688-1000	HR: —	Exchange: Nasdaq
Fax: 206-688-1099	Employees: 82	Symbol: DDIM

Computers - knowledge-based & tool-assisted millennium consulting services

DATA GENERAL CORPORATION

4400 Computer Dr.	CEO: Ronald L. Skates	1995 Sales: $1,159.3 million
Westborough, MA 01580	CFO: Arthur W. DeMelle	1-Yr. Sales Change: 3.5%
Phone: 508-898-5000	HR: Jonathan W. Lane	Exchange: NYSE
Fax: 508-898-4003	Employees: 5,000	Symbol: DGN

Computers - servers & workstations (AViiON), storage systems (CLARiiON), PCs & hardware & software support & maintenance services

 See pages 90–91 for a full profile of this company.

DATA I/O CORPORATION

10525 Willows Rd. NE	CEO: William C. Erxleben	1995 Sales: $66.0 million
Redmond, WA 98073	CFO: Steven M. Gordon	1-Yr. Sales Change: 7.3%
Phone: 206-881-6444	HR: Susan S. Webber	Exchange: Nasdaq
Fax: 206-869-7423	Employees: 401	Symbol: DAIO

Electrical components - electronic IC programming systems & electronic design automation software

DATA PROCESSING RESOURCES CORPORATION

4400 MacArthur Blvd., Ste. 610
Newport Beach, CA 92660
Phone: 714-752-9111
Fax: 714-752-5850

CEO: Mary Ellen Weaver
CFO: Michael A. Piraino
HR: Paulette J. Suiter
Employees: 500

1995 Sales: $49.6 million
1-Yr. Sales Change: 45.0%
Exchange: Nasdaq
Symbol: DPRC

Personnel - information technology staffing services

DATA RACE, INC.

11550 IH-10 West, Ste. 395
San Antonio, TX 78230
Phone: 210-558-1900
Fax: 210-558-1929

CEO: W. B. Barker
CFO: Gregory Skalla
HR: Greg Williamson
Employees: 185

1996 Sales: $17.2 million
1-Yr. Sales Change: (43.4%)
Exchange: Nasdaq
Symbol: RACE

Computers - integral notebook modems; telecommunication servers (MACH TS), bridges (MACHnet) & multiplexers

DATA RESEARCH ASSOCIATES, INC.

1276 N. Warson Rd., PO Box 8495
St. Louis, MO 63132-1806
Phone: 314-432-1100
Fax: 314-993-8927

CEO: Michael J. Mellinger
CFO: Katharine W. Biggs
HR: Maggie Pickering
Employees: 206

1995 Sales: $34.9 million
1-Yr. Sales Change: 37.9%
Exchange: Nasdaq
Symbol: DRAI

Computers - systems integration (Data Research System, INLEX/300 System, MultiLIS System)

DATA STORAGE MARKETING, INC.

5718 Central Ave.
Boulder, CO 80301
Phone: 303-442-4747
Fax: 303-442-7985

CEO: Thomas Ward
CFO: Steve Yoder
HR: Julie Ekberg
Employees: 175

1995 Sales: $115.0 million
1-Yr. Sales Change: 8.5%
Ownership: Privately Held

Retail - wholesale computer components & peripheral equipment; microcomputer manufacturing

DATA SYSTEMS & SOFTWARE INC.

200 Rte. 17
Mahwah, NJ 07430
Phone: 201-529-2026
Fax: 201-529-3163

CEO: George Morgenstern
CFO: George Morgenstern
HR: Elihu Levino
Employees: 915

1995 Sales: $129.8 million
1-Yr. Sales Change: 62.9%
Exchange: Nasdaq
Symbol: DSSI

Computers - consulting & development services; semiconductor manufacturing

DATA SYSTEMS NETWORK CORPORATION

34705 W. Twelve Mile Rd., Ste. 300	CEO: Michael W. Grieves	1995 Sales: $30.5 million
Farmington Hills, MI 48331	CFO: Richard R. Burkhart	1-Yr. Sales Change: 33.2%
Phone: 810-489-7117	HR: Janine Jacobs	Exchange: Nasdaq (SC)
Fax: 810-489-1007	Employees: 55	Symbol: DSYS

Computers - network integration & data-management services

DATA TRANSLATION, INC.

100 Locke Dr.	CEO: Alfred A. Molinari Jr.	1995 Sales: $72.5 million
Marlborough, MA 01752-1192	CFO: Peter Rice	1-Yr. Sales Change: 44.4%
Phone: 508-481-3700	HR: Hillary Barrett	Exchange: Nasdaq
Fax: 508-481-8620	Employees: 347	Symbol: DATX

Computers - digital editing (Media 100), data acquisition & imaging products

DATA TRANSMISSION NETWORK CORPORATION

9110 W. Dodge Rd., Ste. 200	CEO: Roger R. Brodersen	1995 Sales: $62.3 million
Omaha, NE 68114	CFO: Brian L. Larson	1-Yr. Sales Change: 35.1%
Phone: 402-390-2328	HR: Carol Pigg	Exchange: Nasdaq
Fax: 402-390-7188	Employees: 240	Symbol: DTLN

Business services - electronic information & communication services, primarily satellite delivery of time-sensitive information

DATABEAM, INC.

3191 Nicholasville Rd.	CEO: Lee Todd Jr.	1995 Est. Sales: $7.0 mil.
Lexington, KY 40503	CFO: —	1-Yr. Sales Change: 100.0%
Phone: 606-245-3500	HR: Susan Denny	Ownership: Privately Held
Fax: 606-245-3515	Employees: —	

Computers - data-conferencing software

DATAEXPERT CORPORATION

1178 Sonora Ct.	CEO: Bruce Yen	1995 Est. Sales: $175.0 mil.
Sunnyvale, CA 94086-5308	CFO: Jonathan Wang	1-Yr. Sales Change: 2.9%
Phone: 408-737-8880	HR: —	Ownership: Privately Held
Fax: 408-737-8390	Employees: 310	

Retail - wholesale processing boards

DATAFLEX CORPORATION

3920 Park Ave.	CEO: Richard C. Rose	1996 Sales: $472.1 million
Edison, NJ 08820	CFO: Raymond DioGuardi	1-Yr. Sales Change: 72.4%
Phone: 908-321-1100	HR: David Castel	Exchange: Nasdaq
Fax: 908-321-6590	Employees: 811	Symbol: DFLX

Retail - direct marketing of desktop computer equipment & related products supplied primarily by major manufacturers

 See page 278 for a full profile of this company.

DATALOGIX INTERNATIONAL INC.

100 Summit Lake Dr.	CEO: Richard C. Giordanella	1996 Sales: $49.2 million
Valhalla, NY 10595	CFO: Rick L. Smith	1-Yr. Sales Change: 13.9%
Phone: 914-747-2900	HR: Patricia L. Anderson	Exchange: Nasdaq
Fax: 914-747-2987	Employees: 289	Symbol: DLGX

Computers - software for managing the manufacturing, logistics & financial operations of process-manufacturing companies (CIMPRO, DATALOGIX, GEMMS)

DATAMETRICS CORPORATION

21135 Erwin St.	CEO: Sidney E. Wing	1995 Sales: $19.0 million
Woodland Hills, CA 91367	CFO: John J. Van Buren	1-Yr. Sales Change: (24.6%)
Phone: 818-598-6200	HR: Roger DeBruno	Exchange: AMEX
Fax: 818-598-6290	Employees: 171	Symbol: DC

Electronics - high-performance computers & printers for the military

DATAPOINT CORPORATION

8400 Datapoint Dr.	CEO: Asher B. Edelman	1995 Sales: $174.9 million
San Antonio, TX 78229-8500	CFO: Phillip P. Krumb	1-Yr. Sales Change: 1.2%
Phone: 210-593-7000	HR: Angela Cooper	Exchange: NYSE
Fax: 210-593-7946	Employees: 991	Symbol: DPT

Computers - networking, telephone & video communications hardware & software

DATARAM CORPORATION

PO Box 7528	CEO: Robert V. Tarantino	1996 Sales: $107.6 million
Princeton, NJ 08543-7528	CFO: Bernard L. Riley	1-Yr. Sales Change: 4.5%
Phone: 609-799-0071	HR: Linda Colmenares	Exchange: AMEX
Fax: 609-799-6734	Employees: 77	Symbol: DTM

Electronic components - add-in memory products for use with workstations, servers & minicomputers

DATASTREAM SYSTEMS, INC.

1200 Woodriff Rd., Ste. C-40	CEO: Larry G. Blackwell	1995 Sales: $20.3 million
Greenville, SC 29607	CFO: Daniel H. Christie	1-Yr. Sales Change: 95.2%
Phone: 864-297-6775	HR: Diane Newell	Exchange: Nasdaq
Fax: 864-627-7227	Employees: 211	Symbol: DSTM

Computers - Microsoft Windows-based maintenance management software that tracks facilities & equipment maintenance, parts inventories & personnel

DATATREND SERVICES, INC.

1515 Washington St.	CEO: Mark A. Hanson	1995 Sales: $29.3 million
Braintree, MA 02184	CFO: Mark A. Hanson	1-Yr. Sales Change: (19.5%)
Phone: 617-848-6700	HR: Richard Donahue	Exchange: Nasdaq (SC)
Fax: 617-691-1300	Employees: 62	Symbol: DATA

Retail - microcomputers, peripheral components & accessories

DATAWARE TECHNOLOGIES, INC.

222 Third St., Ste. 3300	CEO: Kurt Mueller	1995 Sales: $41.1 million
Cambridge, MA 02142	CFO: Chris Lorch	1-Yr. Sales Change: 26.9%
Phone: 617-621-0820	HR: Sue Martin	Exchange: Nasdaq
Fax: 617-621-0307	Employees: 320	Symbol: DWTI

Computers - retrieval software for CD-ROM applications

 See page 279 for a full profile of this company.

DATAWATCH CORPORATION

234 Ballardvale St.	CEO: Thomas R. Foley	1995 Sales: $16.6 million
Wilmington, MA 01887	CFO: Bruce R. Gardner	1-Yr. Sales Change: 49.5%
Phone: 508-988-9700	HR: Carol Beauchamp	Exchange: Nasdaq
Fax: 508-988-0672	Employees: 72	Symbol: DWCH

Computers - data access, translation & reporting software

DATAWORKS CORPORATION

5910 Pacific Center Blvd., Ste. 300	CEO: Stuart W. Clifton	1995 Sales: $31.5 million
San Diego, CA 92121	CFO: Norm Farquhar	1-Yr. Sales Change: 87.5%
Phone: 619-546-9600	HR: Pam Fettu	Exchange: Nasdaq
Fax: 619-546-9615	Employees: 227	Symbol: DWRX

Computers - software used by manufacturers to reduce order fulfillment cycle times

DAVOX CORPORATION

6 Technology Park Dr.	CEO: Alphonse M. Lucchese	1995 Sales: $37.6 million
Westford, MA 01886-3140	CFO: John J. Connolly	1-Yr. Sales Change: 25.3%
Phone: 508-952-0200	HR: —	Exchange: Nasdaq
Fax: 508-952-0201	Employees: 164	Symbol: DAVX

Telecommunications equipment - management systems for call-center operations

DAW TECHNOLOGIES, INC.

2700 S. 900 West	CEO: Ronald W. Daw	1995 Sales: $70.6 million
Salt Lake City, UT 84119-2418	CFO: David R. Grow	1-Yr. Sales Change: 48.0%
Phone: 801-977-3100	HR: F. Ray Hawkins	Exchange: Nasdaq
Fax: 801-973-6640	Employees: 457	Symbol: DAWK

Computers - cleanroom system manufacturing, installation & servicing; consulting services

DCT SYSTEMS GROUP

305 E. Rosemont Ave	CEO: Chuck Thakkar	1995 Sales: $135.0 million
St. Paul, MN 55117	CFO: Art Peterson	1-Yr. Sales Change: —
Phone: 612-778-0044	HR: Saloni Thakkar	Ownership: Privately Held
Fax: 612-772-8099	Employees: 180	

Retail - PCs

DDL ELECTRONICS, INC.

2151 Anchor Ct.	CEO: Gregory L. Horton	1996 Sales: $33.1 million
Newbury Park, CA 91320	CFO: Richard K. Vitelle	1-Yr. Sales Change: 11.8%
Phone: 805-376-9415	HR: Barbara Casablanca	Exchange: NYSE
Fax: 805-376-9015	Employees: 340	Symbol: DDL

Electrical components - printed circuit boards for use primarily in the computer, communications & instrumentation industries

DECISIONONE CORPORATION

50 E. Swedesford Rd.	CEO: Kenneth Draeger	1996 Sales: $540.2 million
Frazer, PA 19355	CFO: R. Peter Zimmermann	1-Yr. Sales Change: 231.4%
Phone: 610-296-6000	HR: Dwight Wilson	Exchange: Nasdaq
Fax: 610-993-6334	Employees: 5,600	Symbol: DOCI

Computers - computer maintenance & technology support services

DELL COMPUTER CORPORATION

2214 W. Braker Ln., Ste. D	CEO: Michael S. Dell	1996 Sales: $5,296.0 million
Austin, TX 78758-4053	CFO: Thomas J. Meredith	1-Yr. Sales Change: 52.4%
Phone: 512-338-4400	HR: Julie A. Sackett	Exchange: Nasdaq
Fax: 512-728-3330	Employees: 8,400	Symbol: DELL

Computers - PCs (OptiPlex), notebook computers (Latitude) & servers (PowerEdge SP)

 See pages 92–93 for a full profile of this company.

DELPHI GROUP PLC

7 Selsdon Way, City Harbour	CEO: A. H. Reeves	1995 Sales: $270.8 million
London E14 9GL, UK	CFO: J. R. Pinder	1-Yr. Sales Change: 77.1%
Phone: +44-171-850-2000	HR: —	Exchange: London
Fax: +44-171-510-2297	Employees: 483	

Computers - information technology services

DELPHI INFORMATION SYSTEMS, INC.

3501 Algonquin Rd.	CEO: M. Denis Connaghan	1996 Sales: $44.1 million
Rolling Meadows, IL 60008	CFO: John R. Sprieser	1-Yr. Sales Change: (16.8%)
Phone: 847-506-3100	HR: Alan E. Drizd	Exchange: Nasdaq (SC)
Fax: 847-590-8280	Employees: 326	Symbol: DLPH

Computers - automation systems & services for independent property & casualty insurance agencies & brokerages

DELTA COMPUTEC INC.

6647 Old Thompson Rd.	CEO: L. Rodger Loomis	1995 Sales: $30.8 million
Syracuse, NY 13211-2117	CFO: Peter D. Smith	1-Yr. Sales Change: 21.3%
Phone: 315-437-2202	HR: —	Exchange: OTC
Fax: 315-463-8060	Employees: 232	Symbol: DCIS

Computers - LAN/WAN products & services

DELTAPOINT, INC.

2 Harris Ct., Ste. B-1	CEO: John Ambrose	1995 Sales: $4.0 million
Monterey, CA 93940	CFO: Donald B. Witmer	1-Yr. Sales Change: (18.4%)
Phone: 408-648-4000	HR: Beth Ingram	Exchange: Nasdaq (SC)
Fax: 408-648-4020	Employees: 30	Symbol: DTPT

Computers - charting & graphics software

DENDRITE INTERNATIONAL, INC.

1200 Mount Kemble Ave.	CEO: John E. Bailye	1995 Sales: $54.1 million
Morristown, NJ 07960-6797	CFO: Charles Warczakowski	1-Yr. Sales Change: 37.3%
Phone: 201-425-1200	HR: Steve Van Houten	Exchange: Nasdaq
Fax: 201-425-1919	Employees: 527	Symbol: DRTE

Computers - sales management software for the pharmaceutical industry

DENSE-PAC MICROSYSTEMS, INC.

7321 Lincoln Way	CEO: James G. Turner	1996 Sales: $18.0 million
Garden Grove, CA 92641-1428	CFO: William M. Stowell	1-Yr. Sales Change: 56.5%
Phone: 714-898-0007	HR: Erika Keller	Exchange: Nasdaq (SC)
Fax: 714-897-1772	Employees: 93	Symbol: DPAC

Computers - standard & custom monolithic memories & memory/logic/analog modules & subsystems

DESKTOP DATA, INC.

80 Blanchard Rd.	CEO: Donald L. McLagan	1995 Sales: $23.2 million
Burlington, MA 01803	CFO: Edward R. Siegfried	1-Yr. Sales Change: 61.1%
Phone: 617-229-3000	HR: Jessica Wasner	Exchange: Nasdaq
Fax: 617-229-3030	Employees: 130	Symbol: DTOP

Computers - customized, real-time news & information delivered via LAN

DH TECHNOLOGY, INC.

15070 Avenue of Science	CEO: William H. Gibbs	1995 Sales: $98.9 million
San Diego, CA 92128	CFO: Janet W. Shanks	1-Yr. Sales Change: 27.0%
Phone: 619-451-3485	HR: Tracey Sexton	Exchange: Nasdaq
Fax: 619-451-3573	Employees: 1,017	Symbol: DHTK

Computers - specialty printers, data-collection equipment & related printer products

DIALOGIC CORPORATION

1515 Rte. 10	CEO: Howard G. Bubb	1995 Sales: $168.7 million
Parsippany, NJ 07054	CFO: Edward B. Jordan	1-Yr. Sales Change: 32.6%
Phone: 201-993-3000	HR: Steven P. Wentzell	Exchange: Nasdaq
Fax: 201-993-3093	Employees: 685	Symbol: DLGC

Computers - network-interface equipment; call-processing hardware & software

DIAMOND FLOWER ELECTRIC INSTRUMENT CO. (USA) INC.

135 Main Ave.	CEO: David C. Lu	1995 Sales: $168.0 million
Sacramento, CA 95838-2041	CFO: Geng Lin	1-Yr. Sales Change: 1.2%
Phone: 916-568-1234	HR: Sam Lee	Ownership: Privately Held
Fax: 916-568-1233	Employees: 400	

Computers - PCs, motherboards, interface cards, peripherals & scanners

DIAMOND FLOWER (NORTHEAST), INC.

7 Elkins Rd.	CEO: Rocky Liu	1995 Sales: $35.0 million
East Brunswick, NJ 08816-2006	CFO: Connie Jian	1-Yr. Sales Change: 52.2%
Phone: 908-390-2815	HR: —	Ownership: Privately Held
Fax: 908-390-2817	Employees: 87	

Computers - mainframe systems & parts

DIAMOND MULTIMEDIA SYSTEMS, INC.

2880 Junction Ave.	CEO: William J. Schroeder	1995 Sales: $467.6 million
San Jose, CA 95134-1922	CFO: Gary B. Filler	1-Yr. Sales Change: 130.0%
Phone: 408-325-7000	HR: Song Kim	Exchange: Nasdaq
Fax: 408-325-7070	Employees: 747	Symbol: DIMD

Computers - graphics & digital-video accelerators, audio & telephone subsystems & multimedia upgrade kits

 See page 280 for a full profile of this company.

DICKENS DATA SYSTEMS, INC.

1175 Northmeadow Pkwy., Ste. 150	CEO: Gordon Dickens	1996 Sales: $100.0 million
Roswell, GA 30076	CFO: Warren Turner	1-Yr. Sales Change: 98.0%
Phone: 770-475-8860	HR: Nancy Anheir	Ownership: Privately Held
Fax: 770-442-7950	Employees: 130	

Computers - UNIX products for IBM RS/6000 & PS/2

DIEBOLD, INCORPORATED

5995 Mayfair Rd.	CEO: Robert W. Mahoney	1995 Sales: $863.4 million
North Canton, OH 44720-8077	CFO: Gerald F. Morris	1-Yr. Sales Change: 13.6%
Phone: 330-489-4000	HR: Charles B. Scheurer	Exchange: NYSE
Fax: 330-490-4549	Employees: 5,178	Symbol: DBD

Protection - security products & cameras; automatic teller machine manufacturing; product- & system-maintenance services

DIEHL GRAPHSOFT, INC.

10270 Old Columbia Rd., Ste. 100	CEO: Richard Diehl	1996 Sales: $4.9 million
Columbia, MD 21046	CFO: Joseph Schmelzle	1-Yr. Sales Change: (3.9%)
Phone: 410-290-5114	HR: —	Exchange: Nasdaq (SC)
Fax: 410-290-8050	Employees: 29	Symbol: DIEG

Computers - CAD software for Macintosh computers

DIGI INTERNATIONAL INC.

6400 Flying Cloud Dr.	CEO: Ervin F. Kamm Jr.	1995 Sales: $165.0 million
Eden Prairie, MN 55344	CFO: Gerald A. Wall	1-Yr. Sales Change: 26.1%
Phone: 612-943-9020	HR: T. Harrison Tuffy Bryant	Exchange: Nasdaq
Fax: 612-943-5396	Employees: 605	Symbol: DGII

Computers - data communications hardware & software products that deliver connectivity solutions for multiuser environments, LAN & WAN remote access markets & LAN connect markets

DIGITAL BIOMETRICS, INC.

5600 Rowland Rd., Ste. 205	CEO: Jack A. Klingert	1995 Sales: $9.1 million
Minnetonka, MN 55343-4315	CFO: Donald E. Berg	1-Yr. Sales Change: 8.3%
Phone: 612-932-0888	HR: Donald E. Berg	Exchange: Nasdaq
Fax: 612-932-7181	Employees: 60	Symbol: DBII

Optical character recognition - fingerprint recording & identification products based on electro-optical imaging technologies

DIGITAL DESCRIPTOR SYSTEMS, INC.

2010 F. Cabot Blvd. West	CEO: Garrett U. Cohn	1995 Sales: $2.2 million
Langhorne, PA 19047	CFO: —	1-Yr. Sales Change: 57.1%
Phone: 215-752-0963	HR: —	Exchange: Nasdaq (SC)
Fax: 215-752-5910	Employees: 30	Symbol: DDSI

Computers - computer installations, including video digitizing systems

DIGITAL EQUIPMENT CORPORATION

111 Powdermill Rd.	CEO: Robert B. Palmer	1996 Sales: $14,562.8 mil.
Maynard, MA 01754-1499	CFO: Vincent J. Mullarkey	1-Yr. Sales Change: 5.4%
Phone: 508-493-5111	HR: Savino R. Sid Ferrales	Exchange: NYSE
Fax: 508-493-8780	Employees: 59,100	Symbol: DEC

Computers - PCs, workstations & servers, peripherals & software products

 See pages 94–95 for a full profile of this company.

DIGITAL LIGHTWAVE, INC.

601 Cleveland St., 5th Fl.	CEO: Bryan J. Zwan	1995 Sales: $0.0 million
Clearwater, FL 34615	CFO: Beth A. Morris	1-Yr. Sales Change: —
Phone: 813-442-6677	HR: —	Ownership: Privately Held
Fax: 813-462-5660	Employees: 57	

Computers - computer systems that provide information concerning the performance of telecommunications networks & transmission equipment

DIGITAL LINK CORPORATION

217 Humboldt Ct.	CEO: Vinita Gupta	1995 Sales: $44.3 million
Sunnyvale, CA 94089	CFO: Stanley E. Kazmierczak	1-Yr. Sales Change: 25.9%
Phone: 408-745-6200	HR: Diane Mastilock	Exchange: Nasdaq
Fax: 408-745-6250	Employees: 211	Symbol: DLNK

Computers - high-speed digital access WAN products for wide- area networks worldwide

DIGITAL NETWORK ASSOCIATES INC.

110 Wall St., 25th Fl.	CEO: Eric B. Schwartz	1995 Est. Sales: $16.0 mil.
New York, NY 10005	CFO: Joseph B. Goeller	1-Yr. Sales Change: 19.4%
Phone: 212-425-8000	HR: Robert M. Johnson	Ownership: Privately Held
Fax: 212-425-0809	Employees: 40	

Computers - network integration services linking dissimiliar host & client environments

DIGITAL PICTURES

1825 S. Grant St., Ste. 900	CEO: Tom Zito	1995 Sales: $10.0 million
San Mateo, CA 94402	CFO: Mark Carlson	1-Yr. Sales Change: —
Phone: 415-345-5300	HR: N. Brucker	Ownership: Privately Held
Fax: 415-286-8811	Employees: 35	

Computers - live-action interactive CD-ROM games (Corpse Killer, Maximum Surge, Night Trap, Prize Fighter, Quarterback Attack with Mike Ditka, Sewer Shark, Slam City with Scottie Pippen, What's My Story)

 **See page 281 for a full profile of this company.**

DIGITAL SOUND CORPORATION

6307 Carpinteria Ave.	CEO: Mark C. Ozur	1995 Sales: $23.2 million
Carpinteria, CA 93013	CFO: B. Robert Suh	1-Yr. Sales Change: (26.8%)
Phone: 805-566-2000	HR: —	Exchange: Nasdaq
Fax: 805-684-2848	Employees: 131	Symbol: DGSD

Telecommunications equipment - voice information processing systems (InfoMail) used to integrate voice, fax & e-mail messaging services

DIGITAL SYSTEMS INTERNATIONAL, INC.

6464 185th Ave. NE
Redmond, WA 98052-6736
Phone: 206-881-7544
Fax: 206-556-8040

CEO: Patrick S. Howard
CFO: John J. Flavio
HR: Ingrid Rasch
Employees: 342

1995 Sales: $68.0 million
1-Yr. Sales Change: 27.6%
Exchange: Nasdaq
Symbol: DGTL

Telecommunications equipment - telephone-call-processing systems & services

DIGITAL VIDEO SYSTEMS, INC.

2710 Walsh Ave.
Santa Clara, CA 95051
Phone: 408-748-2100
Fax: 408-727-1888

CEO: Edmund Y. Sun
CFO: Janis P. Gemignani
HR: Janis P. Gemignani
Employees: 51

1995 Sales: $3.5 million
1-Yr. Sales Change: (55.1%)
Exchange: Nasdaq
Symbol: DVID

Computers - digital video compression & decompression hardware & software for entertainment, business & educational uses

THE DII GROUP, INC.

6273 Monarch Park Pl., Ste. 200
Niwot, CO 80503
Phone: 303-652-2221
Fax: 303-652-0602

CEO: Ronald R. Budacz
CFO: Carl R. Vertuca Jr.
HR: Connie Renfrew
Employees: 3,500

1995 Sales: $335.4 million
1-Yr. Sales Change: 61.3%
Exchange: Nasdaq
Symbol: DIIG

Electrical products - printed circuit boards, testing software & systems for printed circuit boards & miniature-embedded modules

 See page 282 for a full profile of this company.

DIODES INCORPORATED

3050 E. Hillcrest Dr., Ste. 200
Westlake Village, CA 91362-3154
Phone: 805-446-4800
Fax: 805-446-4850

CEO: David Lin
CFO: Joseph Liu
HR: Patricia Friou
Employees: 51

1995 Sales: $58.2 million
1-Yr. Sales Change: 52.0%
Exchange: AMEX
Symbol: DIO

Electrical components - discrete semiconductor products, including standard, zener & signal diodes, bridge rectifiers, small-signal transistors & transient voltage suppressors

DISC INC.

372 Turquoise Sr.
Milpitas, CA 95035
Phone: 408-934-7000
Fax: 408-934-7007

CEO: J. Richard Ellis
CFO: Henry Madrid
HR: —
Employees: 31

1995 Sales: $6.6 million
1-Yr. Sales Change: 53.5%
Exchange: Nasdaq (SC)
Symbol: DCSR

Computers - optical-disk-storage libraries

DISCREET LOGIC INC.

5505 Boulevard St. Laurent, Ste. 5200	CEO: Richard J. Szalwinski	1996 Sales: $84.0 million
Montreal, QC H2T 1S6, Canada	CFO: Douglas R. Johnson	1-Yr. Sales Change: 30.2%
Phone: 514-272-0525	HR: Garry Blagrave	Exchange: Nasdaq
Fax: 514-272-0585	Employees: 270	Symbol: DSLGF

Computers - digital image processing systems for creating & editing special visual effects for film (Speed, Forrest Gump, Interview with the Vampire) & video

D-LINK SYSTEMS INC.

5 Musick	CEO: Roger Kao	1995 Sales: $38.0 million
Irvine, CA 92718	CFO: Roger Kao	1-Yr. Sales Change: 18.8%
Phone: 714-455-1688	HR: Steven H. Joe	Ownership: Privately Held
Fax: 714-455-2521	Employees: 48	

Computers - LAN products (LANsmart, LANmagic)

DMI, INC.

2501 W. Fifth St.	CEO: Elvin Rose	1995 Sales: $0.2 million
Santa Ana, CA 92703	CFO: Barry K. Sugden Jr.	1-Yr. Sales Change: (50.0%)
Phone: 714-571-1900	HR: —	Exchange: OTC
Fax: 714-571-1909	Employees: 2	Symbol: DMIN

Office automation - workstations (ARS system) that attach to multihost computers to store & retrieve information previously kept on either the host computer or on paper, microfiche, or tapes

DOCUCON, INCORPORATED

7461 Callaghan Rd.	CEO: Edward P. Gistaro	1995 Sales: $11.0 million
San Antonio, TX 78229	CFO: Lori A. Turner	1-Yr. Sales Change: 27.9%
Phone: 210-525-9221	HR: Alice Hopkins	Exchange: Nasdaq (SC)
Fax: 210-525-9484	Employees: 187	Symbol: DOCU

Business services - document conversion to computer-accessible formats; database creation for legal professionals

DOCUMENT SCIENCES CORPORATION

6333 Greenwich Dr., Ste. 100	CEO: Tony N. Domit	1995 Sales: $10.5 million
San Diego, CA 92122	CFO: Barbara E. Amantea	1-Yr. Sales Change: 45.8%
Phone: 619-625-2000	HR: Tiffany Skinner	Exchange: Nasdaq
Fax: 619-625-3031	Employees: 95	Symbol: DOCX

Computers - document automation software (Autograph) for electronic publishing for a variety of industries

DOCUMENTUM, INC.

5671 Gibraltar Dr.
Pleasanton, CA 94588-8547
Phone: 510-463-6800
Fax: 510-463-6850

CEO: Jeffrey A. Miller
CFO: Alan S. Henricks
HR: Joseph P. Gabbert
Employees: 174

1995 Sales: $25.5 million
1-Yr. Sales Change: 145.2%
Exchange: Nasdaq
Symbol: DCTM

Computers - object-oriented client/server document management software

DREXLER TECHNOLOGY CORPORATION

1077 Independence Ave.
Mountain View, CA 94043
Phone: 415-969-7277
Fax: 415-969-6121

CEO: Jerome Drexler
CFO: Steven G. Larson
HR: Margaret Galloway
Employees: 44

1996 Sales: $5.3 million
1-Yr. Sales Change: 65.6%
Exchange: Nasdaq
Symbol: DRXR

Computers - optical data storage products & associated software, including PC-based optical memory cards, optical card data systems, card integration software & system software development tools

DSC COMMUNICATIONS CORPORATION

1000 Coit Rd.
Plano, TX 75075-5813
Phone: 214-519-3000
Fax: 214-519-4122

CEO: James L. Donald
CFO: Gerald F. Montry
HR: John O'Loughlin
Employees: 5,860

1995 Sales: $1,422.0 million
1-Yr. Sales Change: 41.8%
Exchange: Nasdaq
Symbol: DIGI

Telecommunications equipment - digital switching, transmission & private network system products

DSP COMMUNICATIONS, INC.

20300 Stevens Creek Blvd.
Cupertino, CA 95014
Phone: 408-777-2700
Fax: 408-777-2770

CEO: Nathan Hod
CFO: Gerald Dogon
HR: —
Employees: 66

1995 Sales: $40.9 million
1-Yr. Sales Change: 155.6%
Exchange: Nasdaq
Symbol: DSPC

Computers - digital signal processing software & other wireless communications technologies

DSP GROUP, INC.

3120 Scott Blvd.
Santa Clara, CA 95054
Phone: 408-986-4300
Fax: 408-986-4323

CEO: Eli Ayalon
CFO: John P. Goldsberry
HR: Karin Pitcock
Employees: 115

1995 Sales: $50.4 million
1-Yr. Sales Change: 76.2%
Exchange: Nasdaq
Symbol: DSPG

Computers - digital signal processing software & integrated circuits for telephone answering machines & multimedia computer applications

DSP TECHNOLOGY INC.

48500 Kato Rd.
Fremont, CA 94538
Phone: 510-657-7555
Fax: 510-657-7576

CEO: F. Gil Troutman Jr.
CFO: Joe M. Millares Jr.
HR: —
Employees: 71

1996 Sales: $15.5 million
1-Yr. Sales Change: 19.2%
Exchange: Nasdaq
Symbol: DSPT

Electronics - computer-automated measurement & control systems for the transportation & advanced research markets

DST SYSTEMS, INC.

1055 Broadway
Kansas City, MO 64105
Phone: 816-435-1000
Fax: 816-435-8618

CEO: Thomas A. McDonnell
CFO: Kenneth V. Hager
HR: Joan Horan
Employees: 5,000

1995 Sales: $484.1 million
1-Yr. Sales Change: 56.3%
Exchange: NYSE
Symbol: DST

Computers - information processing & computer software services & products, primarily for mutual funds, insurance providers, banks & other financial services organizations

DUN & BRADSTREET SOFTWARE SERVICES

66 Perimeter Center East
Atlanta, GA 30346
Phone: 404-239-2000
Fax: 404-239-2404

CEO: Doug MacIntyre
CFO: Pete Sinisgalli
HR: Ron McKenzie
Employees: 2,000

1995 Sales: $457.4 million
1-Yr. Sales Change: 12.7%
Ownership: Subsidiary

Computers - mainframe software (subsidiary of Dun & Bradstreet)

DUPONT PHOTOMASKS, INC.

100 Texas Ave.
Round Rock, TX 78664
Phone: 512-244-0024
Fax: 512-244-3162

CEO: J. Michael Hardinger
CFO: David S. Gino
HR: Rosemary Parelli
Employees: 1,255

1996 Sales: $213.4 million
1-Yr. Sales Change: 32.1%
Exchange: Nasdaq
Symbol: DPMI

Electrical components - high-purity quartz & glass plates that transfer circuit patterns onto silicon wafers used to make semiconductors

DYCAM INC.

9414 Eton Ave.
Chatsworth, CA 91311
Phone: 818-998-8008
Fax: 818-998-7951

CEO: John A. Edling
CFO: John A. Edling
HR: Dolores Delgado
Employees: 26

1995 Sales: $1.7 million
1-Yr. Sales Change: —
Exchange: AMEX
Symbol: DYC

Computers - digital cameras for use with PCs

DYNAMIC GRAPHICS, INC.

6000 N. Forest Park Dr.
Peoria, IL 61614-3592
Phone: 309-688-8800
Fax: 309-688-5873

CEO: Jayne Mueller
CFO: Matt Smutz
HR: Karen Dennison
Employees: 150

1996 Est. Sales: $15.0 mil.
1-Yr. Sales Change: —
Ownership: Privately Held

Computers - clip art software & subscription services (Clipper, Electronic Print Media Service); graphic design magazines (Step-By-Step Graphics, Clipper Options) & newsletter (Step-By-Step Electronic Design)

DYNAMIC HEALTHCARE TECHNOLOGIES, INC.

101 S. Hall Ln., Ste. 210
Maitland, FL 32751
Phone: 407-875-9991
Fax: 407-875-9915

CEO: Mitchel J. Laskey
CFO: J. A. Terrano
HR: —
Employees: 91

1995 Sales: $8.9 million
1-Yr. Sales Change: 27.1%
Exchange: Nasdaq (SC)
Symbol: DHTI

Computers - hardware & software for the health care industry

DYNAMICS RESEARCH CORPORATION

60 Frontage Rd.
Andover, MA 01810-5498
Phone: 508-475-9090
Fax: 508-475-8205

CEO: Albert Rand
CFO: Douglas R. Potter
HR: John L. Wilkinson
Employees: 1,249

1995 Sales: $103.9 million
1-Yr. Sales Change: 0.9%
Exchange: Nasdaq
Symbol: DRCO

Engineering - computer-based systems development, engineering & support services

DYNAMOTION/ATI CORPORATION

1639 E. Edinger Ave.
Santa Ana, CA 92705
Phone: 714-541-2927
Fax: 714-541-0307

CEO: Jon R. Hopper
CFO: Kirk Waldron
HR: Helen Borden
Employees: 112

1995 Sales: $20.5 million
1-Yr. Sales Change: 28.1%
Exchange: Nasdaq (SC)
Symbol: DYMO

Machinery - semiconductor manufacturing equipment

EA INDUSTRIES, INC.

185 Monmouth Pkwy.
West Long Branch, NJ 07764-9989
Phone: 908-229-1100
Fax: 908-571-0583

CEO: Joseph R. Spalliero
CFO: Stanley O. Jester
HR: Barbara Evenson
Employees: 514

1995 Sales: $77.1 million
1-Yr. Sales Change: 152.8%
Exchange: NYSE
Symbol: EA

Electrical components - integrated-circuit components & assemblies

EAGLE POINT SOFTWARE CORPORATION

4131 Westmark Dr.	CEO: Rodney L. Blum	1996 Sales: $19.2 million
Dubuque, IA 52002-2627	CFO: Dennis J. George	1-Yr. Sales Change: 21.5%
Phone: 319-556-8392	HR: Teresa Davis	Exchange: Nasdaq
Fax: 319-556-5321	Employees: 236	Symbol: EGPT

Computers - application software for engineering, architecture, construction & geographic information systems industries

EARTHLINK NETWORK, INC.

3100 New York Dr., Ste. 201	CEO: Charles G. Betty	1995 Sales: $3.0 million
Pasadena, CA 91107	CFO: Robert E. Johnson	1-Yr. Sales Change: 2,900%
Phone: 818-296-2400	HR: Carol Cross	Ownership: Privately Held
Fax: 818-296-2470	Employees: 376	

Computers - Internet access services (TotalAccess Internet software package)

ECCS, INC.

One Sheila Dr.	CEO: Michael E. Faherty	1995 Sales: $31.2 million
Tinton Falls, NJ 07724	CFO: Jay Disler	1-Yr. Sales Change: (26.9%)
Phone: 908-747-6995	HR: Sharon Wallace	Exchange: Nasdaq (SC)
Fax: 908-747-6542	Employees: 86	Symbol: ECCS

Computers - computer hardware & mass storage products (Space Module, Space Tower), including RAID products (Micro-DFT-1E, Micro-DFT-1R), optical & tape systems (EXAMODULE, DAT Module) & RAM

ECRM INCORPORATED

554 Clark Rd.	CEO: William R. Givens	1995 Sales: $59.3 million
Tewksbury, MA 01876	CFO: Rudolf I. Bunde	1-Yr. Sales Change: 21.8%
Phone: 508-851-0207	HR: Andrea Bunde	Ownership: Privately Held
Fax: 508-851-7016	Employees: 248	

Computers - image processing systems, including imagesetters (AIR75-Advanced Image Recorder), scanners (Autokon) & related software for the printing & publishing industry worldwide

EDIFY CORPORATION

2840 San Tomas Expwy.	CEO: Jeffrey M. Crowe	1995 Sales: $16.0 million
Santa Clara, CA 95051	CFO: Stephanie A. Vinella	1-Yr. Sales Change: 90.5%
Phone: 408-982-2000	HR: Patricia A. Tomlinson	Exchange: Nasdaq
Fax: 408-982-0777	Employees: 173	Symbol: EDFY

Computers - software (Electronic Workforce) that allows companies to communicate with their customers & employees through voice mail, fax, email & the World Wide Web

EDMARK CORPORATION

6727 185th Ave. NE
Redmond, WA 98052-3218
Phone: 206-556-8400
Fax: 206-556-8430

CEO: Sally G. Narodick
CFO: Paul N. Bialek
HR: Diane Coplentz
Employees: 209

1996 Sales: $32.2 million
1-Yr. Sales Change: 41.9%
Exchange: Nasdaq (SC)
Symbol: EDMK

Computers - children's educational software (Millie's Math House, KidDesk) & books

EDUSOFT LTD.

19 Weissburg St.
Tel Aviv 61130, Israel
Phone: +972-3-648-2131
Fax: +972-3-647-8095

CEO: Menachem Hasfari
CFO: Amos Genish
HR: —
Employees: 62

1995 Sales: $11.0 million
1-Yr. Sales Change: 10.0%
Exchange: Nasdaq
Symbol: EDUSF

Computers - educational software covering science, technology (TINA), language (English Discoveries) &
early childhood development

EFFECTIVE MANAGEMENT SYSTEMS, INC.

1200 W. Park Place
Milwaukee, WI 53224
Phone: 414-359-9800
Fax: 414-359-9011

CEO: Michael D. Dunham
CFO: Jeffrey J. Fossum
HR: Jane L. Ruman
Employees: 170

1995 Sales: $29.0 million
1-Yr. Sales Change: 27.8%
Exchange: Nasdaq
Symbol: EMSI

Computers - integrated manufacturing & business-management software

EGGHEAD, INC.

22705 E. Mission
Liberty Lake, WA 99019
Phone: 509-922-7031
Fax: 509-921-7929

CEO: Terence M. Strom
CFO: Edward Wozniak
HR: Kurt S. Conklin
Employees: 2,300

1996 Sales: $403.8 million
1-Yr. Sales Change: (53.2%)
Exchange: Nasdaq
Symbol: EGGS

Retail - personal computer software reseller

 See pages 96–97 for a full profile of this company.

EL CAMINO RESOURCES, LTD.

21051 Warner Center Ln.
Woodland Hills, CA 91364
Phone: 818-226-6600
Fax: 818-226-6787

CEO: David Harmon
CFO: Brian Ofria
HR: Jo Glascock
Employees: 430

1996 Est. Sales: $540.0 mil.
1-Yr. Sales Change: 5.5%
Ownership: Privately Held

Leasing - computer equipment (#1 in US), including IBM mainframe & midrange computers (REAL
Applications), in the US, Canada, Germany, Mexico, Singapore & the UK

ELAMEX S.A. DE C.V.

Av. Insurgentes No. 41-45-B Ote.	CEO: Hector M. Raynal	1995 Sales: $97.5 million
32340 Ciudad Juarez, Chihuahua, Mexico	CFO: Salvador Almeida	1-Yr. Sales Change: 15.0%
Phone: 915-774-8252	HR: —	Exchange: Nasdaq
Fax: —	Employees: 3,865	Symbol: ELAMF

Electrical components - rigid & flexible printed circuit boards, box build final assemblies, plastic overmolding & complex wire assemblies

ELANTEC SEMICONDUCTOR, INC.

1996 Tarob Ct.	CEO: David O'Brien	1995 Sales: $26.9 million
Milpitas, CA 95035	CFO: Terrence W. Plette	1-Yr. Sales Change: 17.5%
Phone: 408-945-1323	HR: Raymond L. Campbell	Exchange: Nasdaq
Fax: 408-945-9305	Employees: 163	Symbol: ELNT

Electrical components - analog integrated circuits for video/multimedia, data processing & telecommunications markets

ELCOM INTERNATIONAL, INC.

10 Oceana Way	CEO: Robert J. Crowell	1995 Sales: $272.8 million
Norwood, MA 02062	CFO: Laurence F. Mulhern	1-Yr. Sales Change: 847.2%
Phone: 617-551-3380	HR: Mary Palengo	Exchange: Nasdaq
Fax: 617-762-1540	Employees: 802	Symbol: ELCO

Computers - interactive electronic commerce software systems

ELECTRO RENT CORPORATION

6060 Sepulveda Blvd.	CEO: Daniel Greenberg	1996 Sales: $141.1 million
Van Nuys, CA 91411-2512	CFO: Craig R. Jones	1-Yr. Sales Change: 16.2%
Phone: 818-786-2525	HR: Peter Shapiro	Exchange: Nasdaq
Fax: 818-786-4354	Employees: 466	Symbol: ELRC

Leasing - test & measurement instruments & microprocessor development systems

ELECTROGLAS INC.

2901 Coronado Dr.	CEO: Curtis S. Wozniak	1995 Sales: $169.2 million
Santa Clara, CA 95054	CFO: Armand J. Stegall	1-Yr. Sales Change: 50.7%
Phone: 408-727-6500	HR: Fran Keegan	Exchange: Nasdaq
Fax: 408-980-4180	Employees: 520	Symbol: EGLS

Machinery - automatic wafer-probing systems used in semiconductor manufacturing equipment

ELECTRONIC ARTS INC.

1450 Fashion Island Blvd.
San Mateo, CA 94404-2064
Phone: 415-571-7171
Fax: 415-513-7160

CEO: Lawrence F. Probst III
CFO: E. Stanton McKee Jr.
HR: E. Stanton McKee Jr.
Employees: 1,500

1996 Sales: $531.9 million
1-Yr. Sales Change: 7.8%
Exchange: Nasdaq
Symbol: ERTS

Computers - interactive entertainment software (Wing Commander IV, Crusader: No Remorse)
& video-game players

 See page 283 for a full profile of this company.

ELECTRONIC DATA SYSTEMS CORPORATION

5400 Legacy Dr.
Plano, TX 75024-3105
Phone: 214-604-6000
Fax: 214-645-6798

CEO: Lester M. Alberthal Jr.
CFO: Joseph M. Grant
HR: G. Stuart Reeves
Employees: 96,000

1995 Sales: $12,422.1 mil.
1-Yr. Sales Change: 23.6%
Exchange: NYSE
Symbol: EDS

Consulting - outsourcing, consulting & system design services

 See pages 98–99 for a full profile of this company.

ELECTRONIC DESIGNS INC.

One Research Dr.
Westborough, MA 01581
Phone: 508-366-5151
Fax: 508-836-4850

CEO: Donald F. McGuinness
CFO: Frank D. Edwards
HR: Sally Baronian
Employees: 127

1995 Sales: $1.6 million
1-Yr. Sales Change: 23.1%
Exchange: Nasdaq
Symbol: EDIX

Electrical components - semiconductor memory circuits & flat panel display products; industrial
applications for synthetic diamond films & coatings

ELECTRONIC RETAILING SYSTEMS INTERNATIONAL, INC.

372 Danbury Rd.
Wilton, CT 06897
Phone: 203-761-7900
Fax: 203-761-9928

CEO: Bruce F. Failing Jr.
CFO: George C. Rough Jr.
HR: Virginia Menz
Employees: 62

1995 Sales: $3.0 million
1-Yr. Sales Change: 25.0%
Exchange: Nasdaq
Symbol: ERSI

Computers - electronic shelf-labeling systems for supermarkets

ELECTRONICS BOUTIQUE, INC.

1345 Enterprise Dr.
West Chester, PA 19380
Phone: 610-430-8100
Fax: 610-430-6574

CEO: Joseph J. Firestone
CFO: John Panichello
HR: Leslie Boris
Employees: 2,000

1996 Est. Sales: $250.0 mil.
1-Yr. Sales Change: 4.2%
Ownership: Subsidiary

Retail - software & video games (over 500 units worldwide: subsidiary of Anam Group)

ELECTRONICS FOR IMAGING, INC.

2855 Campus Dr.	CEO: Dan Avida	1995 Sales: $190.5 million
San Mateo, CA 94403	CFO: David Warner	1-Yr. Sales Change: 46.1%
Phone: 415-286-8600	HR: Janice Smith	Exchange: Nasdaq
Fax: 415-286-8544	Employees: 222	Symbol: EFII

Computers - workstations that connect color copiers with computer networks to enable high-quality printing in short production runs (Fiery Color Servers)

 See page 284 for a full profile of this company.

ELECTROSTAR, INC.

710 N. 600 West	CEO: Kenton K. Alder	1995 Sales: $61.4 million
Logan, UT 84321	CFO: F. G. Burton Jr.	1-Yr. Sales Change: 168.1%
Phone: 801-753-4700	HR: —	Exchange: Nasdaq
Fax: —	Employees: 500	Symbol: ESTR

Electrical components - printed circuit boards

ELEK-TEK, INC.

7350 N. Linder Ave.	CEO: Richard L. Rodriguez	1995 Sales: $338.0 million
Skokie, IL 60077	CFO: Miguel A. Martinez	1-Yr. Sales Change: 10.6%
Phone: 847-677-7660	HR: Jane McCarthy	Exchange: Nasdaq
Fax: 847-677-1081	Employees: 893	Symbol: ELEK

Retail - computer hardware, software & related accessories & supplies; catalog & direct sales

 See page 285 for a full profile of this company.

ELEXSYS INTERNATIONAL, INC.

18522 Von Karman Ave.	CEO: Milan Mandaric	1995 Sales: $104.0 million
Irvine, CA 92715	CFO: Michael S. Shimada	1-Yr. Sales Change: 8.7%
Phone: 714-833-0870	HR: Jess Jimenez	Exchange: Nasdaq (SC)
Fax: 714-474-2338	Employees: 793	Symbol: ELEX

Electrical components - circuit boards & back panels

ELRON ELECTRONIC INDUSTRIES LIMITED

Advanced Technology Ctr., PO Box 1573	CEO: Uzia Galil	1995 Sales: $8.5 million
Haifa 31015, Israel	CFO: Zahava Tavor	1-Yr. Sales Change: (54.1%)
Phone: +212-935-3110	HR: —	Exchange: Nasdaq
Fax: —	Employees: 42	Symbol: ELRNF

Electrical components - semiconductors; medical diagnostic imaging equipment, defense electronics, communications & networking equipment & factory automation equipment

ELTRON INTERNATIONAL, INC.

41 Moreland Rd.
Simi Valley, CA 93065
Phone: 805-579-1800
Fax: 805-579-1808

CEO: Donald K. Skinner
CFO: Daniel C. Toomey Jr.
HR: Bobby Stocking
Employees: 213

1995 Sales: $42.4 million
1-Yr. Sales Change: 142.3%
Exchange: Nasdaq
Symbol: ELTN

Computers - bar-code label printers, software & related accessories

EMC CORPORATION

171 South St.
Hopkinton, MA 01748-9103
Phone: 508-435-1000
Fax: 508-497-6961

CEO: Michael C. Ruettgers
CFO: Colin G. Patteson
HR: Brian P. O'Connor
Employees: 4,100

1995 Sales: $1,921.3 million
1-Yr. Sales Change: 39.5%
Exchange: NYSE
Symbol: EMC

Computers - computer storage & retrieval products

 See pages 100–101 for a full profile of this company.

EMULEX CORPORATION

3535 Harbor Blvd.
Costa Mesa, CA 92626
Phone: 714-662-5600
Fax: 714-241-0792

CEO: Paul F. Folino
CFO: Walter J. McBride
HR: Sadie A. Herrera
Employees: 298

1996 Sales: $51.3 million
1-Yr. Sales Change: (32.1%)
Exchange: Nasdaq
Symbol: EMLX

Computers - network-access servers, printer servers, network software & WAN adapters

EN POINTE TECHNOLOGIES, INC.

5245 Pacific Concourse Dr., Ste. 200
Los Angeles, CA 90045
Phone: 310-725-5200
Fax: 310-725-5289

CEO: Bob Din
CFO: Robert Mercer
HR: Robert Chilman
Employees: 190

1995 Sales: $200.0 million
1-Yr. Sales Change: 81.8%
Exchange: Nasdaq
Symbol: ENPT

Retail - computers & related products & services

ENCAD, INC.

6059 Cornerstone Ct. West
San Diego, CA 92121-3734
Phone: 619-452-0882
Fax: 619-452-0891

CEO: David A. Purcell
CFO: Todd Schmidt
HR: Heather Kile
Employees: 272

1995 Sales: $65.5 million
1-Yr. Sales Change: 49.9%
Exchange: Nasdaq
Symbol: ENCD

Computers - large-format ink-jet color printers & plotters

ENCORE COMPUTER CORPORATION

6901 W. Sunrise Blvd.
Fort Lauderdale, FL 33313-4499
Phone: 954-587-2900
Fax: 954-797-5723

CEO: Kenneth G. Fisher
CFO: T. Mark Morley
HR: Charles S. Anderson
Employees: 694

1995 Sales: $49.3 million
1-Yr. Sales Change: (35.6%)
Exchange: Nasdaq
Symbol: ENCC

Computers - mainframe computers for online transaction processing

ENGINEERING ANIMATION, INC.

2625 N. Loop Dr.
Ames, IA 50010
Phone: 515-296-9908
Fax: 515-296-7025

CEO: Matthew M. Rizai
CFO: Michael K. Jewell
HR: Lisa Hanson
Employees: 190

1995 Sales: $7.8 million
1-Yr. Sales Change: 95.0%
Exchange: Nasdaq
Symbol: EAII

Computers - 3D animation products, including custom animated movies on videotape, videodisc & CD-ROM for the litigation, biomedical & scientific markets; interactive software products & animation software tools

ENLIGHTEN SOFTWARE SOLUTIONS, INC.

999 Baker Way, Ste. 390
San Mateo, CA 94404
Phone: 415-578-0700
Fax: 415-578-0118

CEO: Peter J. McDonald
CFO: Michael A. Morgan
HR: Mena Baloun
Employees: 54

1995 Sales: $6.6 million
1-Yr. Sales Change: (13.2%)
Exchange: Nasdaq
Symbol: SFTW

Computers - software designed to automate the management of computer systems for banking, finance, telecommunications, information technology & other major industries

ENTERACTIVE, INC.

110 W. 40th St., Ste. 2100
New York, NY 10018
Phone: 212-221-6559
Fax: 212-730-6045

CEO: Andrew Gyenes
CFO: Kenneth Gruber
HR: —
Employees: 37

1996 Sales: $0.9 million
1-Yr. Sales Change: 125.0%
Exchange: Nasdaq (SC)
Symbol: ENTR

Computers - interactive multimedia products for the home & school markets

ENTERPRISE SYSTEMS, INC.

1400 S. Wolf Rd.
Wheeling, IL 60090-6524
Phone: 847-537-4800
Fax: 847-537-4866

CEO: Glen E. Tullman
CFO: David B. Mullen
HR: —
Employees: 332

1995 Sales: $33.2 million
1-Yr. Sales Change: 34.4%
Exchange: Nasdaq
Symbol: ESIX

Computers - health care management software

ENTEX INFORMATION SERVICES

6 International Dr.
Rye Brook, NY 10573
Phone: 914-935-3600
Fax: 914-935-3750

CEO: John A. McKenna Jr.
CFO: David I. Chemerow
HR: Phillip R. Johnson
Employees: 5,000

1996 Sales: $2,100.0 million
1-Yr. Sales Change: 42.9%
Ownership: Privately Held

Retail - PCs; PC systems integration

See pages 102–103 for a full profile of this company.

ENVIRONMENTAL SYSTEMS RESEARCH INSTITUTE INC.

380 New York St.
Redlands, CA 92373
Phone: 909-793-2853
Fax: 909-793-5953

CEO: Jack Dangermond
CFO: Tom Pickett
HR: Chuck Becker
Employees: 2,000

1995 Sales: $174.1 million
1-Yr. Sales Change: 31.9%
Ownership: Privately Held

Computers - GIS software; GIS consulting & database construction

ENVISIONS SOLUTIONS TECHNOLOGY INC.

47400 Seabridge Dr.
Fremont, CA 94538
Phone: 800-365-7226
Fax: 510-438-6709

CEO: Jerry Gadbois
CFO: Jerry Gadbois
HR: Carrie Walters
Employees: 30

1995 Sales: $7.8 million
1-Yr. Sales Change: 1.3%
Ownership: Privately Held

Retail - direct marketing of scanner products

EPIC DESIGN TECHNOLOGY, INC.

310 N. Mary Ave.
Sunnyvale, CA 94086
Phone: 408-733-8080
Fax: 408-988-8324

CEO: Sang S. Wang
CFO: Tammy S. Liu
HR: Angela Wanninger
Employees: 127

1995 Sales: $25.0 million
1-Yr. Sales Change: 121.2%
Exchange: Nasdaq
Symbol: EPIC

Computers - simulation & analysis software for integrated circuit design (PathMill, PowerMill, RailMill, TimeMill, Vertue)

EQUINOX SYSTEMS INC.

6851 W. Sunrise Blvd.
Fort Lauderdale, FL 33313
Phone: 954-746-9000
Fax: 954-791-5001

CEO: William A. Dambrackas
CFO: Mark Kacer
HR: Kathy Puziak
Employees: 85

1995 Sales: $20.2 million
1-Yr. Sales Change: 1.0%
Exchange: Nasdaq
Symbol: EQNX

Computers - commmunications interfaces, serial I/O products, multiport boards, expandable I/O subsystems & cluster controllers for connecting serial devices to minicomputers & mainframes

EQUITRAC CORPORATION

836 Ponce de Leon Blvd.	CEO: George P. Wilson	1996 Sales: $33.7 million
Coral Gables, FL 33134	CFO: Scott J. Modist	1-Yr. Sales Change: 8.0%
Phone: 305-442-2060	HR: Kristin Delpape	Exchange: Nasdaq
Fax: 305-442-0687	Employees: 301	Symbol: ETRC

Office automation - automated cost recovery & expense management systems for copiers, printers, fax machines & other office equipment

ESCOM AG

Burgstrasse 27-31	CEO: Helmut Jost	1995 Sales: $1,641.6 million
D-44867 Bochum, Germany	CFO: —	1-Yr. Sales Change: 18.3%
Phone: +49-2327-303-183	HR: —	Exchange: Frankfurt
Fax: +49-2327-948-622	Employees: 1,934	

Computers - PC manufacturing & retail (#2 in Germany)

ESS TECHNOLOGY, INC.

46107 Landing Pkwy.	CEO: Fred S. L. Chan	1995 Sales: $105.7 million
Fremont, CA 94538	CFO: Ralph J. Harms	1-Yr. Sales Change: 216.5%
Phone: 510-226-1088	HR: Stephen Gonia	Exchange: Nasdaq
Fax: 510-226-8868	Employees: 158	Symbol: ESST

Electrical components - integrated mixed signal semiconductor audio solutions (AudioDrive) for multimedia desktop & notebook computer manufacturers

ESTERLINE TECHNOLOGIES CORPORATION

10800 NE Eighth St., Ste. 600	CEO: Wendell P. Hurlbut	1995 Sales: $351.9 million
Bellevue, WA 98004	CFO: Robert W. Stevenson	1-Yr. Sales Change: 19.7%
Phone: 206-453-9400	HR: Marcia J.M. Greenberg	Exchange: NYSE
Fax: 206-453-2916	Employees: 3,499	Symbol: ESL

Machinery - semiconductor manufacturing equipment; measuring & sensing devices for the aerospace industry; meters, switches & indicators & measurement & analysis equipment

ETEC SYSTEMS, INC.

26460 Corporate Ave.	CEO: Stephen E. Cooper	1995 Sales: $82.9 million
Hayward, CA 94545	CFO: Philip J. Koen Jr.	1-Yr. Sales Change: 20.7%
Phone: 510-783-9210	HR: Trisha A. Dohren	Exchange: Nasdaq
Fax: 510-887-2870	Employees: 577	Symbol: ETEC

Machinery - mask pattern generation equipment for the semiconductor industry (#1 worldwide)

E*TRADE GROUP, INC.

4 Embarcadero Place, 2400 Geng Rd.	CEO: Christos M. Cotsakos	1995 Sales: $23.3 million
Palo Alto, CA 94303	CFO: Stephen C. Richards	1-Yr. Sales Change: 113.8%
Phone: 415-842-2500	HR: Robin N. Rosenberg	Exchange: Nasdaq
Fax: 415-842-2575	Employees: 115	Symbol: EGRP

Business services - electronic brokerage services, including automated order placement, portfolio tracking & related market news & other 24-hour information services online & via telephone & interactive TV

EUROPE ONLINE A.S.B.L.

29, route de Thionville	CEO: Candace Johnson	1995 Sales: $0.0 million
L-2911, Luxembourg	CFO: Romain Reuland	1-Yr. Sales Change: —
Phone: +352 297599	HR: —	Ownership: Non-profit
Fax: +352 297601	Employees: —	

Computers - World Wide Web-based consumer online service

EVANS & SUTHERLAND COMPUTER CORPORATION

600 Komas Dr.	CEO: James R. Oyler	1995 Sales: $113.2 million
Salt Lake City, UT 84108	CFO: John T. Lemley	1-Yr. Sales Change: 0.1%
Phone: 801-582-5847	HR: Bob Morishita	Exchange: Nasdaq
Fax: 801-583-9701	Employees: 754	Symbol: ESCC

Computers - flight-training simulation systems, graphic accelerators & software development tools for advanced 3D graphics applications

EVOLUTIONARY TECHNOLOGIES INTERNATIONAL, INC.

4301 Westbank Dr., Bldg. B., Ste. 100	CEO: Katherine Hammer	1995 Sales: $12.0 million
Austin, TX 78746	CFO: Ken Bartley	1-Yr. Sales Change: —
Phone: 512-327-6994	HR: —	Ownership: Privately Held
Fax: 512-327-6117	Employees: 125	

Computers - software that consolidates otherwise incompatible computer systems

EXABYTE CORPORATION

1685 38th St.	CEO: Peter D. Behrendt	1995 Sales: $374.1 million
Boulder, CO 80301	CFO: William L. Marriner	1-Yr. Sales Change: (2.0%)
Phone: 303-442-4333	HR: Sam Trenka	Exchange: Nasdaq
Fax: 303-417-7170	Employees: 1,278	Symbol: EXBT

Computers - data storage equipment & related products & accessories

EXAR CORPORATION

48720 Kato Rd.
Fremont, CA 94538
Phone: 510-668-7000
Fax: 510-668-7001

CEO: George D. Wells
CFO: Ronald W. Guire
HR: Gene Robles
Employees: 500

1996 Sales: $125.8 million
1-Yr. Sales Change: (21.1%)
Exchange: Nasdaq
Symbol: EXAR

Electrical components - analog & mixed-signal integrated circuits

EXCALIBUR TECHNOLOGIES CORPORATION

1921 Gallows Rd., Ste. 200
Vienna, VA 22182
Phone: 703-761-3700
Fax: 703-761-1990

CEO: Patrick C. Condo
CFO: James H. Buchanan
HR: —
Employees: 125

1996 Sales: $18.7 million
1-Yr. Sales Change: 73.1%
Exchange: Nasdaq
Symbol: EXCA

Computers - document imaging & multimedia information retrieval software (RetrievalWare)

EXCITE INC.

1091 N. Shoreline Blvd.
Mountain View, CA 94043
Phone: 415-934-3611
Fax: 415-934-3610

CEO: George Bell
CFO: Richard B. Redding
HR: Nancy Shearer-Schroeder
Employees: 38

1995 Sales: $0.4 million
1-Yr. Sales Change: 300.0%
Exchange: Nasdaq
Symbol: XCIT

Computers - World Wide Web search service (NetSearch), reviews of web sites (NetDirectory), personal information interface (Personal Excite) & regional web search database (City.Net)

EXECUTRAIN CORPORATION

4800 North Point Pkwy.
Alpharetta, GA 30202
Phone: 770-667-7700
Fax: 770-664-2006

CEO: David Deutsch
CFO: Robert Holtackers
HR: Hal Boyd
Employees: 102

1995 Sales: $29.0 million
1-Yr. Sales Change: 31.8%
Ownership: Privately Held

Computers - training & support services

EXIDE ELECTRONICS GROUP, INC.

8609 Six Forks Rd.
Raleigh, NC 27615
Phone: 919-872-3020
Fax: 919-870-3100

CEO: James A. Risher
CFO: Marty R. Kittrell
HR: Nicholas J. Costanza
Employees: 1,700

1995 Sales: $391.0 million
1-Yr. Sales Change: 19.7%
Exchange: Nasdaq
Symbol: XUPS

Electrical products - uninterruptible power systems (#1 worldwide) & related equipment & power management & facilities-monitoring software to provide temporary backup during power outages

EXIGENT INTERNATIONAL, INC.

1225 Evans Rd.	CEO: Jeffrey C. Clift	1996 Sales: $25.3 million
Melbourne, FL 32904-2314	CFO: Don F. Riordan Jr.	1-Yr. Sales Change: 27.8%
Phone: 407-723-3999	HR: Wanda Schollian	Ownership: Privately Held
Fax: 407-676-4510	Employees: 247	

Computers - professional contract computer solutions & systems services (Software Technology, Inc.) for government & industry

EXPERT SOFTWARE, INC.

800 Douglas Rd., Ste. 750	CEO: Kenneth P. Currier	1995 Sales: $27.6 million
Coral Gables, FL 33134-3128	CFO: Charles H. Murphy	1-Yr. Sales Change: 40.1%
Phone: 305-567-9990	HR: Sara Johnson	Exchange: Nasdaq
Fax: 305-443-0786	Employees: 147	Symbol: XPRT

Computers - personal, business productivity & hobbyist software (Home Design 3D, Diet, Forms, Casino)

FACTSET RESEARCH SYSTEMS INC.

One Greenwich Plaza	CEO: Howard E. Wille	1995 Sales: $36.2 million
Greenwich, CT 06830	CFO: Ernest S. Wong	1-Yr. Sales Change: 24.8%
Phone: 203-863-1500	HR: Rick Varney	Exchange: NYSE
Fax: 203-863-1501	Employees: 116	Symbol: FDS

Computers - online database services, including company information, for the financial community

FALCON SYSTEMS INC.

1417 N. Market Blvd.	CEO: Craig Caudill	1995 Sales: $51.8 million
Sacramento, CA 95834-1936	CFO: Patti Thomas	1-Yr. Sales Change: 15.1%
Phone: 916-928-9255	HR: Jim Kangas	Ownership: Privately Held
Fax: 916-928-9355	Employees: 78	

Computers - peripherals & mass storage devices for UNIX systems

FARALLON COMMUNICATIONS, INC.

2470 Mariner Square Loop	CEO: Alan B. Lefkof	1995 Sales: $57.2 million
Alameda, CA 94501	CFO: James A. Clark	1-Yr. Sales Change: 0.4%
Phone: 510-814-5100	HR: Rita Dettore	Exchange: Nasdaq
Fax: 510-814-5002	Employees: 225	Symbol: FRLN

Computers - networking hardware (Etherwave) & software (Timbuktu)

FASTCOMM COMMUNICATIONS CORPORATION

45472 Holiday Dr.	CEO: Peter C. Madsen	1996 Sales: $10.0 million
Sterling, VA 20166	CFO: Mark H. Rafferty	1-Yr. Sales Change: 138.1%
Phone: 703-318-7750	HR: —	Exchange: Nasdaq
Fax: 703-787-4625	Employees: 46	Symbol: FSCX

Telecommunications equipment - digital & analog access products for public & private computer networks

FDP CORP.

2140 S. Dixie Hwy.	CEO: Michael C. Goldberg	1995 Sales: $19.4 million
Miami, FL 33133	CFO: Mark Silverman	1-Yr. Sales Change: 3.7%
Phone: 305-858-8200	HR: Lew Price	Exchange: Nasdaq
Fax: 305-854-6305	Employees: 237	Symbol: FDPC

Computers - life insurance & employee benefit software

FEI COMPANY

7451 NE Evergreen Pkwy.	CEO: Lynwood W. Swanson	1995 Sales: $41.7 million
Hillsboro, OR 97124-5830	CFO: William G. Langley	1-Yr. Sales Change: 87.0%
Phone: 503-640-7500	HR: Michael E. Stabeno	Exchange: Nasdaq
Fax: 503-640-7509	Employees: 132	Symbol: FEIC

Machinery - focused ion beam (FIB) workstations & components used to produce integrated circuits

FENWICK & WEST LLP

2 Palo Alto Sq.	CEO: Frederick R. Chilton	1995 Sales: $51.0 million
Palo Alto, CA 94306	CFO: Patricia M. Rock	1-Yr. Sales Change: 34.9%
Phone: 415-494-0600	HR: Carol Ida	Ownership: Partnership
Fax: 415-494-0674	Employees: 250	

Law firm - provides legal services for the high-tech industry

 See page 286 for a full profile of this company.

FILENET CORPORATION

3565 Harbor Blvd.	CEO: Theodore J. Smith	1995 Sales: $215.5 million
Costa Mesa, CA 92626-1420	CFO: Mark S. St. Clare	1-Yr. Sales Change: 19.9%
Phone: 714-966-3400	HR: Audrey N. Schaeffer	Exchange: Nasdaq
Fax: 714-966-3232	Employees: 1,126	Symbol: FILE

Computers - document storage, retrieval systems & character-recognition products

 See page 287 for a full profile of this company.

FINANZIARIA PER I SISTEMI INFORMATIVI ELETTRONICI S.P.A.

Via Isonzo, 21/b
00198 Rome, Italy
Phone: +39-6-84311
Fax: +39-6-8431-5236

CEO: Pier Paolo Davoli
CFO: —
HR: —
Employees: 8,315

1995 Sales: $1,103.0 million
1-Yr. Sales Change: 19.2%
Ownership: Subsidiary

Computers - IT services & consultancy, software system development & data management; management consulting & training; banking (subsidiary of STET)

FIND/SVP, INC.

625 Avenue of the Americas, 2nd Fl.
New York, NY 10011
Phone: 212-645-4500
Fax: 212-645-7681

CEO: Andrew P. Garvin
CFO: Peter J. Fiorillo
HR: —
Employees: 236

1995 Sales: $28.6 million
1-Yr. Sales Change: 17.2%
Exchange: Nasdaq (SC)
Symbol: FSVP

Consulting & information services

FIRECREST GROUP PLC

5 Stratford Place
London W1N 9AE, UK
Phone: +44-171-409-1214
Fax: +44-171-409-1209

CEO: Roy Capper
CFO: Gregory B. Carvalho
HR: —
Employees: —

1995 Sales: $10.2 million
1-Yr. Sales Change: (8.1%)
Exchange: London

Computers - Internet access services

FIRST SOURCE INTERNATIONAL INC.

7 Journey
Aliso Viejo, CA 92656
Phone: 714-448-7750
Fax: 714-448-7774

CEO: Douglas Dreier
CFO: Donald Snowden
HR: Stacy George
Employees: 75

1995 Sales: $65.0 million
1-Yr. Sales Change: 48.1%
Ownership: Privately Held

Retail - mail-order sales of computer peripherals, including monitors & mice

FIRST USA PAYMENTECH, INC.

1601 Elm St.
Dallas, TX 75201
Phone: 214-849-2000
Fax: 214-849-3748

CEO: Pamela H. Patsley
CFO: David W. Truetzel
HR: Bonnie Johnston
Employees: 831

1996 Sales: $121.2 million
1-Yr. Sales Change: 40.0%
Exchange: NYSE
Symbol: PTI

Financial - credit card transaction processing services

FIRST VIRTUAL HOLDINGS INCORPORATED

11975 El Camino Real, Ste. 300	CEO: Lee Stein	1995 Est. Sales: $18.5 mil.
San Diego, CA 92130	CFO: —	1-Yr. Sales Change: 48.0%
Phone: 619-793-2700	HR: Carey Storm	Ownership: Privately Held
Fax: 619-793-2950	Employees: 88	

Computers - electronic bank accounts that let Internet shoppers pay for products purchased over the network

FISERV, INC.

255 Fiserv Dr.	CEO: George D. Dalton	1995 Sales: $703.4 million
Brookfield, WI 53045	CFO: Kenneth R. Jensen	1-Yr. Sales Change: 31.1%
Phone: 414-879-5000	HR: Jack P. Bucalo	Exchange: Nasdaq
Fax: 414-879-5013	Employees: 8,222	Symbol: FISV

Business services - data-processing & information-management services

 See page 288 for a full profile of this company.

FLASH CREATIVE MANAGEMENT

433 Hackensack Ave., 12th Fl.	CEO: David Blumenthal	1995 Sales: $2.0 million
Hackensack, NJ 07601	CFO: David Blumenthal	1-Yr. Sales Change: —
Phone: 201-489-2500	HR: David Blumenthal	Ownership: Privately Held
Fax: 201-489-6750	Employees: 15	

Computers - consulting services, including business process improvement, strategic information systems development & developer-level training services

FLEXTRONICS INTERNATIONAL LTD.

514 Chai Chee Ln., Ste. 4-13	CEO: Michael E. Marks	1996 Sales: $448.3 million
Bedok Industrial Estate 1646, Singapore	CFO: Goh Chan Peng	1-Yr. Sales Change: 88.8%
Phone: 65-449-5255	HR: —	Exchange: Nasdaq
Fax: 65-448-6040	Employees: 3,994	Symbol: FLEXF

Electrical components - printed circuit board assemblies for the computer, medical, consumer & communications industries

FLIPSIDE COMMUNICATIONS, INC.

1550 Bryant St., Ste. 950	CEO: Anthony Perkins	1995 Est. Sales: $3.0 mil.
San Francisco, CA 94103	CFO: John Hardy	1-Yr. Sales Change: —
Phone: 415-865-2277	HR: —	Ownership: Privately Held
Fax: 415-865-2280	Employees: 38	

Publishing - high technology investment & finance magazine (The Red Herring) & online service (herring.com)

FLUOROWARE INC.

3500 Lyman Blvd.
Chaska, MN 55318
Phone: 612-448-3131
Fax: 612-368-8022

CEO: Dan Quernemoen
CFO: John Villas
HR: Wayne Holtmeier
Employees: 1,000

1995 Sales: $97.0 million
1-Yr. Sales Change: —
Ownership: Privately Held

Electrical components - microelectronics materials & critical fluid management products for the
semiconductor, data storage & flat panel display industries

FOCUS ENHANCEMENTS, INC.

800 W. Cummings Park, Ste. 4500
Woburn, MA 01801
Phone: 617-938-8088
Fax: 617-938-1098

CEO: Thomas L. Massie
CFO: Jeremiah Cole
HR: Jacqui M. Manganaro
Employees: 49

1995 Sales: $17.1 million
1-Yr. Sales Change: (2.8%)
Exchange: Nasdaq (SC)
Symbol: FCSE

Computers - connectivity products, video graphics products & software utilities

FONIX CORPORATION

60 E. South Temple St., Ste. 1225
Salt Lake City, UT 84111
Phone: 801-328-0161
Fax: 801-328-8778

CEO: Stephen M. Studdert
CFO: Roger Dudley
HR: Yvonne Hagen
Employees: 6

1995 Sales: $0.0 million
1-Yr. Sales Change: —
Exchange: Nasdaq (SC)
Symbol: FONX

Computers - communications software, natural language voice recognition technologies using specific-
speech knowledge, proprietary speech modeling

FORCE COMPUTERS INC.

2001 Logic Dr.
San Jose, CA 95124-3456
Phone: 408-369-6000
Fax: 408-371-3382

CEO: Sven Behrendt
CFO: —
HR: Ursula Dinse
Employees: 306

1995 Est. Sales: $105.0 mil.
1-Yr. Sales Change: 7.7%
Ownership: Privately Held

Computers - computer & peripheral boards

FORE SYSTEMS, INC.

174 Thorn Hill Rd.
Warrendale, PA 15086-7586
Phone: 412-772-6600
Fax: 412-772-6500

CEO: Eric C. Cooper
CFO: Thomas J. Gill
HR: Thomas Armour
Employees: 977

1996 Sales: $235.2 million
1-Yr. Sales Change: 211.1%
Exchange: Nasdaq
Symbol: FORE

Computers - ATM networking products; switching systems (Ethernet, Fast Ethernet)

See page 289 for a full profile of this company.

THE FOREFRONT GROUP, INC.

1360 Post Oak Blvd., Ste. 1660	CEO: David Sikora	1995 Sales: $0.3 million
Houston, TX 77056	CFO: Ernest D. Rapp	1-Yr. Sales Change: (40.0%)
Phone: 713-961-1101	HR: Charlotte Howard	Exchange: Nasdaq
Fax: 713-961-1149	Employees: 31	Symbol: FFGI

Computers - software for sharing information simultaneously over the Internet & private
computer networks

FORRESTER RESEARCH, INC.

1033 Massachusetts Ave.	CEO: George F. Colony	1995 Sales: $14.6 million
Cambridge, MA 02138	CFO: David H. Ramsdell	1-Yr. Sales Change: 50.5%
Phone: 617-497-7090	HR: Sherry Marconi	Ownership: Privately Held
Fax: 617-868-0577	Employees: 118	

Business services - research products & services to allow clients to assess the effect of technology on
their businesses

FORSYTHE MCARTHUR ASSOCIATES, INC.

7500 Frontage Rd.	CEO: Richard A. Forsythe	1995 Sales: $151.0 million
Skokie, IL 60077	CFO: Gordon Decker	1-Yr. Sales Change: (5.6%)
Phone: 847-675-8000	HR: Jan Bonnuci	Ownership: Privately Held
Fax: 847-675-2130	Employees: 155	

Leasing - computer, communications & networking equipment

FORTE SOFTWARE, INC.

1800 Harrison St.	CEO: Martin J. Sprinzen	1996 Sales: $30.0 million
Oakland, CA 94612	CFO: Rodger Weismann	1-Yr. Sales Change: 200.0%
Phone: 510-869-3400	HR: Karen Yoneda	Exchange: Nasdaq
Fax: 510-869-3480	Employees: 221	Symbol: FRTE

Computers - software application & management tools for client/server applications

FOURTH SHIFT CORPORATION

7900 International Dr., Ste. 450	CEO: Marion Melvin Stuckey	1995 Sales: $37.2 million
Minneapolis, MN 55425	CFO: David Latzke	1-Yr. Sales Change: (20.7%)
Phone: 612-851-1500	HR: Renee Conklin	Exchange: Nasdaq
Fax: 612-851-1560	Employees: 420	Symbol: FSFT

Computers - accounting & manufacturing management software

FRACTAL DESIGN CORPORATION

335 Spreckels Dr.	CEO: Mark Zimmer	1996 Sales: $21.8 million
Aptos, CA 95003	CFO: Leslie E. Wright	1-Yr. Sales Change: 66.4%
Phone: 408-688-5300	HR: —	Exchange: Nasdaq
Fax: 408-688-0415	Employees: 66	Symbol: FRAC

Computers - software for creating graphic images for editorial, print ads & graphics for TV

FRANKLIN ELECTRONIC PUBLISHERS, INCORPORATED

One Franklin Plaza	CEO: Morton E. David	1996 Sales: $100.8 million
Burlington, NJ 08016	CFO: Kenneth H. Lind	1-Yr. Sales Change: 21.0%
Phone: 609-261-4800	HR: —	Exchange: NYSE
Fax: 609-387-7420	Employees: 310	Symbol: FEP

Publishing - electronic books (#1 worldwide: Spelling Ace, Med-Spell MED-55, Holy Bible - New International Version)

 See page 290 for a full profile of this company.

FRISCO BAY INDUSTRIES LTD.

160 Graveline St.	CEO: Barry E. Katsof	1996 Sales: $17.1 million
St. Laurent, QC H4T 1R7, Canada	CFO: Richard Plamondon	1-Yr. Sales Change: 9.6%
Phone: 514-738-7300	HR: Heather Halickman	Exchange: Nasdaq
Fax: 514-735-7039	Employees: 175	Symbol: FBAYF

Computers - self-service & financial transaction processing systems & computerized time management & integrated security systems, primarily for banks & other financial institutions

FRY'S ELECTRONICS INC.

382 Portage Ave.	CEO: John Fry	1995 Sales: $414.0 million
Palo Alto, CA 94306-2244	CFO: David Fry	1-Yr. Sales Change: 26.6%
Phone: 415-496-6100	HR: Katherine Bleisae	Ownership: Privately Held
Fax: 415-496-6093	Employees: 1,500	

Retail - computer superstores in California

 See page 291 for a full profile of this company.

FSI INTERNATIONAL, INC.

322 Lake Hazeltine Dr.	CEO: Joel A. Elftmann	1995 Sales: $190.4 million
Chaska, MN 55318-1096	CFO: Benno G. Sand	1-Yr. Sales Change: 102.6%
Phone: 612-448-5440	HR: Timothy D. Krieg	Exchange: Nasdaq
Fax: 612-448-2825	Employees: 968	Symbol: FSII

Machinery - microlithography, surface-conditioning & chemical-management equipment used in the manufacture of semiconductors

FTP SOFTWARE, INC.

2 High St.
North Andover, MA 01845
Phone: 508-685-4000
Fax: 508-794-4488

CEO: David H. Zirkle
CFO: John J. Warnock Jr.
HR: Karen A. Wharton
Employees: 740

1995 Sales: $136.4 million
1-Yr. Sales Change: 46.4%
Exchange: Nasdaq
Symbol: FTPS

Computers - internetworking software (PC/TCP)

FUJITSU LIMITED

6-1, Marunouchi 1-chome, Chiyoda-ku
Tokyo 100, Japan
Phone: +81-3-3216-3211
Fax: +81-3-3216-9352

CEO: Tadashi Sekizawa
CFO: —
HR: —
Employees: 164,364

1996 Sales: $35,490.0 mil.
1-Yr. Sales Change: (3.0%)
Exchange: OTC
Symbol: FJTSY

Computers - mainframes, PCs, peripherals, storage systems, file servers & semiconductor gate arrays (#1 in Japan)

 See pages 104–105 for a full profile of this company.

FULCRUM TECHNOLOGIES INC.

785 Carling Ave., Ninth Fl.
Ottawa , ON K1S 5H4, Canada
Phone: 613-238-1761
Fax: 613-238-6921

CEO: Eric K. Goodwin
CFO: Peter C. Reid
HR: Gesie Morin
Employees: 250

1995 Sales: $31.5 million
1-Yr. Sales Change: 59.9%
Exchange: Nasdaq
Symbol: FULCF

Computers - text-retrieval software for CD-ROMs & online databases; product maintenance, consulting & training

FUSION SYSTEMS CORPORATION

7600 Standish Place
Rockville, MD 20855-2798
Phone: 301-251-0300
Fax: 301-279-0578

CEO: Leslie S. Levine
CFO: Joseph F. Greeves
HR: Carol Barnes
Employees: 593

1995 Sales: $109.6 million
1-Yr. Sales Change: 35.8%
Exchange: Nasdaq
Symbol: FUSN

Machinery - ultraviolet curing systems used in semiconductor manufacturing equipment & printing & coating applications

FUTURE SHOP LTD.

1400-1111 W. Georgia St.
Vancouver, BC V6E 4M3, Canada
Phone: 604-689-1804
Fax: 604-681-9258

CEO: Mohammad Ziabakhsh
CFO: Gary Patterson
HR: Janette Stewart
Employees: 3,266

1996 Sales: $959.2 million
1-Yr. Sales Change: 24.0%
Exchange: Toronto

Retail - computers; consumer electronic products; appliances; music software

FUTUREMEDIA PUBLIC LIMITED COMPANY

Media House, Arundel Rd., Walberton
Arundel, West Sussex BN18 OQP, UK
Phone: +44-1-243-555-000
Fax: +44-1-243-555-020

CEO: Peter Copeland
CFO: Philip Lingard
HR: Hilary Channing
Employees: 75

1996 Sales: $5.7 million
1-Yr. Sales Change: (37.4%)
Exchange: OTC
Symbol: FMDAY (ADS)

Computers - interactive multimedia training programs & merchandising systems

GAMETEK INC.

2999 NE 191st St., Ste. 500
North Miami Beach, FL 33180
Phone: 305-935-3995
Fax: 305-932-8651

CEO: James Harris
CFO: R. Lynn Anderson
HR: —
Employees: 52

1995 Sales: $33.9 million
1-Yr. Sales Change: (27.7%)
Exchange: Nasdaq
Symbol: GAME

Computers - interactive entertainment (Saturday Night Live 20th Anniversary CD-ROM), educational & productivity software

GANDALF TECHNOLOGIES INC.

130 Colonnade Rd. South
Nepean, ON K2E 7M4, Canada
Phone: 613-274-6500
Fax: 613-274-6501

CEO: Thomas A. Vassiliades
CFO: Walter R. MacDonald
HR: Jeff Singer
Employees: 812

1996 Sales: $116.5 million
1-Yr. Sales Change: (3.3%)
Exchange: Nasdaq
Symbol: GANDF

Computers - networking hardware & software

GARTNER GROUP, INC.

56 Top Gallant Rd.
Stamford, CT 06904-2212
Phone: 203-964-0096
Fax: 203-316-1100

CEO: Manuel A. Fernandez
CFO: John F. Halligan
HR: Lindon Smith
Employees: 1,175

1995 Sales: $229.2 million
1-Yr. Sales Change: 35.5%
Exchange: Nasdaq
Symbol: GART

Business services - subscription-based research & analysis services

See page 292 for a full profile of this company.

GASONICS INTERNATIONAL CORPORATION

2730 Junction Ave.
San Jose, CA 95134-1909
Phone: 408-944-0212
Fax: 408-473-9509

CEO: Dave Toole
CFO: Jerald P. Shaevitz
HR: Robert Mearns
Employees: 476

1995 Sales: $102.0 million
1-Yr. Sales Change: 53.2%
Exchange: Nasdaq
Symbol: GSNX

Machinery - photoresist removal equipment used in semiconductor manufacturing

GATEWAY 2000, INC.

610 Gateway Dr.	CEO: Theodore W. Waitt	1995 Sales: $3,676.3 million
North Sioux City, SD 57049-2000	CFO: David J. McKittrick	1-Yr. Sales Change: 36.1%
Phone: 605-232-2000	HR: Robert N. Beck	Exchange: Nasdaq
Fax: 605-232-2023	Employees: 9,300	Symbol: GATE

Computers - mail order PCs; portable computers & peripheral products

See pages 106–107 for a full profile of this company.

GATEWAY DATA SCIENCES CORPORATION

3410 E. University Dr., Ste. 100	CEO: Michael M. Gordon	1996 Sales: $23.9 million
Phoenix, AZ 85034	CFO: Vickie B. Jarvis	1-Yr. Sales Change: 15.5%
Phone: 602-968-7000	HR: Vickie B. Jarvis	Exchange: Nasdaq
Fax: 602-437-8230	Employees: 96	Symbol: GDSC

Computers - point-of-sale management, retail merchandising & warehouse automation systems software & related services

GE INFORMATION SERVICES, INC.

401 N. Washington St., VB 2	CEO: Harvey F. Seegers	1995 Sales: $700.0 million
Rockville, MD 20849-6403	CFO: —	1-Yr. Sales Change: —
Phone: 301-340-4568	HR: William J. Conaty	Ownership: Subsidiary
Fax: 301-251-6421	Employees: 2,500	

Business services - electronic commerce services, including transaction, trading management & cash management services (subsidiary of General Electric)

GEAC COMPUTER CORP.

300, 11 Allstate Pkwy.	CEO: Stephen J. Sadler	1996 Sales: $148.0 million
Markham, Ontario L3R 9T8, Canada	CFO: David G. B. Scott	1-Yr. Sales Change: 8.5%
Phone: 905-475-0525	HR: —	Exchange: Toronto
Fax: —	Employees: —	

Computers - software for use by libraries, financial institutions, hotels & property management companies

GENERAL AUTOMATION, INC.

17731 Mitchell North	CEO: Jane Christie	1995 Sales: $14.3 million
Irvine, CA 92714	CFO: John R. Donnelly	1-Yr. Sales Change: (58.8%)
Phone: 714-250-4800	HR: Luanne Crawford	Exchange: AMEX
Fax: 714-752-6772	Employees: 115	Symbol: GA

Computers - product training, system design & site preparation, network-configuration support & disaster-recovery programs; systems integration services

GENERAL DATACOMM INDUSTRIES, INC.

1579 Straits Tpke.
Middlebury, CT 06762-1299
Phone: 203-574-1118
Fax: 203-758-8507

CEO: Charles P. Johnson
CFO: William S. Lawrence
HR: Robert H. Dorion Jr.
Employees: 1,849

1995 Sales: $221.2 million
1-Yr. Sales Change: 4.7%
Exchange: NYSE
Symbol: GDC

Telecommunications equipment - multimedia networks & telecommunications systems

THE GENERAL ELECTRIC COMPANY PLC

One Stanhope Gate
London W1A 1EH, UK
Phone: +44-171-493-8484
Fax: +44-171-493-1974

CEO: Lord Weinstock
CFO: D. B. Newlands
HR: Hon. Sara Morrison
Employees: 82,967

1996 Sales: $9,759.5 million
1-Yr. Sales Change: —
Exchange: OTC
Symbol: GNELY

Electrical products - electronic & power systems; steam turbines & generators; semiconductors; defense electronics; telecommunications equipment

GENERAL MAGIC, INC.

420 N. Mary Ave.
Sunnyvale, CA 94086
Phone: 408-774-4000
Fax: 408-774-4010

CEO: Steve Markman
CFO: Wendy Olszewski
HR: Stephen Hams
Employees: 208

1995 Sales: $14.2 million
1-Yr. Sales Change: 468.0%
Exchange: Nasdaq
Symbol: GMGC

Computers - communications software (Telescript) for hand-held computers

 See page 293 for a full profile of this company.

GENICOM CORPORATION

14800 Conf. Ctr. Dr., Ste. 400, Westfields
Chantilly, VA 22021-3806
Phone: 703-802-9200
Fax: 703-802-9039

CEO: Paul T. Winn
CFO: James C. Gale
HR: Bruce Meyer
Employees: 1,638

1995 Sales: $294.1 million
1-Yr. Sales Change: 25.8%
Exchange: Nasdaq
Symbol: GECM

Computers - impact & non-impact printers, related supplies & sealed relay products

GENRAD, INC.

300 Baker Ave.
Concord, MA 01742-2174
Phone: 508-287-7000
Fax: 508-287-7007

CEO: James F. Lyons
CFO: Daniel F. Harrington
HR: —
Employees: 1,095

1995 Sales: $153.6 million
1-Yr. Sales Change: 6.7%
Exchange: NYSE
Symbol: GEN

Electronics - integrated test & diagnostic systems for the manufacture & maintenance of electronic products

GENSYM CORPORATION

125 Cambridge Park Dr., 5th Fl.
Cambridge, MA 02140
Phone: 617-547-2500
Fax: 617-547-1962

CEO: Lowell B. Hawkinson
CFO: Stephen N. Gregorio
HR: Louise Callahan
Employees: 226

1995 Sales: $28.1 million
1-Yr. Sales Change: 43.4%
Exchange: Nasdaq
Symbol: GNSM

Computers - intelligent real-time software (G2) that can reach conclusions, provide advice & take actions

GENUS, INC.

1139 Karlstad Dr.
Sunnyvale, CA 94089
Phone: 408-747-7120
Fax: 408-747-7199

CEO: William W.R. Elder
CFO: Ernest Quinones
HR: Dawn Newman
Employees: 319

1995 Sales: $100.4 million
1-Yr. Sales Change: 57.9%
Exchange: Nasdaq
Symbol: GGNS

Machinery - advanced semiconductor manufacturing equipment; high-energy ion implantation systems & chemical vapor deposition systems for tungsten-based films

GEOSCIENCE CORPORATION

10500 Westoffice Dr., Ste. 200
Houston, TX 77042-5391
Phone: 713-785-7790
Fax: 713-780-3524

CEO: Richard F. Miles
CFO: Ray F. Thompson
HR: Rena Johnson
Employees: 620

1995 Sales: $84.2 million
1-Yr. Sales Change: 32.8%
Exchange: Nasdaq
Symbol: GSCI

Computers - seismic data acquisition systems, geoscientific software & related products for use worldwide by the oil & gas industry to identify subsurface geologic structures

GEOTEL COMMUNICATIONS CORPORATION

25 Porter Rd.
Littleton, MA 01460
Phone: 508-486-1100
Fax: 508-486-1200

CEO: John C. Thibault
CFO: Timothy J. Allen
HR: Mary Ann Benedetti
Employees: 55

1995 Sales: $1.5 million
1-Yr. Sales Change: —
Ownership: Privately Held

Computers - telecommunications software solutions

GEOWORKS

960 Atlantic Ave.
Alameda, CA 94501
Phone: 510-814-1660
Fax: 510-814-4250

CEO: Gordon E. Mayer
CFO: Daniel L. Sicotte
HR: Darlene Fontaine
Employees: 113

1996 Sales: $5.0 million
1-Yr. Sales Change: 28.2%
Exchange: Nasdaq
Symbol: GWRX

Computers - operating system & application software for consumer computing devices market

GHS, INC.

1350 Piccard Dr., Ste. 360	CEO: Alan Gold	1995 Sales: $4.4 million
Rockville, MD 20850-4307	CFO: —	1-Yr. Sales Change: 83.3%
Phone: 301-417-9808	HR: —	Exchange: Nasdaq (SC)
Fax: 301-926-9088	Employees: 27	Symbol: GHSI

Computers - computerized integrated patient record-based processing systems for ambulatory care facilities & hospitals

GIGA INFORMATION GROUP, INC.

One Kendall Sq., Bldg. 1400W	CEO: Gideon I. Gartner	1995 Sales: $10.7 million
Cambridge, MA 02139	CFO: Richard B. Goldman	1-Yr. Sales Change: —
Phone: 617-577-9595	HR: Don Colanton	Ownership: Privately Held
Fax: 617-871-5098	Employees: 247	

Business services - information, analysis & advice about the information technology industry

GLASGAL COMMUNICATIONS, INC.

151 Veterans Dr.	CEO: Isaac J. Gaon	1996 Sales: $41.8 million
Northvale, NJ 07647	CFO: James M. Caci	1-Yr. Sales Change: 18.7%
Phone: 201-768-8082	HR: Mary Simon	Exchange: Nasdaq (SC)
Fax: 201-768-2947	Employees: 164	Symbol: GLAS

Computers - design, installation & service of computer networks; marketing of datacommunication equipment

GLOBAL COMPUTRONICS, INC.

5003 University Ave. NE	CEO: Kay Kuba	1995 Sales: $10.0 million
Minneapolis, MN 55421	CFO: Sanjay Kuba	1-Yr. Sales Change: 51.5%
Phone: 612-571-2591	HR: Anita Kuba	Ownership: Privately Held
Fax: 612-571-0746	Employees: 17	

Retail - computers & peripheral equipment (d/b/a GCI Systems)

GLOBAL DIRECTMAIL CORPORATION

22 Harbor Park Dr.	CEO: Richard Leeds	1995 Sales: $634.5 million
Port Washington, NY 11050	CFO: Kenneth J. Hall	1-Yr. Sales Change: 31.0%
Phone: 516-625-1555	HR: Lillian Berman	Exchange: NYSE
Fax: 516-625-0038	Employees: 1,693	Symbol: GML

Retail - direct marketing of brand name & private label computer-related products, office products & industrial products (Global, Misco)

GLOBAL INTELLICOM, INC.

747 Third Ave.
New York, NY 10017
Phone: 212-750-3772
Fax: 212-750-2320

CEO: N. Norman Muller
CFO: Michael A. Doris
HR: Elaine Ranieri
Employees: 60

1995 Sales: $30.4 million
1-Yr. Sales Change: 2,071%
Exchange: Nasdaq (SC)
Symbol: GBIT

Retail - distribution & resale of computers, peripherals, software & wireless data communication products

GLOBAL KNOWLEDGE NETWORK, INC.

One Univ. Office Park, 29 Sawyer Rd.
Waltham, MA 02154
Phone: 617-893-6007
Fax: 617-893-7791

CEO: Anthony Craig
CFO: Thomas Crawford
HR: Harry Hutson
Employees: 700

1995 Sales: $150.0 million
1-Yr. Sales Change: —
Ownership: Privately Held

Computers - distribution of courseware developed to train users of Digital Equipment
Corporation's hardware

GLOBAL MED TECHNOLOGIES, INC.

12600 W. Colfax, Ste. A-500
Lakewood, CO 80215
Phone: 303-238-2000
Fax: 303-238-2009

CEO: Michael I. Ruxin
CFO: Bart K. Valdez
HR: Lori Lynn Perry
Employees: 123

1995 Sales: $6.7 million
1-Yr. Sales Change: 34.0%
Ownership: Privately Held

Computers - information management software products & services for the healthcare industry; substance
abuse testing program services

GLOBAL VILLAGE COMMUNICATION, INC.

1144 E. Arques Ave.
Sunnyvale, CA 94086-4602
Phone: 408-523-1000
Fax: 408-523-2287

CEO: Neil Selvin
CFO: James M. Walker
HR: Mary Cravalho
Employees: 297

1996 Sales: $144.5 million
1-Yr. Sales Change: 80.6%
Exchange: Nasdaq
Symbol: GVIL

Computers - data modems & fax cards for Macintosh, Windows, OS/2 & DOS computers

 See page 294 for a full profile of this company.

GLOBALINK, INC.

9302 Lee Highway, 12th Fl.
Fairfax, VA 22031-1208
Phone: 703-273-5600
Fax: 703-273-3866

CEO: Harry E. Hagerty
CFO: Mark Pacewonsky
HR: Jean Ellen Wood
Employees: 90

1995 Sales: $17.6 million
1-Yr. Sales Change: 1.7%
Exchange: Nasdaq (SC)
Symbol: GNK

Computers - software (The Language Assistant Series, Power Translator) for creating draft translations
between English & Spanish, French, German & Italian

GLOBELLE CORPORATION

5101 Orbitor Dr.
Mississauga, Ontario L4W 4V1, Canada
Phone: 800-456-1616
Fax: —

CEO: Geoff Matus
CFO: Chris Rathgeber
HR: Linda Mullenbach
Employees: 160

1995 Sales: $531.7 million
1-Yr. Sales Change: —
Exchange: Toronto

Retail - microcomputer peripherals distribution

GMIS INC.

5 Country View Rd.
Malvern, PA 19355
Phone: 610-296-3838
Fax: 610-640-9876

CEO: Thomas R. Owens
CFO: Timothy M. Leonard
HR: Bradley G. Mousseau
Employees: 222

1995 Sales: $35.8 million
1-Yr. Sales Change: 11.2%
Exchange: Nasdaq
Symbol: GMIS

Computers - computer medical services software for health care payers

GOVERNMENT TECHNOLOGY SERVICES, INC.

4100 Lafayette Center Dr.
Chantilly, VA 22021-0808
Phone: 703-502-2000
Fax: 703-222-5210

CEO: M. Dendy Young
CFO: Peter E. Janke
HR: David Novick
Employees: 348

1995 Sales: $527.0 million
1-Yr. Sales Change: (14.6%)
Exchange: Nasdaq
Symbol: GTSI

Retail - microcomputer products, primarily to the US government

GRAPHIX ZONE, INC.

42 Corporate Park, Ste. 200
Irvine, CA 92714
Phone: 714-833-3838
Fax: 714-833-3990

CEO: Charles R. Cortright Jr.
CFO: Norman Block
HR: Jill Lewis
Employees: 46

1996 Sales: $9.2 million
1-Yr. Sales Change: 170.6%
Exchange: Nasdaq (SC)
Symbol: GZON

Computers - interactive multimedia products & services

GREENTREE SOFTWARE, INC.

201 Boston Post Rd. West, Ste. 201
Marlborough, MA 01752
Phone: 508-460-7997
Fax: 508-460-7830

CEO: George M. Cassidy
CFO: J. Robert Gary
HR: —
Employees: 6

1996 Sales: $0.3 million
1-Yr. Sales Change: (50.0%)
Exchange: OTC
Symbol: GTSW

Computer - purchasing & materials management software (CAP-3, Greentree 4.0)

GRIFFIN TECHNOLOGY INCORPORATED

1133 Corporate Dr.	CEO: Robert S. Urland	1995 Sales: $17.9 million
Farmington, NY 14425	CFO: Joseph A. Murrer	1-Yr. Sales Change: 5.9%
Phone: 716-924-7121	HR: —	Exchange: Nasdaq
Fax: 716-924-1553	Employees: 191	Symbol: GRIF

Computers - microcomputer systems, software & accessories & identification cards

GROUP 1 SOFTWARE, INC.

4200 Parliament Place, Ste. 600	CEO: Robert S. Bowen	1996 Sales: $45.9 million
Lanham, MD 20706-1844	CFO: Charles A. Crew	1-Yr. Sales Change: 21.1%
Phone: 301-731-2300	HR: Trent Lutz	Exchange: Nasdaq
Fax: 301-731-0360	Employees: 227	Symbol: GSOF

Computers - mailing list/list management software

GROUP TECHNOLOGIES CORPORATION

10901 Malcolm McKinley Dr.	CEO: Carl P. McCormick	1995 Sales: $273.6 million
Tampa, FL 33612	CFO: David D. Johnson	1-Yr. Sales Change: (0.2%)
Phone: 813-972-6000	HR: Janis Beal	Exchange: Nasdaq
Fax: 813-972-6704	Employees: 2,260	Symbol: GRTK

Electrical components - complex circuit-card assemblies, subsystems & end-user products

GSE SYSTEMS, INC.

8930 Stanford Blvd.	CEO: William E. Kuhlmann	1995 Sales: $85.3 million
Columbia, MD 21045	CFO: D. Ganesan	1-Yr. Sales Change: 153.9%
Phone: 410-312-3500	HR: Debbie Caddy	Exchange: Nasdaq
Fax: 410-312-3611	Employees: 500	Symbol: GSES

Computers - real-time simulation software, systems & services for the energy & manufacturing industries

GST, INC.

17707 Valley View Ave.	CEO: J. P. Wang	1995 Sales: $36.0 million
Cerritos, CA 90703	CFO: Christine Chou	1-Yr. Sales Change: 12.5%
Phone: 714-739-0106	HR: Christine Chou	Ownership: Privately Held
Fax: 714-670-6404	Employees: 60	

Computers - PC motherboards

GT INTERACTIVE SOFTWARE CORP.

16 E. 40th St.
New York, NY 10016
Phone: 212-726-6500
Fax: 212-726-6590

CEO: Ronald Chaimowitz
CFO: Andrew Gregor
HR: Harry Glanz
Employees: 597

1995 Sales: $204.1 million
1-Yr. Sales Change: 139.6%
Exchange: Nasdaq
Symbol: GTIS

Publishing - interactive entertainment (Doom II, Mortal Kombat 3), edutainment, children's adventure stories (Fatty Bear's Birthday Surprise) & reference software publishing & distribution

 See page 295 for a full profile of this company.

GVC CORPORATION

76 Tunhwa S. Rd., Section 2, 14F
Taipei, Taiwan
Phone: +886-2-755-2888
Fax: +886-2-755-2413

CEO: Chengtai Lin
CFO: —
HR: —
Employees: 1,084

1995 Sales: $662.5 million
1-Yr. Sales Change: —
Exchange: Taipei

Computers - fax modems & PC mother boards

HADCO CORPORATION

12A Manor Pkwy.
Salem, NH 03079
Phone: 603-898-8000
Fax: 603-898-6227

CEO: Andrew E. Lietz
CFO: Timothy P. Losik
HR: Richard P. Saporito
Employees: 2,346

1995 Sales: $265.2 million
1-Yr. Sales Change: 19.7%
Exchange: Nasdaq
Symbol: HDCO

Electrical components - high-density double-sided & complex multilayer printed circuits & backplane assemblies used in the computer, telecommunications & industrial automation industries

HALIFAX CORPORATION

5250 Cherokee Ave.
Alexandria, VA 22312
Phone: 703-750-2202
Fax: 703-658-2411

CEO: Howard C. Mills
CFO: Richard J. Smithson
HR: Douglas L. Randles
Employees: 421

1996 Sales: $47.2 million
1-Yr. Sales Change: 3.5%
Exchange: AMEX
Symbol: HX

Computers - maintenance & installation of computers, communication systems & simulators

HAMBRECHT & QUIST LLP

One Bush St.
San Francisco, CA 94104
Phone: 415-576-3300
Fax: 415-576-3624

CEO: Daniel H. Case III
CFO: Raymond J. Minehan
HR: K. C. Egan
Employees: 500

1995 Sales: $220.0 million
1-Yr. Sales Change: 84.4%
Exchange: NYSE
Symbol: HMQ

Financial - investment banking

 See page 296 for a full profile of this company.

HARBINGER CORPORATION

1055 Lenox Park Blvd.	CEO: C. Tycho Howle	1995 Sales: $23.1 million
Atlanta, GA 30319	CFO: Joel G. Katz	1-Yr. Sales Change: 68.6%
Phone: 404-841-4334	HR: Michael Lieb	Exchange: Nasdaq
Fax: 404-841-4399	Employees: 210	Symbol: HRBC

Computers - electronic data interchange translation software, handling computer-to-computer exchange of business documents

HATHAWAY CORPORATION

8228 Park Meadows Dr.	CEO: Eugene E. Prince	1996 Sales: $35.4 million
Littleton, CO 80124	CFO: Richard D. Smith	1-Yr. Sales Change: (11.1%)
Phone: 303-799-8200	HR: Tracy Montford	Exchange: Nasdaq
Fax: 303-799-8880	Employees: 363	Symbol: HATH

Computers - electronic instrumentation products for power & process industries worldwide; motion control products

HAUPPAUGE DIGITAL, INC.

91 Cabot Ct.	CEO: Kenneth Plotkin	1995 Sales: $11.6 million
Hauppauge, NY 11788	CFO: Gerald Tucciarone	1-Yr. Sales Change: 176.2%
Phone: 516-434-1600	HR: Gerald Tucciarone	Exchange: Nasdaq (SC)
Fax: 516-434-3198	Employees: 45	Symbol: HAUP

Computers - digital video boards for the PC-based digital video market (Win/TV)

HAYES MICROCOMPUTER PRODUCTS, INC.

5835 Peachtree Corners East	CEO: Joseph Formichelli	1995 Sales: $275.0 million
Norcross, GA 30092-3405	CFO: James Jones	1-Yr. Sales Change: 11.4%
Phone: 770-840-9200	HR: Bruce Meyers	Ownership: Privately Held
Fax: 770-441-1213	Employees: 1,100	

Computers - internal/external PC modems (Hayes, Practical Peripherals), connectivity software & ISDN adapters

 See page 297 for a full profile of this company.

HBO & COMPANY

301 Perimeter Center North	CEO: Charles W. McCall	1995 Sales: $495.6 million
Atlanta, GA 30346	CFO: Jay P. Gilbertson	1-Yr. Sales Change: 51.5%
Phone: 770-393-6000	HR: Chris Ramsey	Exchange: Nasdaq
Fax: 770-393-6092	Employees: 2,383	Symbol: HBOC

Computers - health care information systems services

HCIA INC.

300 E. Lombard St.
Baltimore, MD 21202
Phone: 410-332-7532
Fax: 410-576-9429

CEO: George D. Pillari
CFO: Barry C. Offutt
HR: John Robison
Employees: 502

1995 Sales: $48.0 million
1-Yr. Sales Change: 56.4%
Exchange: Nasdaq
Symbol: HCIA

Medical practice management - integrated clinical- & financial-information systems & products

HD SYSTEMS, INC.

1196 Kern Ave.
Sunnyvale, CA 94086
Phone: 408-986-9898
Fax: 408-986-9989

CEO: Paul Hsu
CFO: Richard Chin
HR: Corrine Purcell
Employees: 65

1995 Sales: $24.0 million
1-Yr. Sales Change: (4.0%)
Ownership: Privately Held

Retail - PC clones

HDS NETWORK SYSTEMS, INC.

400 Feheley Dr.
King of Prussia, PA 19406
Phone: 610-277-8300
Fax: 610-275-5739

CEO: Arthur R. Spector
CFO: Scott Holland
HR: —
Employees: 51

1996 Sales: $20.8 million
1-Yr. Sales Change: (4.6%)
Exchange: Nasdaq
Symbol: HDSX

Computers - desktop computer devices, including terminals (X Window)

HEALTH SYSTEMS DESIGN CORPORATION

1330 Broadway
Oakland, CA 94612
Phone: 510-763-2629
Fax: 510-763-2081

CEO: Richard C. Auger
CFO: Richard E. Malone
HR: Ruth Nygaard
Employees: 100

1995 Sales: $6.8 million
1-Yr. Sales Change: 36.0%
Exchange: Nasdaq
Symbol: HSDC

Computers - managed-care information-systems software (Diamond)

HEALTHDYNE INFORMATION ENTERPRISES, INC.

1850 Parkway Place, Ste. 1100
Marietta, GA 30067
Phone: 770-423-8450
Fax: 770-423-8440

CEO: H. Darrell Young
CFO: Joseph G. Bleser
HR: Jim Juett
Employees: 104

1995 Sales: $8.7 million
1-Yr. Sales Change: 8,600%
Exchange: Nasdaq (SC)
Symbol: HDIE

Computers - clinical information system products, tools & services for health care providers

HEALTHEON CORPORATION

87 Encina Ave.
Palo Alto, CA 94301
Phone: 415-614-0200
Fax: 415-614-2250

CEO: David Schnell
CFO: Kallen Chan
HR: Debra Machado
Employees: 55

1995 Sales: $0.0 million
1-Yr. Sales Change: —
Ownership: Privately Held

Computers - Internet-based online health care & benefit information & services

HEI, INC.

1495 Steiger Lake Ln., PO Box 5000
Victoria, MN 55386
Phone: 612-443-2500
Fax: 612-443-2668

CEO: Eugene W. Courtney
CFO: Jerald H. Mortenson
HR: Jerald H. Mortenson
Employees: 135

1996 Sales: $20.7 million
1-Yr. Sales Change: (11.5%)
Exchange: Nasdaq
Symbol: HEII

Electrical components - ultraminiature microelectronic devices & computer pens; heart pacemakers & defibrillators & hearing aids

HELISYS, INC.

24015 Garnier St.
Torrance, CA 90505
Phone: 310-891-0600
Fax: 310-891-0419

CEO: Michael Feygin
CFO: Dave T. Okazaki
HR: —
Employees: 86

1995 Sales: $11.5 million
1-Yr. Sales Change: 105.4%
Exchange: Nasdaq
Symbol: HELI

Computers - rapid prototyping systems & sale of sheet-form materials

HERTZ TECHNOLOGY GROUP, INC.

325 Fifth Ave.
New York, NY 10016-5012
Phone: 212-684-4141
Fax: 212-684-3658

CEO: Eli E. Hertz
CFO: Barry J. Goldsammler
HR: Wendy Freid
Employees: 56

1995 Sales: $11.2 million
1-Yr. Sales Change: 2.8%
Ownership: Privately Held

Computers - microcomputers & related technology services; ergonomically engineered mounting & support structures & technical furniture (Hergo)

HEWLETT-PACKARD COMPANY

3000 Hanover St.
Palo Alto, CA 94304
Phone: 415-857-1501
Fax: 415-857-7299

CEO: Lewis E. Platt
CFO: Robert P. Wayman
HR: F. E. (Pete) Peterson
Employees: 102,300

1995 Sales: $31,519 million
1-Yr. Sales Change: 26.1%
Exchange: NYSE
Symbol: HWP

Computers - PCs, laser printers (LaserJet), test equipment & information storage products, including digital audio tape; medical products, including cardiac ultrasound machines

 See pages 108–109 for a full profile of this company.

HITACHI, LTD.

6, Kanda-Surugadai 4-chome
Tokyo 101, Japan
Phone: +81-3-3258-1111
Fax: +81-3-3258-2375

CEO: Tsutomu Kanai
CFO: —
HR: —
Employees: 331,852

1996 Sales: $76,640 million
1-Yr. Sales Change: (12.6%)
Exchange: NYSE
Symbol: HIT

Diversified operations - mainframes, semiconductors (#2 DRAM maker, flash memory) & test equipment;
heavy machinery; power plants; consumer products

 See pages 110–111 for a full profile of this company.

HMT TECHNOLOGY CORPORATION

1055 Page Ave.
Fremont, CA 94538
Phone: 510-490-3100
Fax: 510-623-9642

CEO: Ronald L. Schauer
CFO: Peter S. Norris
HR: Phyllis Ziakas
Employees: 651

1996 Sales: $194.4 million
1-Yr. Sales Change: 166.7%
Exchange: Nasdaq
Symbol: HMTT

Computers - thin film disks for hard disk drives

HNC SOFTWARE INC.

5930 Cornerstone Ct. West
San Diego, CA 92121-3728
Phone: 619-546-8877
Fax: 619-452-6524

CEO: Robert L. North
CFO: Raymond V. Thomas
HR: Liz Meany
Employees: 152

1995 Sales: $25.2 million
1-Yr. Sales Change: 52.7%
Exchange: Nasdaq
Symbol: HNCS

Computers - software to detect credit/debit card fraud (Falcon), manage merchant risk (Eagle), automate
lending decisions (Colleague) & home valuation (AREAS) & manage retail inventories (SkuPLAN)

HOMECOM COMMUNICATIONS, INC.

3535 Piedmont Rd., Bldg. 14, Ste. 100
Atlanta, GA 30305
Phone: 404-237-4646
Fax: 404-237-3060

CEO: Harvey W. Sax
CFO: Vinod Keni
HR: Vinod Keni
Employees: 42

1995 Sales: $0.3 million
1-Yr. Sales Change: —
Ownership: Privately Held

Computers - software applications & products & Internet & intranet services

HOOVER'S, INC.

1033 La Posada, Ste. 250
Austin, TX 78752
Phone: 512-374-4500
Fax: 512-454-9401

CEO: Patrick J. Spain
CFO: Lynn Atchison
HR: Lynn Atchison
Employees: 48

1996 Sales: $2.6 million
1-Yr. Sales Change: 62.5%
Ownership: Privately Held

Publishing - business reference books (Hoover's Handbooks), online services (Hoover's Online, Hoover's
Business Resources), CD-ROMs & software

HOWTEK, INC.

21 Park Ave.	CEO: David Bothwell	1995 Sales: $20.6 million
Hudson, NH 03051	CFO: Robert Lungo	1-Yr. Sales Change: (15.6%)
Phone: 603-882-5200	HR: Connie Webster	Exchange: Nasdaq
Fax: 603-880-3843	Employees: 116	Symbol: HOWT

Computers - digital image scanners & related software

HPR INC.

245 First St.	CEO: Marcia J. Radosevich	1996 Sales: $28.3 million
Cambridge, MA 02142	CFO: Brian D. Cahill	1-Yr. Sales Change: 54.6%
Phone: 617-679-8000	HR: Maureen Wolfe	Exchange: Nasdaq
Fax: 617-679-8888	Employees: 145	Symbol: HPRI

Computers - clinical database software for health care providers

HUMAN CODE, INC.

1411 West Ave., Ste. 100	CEO: Chipp Walters	1995 Sales: $2.5 million
Austin, TX 78701	CFO: —	1-Yr. Sales Change: —
Phone: 512-477-5455	HR: Bettye Nowlin	Ownership: Privately Held
Fax: 512-477-5456	Employees: 35	

Computers - interactive multimedia products

HUMMER WINBLAD VENTURE PARTNERS

Holice St., Ste. R	CEO: John Hummer	1996 Sales: —
Emeryville, CA 94608	CFO: —	1-Yr. Sales Change: —
Phone: 510-652-8061	HR: —	Ownership: Privately Held
Fax: 510-652-7572	Employees: 3	

Financial - venture capital investment specializing in software companies

HUMMINGBIRD COMMUNICATIONS LTD.

One Sparks Ave.	CEO: Fred Sorkin	1995 Sales: $47.5 million
North York, ON M2H 2W1, Canada	CFO: Inder P. S. Duggal	1-Yr. Sales Change: 94.7%
Phone: 416-496-2200	HR: Mike Wayling	Exchange: Nasdaq
Fax: 416-496-2207	Employees: 240	Symbol: HUMCF

Computers - X server software (software that allows users to access & display, on one workstation, several applications running on different computers across a network)

HUTCHINSON TECHNOLOGY INCORPORATED

40 W. Highland Park	CEO: Jeffrey W. Green	1995 Sales: $300.0 million
Hutchinson, MN 55350	CFO: John A. Ingleman	1-Yr. Sales Change: 25.6%
Phone: 320-587-3797	HR: Rebecca A. Albrecht	Exchange: Nasdaq
Fax: 320-587-1892	Employees: 4,858	Symbol: HTCH

Computers - mechanical suspension assembly arms for hard disk drives

 See page 298 for a full profile of this company.

HYPERION SOFTWARE CORPORATION

900 Long Ridge Rd.	CEO: James A. Perakis	1996 Sales: $172.8 million
Stamford, CT 06902-1247	CFO: Lucy Rae Ricciardi	1-Yr. Sales Change: 26.0%
Phone: 203-703-3000	HR: Paul Avalone	Exchange: Nasdaq
Fax: 203-595-8500	Employees: 1,046	Symbol: HYSW

Computers - enterprise-level financial-management software for client/server environments

 See page 299 for a full profile of this company.

HYUNDAI GROUP

140-2, Kye-Dong, Chongro-ku	CEO: Park Se Yong	1995 Sales: $23,221.2 mil.
Seoul, South Korea	CFO: Park Won-jin	1-Yr. Sales Change: —
Phone: +82-2-746-1114	HR: —	Ownership: Privately Held
Fax: +82-2-741-2341	Employees: 50,000	

Electronics & electrical products - ships & industrial plants, machinery & transportation, steel & metal

I2 TECHNOLOGIES, INC.

909 E. Las Colinas Blvd., 16th Fl.	CEO: Sanjiv S. Sidhu	1995 Sales: $25.9 million
Irving, TX 75039	CFO: David F. Cary	1-Yr. Sales Change: 125.2%
Phone: 214-860-6000	HR: Jeanne Durbin	Exchange: Nasdaq
Fax: 214-860-6060	Employees: 181	Symbol: ITWO

Computers - supply chain management software (Rhythm)

IBIS TECHNOLOGY CORPORATION

32A Cherry Hill Dr.	CEO: Geoffrey Ryding	1995 Sales: $4.6 million
Danvers, MA 01923	CFO: Debra L. Carroll	1-Yr. Sales Change: 43.7%
Phone: 508-777-4247	HR: Peg Donovan	Exchange: Nasdaq (SC)
Fax: 508-777-6570	Employees: 46	Symbol: IBIS

Electronic components - wafers used in the production of semiconductors

ICHAT, INC.

8303 N. Mopac, Bldg. A., Ste. 114	CEO: Mark W. Saul	1995 Sales: $0.1 million
Austin, TX 78759	CFO: Rod MacDonald	1-Yr. Sales Change: —
Phone: 512-349-0339	HR: —	Ownership: Privately Held
Fax: 512-349-0005	Employees: 24	

Computers - Web-based, real-time chat communications software (ROOMS)

ICL PLC

ICL House, One High St., Putney	CEO: T. Keith Todd	1995 Sales: $4,826.0 million
London SW15 1SW, UK	CFO: Peter Kelly	1-Yr. Sales Change: 17.0%
Phone: +44-181-788-7272	HR: Phil Resch	Ownership: Privately Held
Fax: +44-181-785-3936	Employees: 24,000	

Computers - networking hardware, information technology services & application software (owned by Fujitsu & Northern Telecom)

 See pages 112–113 for a full profile of this company.

ID SOFTWARE, INC.

18601 LBJ Fwy., Ste. 615	CEO: Jay Wilbur	1995 Sales: $15.6 million
Mesquite, TX 75150	CFO: Jay Wilbur	1-Yr. Sales Change: 102.6%
Phone: 214-613-3589	HR: Donna Jackson	Ownership: Privately Held
Fax: 214-686-9288	Employees: 13	

Computer - games software (Commander Keen, Doom, Heretic, Quake, Spear of Destiny, Wolfenstein 3-D)

 See page 300 for a full profile of this company.

IDT CORPORATION

294 State St.	CEO: Howard S. Jonas	1996 Sales: $57.7 million
Hackensack, NJ 07601	CFO: Stephen R. Brown	1-Yr. Sales Change: 393.2%
Phone: 201-928-1000	HR: Howard Millendorf	Exchange: Nasdaq
Fax: 201-928-1057	Employees: 337	Symbol: IDTC

Computers - Internet access services & discounted long-distance phone services

IDX SYSTEMS CORPORATION

1400 Shelburne Rd.	CEO: Richard E. Tarrant	1995 Sales: $128.1 million
South Burlington, VT 05403	CFO: John A. Kane	1-Yr. Sales Change: 22.3%
Phone: 802-862-1022	HR: Dean E. Haller	Exchange: Nasdaq
Fax: 802-862-6848	Employees: 1,039	Symbol: IDXC

Computers - health care information systems software for physician groups & medical centers for patient registration, billing, scheduling, managed care & other administrative tasks

IEC ELECTRONICS CORP.

105 Norton St.
Newark, NY 14513-1298
Phone: 315-331-7742
Fax: 315-331-3547

CEO: Roger E. Main
CFO: Timothy J. Kennedy
HR: Joe Schadeberg
Employees: 2,456

1995 Sales: $127.6 million
1-Yr. Sales Change: (2.1%)
Exchange: Nasdaq
Symbol: IECE

Electrical components - printed circuit board assemblies, modems & video enhancement cards

I.I.S. INTELLIGENT INFORMATION SYSTEMS LIMITED

Yokneam Industrial Park, PO Box 110
Yokneam 20692, Israel
Phone: +972-4-989-2077
Fax: +972-4-989-2079

CEO: Jacob Herbst
CFO: Gideon Barak
HR: —
Employees: 450

1995 Sales: $76.5 million
1-Yr. Sales Change: (16.7%)
Exchange: Nasdaq
Symbol: IISLF

Computers - communication, networking & peripheral products

IKOS SYSTEMS, INC.

19050 Pruneridge Ave.
Cupertino, CA 95014
Phone: 408-255-4567
Fax: 408-366-8699

CEO: Ramon A. Nunez
CFO: Joseph W. Rockom
HR: Ray Mendonca
Employees: 130

1995 Sales: $28.6 million
1-Yr. Sales Change: 32.4%
Exchange: Nasdaq
Symbol: IKOS

Computers - logic-simulation systems for ASIC applications

ILC INDUSTRIES, INC.

105 Wilbur Place
New York, NY 11716
Phone: 516-567-5600
Fax: 516-567-6357

CEO: Clifford P. Lane
CFO: Ken Sheedy
HR: Martha Solowey
Employees: 1,100

1995 Est. Sales: $125.0 mil.
1-Yr. Sales Change: 4.2%
Ownership: Privately Held

Electrical components - semiconductors & electronic coils

IMAGEMATRIX CORPORATION

400 S. Colorado Blvd., Ste. 500
Denver, CO 80222
Phone: 303-399-3700
Fax: 303-399-1554

CEO: Gerald E. Henderson
CFO: Keith E. Brue
HR: —
Employees: 31

1995 Sales: $2.0 million
1-Yr. Sales Change: 11.1%
Exchange: Nasdaq (SC)
Symbol: IMCX

Computers - document imaging & workflow systems for HMOs, health insurance companies & for businesses & associations in financial, communications, engineering & other industries

IMATION CORP.

One Imation Place	CEO: William T. Monahan	1995 Sales: $2,245.6 million
Oakdale, MN 55128	CFO: Jill. D. Burchill	1-Yr. Sales Change: (1.5%)
Phone: 612-704-4000	HR: Jacqueline Chase	Exchange: NYSE
Fax: 612-704-4200	Employees: 12,000	Symbol: IMN

Computers - removable magnetic & optical media; color proofing systems (Matchprint); private label film for the amateur photography market; data storage tape cartridges (Travan)

 See pages 114–115 for a full profile of this company.

IMC NETWORKS CORPORATION

16931 Millikan Ave.	CEO: Jerry Roby	1995 Est. Sales: $12.0 mil.
Irvine, CA 92606	CFO: Michael Dailey	1-Yr. Sales Change: 17.6%
Phone: 714-724-1070	HR: Janet Thompson	Ownership: Privately Held
Fax: 714-724-1020	Employees: 44	

Computers - Ethernet bridges, hubs, media converters & repeaters for local area networks

IMNET SYSTEMS, INC.

8601 Dunwoody Place, Ste. 420	CEO: Kenneth D. Rardin	1996 Sales: $26.6 million
Atlanta, GA 30350	CFO: Raymond L. Brown	1-Yr. Sales Change: 212.9%
Phone: 770-998-2200	HR: Michelle Goss	Exchange: Nasdaq
Fax: 770-992-6357	Employees: 181	Symbol: IMNT

Computers - information & document management systems

IMP, INC.

2830 N. First St.	CEO: David A. Laws	1996 Sales: $76.8 million
San Jose, CA 95134-2071	CFO: Charles S. Isherwood	1-Yr. Sales Change: 28.4%
Phone: 408-432-9100	HR: Robert J. Crossley	Exchange: Nasdaq
Fax: 408-434-0335	Employees: 434	Symbol: IMPX

Electrical components - application specific standard ICs, custom memory ICs & silicon foundry services

IN FOCUS SYSTEMS, INC.

27700B SW Parkway Ave.	CEO: John V. Harker	1995 Sales: $202.8 million
Wilsonville, OR 97070-9215	CFO: Michael D. Yonker	1-Yr. Sales Change: 64.7%
Phone: 503-685-8888	HR: Susan L. Thompson	Exchange: Nasdaq
Fax: 503-685-8889	Employees: 391	Symbol: INFS

Computers - liquid crystal display projection panels for use with overhead projectors to project data & video onto a screen either via PCs or a built-in disk drive and presentation software (LiteShow II)

 See page 301 for a full profile of this company.

INACOM CORP.

10810 Farnam Dr.
Omaha, NE 68154
Phone: 402-392-3900
Fax: 402-392-3602

CEO: Bill L. Fairfield
CFO: Dave Guenthner
HR: Larry Fazzini
Employees: 2,196

1995 Sales: $2,200.3 million
1-Yr. Sales Change: 22.2%
Exchange: Nasdaq
Symbol: INAC

Retail - wholesale microcomputer systems, workstations, networking & telecommunications equipment & related products

 See pages 116–117 for a full profile of this company.

INCOMNET, INC.

21031 Ventura Blvd., Ste. 1100
Woodland Hills, CA 91364
Phone: 818-887-3400
Fax: 818-587-5697

CEO: M. Reznick
CFO: Helen Mulliner
HR: Helen Mulliner
Employees: 267

1995 Sales: $86.6 million
1-Yr. Sales Change: 85.0%
Exchange: Nasdaq (SC)
Symbol: ICNT

Computers - networking hardware & software; long-distance telephone services marketing

INDEX STOCK PHOTOGRAPHY, INC.

126 Fifth Ave.
New York, NY 10011
Phone: 212-929-4644
Fax: 212-633-1914

CEO: Bahar Gidwani
CFO: James D. Pyden
HR: Kevin Cooper
Employees: 44

1995 Sales: $2.2 million
1-Yr. Sales Change: 29.4%
Exchange: Nasdaq (SC)
Symbol: ISPI

Photographic equipment & supplies - storage, retrieval & transmission (Telephoto System) of more than one million still images for stock photography users & Internet content providers

INDIVIDUAL, INC.

8 New England Executive Park West
Burlington, MA 01803
Phone: 617-273-6000
Fax: 617-273-6060

CEO: Andy Devereaux
CFO: Bruce D. Glabe
HR: Linda Schofield
Employees: 157

1995 Sales: $20.0 million
1-Yr. Sales Change: 100.0%
Exchange: Nasdaq
Symbol: INDV

Computers - enterprisewide news service (First! for Notes) & agent-based news service (First! for Mosaic) delivered on the Internet

THE INDUS GROUP INC.

60 Spear St.
San Francisco, CA 94105
Phone: 415-904-5000
Fax: 415-904-4949

CEO: Robert W. Felton
CFO: —
HR: Kay Mullins
Employees: 398

1995 Sales: $53.8 million
1-Yr. Sales Change: 75.8%
Exchange: Nasdaq
Symbol: IGRP

Computers - integrated information-management software

INDUSTRIAL TECHNOLOGIES, INC.

One Trefoil Dr.	CEO: Gerald W. Stewart	1995 Sales: $9.1 million
Trumbull, CT 06611	CFO: Joseph Schlig	1-Yr. Sales Change: 37.9%
Phone: 203-268-8000	HR: Nancy Wilkins	Exchange: Nasdaq (SC)
Fax: 203-268-2538	Employees: 46	Symbol: INTI

Computers - sensoring, monitoring, processing & inspection technologies designed to improve industrial operations; standard inspection & industrial-strength computers for harsh conditions

INDUSTRI-MATEMATIK INTERNATIONAL CORP.

Kungsgatan 12-14, Box 7733	CEO: Stig G. Durlow	1995 Sales: $40.0 million
103 95 Stockholm, Sweden	CFO: Lars-Goran Peterson	1-Yr. Sales Change: 44.4%
Phone: +46-8-676-5000	HR: —	Ownership: Privately Held
Fax: —	Employees: 287	

Computers - demand chain management software (System ESS) for order fulfillment & management, distribution logistics, inventory replenishment & demand planning

INFERENCE CORPORATION

101 Rowland Way, Ste. 310	CEO: Peter R. Tierney	1996 Sales: $29.4 million
Novato, CA 94945	CFO: William D. Griffin	1 Yr. Sales Change: 3.2%
Phone: 415-899-0100	HR: Jeanette Bergmann	Exchange: Nasdaq
Fax: 415-899-9080	Employees: 191	Symbol: INFR

Computers - marketing, customer service, financial underwriting & insurance claims analysis software

INFINITY FINANCIAL TECHNOLOGY, INC.

640 Clyde Ct.	CEO: Roger A. Lang	1995 Sales: $24.7 million
Mountain View, CA 94043	CFO: Terry H. Carlitz	1-Yr. Sales Change: 96.0%
Phone: 415-940-6100	HR: Susan Coleman	Ownership: Privately Held
Fax: 415-964-9844	Employees: 133	

Computers - object-oriented, client/server platform & solutions software for financial trading & risk management

INFODATA SYSTEMS INC.

12150 Monument Dr., Ste. 400	CEO: Harry Kaplowitz	1995 Sales: $7.0 million
Fairfax, VA 22033	CFO: David A. Karish	1-Yr. Sales Change: (6.7%)
Phone: 703-934-5205	HR: Dawn Belliveau	Exchange: Nasdaq (SC)
Fax: 703-934-7154	Employees: 56	Symbol: INFD

Computers - text & database management software

INFOMED HOLDINGS, INC

1180 S.W. 36th Ave.
Pompano Beach, FL 33069
Phone: 954-974-0707
Fax: 954-975-3906

CEO: Don Vander Beke
CFO: —
HR: Margie Rosenthal
Employees: 121

1996 Sales: $13.5 million
1-Yr. Sales Change: (6.9%)
Exchange: OTC
Symbol: IMHI

Computers - information systems for health care providers

INFONAUTICS, INC.

900 W. Valley Rd., Ste. 1000
Wayne, PA 19087-1830
Phone: 610-971-8840
Fax: 610-971-8859

CEO: Marvin I. Weinberger
CFO: Ronald A. Berg
HR: Robert Palmer
Employees: 52

1995 Sales: $0.4 million
1-Yr. Sales Change: —
Exchange: Nasdaq
Symbol: INFO

Computers - online reference services, including an Internet search engine (The Electric Library), online general reference library for kids (Homework Helper) & custom online information services

INFONOW CORPORATION

3131 S. Vaughn Way, Ste. 134
Aurora, CO 80014
Phone: 303-368-4646
Fax: 303-695-8238

CEO: Michael W. Johnson
CFO: Kevin Andrew
HR: Nancy Dixon
Employees: 38

1995 Sales: $1.4 million
1-Yr. Sales Change: 40.0%
Exchange: OTC
Symbol: INOW

Computers - electronic distribution system software & related products

INFORMATION BUILDERS, INC.

1250 Broadway, 38th Fl.
New York, NY 10001-3782
Phone: 212-736-4433
Fax: 212-967-6406

CEO: Gerald D. Cohen
CFO: Harry Lerner
HR: Lila Goldberg
Employees: 1,750

1995 Sales: $240.0 million
1-Yr. Sales Change: —
Ownership: Privately Held

Computers - database software (Focus)

INFORMATION MANAGEMENT RESOURCES, INC.

26750 US Hwy. 19 North, Ste. 500
Clearwater, FL 34621
Phone: 813-797-7080
Fax: 813-791-8152

CEO: Satish K. Sanan
CFO: Michael J. Dean
HR: Sunil Subhedar
Employees: 600

1995 Sales: $22.7 million
1-Yr. Sales Change: 61.0%
Ownership: Privately Held

Computers - applications software outsourcing solutions for information technology (IT) departments of businesses

INFORMATION RESOURCE ENGINEERING INC.

8029 Corporate Dr.	CEO: Anthony A. Caputo	1995 Sales: $8.1 million
Baltimore, MD 21236	CFO: David A. Skalitzky	1-Yr. Sales Change: 138.2%
Phone: 410-931-7500	HR: David A. Skalitzky	Exchange: Nasdaq
Fax: 410-931-7524	Employees: 90	Symbol: IREG

Computers - data transmission security software using encryption technology

INFORMATION STORAGE DEVICES, INC.

2045 Hamilton Ave.	CEO: David L. Angel	1995 Sales: $55.5 million
San Jose, CA 95125	CFO: Felix J. Rosengarten	1-Yr. Sales Change: 43.0%
Phone: 408-369-2400	HR: Diane Jacobson	Exchange: Nasdaq
Fax: 408-369-2422	Employees: 122	Symbol: ISDI

Electrical components - integrated circuits used for recording & playing back human voices in greeting cards, games, building security systems & cellular phones

INFORMATION SYSTEMS & SERVICES, INC.

8405 Colesville Rd., Ste. 600	CEO: Bhasker Agarwal	1995 Sales: $6.6 million
Silver Spring, MD 20910	CFO: Bhasker Agarwal	1-Yr. Sales Change: 15.8%
Phone: 301-588-3800	HR: Sarla Bhaskar	Ownership: Privately Held
Fax: 301-588-3986	Employees: 80	

Computers - network development & integration management

INFORMEDICS, INC.

4000 Kruse Way Pl., Bldg. 3, Ste. 300	CEO: John Tortorici	1995 Sales: $5.2 million
Lake Oswego, OR 97035	CFO: Dale E. Conner	1-Yr. Sales Change: (5.5%)
Phone: 503-697-3000	HR: Dale E. Conner	Exchange: Nasdaq (SC)
Fax: 503-697-7671	Employees: 67	Symbol: IMED

Computers - physician practice management software (ClinicManager), blood bank data management software (LifeLine) & pathology data management software (StarPath)

INFORMIX CORPORATION

4100 Bohannon Dr.	CEO: Phillip E. White	1995 Sales: $709.0 million
Menlo Park, CA 94025	CFO: Howard H. Graham	1-Yr. Sales Change: 51.3%
Phone: 415-926-6300	HR: Ira H. Dorf	Exchange: Nasdaq
Fax: 415-926-6564	Employees: 3,219	Symbol: IFMX

Computers - UNIX database management software

 See page 302 for a full profile of this company.

INFOSAFE SYSTEMS, INC.

342 Madison Ave., Ste. 622	CEO: Thomas H. Lipscomb	1995 Sales: $0.1 million
New York, NY 10173	CFO: Alan Alpern	1-Yr. Sales Change: (75.0%)
Phone: 212-867-7200	HR: Alistair Wier	Exchange: Nasdaq (SC)
Fax: 212-867-7227	Employees: 17	Symbol: ISFEA

Computers - secure electronic distribution systems (Infosafe System) for publishers & other information providers to prevent theft of digital information, video, graphics & software

INFOSEEK CORPORATION

2620 Augustine Dr., Ste. 250	CEO: Robert E. Robin Johnson III	1995 Sales: $1.0 million
Santa Clara, CA 95054	CFO: Leonard J. LeBlanc	1-Yr. Sales Change: —
Phone: 408-567-2700	HR: Victoria Blakeslee	Exchange: Nasdaq
Fax: 408-986-1889	Employees: 71	Symbol: SEEK

Computers - World Wide Web search service (Infoseek Guide)

INGRAM MICRO INC.

1600 E. St. Andrew Place	CEO: Jerre L. Stead	1995 Sales: $8,616.9 million
Santa Ana, CA 92705	CFO: Michael J. Grainger	1-Yr. Sales Change: 47.8%
Phone: 714-566-1000	HR: David M. Finley	Ownership: Subsidiary
Fax: 714-566-7733	Employees: 7,604	

Retail - PC wholesaler (#1 in US), including microcomputer hardware, networking equipment & software products (subsidiary of Ingram Industries)

 See pages 118–119 for a full profile of this company.

INNODATA CORPORATION

95 Rockwell Place	CEO: Barry Hertz	1995 Sales: $20.8 million
New York, NY 11217	CFO: Martin Kaye	1-Yr. Sales Change: 45.5%
Phone: 718-625-7750	HR: Jack Cohen	Exchange: Nasdaq
Fax: 718-522-9235	Employees: 3,100	Symbol: INOD

Data collection & systems - data entry & conversion, scanning, indexing & abstracting services

INNOVATIVE TECHNICAL SYSTEMS, INC.

444 Jacksonville Rd., Ste. 200	CEO: William M. Thompson	1996 Sales: $2.8 million
Warminster, PA 18947	CFO: Louis J. Desiderio	1-Yr. Sales Change: 115.4%
Phone: 215-441-5600	HR: Louis J. Desiderio	Exchange: Nasdaq (SC)
Fax: 215-441-3733	Employees: 53	Symbol: ITSY

Computers - proprietary computer integrated facilities management (CIFM) software

INNOVEX, INC.

1313 Fifth St. South	CEO: Thomas W. Haley	1995 Sales: $50.2 million
Hopkins, MN 55343-9904	CFO: Douglas W. Keller	1-Yr. Sales Change: 64.1%
Phone: 612-938-4155	HR: Jack Kilby	Exchange: Nasdaq
Fax: 612-938-7718	Employees: 487	Symbol: INVX

Computers - lead-wire assemblies for heads of hard disk drives (#1 worldwide); indexing & abstracting software for Internet's World Wide Web & for professional writers

INNOVUS CORPORATION

2060 E. 2100 South	CEO: David Mock	1995 Sales: $0.2 million
Salt Lake City, UT 84109	CFO: Gary Wall	1-Yr. Sales Change: —
Phone: 801-487-9388	HR: —	Exchange: Nasdaq (SC)
Fax: 801-484-9561	Employees: 67	Symbol: INUS

Computers - multimedia software for government & corporate clients

INSCI CORP.

2 Westborough Business Park	CEO: David W. Grace	1996 Sales: $7.9 million
Westborough, MA 01581	CFO: John E. Steinkrauss	1-Yr. Sales Change: 9.7%
Phone: 508-870-4000	HR: Jack Steinkrauss	Exchange: Nasdaq (SC)
Fax: 508-870-5585	Employees: 45	Symbol: INSI

Computers - software that uses magnetic, optical & CDR disk storage technologies with hardware systems to archive, index, retrieve, print & fax computer-generated documents

INSIGHT ENTERPRISES, INC.

1912 W. Fourth St.	CEO: Eric J. Crown	1996 Sales: $342.8 million
Tempe, AZ 85281	CFO: Stanley Laybourne	1-Yr. Sales Change: 39.9%
Phone: 602-902-1001	HR: Kaylene Ozmun	Exchange: Nasdaq
Fax: 602-902-1141	Employees: 548	Symbol: NSIT

Retail - microcomputers, peripherals & software for the home, business, government & education markets in the US & Canada

INSIGNIA SOLUTIONS PLC

2200 Lawson Ln.	CEO: Robert P. Lee	1995 Sales: $55.1 million
Santa Clara, CA 94054	CFO: Richard Noling	1-Yr. Sales Change: 39.8%
Phone: 408-327-6000	HR: J. Brezovec	Exchange: Nasdaq
Fax: 408-327-6105	Employees: 265	Symbol: INSGY

Computers - cross-platform software, primaily Macintosh & UNIX, designed to run all Microsoft Windows & MS-DOS applications

INSIGNIA SYSTEMS, INC.

10801 Red Circle Dr.	CEO: G. L. Hoffman	1995 Sales: $15.5 million
Minnetonka, MN 55343	CFO: Ronald W. McClurg	1-Yr. Sales Change: (4.9%)
Phone: 612-930-8200	HR: Deb Price	Exchange: Nasdaq (SC)
Fax: 612-930-8222	Employees: 125	Symbol: ISIG

Computers - sign & label production software & equipment

INSO CORPORATION

31 St. James Ave.	CEO: Steven R. Vana-Paxhia	1995 Sales: $43.4 million
Boston, MA 02116-4101	CFO: Betty J. Savage	1-Yr. Sales Change: 84.7%
Phone: 617-753-6500	HR: Judith Tavano-Finkle	Exchange: Nasdaq
Fax: 617-753-6666	Employees: 176	Symbol: INSO

Computers - proofing, reference & information management software (IntelliScope)

 See page 303 for a full profile of this company.

INTEGRAL SYSTEMS, INC.

5000 Philadelphia Way, Ste. A	CEO: Steven R. Chamberlain	1995 Sales: $10.8 million
Lanham, MD 20706	CFO: Kimberly A. Chamberlain	1-Yr. Sales Change: 20.0%
Phone: 301-731-4233	HR: —	Exchange: Nasdaq (SC)
Fax: 301-731-9606	Employees: 79	Symbol: ISYS

Computers - satellite command & control systems, data processing, simulation & flight-software validation

INTEGRATED CIRCUIT SYSTEMS, INC.

2435 Blvd. of the Generals, PO Box 968	CEO: David W. Sear	1996 Sales: $100.5 million
Valley Forge, PA 19482-0968	CFO: Hock E. Tan	1-Yr. Sales Change: (3.7%)
Phone: 610-630-5300	HR: Thomas Halphen	Exchange: Nasdaq
Fax: 610-666-1099	Employees: 206	Symbol: ICST

Electrical components - integrated circuits that combine analog & digital circuitry; frequency timing generators used in video graphics applications, PC motherboards & peripheral devices

INTEGRATED DEVICE TECHNOLOGY, INC.

2975 Stender Way	CEO: Leonard C. Perham	1996 Sales: $679.5 million
Santa Clara, CA 95054	CFO: William D. Snyder	1-Yr. Sales Change: 60.9%
Phone: 408-727-6116	HR: Thomas B. Wroblewski	Exchange: Nasdaq
Fax: 408-492-8674	Employees: 3,828	Symbol: IDTI

Electrical components - high performance ICs in CMOS & BiCMOS technologies for SRAM components, specialty memory products & logic circuit & RISC microprocessors & subsystems

 See page 304 for a full profile of this company.

INTEGRATED PACKAGING ASSEMBLY CORPORATION

2221 Oakland Rd.	CEO: Victor A. Batinovich	1995 Sales: $20.8 million
San Jose, CA 95131	CFO: Tony Lin	1-Yr. Sales Change: 494.3%
Phone: 408-321-3600	HR: Renae Hogan	Exchange: Nasdaq
Fax: 408-321-3603	Employees: 116	Symbol: IPAC

Electronics - semiconductor packaging foundry

INTEGRATED PROCESS EQUIPMENT CORPORATION

911 Bern Ct.	CEO: Sanjeev R. Chitre	1996 Sales: $184.5 million
San Jose, CA 95112	CFO: Joh S. Hodgson	1-Yr. Sales Change: 108.7%
Phone: 408-436-2170	HR: —	Exchange: Nasdaq (SC)
Fax: 408-436-2179	Employees: 1,042	Symbol: IPEC

Machinery - semiconductor manufacturing equipment

INTEGRATED SILICON SOLUTION, INC.

680 Almanor Ave.	CEO: Jimmy S. M. Lee	1995 Sales: $123.2 million
Sunnyvale, CA 94086-3513	CFO: Gary L. Fischer	1-Yr. Sales Change: 102.6%
Phone: 408-733-4774	HR: Gary L. Fischer	Exchange: Nasdaq
Fax: 408-245-4774	Employees: 311	Symbol: ISSI

Electrical components - random access memory (SRAM) chips & nonvolatile memory integrated circuits used in personal computers, data communications, telecommunications & instrumentation

INTEGRATED SYSTEMS CONSULTING GROUP, INC.

575 E. Swedesford Rd., Ste. 200	CEO: David S. Lipson	1995 Sales: $21.0 million
Wayne, PA 19087	CFO: —	1-Yr. Sales Change: 55.6%
Phone: 610-989-7000	HR: —	Exchange: Nasdaq
Fax: 610-989-7100	Employees: 284	Symbol: ISCG

Computers - consulting services, including client-server architecture, graphical user interface-based applications & cross-platform applications integration

INTEGRATED SYSTEMS, INC.

201 Moffett Park Dr.	CEO: David P. St. Charles	1996 Sales: $84.4 million
Sunnyvale, CA 94089	CFO: Steven Sipowicz	1-Yr. Sales Change: 62.3%
Phone: 408-542-1500	HR: Janice Waterman	Exchange: Nasdaq
Fax: 408-542-1950	Employees: 416	Symbol: INTS

Computers - CAE/CASE software & software for embedded controllers in household & industrial products

INTEGRATED TECHNOLOGY USA, INC.

545 Cedar Ln.	CEO: Alan P. Haber	1995 Sales: $0.8 million
Teaneck, NJ 07666	CFO: Simon M. Kahn	1-Yr. Sales Change: 700.0%
Phone: 201-907-0200	HR: —	Exchange: AMEX
Fax: 201-907-0344	Employees: 15	Symbol: ITH

Computers - products for Internet telephony & computer/telephone integration, including PC keyboards that also function as conventional telephones (CompuNet 2000)

INTEL CORPORATION

2200 Mission College Blvd.	CEO: Andrew S. Grove	1995 Sales: $16,202 million
Santa Clara, CA 95052-8119	CFO: Andy D. Bryant	1-Yr. Sales Change: 40.6%
Phone: 408-765-8080	HR: Kirby A. Dyess	Exchange: Nasdaq
Fax: 408-765-1402	Employees: 41,600	Symbol: INTC

Electrical components - microprocessors, chipsets & motherboards; semiconductors, including flash memory & control chips; supercomputers

 See pages 120–121 for a full profile of this company.

INTELLICORP, INC.

1975 El Camino Real West, Ste. 101	CEO: Kenneth H. Haas	1996 Sales: $11.0 million
Mountain View, CA 94040-2216	CFO: Nancy J. Hiker	1-Yr. Sales Change: (36.8%)
Phone: 415-965-5500	HR: Judy Williams	Exchange: Nasdaq (SC)
Fax: 415-965-5647	Employees: 84	Symbol: INAI

Computers - object-oriented software tools for the design, development & delivery of scalable client/server applications

INTELLIGENT ELECTRONICS, INC.

411 Eagleview Blvd.	CEO: Richard D. Sanford	1996 Sales: $3,588.1 million
Exton, PA 19341-1117	CFO: Thomas J. Coffey	1-Yr. Sales Change: 11.8%
Phone: 610-458-5500	HR: Sherri Haines	Exchange: Nasdaq
Fax: 610-458-6702	Employees: 2,569	Symbol: INEL

Retail - wholesale microcomputer systems, workstations, networking & telecommunications equipment & software

 See pages 122–123 for a full profile of this company.

INTELLIGENT SYSTEMS CORPORATION

4355 Shackleford Rd.	CEO: J. Leland Strange	1995 Sales: $28.2 million
Norcross, GA 30093	CFO: J. Leland Strange	1-Yr. Sales Change: 31.8%
Phone: 770-381-2900	HR: Marcy Powers	Exchange: AMEX
Fax: 770-381-2808	Employees: 285	Symbol: INS

Computers - software distribution; computer training services; ultraclean manufacturing facilities; psychiatric treatment programs

INTELLIGROUP, INC.

517 Rte. One South
Iselin, NJ 08830
Phone: 908-750-1600
Fax: 908-750-1880

CEO: Ashok Pandey
CFO: Robert M. Olanoff
HR: Suzanne Marquez
Employees: 231

1995 Sales: $24.6 million
1-Yr. Sales Change: 261.8%
Exchange: Nasdaq
Symbol: ITIG

Computers - IT services, including enterprise-wide business process solutions, systems integration & custom software development

INTELLIQUEST INFORMATION GROUP, INC.

1250 Capital of Texas Hwy. S., Bldg. 2
Austin, TX 78746
Phone: 512-329-0808
Fax: 512-329-0888

CEO: Peter Zandan
CFO: James Schellhase
HR: Bobbi Garrison
Employees: 113

1995 Sales: $17.0 million
1-Yr. Sales Change: 29.8%
Exchange: Nasdaq
Symbol: IQST

Business services - survey-based market research information for technology companies

INTERACT MEDICAL TECHNOLOGIES CORPORATION

654 Madison Ave., Ste. 1606
New York, NY 10021
Phone: 212-319-3500
Fax: —

CEO: Bruce D. Sturman
CFO: Thomas E. Mignanelli
HR: —
Employees: 25

1995 Sales: $0.3 million
1-Yr. Sales Change: —
Ownership: Privately Held

Computers - software (Preview) that provides three-dimensional models of a patient's anatomy for facilitating minimally invasive surgical procedures

INTERACTION MEDIA CORPORATION

1701 Ponce de Leon Blvd.
Coral Gables, FL 33134
Phone: 305-446-5900
Fax: 305-446-5907

CEO: Harold G. Schenker
CFO: Michael Burnstine
HR: —
Employees: 17

1995 Sales: $0.0 million
1-Yr. Sales Change: —
Exchange: Nasdaq (SC)
Symbol: IKEC

Business - interactive multimedia kiosks through computer touch screen technology

INTERACTIVE FLIGHT TECHNOLOGIES, INC.

3070 W. Post Rd.
Las Vegas, NV 89118
Phone: 702-896-8900
Fax: 702-896-4234

CEO: Michail Itkis
CFO: Robert J. Aten
HR: Robert J. Aten
Employees: 42

1995 Sales: $0.0 million
1-Yr. Sales Change: —
Exchange: Nasdaq
Symbol: FLYT

Computers - in-flight entertainment network equipment & programming, including movies, casino & video arcade games & shopping channels

INTERACTIVE GROUP, INC.

5095 Murphy Canyon Rd.	CEO: Robert C. Vernon	1995 Sales: $33.0 million
San Diego, CA 92123	CFO: Michael D. Reynolds	1-Yr. Sales Change: 15.4%
Phone: 619-560-8525	HR: Doug Fulkerson	Exchange: Nasdaq
Fax: 619-565-8750	Employees: 292	Symbol: INTE

Computers - manufacturers' make-to-order & make-to-stock support software (INFOFLO, Intrepid)

INTERACTIVE, INC.

204 N. Main	CEO: Russ Pohl	1995 Sales: $0.3 million
Humboldt, SD 57035	CFO: Paul Schock	1-Yr. Sales Change: (85.7%)
Phone: 605-363-5117	HR: Carol Flickinger	Exchange: OTC
Fax: 605-363-5102	Employees: 3	Symbol: IACT

Computers - networking & connectivity hardware & software

INTERFACE SYSTEMS, INC.

5855 Interface Dr.	CEO: Garnel "Gene" F. Graber	1995 Sales: $70.2 million
Ann Arbor, MI 48103	CFO: David O. Schupp	1-Yr. Sales Change: 80.0%
Phone: 313-769-5900	HR: —	Exchange: Nasdaq
Fax: 313-769-1047	Employees: 210	Symbol: INTF

Computers - printers, interfaces, specialty data communications systems & printed circuit boards

INTERGRAPH CORPORATION

One Industrial Park	CEO: James W. Meadlock	1995 Sales: $1,098.0 million
Huntsville, AL 35894-0001	CFO: Larry J. Laster	1-Yr. Sales Change: 5.4%
Phone: 205-730-2000	HR: Milford B. French	Exchange: Nasdaq
Fax: 205-730-7898	Employees: 8,400	Symbol: INGR

Computers - CAD/CAM/CAE software, computer graphics systems & industry-specific software, workstations & servers

 See pages 124–125 for a full profile of this company.

INTERLEAF, INC.

62 Fourth Ave.	CEO: Ed Koepfler	1996 Sales: $88.6 million
Waltham, MA 02154	CFO: G. Gordon M. Large	1-Yr. Sales Change: 0.8%
Phone: 617-290-0710	HR: Kate Horsemann	Exchange: Nasdaq
Fax: 617-290-4943	Employees: 674	Symbol: LEAF

Computers - publishing software used in the creation, management & distribution of documents

INTERLINK COMPUTER SCIENCES, INC.

47370 Fremont Blvd.
Fremont, CA 94538
Phone: 510-657-9800
Fax: 510-659-6381

CEO: Charles W. Jepson
CFO: Gloria M. Purdy
HR: Ann Riddle
Employees: 175

1996 Sales: $34.0 million
1-Yr. Sales Change: 25.5%
Exchange: Nasdaq
Symbol: INLK

Computers - business network systems management products (TCPaccess, HARBOR) & services for server connectivity, fault tolerance, integration, backup, archiving, restoration & data & software distribution

INTERLINQ SOFTWARE CORPORATION

11255 Kirkland Way
Kirkland, WA 98033
Phone: 206-827-1112
Fax: 206-827-0927

CEO: Jiri Nechleba
CFO: Stephen A. Yount
HR: Stephen A. Yount
Employees: 150

1996 Sales: $13.1 million
1-Yr. Sales Change: 19.1%
Exchange: Nasdaq
Symbol: INLQ

Computers - PC-based stand-alone & network software products (MortgageWare) for mortgage brokers & bankers, banks, credit unions & savings institutions

INTERMIND CORPORATION

217 Pine St.
Seattle, WA 98101-1500
Phone: 206-812-6000
Fax: 206-812-6377

CEO: David W. Arnold
CFO: Bart Wilson
HR: Brian Rush
Employees: 80

1995 Sales: $0.0 million
1-Yr. Sales Change: —
Ownership: Privately Held

Computers - Internet content provider

INTERNATIONAL BUSINESS MACHINES CORPORATION

One Old Orchard Rd.
Armonk, NY 10504
Phone: 914-765-1900
Fax: 914-288-1147

CEO: Louis V. Gerstner Jr.
CFO: G. Richard Thoman
HR: J. Thomas Bouchard
Employees: 225,347

1995 Sales: $71,940 million
1-Yr. Sales Change: 12.3%
Exchange: NYSE
Symbol: IBM

Computers - mainframes, minis, micros, processors, software & peripherals; information technology consulting, systems integration & development services

 See pages 126–127 for a full profile of this company.

INTERNATIONAL DATA GROUP

One Exeter Plaza, 15th Fl.
Boston, MA 02116
Phone: 617-534-1200
Fax: 617-262-2300

CEO: Patrick J. McGovern
CFO: William P. Murphy
HR: Martha Stephens
Employees: 8,500

1995 Sales: $1,400.0 million
1-Yr. Sales Change: 27.3%
Ownership: Privately Held

Publishing - computer magazines (PC World, Publish, ComputerWorld); market research & trade shows

 See pages 128–129 for a full profile of this company.

INTERNATIONAL MICROCOMPUTER SOFTWARE, INC.

1895 E. Francisco Blvd.	CEO: Martin Sacks	1996 Sales: $25.7 million
San Rafael, CA 94901-5568	CFO: Mark Cosmez	1-Yr. Sales Change: 26.6%
Phone: 415-454-7101	HR: Chris Diesch	Exchange: Nasdaq (SC)
Fax: 415-257-3565	Employees: 144	Symbol: IMSI

Computers - productivity software for small businesses (TurboCAD, FormTool)

INTERNATIONAL NETWORK SERVICES

1213 Innsbruck Dr.	CEO: Donald K. McKinney	1996 Sales: $44.1 million
Sunnyvale, CA 94089	CFO: Kevin J. Laughlin	1-Yr. Sales Change: 184.5%
Phone: 408-542-0100	HR: Steven R. Umphreys	Exchange: Nasdaq
Fax: 408-542-0101	Employees: 425	Symbol: INSS

Computers - services for complex enterprise networks

INTERNATIONAL RECTIFIER CORPORATION

233 Kansas St.	CEO: Derek B. Lidow	1996 Sales: $576.8 million
El Segundo, CA 90245	CFO: Michael P. McGee	1-Yr. Sales Change: 34.5%
Phone: 310-322-3331	HR: Dennis Marchand	Exchange: NYSE
Fax: 310-322-3332	Employees: 3,915	Symbol: IRF

Electrical components - power-regulating semiconductors for power conversion

INTERNATIONAL TELECOMMUNICATION DATA SYSTEMS, INC.

969 High Ridge Rd., Ste. 205	CEO: Charles L. Bakes	1995 Sales: $10.8 million
Stamford, CT 06905	CFO: Mark D. Spitzer	1-Yr. Sales Change: 71.4%
Phone: 203-329-3300	HR: —	Ownership: Privately Held
Fax: 203-323-1314	Employees: 169	

Computers - transactional billing & management information software for the telecommunications industry

INTERPHASE CORPORATION

13800 Senlac	CEO: R. Stephen Polley	1995 Sales: $47.4 million
Dallas, TX 75234	CFO: Robert L. Drury	1-Yr. Sales Change: 16.7%
Phone: 214-919-9000	HR: Paula Jandura	Exchange: Nasdaq
Fax: 214-919-9200	Employees: 193	Symbol: INPH

Computers - networking & mass-storage adapters

INTERPLAY PRODUCTIONS INC.

17922 Fitch Ave.	CEO: Brian Fargo	1996 Sales: $110.0 million
Irvine, CA 92714	CFO: Chuck Camps	1-Yr. Sales Change: 11.1%
Phone: 714-553-6655	HR: Lisa Fisher	Ownership: Privately Held
Fax: 714-252-2820	Employees: 420	

Computers - interactive video game software

INTERPOINT CORPORATION

10301 Willows Rd., PO Box 97005	CEO: Peter H. van Oppen	1995 Sales: $71.1 million
Redmond, WA 98073-9705	CFO: Leslie S. Rock	1-Yr. Sales Change: 29.7%
Phone: 206-882-3100	HR: Shannon Dillingham	Exchange: Nasdaq
Fax: 206-869-7402	Employees: 340	Symbol: INTP

Electrical components - power converter microcircuits

INTERSCIENCE COMPUTER CORPORATION

5171 Clareton Dr.	CEO: Frank J. LaChapelle	1995 Sales: $9.4 million
Agoura Hills, CA 91301	CFO: Michael W. Brennan	1-Yr. Sales Change: (1.1%)
Phone: 818-707-2000	HR: Linda Patchen	Exchange: Nasdaq
Fax: 818-707-1627	Employees: 75	Symbol: INTR

Computers - maintenance services for computers & peripheral equipment

INTERSOLV, INC.

9420 Key West Ave.	CEO: Kevin J. Burns	1996 Sales: $145.3 million
Rockville, MD 20850	CFO: Kenneth A. Sexton	1-Yr. Sales Change: 25.8%
Phone: 301-838-5000	HR: Karen Davis	Exchange: Nasdaq
Fax: 301-838-5064	Employees: 610	Symbol: ISLI

Computers - client/server software development tools

INTERSYSTEMS CORP.

One Memorial Dr.	CEO: Phillip T. Ragon	1995 Sales: $38.2 million
Cambridge , MA 02142	CFO: Phillip T. Ragon	1-Yr. Sales Change: —
Phone: 617-621-0600	HR: —	Ownership: Privately Held
Fax: 617-494-1631	Employees: 165	

Computers - user interface software development facility & database

INTEVAC, INC.

3550 Bassett	CEO: Norman H. Pond	1995 Sales: $42.9 million
Santa Clara, CA 95054-2704	CFO: Charles B. Eddy III	1-Yr. Sales Change: 109.3%
Phone: 408-986-9888	HR: —	Exchange: Nasdaq
Fax: 408-727-5739	Employees: 186	Symbol: IVAC

Computers - static disk sputtering systems

INTIME SYSTEMS INTERNATIONAL, INC.

1655 Palm Beach Blvd., Ste. 200	CEO: William E. Berry	1995 Sales: $7.5 million
West Palm Beach, FL 33401	CFO: Mark Murphy	1-Yr. Sales Change: 29.3%
Phone: 561-478-0022	HR: Lynn Bentley	Exchange: Nasdaq (SC)
Fax: 561-689-4759	Employees: 83	Symbol: TAMSA

Computers - time- & attendance-management software; consulting services

INTRACORP ENTERTAINMENT

501 Brickell Key Dr., 6th Fl.	CEO: Leigh M. Rothschild	1995 Sales: $8.1 million
Miami, FL 33131	CFO: Scott R. Yackee	1-Yr. Sales Change: 131.4%
Phone: 305-373-7700	HR: —	Ownership: Privately Held
Fax: —	Employees: 80	

Computers - entertainment software for PCs, including 3-D action & military strategy simulation games

INTUIT INC.

155 Linfield Ave.	CEO: William V. Campbell	1996 Sales: $552.9 million
Menlo Park, CA 94025	CFO: James J. Heeger	1-Yr. Sales Change: 39.7%
Phone: 415-322-0573	HR: Michael A. Ahearn	Exchange: Nasdaq
Fax: 415-329-2788	Employees: 2,732	Symbol: INTU

Computers - personal finance (Quicken), tax preparation (MacInTax, TurboTax) & related electronic software

 See page 305 for a full profile of this company.

IOMEGA CORPORATION

1821 W. Iomega Way	CEO: Kim B. Edwards	1995 Sales: $326.2 million
Roy, UT 84067	CFO: Leonard C. Purkis	1-Yr. Sales Change: 156.2%
Phone: 801-778-1000	HR: Dan Henrie	Exchange: Nasdaq
Fax: 801-778-3190	Employees: 1,667	Symbol: IOMG

Computers - removable data storage products for back-up & storage on personal computers (Zip drives)

 See page 306 for a full profile of this company.

IPC CORPORATION

IPC Building, 23 Tai Seng Dr.	CEO: Mike Driscoll	1995 Sales: $1,089.2 million
535224, Singapore	CFO: Steve Gunn	1-Yr. Sales Change: —
Phone: +65-744-2688	HR: Debbie Schlager	Exchange: Singapore
Fax: +65-743-0691	Employees: —	

Computers - PCs; direct sales of PCs (IPC Technologies)

IPC INFORMATION SYSTEMS, INC.

Wall Street Plaza, 88 Pine St.	CEO: S. T. Terry Clontz	1995 Sales: $206.3 million
New York, NY 10005-1852	CFO: Gregory Riedel	1-Yr. Sales Change: 26.0%
Phone: 212-825-9060	HR: Jody Tracey	Exchange: Nasdaq
Fax: 212-344-5106	Employees: 598	Symbol: IPCI

Telecommunications equipment - specialized systems for the financial services industry; design & implementation of local & wide area networks for voice, data & video networking

IPL SYSTEMS, INC.

124 Acton St.	CEO: Ronald J. Gellert	1995 Sales: $24.8 million
Maynard, MA 01754	CFO: Eugene F. Tallone	1-Yr. Sales Change: (17.1%)
Phone: 508-461-1000	HR: Eugene F. Tallone	Exchange: Nasdaq
Fax: 508-461-1316	Employees: 85	Symbol: IPLS

Computers - open-architecture storage systems (RAID 5, ESS) for multi-host computer environments

IQ SOFTWARE CORPORATION

3295 River Exchange Dr., Ste. 550	CEO: Charles R. Chitty	1996 Sales: $21.9 million
Norcross, GA 30092-4220	CFO: Michael J. Casey	1-Yr. Sales Change: 9.0%
Phone: 770-446-8880	HR: —	Exchange: Nasdaq
Fax: 770-448-4088	Employees: 156	Symbol: IQSW

Computers - client/server query & reporting tools software (Intelligent Query, IQ Access)

IRVINE SENSORS CORPORATION

3001 Redhill Ave., Bldg. 3	CEO: Kenneth T. Lian	1995 Sales: $8.0 million
Costa Mesa, CA 92626	CFO: John J. Stuart Jr.	1-Yr. Sales Change: 56.9%
Phone: 714-549-8211	HR: David Greenhut	Exchange: Nasdaq (SC)
Fax: 714-557-1260	Employees: 115	Symbol: IRSN

Electrical components - microchip-stacking technology to increase the operating speed of computer systems

ISG INTERNATIONAL SOFTWARE GROUP LTD.

Industrial Park
Technion City, Haifa 32000, Israel
Phone: +972-4-324-536
Fax: +972-4-320-754

CEO: Arie Gonen
CFO: Shlomo Baumgarten
HR: —
Employees: 144

1995 Sales: $12.7 million
1-Yr. Sales Change: 188.6%
Exchange: Nasdaq
Symbol: SISGF

Computers - applications development tools (APTools, CorVision) & applications software (Mancal, Optiview)

ISI SYSTEMS, INC.

2 Tech Dr.
Andover, MA 01810
Phone: 508-682-5500
Fax: 508-686-0130

CEO: Simon N. Garneau
CFO: Martin P. Ford
HR: Lucia Valente
Employees: 550

1995 Sales: $111.7 million
1-Yr. Sales Change: —
Ownership: Subsidiary

Computers - specialized computer processing systems, services & applications software such as rating automation & insurance applications software (subsidiary of Teleglobe)

ISOCOR

3420 Ocean Park Blvd.
Santa Monica, CA 90405-3306
Phone: 310-581-8100
Fax: 310-581-8111

CEO: Andrew De Mari
CFO: Janine M. Bushman
HR: —
Employees: 187

1995 Sales: $16.5 million
1-Yr. Sales Change: 61.8%
Exchange: Nasdaq
Symbol: ICOR

Computers - open, enterprise-wide business document interchange software for corporate, government & telecom organizations

ISTAR INTERNET INC.

250 Albert St., Ste. 202
Ottawa, ON K1P 6M1, Canada
Phone: 613-780-2200
Fax: —

CEO: Rainer N. Paduch
CFO: David Ellis
HR: —
Employees: 55

1996 Sales: $14.1 million
1-Yr. Sales Change: 1,182%
Exchange: Toronto

Computers - Internet access services, including web-based products & services

IVI PUBLISHING INC.

7500 Flying Cloud Dr.
Minneapolis, MN 55344-3739
Phone: 612-996-6000
Fax: 612-966-6001

CEO: Joy A. Solomon
CFO: Thomas P. Skiba
HR: Sherri Calton
Employees: 92

1995 Sales: $12.0 million
1-Yr. Sales Change: 71.4%
Exchange: Nasdaq
Symbol: IVIP

Publishing - health & medical multimedia CD-ROMs (Mayo Clinic series)

JABIL CIRCUIT, INC.

10800 Roosevelt Blvd.
St. Petersburg, FL 33716
Phone: 813-577-9749
Fax: 813-579-8529

CEO: William D. Morean
CFO: Ronald J. Rapp
HR: Fred McCoy
Employees: 2,661

1995 Sales: $559.5 million
1-Yr. Sales Change: 48.9%
Exchange: Nasdaq
Symbol: JBIL

Electrical components - electronic circuit boards & systems for OEMs in the international PC, computer peripheral, communications & automotive markets

 See page 307 for a full profile of this company.

JACK HENRY & ASSOCIATES, INC.

663 Hwy. 60, PO Box 807
Monett, MO 65708
Phone: 417-235-6652
Fax: 417-235-8406

CEO: Michael E. Henry
CFO: Terry W. Thompson
HR: Michael R. Wallace
Employees: 332

1996 Sales: $67.6 million
1-Yr. Sales Change: 46.6%
Exchange: Nasdaq
Symbol: JKHY

Computers - outsourcing & system integration services software for the retail banking industry

J&R COMPUTER WORLD

15 Park Row
New York, NY 10038
Phone: 212-238-9000
Fax: 212-238-9191

CEO: Rachelle Friedman
CFO: Zvi Hirsch
HR: Dean Shilenok
Employees: 615

1995 Est. Sales: $150.0 mil.
1-Yr. Sales Change: 11.1%
Ownership: Privately Held

Retail - computers & peripherals

J.D. EDWARDS & COMPANY

8055 E. Tufts Ave.
Denver, CO 80237
Phone: 303-488-4000
Fax: 303-488-4678

CEO: C. Edward McVaney
CFO: Richard E. Allen
HR: Greg Dixon
Employees: 2,310

1995 Sales: $340.8 million
1-Yr. Sales Change: 41.6%
Ownership: Privately Held

Computers - business development software

JDA SOFTWARE GROUP, INC.

11811 N. Tatum Blvd., Ste. 2000
Phoenix, AZ 85028
Phone: 602-404-5500
Fax: 602-404-5520

CEO: James D. Armstrong
CFO: Thomas M. Proud
HR: Judy Wieler
Employees: 209

1995 Sales: $30.1 million
1-Yr. Sales Change: 26.5%
Exchange: Nasdaq
Symbol: JDAS

Computers - software for retailing organizations (Merchandise Management System)

JETFORM CORPORATION

560 Rochester St., Ste. 500
Ottawa, ON K1S 5K2, Canada
Phone: 613-230-3676
Fax: 613-594-8886

CEO: Abraham E. Ostrovsky
CFO: Kenneth J. Killin
HR: Rosemary Lauren
Employees: 315

1996 Sales: $31.9 million
1-Yr. Sales Change: 75.3%
Exchange: Nasdaq
Symbol: FORMF

Computers - electronic-forms software

JONES EDUCATION NETWORKS, INC.

9697 E. Mineral Ave.
Englewood, CO 80112
Phone: 303-792-3111
Fax: 303-784-8508

CEO: Glenn R. Jones
CFO: Stephanie L. Garcia
HR: —
Employees: 74

1995 Sales: $15.9 million
1-Yr. Sales Change: 59.0%
Ownership: Privately Held

TV production, programming & services - educational programming, products & services (ME/U Knowledge
TV, Jones Computer Network)

JTS CORPORATION

166 Baypointe Pkwy.
San Jose, CA 95134
Phone: 408-468-1800
Fax: 408-468-1801

CEO: Tom Mitchell
CFO: W. Virginia Walker
HR: Margaret Carey
Employees: 1,300

1996 Sales: $18.8 million
1-Yr. Sales Change: —
Exchange: AMEX
Symbol: JTS

Computers - disk drives (Nordic, Palladium); video game systems (Jaguar)

 See page 308 for a full profile of this company.

THE JUDGE GROUP, INC.

2 Bala Plaza, Ste. 800
Bala Cynwyd, PA 19004
Phone: 610-667-7700
Fax: —

CEO: Martin E. Judge Jr.
CFO: Jeffrey J. Andrews
HR: Katharin A. Wiercinski
Employees: 307

1995 Sales: $63.3 million
1-Yr. Sales Change: 39.7%
Ownership: Privately Held

Personnel - provides information technology (IT) & engineering personnel

KEANE, INC.

10 City Sq.
Boston, MA 02129-3798
Phone: 617-241-9200
Fax: 617-241-9507

CEO: John F. Keane
CFO: Wallace A. Cataldo
HR: Edward C. Sugrue
Employees: 5,338

1995 Sales: $382.7 million
1-Yr. Sales Change: 11.1%
Exchange: AMEX
Symbol: KEA

Computers - software design, integration & management services for corporations & health care facilities

KENTEK INFORMATION SYSTEMS, INC.

2945 Wilderness Place	CEO: Philip Shires	1996 Sales: $74.4 million
Boulder, CO 80301	CFO: Craig Lamborn	1-Yr. Sales Change: 6.0%
Phone: 303-440-5500	HR: Deborah Cason	Exchange: Nasdaq
Fax: 303-440-9600	Employees: 271	Symbol: KNTK

Computers - network printers & heavy-duty computers

KEY TRONIC CORPORATION

4424 N. Sullivan Rd.	CEO: Fred Wenninger	1996 Sales: $201.0 million
Spokane, WA 99216	CFO: Ronald F. Klawitter	1-Yr. Sales Change: (3.1%)
Phone: 509-928-8000	HR: Keith C. Clement	Exchange: Nasdaq
Fax: 509-927-5248	Employees: 2,824	Symbol: KTCC

Computers - keyboards (#1 independent manufacturer worldwide), including ergonomic & voice-recognition keyboards; mice (ClikMate) & input devices

 See page 309 for a full profile of this company.

KINETIKS.COM, INC.

700 Rockmead Dr., Ste. 240	CEO: Gregory S. Carr	1995 Sales: $0.0 million
Kingwood, TX 77339	CFO: James C. Waldrop	1-Yr. Sales Change: —
Phone: 713-359-7638	HR: Susan Alexander	Exchange: Nasdaq (SC)
Fax: 713-359-7915	Employees: 46	Symbol: KNET

Computers - develops and markets software programs for use on the World Wide Web offering free information to water sports enthusiasts

KINGSTON TECHNOLOGY CORPORATION

17600 Newhope St.	CEO: John Tu	1995 Sales: $1,300.0 million
Fountain Valley, CA 92708	CFO: Henri Tchen	1-Yr. Sales Change: 62.1%
Phone: 714-435-2600	HR: Daniel Hsu	Ownership: Privately Held
Fax: 714-435-2699	Employees: 450	

Computers - memory, processor & storage add-in peripherals for PCs, notebooks & laser printers; PCMCIA adapters

 See pages 130–131 for a full profile of this company.

KLA INSTRUMENTS CORPORATION

160 Rio Robles, PO Box 49055	CEO: Kenneth Levy	1996 Sales: $694.9 million
San Jose, CA 95161-9055	CFO: Robert J. Boehlke	1-Yr. Sales Change: 57.1%
Phone: 408-468-4200	HR: Virginia J. DeMars	Exchange: Nasdaq
Fax: 408-434-4266	Employees: 2,500	Symbol: KLAC

Machinery - yield-management & process-monitoring systems for semiconductor manufacturing

 See page 310 for a full profile of this company.

KLEINER PERKINS CAUFIELD & BYERS

2750 Sand Hill Rd.
Menlo Park, CA 94025
Phone: 415-233-2750
Fax: 415-233-0300

CEO: E. Floyd Kvamme
CFO: Michael S. Curry
HR: —
Employees: 14

1996 Sales: —
1-Yr. Sales Change: —
Ownership: Privately Held

Financial - venture capital investment

 See page 311 for a full profile of this company.

KNIGHT-RIDDER BUSINESS INFORMATION SERVICES

One Herald Plaza
Miami, FL 33132-1693
Phone: 305-376-3800
Fax: 305-376-3876

CEO: P. Anthony Ridder
CFO: Ross Jones
HR: Mary Jean Connors
Employees: 2,500

1995 Sales: $501.7 million
1-Yr. Sales Change: (2.4%)
Ownership: Subsidiary

Computers - archival business & professional information services (DIALOG, Data-Star & Infomart DIALOG); real-time & archival news; investor relations databases (subsidiary of Knight-Ridder)

KNOWLEDGE ADVENTURE, INC.

1311 Grand Central Ave.
Glendale, CA 91201
Phone: 818-246-4400
Fax: 818-246-5604

CEO: Larry Gross
CFO: Frank Greico
HR: —
Employees: 115

1995 Est. Sales: $39.0 mil.
1-Yr. Sales Change: 11.4%
Ownership: Privately Held

Computers - entertainment & education multimedia software (My First Encyclopedia, 3-D Dinosaur Adventure, Kid's Zoo)

KNOWLEDGEPOINT

1129 Industrial Ave.
Petaluma, CA 94952
Phone: 707-762-0333
Fax: 707-762-0802

CEO: Michael Troy
CFO: Jerri Brown
HR: Diane Pratt
Employees: 24

1995 Est. Sales: $3.0 mil.
1-Yr. Sales Change: (23.1%)
Ownership: Privately Held

Computers - personnel management (Performance Now!), job descriptions (Descriptions Now!) & employee policy manual (Policies Now!) software

KOMAG, INCORPORATED

275 S. Hillview Dr.
Milpitas, CA 95035
Phone: 408-946-2300
Fax: 408-946-1126

CEO: Stephen C. Johnson
CFO: William L. Potts Jr.
HR: —
Employees: 2,915

1995 Sales: $512.2 million
1-Yr. Sales Change: 30.5%
Exchange: Nasdaq
Symbol: KMAG

Computers - thin-film magnetic media on rigid disk platters for hard-disk drives (#1 worldwide)

 See page 312 for a full profile of this company.

KOPIN CORPORATION

695 Myles Standish Blvd.	CEO: John C. Fan	1995 Sales: $17.5 million
Taunton, MA 02780-1042	CFO: Paul J. Mitchell	1-Yr. Sales Change: 18.2%
Phone: 508-824-6696	HR: —	Exchange: Nasdaq
Fax: 508-822-1381	Employees: 89	Symbol: KOPN

Electrical components - integrated circuits & electronic-imaging devices

KRONOS INCORPORATED

460 Fifth Ave.	CEO: Mark S. Ain	1995 Sales: $120.4 million
Waltham, MA 02154	CFO: Paul A. Lacy	1-Yr. Sales Change: 29.6%
Phone: 617-890-3232	HR: Carl Lopes	Exchange: Nasdaq
Fax: 617-890-8768	Employees: 729	Symbol: KRON

Data collection & systems - workplace time, attendance & other data collection systems

KRYSTALTECH INTERNATIONAL INC.

555 W. 57th St., Ste. 1750	CEO: Dan Tochner	1995 Sales: $104.0 million
New York, NY 10017-2925	CFO: Kevin Khoo	1-Yr. Sales Change: 88.7%
Phone: 212-261-0400	HR: —	Ownership: Privately Held
Fax: 212-262-0414	Employees: 55	

Retail - computer parts & peripherals

KULICKE AND SOFFA INDUSTRIES, INC.

2101 Blair Mill Rd.	CEO: C. Scott Kulicke	1995 Sales: $304.5 million
Willow Grove, PA 19090	CFO: Clifford G. Sprague	1-Yr. Sales Change: 75.7%
Phone: 215-784-6000	HR: Mark H. Heeter	Exchange: Nasdaq
Fax: 215-659-7588	Employees: 1,876	Symbol: KLIC

Machinery - semiconductor assembly systems, including wire bonders, dicing saws & die bonders

KURZWEIL APPLIED INTELLIGENCE, INC.

411 Waverly Oaks Rd.	CEO: Thomas E. Brew Jr.	1996 Sales: $9.4 million
Waltham, MA 02154	CFO: Thomas B. Doherty	1-Yr. Sales Change: (24.2%)
Phone: 617-893-5151	HR: Michelle Roccia	Exchange: Nasdaq
Fax: 617-893-6525	Employees: 106	Symbol: KURZ

Computers - automated speech recognition systems software used to create documents & interact with computers by voice

KYOCERA CORPORATION

5-22 Kitainoue-cho, Higashino	CEO: Kensuke Itoh	1996 Sales: $5,965.0 million
Kyoto 607, Japan	CFO: Yuji Itoh	1-Yr. Sales Change: 3.9%
Phone: +81-75-592-3851	HR: —	Exchange: NYSE
Fax: +81-75-501-2194	Employees: 13,162	Symbol: KYO

Ceramics & ceramic products - ceramic integrated-circuit packaging; semiconductor parts; electronic components; optical instruments; consumer-related products

 See pages 132–133 for a full profile of this company.

LAM RESEARCH CORPORATION

4650 Cushing Pkwy.	CEO: Roger D. Emerick	1996 Sales: $1,276.9 million
Fremont, CA 94538	CFO: Henk J. Evenhuis	1-Yr. Sales Change: 57.5%
Phone: 510-659-0200	HR: Henk J. Evenhuis	Exchange: Nasdaq
Fax: 510-572-6454	Employees: 4,500	Symbol: LRCX

Machinery - semiconductor processing equipment (AutoEtch, Rainbow, TCP) for the fabrication of integrated circuits

 See page 313 for a full profile of this company.

LANDMARK GRAPHICS CORPORATION

15150 Memorial Dr.	CEO: Robert P. Peebler	1996 Sales: $187.3 million
Houston, TX 77079-4304	CFO: William H. Seippel	1-Yr. Sales Change: 9.4%
Phone: 713-560-1000	HR: Daniel L. Casaccia	Ownership: Subsidiary
Fax: 713-560-1410	Employees: 1,022	

Computers - geoscientific exploration software (CAEX) & systems for the oil & gas industry (subsidiary of Halliburton)

LANTRONIX CORPORATION

15353 Barranca Pkwy.	CEO: Brad Freeburg	1995 Est. Sales: $35.0 mil.
Irvine, CA 92718	CFO: John Gallogly	1-Yr. Sales Change: 27.3%
Phone: 714-453-3990	HR: —	Ownership: Privately Held
Fax: 714-453-3995	Employees: 60	

Computers - Ethernet connectivity products, including multiprotocol Ethernet print servers & terminal servers

LANVISION SYSTEMS, INC.

10671 Techwoods Circle	CEO: J. Brian Patsy	1996 Sales: $5.0 million
Cincinnati, OH 45242	CFO: Thomas E. Perazzo	1-Yr. Sales Change: 108.3%
Phone: 513-554-6900	HR: —	Exchange: Nasdaq
Fax: 513-769-5959	Employees: 38	Symbol: LANV

Computers - health care information access systems

LAP-TOP SUPERSTORE

600 Worcester Rd., Rte. 9	CEO: Gary Tsai	1995 Sales: $17.5 million
Natick, MA 01760	CFO: Jerry Tsai	1-Yr. Sales Change: —
Phone: 508-650-3616	HR: —	Ownership: Privately Held
Fax: 508-653-4998	Employees: 100	

Retail - IBM-compatible notebook computers & accessories, including carrying cases, PCMCIA cards & communications software

LASERMASTER TECHNOLOGIES, INC.

7156 Shady Oak Rd.	CEO: Melvin L. Masters	1996 Sales: $93.6 million
Eden Prairie, MN 55344	CFO: Randall L. Ruegg	1-Yr. Sales Change: (21.6%)
Phone: 612-941-8687	HR: Mary Paige	Exchange: Nasdaq
Fax: 612-941-8652	Employees: 417	Symbol: LMTS

Computers - wide-format digital color printers, plain-paper typesetters & chemical-free filmsetters for professional applications

LATTICE SEMICONDUCTOR CORPORATION

5555 NE Moore Ct.	CEO: Cyrus Y. Tsui	1996 Sales: $198.2 million
Hillsboro, OR 97124-6421	CFO: Rodney F. Sloss	1-Yr. Sales Change: 37.5%
Phone: 503-681-0118	HR: Terry Dols	Exchange: Nasdaq
Fax: 503-681-0347	Employees: 438	Symbol: LSCC

Electrical components - CMOS Programmable Logic Device (PLD) semiconductors & related development system software (#1 worldwide supplier)

LAWSON SOFTWARE

1300 Godward St.	CEO: William Lawson	1996 Sales: $101.4 million
Minneapolis, MN 55413	CFO: Susan Dub	1-Yr. Sales Change: 34.3%
Phone: 612-379-2633	HR: Wanda Fischer	Ownership: Privately Held
Fax: 612-379-7141	Employees: 750	

Computers - client/server business applications software, including accounting, human resources, procurement & supply chain management software

THE LEAP GROUP, INC.

22 W. Hubbard St.	CEO: R. Steven Lutterbach	1996 Sales: $8.2 million
Chicago, IL 60610	CFO: Peter Vezmar	1-Yr. Sales Change: 74.5%
Phone: 312-494-0300	HR: Nikki Fletcher	Exchange: Nasdaq
Fax: 312-494-0120	Employees: 38	Symbol: LEAP

Business services - design & implementation of brand marketing plans & advertising campaigns through traditional & new media

LEARMONTH & BURCHETT MANAGEMENT SYSTEMS PLC

1800 West Loop South, 6th Fl.
Houston, TX 77027
Phone: 713-625-9300
Fax: 713-625-9487

CEO: John P. Bantleman
CFO: Stephen E. Odom
HR: Gordon Frutiger
Employees: 279

1996 Sales: $41.2 million
1-Yr. Sales Change: 12.9%
Exchange: Nasdaq
Symbol: LBMSY

Computers - client/server management software

LEARNING TREE INTERNATIONAL

6053 W. Century Blvd.
Los Angeles, CA 90045-0028
Phone: 310-417-9700
Fax: 310-417-3418

CEO: David C. Collins
CFO: Gary R. Wright
HR: Angela Sheard
Employees: 288

1995 Sales: $78.8 million
1-Yr. Sales Change: 36.1%
Exchange: Nasdaq
Symbol: LTRE

Computers - education & training of professionals in business & government organizations responsible for
programming, updating & maintaining software

LEASING EDGE CORPORATION

6540 S. Pecos Rd., Ste. 103
Las Vegas, NV 89102
Phone: 702-454-7900
Fax: 702-454-7779

CEO: Michael F. Daniels
CFO: William J. Vargas
HR: —
Employees: 21

1995 Sales: $18.2 million
1-Yr. Sales Change: (8.5%)
Exchange: Nasdaq (SC)
Symbol: LECE

Leasing - computers, telecommunications systems, peripherals, point-of-sale systems & other
related equipment

LEASING SOLUTIONS, INC.

10 Almaden Blvd., Ste. 1500
San Jose, CA 95113-2238
Phone: 408-995-6565
Fax: 408-995-0696

CEO: Hal J. Krauter
CFO: Robert J. Kearns III
HR: Lisa Zane
Employees: 60

1995 Sales: $80.7 million
1-Yr. Sales Change: 34.3%
Exchange: Nasdaq
Symbol: LSSI

Leasing - information-processing & communications equipment, including display stations,
communications controllers, tape & disk products, printers, file servers, database machines &
personal computers

LECTRA SYSTEMES SA

B.P. 34, Chemin de Marticot
33611 Cestas Cedex, France
Phone: +33-56-68-80-00
Fax: +33-56-78-22-72

CEO: D. Harari
CFO: Jerome Viala
HR: —
Employees: 1,195

1995 Sales: $181.2 million
1-Yr. Sales Change: 16.0%
Exchange: Paris

Computers - computer-aided design (CAD/CAM systems) & manufacturing systems for use in the apparel,
footwear, upholstery & automotive industries

LEGACY SOFTWARE, INC.

8521 Reseda Blvd.	CEO: Ariella J. Lehrer	1995 Sales: $0.1 million
Northridge, CA 91324	CFO: William E. Sliney	1-Yr. Sales Change: (50.0%)
Phone: 818-885-5773	HR: Ariella J. Lehrer	Exchange: Nasdaq
Fax: 818-885-5779	Employees: 15	Symbol: LGCY

Computers - edutainment software (CAREER SIM series)

LEGATO SYSTEMS, INC.

3145 Porter Dr.	CEO: Louis C. Cole	1995 Sales: $29.8 million
Palo Alto, CA 94304	CFO: Gary L. Thompson	1-Yr. Sales Change: 81.7%
Phone: 415-812-6000	HR: Andee Treinis	Exchange: Nasdaq
Fax: 415-812-6156	Employees: 113	Symbol: LGTO

Computers - network storage management software (NetWorker)

LEVEL ONE COMMUNICATIONS, INC.

9750 Goethe Rd.	CEO: Robert Pepper	1995 Sales: $78.0 million
Sacramento, CA 95827	CFO: John Kehoe	1-Yr. Sales Change: 66.7%
Phone: 916-855-5000	HR: —	Exchange: Nasdaq
Fax: 916-854-1101	Employees: 319	Symbol: LEVL

Electrical components - transmission networking semiconductors

LEVEL 8 SYSTEMS INC.

382 Main St.	CEO: Robert R. MacDonald	1995 Sales: $10.1 million
Salem, NH 03079	CFO: Joseph J. DiZazzo	1-Yr. Sales Change: 180.6%
Phone: 603-898-9800	HR: —	Exchange: Nasdaq
Fax: 603-898-7554	Employees: 107	Symbol: LVEL

Computers - multiplatform communications software & consulting services (Level 8); manufacturing resource planning software & related support (ProfitKey); retail management software & support (Bizware)

LEXIS-NEXIS

9393 Springboro Pike	CEO: Ira Siegel	1995 Sales: $623.0 million
Miamisburg, OH 45432	CFO: Tim Davies	1-Yr. Sales Change: 12.9%
Phone: 513-865-6800	HR: Larry Fultz	Ownership: Subsidiary
Fax: 513-865-1655	Employees: 4,000	

Computers - electronic information retrieval systems (subsidiary of Reed Elsevier)

LEXMARK INTERNATIONAL GROUP, INC.

740 New Circle Rd. NW
Lexington, KY 40511
Phone: 606-232-2000
Fax: 606-232-2403

CEO: Marvin L. Mann
CFO: Gary E. Morin
HR: Kathleen E. Affeldt
Employees: 7,500

1995 Sales: $2,157.8 million
1-Yr. Sales Change: 16.5%
Exchange: NYSE
Symbol: LXK

Computers - keyboards, laser & ink-jet printers, notebook computers, electric typewriters & associated consumable supplies for the office & home markets

 See pages 134–135 for a full profile of this company.

LG GROUP

20 Yoido-dong, Yongdungpo-gu
Seoul 150, Korea
Phone: +82-2-787-5114
Fax: +82-2-787-7684

CEO: Park Su-Whan
CFO: Yeo Seong-Koo
HR: —
Employees: 20,000

1995 Sales: $13,188.5 mil.
1-Yr. Sales Change: —
Exchange: Korea

Consumer electronics, semiconductors, high-definition television (HDTV) & thin-film transistor liquid crystal displays (LCDs) for laptop computers (Goldstar); precision chemicals; synthetic resins

LIFERATE SYSTEMS, INC.

7210 Metro Blvd.
Edina, MN 55439
Phone: 612-844-0599
Fax: 612-844-0797

CEO: William W. Chorske
CFO: Bruce T. Klein
HR: Terri Pilaczynski
Employees: 12

1995 Sales: $0.2 million
1-Yr. Sales Change: 100.0%
Exchange: Nasdaq (SC)
Symbol: LRSI

Computers - database software for health care providers

LINEAR TECHNOLOGY CORPORATION

1630 McCarthy Blvd.
Milpitas, CA 95035-7487
Phone: 408-432-1900
Fax: 408-434-0507

CEO: Robert H. Swanson Jr.
CFO: Paul Coghlan
HR: Steve Marcey
Employees: 1,638

1996 Sales: $377.8 million
1-Yr. Sales Change: 42.6%
Exchange: Nasdaq
Symbol: LLTC

Electrical components - standard linear integrated circuits for telecommunications equipment, notebook & desktop computers, video & multimedia & computer peripherals

 See page 314 for a full profile of this company.

LIUSKI INTERNATIONAL, INC.

6585 Crescent Dr.
Norcross, GA 30071
Phone: 770-447-9454
Fax: 770-447-8266

CEO: Morries Liu
CFO: Mark Rafuse
HR: Mark Rafuse
Employees: 516

1995 Sales: $395.1 million
1-Yr. Sales Change: 8.2%
Exchange: Nasdaq
Symbol: LSKI

Retail - wholesale peripherals; PC manufacturing (Magitronic)

 See page 315 for a full profile of this company.

LOGAL EDUCATIONAL SOFTWARE AND SYSTEMS, LTD.

125 Cambridge Park Dr.	CEO: Yoel Givol	1995 Sales: $5.1 million
Cambridge, MA 02140	CFO: Aharon Ben-Nun	1-Yr. Sales Change: 142.9%
Phone: 617-491-4440	HR: Milt Bunker	Exchange: Nasdaq
Fax: 617-491-5855	Employees: 80	Symbol: LOGLF

Computers - interactive educational software & laboratory probeware for science & math curricula in high schools & colleges

LOGIC DEVICES INCORPORATED

628 E. Evelyn Ave.	CEO: William J. Volz	1995 Sales: $16.6 million
Sunnyvale, CA 94086	CFO: Todd J. Ashford	1-Yr. Sales Change: 23.0%
Phone: 408-737-3300	HR: Todd J. Ashford	Exchange: Nasdaq
Fax: 408-733-7690	Employees: 49	Symbol: LOGC

Electrical components - digital integrated circuits for computers, video image processing, medical instrumentation, telecommunications & military signal processing applications

LOGIC WORKS, INC.

111 Campus Dr.	CEO: Benjamin C. Cohen	1995 Sales: $30.7 million
Princeton, NJ 08540	CFO: Mark S. Finkel	1-Yr. Sales Change: 130.8%
Phone: 609-514-1177	HR: —	Exchange: Nasdaq
Fax: 609-252-1175	Employees: 162	Symbol: LGWX

Computers - client/server database design & business-process modeling software (ERwin, BPwin)

LOGISTIX

48021 Warm Springs Blvd.	CEO: Stephen Weinstein	1996 Sales: $290.0 million
Fremont, CA 94539	CFO: Dan DePalma	1-Yr. Sales Change: 31.0%
Phone: 510-656-8000	HR: Frank Schneider	Ownership: Privately Held
Fax: 510-438-9486	Employees: 611	

Computers - supply-based services for computers & software

LOGITECH INTERNATIONAL SA

Moulin-du-Choc	CEO: Daniel Borel	1996 Sales: $355.0 million
1122 Romanel-sur-Morges, Switzerland	CFO: Bary Zwarenstein	1-Yr. Sales Change: 17.2%
Phone: +41-21-863-51-11	HR: Marianne Jackson	Exchange: Zurich
Fax: +41-21-863-53-11	Employees: 2,322	

Computers - mice (#1 worldwide), trackballs, pens, joysticks, scanners (Handscanner) & sound products (AudioMan, SoundMan); digital video cameras

 See pages 136–137 for a full profile of this company.

LONE STAR EVALUATION LABORATORIES

Rte. 2
Georgetown, TX 78626
Phone: 512-746-2251
Fax: —

CEO: Ed Curry
CFO: Ed Curry
HR: —
Employees: 3

1995 Est. Sales: $0.8 mil.
1-Yr. Sales Change: —
Ownership: Privately Held

Computers - software that performs security tests on a computer's microprocessor & surrounding chips

LORONIX INFORMATION SYSTEMS, INC.

820 Airport Rd.
Durango, CO 81301
Phone: 970-259-6161
Fax: 970-259-9399

CEO: M. Dean Gilliam
CFO: Jonathan C. Lupia
HR: Lolita Powers
Employees: 70

1995 Sales: $6.8 million
1-Yr. Sales Change: 1.5%
Exchange: Nasdaq
Symbol: LORX

Computers - digital identification & video image management systems software for access control, security, retail point-of-sale, human resource management & other control systems

LOTUS DEVELOPMENT CORPORATION

55 Cambridge Pkwy.
Cambridge, MA 02142
Phone: 617-577-8500
Fax: 617-693-1299

CEO: Michael D. Zisman
CFO: J. Philip Dellasega
HR: —
Employees: 6,000

1995 Sales: $1,150.0 million
1-Yr. Sales Change: 18.5%
Ownership: Subsidiary

Computers - spreadsheet (1-2-3), graphics (Freelance), communications (cc:Mail, Notes) & word processing (Ami Pro) software (subsidiary of IBM)

 See pages 138–139 for a full profile of this company.

LSI LOGIC CORPORATION

1551 McCarthy Blvd.
Milpitas, CA 95035
Phone: 408-433-8000
Fax: 408-434-7715

CEO: Wilfred J. Corrigan
CFO: Albert A. Pimentel
HR: Lewis C. Wallbridge
Employees: 3,870

1995 Sales: $1,267.7 million
1-Yr. Sales Change: 40.6%
Exchange: NYSE
Symbol: LSI

Electrical components - application-specific integrated circuits

 See pages 140–141 for a full profile of this company.

LTX CORPORATION

LTX Park at University Ave.
Westwood, MA 02090
Phone: 617-461-1000
Fax: 617-329-8836

CEO: Roger W. Blethen
CFO: John J. Arcari
HR: Richard Bove
Employees: 944

1996 Sales: $266.5 million
1-Yr. Sales Change: 26.7%
Exchange: Nasdaq
Symbol: LTXX

Electronics - semiconductor test equipment for use by the computer, communications, automotive & consumer electronics industries

LUCASARTS ENTERTAINMENT COMPANY

PO Box 10307	CEO: Jack Sorensen	1995 Est. Sales: $130.0 mil.
San Rafael, CA 94912	CFO: Tom McCarthy	1-Yr. Sales Change: 4.0%
Phone: 415-472-3400	HR: Karen Chelini	Ownership: Privately Held
Fax: 415-662-2460	Employees: 230	

Computers - film production & interactive games software (The Dig, Rebel Assault II, Full Throttle, Indiana Jones)

LYCOS, INC.

293 Boston Post Rd. West	CEO: Robert J. Davis	1995 Sales: $0.0 million
Marlborough, MA 01752	CFO: Edward M. Philip	1-Yr. Sales Change: —
Phone: 508-229-0717	HR: Jon Gilthwell	Exchange: Nasdaq
Fax: 508-229-2866	Employees: 28	Symbol: LCOS

Computers - World Wide Web search service (Lycos Catalog), web site reviews (Point Reviews) & directory of popular web sites (a2z Directory)

MA LABORATORIES

1972 Concourse Dr.	CEO: Abraham Ma	1995 Sales: $497.6 million
San Jose, CA 95131	CFO: Ricky Chao	1-Yr. Sales Change: —
Phone: 408-954-8886	HR: Grace Lee	Ownership: Privately Held
Fax: 408-954-0944	Employees: 200	

Computers - memory modules, CPUs & hard disk drives

COMPAGNIE DES MACHINES BULL SA

68, route de Versailles	CEO: Jean-Marie Descarpentries	1995 Sales: $5,440.0 million
78430 Louveciennes, France	CFO: Camille de Montalivet	1-Yr. Sales Change: (3.0%)
Phone: +33-1-39-66-60-60	HR: Cecile Wright	Exchange: OTC
Fax: +33-1-46-96-90-92	Employees: 24,000	Symbol: CODMY

Computers - mainframes, microcomputers & peripherals

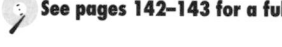 **See pages 142–143 for a full profile of this company.**

THE MACNEAL-SCHWENDLER CORPORATION

815 Colorado Blvd.	CEO: Thomas C. Curry	1996 Sales: $130.5 million
Los Angeles, CA 90041-1777	CFO: Louis A. Greco	1-Yr. Sales Change: 29.6%
Phone: 213-258-9111	HR: Lois Crum	Exchange: NYSE
Fax: 213-259-3838	Employees: 625	Symbol: MNS

Computers - mechanical computer-aided engineering (MCAE) software (#1 worldwide)

MACRO 4 PLC

The Orangery, Turners Hill Rd., Worth
Crawley, West Sussex RH10 4SS, UK
Phone: +44-1-293-886-060
Fax: +44-1-293-886-254

CEO: A. J. Staples
CFO: M. R. Smith
HR: —
Employees: 188

1996 Sales: $40.3 million
1-Yr. Sales Change: 1.0%
Exchange: London

Computers - systems software for IBM & IBM-compatible mainframe & mid-range computers

MACROMEDIA, INC.

600 Townsend St.
San Francisco, CA 94103
Phone: 415-252-2000
Fax: 415-626-0554

CEO: John C. Colligan
CFO: Richard B. Wood
HR: Denise Minaberry
Employees: 396

1996 Sales: $116.7 million
1-Yr. Sales Change: 117.3%
Exchange: Nasdaq
Symbol: MACR

Computers - multimedia software tools (Director, FreeHand, Authorware, Extreme 3D)

 See page 316 for a full profile of this company.

MACRONIX INTERNATIONAL CO., LTD.

No. 3, Creation Rd. III
Hsin Chu, Taiwan
Phone: +886-35-788-888
Fax: —

CEO: Miin Wu
CFO: —
HR: —
Employees: 1,754

1995 Sales: $324.9 million
1-Yr. Sales Change: 56.1%
Exchange: Nasdaq
Symbol: MXICY

Electrical components - nonvolatile memory integrated circuits & mask ROM, EPROM & flash memory
products; audio, network, clock generator & graphic applications devices

MACROTRON AG

Stahlgruberring 28
D-81829 Munich, Germany
Phone: +49-89-420-80
Fax: +49-89-42-95-63

CEO: M. Kaack
CFO: R. Grimm
HR: —
Employees: 500

1995 Sales: $504.0 million
1-Yr. Sales Change: (0.3%)
Exchange: Frankfurt

Retail - wholesale computer products; industrial & testing equipment

MACTEMPS, INC.

54 Church St., Harvard Sq.
Cambridge, MA 02138
Phone: 617-868-6800
Fax: 617-868-6820

CEO: John Chuang
CFO: Nunzio Domilici
HR: Michael Smith
Employees: 8,000

1995 Est. Sales: $60.0 mil.
1-Yr. Sales Change: 42.9%
Ownership: Privately Held

Personnel - temporary employment services for the computer-literate

MADGE NETWORKS N.V.

Polaris Ave. 23
NL-2132 JH Hoofddorp, The Netherlands
Phone: +31-2356-855-24
Fax: +31-2356-855-27

CEO: Robert H. Madge
CFO: Kevin R. Evins
HR: Ivy Ang
Employees: 1,473

1995 Sales: $402.0 million
1-Yr. Sales Change: 88.5%
Exchange: Nasdaq
Symbol: MADGF

Computers - end-to-end switched LAN & WAN solutions for large enterprises integrating data, voice & video across their networks

 See page 317 for a full profile of this company.

MAGIC SOFTWARE ENTERPRISES LTD.

5 Haplada St.
Or Yehuda 60218, Israel
Phone: +972-3-538-9292
Fax: +972-3-7538-9393

CEO: David Assia
CFO: Elan Penn
HR: Yohai Shaked
Employees: 265

1995 Sales: $25.4 million
1-Yr. Sales Change: 18.7%
Exchange: OTC
Symbol: MGICF

Computers - software development tools

MAGNETEK, INC.

26 Century Blvd., PO Box 290159
Nashville, TN 37229-0159
Phone: 615-316-5100
Fax: 615-316-5181

CEO: Ronald N. Hoge
CFO: David P. Reiland
HR: Don Shuster
Employees: 13,000

1996 Sales: $1,161.6 million
1-Yr. Sales Change: (3.4%)
Exchange: NYSE
Symbol: MAG

Electrical products - fluorescent light ballasts, motors, capacitors, uninterruptible power supplies, wire & other electrical products, motors & control systems

MAI SYSTEMS CORPORATION

9600 Jeronimo Rd.
Irvine, CA 92718
Phone: 714-580-0700
Fax: 714-580-2378

CEO: Richard S. Ressler
CFO: Brian W. Kretzmer
HR: Cheryl Moreno
Employees: 630

1995 Sales: $66.3 million
1-Yr. Sales Change: 0.3%
Exchange: AMEX
Symbol: NOW

Computers - information systems, primarily for the gaming & hospitality industries

M.A.I.D PLC

The Comm. Bldg., 48 Leicester Sq.
London WC2H 7DB, UK
Phone: +44-171-930-6900
Fax: +44-171-930-6006

CEO: Daniel M. Wagner
CFO: David G. Mattey
HR: —
Employees: 166

1995 Sales: $20.0 million
1-Yr. Sales Change: 55.0%
Exchange: Nasdaq
Symbol: MAIDY

Computers - online distribution of business information, market research reports, company statistics, stockbroker research analyses & stock market & commodity prices

MANAGED CARE SOLUTIONS, INC.

2510 W. Dunlap
Phoenix, AZ 85021
Phone: 602-943-5660
Fax: 602-943-5512

CEO: Blaine Bergeson
CFO: Michael J. Kennedy
HR: Rita Console
Employees: 306

1996 Sales: $23.2 million
1-Yr. Sales Change: (31.4%)
Exchange: Nasdaq
Symbol: MCSX

Computers - clinical & financial information access software for health-care professionals

MANAGEMENT TECHNOLOGIES, INC.

335 Madison Ave.
New York, NY 10017
Phone: 212-557-0022
Fax: 212-557-6967

CEO: Paul Ekon
CFO: Arthur Milton
HR: Maria Gutierrez
Employees: 223

1996 Sales: $21.3 million
1-Yr. Sales Change: 13.9%
Exchange: Nasdaq (SC)
Symbol: MTCI

Computers - standard international banking applications software packages for DEC computer systems & those using the UNIX operating system

MANATRON, INC.

2970 S. Ninth St.
Kalamazoo, MI 49009
Phone: 616-375-5300
Fax: 616-375-9826

CEO: Paul R. Sylvester
CFO: Paul R. Sylvester
HR: Mary Gephart
Employees: 258

1996 Sales: $23.9 million
1-Yr. Sales Change: (3.6%)
Exchange: Nasdaq
Symbol: MANA

Data collection & systems - computer-based data processing systems, primarily for city, county, and state government agencies

MANCHESTER EQUIPMENT CO., INC.

160 Oser Ave.
New York, NY 11788
Phone: 516-435-1199
Fax: 516-435-2113

CEO: Barry R. Steinberg
CFO: Joseph Looney
HR: Brian Milack
Employees: 222

1996 Sales: $189.7 million
1-Yr. Sales Change: 11.1%
Ownership: Privately Held

Computers - hardware, software & networking products

MANUGISTICS GROUP, INC.

2115 E. Jefferson St.
Rockville, MD 20852-4999
Phone: 301-984-5000
Fax: 301-984-5370

CEO: William M. Gibson
CFO: Peter Q. Repetti
HR: Carl Di Pietro
Employees: 499

1996 Sales: $62.3 million
1-Yr. Sales Change: 26.1%
Exchange: Nasdaq
Symbol: MANU

Computers - supply chain management software to monitor & control manufacturing operations

MAPINFO CORPORATION

One Global View	CEO: Brian D. Owen	1995 Sales: $40.0 million
Troy, NY 12180	CFO: D. Joseph Gersuk	1-Yr. Sales Change: 34.7%
Phone: 518-285-6000	HR: Joseph Clement	Exchange: Nasdaq
Fax: 518-285-7060	Employees: 298	Symbol: MAPS

Computers - desktop mapping software (MapInfo)

MARCAM CORPORATION

95 Wells Ave.	CEO: Michael Quinlan	1995 Sales: $202.3 million
Newton, MA 02159	CFO: George A. Chamberlain III	1-Yr. Sales Change: 17.0%
Phone: 617-965-0220	HR: Heidi Johnson	Exchange: Nasdaq
Fax: 617-965-7273	Employees: 1,093	Symbol: MCAM

Computers - business planning & control software (PRISM, MAPICS, Protean) & services for manufacturing & distribution companies to track production, logistics, maintenance & financial functions

MARIMBA, INC.

445 Sherman Ave.	CEO: Kim Polese	1995 Sales: $0.0 million
Palo Alto, CA 94306	CFO: —	1-Yr. Sales Change: —
Phone: 415-328-5282	HR: —	Ownership: Privately Held
Fax: 415-328-5295	Employees: —	

Computers - Java-based web development & content delivery tools

MARKET GUIDE INC.

2001 Marcus Ave., Ste. South 200	CEO: Homi M. Byramji	1996 Sales: $4.0 million
Lake Success, NY 11042-1011	CFO: Lewis Leonardi	1-Yr. Sales Change: 48.1%
Phone: 516-327-2400	HR: Angela Dimaggio	Exchange: OTC
Fax: 516-327-2425	Employees: 58	Symbol: MARG

Publishing - financial database software and online service that includes financial information for more than 7,300 publicly traded companies

MARSHALL INDUSTRIES

9320 Telstar Ave.	CEO: Robert Rodin	1996 Sales: $1,164.8 million
El Monte, CA 91731-2895	CFO: Henry W. Chin	1-Yr. Sales Change: 15.4%
Phone: 818-307-6000	HR: Les Jones	Exchange: NYSE
Fax: 818-307-6292	Employees: 1,440	Symbol: MI

Electronics - distribution of industrial electronic components, including semiconductors, passive components, connectors & interconnect products, computer systems & peripheral products

MATHSOFT, INC.

101 Main St.
Cambridge, MA 02142-1519
Phone: 617-577-1017
Fax: 617-577-8829

CEO: Charles J. Digate
CFO: Robert P. Orlando
HR: Melisa Kahler
Employees: 118

1996 Sales: $20.8 million
1-Yr. Sales Change: 30.0%
Exchange: Nasdaq
Symbol: MATH

Computers - technical software (Mathcad) & electronic books

MATTSON TECHNOLOGY, INC.

3550 W. Warren Ave.
Fremont, CA 94538
Phone: 510-657-5900
Fax: 510-657-0165

CEO: Brad Mattson
CFO: Richard S. Mora
HR: Sowji Reddy
Employees: 270

1995 Sales: $55.3 million
1-Yr. Sales Change: 182.1%
Exchange: Nasdaq
Symbol: MTSN

Machinery - semiconductor manufacturing equipment

MAXIM INTEGRATED PRODUCTS, INC.

120 San Gabriel Dr.
Sunnyvale, CA 94086
Phone: 408-737-7600
Fax: 408-737-7194

CEO: John F. Gifford
CFO: Michael J. Byrd
HR: Patrick Murray
Employees: 1,987

1996 Sales: $421.6 million
1-Yr. Sales Change: 68.1%
Exchange: Nasdaq
Symbol: MXIM

Electrical components - analog integrated circuits

MAXIMUM STRATEGY, INC.

801 Buckeye Ct.
Milpitas, CA 95035-7408
Phone: 408-383-1600
Fax: 408-383-1616

CEO: Del Masters
CFO: Nadine W. Priestley
HR: Pat Russ
Employees: 36

1995 Sales: $14.1 million
1-Yr. Sales Change: 48.4%
Ownership: Privately Held

Computers - storage systems (Gen5) & file servers (proFILE)

MAXIS, INC.

2121 N. California Blvd., Ste. 600
Walnut Creek, CA 94596-3572
Phone: 510-933-5630
Fax: 510-927-3736

CEO: Samuel L. Poole
CFO: Fred M. Gerson
HR: Deborah L. Gross
Employees: 210

1996 Sales: $55.4 million
1-Yr. Sales Change: 45.4%
Exchange: Nasdaq
Symbol: MXIS

Computers - entertainment & educational software (SimTower, SimCity 2000, SimTown)

 See page 318 for a full profile of this company.

MCAFEE ASSOCIATES, INC.

2710 Walsh Ave., Ste. 200	CEO: William L. Larson	1995 Sales: $90.1 million
Santa Clara, CA 95051	CFO: Prabhat Goyal	1-Yr. Sales Change: 173.9%
Phone: 408-988-3832	HR: Robert J. Schwei	Exchange: Nasdaq
Fax: 408-970-9727	Employees: 250	Symbol: MCAF

Computers - anti-virus software distributed through electronic online bulletin board services; utility software including LAN management software (Saber LAN Workstation)

 See page 319 for a full profile of this company.

MCI SYSTEMHOUSE INC.

50 O'Conner St., Ste. 501	CEO: John R. Oltman	1995 Sales: $892.9 million
Ottawa, ON K1P 6L2, Canada	CFO: William W. Linton	1-Yr. Sales Change: 5.2%
Phone: 613-236-1428	HR: Douglas A. Fumagalli	Ownership: Subsidiary
Fax: 613-563-9896	Employees: 5,189	

Computers - outsourcing & system design services for large computer systems (subsidiary of MCI)

MDL INFORMATION SYSTEMS, INC.

14600 Catalina St.	CEO: Steven D. Goldby	1996 Sales: $61.5 million
San Leandro, CA 94577	CFO: John J. Hanlon	1-Yr. Sales Change: 20.6%
Phone: 510-895-1313	HR: Dan E. Kingman	Exchange: Nasdaq
Fax: 510-614-3622	Employees: 361	Symbol: MDLI

Computers - scientific information management software, chemical information databases & related services for the pharmaceutical, biotechnology, agrochemical & chemical industries

MDY ADVANCED TECHNOLOGIES INC.

21-00 Rte. 208 South	CEO: Galina Datskovsky	1995 Sales: $6.0 million
Fair Lawn, NJ 07410-2605	CFO: David Stott	1-Yr. Sales Change: 50.0%
Phone: 201-797-6676	HR: Roy Strunin	Ownership: Privately Held
Fax: 201-797-6852	Employees: 30	

Computers - consulting, development & network integration

MECHANICAL DYNAMICS, INC.

2301 Commonwealth Blvd.	CEO: M. E. Korybalski	1995 Sales: $21.3 million
Ann Arbor, MI 48105	CFO: James E. Vincke	1-Yr. Sales Change: 30.7%
Phone: 313-994-3800	HR: Linda Moore	Exchange: Nasdaq
Fax: 313-994-6418	Employees: 144	Symbol: MDII

Computers - virtual prototyping software that allows a designer or engineer to design a product by visually & mathematically simulating a product in motion

MECKLERMEDIA CORPORATION

20 Ketchum St.	CEO: Alan M. Meckler	1995 Sales: $14.5 million
Westport, CT 06880	CFO: Christopher S. Cardell	1-Yr. Sales Change: 74.7%
Phone: 203-226-6967	HR: —	Exchange: Nasdaq (SC)
Fax: 203-454-5840	Employees: 80	Symbol: MECK

Publishing - magazines (Internet World, Web Developer, Web Week), books & newspapers , trade shows & seminars

 See page 320 for a full profile of this company.

MECON INC.

200 Porter Dr., Ste. 100	CEO: Vasu R. Devan	1996 Sales: $12.0 million
San Ramon, CA 94583	CFO: David J. Allinson	1-Yr. Sales Change: 34.8%
Phone: 510-838-1700	HR: Judy Axtman	Exchange: Nasdaq
Fax: 510-838-0494	Employees: 101	Symbol: MECN

Computers - operations benchmarking data, information products & decision support software & consulting services for the hospital industry

MEDIA LOGIC, INC.

310 South St.	CEO: William E. Davis Jr.	1996 Sales: $3.6 million
Plainville, MA 02762	CFO: Paul M. O'Brien	1-Yr. Sales Change: (37.9%)
Phone: 508-695-2006	HR: —	Exchange: AMEX
Fax: 508-695-8593	Employees: 74	Symbol: TST

Electronics - certification & evaluation equipment for flexible computer storage media such as floppy disks & magnetic tape

MEDIC COMPUTER SYSTEMS, INC.

8601 Six Forks Rd.	CEO: John P. McConnell	1995 Sales: $143.2 million
Raleigh, NC 27615-2965	CFO: Luanne L. Roth	1-Yr. Sales Change: 33.6%
Phone: 919-847-8102	HR: Jan Guy	Exchange: Nasdaq
Fax: 919-846-1555	Employees: 952	Symbol: MCSY

Computers - business software for physicians' offices

MEDICUS SYSTEMS CORPORATION

One Rotary Ctr., Ste. 400	CEO: Richard C. Jelinek	1996 Sales: $31.1 million
Evanston, IL 60201	CFO: William W. Cowan	1-Yr. Sales Change: (8.0%)
Phone: 847-570-7500	HR: Mary Stewart	Exchange: Nasdaq
Fax: 847-570-7518	Employees: 306	Symbol: MECS

Computers - decision-support software for the health care industry

MEDIRISK, INC.

3565 Piedmont Rd. NE	CEO: Mark A. Kaiser	1995 Sales: $3.7 million
Atlanta, GA 30305-1502	CFO: Kenneth M. Goins Jr.	1-Yr. Sales Change: 27.6%
Phone: 404-364-6700	HR: Lois Rickard	Ownership: Privately Held
Fax: 404-364-6710	Employees: 109	

Computers - databases & related decision-support software & analytical services for the health care industry

MEDIWARE INFORMATION SYSTEMS, INC.

1121 Old Walt Whitman Rd.	CEO: John Frieberg	1995 Sales: $8.1 million
Melville, NY 11747-3005	CFO: Patty Schwartz	1-Yr. Sales Change: (2.4%)
Phone: 516-423-7800	HR: —	Exchange: Nasdaq (SC)
Fax: 516-423-0161	Employees: 72	Symbol: MEDW

Computers - computer-based management information systems for use in various clinical departments of hospitals

MEMC ELECTRONIC MATERIALS, INC.

501 Pearl Dr.	CEO: Roger D. McDaniel	1995 Sales: $886.9 million
St. Peters, MO 63376	CFO: James M. Stolze	1-Yr. Sales Change: 34.2%
Phone: 314-279-5500	HR: Huston E. Sherrill	Exchange: NYSE
Fax: 314-279-5161	Employees: 6,400	Symbol: WFR

Electrical components - silicon wafers used in the production of semiconductors

MEMOREX TELEX N.V.

545 E. John Carpenter Fwy.	CEO: Peter H. Dailey	1996 Sales: $834.1 million
Irving , TX 75062-3931	CFO: David J. Faulkner	1-Yr. Sales Change: (8.3%)
Phone: 972-444-3500	HR: Peg O'Neal	Exchange: Nasdaq
Fax: 972-444-3501	Employees: 4,100	Symbol: MEMXY

Computers - systems integration & data storage

 **See page 321 for a full profile of this company.**

MENLO VENTURES

3000 Sand Hill Rd., Bldg. 4, Ste. 100	CEO: Douglas C. Carlisle	1996 Sales: —
Menlo Park, CA 94025	CFO: Catherine Shaw	1-Yr. Sales Change: —
Phone: 415-854-8540	HR: —	Ownership: Privately Held
Fax: 415-854-7059	Employees: 10	

Financial - venture capital investment

MENTOR GRAPHICS CORPORATION

8005 SW Boeckman Rd.
Wilsonville, OR 97070-7777
Phone: 503-685-7000
Fax: 503-685-1202

CEO: Walden C. Rhines
CFO: R. Douglas Norby
HR: Frank S. Delia
Employees: 2,039

1995 Sales: $384.5 million
1-Yr. Sales Change: 10.4%
Exchange: Nasdaq
Symbol: MENT

Computers - electronic design automation software

 **See page 322 for a full profile of this company.**

MERCURY INTERACTIVE CORPORATION

470 Potrero Ave.
Sunnyvale, CA 95086
Phone: 408-523-9900
Fax: 408-523-9911

CEO: Aryeh Finegold
CFO: Sharlene Abrams
HR: Betty Hardonag
Employees: 296

1995 Sales: $39.5 million
1-Yr. Sales Change: 68.1%
Exchange: Nasdaq
Symbol: MERQ

Computers - testing & quality assurance software

MERIDIAN DATA, INC.

5615 Scotts Valley Dr.
Scotts Valley, CA 95066
Phone: 408-438-3100
Fax: 408-438-6816

CEO: Gianluca U. Rattazzi
CFO: Erik E. Miller
HR: Kathy Freeman
Employees: 88

1995 Sales: $25.3 million
1-Yr. Sales Change: 328.8%
Exchange: Nasdaq
Symbol: MDCD

Computers - CD-ROM network software & hardware

MERISEL, INC.

200 Continental Blvd.
El Segundo, CA 90245-0948
Phone: 310-615-3080
Fax: 310-615-1270

CEO: Dwight A. Steffensen
CFO: James E. Ilson
HR: Carol Baker
Employees: 3,263

1995 Sales: $5,957.0 million
1-Yr. Sales Change: 18.7%
Exchange: Nasdaq
Symbol: MSEL

Retail - wholesale microcomputer hardware & software products

See pages 144–145 for a full profile of this company.

MERIX CORPORATION

1521 Poplar Ln.
Forest Grove, OR 97116
Phone: 503-359-9300
Fax: 800-525-5769

CEO: Deborah A. Coleman
CFO: Joseph H. Howell
HR: Terri L. Timberman
Employees: 889

1996 Sales: $155.6 million
1-Yr. Sales Change: 53.5%
Exchange: Nasdaq
Symbol: MERX

Electrical components - electronic interconnect products including printed circuit boards & integrated circuits

MERKANTILDATA AS

Sinsenvn 47B, PO Box 76 Refstad
N-0513 Oslo, Norway
Phone: +47-22-71-05-50
Fax: +47-22-15-84-33

CEO: Magne Storvik
CFO: C. E. Wollebekk
HR: —
Employees: 640

1995 Sales: $221.5 million
1-Yr. Sales Change: 114.4%
Exchange: Oslo

Computers - systems integration between different networks, operating systems & hardware platforms;
marketing of applications & consulting services

META GROUP, INC.

208 Harbor Dr.
Stamford, CT 06912-0061
Phone: 203-973-6713
Fax: 203-359-8066

CEO: Dale Kutnick
CFO: Bernard F. Denoyer
HR: Denise Ritchie
Employees: 194

1995 Sales: $29.6 million
1-Yr. Sales Change: 57.4%
Exchange: Nasdaq
Symbol: METG

Business services - independent market assessment company, focusing on the computer, communications
& related IT industries

METAMOR TECHNOLOGIES LTD

One N. Franklin, Ste. 1500
Chicago, IL 60606
Phone: 312-638-2667
Fax: 312-251-2998

CEO: Irv Shapiro
CFO: Stan Shapiro
HR: Marcie Newman
Employees: 176

1995 Sales: $13.0 million
1-Yr. Sales Change: 64.6%
Ownership: Privately Held

Computers - systems integration

META-SOFTWARE, INC.

1300 White Oaks Rd.
Campbell, CA 95008
Phone: 408-369-5400
Fax: 408-371-5638

CEO: Shawn M. Hailey
CFO: William C. Smith
HR: Linda Gunther
Employees: 111

1995 Sales: $25.3 million
1-Yr. Sales Change: 28.4%
Exchange: Nasdaq
Symbol: MESW

Computers - simulation & library generation software products for use in integrated circuit design
(HSPICE, MASTER Toolbox)

METATEC CORPORATION

7001 Metatec Blvd.
Dublin, OH 43017
Phone: 614-761-2000
Fax: 614-761-4258

CEO: Jeffrey M. Wilkins
CFO: William H. Largent
HR: Barry Rellaford
Employees: 340

1995 Sales: $39.3 million
1-Yr. Sales Change: 36.0%
Exchange: Nasdaq
Symbol: META

Business services - CD-ROM products & services, including optical disk manufacturing facilities & software
development services for companies with CD-ROM applications

METATOOLS, INC.

6303 Carpinteria Ave.
Carpinteria, CA 93013
Phone: 805-566-6200
Fax: 805-566-6385

CEO: John J. Wilczak
CFO: Terry Kinninger
HR: Kari Zeni
Employees: 100

1995 Sales: $17.6 million
1-Yr. Sales Change: 79.6%
Exchange: Nasdaq
Symbol: MTLS

Computers - graphics (Kai's Power Tools)

METRICOM, INC.

980 University Ave.
Los Gatos, CA 95030-2375
Phone: 408-399-8200
Fax: 408-354-1024

CEO: Robert P. Dilworth
CFO: William D. Swain
HR: Chris Millard
Employees: 200

1995 Sales: $5.8 million
1-Yr. Sales Change: (73.1%)
Exchange: Nasdaq
Symbol: MCOM

Telecommunications equipment - wide area wireless data communication networks

METROLOGIC INSTRUMENTS, INC.

Coles Rd. at Rte. 42
Blackwood, NJ 08012
Phone: 609-228-8100
Fax: 609-228-6673

CEO: C. Harry Knowles
CFO: Thomas E. Mills IV
HR: John Patten
Employees: 303

1995 Sales: $41.6 million
1-Yr. Sales Change: 15.6%
Exchange: Nasdaq
Symbol: MTLG

Optical character recognition - bar code scanning equipment

METROWERKS, INC.

1500 du College, Ste. 210
St. Laurent, Quebec H4L 5G6, Canada
Phone: 604-688-6955
Fax: —

CEO: Gregory Galanos
CFO: Jim Welch
HR: —
Employees: 55

1995 Sales: $5.1 million
1-Yr. Sales Change: 155.0%
Exchange: Nasdaq
Symbol: MTWKF

Computers - software (CodeWarrier) for Macintosh computers

METTERS INDUSTRIES INC.

8200 Greensboro Dr., Ste. 500
McLean, VA 22102
Phone: 703-821-3300
Fax: 703-821-3996

CEO: Samuel Metters
CFO: Eugene Lynch
HR: —
Employees: 475

1995 Sales: $41.9 million
1-Yr. Sales Change: —
Ownership: Privately Held

Computers - systems engineering; software development

MIAMI COMPUTER SUPPLY CORPORATION

3884 Indian Ripple Rd.
Dayton, OH 45440
Phone: 937-429-5211
Fax: 937-429-2085

CEO: Albert L. Schwarz
CFO: Michael E. Peppel
HR: Rosie Fox
Employees: 118

1995 Sales: $43.3 million
1-Yr. Sales Change: 21.3%
Ownership: Privately Held

Computers - computer & office automation supplies & accessories distribution

MICREL, INCORPORATED

1849 Fortune Dr.
San Jose, CA 95131
Phone: 408-944-0800
Fax: 408-944-0970

CEO: Raymond D. Zinn
CFO: Robert J. Barker
HR: Barbara Jenkins
Employees: 344

1995 Sales: $53.0 million
1-Yr. Sales Change: 47.6%
Exchange: Nasdaq
Symbol: MCRL

Electrical components - analog integrated circuits

MICRION CORPORATION

One Corporation Way
Peabody, MA 01960-7990
Phone: 508-531-6464
Fax: 508-531-9648

CEO: Nicholas P. Economou
CFO: David M. Hunter
HR: Sheryl Cherry
Employees: 211

1996 Sales: $39.5 million
1-Yr. Sales Change: 37.2%
Exchange: Nasdaq (SC)
Symbol: MICN

Electronics - focused-ion-beam systems that locate problems during semiconductor production

MICRO COMPONENT TECHNOLOGY, INC.

3850 N. Victoria St.
St. Paul, MN 55126
Phone: 612-482-5100
Fax: 612-482-6492

CEO: Roger E. Gower
CFO: David M. Sugishita
HR: —
Employees: 165

1996 Sales: $22.3 million
1-Yr. Sales Change: (5.5%)
Exchange: Nasdaq (SC)
Symbol: MCTI

Electronics - automated test equipment for semiconductors

MICRO ELECTRONICS INC.

4119 Leap Rd.
Hilliard, OH 43026
Phone: 614-850-3000
Fax: 614-850-3001

CEO: Dale Brown
CFO: James Koehler
HR: Deanna Lyon
Employees: 1,800

1995 Est. Sales: $930.0 mil.
1-Yr. Sales Change: 19.2%
Ownership: Privately Held

Retail - computers (Micro Center); notebook (WinBook) & desktop (PowerSpec) computers;
training services

 See page 323 for a full profile of this company.

MICRO FOCUS GROUP

Speed Ct., 7 Oxford Rd.
Newbury, Berkshire RG14 1PB, UK
Phone: +44-1-635-32646
Fax: +44-1-635-33966

CEO: Brian Reynolds
CFO: Ron Forbes
HR: —
Employees: 708

1996 Sales: $122.0 million
1-Yr. Sales Change: (11.9%)
Exchange: Nasdaq
Symbol: MIFGY

Computers - computer-aided software engineering tools

MICRO LINEAR CORPORATION

2092 Concourse Dr.
San Jose, CA 95131
Phone: 408-433-5200
Fax: 408-432-0295

CEO: Arthur B. Stabenow
CFO: J. Philip Russell
HR: Debra Morton-Padilla
Employees: 251

1995 Sales: $57.4 million
1-Yr. Sales Change: 37.6%
Exchange: Nasdaq
Symbol: MLIN

Electrical components - analog & mixed signal integrated circuits for use in communications, computer & industrial markets

MICRO WAREHOUSE, INC.

535 Connecticut Ave.
Norwalk, CT 06854
Phone: 203-899-4000
Fax: 203-899-4203

CEO: Peter Godfrey
CFO: Steven Purcell
HR: Michael J. Kurtz
Employees: 3,100

1995 Sales: $1,308.0 million
1-Yr. Sales Change: 68.5%
Exchange: Nasdaq
Symbol: MWHS

Retail - mail-order sales of peripheral equipment & software (MacWAREHOUSE, MicroWAREHOUSE)

 See pages 146–147 for a full profile of this company.

MICROAGE, INC.

2400 S. Microage Way
Tempe, AZ 85282-1896
Phone: 602-804-2000
Fax: 602-966-7339

CEO: Jeffrey D. McKeever
CFO: James R. Daniel
HR: Alan R. Lyons
Employees: 2,088

1995 Sales: $2,941.1 million
1-Yr. Sales Change: 32.4%
Exchange: Nasdaq
Symbol: MICA

Retail - wholesale computer hardware & software (COMPAQ, Hewlett-Packard, IBM, Apple); direct sales of computer equipment & services to large corporate accounts

 See pages 148–149 for a full profile of this company.

MICROCHIP TECHNOLOGY INCORPORATED

2355 W. Chandler Blvd.
Chandler, AZ 85224-6199
Phone: 602-786-7200
Fax: 602-899-9210

CEO: Steve Sanghi
CFO: C. Philip Chapman
HR: Michael J. Jones
Employees: 1,400

1996 Sales: $285.9 million
1-Yr. Sales Change: 37.5%
Exchange: Nasdaq
Symbol: MCHP

Electronic components - field-programmable embedded micro-controller semiconductors for the consumer, automotive, office automation, communications & industrial markets

MICROCOM, INC.

500 River Ridge Dr.	CEO: Roland D. Pampel	1996 Sales: $146.0 million
Norwood, MA 02062-5028	CFO: Peter J. Minihane	1-Yr. Sales Change: 56.8%
Phone: 617-551-1000	HR: Bill Cashman	Exchange: Nasdaq
Fax: 617-551-1968	Employees: 405	Symbol: MNPI

Computers - modems, communication software & remote internetworking products

MICRODYNE CORPORATION

3601 Eisenhower Ave.	CEO: Philip T. Cunningham	1995 Sales: $170.1 million
Alexandria, VA 22304	CFO: Christopher M. Maginniss	1-Yr. Sales Change: 67.9%
Phone: 703-329-3700	HR: Paul Sinclair	Exchange: Nasdaq
Fax: 703-329-3722	Employees: 673	Symbol: MCDY

Computers - LAN adapter cards & concentrators, computer networking hardware & software, aerospace telementry receivers for data gathering & analysis & technical services

MICROELECTRONIC PACKAGING, INC.

9350 Trade Place	CEO: Timothy da Silva	1995 Sales: $58.0 million
San Diego, CA 92126	CFO: David A. Hinkle	1-Yr. Sales Change: 37.1%
Phone: 619-530-1660	HR: Teresa Scafate	Exchange: Nasdaq
Fax: 619-530-1661	Employees: 849	Symbol: MPIX

Electrical components - integrated circuits & electronic systems

MICROELECTRONICS & COMPUTER TECHNOLOGY CORPORATION

3500 West Balcones Center Dr.	CEO: John W. McRary	1995 Sales: $45.0 million
Austin, TX 78759	CFO: George J. Roberts	1-Yr. Sales Change: 12.5%
Phone: 512-343-0978	HR: Jeanne Jackson	Ownership: Consortium
Fax: 512-338-3892	Employees: 120	

Computers - high-technology research consortium

 **See page 324 for a full profile of this company.**

MICROFIELD GRAPHICS, INC.

9825 SW Sunshine Ct.	CEO: John B. Conroy	1995 Sales: $5.3 million
Beaverton, OR 97005	CFO: Randall R. Reed	1-Yr. Sales Change: 96.3%
Phone: 503-626-9393	HR: —	Exchange: Nasdaq (SC)
Fax: 503-641-9333	Employees: 40	Symbol: MICG

Computers - electronic white-boards that allow users to record & display on a computer what they write or draw (SoftBoard)

MICROFRAME, INC.

21 Meridian Rd.	CEO: Steve Gray	1996 Sales: $6.3 million
Edison, NJ 08820	CFO: Mark Simmons	1-Yr. Sales Change: (11.3%)
Phone: 908-494-4440	HR: —	Exchange: Nasdaq (SC)
Fax: 908-494-4570	Employees: 37	Symbol: MCFR

Computers - data communications & security devices

MICROGEN HOLDINGS PLC

New Lodge, Drift Rd.	CEO: Douglas N. Lee	1995 Sales: $109.1 million
Windsor, Berkshire SL4 4RQ, UK	CFO: Gerald E. Liddle	1-Yr. Sales Change: 13.4%
Phone: +44-1-344-899-265	HR: —	Exchange: London
Fax: +44-1-344-891-116	Employees: 794	

Computers - specialist services, including management of computer-generated data, computer output microfilming & electronic printing

MICROGRAFX, INC.

1303 Arapaho Rd.	CEO: J. Paul Grayson	1996 Sales: $72.9 million
Richardson, TX 75081	CFO: Gregory A. Peters	1-Yr. Sales Change: 20.7%
Phone: 972-234-1769	HR: Mary Boyd	Exchange: Nasdaq
Fax: 972-994-6475	Employees: 262	Symbol: MGXI

Computers - high-powered graphics software for business, professional & home markets

MICRO-INTEGRATION CORP.

One Science Park	CEO: John A. Parsons	1996 Sales: $7.8 million
Frostburg, MD 21532	CFO: Kenneth R. Tressler	1-Yr. Sales Change: (22.8%)
Phone: 301-689-0800	HR: Kathy Snyder	Exchange: Nasdaq
Fax: 301-689-0808	Employees: 87	Symbol: MINT

Computers - communications links, terminal emulation, application programming interfaces & client/server applications & development tools

MICROLEAGUE MULTIMEDIA, INC.

750 Dawson Dr.	CEO: Neil B. Swartz	1995 Sales: $5.0 million
Newark, DE 19713	CFO: Peter Flanagan	1-Yr. Sales Change: 78.6%
Phone: 302-368-9990	HR: —	Exchange: Nasdaq (SC)
Fax: 302-368-5164	Employees: 54	Symbol: MLMI

Computers - interactive multimedia computer software for entertainment & education

MICROLYTICS, INC.

2 Tobey Village Office Park	CEO: Robert C. Harris Jr.	1995 Sales: $2.8 million
Pittsford, NY 14534	CFO: —	1-Yr. Sales Change: (60.6%)
Phone: 716-248-3875	HR: Carolyn Hotchkiss	Exchange: OTC
Fax: 716-248-5612	Employees: 35	Symbol: MCYX

Publishing - electronic telephone directories (MicroPages), electronic directory assistance products & Internet advertising media

MICRON ELECTRONICS, INC.

900 E. Karcher Rd.	CEO: Joseph M. Daltoso	1995 Sales: $1,000.0 million
Nampa, ID 83687	CFO: T. Erik Oaas	1-Yr. Sales Change: 275.5%
Phone: 208-893-3434	HR: Tresa Ball	Exchange: Nasdaq
Fax: 208-465-8995	Employees: 1,955	Symbol: MUEI

Computers - PCs (Zeos) & contract manufacturing (79% owned by Micron Technology)

MICRON TECHNOLOGY, INC.

8000 S. Federal Way	CEO: Steven R. Appleton	1996 Sales: $3,653.8 million
Boise, ID 83707-0006	CFO: Wilbur G. Stover Jr.	1-Yr. Sales Change: 23.7%
Phone: 208-368-4000	HR: Susan Metzger	Exchange: NYSE
Fax: 208-368-4435	Employees: 8,080	Symbol: MU

Electrical components - integrated circuit memory chips (DRAM, SRAM), complex printed circuit boards & complete PCs

 See pages 150–151 for a full profile of this company.

MICRONICS COMPUTERS, INC.

232 E. Warren Ave.	CEO: Shanker Munshani	1995 Sales: $234.1 million
Fremont, CA 94539-7085	CFO: Robert Mahoney	1-Yr. Sales Change: 43.1%
Phone: 510-651-2300	HR: Ron Victor	Exchange: Nasdaq
Fax: 510-651-5666	Employees: 366	Symbol: MCRN

Computers - advanced system boards for PCs

 See page 325 for a full profile of this company.

MICROS SYSTEMS, INC.

12000 Baltimore Ave.	CEO: A. L. Giannopoulos	1996 Sales: $178.0 million
Beltsville, MD 20705-1291	CFO: Gary C. Kaufman	1-Yr. Sales Change: 58.9%
Phone: 301-210-6000	HR: Cathy Rensel	Exchange: Nasdaq
Fax: 301-210-3334	Employees: 1,289	Symbol: MCRS

Computers - point-of-sale computer systems for hospitality providers

MICROSECONDS INTERNATIONAL INC.

PO Box 201
Rancho Santa Fe, CA 92067
Phone: 619-756-0765
Fax: 619-756-0855

CEO: Dennis Nederlof
CFO: J. Larry Nederlof
HR: —
Employees: 35

1995 Sales: $25.0 million
1-Yr. Sales Change: —
Ownership: Privately Held

Computers - utilities & screen savers for Windows

MICROSEMI CORPORATION

2830 S. Fairview St.
Santa Ana, CA 92704
Phone: 714-979-8220
Fax: 714-557-5989

CEO: Philip Frey Jr.
CFO: David R. Sonksen
HR: James M. Thomas
Employees: 2,309

1995 Sales: $133.9 million
1-Yr. Sales Change: 12.3%
Exchange: Nasdaq
Symbol: MSCC

Electrical components - power semiconductors, surface mount & custom diode assemblies, transistors & silicon controlled rectifiers

MICROSOFT CORPORATION

One Microsoft Way
Redmond, WA 98052-6399
Phone: 206-882-8080
Fax: 206-883-8101

CEO: William H. Gates III
CFO: Michael W. Brown
HR: Michael R. Murray
Employees: 20,561

1996 Sales: $8,671.0 million
1-Yr. Sales Change: 46.1%
Exchange: Nasdaq
Symbol: MSFT

Computers - operating systems (#1 worldwide: MS-DOS, Windows, Windows 95); application & language software, CD-ROMs; online service (Microsoft Network); online publishing; news services (MSNBC)

 See pages 152–153 for a full profile of this company.

MICROS-TO-MAINFRAMES, INC.

614 Corporate Way
Valley Cottage, NY 10989
Phone: 914-268-5000
Fax: 914-268-9695

CEO: Steven H. Rothman
CFO: Frank Wong
HR: Dottie Sloaman
Employees: 96

1996 Sales: $47.3 million
1-Yr. Sales Change: 10.0%
Exchange: Nasdaq (SC)
Symbol: MTMC

Computers - systems integration; hardware & software sales

MICROTEK INTERNATIONAL

No. 6, Industry E. Rd. 3
Hsinchu City, Taiwan
Phone: +886-35-772-155
Fax: +886-35-772-598

CEO: Chenghsiun Hsu
CFO: —
HR: —
Employees: 397

1995 Sales: $158.0 million
1-Yr. Sales Change: —
Exchange: Taipei

Computers - accessories, including image scanners

MICROTEST, INC.

4747 N. 22nd St.	CEO: Richard G. Meise	1995 Sales: $52.5 million
Phoenix, AZ 85016-4708	CFO: Richard R. Douglas	1-Yr. Sales Change: 32.6%
Phone: 602-952-6400	HR: Judy Bourassa	Exchange: Nasdaq
Fax: 602-952-6401	Employees: 187	Symbol: MTST

Computers - network diagnostic tools & enhancement software

MICROTOUCH SYSTEMS, INC.

300 Griffin Brook Park Dr.	CEO: D. Westervelt Davis	1995 Sales: $76.7 million
Methuen, MA 01844-1873	CFO: Geoffrey P. Clear	1-Yr. Sales Change: 30.2%
Phone: 508-659-9000	HR: Annemarie Bell	Exchange: Nasdaq
Fax: 508-659-9100	Employees: 478	Symbol: MTSI

Computers - touch-screen monitors (#1 worldwide: TruePoint Kiosk Monitor)

 See page 326 for a full profile of this company.

MICROWARE SYSTEMS CORP.

1900 NW 114th St.	CEO: Kenneth B. Kaplan	1996 Sales: $23.7 million
Des Moines, IA 50325-7077	CFO: George J. Berry	1-Yr. Sales Change: 25.4%
Phone: 515-224-1929	HR: Sandee Cook	Exchange: Nasdaq
Fax: 515-224-1352	Employees: 210	Symbol: MWAR

Computers - real-time operating systems, network software & development tools for wireless telecommunications, PDAs, CDs & interactive TV

MIDISOFT CORPORATION

1605 NW Sammamish Rd., Ste. 205	CEO: Larry Foster	1995 Sales: $5.4 million
Issaquah, WA 98027	CFO: Melinda Bryden	1-Yr. Sales Change: (6.9%)
Phone: 206-391-3610	HR: —	Exchange: Nasdaq
Fax: 206-391-3422	Employees: 45	Symbol: MIDI

Computers - interactive multimedia audio software

MIDWAY GAMES INC.

3401 N. California Ave.	CEO: Neil D. Nicastro	1996 Sales: $245.4 million
Chicago, IL 60618	CFO: Harold H. Bach Jr.	1-Yr. Sales Change: 36.0%
Phone: 312-961-2222	HR: Mike Sirchio	Ownership: Subsidiary
Fax: 312-961-1099	Employees: 326	

Computers - video games for the coin-operated & home video game markets (Mortal Kombat, NBA Jam, Defender, Pacman, Space Invaders, Centipede, Pong); subsidiary of WMS Industries

MILGRAY ELECTRONICS, INC.

77 Schmitt Blvd.
Farmingdale, NY 11735
Phone: 516-420-9800
Fax: 516-752-9221

CEO: Herbert S. Davidson
CFO: John Tortorici
HR: Gerry Reagen
Employees: 500

1995 Sales: $239.5 million
1-Yr. Sales Change: 31.7%
Exchange: Nasdaq (SC)
Symbol: MGRY

Electrical components - distribution of semiconductors, electromechanical devices, passive components & computer products

MILTOPE GROUP INC.

500 Richardson Rd. South
Hope Hull, AL 36043
Phone: 334-284-8665
Fax: 334-613-6302

CEO: George K. Webster
CFO: James T. Matthews
HR: Edward F. Crowell
Employees: 319

1995 Sales: $65.7 million
1-Yr. Sales Change: (13.1%)
Exchange: Nasdaq
Symbol: MILT

Computers - microcomputers & peripheral equipment for land, sea & air operations for military & commercial customers (#1 in US)

MINDSPRING ENTERPRISES, INC.

1430 W. Peachtree St. NW, Ste. 400
Atlanta, GA 30309
Phone: 404-815-0770
Fax: 404-815-8805

CEO: Charles M. Brewer
CFO: Michael G. Misikoff
HR: K. Anne Peavler
Employees: 101

1995 Sales: $2.2 million
1-Yr. Sales Change: 2,100%
Exchange: Nasdaq
Symbol: MSPG

Computers - Internet access provider serving the southeastern US

MISSION RESEARCH CORPORATION

735 State St.
Santa Barbara, CA 93101
Phone: 805-963-8761
Fax: 805-962-8530

CEO: Steve Gutsche
CFO: John Lishman
HR: —
Employees: 360

1995 Sales: $53.0 million
1-Yr. Sales Change: 10.4%
Ownership: Privately Held

Computers - communications & radar systems; optical sensors & systems

MISYS PLC

Burleigh House, Chapel Oak
Salford Priors, Worcs. WR11 5SH, UK
Phone: +44-1-386-871-373
Fax: +44-1-386-871-045

CEO: P. S. S. Macpherson
CFO: R. K. Graham
HR: —
Employees: 3,441

1996 Sales: $430.3 million
1-Yr. Sales Change: 76.6%
Exchange: London

Computers - application software products; data & transaction processing services

MIZAR, INC.

2410 Luna Rd., Ste. 132	CEO: David H. Irwin	1996 Sales: $14.1 million
Carrollton, TX 75006	CFO: C. D. Brockenbush	1-Yr. Sales Change: 0.7%
Phone: 972-277-4600	HR: —	Exchange: Nasdaq
Fax: 972-277-4666	Employees: 46	Symbol: MIZR

Computers - multiprocessor computing board-level products, subsystems & systems

MLC HOLDINGS, INC.

11150 Sunset Hills Rd., Ste. 110	CEO: Phillip G. Norton	1996 Sales: $34.8 million
Reston, VA 20190-5321	CFO: Bruce M. Bowen	1-Yr. Sales Change: (5.7%)
Phone: 703-834-5710	HR: Sandy Reed	Ownership: Privately Held
Fax: 703-834-5718	Employees: 47	

Leasing - information technology equipment, including personal computers, client server systems, networks, mainframe computer equipment & telecommunications equipment & software

MODACAD, INC.

1954 Cotner Ave.	CEO: Joyce Freedman	1995 Sales: $1.9 million
Los Angeles, CA 90025	CFO: Lee Freedman	1-Yr. Sales Change: (26.9%)
Phone: 310-312-6632	HR: —	Exchange: Nasdaq (SC)
Fax: 310-444-9577	Employees: 37	Symbol: MODA

Computers - virtual reality, rendering & modeling software for industrial design & retail customers, primarily in the apparel, textile, home furnishings & home design industries

MOSCOM CORPORATION

3750 Monroe Ave.	CEO: Albert J. Montevecchio	1995 Sales: $17.6 million
Pittsford, NY 14534	CFO: Paul A. Lipari	1-Yr. Sales Change: 23.1%
Phone: 716-381-6000	HR: —	Exchange: Nasdaq
Fax: 716-383-6800	Employees: 181	Symbol: MSCM

Telecommunications equipment - call-accounting products, which are used by organizations to control telecommunications usage & expenses

MOSEL VITELIC CORPORATION

One Creation Rd.	CEO: Hsing Tuan	1995 Sales: $540.0 million
Hsinchu City, Taiwan	CFO: Janny Lu	1-Yr. Sales Change: 89.5%
Phone: 886-35-783344	HR: Mary Fisher	Ownership: Privately Held
Fax: 886-35-792838	Employees: 2,370	

Electrical components - DRAMs, SRAMs, Video RAMs, DRAM memory modules & specialty memories to the worldwide computer graphics, data storage, telecommunications, & computer peripheral markets

MOTOROLA, INC.

1303 E. Algonquin Rd.	CEO: Gary L. Tooker	1995 Sales: $27,037 million
Schaumburg, IL 60196	CFO: Carl F. Koenemann	1-Yr. Sales Change: 21.5%
Phone: 847-576-5000	HR: Glenn A. Gienko	Exchange: NYSE
Fax: 847-576-8003	Employees: 142,000	Symbol: MOT

Electrical products - wireless communications products (#1 worldwide: cellular telephone, paging & two-way radio) & electronic equipment, systems & components

 See pages 154–155 for a full profile of this company.

MRV COMMUNICATIONS, INC.

8917 Fullbright Ave.	CEO: Noam Lotan	1995 Sales: $39.2 million
Chatsworth, CA 91311-6124	CFO: Edmund Glazer	1-Yr. Sales Change: 124.0%
Phone: 818-773-9044	HR: Edmund Glazer	Exchange: Nasdaq
Fax: 818-773-0261	Employees: 207	Symbol: MRVC

Electrical components - semiconductor laser diodes, light-emitting diodes, fiber-optic systems & switching hubs for Ethernet networks

MSI ELECTRONICS INC.

31-00 47th Ave.	CEO: Albert Lederman	1995 Sales: $0.7 million
Long Island City, NY 11101	CFO: Albert Lederman	1-Yr. Sales Change: (36.4%)
Phone: 718-937-3330	HR: —	Exchange: OTC
Fax: 718-937-3499	Employees: 16	Symbol: MSIE

Electrical components - semiconductor diodes & electronic instruments designed to measure the properties of semiconductors; hardware & software for telephone switching systems

MTI TECHNOLOGY CORPORATION

4905 E. La Palma Ave.	CEO: Earl Pearlman	1996 Sales: $131.9 million
Anaheim, CA 92807	CFO: Dale Boyd	1-Yr. Sales Change: 3.6%
Phone: 714-970-0300	HR: Kathie Nichols	Exchange: Nasdaq
Fax: 714-693-2202	Employees: 600	Symbol: MTIC

Computers - data storage & management software for use on various network environments

MULTICOM PUBLISHING, INC.

1100 Olive Way	CEO: Tamara L. Attard	1996 Sales: $7.1 million
Seattle, WA 98101	CFO: Ellen R. M. Boyer	1-Yr. Sales Change: 82.1%
Phone: 206-622-5530	HR: —	Exchange: Nasdaq (SC)
Fax: 206-622-4380	Employees: 64	Symbol: MNET

Computers - home/family/lifestyle multimedia products delivered through CD-ROMs, the Internet, the World Wide Web, online services, TV-based systems, interactive kiosks & laptop PC presentations

MULTIMEDIA GAMES, INC.

7335 S. Lewis Ave., Ste. 302	CEO: Gordon T. Graves	1995 Sales: $17.1 million
Tulsa, OK 74136	CFO: Mike Howard	1-Yr. Sales Change: 1,121%
Phone: 918-494-0576	HR: —	Exchange: Nasdaq (SC)
Fax: 918-501-0043	Employees: 57	Symbol: MGAM

Computers - interactive, multimedia communications & data processing services & products for the gaming & entertainment industries

MULTI-MEDIA TUTORIAL SERVICE

205 Kings Hwy.	CEO: Morris Berger	1996 Sales: $9.2 million
Brooklyn, NY 11223	CFO: Robert Selevan	1-Yr. Sales Change: 100.0%
Phone: 718-234-0404	HR: —	Exchange: Nasdaq (SC)
Fax: 718-234-0550	Employees: 90	Symbol: MMTS

Computers - tutorial & educational programs in videotape & CD-ROM formats

MULTIPLE ZONES INTERNATIONAL, INC.

707 S. Grady Way	CEO: Victor J. Melfi Jr.	1995 Sales: $242.6 million
Renton, WA 98055-3233	CFO: Peter J. Biere	1-Yr. Sales Change: 113.7%
Phone: 206-430-3000	HR: Annette Gregorich	Exchange: Nasdaq
Fax: 206-430-3626	Employees: 560	Symbol: MZON

Computers - direct marketing through catalogs (The Mac Zone, The PC Zone) of hardware, software, peripherals & accessories for Macintosh- & IBM-compatible computers

MULTI-TECH SYSTEMS, INC.

2205 Woodale Dr.	CEO: Raghu Sharma	1995 Est. Sales: $125.0 mil.
Mounds View, MN 55112	CFO: Steve Giebler	1-Yr. Sales Change: 21.4%
Phone: 612-785-3500	HR: Kathy Higby	Ownership: Privately Held
Fax: 612-785-9874	Employees: 400	

Computers - data communications equipment, including desktop modems, internal PC modems, communications servers & related products

MUSTANG SOFTWARE, INC.

6200 Lake Ming Rd.	CEO: James A. Harrer	1995 Sales: $4.8 million
Bakersfield, CA 93306	CFO: Donald M. Leonard	1-Yr. Sales Change: —
Phone: 805-873-2500	HR: Lynn Wright	Exchange: Nasdaq
Fax: 805-873-2599	Employees: 65	Symbol: MSTG

Computers - e-mail exchange, file transfer & fax software (Wildcat! BBS, QmodemPro, Off-Line Xpress)

M-WAVE, INC.

216 Evergreen St.	CEO: Joseph A. Turek	1995 Sales: $29.5 million
Bensenville, IL 60106	CFO: Paul H. Schmitt	1-Yr. Sales Change: 5.4%
Phone: 708-860-9542	HR: —	Exchange: Nasdaq
Fax: 708-860-5350	Employees: 187	Symbol: MWAV

Electrical components - Teflon-coated high-frequency printed circuit boards & microwave-frequency components

MYLEX CORPORATION

34551 Ardenwood Blvd.	CEO: Albert E. Montross	1995 Sales: $100.4 million
Fremont, CA 94555	CFO: Colleen Gray	1-Yr. Sales Change: 60.6%
Phone: 510-796-6100	HR: Joe Schmidt	Exchange: Nasdaq
Fax: 510-745-7654	Employees: 193	Symbol: MYLX

Computers - data-storage devices & computer-system boards

MYSOFTWARE COMPANY

2197 E. Bayshore Rd.	CEO: David P. Mans	1995 Sales: $13.4 million
Palo Alto, CA 94303	CFO: David P. Mans	1-Yr. Sales Change: 45.7%
Phone: 415-473-3600	HR: —	Exchange: Nasdaq
Fax: 415-325-3106	Employees: 48	Symbol: MYSW

Computers - task-specific software applications for small business & home based businesses

N2K INC.

55 Broad St., 10th Fl.	CEO: Lawrence L. Rosen	1995 Sales: $11.1 million
New York, NY 10004	CFO: Bruce Johnson	1-Yr. Sales Change: (2.6%)
Phone: 212-378-5555	HR: Rich Harris	Ownership: Privately Held
Fax: 212-742-1755	Employees: 108	

Computers - entertainment, information & merchandising Web sites (Music Boulevard, Jazz Central Station, Rocktropolis) & sites for individual artists (David Bowie, The Rolling Stones)

NAI TECHNOLOGIES, INC.

2405 Trade Centre Ave.	CEO: Robert A. Carlson	1995 Sales: $60.0 million
Longmont, CO 80503-7602	CFO: Richard A. Schneider	1-Yr. Sales Change: 10.1%
Phone: 303-776-5674	HR: Len Stanton	Exchange: Nasdaq
Fax: 303-776-5484	Employees: 390	Symbol: NATL

Computers - rugged computers & peripheral equipment; telecommunications products, including test equipment

NAM TAI ELECTRONICS

16 Hung To Rd., Kwun Tong
Kowloon, Hong Kong
Phone: +852-341-0273
Fax: +852-341-4164

CEO: Ming Kown Koo
CFO: Mark Waslen
HR: —
Employees: 2,300

1995 Sales: $121.2 million
1-Yr. Sales Change: 25.5%
Exchange: Nasdaq
Symbol: NTAIF

Electronics - digital consumer electronics, including calculators, translators, spell checkers, dictionaries, typewriters & scales; digital thermometers & blood-pressure meters

NANOMETRICS INCORPORATED

310 DeGuigne Dr.
Sunnyvale, CA 94086
Phone: 408-746-1600
Fax: 408-720-0196

CEO: Vincent J. Coates
CFO: Paul B. Nolan
HR: —
Employees: 100

1995 Sales: $22.8 million
1-Yr. Sales Change: 67.6%
Exchange: Nasdaq
Symbol: NANO

Electronics - optical microscope-based measurement & inspection stations to monitor the fabrication of integrated circuits on wafers, flat panel displays & recording heads

NASHUA CORPORATION

44 Franklin St.
Nashua, NH 03061-2002
Phone: 603-880-2323
Fax: 603-880-5671

CEO: Gerald G. Garbacz
CFO: Daniel M. Junius
HR: Bruce Wright
Employees: 3,234

1995 Sales: $452.2 million
1-Yr. Sales Change: (5.5%)
Exchange: NYSE
Symbol: NSH

Office equipment & supplies - imaging supplies, including toners, developers, remanufactured laser printer cartridges, facsimile paper, copy paper & labels; precision machined parts for computer disks; photofinishing services

NAT SYSTEMS INTERNATIONAL, INC.

1420 Spring Hill Rd.
McLean, VA 22102
Phone: 703-760-0900
Fax: 703-760-9810

CEO: John F. Burton
CFO: Kenneth J. Tarpey
HR: —
Employees: 300

1995 Sales: $29.3 million
1-Yr. Sales Change: 55.0%
Ownership: Privately Held

Computers - adaptable & integrated software for developing, deploying & maintaining enterprise client/server applications

NATIONAL BUSINESS GROUP INC.

2840 Mt. Wilkinson Pkwy., Ste. 200
Atlanta, GA 30339
Phone: 770-319-8300
Fax: 770-319-1416

CEO: Rich Basich
CFO: James W. Hughes
HR: James W. Hughes
Employees: 49

1995 Sales: $14.8 million
1-Yr. Sales Change: 3.5%
Ownership: Privately Held

Computers - connectivity hardware & software

NATIONAL COMPUTER SYSTEMS, INC.

11000 Prairie Lakes Dr.	CEO: Russell A. Gullotti	1996 Sales: $359.0 million
Eden Prairie, MN 55344	CFO: Jeffrey W. Taylor	1-Yr. Sales Change: 6.6%
Phone: 612-829-3000	HR: Richard L. Poss	Exchange: Nasdaq
Fax: 612-829-3167	Employees: 2,700	Symbol: NLCS

Optical character recognition - optical mark-scanning systems used to read pencil marks

NATIONAL DATA CORPORATION

National Data Plaza	CEO: Robert A. Yellowlees	1995 Sales: $242.0 million
Atlanta, GA 30329-2010	CFO: Jerry W. Braxton	1-Yr. Sales Change: 18.6%
Phone: 404-728-2000	HR: Donald L. Howard	Exchange: NYSE
Fax: 404-728-2551	Employees: 1,900	Symbol: NDC

Financial - credit card sales approval services; debit card, check approval & electronic payment & filing processing

NATIONAL EDUCATION CORPORATION

18400 Von Karman Ave.	CEO: Sam Yau	1995 Sales: $258.6 million
Irvine, CA 92715	CFO: Keith K. Ogata	1-Yr. Sales Change: 7.0%
Phone: 714-474-9400	HR: Lori Grigg	Exchange: NYSE
Fax: 714-474-9488	Employees: 2,000	Symbol: NEC

Schools - computer training (ICS Learning Systems); vocational & technical schools (National Education Training); educational materials publisher (Steck-Vaughn)

NATIONAL HEALTH ENHANCEMENT SYSTEMS, INC.

3200 N. Central Ave., Ste. 1750	CEO: Gregory J. Petras	1996 Sales: $16.9 million
Phoenix, AZ 85012	CFO: Jeffrey T. Zywicki	1-Yr. Sales Change: 29.0%
Phone: 602-230-7575	HR: Laurinda Bess	Exchange: Nasdaq (SC)
Fax: 602-274-6158	Employees: 160	Symbol: NHES

Computers - health-care-related software

NATIONAL INSTRUMENTS CORPORATION

6504 Bridge Point Pkwy.	CEO: James J. Truchard	1995 Sales: $164.8 million
Austin, TX 78730-5039	CFO: Joel B. Rollins	1-Yr. Sales Change: 29.8%
Phone: 512-794-0100	HR: Mark Finger	Exchange: Nasdaq
Fax: 512-794-8411	Employees: 1,062	Symbol: NATI

Computers - computer-based instrumentation software

NATIONAL SEMICONDUCTOR CORPORATION

2900 Semiconductor Dr.	CEO: Brian Halla	1996 Sales: $2,623.1 million
Santa Clara, CA 95051	CFO: Donald MacLeod	1-Yr. Sales Change: 10.2%
Phone: 408-721-5000	HR: Richard A. Wilson	Exchange: NYSE
Fax: 408-739-9803	Employees: 22,400	Symbol: NSM

Electrical components - analog & digital semiconductors, memory products, embedded microprocessors & specialized security microchips

 See pages 156–157 for a full profile of this company.

NATIONAL TECHTEAM, INC.

22000 Garrison Ave.	CEO: William F. Coyro Jr.	1995 Sales: $41.8 million
Dearborn, MI 48124-2306	CFO: Lawrence A. Mills	1-Yr. Sales Change: 38.4%
Phone: 313-277-2277	HR: Kris Munroe	Exchange: Nasdaq
Fax: 313-277-6409	Employees: 1,056	Symbol: TEAM

Computers - computer support, training, consulting, systems integration & other services

NATURAL MICROSYSTEMS CORPORATION

8 Erie Dr.	CEO: Robert Schechter	1995 Sales: $32.8 million
Natick, MA 01760	CFO: John F. Kennedy	1-Yr. Sales Change: 92.9%
Phone: 508-650-1300	HR: Christine Wheeler	Exchange: Nasdaq
Fax: 508-650-1352	Employees: 129	Symbol: NMSS

Computers - integrated hardware & software products used to develop link PCs & public telephone networks

NAVARRE CORPORATION

7400 49th Ave. North	CEO: Eric H. Paulson	1996 Sales: $158.4 million
New Hope, MN 55428	CFO: Charles E. Cheney	1-Yr. Sales Change: 32.6%
Phone: 612-535-8333	HR: Margot McManus	Exchange: Nasdaq
Fax: 612-533-2156	Employees: 131	Symbol: NAVR

Wholesale distribution - prerecorded music & PC software

NAVIGATION TECHNOLOGIES CORPORATION

740 E. Arques Ave.	CEO: T. Russell Shields	1995 Sales: $3.7 million
Sunnyvale, CA 94086	CFO: Thomas A. Lerone	1-Yr. Sales Change: 48.0%
Phone: 408-737-3200	HR: Karen Elam	Ownership: Privately Held
Fax: 408-737-3280	Employees: 1,103	

Computers - navigable database for use with in-vehicle software & hardware systems that use global positioning satellite (GPS) technology

NCR CORPORATION

1700 S. Patterson Blvd.	CEO: Lars Nyberg	1995 Sales: $8,160.0 million
Dayton, OH 45479	CFO: John L. Giering	1-Yr. Sales Change: (3.5%)
Phone: 513-445-2078	HR: Richard H. Evans	Ownership: Division
Fax: 513-445-1893	Employees: 37,900	

Computers - commercial database systems, automated teller machines, financial processing systems, networking management systems & tools, multiprocessing systems (division of AT&T)

 See pages 158–159 for a full profile of this company.

NCUBE CORPORATION

110 Marsh Dr.	CEO: Ronald A. Dilbeck	1995 Est. Sales: $40.0 mil.
Foster City, CA 94404-1184	CFO: Alan Beauchamp	1-Yr. Sales Change: —
Phone: 415-593-9000	HR: Sandra Chroman	Ownership: Privately Held
Fax: 415-508-5408	Employees: 160	

Computers - massively parallel computers

 See page 327 for a full profile of this company.

NEC CORPORATION

7-1, Shiba 5-chome, Minato-ku	CEO: Hisashi Kaneko	1996 Sales: $41,376.0 mil.
Tokyo 108-01, Japan	CFO: Yoshihiro Suzuki	1-Yr. Sales Change: (4.5%)
Phone: +81-3-3454-1111	HR: Hirokazu Akiyama	Exchange: Nasdaq
Fax: +81-3-3798-1510	Employees: 152,719	Symbol: NIPNY

Electrical components - semiconductors, PCs & other operations (89 subsidiaries in Japan & in 30 other countries)

 See pages 160–161 for a full profile of this company.

NEMATRON CORPORATION

5840 Interface Dr.	CEO: Frank G. Logan III	1995 Sales: $17.6 million
Ann Arbor, MI 48103	CFO: —	1-Yr. Sales Change: 15.0%
Phone: 313-994-0591	HR: Barbara Harrigan	Exchange: Nasdaq
Fax: 313-994-8074	Employees: 100	Symbol: NEMA

Computers - industrial workstations for factories, including electronic displays, keyboards & software

NEOSTAR RETAIL GROUP, INC.

2250 William D. Tate Ave.	CEO: James B. McCurry	1996 Sales: $513.5 million
Grapevine, TX 76051	CFO: Opal P. Ferraro	1-Yr. Sales Change: 1.9%
Phone: 817-424-2000	HR: Michael A. Ivanich	Exchange: Nasdaq
Fax: 817-424-2002	Employees: 7,100	Symbol: NEOS

Retail - personal computer software (Babbage's, Software Etc.)

 See page 328 for a full profile of this company.

NETCOM ON-LINE COMMUNICATION SERVICES, INC.

3031 Tisch Way, 2nd Fl.	CEO: David W. Garrison	1995 Sales: $52.4 million
San Jose, CA 95128	CFO: Clifton T. Weatherford	1-Yr. Sales Change: 322.6%
Phone: 408-556-3233	HR: Irene Meister	Exchange: Nasdaq
Fax: 408-556-3250	Employees: 508	Symbol: NETC

Computers - Internet service provider & web browser software (NetCruiser)

See page 329 for a full profile of this company.

NETCOUNT, LLC

1645 N. Vine St., Level 4	CEO: Paul Grant	1995 Sales: $0.0 million
Los Angeles, CA 90028	CFO: Jim Spence	1-Yr. Sales Change: —
Phone: 213-848-5480	HR: —	Ownership: Privately Held
Fax: 213-848-5750	Employees: 25	

Computers - Web site activity measurement services

NETEGRITY, INC.

90 Industrial Park Rd.	CEO: Barry N. Bycoff	1996 Sales: $56.1 million
Hingham, MA 02043	CFO: James O'Connor	1-Yr. Sales Change: 41.3%
Phone: 617-740-0101	HR: Sylvia Sprague	Exchange: Nasdaq (SC)
Fax: 617-740-0064	Employees: 102	Symbol: NETE

Retail - mail-order sales of business productivity, engineering & scientific hardware & software (The Programmer's Shop, Personal Computing Tools, SDC Communications, CD Select)

NETFRAME SYSTEMS INCORPORATED

1545 Barber Ln.	CEO: Robert L. Puette	1995 Sales: $76.4 million
Milpitas, CA 95035	CFO: David S. Dury	1-Yr. Sales Change: (14.3%)
Phone: 408-944-0600	HR: Vivian M. Golub	Exchange: Nasdaq
Fax: 408-944-0111	Employees: 284	Symbol: NETF

Computers - departmental & enterprise network servers, fault-tolerant servers (ClusterServer) & messaging systems (Concerto)

NETMANAGE, INC.

10725 N. De Anza Blvd.	CEO: Zvi Alon	1995 Sales: $125.4 million
Cupertino, CA 95014	CFO: Walter D. Amaral	1-Yr. Sales Change: 103.6%
Phone: 408-973-7171	HR: Pat Roboostoff	Exchange: Nasdaq
Fax: 408-257-6405	Employees: 318	Symbol: NETM

Computers - internetworking software & tools (Internet Chameleon, ECCO)

NETOBJECTS, INC.

2055 Woodside Rd.
Redwood City, CA 94061
Phone: 415-562-0285
Fax: 415-562-0288

CEO: Samir Arora
CFO: —
HR: —
Employees: —

1995 Sales: $0.0 million
1-Yr. Sales Change: —
Ownership: Privately Held

Computers - Web authoring software (Fusion, NetObjects Site Publisher)

NETPLEX GROUP INC.

175 Community Dr.
Great Neck, NY 11021
Phone: 516-829-1883
Fax: 516-829-5001

CEO: Howard Davis
CFO: Maria Bruzzese
HR: —
Employees: 22

1995 Sales: $0.4 million
1-Yr. Sales Change: (20.0%)
Exchange: OTC
Symbol: NTPL

Computers - software applications for the office automation market, including electronic messaging & networking gateway products

NETRIX CORPORATION

13595 Dulles Technology Dr.
Herndon, VA 22071
Phone: 703-742-6000
Fax: 703-742-4048

CEO: Charles W. Stein
CFO: Richard G. Tennant
HR: —
Employees: 278

1995 Sales: $48.2 million
1-Yr. Sales Change: (8.0%)
Exchange: Nasdaq
Symbol: NTRX

Telecommunications equipment - integrated networking equipment & related management software for combined data, voice & image networks

NETS INC.

25 First St.
Cambridge, MA 02141
Phone: 617-252-5000
Fax: 617-252-5551

CEO: Jim Manzi
CFO: Mike Stubler
HR: Russ Campanello
Employees: 150

1995 Est. Sales: $25.0 mil.
1-Yr. Sales Change: —
Ownership: Privately Held

Computers - Internet-based commerce system that links sellers & buyers (Industry.Net); Internet business-information service (AT&T Business Network)

NETSCAPE COMMUNICATIONS CORPORATION

501 E. Middlefield Rd.
Mountain View, CA 94043
Phone: 415-254-1900
Fax: 415-528-4125

CEO: James L. Barksdale
CFO: Peter L. S. Currie
HR: Kandis Malefyt
Employees: 725

1995 Sales: $80.7 million
1-Yr. Sales Change: 11,429%
Exchange: Nasdaq
Symbol: NSCP

Computers - Internet navigation software (Netscape Navigator), Website server software & transaction security software

 See page 330 for a full profile of this company.

NETSMART TECHNOLOGIES, INC.

146 Nassau Ave.	CEO: Lewis S. Schiller	1995 Sales: $7.4 million
Islip, NY 11751	CFO: Anthony F. Grisanti	1-Yr. Sales Change: 155.2%
Phone: 516-968-2000	HR: —	Exchange: Nasdaq (SC)
Fax: 516-968-2123	Employees: 66	Symbol: NTST

Computers - networking software, smart cards (CardSmart System)

NETSOLVE INCORPORATED

9130 Jollyville Rd., Ste. 200	CEO: Craig Tysdal	1996 Sales: $24.0 million
Austin, TX 78759-7475	CFO: Kenneth C. Kieley	1-Yr. Sales Change: 23.1%
Phone: 512-795-3000	HR: Jenny Voight	Ownership: Privately Held
Fax: 512-795-3008	Employees: 70	

Computers - wide-area internetworking outsourcing services, including network design, equipment installation & network management

NETVANTAGE, INC.

1800 Stewart St., Ste. R	CEO: Stephen Rizzone	1995 Sales: $1.3 million
Santa Monica, CA 90404	CFO: Thomas V. Baker	1-Yr. Sales Change: 1,200%
Phone: 310-828-9898	IIR: Thomas V. Baker	Exchange: Nasdaq (SC)
Fax: 310-828-2553	Employees: 39	Symbol: NETVA

Computers - Ethernet switching devices

NETWORK APPLIANCE CORPORATION

319 N. Bernardo Ave.	CEO: Daniel Warmenhoven	1996 Sales: $46.6 million
Mountain View, CA 94043	CFO: Michael J. McCloskey	1-Yr. Sales Change: 214.9%
Phone: 415-428-5100	HR: Chris Carlton	Exchange: Nasdaq
Fax: 415-428-5151	Employees: 103	Symbol: NTAP

Computers - network data storage devices

NETWORK COMPUTING DEVICES, INC.

350 N. Bernardo Ave.	CEO: Robert G. Gilbertson	1995 Sales: $142.0 million
Mountain View, CA 94043	CFO: Jack A. Bradley	1-Yr. Sales Change: (11.7%)
Phone: 415-694-0650	HR: JoAnn Rogers	Exchange: Nasdaq
Fax: 415-961-7711	Employees: 359	Symbol: NCDI

Computers - X terminals & server software (PC Xware), e-mail & messaging software for open systems (Z-Mail) & networking software (NCDware)

THE NETWORK CONNECTION, INC.

1324 Union Hill Rd.
Alpharetta, GA 30201
Phone: 770-751-0889
Fax: 770-751-1884

CEO: Wilbur Riner
CFO: Bryan Carr
HR: —
Employees: 26

1995 Sales: $3.8 million
1-Yr. Sales Change: (20.8%)
Exchange: Nasdaq (SC)
Symbol: TNCX

Computers - high-performance file servers & work stations

NETWORK EQUIPMENT TECHNOLOGIES, INC.

800 Saginaw Dr.
Redwood City, CA 94063
Phone: 415-366-4400
Fax: 415-366-5675

CEO: Joseph J. Francesconi
CFO: Craig M. Gentner
HR: Roger A. Barney
Employees: 1,318

1996 Sales: $338.9 million
1-Yr. Sales Change: 19.3%
Exchange: NYSE
Symbol: NWK

Computers - digital communication products for wide-area networks (IDNX, FrameXpress, SONET Transmission Manager)

NETWORK GENERAL CORPORATION

4200 Bohannon Dr.
Menlo Park, CA 94025
Phone: 415-473-2000
Fax: 415-321-0855

CEO: Leslie G. Denend
CFO: James T. Richardson
HR: Sally Takemoto
Employees: 721

1996 Sales: $188.8 million
1-Yr. Sales Change: 35.1%
Exchange: Nasdaq
Symbol: NETG

Computers - local area network analysis software

NETWORK IMAGING CORPORATION

500 Huntmar Park Dr.
Herndon, VA 22070-5100
Phone: 703-478-2260
Fax: 703-478-0147

CEO: James Leto
CFO: Jorge Forgues
HR: Karen Alden
Employees: 333

1995 Sales: $69.2 million
1-Yr. Sales Change: 3.3%
Exchange: Nasdaq
Symbol: IMGX

Computers - graphics software products & applications

NETWORK PERIPHERALS INC.

1371 McCarthy Blvd.
Milpitas, CA 95035
Phone: 408-321-7300
Fax: 408-321-9218

CEO: Pauline L. Alker
CFO: Truman Cole
HR: Myra Mauricio
Employees: 104

1995 Sales: $47.1 million
1-Yr. Sales Change: 40.6%
Exchange: Nasdaq
Symbol: NPIX

Computers - local area network management hardware & software

NETWORK SIX, INC.

475 Kilvert St.	CEO: Kenneth C. Kirsch	1995 Sales: $21.0 million
Warwick, RI 02886	CFO: Bryan M. Gleason	1-Yr. Sales Change: (0.9%)
Phone: 401-732-9000	HR: Maryellen Budria	Exchange: Nasdaq
Fax: 401-732-9009	Employees: 150	Symbol: NWSS

Computers - consulting & system integration services to government agencies that deliver social services

NEW DIMENSION SOFTWARE, INC.

Devora Hanevia St., Bldg. 7, 5C Atidim	CEO: Roni A. Einav	1995 Sales: $35.7 million
Tel Aviv 61430, Israel	CFO: Isaac Zion	1-Yr. Sales Change: 26.6%
Phone: +972-3-645-1111	HR: —	Exchange: Nasdaq
Fax: +972-3-645-1100	Employees: 285	Symbol: DDDDF

Data collection & systems - data systems automation software

NEW IMAGE INDUSTRIES INC.

2283 Cosmos Ct.	CEO: Dewey F. Edmunds	1996 Sales: $37.1 million
Carlsbad, CA 92009	CFO: Hal Orr	1-Yr. Sales Change: 17.4%
Phone: 619-930-9900	HR: Tracy Chandler	Exchange: Nasdaq
Fax: 619-930-9999	Employees: 162	Symbol: NIIS

Medical instruments - dental video cameras & computer-imaging systems

NEW PARADIGM SOFTWARE CORPORATION

335 Madison Ave.	CEO: Mark Blundell	1996 Sales: $0.4 million
New York, NY 10017	CFO: Mark Blundell	1-Yr. Sales Change: 300.0%
Phone: 212-557-0933	HR: Lauren Gray	Exchange: Nasdaq (SC)
Fax: 212-557-0935	Employees: 18	Symbol: NPSC

Computers - enterprise-wide system integration software (Copernicus)

NEWBRIDGE NETWORKS CORPORATION

600 March Rd.	CEO: Terence H. Matthews	1996 Sales: $676.6 million
Kanata, ON K2K 2E6, Canada	CFO: Peter D. Charbonneau	1-Yr. Sales Change: 14.6%
Phone: 613-591-3600	HR: Michael Gaffney	Exchange: NYSE
Fax: 613-591-3680	Employees: 3,400	Symbol: NN

Computers - multimedia networking products for LAN & WAN applications

 **See page 331 for a full profile of this company.**

NEXT SOFTWARE, INC.

900 Chesapeake Dr.	CEO: Steven Jobs	1995 Sales: $46.0 million
Redwood City, CA 94063	CFO: Dominique Trempont	1-Yr. Sales Change: (7.4%)
Phone: 415-366-0900	HR: Paul Bianchi	Ownership: Privately Held
Fax: 415-780-3929	Employees: 280	

Computers - object-oriented software, including operating systems (NEXTSTEP) and programming tools

 See page 332 for a full profile of this company.

NICHOLS RESEARCH CORPORATION

4040 S. Memorial Pkwy.	CEO: Chris H. Horgen	1995 Sales: $170.3 million
Huntsville, AL 35802-1326	CFO: Allen E. Dillard	1-Yr. Sales Change: 18.9%
Phone: 205-883-1140	HR: Scott Parker	Exchange: Nasdaq
Fax: 205-880-0367	Employees: 1,336	Symbol: NRES

Engineering - information & computer technology & R&D services for the US Department of Defense

NINTENDO CO., LTD.

60 Fukuine Kamitakamatsu-cho	CEO: Hiroshi Yamauchi	1996 Sales: $3,337.0 million
Kyoto 605, Japan	CFO: —	1-Yr. Sales Change: (28.5%)
Phone: +81-75-541-6111	HR: —	Exchange: OTC
Fax: +81-75-531-7996	Employees: 952	Symbol: NTDOY

Computers - interactive entertainment hardware (Virtual Boy, Nintendo Ultra 64) & software (Super NES, Game Boy)

 See pages 162–163 for a full profile of this company.

NOBODY BEATS THE WIZ

1300 Federal Blvd.	CEO: Lawrence Jemal	1996 Est. Sales: $1,000 mil.
Carteret, NJ 07008	CFO: Stan Berg	1-Yr. Sales Change: 5.3%
Phone: 908-602-1900	HR: Bob Brummer	Ownership: Privately Held
Fax: 908-634-6856	Employees: 4,300	

Retail - consumer electronics superstores in the NY metro area

NORAND CORPORATION

550 Second St. SE	CEO: N. Robert Hammer	1995 Sales: $217.9 million
Cedar Rapids, IA 52401	CFO: Don Rowley	1-Yr. Sales Change: 12.9%
Phone: 319-369-3100	HR: James Harrington	Exchange: Nasdaq
Fax: 319-369-3453	Employees: 977	Symbol: NRND

Data collection & systems - wireless data-collection systems (Pen*Key) for retail & other applications

NORTH STAR UNIVERSAL, INC.

5353 Wayzata Blvd., Ste. 610	CEO: Jeffrey J. Michael	1995 Sales: $54.9 million
Minneapolis, MN 55416-1335	CFO: Peter E. Flynn	1-Yr. Sales Change: (40.5%)
Phone: 612-546-7500	HR: Gail Ellingson	Exchange: Nasdaq
Fax: 612-540-9100	Employees: 379	Symbol: NSRU

Diversified operations - computer cable; IBM & IBM-compatible computer refurbishing; food processing; climate-control equipment for off-road vehicles

NORWEST VENTURE CAPITAL

2800 Piper Jaffray Tower, 222 S. 9th St.	CEO: Daniel J. Haggerty	1996 Sales: —
Minneapolis, MN 55402-3388	CFO: John P. Whaley	1-Yr. Sales Change: —
Phone: 612-667-1650	HR: Patti Reskin	Ownership: Privately Held
Fax: 612-667-1660	Employees: 25	

Financial - equity investments in start-up businesses, emerging growth companies, management buyouts, acquisitions & corporate recapitalizations

NOVADIGM, INC.

One International Blvd., Ste 200	CEO: Albion J. Fitzgerald	1996 Sales: $25.0 million
Mahwah, NJ 07495	CFO: Wallace D. Ruiz	1-Yr. Sales Change: 168.8%
Phone: 201-512-1000	HR: —	Exchange: Nasdaq
Fax: 201-512-1452	Employees: 92	Symbol: NVDM

Computers - networking & connectivity system management software

NOVAQUEST INFOSYSTEMS, INC.

19950 Mariner Ave.	CEO: Asif Hudani	1995 Sales: $142.0 million
Torrance, CA 90503	CFO: Don Peterson	1-Yr. Sales Change: 16.4%
Phone: 310-214-4200	HR: Trina Hunter	Ownership: Privately Held
Fax: 310-214-4387	Employees: 170	

Retail - microcomputer hardware, software & networking products; related support services

NOVELL, INC.

1555 N. Technology Way	CEO: John A. Young	1995 Sales: $2,041.2 million
Orem, UT 84057	CFO: James R. Tolonen	1-Yr. Sales Change: 2.2%
Phone: 801-222-6000	HR: Jennifer Konecny-Costa	Exchange: Nasdaq
Fax: 801-222-7077	Employees: 7,272	Symbol: NOVL

Computers - network software (NetWare) & Internet access tools (Corsair 3D, Ferret)

 **See pages 164–165 for a full profile of this company.**

NOVELLUS SYSTEMS INC

3970 N. First St.
San Jose, CA 95134
Phone: 408-943-9700
Fax: 408-943-3422

CEO: Richard S. Hill
CFO: William J. Wall
HR: Linus Cordes
Employees: 790

1995 Sales: $373.7 million
1-Yr. Sales Change: 66.3%
Exchange: Nasdaq
Symbol: NVLS

Machinery - chemical vapor deposition systems (Concept Two Sequel-S, Dual Sequel, Concept One Maxus)
for the manufacture of multilevel integrated circuits

 See page 333 for a full profile of this company.

NTN COMMUNICATIONS, INC.

5966 La Place Ct.
Carlsbad, CA 92008
Phone: 619-438-7400
Fax: 619-438-7470

CEO: Patrick J. Downs
CFO: Gerald Sokol Jr.
HR: Genice Eichert
Employees: 275

1995 Sales: $31.8 million
1-Yr. Sales Change: 29.3%
Exchange: AMEX
Symbol: NTN

TV production & programming - interactive subscription-based TV network (NTN Network); interactive
software & video games

NU HORIZONS ELECTRONIC CORP.

6000 New Horizons Blvd.
Amityville, NY 11701
Phone: 516-226-6000
Fax: 516-226-5505

CEO: Irving Lubman
CFO: Paul Durando
HR: Pattie Englert
Employees: 400

1996 Sales: $202.8 million
1-Yr. Sales Change: 55.6%
Exchange: Nasdaq
Symbol: NUHC

Electronics - distribution of high-technology active & passive electronic components

NUMBER NINE VISUAL TECHNOLOGY CORPORATION

18 Hartwell Ave.
Lexington, MA 02173
Phone: 617-674-0009
Fax: 617-674-2919

CEO: Andrew Najda
CFO: Daniel W. Muehl
HR: —
Employees: 144

1995 Sales: $116.8 million
1-Yr. Sales Change: 76.4%
Exchange: Nasdaq
Symbol: NINE

Computer - video- & graphic-accelerator subsystems, chips & software

N-VISION, INC.

7680 Old Springhouse Rd.
McLean, VA 22102
Phone: 703-506-8808
Fax: 703-903-0455

CEO: Delmar J. Lewis
CFO: Robert B. Hamilton
HR: Preston Evers
Employees: 11

1995 Sales: $0.6 million
1-Yr. Sales Change: (60.0%)
Exchange: Nasdaq (SC)
Symbol: NVSN

Computers - flight simulation, industrial design, entertainment, medicine, training & education virtual
reality software & systems for commercial, industrial & military use

OACIS HEALTHCARE HOLDING CORP.

100 Drakes Landing Rd., Ste. 100	CEO: Jim McCord	1995 Sales: $13.6 million
Greenbrae, CA 94904	CFO: Sephen Ghiglieri	1-Yr. Sales Change: 138.6%
Phone: 415-925-0121	HR: Jay Allen	Exchange: Nasdaq
Fax: 415-925-4610	Employees: 157	Symbol: OCIS

Computers - flexible, open architecture information systems for hospitals & health care delivery systems

OAK TECHNOLOGY, INC.

139 Kifer Ct.	CEO: David D. Tsang	1996 Sales: $248.0 million
Sunnyvale, CA 94086	CFO: Sidney S. Faulkner	1-Yr. Sales Change: 123.4%
Phone: 408-737-0888	HR: Malinda Law	Exchange: Nasdaq
Fax: 408-737-3838	Employees: 291	Symbol: OAKT

Computers - multimedia semiconductors, CD-ROM controllers & MPEG video decoders for use in optical-storage, compression, imaging, video, & PC audio applications

OBJECT DESIGN, INC.

25 Mall Rd.	CEO: Robert N. Goldman	1995 Sales: $32.7 million
Burlington, MA 01803-4100	CFO: Lacey P. Brandt	1-Yr. Sales Change: 28.2%
Phone: 617-674-5000	HR: Andrea Johnson	Exchange: Nasdaq
Fax: 617-674-5010	Employees: 204	Symbol: ODIS

Computers - database management systems (ObjectStore, Internet Solution Suite, DBconnect) & related tools for building & deploying Internet, Intranet & other applications

OBJECTIVE SYSTEMS INTEGRATORS, INC.

100 Blue Ravine Rd.	CEO: Joseph T. Ambrozy	1996 Sales: $55.9 million
Folsom, CA 95630	CFO: Gayety W. Hirahara	1-Yr. Sales Change: 55.3%
Phone: 916-353-2400	HR: Becky Wagner	Exchange: Nasdaq
Fax: 916-353-2424	Employees: 328	Symbol: OSII

Computers - client/server software solutions for network operations support & management

OBJECTSOFT CORPORATION

433 Hackensack Ave., Plaza III	CEO: George J. Febish	1995 Sales: $0.6 million
Hackensack, NJ 07601	CFO: George J. Febish	1-Yr. Sales Change: (25.0%)
Phone: 201-343-9100	HR: —	Ownership: Privately Held
Fax: 201-343-0056	Employees: 9	

Computers - information & transaction-based services provided through public access kiosks over private networks (SmartStreet)

OCTUS, INC.

PO Box 232397
San Diego, CA 92193-2397
Phone: 619-268-5140
Fax: 619-268-5175

CEO: John C. Belden
CFO:
HR: Jim B. Donley
Employees: 2

1995 Sales: $1.5 million
1-Yr. Sales Change: 25.0%
Exchange: OTC
Symbol: OCTS

Computers - computer & telephone integration software

OKI ELECTRIC INDUSTRY COMPANY, LIMITED

7-12,Toranomon 1-chome, Minato-ku
Tokyo 105, Japan
Phone: +81-3-3501-3111
Fax: +81-3-3581-5522

CEO: Shiko Sawamura
CFO: —
HR: —
Employees: 21,718

1996 Sales: $6,977.0 million
1-Yr. Sales Change: (4.4%)
Exchange: Tokyo

Computers - laser printers, PCs, POS systems, ASIC-memory-microprocessor integrated circuits, cellular phones, modems, fax machines & PBX systems

 **See pages 166–167 for a full profile of this company.**

OLICOM A/S

Nybrovej 114
DK-2800 Lyngby, Denmark
Phone: +45-45-27-00-00
Fax: +45-45-27-01-01

CEO: Lars Stig Nielsen
CFO: Peter K. Ryaa
HR: —
Employees: 200

1995 Sales: $127.5 million
1-Yr. Sales Change: 12.2%
Exchange: Nasdaq
Symbol: OLCMF

Computers - Token-Ring & Ethernet local area network software & hardware

OLIVETTI S.P.A.

Via Jervis 77
10015 Ivrea, Italy
Phone: +39-125-52-5
Fax: +39-125-52-20-08

CEO: Francesco Caio
CFO: Angelo Fornasari
HR: —
Employees: 30,120

1995 Sales: $6,208.0 million
1-Yr. Sales Change: 11.5%
Exchange: OTC
Symbol: OLIVY

Computers - electronic equipment, systems & printers, including special systems, smart cards, modules & networks & printed circuits; office furniture & fittings

 **See pages 168–169 for a full profile of this company.**

OMNI MULTIMEDIA GROUP, INC.

50 Howe Ave.
Millbury, MA 01527
Phone: 508-865-4451
Fax: 508-865-1853

CEO: Paul F. Johnson
CFO: Robert E. Lee
HR: —
Employees: 117

1996 Sales: $18.9 million
1-Yr. Sales Change: 101.1%
Exchange: AMEX
Symbol: OMG

Computers - software duplication for financial & insurance services; CD-ROM multimedia catalog

ON TECHNOLOGY CORPORATION

One Cambridge Ctr.	CEO: Christopher A. Risley	1995 Sales: $44.1 million
Cambridge, MA 02142-1604	CFO: John M. Bogdan	1-Yr. Sales Change: 70.9%
Phone: 617-374-1400	HR: —	Exchange: Nasdaq
Fax: 617-374-1433	Employees: 186	Symbol: ONTC

Computers - networking software for heterogeneous networks

ONESOURCE INFORMATION SERVICES INC.

150 Cambridge Park Dr.	CEO: Dan Schimmel	1995 Sales: $30.0 million
Cambridge, MA 02140	CFO: Roy Landon	1-Yr. Sales Change: —
Phone: 617-441-7000	HR: —	Ownership: Privately Held
Fax: 617-441-7058	Employees: 200	

Computers - business information databases on CD-ROM and the Internet

ONEWAVE, INC.

One Arsenal Marketplace	CEO: Klaus P. Besier	1995 Sales: $6.1 million
Watertown, MA 02172	CFO: Mark Gallagher	1-Yr. Sales Change: —
Phone: 617-923-6500	HR: David Kimmelman	Exchange: Nasdaq
Fax: 617-923-6565	Employees: 102	Symbol: OWAV

Computers - Web-enabled software for mission-critical business applications across an organization's disparate IT system & applications extended to Intranets & the Internet

ONLINE SYSTEM SERVICES, INC.

1800 Glenarm Place, Ste. 800	CEO: R. Steven Adams	1995 Sales: $0.4 million
Denver, CO 80202	CFO: —	1-Yr. Sales Change: —
Phone: 303-296-9200	HR: —	Exchange: Nasdaq (SC)
Fax: 303-295-3584	Employees: 24	Symbol: WEBB

Computers - World Wide Web site development, marketing & sales

ONTRAK SYSTEMS, INC.

1753 S. Main St.	CEO: James W. Bagley	1996 Sales: $55.8 million
Milpitas, CA 95035	CFO: Patrick C. O'Connor	1-Yr. Sales Change: 114.6%
Phone: 408-262-5200	HR: Amy Buck	Exchange: Nasdaq
Fax: 408-952-5441	Employees: 323	Symbol: ONTK

Electrical components - semiconductor equipment that cleans silicon wafers

OPAL, INC.

2903 Bunker Hill Ln., Ste. 103
Santa Clara, CA 95054
Phone: 408-727-6060
Fax: 408-727-6332

CEO: Rafi Yizhar
CFO: Henry Schwarzbaum
HR: Laura Higbie
Employees: 224

1995 Sales: $44.7 million
1-Yr. Sales Change: 81.7%
Exchange: Nasdaq
Symbol: OPAL

Electronics - inspection systems for the integrated circuit manufacturing process

OPEN ENVIRONMENT CORPORATION

25 Travis St.
Boston, MA 02134
Phone: 617-562-0900
Fax: 617-562-5942

CEO: Nathan P. Morton
CFO: James J. Driscoll
HR: Juanita Duserick
Employees: 214

1995 Sales: $31.1 million
1-Yr. Sales Change: 120.6%
Exchange: Nasdaq
Symbol: OPEN

Computers - client/server software development tools

OPEN MARKET, INC.

245 First St.
Cambridge, MA 02142
Phone: 617-621-9500
Fax: 617-621-1703

CEO: Gary B. Eichorn
CFO: Regina O. Sommer
HR: Joanne C. Conrad
Employees: 257

1995 Sales: $1.8 million
1-Yr. Sales Change: —
Exchange: Nasdaq
Symbol: OMKT

Computers - software for business-to-consumer, business-to-business & intra-enterprise (Intranet)
Internet commerce

OPEN TEXT CORPORATION

180 Columbia St. West, Ste. 2110
Waterloo, ON N2L 3L3, Canada
Phone: 519-888-7111
Fax: 519-888-0677

CEO: P. Thomas Jenkins
CFO: William N. Stirlen
HR: —
Employees: 133

1996 Sales: $10.0 million
1-Yr. Sales Change: 300.0%
Exchange: Nasdaq
Symbol: OTEXF

Computers - software for use on LANs, WANs & the Internet to find electronically stored information

OPENVISION TECHNOLOGIES, INC.

7133 Koll Center Pkwy., Ste. 200
Pleasanton, CA 94566
Phone: 510-426-6400
Fax: 510-426-6486

CEO: Geoffrey W. Squire
CFO: Kenneth E. Lonchar
HR: Sonia Gril
Employees: 220

1996 Sales: $29.9 million
1-Yr. Sales Change: 61.6%
Exchange: Nasdaq
Symbol: OPVN

Computers - client/server systems management software (AXXiON) for storage, operations & security

OPTI, INC.

2525 Walsh Ave.	CEO: Jerry Chang	1995 Sales: $163.7 million
Santa Clara, CA 95051	CFO: David Zacarias	1-Yr. Sales Change: 22.1%
Phone: 408-980-8178	HR: Steve Rowe	Exchange: Nasdaq
Fax: 408-980-8860	Employees: 224	Symbol: OPTI

Electrical components - core logic chipsets for 32-bit & 64-bit PC market

OPTICAL COATING LABORATORY, INC.

2789 Northpoint Pkwy.	CEO: Herbert M. Dwight Jr.	1995 Sales: $169.4 million
Santa Rosa, CA 95407-7397	CFO: John M. Markovich	1-Yr. Sales Change: 28.5%
Phone: 707-545-6440	HR: William C. Burgess	Exchange: Nasdaq
Fax: 707-525-7410	Employees: 1,410	Symbol: OCLI

Electrical products - multilayer optical thin-film coated components for the aerospace, computer, telecommunication & defense industries

OPTICAL DATA SYSTEMS, INC.

1101 E. Arapaho Rd.	CEO: G. Ward Paxton	1995 Sales: $111.5 million
Richardson, TX 75081	CFO: Timothy W. Kinnear	1-Yr. Sales Change: 28.8%
Phone: 972-234-6400	HR: Donna J. Combs	Exchange: Nasdaq
Fax: 972-234-1467	Employees: 230	Symbol: ODSI

Computers - networking hubs (Infinity), bridges & routers

OPTIKA IMAGING SYSTEMS, INC.

5755 Mark Dabling Blvd., Ste. 100	CEO: Mark K. Ruport	1995 Sales: $10.5 million
Colorado Springs, CO 80919	CFO: Steven M. Johnson	1-Yr. Sales Change: 12.9%
Phone: 719-548-9800	HR: Les Brown	Exchange: Nasdaq
Fax: 719-531-7915	Employees: 119	Symbol: OPTK

Computers - document imaging & automated workflow transaction processing software (FilePower Suite) for paper-intensive industries, including health care, financial services, insurance & retail

ORACLE CORPORATION

500 Oracle Pkwy.	CEO: Lawrence J. Ellison	1996 Sales: $4,223.3 million
Redwood City, CA 94065	CFO: Jeffrey O. Henley	1-Yr. Sales Change: 42.3%
Phone: 415-506-7000	HR: Phillip E. Wilson	Exchange: Nasdaq
Fax: 415-506-7200	Employees: 16,882	Symbol: ORCL

Computers - database management systems software (#1 worldwide), network products & productivity tools

 See pages 170–171 for a full profile of this company.

ORBOTECH LTD.

New Industrial Zone, PO Box 215	CEO: Yochai Richter	1995 Sales: $129.5 million
Yavne 70651, Israel	CFO: Dan Falk	1-Yr. Sales Change: 9.7%
Phone: +972-8-428-533	HR: Eitan Ben-Sinai	Exchange: Nasdaq
Fax: +972-8-438-769	Employees: 262	Symbol: ORBKF

Machinery - computerized electro-optical systems for inspecting & indentifying defects in printed circuit boards & LCDs; engineering & tooling-generation systems & laser plotters

ORCAD, INC.

9300 SW Nimbus Ave.	CEO: Michael F. Bosworth	1995 Sales: $13.7 million
Beaverton, OR 97008	CFO: Tom Cusick	1-Yr. Sales Change: 39.8%
Phone: 503-671-9500	HR: Linda Browning	Exchange: Nasdaq
Fax: 503-671-9501	Employees: 104	Symbol: OCAD

Computers - Windows-based software products

ORGANIC ONLINE

520 Third St.	CEO: Jonathan Nelson	1995 Est. Sales: $3.0 mil.
San Francisco, CA 94107	CFO: Jeff D. Davids	1-Yr. Sales Change: 200.0%
Phone: 415-284-6888	HR: Regina Brown	Ownership: Privately Held
Fax: 415-284-6891	Employees: 35	

Advertising agency specializing in developing corporate web sites

ORIGIN B.V.

Euclideslaan 2	CEO: Geoffrey Carroll	1995 Sales: $1,200.0 million
NL 3584 BN Utrecht, The Netherlands	CFO: Wil C. J. T. van Gorp	1-Yr. Sales Change: 39.5%
Phone: +31-30-586800	HR: Mattjis Kropholler	Ownership: Privately Held
Fax: +31-30-2586710	Employees: 9,772	

Consulting - IT services to large & medium-sized companies & government organizations, including automation development & consultancy services (82.4% owned by Philips Electronics N.V.)

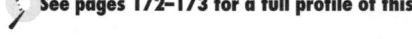 **See pages 172–173 for a full profile of this company.**

OSHAP TECHNOLOGIES LTD.

Delta House, 16 Hagalim Ave.	CEO: Shlomo Dovrat	1995 Sales: $38.2 million
Herzliya 46733, Israel	CFO: Avi Zeevi	1-Yr. Sales Change: 38.4%
Phone: +972-9-594-894	HR: —	Exchange: Nasdaq
Fax: +972-9-594-898	Employees: 285	Symbol: OSHSF

Computers - computer aided production engineering (CAPE) software; information switching software for the financial market

OVID TECHNOLOGIES, INC.

333 Seventh Ave.	CEO: Mark L. Nelson	1995 Sales: $29.3 million
New York, NY 10001	CFO: Jerry P. McAuliffe	1-Yr. Sales Change: 32.0%
Phone: 212-563-3006	HR: Beatriz Abreu	Exchange: Nasdaq
Fax: 212-563-3784	Employees: 168	Symbol: OVID

Database collection & systems - electronic information retrieval services to major medical centers in the US & Canada

OZEMAIL LIMITED

39 Herbert St., St. Leonards	CEO: Sean Howard	1995 Sales: $6.6 million
2065 Sydney, Australia	CFO: John Worton	1-Yr. Sales Change: —
Phone: +61-2-391-0400	HR: —	Exchange: Nasdaq
Fax: +61-2-437-5888	Employees: 134	Symbol: OZEMY

Computers - Internet & consulting services in Australia & New Zealand

P & P PLC

Todd Hall Rd., Haslingden	CEO: David R. Southworth	1995 Sales: $524.1 million
Rossendale, Lancashire BB4 5HU, UK	CFO: John D. Atkin	1-Yr. Sales Change: 26.9%
Phone: +44-1-706-217-744	HR: —	Exchange: London
Fax: +44-1-706-211-401	Employees: 1,243	

Computers - computer desktop hardware & software; computer communications

PACE HEALTH MANAGEMENT SYSTEMS, INC.

1025 Ashworth Rd., Ste. 420	CEO: Mark J. Emkjer	1995 Sales: $2.1 million
West Des Moines, IA 50265	CFO: Roger D. Huseman	1-Yr. Sales Change: 425.0%
Phone: 515-222-1717	HR: —	Exchange: Nasdaq (SC)
Fax: 515-222-1716	Employees: 50	Symbol: PCES

Computers - point-of-care clinical software that automates the recording, retrieval & management of patient care information

PACIFIC ANIMATED IMAGING CORP.

326 First St., Ste. 100	CEO: John J. Cadigan	1995 Sales: $0.7 million
Annapolis, MD 21403	CFO: Suzanne C. Brown	1-Yr. Sales Change: (12.5%)
Phone: 410-263-7761	HR: —	Exchange: Nasdaq (SC)
Fax: 410-280-6013	Employees: 24	Symbol: PAID

Computers - interactive computer-animated graphics for training applications; consumer software for teaching scientific concepts

PACKARD BELL ELECTRONICS, INC.

One Packard Bell Way	CEO: Beny Alagem	1995 Sales: $4,600.0 million
Sacramento, CA 95828-0903	CFO: Phil Handley	1-Yr. Sales Change: 53.3%
Phone: 916-388-0101	HR: Karen Schmidt	Ownership: Privately Held
Fax: 916-388-1109	Employees: 5,000	

Computers - PC-compatible desktop computers, notebooks, peripherals & multimedia PCs

 See pages 174–175 for a full profile of this company.

THE PANDA PROJECT, INC.

5201 Congress Ave., Ste. C-100	CEO: Stanford W. Crane Jr.	1996 Sales: $0.9 million
Boca Raton, FL 33487	CFO: Robert Bowman	1-Yr. Sales Change: 200.0%
Phone: 561-994-2300	HR: Diane Charpentier	Exchange: Nasdaq (SC)
Fax: 561-994-0191	Employees: 139	Symbol: PNDA

Electrical components - chip packages which house & protect semiconductor components (Spider Pack)

PAPYRUS ASSOCIATES, INC.

21 Wayside Rd.	CEO: William E. Kania	1996 Sales: $2.0 million
Westborough, MA 01581	CFO: Brian Mottershead	1-Yr. Sales Change: —
Phone: 508-836-5443	HR: —	Ownership: Privately Held
Fax: 800-877-3934	Employees: 10	

Computers - handwriting recognition software & pen computing applications for Pen PCs, PDAs, 2-way pagers & communicators

PAR TECHNOLOGY CORPORATION

PAR Tech. Park, 8383 Seneca Tpke.	CEO: John W. Sammon Jr.	1995 Sales: $107.4 million
New Hartford, NY 13413-4991	CFO: Ronald J. Casciano	1-Yr. Sales Change: 13.7%
Phone: 315-738-0600	HR: Ken Giffune	Exchange: NYSE
Fax: 315-738-0411	Employees: 822	Symbol: PTC

Computers - transaction processing systems; point-of-sale systems for restaurants; industrial data collection systems; image processing for ophthalmic & food processing; computer systems for the military

PARADIGM TECHNOLOGY, INC.

71 Vista Montana	CEO: Michael Gulett	1995 Sales: $51.9 million
San Jose, CA 95134	CFO: Robert C. McClelland	1-Yr. Sales Change: 63.2%
Phone: 408-954-0500	HR: Dennis McDonald	Exchange: Nasdaq
Fax: 408-954-8913	Employees: 211	Symbol: PRDM

Electrical components - static random-access memory (SRAM) chips for computer workstations & telecommunications equipment

PARAMETRIC TECHNOLOGY CORPORATION

128 Technology Dr.
Waltham, MA 02154
Phone: 617-398-5000
Fax: 617-398-6000

CEO: Steven C. Walske
CFO: Edwin J. Gillis
HR: Carl Ockerbloom
Employees: 1,960

1995 Sales: $394.3 million
1-Yr. Sales Change: 61.4%
Exchange: Nasdaq
Symbol: PMTC

Computers - computer-aided design, manufacturing & engineering software (Pro/ENGINEER)

 See page 334 for a full profile of this company.

PARAMOUNT FINANCIAL CORPORATION

100 Crossways Park West, Ste. 205
Woodbury, NY 11797-2012
Phone: 516-921-3399
Fax: 516-938-3995

CEO: Jeffrey Nortman
CFO: Paul Vecker
HR: —
Employees: 7

1995 Sales: $33.1 million
1-Yr. Sales Change: 18.2%
Exchange: Nasdaq
Symbol: PARA

Leasing - computers & other high-technology equipment

PARAVANT COMPUTER SYSTEMS, INC.

780 S. Apollo Blvd., Atrium One
Melbourne, FL 32901
Phone: 407-727-3672
Fax: 407-725-0496

CEO: Krishan K. Joshi
CFO: Kevin Bartczak
HR: —
Employees: 60

1995 Sales: $8.7 million
1-Yr. Sales Change: 11.5%
Exchange: Nasdaq
Symbol: PVAT

Computers - portable computers & communications interfaces for the military, government & commercial markets

PARCPLACE-DIGITALK, INC.

999 E. Arques Ave.
Sunnyvale, CA 94086
Phone: 408-481-9090
Fax: 408-481-9095

CEO: William P. Lyons
CFO: Carolyn V. Aver
HR: Kathy Schmidt
Employees: 230

1996 Sales: $49.6 million
1-Yr. Sales Change: 26.9%
Exchange: Nasdaq
Symbol: PARQ

Computers - object-oriented software development tools

PARITY SYSTEMS INC.

110 Knowles Dr.
Los Gatos, CA 95030-1828
Phone: 408-378-1000
Fax: 408-378-1022

CEO: Norbert Witt
CFO: Nick Ward
HR: Sally Seales
Employees: 64

1995 Sales: $32.0 million
1-Yr. Sales Change: 6.7%
Ownership: Privately Held

Computers - memory products & SCSI storage devices for UNIX/RISC workstations & servers

PARK ELECTROCHEMICAL CORP.

5 Dakota Dr.	CEO: Jerry Shore	1996 Sales: $313.0 million
Lake Success, NY 11042	CFO: Paul R. Shackford	1-Yr. Sales Change: 23.7%
Phone: 516-354-4100	HR: —	Exchange: NYSE
Fax: 516-354-4128	Employees: 2,240	Symbol: PKE

Electrical components - advanced laminates & semi-finished circuit boards; bathtub spouts, shower heads & faucet housings; specialty resins for aerospace, military, recreational & telecommunications products

THE PAUL ALLEN GROUP

110 110th Ave. NE, Ste. 530	CEO: Vern Raburn	1996 Sales: —
Bellevue, WA 98004	CFO: Frank Kraus	1-Yr. Sales Change: —
Phone: 206-453-6101	HR: Pam Faber	Ownership: Privately Held
Fax: 206-453-1985	Employees: 10	

Financial - investments in high-tech companies, including Asymetrix Corp. (100%), DreamWorks SKG (18.5%), Portland Trail Blazers (100%), Starwave Corp. (100%) & Ticketmaster Corp. (80%)

 See page 335 for a full profile of this company.

PAVILION TECHNOLOGIES

11100 Metric Blvd., Ste. 700	CEO: Ron Riedesel	1995 Sales: $10.0 million
Austin, TX 78758-4018	CFO: —	1-Yr. Sales Change: —
Phone: 512-438-1400	HR: —	Ownership: Privately Held
Fax: 512-438-1401	Employees: 103	

Computers - software used to create virtual models of manufacturing environments

PC AND MAC CONNECTION INC.

6 Mill St.	CEO: Patricia Gallup	1995 Est. Sales: $225.0 mil.
Marlow, NH 03456	CFO: Ron Karuoski	1-Yr. Sales Change: 12.5%
Phone: 603-446-3383	HR: Ronda Farrington	Ownership: Privately Held
Fax: 603-446-7796	Employees: 750	

Retail - mail order PCs & peripherals

PC DOCS GROUP INTERNATIONAL INC.

85 Scarsdale Rd.	CEO: Rubin I. Osten	1996 Sales: $58.4 million
Toronto, ON M3B 2R2, Canada	CFO: P. Ian Reece	1-Yr. Sales Change: 70.3%
Phone: 416-445-4823	HR: —	Exchange: Nasdaq
Fax: 416-445-6228	Employees: 325	Symbol: DOCSF

Computers - document management software (PC DOCS Open) for client/server environments; legal information management software (CMS OPEN, LawPack)

PC QUOTE, INC.

300 S. Wacker Dr., Ste. 300	CEO: Louis J. Morgan	1995 Sales: $13.4 million
Chicago, IL 60606	CFO: Richard F. Chappetto	1-Yr. Sales Change: 3.9%
Phone: 312-913-2800	HR: Darlene Czaja	Exchange: AMEX
Fax: 312-913-2900	Employees: 78	Symbol: PQT

Financial - electronic stock quotation service

PC SERVICE SOURCE, INC.

2350 Valley View Ln.	CEO: Mark Hilz	1995 Sales: $68.7 million
Dallas, TX 75234	CFO: Brian R. Ervine	1-Yr. Sales Change: 62.4%
Phone: 214-406-8583	HR: Mary Zapata	Exchange: Nasdaq
Fax: 214-406-9081	Employees: 360	Symbol: PCSS

Electronics - distribution of repair parts for PCs & related peripherals; inventory management & outsourcing services

PC WAREHOUSE INVESTMENT, INC.

174 State Rte. 17 North	CEO: Robin Lu	1995 Sales: $149.0 million
Rochelle Park, NJ 07662	CFO: Sean Chen	1-Yr. Sales Change: (3.9%)
Phone: 201-587-9600	HR: Suzanne Tseng	Ownership: Privately Held
Fax: 201-587-1734	Employees: 149	

Retail - PCs & software

PEAK TECHNOLOGIES GROUP, INC.

9200 Berger Rd.	CEO: Nicholas R. H. Toms	1995 Sales: $184.6 million
Columbia, MD 21046	CFO: Edward A. Stevens	1-Yr. Sales Change: 61.8%
Phone: 410-312-6000	HR: Mike Bush	Exchange: Nasdaq
Fax: 410-312-6065	Employees: 813	Symbol: PEAK

Optical character recognition - industrial bar code systems

PEAPOD, INC.

1033 University Place	CEO: Andrew Parkinson	1995 Est. Sales: $20.0 mil.
Evanston, IL 60201	CFO: Dave Beedie	1-Yr. Sales Change: —
Phone: 847-492-8900	HR: Toya Campbell	Ownership: Privately Held
Fax: 847-492-0172	Employees: 450	

Retail - online shopping service that delivers groceries in Chicago & San Francisco

PEERLESS SYSTEMS CORPORATION

2381 Rosecrans Ave.
El Segundo, CA 90245
Phone: 310-536-0908
Fax: 310-536-0058

CEO: Edward A. Gavaldon
CFO: Hoshi Printer
HR: Jan Bowler
Employees: 85

1995 Sales: $10.4 million
1-Yr. Sales Change: 11.8%
Exchange: Nasdaq
Symbol: PRLS

Computers - software-based embedded imaging systems for original equipment manufacturers of digital document products

PEGASYSTEMS INC.

101 Main St.
Cambridge, MA 02142
Phone: 617-374-9600
Fax: 617-374-9620

CEO: Alan Trefler
CFO: Ira Vishner
HR: Michelle Kennan
Employees: 160

1995 Sales: $22.2 million
1-Yr. Sales Change: 36.2%
Exchange: Nasdaq
Symbol: PEGA

Computers - customer service management software used by banks, mutual funds & credit card organizations to automate customer interactions across transaction-intensive enterprises

PEN INTERCONNECT, INC.

2351 S. 2300 West
Salt Lake City, UT 84119
Phone: 801-973-6090
Fax: 801-977-3887

CEO: James S. Pendleton
CFO: Wayne R. Wright
HR: Deleene Counter
Employees: 360

1995 Sales: $15.0 million
1-Yr. Sales Change: 127.3%
Exchange: Nasdaq
Symbol: PENC

Electrical connectors - custom cable interconnections for OEMs in the computer, telecommunications & testing industries

PENRIL DATACOMM NETWORKS, INC.

1300 Quince Orchard Blvd.
Gaithersburg, MD 20878
Phone: 301-417-0552
Fax: 301-948-5761

CEO: Henry D. Epstein
CFO: Richard S. Rose
HR: Debbie VanCoutren
Employees: 324

1995 Sales: $58.2 million
1-Yr. Sales Change: (21.1%)
Exchange: Nasdaq
Symbol: PNRL

Computers - data-communication network systems & specialized electronic instruments

PEOPLESOFT, INC.

4440 Rosewood Dr.
Pleasanton, CA 94588
Phone: 510-225-3000
Fax: 510-225-3100

CEO: David A. Duffield
CFO: Ronald E. F. Codd
HR: Larry Butler
Employees: 1,341

1995 Sales: $227.6 million
1-Yr. Sales Change: 101.6%
Exchange: Nasdaq
Symbol: PSFT

Computers - human resource & financial administration client/server software, including accounts payable/receivable, benefits adminstration, financial systems, payroll & project costing software

 See page 336 for a full profile of this company.

PERCON INCORPORATED

1720 Willow Creek Circle, Ste. 530	CEO: Michael P. Coughlin	1995 Sales: $12.7 million
Eugene, OR 97402-9171	CFO: G. Scott Purcell	1-Yr. Sales Change: 35.1%
Phone: 541-344-1189	HR: Rebecca Plant	Exchange: Nasdaq
Fax: 541-344-1399	Employees: 68	Symbol: PRCN

Computers - bar code reading products, including fixed station decoders & portable data terminals for automatic identification & data collection

PERFORMANCE TECHNOLOGIES, INCORPORATED

315 Science Pkwy.	CEO: Charles E. Maginness	1995 Sales: $17.9 million
Rochester, NY 14620	CFO: Dorrance W. Lamb	1-Yr. Sales Change: 42.1%
Phone: 716-256-0200	HR: —	Exchange: Nasdaq
Fax: 716-256-0791	Employees: 101	Symbol: PTIX

Computers - networking & data storage interface system products, including local & wide area interface adapters, communications servers & mass storage interface products

PERICOM SEMICONDUCTOR CORPORATION

2380 Bering Dr.	CEO: Alex Hui	1995 Sales: $42.0 million
San Jose, CA 95131	CFO: Patrick Brennan	1-Yr. Sales Change: —
Phone: 408-435-0800	HR: —	Ownership: Privately Held
Fax: 408-321-0933	Employees: 120	

Electrical components - digital & mixed-signal integrated circuits

PERLE SYSTEMS LIMITED

60 Renfrew Dr.	CEO: Joseph E. Perle	1996 Sales: $33.7 million
Markham, ON L3R OE1, Canada	CFO: J. Douglas Langford	1-Yr. Sales Change: —
Phone: 905-475-8885	HR: Natasha Avsenik	Exchange: Nasdaq (SC)
Fax: 905-475-8646	Employees: 179	Symbol: PERLF

Computers - communication controllers & emulation cards used with IBM midrange computers

PEROT SYSTEMS CORPORATION

12377 Merit Dr., Ste. 1100	CEO: James A. Cannavino	1995 Sales: $350.0 million
Dallas, TX 75251	CFO: John Vonesh	1-Yr. Sales Change: 9.4%
Phone: 214-383-5600	HR: Carol Barnett	Ownership: Privately Held
Fax: 214-383-4157	Employees: 2,400	

Computers - systems integration & consulting services & custom software design

See page 337 for a full profile of this company.

PERSONAL COMPUTER PRODUCTS, INC.

10865 Rancho Bernardo Rd.
San Diego, CA 92127
Phone: 619-487-8411
Fax: 619-487-5809

CEO: Edward W. Savarese
CFO: Gary B. Berg
HR: —
Employees: 53

1996 Sales: $11.6 million
1-Yr. Sales Change: (19.4%)
Exchange: OTC
Symbol: PCPI

Computers - firmware (software embedded in memory chips), circuit boards, application-specific integrated circuits (ASICs) & software for use in computer imaging devices

PERVASIVE SOFTWARE INC.

8834 Capital of Texas Hwy. N. Ste. 300
Austin, TX 78759
Phone: 512-794-1719
Fax: 512-794-1778

CEO: Ron R. Harris
CFO: —
HR: Meiling Newman
Employees: 150

1996 Sales: $15.0 million
1-Yr. Sales Change: 50.0%
Ownership: Privately Held

Computers - database software (Btrieve) that allows users to store, retrieve & sort information rapidly over a personal computer network

PHOENIX INTERNATIONAL LTD., INC.

900 Winderley Place, Ste. 140
Maitland, FL 32751
Phone: 407-667-0033
Fax: 407-667-0133

CEO: Bahram Yusefzadeh
CFO: Clay E. Scarborough
HR: Dahlia Joseph
Employees: 91

1995 Sales: $0.4 million
1-Yr. Sales Change: —
Exchange: Nasdaq
Symbol: PHXX

Computers - enterprise-wide client/server software for the financial services industry, primarily middle-market banks

PHOENIX TECHNOLOGIES LTD.

2770 De La Cruz Blvd.
Santa Clara, CA 95050-2624
Phone: 408-654-9000
Fax: 408-452-1985

CEO: Jack Kay
CFO: Robert J. Riopel
HR: Judith A. Sundue
Employees: 362

1995 Sales: $49.9 million
1-Yr. Sales Change: (42.1%)
Exchange: Nasdaq
Symbol: PTEC

Computers - system software for PC, PC peripheral equipment & system boards manufacturers

PHOTOCIRCUITS CORPORATION

31 Sea Cliff Ave.
New York, NY 11542
Phone: 516-674-1000
Fax: 516-674-1383

CEO: John Endee
CFO: James Zerby
HR: Robert Potorski
Employees: 2,400

1995 Sales: $265.0 million
1-Yr. Sales Change: 12.8%
Ownership: Privately Held

Electrical components - printed circuit boards

PHOTRONICS, INC.

1061 E. Indiantown Rd.
Jupiter, FL 33477
Phone: 561-747-4163
Fax: 561-747-1432

CEO: Constantine Deno Macricostas
CFO: Robert J. Bollo
HR: Jeffrey P. Moonan
Employees: 684

1995 Sales: $125.3 million
1-Yr. Sales Change: 53.2%
Exchange: Nasdaq
Symbol: PLAB

Electrical components - photomasks (quartz plates) used to manufacture semiconductor wafers

PHYSICIAN COMPUTER NETWORK, INC.

1200 American Rd.
Morris Plains, NJ 07950
Phone: 201-490-3100
Fax: 201-490-3101

CEO: Henry Green
CFO: Thomas Wraback
HR: Hank Halat
Employees: 640

1995 Sales: $41.8 million
1-Yr. Sales Change: 103.9%
Exchange: Nasdaq
Symbol: PCNI

Computers - physician practice-management software

PINNACLE MICRO, INC.

19 Technology Dr.
Irvine, CA 92718
Phone: 714-789-3000
Fax: 714-789-3150

CEO: Lawrence Goelman
CFO: Roger Hay
HR: Chuck McGee
Employees: 185

1995 Sales: $81.8 million
1-Yr. Sales Change: 25.1%
Exchange: Nasdaq
Symbol: PNCL

Computers - optical storage drive peripherals for general data storage

 See page 338 for a full profile of this company.

PIONEER-STANDARD ELECTRONICS, INC.

4800 E. 131st St.
Cleveland, OH 44105
Phone: 216-587-3600
Fax: 216-587-3906

CEO: James L. Bayman
CFO: John V. Goodger
HR: Linda Brown
Employees: 1,399

1996 Sales: $1,105.3 million
1-Yr. Sales Change: 32.8%
Exchange: Nasdaq
Symbol: PIOS

Electronics - distribution of semiconductors, computer products & passive & electromechanical components to OEMs, research labs & government agencies

PIXAR

1001 W. Cutting Blvd.
Richmond, CA 94804
Phone: 510-236-4000
Fax: 510-236-0388

CEO: Steven P. Jobs
CFO: Lawrence B. Levy
HR: Lisa Ellis
Employees: 167

1995 Sales: $12.1 million
1-Yr. Sales Change: 116.1%
Exchange: Nasdaq
Symbol: PIXR

Motion pictures & services - digital animated features (Toy Story), CD-ROM titles & related products

 See page 339 for a full profile of this company.

PLAINTREE SYSTEMS INC.

9 Hillside Ave.
Waltham, MA 02154
Phone: 617-290-5800
Fax: 617-290-0963

CEO: Bruce V. Walter
CFO: Thomas J. Branca
HR: —
Employees: 108

1996 Sales: $31.4 million
1-Yr. Sales Change: 15.4%
Ownership: Privately Held

Computers - networking & connectivity equipment for local area networks (LAN)

PLANNING SCIENCES INTERNATIONAL PLC

St. George's Rd., Wimbledon
London SW19 4EU, UK
Phone: +44-181-971-4000
Fax: —

CEO: Paul R. Rolph
CFO: Anthony K. Fox
HR: —
Employees: 121

1995 Sales: $10.8 million
1-Yr. Sales Change: 77.0%
Exchange: London

Computers - client/server decision support software (Gentia) for business planning & decision making

PLASMA & MATERIALS TECHNOLOGIES, INC.

9255 Deering Ave.
Chatsworth, CA 91311
Phone: 818-886-8000
Fax: 818-775-1226

CEO: Gregor A. Campbell
CFO: John W. LaValle
HR: Kerrin Turrow
Employees: 144

1995 Sales: $21.3 million
1-Yr. Sales Change: 102.9%
Exchange: Nasdaq
Symbol: PMAT

Machinery - high-density low pressure plasma sources, process modules & plasma processing systems for etch & chemical vapor deposition applications for the semiconductor & thin film industries worldwide

PLASMA-THERM, INC.

9509 International Ct.
St. Petersburg, FL 33716
Phone: 813-577-4999
Fax: 813-577-6844

CEO: Ronald H. Deferrari
CFO: Stacy L. Wagner
HR: Barbie Taylor
Employees: 148

1995 Sales: $29.6 million
1-Yr. Sales Change: 27.0%
Exchange: Nasdaq (SC)
Symbol: PTIS

Machinery - semiconductor & flat panel display manufacturing equipment

PLATINUM SOFTWARE CORPORATION

195 Technology Dr.
Irvine, CA 92718-2402
Phone: 714-453-4000
Fax: 714-453-4091

CEO: L. George Klaus
CFO: Michael J. Simmons
HR: Nancy Orr
Employees: 333

1996 Sales: $40.6 million
1-Yr. Sales Change: (27.8%)
Exchange: Nasdaq
Symbol: PSQL

Computers - integrated financial applications software (Platinum for Windows, Platinum SQL Enterprise, Platinum SQL NT)

PLATINUM TECHNOLOGY, INC.

1815 S. Meyers Rd.	CEO: Andrew J. Filipowski	1995 Sales: $275.9 million
Oakbrook Terrace, IL 60181	CFO: Michael P. Cullinane	1-Yr. Sales Change: 188.3%
Phone: 708-620-5000	HR: Jennifer Werneke	Exchange: Nasdaq
Fax: 708-691-0710	Employees: 3,300	Symbol: PLAT

Computers - database management software for mainframes

 See page 340 for a full profile of this company.

PLEXUS CORP.

55 Jewelers Park Dr.	CEO: Peter Strandwitz	1995 Sales: $283.1 million
Neenah, WI 54957-0156	CFO: Thomas B. Sabol	1-Yr. Sales Change: 16.7%
Phone: 414-722-3451	HR: —	Exchange: Nasdaq
Fax: 414-751-3234	Employees: 2,350	Symbol: PLXS

Electrical components - test equipment, electronic meters, printed circuit boards & other electronic products

PNY ELECTRONICS, INC.

200 Anderson Ave.	CEO: Gadi Cohen	1995 Sales: $500.0 million
Moonachie, NJ 07074	CFO: Luke Beshar	1-Yr. Sales Change: 70.6%
Phone: 201-438-6300	HR: Miriam Brilleman	Ownership: Privately Held
Fax: 201-438-9144	Employees: 450	

Computers - memory boards

POINTCAST, INCORPORATED

10101 N. De Anza Blvd.	CEO: Christopher R. Hassett	1995 Sales: $0.0 million
Cupertino, CA 95014	CFO: John P. Jewett	1-Yr. Sales Change: —
Phone: 408-253-0894	HR: —	Ownership: Privately Held
Fax: 408-253-1062	Employees: —	

Computers - personalized news, stock quotes, weather & other information services broadcast via the Internet (The PointCast Network)

POLICY MANAGEMENT SYSTEMS CORPORATION

One PMSC Ctr.	CEO: G. Larry Wilson	1995 Sales: $537.3 million
Blythewood, SC 29016	CFO: Timothy V. Williams	1-Yr. Sales Change: 9.1%
Phone: 803-735-4000	HR: G. C. Pundt	Exchange: NYSE
Fax: 803-735-5544	Employees: 4,655	Symbol: PMS

Computers - insurance industry software & services

 See page 341 for a full profile of this company.

POLYPHASE CORPORATION

16885 Dallas Pkwy., Ste. 400
Dallas, TX 75248
Phone: 214-732-0010
Fax: 214-732-6430

CEO: Paul A. Tanner
CFO: William E. Shatley
HR: Paul A. Tanner
Employees: 832

1995 Sales: $102.0 million
1-Yr. Sales Change: 308.0%
Exchange: AMEX
Symbol: PLY

Computers - networking & connectivity hardware, inclduing transformers, inductors & filters; timber & logging equipment distribution

POMEROY COMPUTER RESOURCES, INC.

1840 Airport Exchange Blvd., Ste. 240
Erlanger, KY 41018
Phone: 606-282-7111
Fax: 606-283-8281

CEO: David B. Pomeroy
CFO: Edwin S. Weinstein
HR: Kim Garner
Employees: 441

1995 Sales: $144.6 million
1-Yr. Sales Change: 28.9%
Exchange: Nasdaq
Symbol: PMRY

Retail - value-added reseller of PCs & peripherals

POPPE TYSON, INC.

40 W. 23rd St.
New York, NY 10010-5201
Phone: 212-727-5600
Fax: 212-727-5662

CEO: Fergus O'Daly Jr.
CFO: Steven M. Blondy
HR: Barbra Sgro
Employees: 365

1996 Sales: $19.0 million
1-Yr. Sales Change: 71.2%
Ownership: Privately Held

Business services - marketing services using traditional media & the Internet, CD-ROMs & digital diskettes

PORTFOLIO ACQUISITION CORPORATION

1500 Broadway
New York, NY 10036
Phone: 212-302-4000
Fax: 212-302-0393

CEO: Jose E. Rodriguez
CFO: Jose E. Rodriguez
HR: Jose E. Rodriguez
Employees: 14

1995 Sales: $89.3 million
1-Yr. Sales Change: 8.0%
Ownership: Privately Held

Leasing - computers

POWER COMPUTING CORPORATION

12337 Technology Blvd.
Austin, TX 78727-6104
Phone: 512-258-1350
Fax: 512-250-3390

CEO: Steve Kahng
CFO: Song Kim
HR: Kay Secord
Employees: 300

1996 Sales: $250.0 million
1-Yr. Sales Change: —
Ownership: Privately Held

Computers - Apple Macintosh clones

See page 342 for a full profile of this company.

POWERCERV CORPORATION

400 N. Ashley Dr., Ste. 2700	CEO: Harold R. Ross	1995 Sales: $28.2 million
Tampa, FL 33602	CFO: Gerald Wicker	1-Yr. Sales Change: 115.3%
Phone: 813-226-2600	HR: Nancy Cahall	Exchange: Nasdaq
Fax: 813-222-0886	Employees: 324	Symbol: PCRV

Computers - client/server development tools (PowerPerformance Series), application products & services for businesses

PRAEGITZER INDUSTRIES INC.

1270 S E Monmouth Cut-off Rd.	CEO: Robert Praegitzer	1996 Sales: $95.1 million
Dallas, OR 97338-9532	CFO: —	1-Yr. Sales Change: 63.7%
Phone: 503-623-9273	HR: —	Exchange: Nasdaq
Fax: —	Employees: 1,036	Symbol: PGTZ

Electrical components - printed circuit boards for computer, telecommunications & contract manufacturers

PRC INC.

1500 PRC Dr.	CEO: James J. Leto	1995 Sales: $720.0 million
McLean, VA 22102	CFO: John Becka	1-Yr. Sales Change: (18.5%)
Phone: 703-556-1000	HR: Robert A. Waters	Ownership: Subsidiary
Fax: 703-556-1174	Employees: 6,850	

Computers - systems integration, primarily for US government clients (subsidiary of Litton Industries); subsidiary of Black & Decker

PRECISION SYSTEMS, INC.

11800 30th Ct. North	CEO: Russell I. Pillar	1995 Sales: $21.5 million
St. Petersburg, FL 33716	CFO: John R. Hindman	1-Yr. Sales Change: 121.6%
Phone: 813-572-9300	HR: Debbie Simon	Exchange: Nasdaq (SC)
Fax: 813-313-6593	Employees: 129	Symbol: PSYS

Telecommunications equipment - network-based interactive communications systems utilizing interactive call processing software for wired & wireless communications

PREMENOS TECHNOLOGY CORP.

1000 Burnett Ave., 2nd Fl.	CEO: Daniel M. Federman	1995 Sales: $25.5 million
Concord, CA 94520	CFO: H. Ward Wolff	1-Yr. Sales Change: 27.5%
Phone: 510-602-2000	HR: —	Exchange: Nasdaq
Fax: 510-602-2024	Employees: 193	Symbol: PRMO

Computers - electronic data interchange software for electronic commerce

PREMISYS COMMUNICATIONS, INC.

48664 Milmont Dr.	CEO: Raymond C. Lin	1996 Sales: $73.9 million
Fremont, CA 94538	CFO: Riley R. Willcox	1-Yr. Sales Change: 139.2%
Phone: 510-353-7600	HR: Ann Mazzini	Exchange: Nasdaq
Fax: 510-353-7601	Employees: 117	Symbol: PRMS

Telecommunications equipment - integrated multiple access products for telecommunications providers

PRI AUTOMATION, INC.

805 Middlesex Tpke.	CEO: Mordechai Wiesler	1995 Sales: $64.0 million
Billerica, MA 01821-3986	CFO: John J. Schickling	1-Yr. Sales Change: 76.3%
Phone: 508-663-8555	HR: Diane M. DeLucia	Exchange: Nasdaq
Fax: 508-671-5486	Employees: 424	Symbol: PRIA

Industrial automation & robotics - semiconductor factory-automation systems

PRIMARK CORPORATION

1000 Winter St., Ste. 4300N	CEO: Joseph E. Kasputys	1995 Sales: $617.3 million
Waltham, MA 02154	CFO: Stephen H. Curran	1-Yr. Sales Change: 29.4%
Phone: 617-466-6611	HR: Diane Robesen	Exchange: NYSE
Fax: 617-890-6187	Employees: 5,131	Symbol: PMK

Computers - online & software-based financial information services (Datastream, Disclosure); real-time, value-added weather data & imagery systems & software (WSI)

PRIMAVERA SYSTEMS INC.

2 Bala Plaza	CEO: Joel M. Koppelman	1995 Sales: $30.0 million
Bala Cynwyd, PA 19004	CFO: Bob Corey	1-Yr. Sales Change: 30.4%
Phone: 610-667-8600	HR: Gene Eckenrode	Ownership: Privately Held
Fax: 610-660-5857	Employees: 205	

Computers - project management software

PRINTRONIX, INC.

17500 Cartwright Rd., PO Box 19559	CEO: Robert A. Kleist	1996 Sales: $159.3 million
Irvine, CA 92713	CFO: George L. Harwood	1-Yr. Sales Change: 8.7%
Phone: 714-863-1900	HR: Juli A. Mathews	Exchange: Nasdaq
Fax: 714-660-8682	Employees: 885	Symbol: PTNX

Computers - medium- & high-speed printers; line-matrix printers for heavy-duty jobs, laser printers for office networks & form & label makers (Intelligent Graphics Processors)

PRISM GROUP, INC.

15530 Woodinville-Redmond Rd.	CEO: K. C. Aly	1995 Sales: $20.5 million
Woodinville, WA 98072	CFO: Gary M. Cully	1-Yr. Sales Change: (25.2%)
Phone: 206-881-1609	HR: —	Exchange: Nasdaq (SC)
Fax: 206-488-1807	Employees: 315	Symbol: PRSMC

Computers - order-processing, manufacturing & product-delivery software

PRISM SOLUTIONS, INC.

1000 Hamlin Ct.	CEO: James W. Ashbrook	1995 Sales: $17.8 million
Sunnyvale, CA 94089	CFO: Samuel Hedgpeth III	1-Yr. Sales Change: 117.1%
Phone: 408-752-1888	HR: Jerry Harmon	Exchange: Nasdaq
Fax: 408-752-1875	Employees: 154	Symbol: PRZM

Computers - database management software (Prism Warehouse Manager, Prism Directory Manager)

PROCOM TECHNOLOGY, INC.

2181 Dupont Dr.	CEO: Alex Razmjoo	1995 Sales: $45.0 million
Irvine, CA 92715	CFO: Alex Aydin	1-Yr. Sales Change: 25.0%
Phone: 714-852-1000	HR: Atashe Aydin	Ownership: Privately Held
Fax: 714-852-1221	Employees: 150	

Computers - redundant arrays of independent disks (RAID) storage systems & CD Servers

PRODIGY SERVICES COMPANY

445 Hamilton Ave.	CEO: Paul DeLacey	1995 Sales: $220.0 million
White Plains, NY 10601	CFO: J. Mark Hattendorf	1-Yr. Sales Change: 10.0%
Phone: 914-448-8000	HR: Nicolas Lapko	Ownership: Privately Held
Fax: 914-448-8083	Employees: 485	

Computers - online consumer information services, including reference databases, financial information, travel services & Internet access

 See page 343 for a full profile of this company.

PROGRAMART CORP.

124 Mount Auburn St.	CEO: John E. Thron	1995 Sales: $34.3 million
Cambridge, MA 02138	CFO: Robert Morse	1-Yr. Sales Change: —
Phone: 617-661-3020	HR: William Mrachek	Ownership: Privately Held
Fax: 617-498-4010	Employees: 176	

Computers - engineering, performance measurement & analysis software

PROGRAMMER'S PARADISE, INC.

1163 Shrewsbury Ave
Shrewsbury, NJ 07702-4321
Phone: 908-389-8950
Fax: 908-389-9227

CEO: Roger Paradis
CFO: John P. Broderick
HR: Claudia Corbalis
Employees: 66

1995 Sales: $93.3 million
1-Yr. Sales Change: 30.9%
Exchange: Nasdaq
Symbol: PROG

Retail - direct marketing of computer software

PROGRESS SOFTWARE CORPORATION

14 Oak Park
Bedford, MA 01730
Phone: 617-280-4000
Fax: 617-280-4095

CEO: Joseph W. Alsop
CFO: Bud Robertson
HR: Robert H. Glaudel
Employees: 1,105

1995 Sales: $180.1 million
1-Yr. Sales Change: 29.4%
Exchange: Nasdaq
Symbol: PRGS

Computers - database management software products & services for development & deployment of
application software

 See page 344 for a full profile of this company.

PROJECT SOFTWARE & DEVELOPMENT, INC.

20 University Rd.
Cambridge, MA 02138
Phone: 617-661-1444
Fax: 617-661-1144

CEO: Robert L. Daniels
CFO: Paul D. Birch
HR: Margaret Brook
Employees: 243

1995 Sales: $46.3 million
1-Yr. Sales Change: 37.8%
Exchange: Nasdaq
Symbol: PSDI

Computers - enterprise-wide, client/server maintenance applications & management systems for businesses,
government agencies & other organizations

PROLOGIC MANAGEMENT SYSTEMS, INC.

2731 E. Elvira St.
Tucson, AZ 85706
Phone: 520-741-1001
Fax: 520-741-1007

CEO: James M. Heim
CFO: William E. Wallin
HR: —
Employees: 30

1996 Sales: $2.6 million
1-Yr. Sales Change: 188.9%
Exchange: AMEX
Symbol: PRLO

Computers - applications software & systems integration services

PROPHET 21, INC.

19 W. College Ave.
Yardley, PA 19067
Phone: 215-493-8900
Fax: 215-321-8008

CEO: John E. Meggitt
CFO: Charles L. Boyle III
HR: Carol Frymire
Employees: 235

1996 Sales: $33.1 million
1-Yr. Sales Change: 6.1%
Exchange: Nasdaq
Symbol: PXXI

Computers - online business management software (Prophet 21 XL)

PROTEON, INC.

9 Technology Dr.
Westborough, MA 01581
Phone: 508-898-2800
Fax: 508-898-3334

CEO: Daniel J. Capone
CFO: Joseph A. DiGiantommaso
HR: Michelle Schoellkopf
Employees: 231

1995 Sales: $75.3 million
1-Yr. Sales Change: (19.8%)
Exchange: Nasdaq
Symbol: PTON

Computers - token ring network & internetworking systems

PROTOSOURCE CORPORATION

2580 W. Shaw
Fresno, CA 93711
Phone: 209-448-8040
Fax: 209-448-8050

CEO: Charles T. Howard
CFO: Steven L. Wilson
HR: Amy DeFendis
Employees: 55

1995 Sales: $1.8 million
1-Yr. Sales Change: —
Exchange: Nasdaq (SC)
Symbol: PSCO

Computers - agri-business accounting, product tracking & billing system software

PROXIMA CORPORATION

9440 Carroll Park Dr.
San Diego, CA 92121-2298
Phone: 619-457-5500
Fax: 619-457-9647

CEO: John E. Rehfeld
CFO: Dennis A. Whittler
HR: Frank Drdek
Employees: 689

1996 Sales: $159.8 million
1-Yr. Sales Change: 17.7%
Exchange: Nasdaq
Symbol: PRXM

Computers - LCD projection equipment (ColorWorks, Cyclops, Multimode, Proxima Ovation, Versa Color)

PSC INC.

675 Basket Rd.
Webster, NY 14580-0448
Phone: 716-265-1600
Fax: 716-265-1689

CEO: L. Michael Hone
CFO: William J. Woodard
HR: Mary A. Gallahan
Employees: 500

1995 Sales: $87.5 million
1-Yr. Sales Change: 44.9%
Exchange: Nasdaq
Symbol: PSCX

Optical character recognition - bar code scanning equipment, handheld & fixed position laser-based scanners & scan engines

PSINET, INC.

510 Huntmar Park Dr.
Herndon, VA 22070
Phone: 703-904-4100
Fax: 703-904-4200

CEO: William L. Schrader
CFO: Harold Wills
HR: David Mann
Employees: 629

1995 Sales: $38.7 million
1-Yr. Sales Change: 154.6%
Exchange: Nasdaq
Symbol: PSIX

Computers - Internet services to businesses

 See page 345 for a full profile of this company.

PSION

Alexander House, 85 Frampton St.
London NW8 8NQ, UK
Phone: +44-171-262-55-580
Fax: +44-171-258-7340

CEO: David Potter
CFO: M. G. Langley
HR: —
Employees: 651

1995 Sales: $140.0 million
1-Yr. Sales Change: 46.0%
Exchange: London

Computers - handheld (#1 worldwide: the Organiser)

PULSAR DATA SYSTEMS, INC.

5000 Philadelphia Way
Lanham, MD 20706-4414
Phone: 301-459-2650
Fax: 301-306-0618

CEO: William W. Davis Sr.
CFO: William W. Davis Sr.
HR: Richard Pagnotta
Employees: 144

1995 Sales: $165.1 million
1-Yr. Sales Change: —
Ownership: Privately Held

Retail - wholesale computers

PUMA TECHNOLOGY, INC.

2940 N. First St.
San Jose, CA 95134
Phone: 408-321-7650
Fax: 408-433-2212

CEO: Bradley A. Rowe
CFO: M. Bruce Nakao
HR: Mitzi Zenger
Employees: 79

1996 Sales: $7.7 million
1-Yr. Sales Change: 755.6%
Ownership: Privately Held

Computers - mobile data exchange software (TranXit)

PURE ATRIA CORP.

1309 S. Mary Ave.
Sunnyvale, CA 94087
Phone: 408-720-1600
Fax: 408-720-9200

CEO: Reed Hastings
CFO: Chuck Bay
HR: Patty McCord
Employees: 199

1995 Sales: $44.0 million
1-Yr. Sales Change: 141.8%
Exchange: Nasdaq
Symbol: PASW

Computers - quality assurance software for building applications for the UNIX operating system (Purify, Quantify, PureCoverage, PureLink, Pure DDTS)

QC OPTICS, INC.

154 Middlesex Tpke.
Burlington, MA 01803
Phone: 617-272-4949
Fax: 617-273-0431

CEO: Eric T. Chase
CFO: John R. Freeman
HR: Marsha Olsen
Employees: —

1995 Sales: $10.4 million
1-Yr. Sales Change: 23.8%
Ownership: Privately Held

Electrical components - laser-based defect detection systems for the semiconductor, flat panel display & computer hard disk markets

QLOGIC CORPORATION

3545 Harbor Blvd.	CEO: H. K. Desai	1996 Sales: $53.8 million
Costa Mesa, CA 92626	CFO: Thomas R. Anderson	1-Yr. Sales Change: (6.8%)
Phone: 714-438-2200	HR: Bill Graves	Exchange: Nasdaq
Fax: 714-668-6950	Employees: 63	Symbol: QLGC

Electrical components - integrated circuits & subsystems for data storage

QMS, INC.

One Magnum Pass	CEO: James L. Busby	1995 Sales: $259.7 million
Mobile, AL 36618	CFO: James K. Doan	1-Yr. Sales Change: (11.3%)
Phone: 334-633-4300	HR: Gregory R. Jones	Exchange: NYSE
Fax: 334-633-0013	Employees: 1,194	Symbol: AQM

Computers - desktop & networked intelligent print systems, color laser printers (QMS magicolor), adapter cards & software (CrownNet)

QUAD SYSTEMS CORPORATION

2 Electronic Dr.	CEO: David W. Smith	1995 Sales: $62.6 million
Horsham, PA 19044	CFO: Anthony R. Drury	1-Yr. Sales Change: 23.2%
Phone: 215-657-6202	HR: Craig Walker	Exchange: Nasdaq
Fax: 215-657-5013	Employees: 178	Symbol: QSYS

Machinery - printed circuit board surface-mount assembly equipment

QUALCOMM INCORPORATED

6455 Lusk Blvd.	CEO: Irwin Mark Jacobs	1995 Sales: $386.6 million
San Diego, CA 92121-2779	CFO: Anthony S. Thornley	1-Yr. Sales Change: 42.3%
Phone: 619-587-1121	HR: Daniel L. Sullivan	Exchange: Nasdaq
Fax: 619-658-2501	Employees: 3,167	Symbol: QCOM

Telecommunications equipment - two-way mobile satellite communication & tracking systems; electronic mail software (Eudora); code division multiple access (CDMA) & other advanced communications systems

QUALITY SEMICONDUCTOR, INC.

851 Martin Ave.	CEO: R. Paul Gupta	1995 Sales: $46.2 million
Santa Clara, CA 95050-2903	CFO: Stephen H. Vonderach	1-Yr. Sales Change: 24.9%
Phone: 408-450-8000	HR: Steve Gonia	Exchange: Nasdaq
Fax: 408-496-0773	Employees: 137	Symbol: QUAL

Electrical components - high performance logic & logic-intensive specialty memory semiconductor products

QUALITY SYSTEMS, INC.

17822 E. 17th St.	CEO: Sheldon Razin	1996 Sales: $16.7 million
Tustin, CA 92680	CFO: Robert G. McGraw	1-Yr. Sales Change: 39.2%
Phone: 714-731-7171	HR: Alison Razin	Exchange: Nasdaq
Fax: 714-731-9494	Employees: 110	Symbol: QSII

Computers - software systems for health care

QUANTUM CORPORATION

500 McCarthy Blvd.	CEO: Michael A. Brown	1996 Sales: $4,422.7 million
Milpitas, CA 95035	CFO: Joseph T. Rodgers	1-Yr. Sales Change: 31.3%
Phone: 408-894-4000	HR: Deborah E. Barber	Exchange: Nasdaq
Fax: 408-894-3218	Employees: 7,036	Symbol: QNTM

Computers - disk drives (Trailblazer, Fireball, Bigfoot, Atlas)

 See pages 176–177 for a full profile of this company.

QUARK, INC.

1800 Grant St.	CEO: Farhad Fred Ebrahimi	1995 Est. Sales: $200.0 mil.
Denver, CO 80203	CFO: Kenneth J. Collins	1-Yr. Sales Change: 19.0%
Phone: 303-894-8888	HR: D. Witonsky	Ownership: Privately Held
Fax: 303-894-3399	Employees: 600	

Computers - desktop publishing software (Quark XPress) & multilingual electronic publishing software (QuarkXPress Passport)

 See page 346 for a full profile of this company.

QUARTERDECK CORPORATION

13160 Mindanao Way	CEO: King R. Lee & A. Tikhman	1995 Sales: $70.7 million
Marina del Rey, CA 90292-9705	CFO: Frank R. Greico	1-Yr. Sales Change: 163.8%
Phone: 310-309-3700	HR: Teresa Hammond	Exchange: Nasdaq
Fax: 310-309-4218	Employees: 532	Symbol: QDEK

Computers - multitasking, windowing & memory management software; software erasing utility program (Clean-Sweep); telecommunications & Internet applications & systems

See page 347 for a full profile of this company.

QUICKTURN DESIGN SYSTEMS INC.

440 Clyde Ave.	CEO: Keith R. Lobo	1995 Sales: $81.8 million
Mountain View, CA 94043-2232	CFO: Raymond K. Ostby	1-Yr. Sales Change: 24.9%
Phone: 415-967-3300	HR: Renate Dietz	Exchange: Nasdaq
Fax: 415-967-3199	Employees: 272	Symbol: QKTN

Electronics - logic-chip test equipment

KEY COMPUTER COMPANIES

QUOTE.COM, INC.

3375 Scott Blvd., Ste. 300	CEO: Chris Cooper	1995 Est. Sales: $5.0 mil.
Santa Clara, CA 95054	CFO: Jeff Tang	1-Yr. Sales Change: —
Phone: 408-327-0700	HR: —	Ownership: Privately Held
Fax: 408-327-0707	Employees: 5	

Computers - online financial information service, including stock quotes and financial information

RACAL ELECTRONICS PLC

Western Rd.	CEO: David C. Elsbury	1996 Sales: $1,617.0 million
Bracknell, Berkshire RG12 1RG, UK	CFO: J. M. Kaye	1-Yr. Sales Change: 4.9%
Phone: +44-1-344-481-222	HR: —	Exchange: London
Fax: +44-1-344-541-19	Employees: 12,855	

Telecommunications equipment - equipment for security, data communication, network services & radio communication

> **See pages 178–179 for a full profile of this company.**

RACOTEK, INC.

7301 Ohms Ln.	CEO: Mike Fabiaschi	1995 Sales: $6.1 million
Minneapolis, MN 55439-1472	CFO: James E. Flaherty	1-Yr. Sales Change: 52.5%
Phone: 612-832-9800	HR: Kay Lee	Exchange: Nasdaq
Fax: 612-832-9383	Employees: 117	Symbol: RACO

Telecommunications equipment - wireless computing software that extends corporate information systems to people in the field

RADISYS CORPORATION

15025 SW Koll Pkwy	CEO: Glenford J. Myers	1995 Sales: $35.0 million
Beaverton, OR 97006	CFO: Brian Turner	1-Yr. Sales Change: 73.3%
Phone: 503-646-1800	HR: Mark Skiba	Exchange: Nasdaq
Fax: 503-646-1850	Employees: 154	Symbol: RSYS

Computers - embedded microcomputers for automation, telecommunications & medical devices, transportation, test & measurement & retail management applications

RADIUS INC.

215 Moffett Park Dr.	CEO: Charles W. Berger	1995 Sales: $308.1 million
Sunnyvale, CA 94089	CFO: Dennis J. Dunnigan	1-Yr. Sales Change: (5.1%)
Phone: 408-541-6100	HR: Dawn Thompson	Exchange: Nasdaq
Fax: 408-541-6150	Employees: 237	Symbol: RDUSC

Computers - color publishing & digital video computer products, including video systems & software, high resolution color reference displays & Macintosh-compatible computer systems

> **See page 348 for a full profile of this company.**

RAINBOW TECHNOLOGIES, INC.

50 Technology Dr.
Irvine, CA 92718-
Phone: 714-450-7300
Fax: 714-450-7450

CEO: Walter W. Straub
CFO: Patrick E. Fevery
HR: Karen Brown
Employees: 270

1995 Sales: $66.3 million
1-Yr. Sales Change: 72.2%
Exchange: Nasdaq
Symbol: RNBO

Computers - software-protection products (NetSentinel, SentinelEve3, SentinelSuperPro)

RAMTRON INTERNATIONAL CORPORATION

1850 Ramtron Dr.
Colorado Springs, CO 80921
Phone: 719-481-7000
Fax: 719-481-9294

CEO: L. David Sikes
CFO: Richard L. Mohr
HR: Bob Massie
Employees: 88

1995 Sales: $28.9 million
1-Yr. Sales Change: 41.7%
Exchange: Nasdaq
Symbol: RMTR

Electrical components - specialty high-performance semiconductor memory devices (ferroelectric random access memory & high-speed dynamic random access memory)

RAND MCNALLY & COMPANY

8255 N. Central Park Ave.
Skokie, IL 60076-2970
Phone: 847-329-8100
Fax: 847-673-0539

CEO: Andrew McNally IV
CFO: James J. Habschmidt
HR: Kurt D. Steele
Employees: 4,650

1995 Sales: $468.5 million
1-Yr. Sales Change: 7.0%
Ownership: Privately Held

Publishing - geographic information books, including travel guide CD-ROMs (TripMaker); computer services; airline & surface transportation tickets & baggage tags; labels, tags & cards for automated systems

RAPTOR SYSTEMS, INC.

69 Hickory Dr.
Waltham, MA 02154
Phone: 617-487-7700
Fax: 617-487-6755

CEO: Robert A. Steinkrauss
CFO: Robert H. Fincke
HR: —
Employees: 58

1995 Sales: $3.9 million
1-Yr. Sales Change: 1,850%
Exchange: Nasdaq
Symbol: RAPT

Computers - network security software products

RASTER GRAPHICS, INC.

3025 Orchard Pkwy.
San Jose, CA 95134
Phone: 408-232-4000
Fax: 408-232-4100

CEO: Rakesh Kumar
CFO: Dennis R. Mahoney
HR: Lynne Reynolds
Employees: 146

1995 Sales: $26.0 million
1-Yr. Sales Change: 97.0%
Exchange: Nasdaq
Symbol: RGFX

Computers - large-format color printers (Digital Color Station) & software (PosterShop)

RATIONAL SOFTWARE CORPORATION

2800 San Tomas Expwy.
Santa Clara, CA 95051-0951
Phone: 408-496-3600
Fax: 408-496-3636

CEO: Paul D. Levy
CFO: Robert T. Bond
HR: Burr Gibbons
Employees: 533

1996 Sales: $91.1 million
1-Yr. Sales Change: 25.0%
Exchange: Nasdaq
Symbol: RATL

Computers - software development tools & services

RAXCO, INC.

2440 Research Blvd.
Rockville, MD 20850
Phone: 301-258-2620
Fax: 301-330-5756

CEO: Richard Lefebvre
CFO: —
HR: —
Employees: 270

1995 Sales: $36.0 million
1-Yr. Sales Change: —
Ownership: Privately Held

Computers - systems management software (Disk Defragmenter, Defragmenting for Open Files, Disk Caching Software, Dynamic System Tuner, Help Desk Software, Asset Management Software)

READ-RITE CORPORATION

345 Los Coches St.
Milpitas, CA 95035
Phone: 408-262-6700
Fax: 408-956-3205

CEO: Cyril J. Yansouni
CFO: John T. Kurtzweil
HR: Sherry F. McVicar
Employees: 23,074

1995 Sales: $1,003.0 million
1-Yr. Sales Change: 57.1%
Exchange: Nasdaq
Symbol: RDRT

Computers - thin-film magnetic read-write heads for hard disks (#1 worldwide); headstack assemblies & heads for tape drives

 See pages 180–181 for a full profile of this company.

RED BRICK SYSTEMS, INC.

485 Alberto Way
Los Gatos, CA 95032
Phone: 408-399-3200
Fax: 408-399-3277

CEO: Christopher G. Erickson
CFO: Robert C. Hausmann
HR: Peggy J. DeLeon
Employees: 134

1995 Sales: $20.6 million
1-Yr. Sales Change: 142.4%
Exchange: Nasdaq
Symbol: REDB

Computers - client/server relational database management system software, servers & administration tools for data warehouse applications

THE REGISTRY, INC.

189 Wells Ave.
Newton, MA 02159
Phone: 617-527-6886
Fax: 617-965-4807

CEO: G. Drew Conway
CFO: Robert E. Foley
HR: Linda Krentzman
Employees: 447

1996 Sales: $145.6 million
1-Yr. Sales Change: 47.5%
Exchange: Nasdaq
Symbol: REGI

Personnel - information technology staffing & management consulting services

REMEDY CORPORATION

1505 Salado Dr.	CEO: Lawrence L. Garlick	1995 Sales: $40.1 million
Mountain View, CA 94043-1110	CFO: George A. de Urioste	1-Yr. Sales Change: 102.5%
Phone: 415-903-5200	HR: Kara Finn	Exchange: Nasdaq
Fax: 415-903-9001	Employees: 129	Symbol: RMDY

Computers - help desk & support automation software

RENAISSANCE SOLUTIONS, INC.

55 Old Bedford Rd.	CEO: David P. Norton	1995 Sales: $22.6 million
Lincoln, MA 01773	CFO: George A. McMillan	1-Yr. Sales Change: 75.2%
Phone: 617-259-8833	HR: Timothy Riley	Exchange: Nasdaq
Fax: 617-259-0565	Employees: 118	Symbol: RENS

Consulting - management consulting & client/server systems integration services

REPTRON ELECTRONICS, INC.

14401 McCormick Dr.	CEO: Michael L. Musto	1995 Sales: $223.3 million
Tampa, FL 33626-3046	CFO: Paul J. Plante	1-Yr. Sales Change: 36.2%
Phone: 813-854-2351	HR: Tom Ginnetti	Exchange: Nasdaq
Fax: 813-855-1697	Employees: 590	Symbol: REPT

Electronics - distribution of semiconductors, passive products & electromechanical components

RESEARCH ENGINEERS, INC.

22700 Savi Ranch Pkwy.	CEO: Amrit K. Das	1996 Sales: $7.3 million
Yorba Linda, CA 92687	CFO: Brian Paul	1-Yr. Sales Change: 49.0%
Phone: 714-974-2500	HR: —	Exchange: Nasdaq
Fax: 714-974-4771	Employees: 77	Symbol: RENG

Computers - stand-alone & network-based engineering software

RESTRAC, INC.

3 Allied Dr.	CEO: Lars D. Perkins	1995 Sales: $15.0 million
Dedham, MA 02026	CFO: Cynthia G. Eades	1-Yr. Sales Change: 54.6%
Phone: 617-320-5600	HR: Brett Costello	Exchange: Nasdaq
Fax: 617-320-5630	Employees: 125	Symbol: RTRK

Computers - human resource staffing software for automating workforce recruitment, selection & placement

RETIX

4640 Admiralty Way, North Tower	CEO: Joe Stephan	1995 Sales: $38.8 million
Marina del Rey, CA 90292-6695	CFO: Steven Waszak	1-Yr. Sales Change: (34.3%)
Phone: 310-828-3400	HR: Ken Zabel	Exchange: Nasdaq
Fax: 310-828-2255	Employees: 344	Symbol: RETX

Computers - networking systems & software, including multiprotocol routers (ROUTERXchange) & Ethernet switches (SWITCHStak)

REUTERS HOLDINGS PLC

85 Fleet St.	CEO: Peter J. D. Job	1995 Sales: $4,188.0 million
London EC4P 4AJ, UK	CFO: Robert O. "Rob" Rowley	1-Yr. Sales Change: 15.9%
Phone: +44-171-250-1122	HR: Patrick A. V. Mannix	Exchange: Nasdaq
Fax: +44-171-510-5896	Employees: 14,348	Symbol: RTRSY

Business services - gathering & electronic supply of financial data, news, historical databases & information-management systems

THE REYNOLDS AND REYNOLDS COMPANY

115 S. Ludlow St.	CEO: David R. Holmes	1995 Sales: $910.9 million
Dayton, OH 45402	CFO: Dale L. Medford	1-Yr. Sales Change: 12.6%
Phone: 513-443-2000	HR: Tom Momchilov	Exchange: NYSE
Fax: 513-449-4416	Employees: 6,036	Symbol: REY

Paper - business forms; computer software & services for the automotive sales & health care industries

RICOH COMPANY, LTD.

15-5, Minami-Aoyama 1-chome	CEO: Masamitu Sakurai	1996 Sales: $10,258.0 mil.
Minato-ku, Tokyo 107, Japan	CFO: —	1-Yr. Sales Change: (10.5%)
Phone: +81-3-3479-3111	HR: Ted Graske	Exchange: Tokyo
Fax: +81-3-3403-1578	Employees: 50,000	

Office automation - equipment such as copiers, facsimile machines, data processing systems & related supplies; electronic devices & photographic equipment

RIMAGE CORPORATION

7725 Washington Ave. South	CEO: David J. Suden	1995 Sales: $51.5 million
Minneapolis, MN 55439-2423	CFO: John D. Wylie	1-Yr. Sales Change: 103.6%
Phone: 612-944-8144	HR: Renee Dallman	Exchange: Nasdaq
Fax: 612-944-7808	Employees: 268	Symbol: RIMG

Computers - diskette, digital tape & CD-ROM duplication & finishing equipment

RIVA GROUP PLC

Crompton House, Barrs Fold Rd.
Westhoughton, Bolton BL5 3XP, UK
Phone: +44-1-204-871-300
Fax: +44-1-204-871-301

CEO: T. A. Milne
CFO: P. A. Briggs
HR: —
Employees: 834

1995 Sales: $113.0 million
1-Yr. Sales Change: 24.4%
Exchange: London

Computers - electronic data processing equipment; supply to food retailers

RMS TECHNOLOGIES INCORPORATED

5 Eves Dr.
Marlton, NJ 08053-5775
Phone: 609-596-5775
Fax: 609-596-0729

CEO: David W. Huggins
CFO: Joseph J. Rita
HR: Harry Dingler
Employees: 1,000

1995 Sales: $95.0 million
1-Yr. Sales Change: —
Ownership: Privately Held

Computers - data transfer consulting services, primarily to the US government

ROCKET SCIENCE GAMES INC.

139 Townsend St., Ste. 100
San Francisco, CA 94107
Phone: 415-442-5000
Fax: 415-442-5001

CEO: Steven Gary Blank
CFO: Richard Booroojian
HR: Debbie Kerlin
Employees: 65

1995 Est. Sales: $5.0 mil.
1-Yr. Sales Change: 42.9%
Ownership: Privately Held

Computers - CD-ROM games (Loadstar, Cadillacs & Dinosaurs); CD-ROM speed acceleration technology

ROCKY MOUNTAIN INTERNET, INC.

1800 Glenarm Pl., Ste 1100
Denver, CO 80202
Phone: 303-672-0700
Fax: 303-672-0711

CEO: Roy J. Dimoff
CFO: D. Kirk Roberts
HR: —
Employees: —

1995 Sales: $1.2 million
1-Yr. Sales Change: 300.0%
Exchange: Nasdaq (SC)
Symbol: RMII

Computers - regional full-service Internet access provider, dial-up, dedicated accounts & software solutions

ROGUE WAVE SOFTWARE, INC.

850 SW 35th St.
Corvallis, OR 97333
Phone: 541-754-3010
Fax: 541-753-1912

CEO: Thomas Keffer
CFO: Robert M. Holburn Jr.
HR: Hazel Stratton
Employees: 176

1995 Sales: $11.9 million
1-Yr. Sales Change: 65.3%
Ownership: Privately Held

Computers - provider of object-oriented software & related tools

ROM TECH, INC.

2000 Cabot Blvd. West, Ste. 110	CEO: Joseph A. Falsetti	1996 Sales: $3.1 million
Langhorne, PA 19047	CFO: Gerald W. Klein	1-Yr. Sales Change: 181.8%
Phone: 215-750-6606	HR: —	Exchange: Nasdaq
Fax: 215-750-3722	Employees: 14	Symbol: ROMT

Computers - multimedia software for consumer, educational & business applications

ROSS SYSTEMS, INC.

555 Twin Dolphin Dr.	CEO: Dennis V. Vohs	1996 Sales: $68.3 million
Redwood City, CA 94065	CFO: James A. Watts Jr.	1-Yr. Sales Change: (4.2%)
Phone: 415-593-2500	HR: Alan Cole	Exchange: Nasdaq
Fax: 415-592-9364	Employees: 440	Symbol: ROSS

Computers - enterprise-wide business software & related services (Renaissance CS Financial Series, Renaissance CS PROMIX Manufacturing Series & Renaissance CS Human Resource Series)

ROSS TECHNOLOGY, INC.

5316 Hwy. 290 West, Ste. 500	CEO: Roger D. Ross	1996 Sales: $100.8 million
Austin, TX 78735-8930	CFO: David A. Zeleniak	1-Yr. Sales Change: 158.5%
Phone: 512-892-7802	HR: Jim Tramel	Exchange: Nasdaq
Fax: 512-892-3036	Employees: 134	Symbol: RTEC

Electrical components - microprocessors & semiconductor products for SPARC workstations, servers & embedded applications; majority owned by Fujitsu

RSA DATA SECURITY, INC.

100 Marine Pkwy.	CEO: James Bidzos	1995 Sales: $11.6 million
Redwood City, CA 94065	CFO: Kathy Conrow	1-Yr. Sales Change: 16.0%
Phone: 415-595-8782	HR: —	Ownership: Subsidiary
Fax: 415-595-1873	Employees: 50	

Computers - encryption, network & security products (subsidiary of Security Dynamics Technologies)

RWD TECHNOLOGIES, INC.

10480 Little Patuxent Pkwy.	CEO: Robert W. Deutsch	1995 Sales: $47.1 million
Columbia, MD 21044-3530	CFO: Ronald E. Holtz	1-Yr. Sales Change: 60.2%
Phone: 410-730-4377	HR: Jan P. Keller	Ownership: Privately Held
Fax: 410-964-0039	Employees: 522	

Computers - training & documentation services, performance support & manufacturing production systems

S3 INCORPORATED

2770 San Tomas Expwy.
Santa Clara, CA 95051-0968
Phone: 408-980-5400
Fax: 408-980-5444

CEO: Gary J. Johnson
CFO: George A. Hervey
HR: Cecilia A. Hayes
Employees: 449

1995 Sales: $316.3 million
1-Yr. Sales Change: 125.4%
Exchange: Nasdaq
Symbol: SIII

Computers - graphics accelerator systems (S3 Vision/VA, Vision964) & video MPEG accelerators

 See page 349 for a full profile of this company.

SAF T LOK, INC.

4152 Blue Heron Blvd. West, Ste. 118
Riviera Beach, FL 33404
Phone: 561-844-3348
Fax: 561-844-3699

CEO: Steven M. Crane
CFO: Cynthia T. Gilbert
HR: —
Employees: 8

1995 Sales: $0.4 million
1-Yr. Sales Change: (77.8%)
Exchange: Nasdaq (SC)
Symbol: LOCK

Computers - PC-based video editing systems (AmiLink, UniSuite)

SAFEGUARD SCIENTIFICS, INC.

435 Devon Park Dr.
Wayne, PA 19087
Phone: 610-293-0600
Fax: 610-293-0601

CEO: Warren V. Musser
CFO: Gerald M. Wilk
HR: Gerald M. Hogan
Employees: 3,600

1995 Sales: $1,546.0 million
1-Yr. Sales Change: 7.5%
Exchange: NYSE
Symbol: SFE

Financial - investment in high-tech companies (MulyiGen, Tangram Enterprise Solutions, Cambridge Technology Partners)

THE SAGE GROUP PLC

Sage House, Benton Park Rd.
Newcastle upon Tyne NE7 7LZ, UK
Phone: +44-1-91-201-3000
Fax: +44-1-91-201-0308

CEO: Paul A. Walker
CFO: Aiden Hughes
HR: Rupert Wyndham
Employees: 1,325

1995 Sales: $161.8 million
1-Yr. Sales Change: 141.5%
Exchange: London

Computers - accounting & legal software & related products

SAMSUNG GROUP

CPO Box 1580
Seoul, Korea
Phone: +82-2-724-0361
Fax: +82-2-724-0198

CEO: Song Bo Soon
CFO: Seong Bea Kim
HR: Robert Schachter
Employees: 206,407

1995 Sales: $78,100.0 mil.
1-Yr. Sales Change: 19.9%
Ownership: Privately Held

Diversified operations - #1 global memory chip maker; plain-paper fax engines; video monitors; hard drives; cellular phones, high-definition projection TV & HDTV picture tubes

 See pages 182–183 for a full profile of this company.

SAND TECHNOLOGY SYSTEMS INTERNATIONAL, INC.

4141 Sherbrooke St. West, Ste. 410	CEO: Arthur G. Ritchie	1995 Sales: $11.5 million
Westmount, QC H3Z 1B8, Canada	CFO: Susan Waxman	1-Yr. Sales Change: (29.9%)
Phone: 514-939-3477	HR: —	Exchange: Nasdaq
Fax: 514-939-2042	Employees: 40	Symbol: SNDCF

Computers - sales & service of mainframe peripheral products manufactured by Hitachi Ltd.

SANDISK CORPORATION

140 Caspian Ct.	CEO: Eli Harari	1995 Sales: $62.8 million
Sunnyvale, CA 94089	CFO: Cindy Burgdorf	1-Yr. Sales Change: 77.4%
Phone: 408-542-0500	HR: Marianne Jackson	Exchange: Nasdaq
Fax: 408-542-0403	Employees: 255	Symbol: SNDK

Electronics - flash memory data storage products

 See page 350 for a full profile of this company.

SANMINA CORPORATION

355 Trimble Rd.	CEO: Jure Sola	1995 Sales: $167.8 million
San Jose, CA 95131	CFO: Randy W. Furr	1-Yr. Sales Change: 45.8%
Phone: 408-435-8444	HR: Sylvia Norris	Exchange: Nasdaq
Fax: 408-943-1401	Employees: 703	Symbol: SANM

Electrical components - assemblies, subassemblies & multilayered printed circuit boards

THE SANTA CRUZ OPERATION, INC.

400 Encinal St.	CEO: Alok Mohan	1995 Sales: $199.3 million
Santa Cruz, CA 95060	CFO: John Jarvis	1-Yr. Sales Change: 8.3%
Phone: 408-425-7222	HR: Jack Moyer	Exchange: Nasdaq
Fax: 408-458-4227	Employees: 1,128	Symbol: SCOC

Computers - UNIX-based operating system software, client/server software & related tools for retail, finance, telecommunications & government operations

 See page 351 for a full profile of this company.

SAP AG

Neurottstrasse 16	CEO: Paul Wahl	1995 Sales: $1,875.0 million
69190 Walldorf, Germany	CFO: —	1-Yr. Sales Change: 58.6%
Phone: +49-6227-34-0	HR: —	Exchange: Frankfurt
Fax: +49-6227-34-12-82	Employees: 6,857	

Computers - data processing systems, applications & products

 See pages 184–185 for a full profile of this company.

SAPIENS INTERNATIONAL CORPORATION N.V.

de Ruyterkade 58A, PO Box 837
Curacao, Netherlands Antilles
Phone: +2011-599-96-613277
Fax: +2011-311-8201-9088

CEO: Ron Zuckerman
CFO: Moti Weiss
HR: —
Employees: 395

1995 Sales: $39.9 million
1-Yr. Sales Change: 7.5%
Exchange: Nasdaq
Symbol: SPNSF

Computers - rapid application development software

SAPIENT CORPORATION

One Memorial Dr.
Cambridge, MA 02142
Phone: 617-621-0200
Fax: 617-621-1300

CEO: Jerry A. Greenberg
CFO: Susan D. Johnson
HR: —
Employees: 263

1995 Sales: $21.9 million
1-Yr. Sales Change: 133.0%
Exchange: Nasdaq
Symbol: SAPE

Computers - process engineering & software applications (QUADD methodology) implemented by facilitators for large, information-intensive organization problem solving applications

SARCOM INC.

530 C Lakeview Plaza Blvd.
Worthington, OH 43085
Phone: 614-431-2228
Fax: 614-841-2345

CEO: Randy Wilcox
CFO: Pete Struzzi
HR: Betsy Kramer
Employees: 710

1995 Sales: $200.0 million
1-Yr. Sales Change: 100.0%
Ownership: Privately Held

Retail - computers

SAS INSTITUTE INC.

SAS Campus Dr.
Cary, NC 27513
Phone: 919-677-8000
Fax: 919-677-8123

CEO: James H. Goodnight
CFO: Greyson Quarles
HR: David Russo
Employees: 3,683

1995 Sales: $562.4 million
1-Yr. Sales Change: 16.7%
Ownership: Privately Held

Computers - integrated applications software

 See pages 186–187 for a full profile of this company.

SAVILLE SYSTEMS PLC

IDA Business Park
Dangan, Galway, Ireland
Phone: +353-91-526-611
Fax: —

CEO: John J. Boyle III
CFO: Marc J. Venator
HR: —
Employees: 347

1995 Sales: $30.3 million
1-Yr. Sales Change: 50.7%
Exchange: Nasdaq
Symbol: SAVLY

Computers - software that collects price & customer usage for local, long-distance & wireless telecommunications service providers

SAYERS COMPUTER SOURCE

1150 Feehanville Dr.	CEO: Gale Sayers	1995 Sales: $55.0 million
Mount Prospect, IL 60056	CFO: Ann Chiodo	1-Yr. Sales Change: 3.8%
Phone: 847-391-4040	HR: Jeanette Kratz	Ownership: Privately Held
Fax: 847-294-0750	Employees: 70	

Retail - computer hardware & software distribution; systems integration services

SAZTECH INTERNATIONAL, INC.

43 Manning Rd.	CEO: Gary N. Abernathy	1996 Sales: $10.9 million
Billerica, MA 01821-3966	CFO: Thomas K. O'Loughlin	1-Yr. Sales Change: (19.9%)
Phone: 508-262-9600	HR: Keith Meyer	Exchange: OTC
Fax: 508-262-9800	Employees: 191	Symbol: SAZZ

Computers - information conversion from paper to computer-usable formats

SBE, INC.

4550 Norris Canyon Rd.	CEO: William B. Heye Jr.	1995 Sales: $19.4 million
San Ramon, CA 94583-1369	CFO: Timothy J. Repp	1-Yr. Sales Change: (14.5%)
Phone: 510-355-2000	HR: Amy Hammer	Exchange: Nasdaq
Fax: 510-355-2020	Employees: 162	Symbol: SBEI

Computers - networking systems & products; VMEbus, PC-bus & Multibus systems

SC&T INTERNATIONAL, INC.

3837 E. Lasalle St.	CEO: James Copland	1996 Sales: $3.8 million
Phoenix, AZ 85040	CFO: Timothy Stocker	1-Yr. Sales Change: 8.6%
Phone: 602-470-1334	HR: —	Exchange: Nasdaq (SC)
Fax: 602-470-1507	Employees: 10	Symbol: SCTI

Computers - peripheral equipment, including multimedia stereo keyboards & CD-ROM audio cables

SCANGRAPHICS, INC.

700 Abbott Dr.	CEO: Andrew E. Trolio	1995 Sales: $5.0 million
Broomall, PA 19008-4373	CFO: Joseph N. Battista	1-Yr. Sales Change: 108.3%
Phone: 610-328-1040	HR: Victoria Franchetti	Exchange: Nasdaq (SC)
Fax: 610-543-6257	Employees: 55	Symbol: SCNG

Computers - imaging equipment & software (FRIENDS, SRV/SGE software); scanners, printers, plotters & interfaces

SCAN-OPTICS, INC.

22 Prestige Park Circle
East Hartford, CT 06108
Phone: 860-289-6001
Fax: 860-289-9034

CEO: Richard I. Tanaka
CFO: Michael J. Villano
HR: Marianna Emanuelson
Employees: 269

1995 Sales: $42.1 million
1-Yr. Sales Change: (4.1%)
Exchange: Nasdaq
Symbol: SOCR

Computers - information-processing systems

SCANSOURCE, INC.

6 Logue Ct., Ste. G
Greenville, SC 29615
Phone: 864-288-2432
Fax: 864-288-1165

CEO: Steven H. Owings
CFO: Jeffery A. Bryson
HR: Jeffery A. Bryson
Employees: 52

1996 Sales: $55.7 million
1-Yr. Sales Change: 62.9%
Exchange: Nasdaq (SC)
Symbol: SCSC

Wholesale distribution - bar code equipment, scanners, receipt printers & magnetic stripe readers

SCB COMPUTER TECHNOLOGY

1365 W. Brierbrook Rd.
Memphis, TN 38138
Phone: 901-754-6577
Fax: 901-754-8463

CEO: Ben C. Bryant Jr.
CFO: Gordon L. Bateman
HR: —
Employees: 600

1996 Sales: $48.7 million
1-Yr. Sales Change: 45.8%
Exchange: Nasdaq
Symbol: SCBI

Personnel - outsourcing of information systems management & operations

SCI SYSTEMS, INC.

2101 W. Clinton Ave.
Huntsville, AL 35805
Phone: 205-882-4800
Fax: 205-882-4804

CEO: Olin B. King
CFO: Ronald G. Sibold
HR: Francis X. Henry
Employees: 13,185

1995 Sales: $2,673.8 million
1-Yr. Sales Change: 44.3%
Exchange: Nasdaq
Symbol: SCIS

Electrical components - electronic circuitry, systems, subsystems & other assemblies; aerospace & defense products

 See pages 188–189 for a full profile of this company.

SCIENCE APPLICATIONS INTERNATIONAL CORPORATION

10260 Campus Point Dr.
San Diego, CA 92121
Phone: 619-546-6000
Fax: 619-546-6634

CEO: J. Robert Beyster
CFO: William A. Roper
HR: Bernard Theull
Employees: 20,500

1995 Sales: $1,922.0 million
1-Yr. Sales Change: 15.0%
Ownership: Privately Held

Engineering - R&D services, systems integration

 See pages 190–191 for a full profile of this company.

SCIENTIFIC SOFTWARE-INTERCOMP, INC.

1801 California St., Ste. 295	CEO: George Steel	1995 Sales: $24.1 million
Denver, CO 80202	CFO: E. S. Wittman	1-Yr. Sales Change: (13.6%)
Phone: 303-292-1111	HR: Ned Fraizer	Exchange: OTC
Fax: 303-293-0261	Employees: 147	Symbol: SSFT

Computers - software licenses; engineering consulting services

SCITEX CORPORATION LTD.

Hamada St., Industrial Park	CEO: Yoav Z. Chelouche	1995 Sales: $728.9 million
Herzlia B 46103, Israel	CFO: Giora Bitan	1-Yr. Sales Change: 3.5%
Phone: +972-9-597-222	HR: Ilan Gonen	Exchange: Nasdaq
Fax: +972-9-502-922	Employees: 3,600	Symbol: SCIXF

Computers - digital visual-information communication systems, including electronic prepress, digital printing, video editing & digital photography products

 See pages 192–193 for a full profile of this company.

SCOPUS TECHNOLOGY, INC.

1900 Powell St., Ste. 700	CEO: Ori Sasson	1996 Sales: $28.6 million
Emeryville, CA 94608	CFO: William C. Leetham	1-Yr. Sales Change: 86.9%
Phone: 510-597-5800	HR: Lori Allen	Exchange: Nasdaq
Fax: 510-428-1027	Employees: 161	Symbol: SCOP

Computers - customer information-management software (Scopus SupportTEAM, Scopus QualityTEAM, Scopus SalesTEAM, Scopus ServiceTEAM)

SCRIBONA AB

Box 1374, Sundbybergsvagen 1	CEO: Orjan Hakanson	1995 Sales: $910.0 million
S-171 27 Solna, Sweden	CFO: Lennart Bernard	1-Yr. Sales Change: 71.7%
Phone: +46-8-734-34-00	HR: —	Exchange: Stockholm
Fax: +46-8-27-84-25	Employees: 1,801	

Retail - wholesale computer products, office supplies & machines

SDL, INC.

80 Rose Orchard Way	CEO: Donald R. Scifres	1995 Sales: $53.9 million
San Jose, CA 95134-1365	CFO: Gregory C. Lindholm	1-Yr. Sales Change: 63.3%
Phone: 408-943-9411	HR: Donald R. Scifres	Exchange: Nasdaq
Fax: 408-943-1258	Employees: 206	Symbol: SDLI

Electrical components - semiconductor optoelectronic-integrated circuits & high-powered semiconductor lasers

SEACHANGE INTERNATIONAL, INC.

124 Acton St.	CEO: William C. Styslinger III	1995 Sales: $23.2 million
Maynard, MA 01754	CFO: Joseph S. Tibbetts Jr.	1-Yr. Sales Change: 307.0%
Phone: 508-897-0100	HR: Nancy Kittredge	Ownership: Privately Held
Fax: 508-897-0132	Employees: 95	

Computers - software-based products used to manage, store & distribute digital video for cable TV operators & telecommunications companies

SEAGATE TECHNOLOGY, INC.

920 Disc Dr.	CEO: Alan F. Shugart	1996 Sales: $8,588.3 million
Scotts Valley, CA 95066	CFO: Donald L. Waite	1-Yr. Sales Change: 89.2%
Phone: 408-438-6550	HR: Annette Surtees	Exchange: NYSE
Fax: 408-438-6172	Employees: 87,000	Symbol: SEG

Computers - rigid magnetic disk drives & other computer memory components (#1 worldwide), including flash memory storage products

 See pages 194–195 for a full profile of this company.

SECURE COMPUTING CORPORATION

2675 Long Lake Rd.	CEO: Kermit M. Beseke	1995 Sales: $20.7 million
Roseville, MN 55113	CFO: Timothy P. McGurran	1-Yr. Sales Change: 36.2%
Phone: 612-628-2700	HR: —	Exchange: Nasdaq
Fax: 612-628-2701	Employees: 276	Symbol: SCUR

Computers - network security software (#1 worldwide: Sidewinder)

SECURITY DYNAMICS TECHNOLOGIES, INC.

One Alewife Ctr.	CEO: Charles R. Stuckey Jr.	1995 Sales: $33.6 million
Cambridge, MA 02140	CFO: Arthur W. Coviello Jr.	1-Yr. Sales Change: 90.9%
Phone: 617-547-7820	HR: Vivian Vitale	Exchange: Nasdaq
Fax: 617-354-8836	Employees: 162	Symbol: SDTI

Computers - security & access software (SecurID Card, ACE-Server)

 See page 352 for a full profile of this company.

SECURITY FIRST NETWORK BANK

2957 Clairmont Rd., Ste. 280	CEO: James S. Mahan III	1995 Sales: $4.6 million
Atlanta, GA 30329	CFO: Robert F. Stockwell	1-Yr. Sales Change: (19.3%)
Phone: 404-679-3200	HR: Kahlila M. Klingler	Exchange: Nasdaq
Fax: 404-679-3210	Employees: 42	Symbol: SFNB

Financial - traditional banking services over the Internet (Virtual Bank Manager)

SEEQ TECHNOLOGY INCORPORATED

47200 Bayside Pkwy.
Fremont, CA 94538
Phone: 510-226-7400
Fax: 510-657-2837

CEO: Phillip J. Salsbury
CFO: Robert O. Hersh
HR: Pat Reno
Employees: 67

1995 Sales: $22.5 million
1-Yr. Sales Change: 4.7%
Exchange: Nasdaq
Symbol: SEEQ

Electrical components - data communication controllers (Ethernet), chip sets (AutoDUPLEX Ethernet), encoders & decoders, CMOS transceivers & networking modules

SEER TECHNOLOGIES, INC.

8000 Regency Pkwy.
Cary, NC 27511
Phone: 919-380-5000
Fax: 919-469-1910

CEO: Thomas A. Wilson
CFO: Mark J. Baric
HR: Irene Wong
Employees: 797

1995 Sales: $117.2 million
1-Yr. Sales Change: 41.7%
Exchange: Nasdaq
Symbol: SEER

Computers - client/server software development tools

SEGA ENTERPRISES, LTD.

2-12, Haneda 1-chome, Ohta-ku
Tokyo 144, Japan
Phone: +81-3-5736-7034
Fax: +81-3-5736-7058

CEO: Hayao Nakayama
CFO: Shinobu Toyoda
HR: Steve Goveia
Employees: 3,758

1996 Sales: $3,227.6 million
1-Yr. Sales Change: (13.5%)
Exchange: OTC
Symbol: SEGNY

Computers - home video game systems (SegaSaturn), electronic learning aids for children (PICO), game software (Virtua Fighter), amusement machines (Daytona USA) & amusement centers (Galbo, Joypolis)

 See pages 196–197 for a full profile of this company.

SEGUE SOFTWARE, INC.

1320 Centre St.
Newton Centre, MA 02159
Phone: 617-796-1000
Fax: 617-796-1610

CEO: Elisabeth Elterman
CFO: J. J. Bingenheimer
HR: Betsy Rudnick
Employees: 85

1995 Sales: $11.1 million
1-Yr. Sales Change: 73.4%
Exchange: Nasdaq
Symbol: SEGU

Computers - automated testing products & consulting services for organizations developing client/server & Internet-based software

SEMATECH, INC.

2706 Montopolis Dr.
Austin, TX 78741-6499
Phone: 512-356-3500
Fax: 512-356-3086

CEO: William J. Spencer
CFO: Dan Damon
HR: Mike Foster
Employees: 600

1996 Sales: —
1-Yr. Sales Change: —
Ownership: Consortium

Engineering - R&D services, semiconductor technology

 See page 353 for a full profile of this company.

SEMICONDUCTOR LASER INTERNATIONAL CORPORATION

148 Vestal Pkwy. East	CEO: Geoffrey T. Burnham	1995 Sales: $0.0 million
Vestal, NY 13850	CFO: —	1-Yr. Sales Change: —
Phone: 607-754-0112	HR: —	Exchange: Nasdaq (SC)
Fax: 607-754-5974	Employees: 6	Symbol: SLIC

Electrical components - semiconductors

SEMITOOL, INC.

655 W. Reserve Dr.	CEO: Raymon F. Thompson	1995 Sales: $115.3 million
Kalispell, MT 59901	CFO: John W. Sullivan	1-Yr. Sales Change: 107.0%
Phone: 406-752-2107	HR: Vicki Billmayer	Exchange: Nasdaq
Fax: 406-752-5522	Employees: 1,098	Symbol: SMTL

Machinery - batch & single substrate spray chemical processing tools, thermal processing equipment & wafer-carrier cleaning systems used in the fabrication of semiconductors

SEQUENT COMPUTER SYSTEMS, INC.

15450 SW Koll Pkwy.	CEO: Karl Casey Powell Jr.	1995 Sales: $540.3 million
Beaverton, OR 97006-6063	CFO: Robert S. Gregg	1-Yr. Sales Change: 19.9%
Phone: 503-626-5700	HR: Diane M. Williams	Exchange: Nasdaq
Fax: 503-578-9890	Employees: 2,129	Symbol: SQNT

Computers - multiprocessing UNIX-based systems & relational database-management software (RDBMS)

 See page 354 for a full profile of this company.

SEQUOIA SYSTEMS, INC.

400 Nickerson Rd.	CEO: J. Michael Stewart	1996 Sales: $102.2 million
Marlborough, MA 01752	CFO: Richard B. Goldman	1-Yr. Sales Change: (1.7%)
Phone: 508-480-0800	HR: Don Colanton	Exchange: Nasdaq
Fax: 508-481-8740	Employees: 396	Symbol: SEQS

Computers - fault-tolerant PCs used primarily for online transaction processing

SERCO GROUP PLC

Serco House, Hayes Rd.	CEO: G. G. Gray	1995 Sales: $500.2 million
Southhall, Middlesex UB2 5NJ, UK	CFO: D. E. Perkins	1-Yr. Sales Change: 22.8%
Phone: +44-1-81-843-2411	HR: —	Exchange: London
Fax: +44-1-81-843-3907	Employees: 10,791	

Computers - facilities management, operation & maintenance; systems engineering & project management support

SGS-THOMSON MICROELECTRONICS N.V.

165, rue Edouard Branly	CEO: Pasquale Pistorio	1995 Sales: $3,554.4 million
01630 Saint Genis Pouilly, France	CFO: Maurizio Ghirga	1-Yr. Sales Change: 34.6%
Phone: +33-50-40-26-40	HR: Alain Dutheil	Exchange: NYSE
Fax: +33-50-40-28-60	Employees: 25,523	Symbol: STM

Electrical components - semiconductors (#2 in Europe)

 See pages 198–199 for a full profile of this company.

SHARED MEDICAL SYSTEMS CORPORATION

51 Valley Stream Pkwy.	CEO: Marvin S. Cadwell	1995 Sales: $650.6 million
Malvern, PA 19355	CFO: Terrence W. Kyle	1-Yr. Sales Change: 18.1%
Phone: 610-219-6300	HR: Doug Lawrence	Exchange: Nasdaq
Fax: 610-219-3124	Employees: 4,826	Symbol: SMED

Medical practice management - computer-based information-processing systems & services

SHARP CORPORATION

22-22 Nagaike-cho, Abeno-ku	CEO: Haruo Tsuji	1996 Sales: $17,102.2 mil.
Osaka 545, Japan	CFO: Yoshio Nagaike	1-Yr. Sales Change: (7.0%)
Phone: +81-6-621-1221	HR: Manfred Edelman	Exchange: OTC
Fax: +81-6-627-1759	Employees: 42,883	Symbol: SHCAY

Consumer electronics - TV, video & audio equipment, information tools & electronic components (calculators, copiers, scanners), computers & home appliances

SHEPHERD SURVEILLANCE SOLUTIONS, INC.

3420 E. Third Ave.	CEO: Sergio Magistri	1995 Sales: $9.7 million
Foster City, CA 94404	CFO: Curtis P. DiSibio	1-Yr. Sales Change: —
Phone: 415-578-1930	HR: Gail Sines	Exchange: Nasdaq
Fax: 415-578-0930	Employees: 69	Symbol: SSSI

Protection - computer tomography based systems (CTX 5000) for automated detection of explosive devices in baggage, parcels & freight

SHIVA CORPORATION

28 Crosby Dr.	CEO: Frank A. Ingari	1995 Sales: $117.7 million
Bedford, MA 01730	CFO: Cynthia M. Deysher	1-Yr. Sales Change: 182.9%
Phone: 617-270-8300	HR: Jane Callanan	Exchange: Nasdaq
Fax: 617-270-8599	Employees: 486	Symbol: SHVA

Computers - networking hardware & software (LanRover)

 See page 355 for a full profile of this company.

SI DIAMOND TECHNOLOGY, INC.

2435 North Blvd.	CEO: Marc Eller	1995 Sales: $3.0 million
Houston, TX 77098	CFO: Lawrence K. King	1-Yr. Sales Change: 57.9%
Phone: 713-529-9040	HR: Marijane Ensminger	Exchange: Nasdaq (SC)
Fax: 713-529-1147	Employees: 113	Symbol: SIDT

Electrical components - thin-film diamond coatings & related products, including flat-panel displays

SIDUS SYSTEMS INC.

66 Leek Crescent	CEO: Henry Kalisky	1995 Sales: $186.0 million
Richmond Hill, ON L4B 1J7, Canada	CFO: Reg Tiessen	1-Yr. Sales Change: 19.8%
Phone: 905-882-1600	HR: —	Exchange: Toronto
Fax: 905-882-2430	Employees: 250	

Computers - systems integrator, designer & custom manufacturer of high-end personal computers & workstations

SIEBEL SYSTEMS, INC.

4005 Bohannon Dr.	CEO: Thomas M. Siebel	1995 Sales: $8.0 million
Menlo Park, CA 94025	CFO: Justin R. Dooley	1-Yr. Sales Change: 7,900%
Phone: 415-329-6500	HR: Les Cundall	Exchange: Nasdaq
Fax: 415-329-6511	Employees: 103	Symbol: SEBL

Computers - sales & marketing information software

SIEMENS AG

Wittelsbacherplatz 2	CEO: Heinrich von Pierer	1995 Sales: $61,641.0 mil.
D-80333 Munich, Germany	CFO: Karl-Hermann Baumann	1-Yr. Sales Change: 12.9%
Phone: +49-89-2-34-28-12	HR: Werner Maly	Exchange: OTC
Fax: +49-89-2-34-28-25	Employees: 373,000	Symbol: SMAWY

Diversified operations - information systems & components (Siemens Nixdorf); telecommunications; medical & power plant engineering products; lighting; transportation & automotive systems

 See pages 200–201 for a full profile of this company.

SIERRA SEMICONDUCTOR CORPORATION

2075 N. Capitol Ave.	CEO: James V. Diller	1995 Sales: $188.7 million
San Jose, CA 95132	CFO: Glenn C. Jones	1-Yr. Sales Change: 73.8%
Phone: 408-263-9300	HR: George Antennuci	Exchange: Nasdaq
Fax: 408-263-1969	Employees: 474	Symbol: SERA

Electrical components - integrated mixed signal ICs, peripheral & graphics controllers, voice/modem/fax ICs & voice synthesis & recognition systems

SIGMA CIRCUITS, INC.

393 Mathew St.
Santa Clara, CA 95050
Phone: 408-727-9169
Fax: 408-727-0319

CEO: B. Kevin Kelly
CFO: Philip S. Bushnell
HR: Lee Ann Vriend
Employees: 740

1996 Sales: $87.7 million
1-Yr. Sales Change: 82.0%
Exchange: Nasdaq
Symbol: SIGA

Electrical components - printed circuit boards, back-plane assemblies, subassemblies & flexible circuits

SIGMA DESIGNS, INC.

46501 Landing Pkwy.
Fremont, CA 94538
Phone: 510-770-0100
Fax: 510-770-2640

CEO: Thinh Q. Tran
CFO: Q. Binh Trinh
HR: Carol Sedore
Employees: 60

1996 Sales: $26.4 million
1-Yr. Sales Change: (39.6%)
Exchange: Nasdaq
Symbol: SIGM

Computers - multimedia & imaging display systems for use with PCs

SIGMATRON INTERNATIONAL, INC.

2201 Landmeier Rd.
Elk Grove Village, IL 60007
Phone: 847-956-8000
Fax: 847-956-8082

CEO: Gary R. Fairhead
CFO: Linda K. Blake
HR: Nancy Geiser
Employees: 1,395

1996 Sales: $69.6 million
1-Yr. Sales Change: 53.6%
Exchange: Nasdaq
Symbol: SGMA

Electrical components - printed circuit boards & turnkey electronic products

SIGNAL TECHNOLOGY CORPORATION

955 Benecia Ave.
Sunnyvale, CA 94086
Phone: 408-730-6318
Fax: 408-245-3396

CEO: Dale L. Peterson
CFO: John H. Wellman
HR: Gloria L. Duran
Employees: 894

1995 Sales: $89.7 million
1-Yr. Sales Change: (3.7%)
Exchange: AMEX
Symbol: STZ

Electronics - components & subsystems used in advanced military, intelligence & commercial applications

SILICON GRAPHICS, INC.

2011 N. Shoreline Blvd.
Mountain View, CA 94043
Phone: 415-960-1980
Fax: 415-390-6220

CEO: Edward R. McCracken
CFO: Stanley J. Meresman
HR: Kirk Froggatt
Employees: 6,300

1996 Sales: $2,921.3 million
1-Yr. Sales Change: 31.1%
Exchange: NYSE
Symbol: SGI

Computers - graphics hardware & software, interactive 3D graphics, digital media & multiprocessing

 See pages 202–203 for a full profile of this company.

SILICON STORAGE TECHNOLOGY, INC.

1171 Sonora Ct.	CEO: Bing Yeh	1995 Sales: $39.5 million
Sunnyvale, CA 94086	CFO: Michael J. Praisner	1-Yr. Sales Change: 863.4%
Phone: 408-735-9110	HR: Steve Remmel	Exchange: Nasdaq
Fax: 408-735-9036	Employees: 94	Symbol: SSTI

Computers - memory devices (Flash) for medium-density components such as CD-ROM drives & portable electronic devices

SILICON VALLEY BANCSHARES

3003 Tasman Dr.	CEO: John C. Dean	1995 Sales: $113.8 million
Santa Clara, CA 95054-1191	CFO: Glen Blackmon	1-Yr. Sales Change: 42.3%
Phone: 408-654-7282	HR: Glen G. Simmons	Exchange: Nasdaq
Fax: 408-383-5298	Employees: 348	Symbol: SIVB

Banks - provides banking services for the high-tech industry

 See page 356 for a full profile of this company.

SILICON VALLEY GROUP, INC.

2240 Ringwood Ave.	CEO: Papken S. Der Torossian	1995 Sales: $462.0 million
San Jose, CA 95131	CFO: Russell G. Weinstock	1-Yr. Sales Change: 44.4%
Phone: 408-434-0500	HR: Boris Lipkin	Exchange: Nasdaq
Fax: 408-434-0216	Employees: 2,653	Symbol: SVGI

Machinery - semiconductor manufacturing equipment

 See page 357 for a full profile of this company.

SILICON VALLEY RESEARCH, INC.

6360 San Ignacio Ave.	CEO: Glenn E. Abood	1996 Sales: $10.9 million
San Jose, CA 95119	CFO: Stephen J. Burdoin	1-Yr. Sales Change: 31.3%
Phone: 408-361-0333	HR: —	Exchange: Nasdaq
Fax: 408-361-0330	Employees: 60	Symbol: SVRI

Computers - electronic design automation software tools for the development of ASICs & custom integrated circuits

SILICONIX INCORPORATED

2201 Laurelwood Rd.	CEO: Richard J. Kulle	1995 Sales: $250.3 million
Santa Clara, CA 95056-0951	CFO: Jurgen F. Biehn	1-Yr. Sales Change: 27.4%
Phone: 408-988-8000	HR: Vickie Ruiz	Exchange: Nasdaq
Fax: 408-970-3950	Employees: 1,269	Symbol: SILI

Electrical components - power & analog semiconductor products, power transistors & integrated circuits for power management & motion control in computers, automobiles & communications systems

 See page 358 for a full profile of this company.

SIMPLE TECHNOLOGY INC.

3001 Daimler St.	CEO: Manouch Moshnayedi	1995 Sales: $210.0 million
Santa Ana, CA 92705	CFO: Daniel Moses	1-Yr. Sales Change: 112.8%
Phone: 714-476-1180	HR: Kathy Herold	Ownership: Privately Held
Fax: 714-476-1209	Employees: 360	

Computers - memory upgrades & PC cards

SIMTEK CORPORATION

1465 Kelly Johnson Blvd., Ste. 301	CEO: Richard Petriz	1995 Sales: $2.6 million
Colorado Springs, CO 80920	CFO: Richard Petritz	1-Yr. Sales Change: 116.7%
Phone: 719-531-9444	HR: Kim Carothers	Exchange: OTC
Fax: 719-531-9481	Employees: 16	Symbol: SRAM

Electrical components - nonvolatile static random-access memory (nvSRAM) semiconductors

SIMULATION SCIENCES INC.

601 Valencia Ave., Ste. 100	CEO: Charles R. Harris	1995 Sales: $33.1 million
Brea, CA 92823	CFO: L. Ronald Trepp	1-Yr. Sales Change: 17.0%
Phone: 714-579-0412	HR: Daniel T. Nichols	Ownership: Privately Held
Fax: 714-579-0197	Employees: 243	

Computers - commercial simulation software & related services

SIMWARE INC.

2 Gurdwara Rd.	CEO: William G. Breen	1996 Sales: $13.0 million
Ottawa, ON K2E 1A2, Canada	CFO: Michael R. Peckham	1-Yr. Sales Change: (7.8%)
Phone: 613-727-1779	HR: —	Exchange: Nasdaq
Fax: —	Employees: 130	Symbol: SIMWF

Computers - local area network administration & connectivity software (A2B) for remote or mobile end-users

SIPEX CORPORATION

22 Linnell Circle	CEO: James E. Donegan	1995 Sales: $30.0 million
Billerica, MA 01821	CFO: Frank R. DiPietro	1-Yr. Sales Change: 31.6%
Phone: 508-667-8700	HR: —	Exchange: Nasdaq
Fax: 508-667-8310	Employees: 239	Symbol: SIPX

Electrical components - analog integrated circuits

SIRIUS PUBLISHING INCORPORATED

7320 E. Butherus Dr., Ste. 100	CEO: Richard Gnant	1995 Sales: $21.6 million
Scottsdale, AZ 85260	CFO: Robert Tierney	1-Yr. Sales Change: 1.4%
Phone: 602-951-3288	HR: Marilyn McChristy	Ownership: Privately Held
Fax: 602-951-3884	Employees: 55	

Computers - 5-foot & 6-foot bundles of CD-ROMs; music, entertainment & multimedia software publishing (Treasure Quest, Triple Play)

SK TECHNOLOGIES CORPORATION

1650 S. Dixie Hwy.	CEO: Calvin S. Shoemaker	1996 Sales: $0.6 million
Boca Raton, FL 33432	CFO: Melvin T. Goldberger	1-Yr. Sales Change: 20.0%
Phone: 561-393-7540	HR: —	Exchange: Nasdaq (SC)
Fax: 561-395-2499	Employees: 27	Symbol: SKTC

Computers - point-of-purchase & store management software for retail industry

GROUPE SLIGOS

Ile-de-France-3, place de la Pyramide	CEO: Henri Pascaud	1995 Sales: $879.2 million
92067 Paris Cedex 49, France	CFO: Frederic Brunet	1-Yr. Sales Change: 14.4%
Phone: +33-1-49-00-90-00	HR: —	Exchange: Paris
Fax: +33-1-47-73-07-63	Employees: 6,347	

Computers - information systems for computer service companies

 See page 359 for a full profile of this company.

SMART MODULAR TECHNOLOGIES, INC.

4305 Cushing Pkwy.	CEO: Ajay Shah	1995 Sales: $274.6 million
Fremont, CA 94538	CFO: Lata Krishnan	1-Yr. Sales Change: 67.6%
Phone: 510-623-1231	HR: Misha Wyatt	Exchange: Nasdaq
Fax: 510-623-1434	Employees: 354	Symbol: SMOD

Computers - memory devices for PCs & workstations; modems

 See page 360 for a full profile of this company.

SMARTFLEX SYSTEMS, INC.

14312 Franklin Ave.	CEO: William L. Healey	1995 Sales: $125.3 million
Tustin, CA 92680	CFO: Alfred B. Castleman	1-Yr. Sales Change: 64.9%
Phone: 714-838-8737	HR: Sherrie L. Suski	Exchange: Nasdaq
Fax: 714-573-6918	Employees: 868	Symbol: SFLX

Electrical components - flexible interconnect assemblies

SMARTSERV ONLINE, INC.

Metro Center, One Station Place
Stamford, CT 06902
Phone: 203-353-5950
Fax: 203-353-5962

CEO: Sebastian Cassetta
CFO: Thomas Haller
HR: —
Employees: 18

1996 Sales: $0.0 million
1-Yr. Sales Change: —
Exchange: Nasdaq (SC)
Symbol: SSOL

Computers - real-time information & transaction services for telephone companies & financial & other business institutions

SMITH MICRO SOFTWARE, INC.

51 Columbia
Aliso Viejo, CA 92656
Phone: 714-362-5800
Fax: 714-362-2300

CEO: William W. Smith Jr.
CFO: Robert E. Grice
HR: Christine Gonzales
Employees: 70

1995 Sales: $18.0 million
1-Yr. Sales Change: 73.1%
Exchange: Nasdaq
Symbol: SMSI

Computers - data, fax & voice communication PC software, primarily to modem manufacturers

SOCKET COMMUNICATIONS, INC.

6500 Kaiser Dr.
Fremont, CA 94555
Phone: 510-744-2700
Fax: 510-744-2727

CEO: Martin S. Levetin
CFO: David W. Dunlap
HR: David W. Dunlap
Employees: 31

1995 Sales: $4.5 million
1-Yr. Sales Change: 45.2%
Exchange: Nasdaq (SC)
Symbol: SCKT

Computers - data communications hardware for the mobile computer market, including paging devices (PageCard Wireless Messaging System) & Ethernet adapters (Socket EA)

SOFTBANK CORP.

24-1, Nihonbashi Hakozaki-cho
Chuo-ku, Tokyo 103, Japan
Phone: +81-3-5642-8000
Fax: +81-3-5641-3401

CEO: Masayoshi Son
CFO: Yoshitaka Kitao
HR: Toshitada Kobayashi
Employees: 4,375

1996 Sales: $1,595.0 million
1-Yr. Sales Change: 42.5%
Exchange: Tokyo

Business services - computer trade show organizer (Comdex); wholesale software; computer magazine publishing (Ziff-Davis)

 See pages 204–205 for a full profile of this company.

SOFTDESK, INC.

7 Liberty Hill Rd.
Henniker, NH 03242
Phone: 603-428-5000
Fax: 603-428-5325

CEO: David C. Arnold
CFO: John A. Rogers
HR: Robin Pullo
Employees: 273

1995 Sales: $41.7 million
1-Yr. Sales Change: 73.8%
Exchange: Nasdaq
Symbol: SDSK

Computers - CAD software for professionals in the architecture, engineering & construction industries

SOFTECH, INC.

460 Totten Pond Rd.	CEO: Norman L. Rasmussen	1996 Sales: $13.7 million
Waltham, MA 02154-1960	CFO: Joseph P. Mullaney	1-Yr. Sales Change: (72.5%)
Phone: 617-890-6900	HR: Jean Croteaux	Exchange: Nasdaq
Fax: 617-890-6055	Employees: 39	Symbol: SOFT

Computers - software design & implementation; systems engineering & integration

SOFTKEY INTERNATIONAL INC.

One Athenaeum St.	CEO: Michael J. Perik	1995 Sales: $167.0 million
Cambridge, MA 02142	CFO: R. Scott Murray	1-Yr. Sales Change: 37.7%
Phone: 617-494-1200	HR: Mary De Saint Croix	Exchange: Nasdaq
Fax: 617-225-0318	Employees: 775	Symbol: SKEY

Computers - word processing, education & entertainment software (The Trail Family, The Mathkeys Family, The GeoGraph Family)

 See page 361 for a full profile of this company.

SOFTMART, INC.

467 Creamery Way	CEO: A. Richard Sloane	1995 Est. Sales: $100.0 mil.
Exton, PA 19341-2508	CFO: Joe Alberici	1-Yr. Sales Change: 25.0%
Phone: 610-524-7440	HR: Brenda Reis	Ownership: Privately Held
Fax: 610-363-1438	Employees: 550	

Retail - business software, networks, peripherals & consulting services to the corporate, consumer & government markets

SOFTNET SYSTEMS, INC.

717 Forest Ave.	CEO: John Jellinek	1995 Sales: $21.3 million
Lake Forest, IL 60045	CFO: Martin A. Koehler	1-Yr. Sales Change: 121.9%
Phone: 847-793-2000	HR: Emily Harder	Exchange: AMEX
Fax: 847-793-2005	Employees: 263	Symbol: SOF

Computers - imaging processing systems for hospital documents; telecommunication products

SOFTQUAD INTERNATIONAL, INC.

56 Aberfoyle Crescent, 5th Fl.	CEO: David J. Gurney	1995 Sales: $7.9 million
Toronto, ON M8X 2W4, Canada	CFO: Selwyn Wener	1-Yr. Sales Change: 88.1%
Phone: 416-239-4801	HR: Janis Haydar	Exchange: Nasdaq
Fax: 416-239-7105	Employees: 105	Symbol: SWEBF

Computers - HTML & SGML publishing tools for the World Wide Web & corporate intranets

SOFTWARE 2000, INC.

25 Communications Way
Hyannis, MA 02601
Phone: 508-778-2000
Fax: 508-775-3764

CEO: Robert A. Pemberton
CFO: Daniel J. Kossmann
HR: Susan O'Connor
Employees: 449

1995 Sales: $63.2 million
1-Yr. Sales Change: 11.3%
Exchange: Nasdaq
Symbol: SFWR

Computers - financial, human resources & environmental management software for IBM AS/400

SOFTWARE AG

Uhlandstrasse 12
D-64297 Darmstadt, Germany
Phone: +49-6151-92-0
Fax: +49-6151-92-1191

CEO: Erwin W. Koenigs
CFO: —
HR: William Cripe
Employees: 2,800

1995 Sales: $552.0 million
1-Yr. Sales Change: 3.6%
Ownership: Privately Held

Computers - database management software (ADABAS) & client/server & applications engineering software (ENTIRE) for mainframe & midrange computers; Germany's second largest software company

 See page 362 for a full profile of this company.

SOFTWARE ARTISTRY, INC.

9449 Priority Way West Dr.
Indianapolis, IN 46240
Phone: 317-843-1663
Fax: 317-843-7477

CEO: W. Scott Webber
CFO: Stephen R. Head
HR: Kimberly D. Kean
Employees: 113

1995 Sales: $25.6 million
1-Yr. Sales Change: 74.1%
Exchange: Nasdaq
Symbol: SWRT

Computers - customer support software (Expert Advisor)

SOFTWARE ENGINEERING OF AMERICA INC.

1230 Hempstead Turnpike
Franklin Square, NY 11010
Phone: 516-328-7000
Fax: 516-354-4015

CEO: Salvatore Simeone
CFO: John Chase
HR: John Chase
Employees: 325

1995 Sales: $94.6 million
1-Yr. Sales Change: —
Ownership: Privately Held

Computers - operations automation, help desk automation & application development

SOFTWARE PUBLISHERS ASSOCIATION

1730 M St. NW, Ste. 700
Washington, DC 20036-4510
Phone: 202-452-1600
Fax: 202-223-8756

CEO: Ken Wasch
CFO: Tom Meldrum
HR: Katrina Styles
Employees: 65

1995 Sales: $10.4 million
1-Yr. Sales Change: 6.1%
Ownership: Trade assn.

Computers - not-for-profit trade association of publishers, developers, distributors, retailers & consultants for the computer software industry

SOFTWARE PUBLISHING CORPORATION

111 N. Market St.	CEO: Irfan Salim	1995 Sales: $31.4 million
San Jose, CA 95113	CFO: Miriam K. Frazer	1-Yr. Sales Change: (48.9%)
Phone: 408-537-3000	HR: Mickey Satterwhite	Exchange: Nasdaq
Fax: 408-537-3500	Employees: 210	Symbol: SPCO

Computers -word processing (Professional Write), database (Superbase) & graphics (Harvard Graphics) software

SOFTWARE SPECTRUM, INC.

2140 Merritt Dr.	CEO: Judy O. Sims	1996 Sales: $398.5 million
Garland, TX 75041	CFO: Deborah A. Nugent	1-Yr. Sales Change: 13.2%
Phone: 972-840-6600	HR: Sue Zurber	Exchange: Nasdaq
Fax: 972-864-7878	Employees: 835	Symbol: SSPE

Retail - microcomputer business software

 See page 363 for a full profile of this company.

SOLECTRON CORPORATION

777 Gibraltar Dr.	CEO: Koichi Nishimura	1995 Sales: $2,066.0 million
Milpitas, CA 95035	CFO: Susan S. Wang	1-Yr. Sales Change: 41.8%
Phone: 408-957-8500	HR: Thomas Morelli	Exchange: NYSE
Fax: 408-956-6075	Employees: 11,049	Symbol: SLR

Electrical components - printed circuit boards & other electrical products

 See pages 206–207 for a full profile of this company.

SOLITRON DEVICES, INC.

3301 Electronics Way	CEO: Shevach Saraf	1996 Sales: $6.7 million
West Palm Beach, FL 33407	CFO: Tom Ruth	1-Yr. Sales Change: 6.3%
Phone: 561-848-4311	HR: Linda Petteruti	Exchange: Nasdaq (SC)
Fax: 561-881-5652	Employees: 100	Symbol: SODI

Electrical components - semiconductor components & related devices

SOLOPOINT, INC.

130-B Knowles Dr.	CEO: Edward M. Esber Jr.	1995 Sales: $0.0 million
Los Gatos, CA 95030	CFO: Edward M. Esber Jr.	1-Yr. Sales Change: —
Phone: 408-364-8850	HR: —	Exchange: Nasdaq (SC)
Fax: 408-364-1724	Employees: —	Symbol: SLPT

Computers - voice communication devices that integrate phones, pagers, voice mail & faxes (SoloCall Smart Center) & turn cellular phones into extensions of home or office phones (SoloCall SmartMonitor)

SONIC SOLUTIONS

101 Rowland Way
Novato, CA 94945
Phone: 415-893-8000
Fax: 415-893-8008

CEO: Robert J. Doris
CFO: A. Clay Leighton
HR: —
Employees: 75

1996 Sales: $13.9 million
1-Yr. Sales Change: (31.2%)
Exchange: Nasdaq
Symbol: SNIC

Computers - digital audio workstations for professional applications

SONY CORPORATION

7-35, Kitashinagawa 6-chome
Shinagawa-ku, Tokyo 141, Japan
Phone: +81-3-5448-2111
Fax: +81-3-5448-2244

CEO: Norio Ohga
CFO: Tsunao Hashimoto
HR: —
Employees: 138,000

1996 Sales: $47,581.5 mil.
1-Yr. Sales Change: 6.3%
Exchange: NYSE
Symbol: SNE

Audio & video home products - TVs, VCRs, CD players & tape recorders; semiconductors, telephone &
telecommunications equipment & computers; music & motion picture operations

SOUND SOURCE INTERACTIVE INC.

2985 E. Hillcrest Dr., Ste. A
West Lake Village, CA 91362
Phone: 805-494-9996
Fax: 805-379-3446

CEO: Vincent J. Bitetti
CFO: U. E. Gottschling
HR: —
Employees: 31

1996 Sales: $2.3 million
1-Yr. Sales Change: 4.5%
Exchange: Nasdaq (SC)
Symbol: SSII

Computers - educational & entertainment software (Interactive Movie Books)

SOURCE SERVICES CORPORATION

5580 LBJ Fwy., Ste. 300
Dallas, TX 75240
Phone: 972-385-3002
Fax: 972-385-7003

CEO: D. Les Ward
CFO: Richard DuPont
HR: Dawn Reyes
Employees: 2,600

1995 Sales: $141.8 million
1-Yr. Sales Change: 57.4%
Exchange: Nasdaq
Symbol: SRSV

Personnel - permanent & temporary placement of professionals in the legal, information technology,
consulting, accounting & finance, software engineering & health care services industries

SOURCE TECHNOLOGIES, INC.

628 Griffith Rd.
Charlotte, NC 28217
Phone: 704-522-8500
Fax: 704-522-7533

CEO: Miles Busby
CFO: Gordon Friedrich
HR: Gordon Friedrich
Employees: 44

1995 Sales: $21.8 million
1-Yr. Sales Change: 11.2%
Ownership: Privately Held

Computers - printers

SOUTHLAND MICRO SYSTEMS INC.

11 Musick
Irvine, CA 92718
Phone: 714-380-1958
Fax: 714-380-0995

CEO: John Meehan
CFO: Joe Meehan
HR: Connie Cole
Employees: 125

1995 Est. Sales: $150.0 mil.
1-Yr. Sales Change: 50.0%
Ownership: Privately Held

Computers - memory products

SPACETEC IMC CORPORATION

600 Suffolk St.
Lowell, MA 01854-3629
Phone: 508-970-0330
Fax: 508-970-0199

CEO: Dennis Gain
CFO: Linda S. Linsalata
HR: —
Employees: 59

1996 Sales: $8.1 million
1-Yr. Sales Change: 47.3%
Exchange: Nasdaq
Symbol: SIMC

Computers - 3-D interactive motion control systems & software

SPANLINK COMMUNICATIONS

One Main St. SE
Minneapolis, MN 55414
Phone: 612-362-8000
Fax: 612-362-8335

CEO: Brett A. Shockley
CFO: Patrick P. Irestone
HR: Kris Taylor
Employees: 48

1995 Sales: $4.3 million
1-Yr. Sales Change: (6.5%)
Exchange: Nasdaq (SC)
Symbol: SPLK

Computers - software & services (ExtraAgent, WebCall, VoiceSuite, ExtraPage Information System, SelectSolutions) that link business computer systems, telecommunications systems & the Internet

SPECTRUM HOLOBYTE, INC.

2490 Mariner Square Loop, Ste. 100
Alameda, CA 94501
Phone: 510-522-3584
Fax: 510-522-9305

CEO: Stephen M. Race
CFO: Richard A. Gelhaus
HR: Peggy DeLeon
Employees: 378

1996 Sales: $59.7 million
1-Yr. Sales Change: (29.3%)
Exchange: Nasdaq
Symbol: SBYT

Computers - entertainment software (F-15 Strike Eagle, Tetris)

SPECTRUM SIGNAL PROCESSING, INC.

8525 Baxter Place, 100 Production Ct.
Burnaby, BC V5A 4V7, Canada
Phone: 604-421-5422
Fax: 604-421-1764

CEO: Barry Jinks
CFO: Martin McConnell
HR: —
Employees: 100

1995 Sales: $18.9 million
1-Yr. Sales Change: 3.8%
Exchange: Nasdaq
Symbol: SSPIF

Electrical components - digital signal processing development & embedded systems

SPEEDFAM INTERNATIONAL, INC.

7406 W. Detroit
Chandler, AZ 85226
Phone: 602-961-2175
Fax: 602-961-7577

CEO: James N. Farley
CFO: Roger K. Marach
HR: Kathy Hanson
Employees: 382

1996 Sales: $120.2 million
1-Yr. Sales Change: 101.0%
Exchange: Nasdaq
Symbol: SFAM

Machinery - precision surface-processing systems for fabrication of thin film memory disk
media & semiconductors

SPIRE CORPORATION

One Patriots Park
Bedford, MA 01730-2396
Phone: 617-275-6000
Fax: 617-275-7470

CEO: Roger G. Little
CFO: Richard S. Gregorio
HR: Richard S. Gregorio
Employees: 122

1995 Sales: $17.5 million
1-Yr. Sales Change: (4.9%)
Exchange: Nasdaq
Symbol: SPIR

Electrical components - compound semiconductor wafers & devices & photovoltaic-module
manufacturing equipment

SPLASH TECHNOLOGY HOLDINGS, INC.

555 Del Rey Ave.
Sunnyvale, CA 94086
Phone: 408-328-6300
Fax: 408-328-6380

CEO: Kevin K. Macgillivray
CFO: Joan P. Platt
HR: Bridget Clark
Employees: 40

1995 Sales: $30.5 million
1-Yr. Sales Change: 86.0%
Ownership: Privately Held

Computers - color servers that link desktop computers & digital color laser copiers for networked
color printing

SPORTS SCIENCES, INC.

2075 Case Pkwy. South
Twinsburg, OH 44087
Phone: 216-963-0660
Fax: 216-963-0661

CEO: John D. Lipps
CFO: Nicholas J. Chuma
HR: —
Employees: 7

1995 Sales: $1.4 million
1-Yr. Sales Change: (65.0%)
Exchange: OTC
Symbol: SSCI

Computers - graphics & video software, including interactive electronic game simulators for the consumer
electronics industry (Pro Swing, TeeV Golf, Batter Up, PC Golf)

SPORTSLINE USA, INC.

6340 NW Fifth Way
Fort Lauderdale, FL 33309
Phone: 954-351-2120
Fax: 954-351-9175

CEO: Michael Levy
CFO: Ron Tolliver
HR: Randall Hafer
Employees: 120

1996 Sales: $2.5 million
1-Yr. Sales Change: 1,150%
Ownership: Privately Held

Computers - online interactive sports information service

SPSS INC.

444 N. Michigan Ave.
Chicago, IL 60611
Phone: 312-329-2400
Fax: 312-329-3558

CEO: Jack Noonan
CFO: Edward Hamburg
HR: Theresa A. Dear
Employees: 439

1995 Sales: $63.0 million
1-Yr. Sales Change: 21.6%
Exchange: Nasdaq
Symbol: SPSS

Computers - statistical software which provides data management, statistical analysis, reporting & presentation capabilities

SPYGLASS, INC.

1240 E. Diehl Rd.
Naperville, IL 60563
Phone: 708-505-1010
Fax: 708-505-4944

CEO: Douglas P. Colbeth
CFO: Gary Vilchick
HR: Lee Nelson
Employees: 73

1995 Sales: $10.4 million
1-Yr. Sales Change: 188.9%
Exchange: Nasdaq
Symbol: SPYG

Computers - software (Mosaic) for the World Wide Web

SQA, INC.

One Burlington Woods
Burlington, MA 01803
Phone: 617-229-3500
Fax: 617-229-3780

CEO: Ronald Nordin
CFO: Kenneth Tarpey
HR: —
Employees: 85

1995 Sales: $12.9 million
1-Yr. Sales Change: 186.7%
Exchange: Nasdaq
Symbol: SQAX

Computers - automated testing & quality management software for Windows-based client/server applications

SRI INTERNATIONAL

333 Ravenswood Ave.
Menlo Park, CA 94025-3493
Phone: 415-326-6200
Fax: 415-326-5512

CEO: William P. Sommers
CFO: John J. Oakson
HR: Stephen McElfresh
Employees: 1,900

1995 Est. Sales: $315.0 mil.
1-Yr. Sales Change: 1.0%
Ownership: Nonprofit org.

Engineering - contract research in engineering, science, technology, business & policy

SS&C TECHNOLOGIES, INC.

Corporate Place, 705 Bloomfield Ave.
Bloomfield, CT 06002
Phone: 860-242-7887
Fax: 860-242-8897

CEO: William C. Stone
CFO: John S. Wieczorek
HR: Kathy Whelihan
Employees: 195

1995 Sales: $18.8 million
1-Yr. Sales Change: 102.2%
Exchange: Nasdaq
Symbol: SSNC

Computers - client-server-based software (CAMRA, FILMS, PTS, FOTOS) & related consulting services for investment management within the financial services industry

STAC, INC.

12636 High Bluff Dr.	CEO: Gary W. Clow	1995 Sales: $45.8 million
San Diego, CA 92130-2093	CFO: John R. Witzel	1-Yr. Sales Change: 46.3%
Phone: 619-794-4300	HR: Sharon Worden	Exchange: Nasdaq
Fax: 619-794-4572	Employees: 180	Symbol: STAC

Computers - real-time data compression software (Stacker) & other software products (ReachOut Remote Control, CD-QuickShare)

STANDARD MICROSYSTEMS CORPORATION

80 Arkay Dr.	CEO: Paul Richman	1996 Sales: $341.9 million
Hauppauge, NY 11788	CFO: Anthony M. D'Agostino	1-Yr. Sales Change: (9.7%)
Phone: 516-435-6000	HR: Andrew Solowey	Exchange: Nasdaq
Fax: 516-273-5550	Employees: 864	Symbol: SMSC

Computers - local area network interface hardware & VLSI circuitry

STAR TECHNOLOGIES, INC.

515 Shaw Rd.	CEO: Robert C. Compton	1996 Sales: $4.3 million
Sterling, VA 20166	CFO: Edward J. Larese	1-Yr. Sales Change: (80.1%)
Phone: 703-689-4400	HR: Stan Surrette	Exchange: Nasdaq
Fax: 703-478-3600	Employees: 45	Symbol: STRR

Computers - image & signal processing computers for medical topography

STARFISH SOFTWARE

1700 Green Hills Rd.	CEO: Philippe Kahn	1995 Sales: $7.8 million
Scotts Valley, CA 95066	CFO: Norman Cheung	1-Yr. Sales Change: —
Phone: 408-461-5800	HR: Norman Cheung	Ownership: Privately Held
Fax: 408-461-5900	Employees: 30	

Computers - time-management software (Sidekick, Dashboard)

STARWAVE CORPORATION

13810 SE Eastgate Way	CEO: Michael Slade	1995 Est. Sales: $15.0 mil.
Bellevue, WA 98005	CFO: Ed Harris	1-Yr. Sales Change: 200.0%
Phone: 206-957-2000	HR: Barbara Thompson	Ownership: Privately Held
Fax: 206-957-2009	Employees: 221	

Computers - online services, including sports (ESPNET SportsZone), entertainment (Mr. Showbiz), game network (Castle Infinity), adventure & travel (Outside Online), family-oriented (Family Planet)

STATE OF THE ART, INC.

56 Technology South
Irvine, CA 92718
Phone: 714-753-1222
Fax: 714-753-1859

CEO: David W. Hanna
CFO: Joseph R. Armstrong
HR: Rosemary Schub
Employees: 313

1995 Sales: $46.1 million
1-Yr. Sales Change: 23.6%
Exchange: Nasdaq
Symbol: SOTA

Computers - accounting & financial management software for PCs & personal digital assistants (M*A*S 90 Evolution/2)

STB SYSTEMS, INC.

1651 N. Glenville Dr.
Richardson, TX 75081
Phone: 972-234-8750
Fax: 972-234-1306

CEO: William E. Ogle
CFO: James L. Hopkins
HR: Sherri Wolf
Employees: 913

1995 Sales: $129.6 million
1-Yr. Sales Change: 44.3%
Exchange: Nasdaq
Symbol: STBI

Computers - graphics adapters for single- & multimonitor configurations, primarily in IBM-compatible PCs

STERLING COMMERCE, INC.

8080 N. Central Expwy., Ste. 1100
Dallas, TX 75206
Phone: 214-891-8680
Fax: 214-739-0535

CEO: Sterling L. Williams
CFO: Jeannette P. Meier
HR: —
Employees: 1,009

1995 Sales: $191.9 million
1-Yr. Sales Change: 23.1%
Exchange: NYSE
Symbol: SE

Computers - electronic commerce software & network services for business-to-business communications & transactions

STERLING ELECTRONICS CORPORATION

4201 Southwest Fwy., PO Box 1229
Houston, TX 77251-1229
Phone: 713-627-9800
Fax: 713-629-3938

CEO: Ronald S. Spolane
CFO: Mac McConnell
HR: Sheila Babin
Employees: 655

1996 Sales: $322.1 million
1-Yr. Sales Change: 32.9%
Exchange: NYSE
Symbol: SEC

Electronics - distribution of electronic components

STERLING INFORMATION GROUP

515 Capital of Texas Hwy. South
Austin, TX 78746-4305
Phone: 512-327-0090
Fax: 512-327-0197

CEO: Chip Wolfe
CFO: Michael Haney
HR: Leslie Martinich
Employees: 70

1995 Sales: $6.3 million
1-Yr. Sales Change: 70.3%
Ownership: Privately Held

Computers - software consulting services

STERLING SOFTWARE, INC.

8080 N. Central Expwy., Ste. 1100	CEO: Sterling L. Williams	1995 Sales: $588.2 million
Dallas, TX 75206-1895	CFO: Jeannette P. Meier	1-Yr. Sales Change: 24.3%
Phone: 214-891-8600	HR: —	Exchange: NYSE
Fax: 214-739-0535	Employees: 3,700	Symbol: SSW

Computers - software products & services for the electronic commerce & systems & applications management software markets; technical professional services for the federal government

 See page 364 for a full profile of this company.

STM WIRELESS, INC.

One Mauchly	CEO: Emil Youssefzadeh	1995 Sales: $37.1 million
Irvine, CA 92718	CFO: Preston Romm	1-Yr. Sales Change: 41.1%
Phone: 714-753-7864	HR: Sandi Porralas	Exchange: Nasdaq
Fax: 714-753-1122	Employees: 200	Symbol: STMI

Telecommunications equipment - two-way earth stations, hub equipment & software, transceivers, modems & other networking products

STORAGE COMPUTER CORPORATION

11 Riverside St.	CEO: Ted Goodlander	1995 Sales: $23.1 million
Nashua, NH 03062-1373	CFO: Ted Goodlander	1-Yr. Sales Change: 59.3%
Phone: 603-880-3005	HR: Theda McGrath	Exchange: AMEX
Fax: 603-889-7232	Employees: 22	Symbol: SOS

Computers - disk storage systems & solid state data storage

STORAGE TECHNOLOGY CORPORATION

2270 S. 88th St.	CEO: David E. Weiss	1995 Sales: $1,929.5 million
Louisville, CO 80028-4309	CFO: David E. Lacey	1-Yr. Sales Change: 18.7%
Phone: 303-673-5151	HR: Laurie Dodd	Exchange: NYSE
Fax: 303-673-2296	Employees: 10,000	Symbol: STK

Computers - information storage & retrieval systems & networking products

 See pages 208–209 for a full profile of this company.

STORMEDIA, INC.

390 Reed St.	CEO: Michael E. Oxsen	1995 Sales: $161.5 million
Santa Clara, CA 95050	CFO: Stephen M. Abely	1-Yr. Sales Change: 97.4%
Phone: 408-988-1409	HR: Judy Kelley	Exchange: Nasdaq
Fax: 408-727-9814	Employees: 720	Symbol: STMD

Electrical components - thin film disks for hard disk drives

STRATASYS, INC.

14950 Martin Dr.	CEO: S. Scott Crump	1995 Sales: $10.3 million
Eden Prairie, MN 55344-2020	CFO: S. Scott Crump	1-Yr. Sales Change: 171.1%
Phone: 612-937-3000	HR: Cari Feik	Exchange: Nasdaq (SC)
Fax: 612-937-0070	Employees: 81	Symbol: SSYS

Engineering - rapid prototyping hardware & software that create physical models from CAD workstations

STRATUS COMPUTER, INC.

55 Fairbanks Blvd.	CEO: William E. Foster	1995 Sales: $587.9 million
Marlborough, MA 01752	CFO: Robert E. Donahue	1-Yr. Sales Change: 2.0%
Phone: 508-460-2000	HR: John F. Young	Exchange: NYSE
Fax: 508-481-8945	Employees: 2,441	Symbol: SRA

Computers - continuously available hardware-based fault-tolerant computer systems & related software & services

 See page 365 for a full profile of this company.

STREAM INTERNATIONAL INC.

105 Rosemont Rd.	CEO: Terry Leahy	1995 Sales: $1,433.0 million
Westmont, MA 02090	CFO: Gene Morphis	1-Yr. Sales Change: 16.7%
Phone: 617-751-1000	HR: John McMahon	Ownership: Privately Held
Fax: 617-751-7751	Employees: 7,500	

Computers - software upgrades & training to corporations; software & manual production for software manufacturers

STREAMLOGIC CORPORATION

21329 Nordhoff St.	CEO: J. Larry Smart	1995 Sales: $211.3 million
Chatsworth, CA 91311	CFO: Lee Hilbert	1-Yr. Sales Change: (39.0%)
Phone: 818-701-8400	HR: Nancy Tullos	Exchange: Nasdaq
Fax: 818-701-8410	Employees: 2,069	Symbol: STLC

Computers - data storage subsystems and software

STRUCTURAL DYNAMICS RESEARCH CORPORATION

2000 Eastman Dr.	CEO: Albert F. Peter	1995 Sales: $204.1 million
Milford, OH 45150-2740	CFO: Jeffrey J. Vorholt	1-Yr. Sales Change: 21.9%
Phone: 513-576-2400	HR: Bryan M. Valentine	Exchange: Nasdaq
Fax: 513-576-2734	Employees: 1,100	Symbol: SDRC

Computers - CAE software for mechanical design automation & product data management

SUBMICRON SYSTEMS CORPORATION

6330 Hedgewood Dr., Ste. 150
Allentown, PA 18106
Phone: 610-391-9200
Fax: 610-391-1982

CEO: David F. Levy
CFO: R. G. Holmes
HR: Amy Anderson
Employees: 681

1995 Sales: $117.7 million
1-Yr. Sales Change: 114.8%
Exchange: Nasdaq
Symbol: SUBM

Machinery - semiconductor manufacturing equipment

SULCUS COMPUTER CORPORATION

Sulcus Centre, 41 N. Main St.
Greensburg, PA 15601
Phone: 412-836-2000
Fax: 412-836-1440

CEO: Joel Nagelmann
CFO: H. Richard Howie
HR: Nadine Greimer
Employees: 408

1995 Sales: $46.0 million
1-Yr. Sales Change: 6.7%
Exchange: AMEX
Symbol: SUL

Computers - legal, real estate, restaurant & hotel management systems & software

SUMMIT DESIGN, INC.

9305 SW Gemini Dr.
Beaverton, OR 97008
Phone: 503-643-9281
Fax: 503-646-4954

CEO: Larry J. Gerhard
CFO: C. Albert Koob
HR: Sharon Beinlich
Employees: 118

1995 Sales: $14.1 million
1-Yr. Sales Change: 8.5%
Ownership: Privately Held

Computers - graphical design entry, verification & simulation design-to-test software

SUMMIT MEDICAL SYSTEMS, INC.

One Carlson Pkwy.
Minneapolis, MN 55447
Phone: 612-473-3250
Fax: 612-473-8534

CEO: Kevin R. Green
CFO: Anthony W. Rees
HR: Kathy Pinger
Employees: 150

1995 Sales: $13.8 million
1-Yr. Sales Change: 68.3%
Exchange: Nasdaq
Symbol: SUMT

Computers - database software for the health care industry

SUN MICROSYSTEMS, INC.

2550 Garcia Ave.
Mountain View, CA 94043-1100
Phone: 415-960-1300
Fax: 415-969-9131

CEO: Scott G. McNealy
CFO: Michael E. Lehman
HR: Kenneth M. Alvares
Employees: 17,400

1996 Sales: $7,094.8 million
1-Yr. Sales Change: 20.2%
Exchange: Nasdaq
Symbol: SUNW

Computers - UNIX-based workstations (#1 worldwide), Internet servers & operating & productivity software

 **See pages 210–211 for a full profile of this company.**

SUNGARD DATA SYSTEMS INC.

1285 Drummers Ln.	CEO: James L. Mann	1995 Sales: $532.6 million
Wayne, PA 19087	CFO: Michael J. Ruane	1-Yr. Sales Change: 21.8%
Phone: 610-341-8700	HR: Donna J. Pedrick	Exchange: Nasdaq
Fax: 610-341-8739	Employees: 2,900	Symbol: SNDT

Computers - investment support services; disaster recovery services for computers shut down by natural or man-made catastrophes

SUNQUEST INFORMATION SYSTEMS, INC.

4801 E. Broadway Blvd.	CEO: Sidney A. Goldblatt	1995 Sales: $61.5 million
Tucson, AZ 85711	CFO: Nina M. Dmetruk	1-Yr. Sales Change: (1.8%)
Phone: 520-570-2000	HR: Marsha Morgan	Exchange: Nasdaq
Fax: 520-570-2494	Employees: 563	Symbol: SUNQ

Computers - health care information systems, including departmental clinical, clinical repository & managed care systems for large & mid-sized hospitals, clinics & other facilities

SUPERCOM, INC.

410 S. Abbott Ave.	CEO: James Fang	1996 Sales: $565.0 million
Milpitas, CA 95035-5257	CFO: Gabrielle Tetreault	1-Yr. Sales Change: 32.9%
Phone: 408-456-8888	HR: B. B. Sato	Ownership: Privately Held
Fax: 408-263-3003	Employees: 375	

Retail - personal computers, accessories & home entertainment

SUPERCONDUCTOR TECHNOLOGIES INC.

460 Ward Dr., Ste. F	CEO: Daniel C. Hu	1995 Sales: $7.6 million
Santa Barbara, CA 93111-2310	CFO: James G. Evans Jr.	1-Yr. Sales Change: 38.2%
Phone: 805-683-7646	HR: Cherie Welsh	Exchange: Nasdaq
Fax: 805-967-0342	Employees: 62	Symbol: SCON

Electrical components - superconductor manufacturing materials, circuit designs & cooling techniques

SUPERTEX, INC.

1350 Bordeaux Dr.	CEO: Henry C. Pao	1996 Sales: $42.8 million
Sunnyvale, CA 94089	CFO: Henry C. Pao	1-Yr. Sales Change: 34.6%
Phone: 408-744-0100	HR: Melba Stathis	Exchange: Nasdaq
Fax: 408-734-5247	Employees: 256	Symbol: SUPX

Electrical components - high voltage semiconductor products & power transistors & ICs

SYBASE, INC.

6475 Christie Ave.	CEO: Mitchell E. Kertzman	1995 Sales: $956.6 million
Emeryville, CA 94608	CFO: Jack L. Acosta	1-Yr. Sales Change: 37.9%
Phone: 510-596-3500	HR: Juanita Lott	Exchange: Nasdaq
Fax: 510-658-9441	Employees: 5,865	Symbol: SYBS

Computers - database management software & services for building online, enterprisewide information systems

 See page 366 for a full profile of this company.

SYKES ENTERPRISES, INC.

100 N. Tampa St., Ste. 3900	CEO: John H. Sykes	1995 Sales: $63.1 million
Tampa, FL 33062	CFO: Scott J. Bendert	1-Yr. Sales Change: 246.7%
Phone: 813-274-1000	HR: John D. Bray	Exchange: Nasdaq
Fax: 813-273-0148	Employees: 1,973	Symbol: SYKE

Personnel - information technology outsourcing services

SYMANTEC CORPORATION

10201 Torre Ave.	CEO: Gordon E. Eubanks Jr.	1996 Sales: $454.4 million
Cupertino, CA 95014-2132	CFO: Robert R. B. Dykes	1-Yr. Sales Change: 35.7%
Phone: 408-253-9600	HR: Joe Shepela	Exchange: Nasdaq
Fax: 408-253-3446	Employees: 2,200	Symbol: SYMC

Computers - information management, productivity-enhancement & development software (Norton Utilities)

 See page 367 for a full profile of this company.

SYMBOL TECHNOLOGIES, INC.

One Symbol Plaza	CEO: Jerome Swartz	1995 Sales: $555.2 million
Holtsville, NY 11742-1300	CFO: Thomas G. Amato	1-Yr. Sales Change: 19.3%
Phone: 516-738-2400	HR: Allen C. Creveling	Exchange: NYSE
Fax: 516-738-4704	Employees: 2,400	Symbol: SBL

Optical character recognition - bar-code-based data collection systems

SYMIX SYSTEMS, INC.

2800 Corporate Exchange Dr.	CEO: Lawrence J. Fox	1996 Sales: $45.8 million
Columbus, OH 43231	CFO: Lawrence W. DeLeon	1-Yr. Sales Change: 7.0%
Phone: 614-523-7000	HR: Robert D. Williams	Exchange: Nasdaq
Fax: 614-895-2504	Employees: 336	Symbol: SYMX

Computers - accounting & management software

SYNC RESEARCH, INC.

7 Studebaker	CEO: John H. Rademaker	1995 Sales: $23.2 million
Irvine, CA 92718	CFO: Ronald J. Scioscia	1-Yr. Sales Change: 95.0%
Phone: 714-588-2070	HR: Joan Gosewisch	Exchange: Nasdaq
Fax: 714-460-4481	Employees: 92	Symbol: SYNX

Computers - networking products that adapt IBM Systems Architecture networks to switched WAN services

SYNERGY SEMICONDUCTOR CORPORATION

3450 Central Expwy.	CEO: Thomas D. Mino	1995 Sales: $25.7 million
Santa Clara, CA 95051	CFO: T. Olin Nichols	1-Yr. Sales Change: 34.6%
Phone: 408-730-1313	HR: —	Ownership: Privately Held
Fax: 408-737-0831	Employees: 185	

Electrical components - digital & mixed-signal integrated circuits for use in system applications, time-clock generators for workstations & telecommunication systems & in local- & wide-area networks

SYNOPSYS, INC.

700 E. Middlefield Rd.	CEO: Aart J. de Geus	1995 Sales: $265.5 million
Mountain View, CA 94043-4033	CFO: A. Brooke Seawell	1-Yr. Sales Change: 35.5%
Phone: 415-962-5000	HR: Sally DeStefano	Exchange: Nasdaq
Fax: 415-965-8637	Employees: 1,388	Symbol: SNPS

Computers - electronic design automation & logic simulation software

 See page 368 for a full profile of this company.

SYNTELLECT INC.

1000 Holcomb Woods Pkwy., Bldg. 410A	CEO: J. Lawrence Bradner	1995 Sales: $33.5 million
Roswell, GA 30076-2585	CFO: Neal L. Miller	1-Yr. Sales Change: (26.2%)
Phone: 770-587-0700	HR: —	Exchange: Nasdaq
Fax: 770-587-0589	Employees: 234	Symbol: SYNL

Telecommunications equipment - voice & information processing systems & application software, including interactive voice response & predictive dialing technology

SYQUEST TECHNOLOGY, INC.

47071 Bayside Pkwy.	CEO: Edwin L. Harper	1995 Sales: $299.5 million
Fremont, CA 94538	CFO: James E. Graber	1-Yr. Sales Change: 35.5%
Phone: 510-226-4000	HR: Robert E. Lyon	Exchange: Nasdaq
Fax: 510-226-4100	Employees: 2,409	Symbol: SYQT

Computers - removable hard-disk cartridges & drives

 See page 369 for a full profile of this company.

SYSTEM SOFTWARE ASSOCIATES, INC.

500 W. Madison St., 32nd Fl.	CEO: Roger E. Covey	1995 Sales: $394.4 million
Chicago, IL 60661	CFO: Joseph J. Skadra	1-Yr. Sales Change: 17.9%
Phone: 312-258-6000	HR: Mark Ugol	Exchange: Nasdaq
Fax: 312-474-7500	Employees: 2,000	Symbol: SSAX

Computers - business-application, maintenance-management, CASE & electronic-data-interchange software

 See page 370 for a full profile of this company.

SYSTEMS & COMPUTER TECHNOLOGY CORPORATION

4 Country View Rd.	CEO: Michael J. Emmi	1995 Sales: $176.1 million
Malvern, PA 19355	CFO: Eric Haskell	1-Yr. Sales Change: 18.8%
Phone: 610-647-5930	HR: Susan R. Sheridan	Exchange: Nasdaq
Fax: 610-640-5102	Employees: 1,500	Symbol: SCTC

Computers - facilities-management services & administrative-application software

SYSTEMSOFT CORPORATION

2 Vision Dr.	CEO: Robert F. Angelo	1996 Sales: $24.6 million
Natick, MA 01760	CFO: David P. Sommers	1-Yr. Sales Change: 61.8%
Phone: 508-651-0088	HR: Randi Nichols	Exchange: Nasdaq
Fax: 508-651-8188	Employees: 138	Symbol: SYSF

Computers - PC Cards & related system-level software for laptops, notebooks, subnotebooks & personal computing devices

 See page 371 for a full profile of this company.

TAD RESOURCES INTERNATIONAL, INC.

639 Massachusetts Ave.	CEO: James S. Davis	1995 Est. Sales: $1,200 mil.
Cambridge, MA 02139	CFO: Richard Chipman	1-Yr. Sales Change: 56.3%
Phone: 617-868-1650	HR: —	Ownership: Privately Held
Fax: 617-492-1432	Employees: 35,000	

Personnel - temporary technical employment services; contract engineering services

TADPOLE TECHNOLOGY PLC

Unit 330, Cambridge Science Park	CEO: George Grey	1995 Sales: $38.3 million
Cambridge CB4 4WQ, UK	CFO: Robert Booth	1-Yr. Sales Change: (25.5%)
Phone: +44-1-223-428-200	HR: —	Exchange: London
Fax: +44-1-223-428-201	Employees: 211	

Computers - portable workstations & specialty components

TAITRON COMPONENTS INCORPORATED

25202 Anza Dr.
Santa Clarita, CA 91355
Phone: 805-257-6060
Fax: 805-257-6415

CEO: Stewart Wang
CFO: David M. Turner
HR: Kenneth Bloomfield
Employees: 51

1995 Sales: $35.9 million
1-Yr. Sales Change: 45.9%
Exchange: Nasdaq
Symbol: TAIT

Electronics - distribution of transistors, diodes & other discrete semiconductors to other electronics distributors & to OEMs

TAIWAN SEMICONDUCTOR MANUFACTURING COMPANY LTD.

No. 121, Park Ave. III
Hsin-chu, Taiwan
Phone: +886-35-780221
Fax: +886-35-781546

CEO: Donald W. Brooks
CFO: —
HR: —
Employees: 3,412

1995 Sales: $1,053.7 million
1-Yr. Sales Change: 41.6%
Exchange: Taipei

Electrical components - 6-inch wafers for other semiconductor companies, including IC design houses, vertically integrated IC firms & systems companies

TALX CORPORATION

1850 Borman Ct.
St. Louis, MO 63146
Phone: 314-434-0046
Fax: 314-434-9205

CEO: William W. Canfield
CFO: Craig N. Cohen
HR: Kathy Lahrmann
Employees: 133

1996 Sales: $13.5 million
1-Yr. Sales Change: 36.4%
Ownership: Privately Held

Computers - interactive communications solutions using computer telephony to integrate interactive voice response, facsimile, e-mail, Internet & corporate Intranet technologies

TANDBERG DATA A/S

Kjelsasveien 161, PO Box 134
N-0411 Oslo, Norway
Phone: +47-22-18-90-90
Fax: +47-22-18-95-50

CEO: Jon Schjold
CFO: Geir L. Sagen
HR: —
Employees: 758

1995 Sales: $198.6 million
1-Yr. Sales Change: 8.8%
Exchange: Oslo

Computers - data storage products, including high-capacity data cartridge equipment (#1 worldwide)

TANDEM COMPUTERS INCORPORATED

19333 Vallco Pkwy.
Cupertino, CA 95014-2599
Phone: 408-285-6000
Fax: 408-285-0035

CEO: Roel Pieper
CFO: David J. Rynne
HR: Philip Johnson
Employees: 8,380

1995 Sales: $2,285.0 million
1-Yr. Sales Change: 8.4%
Exchange: NYSE
Symbol: TDM

Computers - available, open & parallel processing computer systems, client/server solutions & enterprise networks

 See pages 212–213 for a full profile of this company.

TANDY CORPORATION

1800 One Tandy Center	CEO: John V. Roach	1995 Sales: $5,839.1 million
Fort Worth, TX 76102	CFO: Dwain H. Hughes	1-Yr. Sales Change: 18.1%
Phone: 817-390-3700	HR: George Berger	Exchange: NYSE
Fax: 817-390-2647	Employees: 49,300	Symbol: TAN

Retail - consumer electronics (Radio Shack, Computer City, McDuff, VideoConcepts, The Edge, Incredible Universe)

 See pages 214–215 for a full profile of this company.

TANGRAM ENTERPRISE SOLUTIONS, INC.

5511 Capital Center Dr., Ste. 400	CEO: W. Christopher Jesse	1995 Sales: $12.5 million
Raleigh, NC 27606	CFO: Nancy M. Dunn	1-Yr. Sales Change: (2.3%)
Phone: 919-851-6000	HR: Susan Smith-Morris	Exchange: Nasdaq (SC)
Fax: 919-851-6004	Employees: 98	Symbol: TESI

Computers - asset tracking & electronic software distribution for organizations worldwide

TATUNG CO.

22 Chungshan North Rd., Sec. 3	CEO: Lin Weishan	1995 Sales: $3,000.0 million
Taipei 104, Taiwan	CFO: —	1-Yr. Sales Change: —
Phone: +886-2-592-5252	HR: —	Exchange: Taiwan
Fax: +886-2-591-5185	Employees: 19,491	

Computers - cathode ray tubes, personal computers & mice

 See pages 216–217 for a full profile of this company.

TCSI CORPORATION

2121 Allston Way	CEO: Roger A. Strauch	1995 Sales: $55.4 million
Berkeley, CA 94704-1301	CFO: Paul A. Farmer	1-Yr. Sales Change: 37.5%
Phone: 510-649-3700	HR: Dennis Heller	Exchange: Nasdaq
Fax: 510-649-3500	Employees: 288	Symbol: TCSI

Computers - object-oriented telecommunications software for monitoring networks, rerouting traffic & integrating different telecom services more efficiently

TECH DATA CORPORATION

5350 Tech Data Dr.	CEO: Steven A. Raymund	1996 Sales: $3,086.6 million
Clearwater, FL 34620	CFO: Jeffery P. Howells	1-Yr. Sales Change: 27.6%
Phone: 813-539-7429	HR: Lawrence W. Hamilton	Exchange: Nasdaq
Fax: 813-538-7054	Employees: 2,625	Symbol: TECD

Retail - wholesale networking, mass storage, peripherals, hardware & software products for value-added resellers & computer retailers in the US, Canada, France, Latin America & the Caribbean

 See pages 218–219 for a full profile of this company.

TECHDYNE, INC.

2230 W. 77th St.	CEO: Barry Pardon	1995 Sales: $30.4 million
Hialeah, FL 33016	CFO: —	1-Yr. Sales Change: —
Phone: 305-556-9210	HR: —	Exchange: Nasdaq (SC)
Fax: —	Employees: 296	Symbol: TCDN

Electronics - electromechanical electronic & plastic injection-molded components, including molded cable wires, wire harness assemblies & printed circuit boards

TECHFORCE CORPORATION

15950 Bay Vista Dr.	CEO: John A. Koehler	1995 Sales: $49.2 million
Clearwater, FL 34620	CFO: Jerrel W. Kee	1-Yr. Sales Change: 60.3%
Phone: 813-532-3600	HR: Lynn Henderson	Exchange: Nasdaq
Fax: 813-532-3980	Employees: 441	Symbol: TFRC

Computers - integrated network support

TECHNOLOGY MODELING ASSOCIATES, INC.

595 Lawrence Expwy	CEO: Roy E. Jewell	1995 Sales: $12.6 million
Sunnyvale, CA 94086	CFO: Bennet L. Weintraub	1-Yr. Sales Change: 4.1%
Phone: 408-328-0930	HR: Angelica Arellano	Exchange: Nasdaq
Fax: 408-328-0940	Employees: 69	Symbol: TMAI

Computers - provides physical simulation software to support integrated circuit design & manufacturing

TECHNOLOGY SOLUTIONS COMPANY

205 N. Michigan Ave., Ste. 1500	CEO: John T. Kohler	1996 Sales: $97.6 million
Chicago, IL 60601	CFO: Martin T. Johnson	1-Yr. Sales Change: 48.3%
Phone: 312-861-9600	HR: Debbie Steele	Exchange: Nasdaq
Fax: 312-861-9601	Employees: 423	Symbol: TSCC

Computers - consulting & systems integration services

TECNOMATIX TECHNOLOGIES LTD.

Delta House, 16 Hagalim Ave.	CEO: Shlomo Dovrat	1995 Sales: $33.4 million
Herzliya 46733, Israel	CFO: Naftali Idan	1-Yr. Sales Change: 42.7%
Phone: +972-9-594777	HR: —	Exchange: Nasdaq
Fax: +972-9-544402	Employees: 195	Symbol: TCNOF

Computers - automated manufacturing system software for UNIX-based 3D graphics workstations

TEGAL CORPORATION LTD.

2201 S. McDowell Blvd.	CEO: Robert V. Hery	1996 Sales: $62.0 million
Petaluma, CA 94955-6020	CFO: David Curtis	1-Yr. Sales Change: 39.0%
Phone: 707-763-5600	HR: Diane Walsh	Exchange: Nasdaq
Fax: 707-763-0436	Employees: 256	Symbol: TGAL

Machinery - plasma-etch systems used in integrated circuit fabrication

TEKTRONIX, INC.

26600 SW Parkway Ave.	CEO: Jerome J. Meyer	1996 Sales: $1,768.9 million
Wilsonville, OR 97070	CFO: Carl W. Neun	1-Yr. Sales Change: 20.2%
Phone: 503-627-7111	HR: Bob Baughman	Exchange: NYSE
Fax: 503-627-5502	Employees: 7,619	Symbol: TEK

Electronics - measuring instruments, color printing & imaging, video editing systems, network displays

 See pages 220–221 for a full profile of this company.

TELCO SYSTEMS, INC.

63 Nahatan St.	CEO: William B. Smith	1995 Sales: $89.1 million
Norwood, MA 02062-4996	CFO: John A. Ruggiero	1-Yr. Sales Change: (11.3%)
Phone: 617-551-0300	HR: —	Exchange: Nasdaq
Fax: 617-551-0534	Employees: 436	Symbol: TELC

Telecommunications equipment - fiber optic transmission equipment, customer premises network access equipment & internetworking equipment for the telecommunications industry

TELCOM SEMICONDUCTOR, INC.

1300 Terra Bella Ave.	CEO: Phillip M. Drayer	1995 Sales: $39.0 million
Mountain View, CA 94039	CFO: R. Michael O'Malley	1-Yr. Sales Change: 59.2%
Phone: 415-968-9252	HR: Diane Drew	Exchange: Nasdaq
Fax: 415-940-9633	Employees: 322	Symbol: TLCM

Electrical components - analog integrated circuits for industrial, communications, computer, automotive & medical markets

TELEBIT CORPORATION

One Executive Dr.	CEO: James D. Norrod	1995 Sales: $55.9 million
Chelmsford, MA 01824	CFO: Brian D. Cohen	1-Yr. Sales Change: (26.6%)
Phone: 508-441-2181	HR: Joe Musumano	Exchange: Nasdaq
Fax: 508-656-9304	Employees: 288	Symbol: TBIT

Telecommunications equipment - high performance wide area network (WAN) access products

TELECHIPS CORPORATION

6880 S. McCarran Blvd.	CEO: C. A. Burns	1995 Sales: $0.0 million
Reno, NV 89509	CFO: N. B. Caldwell	1-Yr. Sales Change: (100%)
Phone: 702-824-5555	HR: —	Exchange: Nasdaq (SC)
Fax: 702-824-0000	Employees: 33	Symbol: TCHP

Computers - interactive computer-telephone equipment & related software (ThinPhone)

TELEPAD CORPORATION

380 Herndon Pkwy., Ste 1900	CEO: Donald W. Barrett	1995 Sales: $2.6 million
Herndon, VA 22070	CFO: Robert Russell	1-Yr. Sales Change: (55.2%)
Phone: 703-834-9000	HR: —	Exchange: OTC
Fax: 703-834-1235	Employees: 27	Symbol: TPADA

Telecommunications equipment - hardware & software products designed for information processing & communication needs of mobile & remote field workers (TelePad SL)

TELESCAN, INC.

10550 Richmond Ave., Ste. 250	CEO: David L. Brown	1995 Sales: $14.0 million
Houston, TX 77042	CFO: Karen R. Fohn	1-Yr. Sales Change: 33.3%
Phone: 713-588-9700	HR: Brigette Dewhurst	Exchange: Nasdaq (SC)
Fax: 713-588-9797	Employees: 153	Symbol: TSCN

Computers - online financial information services, including databases & software for individual, corporate & institutional customers

TELESENSORY CORPORATION

455 N. Bernardo Ave.	CEO: Larry Israel	1995 Sales: $30.7 million
Mountain View, CA 94043	CFO: Robert W. Kamenski	1-Yr. Sales Change: 11.2%
Phone: 415-960-0920	HR: Janice Rommel	Ownership: Privately Held
Fax: 415-969-9064	Employees: 179	

Computers - electronic & computer-based products for people with severe visual disabilities, including video magnifiers & braille-related devices (PowerBraille, ScreenPower)

TELEVIDEO SYSTEMS, INC.

2345 Harris Way	CEO: K. Philip Hwang	1995 Sales: $16.9 million
San Jose, CA 95161	CFO: K. David Kim	1-Yr. Sales Change: 28.0%
Phone: 408-954-8333	HR: —	Exchange: Nasdaq
Fax: 408-954-0622	Employees: 69	Symbol: TELV

Computers - computer monitors & terminals, multimedia products & disk-controller products

TELIDENT, INC.

One Main St. SE, Ste. 85	CEO: Michael J. Miller	1996 Sales: $2.5 million
Minneapolis, MN 55414	CFO: John Kromer	1-Yr. Sales Change: 8.7%
Phone: 612-623-0911	HR: John Kromer	Exchange: Nasdaq (SC)
Fax: 612-623-0944	Employees: 32	Symbol: TLDT

Computers - networking & connectivity, equipment & software which provide exact locations of 911 calls; switching, selective routing & data interfacing capabilities

TELLABS, INC.

4951 Indiana Ave.	CEO: Michael J. Birck	1995 Sales: $635.2 million
Lisle, IL 60532	CFO: Peter A. Guglielmi	1-Yr. Sales Change: 28.5%
Phone: 708-969-8800	HR: Dan Stolle	Exchange: Nasdaq
Fax: 708-512-8202	Employees: 2,814	Symbol: TLAB

Telecommunications equipment - voice & data transmission products, primarily for telephone & long distance service providers

TELLURIAN, INC.

15 Industrial Ave.	CEO: Ronald Swallow	1995 Sales: $0.5 million
Upper Saddle River, NJ 07458	CFO: Stuart French	1-Yr. Sales Change: —
Phone: 201-818-6767	HR: Stuart French	Ownership: Privately Held
Fax: 201-818-2290	Employees: 9	

Computers - virtual reality products, including image generators (AT-200 Image Generator), related software, helmets & motion systems

TELXON CORPORATION

3330 W. Market St.	CEO: Robert F. Meyerson	1996 Sales: $486.5 million
Akron, OH 44333	CFO: Kenneth W. Haver	1-Yr. Sales Change: 28.2%
Phone: 330-867-3700	HR: Meg Pais	Exchange: Nasdaq
Fax: 330-869-2240	Employees: 1,850	Symbol: TLXN

Computers - portable & wireless transaction systems

TENCOR INSTRUMENTS

2400 Charleston Rd.	CEO: Jon D. Tompkins	1995 Sales: $330.2 million
Mountain View, CA 94043	CFO: Bruce R. Wright	1-Yr. Sales Change: 81.1%
Phone: 415-969-6767	HR: Bruce R. Wright	Exchange: Nasdaq
Fax: 415-968-9482	Employees: 1,311	Symbol: TNCR

Machinery - semiconductor manufacturing equipment

 See page 372 for a full profile of this company.

TENERA, INC.

One Market, Spear Tower, Ste. 1850	CEO: Michael D. Thomas	1995 Sales: $25.5 million
San Francisco, CA 94105-1018	CFO: Jeffrey R. Hazarian	1-Yr. Sales Change: 8.1%
Phone: 415-536-4744	HR: Brad Gettis	Exchange: AMEX
Fax: 415-536-4714	Employees: 238	Symbol: TNR

Computers - integrated management & software services for electric utilities, government agencies & large transporation corporations

TERA COMPUTER COMPANY

2815 Eastlake Ave. East	CEO: James E. Rottsolk	1995 Sales: $0.1 million
Seattle, WA 98102-3027	CFO: James E. Rottsolk	1-Yr. Sales Change: —
Phone: 206-325-0800	HR: Kerri Wood	Exchange: Nasdaq (SC)
Fax: 206-325-2433	Employees: 66	Symbol: TERA

Computers - general purpose parallel computer systems for scientific & engineering applications, such as simulation & visualization of mechanical, biochemical, database mining & computer aided design

TERADYNE, INC.

321 Harrison Ave.	CEO: Alexander V. d'Arbeloff	1995 Sales: $1,191.0 million
Boston, MA 02118	CFO: Owen W. Robbins	1-Yr. Sales Change: 75.8%
Phone: 617-482-2700	HR: James Dawson	Exchange: NYSE
Fax: 617-422-2910	Employees: 5,200	Symbol: TER

Electronics - semiconductor, circuit board & telecommunications test equipment & backplane connection systems

 See pages 222–223 for a full profile of this company.

TEXAS INSTRUMENTS INCORPORATED

13500 N. Central Expwy.	CEO: Thomas J. Engibous	1995 Sales: $13,128.0 mil.
Dallas, TX 75243	CFO: William A. Aylesworth	1-Yr. Sales Change: 27.3%
Phone: 972-995-2011	HR: Charles F. Nielson	Exchange: NYSE
Fax: 972-995-4360	Employees: 59,574	Symbol: TXN

Electrical components - semiconductors, radar & navigation systems, avionics & surveillance equipment; notebook computers (TravelMate 5000 series), calculators & printers; electronic sensors & controls

 See pages 224–225 for a full profile of this company.

THINK NEW IDEAS, INC.

45 W. 36th St.	CEO: Scott Mednick	1996 Sales: $12.1 million
New York, NY 10018	CFO: Melvin Epstein	1-Yr. Sales Change: 17.5%
Phone: 212-629-6800	HR: —	Ownership: Privately Held
Fax: 212-629-6850	Employees: 98	

Business services - marketing & communications solutions using Internet and intranet capabilities

THINKING MACHINES CORPORATION

14 Crosby Dr.	CEO: Robert L. Doretti	1995 Sales: $30.0 million
Bedford, MA 01730	CFO: Robert LaBossiere	1-Yr. Sales Change: (25.2%)
Phone: 617-276-0400	HR: Robert LaBossiere	Ownership: Privately Held
Fax: 617-276-0444	Employees: 180	

Computers - software development tools for parallel computing & parallel processing servers

THINKING TOOLS, INC.

One Lower Ragsdale Dr., I-250	CEO: John Hiles	1995 Sales: $1.3 million
Monterey, CA 93940	CFO: —	1-Yr. Sales Change: 62.5%
Phone: 408-373-8688	HR: Marianne Marinovich	Ownership: Privately Held
Fax: 408-373-7020	Employees: 15	

Computers - PC-based business simulation software programs

T-HQ, INC.

5016 N. Pkwy. Calabasas, Ste. 100	CEO: Brian J. Farrell	1995 Sales: $33.3 million
Calabasas, CA 91302	CFO: Stefan Dietrich	1-Yr. Sales Change: 150.4%
Phone: 818-591-1310	HR: Mary Nelson Garrett	Exchange: Nasdaq (SC)
Fax: 818-591-1615	Employees: 43	Symbol: TOYH

Computers - interactive entertainment software (Ren & Stimpy, Sports Illustrated)

THRUSTMASTER, INC.

10150 SW Nimbus Ave.	CEO: Stephen A. Aanderud	1995 Sales: $19.4 million
Tigard, OR 97223-4337	CFO: Kent E. Koski	1-Yr. Sales Change: 42.6%
Phone: 503-639-3200	HR: Julie Leutschaft	Exchange: Nasdaq
Fax: 503-620-8094	Employees: 96	Symbol: TMSR

Computers - game simulation equipment including flight sticks, rudder pedals & throttle controls for flight simulation

TIBURON SYSTEMS, INC.

1290 Parkmoor Ave.	CEO: Jere W. Patterson	1996 Sales: $24.0 million
San Jose, CA 95126	CFO: Roger Laux	1-Yr. Sales Change: 4.8%
Phone: 408-293-4400	HR: Cindy Arthur	Ownership: Privately Held
Fax: 408-293-9090	Employees: 165	

Computers - defense applications software & systems related to command, control & communications, including tactical data fusion & display

TIMBERLINE SOFTWARE CORPORATION

9600 SW Nimbus Ave.	CEO: John Gorman	1995 Sales: $24.8 million
Beaverton, OR 97008-7163	CFO: Thomas P. Cox	1-Yr. Sales Change: 14.8%
Phone: 503-626-6775	HR: —	Exchange: Nasdaq
Fax: 503-641-7498	Employees: 197	Symbol: TMBS

Computers - accounting & financial management software for the construction, property management, architecture & engineering industries

TIMELINE, INC.

3055 112th Ave. NE, Ste. 106	CEO: John W. Calahan	1996 Sales: $5.0 million
Bellevue, WA 98004-2067	CFO: Charles R. Osenbaugh	1-Yr. Sales Change: 42.9%
Phone: 206-822-3140	HR: Paula McGee	Exchange: Nasdaq (SC)
Fax: 206-822-1120	Employees: 53	Symbol: TMLN

Computers - financial management software (Open General Ledger)

TOSHIBA CORPORATION

1-1, Shibaura 1-chome, Minato-ku	CEO: Taizo Nishimuro	1996 Sales: $48,303.0 mil.
Tokyo 105-01, Japan	CFO: —	1-Yr. Sales Change: (10.3%)
Phone: +81-3-3457-2105	HR: —	Exchange: Tokyo
Fax: +81-3-3456-4776	Employees: 190,000	

Diversified operations - information systems & equipment, such as PCs & portable PCs; telecommunication systems; satellite development; medical equipment; semiconductors; LCDs

 See pages 226–227 for a full profile of this company.

TOUCHSTONE SOFTWARE CORPORATION

2124 Main St.	CEO: C. Shannon Jenkins	1995 Sales: $9.4 million
Huntington Beach, CA 92648	CFO: Ronald Maas	1-Yr. Sales Change: 30.6%
Phone: 714-969-7746	HR: Shan Dabiri	Exchange: Nasdaq
Fax: 714-960-1886	Employees: 53	Symbol: TSSW

Computers - PC utility software (CheckIt)

TRANSACTION SYSTEMS ARCHITECTS, INC.

330 S. 108th Ave.	CEO: William E. Fisher	1995 Sales: $114.9 million
Omaha, NE 68154-2684	CFO: Gregory J. Duman	1-Yr. Sales Change: 23.7%
Phone: 402-390-7600	HR: Jeff Brown	Exchange: Nasdaq
Fax: 402-330-8548	Employees: 880	Symbol: TSAI

Computers - financial transaction management software

TRANSITION SYSTEMS, INC.

One Boston Place
Boston, MA 02108
Phone: 617-723-4222
Fax: 617-723-4224

CEO: Robert F. Raco
CFO: Robert E. Kinney
HR: Fred Delgizzo
Employees: 136

1995 Sales: $27.4 million
1-Yr. Sales Change: 11.8%
Exchange: Nasdaq
Symbol: TSIX

Computers - decision support software for the healthcare industry

THE TRANSLATION GROUP, LTD

7703 Maple Ave.
Pennsauken, NJ 08109
Phone: 609-663-8600
Fax: 609-663-2022

CEO: Charles D. Cascio
CFO: Michael C. Cascio
HR: Charles D. Cascio
Employees: 99

1996 Sales: $2.6 million
1-Yr. Sales Change: 23.8%
Ownership: Privately Held

Business services - translation of conventional documents & software written in one language into other languages

TRANSNET CORPORATION

45 Columbia Rd.
Somerville, NJ 08876-3576
Phone: 908-253-0500
Fax: 908-253-0600

CEO: Steven J. Wilk
CFO: John J. Wilk
HR: Susan Wilk
Employees: 131

1996 Sales: $64.2 million
1-Yr. Sales Change: 14.2%
Exchange: Nasdaq
Symbol: TRNT

Retail - wholesale hardware & software, including LANs, PCs & peripheral equipment, software & supplies

TRANSWITCH CORPORATION

8 Progress Dr.
Shelton, CT 06484
Phone: 203-929-8810
Fax: 203-926-9453

CEO: Santanu Das
CFO: Michael F. Stauff
HR: Michael McCoy
Employees: 80

1995 Sales: $17.5 million
1-Yr. Sales Change: 44.6%
Exchange: Nasdaq
Symbol: TXCC

Electrical components - mixed-signal semiconductors for networking applications

TRIAD SYSTEMS CORPORATION

3055 Triad Dr.
Livermore, CA 94550
Phone: 510-449-0606
Fax: 510-455-6917

CEO: James R. Porter
CFO: Stanley F. Marquis
HR: Thomas O'Malley
Employees: 1,453

1995 Sales: $175.1 million
1-Yr. Sales Change: 4.7%
Exchange: Nasdaq
Symbol: TRSC

Computers - information management tools for the automotive aftermarket & hardgoods distribution markets

TRIANGLE TECHNOLOGIES, INC.

1441 Branding Ln., Ste. 260	CEO: James Wolande	1995 Sales: $11.0 million
Downers Grove, IL 60515	CFO: James Wolande	1-Yr. Sales Change: 57.1%
Phone: 708-969-8200	HR: Donna Cullen	Ownership: Privately Held
Fax: 708-969-8201	Employees: 24	

Computers - local- & wide-area networks (LANs & WANs) & data communication services

TRICORD SYSTEMS, INC.

2800 Northwest Blvd.	CEO: John J. Mitcham	1995 Sales: $60.2 million
Plymouth, MN 55441	CFO: Gregory T. Barnum	1-Yr. Sales Change: (25.8%)
Phone: 612-557-9005	HR: Mika Kunz	Exchange: Nasdaq
Fax: 612-557-8403	Employees: 211	Symbol: TRCD

Computers - enterprise network servers for workgroup & small departments (PowerFrame DS Series, PowerFrame Model 20) & large departments or divisions (PowerFrame ES4000, PowerFrame ES5000, PowerFrame Model 30/40)

TRIDENT MICROSYSTEMS, INC.

189 N. Bernardo Ave.	CEO: Frank C. Lin	1996 Sales: $168.1 million
Mountain View, CA 94043-5203	CFO: James T. Lindstrom	1-Yr. Sales Change: 57.4%
Phone: 415-691-9211	HR: Sandra Cancela	Exchange: Nasdaq
Fax: 415-691-9260	Employees: 308	Symbol: TRID

Computers - integrated circuit graphics & multimedia products for IBM-compatible PCs, including graphical user interface accelerators, graphics controllers & video processors

TRIDEX CORPORATION

61 Wilton Rd.	CEO: Seth M. Lukash	1995 Sales: $54.7 million
Westport, CT 06880	CFO: Richard L. Cote	1-Yr. Sales Change: 62.3%
Phone: 203-226-1144	HR: Thomas F. Curtin Jr.	Exchange: Nasdaq
Fax: 203-226-8806	Employees: 422	Symbol: TRDX

Computers - specialty printers, printer mechanisms & data processing terminals

TRILOBYTE, INC.

1225 Crater Lake Ave.	CEO: Rob Landeros	1995 Est. Sales: $5.0 mil.
Medford, OR 97501	CFO: —	1-Yr. Sales Change: —
Phone: 541-857-0614	HR: Diane Moses	Ownership: Privately Held
Fax: 541-857-0616	Employees: 45	

Computers - CD-ROM games (The 7th Guest, The 11th Hour; The Sequel to The 7th Guest)

TRILOGY DEVELOPMENT GROUP

6034 W. Courtyard Dr.
Austin, TX 78730
Phone: 512-794-5900
Fax: 512-794-8900

CEO: Joe Liemandt
CFO: Wade Monroe
HR: Monica Reed
Employees: 200

1995 Est. Sales: $70.0 mil.
1-Yr. Sales Change: —
Ownership: Privately Held

Computers - sales & marketing software (Selling Chain)

TRIMBLE NAVIGATION LIMITED

645 N. Mary Ave.
Sunnyvale, CA 94086
Phone: 408-481-8000
Fax: 408-481-6860

CEO: Charles R. Trimble
CFO: John H. Barnet
HR: Angela Kupps
Employees: 749

1995 Sales: $235.4 million
1-Yr. Sales Change: 34.0%
Exchange: Nasdaq
Symbol: TRMB

Electronics - instruments & systems that use the satellite-based Global Position System (GPS) for determining precise geographic location

TRINITECH SYSTEMS, INC.

Stamford Harbor Park, 333 Ludlow St.
Stamford, CT 06902
Phone: 203-425-8000
Fax: 203-425-8100

CEO: Peter K. Hansen
CFO: William E. Alvarez Jr.
HR: —
Employees: 28

1995 Sales: $5.0 million
1-Yr. Sales Change: 51.5%
Exchange: AMEX
Symbol: TSI

Computers - ticketless trading systems & related equipment for the financial industry (Trinitech TouchPad)

TRIO TECH INTERNATIONAL

355 Parkside Dr.
San Fernando, CA 91340-3036
Phone: 818-365-9200
Fax: 818-365-8210

CEO: S. W. Yong
CFO: Victor Ting
HR: Maria Chittim
Employees: 684

1996 Sales: $23.2 million
1-Yr. Sales Change: 19.0%
Exchange: Nasdaq (SC)
Symbol: TRTC

Electronics - semiconductor test equipment & services

TRIPOS, INC.

1699 S. Hanley Rd.
St. Louis, MO 63144
Phone: 314-647-1099
Fax: 314-647-9241

CEO: John P. McAlister III
CFO: Colleen A. McDonnell
HR: David Summers
Employees: 136

1995 Sales: $21.1 million
1-Yr. Sales Change: 7.7%
Exchange: Nasdaq
Symbol: TRPS

Computers - software that aids in the discovery of new pharmaceutical & chemical compounds

TRIQUINT SEMICONDUCTOR, INC.

3625A SW Murray Blvd.
Beaverton, OR 97005
Phone: 503-644-3535
Fax: 503-644-3198

CEO: Steven J. Sharp
CFO: Joseph I. Martin
HR: Nancy Andrews
Employees: 191

1995 Sales: $45.9 million
1-Yr. Sales Change: 51.5%
Exchange: Nasdaq
Symbol: TQNT

Electrical components - high-speed gallium arsenide analog & mixed signal ICs for the wireless communications, telecommunications & computing markets

TRITEAL CORPORATION

2011 Palomar Airport Rd.
Carlsbad, CA 92009
Phone: 619-930-2077
Fax: 619-930-2074

CEO: Jeffrey D. Witous
CFO: Arthur S. Budman
HR: Darcy Lynn
Employees: 92

1996 Sales: $8.2 million
1-Yr. Sales Change: 100.0%
Exchange: Nasdaq
Symbol: TEAL

Computers - general application, desktop system software & integrated applications

TRO LEARNING, INC.

1721 Moon Lake Blvd., Ste. 555
Hoffman Estates, IL 60694
Phone: 847-781-7800
Fax: 847-781-7835

CEO: William R. Roach
CFO: Sharon Fierro
HR: Pat Hawver
Employees: 279

1995 Sales: $37.3 million
1-Yr. Sales Change: 31.3%
Exchange: Nasdaq
Symbol: TUTR

Computers - microcomputer-based interactive learning systems (PLATO) for education & instructional use by schools, colleges, the military, airlines & correctional institutions

TRUEVISION, INC.

2500 Walsh Ave.
Santa Clara, CA 95051
Phone: 408-562-4200
Fax: 408-562-4066

CEO: Louis J. Doctor
CFO: R. John Curson
HR: Mary A. Lemons
Employees: 180

1996 Sales: $71.5 million
1-Yr. Sales Change: 7.8%
Exchange: Nasdaq
Symbol: TRUV

Computers - photo-realistic imaging systems; broadcast video production, imaging & multimedia solutions (Truevision)

TRUSTED INFORMATION SYSTEMS, INC.

3060 Washington Rd.
Glenwood, MD 21738
Phone: 301-854-6889
Fax: 301-854-5363

CEO: Stephen T. Walker
CFO: Ronald W. Kaiser
HR: Linda Ulrich
Employees: 203

1995 Sales: $18.1 million
1-Yr. Sales Change: 38.2%
Ownership: Privately Held

Computers - security products (Gauntlet) for protecting computer networks, including Internet-based systems, internal networks, individual workstations & laptops

TSENG LABS, INC.

6 Terry Dr.	CEO: Jack Tseng	1995 Sales: $39.3 million
Newtown, PA 18940	CFO: Mark H. Karsch	1-Yr. Sales Change: (51.3%)
Phone: 215-968-0502	HR: Barbara J. Hawkins	Exchange: Nasdaq
Fax: 215-860-7713	Employees: 95	Symbol: TSNG

Electrical components - video graphics microchips, adapters & controllers for PCs

TSR, INC.

400 Oser Ave., Ste. 400	CEO: Joseph F. Hughes	1996 Sales: $31.8 million
Hauppauge, NY 11788	CFO: John G. Sharkey	1-Yr. Sales Change: 19.1%
Phone: 516-231-0333	HR: —	Exchange: Nasdaq
Fax: 516-435-1428	Employees: 243	Symbol: TSRI

Computers - programming services & database management

TTR INC.

2 Hanagar St.	CEO: Marc D. Tokayer	1995 Sales: $0.0 million
Kfar Saba 44425, Israel	CFO: Marc D. Tokayer	1-Yr. Sales Change: —
Phone: +972-9-766-2393	HR:	Ownership: Privately Held
Fax: —	Employees: 10	

Computers - software security products used to prevent the unauthorized reproduction & use of software programs

TULIP COMPUTERS N V

Hambakenwetering 2, NL-5231 DC	CEO: F. Hetzenauer	1995 Sales: $332.0 million
Hertogenbosch, The Netherlands	CFO: —	1-Yr. Sales Change: 26.4%
Phone: +31-73-405333	HR: —	Exchange: Amsterdam
Fax: +31-73-421915	Employees: 652	

Computers - microcomputer systems, including active network components & operating systems

TWINHEAD CORP.

1537 Centre Pointe Dr.	CEO: Stanley Chiang	1995 Sales: $27.0 million
Milpitas, CA 95035	CFO: Tony Hua	1-Yr. Sales Change: 3.8%
Phone: 408-945-0808	HR: Tony Hua	Ownership: Privately Held
Fax: 408-945-1080	Employees: 55	

Computers - notebook & desktop PCs

TYLAN GENERAL, INC.

9577 Chesapeake Dr.	CEO: David J. Ferran	1995 Sales: $75.8 million
San Diego, CA 92123	CFO: David L. Stone	1-Yr. Sales Change: 57.6%
Phone: 619-571-1222	HR: Michal A. Chick	Exchange: Nasdaq
Fax: 619-576-1703	Employees: 437	Symbol: TYGN

Machinery - semiconductor manufacturing equipment

ULTRADATA CORPORATION

5020 Franklin Dr.	CEO: Nigel Gallop	1995 Sales: $31.1 million
Pleasanton, CA 94588-3354	CFO: —	1-Yr. Sales Change: 21.0%
Phone: 510-463-8356	HR: Brigit Garabedian	Exchange: Nasdaq
Fax: 510-463-0394	Employees: 238	Symbol: ULTD

Computers - advanced database management software

ULTRADATA SYSTEMS, INC.

9375 Dielman Industrial Dr.	CEO: Monte Ross	1995 Sales: $10.1 million
St. Louis, MO 63132	CFO: Monte Ross	1-Yr. Sales Change: 57.8%
Phone: 314-997-2250	HR: Marty Ross	Exchange: Nasdaq
Fax: 314-997-1281	Employees: 28	Symbol: ULTR

Electrical products - hand-held electronic travel & leisure guides (Road Whiz, Greensfinder, Otis—The RV Navigator)

ULTRATECH STEPPER, INC.

3050 Zanker Rd.	CEO: Arthur W. Zafiropoulo	1995 Sales: $157.8 million
San Jose, CA 95134	CFO: William G. Leunis III	1-Yr. Sales Change: 72.8%
Phone: 408-321-8835	HR: —	Exchange: Nasdaq
Fax: 408-577-3379	Employees: 562	Symbol: UTEK

Machinery - photolithography equipment used to manufacture semiconductors

UNICOMP, INC.

1800 Sandy Plains Pkwy., Ste. 305	CEO: Stephen A. Hafer	1996 Sales: $21.3 million
Marietta, GA 30066	CFO: Roger Maloch	1-Yr. Sales Change: 19.7%
Phone: 770-424-3684	HR: —	Exchange: Nasdaq
Fax: 770-424-5558	Employees: 198	Symbol: UCMP

Computers - hardware & software installation & services; public-address system sales

UNIFY CORPORATION

181 Metro Dr., Ste. 300
San Jose, CA 95110
Phone: 408-467-4500
Fax: 408-467-4511

CEO: Reza Mikailli
CFO: Susan Salvesen
HR: Doreen Paige
Employees: 190

1996 Sales: $30.2 million
1-Yr. Sales Change: 4.9%
Exchange: Nasdaq
Symbol: UNFY

Computers - client/server application development tools (Unify VISION, Accell/SQL, Unify 2000)

UNISON SOFTWARE, INC.

5101 Patrick Henry Dr.
Santa Clara, CA 95054
Phone: 408-988-2800
Fax: 408-988-2236

CEO: Don H. Lee
CFO: Richard J. Armitage
HR: Salwa Kawash
Employees: 174

1996 Sales: $30.0 million
1-Yr. Sales Change: 52.3%
Exchange: Nasdaq
Symbol: UNSN

Computers - network systems management software for distributed, heterogeneous computing environments (Maestro, Load Balancer)

UNISYS CORPORATION

Township Line & Union Meeting Rds.
Blue Bell, PA 19422-9945
Phone: 215-986-4011
Fax: 215-986-2312

CEO: James A. Unruh
CFO: —
HR: David O. Aker
Employees: 37,400

1995 Sales: $6,202.3 million
1-Yr. Sales Change: (16.2%)
Exchange: NYSE
Symbol: UIS

Computers - network servers, peripherals, workstations, software & systems-integration & equipment-maintenance services

 See pages 228–229 for a full profile of this company.

UNITED SYSTEMS TECHNOLOGY, INC.

3021 Gateway Dr., Ste. 240
Irving, TX 75063
Phone: 972-518-0728
Fax: 972-580-8280

CEO: Thomas E. Gibbs
CFO: Randall L. McGee
HR: —
Employees: 27

1995 Sales: $1.8 million
1-Yr. Sales Change: (21.7%)
Exchange: OTC
Symbol: USTI

Computers - financial, general administration, public works, civil processing & public safety software products for state, county & local governments

UNITRODE CORPORATION

7 Continental Blvd.
Merrimack, NH 03054
Phone: 603-424-2410
Fax: 603-429-8771

CEO: Robert L. Gable
CFO: Cosmo S. Trapani
HR: Patrick J. Moquin
Employees: 620

1996 Sales: $118.5 million
1-Yr. Sales Change: 22.0%
Exchange: NYSE
Symbol: UTR

Electrical components - analog microcircuits, power supplies & power management analog ICs for switching power supplies

UNIVERSAL DISPLAY CORPORATION

1221 Centennial Rd.	CEO: Sherwin I. Seligsohn	1995 Sales: $0.1 million
Penn Valley, PA 19072	CFO: Sidney D. Rosenblatt	1-Yr. Sales Change: —
Phone: 215-229-4435	HR: —	Exchange: Nasdaq (SC)
Fax: 215-229-4114	Employees: 3	Symbol: PANL

Electrical components - research & development of organic light emitting diode technology for use in full color, flat panel, emissive light displays

UOL PUBLISHING, INC.

105 W. Broad St., Ste. 301	CEO: Narasimhan P. Kannan	1995 Sales: $0.5 million
Falls Church, VA 22046	CFO: Leonard P. Kurtzman	1-Yr. Sales Change: (37.5%)
Phone: 703-533-7500	HR: —	Ownership: Privately Held
Fax: 703-532-3929	Employees: 41	

Computers - educational courseware for the online education & training market

UPSIDE PUBLISHING CO.

2015 Pioneer Ct.	CEO: Susan E. Scott	1995 Est. Sales: $3.0 mil.
San Mateo, CA 94403	CFO: —	1-Yr. Sales Change: 30.4%
Phone: 415-377-0950	HR: —	Ownership: Privately Held
Fax: 415-377-1962	Employees: 27	

Publishing - business magazine (Upside) for high-tech company executives

U.S. ROBOTICS CORPORATION

8100 N. McCormick Blvd.	CEO: Casey G. Cowell	1995 Sales: $889.3 million
Skokie, IL 60076-2999	CFO: Mark Remissong	1-Yr. Sales Change: 134.8%
Phone: 847-982-5010	HR: Elizabeth S. Ryan	Exchange: Nasdaq
Fax: 847-933-5551	Employees: 3,347	Symbol: USRX

Computers - modems, wide- & local-area network hubs (Courier, Megahertz, Sportster, Total Control, WorldPort) & Ethernet adapter cards

 See page 373 for a full profile of this company.

US SERVIS, INC.

414 Eagle Rock Ave.	CEO: Graham O. King	1996 Sales: $16.2 million
West Orange, NJ 07052	CFO: Michael B. Loscalzo	1-Yr. Sales Change: 1.2%
Phone: 201-731-9252	HR: Twyla Bruce	Exchange: Nasdaq
Fax: 201-243-9774	Employees: 224	Symbol: USRV

Computers - business management services & information systems for physicians & physician delivery systems & hospital ambulatory departments

USCS INTERNATIONAL, INC.

2969 Prospect Park Dr.	CEO: James C. Castle	1995 Sales: $229.3 million
Rancho Cordova, CA 95670-6148	CFO: Douglas L. Shurtleff	1-Yr. Sales Change: 21.5%
Phone: 916-636-4500	HR: Kimberley Silvers	Exchange: Nasdaq
Fax: 916-636-4530	Employees: 1,943	Symbol: USCS

Computers - customer management software & services for the global communications industry, including cable TV, wireless & land-line telephony & direct-broadcast satellite clients

USDATA CORPORATION

2435 N. Central Expwy.	CEO: William G. Moore Jr.	1995 Sales: $44.4 million
Richardson, TX 75080-2722	CFO: Jay Shipowitz	1-Yr. Sales Change: (37.5%)
Phone: 972-680-9700	HR: Bonnie Johnston	Exchange: Nasdaq
Fax: 972-669-9557	Employees: 218	Symbol: USDC

Computers - automation software tools for monitoring manufacturing & automated processes; consulting & maintenance services

USER TECHNOLOGY ASSOCIATES, INC.

4301 N. Fairfax Dr., Ste. 400	CEO: Yong K. Kim	1995 Sales: $37.5 million
Arlington, VA 22203-1628	CFO: —	1-Yr. Sales Change: 29.3%
Phone: 703-522-5132	HR: Paul Bonolis	Ownership: Privately Held
Fax: 703-522-6457	Employees: 475	

Computers - acquisition & program management; local & wide area networks; business process reengineering; information resource management; engineering & logistics

U-TRON TECHNOLOGIES, INC.

47448 Fremont Blvd.	CEO: Steve Chen	1995 Sales: $100.0 million
Fremont, CA 94538	CFO: Kathy Tseng	1-Yr. Sales Change: 25.0%
Phone: 510-656-3600	HR: Emily Tsai	Ownership: Privately Held
Fax: 510-656-1688	Employees: 62	

Retail - wholesale PCs

VANSTAR CORPORATION

5964 W. Las Positas Blvd.	CEO: William Y. Tauscher	1996 Sales: $1,804.8 million
Pleasanton, CA 94588	CFO: Jeffrey S. Rubin	1-Yr. Sales Change: 52.0%
Phone: 510-734-4000	HR: Judith Marshall	Exchange: NYSE
Fax: 510-734-4802	Employees: 4,100	Symbol: VST

Computers - customized, integrated solutions for PC network infrastructures, primarily for Fortune 1000 companies & other large enterprises

 See pages 230–231 for a full profile of this company.

THE VANTIVE CORPORATION

2455 Augustine Dr.
Santa Clara, CA 95054
Phone: 408-982-5700
Fax: 408-982-5710

CEO: John R. Luongo
CFO: Kathleen Murphy
HR: Holly Rail
Employees: 139

1995 Sales: $25.0 million
1-Yr. Sales Change: 145.1%
Exchange: Nasdaq
Symbol: VNTV

Computers - customer interaction applications software

VARIAN ASSOCIATES, INC.

3050 Hansen Way
Palo Alto, CA 94304-1000
Phone: 415-493-4000
Fax: 415-493-0307

CEO: J. Tracy O'Rourke
CFO: Robert A. Lemos
HR: Ernest M. Felago
Employees: 6,900

1995 Sales: $1,575.7 million
1-Yr. Sales Change: 1.5%
Exchange: NYSE
Symbol: VAR

Machinery - semiconductor manufacturing equipment; radiation equipment for cancer therapy & industrial inspections; analytical instruments, electron tubes, vacuum equipment & leak detectors

VEKTRON INTERNATIONAL, INC.

2100 N. Highway 360, Ste. 1904
Grand Prairie, TX 75050
Phone: 972-606-0280
Fax: 972-606-1278

CEO: Mark Ozkan
CFO: —
HR: —
Employees: 50

1995 Sales: $25.0 million
1-Yr. Sales Change: 73.6%
Ownership: Privately Held

Retail - mail-order computers & peripheral components

VERILINK CORPORATION

145 Baytech Dr.
San Jose, CA 95134
Phone: 408-945-1199
Fax: 408-945-3823

CEO: Leigh S. Belden
CFO: Timothy G. Conley
HR: —
Employees: 171

1996 Sales: $41.6 million
1-Yr. Sales Change: 32.5%
Exchange: Nasdaq
Symbol: VRLK

Computers - access products (Access System 2000, Advanced Programmable Architecture) for telecommunications network service providers & corporate end users

VERITAS SOFTWARE CORPORATION

1600 Plymouth St.
Mountain View, CA 94043
Phone: 415-335-8000
Fax: 415-335-8050

CEO: Mark Leslie
CFO: —
HR: Susan Chan
Employees: 87

1995 Sales: $24.1 million
1-Yr. Sales Change: 59.6%
Exchange: Nasdaq
Symbol: VRTS

Computers - open-system software for data management

VERITY, INC.

894 Ross Dr.	CEO: Philippe F. Courtot	1996 Sales: $30.7 million
Sunnyvale, CA 94089	CFO: Donald C. McCauley	1-Yr. Sales Change: 93.1%
Phone: 415-960-7600	HR: Rima Touma	Exchange: Nasdaq
Fax: 415-541-1600	Employees: 152	Symbol: VRTY

Computers - software tools & applications to search, filter & disseminate textual information residing on enterprise networks, online services, the Internet, CD-ROM & other electronic media

VERSANT OBJECT TECHNOLOGY CORP.

1380 Willow Rd.	CEO: David Banks	1995 Sales: $11.9 million
Menlo Park, CA 94025	CFO: Richard I. Kadet	1-Yr. Sales Change: 45.1%
Phone: 415-329-7500	HR: —	Exchange: Nasdaq
Fax: 415-325-2380	Employees: 81	Symbol: VSNT

Computers - services, object-oriented database management technology specifically for the telecommunctions industry

VERTEQ, INC.

1241 E. Dyer Rd.	CEO: Keith R. Norby	1995 Sales: $44.0 million
Santa Ana, CA 92705	CFO: Fred G. Wolfrum	1-Yr. Sales Change: 81.8%
Phone: 714-708-0330	HR: —	Ownership: Privately Held
Fax: —	Employees: 432	

Machinery - wet processing equipment used in wafer cleaning, etching & stripping applications in the semiconductor industry

VERTEX INDUSTRIES INC.

23 Carol St., PO Box 996	CEO: James Q. Maloy	1995 Sales: $3.1 million
Clifton, NJ 07014-0996	CFO: Ronald Byer	1-Yr. Sales Change: (22.5%)
Phone: 201-777-3500	HR: Eleanor L. Morris	Exchange: Nasdaq (SC)
Fax: 201-472-0814	Employees: 37	Symbol: VETX

Data collection & systems - identification-verification systems, automated card readers, encoders & decoders for credit & debit cards & badges

VIASOFT, INC.

3033 N. 44th St., Ste. 101	CEO: Steven D. Whiteman	1996 Sales: $43.6 million
Phoenix, AZ 85018	CFO: —	1-Yr. Sales Change: 40.6%
Phone: 602-952-0050	HR: Nancy Mattson	Exchange: Nasdaq
Fax: 602-840-4068	Employees: 266	Symbol: VIAS

Computers - software tools & consulting services for managing COBOL application programs

VICTORMAXX TECHNOLOGIES, INC.

510 Lake Cook Rd., Ste. 100
Deerfield, IL 60015
Phone: 847-267-0007
Fax: 847-267-0037

CEO: Richard H. Currie
CFO: Glenn Petersen
HR: —
Employees: 24

1995 Sales: $0.7 million
1-Yr. Sales Change: —
Exchange: Nasdaq (SC)
Symbol: VMAX

Computers - virtual reality products, primarily headsets (CyberMaxx) for home use

VIDEO DISPLAY CORPORATION

1868 Tucker Industrial Dr.
Tucker, GA 30084
Phone: 770-938-2080
Fax: 770-493-3903

CEO: Ronald D. Ordway
CFO: Carol D. Franklin
HR: —
Employees: 476

1996 Sales: $48.1 million
1-Yr. Sales Change: (0.6%)
Exchange: Nasdaq
Symbol: VIDE

Electronics - cathode ray tubes

VIDEOSERVER, INC.

63 Third Ave.
Burlington, MA 01803
Phone: 617-229-2000
Fax: 617-505-2101

CEO: Robert L. Castle
CFO: Stephen J. Nill
HR: Carol Raymond
Employees: 133

1995 Sales: $28.2 million
1-Yr. Sales Change: 80.8%
Exchange: Nasdaq
Symbol: VSVR

Computers - networking equipment & associated software for multimedia conferencing over wide area networks (Multimedia Conference Servers)

VIEWLOGIC SYSTEMS, INC.

293 Boston Post Rd. West
Marlborough, MA 01752
Phone: 508-480-0881
Fax: 508-480-0882

CEO: Alain J. Hanover
CFO: Ronald R. Benanto
HR: Eugene C. Connolly
Employees: 561

1995 Sales: $121.0 million
1-Yr. Sales Change: 2.0%
Exchange: Nasdaq
Symbol: VIEW

Computers - productivity-enhancing software tools for engineers to use in the design of advanced electronic products

VIEWSONIC CORPORATION

20480 E. Business Pkwy.
Walnut, CA 91789
Phone: 909-869-7976
Fax: 909-869-7958

CEO: James Chu
CFO: Jerry Kanaly
HR: Joanne Thielen
Employees: 200

1995 Sales: $263.0 million
1-Yr. Sales Change: 31.5%
Ownership: Privately Held

Retail - wholesale monitors (ViewSonic) & video controller cards

VIEWSTAR CORPORATION

1101 Marina Village Pkwy.
Alameda, CA 94501
Phone: 510-337-2000
Fax: 510-337-2222

CEO: Kamran Kheirolomoom
CFO: Robert I. Pender Jr.
HR: Alan Chin
Employees: 147

1995 Sales: $25.2 million
1-Yr. Sales Change: 10.5%
Ownership: Privately Held

Computers - document management & workflow process automation software over LANs & WANs

VIISAGE TECHNOLOGY, INC

531 Main St.
Acton, MA 01720
Phone: 508-263-8365
Fax: 508-263-3358

CEO: Robert C. Hughes
CFO: William A. Marshall
HR: Marilyn Cronin
Employees: 42

1995 Sales: $11.2 million
1-Yr. Sales Change: 761.5%
Ownership: Privately Held

Computers - turnkey digital identification systems intended to deter fraud & reduce customers' indentification program costs using facial images, demographic informaation & other biological features

VIKING COMPONENTS

100 Columbia St.
Laguna Hills, CA 94086
Phone: 714-643-7255
Fax: 714-643-7250

CEO: Glen McCusker
CFO: Joe Stafford
HR: Kerri Brechbiel
Employees: 200

1995 Sales: $264.0 million
1-Yr. Sales Change: 48.9%
Ownership: Privately Held

Computers - memory products (SIM boards)

VISHAY INTERTECHNOLOGY, INC.

63 Lincoln Hwy.
Malvern, PA 19355-2120
Phone: 610-644-1300
Fax: 610-296-0657

CEO: Felix Zandman
CFO: Richard N. Grubb
HR: William J. Spires
Employees: 18,000

1995 Sales: $1,224.4 million
1-Yr. Sales Change: 24.0%
Exchange: NYSE
Symbol: VSH

Electronics - passive components, including resistors, capacitors & inductors

 See pages 232–233 for a full profile of this company.

VISIGENIC SOFTWARE, INC.

951 Mariner's Island Blvd., Ste. 460
San Mateo, CA 94404
Phone: 415-286-1900
Fax: 415-286-2464

CEO: Roger J. Sippl
CFO: Glenn C. Myers
HR: Sally Goodyear
Employees: 90

1996 Sales: $5.6 million
1-Yr. Sales Change: 409.1%
Exchange: Nasdaq
Symbol: VSGN

Computers - software for database-independent access & connectivity to distributed databases, the Internet, intranet & enterprise computing environments

VISIO CORPORATION

520 Pike St., Ste. 1800
Seattle, WA 98101-4001
Phone: 206-521-4500
Fax: 206-521-4501

CEO: Jeremy A. Jaech
CFO: Marty Chilberg
HR: Susan Slaton
Employees: 147

1995 Sales: $34.2 million
1-Yr. Sales Change: 66.0%
Exchange: Nasdaq
Symbol: VSIO

Computers - business drawing & diagramming software

VISIONEER, INC.

2860 W. Bayshore Rd.
Palo Alto, CA 94303
Phone: 415-812-6400
Fax: 415-855-9750

CEO: Michael A. McConnell
CFO: Geoffrey C. Darby
HR: —
Employees: 99

1995 Sales: $37.3 million
1-Yr. Sales Change: 856.4%
Exchange: Nasdaq
Symbol: VSNR

Computers - intelligent paper input systems (PaperPort) that allow imaging, manipulation, distribution & storage of paper-based information

VISIONTEK INC.

1175 Lakeside Dr.
Gurnee, IL 60031
Phone: 847-360-7500
Fax: 847-360-7401

CEO: Mark Polinsky
CFO: Craig Gutmann
HR: Michele Feldman
Employees: 270

1995 Sales: $280.0 million
1-Yr. Sales Change: (6.8%)
Ownership: Privately Held

Computers - PC & printer memory upgrades

VISTA INFORMATION SOLUTIONS, INC.

5060 Shoreham Place
San Diego, CA 92122
Phone: 619-450-6100
Fax: 619-450-6195

CEO: Thomas R. Gay
CFO: E. Steve Hamilton
HR: Frankie Campe
Employees: 176

1995 Sales: $7.8 million
1-Yr. Sales Change: 766.7%
Exchange: Nasdaq (SC)
Symbol: VINF

Business services - geodemographic data files, marketing software & custom mapping services

VITALCOM INC.

15222 Del Amo Ave.
Tustin, CA 92680
Phone: 714-546-0147
Fax: 714-571-3945

CEO: David L. Schlotterbeck
CFO: Shelley B. Thunen
HR: Albert G. Sack
Employees: 147

1995 Sales: $24.0 million
1-Yr. Sales Change: 40.4%
Exchange: Nasdaq
Symbol: VCOM

Computers - communication networks & software that acquires, interprets & distributes physiologic data generated from point-of-care patient monitors in health care facilities

VITECH AMERICA, INC.

8807 NW 23rd St.
Miami, FL 33172
Phone: 305-477-1161
Fax: 305-477-1379

CEO: Georges C. St. Laurent III
CFO: Mitchell Asher
HR: Linda Odon
Employees: 240

1995 Sales: $48.5 million
1-Yr. Sales Change: 178.7%
Ownership: Privately Held

Computers - manufacture & distribution of computer equipment & related products in the Federal Republic of Brazil

VITESSE SEMICONDUCTOR CORPORATION

741 Calle Plano
Camarillo, CA 93012
Phone: 805-388-3700
Fax: 805-389-7188

CEO: Louis R. Tomasetta
CFO: Eugene F. Hovanec
HR: Jeanne Johnson
Employees: 225

1995 Sales: $42.9 million
1-Yr. Sales Change: 19.8%
Exchange: Nasdaq
Symbol: VTSS

Electrical components - digital gallium arsenide ICs used in products for the communications, test & instrumentation, computing & defense markets

VITRONICS CORPORATION

One Forbes Rd., Newmarket Ind. Park
Newmarket, NH 03857-2099
Phone: 603-659-6550
Fax: 603-659-7194

CEO: James J. Mansfield Jr.
CFO: James J. Mansfield Jr.
HR: Lorraine D. Giordano
Employees: 128

1995 Sales: $23.5 million
1-Yr. Sales Change: 35.8%
Exchange: AMEX
Symbol: VTC

Machinery - state-of-the-art thermal processing systems for soldering surface-mounted electronic components to printed circuit boards & cleaning of the finished assembly

VITT MEDIA INTERNATIONAL, INC.

114 Sixth Ave.
New York , NY 10036
Phone: 212-921-0500
Fax: 212-455-0519

CEO: John Power
CFO: Ron Shapiro
HR: Ron Shapiro
Employees: 130

1995 Est. Sales: $400.0 mil.
1-Yr. Sales Change: (11.1%)
Ownership: Privately Held

Business services - media planning, buying & syndication; online research & status reports service (Vitt Online)

VLSI TECHNOLOGY, INC.

1109 McKay Dr.
San Jose, CA 95131
Phone: 408-434-3100
Fax: 408-263-2511

CEO: Alfred J. Stein
CFO: Gregory K. Hinckley
HR: Eugene E. Tange
Employees: 2,986

1995 Sales: $719.9 million
1-Yr. Sales Change: 22.6%
Exchange: Nasdaq
Symbol: VLSI

Electrical components - specialized semiconductors; ASICs, ASSPs, microprocessors & data security & software development tools for chip designers

 See page 374 for a full profile of this company.

VMARK SOFTWARE, INC.

50 Washington St.
Westborough, MA 01581-1021
Phone: 508-366-3888
Fax: 508-366-3669

CEO: Robert M. Morrill
CFO: Charles F. Kane
HR: Sally N. Burke
Employees: 456

1995 Sales: $68.4 million
1-Yr. Sales Change: 51.3%
Exchange: Nasdaq
Symbol: VMRK

Computers - database management systems (UniVerse) & related UNIX software for the client/server
business solutions market

VOBIS MICROCOMPUTER AG

Carlo-Schmid Strasse 12
52146 Wurselen, Germany
Phone: +49-241-500-081
Fax: +49-241-534-939

CEO: Theo Lieven
CFO: —
HR: —
Employees: 2,500

1995 Sales: $2,130.6 million
1-Yr. Sales Change: 24.1%
Exchange: Frankfurt

Computers - PCs (#1 in Germany)

VOCALTEC LTD.

One Maskit St.
Herzliya 46733, Israel
Phone: +972-9-562-121
Fax: +972-9-561-867

CEO: Elon A. Ganor
CFO: Yahal Zilka
HR: —
Employees: 47

1995 Sales: $2.5 million
1-Yr. Sales Change: 525.0%
Exchange: Nasdaq
Symbol: VOCLF

Computers - communication software for real-time voice communication & audio broadcasting over the
Internet (Internet Phone, Internet Wave)

VOICE IT WORLDWIDE, INC.

2643 Midpoint Dr., Ste. A
Fort Collins, CO 86525
Phone: 970-221-1705
Fax: 970-221-2058

CEO: Michelle Morgan
CFO: —
HR: —
Employees: 25

1995 Sales: $15.6 million
1-Yr. Sales Change: 160.0%
Exchange: Nasdaq (SC)
Symbol: MEMO

Computers - personal consumer electronic products, including personal note recorders (Voice It)

VOLT INFORMATION SCIENCES, INC.

1221 Avenue of the Americas
New York, NY 10020-1579
Phone: 212-704-2400
Fax: 212-704-2424

CEO: William Shaw
CFO: James J. Groberg
HR: Norma Kraus
Employees: 26,800

1995 Sales: $907.4 million
1-Yr. Sales Change: 23.5%
Exchange: Nasdaq
Symbol: VOLT

Personnel - engineering, design, data processing, scientific & technical support personnel; computerized
image-setting & publishing equipment & software

V-ONE CORPORATION

1803 Research Blvd., Ste. 305	CEO: James F. Chen	1995 Sales: $1.1 million
Rockville, MD 20850	CFO: Chansothi Um	1-Yr. Sales Change: 1,000%
Phone: 301-838-8900	HR: Dan Davis	Ownership: Privately Held
Fax: 301-838-8909	Employees: 52	

Computers - network security products, including smart cards, firewalls & encryption software for businesses' electronic transactions & information exchange via private networks & the Internet

 See page 375 for a full profile of this company.

VOXWARE, INC.

305 College Rd. East	CEO: Michael Goldstein	1996 Sales: $1.6 million
Princeton, NJ 08540	CFO: Kenneth H. Traub	1-Yr. Sales Change: —
Phone: 609-514-4100	HR: Liz O'Connell	Ownership: Privately Held
Fax: 609-514-4101	Employees: 58	

Computers - digital speech processing technologies which allow the high quality reproduction of speech while requiring very low communications bandwith & processing power (MetaVoice)

THE VOYAGER COMPANY

578 Broadway, Ste. 406	CEO: Robert Stein	1995 Sales: $12.0 million
New York, NY 10012	CFO: Jonathan Turell	1-Yr. Sales Change: —
Phone: 212-431-5199	HR: —	Ownership: Privately Held
Fax: 212-431-5799	Employees: 85	

Publishing - laserdisc movies (The Criterion Collection), CD-ROMs (The Complete Maus, A Hard Day's Night) & interactive books (The Complete Hitchhiker's Guide to the Galaxy, Jurassic Park)

WAGGENER EDSTROM

6915 SW Macadam Ave., Ste. 300	CEO: Melissa Waggener	1995 Sales: $27.0 million
Portland, OR 97219-2396	CFO: Pamela Edstrom	1-Yr. Sales Change: 63.6%
Phone: 503-245-0905	HR: Michael Bigelow	Ownership: Privately Held
Fax: 503-244-7261	Employees: 196	

Business services - public relations for computer companies

 See page 376 for a full profile of this company.

WALKER INTERACTIVE SYSTEMS, INC.

303 Second St.	CEO: Leonard Y. Liu	1995 Sales: $58.9 million
San Francisco, CA 94107	CFO: Bruce C. Pollock	1-Yr. Sales Change: (15.6%)
Phone: 415-495-8811	HR: Wallace E. Breitman	Exchange: Nasdaq
Fax: 415-957-1711	Employees: 428	Symbol: WALK

Computers - business & financial management software for mainframes

WALKER RICHER & QUINN INC.

1500 Dexter Ave N.
Seattle, WA 98109-3051
Phone: 206-217-7500
Fax: 206-217-0380

CEO: Doug Walker
CFO: Gerry Smith
HR: Norris Palmanleer
Employees: 525

1995 Sales: $111.6 million
1-Yr. Sales Change: 25.0%
Ownership: Privately Held

Computers - software to connect open & proprietary systems

WALL DATA, INCORPORATED

17769 NE 78th Pl.
Redmond, WA 98052-4992
Phone: 206-814-9255
Fax: 206-814-4300

CEO: James Simpson
CFO: Richard Van Hoesen
HR: Fran Safier
Employees: 783

1995 Sales: $110.7 million
1-Yr. Sales Change: 9.4%
Exchange: Nasdaq
Symbol: WALL

Computers - Windows-based connectivity software (Rumba, Salsa)

 See page 377 for a full profile of this company.

WANDEL & GOLTERMANN TECHNOLOGIES, INC.

1030 Swabia Ct.
Research Triangle Park, NC 27709-3585
Phone: 919-941-5730
Fax: 919-941-9160

CEO: Richard E. Pospisil
CFO: Adelbert Kuthe
HR: Matt Weitz
Employees: 223

1995 Sales: $45.3 million
1-Yr. Sales Change: 11.3%
Exchange: Nasdaq
Symbol: WGTI

Computers - test, measurement, diagnostic & monitoring products for local & wide area data
telecommunication networks for use by operators of telecommunication & data transmission systems

WANDERLUST INTERACTIVE, INC.

598 Broadway
New York, NY 10001
Phone: 212-966-8887
Fax: 212-431-8807

CEO: Catherine Winchester
CFO: Brian Fisher
HR: —
Employees: 26

1996 Sales: $0.1 million
1-Yr. Sales Change: —
Exchange: Nasdaq (SC)
Symbol: LUST

Computers - education & entertainment software (Intelligent Fun & Games)

WANG LABORATORIES, INC.

600 Technology Park Dr.
Billerica, MA 01821-4130
Phone: 508-967-5000
Fax: 508-967-0436

CEO: Joseph M. Tucci
CFO: Franklyn A. Caine
HR: Franklyn A. Caine
Employees: 7,900

1996 Sales: $1,089.8 million
1-Yr. Sales Change: 15.2%
Exchange: Nasdaq
Symbol: WANG

Computers - workflow, imaging, document management & related software applications for client/server
open systems; integration & support services for office networks worldwide

 See pages 234–235 for a full profile of this company.

WATKINS-JOHNSON COMPANY

3333 Hillview Ave.	CEO: W. Keith Kennedy Jr.	1995 Sales: $387.0 million
Palo Alto, CA 94304-1223	CFO: Scott G. Buchanan	1-Yr. Sales Change: 16.4%
Phone: 415-493-4141	HR: Don Aldrich	Exchange: NYSE
Fax: 415-813-2402	Employees: 2,180	Symbol: WJ

Wholesale distribution - semiconductor manufacturing equipment; subassemblies & tranceivers for wireless communications; military eavesdropping equipment, including radio-frequency electronics

WAVE SYSTEMS CORP.

540 Madison Ave., 38th Fl.	CEO: Peter J. Sprague	1995 Sales: $0.1 million
New York, NY 10022	CFO: Thomas R. Dilk	1-Yr. Sales Change: —
Phone: 212-755-3282	HR: Thomas R. Dilk	Exchange: Nasdaq
Fax: 212-755-3436	Employees: 41	Symbol: WAVX

Computers - encryption systems & electronic information metering (WaveMeter)

WAVE TECHNOLOGIES INTERNATIONAL, INC.

10845 Olive Blvd., Ste. 250	CEO: Kenneth W. Kousky	1996 Sales: $24.4 million
St. Louis, MO 63141	CFO: J. Michael Bowles	1-Yr. Sales Change: 35.6%
Phone: 314-995-5767	HR: Diane Kisker	Exchange: Nasdaq
Fax: 314-995-3894	Employees: 217	Symbol: WAVT

Computers - training & instructional services & products related to information technologies including telecommunications, client-server systems & the Internet

WEBSECURE, INC.

1711 Broadway	CEO: Robert Kuzara	1995 Sales: $0.0 million
Saugus, MA 01906	CFO: Carole Ouellette	1-Yr. Sales Change: —
Phone: 617-867-2300	HR: Karyn Anderson	Ownership: Privately Held
Fax: 617-867-2739	Employees: 21	

Computers - Internet access & support services for secure commercial transactions & communications over the Internet

WEITEK CORPORATION

1060 E. Arques Ave.	CEO: Richard H. Bohnet	1995 Sales: $17.6 million
Sunnyvale, CA 94086	CFO: Barry L. Cox	1-Yr. Sales Change: (38.2%)
Phone: 408-738-8400	HR: Stephen J. Gillis	Exchange: OTC
Fax: 408-738-1185	Employees: 73	Symbol: WWTK

Electrical products - integrated circuits (Unified Memory Architecture chipsets) & software development tools

WESTERN DIGITAL CORPORATION

8105 Irvine Center Dr.	CEO: Charles A. Haggerty	1996 Sales: $2,865.2 million
Irvine, CA 92718	CFO: Duston M. Williams	1-Yr. Sales Change: 34.5%
Phone: 714-932-5000	HR: Scott T. Hughes	Exchange: NYSE
Fax: 714-932-6096	Employees: 9,628	Symbol: WDC

Computers - hard-disk drives, graphics chip sets & add-in cards for enhanced video graphics

 See pages 236–237 for a full profile of this company.

WESTERN MICRO TECHNOLOGY, INC.

254 W. Hacienda Ave.	CEO: P. Scott Munro	1995 Sales: $106.5 million
Campbell, CA 95008	CFO: Jim Dorst	1-Yr. Sales Change: (10.7%)
Phone: 408-341-4781	HR: Bob O'Reilly	Exchange: Nasdaq
Fax: 408-341-4762	Employees: 103	Symbol: WSTM

Electronics - parts distribution & technical support

WHITE PINE SOFTWARE, INC.

40 Simon St.	CEO: Howard R. Berke	1995 Sales: $7.2 million
Nashua, NH 03060	CFO: Richard M. Darer	1-Yr. Sales Change: —
Phone: 603-886-9050	HR: —	Ownership: Privately Held
Fax: 603-886-9051	Employees: 117	

Computers - multiplatform desktop connectivity software for worldwide video & audio communication & data collaboration, including videoconferencing software (Enhanced CU-SeeMe, White Pine Reflector)

WHITTMAN-HART, INC.

311 S. Wacker Dr., Ste. 3500	CEO: Robert F. Bernard	1995 Sales: $49.8 million
Chicago, IL 60606	CFO: Kevin M. Gaskey	1-Yr. Sales Change: 68.8%
Phone: 312-922-9200	HR: Susan B. Reardon	Exchange: Nasdaq
Fax: 312-913-3300	Employees: 775	Symbol: WHIT

Computers - systems integration, information technology planning, software development & implementation, business process re-engineering, networking, workgroup & electronic commerce solutions

WILSON SONSINI GOODRICH & ROSATI

650 Page Mill Rd.	CEO: Alan Austin	1996 Sales: $114.1 million
Palo Alto, CA 94304-1050	CFO: Harvey Schloss	1-Yr. Sales Change: 12.7%
Phone: 415-493-9300	HR: Lynette Baranski	Ownership: Partnership
Fax: 415-493-6811	Employees: 726	

Corporate & securities law, litigation & intellectual property (#1 Silicon Valley law firm)

 See page 378 for a full profile of this company.

WILTEK, INC.

542 Westport Ave.	CEO: Boris Frenkiel	1995 Sales: $4.9 million
Norwalk, CT 06851-4492	CFO: Cindy Elwood	1-Yr. Sales Change: 6.5%
Phone: 203-853-7400	HR: —	Exchange: OTC
Fax: 203-846-3177	Employees: 32	Symbol: WLTK

Telecommunications services - worldwide message & data communications services allowing otherwise incompatible terminals, computers & communications networks to send & receive information

WIND RIVER SYSTEMS, INC.

1010 Atlantic Ave.	CEO: Ronald A. Abelmann	1996 Sales: $44.0 million
Alameda, CA 94501	CFO: Richard W. Kraber	1-Yr. Sales Change: 37.1%
Phone: 510-748-4100	HR: Kathy Doyle	Exchange: Nasdaq
Fax: 510-814-2010	Employees: 208	Symbol: WIND

Computers - operating systems & development tools for use in creation of embedded real-time software applications

 See page 379 for a full profile of this company.

WINTHROP RESOURCES CORPORATION

1015 Opus Ctr., 9900 Bren Rd. East	CEO: John L. Morgan	1995 Sales: $68.8 million
Minnetonka, MN 55343	CFO: Kirk A. MacKenzie	1-Yr. Sales Change: (1.6%)
Phone: 612-936-0226	HR: Kim Thompson	Exchange: Nasdaq
Fax: 612-936-0201	Employees: 36	Symbol: WINR

Leasing - computer systems & other equipment, including data processing equipment, point-of-sale devices, telecommunications equipment & office automation equipment.

WIRED VENTURES, INC.

520 Third St., 4th Fl.	CEO: Louis Rossetto	1995 Sales: $25.3 million
San Francisco, CA 94107-1815	CFO: Jeffrey Simon	1-Yr. Sales Change: 175.0%
Phone: 415-222-6200	HR: —	Ownership: Privately Held
Fax: 415-222-6209	Employees: 284	

Publishing - magazine (Wired); WWW site (HotWired Internet)

 See page 380 for a full profile of this company.

WIZ TECHNOLOGY, INC.

32951 Calle Perfecto	CEO: Mar-Jeanne Tendler	1995 Sales: $3.7 million
San Juan Capistrano, CA 92675	CFO: Billie Jolson	1-Yr. Sales Change: 270.0%
Phone: 714-443-3000	HR: Carmen Walsh	Exchange: AMEX
Fax: 714-443-2333	Employees: 30	Symbol: WIZ

Retail - shareware & other software (The $5 Computer Software Store) available through portable displays in grocery chains, airport gift shops, discount & computer stores

CEO: Dirk I. Gates
CFO: Jerry N. Ulrich
HR: Ken Bauer
Employees: 500

1995 Sales: $126
1-Yr. Sales Chang
Exchange: Nasdaq
Symbol: XIRC

e, parallel port & PC LAN adapters, multifunction PC card modems

NC.

CEO: Richard G. Ellenberger
CFO: Stephanie D. Cohen
HR: Sherri Haines
Employees: 1,033

1995 Sales: $79.9 milli
1-Yr. Sales Change: 56.
Ownership: Privately He

ity solutions used to integrate computing & communications devices & equipment
ions & systems

N

Dr., Ste. 120
5108
9000
565

CEO: Lawrence W. McGraw
CFO: William J. Birmingham
HR: Dee Larson
Employees: 18

1995 Sales: $0.4 million
1-Yr. Sales Change: 33.3%
Exchange: Nasdaq (SC)
Symbol: XOXC

cientific, geometric computing software which encompasses the entire body of geometry
al characteristics to visual data

STEMS, INC.

Hwy. 35
n, NJ 07724
08-389-3900
8-389-8823

CEO: Roy B. Andersen Jr.
CFO: Robert S. Vaters
HR: Jane Droge
Employees: 490

1995 Sales: $55.7 million
1-Yr. Sales Change: 34.5%
Exchange: Nasdaq
Symbol: XPED

ss services - fax distribution service (Fax Broadcast); gateway messaging services

LAN CORPORATION

679 W. Agoura Rd.
labasas, CA 91302
one: 818-880-3500
: 818-880-3505

CEO: Steve Y. Kim
CFO: —
HR: Andrew Jentis
Employees: 257

1995 Sales: $29.7 million
1-Yr. Sales Change: 7,325%
Exchange: Nasdaq
Symbol: XYLN

nputers - switching systems (OmniSwitch, PizzaSwitch) for improving network performance

WIZTEC SOLUTIONS LTD.

39 Hagalim St.	CEO: Yaron Polak	1995 Sales: $5.7 million
Herzlia 46725, Israel	CFO: Daniel Cynovich	1-Yr. Sales Change: 338.5%
Phone: +972-9-598-740	HR: —	Exchange: Nasdaq
Fax: —	Employees: 40	Symbol: WIZTF

Computers - subscriber management software (Wizard) for subscription TV operators

WOLFF NEW MEDIA LLC

520 Madison Ave., 11th Fl.	CEO: Michael Wolff	1995 Sales: $5.0 million
New York, NY 10022	CFO: Joseph Cohen	1-Yr. Sales Change: 127.3%
Phone: 212-308-8100	HR: Carol Lappin	Ownership: Privately Held
Fax: 212-308-8837	Employees: 35	

Publishing - Internet guidebooks (Net Chat, Net Games, Net Guide, Net Money, Net Trek); Internet directory (YPN); consulting

WONDERWARE CORPORATION

100 Technology Dr.	CEO: Roy H. Slavin	1995 Sales: $55.0 million
Irvine, CA 92718	CFO: Sam M. Auriemma	1-Yr. Sales Change: 54.1%
Phone: 714-727-3200	HR: Teresa Horton	Exchange: Nasdaq
Fax: 714-727-3270	Employees: 192	Symbol: WNDR

Computers - software for industrial automation, including manufacturing execution systems (MES) software; input-output drivers; connectivity software

WORKGROUP TECHNOLOGY CORPORATION

81 Hartwell Ave.	CEO: James M. Carney	1996 Sales: $10.5 million
Lexington, MA 02173	CFO: George R. McHorney	1-Yr. Sales Change: 128.3%
Phone: 617-674-2000	HR: Ruth Rooney	Exchange: Nasdaq
Fax: 617-674-0034	Employees: 79	Symbol: WKGP

Computers - client/server product data management software (CMS)

WORLDS INC.

605 Market St., 14th Fl.	CEO: Dave Gobel	1995 Est. Sales: $5.0 mil.
San Francisco, CA 94105	CFO: Mark Brown	1-Yr. Sales Change: 900.0%
Phone: 415-281-1300	HR: —	Ownership: Privately Held
Fax: 415-284-9483	Employees: 90	

Computers - on-screen entertainment & networking software for seriously ill children (Starbright World); Internet messaging software (Worlds Chat)

WORLDTALK COMMUNICATIONS CORPORATION

5155 Old Ironsides Dr.	CEO: Mark A. Jung	1995 Sales: $6.7 million
Santa Clara, CA 95054	CFO: Stephen R. Bennion	1-Yr. Sales Change: 52.3%
Phone: 408-567-1500	HR: —	Exchange: Nasdaq
Fax: 408-567-1501	Employees: 60	Symbol: WTLK

Computers - directory-based software linking electronic mail & groupware systems

WYLE ELECTRONICS

15370 Barranca Pkwy.	CEO: Ralph Ozorkiewicz	1995 Sales: $1,077.5 million
Irvine, CA 92718	CFO: R. Van Ness Holland Jr.	1-Yr. Sales Change: 36.0%
Phone: 714-753-9953	HR: Randall J. Kirner	Exchange: NYSE
Fax: 714-753-9870	Employees: 1,248	Symbol: WYL

Electronics - distribution of semiconductors & computer systems & related value-added services

WYSE TECHNOLOGY INC.

3471 N. First St.	CEO: Doug Chance	1996 Est. Sales: $300.0 mil.
San Jose, CA 95134-1803	CFO: Ken Czaja	1-Yr. Sales Change: 3.4%
Phone: 408-473-1200	HR: Frederick M. Chancellor	Ownership: Privately Held
Fax: 408-473-1222	Employees: 1,400	

Computers - terminals, PCs, monitors & UNIX systems

 See page 381 for a full profile of this company.

XCELLENET, INC.

5 Concourse Pkwy., Ste. 850	CEO: Dennis M. Crumpler	1995 Sales: $34.1 million
Atlanta, GA 30328	CFO: Sidney V. Sack	1-Yr. Sales Change: 26.8%
Phone: 770-804-8100	HR: Joel A. Miller	Exchange: Nasdaq
Fax: 770-804-8102	Employees: 250	Symbol: XNET

Computers - client/server system development software for remote & mobile business transactions (RemoteWare)

XEIKON N.V.

Vredebaan 72	CEO: L. De Schamphelaere	1995 Sales: $81.1 million
2640 Mortsel, Belgium	CFO: Marc Blanpain	1-Yr. Sales Change: 289.9%
Phone: +32-3-443-1311	HR: —	Exchange: Nasdaq
Fax: —	Employees: 163	Symbol: XEIKY

Computers - digital color printing systems for the short run color printing market

XEROX CORPORATION

800 Long Ridge Rd.
Stamford, CT 06904
Phone: 203-968-3000
Fax: 203-968-4559

Office equipment & supplies - electrostatic printers, multifunct.

 See pages 238–239 for a full

XICOR, INC.

1511 Buckeye Dr.
Milpitas, CA 95035
Phone: 408-432-8888
Fax: 408-432-0640

HR:
Em

Electrical components - reprogrammable & non controlled potentiometers

XILINX, INC.

2100 Logic Dr.
San Jose, CA 95124-3400
Phone: 408-559-7778
Fax: 408-559-7114

CEO: Willem P.
CFO: Gordon M.
HR: Christine C. T
Employees: 1,201

Electrical components - field-programmable gate arrays & logic

 See page 382 for a full profile of this company.

XIONICS DOCUMENT TECHNOLOGIES, INC.

70 Blanchard Rd.
Burlington, MA 01803
Phone: 617-229-7000
Fax: 617-229-7119

CEO: Robert E. Gilkes
CFO: Gerard T. Feeney
HR: John W. Devine III
Employees: 168

Computers - peripheral equipment, including printers, copiers & scanners

XIOX CORPORATION

577 Airport Blvd., Ste. 700
Burlingame, CA 94010
Phone: 415-375-8188
Fax: 415-342-1139

CEO: William H. Welling
CFO: Melanie D. Reid
HR: —
Employees: 53

Computers - telecommunications-management software systems

XIRCOM, INC.

2300 Corporate Center Dr.
Thousand Oaks, CA 91320-1420
Phone: 805-376-9300
Fax: 805-376-9311

Computers - network hardwa

XLCONNECT SOLUTIONS,

411 Eagleview Blvd.
Exton, PA 19341
Phone: 610-458-5500
Fax: 610-458-6734

Computers - connecti
with software applica

XOX CORPORATION

1450 Energy Par
Saint Paul, MN
Phone: 612-645
Fax: 612-645-9

Computers -
adding physic

WIZTEC SOLUTIONS LTD.

39 Hagalim St.	CEO: Yaron Polak	1995 Sales: $5.7 million
Herzlia 46725, Israel	CFO: Daniel Cynovich	1-Yr. Sales Change: 338.5%
Phone: +972-9-598-740	HR: —	Exchange: Nasdaq
Fax: —	Employees: 40	Symbol: WIZTF

Computers - subscriber management software (Wizard) for subscription TV operators

WOLFF NEW MEDIA LLC

520 Madison Ave., 11th Fl.	CEO: Michael Wolff	1995 Sales: $5.0 million
New York, NY 10022	CFO: Joseph Cohen	1-Yr. Sales Change: 127.3%
Phone: 212-308-8100	HR: Carol Lappin	Ownership: Privately Held
Fax: 212-308-8837	Employees: 35	

Publishing - Internet guidebooks (Net Chat, Net Games, Net Guide, Net Money, Net Trek); Internet directory (YPN); consulting

WONDERWARE CORPORATION

100 Technology Dr.	CEO: Roy H. Slavin	1995 Sales: $55.0 million
Irvine, CA 92718	CFO: Sam M. Auriemma	1-Yr. Sales Change: 54.1%
Phone: 714-727-3200	HR: Teresa Horton	Exchange: Nasdaq
Fax: 714-727-3270	Employees: 192	Symbol: WNDR

Computers - software for industrial automation, including manufacturing execution systems (MES) software; input-output drivers; connectivity software

WORKGROUP TECHNOLOGY CORPORATION

81 Hartwell Ave.	CEO: James M. Carney	1996 Sales: $10.5 million
Lexington, MA 02173	CFO: George R. McHorney	1-Yr. Sales Change: 128.3%
Phone: 617-674-2000	HR: Ruth Rooney	Exchange: Nasdaq
Fax: 617-674-0034	Employees: 79	Symbol: WKGP

Computers - client/server product data management software (CMS)

WORLDS INC.

605 Market St., 14th Fl.	CEO: Dave Gobel	1995 Est. Sales: $5.0 mil.
San Francisco, CA 94105	CFO: Mark Brown	1-Yr. Sales Change: 900.0%
Phone: 415-281-1300	HR: —	Ownership: Privately Held
Fax: 415-284-9483	Employees: 90	

Computers - on-screen entertainment & networking software for seriously ill children (Starbright World); Internet messaging software (Worlds Chat)

WORLDTALK COMMUNICATIONS CORPORATION

5155 Old Ironsides Dr.	CEO: Mark A. Jung	1995 Sales: $6.7 million
Santa Clara, CA 95054	CFO: Stephen R. Bennion	1-Yr. Sales Change: 52.3%
Phone: 408-567-1500	HR: —	Exchange: Nasdaq
Fax: 408-567-1501	Employees: 60	Symbol: WTLK

Computers - directory-based software linking electronic mail & groupware systems

WYLE ELECTRONICS

15370 Barranca Pkwy.	CEO: Ralph Ozorkiewicz	1995 Sales: $1,077.5 million
Irvine, CA 92718	CFO: R. Van Ness Holland Jr.	1-Yr. Sales Change: 36.0%
Phone: 714-753-9953	HR: Randall J. Kirner	Exchange: NYSE
Fax: 714-753-9870	Employees: 1,248	Symbol: WYL

Electronics - distribution of semiconductors & computer systems & related value-added services

WYSE TECHNOLOGY INC.

3471 N. First St.	CEO: Doug Chance	1996 Est. Sales: $300.0 mil.
San Jose, CA 95134-1803	CFO: Ken Czaja	1-Yr. Sales Change: 3.4%
Phone: 408-473-1200	HR: Frederick M. Chancellor	Ownership: Privately Held
Fax: 408-473-1222	Employees: 1,400	

Computers - terminals, PCs, monitors & UNIX systems

 See page 381 for a full profile of this company.

XCELLENET, INC.

5 Concourse Pkwy., Ste. 850	CEO: Dennis M. Crumpler	1995 Sales: $34.1 million
Atlanta, GA 30328	CFO: Sidney V. Sack	1-Yr. Sales Change: 26.8%
Phone: 770-804-8100	HR: Joel A. Miller	Exchange: Nasdaq
Fax: 770-804-8102	Employees: 250	Symbol: XNET

Computers - client/server system development software for remote & mobile business transactions (RemoteWare)

XEIKON N.V.

Vredebaan 72	CEO: L. De Schamphelaere	1995 Sales: $81.1 million
2640 Mortsel, Belgium	CFO: Marc Blanpain	1-Yr. Sales Change: 289.9%
Phone: +32-3-443-1311	HR: —	Exchange: Nasdaq
Fax: —	Employees: 163	Symbol: XEIKY

Computers - digital color printing systems for the short run color printing market

XEROX CORPORATION

800 Long Ridge Rd.	CEO: Paul A. Allaire	1995 Sales: $16,611.0 mil.
Stamford, CT 06904	CFO: Barry D. Romeril	1-Yr. Sales Change: (6.9%)
Phone: 203-968-3000	HR: Hector J. Motroni	Exchange: NYSE
Fax: 203-968-4559	Employees: 85,200	Symbol: XRX

Office equipment & supplies - document-processing products, including black-and-white copiers, ink-jet & electrostatic printers, multifunction & facsimile products, scanners & PC & workstation software

 See pages 238–239 for a full profile of this company.

XICOR, INC.

1511 Buckeye Dr.	CEO: Raphael Klein	1995 Sales: $113.6 million
Milpitas, CA 95035	CFO: Klaus G. Hendig	1-Yr. Sales Change: 9.9%
Phone: 408-432-8888	HR: Madga Madriz	Exchange: Nasdaq
Fax: 408-432-0640	Employees: 641	Symbol: XICO

Electrical components - reprogrammable & nonvolatile semiconductor memory devices & electronically controlled potentiometers

XILINX, INC.

2100 Logic Dr.	CEO: Willem P. Roelandts	1996 Sales: $560.8 million
San Jose, CA 95124-3400	CFO: Gordon M. Steel	1-Yr. Sales Change: 57.9%
Phone: 408-559-7778	HR: Christine C. Taylor	Exchange: Nasdaq
Fax: 408-559-7114	Employees: 1,201	Symbol: XLNX

Electrical components - field-programmable gate arrays & logic devices

 See page 382 for a full profile of this company.

XIONICS DOCUMENT TECHNOLOGIES, INC.

70 Blanchard Rd.	CEO: Robert E. Gilkes	1996 Sales: $23.8 million
Burlington, MA 01803	CFO: Gerard T. Feeney	1-Yr. Sales Change: 52.6%
Phone: 617-229-7000	HR: John W. Devine III	Exchange: Nasdaq
Fax: 617-229-7119	Employees: 168	Symbol: XION

Computers - peripheral equipment, including printers, copiers & scanners

XIOX CORPORATION

577 Airport Blvd., Ste. 700	CEO: William H. Welling	1995 Sales: $6.8 million
Burlingame, CA 94010	CFO: Melanie D. Reid	1-Yr. Sales Change: (9.3%)
Phone: 415-375-8188	HR: —	Exchange: Nasdaq (SC)
Fax: 415-342-1139	Employees: 53	Symbol: XIOX

Computers - telecommunications-management software systems

XIRCOM, INC.

2300 Corporate Center Dr.
Thousand Oaks, CA 91320-1420
Phone: 805-376-9300
Fax: 805-376-9311

CEO: Dirk I. Gates
CFO: Jerry N. Ulrich
HR: Ken Bauer
Employees: 500

1995 Sales: $126.6 million
1-Yr. Sales Change: (3.8%)
Exchange: Nasdaq
Symbol: XIRC

Computers - network hardware, parallel port & PC LAN adapters, multifunction PC card modems

XLCONNECT SOLUTIONS, INC.

411 Eagleview Blvd.
Exton, PA 19341
Phone: 610-458-5500
Fax: 610-458-6734

CEO: Richard G. Ellenberger
CFO: Stephanie D. Cohen
HR: Sherri Haines
Employees: 1,033

1995 Sales: $79.9 million
1-Yr. Sales Change: 56.7%
Ownership: Privately Held

Computers - connectivity solutions used to integrate computing & communications devices & equipment with software applications & systems

XOX CORPORATION

1450 Energy Park Dr., Ste. 120
Saint Paul, MN 55108
Phone: 612-645-9000
Fax: 612-645-9565

CEO: Lawrence W. McGraw
CFO: William J. Birmingham
HR: Dee Larson
Employees: 18

1995 Sales: $0.4 million
1-Yr. Sales Change: 33.3%
Exchange: Nasdaq (SC)
Symbol: XOXC

Computers - scientific, geometric computing software which encompasses the entire body of geometry adding physical characteristics to visual data

XPEDITE SYSTEMS, INC.

446 State Hwy. 35
Eatontown, NJ 07724
Phone: 908-389-3900
Fax: 908-389-8823

CEO: Roy B. Andersen Jr.
CFO: Robert S. Vaters
HR: Jane Droge
Employees: 490

1995 Sales: $55.7 million
1-Yr. Sales Change: 34.5%
Exchange: Nasdaq
Symbol: XPED

Business services - fax distribution service (Fax Broadcast); gateway messaging services

XYLAN CORPORATION

26679 W. Agoura Rd.
Calabasas, CA 91302
Phone: 818-880-3500
Fax: 818-880-3505

CEO: Steve Y. Kim
CFO: —
HR: Andrew Jentis
Employees: 257

1995 Sales: $29.7 million
1-Yr. Sales Change: 7,325%
Exchange: Nasdaq
Symbol: XYLN

Computers - switching systems (OmniSwitch, PizzaSwitch) for improving network performance

XYVISION, INC.

101 Edgewater Dr.
Wakefield, MA 01880-1291
Phone: 617-245-4100
Fax: 617-246-6209

CEO: Thomas H. Conway
CFO: Gene Seneta
HR: Michael Borin
Employees: 155

1996 Sales: $22.4 million
1-Yr. Sales Change: (8.9%)
Exchange: OTC
Symbol: XYVI

Computers - open-architecture publishing software

YAHOO! INC.

3400 Central Expressway, Ste. 201
Santa Clara, CA 95051
Phone: 408-731-3300
Fax: 408-731-3301

CEO: Timothy Koogle
CFO: Gary Valenzuela
HR: —
Employees: 39

1995 Sales: $1.4 million
1-Yr. Sales Change: —
Exchange: Nasdaq
Symbol: YHOO

Computers - World Wide Web search service (Yahoo!), web guide for children (Yahooligans!), country-specific web guides (Yahoo! Japan) & online & print magazine with Ziff-Davis (Yahoo! Internet Life)

 See page 383 for a full profile of this company.

YIELDUP INTERNATIONAL CORPORATION

117 Easy St.
Mountain View, CA 94043
Phone: 415-964-0100
Fax: 415-940-4388

CEO: Raj Mohindra
CFO: Scott M. Gibson
HR: Scott Gibson
Employees: 25

1995 Sales: $1.1 million
1-Yr. Sales Change: 266.7%
Exchange: Nasdaq (SC)
Symbol: YILD

Machinery - semiconductor manufacturing equipment

YOUNG MINDS, INCORPORATED

1906 Orange Tree Ln., Ste. 220
Redlands, CA 92374
Phone: 909-335-5780
Fax: 909-335-8751

CEO: David H. Cote
CFO: Andrew J. Young
HR: Debbie Blaze
Employees: 54

1995 Sales: $7.1 million
1-Yr. Sales Change: (6.6%)
Ownership: Privately Held

Computers - software products, embedded controllers & related services for creating, storing & accessing CD-ROM discs

ZEBRA TECHNOLOGIES CORPORATION

333 Corporate Woods Pkwy.
Vernon Hills, IL 60061-3109
Phone: 847-634-6700
Fax: 847-634-1830

CEO: Edward L. Kaplan
CFO: Charles R. Whitchurch
HR: Ellen Barnes
Employees: 627

1995 Sales: $148.6 million
1-Yr. Sales Change: 38.7%
Exchange: Nasdaq
Symbol: ZBRA

Optical character recognition - bar code printers & related equipment

ZENITH CONTROLS, INC.

830 W. 40th St.	CEO: Arthur Coren	1995 Sales: $33.9 million
Chicago, IL 60609	CFO: Bob Doherty	1-Yr. Sales Change: 12.3%
Phone: 312-247-6400	HR: Pat Schopper	Ownership: Privately Held
Fax: 312-247-7805	Employees: 283	

Electrical components - power switching systems & control equipment

ZIFF-DAVIS PUBLISHING COMPANY

One Park Ave.	CEO: Eric Hippeau	1995 Est. Sales: $950.0 mil.
New York, NY 10016-5801	CFO: Tim O'Brien	1-Yr. Sales Change: 11.5%
Phone: 212-503-3500	HR: Rajna Brown	Ownership: Subsidiary
Fax: 212-503-4599	Employees: 2,700	

Publishing - computer magazine publisher (#1 in US: PC Magazine, PC Week, Computer Shopper); TV programming; online services (ZiffNet) & CD-ROMs; subsidiary of SOFTBANK

 See pages 240–241 for a full profile of this company.

ZILOG, INC.

210 E. Hacienda Ave.	CEO: Edgar A. Sack	1995 Sales: $265.1 million
Campbell, CA 95008-6600	CFO: Robert E. Collins	1-Yr. Sales Change: 13.6%
Phone: 408-370-8000	HR: Sally M. Baumwell	Exchange: NYSE
Fax: 408-370-8056	Employees: 1,574	Symbol: ZLG

Electrical components - integrated circuits for the data communication, consumer-product, computer & other industries

 See page 384 for a full profile of this company.

ZING TECHNOLOGIES, INC.

115 Stevens Ave.	CEO: Robert E. Schrader	1996 Sales: $26.0 million
Valhalla, NY 10595	CFO: Martin S. Fawer	1-Yr. Sales Change: 15.0%
Phone: 914-747-7474	HR: Michelle Mastrapolo	Exchange: Nasdaq
Fax: 914-747-2316	Employees: 186	Symbol: ZING

Electronics - power semiconductor multi-chip modules & packaged semiconductor components for military & industrial use

ZITEL CORPORATION

47211 Bayside Pkwy.	CEO: Jack H. King	1995 Sales: $23.7 million
Fremont, CA 94538-6517	CFO: Henry C. Harris	1-Yr. Sales Change: 35.4%
Phone: 510-440-9600	HR: Eva Santillan	Exchange: Nasdaq
Fax: 510-440-9696	Employees: 92	Symbol: ZITL

Computers - data-storage subsystems, disk drives, performance-enhancement components & interface boards

ZOOM TELEPHONICS, INC.

207 South St.	CEO: Frank B. Manning	1995 Sales: $97.0 million
Boston, MA 02111	CFO: Steven T. Shedd	1-Yr. Sales Change: 42.2%
Phone: 617-423-1072	HR: Marty Levin	Exchange: Nasdaq
Fax: 617-338-5015	Employees: 251	Symbol: ZOOM

Computers - data & fax modems, speed dialers (Hotshot) & voice/data processors

 See page 385 for a full profile of this company.

ZORAN CORPORATION

2041 Mission College Blvd.	CEO: Levy Gerzberg	1995 Sales: $20.1 million
Santa Clara, CA 95054	CFO: —	1-Yr. Sales Change: 148.1%
Phone: 408-986-1314	HR: —	Exchange: Nasdaq
Fax: 408-986-1240	Employees: 61	Symbol: ZRAN

Computers - VLSI products for MPEG-1 & JPEG-based multimedia computing & audio compression applications

ZYCAD CORPORATION

47100 Bayside Pkwy.	CEO: Phillips W. Smith	1995 Sales: $51.1 million
Fremont, CA 94538	CFO: Peter J. Cassidy	1-Yr. Sales Change: 2.0%
Phone: 510-623-4400	HR: Lynn Nistler	Exchange: Nasdaq
Fax: 510-623-4550	Employees: 219	Symbol: ZCAD

Electronics - design verification, rapid prototyping & test analysis systems for high-performance electronic systems

ZYCON CORPORATION

445 El Camino Real	CEO: Ronald H. Donati	1995 Sales: $180.9 million
Santa Clara, CA 95050	CFO: Kenneth R. Shilling	1-Yr. Sales Change: 21.2%
Phone: 408-241-9900	HR: Brenda Mora	Exchange: Nasdaq
Fax: 408-241-9527	Employees: 1,661	Symbol: ZCON

Electrical components - multilayer printed circuit boards for OEMs & contract manufacturers of electronic equipment

ZYTEC CORPORATION

7575 Market Place Dr.	CEO: Ronald D. Schmidt	1995 Sales: $170.5 million
Eden Prairie, MN 55344	CFO: John B. Rogers	1-Yr. Sales Change: 33.1%
Phone: 612-941-1100	HR: Patrick Vincelli	Exchange: Nasdaq
Fax: 612-941-1100	Employees: 1,241	Symbol: ZTEC

Electrical components - custom electric-power supplies

COMPUTER **The Indexes**

Princeton
Bureau of Electronic
Publishing, Inc. 429
Dataram Corporation 465
Logic Works, Inc. 542
Voxware, Inc. 670

Rochelle Park
PC Warehouse Investment,
Inc. 590

Rutherford
Computron Software, Inc.
452

Shrewsbury
Programmer's Paradise,
Inc. 601

Somerville
TransNet Corporation 654

Teaneck
Integrated Technology USA,
Inc. 523

Tinton Falls
ECCS, Inc. 478

Trenton
Base Ten Systems, Inc. 419

Upper Saddle River
Tellurian, Inc. 650

Warren
ANADIGICS, Inc. 403

West Long Branch
EA Industries, Inc. 477

West Orange
US Servis, Inc. 661

NEW YORK
Amityville
Nu Horizons Electronic
Corp. 579

Armonk
International Business
Machines Corporation
126, 526

Bohemia
Computer Concepts Corp.
449

Brooklyn
Multi-Media Tutorial
Service 566

Buffalo
Barrister Information
Systems Corporation 419
Computer Task Group,
Incorporated 451

Farmingdale
Blue Chip Computerware,
Inc. 424
Milgray Electronics, Inc.
563

Farmington
Griffin Technology
Incorporated 504

Franklin Square
Software Engineering of
America Inc. 630

Glen Cove
Acclaim Entertainment,
Inc. **245**, 390

Great Neck
Avnet, Inc. **52**, 417
Netplex Group Inc. 573

Hauppauge
Compositech Ltd. 447
Hauppauge Digital, Inc.
506
Standard Microsystems
Corporation 636
TSR, Inc. 658

Holtsville
Symbol Technologies, Inc.
642

Islandia
Computer Associates
International, Inc. **80**,
449

Islip
Netsmart Technologies,
Inc. 574

Lake Success
Comforce Corporation 447
Market Guide Inc. 548
Park Electrochemical Corp.
589

Manhasset
CMP Publications, Inc. **68**,
444

Melville
Arrow Electronics, Inc. **48**,
409
Mediware Information
Systems, Inc. 552

New Hartford
PAR Technology
Corporation 587

New York
Advanced Voice Technology
394
Alpha Technologies Group,
Inc. 397
Aristo International
Corporation 409
Bell Technology Group Ltd.
421
Bloomberg L.P. 423
BoxHill Systems
Corporation 426

Byron Preiss Multimedia
Company, Inc. 429
Computer Generated
Solutions, Inc. 449
Digital Network Associates
Inc. 472
Enteractive, Inc. 484
FIND/SVP, Inc. 491
Global Intellicom, Inc. 502
GT Interactive Software
Corp. **295**, 505
Hertz Technology Group,
Inc. 508
ILC Industries, Inc. 513
Index Stock Photography,
Inc. 515
Information Builders, Inc.
517
Infosafe Systems, Inc. 519
Innodata Corporation 519
Interact Medical
Technologies Corporation
524
IPC Information Systems,
Inc. 530
J&R Computer World 532
Krystaltech International
Inc. 536
Management Technologies,
Inc. 547
Manchester Equipment Co.,
Inc. 547
N2K Inc. 567
New Paradigm Software
Corporation 576
Ovid Technologies, Inc.
586
Photocircuits Corporation
593
Poppe Tyson, Inc. 597
Portfolio Acquisition
Corporation 597
THINK New Ideas, Inc. 651
Vitt Media International,
Inc. 668
Volt Information Sciences,
Inc. 669
The Voyager Company 670
Wanderlust Interactive, Inc.
671
Wave Systems Corp. 672
Wolff New Media LLC 675
Ziff-Davis Publishing
Company **240**, 680

Newark
IEC Electronics Corp. 513

Northport
ATEC Group, Inc. 413

Godzilla 132
Goelman, Lawrence 338
Goffney, Eric V. 329
Golden, James 307
Golden, Stephen P. 385
Goldman, Hal 285
Goldman, Morton 285
Goldman, Neal 139
Goldsberry, Gary L. 117
Goldstar 182
Goldwasser, Ralph A. 260
Gonen, Ilan 193
Gooch, Lowell Thomas 209
Goodbye, Galaxy! 300
Goodnight, James H. 186, 187
Goodrich, John 378
GoodTimes Home Video 295
Goodyear Tire & Rubber 252
Gordon, Donald M. 267
Gordon, Tica 270
Gordon, William B. 283
Goulden, David 235
Goveia, Steve 197
Government Express! Center 275
Goyal, Prabhat 319
Graber, James E. 369
Graczyk, Beatrice A. 298
Graham Magnetics 250
Graham, Howard H. 302
Graham, Robert 333
Graham, Roy 381
Grainger, Michael J. 119
Granite Computer Products 278
Granite Systems 210
Grant, Joseph M. 99
Grant, Larry 374
Graphics Blaster 88
Graphics Communications 138
Grass Valley Group 220
Gray, Derek J. 31
Grayson, George 244
Grayson, George D. 244
The Great Word Adventure 244
Green, Jeffrey W. 298
Green, Michael I. 289
Green, Roger 48
Green, Shawn 300
Green, Thomas B. 93
Greenbar archiving software 287

Greendale, Christopher H. 265
Gregg, Robert S. 354
Gregor, Andrew 295
Greguras, Fred M. 286
Greico, Frank R. 347
Grenex 194
Gresham, Robert L. 341
Greyhound Lines 354
GRiD Systems 66, 214
Griffin, John J. 247
Griffin, Matthew 96
Griffiths, Jeff 41
Grolier's Academic American Encyclopedia 79
Gross, Deborah L. 318
Gross, Loren D. 65
Gross, Paul H. 57
Grossman, Peter 97
Grotstein, Josh 343
Ground Zero Texas 281
GroupWise groupware 164
Grove, Andrew S. 120, 121
Growney, Robert L. 155
GrR HomeNet Corp. 196
Grubb, Richard N. 233
GT Interactive Software Corp. **295**, 300
GTE 172, 200, 212, 222, 337
Gudonis, Paul R. 260
Guenon, Jacquard W. 380
Guenthner, Dave 117
Guerra, Rebecca 31
Guggenheim, Ralph J. 339
Gulf Oil 190
Gulick, Paul 301
Gullet, Jan L. 263
Gumby, T.F. 244
GummiSavers 339
Gupta Corp. 80
Gutsch, Hans W. 73
Gyenes, Lawrence A. 79

H

Haden, Rodney D. 263
Haefner, Walter 80
Hagen Computer Systems 278
Haggerty, Charles A. 237
Haines, Sherri 123
Hakunetsusha & Company 226
Hald, Alan P. 148, 149
Hale, Alan P. 277
Hall, David W. 75
Hall, Tom 300

Halla, Brian L. 141
Hallam, Thomas F. 49
Halligan, John F. 292
Hallmark Connections 37
Hall-Mark Electronics 52
Haloid Company 238
Halpin, James F. 76, 77
Halske, Johann 200
Halter, John E. 223
Hambly, Lawrence W. 211
Hambrecht & Quist LLP (H&Q) **296**
Hambrecht, William R. 296
Hamilton, Anthony 52
Hamilton Electro 52
Hamilton Hallmark 52, 53
Hamilton, Lawrence W. 219
Hamm, John D. 246
Hammer Technologies 222
Hammond, Mike 106
Hammond, Teresa 347
Hams, Stephen 293
Hancock, David 110, 111
Hancock, Ellen 45
Hancock, Larry J. 297
Handbook subnotebook computer 106
Handley, Phil 175
H&R Block 78
Hanigal, Benny 317
Hanley, James G. 338
Hanley, Peter 333
Hannon, Cyril F. 141
Hans Vision 89
Hansen, Paul G. 246
Hara, Iwao 111
Haran, Pranatharthi 360
Harari, Eli 324
Harbinger Corp. 370
Harbinger*EDI Services 335
Harczak, Harry J. Jr. 267
Hardcard disk 176
Hardesty, Kenneth S. 369
Harding, Richard H. 356
Harker, John V. 301
Harley Davidson 43
Harman International 72
Harmon, Bill 337
Harmonix series 101
Haroian, Gary 365
Harper, Edwin L. 369
Harper, Robin D. 318
Harrell, Samuel 310
Harris Corp. 257, 324
Harris, Keith M. 348
Harris, William H. Jr. 305

The search ˅engine is over.

Find out what's on in cyberspace®

www.ypn.com